Street by Stree

C000002112

MANCHESTER

BOLTON, BURY, OLDHAM, ROCHDALE, SALFORD, STOCKPORT

Altrincham, Ashton-under-Lyne, Hazel Grove, Littleborough,
Middleton, Partington, Ramsbottom, Sale, Stretford, Wilmslow

1st edition May 2001

© Automobile Association Developments
Limited 2001

This product includes map data licensed from
Ordnance Survey® with the permission of the
Controller of Her Majesty's Stationery Office.
© Crown copyright 2000. All rights reserved.
Licence No: 399221.

Published by AA Publishing (a trading name of
Automobile Association Developments
Limited, whose registered office is Norfolk House,
Priestley Road, Basingstoke, Hampshire, RG24 9NY.
Registered number 1878835).

Mapping produced by the Cartographic
Department of The Automobile Association.

A CIP Catalogue record for this book is
available from the British Library.

Printed by G. Canale & C. S.P.A., Torino, Italy

The contents of this atlas are believed to be correct
at the time of the latest revision. However, the
publishers cannot be held responsible for loss
occasioned to any person acting or refraining
from action as a result of any material in this atlas,
nor for any errors, omissions or changes in
such material. The publishers would welcome
information to correct any errors or omissions
and to keep this atlas up to date. Please write to
Publishing, The Automobile Association, Fanum
House, Basing View, Basingstoke, Hampshire,
RG21 4EA.

Ref: MD043

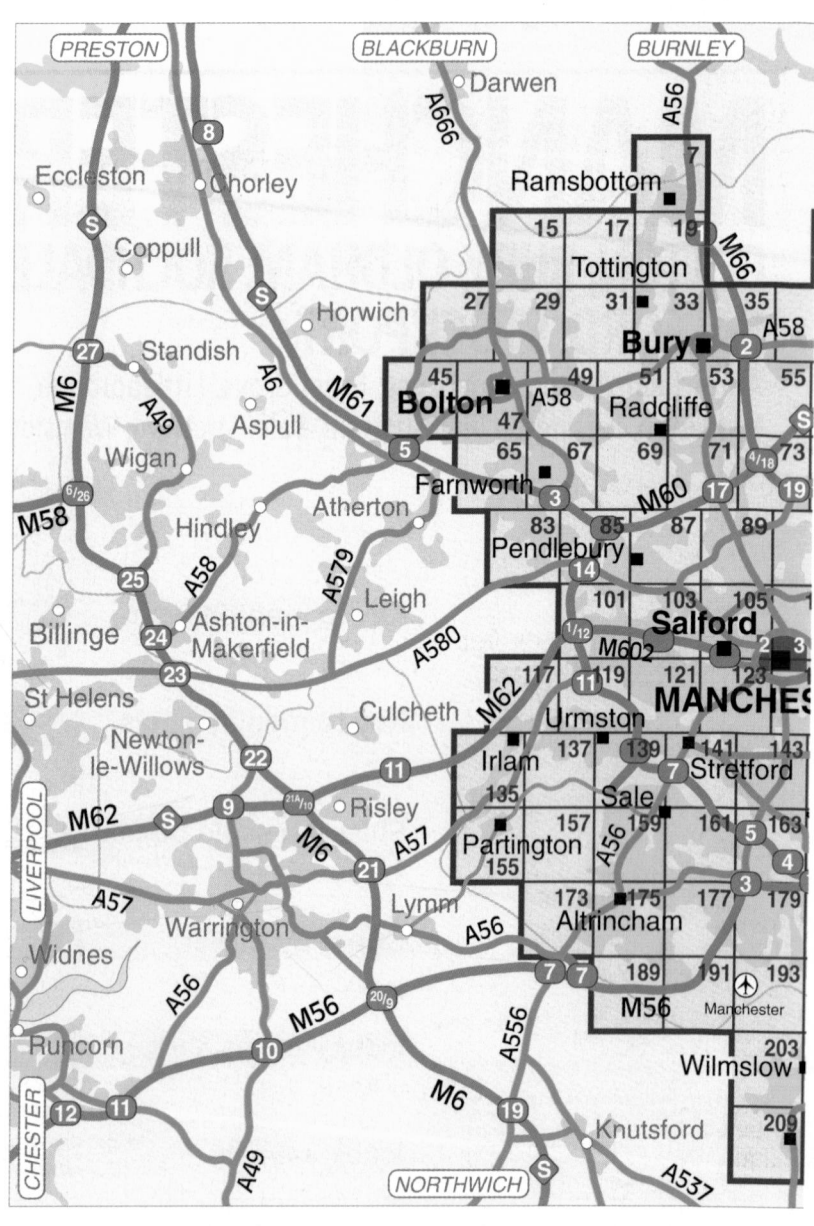

Enlarged scale pages 1:10,000 6.3 inches to 1 mile

0		1/4		miles		1/2	

0	1/4	1/2	kilometres	3/4	1

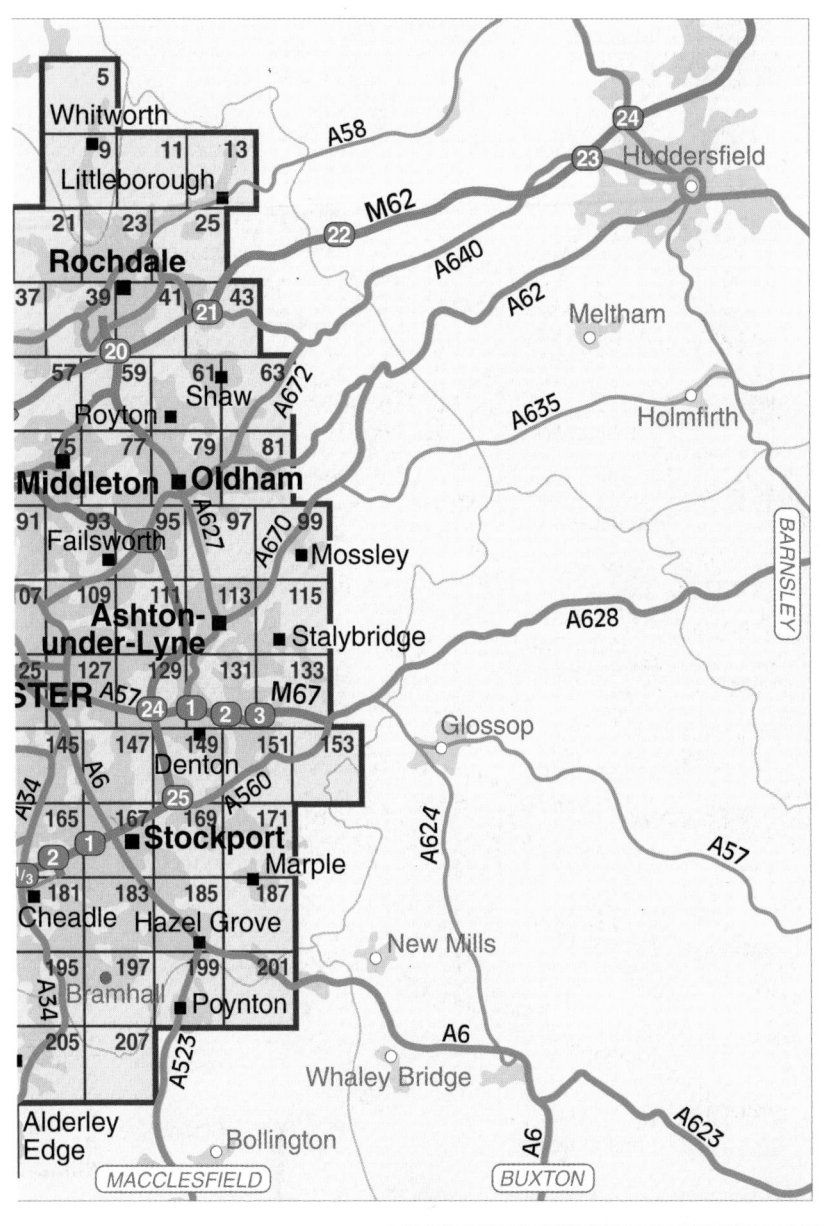

3.6 inches to 1 mile **Scale of main map pages** **1:17,500**

| 0 | | 1/2 | | miles | | 1 |
| 0 | 1/2 | | 1 | kilometres | 1 1/2 |

iv

Junction 9	Motorway & junction	P+🚌	Park & Ride
Services	Motorway service area	🚌	Bus/coach station
	Primary road single/dual carriageway		Railway & main railway station
Services	Primary road service area		Railway & minor railway station
	A road single/dual carriageway	⊖	Underground station
	B road single/dual carriageway	⊖	Light railway & station
	Other road single/dual carriageway	+++++++	Preserved private railway
	Restricted road	_LC_	Level crossing
	Private road	•—•—•	Tramway
← ←	One way street	- - - - - -	Ferry route
	Pedestrian street	....	Airport runway
	Track/ footpath	- · - · - ·	Boundaries- borough/ district
	Road under construction	▼▼▼▼▼▼▼	Mounds
}= = ={	Road tunnel	**93**	Page continuation 1:17,500
P	Parking	**7**	Page continuation to enlarged scale 1:10,000

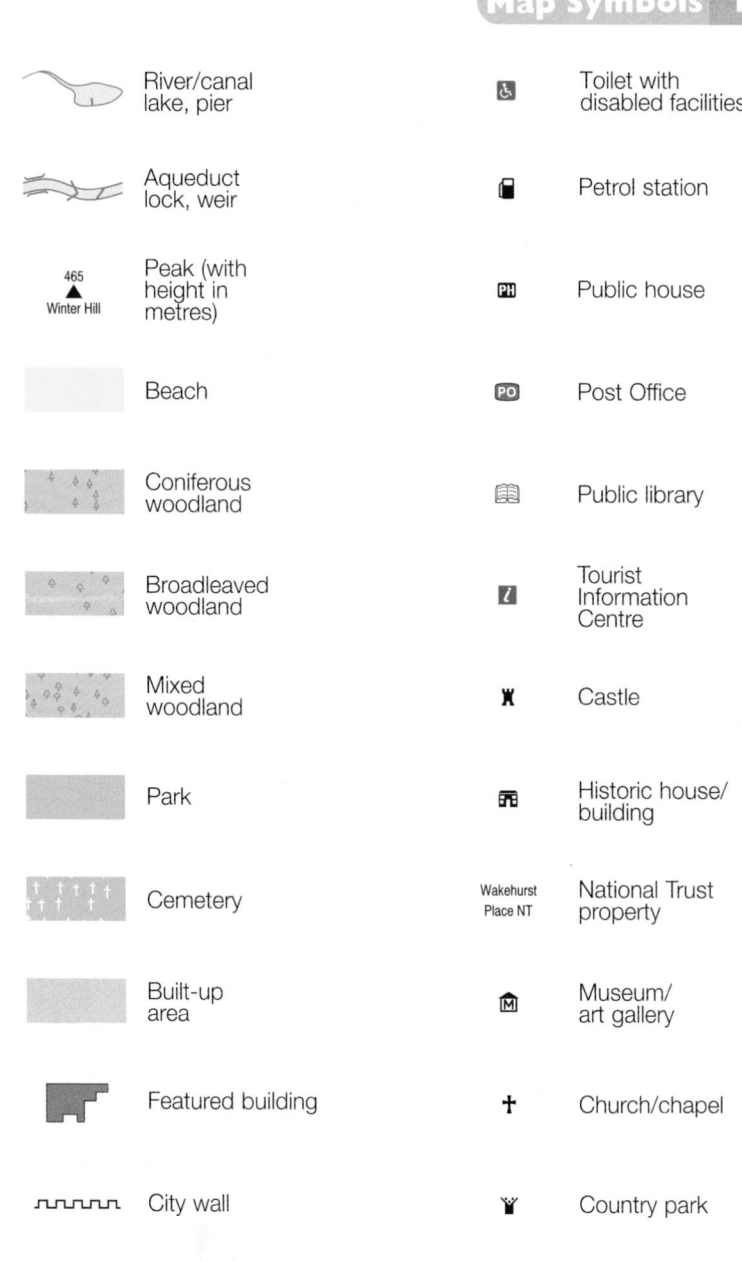

	River/canal lake, pier		Toilet with disabled facilities
	Aqueduct lock, weir		Petrol station
465 ▲ Winter Hill	Peak (with height in metres)	PH	Public house
	Beach	PO	Post Office
	Coniferous woodland		Public library
	Broadleaved woodland	*i*	Tourist Information Centre
	Mixed woodland	✗	Castle
	Park		Historic house/ building
	Cemetery	Wakehurst Place NT	National Trust property
	Built-up area	M	Museum/ art gallery
	Featured building	†	Church/chapel
⌐⌐⌐⌐⌐	City wall	⅄	Country park
A&E	Accident & Emergency hospital		Theatre/ performing arts
	Toilet		Cinema

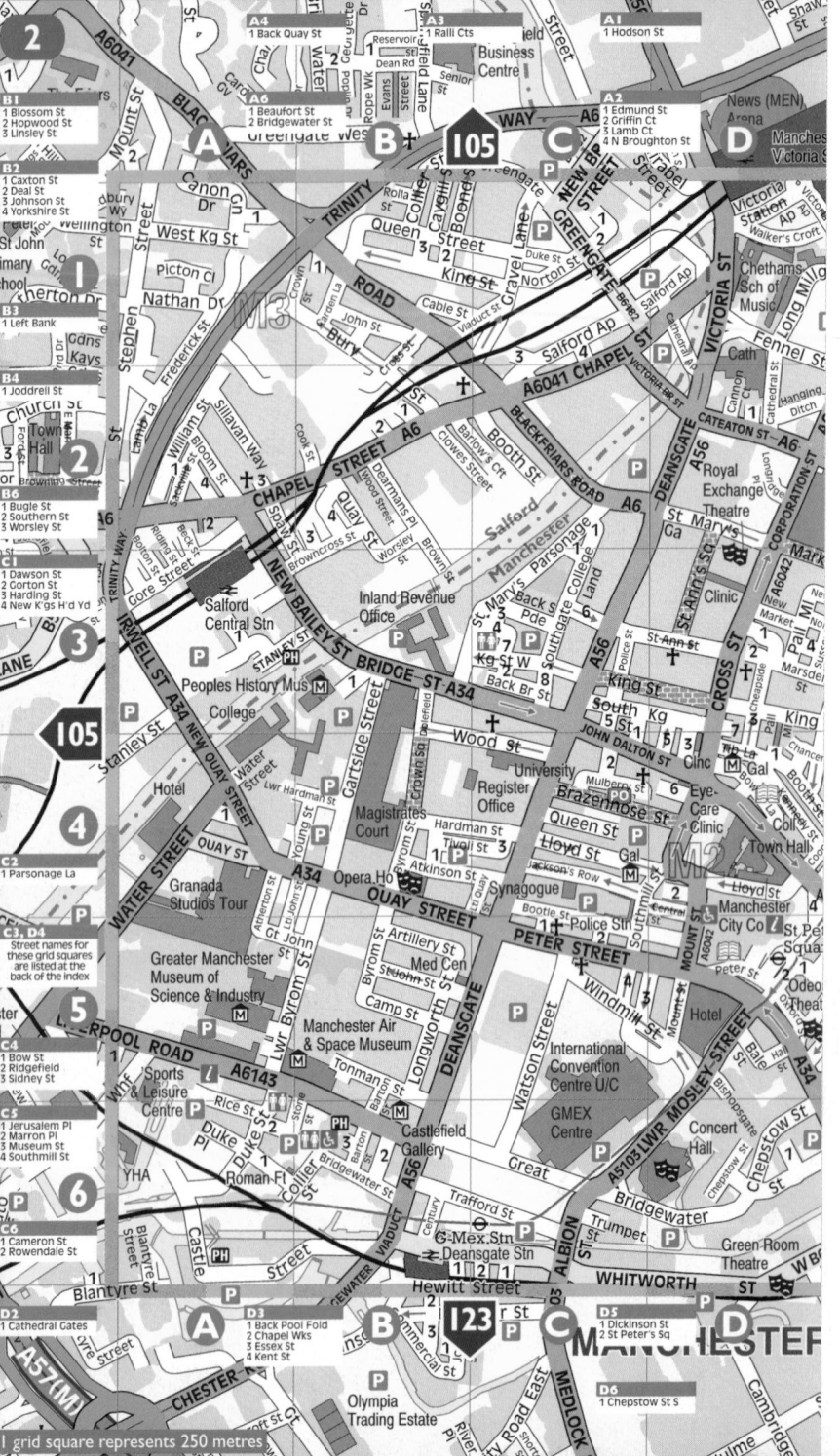

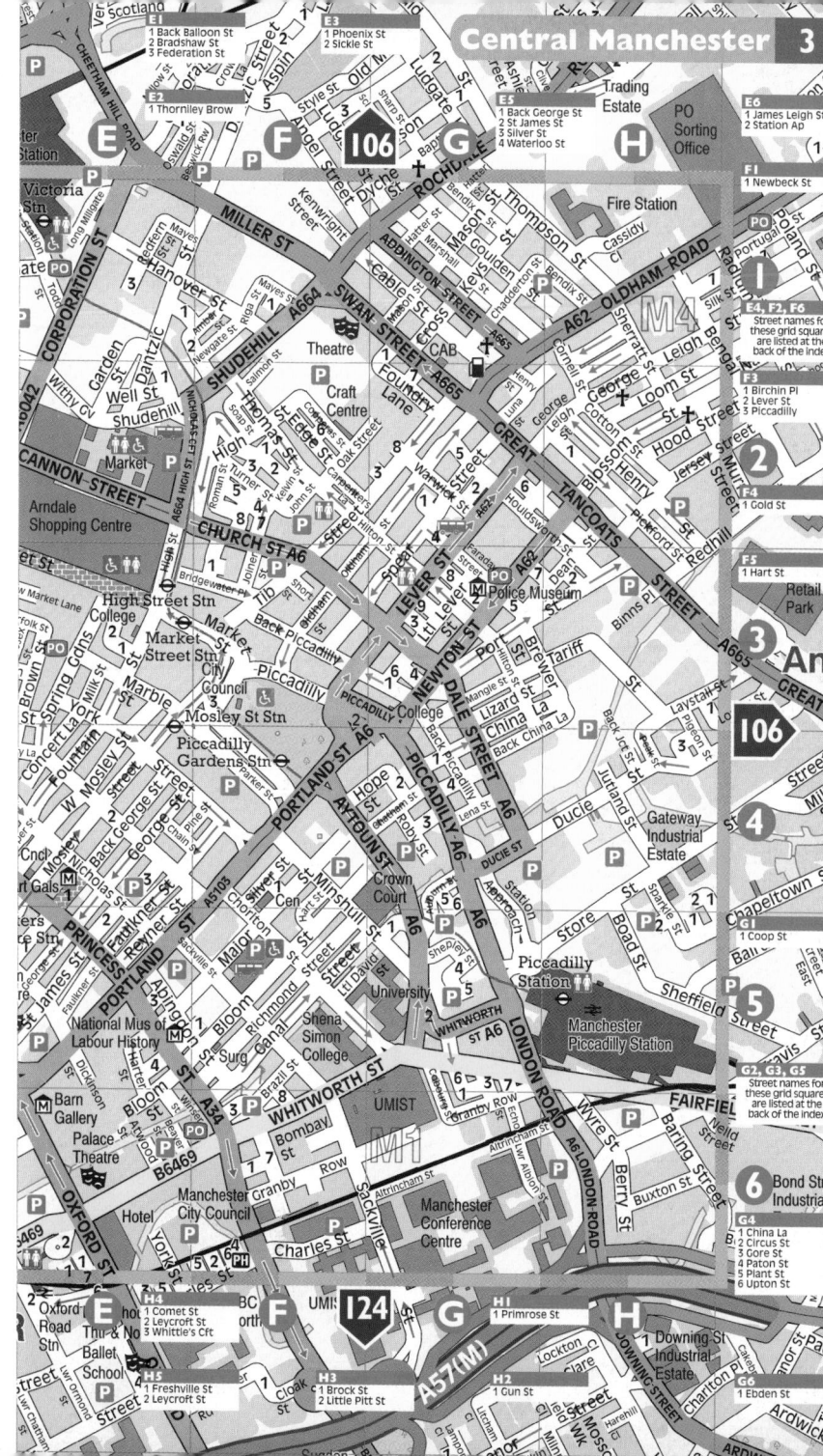

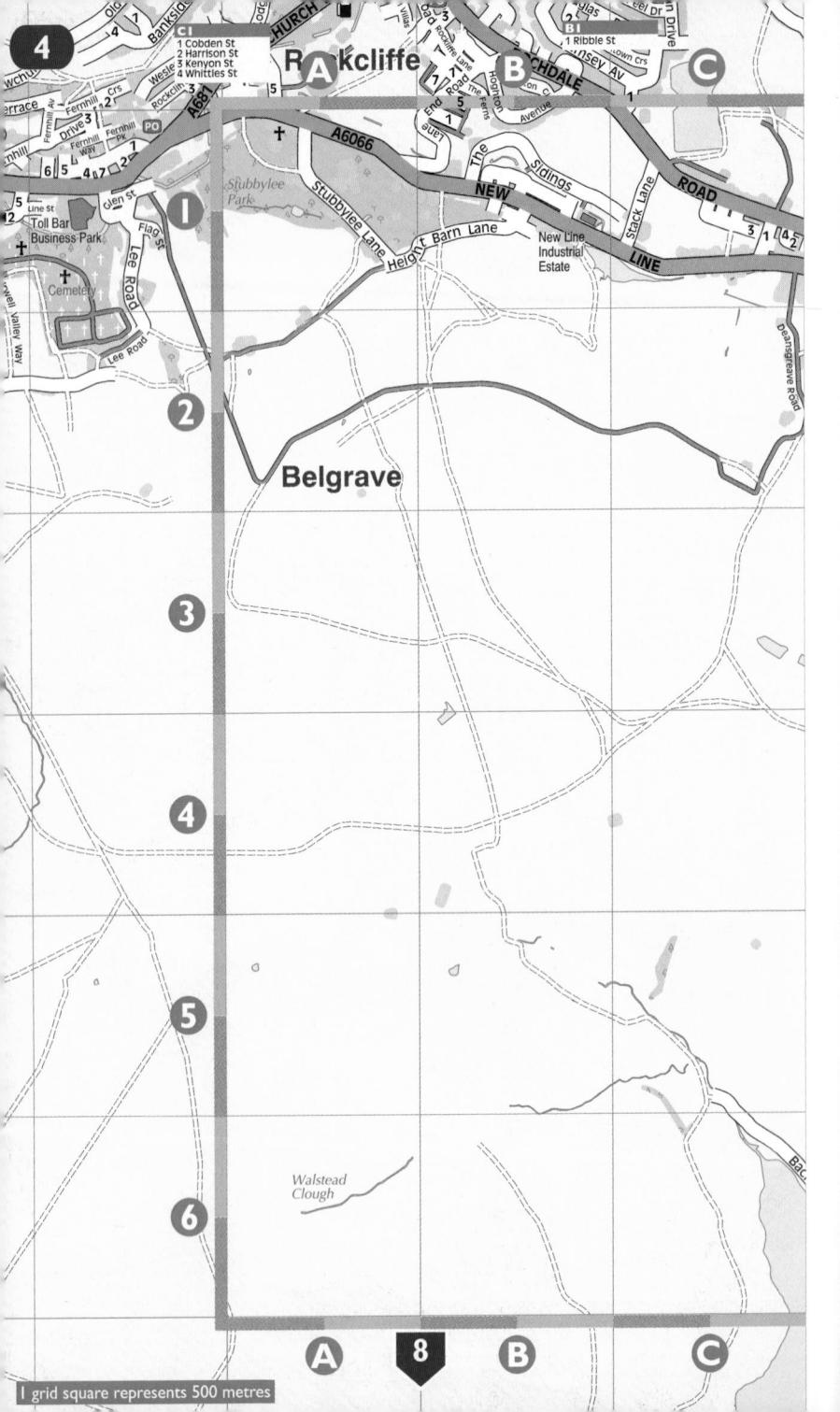

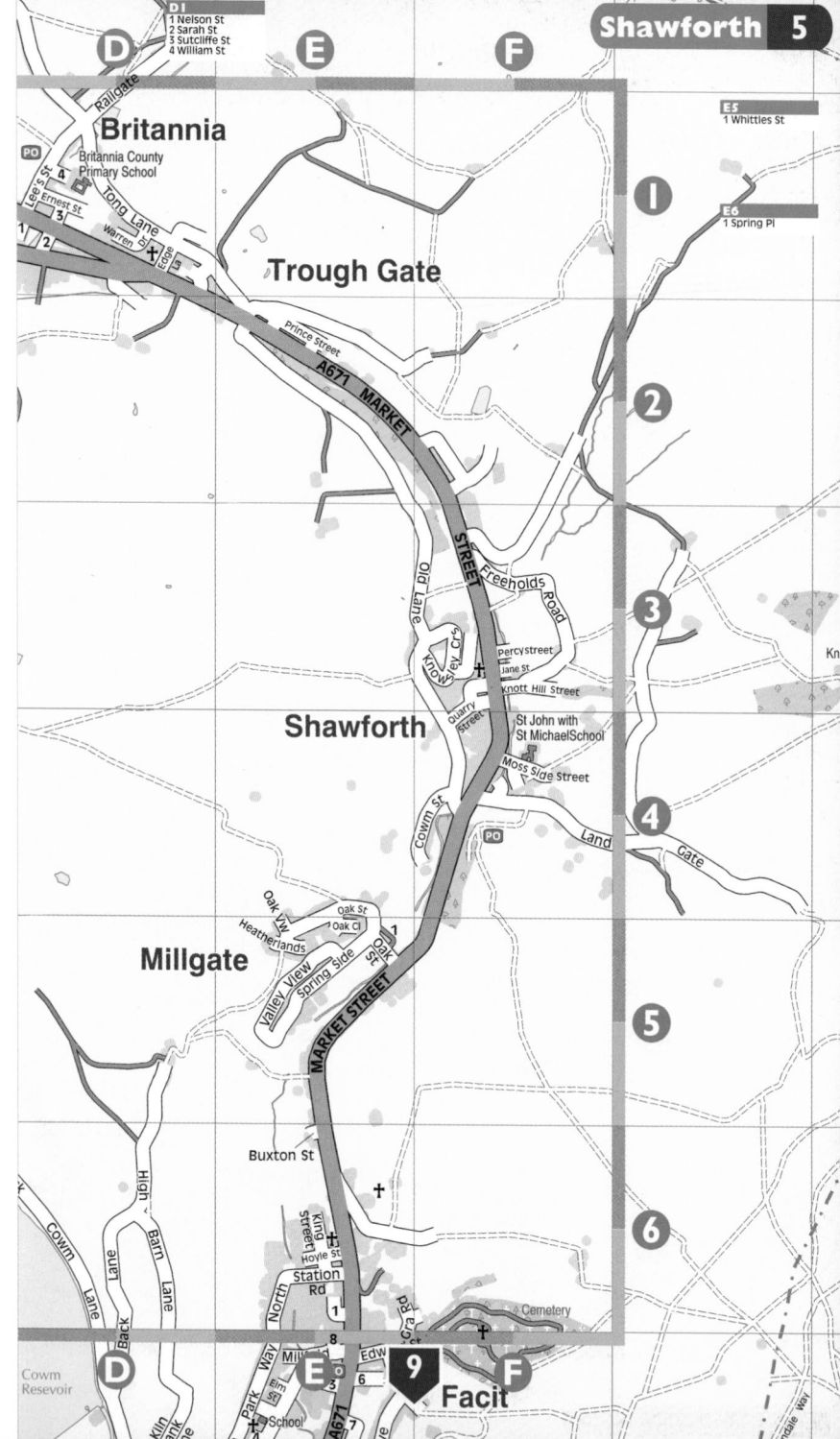

D1
1 Nelson St
2 Sarah St
3 Sutcliffe St
4 William St

D **E** **F**

Raligate

Britannia

PO

Britannia County
Primary School

Lee St
Ernest St
Tong Lane
Warren Br
Edge La

Trough Gate

Prince Street

A671 MARKET

E5
1 Whittles St

1

E6
1 Spring Pl

2

STREET

Freeholds Road

Old Lane

South View Crs
Knoll

Percy street
Jane st

3

Kn

Knott Hill Street

Shawforth

Quarry Street

St John with
St Michael School

Moss Side Street

4

Cowm St

PO

Land Gate

Oak Vw

Oak St
Oak Cl

Heatherlands

Millgate

Valley View
Spring Side

Oak Crs

7

MARKET STREET

5

Buxton St

†

6

King Street
Hoyle St

†

Station Rd

Cowm Lane

High Barn Lane

Back Lane

Kiln Bank

D **E** **F**

North Way
Park Way
Mill St
Elm St

School

A671

Edw

Craig Rd

Cemetery

†

9 **Facit**

Cowm
Reservoir

ndale Way

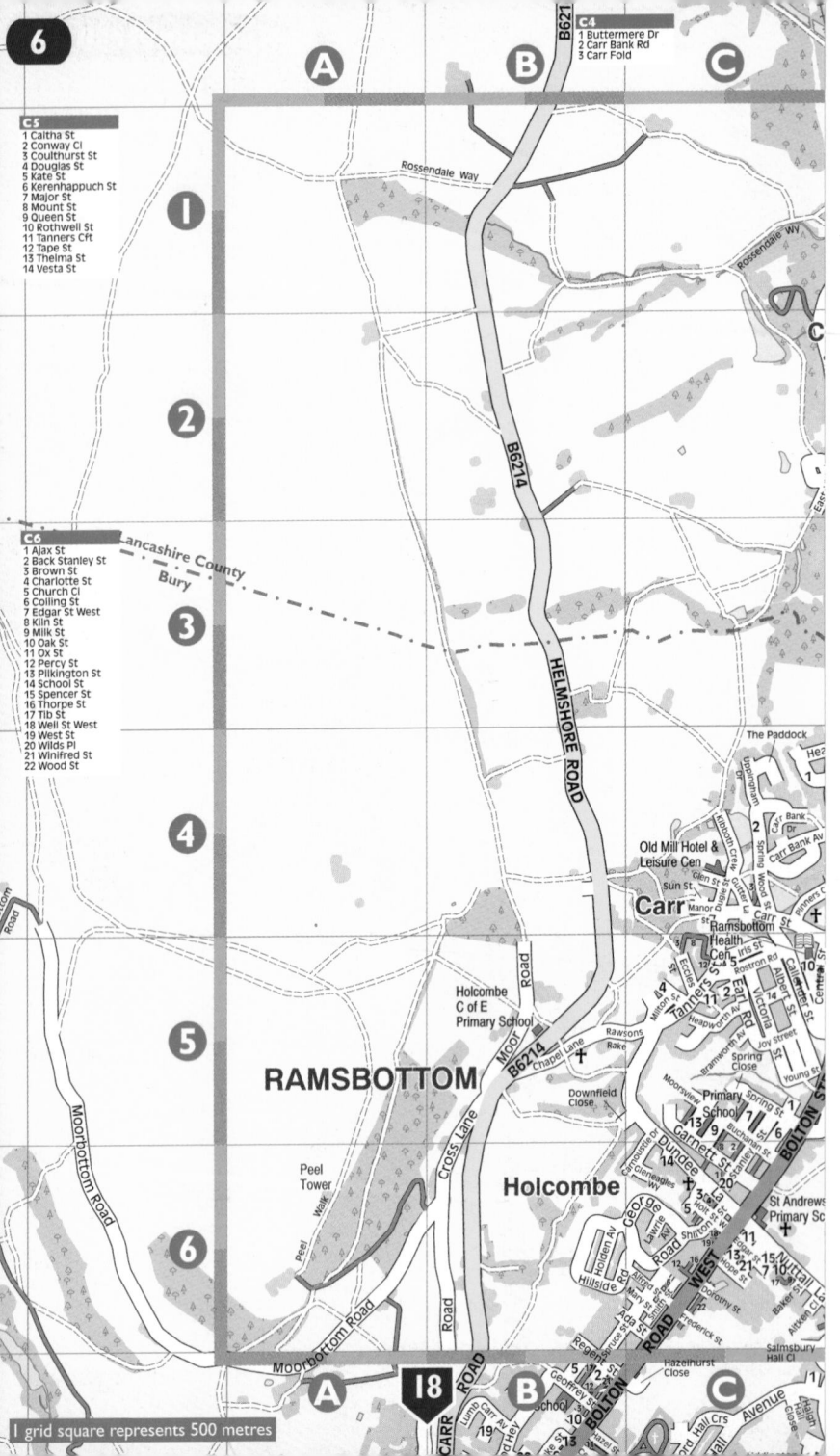

6

C5
1 Caltha St
2 Conway Cl
3 Coulthurst St
4 Douglas St
5 Kate St
6 Kerenhappuch St
7 Major St
8 Mount St
9 Queen St
10 Rothwell St
11 Tanners Cft
12 Tape St
13 Thelma St
14 Vesta St

C6
1 Ajax St
2 Back Stanley St
3 Brown St
4 Charlotte St
5 Church Cl
6 Coiling St
7 Edgar St West
8 Kiln St
9 Milk St
10 Oak St
11 Ox St
12 Percy St
13 Pilkington St
14 School St
15 Spencer St
16 Thorpe St
17 Tib St
18 Well St West
19 West St
20 Wilds Pl
21 Winifred St
22 Wood St

C4
1 Buttermere Dr
2 Carr Bank Rd
3 Carr Fold

B621

B6214

Rossendale Way

Rossendale Wy

Lancashire County

Bury

HELMSHORE ROAD

The Paddock

Old Mill Hotel & Leisure Cen

Carr

Ramsbottom Health Cen

Moor Road

Holcombe C of E Primary School

B6214

Chapel Lane

Rawsons Rake

Tanners

Victoria

Downfield Close

Primary School

RAMSBOTTOM

Cross Lane

BOLTON

Peel Tower

Peel Way

Holcombe

Dundee

George

St Andrews Primary Sc

Hillside

ROAD

WEST

Holden Av

Moorbottom Road

Ramsbottom Road

Road

Moorbottom Road

18

CARR ROAD

A

B

BOLTON

C

Hazelhurst Close

Salmsbury Hall Cl

Avenue

A **B** **C**

I **2** **3** **4** **5** **6**

I grid square represents 500 metres

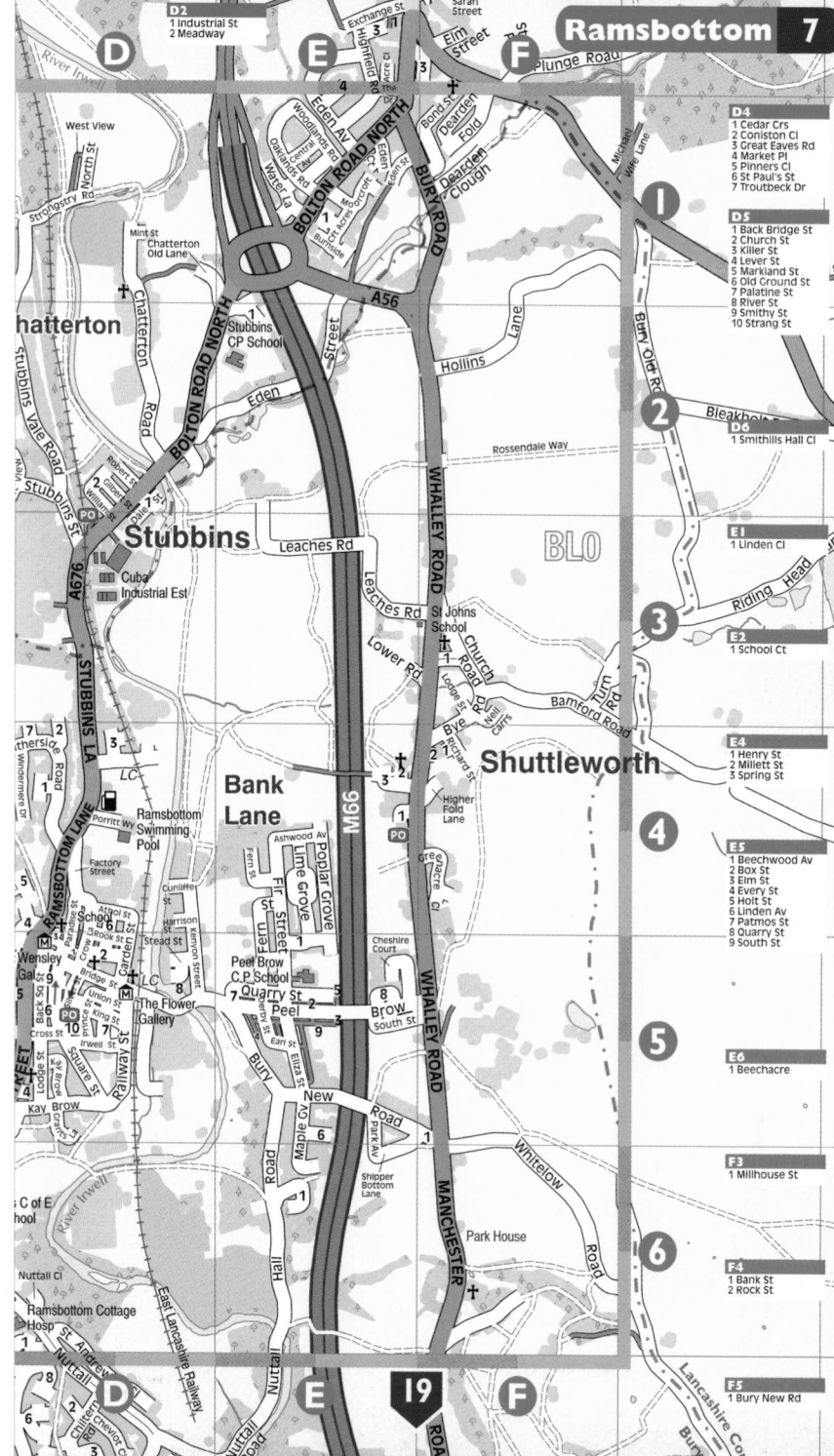

D2
1 Industrial St
2 Meadway

D4
1 Cedar Crs
2 Coniston Cl
3 Great Eaves Rd
4 Market Pl
5 Pinners Cl
6 St Paul's St
7 Troutbeck Dr

D5
1 Back Bridge St
2 Church St
3 Killer St
4 Lever St
5 Markland St
6 Old Ground St
7 Palatine St
8 River St
9 Smithy St
10 Strang St

D6
1 Smithills Hall Cl

E1
1 Linden Cl

E2
1 School Ct

E4
1 Henry St
2 Millett St
3 Spring St

E5
1 Beechwood Av
2 Box St
3 Elm St
4 Every St
5 Holt St
6 Linden Av
7 Patmos St
8 Quarry St
9 South St

E6
1 Beechacre

F3
1 Millhouse St

F4
1 Bank St
2 Rock St

F5
1 Bury New Rd

West View

Chatterton

Stubbins

Cuba
Industrial Est

Bank Lane

Ramsbottom Swimming Pool

Shuttleworth

BLO

Rossendale Way

Leaches Rd

Lower Rd

St Johns School

Peel Brow C.P School

The Flower Gallery

Cheshire Court

Brow South Rd

Park House

Ramsbottom Cottage Hosp

East Lancashire Railway

Lancashire Cou

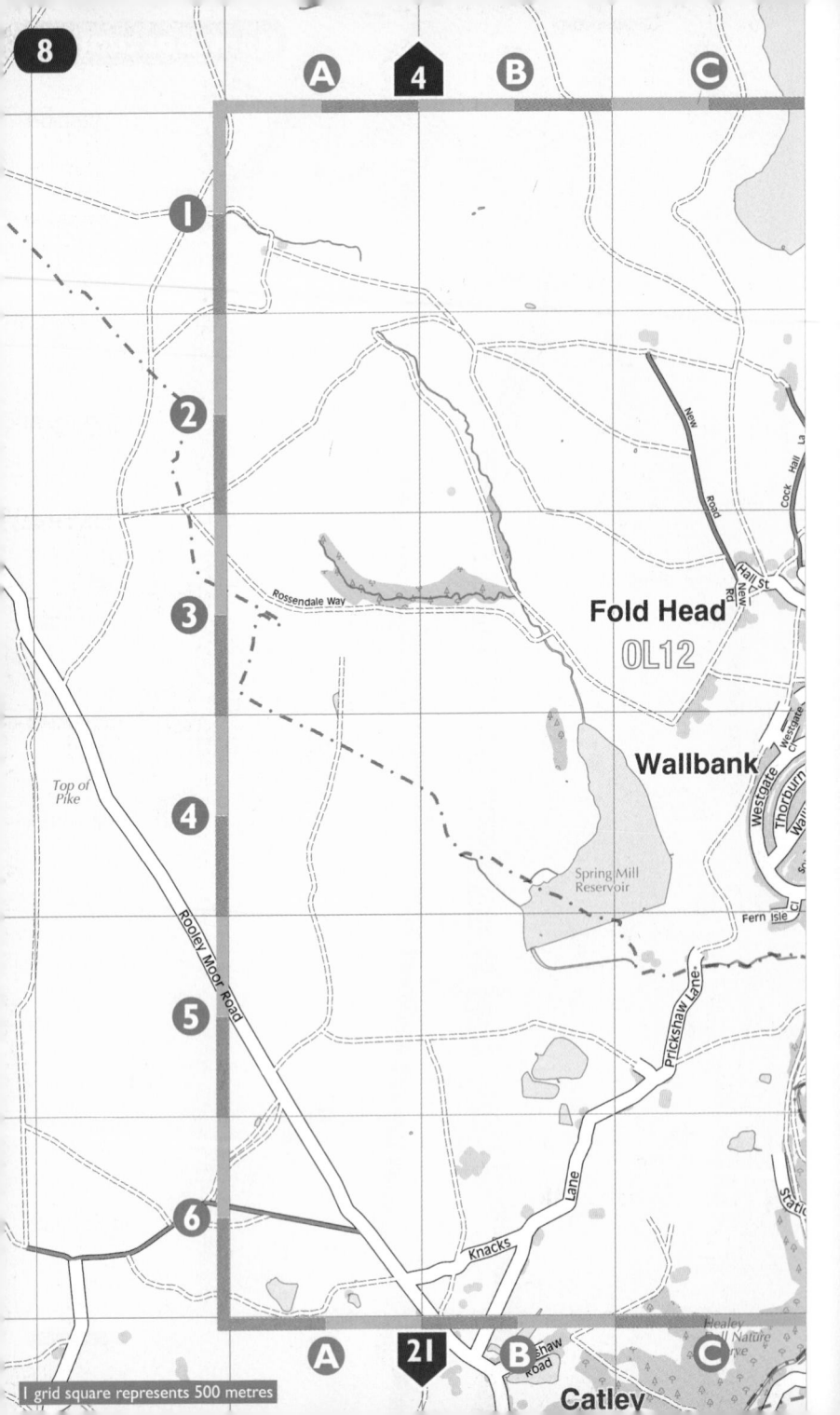

8

A 4 B C

1

2

3 Rossendale Way Fold Head OL12

Wallbank

Top of Pike

4 Spring Mill Reservoir

Fern Isle

5

Rooley Moor Road

Prickshaw Lane

6 Knacks Lane Healey Nature Reserve

A 21 B Shaw Road C

Catley

1 grid square represents 500 metres

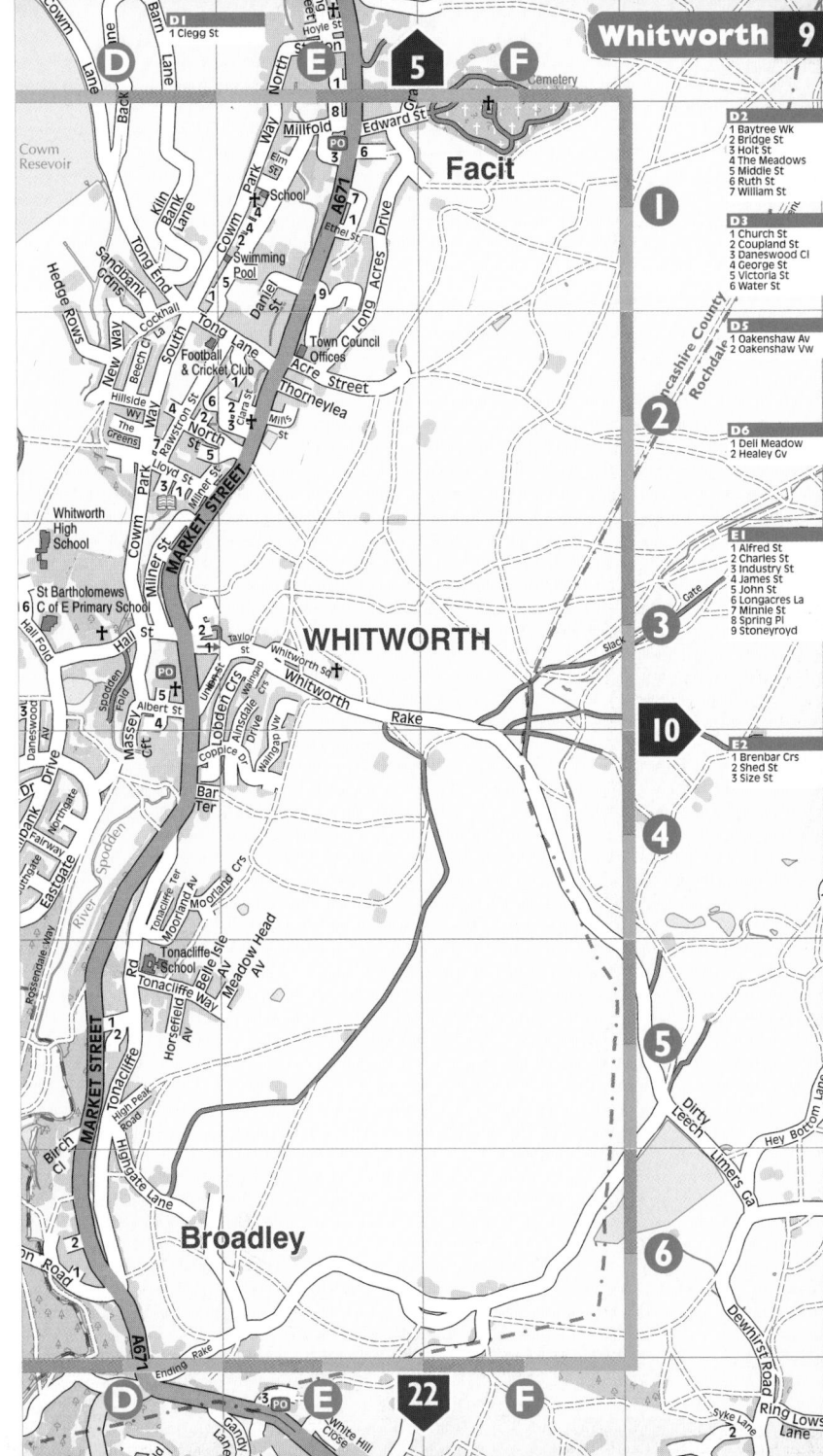

Cowm Reservoir

Facit

WHITWORTH

Broadley

Whitworth High School

St Bartholomews C of E Primary School

Town Council Offices

Football & Cricket Club

Swimming Pool

Cemetery

Lancashire County / Rochdale

MARKET STREET

A671

River Spodden

Whitworth Rake

A   B   C

Cemetery

Facit

1

Rossendale Way

Lancashire County
Rochdale

2

3

Gate

Slack

9

ke

4

Hard Lane

Watergove
Reservoir

Barn Field Lane

Lower House Lane

Bent La

Old

Clough House Lane

5

Hey Bottom Lane

Dirty Leech

Limers Ga

Hey Bottom Lane

Rydings Lane

6

Dewhirst Road

Ring Lows Lane

A   B   C

Lane

23

Ring Lows Lane

Great

Smallbridge
St Johns
C of E School

Rydings School

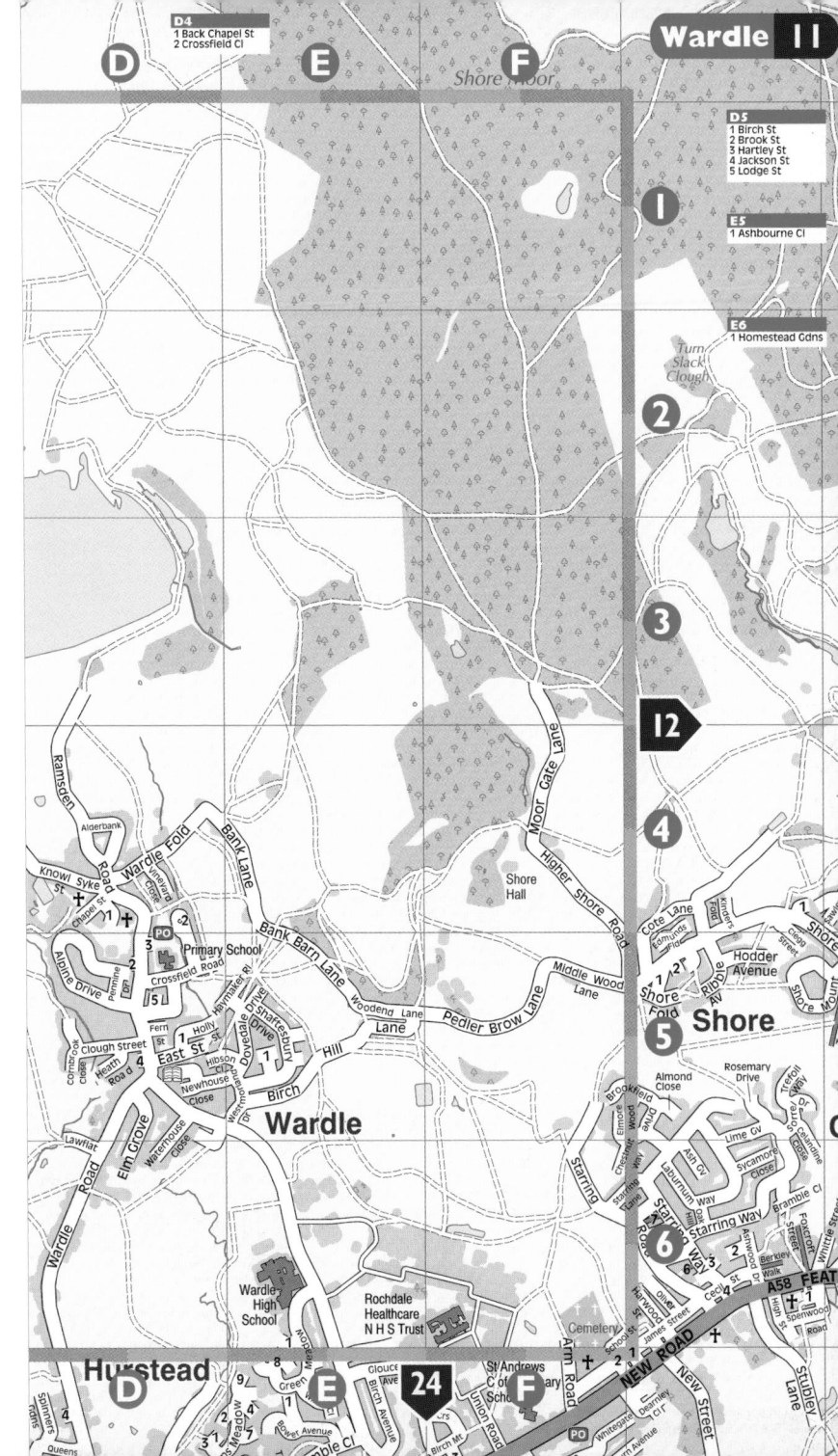

D4
1 Back Chapel St
2 Crossfield Cl

Shore Moor

D
E
F

D5
1 Birch St
2 Brook St
3 Hartley St
4 Jackson St
5 Lodge St

1

E5
1 Ashbourne Cl

E6
1 Homestead Gdns

Turn
Slack
Clough

2

3

12

4

Ramsden Road

Alderbank

Wardle Fold

Bank Lane

Knowl Syke St

Chapel St

PO

Primary School

Crossfield Road

Bank Barn Lane

Moor Gate Lane

Higher Shore Road

Shore
Hall

Cote Lane

Shore
Fold

Edmunds

Ribble Av

Hodder
Avenue

Shore
Mount

Shore

5

Shore

Alpine Drive

Pennine Dr

Fern St

Holly

East St

Haymaker Rl

Snaftesbury

Dovedale Drive

Middle Wood
Lane

Pedler Brow Lane

Woodend Lane

Westminster

Lane

Hill

Comm Crok Close

Heath
Road

Clough Street

Hibson

Newhouse
Close

Birch

Wardle

Brookfield

Almond
Close

Rosemary
Drive

Trefoil

Clementine

Fouracre
Street

Whittle Street

Lawflat

Elm Grove

Waterhouse
Close

Wardle
Road

Starling

Brookfield

Emmott

Crescent

Starling
Way

Laburnum Way

Ash Gr

Starling
Lane

Lime Gv

Sycamore
Close

Bramble Cl

C

6

Starring Way

Arnwood Dr

Berkley

Cecil St

A58 FEAT

Spenwood

High St

Whitle Cl

Stubley
Lane

Wardle
High
School

Rochdale
Healthcare
N H S Trust

Cemetery

Arm Road

School

New Road

James Street

Dearnley

New Street

Hurstead

D

Green

Glouce
Ave

Birch Avenue

24

St Andrews
C of E Primary
School

Union Road

Birch Mt

New Road

PO

Whitegate

Spenwood

Solinners

Meadow

Queens

Bower Avenue

Mole Cl

E

F

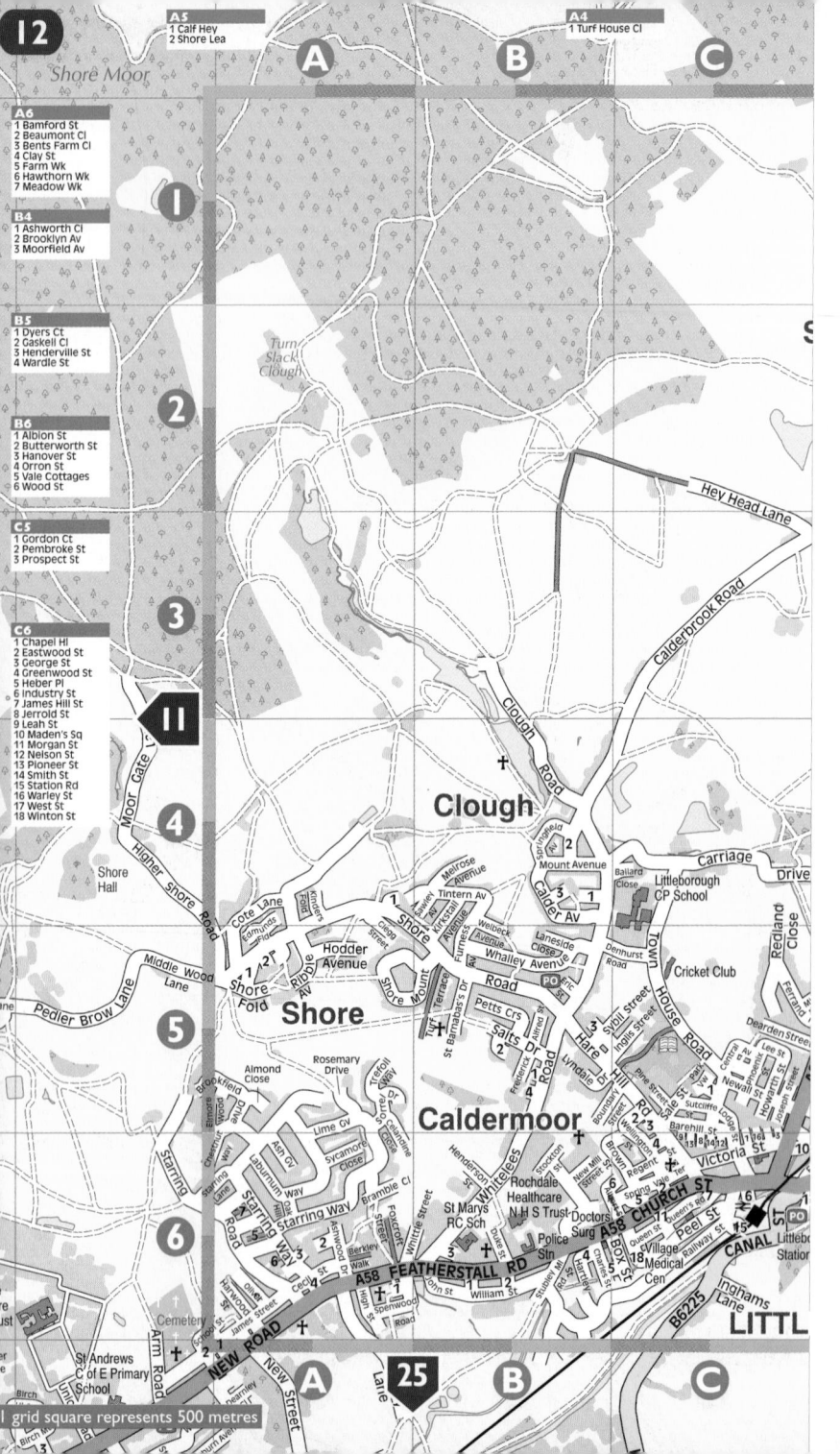

12

Shore Moor

A5
1 Calf Hey
2 Shore Lea

A4
1 Turf House Cl

A   B   C

A6
1 Bamford St
2 Beaumont Cl
3 Bents Farm Cl
4 Clay St
5 Farm Wk
6 Hawthorn Wk
7 Meadow Wk

B4
1 Ashworth Cl
2 Brooklyn Av
3 Moorfield Av

I

B5
1 Dyers Ct
2 Gaskell Cl
3 Henderville St
4 Wardle St

Turn
Slack
Clough

2

B6
1 Albion St
2 Butterworth St
3 Hanover St
4 Orron St
5 Vale Cottages
6 Wood St

Hey Head Lane

Calderbrook Road

C5
1 Gordon Ct
2 Pembroke St
3 Prospect St

3

C6
1 Chapel Hl
2 Eastwood St
3 George St
4 Greenwood St
5 Heber Pl
6 Industry St
7 James Hill St
8 Jerrold St
9 Leah St
10 Maden's Sq
11 Morgan St
12 Nelson St
13 Pioneer St
14 Smith St
15 Station Rd
16 Warley St
17 West St
18 Winton St

II

4

Clough Road

Clough

Mount Avenue

Carriage Drive

Ballard Close

Littleborough
CP School

Shore Hall

Higher Shore Road

Cote Lane

Melrose Avenue

Tintern Av

Calder Av

Redland Close

Cricket Club

Town House Road

Middle Wood Lane

Shore Fold

Hodder Avenue

Whalley Avenue

Laneside Close

Dearden Street

Shore

Pedler Brow Lane

5

Shore Mount

Road

Petts Crs

Saits Dr

Hare Hill

Sybil Street

Caldermoor

Rosemary Drive

Almond Close

Lyndale Dr

Victoria St

6

Starring Road

Starring Way

Lime Gv

Sycamore Close

Bramble Cl

St Marys
RC Sch

Rochdale
Healthcare
N H S Trust

Police
Stn

Doctors
Surg

Village
Medical
Cen

A58 CHURCH ST

CANAL

Station

Cemetery

St Andrews
C of E Primary
School

A58 FEATHERSTALL RD

NEW ROAD

New Street

25

B6225

Inghams Lane

LITTL

A   B   C

I grid square represents 500 metres

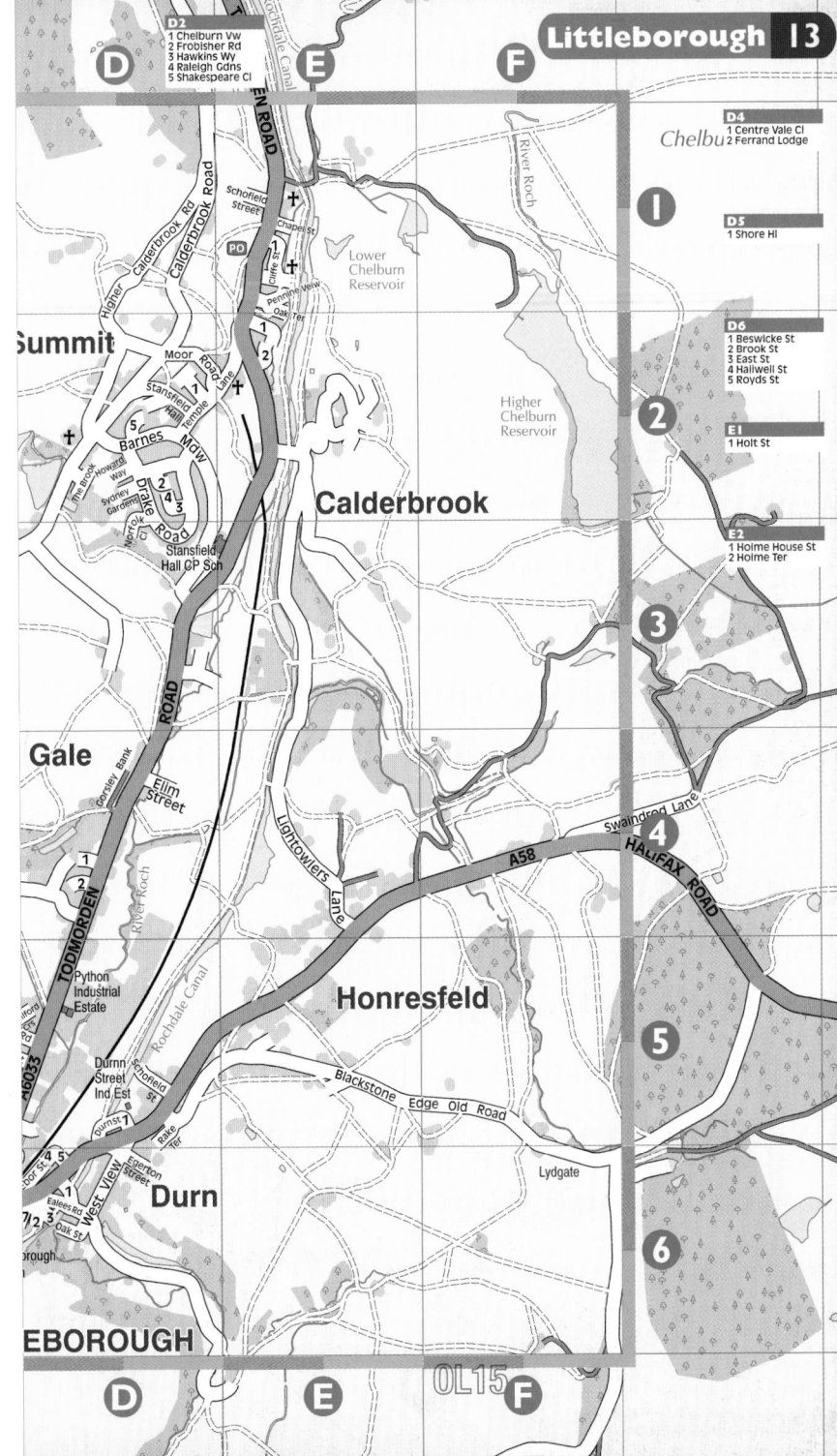

D2
1 Chelburn Vw
2 Frobisher Rd
3 Hawkins Wy
4 Raleigh Gdns
5 Shakespeare Cl

D4
1 Centre Vale Cl
2 Ferrand Lodge

D5
1 Shore Hl

D6
1 Beswicke St
2 Brook St
3 East St
4 Hallwell St
5 Royds St

E1
1 Holt St

E2
1 Holme House St
2 Holme Ter

Chelbu

Summit

Schofield Street

Chapel St

Cliffe St

PO

Pennine View

Oak Ter

Moor

Road Lane

Stansfield Hall Temple

Barnes Mdw

The Brook

Howard Way

Sydney Gardens

Drake Road

Norfo...

Stansfield Hall CP Sch

Lower Chelburn Reservoir

Higher Chelburn Reservoir

River Roch

Calderbrook

Calderbrook Road

Higher Calderbrook Rd

GREEN ROAD

Gale

Gorsley Bank

Elim Street

River Roch

TODMORDEN ROAD

Lightowlers Lane

Swaindrod Lane

A58 HALIFAX ROAD

Honresfeld

Python Industrial Estate

Durn Street Ind Est

Schofield St

Durnst

Rochdale Canal

Blackstone Edge Old Road

Rake Ter

Egerton Street

WEST VIEW

Ealees Rd

Oak St

Durn

Lydgate

A6033

...borough

EBOROUGH

OL15

D E F

I

2

3

4

5

6

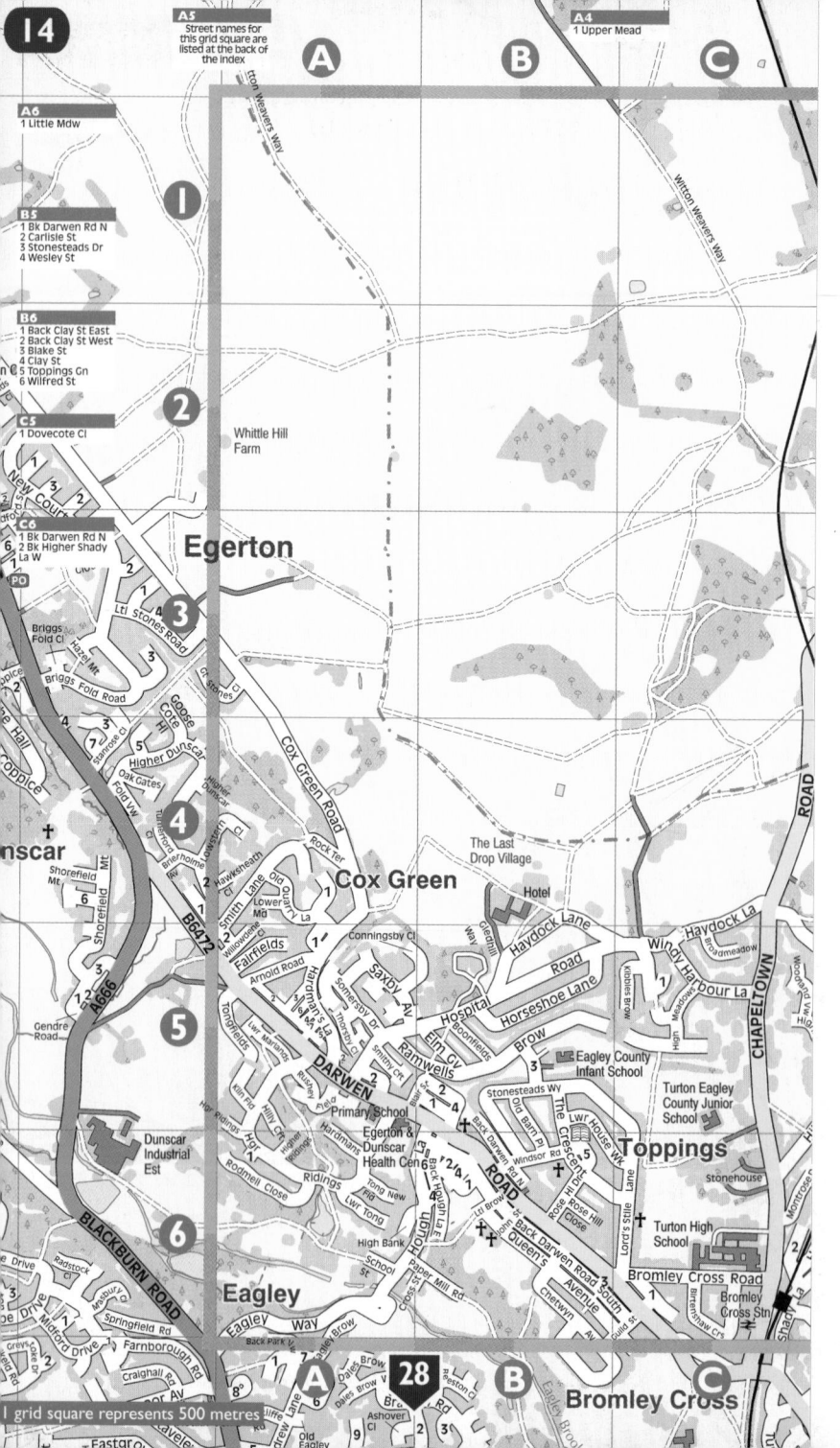

14

Whittle Hill
Farm

Egerton

Witton Weavers Way

Itton Weavers Way

Briggs
Fold Cl

Briggs Fold Road

Hazel Mt

Goose
Cote
Hill

Higher Dunscar

Oak Gates

Starrose Cl

Old Tw

nscar

Shorefield
Mt

Shorefield

Gendre
Road

Dunscar
Industrial
Est

BLACKBURN ROAD

Eagley

Cox Green Road

Rock Ter

Hawksheath
Cl

Smith
Lane

Lowery
Mdw

Old
Quarry La

Willowdene

Fairfields

Arnold Road

Conningsby Cl

Tonge Fold

Lwr Marlands

Hardman's Fld

Somersby Dr

Saxby Av

Thorpe Dr

Rushey
Field

Kiln Fld

Higher Ridings

Hgt

The Last
Drop Village

Gladman
Way

Haydock Lane

Hospital
Road

Horseshoe Lane

Rosenfields

Elm Gv

Ramwells

Smithy Cft

Haydock La
Broadmeadow

Windy Harbour La

Kibbles Brow

High
Meadow

Hotel

Brow

3

Eagley County
Infant School

Stonesteads Wy

Old Barn Rd

The Crescent

Lwr House Wk

Windsor Rd

5

Turton Eagley
County Junior
School

Toppings

Stonehouse

CHAPELTOWN ROAD

ROAD

DARWEN

Primary School

Egerton &
Dunscar
Health Cen

Rodmell Close

Hardman

Ridings

Lwr Tong

Tong New

High Bank

School
St

Back Hough La

Lwr Brow

Back Darwen Road South

Queen's

Paper Mill Rd

Cross Hough

Eagley
Way

Back Park V

Dales Brow

Eagley Brow

28

Ashover
Cl

Rose Hill
Close

Chetwyn
Av

Avenue

Lord's Stile
Lane

Turton High
School

Bromley Cross Road

Bromley
Cross Stn

Birtenshaw La

Shad

Bromley Cross

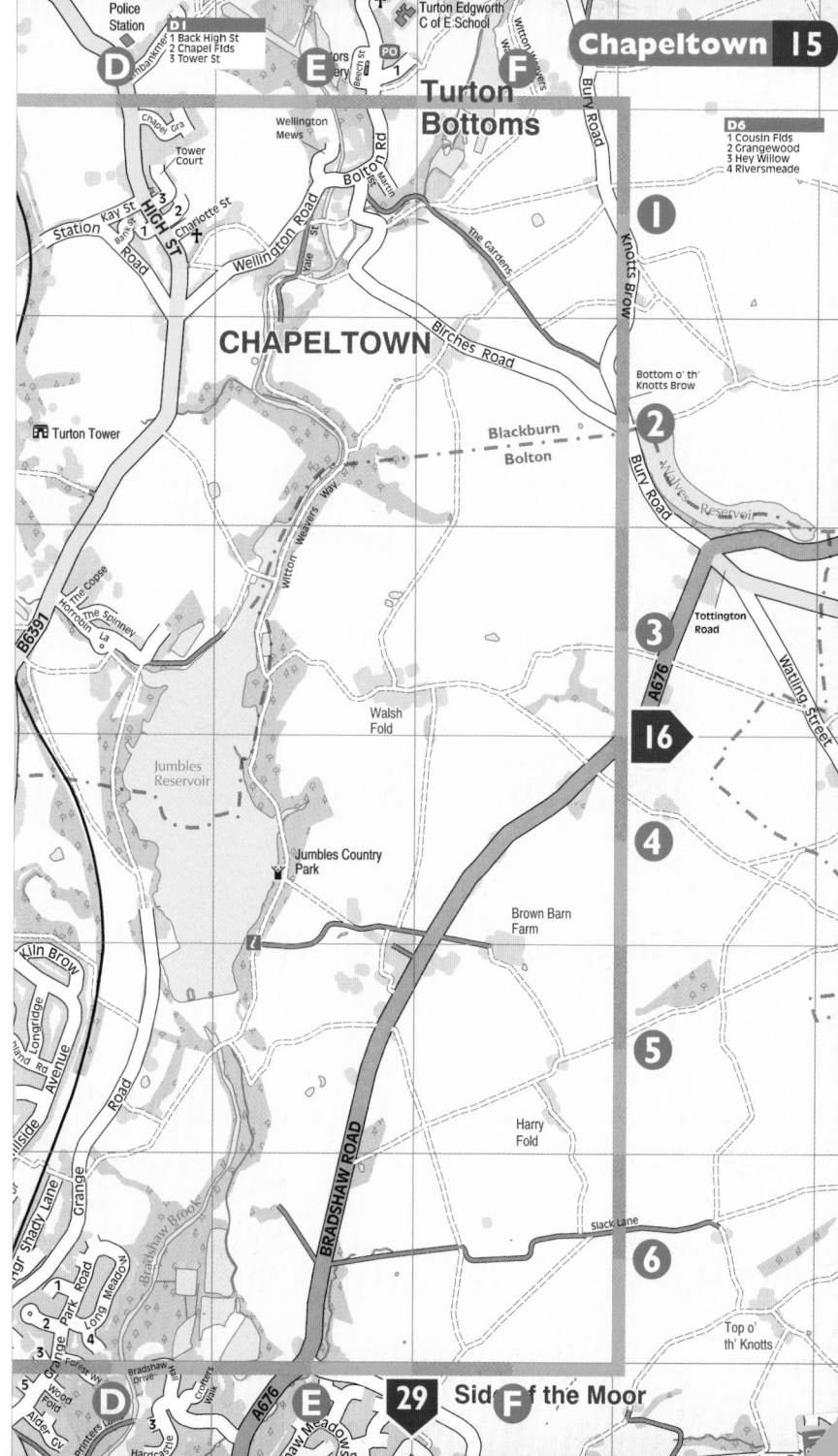

Police Station

D1
1 Back High St
2 Chapel Flds
3 Tower St

Turton Edgworth C of E. School

D6
1 Cousin Flds
2 Grangewood
3 Hey Willow
4 Riversmeade

Turton Bottoms

Witton Weavers

Bury Road

Wellington Mews

Chapel Gra

Tower Court

HIGH ST

Kay St
Bank St

Charlotte St

Station Road

Wellington Road

Bolton Road

Yale St

The Gardens

Knotts Brow

CHAPELTOWN

Birches Road

Turton Tower

Blackburn
Bolton

Bottom o' th'
Knotts Brow

Witton Weavers Way

B6391

The Copse
Horrobin La
The Spinney

Wayoh Reservoir

Bury Road

Tottington Road

A676

Watling Street

Jumbles Reservoir

Walsh Fold

16

Jumbles Country Park

Brown Barn Farm

Klin Brow

Longtidge
Avenue

Road

Hillside

Grange Lane

Bradshaw Brook

Bradshaw Drive

Hardcastle

Crofters Walk

Bradshaw Hall

BRADSHAW ROAD

Harry Fold

Slack Lane

Top o'
th' Knotts

Grange Park Road

Long Meadow

Wood Fold

Alder Cv

Printers

A676

Shaw Meadows

29 Side of the Moor

Turton Bottoms

16

Turton Edgworth School

Witton Weavers Way

Bury Road

The Gardens

Birches Road

Knotts Brow

Bottom o' th' Knotts Brow

Blackburn Bolton

Bury Road

Well' Reservoir

RAMSBOTTOM ROAD

Higher House Farm

Hawkshaw Lane

Quarlton Dr

Croichbank

Troutbeck Close

Two Brooks Lane

Tottington Road

B6213

TURTON ROAD

A676

15

Brown Barn Farm

Watling Street

Affetside
✝

Harry Fold

Slack Lane

Bury Bolton

Top o' th' Knotts

Watling Street

Side of the Moor

Ⓐ **30** Ⓑ Ⓒ

grid square represents 500 metres

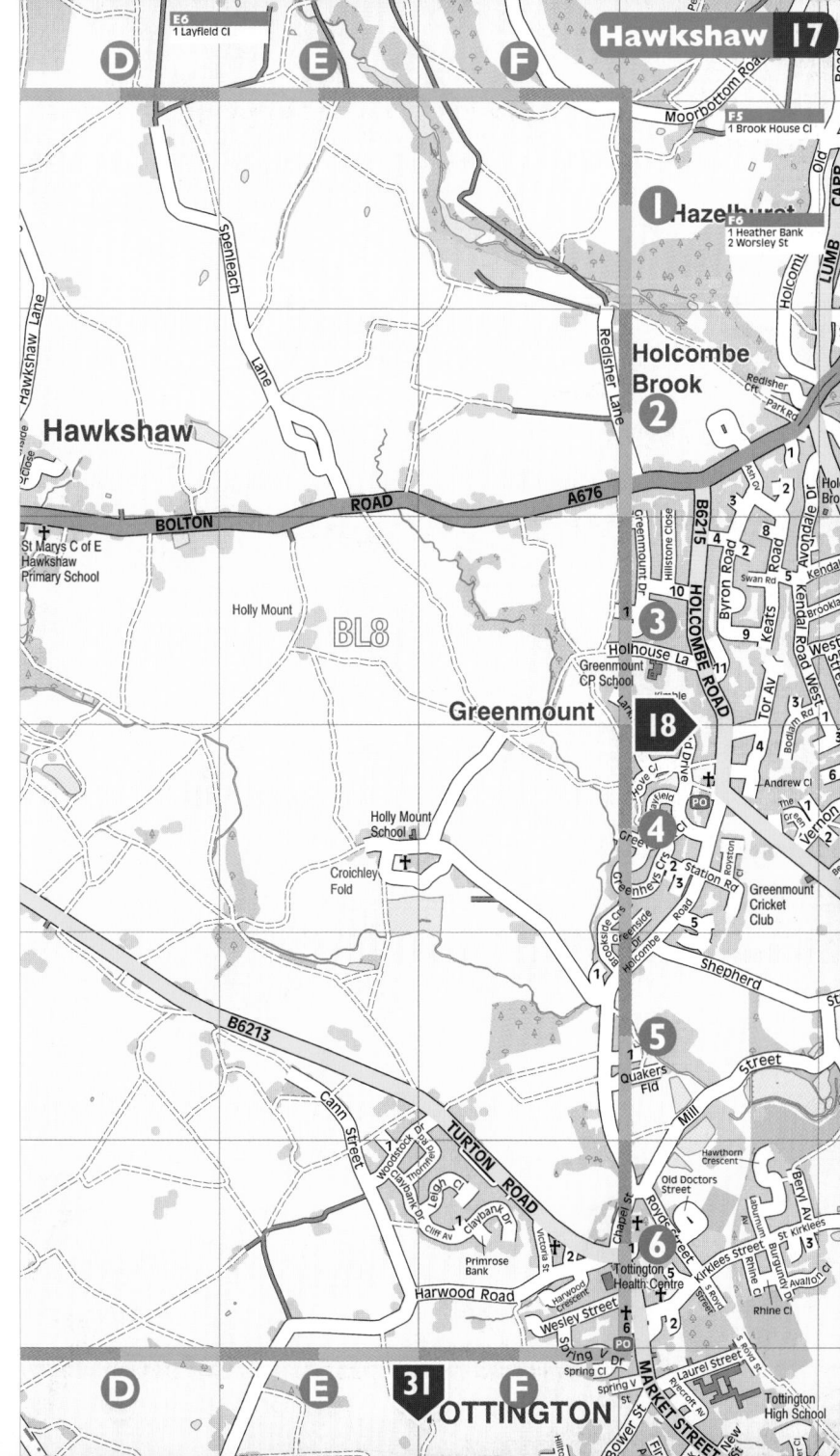

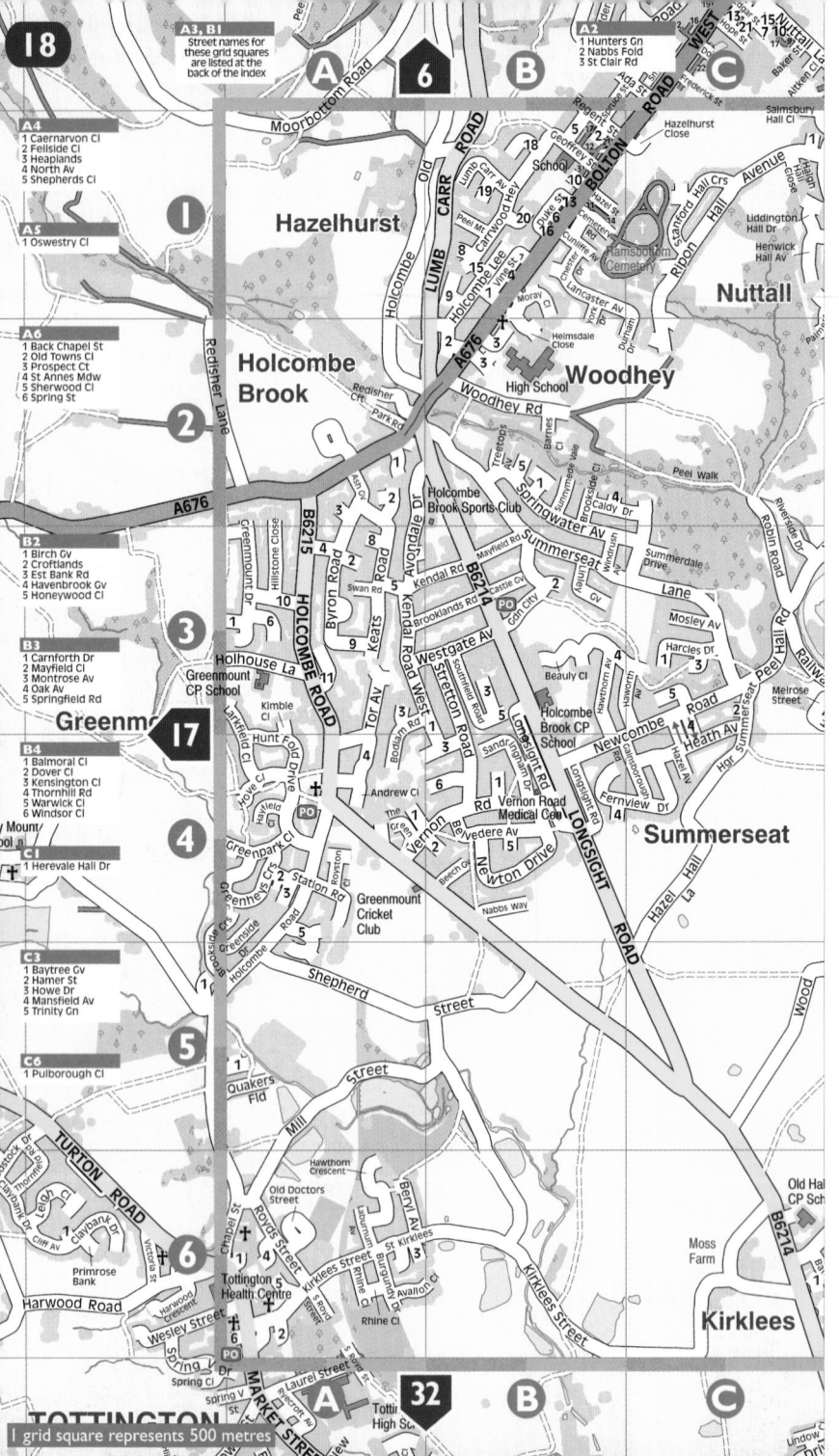

18

A3, B1
Street grid names for
these grid squares
are listed at the
back of the index

A 6 B C

A4
1 Caernarvon Cl
2 Fellside Cl
3 Heaplands
4 North Av
5 Shepherds Cl

A2
1 Hunters Gn
2 Nabbs Fold
3 St Clair Rd

A5
1 Oswestry Cl

A6
1 Back Chapel St
2 Old Towns Cl
3 Prospect Ct
4 St Annes Mdw
5 Sherwood Cl
6 Spring St

B2
1 Birch Gv
2 Croftlands
3 Est Bank Rd
4 Havenbrook Gv
5 Honeywood Cl

B3
1 Carnforth Dr
2 Mayfield Cl
3 Montrose Av
4 Oak Av
5 Springfield Rd

B4
1 Balmoral Cl
2 Dover Cl
3 Kensington Cl
4 Thornhill Rd
5 Warwick Cl
6 Windsor Cl

C1
1 Herevale Hall Dr

C3
1 Baytree Gv
2 Hamer St
3 Howe Dr
4 Mansfield Av
5 Trinity Gn

C6
1 Pulborough Cl

Hazelhurst

Holcombe
Brook

Greenm   **17**

Greenmount
CP School

Nuttall

Woodhey

High School

Summerseat

TOTTINGTON

A 32 B C

1 grid square represents 500 metres

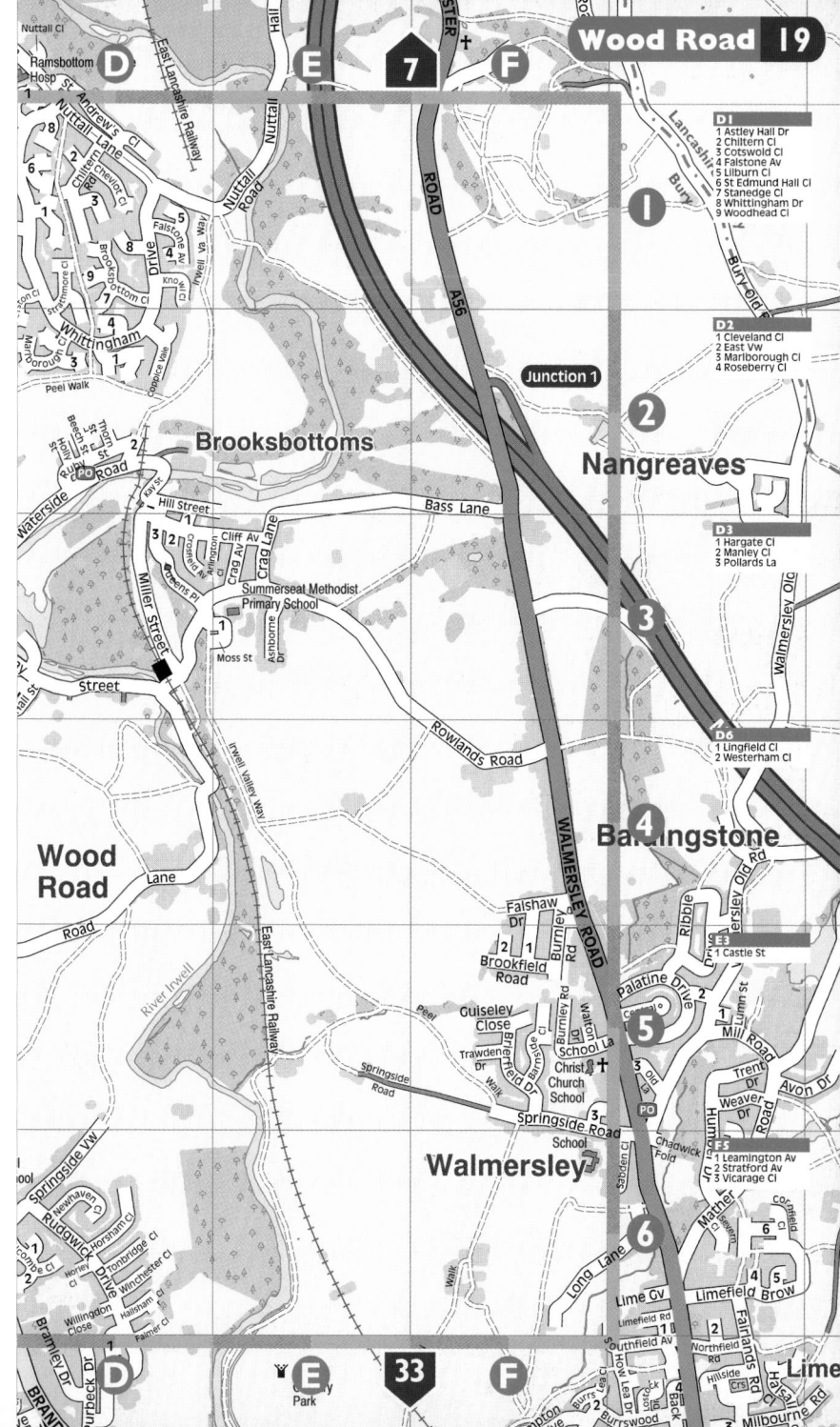

Nuttall Cl
Ramsbottom
Hosp

D

East Lancashire Railway

St Andrew's Cl
Nuttall Lane

Chiltern Cl
Cheviat Cl

Falstone Av
Drive
Brooksbottom Cl

Whittingham

Streetmore Cl
Whittingham Cl
Marlborough

Peel Walk

Thom St
Beech St
Ruby St
Rudby St

E

Nuttall Road
Nuttall Hall

7

F

ROAD
A56

Wood Road `19`

D1
1 Astley Hall Dr
2 Chiltern Cl
3 Cotswold Cl
4 Falstone Av
5 Lilburn Cl
6 St Edmund Hall Cl
7 Stanedge Cl
8 Whittingham Dr
9 Woodhead Cl

Lancashire
Bury
Bury Old Rd

I

D2
1 Cleveland Cl
2 East Vw
3 Marlborough Cl
4 Roseberry Cl

2

Nangreaves

Po

Road

Waterside

Brooksbottoms

Hill Street
Cliff Av
Crossfield Av
Crag Av
Crag Lane
Queens Pl

Bass Lane

Miller Street

Summerseat Methodist
Primary School

Moss St

Ashborne Dr

Street

Irwell Valley Way

**Wood
Road**

Lane

Road

River Irwell

East Lancashire Railway

Peel

Springside
Road

Walmersley Old Rd

3

D3
1 Hargate Cl
2 Manley Cl
3 Pollards La

Walmersley Old

D6
1 Lingfield Cl
2 Westerham Cl

Ba...ingstone

4

WALMERSLEY ROAD

Falshaw
Dr

Burnley Rd

**Brookfield
Road**
2 1

Guiseley
Close

Brierfield Dr
Barnside
Trawden Dr

Burnley Rd

Walton
School La

Christ
Church
School

Springside Road

School

Walmersley

Ribble

E3
1 Castle St

Palatine Drive

Lumn St

Mill Road

Trent
Dr
Weaver
Dr

Humber

Avon Dr
Road

5

PO

Chadwick
Fold

Sabden Cl

F5
1 Leamington Av
2 Stratford Av
3 Vicarage Cl

Mather

cornfield

Severn

6

6

Long Lane

Lime Gv

Limefield Rd

Southfield Av

Limefield **Brow**

4 5

Fairlands
Rd
Northfield
Rd
Hillside
Crs

Lime

Hazel

Milbourne

Springside Vw

Newhaven

Rudgwick

Horsham
Drive

Tonbridge
Cl
Winchester Cl

Willingdon
Close
Hailsham
Cl
Palmer Cl

Horley Cl

Bramley Dr

BRAND...

Purbeck Dr

D

E
Country
Park

33

F

Burrswood

Back

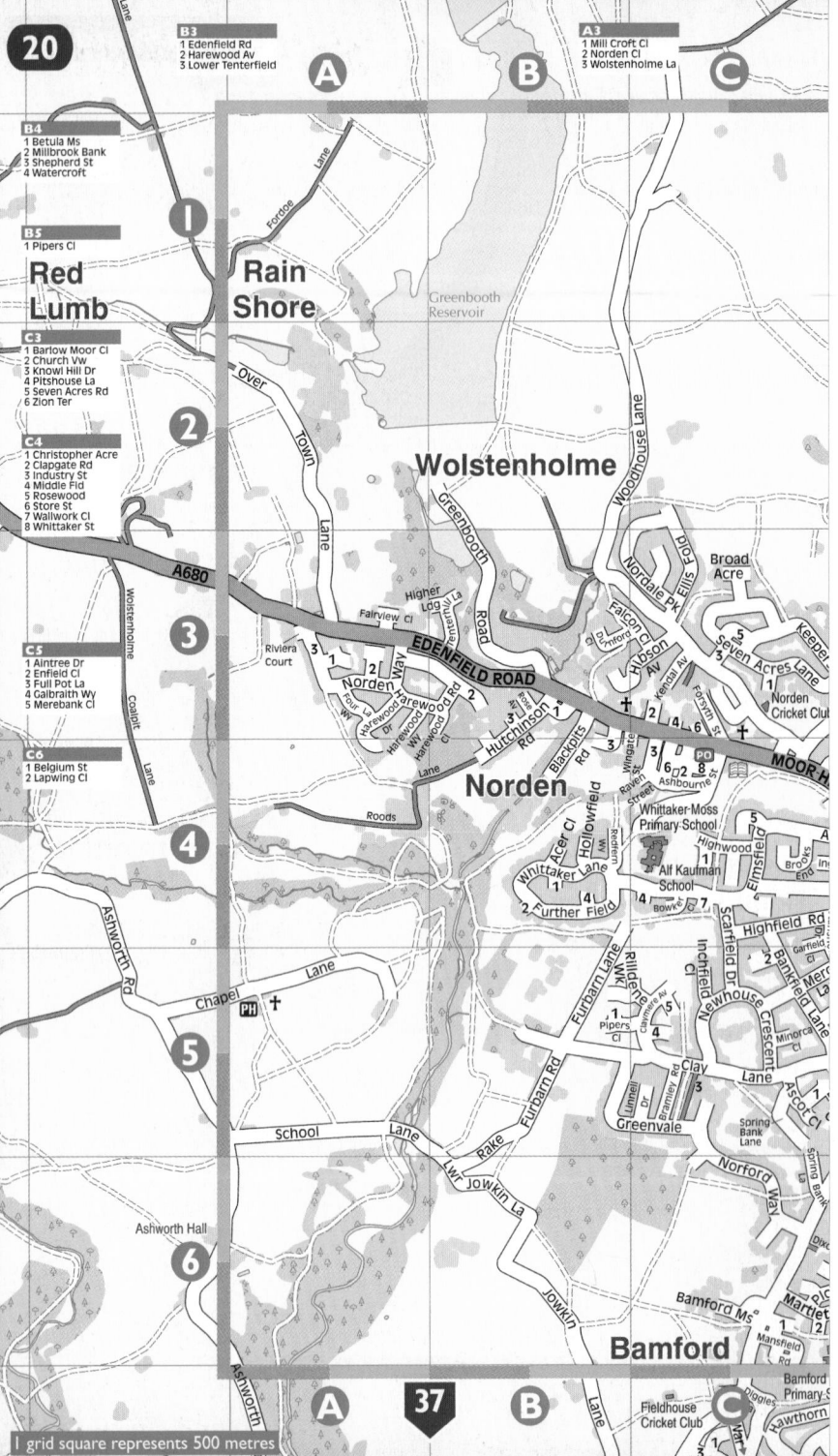

B3
1 Edenfield Rd
2 Harewood Av
3 Lower Tenterfield

A3
1 Mill Croft Cl
2 Norden Cl
3 Wolstenholme La

B4
1 Betula Ms
2 Millbrook Bank
3 Shepherd St
4 Watercroft

B5
1 Pipers Cl

Red Lumb

Rain Shore

Greenbooth Reservoir

C3
1 Barlow Moor Cl
2 Church Vw
3 Knowl Hill Dr
4 Pitshouse La
5 Seven Acres Rd
6 Zion Ter

C4
1 Christopher Acre
2 Clapgate Rd
3 Industry St
4 Middle Fld
5 Rosewood
6 Store St
7 Wallwork Cl
8 Whittaker St

Wolstenholme

Broad Acre

Seven Acres Lane

Norden Cricket Club

C5
1 Aintree Dr
2 Enfield Cl
3 Full Pot La
4 Galbraith Wy
5 Merebank Cl

EDENFIELD ROAD

Norden

MOOR

C6
1 Belgium St
2 Lapwing Cl

Whittaker Moss Primary School

Alf Kaufman School

Highfield Rd

Pipers Cl

Clay Lane

Greenvale

Spring Bank Lane

Norford Way

School Lane

Ashworth Hall

Bamford Ms

Bamford

Fieldhouse Cricket Club

Bamford Primary

1 grid square represents 500 metres

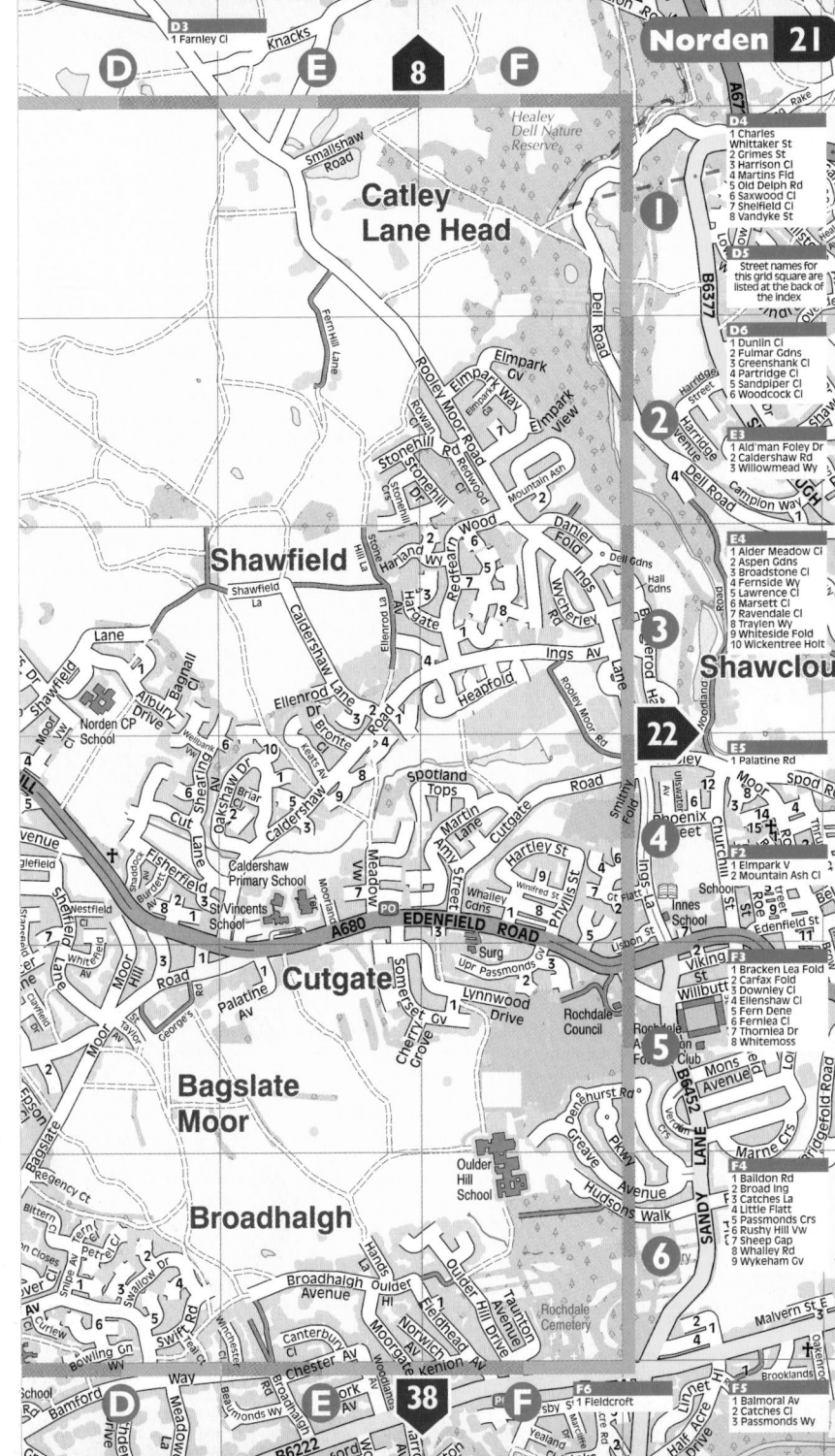

Knacks

D3
1 Farnley Cl

Healey
Dell Nature
Reserve

Smallshaw
Road

**Catley
Lane Head**

Dell Road

Fern Hill Lane

Elmpark
Gv

Elmpark Way

Elmpark View

Rooley Moor Road

Rowan Dr

Elmpark Wy

Stonehill Rd

Redwood

Mountain Ash

Stonehill Dr

Stonehill

Daniel
Fold

Dell Gdns

Shawfield

Stone La

Harland Av

Redfearn Wood

Hargate

Wycherley Rd

Ings

Hall
Gdns

Shawfield
La

Ellenrod Lane

Ings Av

Rooley Moor Rd

Lane

Caldershaw Lane

Ellenrod
Dr

Bronte
Road

Heapfold

Bagnall

Albury
Drive

**Norden CP
School**

Westbank

Shearing

Oakshaw Dr

Briar
Cl

Caldershaw

Kents Av

Spotland
Tops

Cutgate
Road

Smithy
Fold

Moor

Shawfield

Fisherfield

Shaddock

Burnet

Cut Lane

Meadow
Vw

Moorlands

Martin
Lane

Amy Street

Hartley St

Phyllis St

Gt Flatt

**Caldershaw
Primary School**

TSB

Whalley
Gdns

Winifred St

Winfred St

Lisbon St

Innes
School

A680

PO

EDENFIELD ROAD

Surg

Edenfield St

School

Westfield

Sheffield Cl

Whitefield Cl

Moor Hill
Road

Palatine
Av

Taylor

St Georges

Upr Passmonds

Lynnwood
Drive

Cutgate

Somerset
Gv

Cherry
Grove

**Rochdale
Council**

Rochdale
AFC
Football
Club

Viking
St

Willbutt

Mons
Avenue

**Bagslate
Moor**

Bagslate

Regency Ct

Denehurst Rd

Greave Pkwy

Vernon

Marne Crs

Broadhalgh

Bittern

Swift Rd

Swallow Dr

Snipe Av

Petrel

Curlew

**Oulder Hill
School**

Hudsons Walk

Greave Avenue

Broadhalgh
Avenue

Oulder
Hl

Oulder Hill Drive

Fieldhead

Norwich Av

Moorgate

Kenion

Taunton
Avenue

**Rochdale
Cemetery**

Bamford

Thenden
Drive

Greenfield

Bowling Gn

Swift Rd

Winchester

Canterbury
Av

Chester Av

Moorgate Av

Woodland

York
Av

B6222

Lowerford

Bealmonds Wy

Yealand

Tinks

Martlett

Brooklands

Half Acre
Drive

Malvern St E

Shawclough

A67

B6377

B6452

Sandy Lane

Churchill St

Phoenix Street

Spod

D E 8 F

I 2 3 22 4 5 6

38 D E F

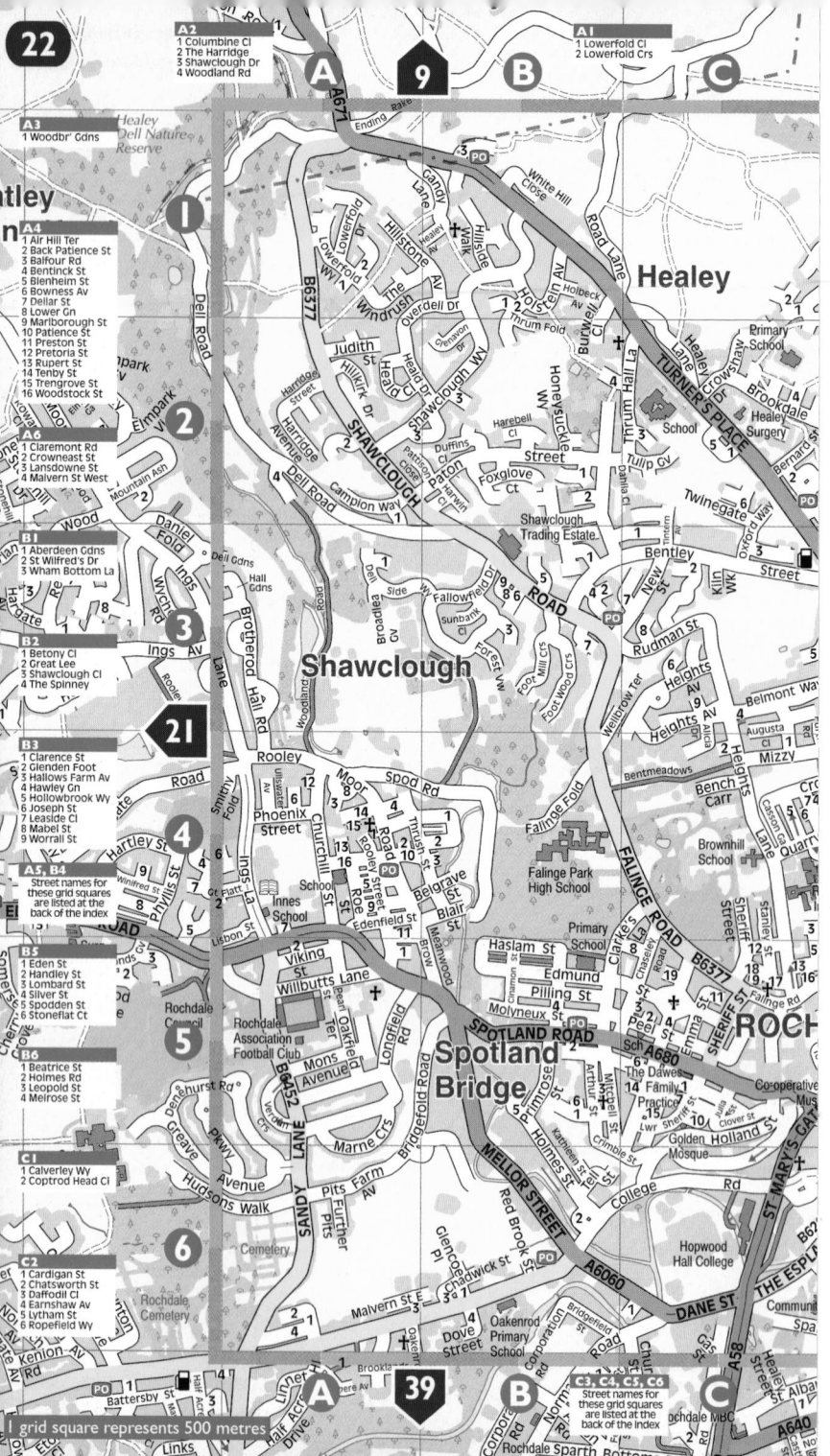

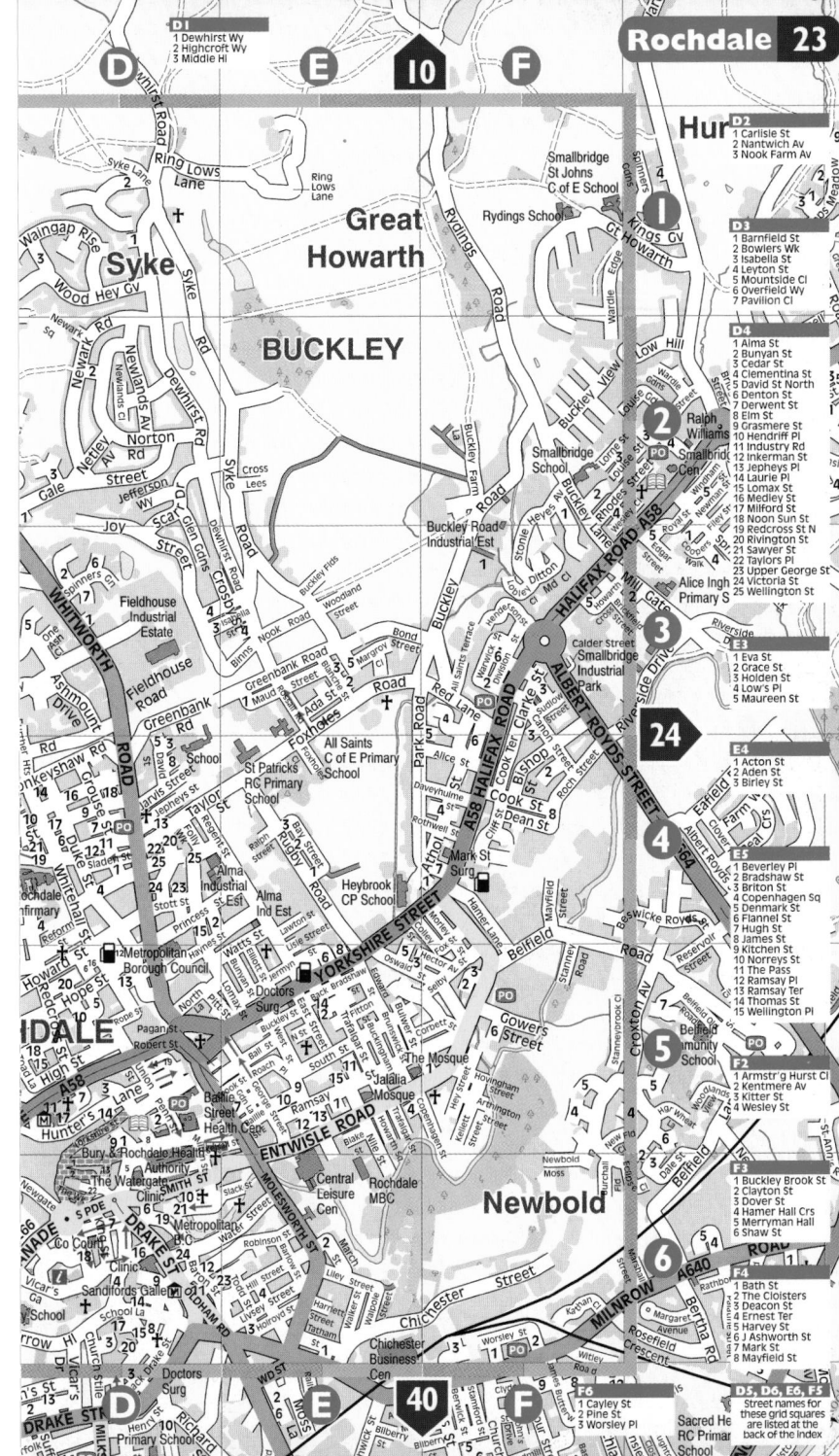

I grid square represents 500 metres

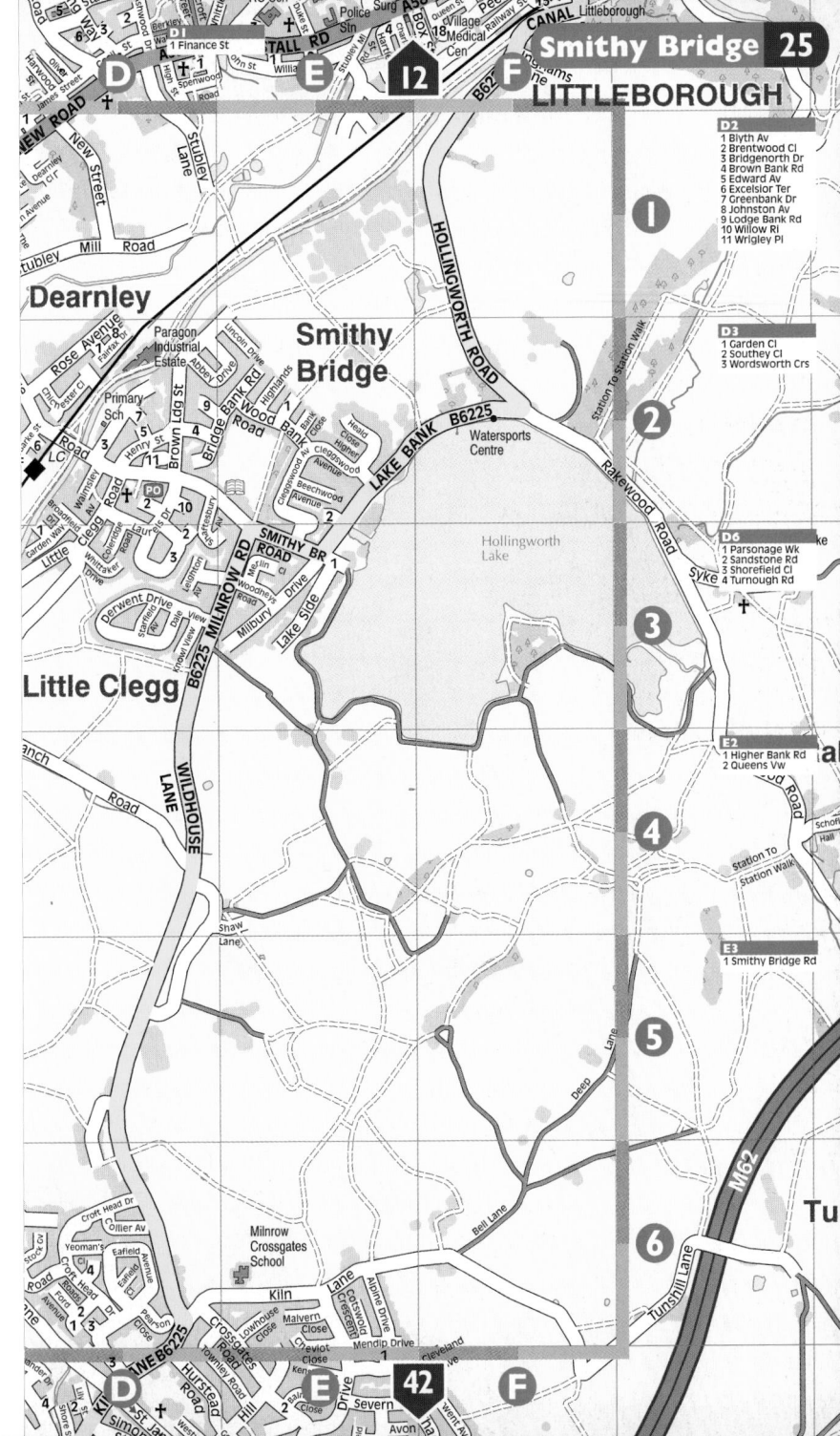

LITTLEBOROUGH

D2
1 Blyth Av
2 Brentwood Cl
3 Bridgenorth Dr
4 Brown Bank Rd
5 Edward Av
6 Excelsior Ter
7 Greenbank Dr
8 Johnston Av
9 Lodge Bank Rd
10 Willow Rl
11 Wrigley Pl

D3
1 Garden Cl
2 Southey Cl
3 Wordsworth Crs

D6
1 Parsonage Wk
2 Sandstone Rd
3 Shorefield Cl
4 Turnough Rd

E2
1 Higher Bank Rd
2 Queens Vw

E3
1 Smithy Bridge Rd

Dearnley

Smithy Bridge

Little Clegg

Hollingworth Lake

Watersports Centre

Milnrow Crossgates School

M62

Tu

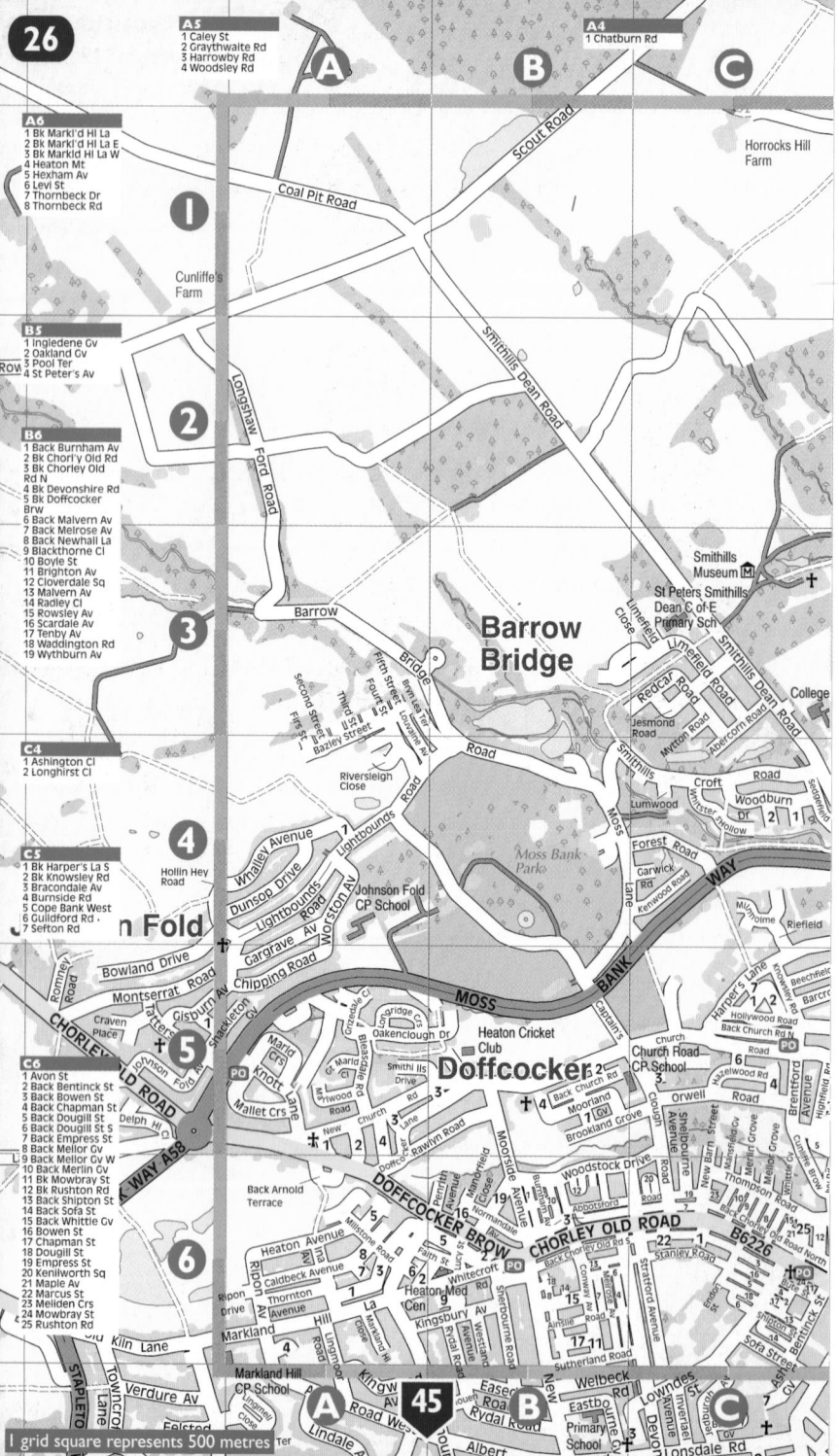

26

A6
1 Bk Markl'd Hl La
2 Bk Markl'd Hl La E
3 Bk Markld Hl La W
4 Heaton Mt
5 Hexham Av
6 Levi St
7 Thornbeck Dr
8 Thornbeck Rd

B5
1 Ingledene Gv
2 Oakland Gv
3 Pool Ter
4 St Peter's Av

B6
1 Back Burnham Av
2 Bk Chorl'y Old Rd
3 Bk Chorley Old Rd N
4 Bk Devonshire Rd
5 Bk Doffcocker Brw
6 Back Malvern Av
7 Back Melrose Av
8 Back Newhall La
9 Blackthorne Cl
10 Boyle St
11 Brighton Av
12 Cloverdale Sq
13 Malvern Av
14 Radley Cl
15 Rowsley Av
16 Scardale Av
17 Tenby Av
18 Waddington Rd
19 Wythburn Av

C4
1 Ashington Cl
2 Longhirst Cl

C5
1 Bk Harper's La S
2 Bk Knowsley Rd
3 Bracondale Av
4 Burnside Rd
5 Cope Bank West
6 Guildford Rd
7 Sefton Rd

C6
1 Avon St
2 Back Bentinck St
3 Back Bowen St
4 Back Chapman St
5 Back Dougill St
6 Back Dougill St S
7 Back Empress St
8 Back Mellor Gv
9 Back Mellor Gv W
10 Bk Merlin Gv
11 Bk Mowbray St
12 Bk Rushton Rd
13 Back Shipton St
14 Back Sofa St
15 Back Whittle Gv
16 Bowen St
17 Chapman St
18 Dougill St
19 Empress St
20 Kenilworth Sq
21 Maple Av
22 Marcus St
23 Meliden Crs
24 Mowbray St
25 Rushton Rd

Horrocks Hill Farm

Coal Pit Road

Scout Road

Cunliffe's Farm

Smithills Dean Road

Longshaw

Ford Road

Smithills Museum

St Peters Smithills Dean C of E Primary Sch

Barrow

Limefield Close

Redcar

Limefield Road

Smithills Dean Road

College

Jesmond Road

Myston Road

Abercorn Road

Barrow Bridge

Bridge

Bury Lea Ter

Firth Street

Fourth St

Third St

Lowaine

Second Street

Bayley Street

First St

Riversleigh Close

Road

Croft

Road

Lumwood

Winster Hollow

Woodburn Dr

Moss Bank Park

Forest Road

Garwick Rd

Kenwood Road

Hollin Hey Road

Whaley Avenue

Dunsop Drive

Lightbounds

Lightbounds Road

Gargrave Av

Wolston Av

Chipping Road

Johnson Fold CP School

Moss Lane

Captain's La

MOSS BANK WAY

Riefield

Milnthorpe

Beechfield

Barcr

n Fold

Bowland Drive

Montserrat Road

Gisburn Av

Shackleton Cl

Oakenclough Dr

Maria Crs

Maria Crs

Harwood Rd

Bleasdale Rd

Church

Heaton Cricket Club

Church Road CP School

Harper's Lane

Hollywood Road

Back Church Rd N

PO

Romney Road

Tattersall

Craven Place

Delph Hl

Knott La

Mallet Crs

New

Smithills Drive

Rd

Doffcocker

Back Church Rd

Moorland

Gv

Brookland Grove

Clough Avenue

Orwell

Road

Shelbourne Avenue

Brentford Avenue

Mellor Grove

Highfield Road

Conner Brow

Back Arnold Terrace

New

Church Lane

Rawlyn Road

Moorside Avenue

Woodstock Drive

Abbotsford Road

Jam Street

Mansfield Grove

Thompson Avenue

Oldham Gv

Road

Road North

DOFFCOCKER BROW

Heaton Avenue

Ripon

Caldbeck Avenue

Milnrow Road

Farm La

Whitecroft

Normandale

Manthorpe Close

Hawthorn Close

Sherbourne Avenue

Back Chorley Old Rd

CHORLEY OLD ROAD

Stratford Avenue

Stanley Road

B6226

PO

Sofa Street

Thornton Avenue

Ripon Drive

Heaton Med Cen

Kingsbury Avenue

La

Westland Avenue

Rydal Road

Ainslie Road

Sutherland Road

Bentinck St

Markland Hill

Kiln Lane

Towncroft

Stapleto Lane

Verdure Av

Markland Hill CP School

Kingw Av

Lindale Av

45

Felsted

Lindale

Close

Ter

Easedale Road

Rydal Road

A

Eastbank Primary School

Welbeck Rd

Lonsdale Road

Lowndes Inverlael

Devonsh

Albert

Road

B

C

I grid square represents 500 metres

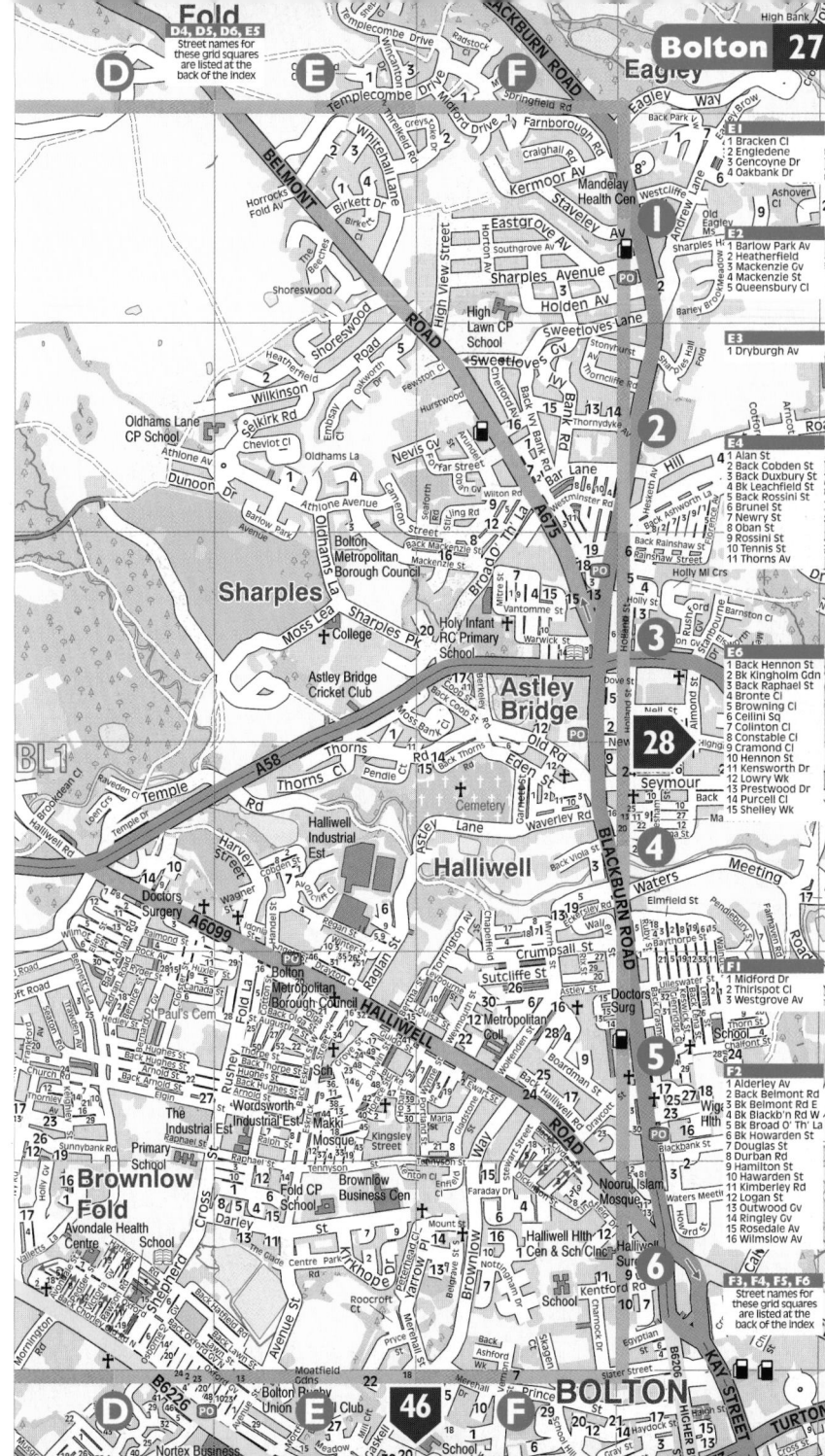

Fold
D4, D5, D6, E5
Street names for
these grid squares
are listed at the
back of the Index

High Bank

Eagley

E1
1 Bracken Cl
2 Engledene
3 Gencoyne Dr
4 Oakbank Dr

E2
1 Barlow Park Av
2 heatherfield
3 Mackenzie Gv
4 Mackenzie St
5 Queensbury Cl

E3
1 Dryburgh Av

E4
1 Alan St
2 Back Cobden St
3 Back Duxbury St
4 Bk Leachfield St
5 Back Rossini St
6 Brunel St
7 Newry St
8 Oban St
9 Rossini St
10 Tennis St
11 Thorns Av

E5
1 Back Hennon St
2 Bk Kingholm Gdn
3 Back Raphael St
4 Bronte Cl
5 Browning Cl
6 Ceilini Sq
7 Colinton Cl
8 Constable Cl
9 Cramond Cl
10 Hennon St
11 Kensworth Dr
12 Lowry Wk
13 Prestwood Dr
14 Purcell Cl
15 Shelley Wk

F1
1 Midford Dr
2 Thirlspot Cl
3 Westgrove Av

F5
1 Alderley Av
2 Back Belmont Rd
3 Bk Belmont Rd E
4 Bk Blackb'n Rd W
5 Bk Broad O' Th' La
6 Bk Howarden St
7 Douglas St
8 Durban St
9 Hamilton St
10 Hawarden St
11 Kimberley Rd
12 Logan St
13 Outwood Gv
14 Ringley Gv
15 Rosedale Av
16 Wilmslow Av

F3, F4, F5, F6
Street names for
these grid squares
are listed at the
back of the index

Sharples

Astley Bridge

Halliwell

Brownlow Fold

BOLTON

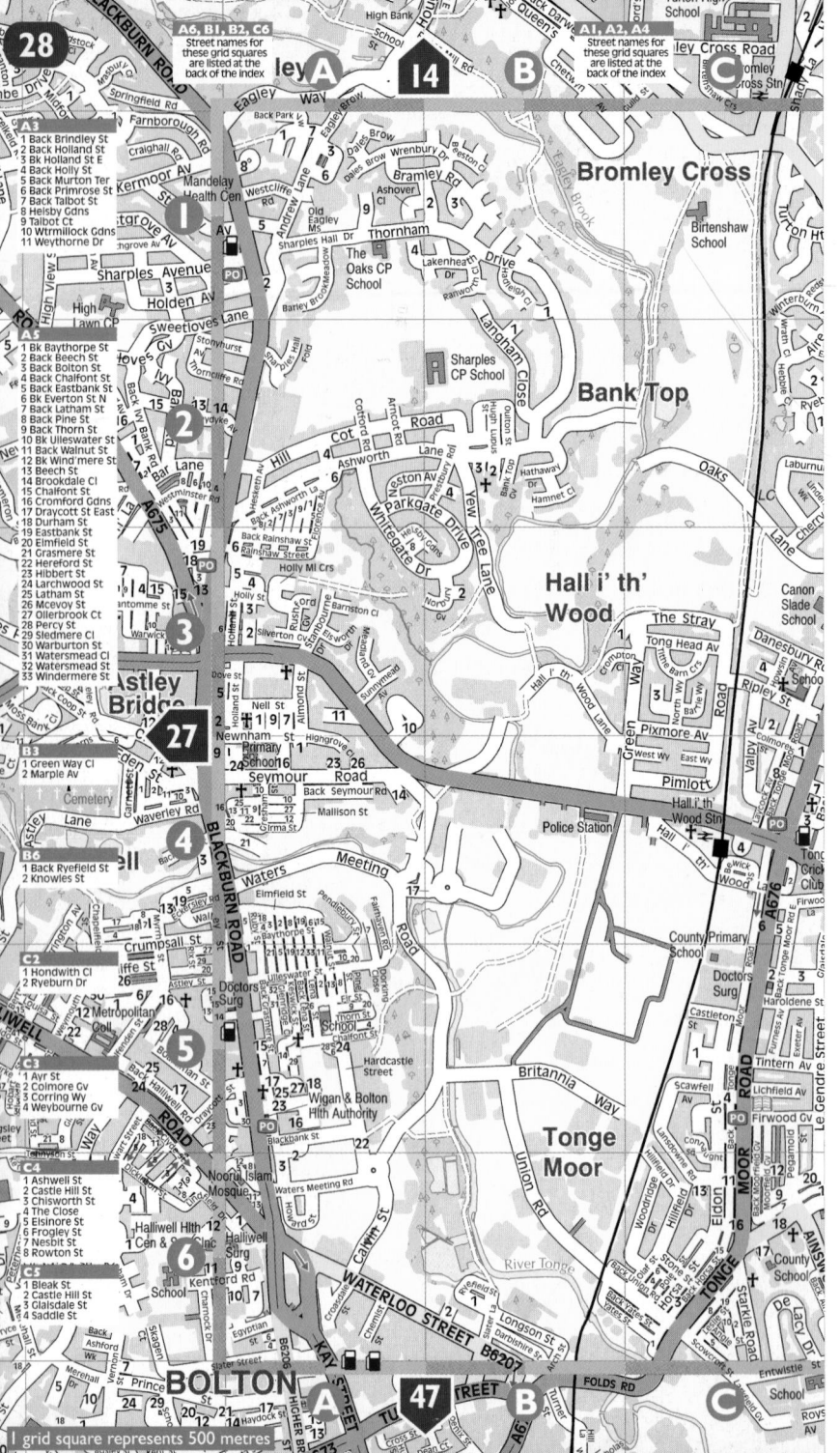

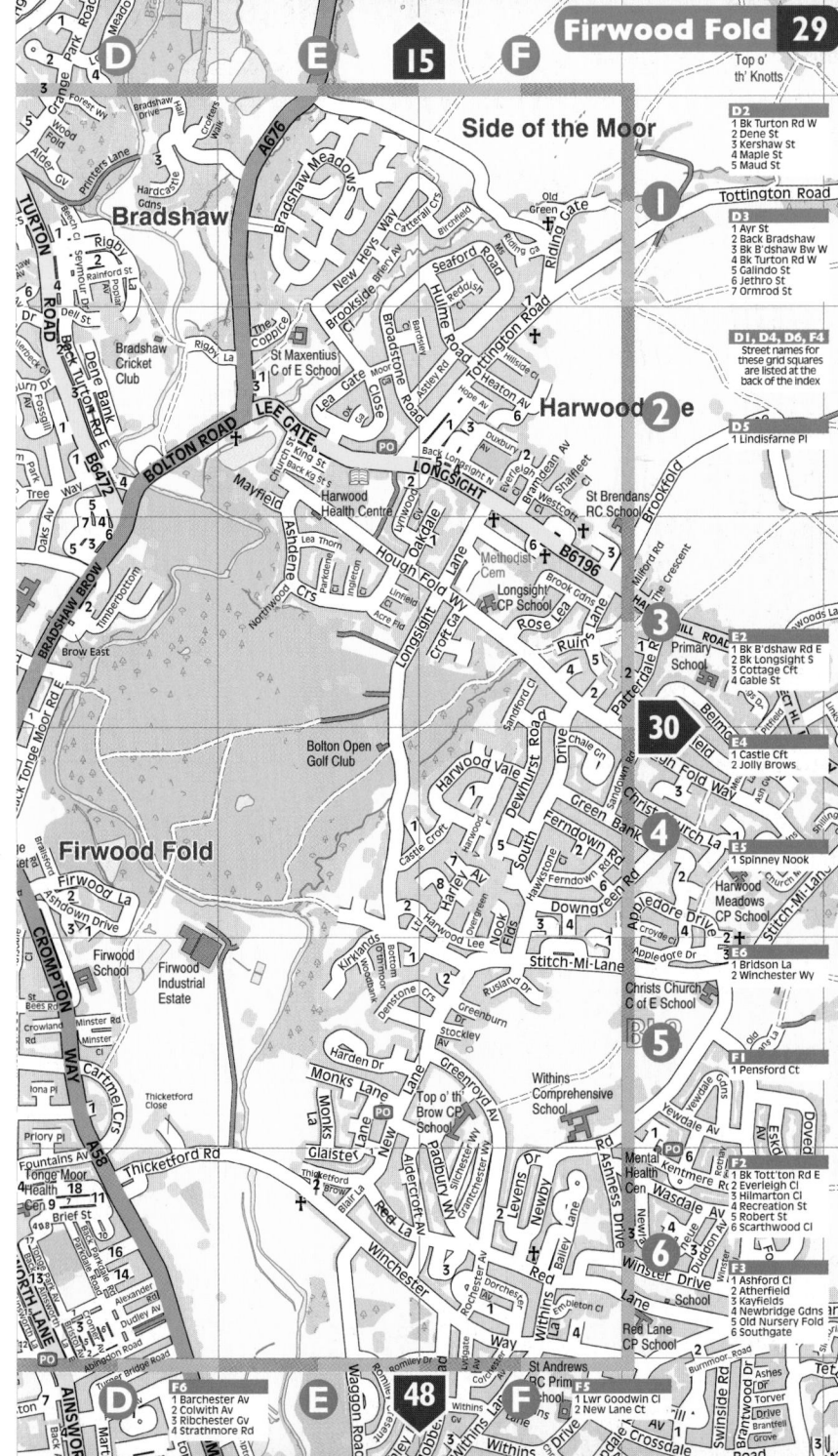

15

Top o' th' Knotts

Side of the Moor

Tottington Road

1

Bradshaw

Bradshaw Cricket Club

St Maxentius C of E School

Harwood **2** e

Harwood Health Centre

LONGSIGHT

St Brendans RC School

Mayfield

Methodist Cem

Longsight CP School

Primary School

3

30

Bolton Open Golf Club

4

Harwood Meadows CP School

Firwood Fold

Harwood Vale

Firwood School

Firwood Industrial Estate

Stitch-Mi-Lane

Christs Church C of E School

5

Thicketford Close

Monks Lane

Top o' th' Brow CP School

Withins Comprehensive School

Mental Kentmere Health Cen

6

Thicketford Rd

Glaister

Winchester

Red Lane CP School

St Andrews RC Prim

D   **E**   **48**   **F**

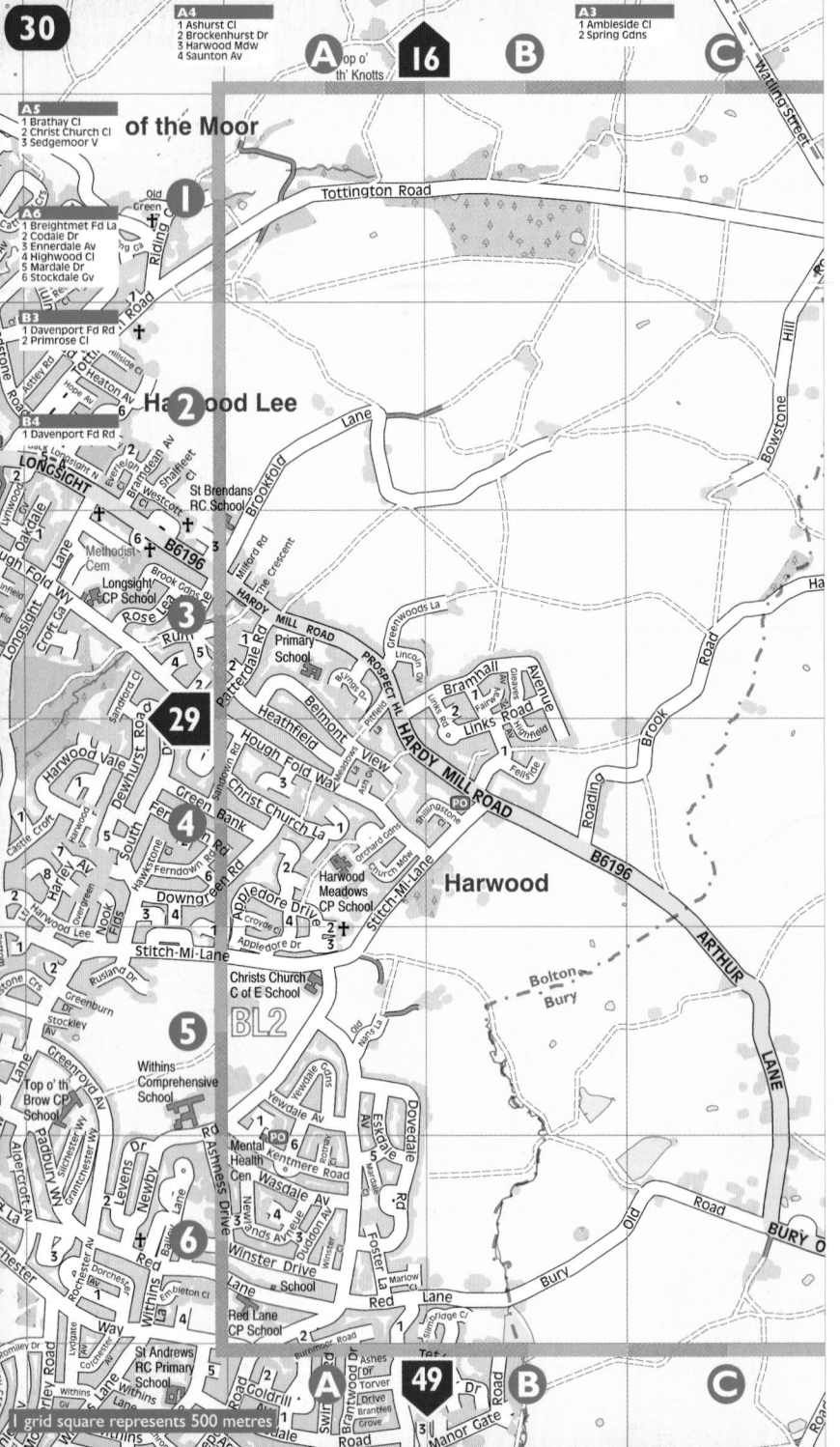

A4
1 Ashurst Cl
2 Brockenhurst Dr
3 Harwood Mdw
4 Saunton Av

A3
1 Ambleside Cl
2 Spring Gdns

A5
1 Brathay Cl
2 Christ Church Cl
3 Sedgemoor V

of the Moor

A6
1 Breightmet Fd La
2 Codale Dr
3 Ennerdale Av
4 Highwood Cl
5 Mardale Dr
6 Stockdale Gv

B3
1 Davenport Fd Rd
2 Primrose Cl

B4
1 Davenport Fd Rd

op o'
th' Knotts

16

Tottington Road

Watling Street

Bowstone Hill

Harwood Lee

Lane

LONGSIGHT

St Brendans
RC School

Brookfold

B6196

Methodist
Cem

Longsight
CP School

Rose La

Greenwoods La

HARDY MILL ROAD

Primary
School

PROSPECT HL

Bramhall

Links Road

Avenue

Brook Road

Roading Road

29

Heathfield

Belmont

View

HARDY MILL ROAD

B6196

ARTHUR LANE

Hough Fola Way

Christ Church La

Green Bank

PO

Harwood

Appledore Drive

Harwood
Meadows
CP School

Stitch-Mi-Lane

Harwood Vale

Dewhurst Road

Downgreen Rd

Stitch-Mi-Lane

Bolton
Bury

Christs Church
C of E School

BL2

Withins
Comprehensive
School

Top o' th
Brow CP
School

Greenroyd Av

Yewdale Gdns

Yewdale Av

Dovedale

Escdale Rd

Bury Old

Road

Mental
Health
Cen

PO

Kentmere Road

Wasdale Av

Duddon Av

Foster Rd

Aldercroft Av

Padbury Wy

Levens Dr

Newby

Ashness Drive

Winster Drive

Bury

Road

Old

Road

Red Lane
CP School

Red Lane

St Andrews
RC Primary
School

Brantwood Dr

Ashes
Dr

Torver
Drive

Brantfell
Grove

49

Manor Gate Road

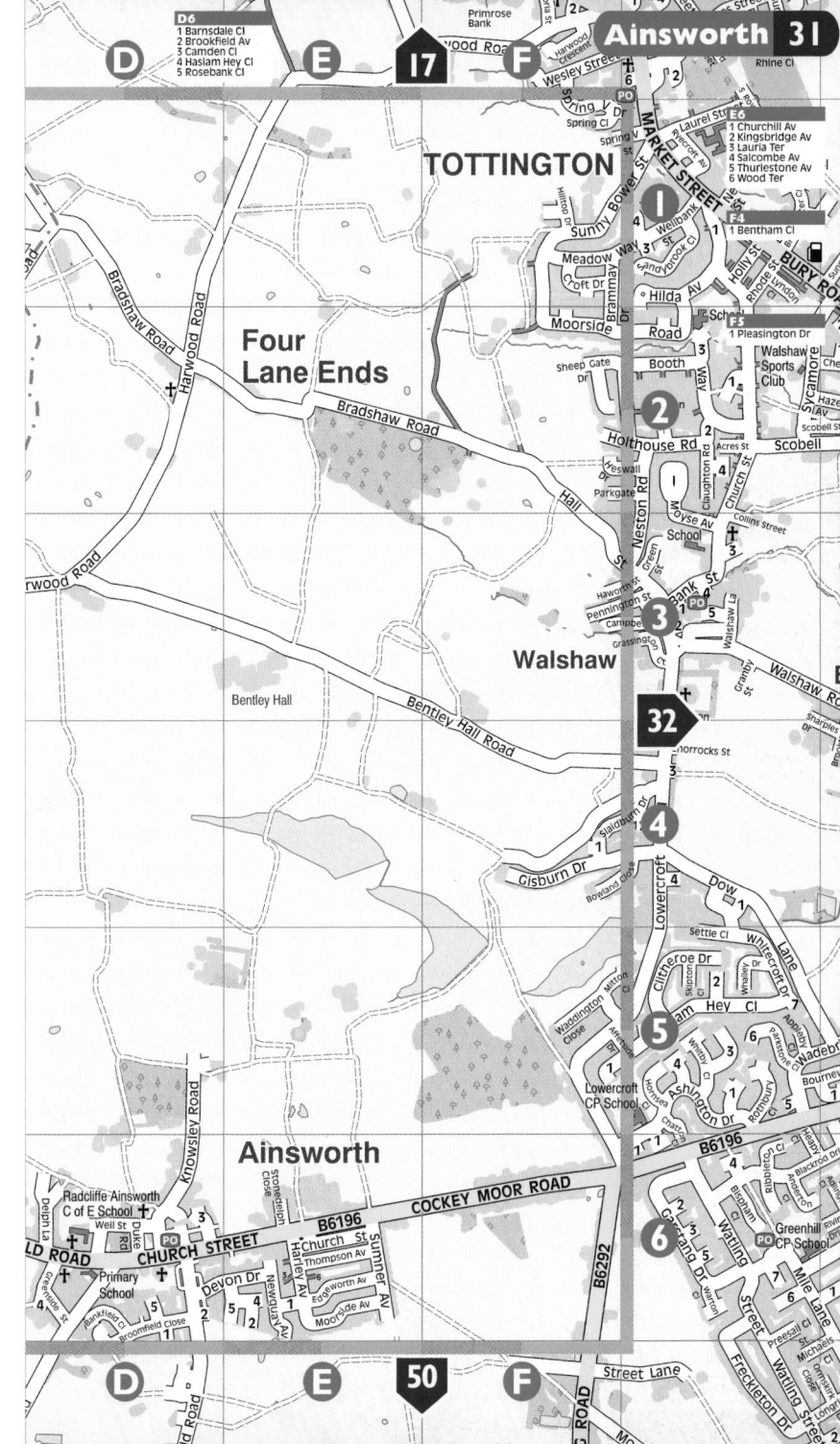

D6
1 Barnsdale Cl
2 Brookfield Av
3 Camden Cl
4 Haslam Hey Cl
5 Rosebank Cl

D **E** **17** **F**

Primrose Bank

Harwood Crescent
Wood Road
Wesley Street
Spring Cl
Spring Cl

Rhine Cl
Street
Old Rd

Ainsworth **31**

Laurel St
I4
1 Churchill Av
2 Kingsbridge Av
3 Lauria Ter
4 Salcombe Av
5 Thurlestone Av
6 Wood Ter

TOTTINGTON

Sunny Bower St
Brammay Way
Hilton Dr
Meadow Croft Dr
Sand Parock Cl
Wellbank St
Hilda Av

I

Holly Av
Rhode St
Lyndon St

BURY ROAD

F4
1 Bentham Cl

F5
1 Pleasington Dr

Sycamore

**Four
Lane Ends**

Moorside
Sheep Gate Dr

Booth
Road

Way

Walshaw
Sports
Club

Chest

Hazel Av

Scobell St

Bradshaw Road

2

Holthouse Rd
Acres St

Scobell

Bradshaw Road

Hall St

Weswall
Pargate
Neston Rd

Claughton Rd

Church St

Collins Street

Moyse Av
School

Arwood Road

Haworth St
Pennington St
Campbe
Grassington

Green St

Bank St
PO
Walshaw La

3

Granby St

Walshaw Rd

B

Walshaw

Bentley Hall

Bentley Hall Road

32

Sharples St
Broadmeadow

Thorrocks St

Staldburn Dr

4

Gisburn Dr
Bowland Grove
Lowercroft
Settle Cl

Dow

Whitecroft Dr
Lane

Clitheroe Dr
Skipton Cl
am Hey Cl

Whitby
Appley

5

Ashington Dr
Whalley
Rothbury

Nadebri

Lowercroft
CP School

Horsea

Bournevil

6

B6196
Bisham
Ribchester

Blackford Drive

Garstang Dr
Watling Street

Greenhill
CP School

Ainsworth

Knowsley Road

Stoneleigh Close

COCKEY MOOR ROAD

Radcliffe Ainsworth
C of E School
Delph La
Well St
PO
Duke Rd

CHURCH STREET
Church St

Thompson Av
Sumner Av

B6196

B6292

Primary
School

Devon Dr
Edgeworth Av
Moorside Av
Newquay Av

Bankfield
Broomfield Close

Mile Lane
St Michaels

Preesall Cl

Watling Street
Freckleton Dr
Longf

D **E** **50** **F**

ld Road
G ROAD
Street Lane
Moo

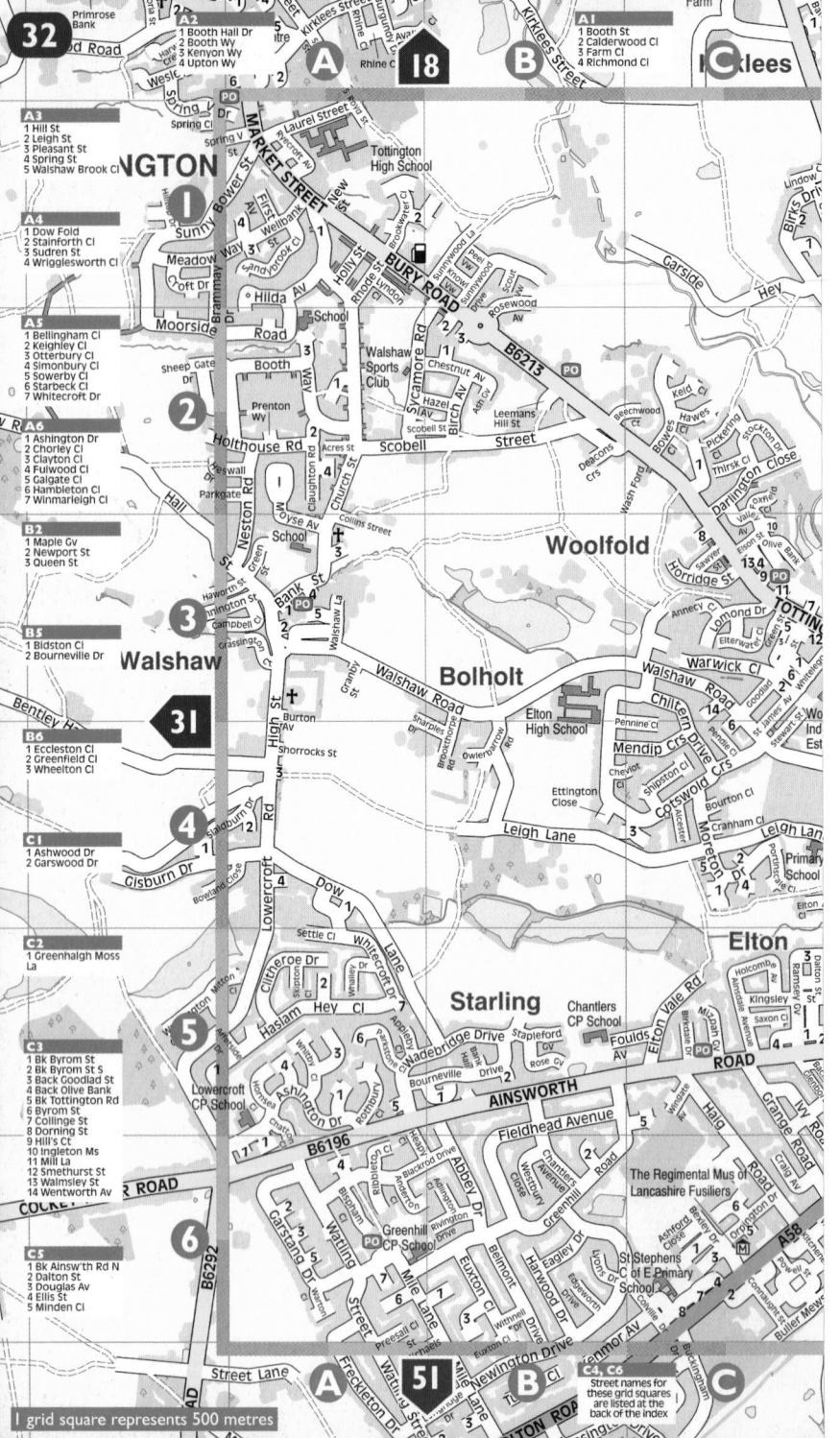

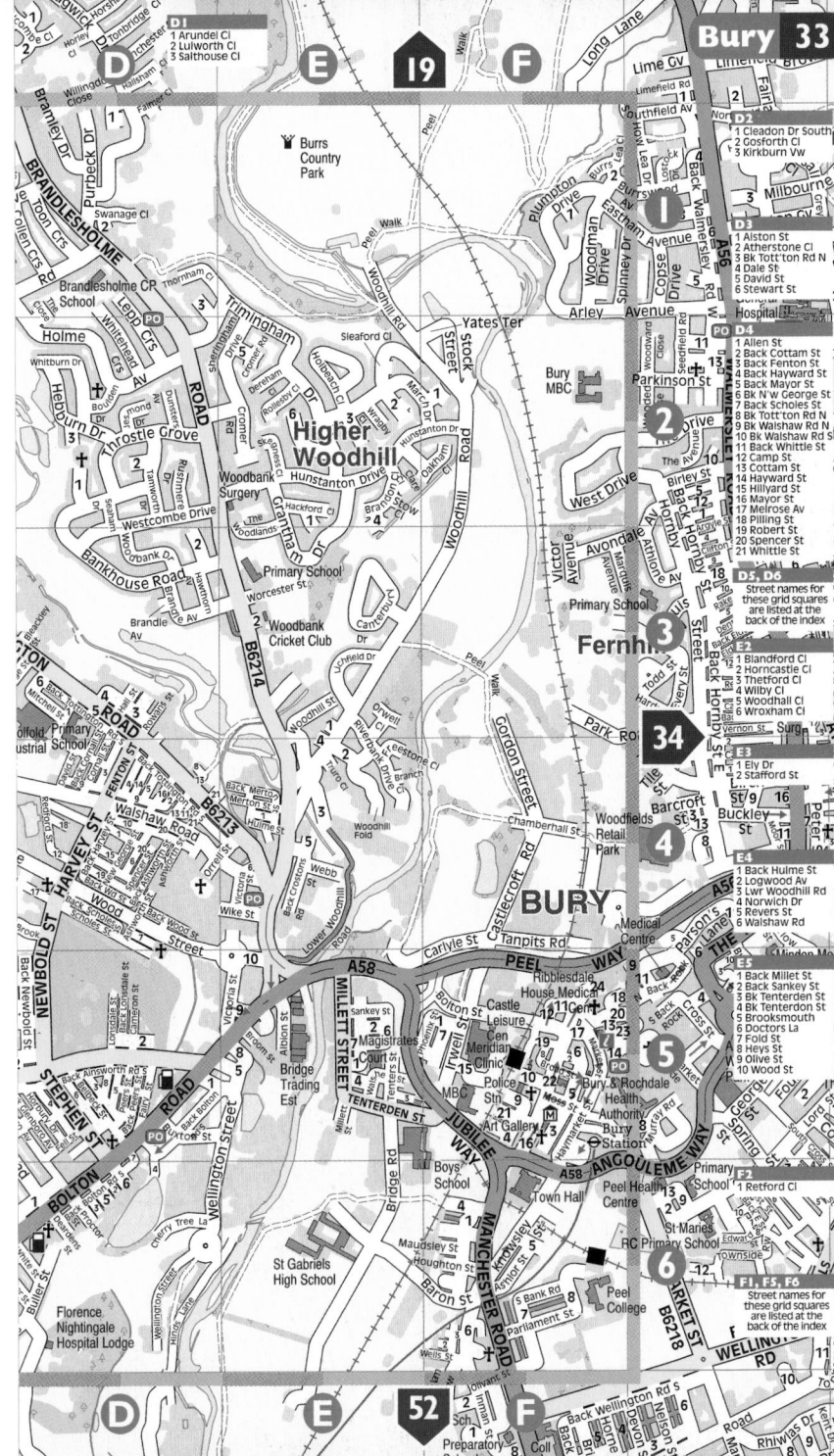

Burrs
Country
Park

Brandlesholme CP
School

Holme

Higher
Woodhill

Woodbank
Surgery

Brandle
Av

Woodbank
Cricket Club

Primary School

Primary School

Bury
MBC

Fernh...

West Drive

Surg

34

Woodfields
Retail
Park

BURY

Woodhill
Fold

Medical
Centre

Ribblesdale
House Medical
Cen

Castle
Leisure
Cen

Magistrates
Court

Meridian
Clinic

Police
Stn

MBC

Art Gallery

Bury & Rochdale
Health
Authority
Bury
Station

Bridge
Trading
Est

Boys
School

Town Hall

Peel Health
Centre

Primary
School

St Maries
RC Primary School

St Gabriels
High School

Maudsley
St

Peel
College

Florence
Nightingale
Hospital Lodge

St Bank Rd

Parliament St

Preparatory
School

Bury
Coll

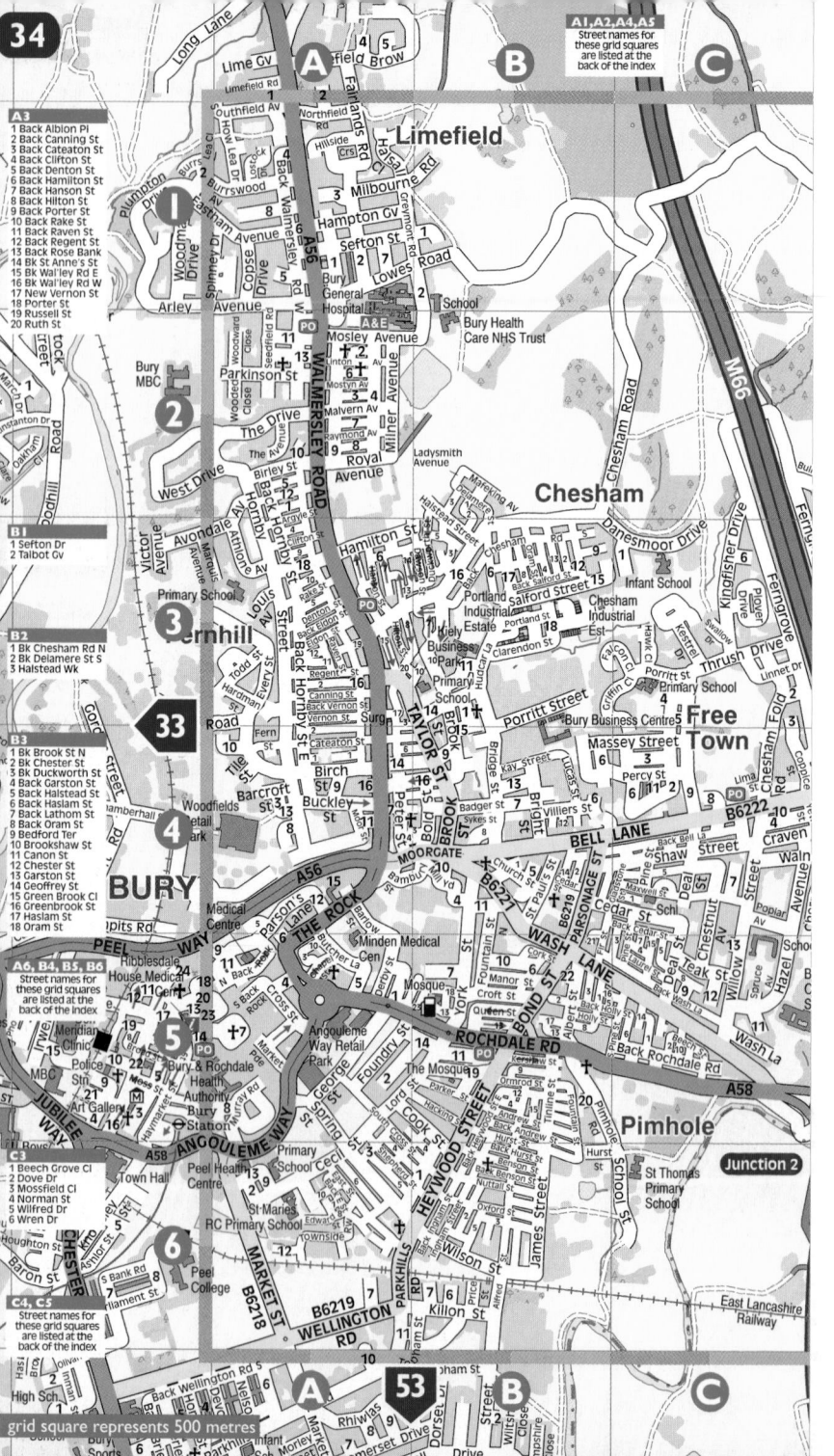

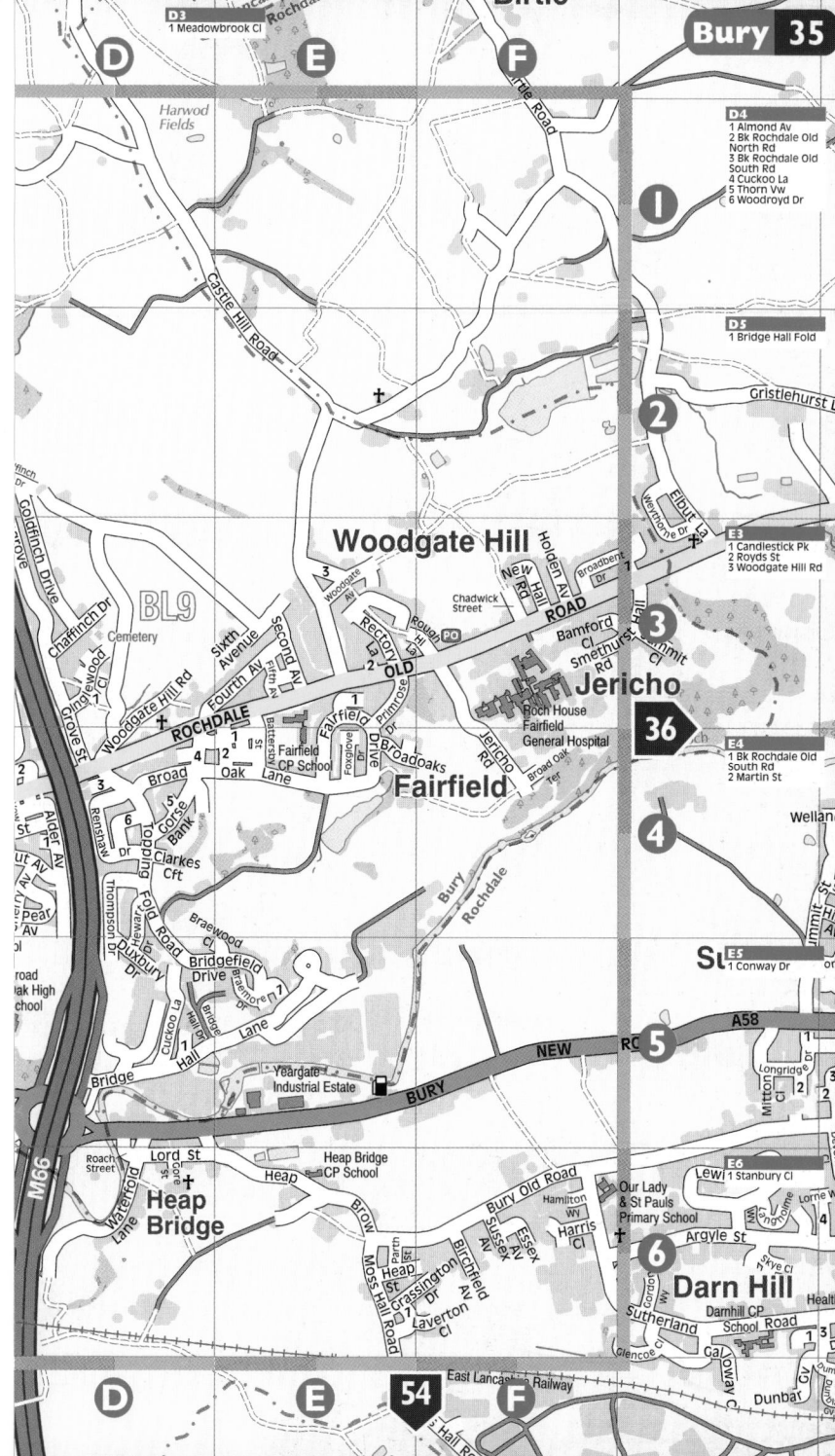

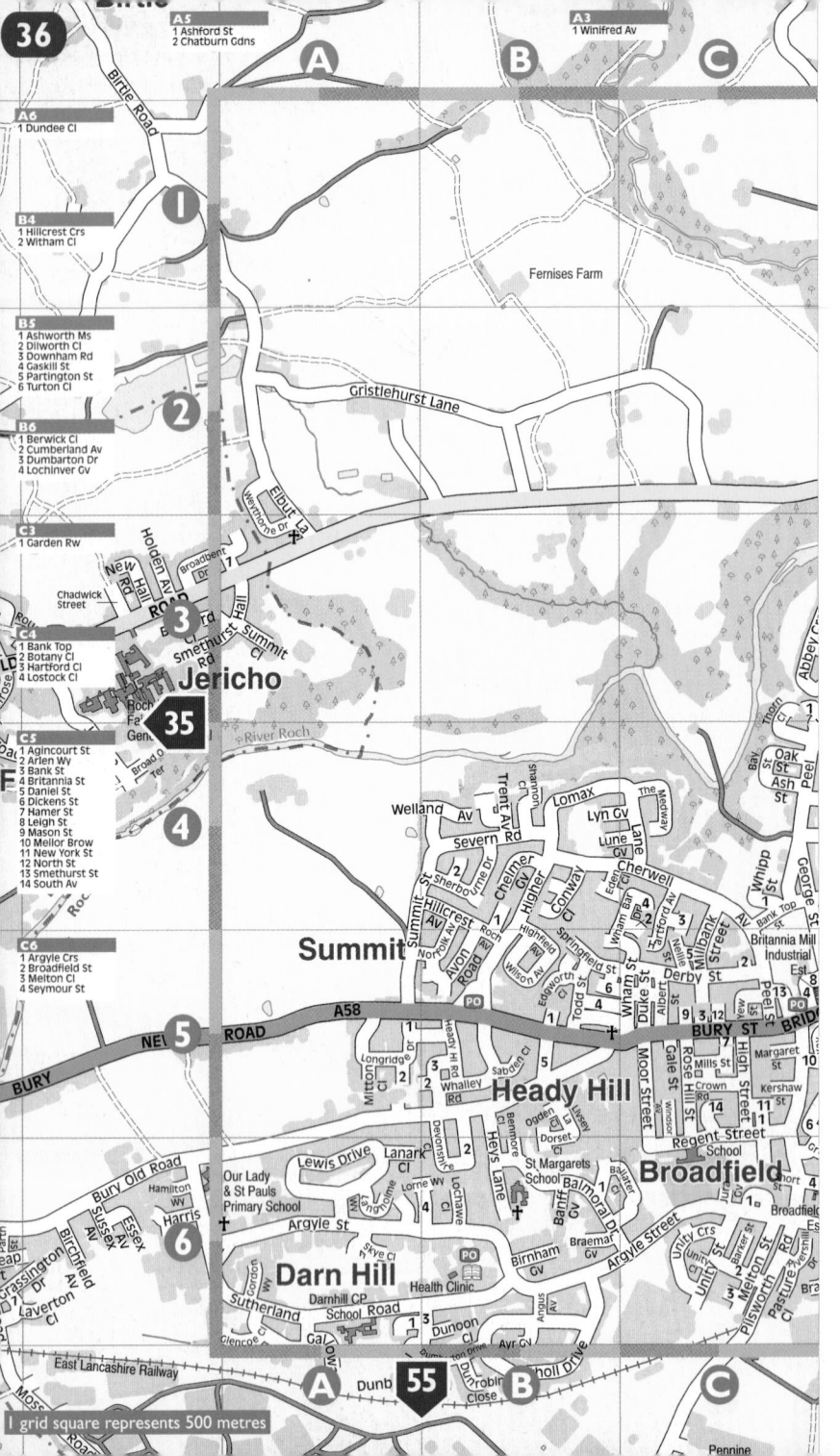

36

Birtle

A5
1 Ashford St
2 Chatburn Gdns

A3
1 Winifred Av

A6
1 Dundee Cl

B4
1 Hillcrest Crs
2 Witham Cl

Fernises Farm

B5
1 Ashworth Ms
2 Dilworth Cl
3 Downham Rd
4 Gaskill St
5 Partington St
6 Turton Cl

Gristlehurst Lane

B6
1 Berwick Cl
2 Cumberland Av
3 Dumbarton Dr
4 Lochinver Gv

C3
1 Garden Rw

Chadwick
Street

C4
1 Bank Top
2 Botany Cl
3 Hartford Cl
4 Lostock Cl

Jericho

River Roch

C5
1 Agincourt St
2 Arlen Wy
3 Bank St
4 Britannia St
5 Daniel St
6 Dickens St
7 Hamer St
8 Leigh St
9 Mason St
10 Mellor Brow
11 New York St
12 North St
13 Smethurst St
14 South Av

Welland

Summit

C6
1 Argyle Crs
2 Broadfield St
3 Melton Cl
4 Seymour St

A58 ROAD

Heady Hill

Broadfield

Our Lady
& St Pauls
Primary School

St Margarets
School

Darn Hill

Health Clinic

East Lancashire Railway

55

1 grid square represents 500 metres

Pennine

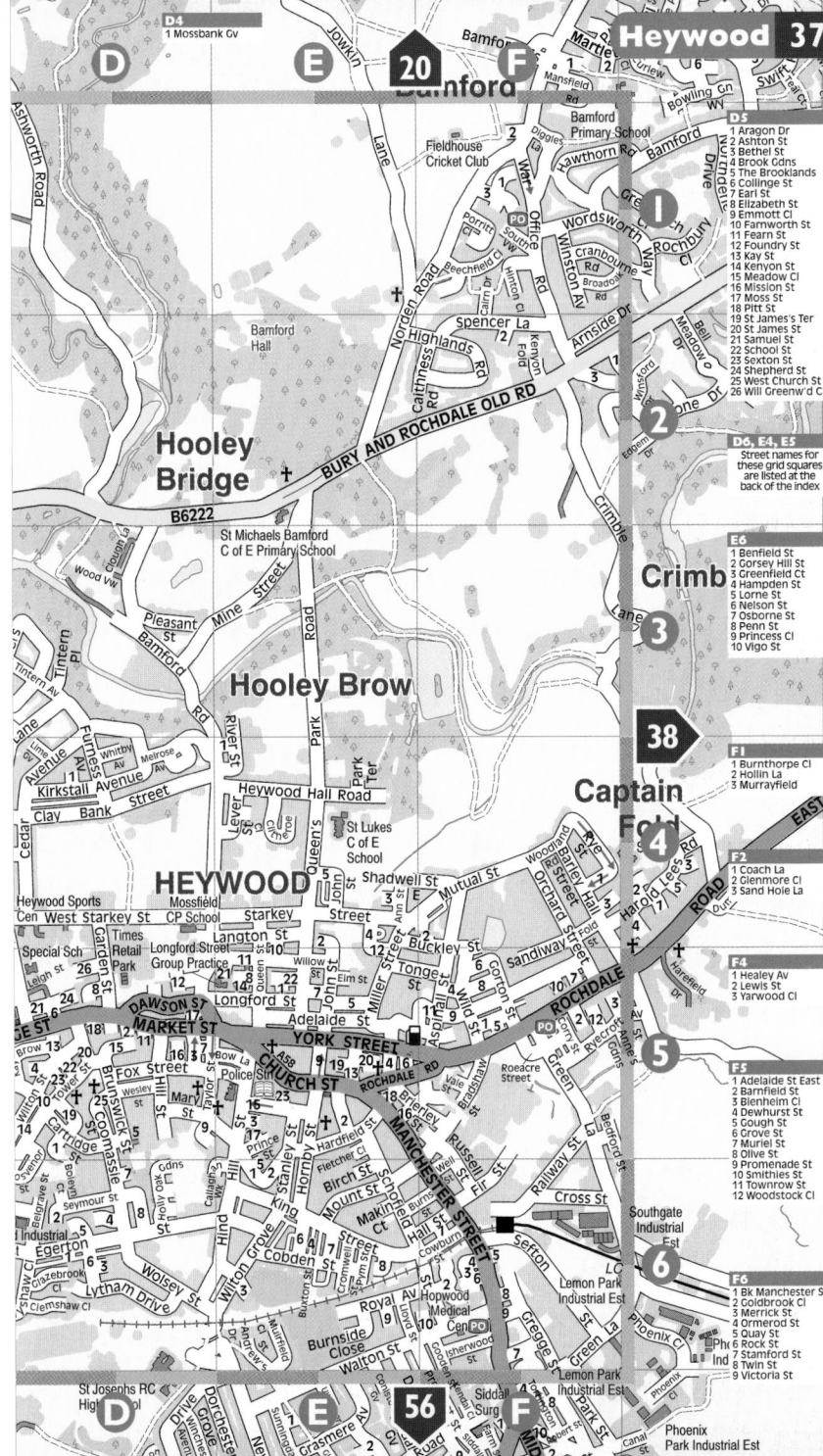

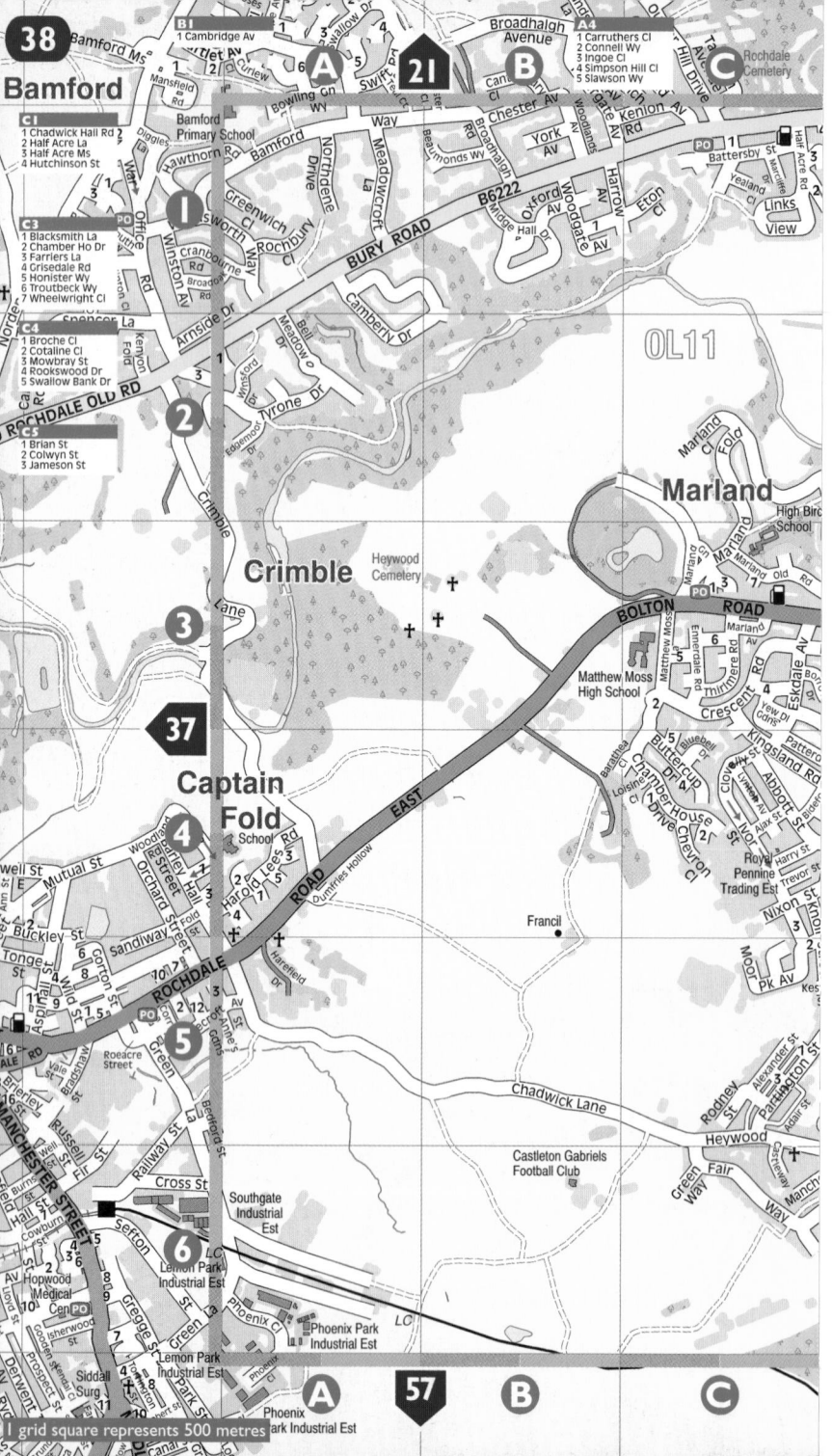

38
Bamford

21

B1
1 Cambridge Av

A4
1 Carruthers Cl
2 Connell Wy
3 Ingoe Cl
4 Simpson Hill Cl
5 Slawson Wy

C1
1 Chadwick Hall Rd
2 Half Acre La
3 Half Acre Ms
4 Hutchinson St

C3
1 Blacksmith La
2 Chamber Ho Dr
3 Farriers La
4 Grisedale Rd
5 Honister Wy
6 Troutbeck Wy
7 Wheelwright Cl

C4
1 Broche Cl
2 Cotaline Cl
3 Mowbray St
4 Rookswood Dr
5 Swallow Bank Dr

C5
1 Brian St
2 Colwyn St
3 Jameson St

Bamford Primary School

BURY ROAD B6222

OL11

Marland

High Bird School

Crimble
Heywood Cemetery

BOLTON ROAD

Matthew Moss High School

37

Captain Fold

ROAD EAST

ROCHDALE

Francil

Chadwick Lane

Castleton Gabriels Football Club

Heywood

Southgate Industrial Est

Lemon Park Industrial Est

Phoenix Park Industrial Est

Lemon Park Industrial Est

57

A   **B**   **C**

Phoenix Park Industrial Est

1 grid square represents 500 metres

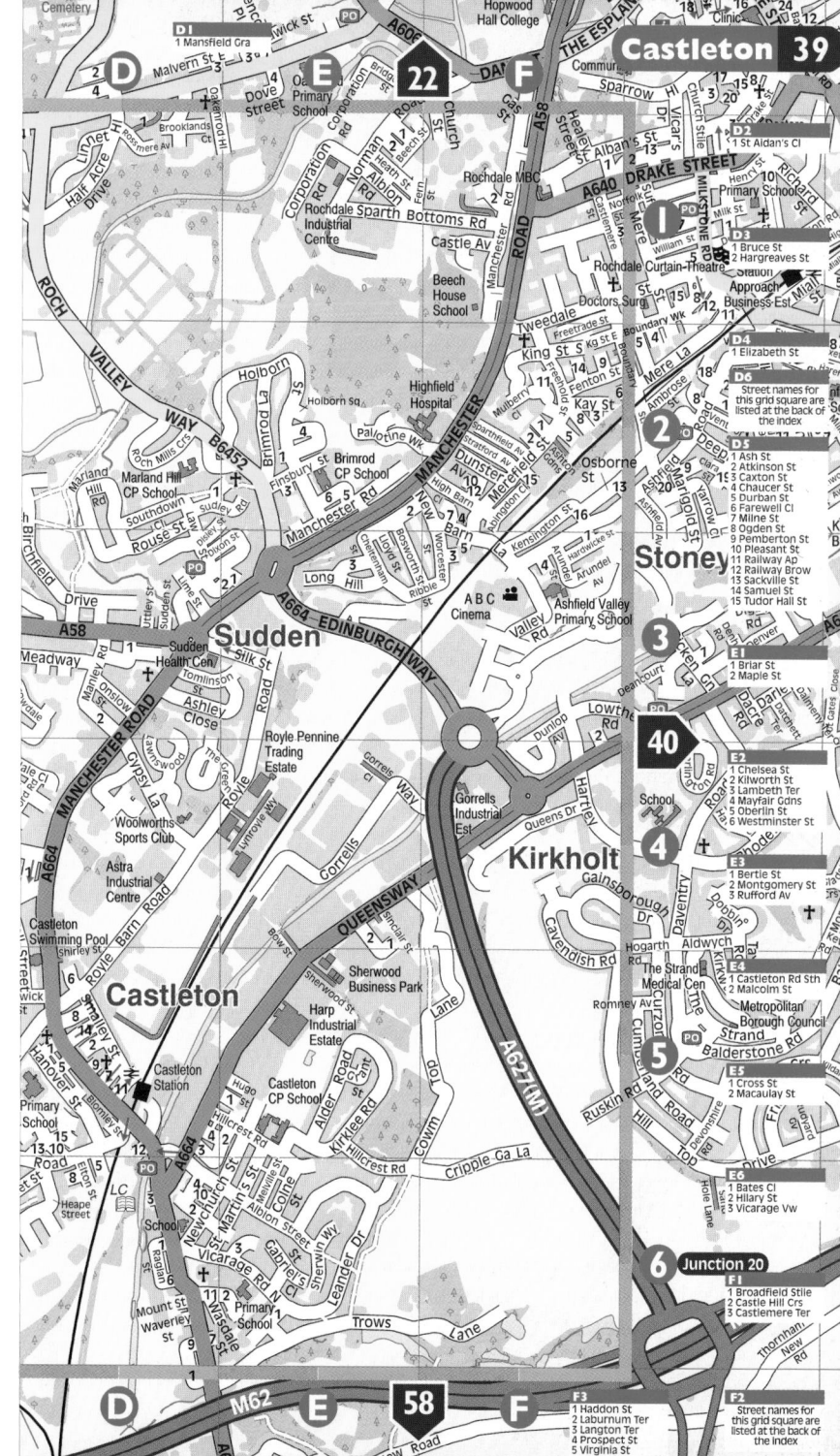

Cemetery

Hopwood Hall College

THE ESPLAN

Communi

22

Sparrow Hi

DI
1 Mansfield Gra

Malvern St

D

Dove Street

E

Oak Primary School

Bridge St

Church St

Vicar's

D2
1 St Aidan's Cl

Brooklands Ct

Bossmere Av

Linnet H

Half Acre Drive

Corporation Rd

Norman Rd

Albion St

Heath St

Beech St

Rochdale MBC

A640 DRAKE STREET

Church Stile

Henry St 10

Richard

D2

158

Milk St

Rochdale Sparth Bottoms Industrial Centre

Sparth Bottoms Rd

Castle Av

Manchester Rd

Norfolk St

Primary School

William St

D3
1 Bruce St
2 Hargreaves St

Rochdale Curtain Theatre

Station Approach Business Est.

Beech House School

Doctors Surg

Tweedale

Freetrade St

Boundary Wk

D4
1 Elizabeth St

Holborn

Brimrod La

Highfield Hospital

King St 5

Kg St 5

Fenton St

Freetrade St

Mere La

Ambrose

D6
Street names for this grid square are listed at the back of the index

Holborn Sq

Pallotine Wk

Mulberry

Kay St

8

3

Finsbury St

Brimrod CP School

Stratford Av

Meterfield

Sparthmill

High Barn

New Barn

Osborne St

13

Deep

D5
1 Ash St
2 Atkinson St
3 Caxton St
4 Chaucer St
5 Durban St
6 Farewell Cl
7 Milne St
8 Ogden St
9 Pemberton St
10 Pleasant St
11 Railway Ap
12 Railway Brow
13 Sackville St
14 Samuel St
15 Tudor Hall St

Marland Hill CP School

Roch Mills Crs

Dunster

Manchester Rd

Bosworth St

Lloyd St

Cheltenham St

Ribble

Worcester St

Kensington St

Hardwicke St

2

Ashfield

Marigold St

Yarrow

Stoney

Southdown

Rouse St

Low St

Long Hill

Arundel

Arundel St

3

E1
1 Briar St
2 Maple St

Birchfield Drive

Uttley St

A58 A664 EDINBURGH WAY

Sudden

Silk St

ABC Cinema

Ashfield Valley Primary School

Valley Rd

Bracken Cl

Rd

Denver

A66

Meadway

Manley Rd

Onslow Rd

Tomlinson

Ashley Close

Royle Pennine Trading Estate

The Green

Dunlop Av

Lowthorpe Rd

40

Oar Dart Rd

E2
1 Chelsea St
2 Kilworth St
3 Lambeth St
4 Mayfair Gdns
5 Oberlin St
6 Westminster St

Woolworths Sports Club

Gypsy La

Lynrowe Wy

Correls La

Way

Correls

Gorrells Industrial Est

Queens Dr

Hartley

School

Rode

4

E3
1 Bertie St
2 Montgomery St
3 Rufford Av

Astra Industrial Centre

Royle Barn Road

Kirkholt

Gainsborough

Bertie St

Castleton Swimming Pool

Shirley St

QUEENSWAY

Sinclair St

Bow St

Sherwood Business Park

Cavendish Rd

Daventry

Dobhi Rd

Aldwych

Kew Rd

Castleton

Hanover St

Blomley St

Harp Industrial Estate

Sherwood St

Grant St

Lane

Hogarth

The Strand Medical Cen

Romney Av

Curzon

E4
1 Castleton Rd Sth
2 Malcolm St

Metropolitan Borough Council

Strand

5

Primary School

13.10

Elm St

Heape Street

Hanover St

Castleton Station

Castleton CP School

Hugo St

Alder Rd

Kirklee Rd

Hillcrest Rd

Cowm

A627(M)

Cumberland Road

Ruskin Rd

Hill

Balderstone Rd

E5
1 Cross St
2 Macaulay St

Cross St

Top

E6
1 Bates Cl
2 Hilary St
3 Vicarage Vw

Raglan St

LC

Newchurch St

Martin St

Melville St

Colne St

Albion Street

Sherwin Wy

Gabriel's Rd

Leander Dr

Hillcrest Rd

Cripple Ga La

Drive

Hole Lane

6 Junction 20

F1
1 Broadfield Stile
2 Castle Hill Crs
3 Castlemere Ter

School

Mount St

Waverley St

Vicarage Rd N

Primary School

Wasdale

Trows

Lane

Thornham New Rd

D

E

58

F

F2
1 Haddon St
2 Laburnum Ter
3 Langton Ter
4 Prospect St
5 Virginia St

F2
Street names for this grid square are listed at the back of the index

New Road

M62

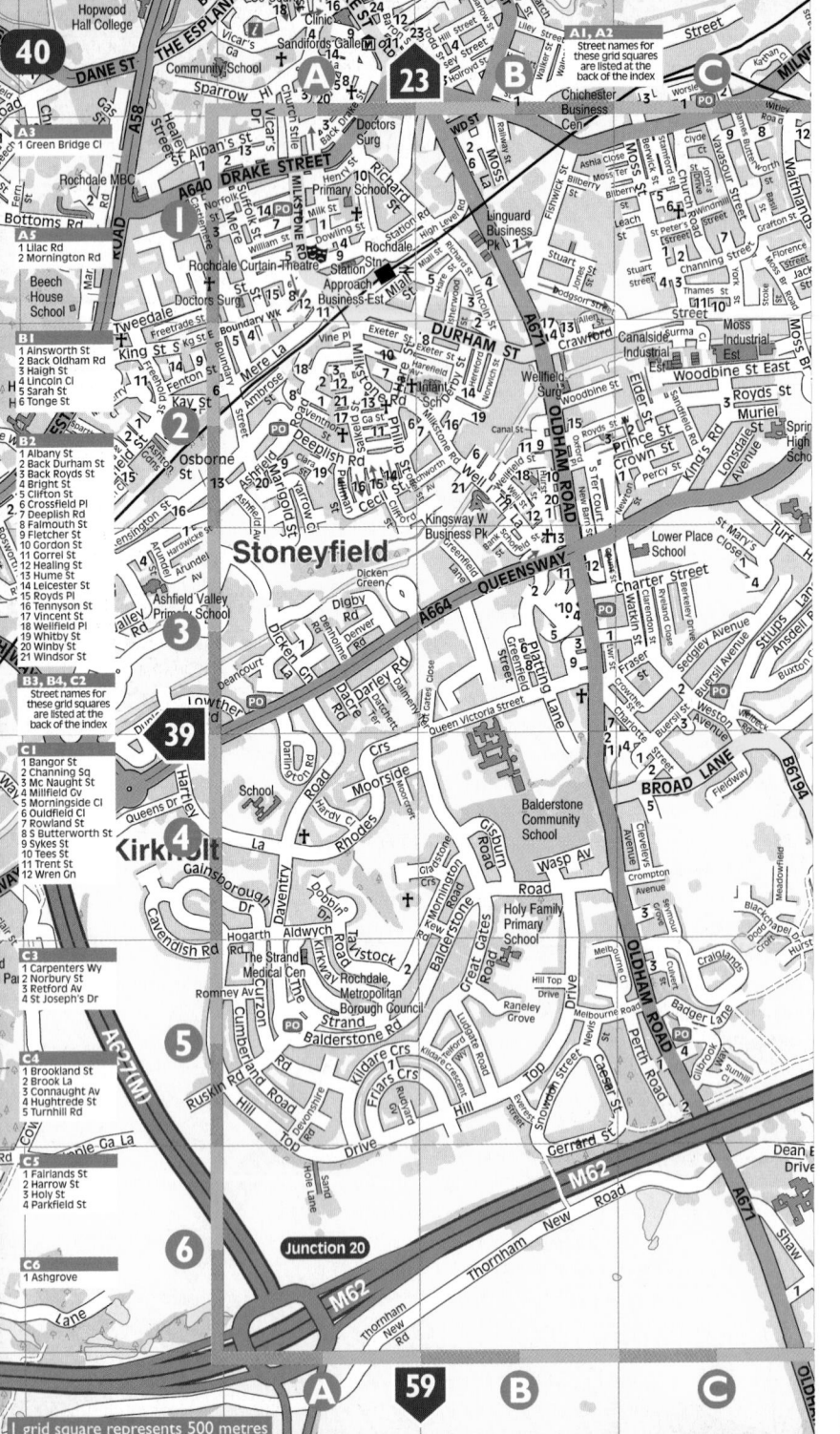

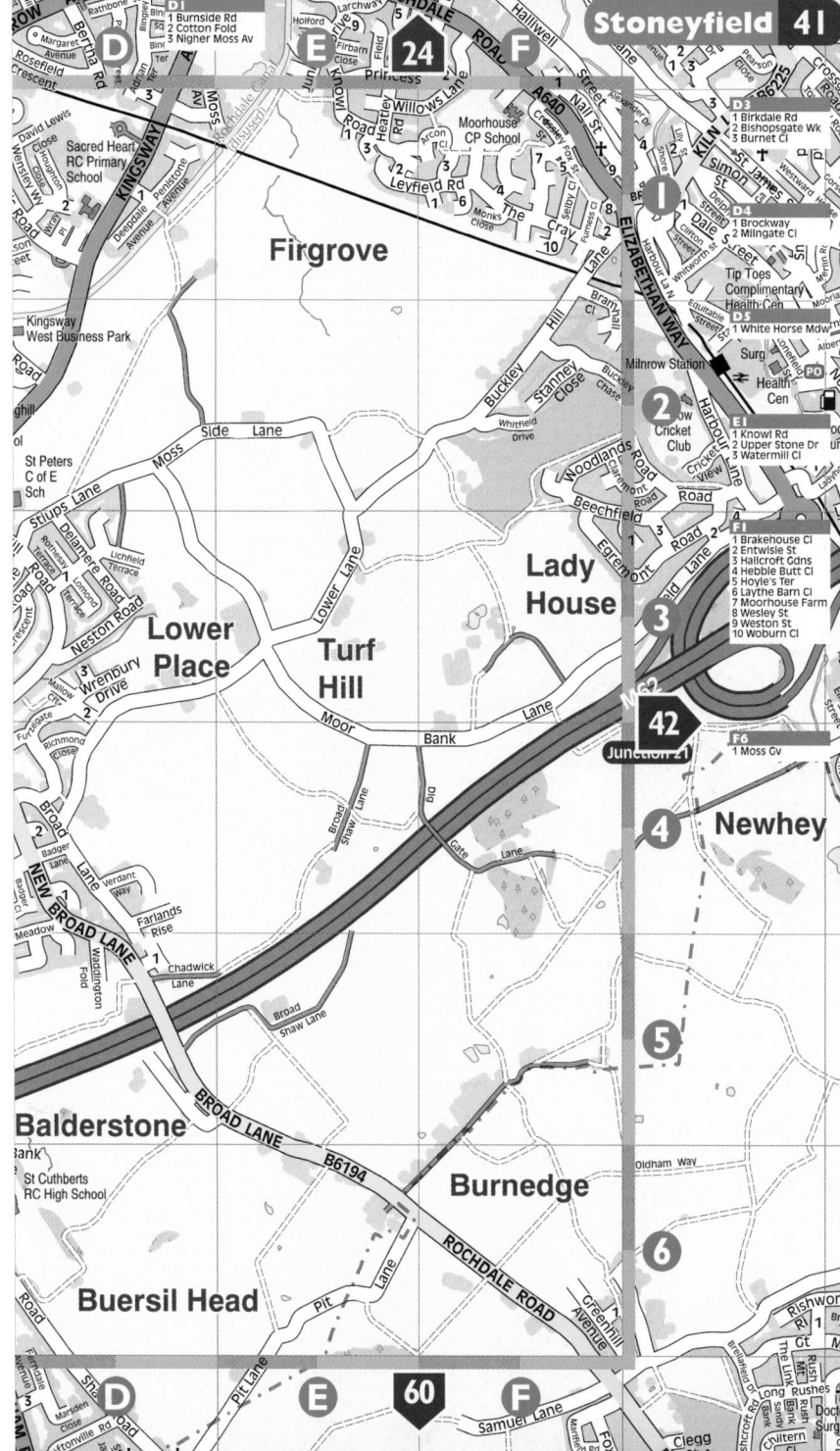

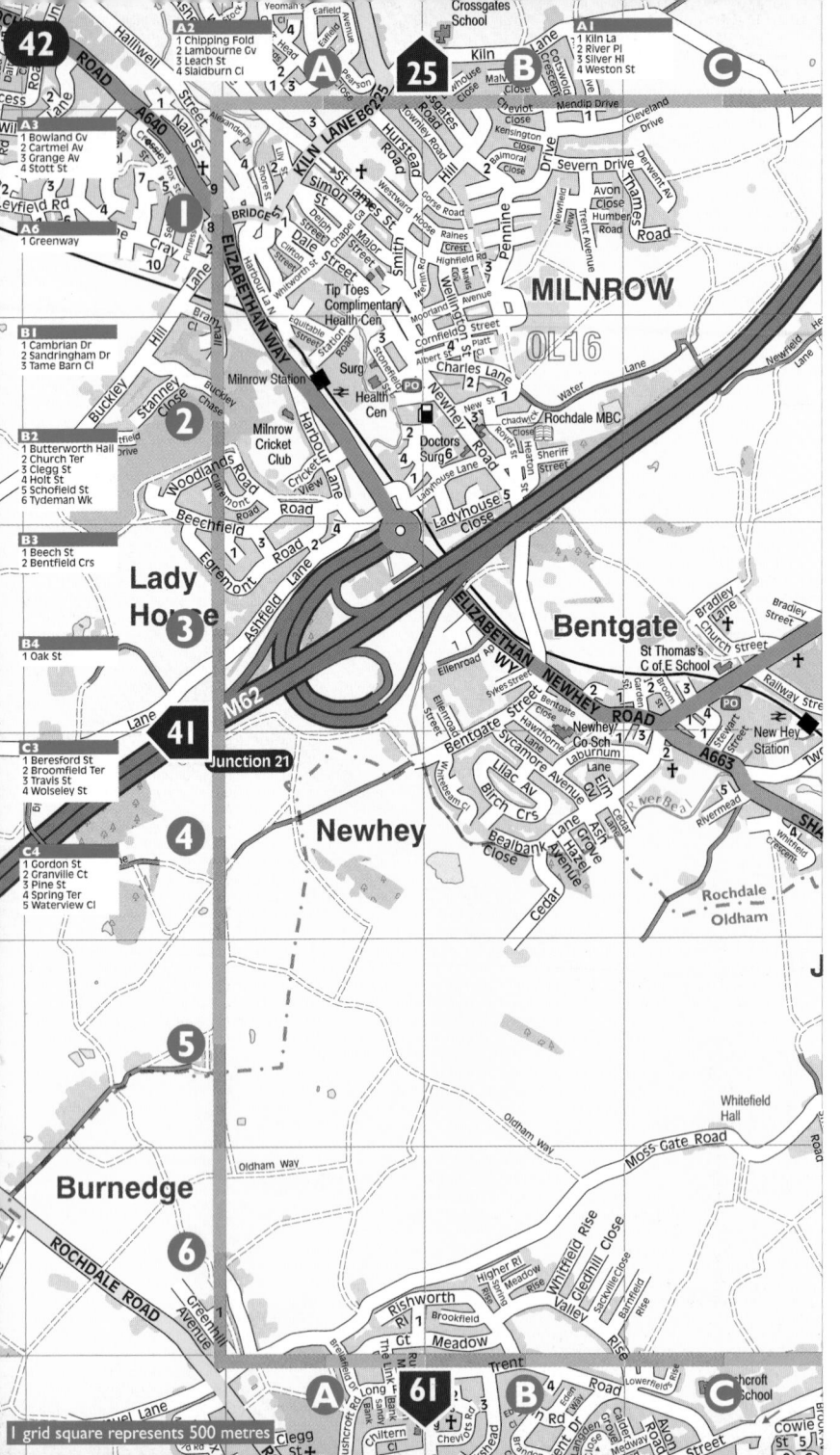

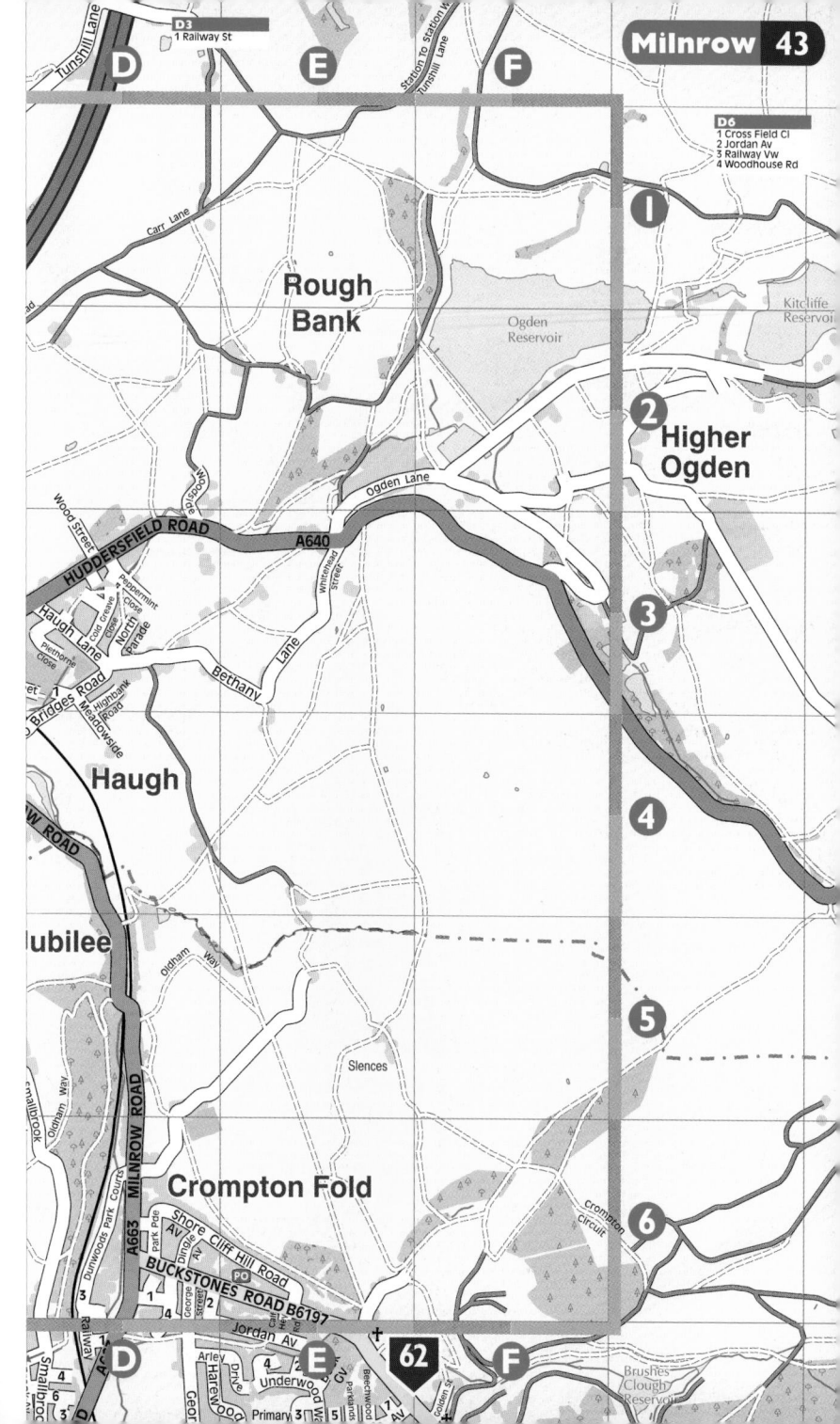

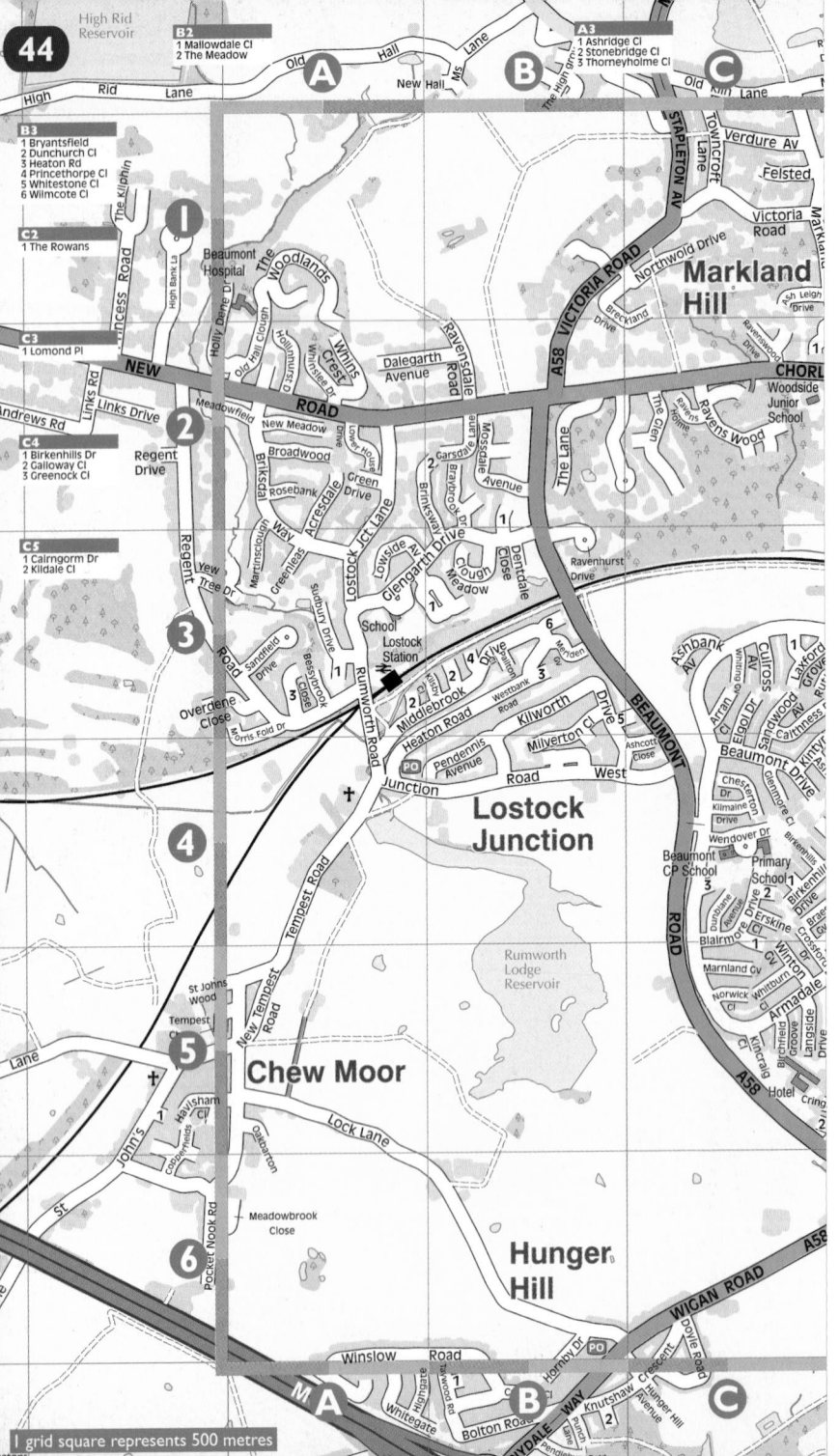

44

High Rid Lane
Old Hall Lane
New Hall

A **B** **C**

Stapleton Av
Towncroft Lane
Verdure Av
Felsted
Victoria Road

Markland Hill

Princess Road
The Kliphin
High Bank La
Beaumont Hospital
The Woodlands
Whins Crest
Holly Dene Dr
Old Hall Clough
Hollinhurst Dr
Ravensdale Road
Dalegarth Avenue

A58 VICTORIA ROAD
Northwold Drive
Breckland Drive

CHORL
Woodside Junior School

NEW ROAD
Meadowfield
New Meadow
Broadwood
Rosebank
Green Drive
Martinscough Way
Greenleas
Lostock Jct Lane
Acresdale
Briksdal
Lowside Av
Brinksway Drive
Glengarth Drive
Carsdale
Braybrook Dr
Mossdale Avenue
Dentdale Close
Clough Meadow

Regent Drive

The Lane
The Glen
Ravens Wood
Elvens Home

Ravenshurst Drive

Regent Road
Yew Tree Dr
Sudbury Drive
Sandfield Drive
Bessbrook Close
School
Lostock Station
Middlebrook
Heaton Road
Pendennis Avenue
PO
Clive Drive
Hulton Dr
Marsden
Westbank Road
Kilworth
Milverton Road West
Ashcott Close

BEAUMONT ROAD
Ashbank Av
Culross Av
Lyxford Grove
Whiting Gv
Arran Av
Elgol Cl
Sandwood Av
Caithness
Kintyre
Beaumont Drive
Chesterton Dr
Kilmaine Drive
Wendover Dr
Glenmore Cl
Birkenhills Drive
Erskine Cl
Crossford Cl
Winton
Gv
Armadale
Landside
Cring

Overdene Close
Sarrys Fold Dr

Rumworth Road

Junction

Lostock Junction

Tempest Road

Beaumont CP School
Beaumont Primary School
Durdsune Clematic
Blairmore Cl
Marnland Gv
Norwich Cl
Whitburn Cl
Kincraig Cl
Kinross Groove

New Tempest Road
St Johns Wood
Tempest Cl

Rumworth Lodge Reservoir

5

Chew Moor
Mavisham Cl
Cobblefields
Oakbarton
Lock Lane

A58
Hotel

Johns St
Lane
Pocket Nook Rd
Meadowbrook Close

6

Hunger Hill

WIGAN ROAD
Dovle Road
Crescent
Knutshaw Hunger Hill Avenue

Winslow Road
Taywood Rd
Hornby Dr
PO

M A **B** **C**
Bolton Road
YNDALE WAY
Whitegate
Knutshaw
Pendlebury

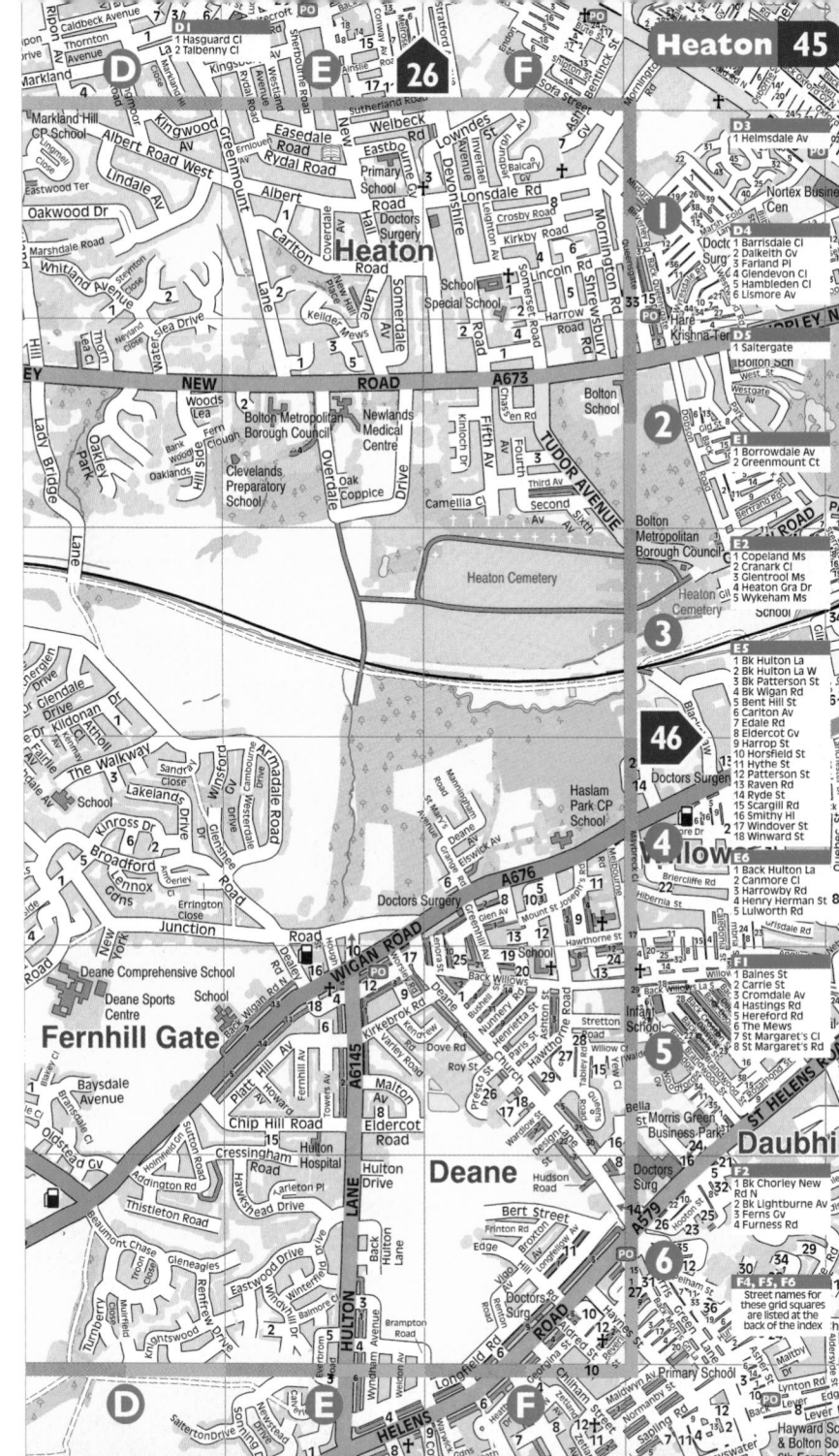

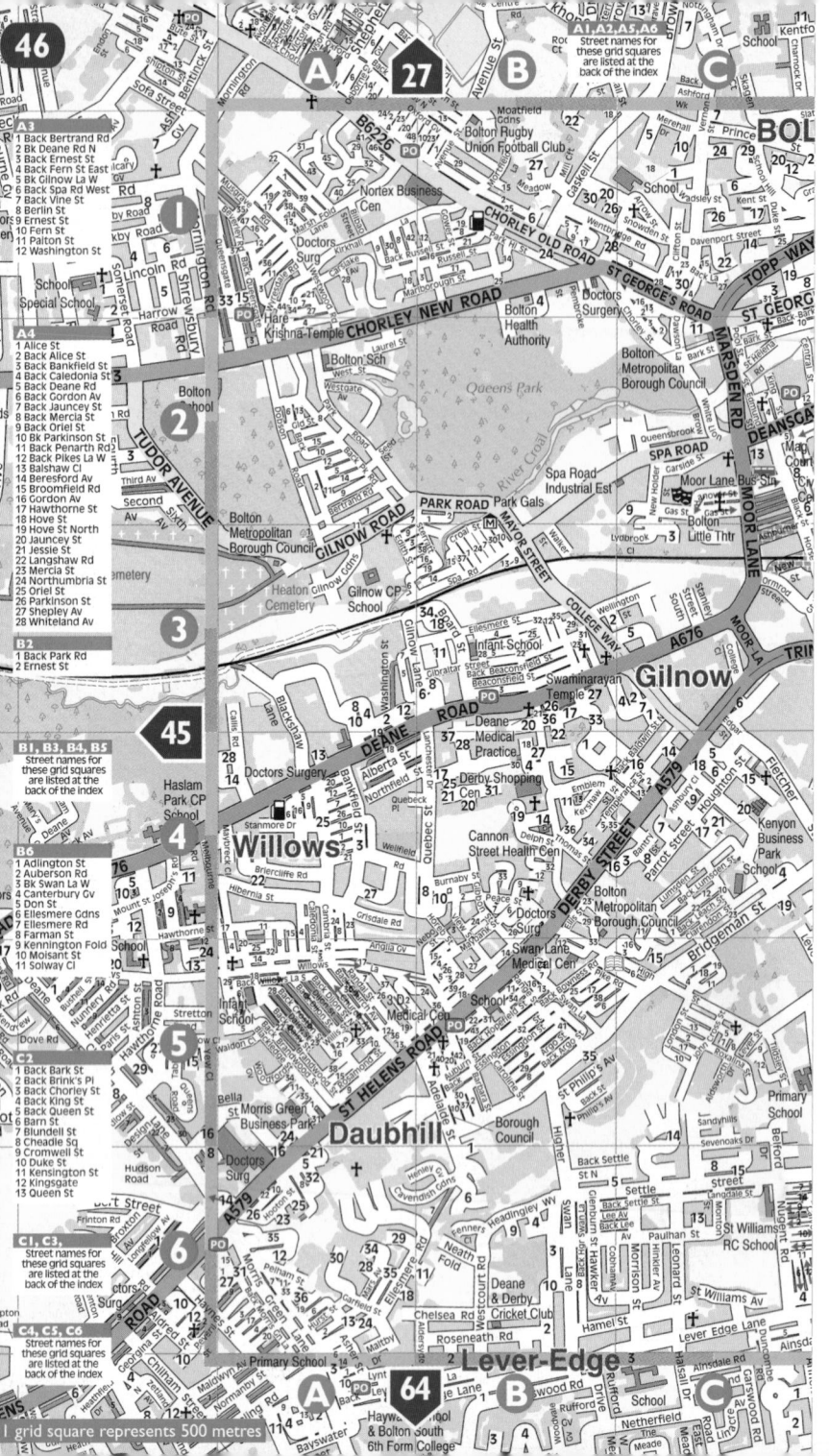

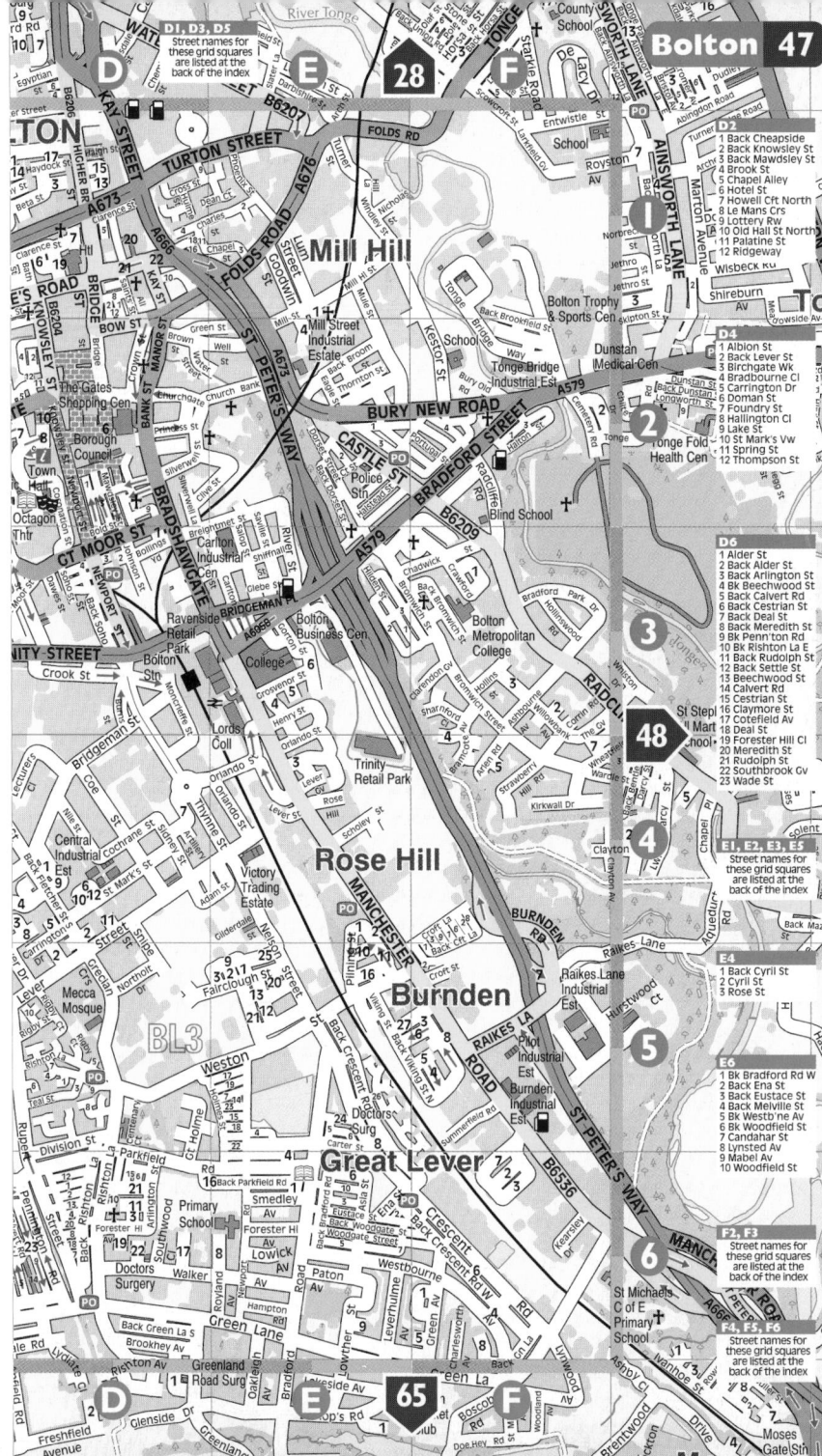

Mill Hill

Rose Hill

Burnden

Great Lever

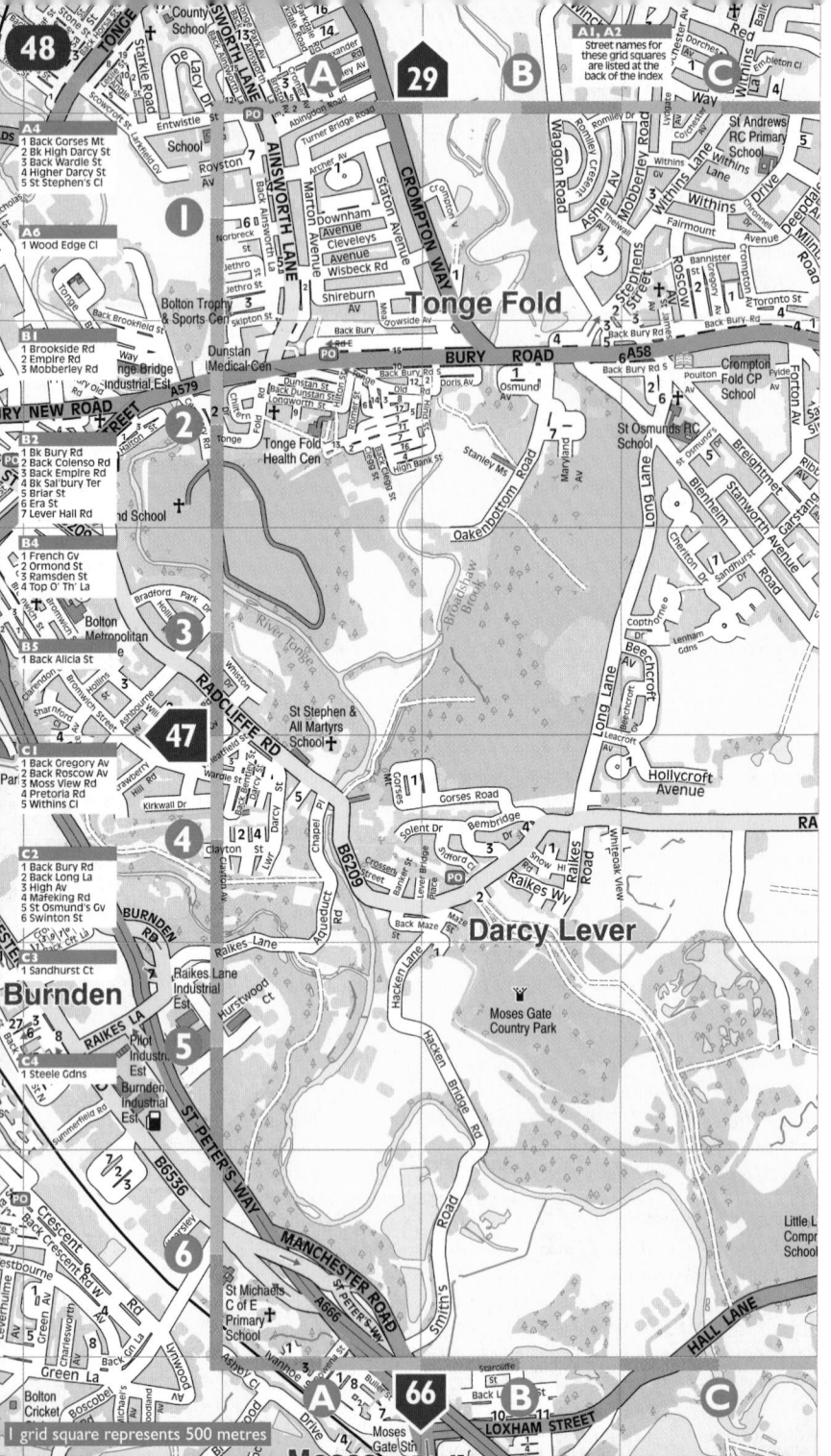

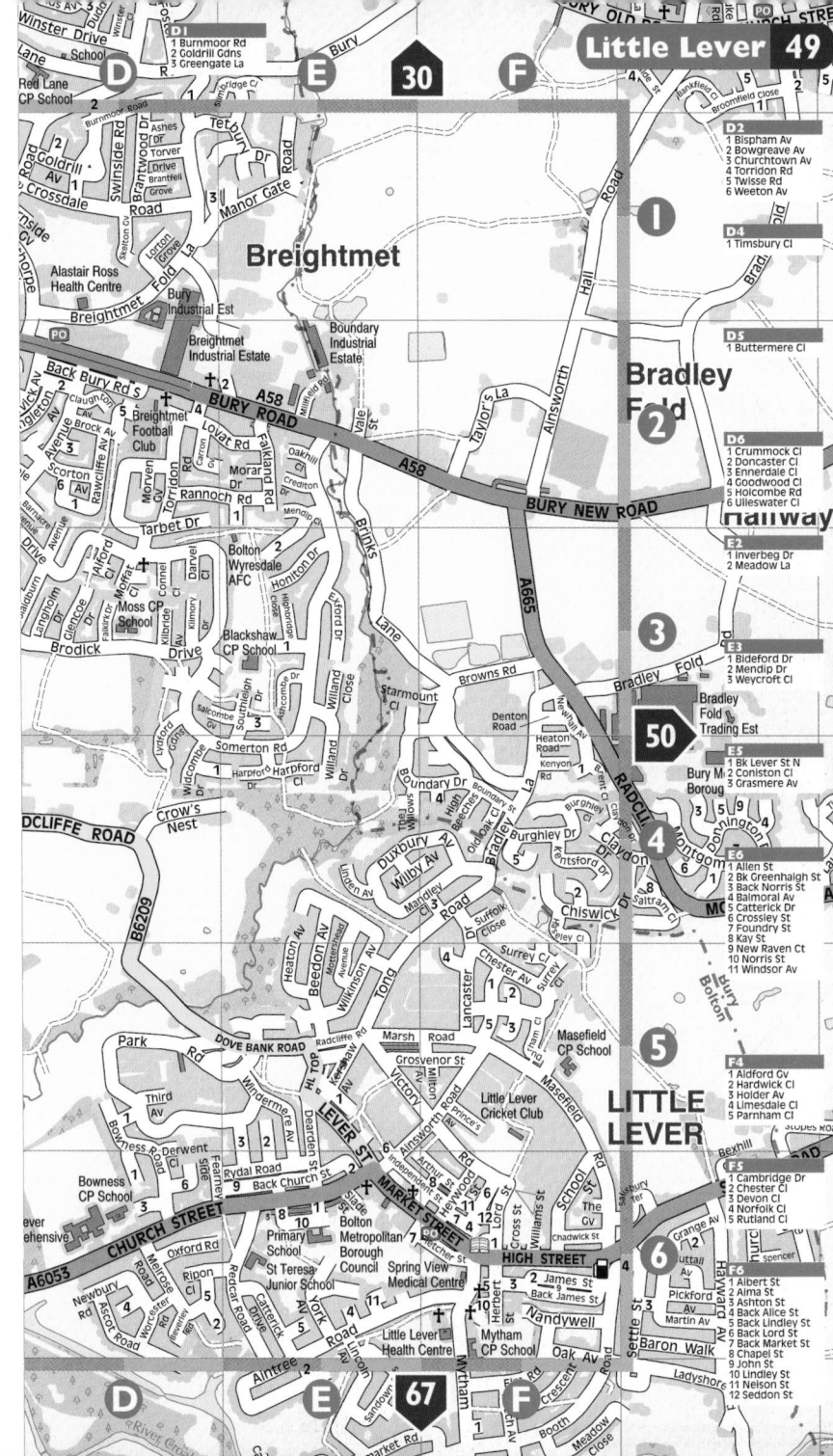

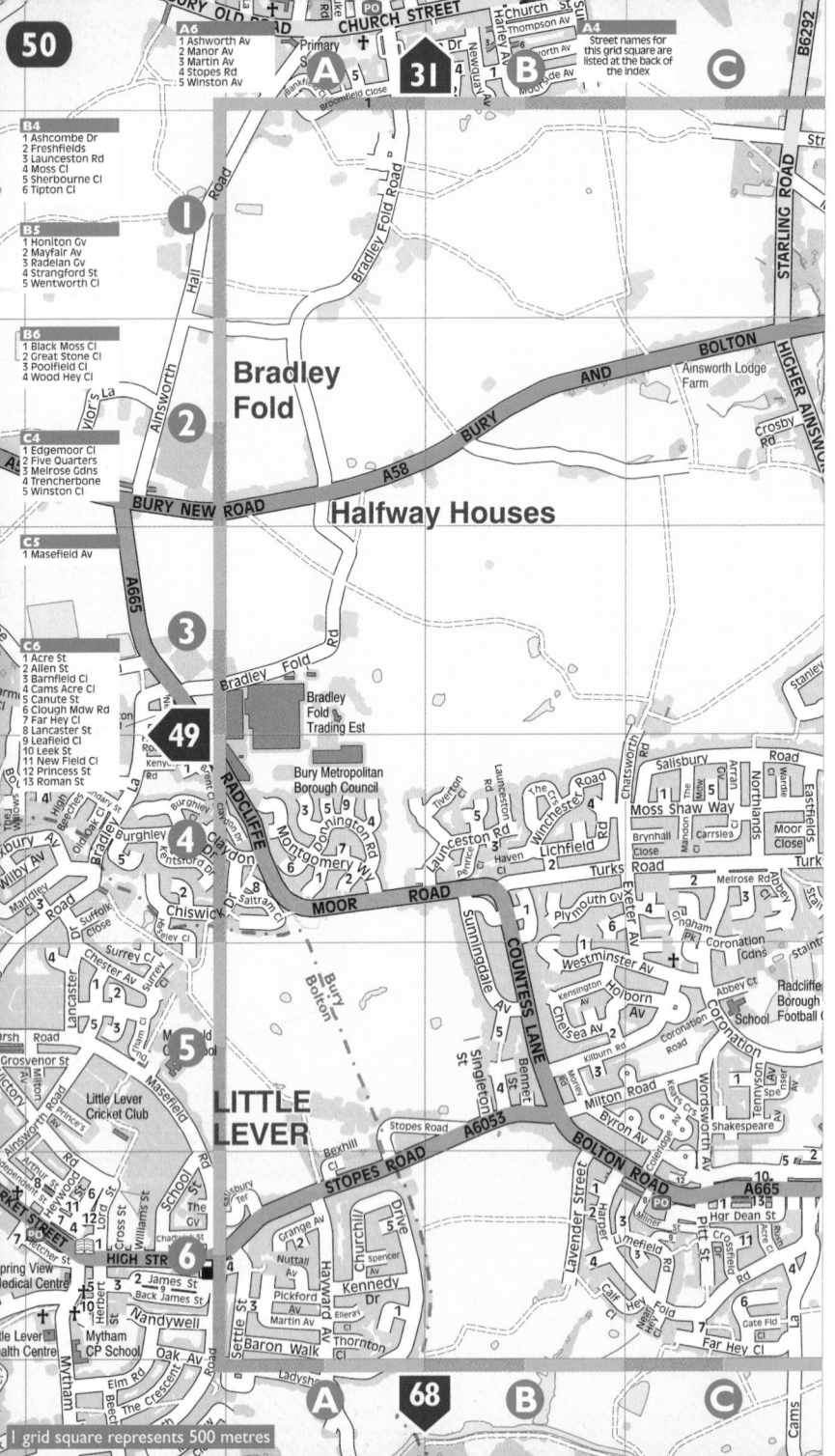

50

Street names for this grid square are listed at the back of the index

Bradley Fold

Halfway Houses

Bradley Fold Trading Est

Bury Metropolitan Borough Council

LITTLE LEVER

Little Lever Cricket Club

Ainsworth Lodge Farm

Radcliffe Borough Football C

Radcliffe Borough School

Spring View Medical Centre

Mytham CP School

le Lever Health Centre

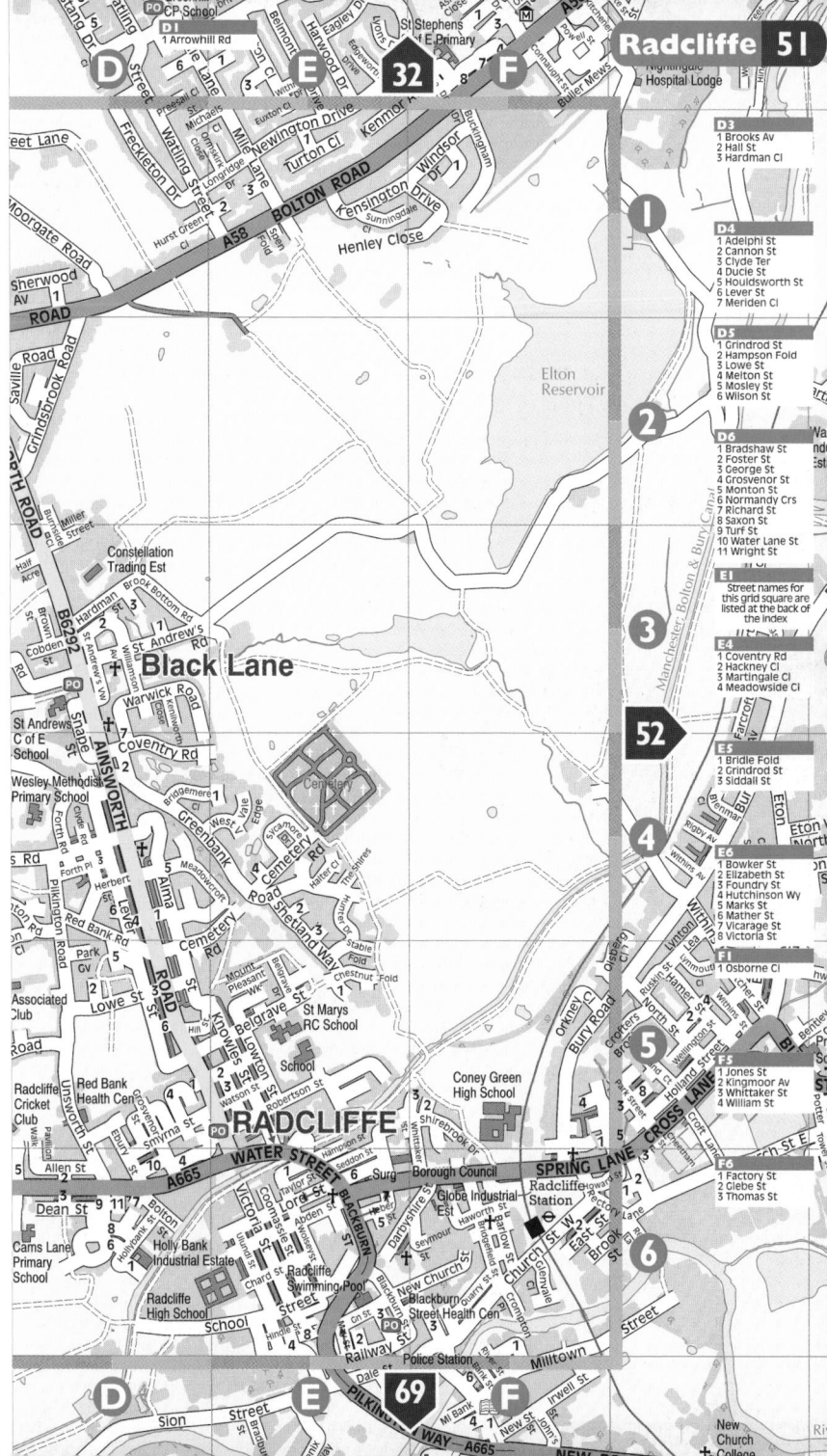

D1
1 Arrowhill Rd

32

D3
1 Brooks Av
2 Hall St
3 Hardman St

I

D4
1 Adelphi St
2 Cannon St
3 Clyde Ter
4 Ducie St
5 Houldsworth St
6 Lever St
7 Meriden Cl

D5
1 Grindrod St
2 Hampson Fold
3 Lowe St
4 Melton St
5 Mosley St
6 Wilson St

2

D6
1 Bradshaw St
2 Foster St
3 George St
4 Grosvenor St
5 Monton St
6 Normandy Crs
7 Richard St
8 Saxon St
9 Turf St
10 Water Lane St
11 Wright St

E1
Street names for
this grid square are
listed at the back of
the index

3

E4
1 Coventry Rd
2 Hackney Cl
3 Martingale Cl
4 Meadowside Cl

52

E5
1 Bridle Fold
2 Grindrod St
3 Siddall St

4

E6
1 Bowker St
2 Elizabeth St
3 Foundry St
4 Hutchinson Wy
5 Marks St
6 Mather St
7 Vicarage St
8 Victoria St

F1
1 Osborne Cl

5

F5
1 Jones St
2 Kingmoor Av
3 Whittaker St
4 William St

F6
1 Factory St
2 Glebe St
3 Thomas St

6

Black Lane

Constellation
Trading Est

St Andrew's
C of E
School

Wesley Methodist
Primary School

Cemetery

Associated
Club

Radcliffe
Cricket
Club

Red Bank
Health Cen

RADCLIFFE

Coney Green
High School

St Marys
RC School

Cams Lane
Primary
School

Holly Bank
Industrial Estate

Radcliffe
High School

Radcliffe
Swimming Pool

Blackburn
Street Health Cen

Globe Industrial
Est

Borough Council

Radcliffe
Station

Police Station

69

New
Church
College

Elton
Reservoir

St Stephens
E Primary

Henley Close

Nightingale
Hospital Lodge

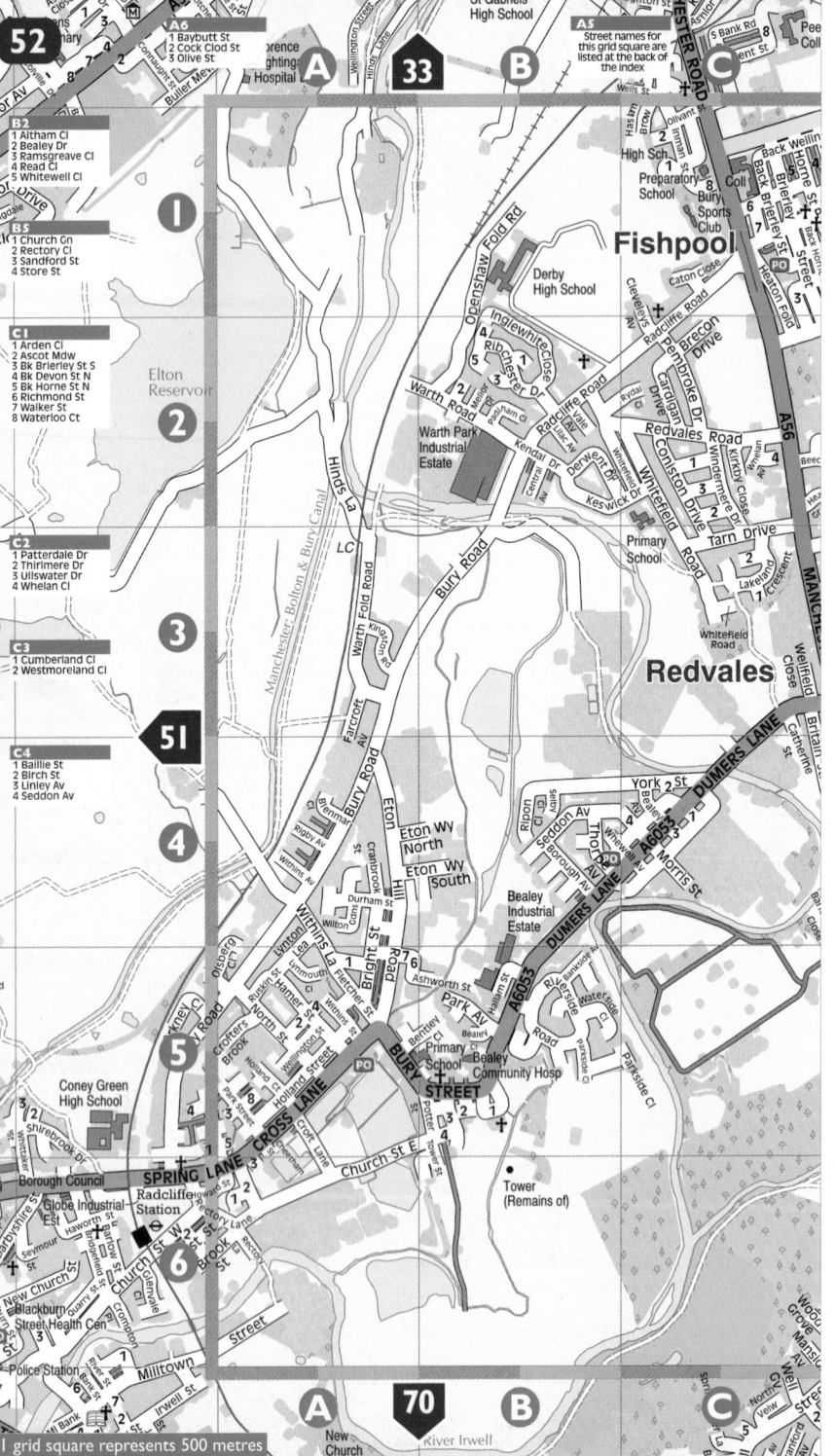

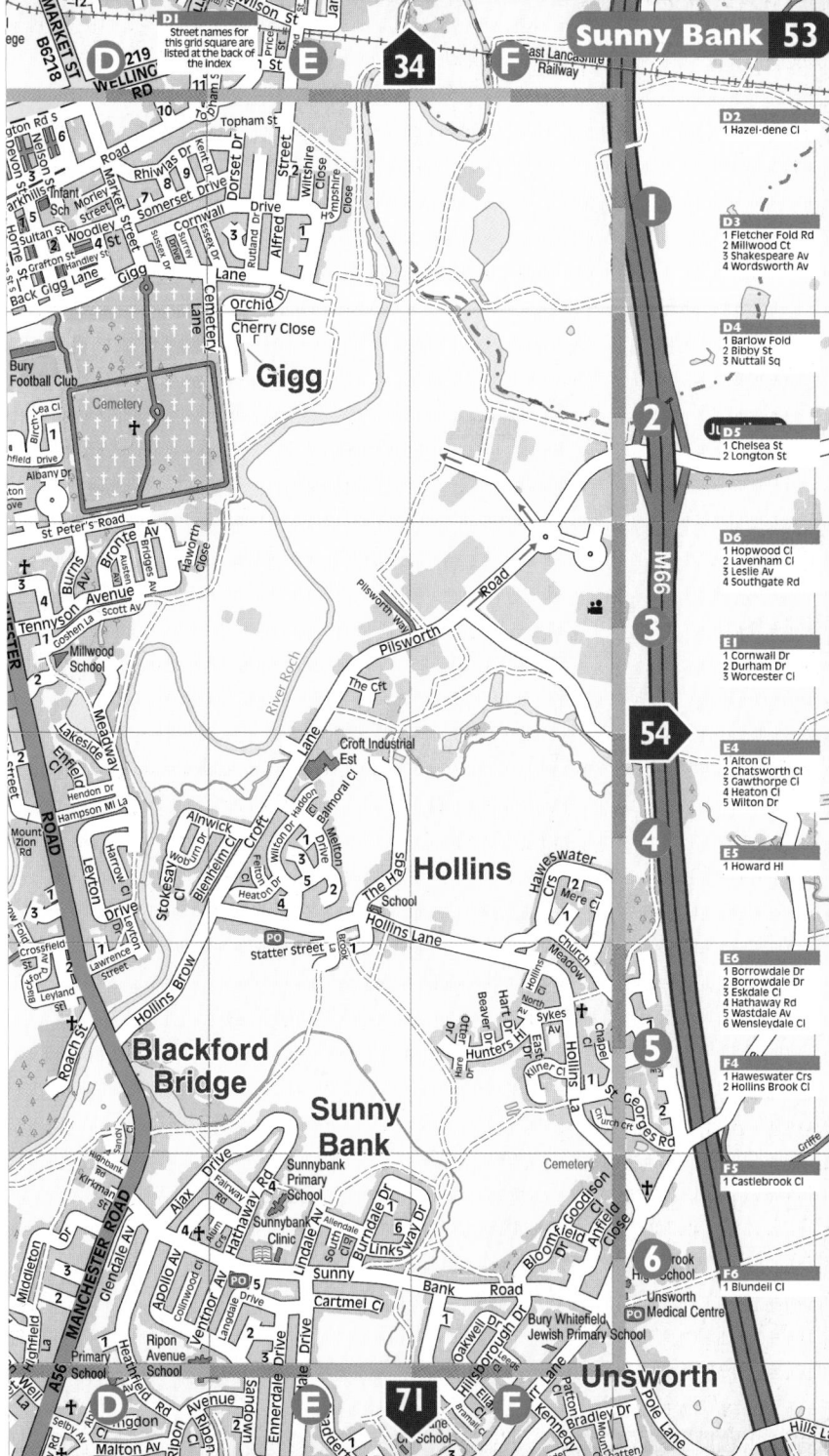

East Lancashire Railway

D1
Street names for this grid square are listed at the back of the index

D2
1 Hazel-dene Cl

D3
1 Fletcher Fold Rd
2 Millwood Ct
3 Shakespeare Av
4 Wordsworth Av

D4
1 Barlow Fold
2 Bibby St
3 Nuttall Sq

D5
1 Chelsea St
2 Longton St

D6
1 Hopwood Cl
2 Lavenham Cl
3 Leslie Av
4 Southgate Rd

E1
1 Cornwall Dr
2 Durham Dr
3 Worcester Cl

E4
1 Alton Cl
2 Chatsworth Cl
3 Cawthorpe Cl
4 Heaton Cl
5 Wilton Dr

E5
1 Howard Hl

E6
1 Borrowdale Dr
2 Borrowdale Dr
3 Eskdale Cl
4 Hathaway Rd
5 Wastdale Av
6 Wensleydale Cl

F4
1 Haweswater Crs
2 Hollins Brook Cl

F5
1 Castlebrook Cl

F6
1 Blundell Cl

Gigg

Bury Football Club

Cemetery

M66

Hollins

Blackford Bridge

Sunny Bank

Hollins Lane

Sunnybank Primary School

Sunnybank Clinic

Ripon Avenue School

Bury Whitefield Jewish Primary School

Unsworth Medical Centre

Unsworth

Cemetery

Croft Industrial Est

Millwood School

Pilsworth Way

Pilsworth

River Roch

The Cft

Manchester Road

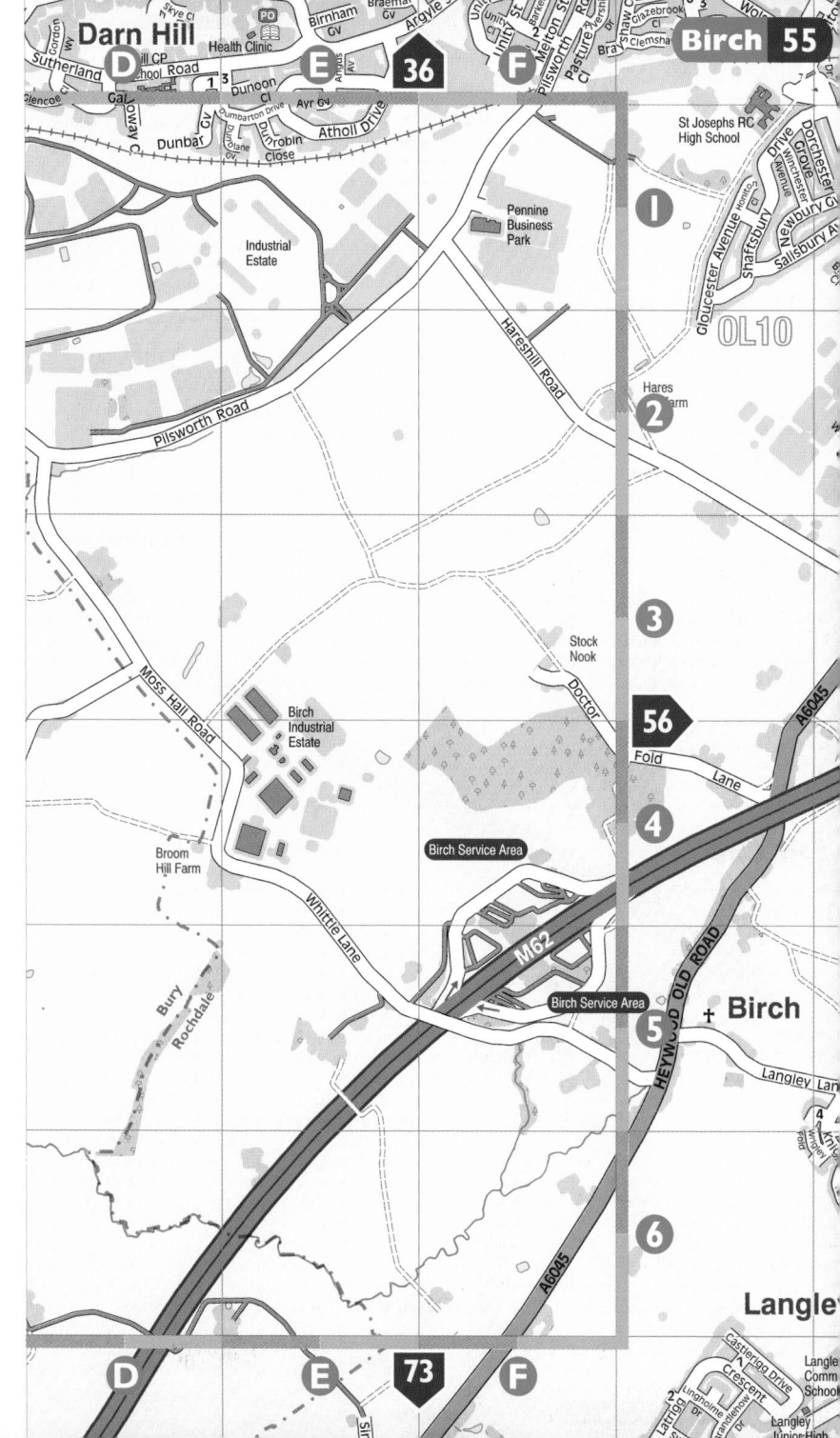

Darn Hill

Health Clinic

Sutherland

Gordon

Glencoe

Gal...

Hill CP
School Road

Dunbar GV

Dunoon
Cl

Ayr Gv

Cumbarton Drive

Durobin
Close

Skye Cl

Birnham
GV

Argyle

Braema...
Gv

Atholl Drive

36

Unity St

Melton St

Pilsworth Rd

Pasture Cl

Bra...

Clemsha...

St Josephs RC
High School

Dorchester

Grove

Winchester

Shaftsbury
Drive

Newbury
Avenue

Horton

Gloucester Avenue

Salisbury Av

OL10

Pennine
Business
Park

Industrial
Estate

Pilsworth Road

Hareshill Road

Hares
Farm

2

3

Stock
Nook

Doctor

56

Fold
Lane

A6045

Moss Hall Road

Birch
Industrial
Estate

4

Broom
Hill Farm

Birch Service Area

Whittle Lane

M62

Birch Service Area

HEYWOOD OLD ROAD

+ Birch

Langley Lan

5

Bury
Rochdale

6

A6045

Langle

Castlerigg Drive

Crescent

Langle
Comm
School

Langley
Junior High

D

E

73

F

Lingholme

Latrigg

Stainen...

Dr

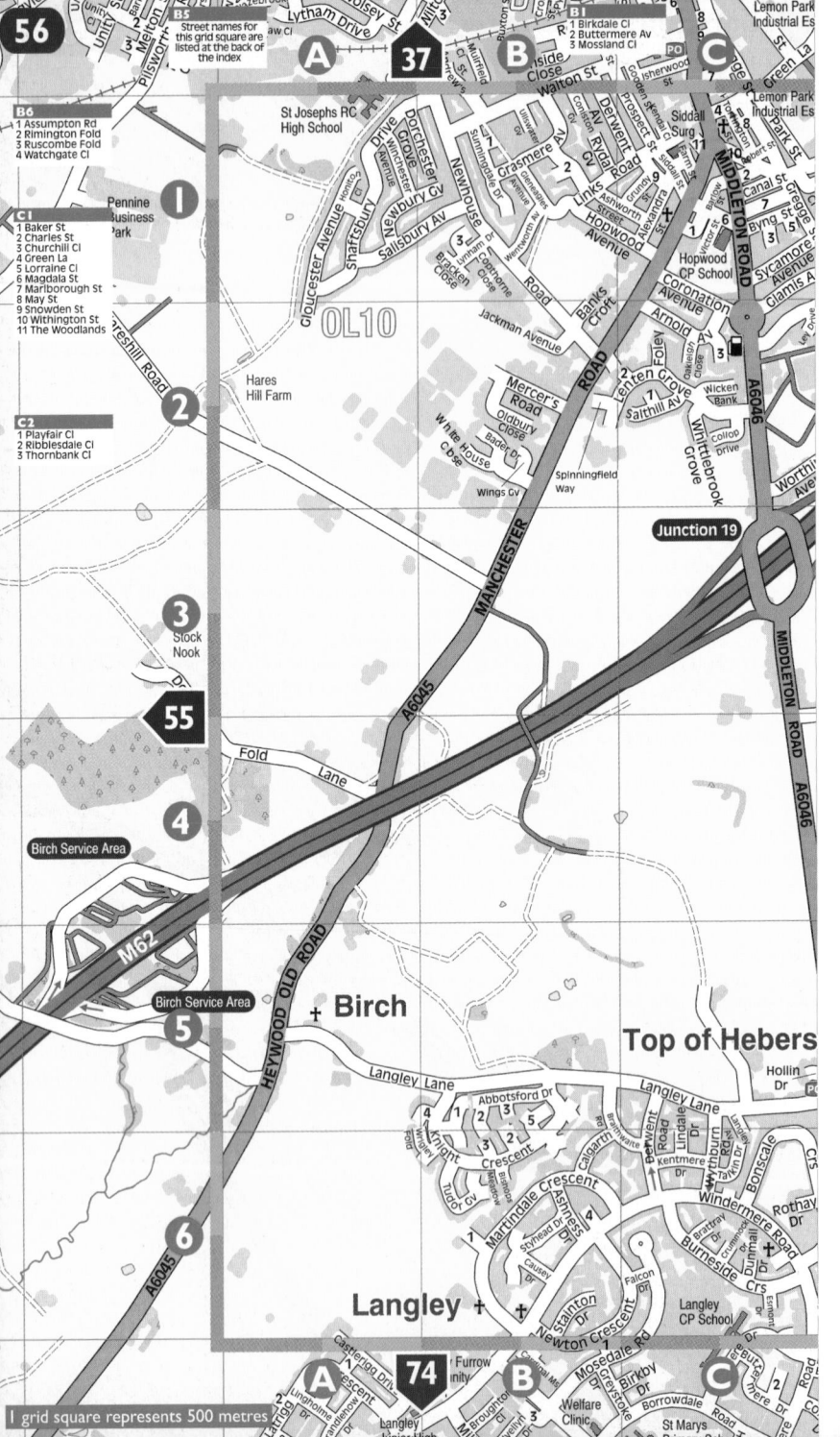

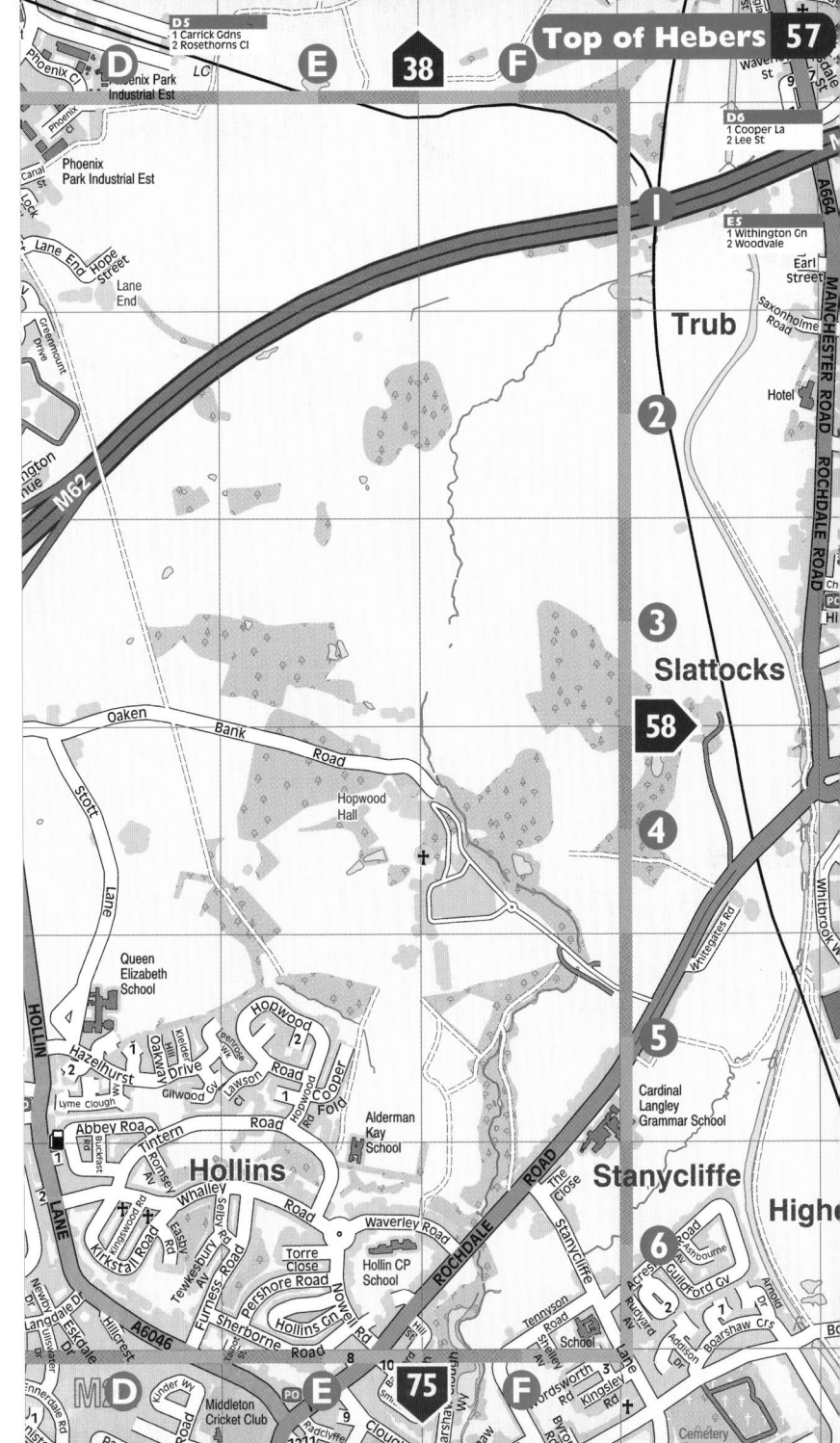

D

E

38

F

D5
1 Carrick Gdns
2 Rosethorns Cl

LC

Phoenix Cl

Phoenix Park
Industrial Est

Phoenix
Cl

Waverley
St

9

D6
1 Cooper La
2 Lee St

A664

Phoenix
Park Industrial Est

Canal
St

Lane End

Hope
Street

Lane
End

Greenmount
Drive

ngton
Avenue

M62

Stott Lane

Oaken Bank Road

Hopwood
Hall

Queen
Elizabeth
School

Hazelhurst

Hollin

Kielder
Hill

Oakway

Gilvood Cv.

Lyme Clough

Abbey Road

Tintern

Whalley Road

Kirkstall Road

Easby
Rd.

Tewkesbury Av.

Newby
Dr.

Langdale Rd.

Eskdale

Hillcrest

A6046

Kinder Wy

Middleton
Cricket Club

Hopwood
Road

Lawson Cu.

Hopwood
Road

Cooper
Ford

Road

Alderman
Kay
School

Hollins

Furness
Road

Pershore Road

Sherborne Road

Romsey
Av.

Aldis

Torre
Close

Waverley Road

Hollin CP
School

Nowell Rd.

Hollins Gn.

ROCHDALE ROAD

The
Close

Stanycliffe

Stanycliffe Lane

Tennyson
Road

Shelley Av.

School

Trub

E5
1 Withington Gn
2 Woodvale

Earl
Street

saxonholme
Road

Hotel

MANCHESTER ROAD

ROCHDALE ROAD

Ch

PC

Hi

Whitbrook W.

Slattocks

58

Whitegates Rd

Cardinal
Langley
Grammar School

Cullyford Gv.

Ashbourne
Road

Acres
Rd.

Rudyard

Boarshaw Crs.

Arnold
Dr.

Addison

High

Wordsworth Rd.

Kingsley
Rd.

Byron

Cemetery

M

D

PO

E

75

F

B

2

3

4

5

6

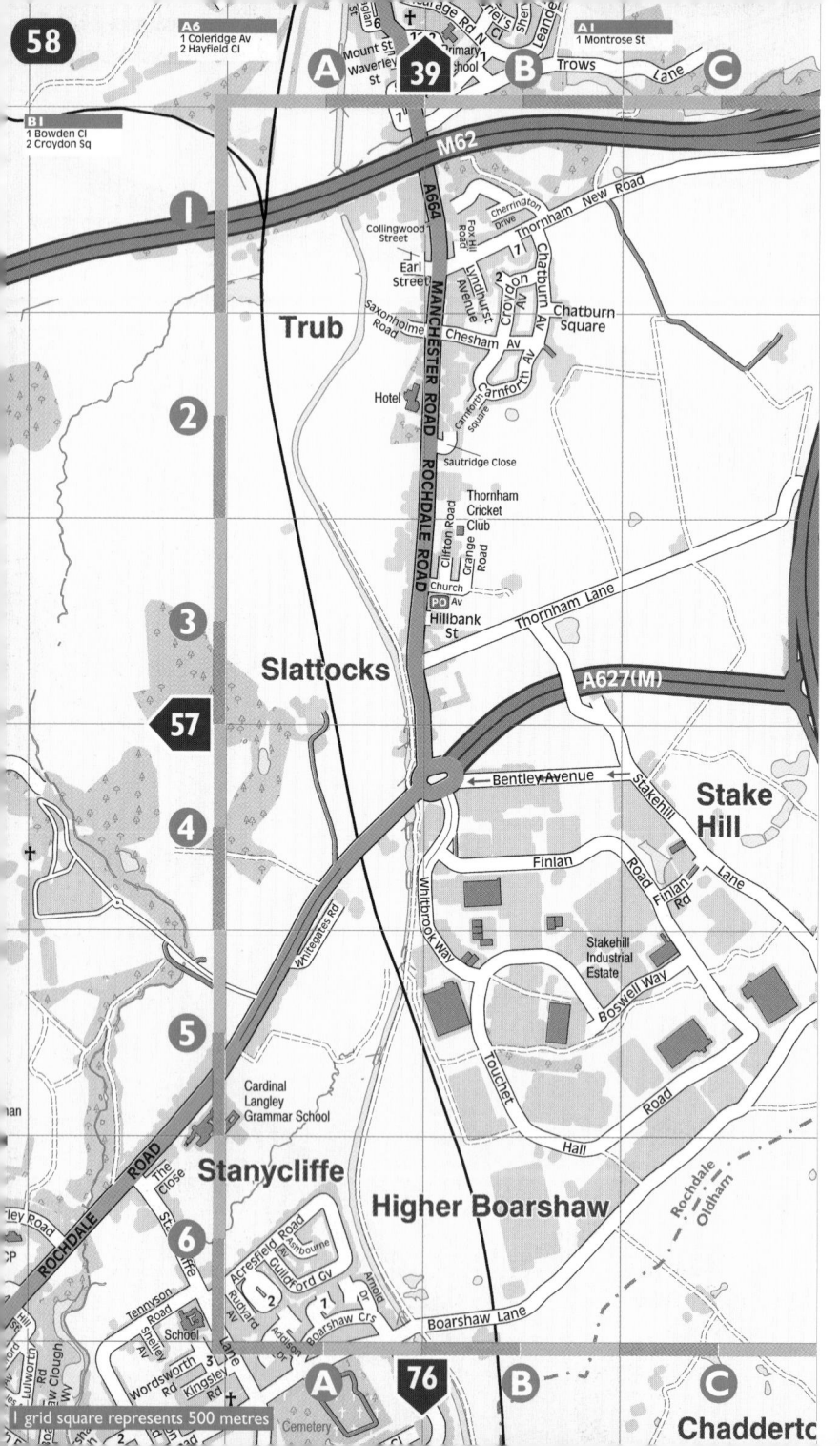

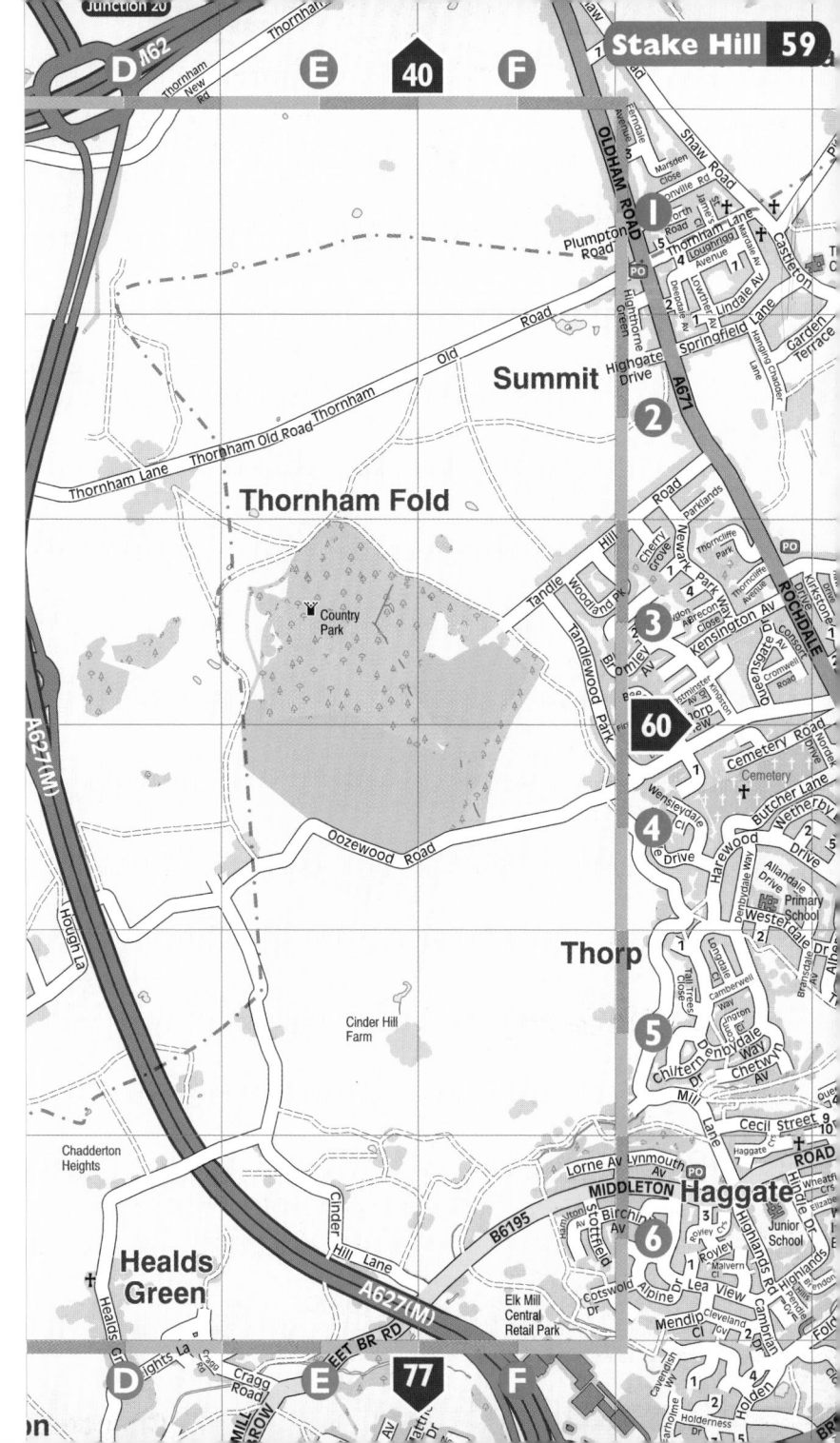

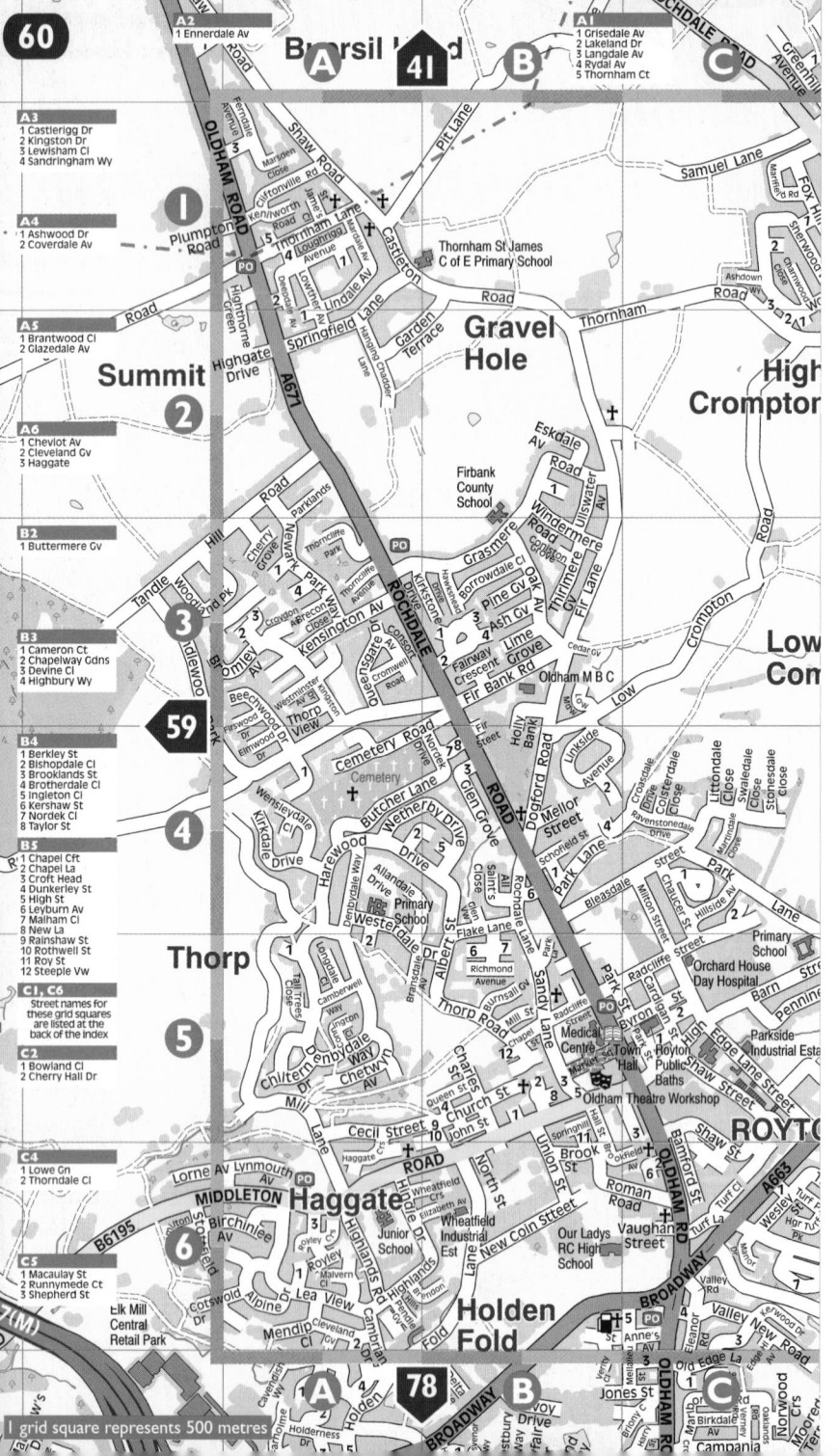

I grid square represents 500 metres

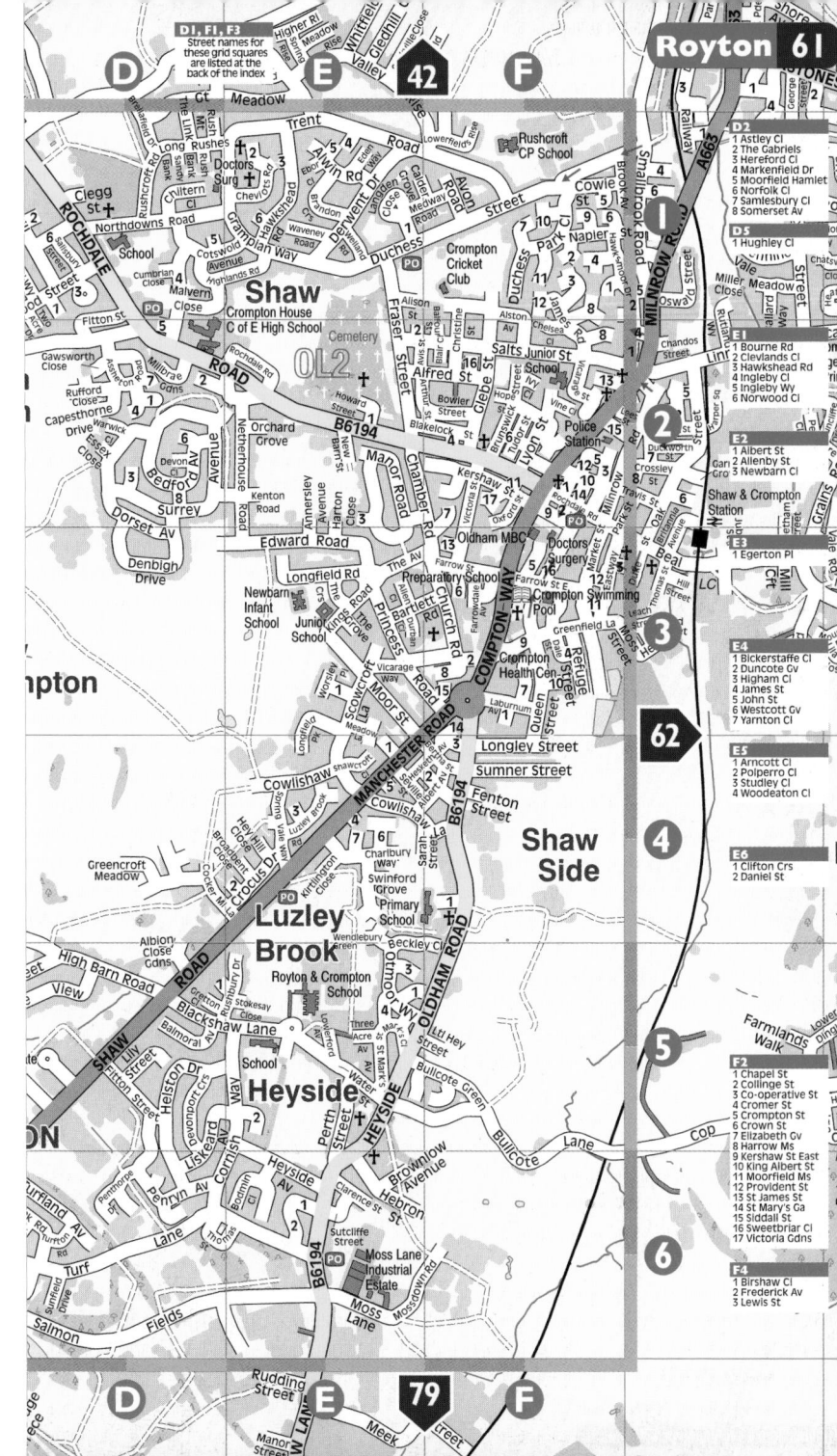

D1, F1, F3
Street names for these grid squares are listed at the back of the index

42

79

62

D2
1 Astley Cl
2 The Gabriels
3 Hereford Cl
4 Markenfield Dr
5 Moorfield Hamlet
6 Norfolk Cl
7 Samlesbury Cl
8 Somerset Av

D5
1 Hughley Cl

E1
1 Bourne Rd
2 Clevlands Cl
3 Hawkshead Rd
4 Ingleby Cl
5 Ingleby Wy
6 Norwood Cl

E2
1 Albert St
2 Allenby St
3 Newbarn Cl

E3
1 Egerton Pl

E4
1 Bickerstaffe Cl
2 Duncote Gv
3 Higham St
4 James St
5 John St
6 Westcott Gv
7 Yarnton

E5
1 Arncott Cl
2 Polperro Cl
3 Studley Cl
4 Woodeaton Cl

E6
1 Clifton Crs
2 Daniel St

F2
1 Chapel St
2 Collinge St
3 Co-operative St
4 Cromer St
5 Crompton St
6 Crown St
7 Elizabeth Gv
8 Harrow Ms
9 Kershaw St East
10 King Albert St
11 Moorfield Ms
12 Provident St
13 St James St
14 St Mary's Ga
15 Siddall St
16 Sweetbriar Cl
17 Victoria Gdns

F4
1 Birshaw Cl
2 Frederick Av
3 Lewis St

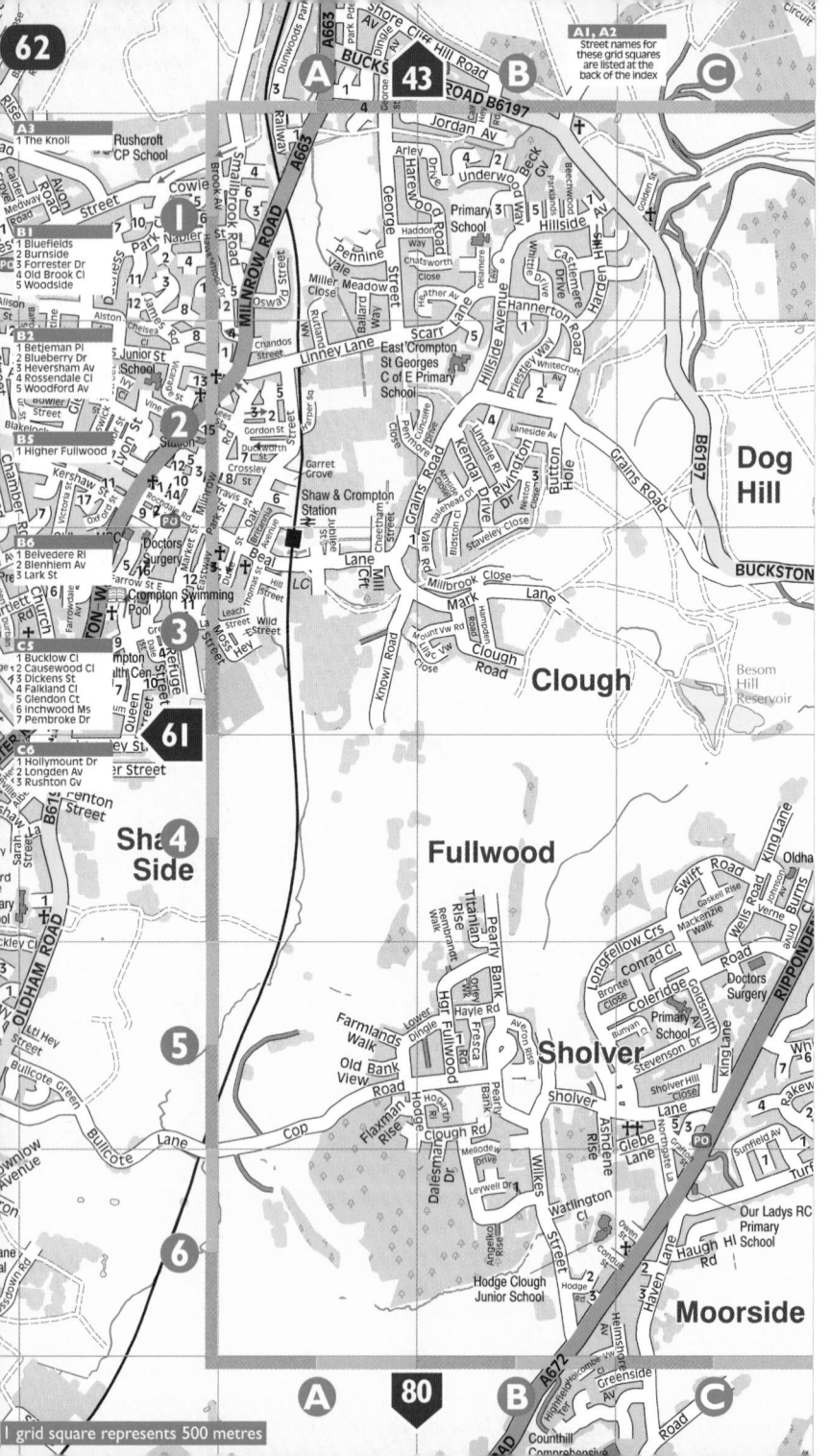

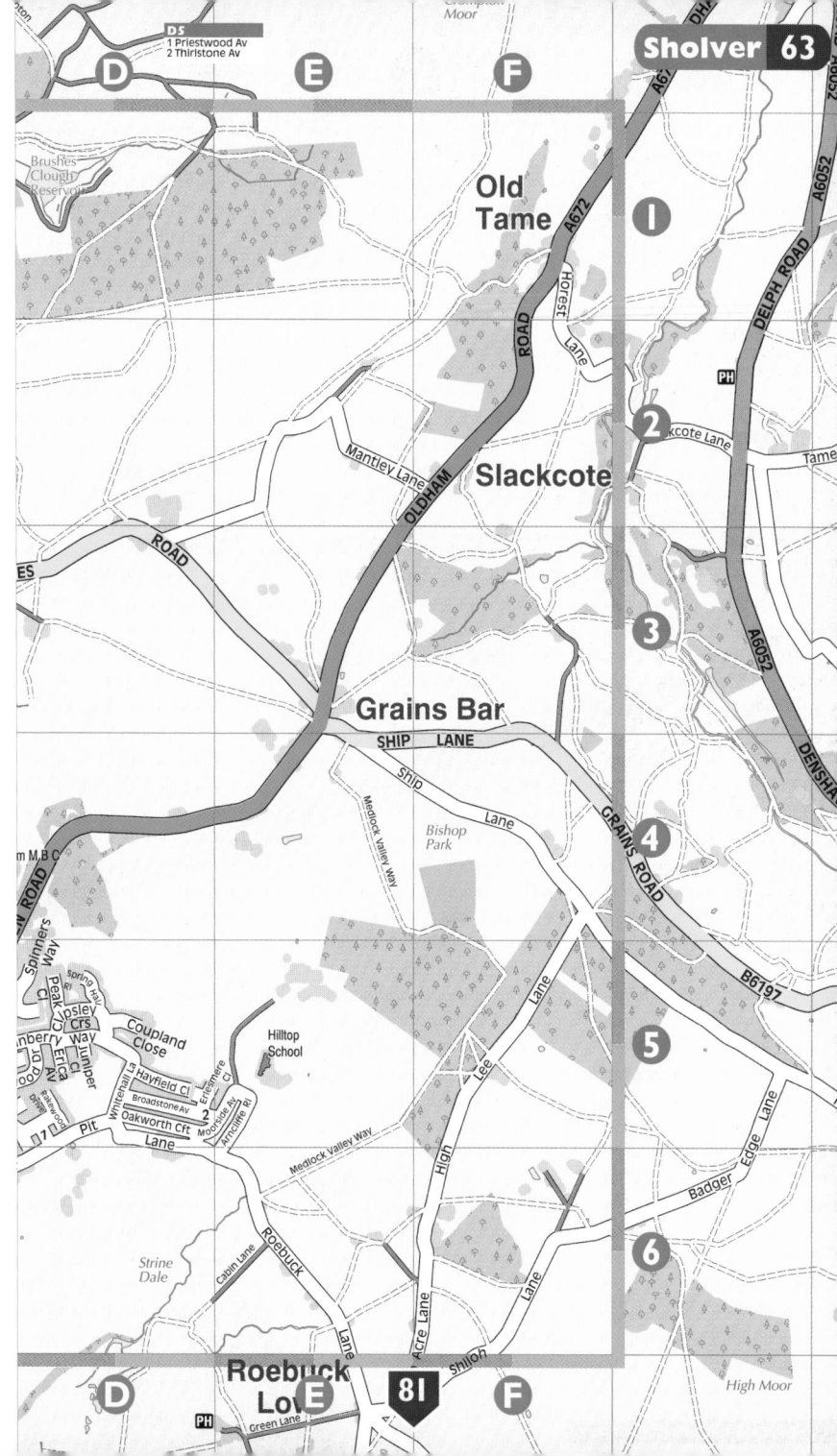

D5
1 Priestwood Av
2 Thirlstone Av

D

E

F

Compton
Moor

Brushes
Clough
Reservoir

Old
Tame

A672

Horest Lane

A67

DELPH ROAD

A6052

A6052

1

PH

2

ckcote Lane

Tame

Mantley Lane

OLDHAM ROAD

Slackcote

ROAD

ES

A6052

DENSHAW

3

Grains Bar

SHIP LANE

Ship Lane

Medlock Valley Way

*Bishop
Park*

GRAINS ROAD

4

B6197

m M.B.C

NEW ROAD

Spinners

View

Peak Cl

Lipsley

Crs

spring Trail

Juniper

Cl

Erica

Av

nberry

Way

xford Rd

Coupland
Close

Whitehall La

Hayfield Cl

Broadstone Av

Moorside Av

Ennesmere Cl

Arncliffe Rd

Hilltop
School

Lee Lane

5

Oakworth Cft

Pit

Lane

Medlock Valley Way

High Lane

Badger

Edge Lane

6

*Strine
Dale*

Cabin Lane

Roebuck Lane

Acre Lane

Shiloh

High Moor

D

**Roebuck
Lo**

E

81

F

PH

Green Lane

64

46

A1
street names for
this grid square are
listed at the back of
the index

B1
1 Hurlston Rd
2 Roseneath Gv
3 Woodvale Dr
4 Woodvale Gdns

B5
1 Clarke Crs
2 Spiningdale

C1
1 Childwall Cl
2 Duncombe Rd
3 Lever Edge La

C3
1 Ennerdale Gv
2 Stanley Rd
3 Thirlmere Gv
4 Whins Av

C4
1 Crummock Rd
2 Elterwater Rd
3 Loweswater Rd

C6
1 Belcroft Gv
2 Co-operative St
3 Highgate Dr
4 Manorial Dr
5 Rothwell Crs

Lever-Edge

Hayward School
& Bolton South
6th Form College

Primary School

Hayward
Sports
Centre

Edge Fold

Hollins

PLODDER LANE

B6199

Watergate Lane

M61

FORD ROAD

Watergate
Dr

Junction 4
WATERGATE LANE

M61

Israel's
Farm

Rosemary Lane

Back Lane

SALFORD ROAD

A6

Leadbeater
Farm

Worsley
Wharton
School

Greenheys

MANCHESTER ROAD

Worsley
Trading
Estate

Little Hulton
Cricket Club

Worsley
Trading
Estate

A   **B**   **C**

1 grid square represents 500 metres

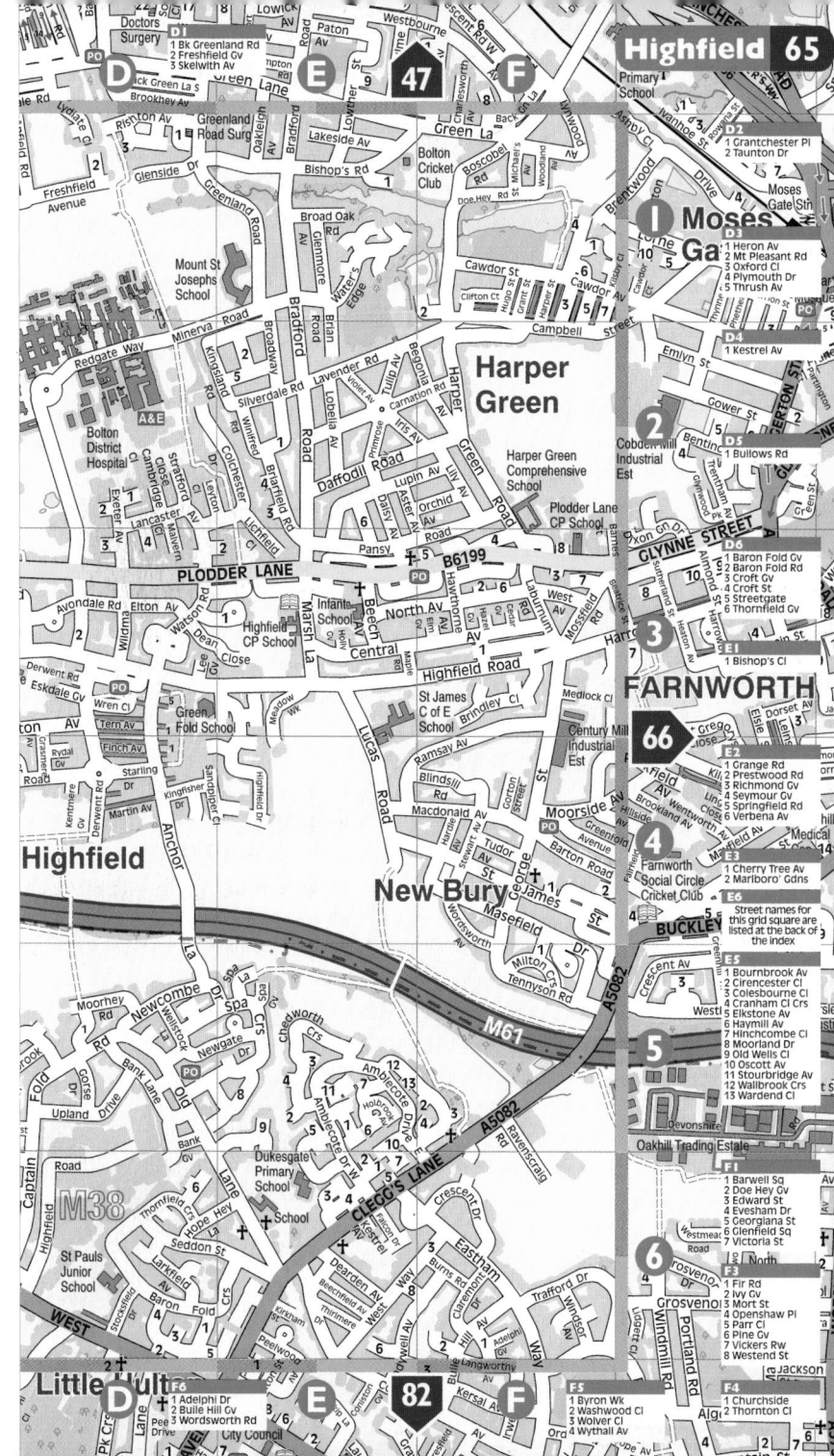

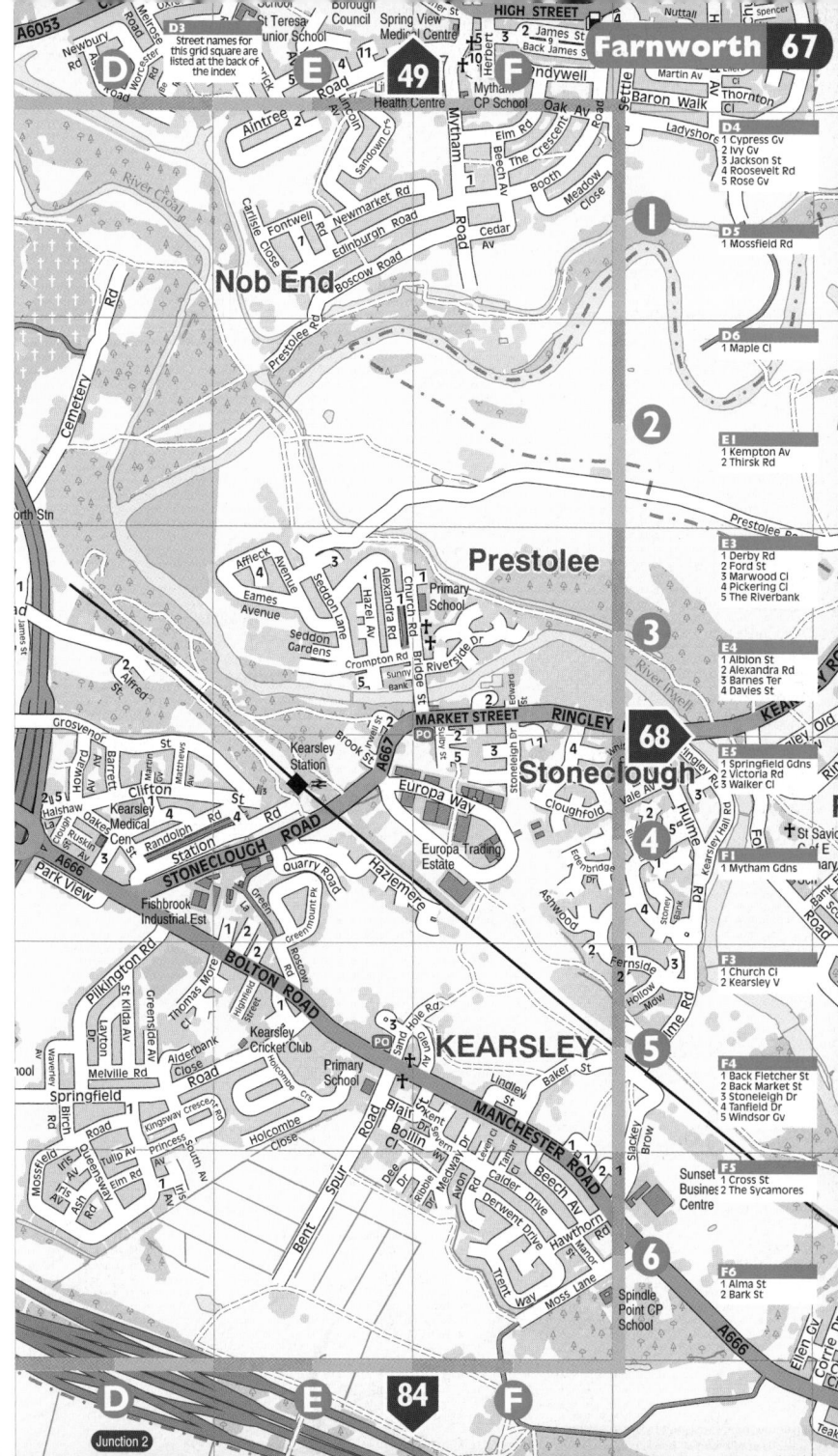

A6053

Newbury Rd

Worcester Rd

D

St Teresa's Junior School

Borough Council

Spring View Medical Centre

HIGH STREET

James St
Back James St

Herbert

E

11

F

49
Health Centre

Mytham CP School

Aintree

River Croal

Nob End

Fontwell

Carlisle

Newmarket Rd

Edinburgh Road

Boscow Road

Cedar Av

Prestolee Rd

Cemetery Rd

Prestolee

Affleck Avenue

Eames Avenue

Seddon Lane

Seddon Gardens

Hazel Av

Alexandra Rd

Church Rd

Primary School

Crompton Rd

Bridge St

Riverside Dr

Sunny Bank

Edward St

MARKET STREET

RINGLEY

Stonecleigh Dr

Cloughfold

Stoneclough

Kearsley Station

A667

Brook St

Europa Way

Europa Trading Estate

Grosvenor

Howard St

Barrett St

Martin St

Matthews St

Clifton St

Halshaw Oaks

Kearsley Medical Cen

Randolph Rd

Station Rd

Park View

A666

STONECLOUGH ROAD

Quarry Road

Hazlemere

Fishbrook Industrial Est

BOLTON ROAD

Greenmount Pk

Boscow

Pilkington Rd

St Kilda Av

Layton

Thomas More Cl

Greenside Av

Alderbank Close

Road

Kearsley Cricket Club

Holcombe Crs

PO

Sand Hole Rd

KEARSLEY

Primary School

Blair

Bollin

Kingsway Cresc

Springfield

Mossfield Rd

Iris Av

Pennysway

Elm Rd

Princess Av

South Av

Spur Rd

Bent

Dee Dr

Avon Rd

Calder Drive

Derwent Drive

Undlew St

MANCHESTER ROAD

Beech Av

Baker St

Hawthorn

Trent Way

Moss Lane

St Saviour C of E

Kearsley Hall Rd

Hulme Rd

Vale Av

Greenbridge Dr

Ashwood

Fernside

Hollow Mow

Lime Rd

Stoney

Slackey Brow

Sunset Business Centre

Spindle Point CP School

A666

Ladyshore

D4
1 Cypress Gv
2 Ivy Gv
3 Jackson St
4 Roosevelt Rd
5 Rose Gv

D5
1 Mossfield Rd

D6
1 Maple Cl

E1
1 Kempton Av
2 Thirsk Rd

E3
1 Derby Rd
2 Ford St
3 Marwood Cl
4 Pickering Cl
5 The Riverbank

E4
1 Albion St
2 Alexandra Rd
3 Barnes Ter
4 Davies St

E5
1 Springfield Gdns
2 Victoria Rd
3 Walker Cl

E1
1 Mytham Gdns

F3
1 Church Cl
2 Kearsley V

F4
1 Back Fletcher St
2 Back Market St
3 Stoneleigh Dr
4 Tanfield Dr
5 Windsor Gv

F5
1 Cross St
2 The Sycamores

F6
1 Alma St
2 Bark St

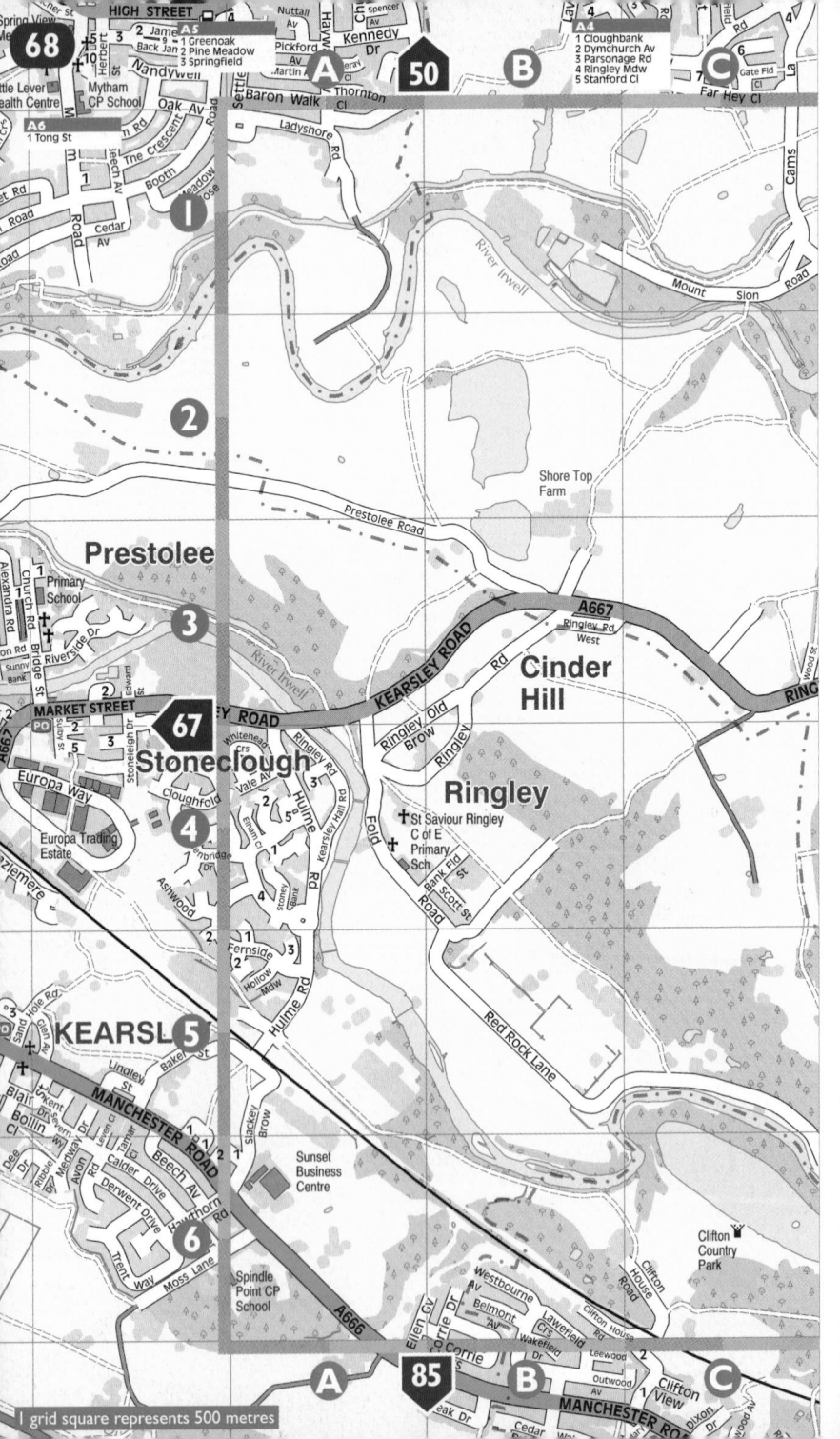

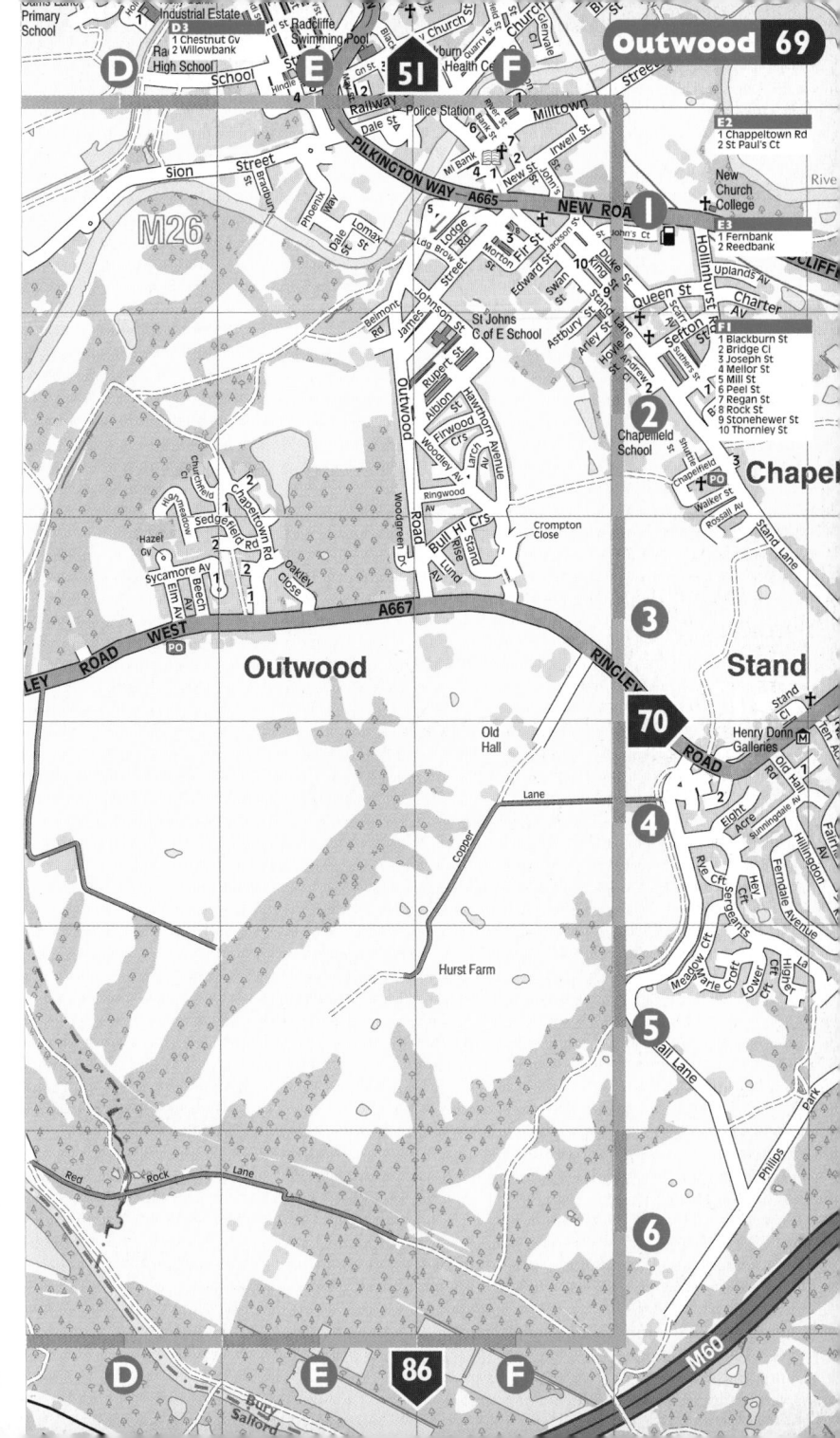

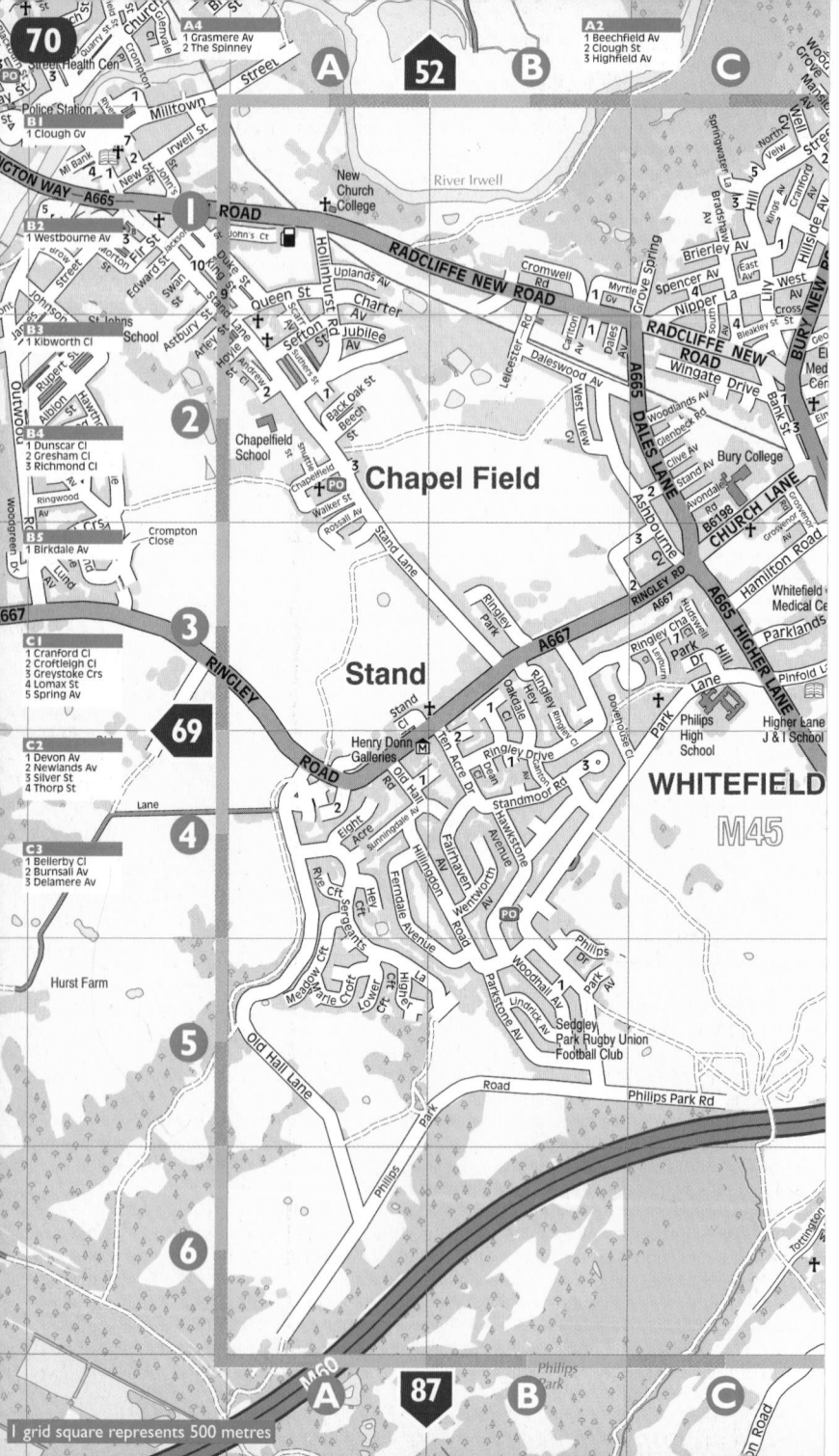

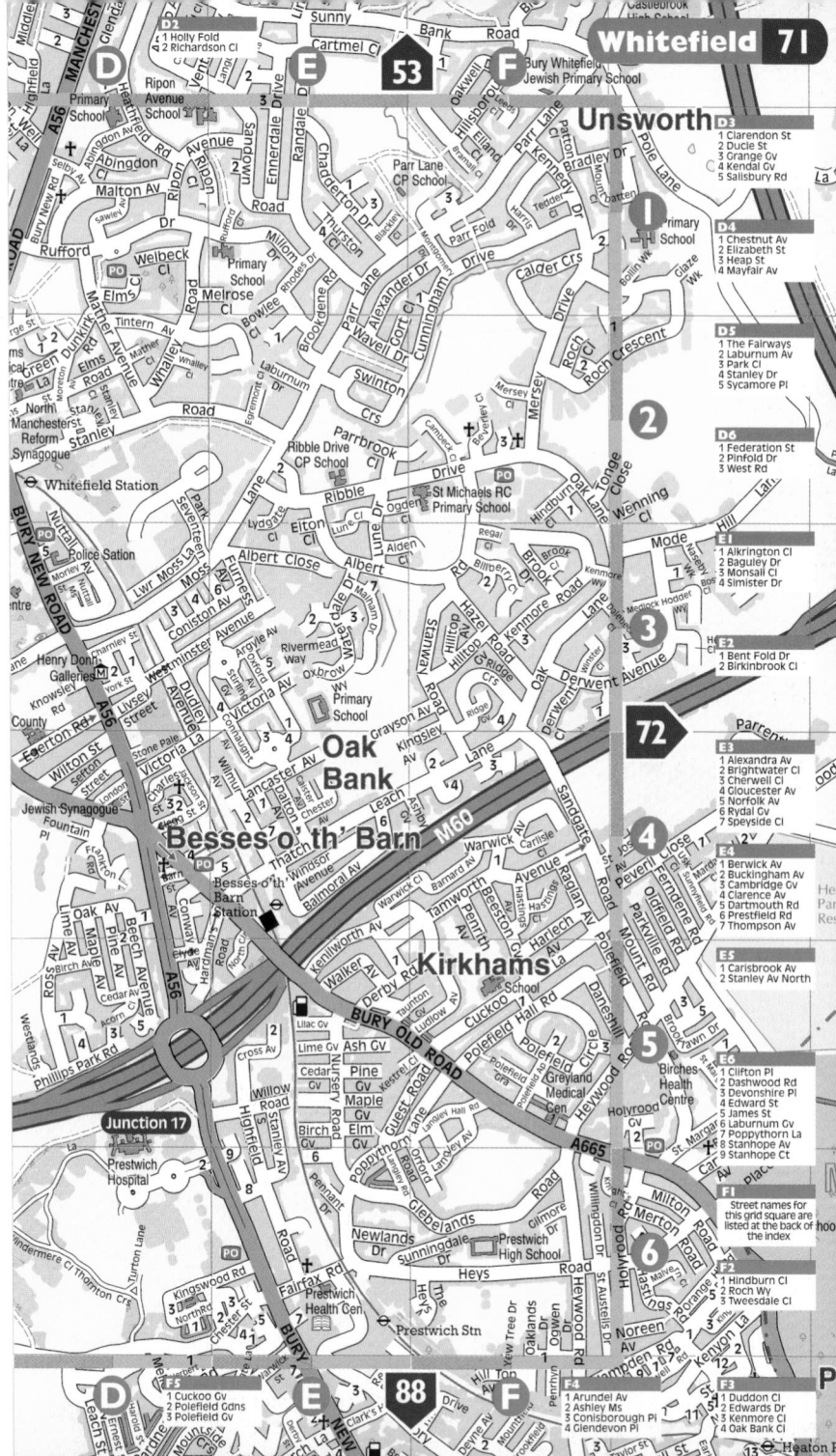

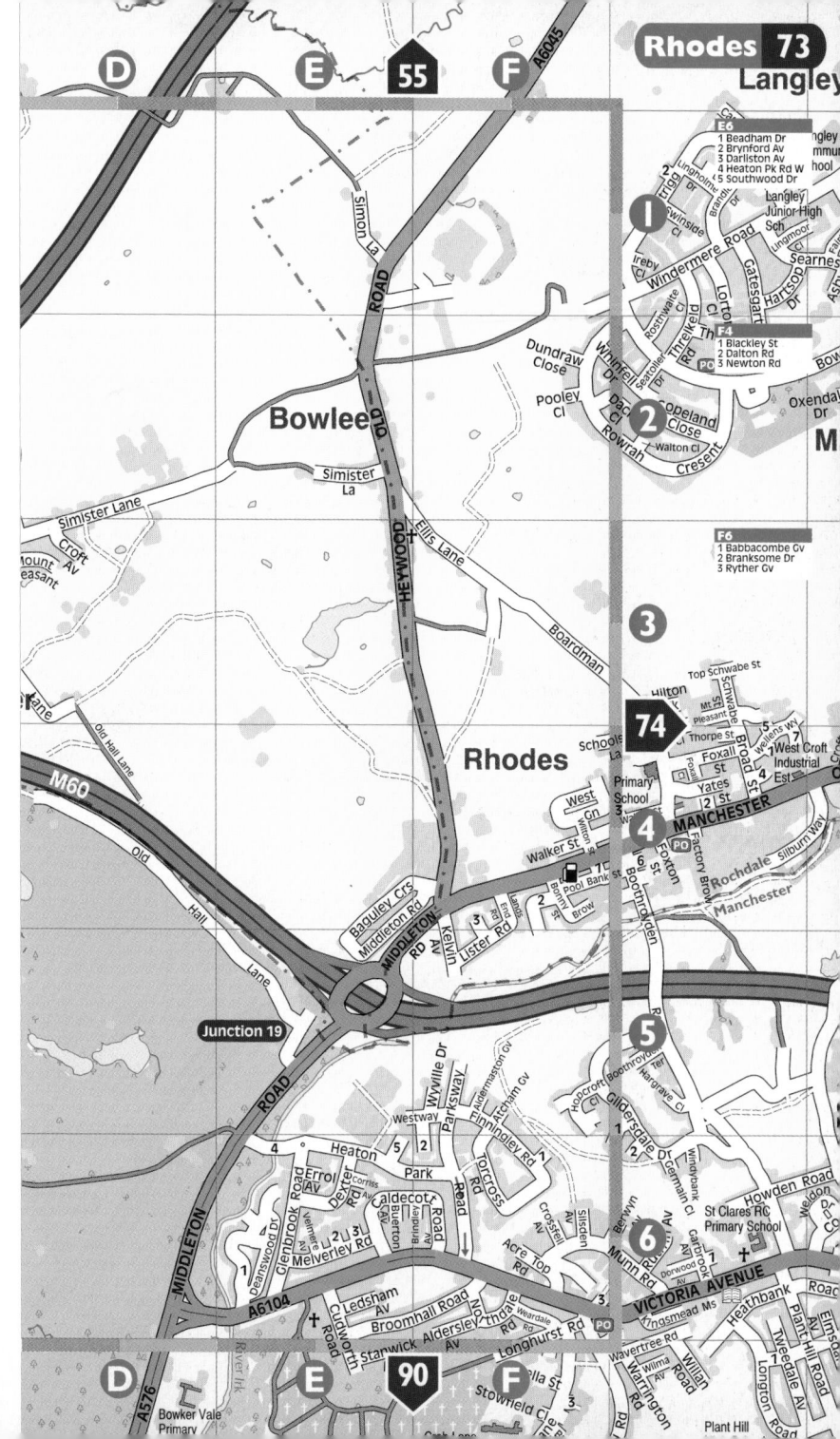

D E 55 F A6045

E6
1 Beadham Dr
2 Brynford Av
3 Darliston Av
4 Heaton Pk Rd W
5 Southwood Dr

Langley
Communi
School

Langley
Junior High
Sch

Searnes

F4
1 Blackley St
2 Dalton Rd
3 Newton Rd

Windermere Road

Gatesgart

Harrsop

Dr

Ash

Bow

Oxendal
Dr

M

Dundraw
Close

Pooley
Cl

Rowrah

Whinfell
Dr

Thelkel

Scandale

Dacre
Cl

Copeland
Close

Walton Cl

Cresent

Bowlee

OLD

HEYWOOD

ROAD

Simon La

Simister
La

Simister Lane

Ellis Lane

Croft
Av

Mount
Pleasant

ane

Old Hall Lane

Boardman

F6
1 Babbacombe Gv
2 Branksome Dr
3 Ryther Gv

3

Rhodes

Top Schwabe St

Schwabe

Hilton

Mt
Pleasant

Thorpe St

Schools
La

74

Broad St

Wellens Wy

West Croft
Industrial
Est

Foxall
St

Yates
St

West
Grn

Primary
School

2 St

MANCHESTER

4

Foxton

PO

Factory Brow

Rochdale Silburn Way

Manchester

Walker St

Pool Bank

Brony
St

Bootholden

Brony
Brow

Lister Rd

Kelvin
Av

Land

End

M60

Old

Hall

Lane

Baguley Crs

Middleton Rd

MIDDLETON

RD

Junction 19

5

HighCroft
Cl

Boothroyd

Hargrave Cl

Gilderscale Dr

Wyville Dr

Parksway

Ackermaston Gv

Afton Gv

Finningley Rd

Westway

Heaton

Park

Errol
Av

Dexter
Rd

Corliss

Caldecot
Av

Buerton

Torcross

Crossield
Rd

Acre Top
Rd

Slisden

Whitebank

Germain Cl

Berwyn

Garbrook
Av

Derwood
Av

Howden Road

St Clares RC
Primary School

Munn Rd

Victoria Avenue

Healthbank

Plant Hill Road

Roac

Elmsfie

MIDDLETON

ROAD

A576

A6104

Glenbrook Dr

Deanswood Dr

Valmere

Melverley Rd

Ledsham
Av

Cudworth
Road

Broomhall Road

Stanwick

Aldersley
Av

Weardale

Thorndale

Rd

PO

Longhurst

Kingsmead Ms

Wavertree Rd

Willan

Warrington

Wilma

Longton
Road

Twedale Av

Plant Hill

D E 90 F

Bowker Vale
Primary

River Irk

Bella St

Stowfield Cl

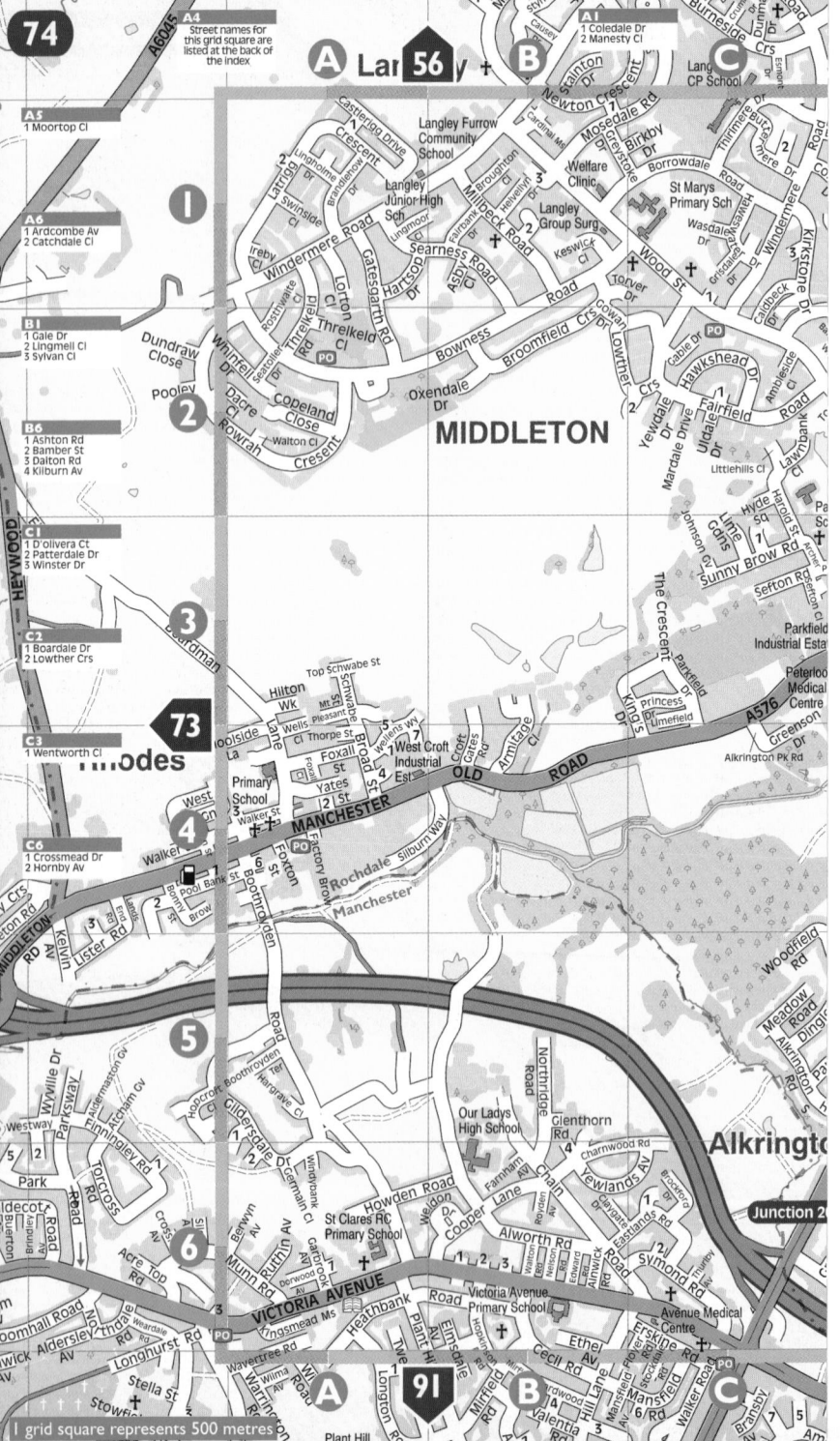

A Lan **56** y **B** **C**

A4
Street names for
this grid square are
listed at the back of
the index

A1
1 Coledale Dr
2 Manesty Cl

A5
1 Moortop Cl

A6
1 Ardcombe Av
2 Catchdale Cl

B1
1 Gale Dr
2 Lingmell Cl
3 Sylvan Cl

B6
1 Ashton Rd
2 Bamber St
3 Dalton Rd
4 Kilburn Av

C1
1 D'olivera Ct
2 Patterdale Dr
3 Winster Dr

C2
1 Boardale Dr
2 Lowther Crs

C3
1 Wentworth Cl

C6
1 Crossmead Dr
2 Hornby Av

MIDDLETON

73

Rhodes

MANCHESTER

OLD ROAD

Rochdale

Manchester

Alkrington

Junction 20

Our Ladys
High School

St Clares RC
Primary School

Victoria Avenue
Primary School

Avenue Medical
Centre

A **91** **B** **C**

1 grid square represents 500 metres

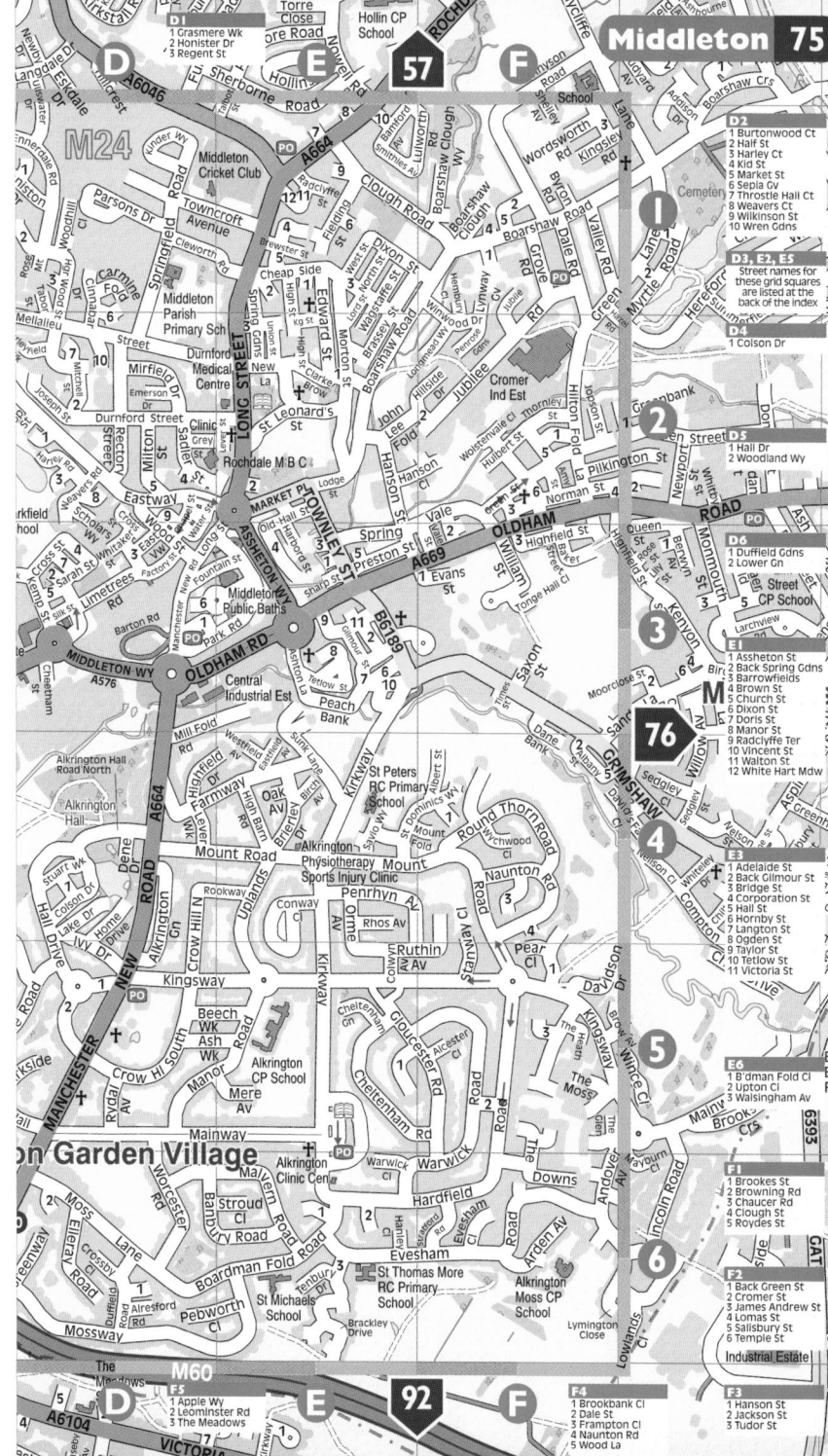

M24

Middleton Cricket Club

Middleton Parish Primary Sch

Durnford Medical Centre

Rochdale M B C

Middleton Public Baths

Central Industrial Est

Alkrington Hall Road North

Alkrington Hall

St Peters RC Primary School

Alkrington Physiotherapy Sports Injury Clinic

Alkrington CP School

Alkrington Clinic Cen

on Garden Village

Alkrington Moss CP School

St Thomas More RC Primary School

St Michaels School

Mossway

The Meadows

M60

VICTORIA

Hollin CP School

Cromer Ind Est

D2
1 Burtonwood Ct
2 Half St
3 Harley Ct
4 Kid St
5 Market St
6 Sepia Gv
7 Throstle Hall Ct
8 Weavers Ct
9 Wilkinson St
10 Wren Gdns

D3, E2, E5
Street names for these grid squares are listed at the back of the index

D4
1 Colson Dr

D5
1 Hall Dr
2 Woodland Wy

D6
1 Duffield Gdns
2 Lower Gn

E
1 Assheton St
2 Back Spring Gdns
3 Barrowfields
4 Brown St
5 Church St
6 Dixon St
7 Doris St
8 Manor St
9 Radcliffe Ter
10 Vincent St
11 Walton St
12 White Hart Mdw

E3
1 Adelaide St
2 Back Gilmour St
3 Bridge St
4 Corporation St
5 Hall St
6 Hornby St
7 Langton St
8 Ogden St
9 Taylor St
10 Tetlow St
11 Victoria St

E6
1 B'dman Fold Cl
2 Upton Cl
3 Walsingham Av

F1
1 Brookes St
2 Browning Rd
3 Chaucer Rd
4 Clough St
5 Roydes St

F2
1 Back Green St
2 Cromer St
3 James Andrew St
4 Lomas St
5 Salisbury St
6 Temple St

Industrial Estate

F3
1 Hanson St
2 Jackson St
3 Tudor St

F4
1 Brookbank Cl
2 Dale St
3 Frampton Cl
4 Naunton Rd
5 Wood La

D
1 Grasmere Wk
2 Honister Dr
3 Regent St

D (bottom)
1 Apple Wy
2 Leominster Rd
3 The Meadows

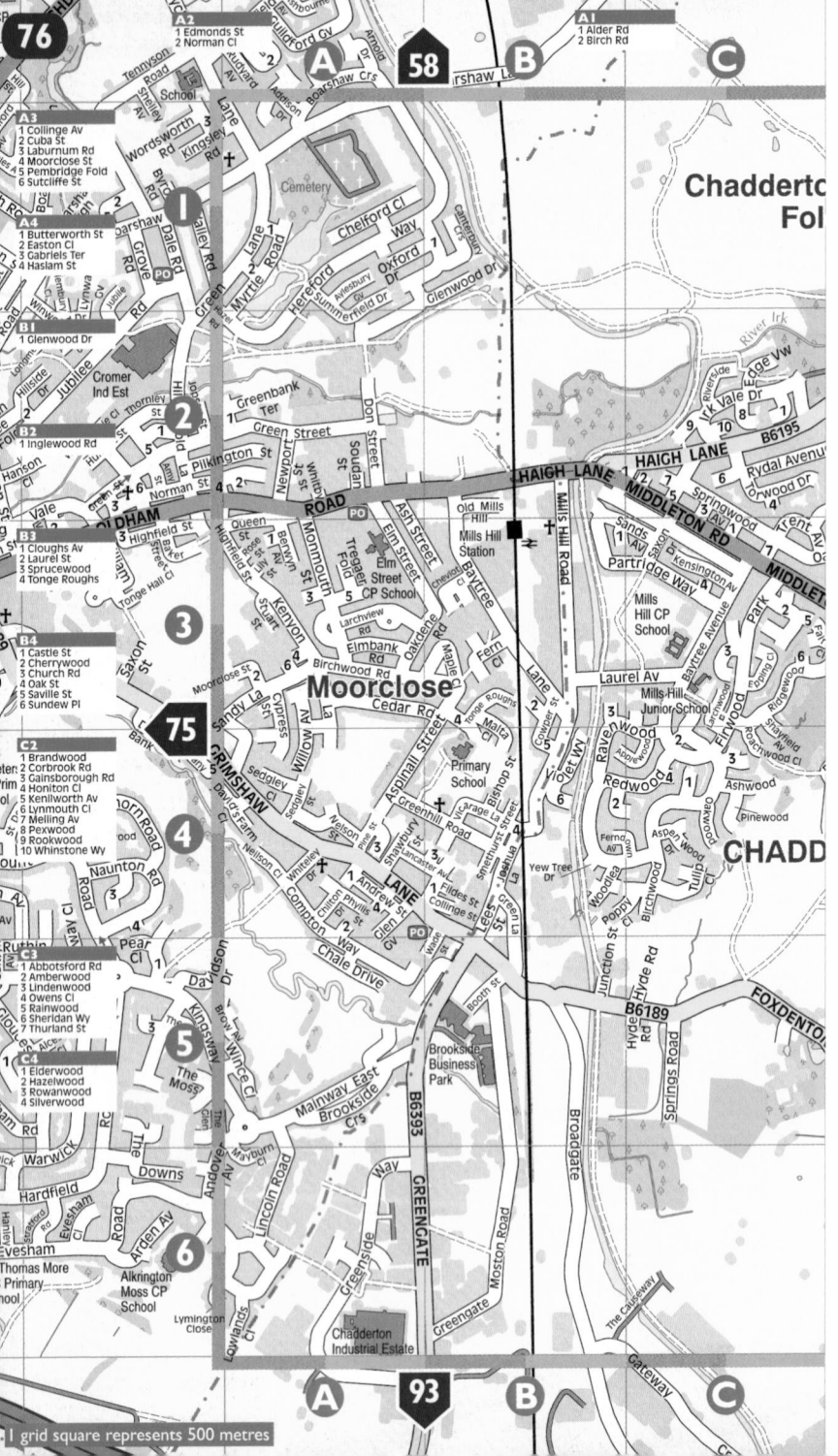

A2
1 Edmonds St
2 Norman Cl

A1
1 Alder Rd
2 Birch Rd

58

A3
1 Collinge Av
2 Cuba St
3 Laburnum Rd
4 Moorclose St
5 Pembridge Fold
6 Sutcliffe St

A4
1 Butterworth St
2 Easton Cl
3 Gabriels Ter
4 Haslam St

B
1 Glenwood Dr

B2
1 Inglewood Rd

B3
1 Cloughs Av
2 Laurel St
3 Sprucewood
4 Tonge Roughs

B4
1 Castle St
2 Cherrywood
3 Church Rd
4 Oak St
5 Saville St
6 Sundew Pl

C2
1 Brandwood
2 Corbrook Rd
3 Gainsborough Rd
4 Honiton Cl
5 Kenilworth Av
6 Lynmouth Cl
7 Melling Av
8 Foxwood
9 Rockwood
10 Whinstone Wy

C
1 Abbotsford Rd
2 Amberwood
3 Lindenwood
4 Owens Cl
5 Rainwood
6 Sheridan Wy
7 Thurland St

C4
1 Elderwood
2 Hazelwood
3 Rowanwood
4 Silverwood

Chaddertor
Fol

River Irk

Moorclose

Mills CP School

Mills Hill Junior School

CHADD

Brookside Business Park

Chadderton Industrial Estate

Thomas More Primary School

Alkrington Moss CP School

93

1 grid square represents 500 metres

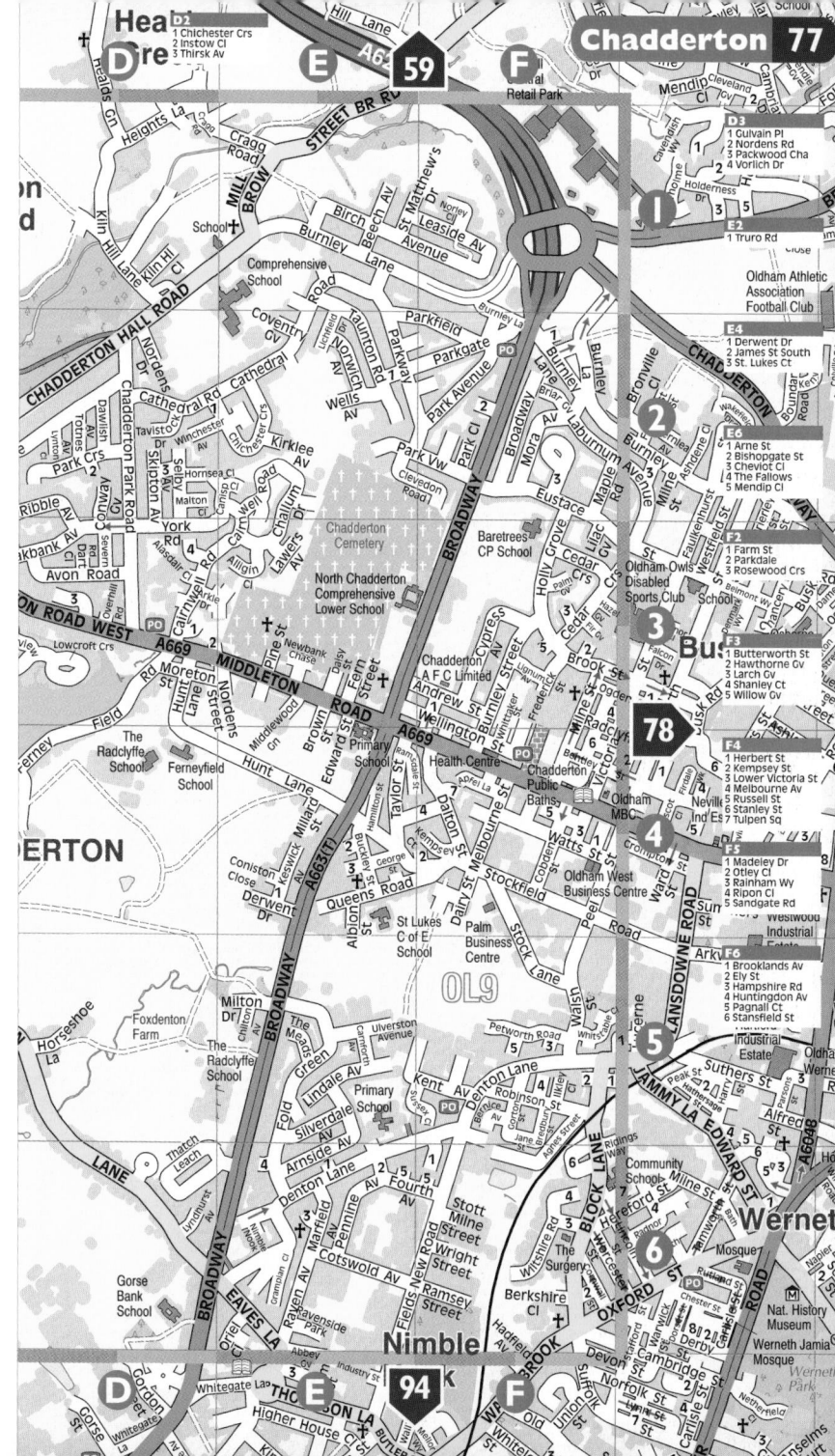

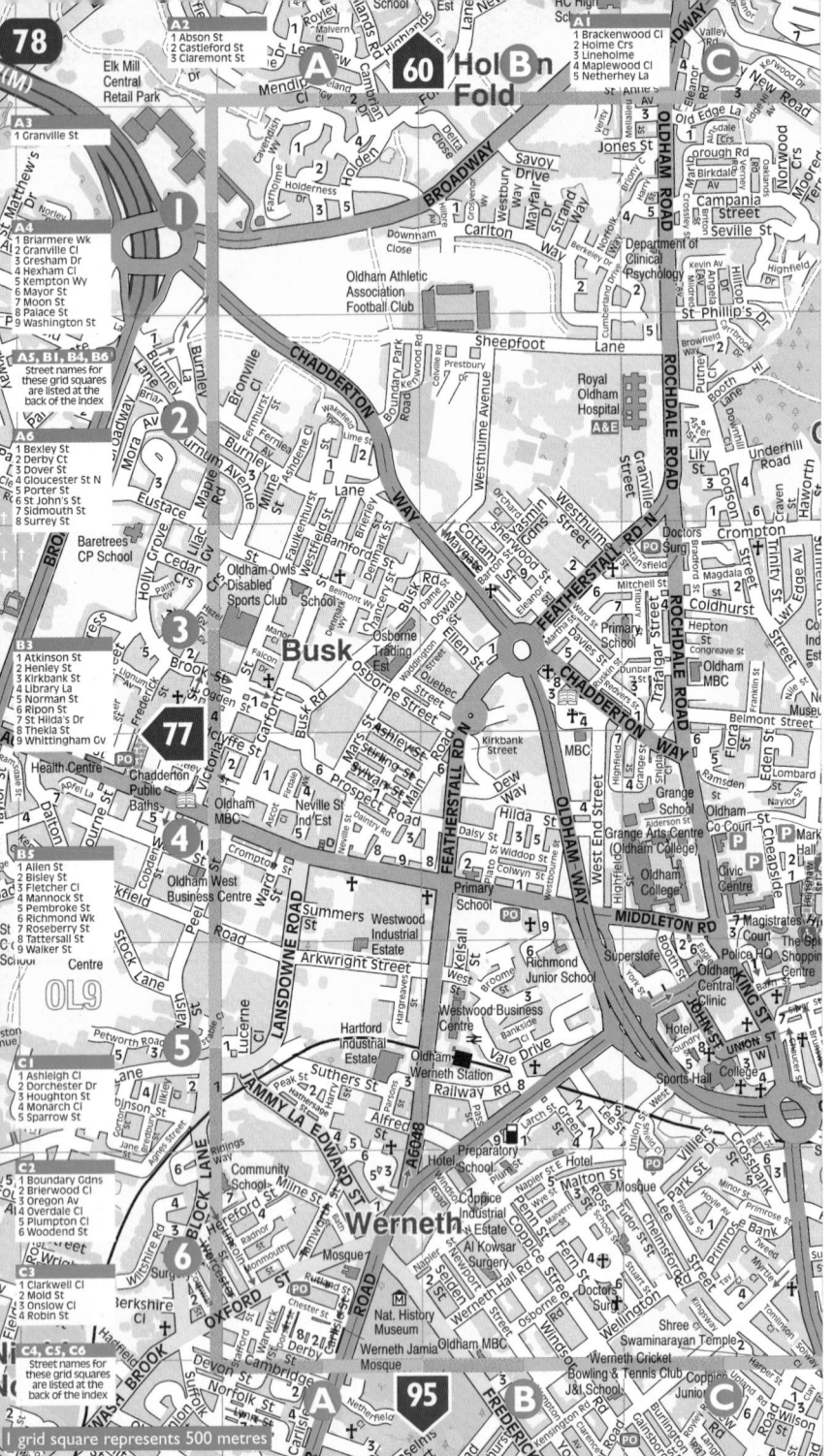

Holl**B**n
Fold

1 grid square represents 500 metres

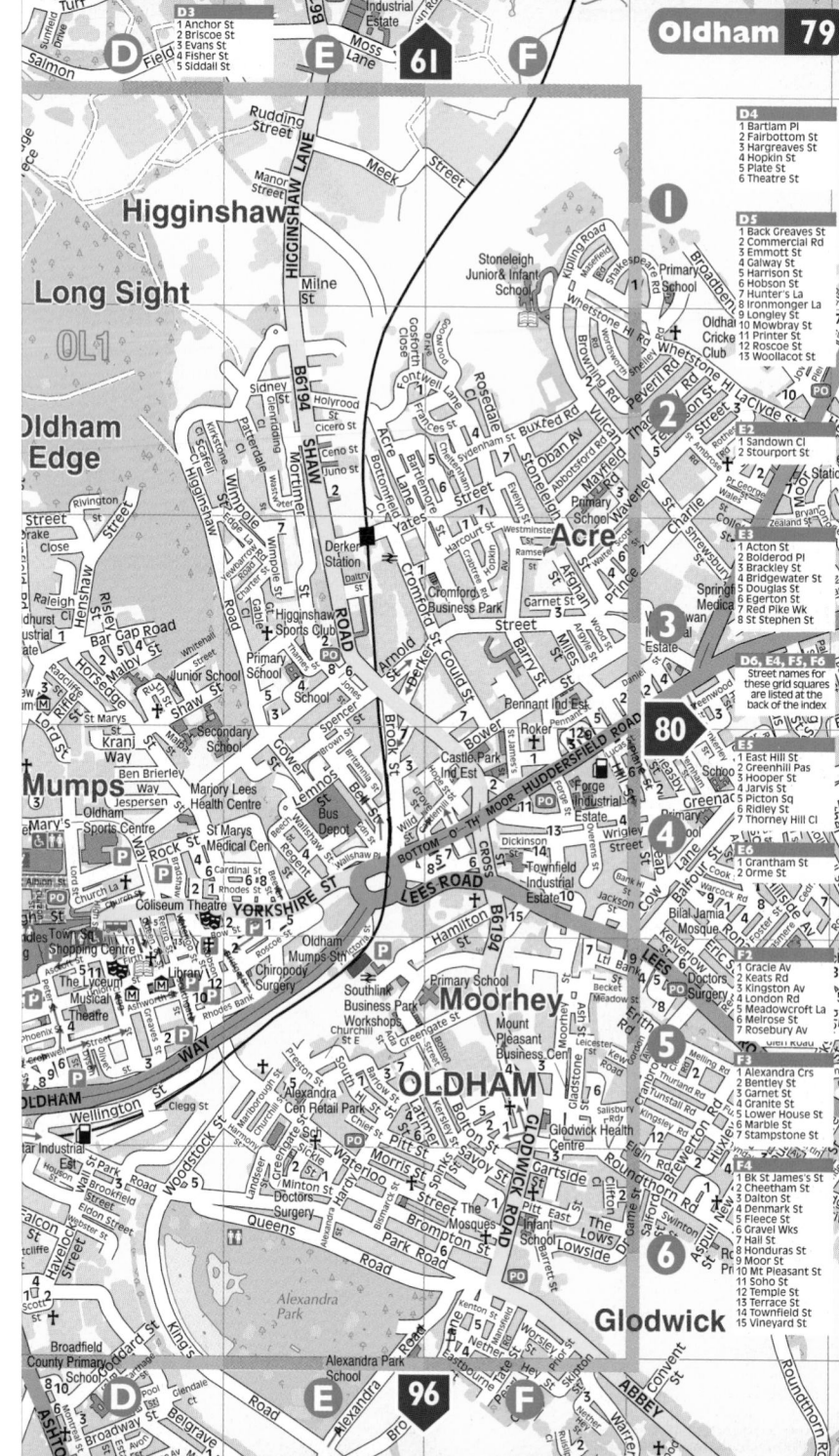

Turf
Sunfield Drive
salmon
Field

Industrial Estate
Moss Lane

61

D **E** **F**

Rudding Street
Manor Street
Meek Street

I

Higginshaw
Milne St
Stoneleigh Junior & Infant School
Primary School
Kipling Road
Shakespeare Rd
Whetstone Hl Rd
Browning Rd
Peveril Rd
Broadbent St
Oldham Cricket Club

Long Sight
OL1
Oldham Edge

Sidney St
Glenridding St
Holyrood St
Cicero St
Ceno St
Juno St
Fontwell Lane
Cosorth St
Acre Lane
Bartlemore Ct
Frances St
Rosedale
Buxted Rd
Oban Av
Mayfield Rd
Vulcan St
Waverley St
Charlie
Shrewsbury Rd
Laclyde St

2

Station

Rivington St
Drake Close
Raleigh St
Henshaw St
Bar Gap Road
Horsedge St
Shaw St
Malby St
Kran Way

Wimpole St
Kilvert St
Pattersdale St
Shaw St
Mortimer St
Higginshaw Road
Junior School
Primary School
Secondary School
Derker Station
Higginshaw Sports Club
Cromford Business Park
Yates St
Harcourt St
Union St
Ramsey St
Westminster St
Garnet St
Arnold St
Brook St
Spencer St
Lemnos St

Acre

Primary School
Evelyn St
Argan St
Prince St
Miles St
Barry St

3

Spring Medical
St Swan
Estate

80

Mumps
Ben Brierley Way
Jespersen St
Marjory Lees Health Centre
St Marys Medical Cen
Oldham Bus Depot

Pennant Ind Est
Roker St
Bower St
Castle Park Ind Est
Forge Industrial Estate
Wrigley St
Greenacre Lane

4

Primary School

St Marys
Oldham Sports Centre
Coliseum Theatre
YORKSHIRE
Town Hall
Shopping Centre
The Lyceum
Musical
Theatre
Library
Oldham Mumps Sth
Chiropody Surgery
Rhodes Bank

Dickinson St
Townfield Industrial Estate
Jackson St
Bilal Jamia Mosque

Hamilton St
Southlink Business Park Workshops
Churchill St E
Moorhey
Mount Pleasant Business Cent

Becket Meadow St
Doctors Surgery

5

OLDHAM
Wellington St
Clegg St

Alexandra Cen Retail Park
Morris St
Pitt St
Waterloo St
Doctors Surgery
Queens
Glodwick Health Centre
Roundthorn Rd

6

Broadfield County Primary School
Ashton
Broadway
Belgrave

Alexandra Park
Alexandra Park School

96

D **E** **F**

Glodwick

Abbey
Roundthorn Rd

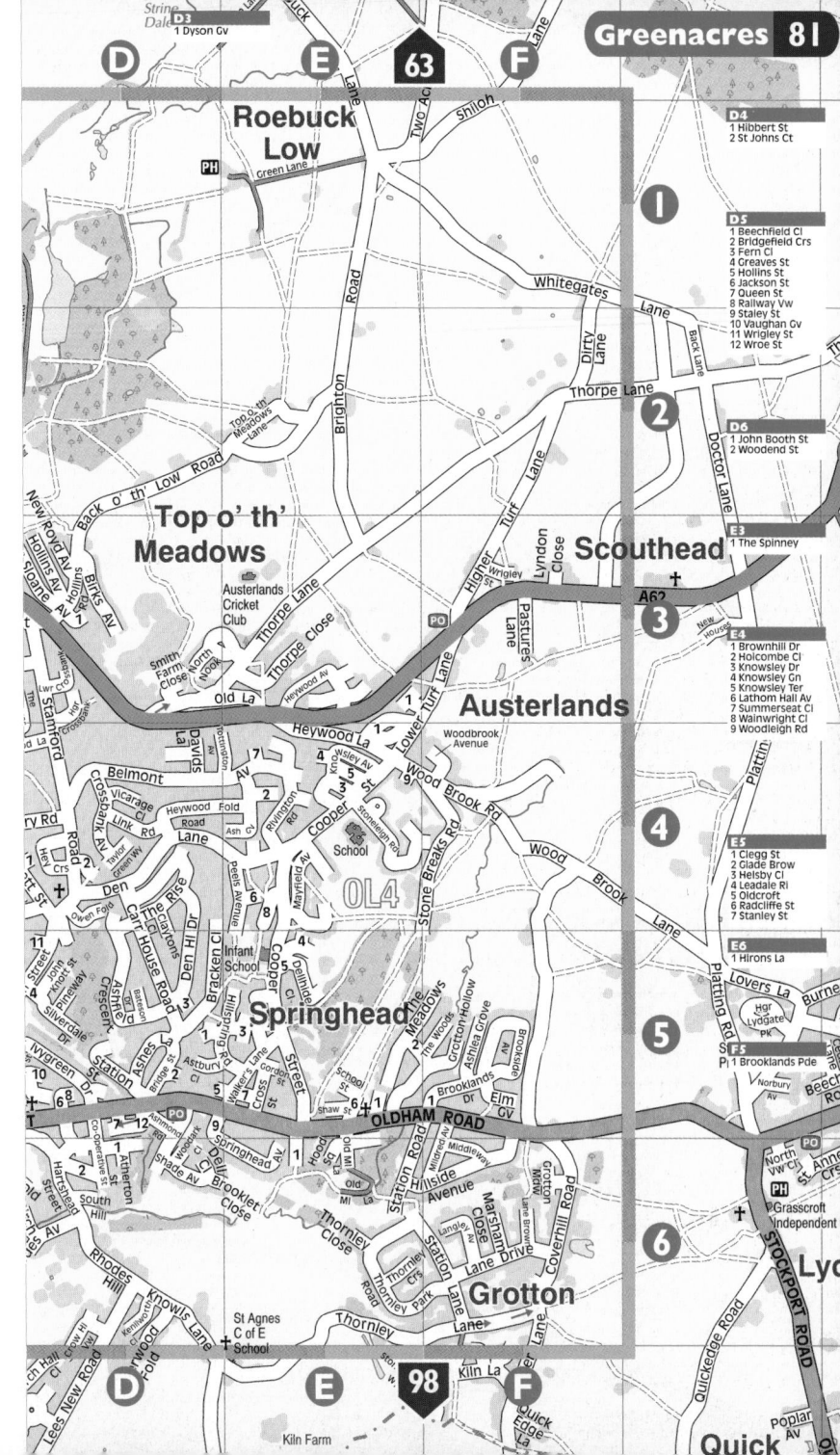

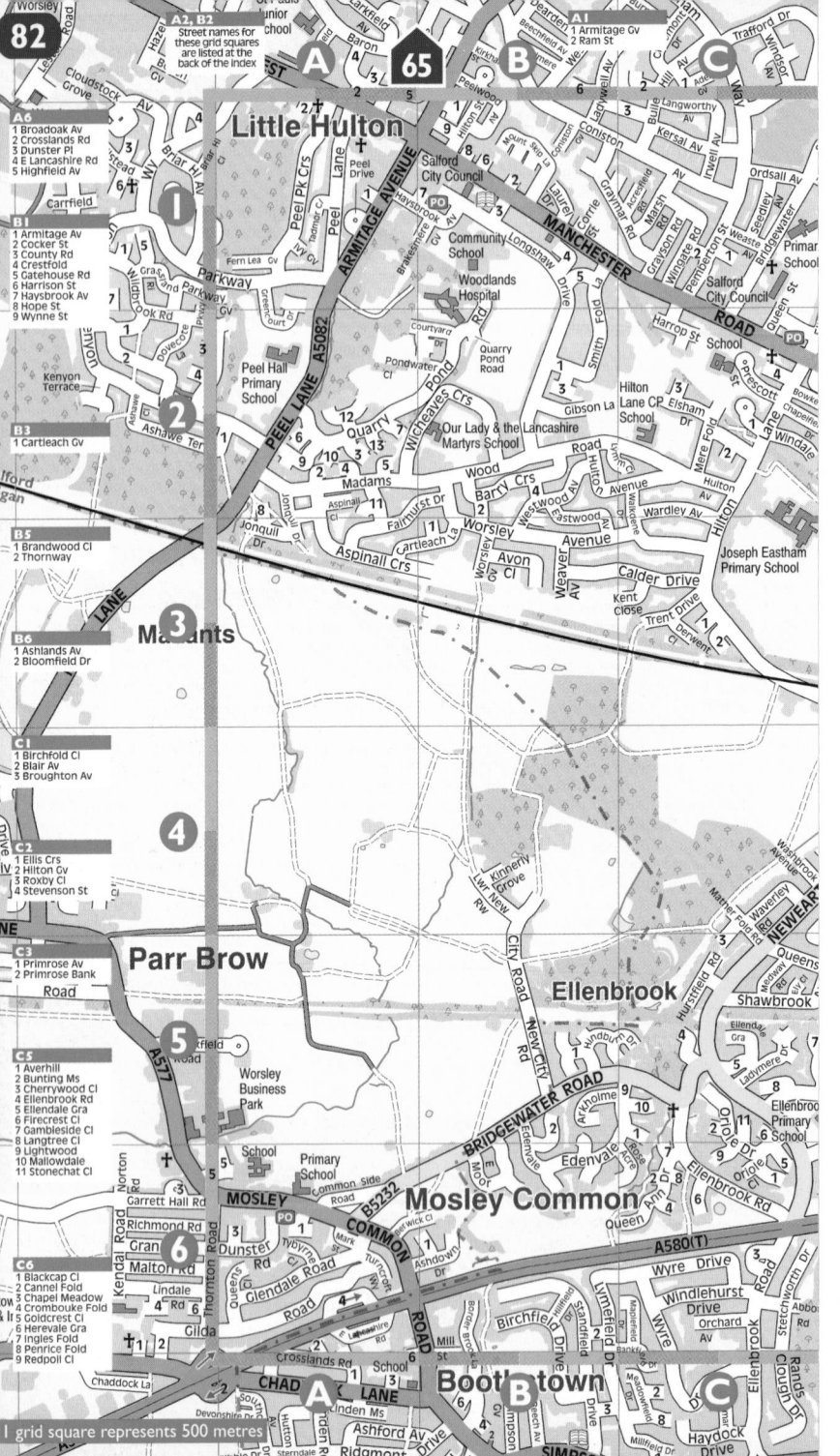

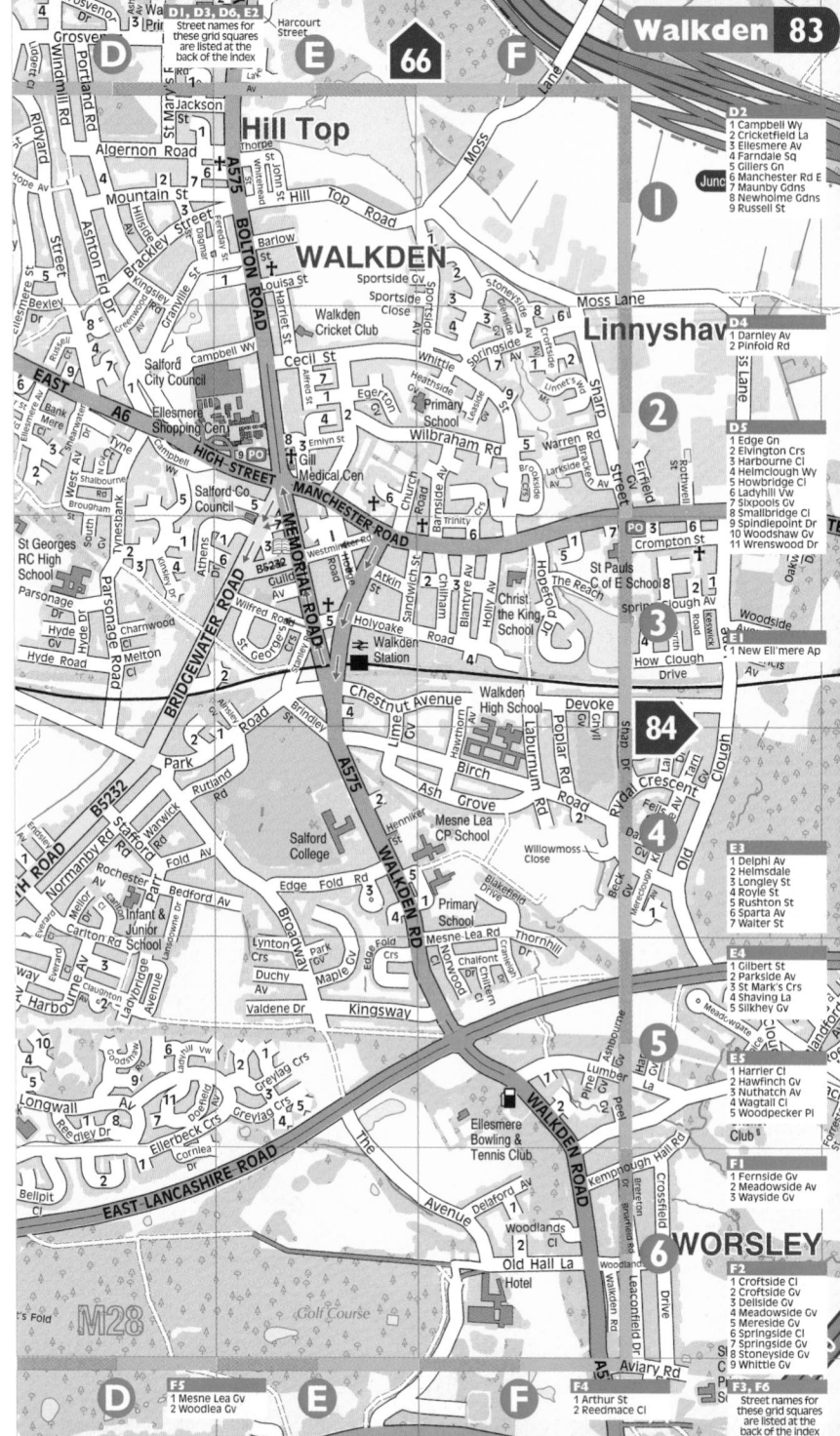

Hill Top

WALKDEN

Linnyshav

WORSLEY

LEIGH   ROAD

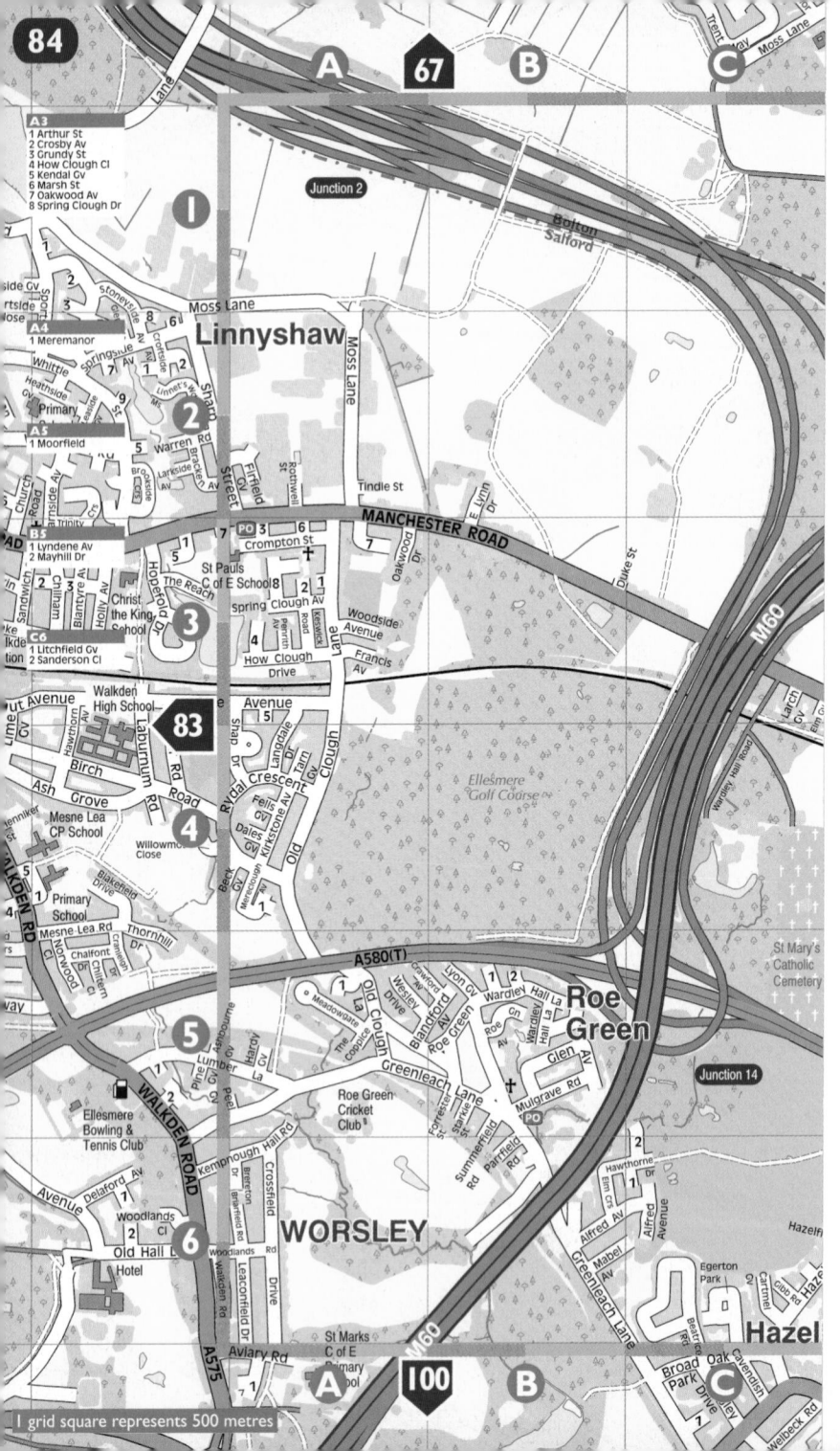

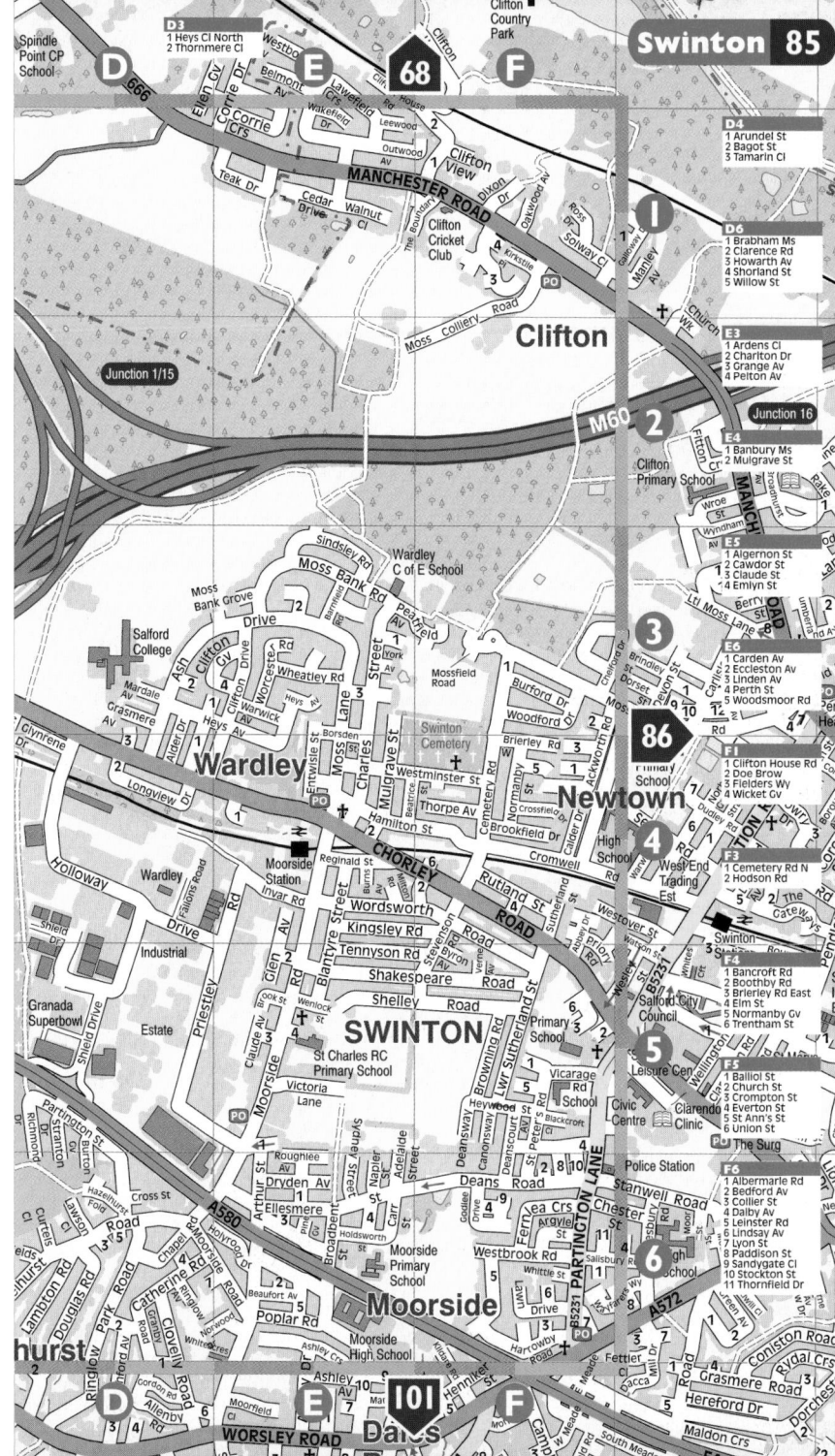

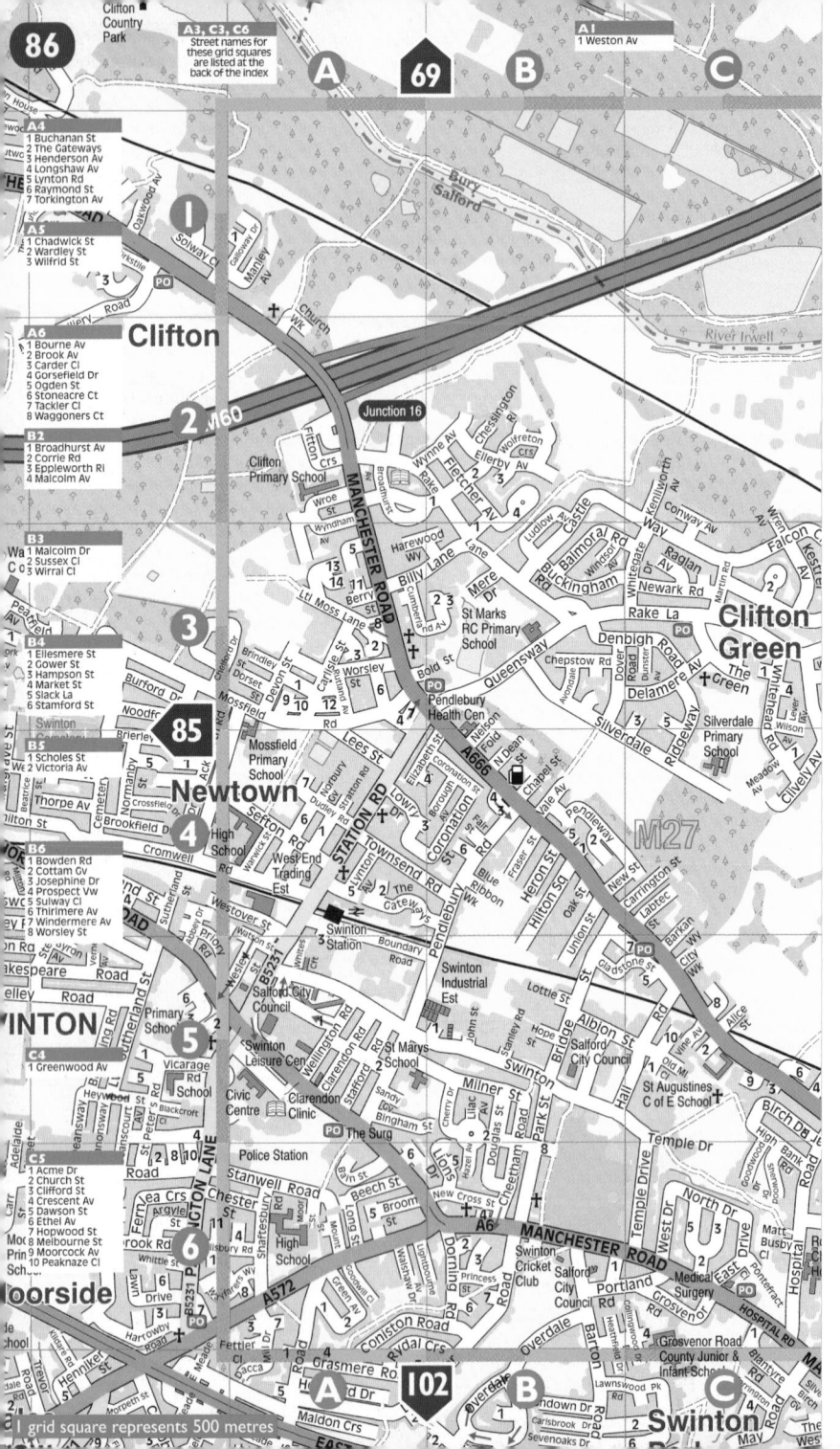

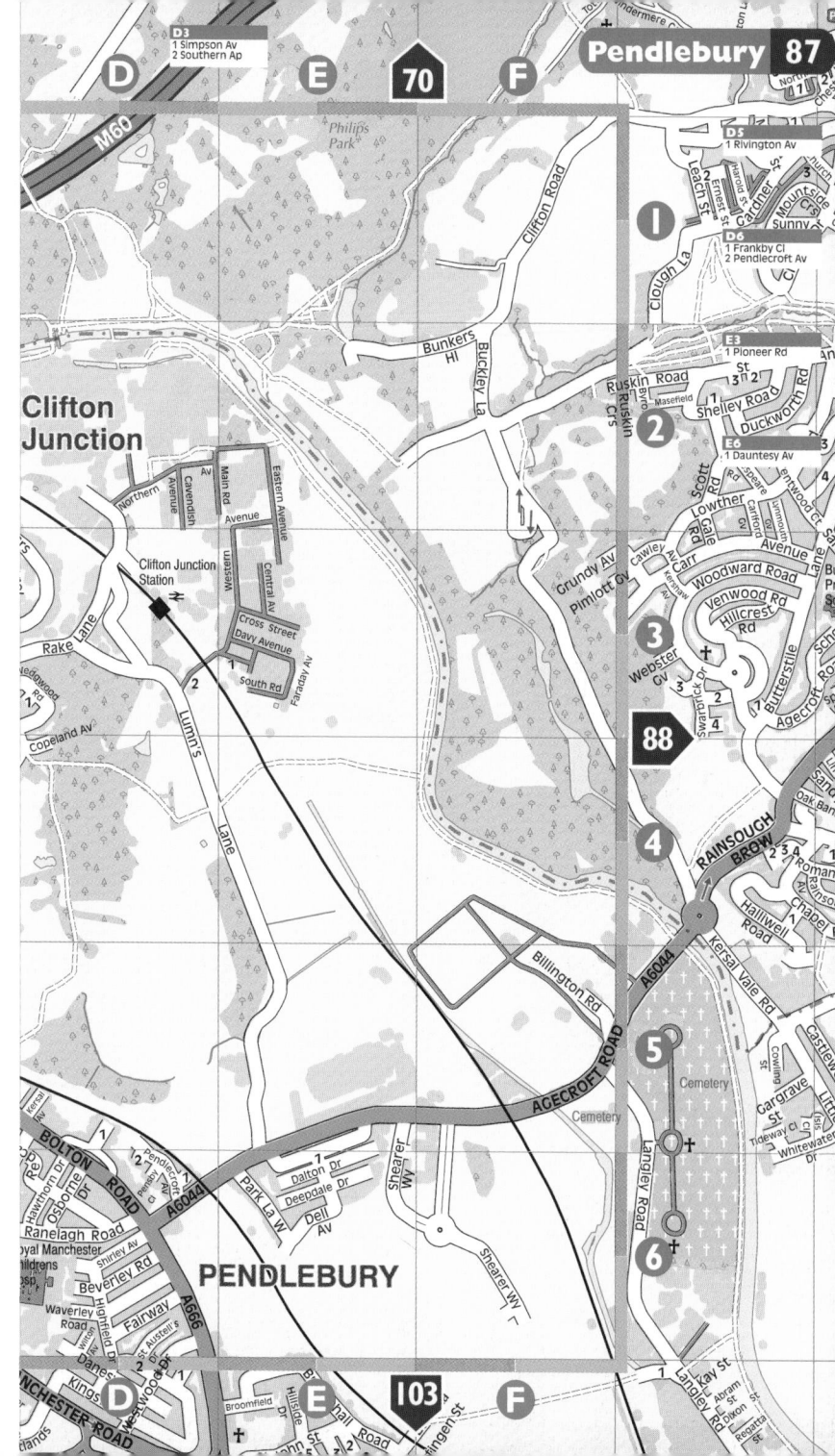

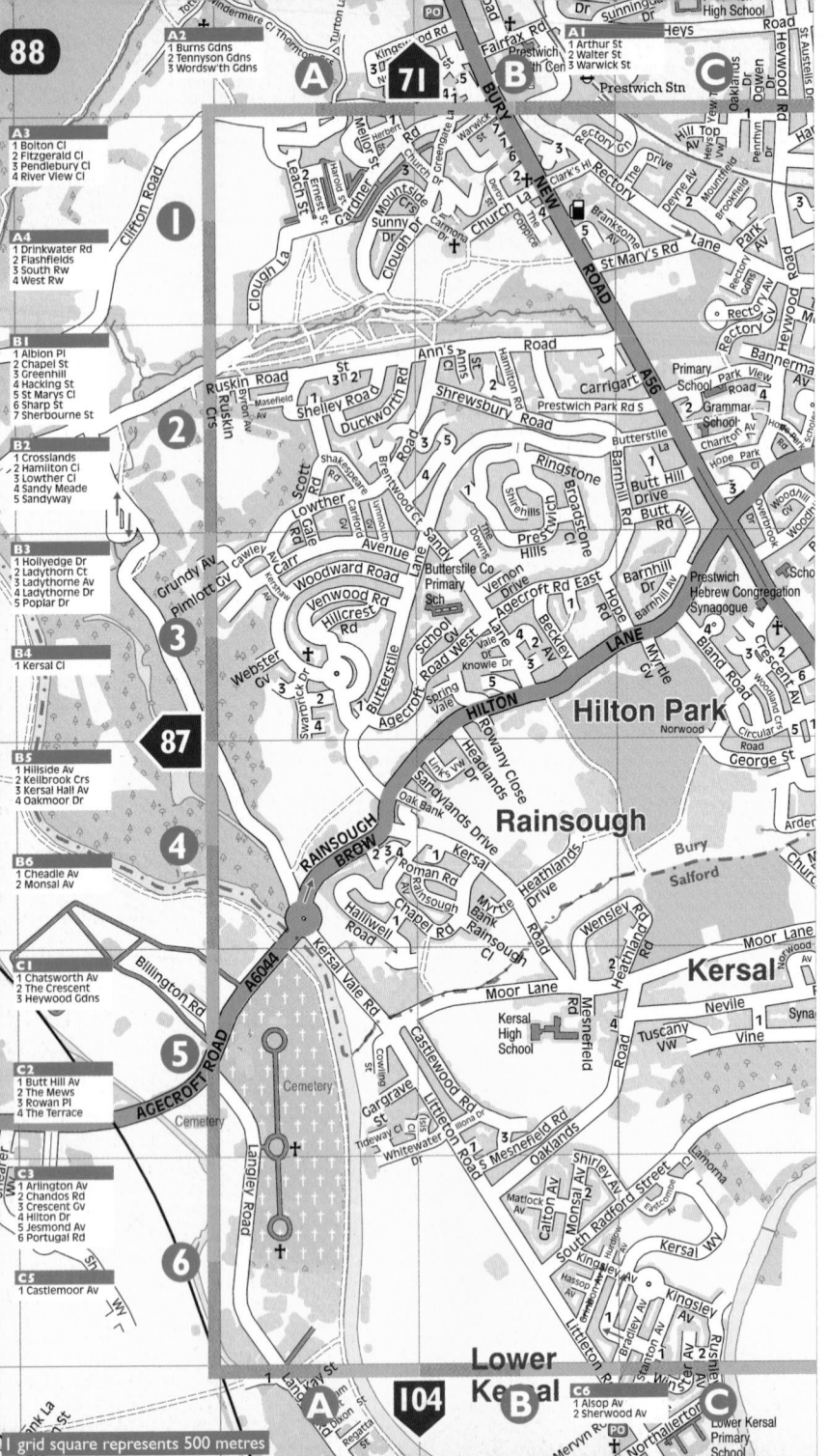

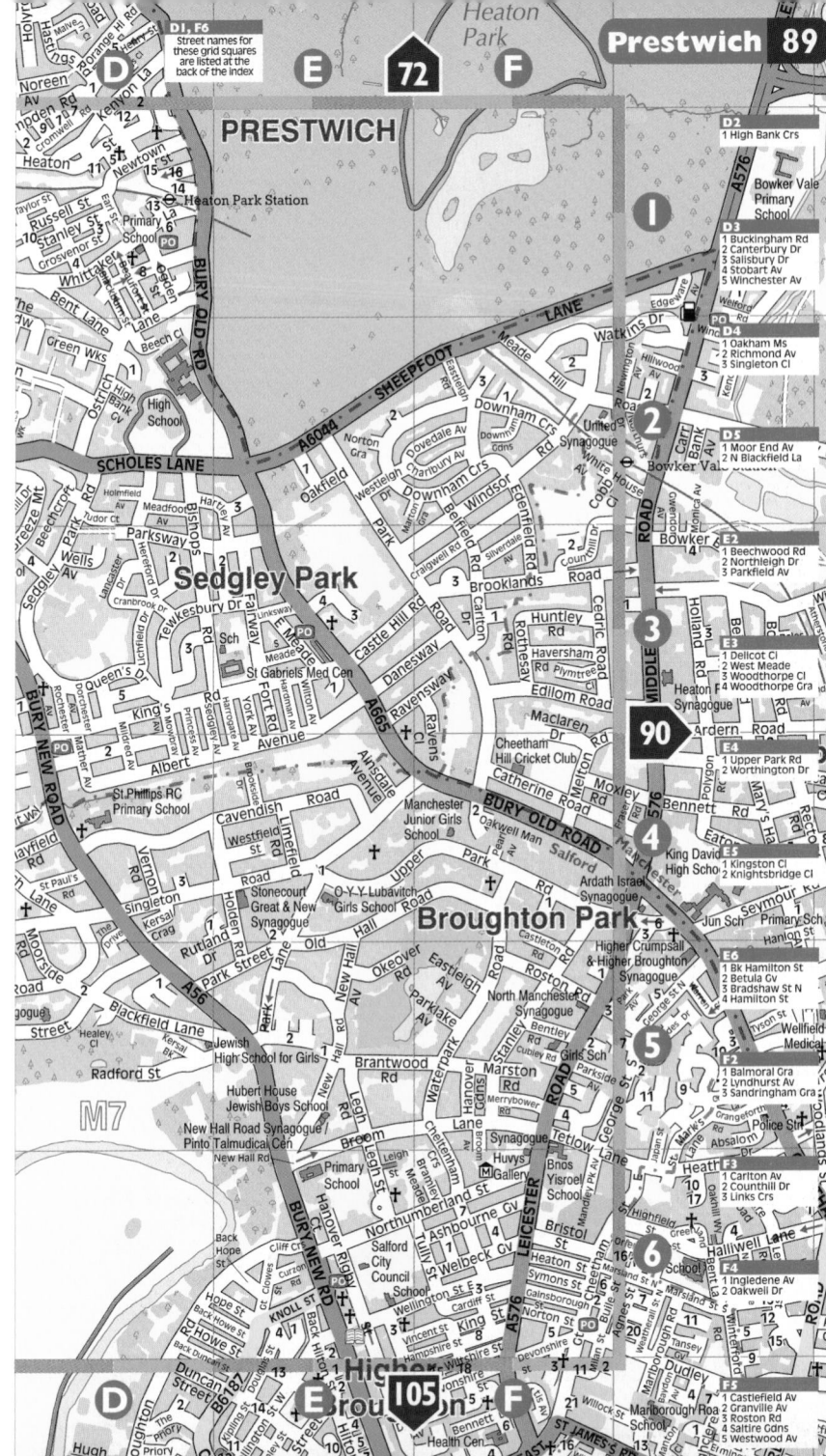

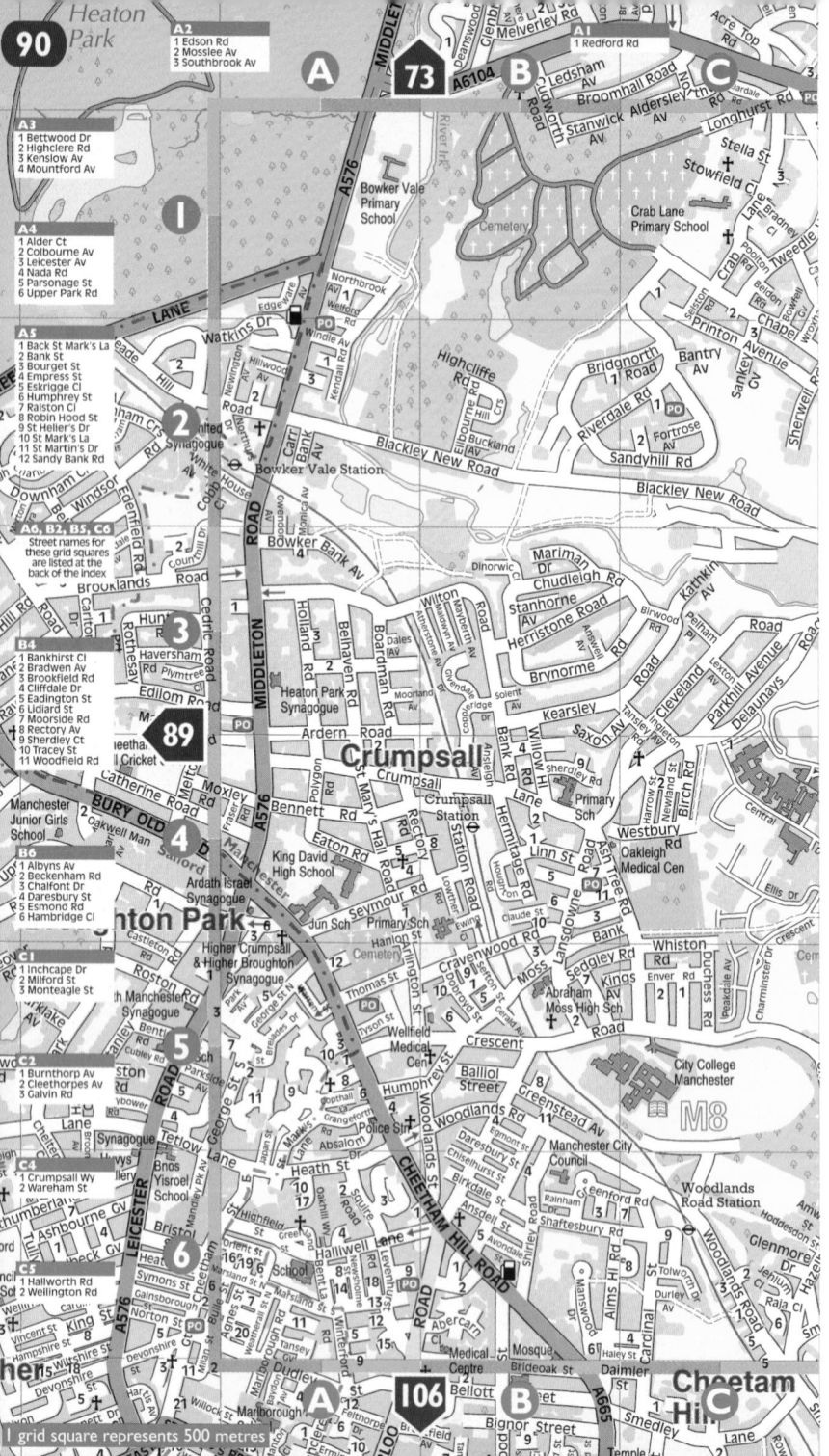

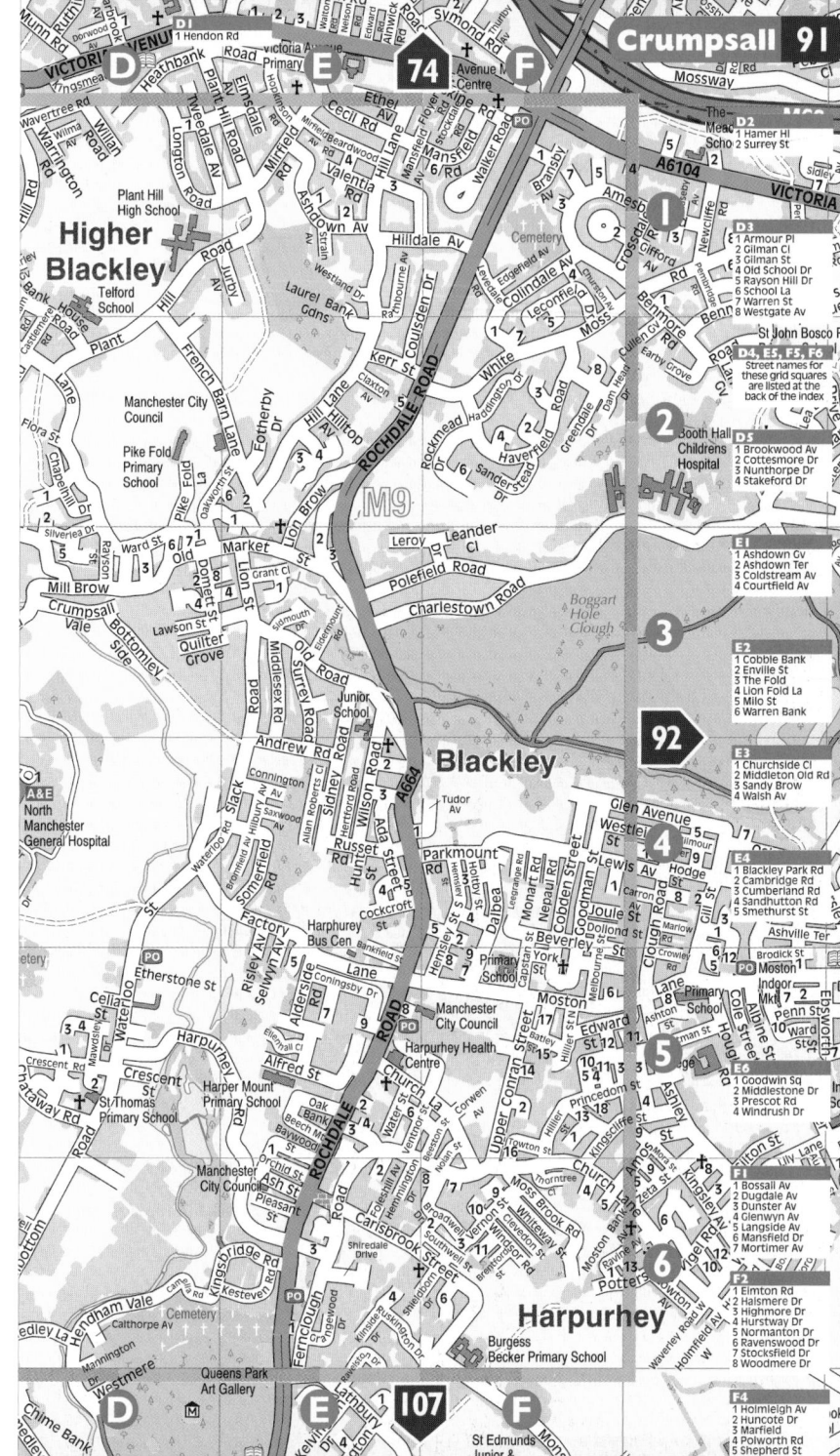

Higher Blackley

Blackley

Harpurhey

VICTORIA

1 Hendon Rd

Plant Hill High School

Telford School

Manchester City Council

Pike Fold Primary School

Mill Brow

Crumpsall Vale

North Manchester General Hospital

Andrew Rd

Junior School

Harpurhey Bus Cen

Etherstone St

St Thomas Primary School

Harper Mount Primary School

Manchester City Council

Manchester City Council

Harpurhey Health Centre

Tudor Av

Queens Park Art Gallery

Burgess Becker Primary School

St Edmunds Junior & Infant School

Cemetery

Booth Hall Childrens Hospital

Boggart Hole Clough

St John Bosco RC

D2
1 Hamer Hl
2 Surrey St

D3
1 Armour Pl
2 Gilman Cl
3 Gilman St
4 Old School Dr
5 Rayson Hill Dr
6 School La
7 Warren St
8 Westgate Av

D4, E5, F5, F6
Street names for these grid squares are listed at the back of the index

D5
1 Brookwood Av
2 Cottesmore Dr
3 Nunthorpe Dr
4 Stakeford Dr

E1
1 Ashdown Gv
2 Ashdown Ter
3 Coldstream Av
4 Courtfield Av

E2
1 Cobble Bank
2 Enville St
3 The Fold
4 Lion Fold La
5 Milo St
6 Warren Bank

E3
1 Churchside Cl
2 Middleton Old Rd
3 Sandy Brow
4 Walsh Av

E4
1 Blackley Park Rd
2 Cambridge Rd
3 Cumberland Rd
4 Sandhutton Rd
5 Smethurst St

E6
1 Goodwin Sq
2 Middlestone Dr
3 Prescot Rd
4 Windrush Dr

F1
1 Bossall Av
2 Dugdale Av
3 Dunster Av
4 Glenwyn Av
5 Langside Av
6 Mansfield Dr
7 Mortimer Av

F3
1 Eimton Rd
2 Halsmere Dr
3 Highmore Dr
4 Hurstway Dr
5 Normanton Dr
6 Ravenswood Dr
7 Stocksfield Dr
8 Woodmere Dr

F4
1 Holmleigh Av
2 Huncote Dr
3 Marfield
4 Polworth Rd
5 Shepherd St

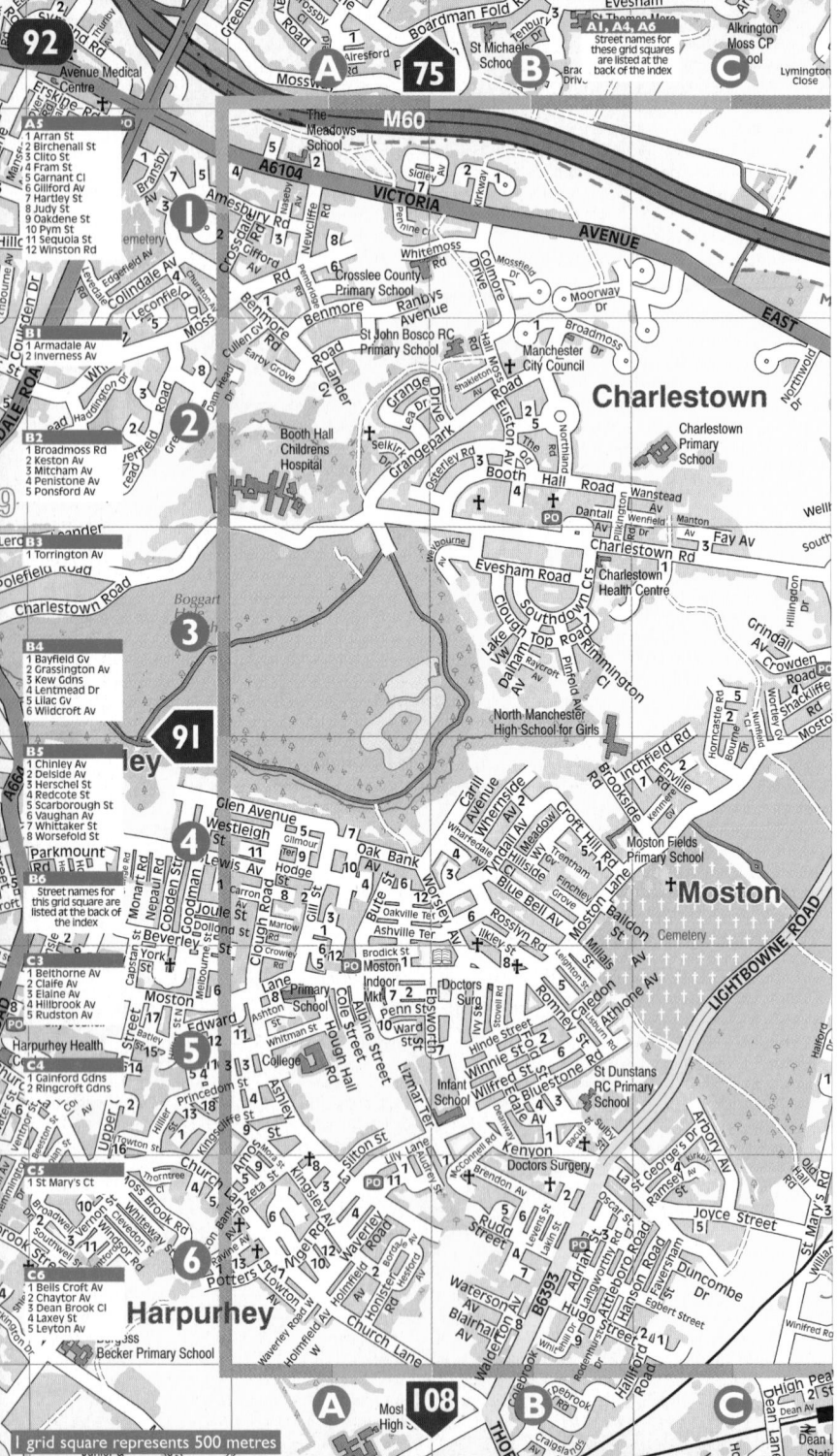

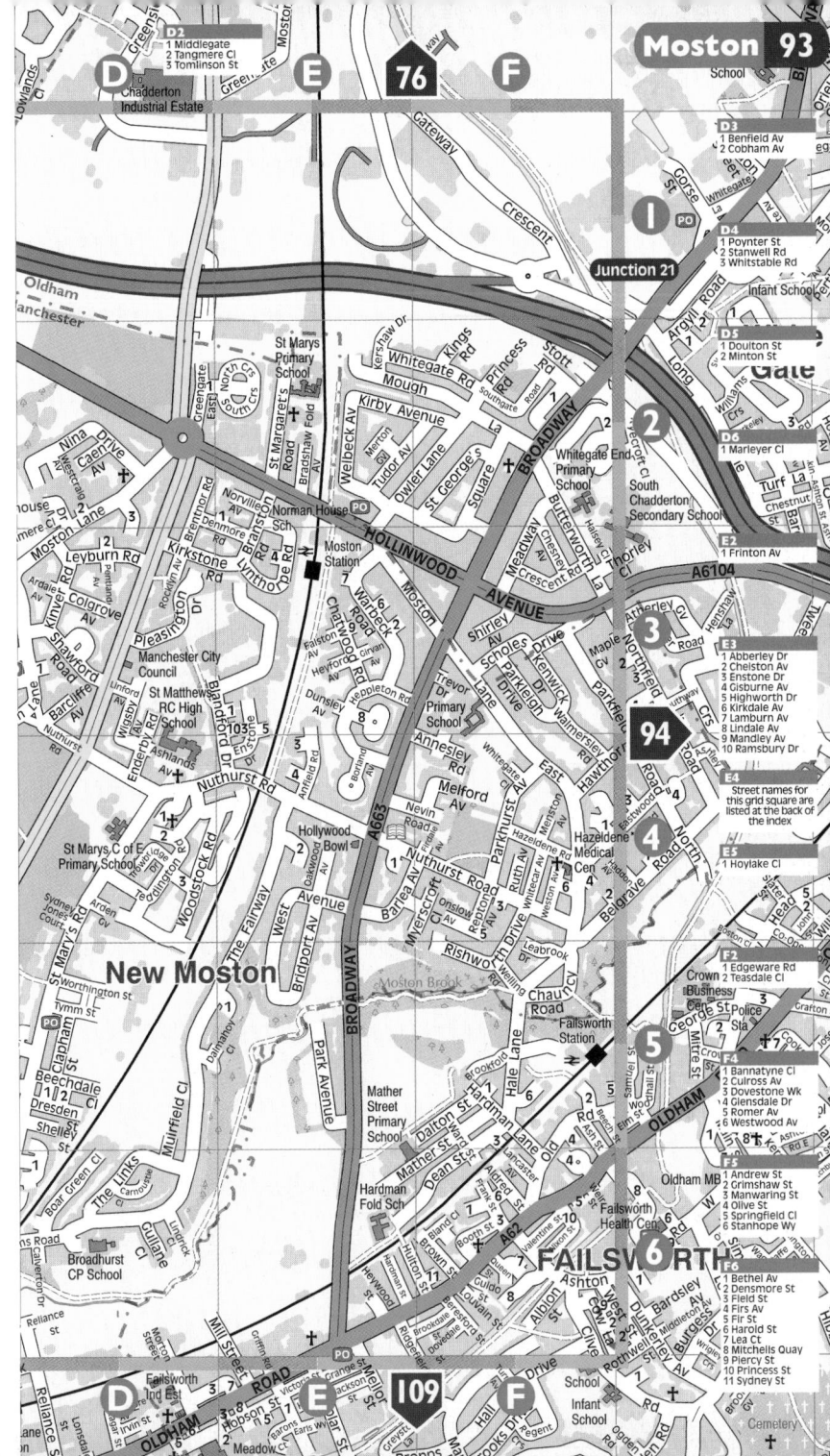

76

109

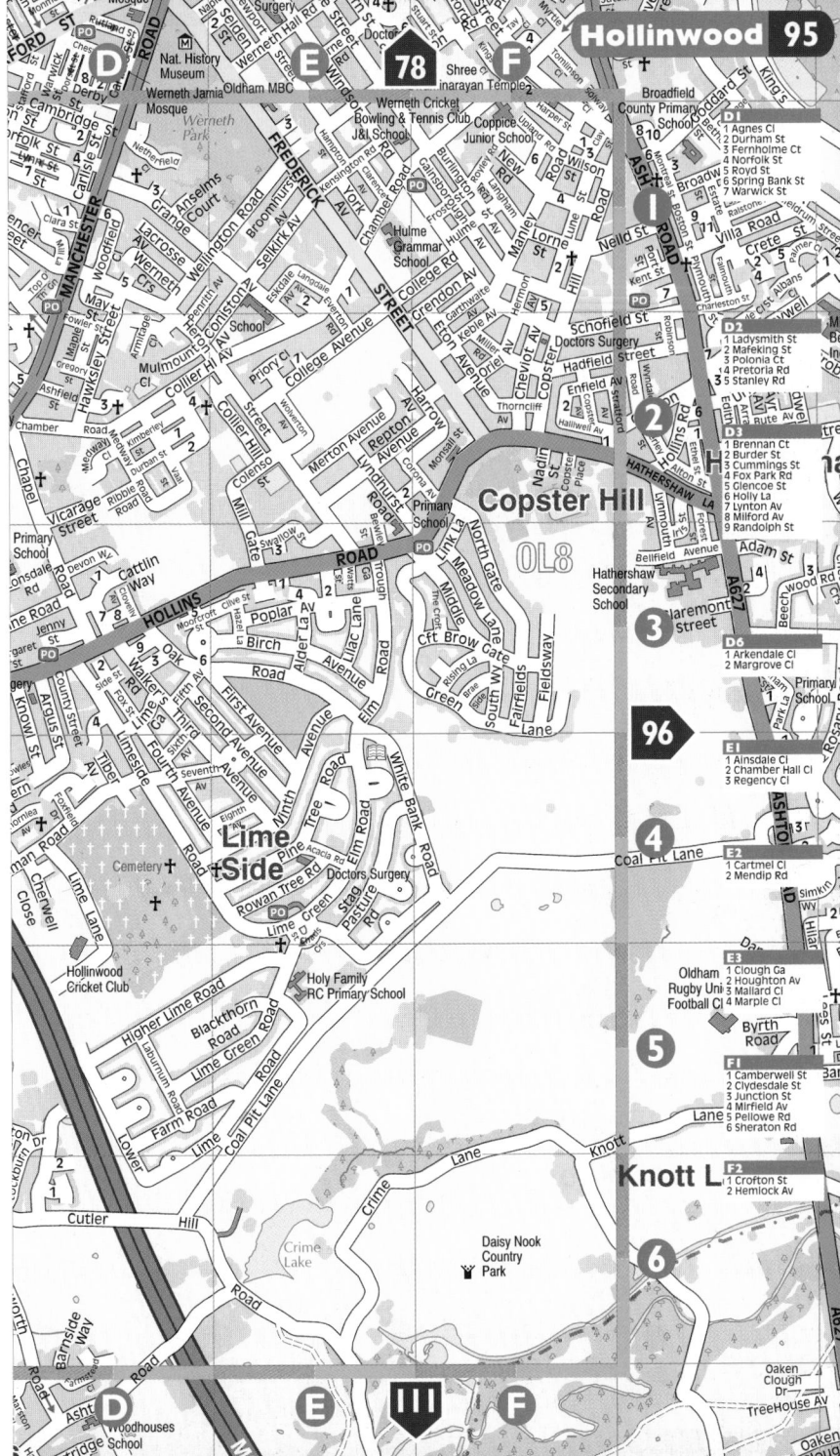

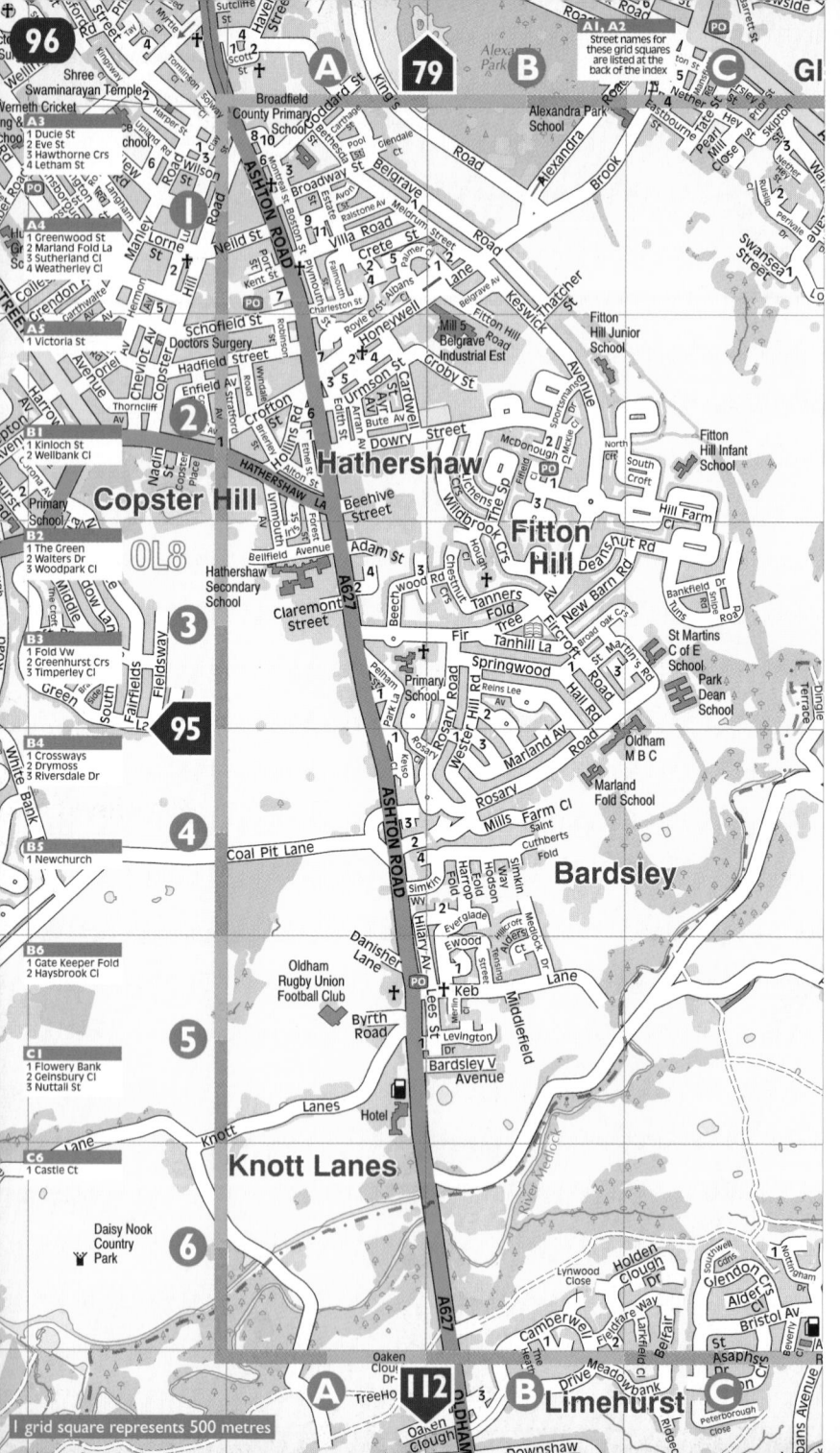

1 grid square represents 500 metres

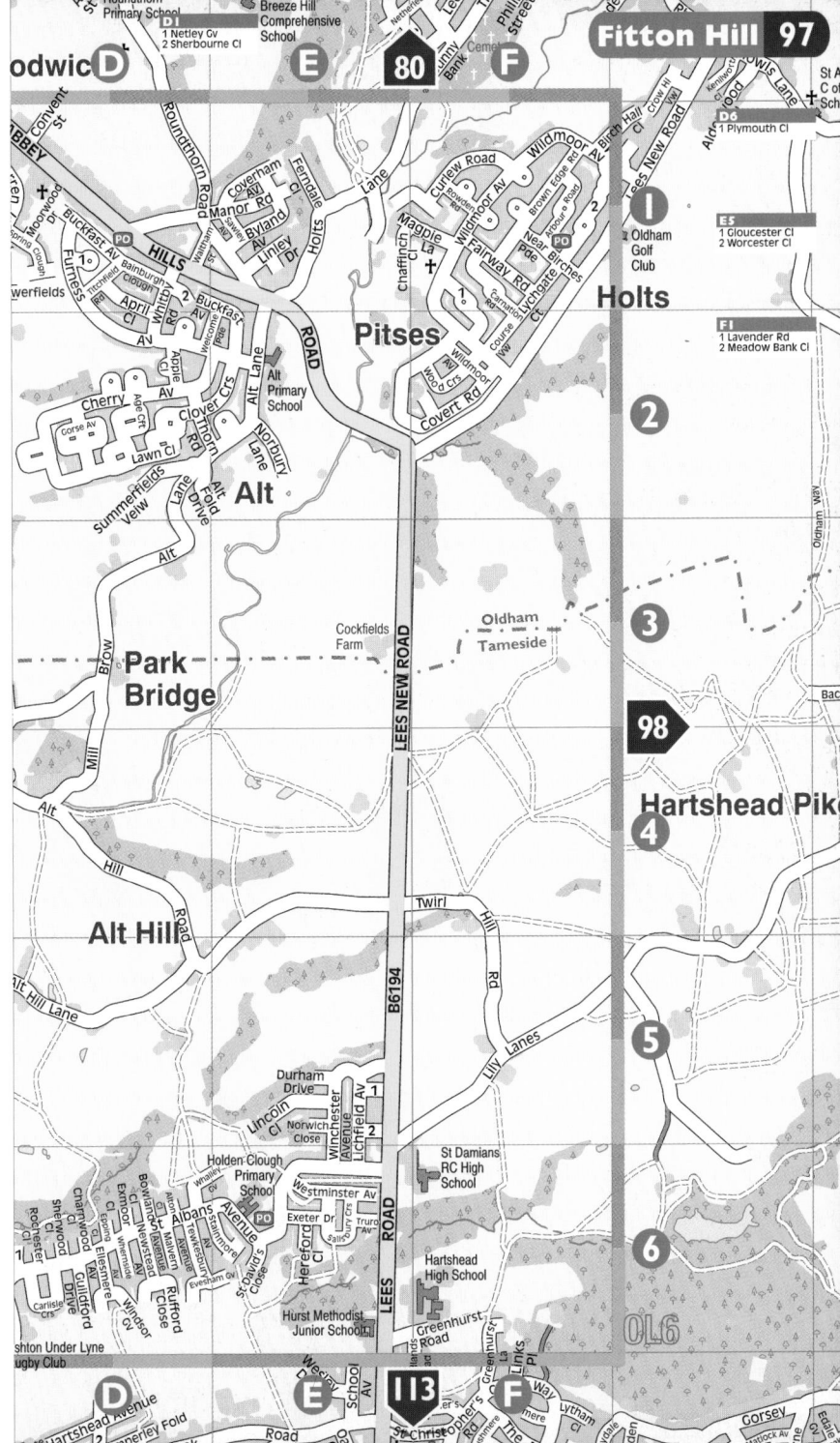

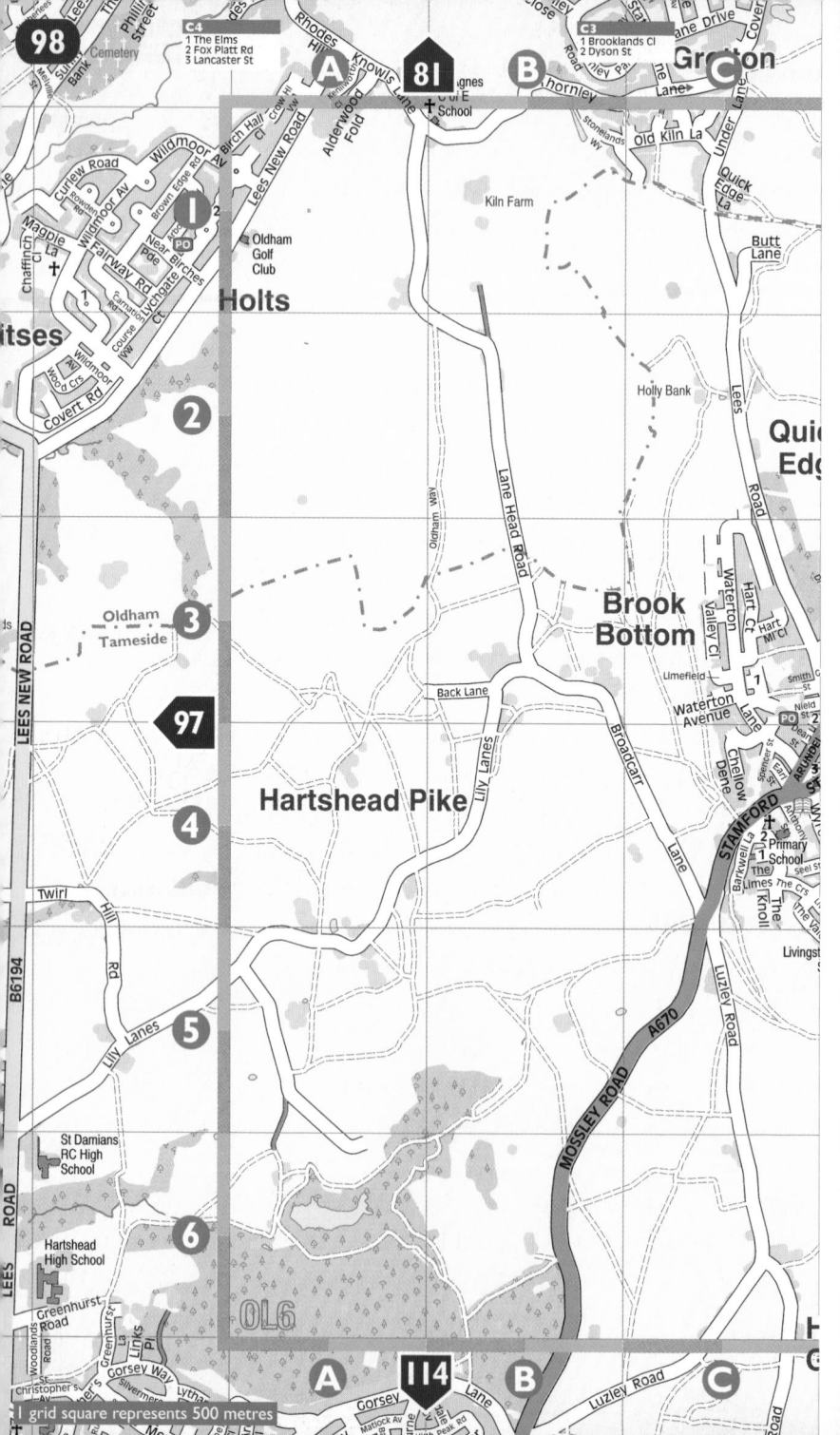

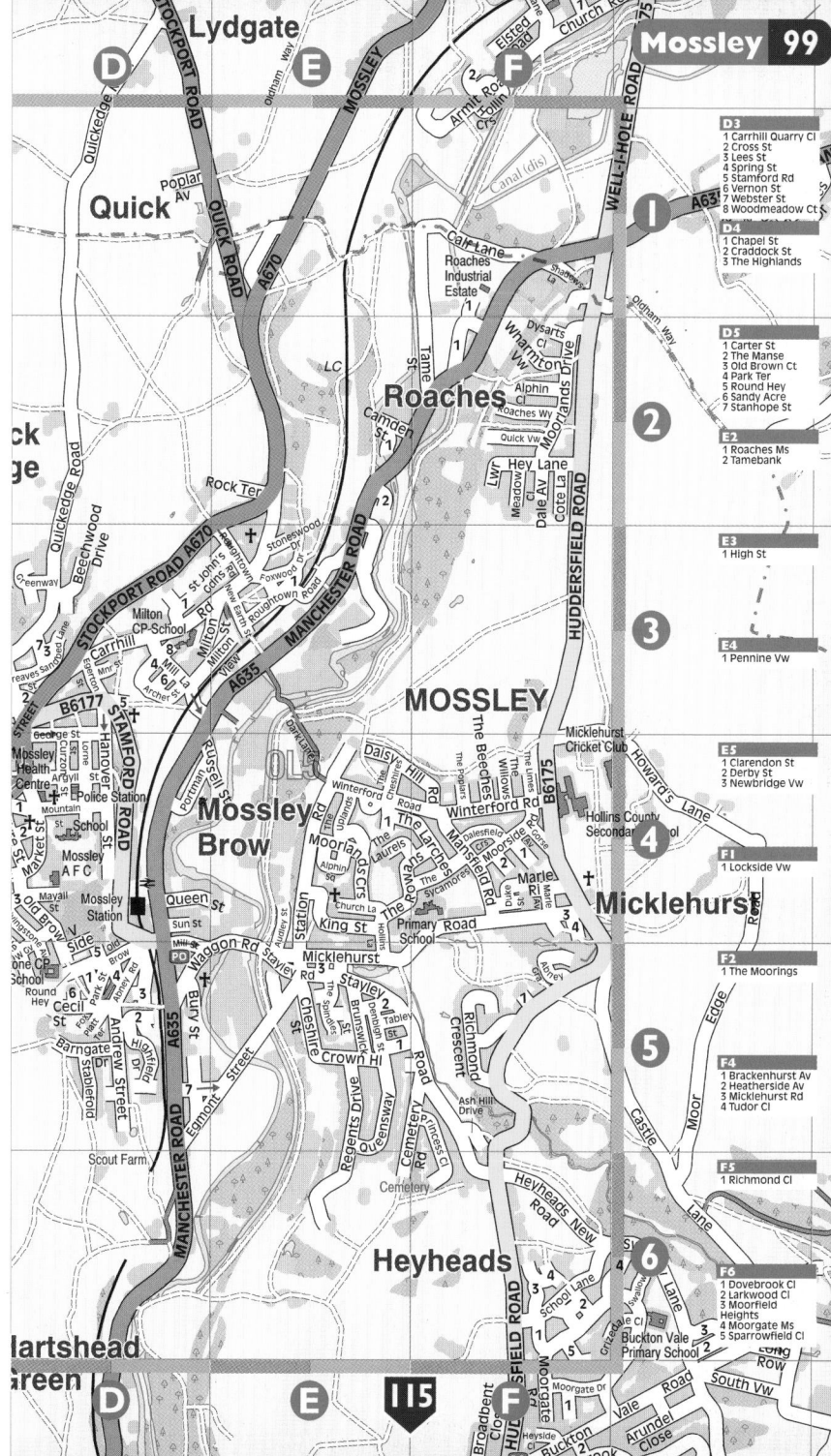

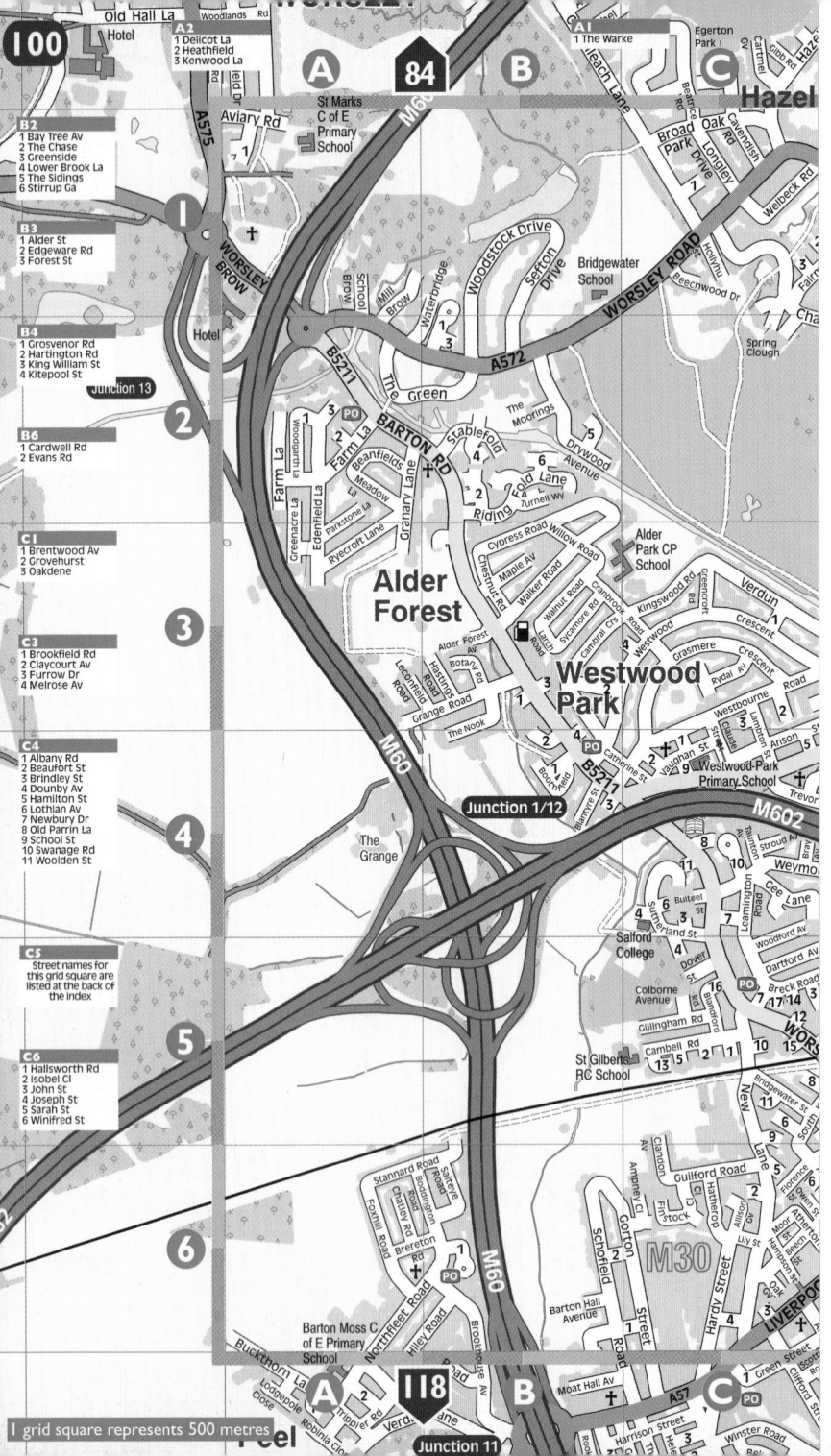

Old Hall La — Woodlands

Hotel

A
84
B
C1
1 The Warke
C

Egerton Park

Hazel

St Marks C of E Primary School

Aviary Rd

B2
1 Bay Tree Av
2 The Chase
3 Greenside
4 Lower Brook La
5 The Sidings
6 Stirrup Ga

Broad Park
Oak
Longley
Drive
Welbeck Rd

Beechwood Dr

B3
1 Alder St
2 Edgeware Rd
3 Forest St

Woodstock Drive
Sefton Drive
Bridgewater School
WORSLEY ROAD

Mill Brow
Waterbridge

B4
1 Grosvenor Rd
2 Hartington Rd
3 King William St
4 Kitepool St

Junction 13

Hotel

School Brow

B5211
The Green
A572

Spring Clough

B6
1 Cardwell Rd
2 Evans Rd

PO
BARTON RD
Stablefold
The Moorings
Drywood Avenue

Farm La
Woodgarth La
Beanfields
Meadow La
Granary Lane
Stablefold
Cold Lane
Turnell Wy

C1
1 Brentwood Av
2 Grovehurst
3 Oakdene

Greenacre La
Edenfield La
Parkstone La
Ryecroft Lane
Cypress Road
Willow Road
Maple Av
Walker Road
Cranbrook Road
Kingswood Rd
Greencroft Rd
Verdun

Riding

Alder Park CP School
Grasmere
Crescent

C3
1 Brookfield Rd
2 Claycourt Av
3 Furrow Dr
4 Melrose Av

Alder Forest

Chestnut Rd
Walnut Road
Sycamore Rd
Cambrai Crs
Westwood
Rydal Av
Road
Westbourne

C4
1 Albany Rd
2 Beaufort St
3 Brindley St
4 Dounby Av
5 Hamilton St
6 Lothian Av
7 Newbury Dr
8 Old Parrin La
9 School St
10 Swanage Rd
11 Woollen St

Alder Forest Av
Hastings Road
Leamfield Road
Grange Road
Botany Av
The Nook
Book Fields
Anson
Trevor

Westwood Park

PO
Catherine st
Vaughan St
Citadel
Liverpool St
Anson

B5211
Westwood Park Primary School

Junction 1/12

M602

The Grange

Taunton Road
Stroud Av
Weymo
Leamington
Cee Lane
Woodford Av
Dartford Av

Buttleet Sutherland st
Dover St
Breck Road
WORS

Salford College

Colborne Avenue

Gillingham Rd
PO

C5
Street names for this grid square are listed at the back of the index

St Gilbert's RC School
Cambell Rd
Bridgewater
New Lane

C6
1 Hallsworth Rd
2 Isobel Cl
3 John St
4 Joseph St
5 Sarah St
6 Winifred St

Stannard Road
Batleye Road
Boddington
Chatley Rd
Foxhill Road
Brereton
PO

Guildford Road
Hatherop
Gorton
Schofield
Clanton
Ampere Cl
Fir Stock
Lily St
Moor Hatt
LIVERPOO

M30

M60

Barton Hall Avenue

Barton Moss C of E Primary School

Buckthorn La
Lodgepole Close
Tipple Rd
Verda Lane
Robina Close
Northfleet Road
Hilley Road
Brookhouse Av

Moat Hall Av

Harrison street
Winster Road
Clifford Rd

A
118
B
A57
C
PO

Junction 11

Peel

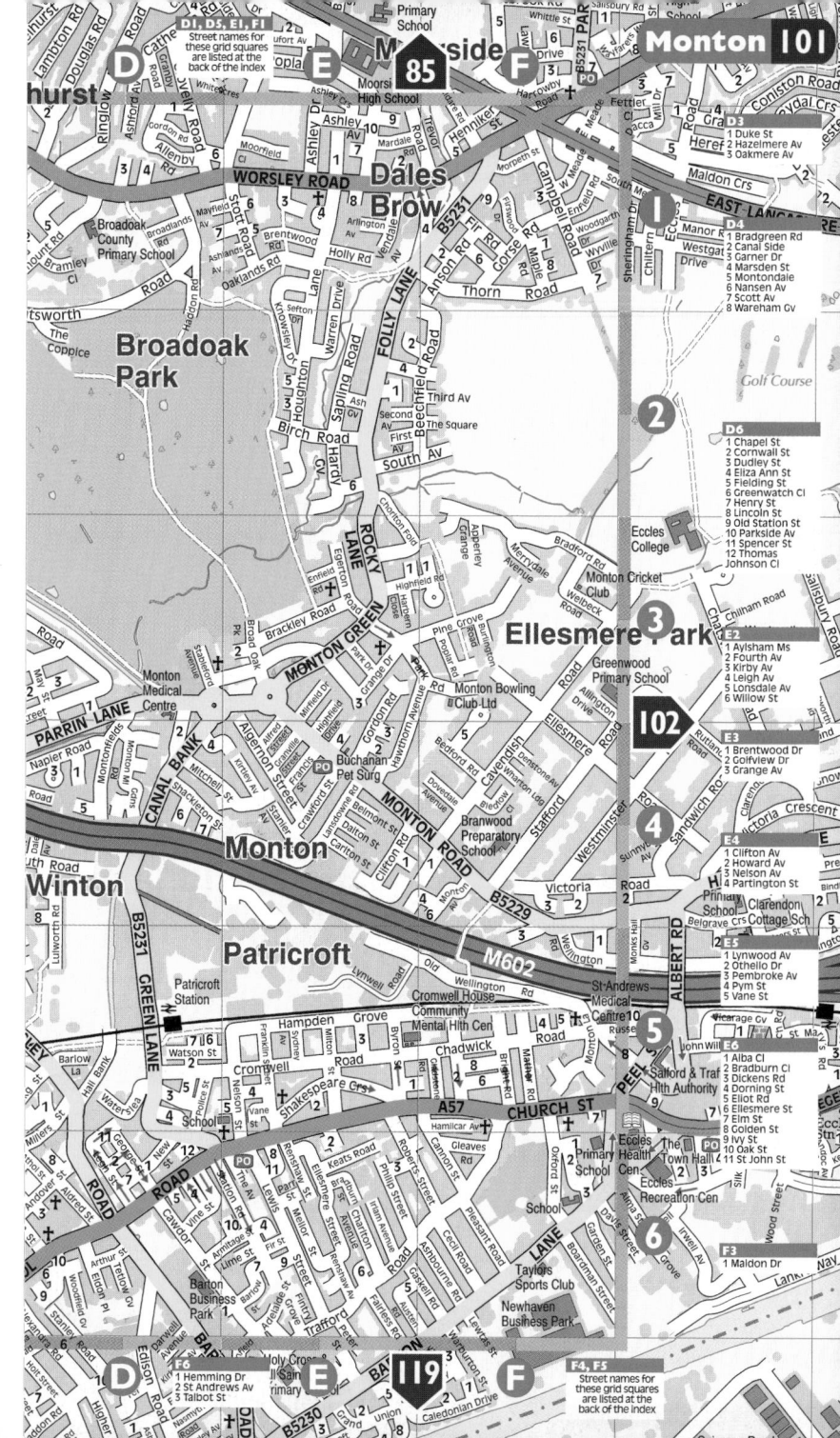

Primary School

Morrside High School

85

D D E Monton F

DI, DS, EI, FI
Street names for these grid squares are listed at the back of the index

Coniston Road

WORSLEY ROAD

Dales Brow

EAST LANCS

D1
1 Duke St
2 Hazelmere Av
3 Oakmere Av

Maldon Crs

Broadoak County Primary School

FOLLY LANE

The coppice

Broadoak Park

Third Av

Second Av

First Av

The Square

South Av

Golf Course

I1
1 Bradgreen Rd
2 Canal Side
3 Garner Dr
4 Marsden St
5 Montondale
6 Nansen Av
7 Scott Av
8 Wareham Gv

2

D6
1 Chapel St
2 Cornwall St
3 Dudley St
4 Eliza Ann St
5 Fielding St
6 Greenwatch Cl
7 Henry St
8 Lincoln St
9 Old Station St
10 Parkside Av
11 Spencer St
12 Thomas Johnson Cl

ROCKY LANE

MONTON GREEN

BRACKLEY ROAD

Eccles College

Monton Cricket Club

3 Ellesmere Park

Greenwood Primary School

E3
1 Aylsham Ms
2 Fourth Av
3 Kirby Av
4 Leigh Av
5 Lonsdale Av
6 Willow St

102

Monton Medical Centre

Monton Bowling Club Ltd

E4
1 Brentwood Cl
2 Golfview Dr
3 Grange Av

PARRIN LANE

CANAL BANK

Napier Road

Buchanan Pet Surg

MONTON ROAD

Branwood Preparatory School

Victoria Crescent

4

E4
1 Clifton Av
2 Howard Av
3 Nelson Av
4 Partington St

Monton

Winton

Clarendon Cottage Sch

Belgrave Crs

E5
1 Lynwood Av
2 Othello Dr
3 Pembroke Av
4 Pym St
5 Vane St

Patricroft

M602

St Andrews Medical Centre

ALBERT RD

Vicarage Gv

E6
1 Alba St
2 Bradburn Cl
3 Dickens Rd
4 Dorning St
5 Eliot Rd
6 Ellesmere St
7 Elm St
8 Golden St
9 Ivy St
10 Oak St
11 St John St

Patricroft Station

GREEN LANE

Cromwell House Community Mental Hlth Cen

Chadwick Road

A57 CHURCH ST

5

PEEL

Salford & Traf Hlth Authority

Barlow La

Shakespeare Crs

Hamilcar Av

Gleaves Rd

Eccles Primary School

Eccles Health Cen

The Town Hall

PO

Eccles Recreation Cen

6

F3
1 Maldon Dr

Barton Business Park

Taylors Sports Club

Newhaven Business Park

BARTON LANE

D **F6**
1 Hemming Dr
2 St Andrews Av
3 Talbot St

E **119** F

F4, F5
Street names for these grid squares are listed at the back of the index

Caledonian Drive

Guinness Road

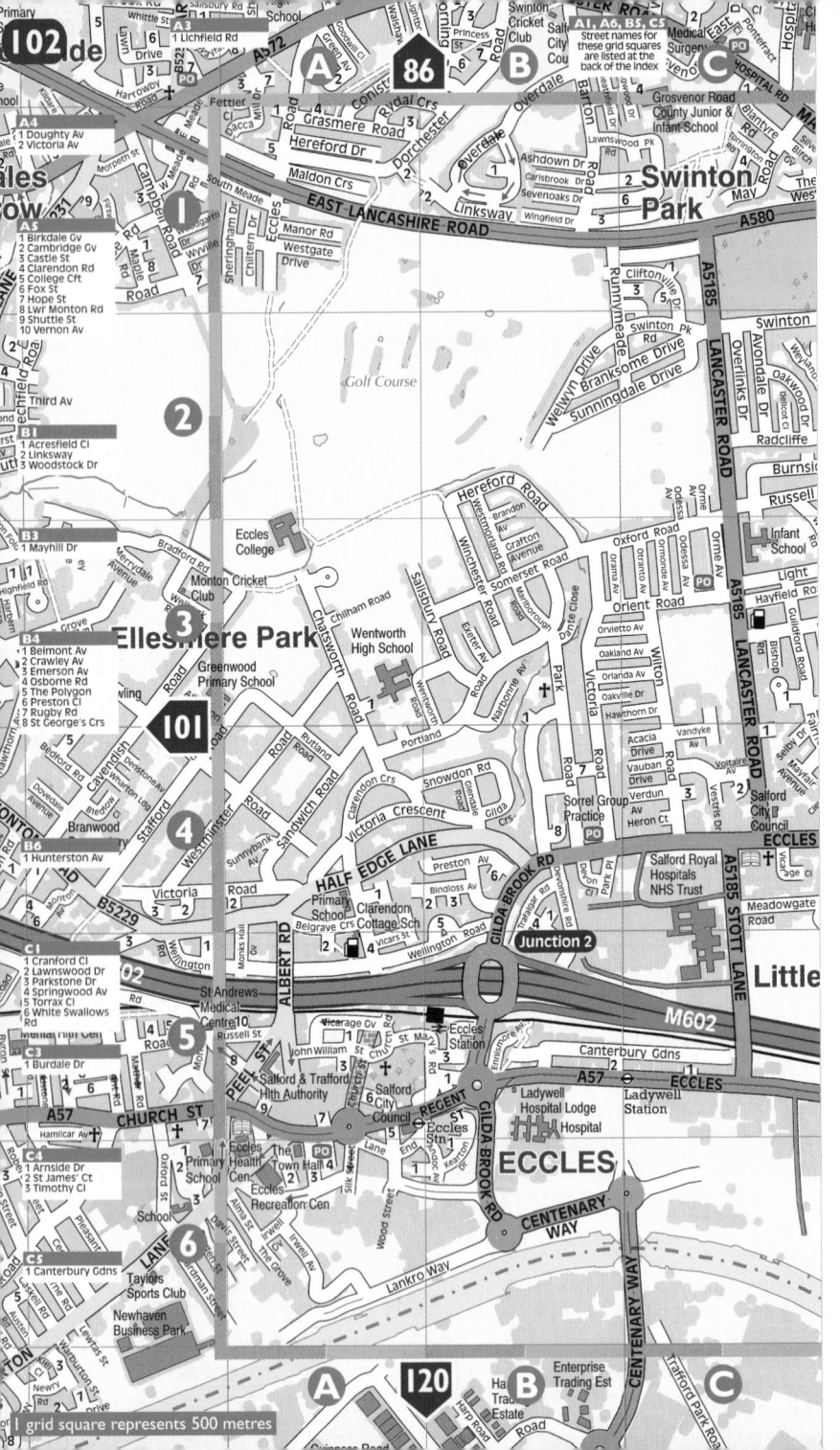

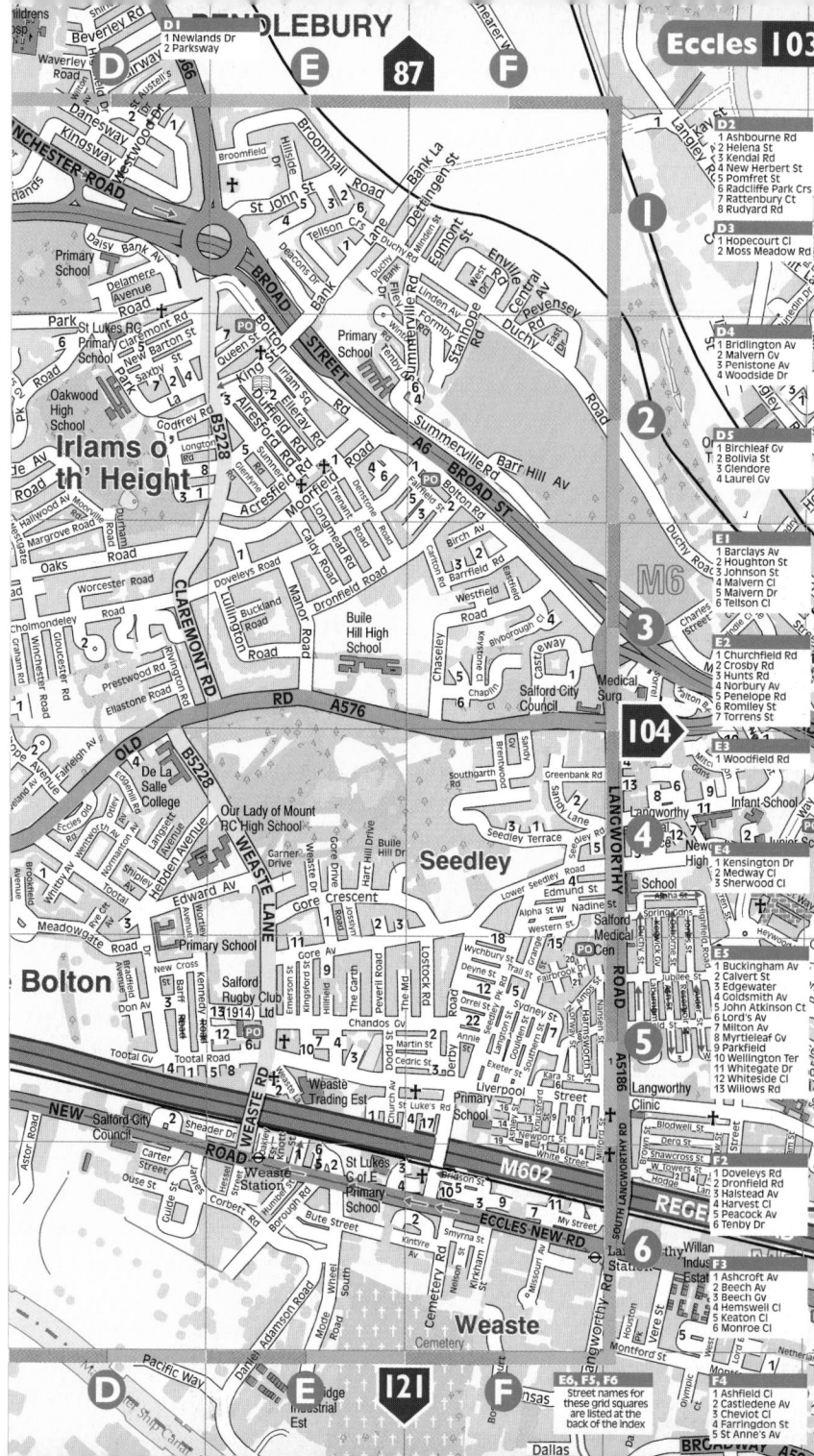

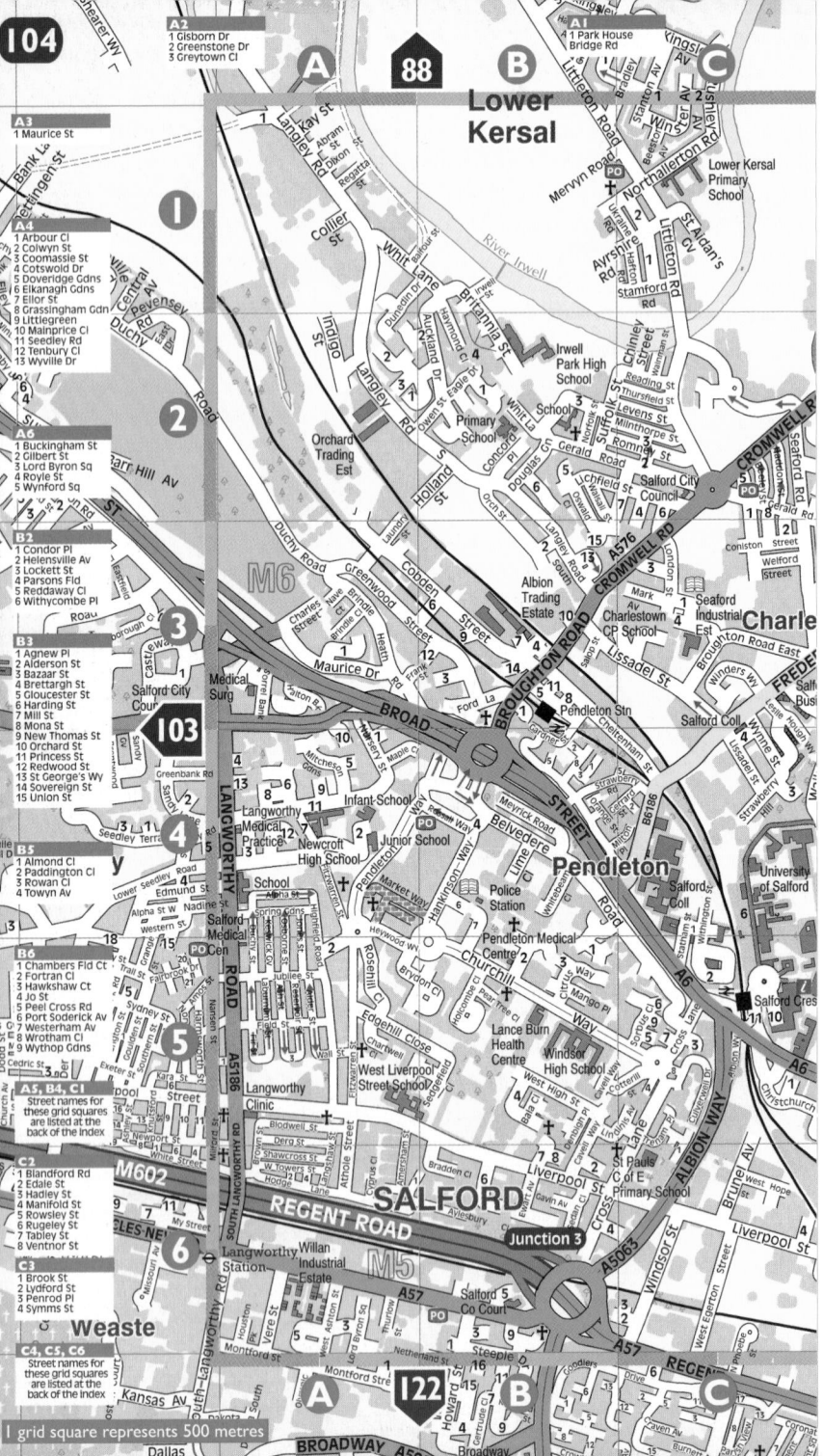

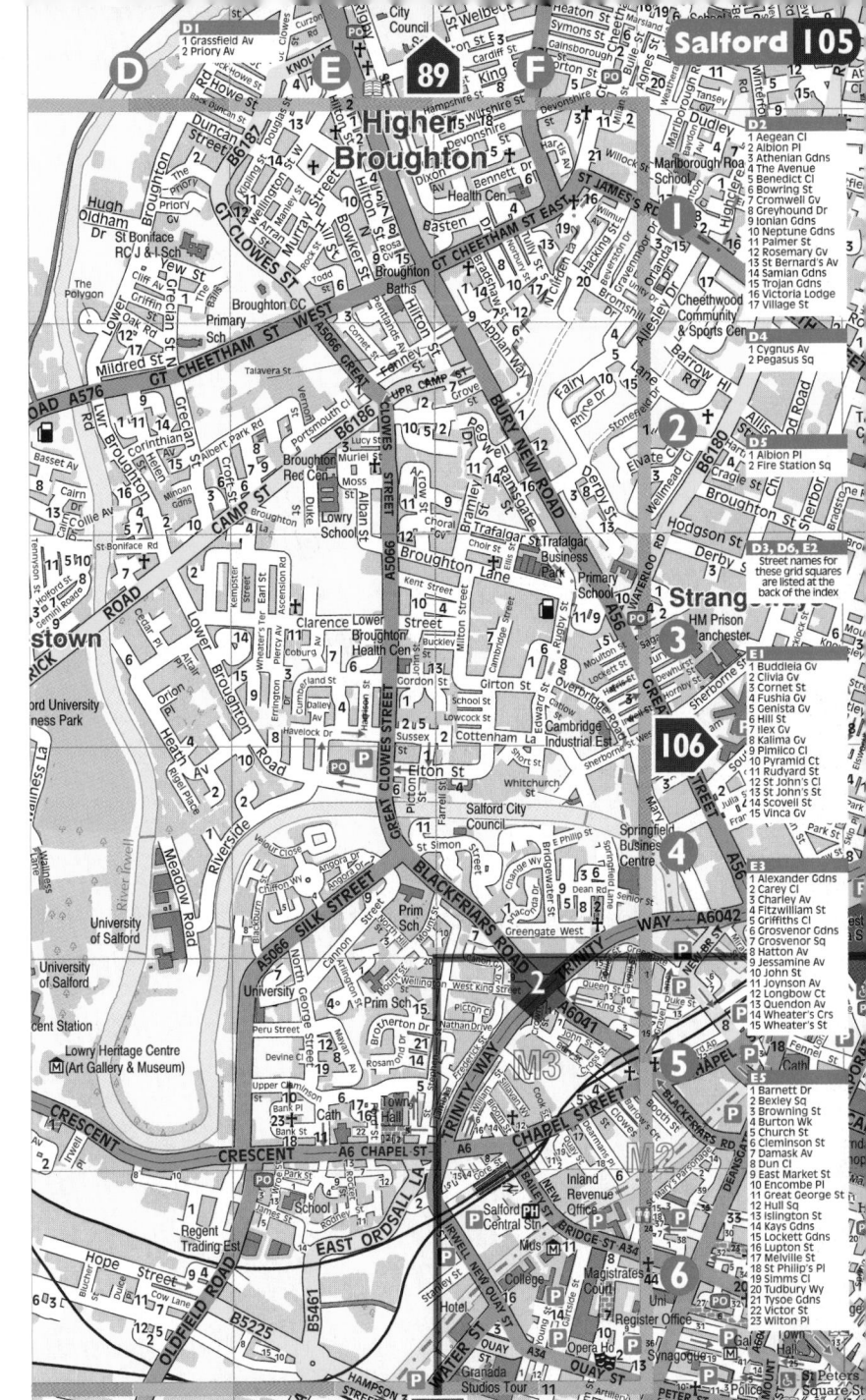

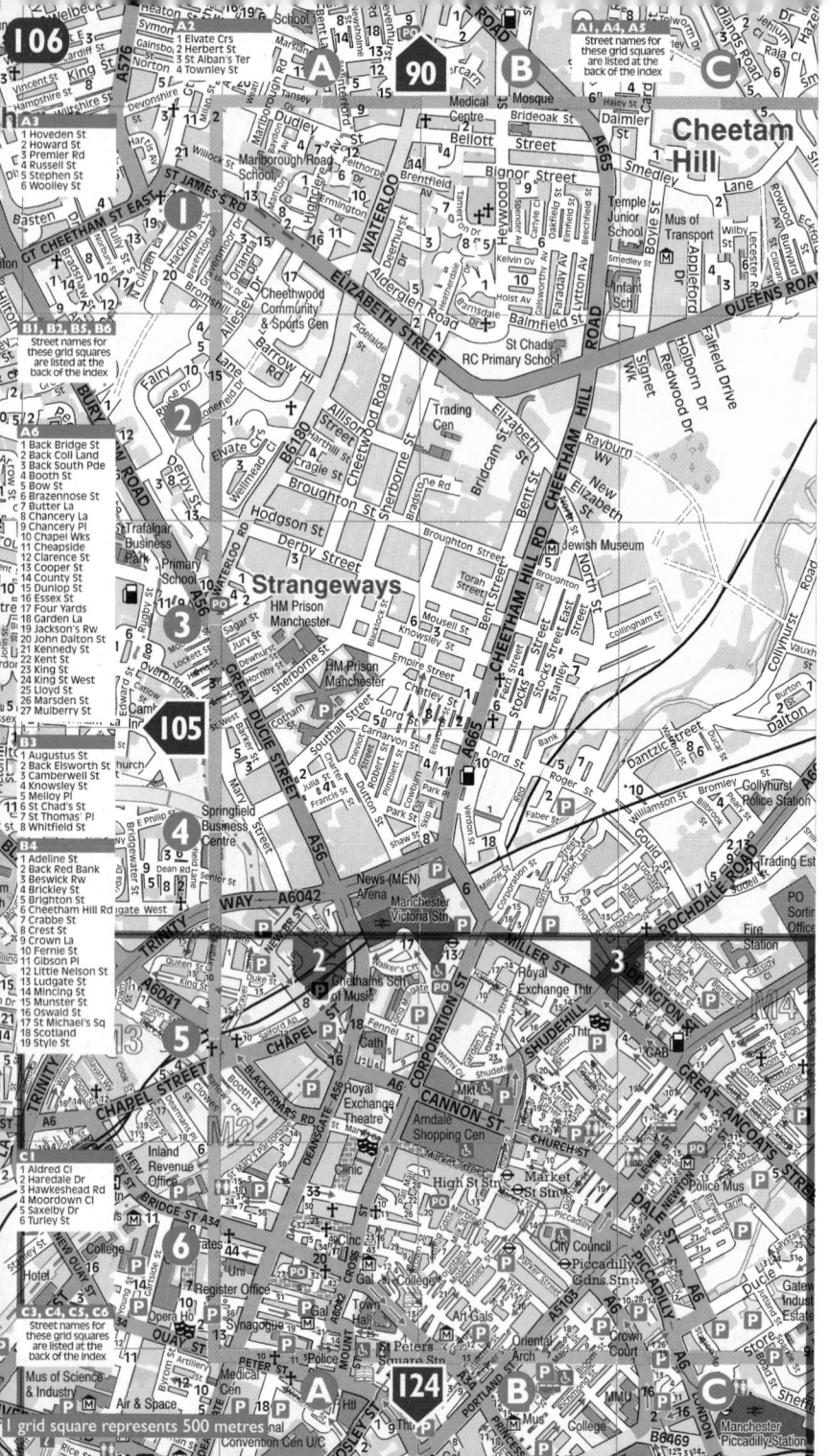

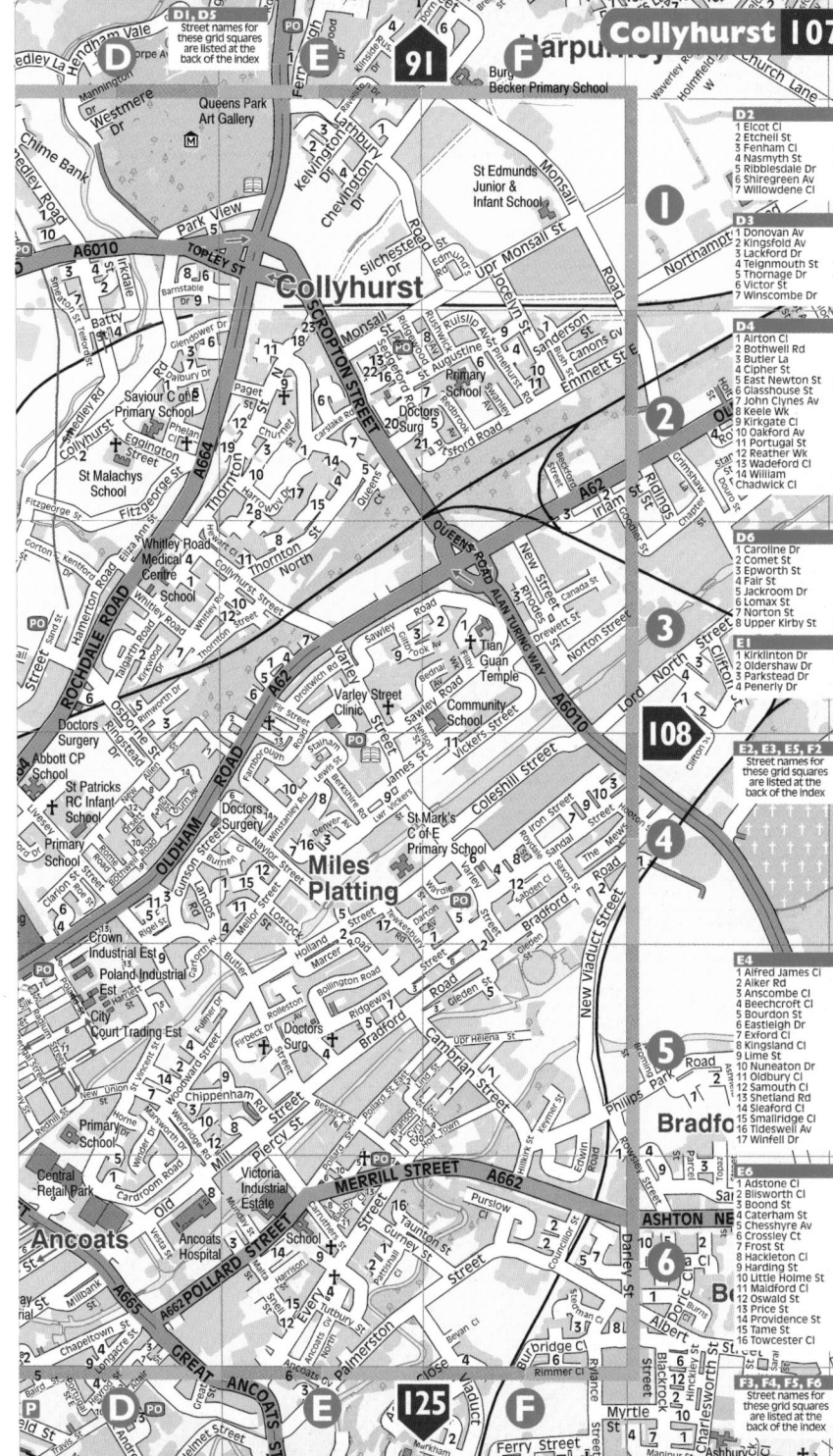

Collyhurst 107

D1, D5
Street names for these grid squares are listed at the back of the index

D2
1 Elcot Cl
2 Etchell St
3 Fenham Cl
4 Nasmyth St
5 Ribblesdale Dr
6 Shiregreen Av
7 Willowdene Cl

D3
1 Donovan Av
2 Kingsfold Av
3 Lackford Dr
4 Teignmouth St
5 Thornage Dr
6 Victor St
7 Winscombe Dr

D4
1 Airton Cl
2 Bothwell Rd
3 Butler La
4 Cipher St
5 East Newton St
6 Glasshouse St
7 John Clynes Av
8 Keele Wk
9 Kirkgate Cl
10 Oakford Av
11 Portugal St
12 Reather Wk
13 Wadeford Cl
14 William Chadwick Cl

D6
1 Caroline Dr
2 Comet St
3 Epworth St
4 Fair St
5 Jackroom Dr
6 Lomax St
7 Norton St
8 Upper Kirby St

E1
1 Kirklinton Dr
2 Oldershaw Dr
3 Parkstead Dr
4 Penerly Dr

E2, E3, E5, F2
Street names for these grid squares are listed at the back of the index

E4
1 Alfred James Cl
2 Alker Rd
3 Anscombe Cl
4 Beechcroft Cl
5 Bourdon St
6 Eastleigh Dr
7 Exford Cl
8 Kingsland Cl
9 Lime St
10 Nuneaton Dr
11 Oldbury Cl
12 Samouth Cl
13 Shetland Rd
14 Sleaford Cl
15 Smallridge Cl
16 Tideswell Av
17 Winfell Dr

E6
1 Adstone Cl
2 Blisworth Cl
3 Boond St
4 Caterham St
5 Chessture Av
6 Crossley Ct
7 Frost St
8 Hackleton Cl
9 Harding St
10 Little Holme St
11 Maldford Cl
12 Oswald St
13 Price St
14 Providence St
15 Tame St
16 Towcester Cl

F3, F4, F5, F6
Street names for these grid squares are listed at the back of the index

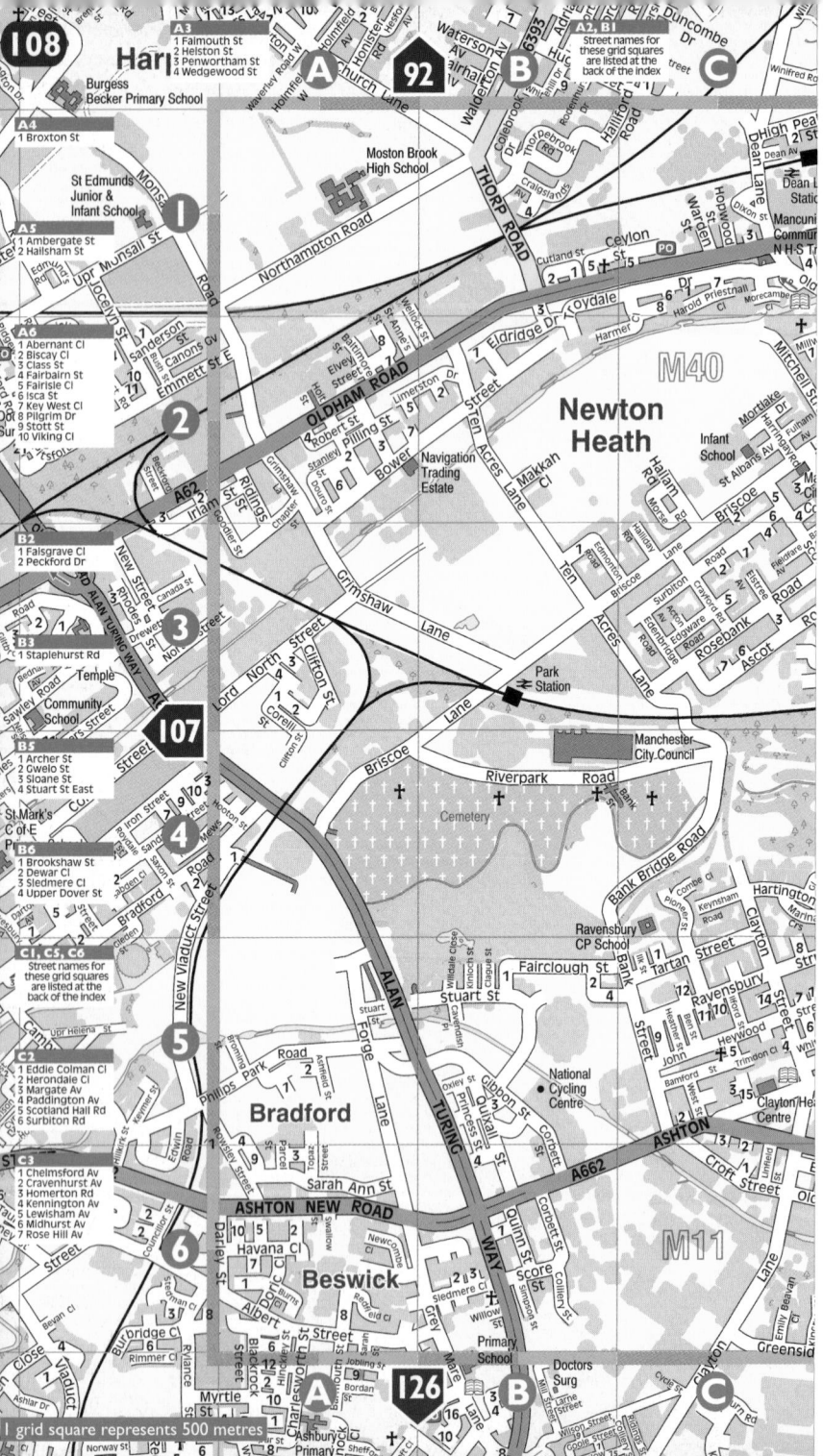

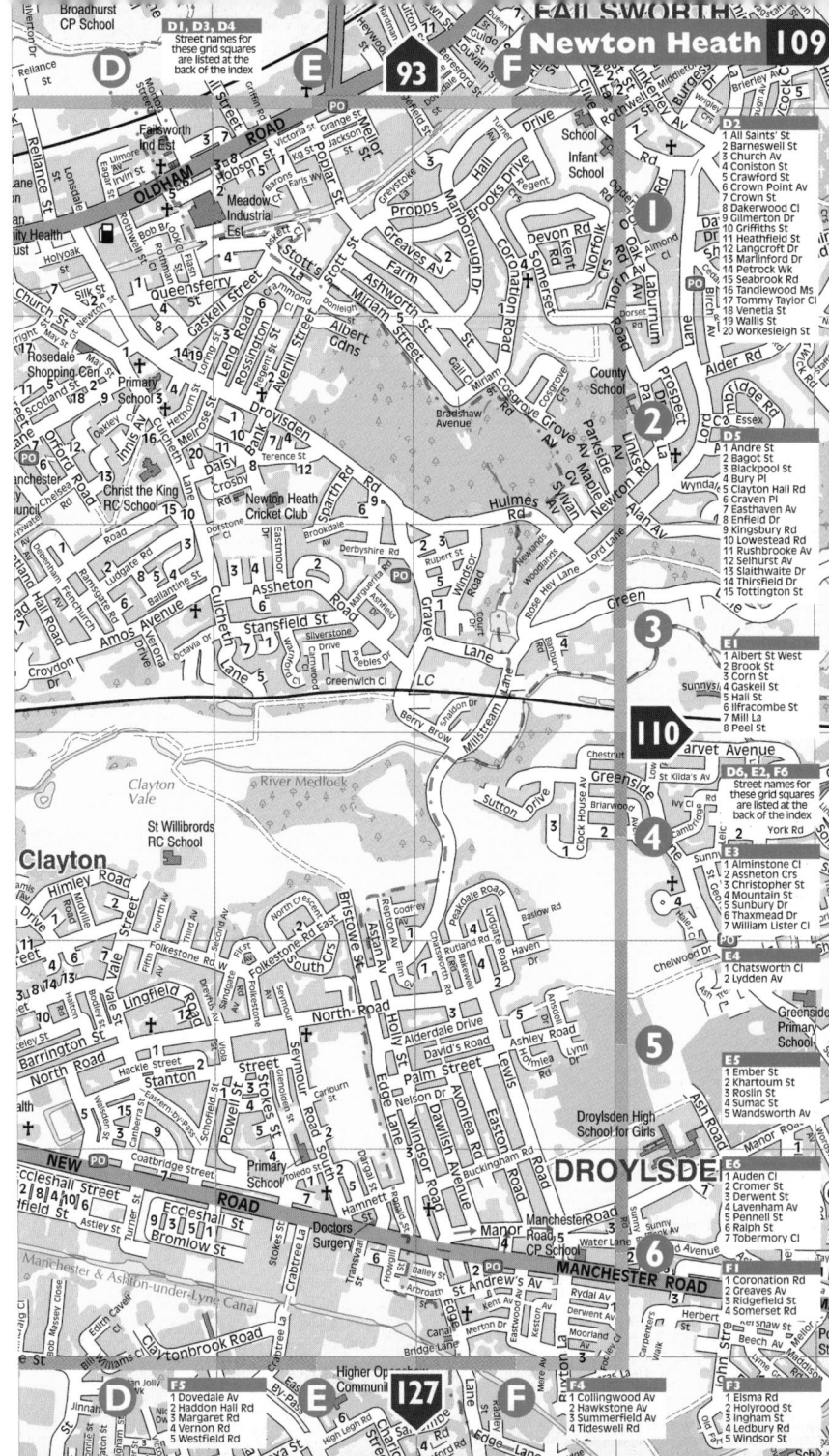

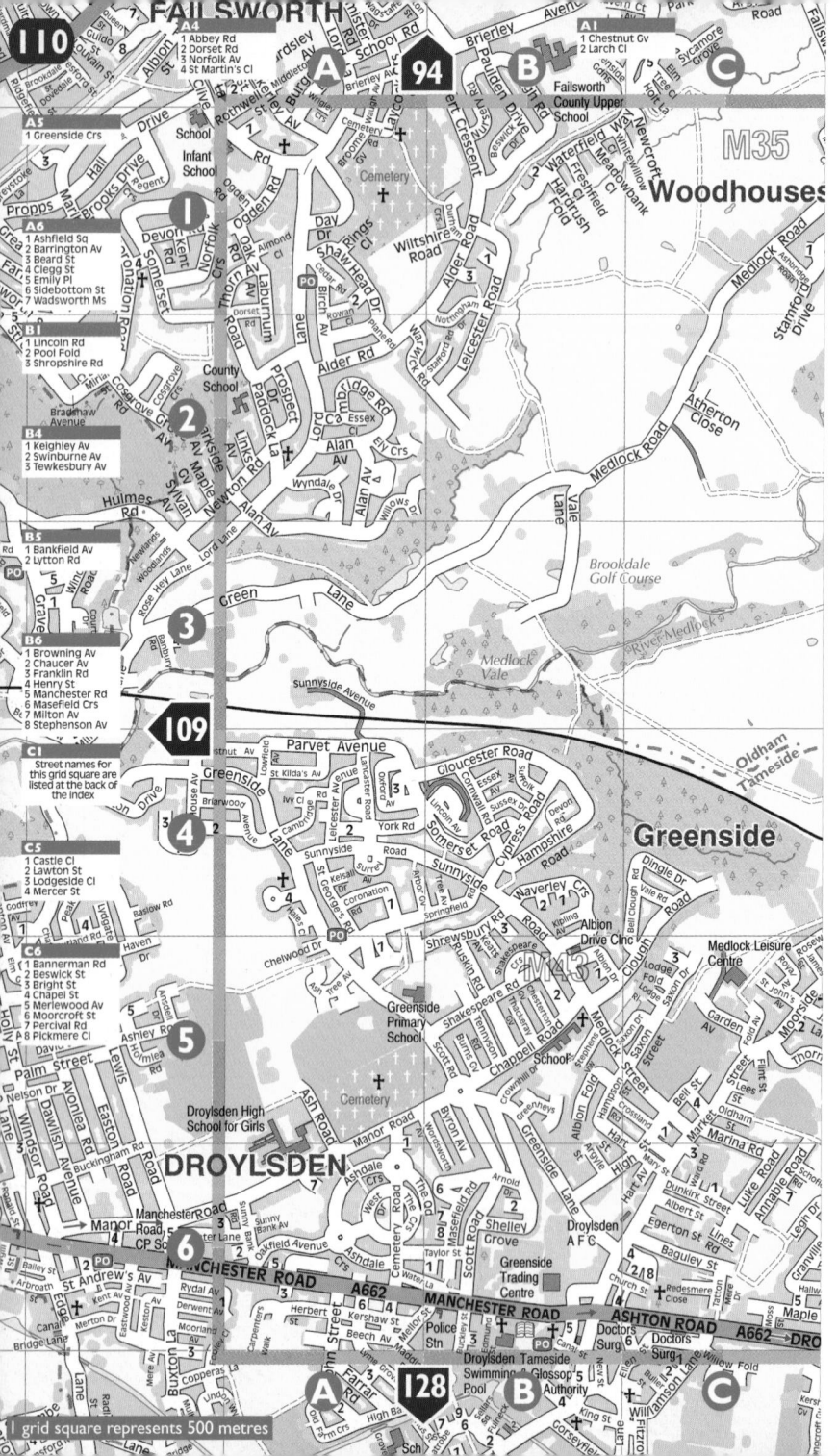

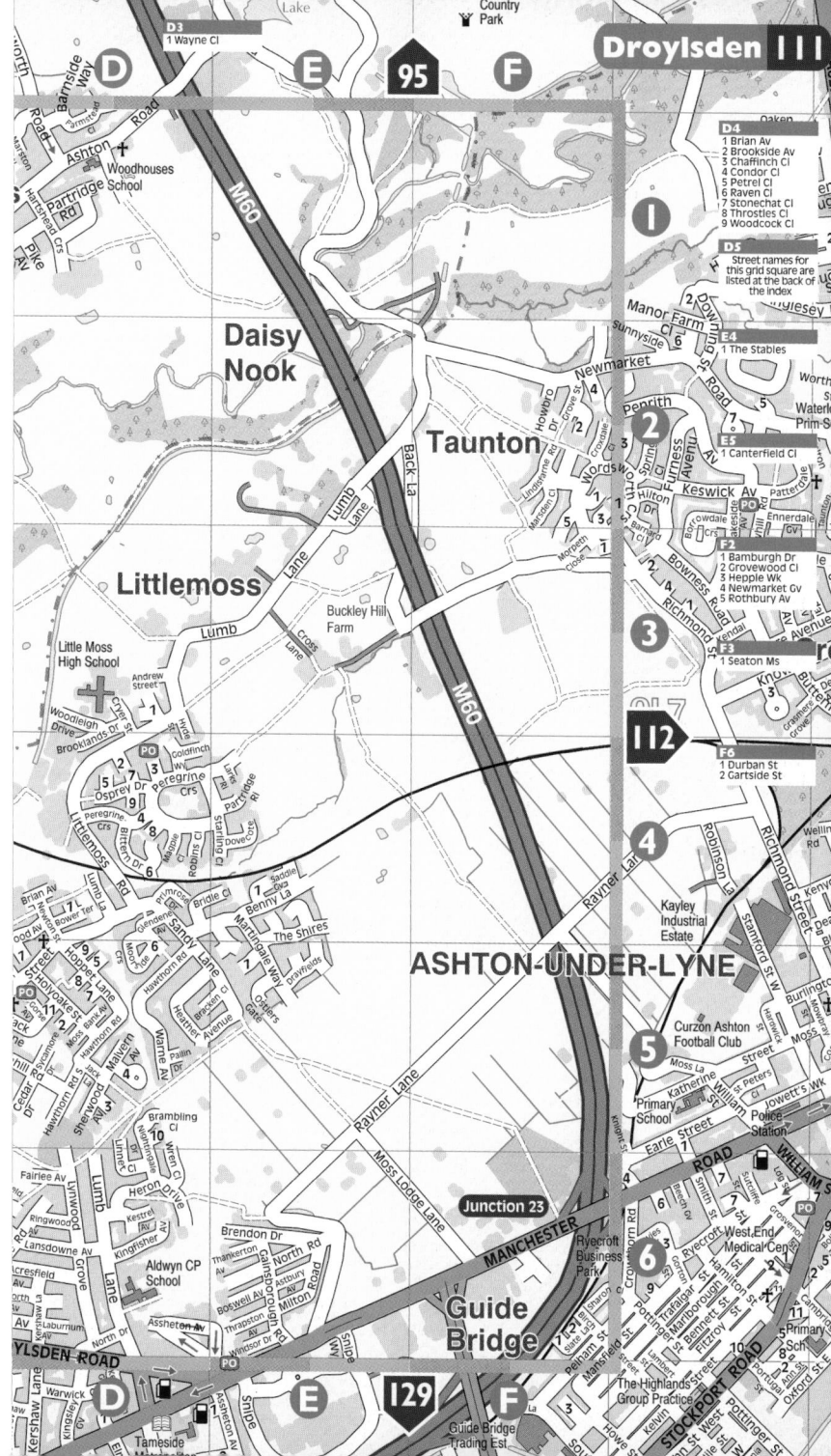

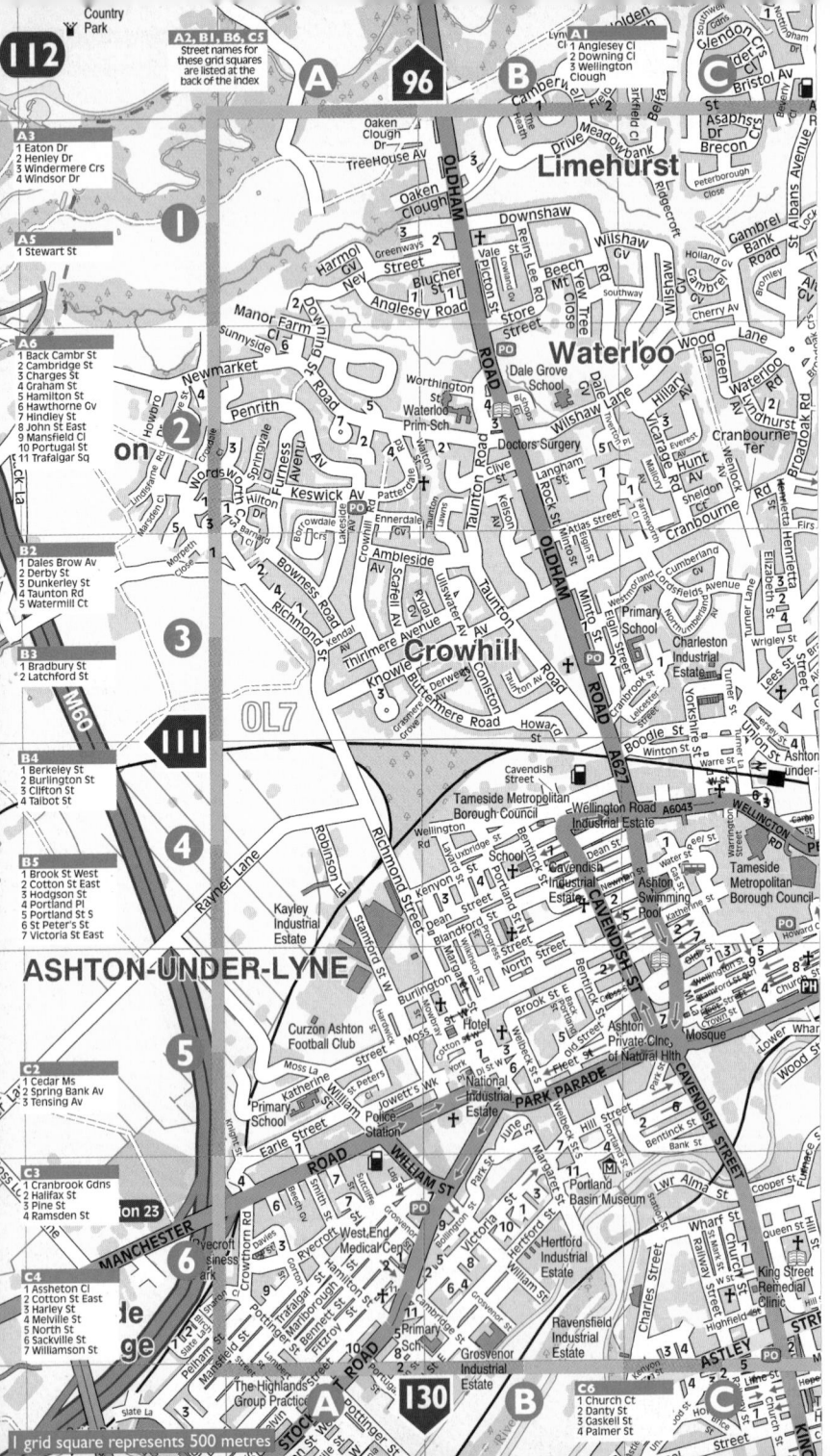

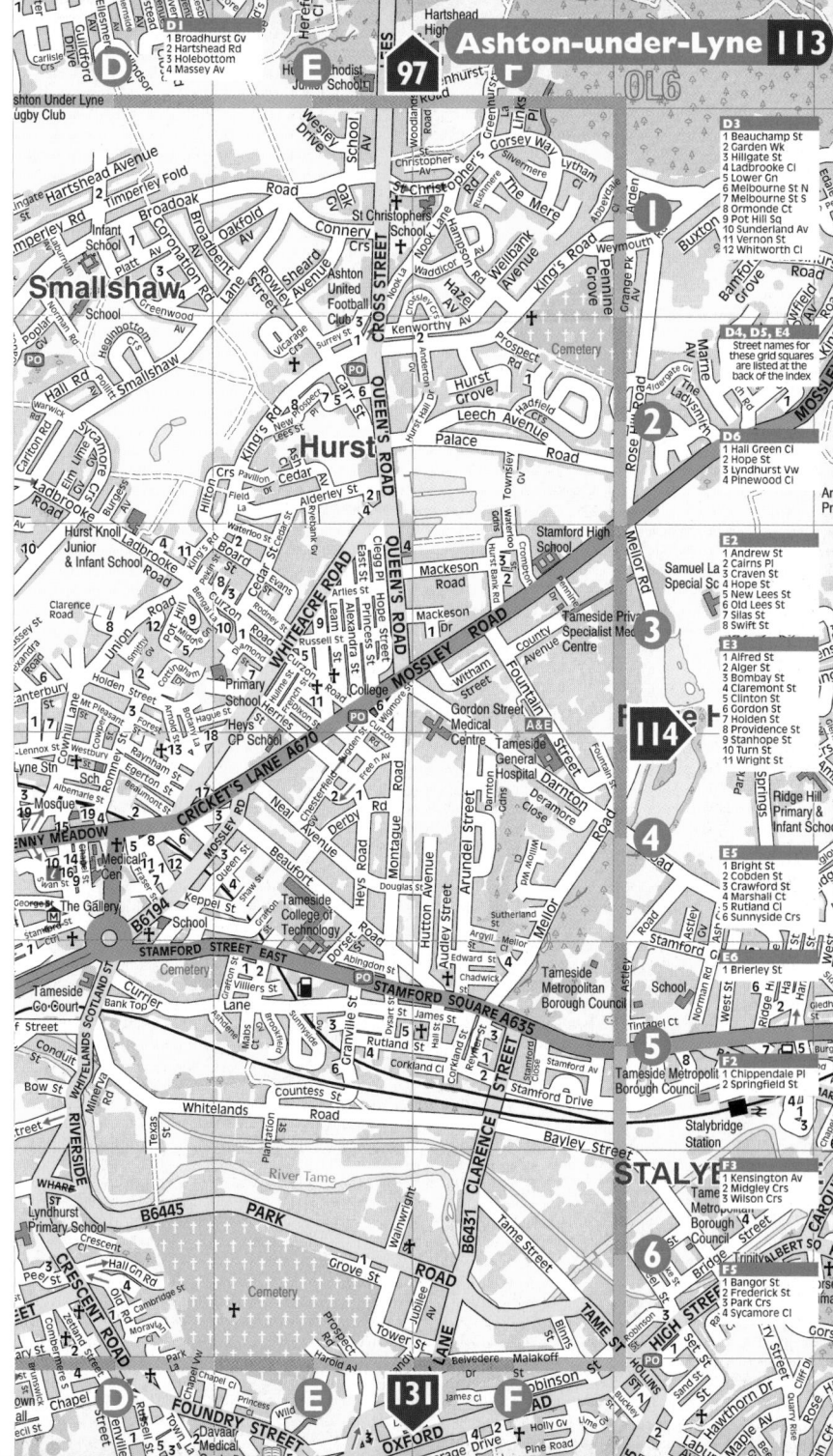

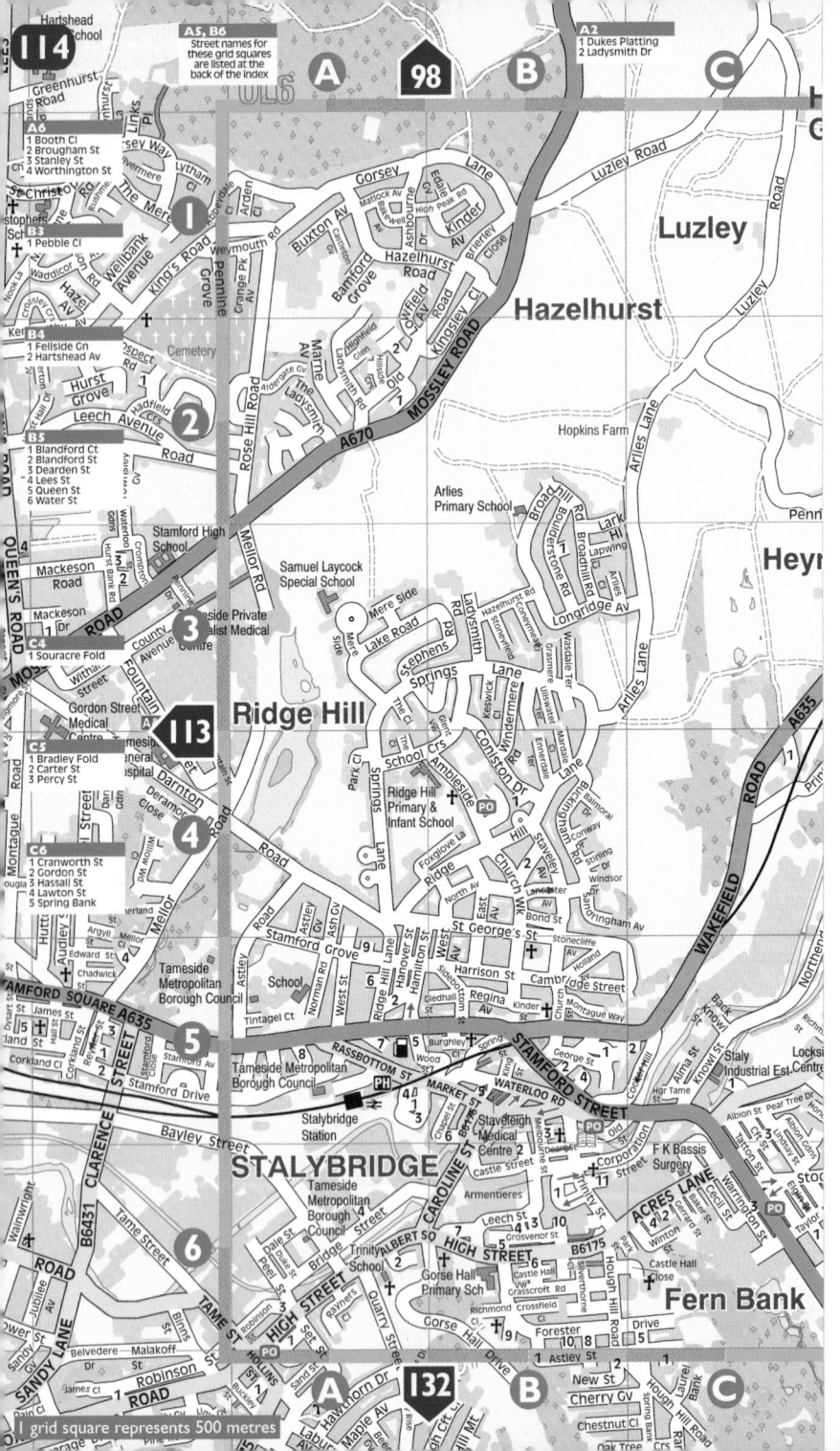

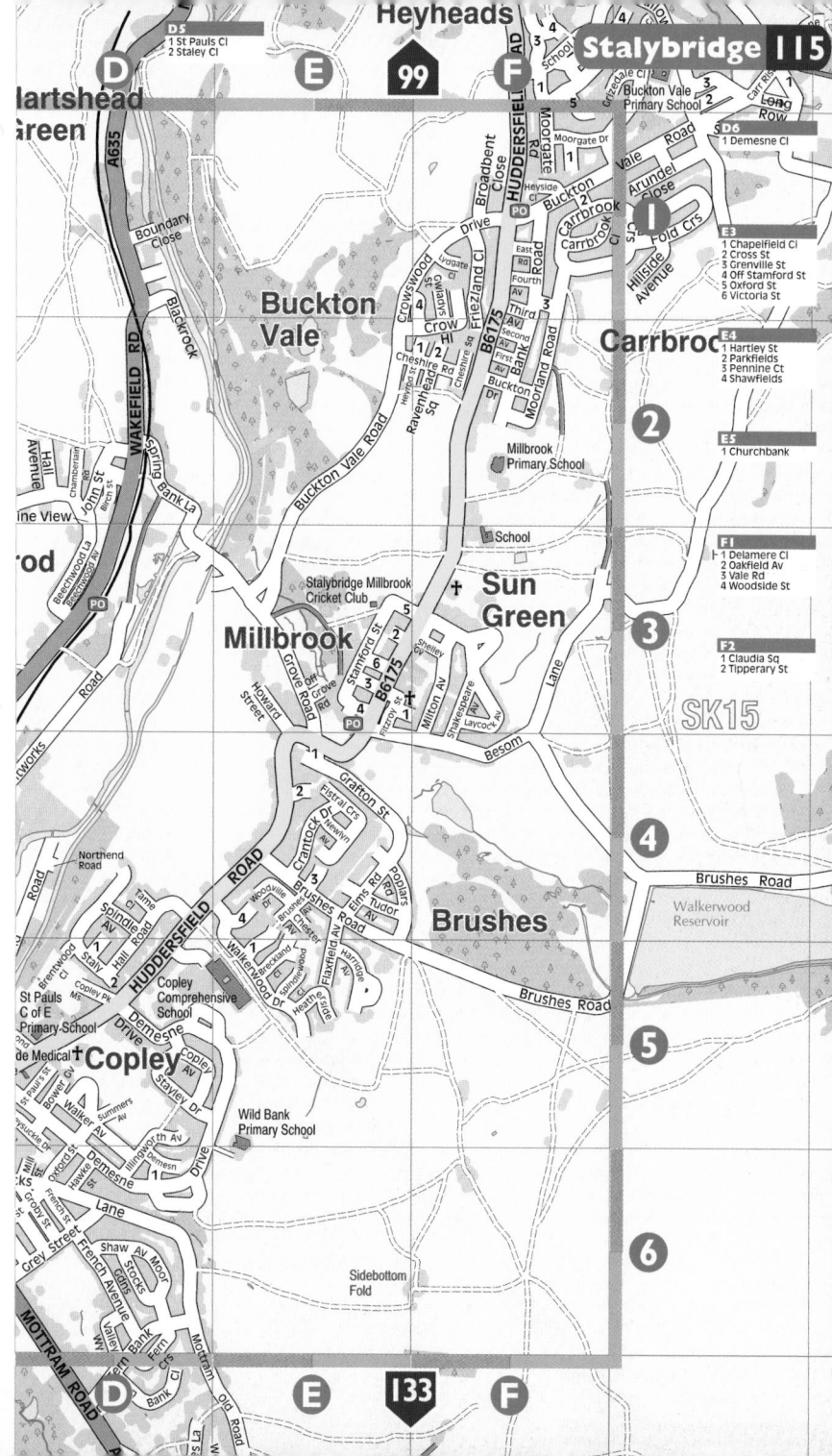

D5
1 St Pauls Cl
2 Staley Cl

D   **E**   **99**   **F**

D6
1 Demesne Cl

Hartshead Green

A635

Boundary Close

Blackrock

Spring Bank La

Buckton Vale

Buckton Vale Road

Millbrook Primary School

School

E3
1 Chapelfield Cl
2 Cross St
3 Grenville St
4 Off Stamford St
5 Oxford St
6 Victoria St

Carrbrook

E4
1 Hartley St
2 Parkfields
3 Pennine Ct
4 Shawfields

E5
1 Churchbank

Buckton Vale Primary School

Hillside Avenue

Arundel Close

Fold Crs

I

2

Sun Green

F1
1 Delamere Cl
2 Oakfield Av
3 Vale Rd
4 Woodside St

F2
1 Claudia Sq
2 Tipperary St

SK15

3

Millbrook

Stalybridge Millbrook Cricket Club

Howard Street

Grove Road

Stamford St

B6175

Besom Lane

4

Grafton St

Crantock Dr

Brushes Road

Walkerwood Reservoir

Brushes

Brushes Road

5

Northend Road

Huddersfield Road

Copley Comprehensive School

St Pauls C of E Primary School

Medical

Copley

Demesne Drive

Staveley Dr

Wild Bank Primary School

6

Shaw Av

French Avenue

Sidebottom Fold

Mottram Road

D   **E**   **133**   **F**

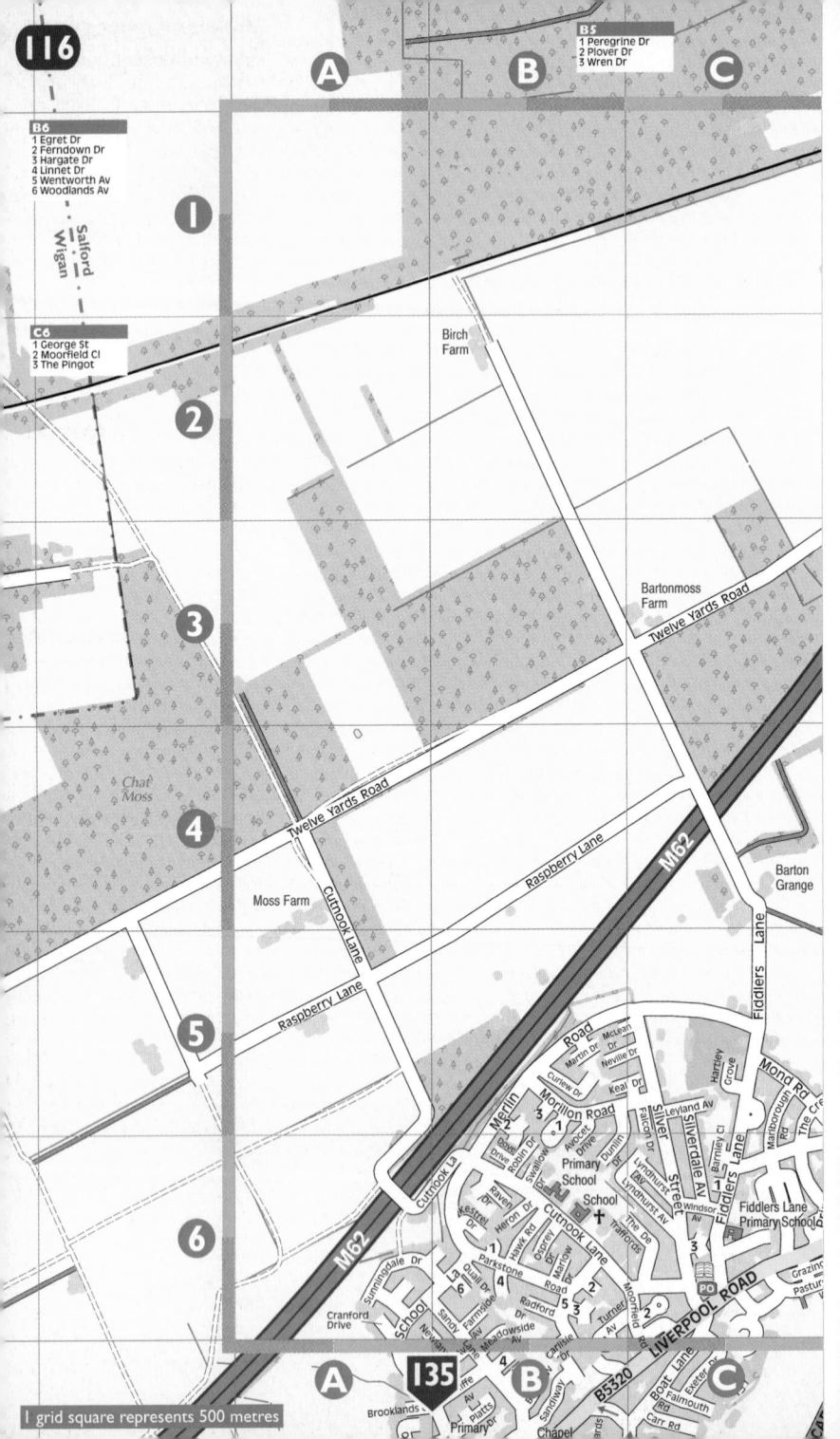

116

B5
1 Peregrine Dr
2 Plover Dr
3 Wren Dr

B6
1 Egret Dr
2 Ferndown Dr
3 Hargate Dr
4 Linnet Dr
5 Wentworth Av
6 Woodlands Av

Salford
Wigan

C6
1 George St
2 Moorfield Cl
3 The Pingot

A
B
C

I

2

3

4

5

6

Birch
Farm

Bartonmoss
Farm

Twelve Yards Road

Twelve Yards Road

Raspberry Lane

M62

Barton
Grange

Chat
Moss

Moss Farm

Cutnook Lane

Raspberry Lane

Fiddlers Lane

M62

Cranford
Drive

Road
McLean
Martin Dr
Neville Dr
Curlew Dr
Keal Dr
Merlin
Morillon Road
Avocet Drive
Robin Dr
Swallow
Dunlin
Primary
School
Kestrel Dr
Raven Dr
Heron Dr
Hawk Rd
Osprey
Harlow
Parkstone
Quail Rd
Sandy
Farndale
Meadowside Av
Carlisle
Radford Dr
Turner Av
Cutnook Lane
Leyland Av
Falcon Dr
Lyndhurst Av
Lyndhurst Av
Windsor
The De
Trafford
Silver Street
Silverdale Av
Barnley Cl
Grove
Hartley
Marlborough Rd
Mond Rd
The Cres
Fiddlers Lane
Fiddlers Lane
Primary School
PO
LIVERPOOL ROAD
Moorfield
Grazing
Pasture
Sunningdale Dr
School
Newton
Platts
Chapel
Brooklands
Primary
135
B5320
Boat La
Exeter Dr
Falmouth
Carr Rd

A
135
B
C

I grid square represents 500 metres

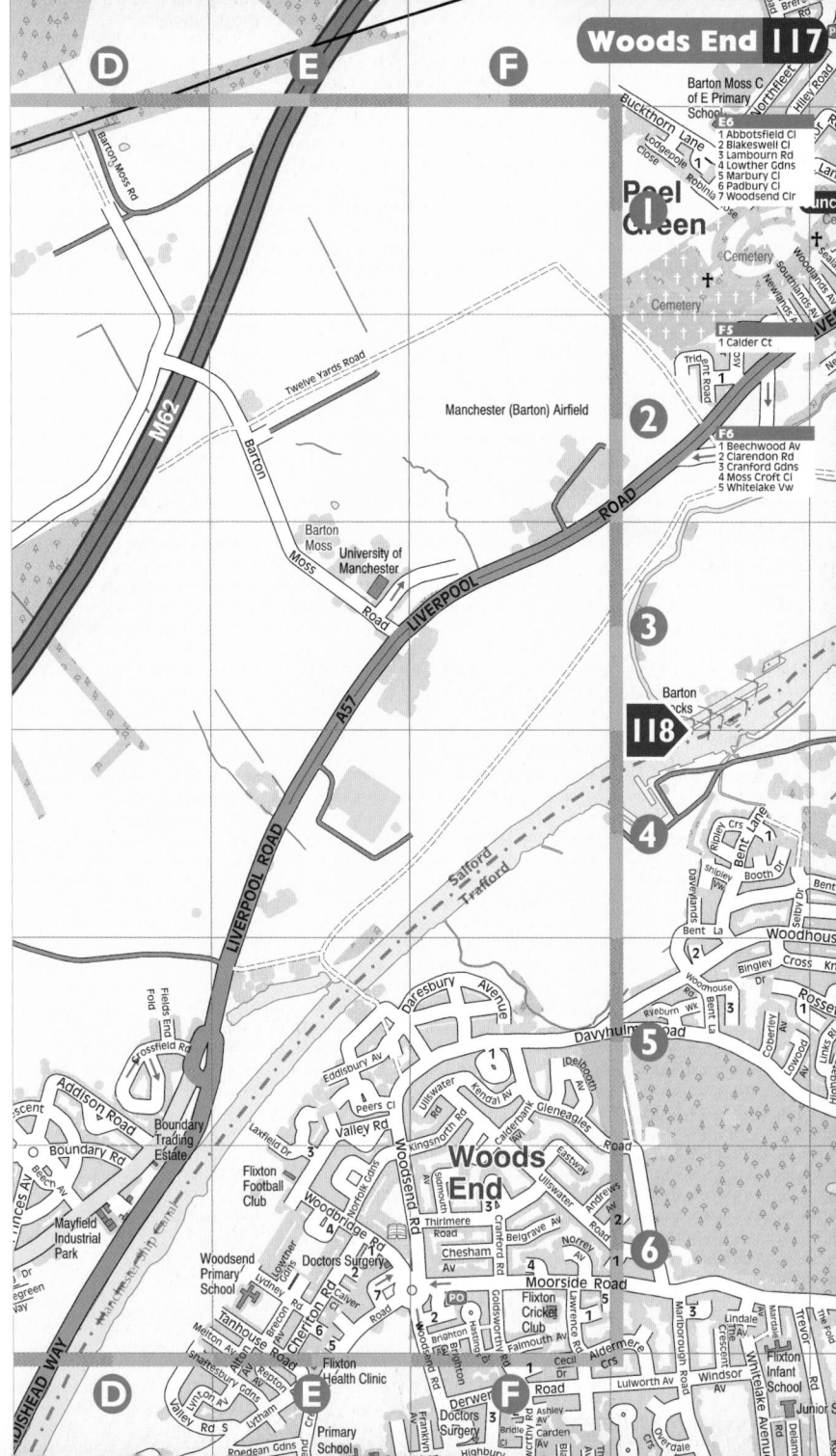

Barton Moss C
of E Primary
School

Buckthorn Lane

E6
1 Abbotsfield Cl
2 Blakeswell Cl
3 Lambourn Rd
4 Lowther Gdns
5 Marbury Cl
6 Padbury Cl
7 Woodsend Cir

Peel Green

Cemetery

Cemetery

F5
1 Calder Ct

Trident Road

F6
1 Beechwood Av
2 Clarendon Rd
3 Cranford Gdns
4 Moss Croft Cl
5 Whitelake Vw

Twelve Yards Road

Manchester (Barton) Airfield

Barton Moss Road

University of Manchester

M62

Barton

Barton Moss Road

LIVERPOOL ROAD

A57

Barton Docks

118

Bent Lane

Ripley Crs

Shipley Vw

Daveylands

Booth Dr

Bent La

Woodhouse

Salford Trafford

Woodhouse Dr

Bingley Cross

Ryeburn Wk

Bent La

Rosset

Davyhulme Road

Daresbury Avenue

Eddisbury Av

Peers Cl

Valley Rd

Laxfield Dr

Ullswater Kendal Av

Kingsnorth Rd

Delroy

Gleneagles Road

Calderbank Wy

Eastway

Fields End Fold

Crossfield Rd

Addison Road

Boundary Rd

Boundary Trading Estate

Mayfield Industrial Park

Flixton Football Club

Woodbridge Rd

Norfolk Gdns

Woodsend Rd

Thirlmere Road

Woods End

Ullswater

Andrews Av

Norrey Av

Chesham Av

Cranford Rd

Belgrave Av

Woodsend Primary School

Doctors Surgery

Calver Road

Cherton Rd

Tanhouse Road

Moorside Road

Flixton Cricket Club

Lawrence Rd

Lindale

Marlborough Rd

The Crescent

Flixton Infant School

Trevor

Melton Av

Rapton

Brecon Av

Flixton Health Clinic

PO

Goldsworthy Rd

Hastings

Brighton

Woodsend Rd

Falmouth Av

Cecil Dr

Aldermere Crs

Lulworth Av

Windsor Av

Overdale

Whitelake Avenue

Delamere

MOSHEAD WAY

Shaftesbury Gdns

Valley Rd S

Lytham

Roedean Gdns

Primary School

Derwent Doctors Surgery

Frankyn

Bridle Rd

Ashley Av

Carden Av

Highbury

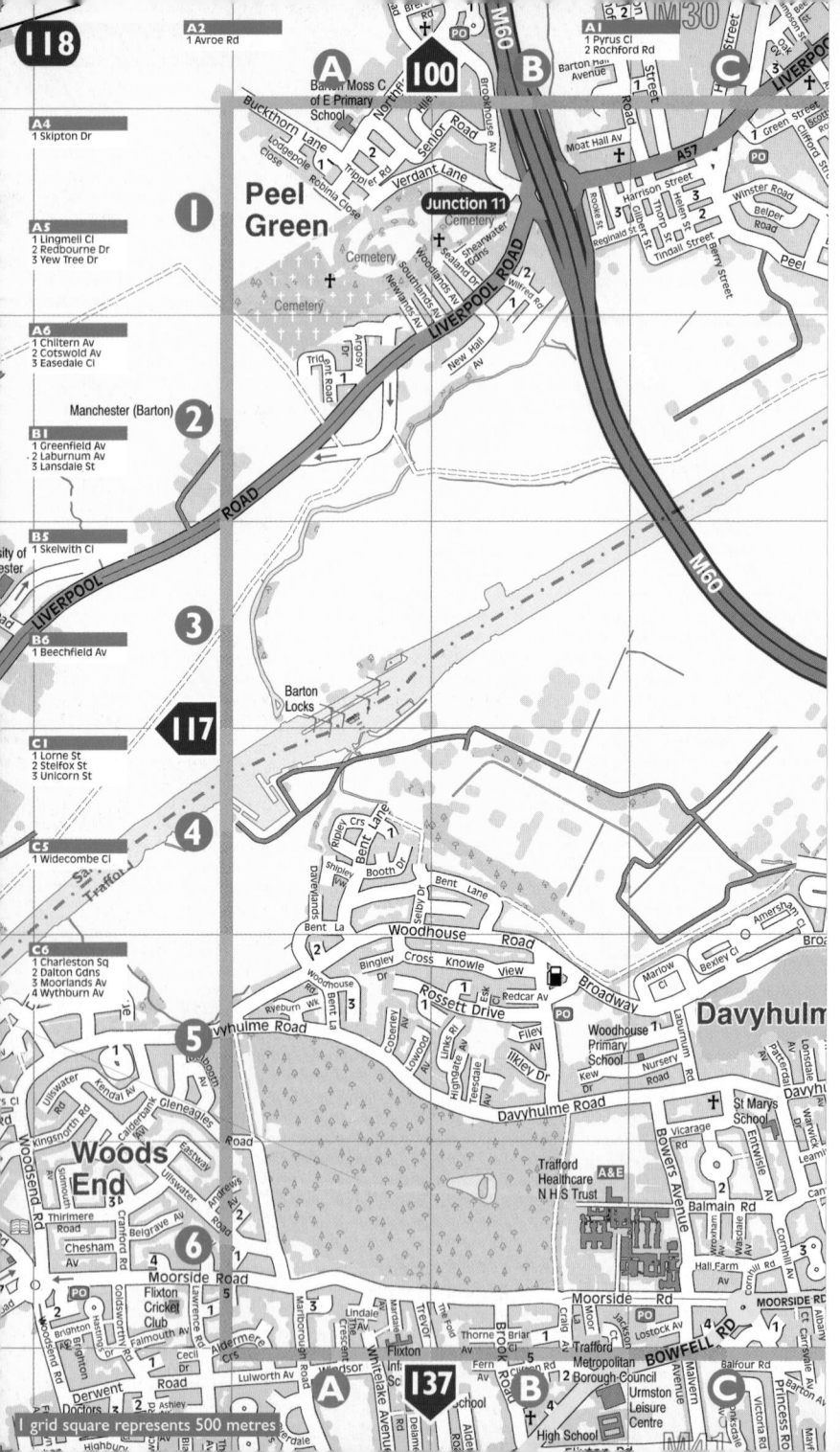

A2
1 Avroe Rd

A
1 Pyrus Cl
2 Rochford Rd

A4
1 Skipton Dr

A
Barton Moss C
of E Primary
School

100

B

C

LIVERPOOL

Street

M30

M60

Buckthorn Lane

Lodgepole Close
Robinia Close
Trippier Rd
Verdant Lane

Barton Hall
Avenue

Moat Hall Av

Green Road

A57

Peel
Green

Junction 11

Harrison Street

Winster Road
Belper
Road

A5
1 Lingmell Cl
2 Redbourne Dr
3 Yew Tree Dr

I

Cemetery

Clearwater

Rooke St
Reginald St

Thorp St
Gilbert St

Tindall Street
Berry Street

A6
1 Chiltern Av
2 Cotswold Av
3 Easedale Cl

Cemetery

Woodlands Dr
Sealand Gdns
Southlands Av
Wilfred Rd

Peel

Cemetery

Newlands Av

Nenmarsh Av

LIVERPOOL ROAD

Manchester (Barton)

2

Argosy Dr

New Hall
Av

B1
1 Greenfield Av
2 Laburnum Av
3 Lansdale St

Trident Road

ROAD

M60

B5
1 Skelwith Cl

LIVERPOOL

B6
1 Beechfield Av

3

Trafford

117

Barton
Locks

C1
1 Lorne St
2 Stelfox St
3 Unicorn St

4

Bent Lane

Ripley Crs

Davey Lands
Shipley Vw
Booth Dr

C5
1 Widecombe Cl

Bent La

Woodhouse

Road

Bent Lane

Amersham St
Broad

C6
1 Charleston Sq
2 Dalton Gdns
3 Moorlands Av
4 Wythburn Av

Woodhouse

Bingley Dr
Cross Knowle
View

Ryeburn Wk

Bent Lane

Rossett Drive

Redcar Av

Marlow
Cl

Bexley Cl

Davyhulm

PO

vyhulme Road

Coberley

Links Rd
Hightgate
Kirkwood

Esk Dr

Filey Dr
Ilkley Dr
Teesdale

Woodhouse
Primary
School

Laburnum Dr
Nursery
Road

Davy

5

Ullswater

Kendal Av

Gleneagles

Calderbank
Road

Eastway
Ullswater

Andrews

Road

Filey V
Kew
Dr

St Marys
School

Warwick

Woods
End

Kingsnorth Rd

Cranford Av

Road

Davyhulme Road

Vicarage
Rd

Entwisle

Davy

Thirlmere
Road

Belgrave Av

Trafford
Healthcare
N H S Trust

A&E

Bowers Avenue

Balmain Rd

Chesham
Av

6

Moorside Road

Flixton
Cricket
Club

Falmouth Av

Aldermere Crs

Marlborough Rd

Lindale
The
Crescent

Trevor Rd
Thorne Rd

Craig Rd

Moor
Jackson

Moorside Rd

Hall Farm
Av

MOORSIDE RD

Brighton
Dr

Goldsworthy Rd

Cecil
Dr

Lulworth Av

Fern Rd

Trafford
Metropolitan
Borough Council

Lostock Av

BOWFELL RD

Balfour Road

Windsor
Road

A

137

Flixton

Whitelake Avenue

B

Urmston
Leisure
Centre

C

High School

M41

D, E4
Street names for these grid squares are listed at the back of the index

D

E

101

F

Taylors
Sports Club
Raven
Business Park

Arthur Ter

Holy Cross &
All Saints R C
Primary School

BARTON

ROAD

Newcroft
Union

Caledonian Drive

I

D4
1 Arran Gdns
2 Broadway Cl
3 Wycombe Cl

Guinness Road
Trad

D5
1 Mirfield Dr

Astra
Business
Park

Barton Upon
Irwell

B5230

Chapel Pl

Twining Rd

Beacon Rd

ROAD

WEST

D6
1 Bendemeer
2 Bransford Rd
3 Broad Lea
4 Burnham Dr
5 Highfield Dr
6 Marshbrook Rd
7 Thurlestone Dr
8 Woodlands

Langland Drive

ASHBURTON

Robson Avenue

Taylor Road

North Avenue

2 e
ding
Estate

E1
1 Caldon Cl
2 Castlerea Cl
3 Fountain St
4 Keadby Cl
5 Kilrush Av
6 Mee's Sq
7 Rockhouse Cl
8 Wharfside Av

Dumplington

Old Barton Road

BARTON-REDCLYFFE RD

BARTON DOCK RD

Traders
Avenue

Phoenix
Wy

3

E5
1 Seabrook Crs

The Trafford Centre

120

Mercury
Way

Cobalt Av

E6
1 Rowan Av

Junction 10

M60

Benbecula Way

Harris

Lewis

Barra

Moss Lane

DOCK ROAD

WAY

4

F1
1 Blisworth Av
2 Braunston Cl
3 Hazelmere Cl

Rivers Lane

Stroma
Wy

Orkney

Shetland

Iona Way

Hoy
Dr

Skye Road

Coll Drive

Jura
Dr

St Modwen

PARK

Newbury
Dr

Dennington Dr

Kingsway Park

Queensway

George H Carnall
Leisure Centre

School

Junction 9

F6
1 Cavendish Rd
2 Chester Av
3 Durham Av
4 Lancaster Av
5 Pangbourne Av
6 Rowland Av
7 Trafford Av
8 York Av

Primary School

Crofts Bank

LOSTOCK RD

B5158

Conway Road

LOSTOCK

ROAD

URMSTON

Audley

Dalton

Berk

5

Primary School

M60

Barton Road

Hulme Road

B5214 CROFTS BANK ROAD

Westminster Rd

Tewkesbury

Rochester

Litchford Rd

Hartford Rd

Beverley

Aylesbury Av

Guildford Rd

Burford

Whalley

Webster

Ely Av

Lincoln Av

Norwich Rd

Glastonbury

Road

Canterbury

Rd

Furness Road

Royston
Road

Canterbury Road
Surg

Wellingford Rd

Rigby

Selby Cl

6

Primary School

Fountains

Road

Cemetery

Canterbury Road
Junior & Infant
School

Newstead Road

Kirkstall Road

Abingdon Rd

Chatsworth

Winchester Road

Haworth Cl

Abbey Cl

Sandsend Rd

Heston
Dr

Denstone
Av

Winchester Rd

Moss

Foxdenton Dr

Urmston
Grammar
School

Sylvan
Av

Derby Road

Granville

Westbourne

138

Eastw

Richmond
Gladstone
Rd

Mount Drive

Humbr

Infant School

Hereford

Sumner
Wy

Alliston House
Doctors
Surg

Medical

St Antony
High School

Hilrose Av

Southbourne

D

E

F

I grid square represents 500 metres

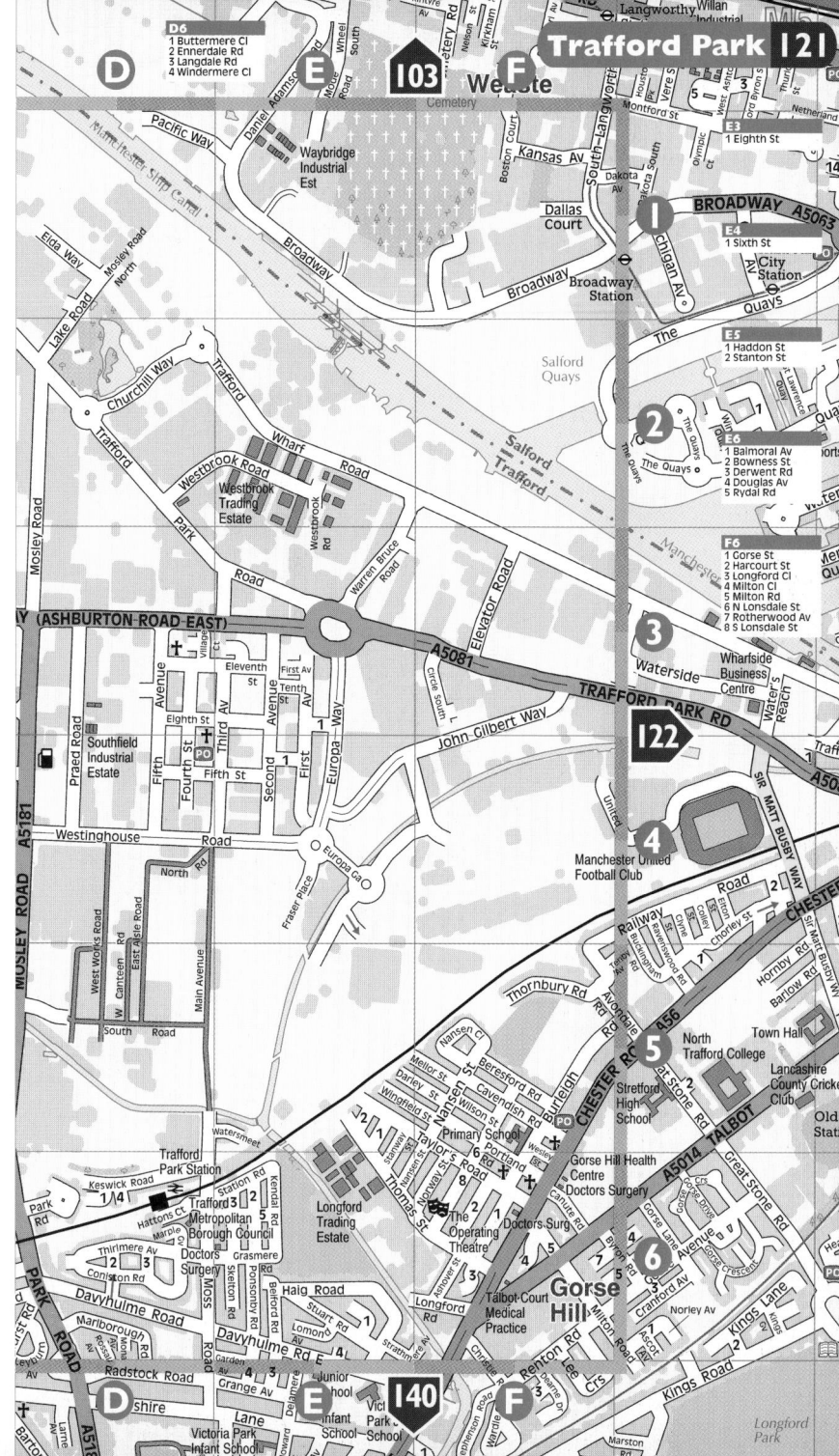

D6
1 Buttermere Cl
2 Ennerdale Rd
3 Langdale Rd
4 Windermere Cl

D **E** 103 **F** Webste

E3
1 Eighth St

Langworthy Willan Industrial

Pacific Way

Daniel Adamson

Waybridge Industrial Est

Wheel Road

Midge Rd

Cemetery

Kirkham St

Nelson St

Boston Court

Kansas Av

South Langworthy

Montford St

Vere S

Houston Ct

West Ashto

3 Byron St

Thurlow St

Netherland St

Dallas Court

Dakota Av

Dakota South

Olympic Ct

14

Manchester Ship Canal

Broadway

Broadway

Michigan Av

I BROADWAY A5063

Broadway Station

Broadway

The Quays

City Station

E4
1 Sixth St

Elda Way

Mosley Road North

Lake Road

Trafford

Churchill Way

Trafford

Salford Quays

E5
1 Haddon St
2 Stanton St

Mosley Road

Wharf Road

Westbrook Road

Westbrook Trading Estate

Westbrook Rd

Park Road

Warren Bruce Road

Salford Trafford

Manchester

The Quays

2

The Quays

The Quays

Quay

Sports

E6
1 Balmoral Av
2 Bowness St
3 Derwent Rd
4 Douglas Av
5 Rydal Rd

Y (ASHBURTON-ROAD EAST)

Village

Eleventh St

Tenth St

First Av

Eighth St

A5081

Circle South

Elevator Road

A5081

Waterside

TRAFFORD PARK RD

Wharfside Business Centre

Water's Reach

F6
1 Gorse St
2 Harcourt St
3 Longford Cl
4 Milton Cl
5 Milton Rd
6 N Lonsdale St
7 Rotherwood Av
8 S Lonsdale St

Merc
Qua

Ci

Traffo

A508

3

Avenue

Third Av

Fifth St

Fifth Road

Fourth St

Second

First

Europa Way

John Gilbert Way

Praed Road

Southfield Industrial Estate

Westinghouse Road

West Works Road

W Canteen Rd

East Aisle Road

North Road

Main Avenue

South Road

Europa Ga

Fraser Place

MUSLEY ROAD A5181

Manchester United Football Club

United Road

Railway

Buckingham Rd

Ravenwood Rd

Elton St

Coke St

Cole Rd

Chorley St

Road

SIR MATT BUSBY WAY

CHESTER

Sir Matt Busby Way

Hornby R

Barlow Rd

122

4

Thornbury Rd

Avondale

Rd

A56

2

Watermeet

Trafford Park Station

Keswick Road

Park Rd

Hattons Ct

Trafford Metropolitan Borough Council Doctors Surgery

Station Rd

Kendal Rd

Marple

Grasmere

Skelton Rd

Ponsonby Rd

Beresford Rd

Nansen Cl

Mellor St

Darley St

Wilson St

Cavendish St

Wingfield Av

Stanway Rd

Taylor's Rd

Portland

Nansen Rd

Westo

Nansen St

Burleigh

Great Stone Rd

PO

Stretford High School

North Trafford College

5

Town Hall

Lancashire County Cricket Club

Old T Statio

Longford Trading Estate

The Operating Theatre

Doctors Surg

Gorse Hill Health Centre Doctors Surgery

CHESTER RD A5014

Gorse Lane

Gorse Drive

Henric

Gorse Dale

Head

Thirlmere Av

Coniston Rd

Davyhulme Road

Marlborough Av

Radstock Road

PARK ROAD A5181

Moss

Bereford Rd

Haig Road

Stuart Rd

Lomon

Davyhulme Rd E

Garden

Grange Av

Delamere

Lane

Longford Rd

Strathmere Av

Talbot Court Medical Practice

Doctors Surg

Gorse Hill

Milton Rd

Renton Rd

Lee

Christie Rd

Byron Av

Cranford Av

Norley Av

Great Stone Rd

Kings Lane

Cranford Av

6

PO

TALBOT

A5014

Victoria Park Infant School

Junior School

E Infant School

Park Infant School

140 **F**

Vict Park School

Mardale

Marston

Kings Road

Wardle

Longford Park

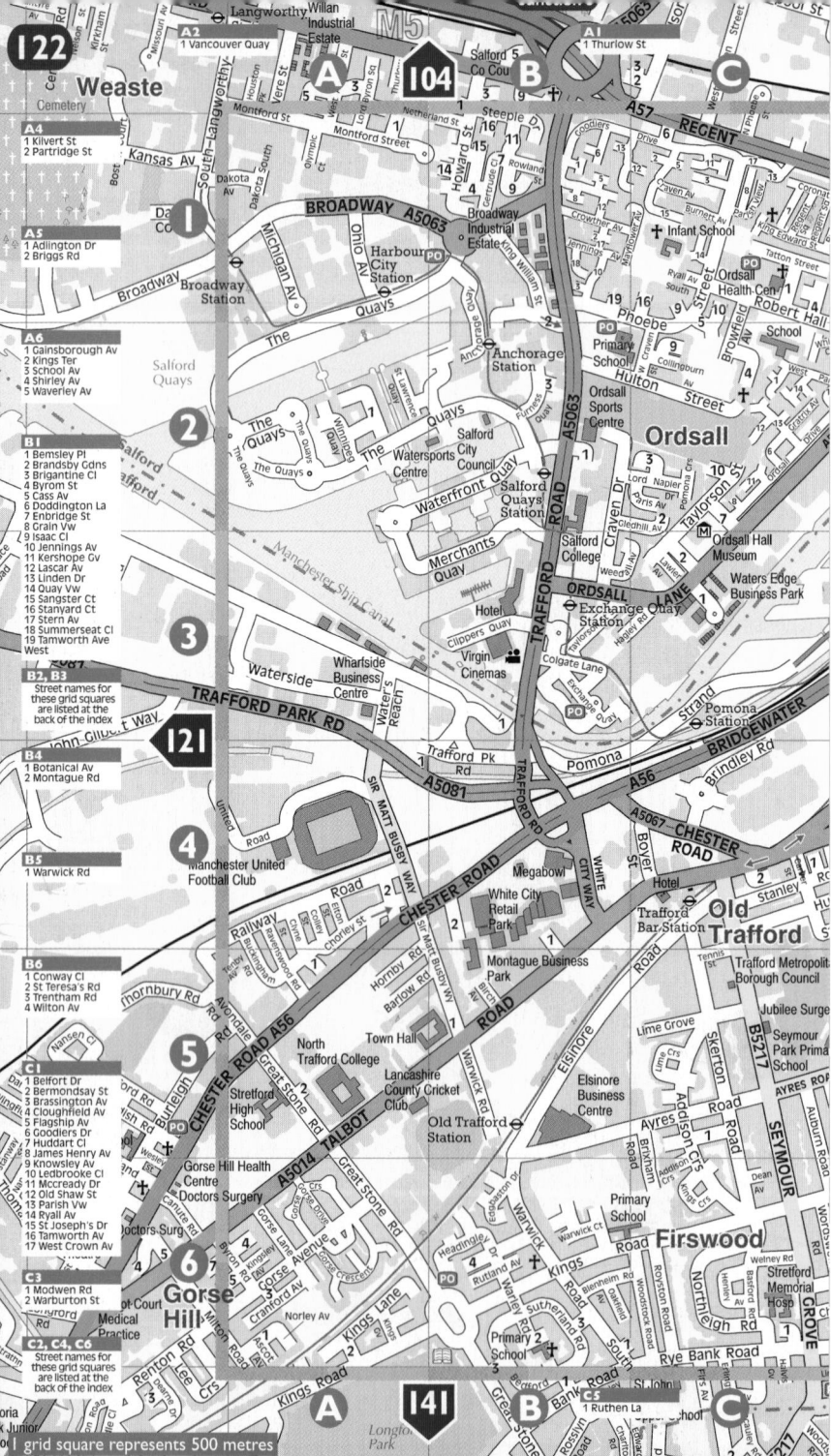

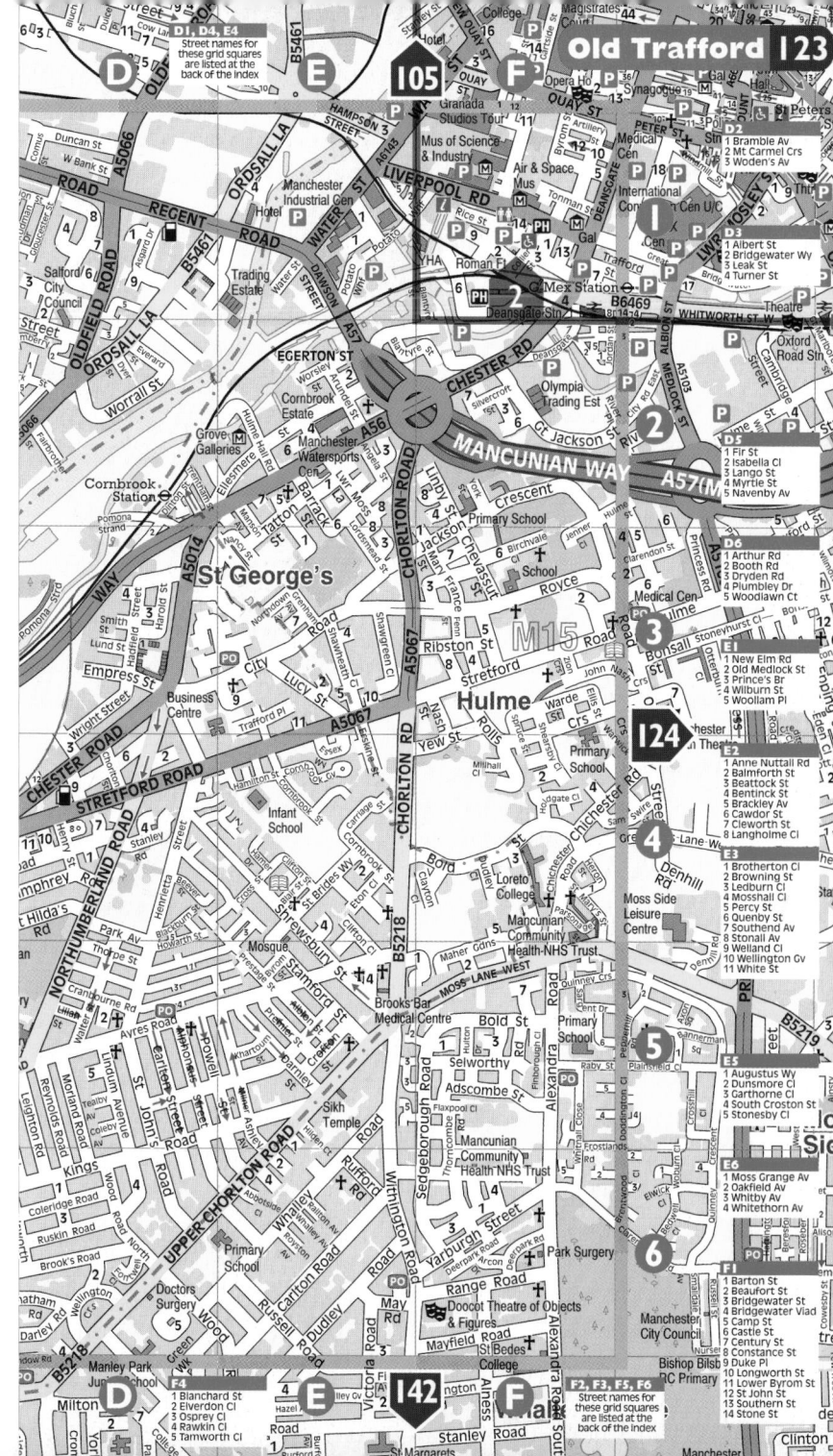

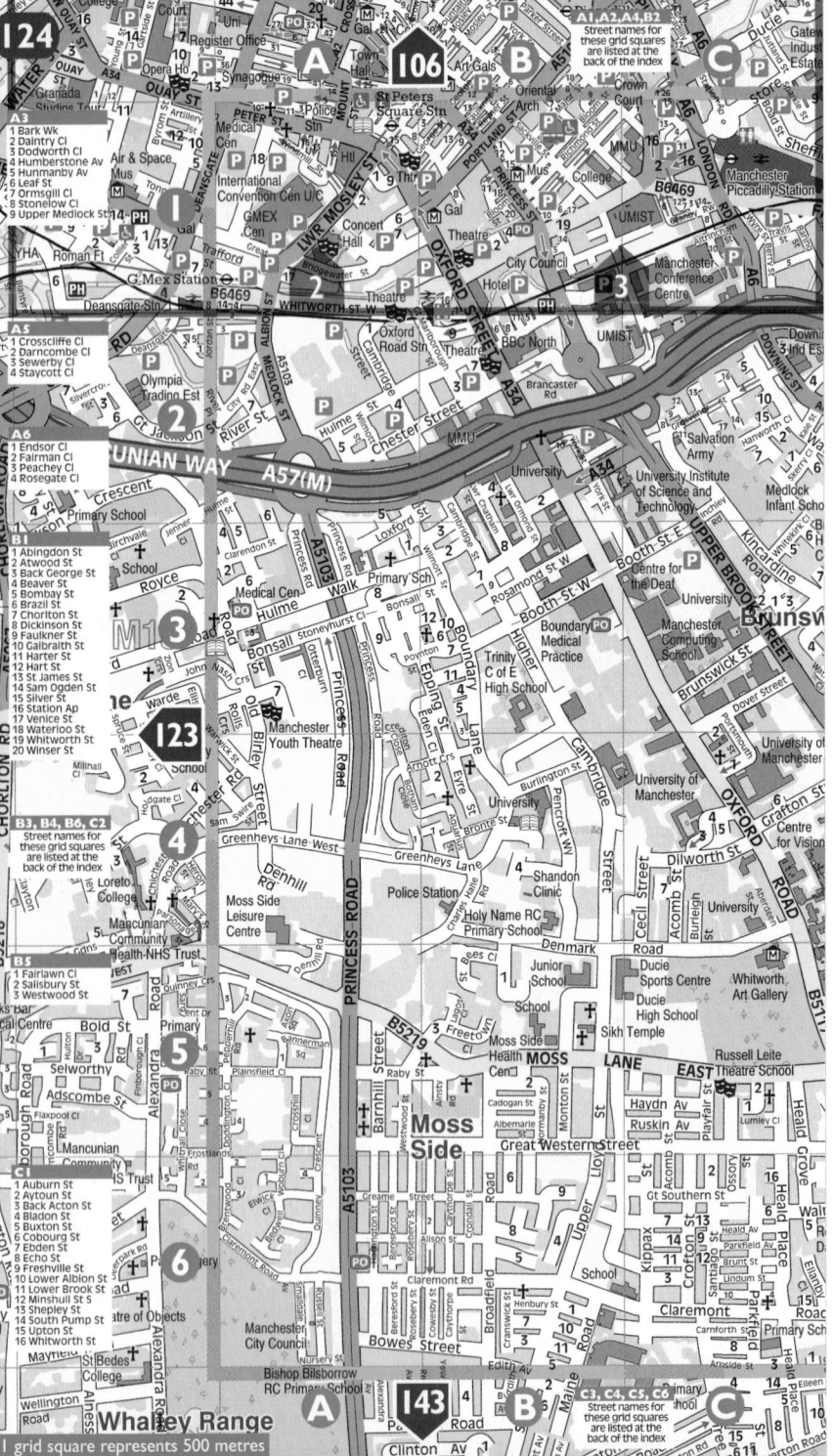

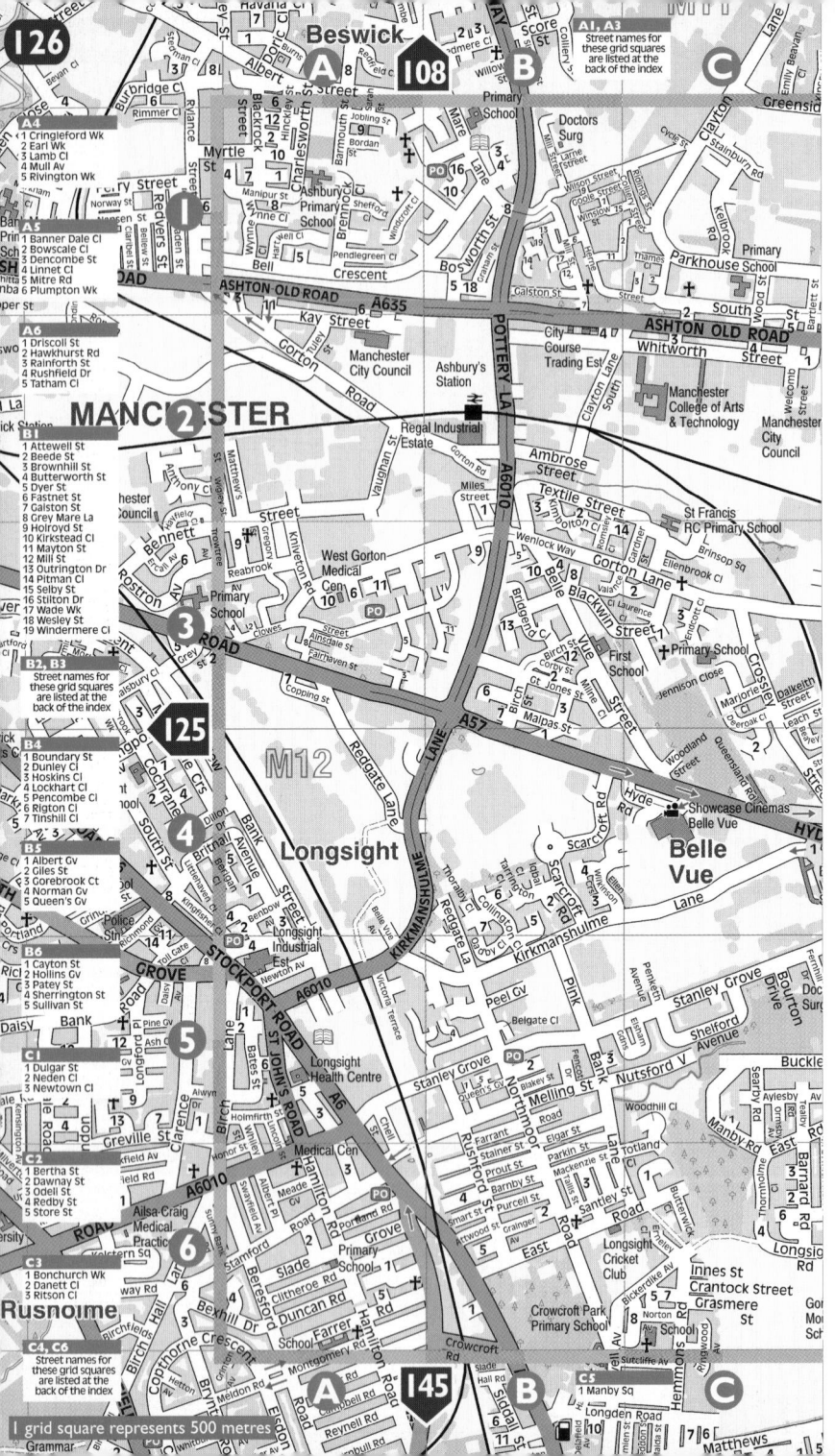

Beswick

A1, A3
Street names for
these grid squares
are listed at the
back of the index

MANCHESTER

Rusholme

Longsight

Belle Vue

Showcase Cinemas
Belle Vue

M12

1 grid square represents 500 metres

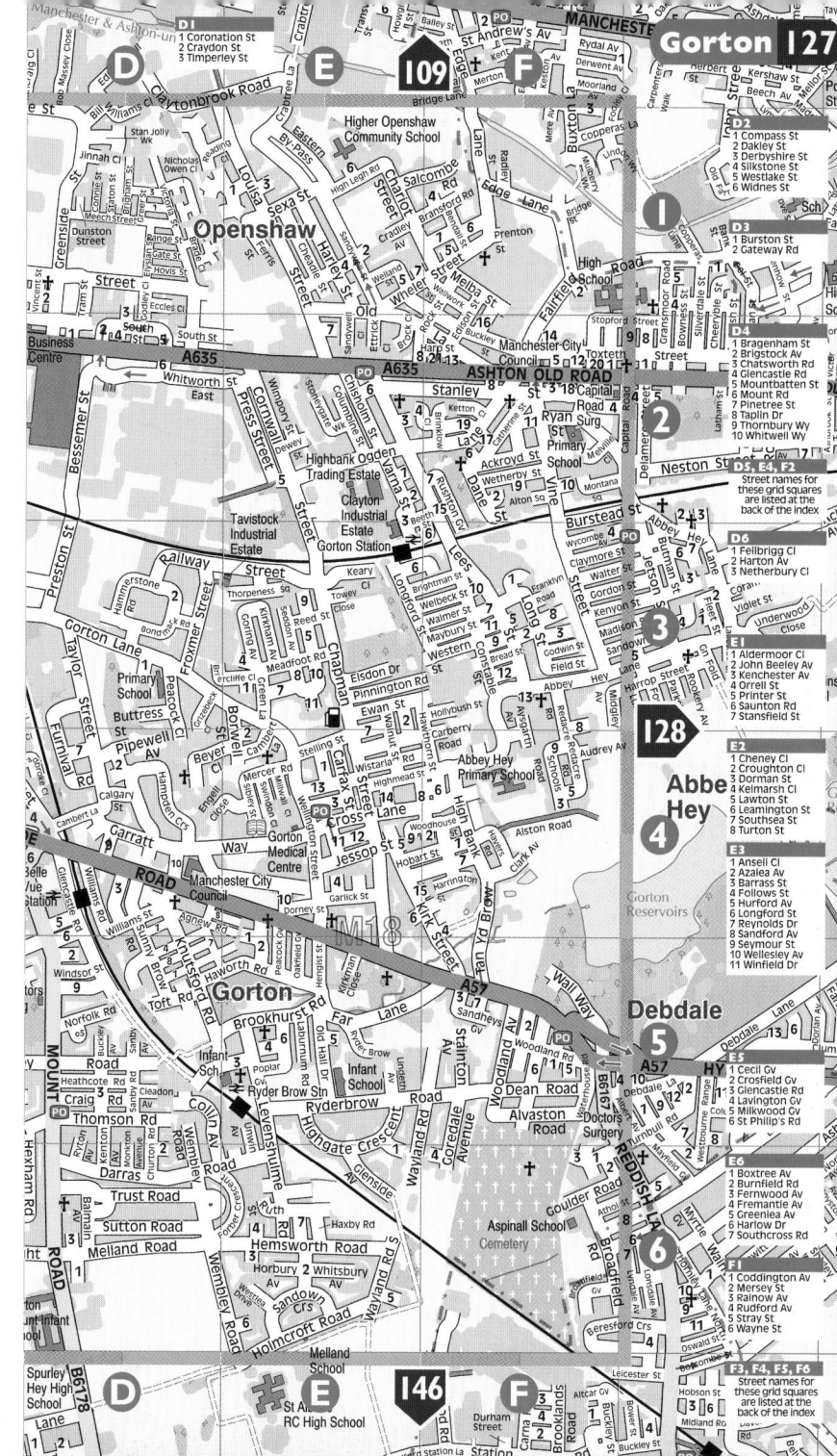

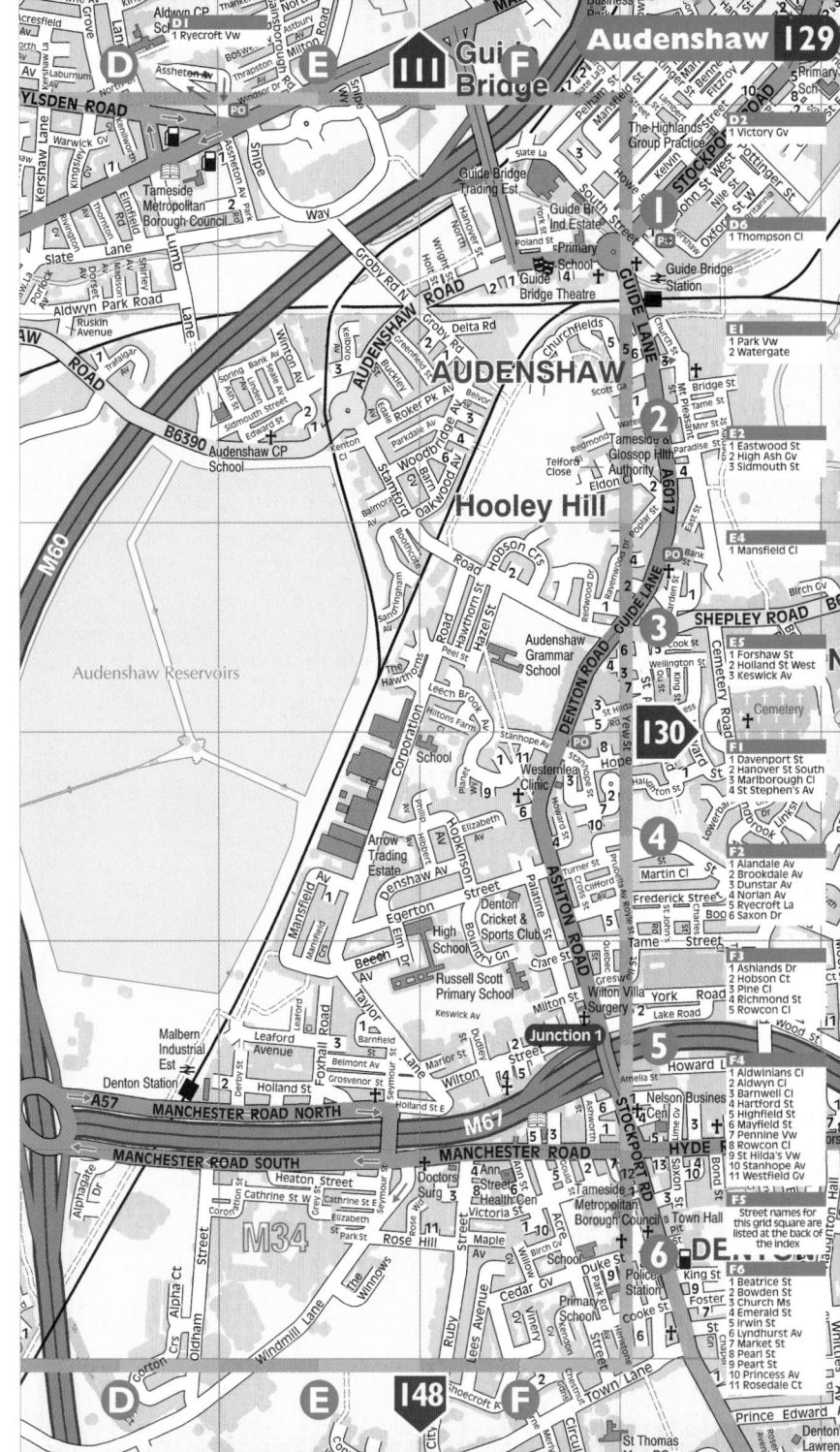

D E F

Guide Bridge

Aldwyn CP School
1 Ryecroft Vw

YLSDEN ROAD

Tameside Metropolitan Borough Council

AUDENSHAW

Hooley Hill

Audenshaw CP School

B6390

Audenshaw Reservoirs

M60

Guide Bridge Trading Est

Guide Bridge Ind Estate

Primary School

Guide Bridge Theatre

Guide Bridge Station

The Highlands Group Practice

STOCKPORT

D2
1 Victory Gv

D6
1 Thompson Cl

E1
1 Park Vw
2 Watergate

E2
1 Eastwood St
2 High Ash Gv
3 Sidmouth St

E4
1 Mansfield Cl

SHEPLEY ROAD

E5
1 Forshaw St
2 Holland St West
3 Keswick Av

Cemetery

E6
1 Davenport St
2 Hanover St South
3 Marlborough Cl
4 St Stephen's Av

130

1 Alandale Av
2 Brookdale Av
3 Dunstar Av
4 Norlan Av
5 Ryecroft La
6 Saxon Dr

F2
1 Ashlands Dr
2 Hobson Ct
3 Pine Ct
4 Richmond St
5 Rowcon Cl

Audenshaw Grammar School

Westernlea Clinic

Arrow Trading Estate

Denton Cricket & Sports Club

Russell Scott Primary School

High School

Malbern Industrial Est

Denton Station

A57

Leaford Avenue

Junction 1

York Road

Wilton Villa Surgery

Lake Road

Howard L

MANCHESTER ROAD NORTH

M67

MANCHESTER ROAD SOUTH

MANCHESTER ROAD

M34

Doctors Surg

Tameside Metropolitan Borough Council

Town Hall

HYDE R

F4
1 Aldwinians Cl
2 Aldwyn Cl
3 Barnwell Cl
4 Hartford St
5 Highfield St
6 Mayfield St
7 Pennine Vw
8 Rowcon Cl
9 St Hilda's Vw
10 Stanhope Av
11 Westfield Gv

Nelson Business Cen

Street names for this grid square are listed at the back of the index

DE

Health Cen

Victoria R

Rose Hill

Primary School

Police Station

King St

Foster

F5
1 Beatrice St
2 Bowden St
3 Church Ms
4 Emerald St
5 Irwin St
6 Lyndhurst Av
7 Market St
8 Pearl St
9 Pearl St
10 Princess Av
11 Rosedale Cl

148

St Thomas More RC

Prince Edward

Denton Lawrence Cricket

D E F

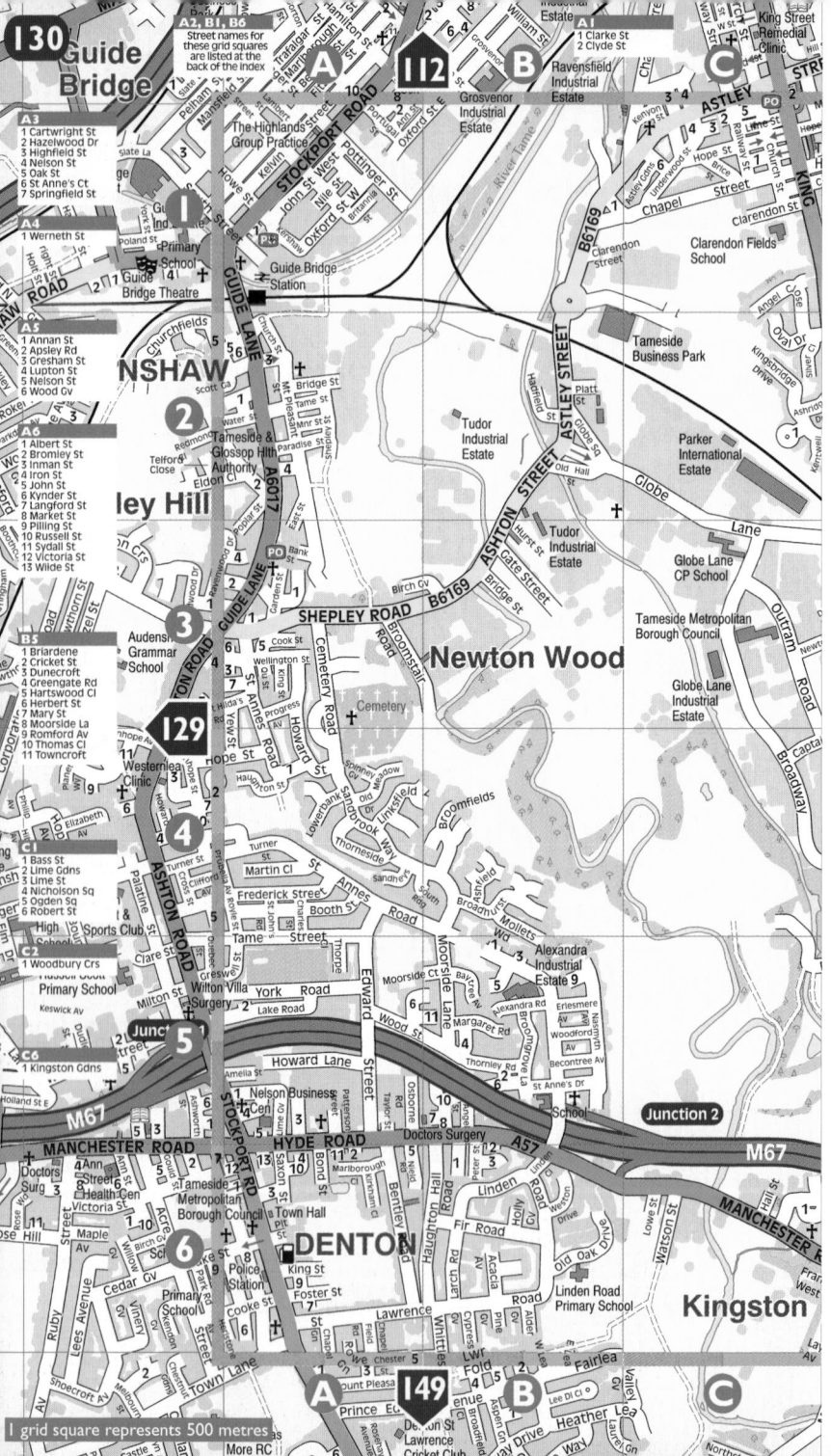

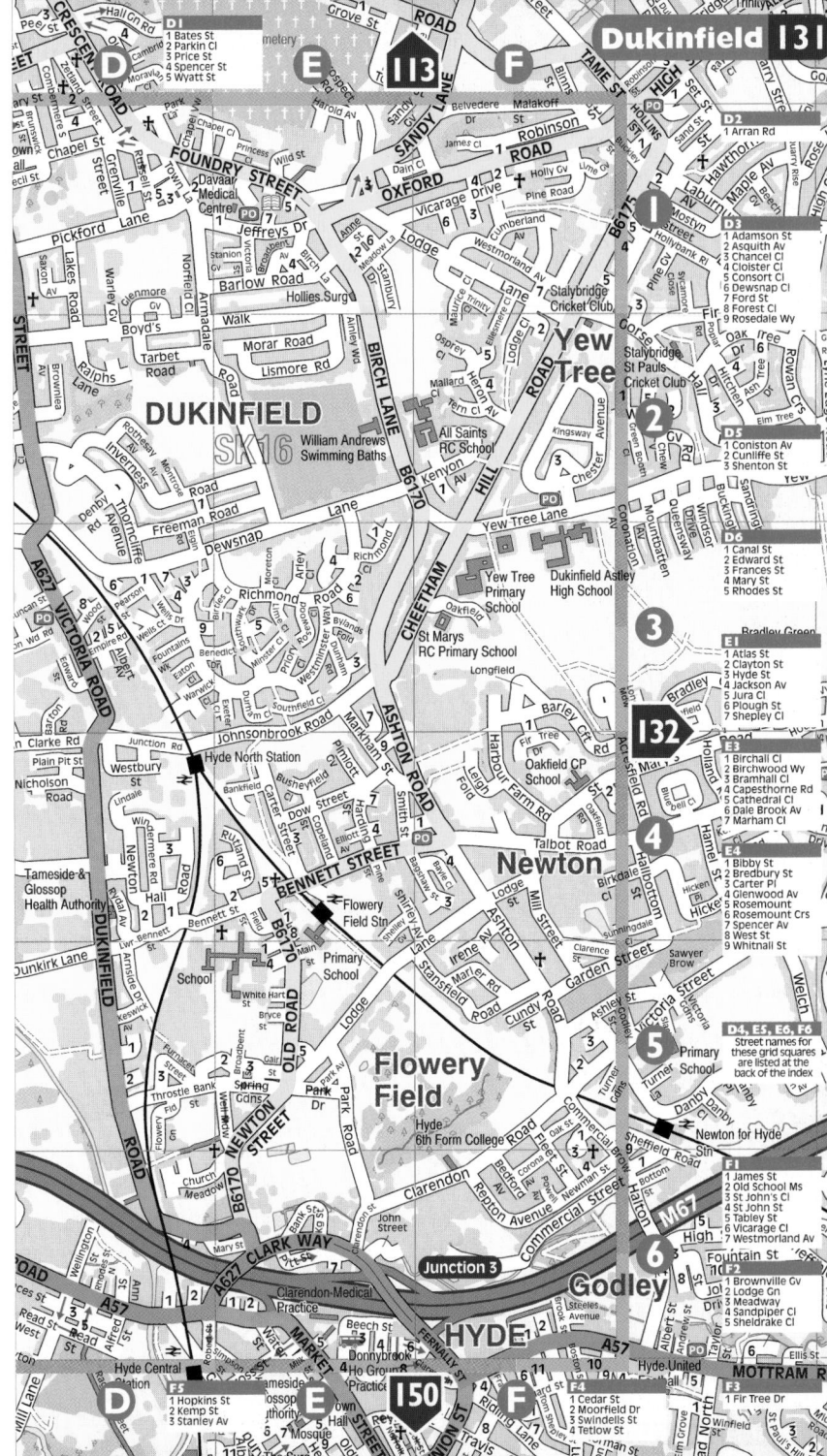

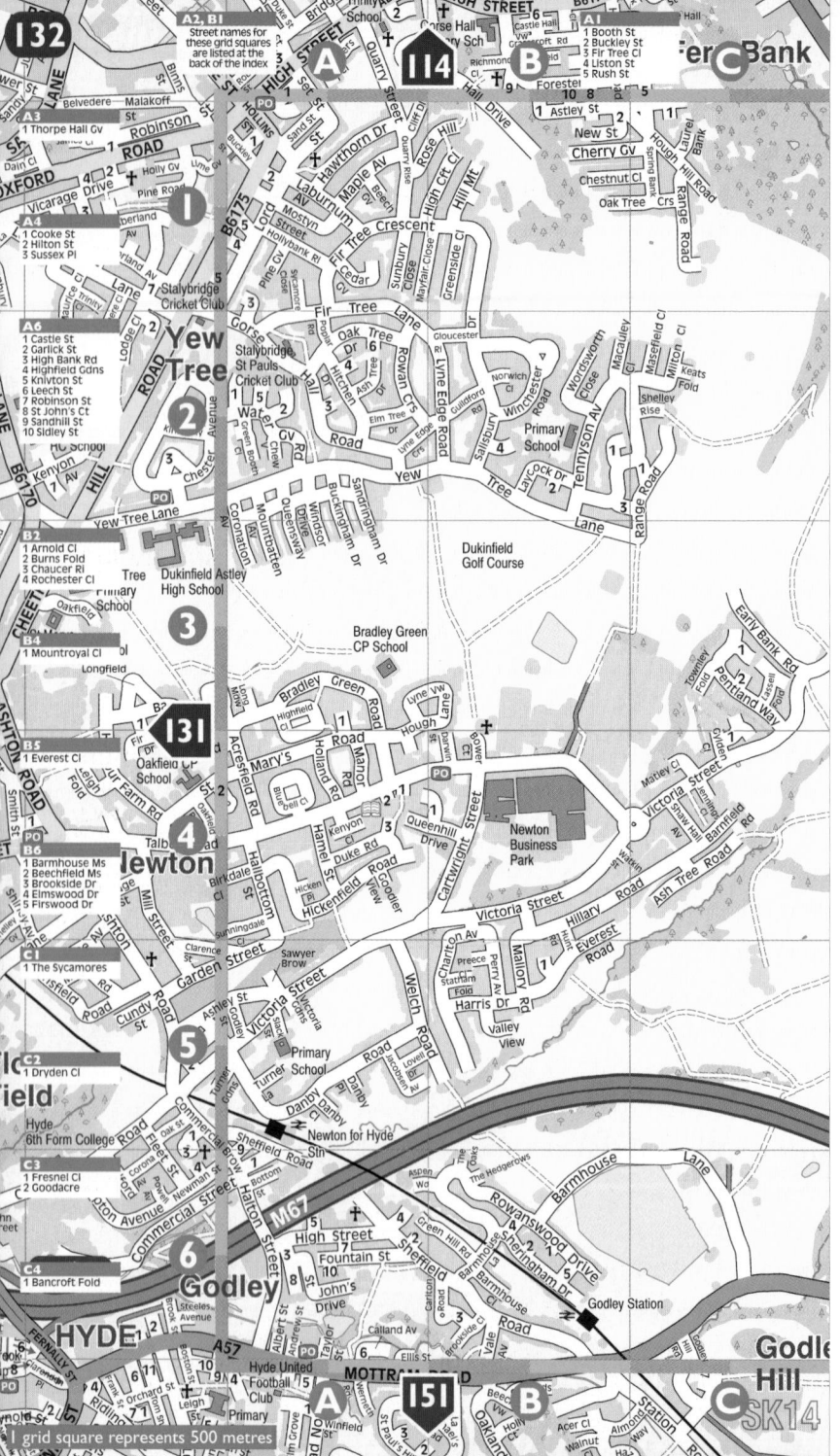

A2, B1
Street names for
these grid squares
are listed at the
back of the index

A1
1 Booth St
2 Buckley St
3 Fir Tree Cl
4 Liston St
5 Rush St

er Bank

HIGH STREET

114

A1
1 Thorpe Hall Gv

Robinson
ROAD

A4
1 Cooke St
2 Hilton St
3 Sussex Pl

1

Stalybridge
Cricket Club

A6
1 Castle St
2 Garlick St
3 High Bank Rd
4 Highfield Gdns
5 Knivton St
6 Leech St
7 Robinson St
8 St John's Ct
9 Sandhill St
10 Sidley St

**Yew
Tree**

2

Stalybridge
St Pauls
Cricket Club

Primary
School

Dukinfield
Golf Course

B2
1 Arnold Cl
2 Burns Fold
3 Chaucer Ri
4 Rochester Cl

Dukinfield Astley
High School

3

Bradley Green
CP School

B4
1 Mountroyal Cl

131

Oakfield CP
School

B5
1 Everest Cl

4

Newton

Newton
Business
Park

B6
1 Barmhouse Ms
2 Beechfield Ms
3 Brookside Dr
4 Elmswood Dr
5 Firswood Dr

C1
1 The Sycamores

Victoria Street

Everest Road

C2
1 Dryden Cl

field

5

Primary
School

Hyde
6th Form College

C3
1 Fresnel Cl
2 Goodacre

Newton for Hyde
Stn

M67

The Hedgerows

Barmhouse

C4
1 Bancroft Fold

6

Godley

High Street

Fountain St

Godley Station

HYDE

A57

MOTTRAM ROAD

Hyde United
Football Club

151

**Godley
Hill**

A

B

C SK14

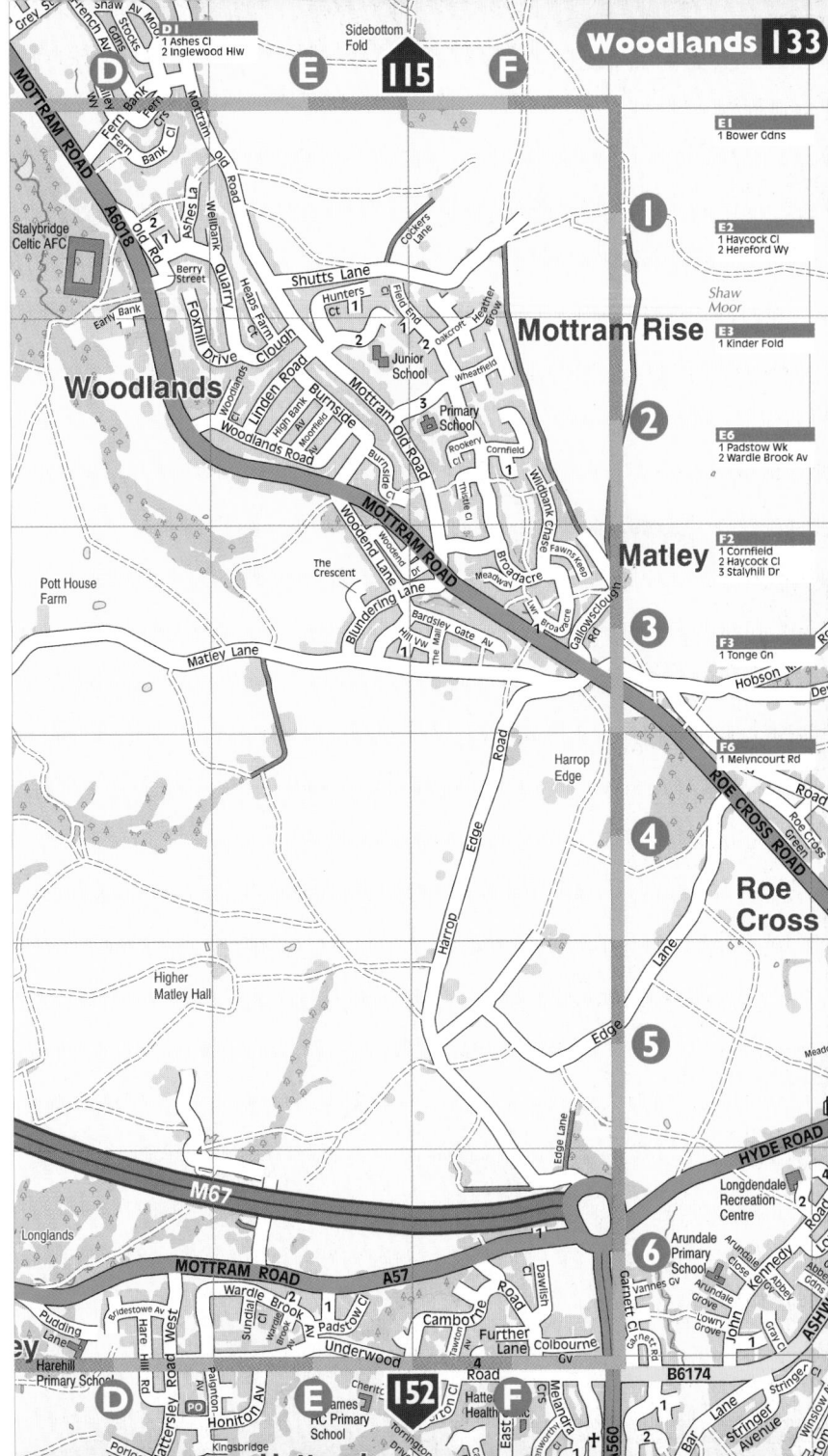

D1
1 Ashes Cl
2 Inglewood Hlw

Sidebottom
Fold

115

E1
1 Bower Gdns

Grey St
French Av
Shaw Av Moo
Stocks Gdns

D

E

F

MOTTRAM ROAD
A6018

Fern Bank
Wiley
Fern Bank
Fern
Bank
Crs
Fern Bank Ct

Mottram Old Road

Stalybridge
Celtic AFC

E2
1 Haycock Cl
2 Hereford Wy

Cockers Lane

Ashes La
Old Rd
Wellbank

Shaw
Moor

Berry
Street

Heaps Farm Ct

Quarry

Early Bank

Shutts Lane

Field End

Heather Brow

Mottram Rise

E3
1 Kinder Fold

Hunters
Ct 1

Oakcroft

Foxhill Drive

Clough

Junior
School

Woodlands
High Bank
Moorend Av

Wheatfield

2

Woodlands

Linden Road

Mottram Old Road

Burnside

Primary
School

3

Cornfield

E6
1 Padstow Wk
2 Wardle Brook Av

Woodlands Road

Burnside Rd

Rookery
Cl

Thistle Cl

Wildbank Chase

1

MOTTRAM ROAD

Pott House
Farm

The
Crescent

Woodend Lane

Woodend Dr

Broadacre

Fawns Keep

Meadway

Broadacre

Matley

F2
1 Cornfield
2 Haycock Cl
3 Stallyhill Dr

Blundering Lane

Bardsley Gate
Av

The Mall

Hill Vw

1

Broadacre Vw

Callowsclough Rd

3

F3
1 Tonge Gn

Matley Lane

Hobson Wy

Dew

Harrop
Edge

Harrop Road

Edge Road

F6
1 Melyncourt Rd

Road

ROE CROSS ROAD

Roe Cross
Green

4

Higher
Matley Hall

Lane

**Roe
Cross**

Edge Road

5

Meadow

M67

HYDE ROAD

Longlands

Longdendale
Recreation
Centre

Edge Lane

Arundale Close
Kennedy

6

Arundale
Primary
School

Arundale
Grove

John

Lon

Road

MOTTRAM ROAD
A57

Road

Dawlish

Lowry
Grove

Kennedy

ASHWO

ey

Pudding
Lane

Bridestowe Av

Hare Hill Rd

Palmerston

Sundial
Cl

Wardle Brook Av

Padstow Cl

1

2

Camborne

Tawton Rd

Further
Road

Colbourne
Gv

Vannes Gv

Garnett Rd

John Grove
Gray Ct

ST

Harehill
Primary School

Hattersley Road West

PO

Honiton Av

Cheriton
Rd

Lowry Grove

152

Eames
RC Primary
School

Hatte
Health

Melandra
Crs

East
Lane

Bar
Lane

Stringer
Avenue

Winslow

D

E

F

B6174

Poring

Kingsbridge

Torrington
Drive

560

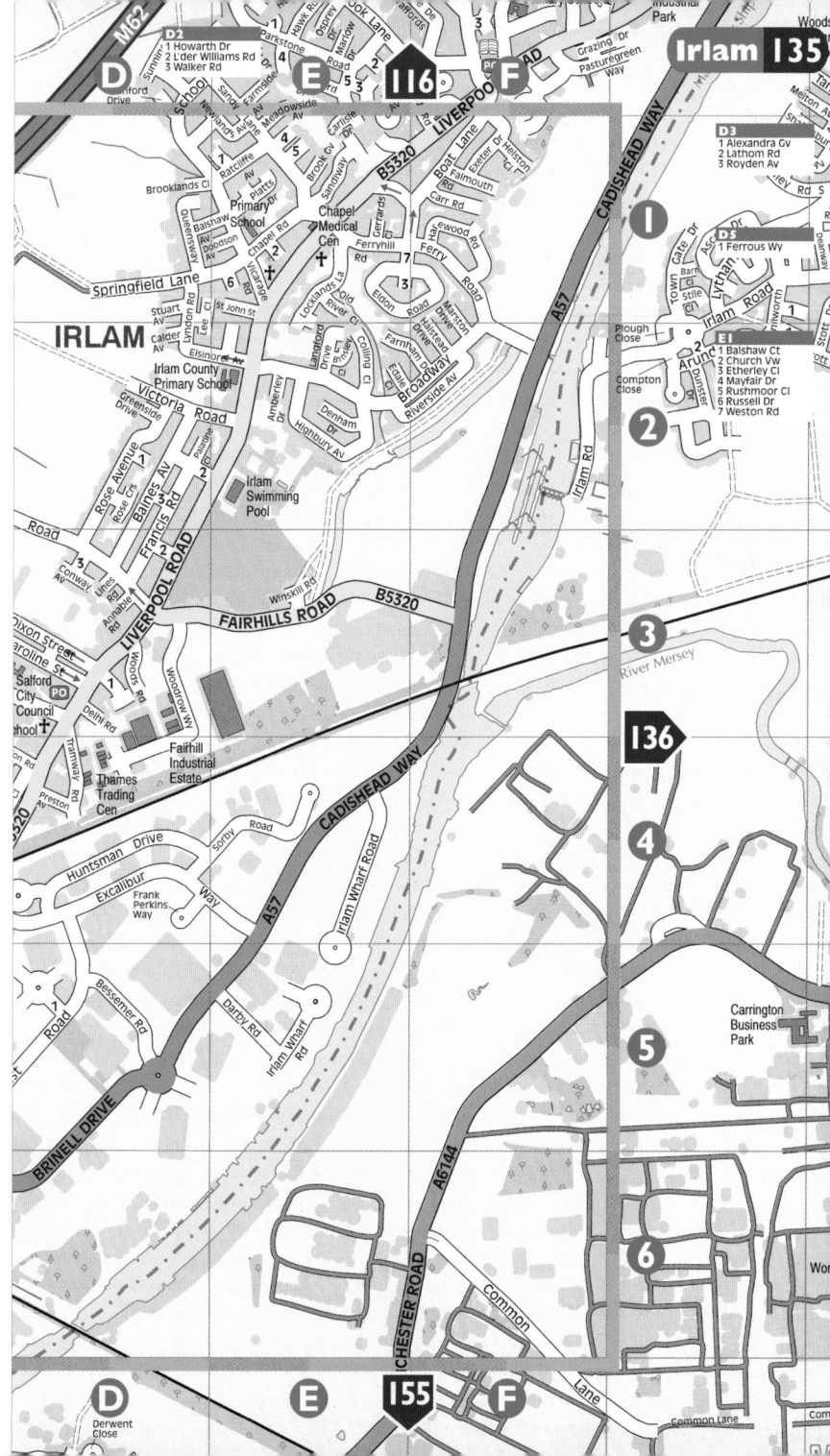

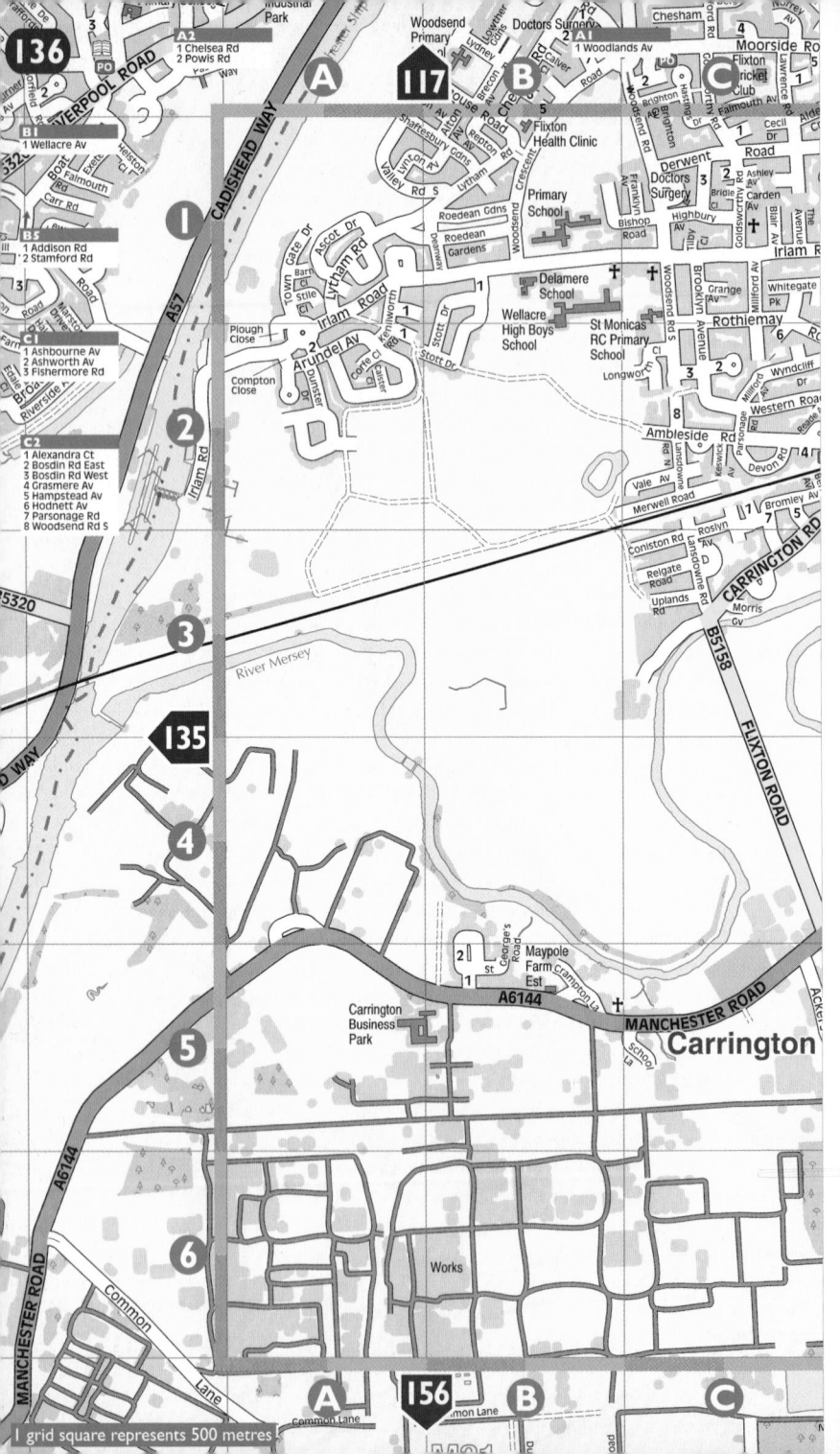

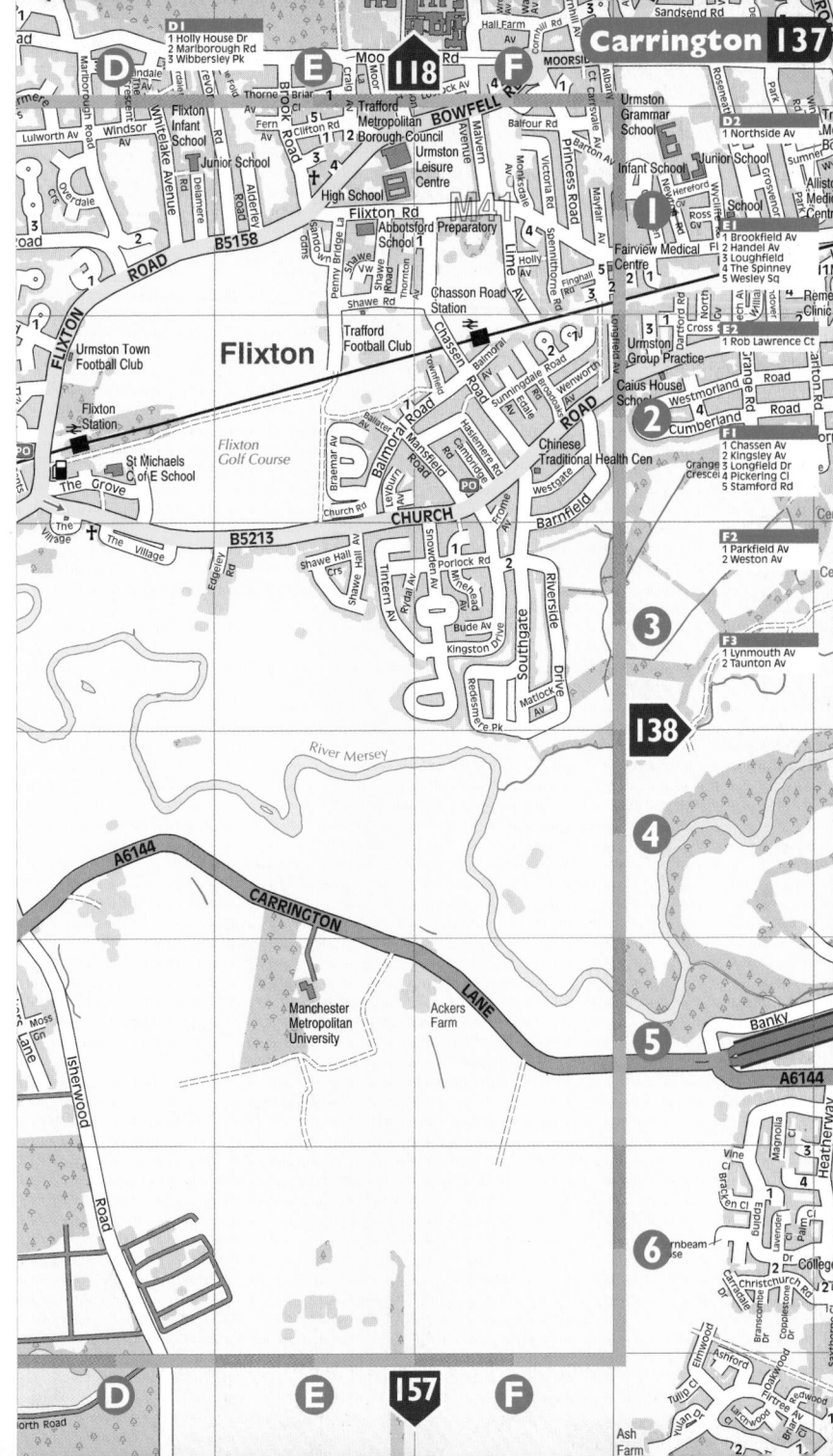

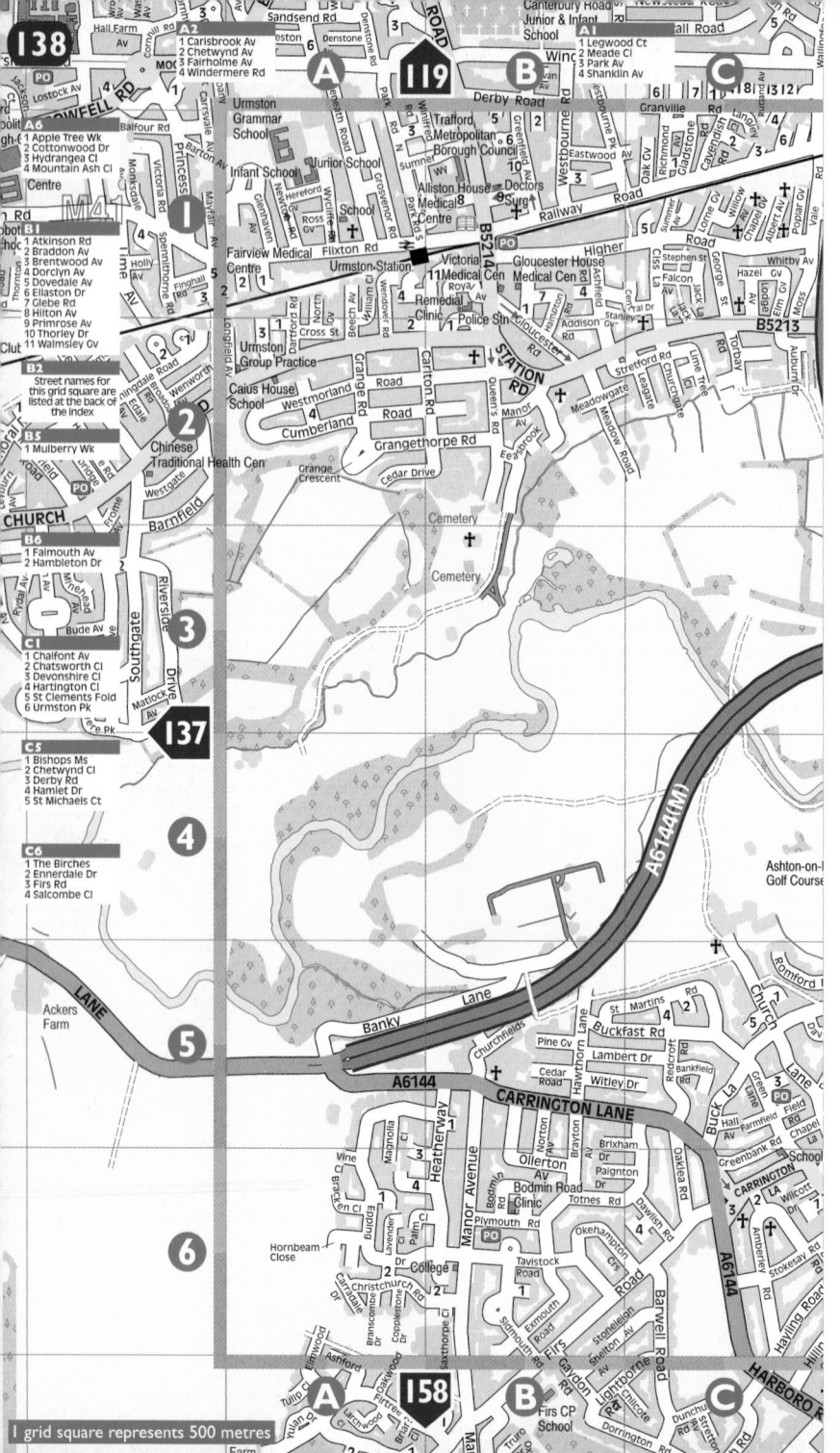

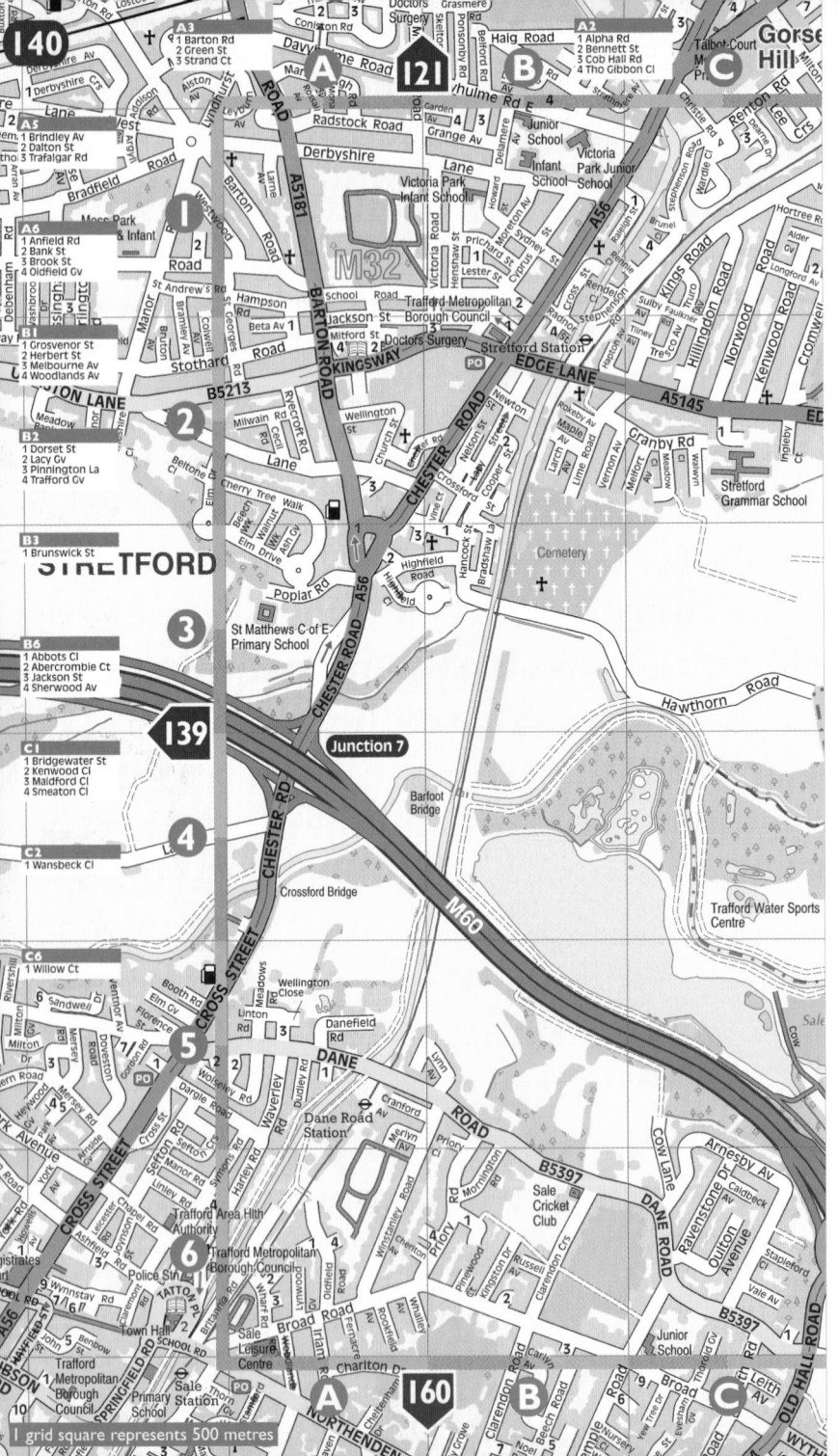

I grid square represents 500 metres

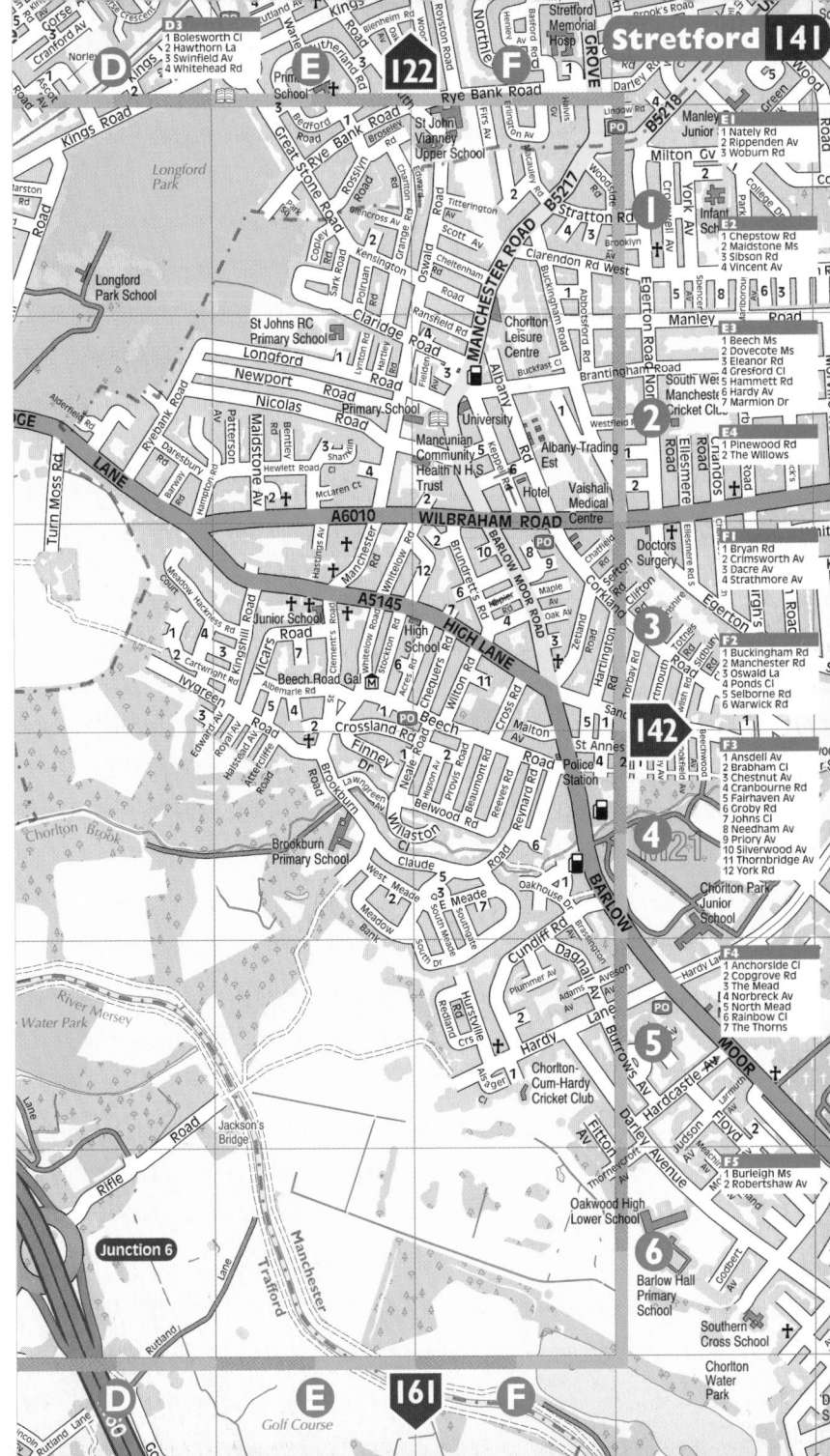

D1
1 Bolesworth Cl
2 Hawthorn La
3 Swinfield Av
4 Whitehead Rd

E1
1 Nately Rd
2 Rippenden Av
3 Woburn Rd

I1
1 Chepstow Rd
2 Maidstone Ms
3 Sibson Rd
4 Vincent Av

1 Beech Ms
2 Dovecote Ms
3 Eleanor Rd
4 Gresford Cl
5 Hammett Rd
6 Marmion Dr

E2
1 Pinewood Rd
2 The Willows

E1
1 Bryan Rd
2 Crimsworth Av
3 Dacre Av
4 Strathmore Av

F2
1 Buckingham Rd
2 Manchester Rd
3 Oswald La
4 Ponds Cl
5 Selborne Rd
6 Warwick Rd

F3
1 Ansdell Av
2 Brabham Cl
3 Chestnut Av
4 Cranbourne Rd
5 Fairhaven Rd
6 Groby Rd
7 Johns Cl
8 Needham Av
9 Priory Av
10 Silverwood Cl
11 Thornbridge Av
12 York Rd

F4
1 Anchorside Cl
2 Copgrove Rd
3 The Mead
4 Norbreck Av
5 North Mead
6 Rainbow Cl
7 The Thorns

F5
1 Burleigh Ms
2 Robertshaw Av

Longford Park

Longford Park School

St John Vianney Upper School

Stretford Memorial Hosp

Chorlton Leisure Centre

University

Mancunian Community Health N H S Trust

Albany Trading Est

Hotel

Vaishali Medical Centre

Doctors Surgery

St Johns RC Primary School

Longford Primary School

Junior School

Beech Road Gal

High School

South West Manchester Cricket Club

St Annes Police Station

Chorlton Park Junior School

Brookburn Primary School

Chorlton-Cum-Hardy Cricket Club

River Mersey Water Park

Jackson's Bridge

Junction 6

Oakwood High Lower School

Barlow Hall Primary School

Southern Cross School

Chorlton Water Park

Golf Course

WILBRAHAM ROAD

HIGH LANE

BARLOW MOOR ROAD

MANCHESTER ROAD

Rye Bank Road

Kings Road

Turn Moss Rd

Darley Avenue

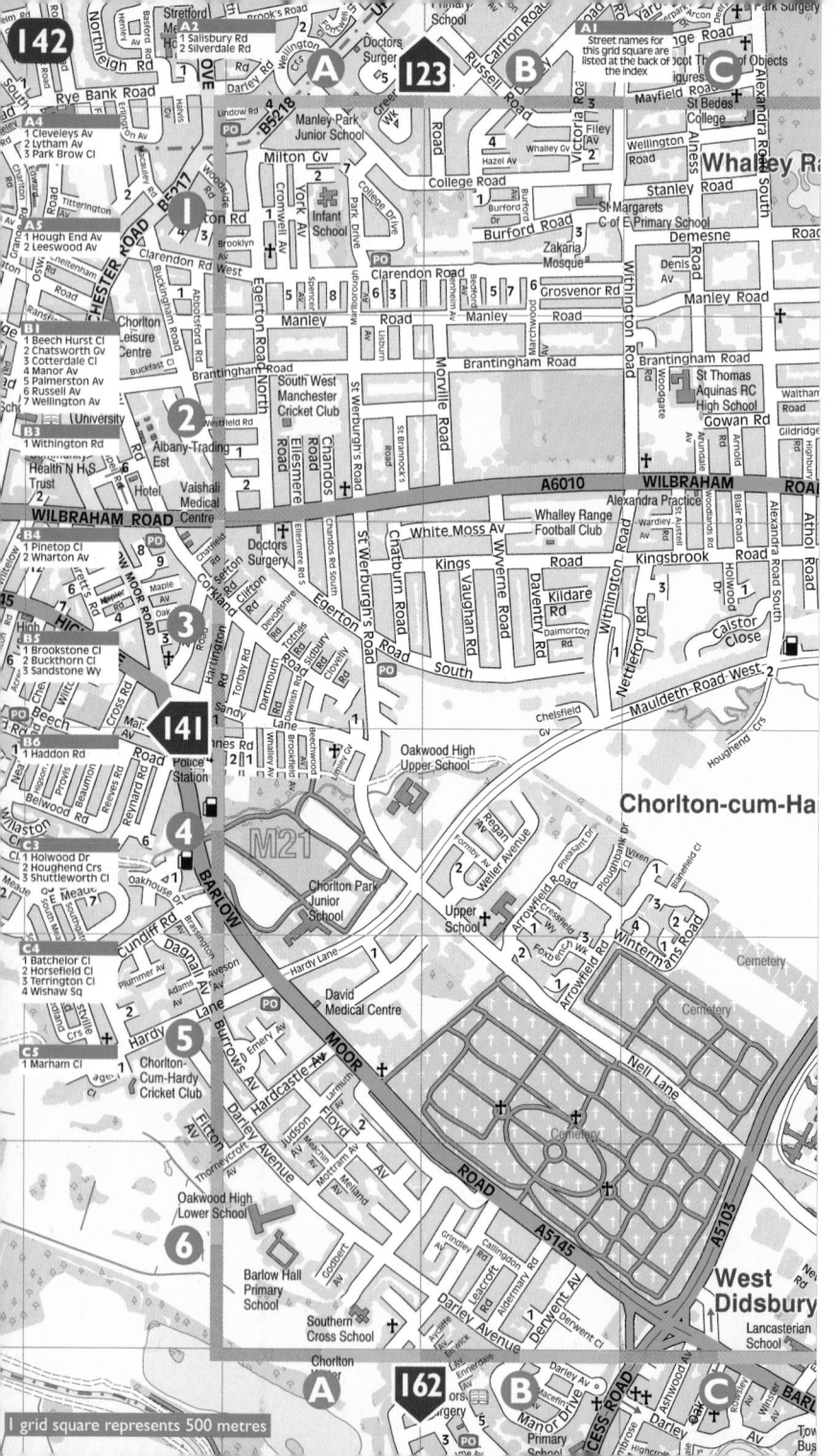

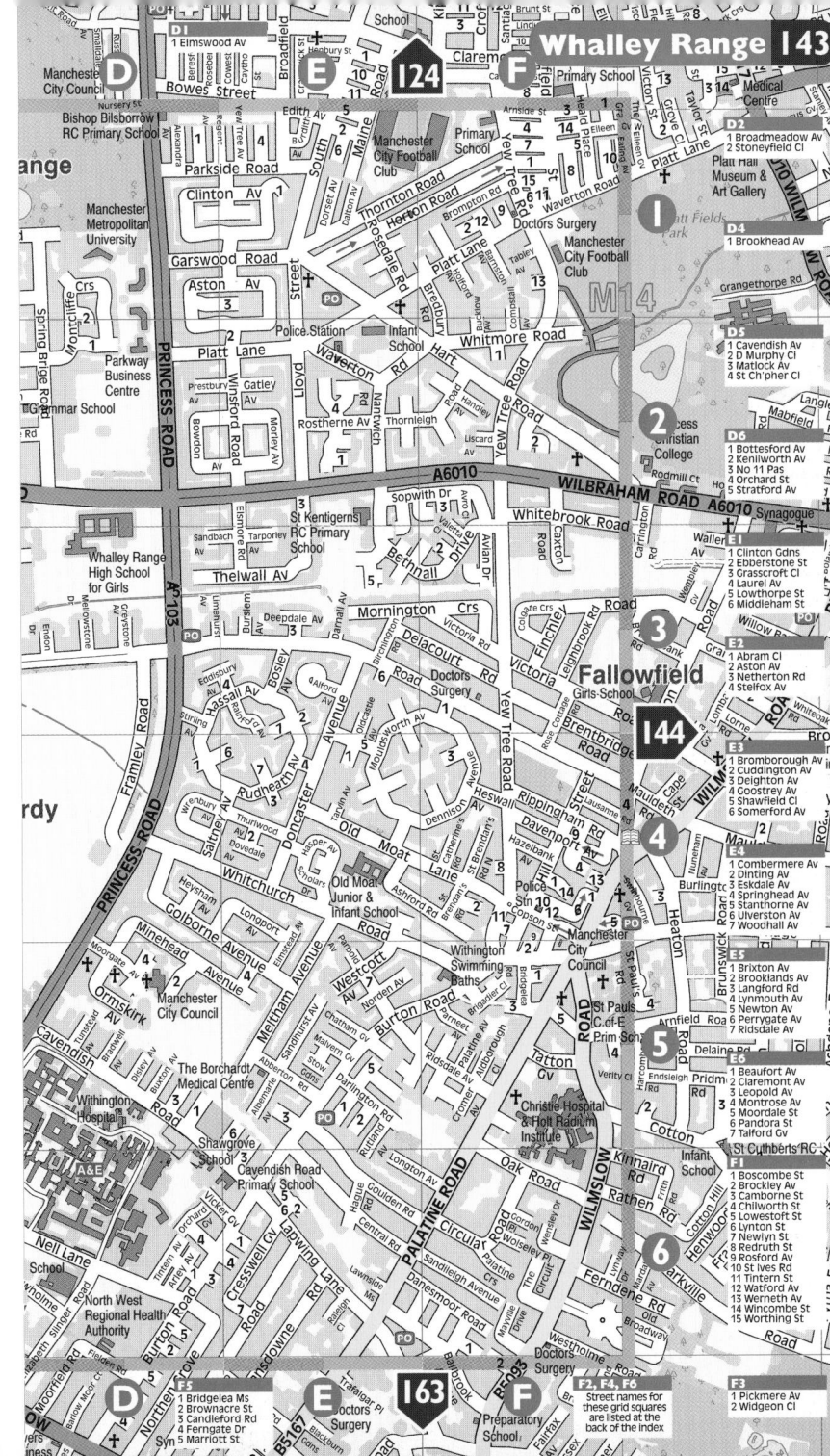

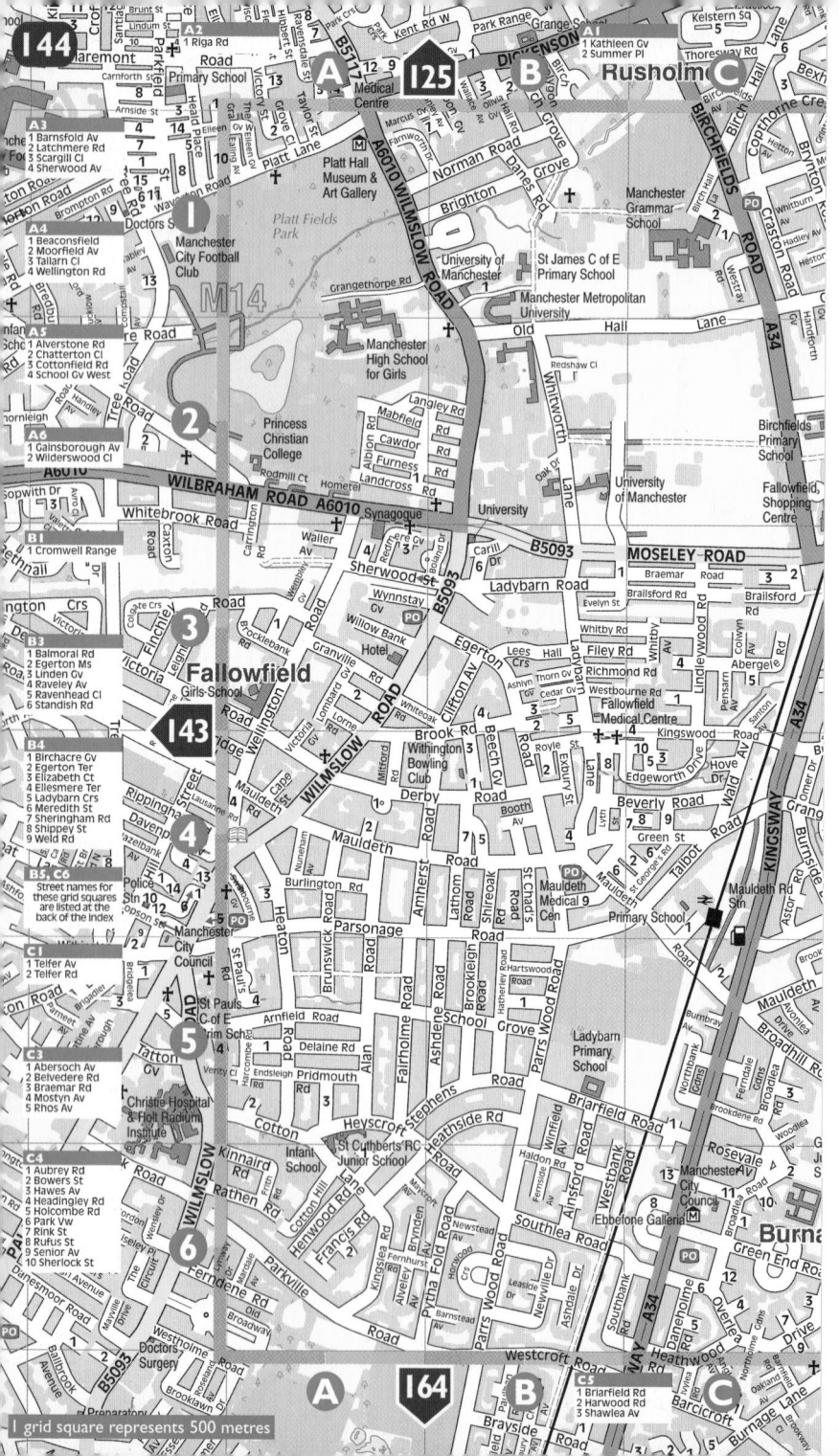

144

A2
1 Riga Rd

125

B

Rusholm

C

A1
1 Kathleen Gv
2 Summer Pl

A2
1 Barnsfold Av
2 Latchmere Rd
3 Scargill Cl
4 Sherwood Av

A4
1 Beaconsfield
2 Moorfield Av
3 Tailarn Cl
4 Wellington Rd

I

Manchester
City Football
Club

M14

A5
1 Alverstone Rd
2 Chatterton Cl
3 Cottonfield Rd
4 School Gv West

2

A6
1 Gainsborough Av
2 Wilderswood Cl

WILBRAHAM ROAD A6010

B1
1 Cromwell Range

Platt Hall
Museum &
Art Gallery

Platt Fields
Park

Manchester
High School
for Girls

Princess
Christian
College

University of
Manchester

St James C of E
Primary School

Manchester Metropolitan
University

Manchester
Grammar
School

University
of Manchester

Fallowfield,
Shopping
Centre

Birchfields
Primary
School

MOSELEY ROAD

3

Fallowfield
Girls School

143

B3
1 Balmoral Rd
2 Egerton Ms
3 Linden Gv
4 Raveley Av
5 Ravenhead Cl
6 Standish Rd

B4
1 Birchacre Gv
2 Egerton Ter
3 Elizabeth Ter
4 Ellesmere Ter
5 Ladybarn Crs
6 Meredith St
7 Sheringham Rd
8 Shippey St
9 Weld Rd

4

B5, C6
Street names for
these grid squares
are listed at the
back of the index

Police
Stn

Manchester
City Council

C1
1 Telfer Av
2 Telfer Rd

5

St Pauls
C of E
Prim Schol

C3
1 Abersoch Av
2 Belvedere Rd
3 Braemar Rd
4 Mostyn Av
5 Rhos Av

Christie Hospital
& Holt Radium
Institute

Ladybarn
Primary
School

C4
1 Aubrey Rd
2 Bowers St
3 Hawes Av
4 Headingley Rd
5 Holcombe Rd
6 Park Vw
7 Rink St
8 Rufus St
9 Senior Av
10 Sherlock St

Infant
School

St Cuthberts RC
Junior School

6

Manchester
City Council

Ebbelone Galleria

Burna

A

164

B

C

C5
1 Briarfield Rd
2 Harwood Rd
3 Shawlea Av

I grid square represents 500 metres

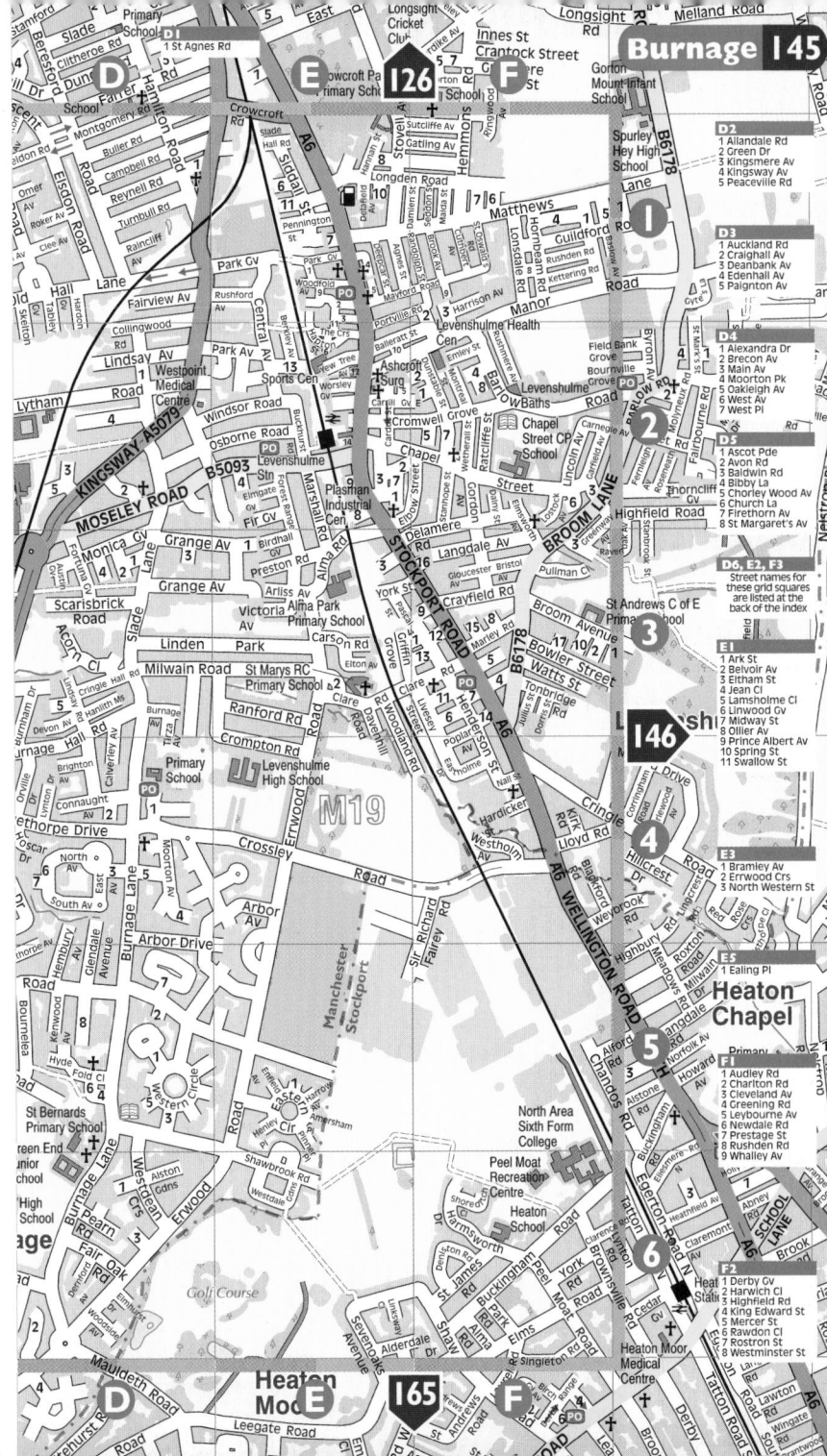

126

F

D

E

I

D2
1 Allandale Rd
2 Green Dr
3 Kingsmere Av
4 Kingsway Av
5 Peaceville Rd

D3
1 Auckland Rd
2 Craighall Av
3 Deanbank Av
4 Edenhall Av
5 Paignton Av

D4
1 Alexandra Dr
2 Brecon Av
3 Main Av
4 Moorton Pk
5 Oakleigh Av
6 West Av
7 West Pl

2

D5
1 Ascot Pde
2 Avon Rd
3 Baldwin Rd
4 Bibby La
5 Chorley Wood Av
6 Church La
7 Firethorn Av
8 St Margaret's Av

D6, E2, F3
Street names for
these grid squares
are listed at the
back of the index

3

E1
1 Ark St
2 Belvoir Av
3 Eltham St
4 Jean Cl
5 Lamsholme Cl
6 Linwood Gv
7 Midway St
8 Ollier Av
9 Prince Albert Av
10 Spring St
11 Swallow St

146

4

E3
1 Bramley Av
2 Errwood Crs
3 North Western St

E5
1 Ealing Pl

Heaton
Chapel

5

1 Audley Rd
2 Charlton Rd
3 Cleveland Av
4 Creering Rd
5 Leybourne Av
6 Newdale Rd
7 Prestage St
8 Rushden Rd
9 Whalley Av

6

F2
1 Derby Gv
2 Harwich Cl
3 Highfield Rd
4 King Edward St
5 Mercer St
6 Rawdon Cl
7 Rostron St
8 Westminster St

D

E

165

F

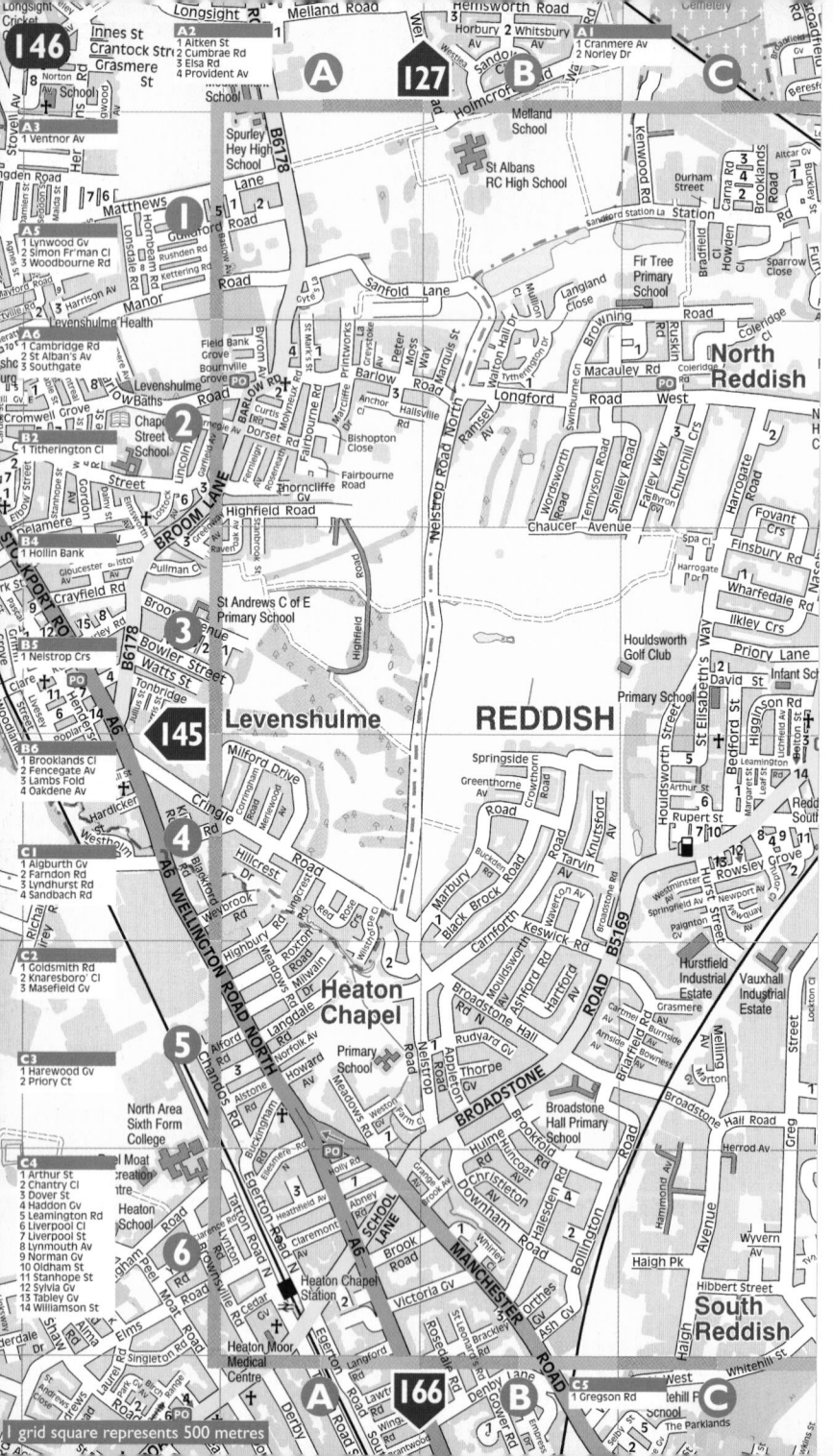

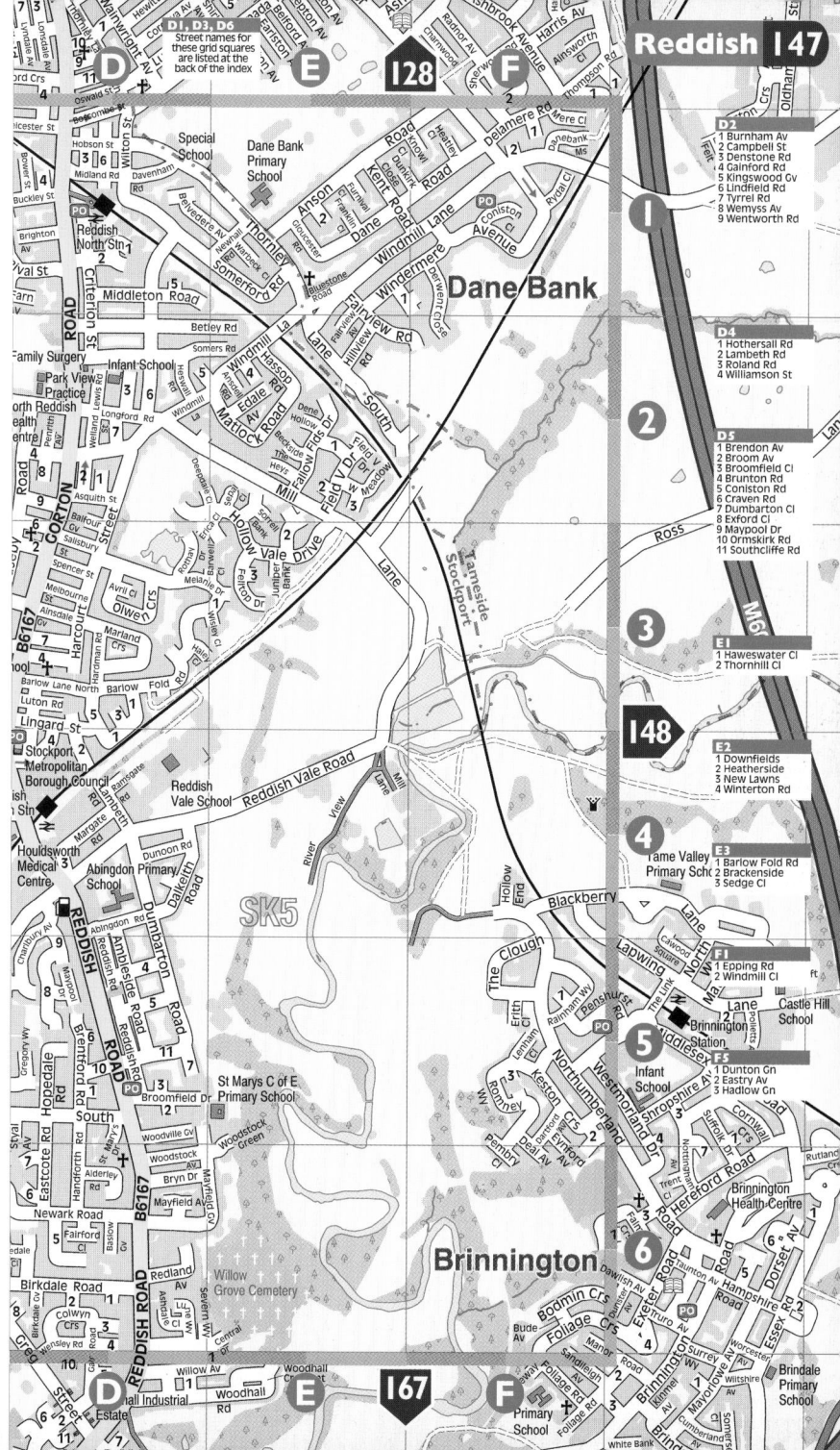

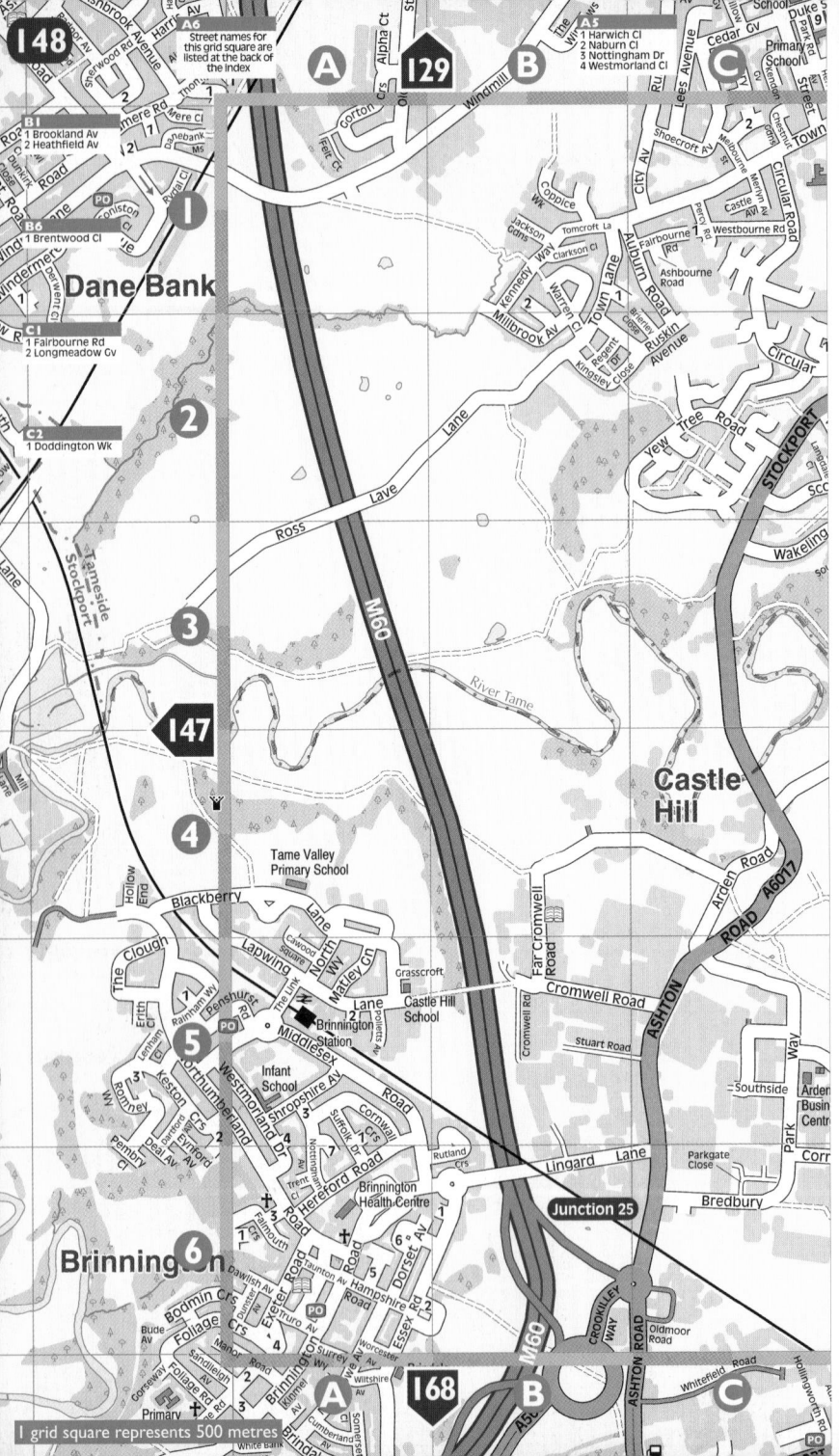

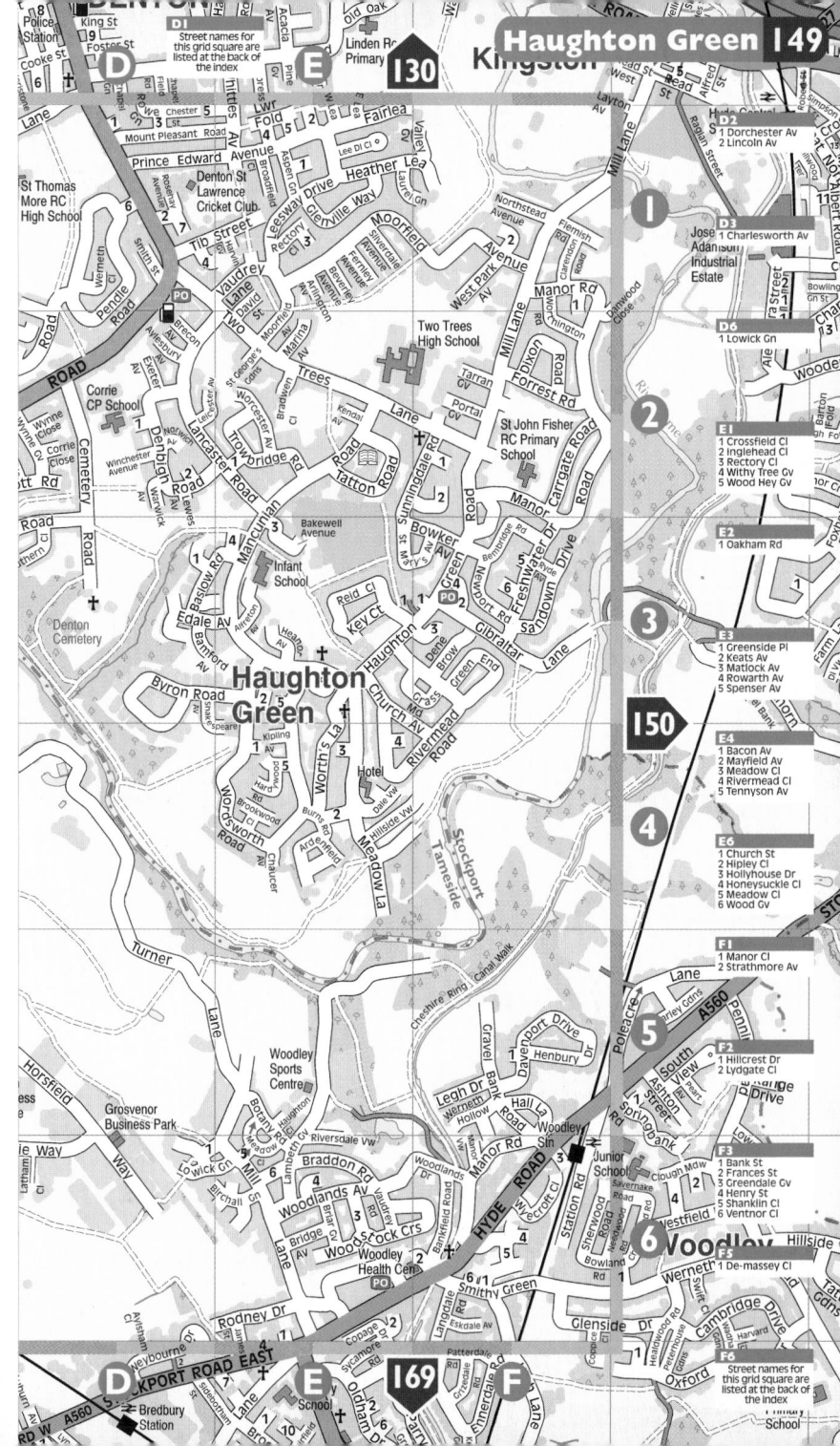

130

150

169

Kingston

D1
Street names for this grid square are listed at the back of the index

D7
1 Dorchester Av
2 Lincoln Av

D3
Jose
Adamson
Industrial
Estate
1 Charlesworth Av

D6
1 Lowick Gn

E1
1 Crossfield Cl
2 Inglehead Cl
3 Rectory Cl
4 Withy Tree Gv
5 Wood Hey Gv

E2
1 Oakham Rd

E3
1 Greenside Pl
2 Keats Av
3 Matlock Av
4 Rowarth Av
5 Spenser Av

E4
1 Bacon Av
2 Mayfield Av
3 Meadow Cl
4 Rivermead Cl
5 Tennyson Av

E6
1 Church St
2 Hipley Cl
3 Hollyhouse Dr
4 Honeysuckle Cl
5 Meadow Cl
6 Wood Gv

F1
1 Manor Cl
2 Strathmore Av

F2
1 Hillcrest Dr
2 Lydgate Cl

F3
1 Bank St
2 Frances St
3 Creendale Gv
4 Henry St
5 Shanklin Cl
6 Ventnor Cl

F5
1 De-massey Cl

F6
Street names for this grid square are listed at the back of the index

Woodley

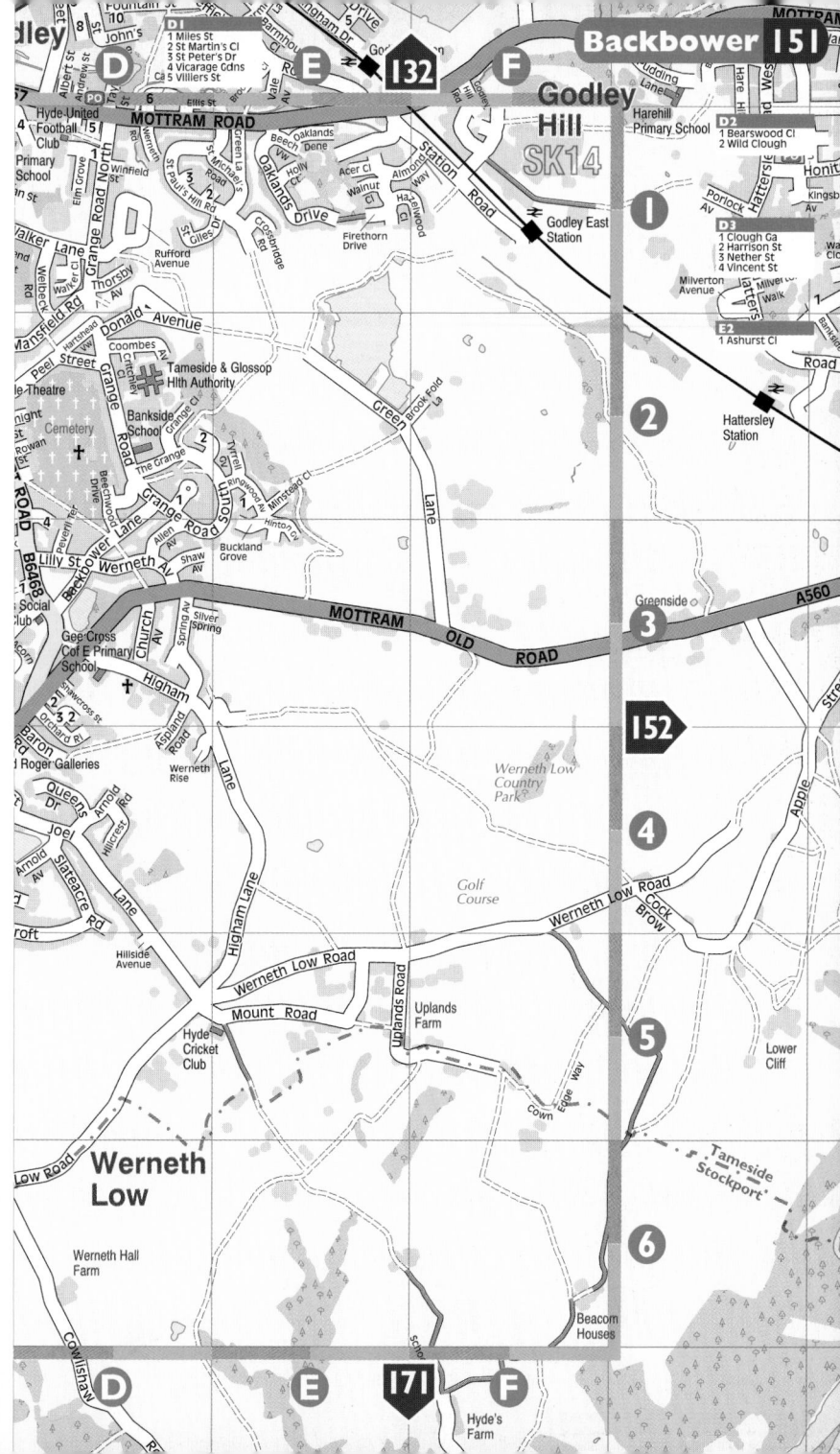

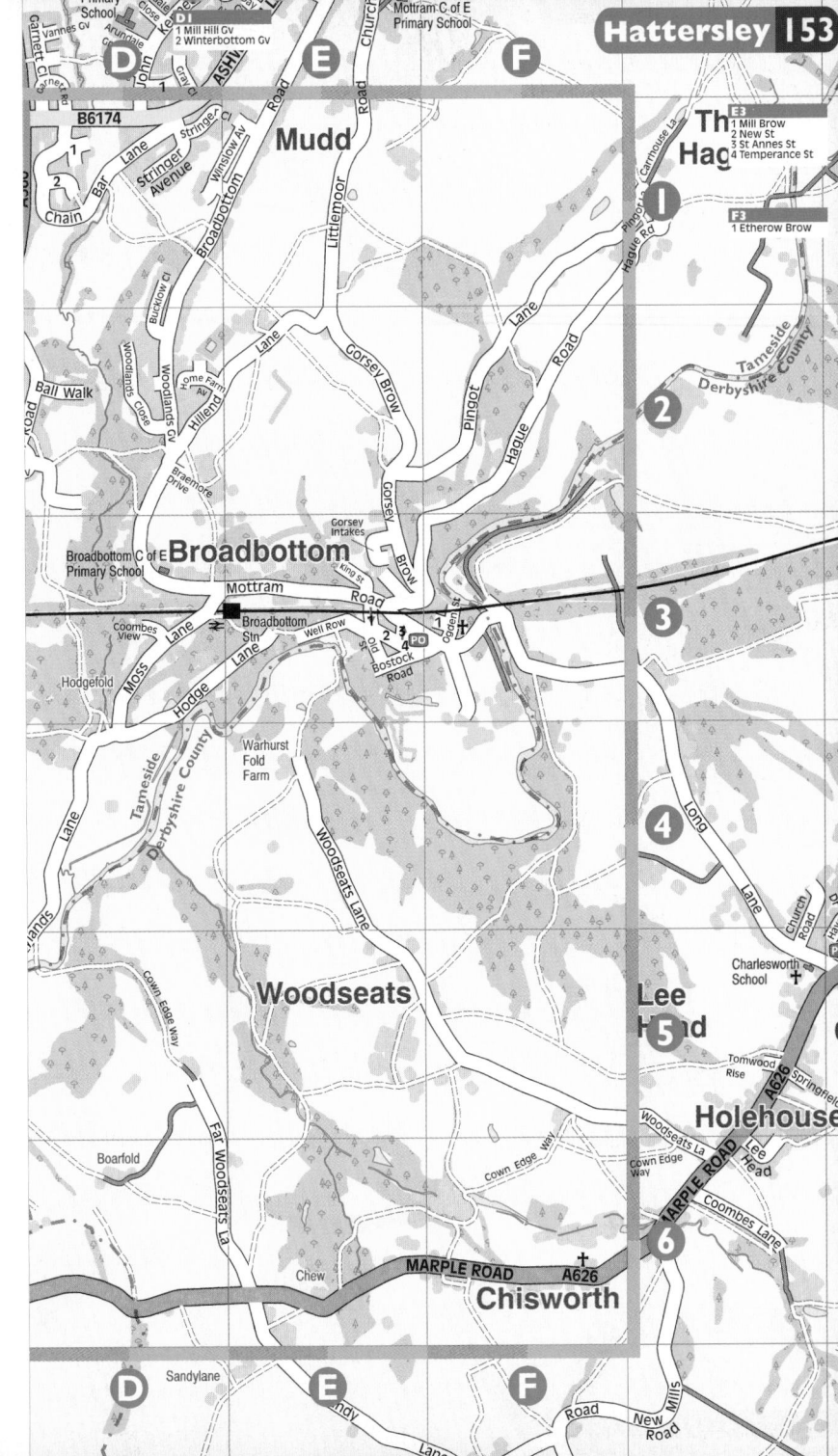

Mottram C of E
Primary School

D1
1 Mill Hill Gv
2 Winterbottom Gv

E3
Th
Hag
1 Mill Brow
2 New St
3 St Annes St
4 Temperance St

F3
1 Etherow Brow

B6174

Garnett Close
Vannes Gv
Arundale
John
Croft

ASHW

Church Road

School

Bar Lane
Chain
Stringer
Lane
Stringer
Stringer Avenue
Winslow Av
Broadbottom
Road
Littlemoor
Lane

Mudd

Pingot La
Carnhouse La
Hague Rd

Woodlands Gv
Bucklow Cl
Home Farm
Av
Hillend
Woodlands Close
Lane
Gorsey Brow

Ball Walk
Braemore
Drive

Tameside
Derbyshire County

Pingot Lane
Hague Road

Gorsey Brow
Gorsey Intakes

Broadbottom C of E
Primary School

Broadbottom

King St
Mottram Road
Coombes
View
Lane
Broadbottom
Stn
Well Row
Lane
Moss
Lane
Hodgefold
Hodge Lane
Old
Old
Bostock
Road
1
Ogden St
PO
2 3
4
†

Tameside
Derbyshire County

Warhurst
Fold
Farm

Woodseats Lane

Long Lane

Charlesworth
School †

**Lee
Head**

Cown Edge Way

Woodseats

Tomwood
Rise

A626 Springfield

Church Road

Hyd

Woodseats La
Cown Edge
Way
Lee
Head

Holehouse

Boarfold
Far Woodseats La

MARPLE ROAD

Coombes Lane

Chew

Cown Edge Way

MARPLE ROAD A626
†

Chisworth

Sandylane

Road
New
Road
Mills
Lane

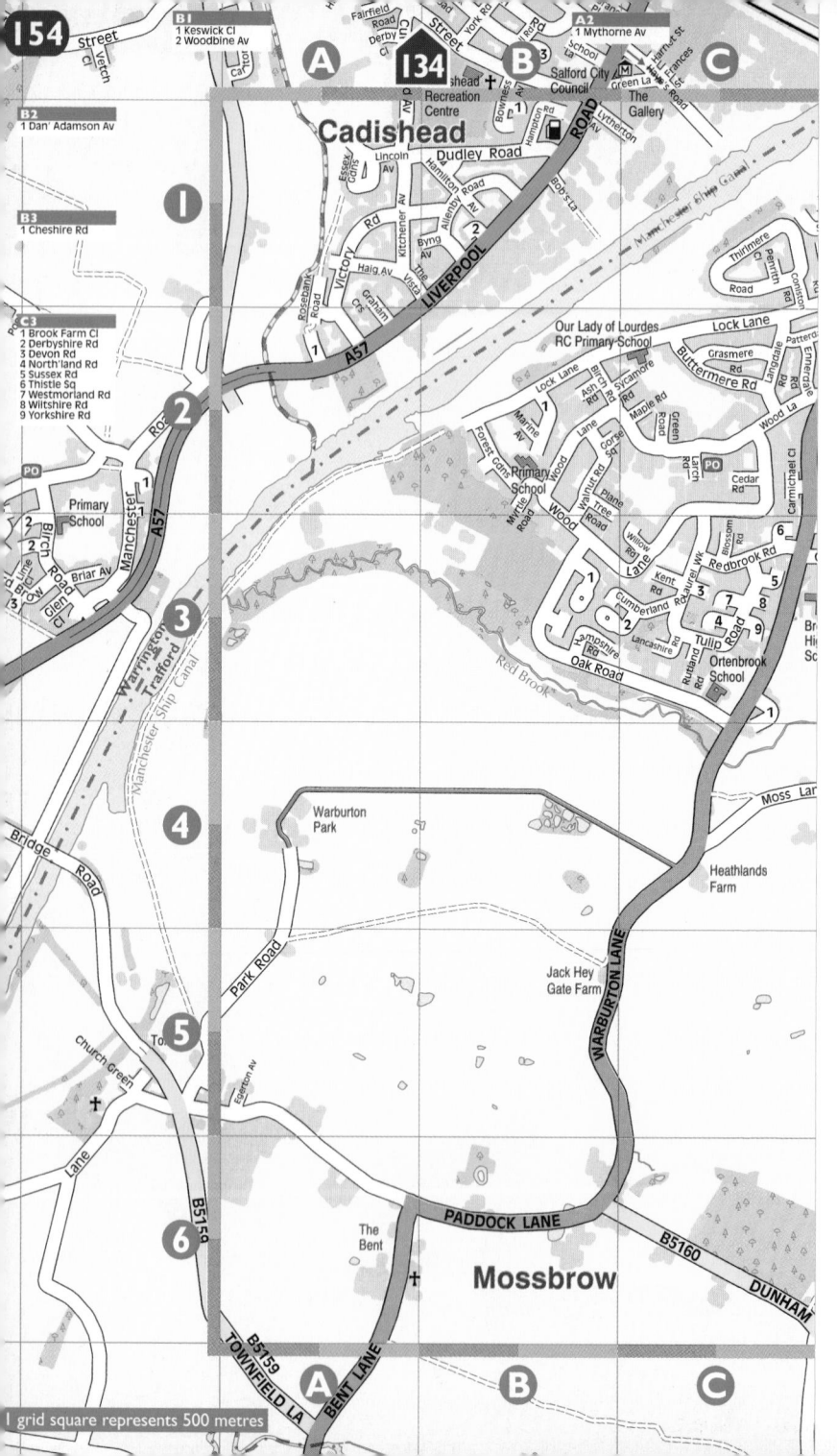

B1
1 Keswick Cl
2 Woodbine Av

B2
1 Dan' Adamson Av

B3
1 Cheshire Rd

C3
1 Brook Farm Cl
2 Derbyshire Rd
3 Devon Rd
4 North'land Rd
5 Sussex Rd
6 Thistle Sq
7 Westmorland Rd
8 Wiltshire Rd
9 Yorkshire Rd

134

Fairfield Road
Derby
Cul
York Rd
Rd
Street

A2
1 Mythorne Av

Salford City
Council

The
Gallery

School La
Green La
Garnet St
Frances

Cadishead

Dudley Road

Recreation
Centre

Bowness
Hamlet Rd
Lytherton

LIVERPOOL ROAD

Essex
Gdns
Lincoln
Av
Hamilton Road
Allenby Rd
Byng Av
La Vista

Victory Rd
Kitchener Rd

Haig Av
Graham Cres

Rosebank Road

Our Lady of Lourdes
RC Primary School

Lock Lane

A57

Thirlmere
Penrith
Road

Compton
Road

Grasmere
Rd
Buttermere Rd
Langdale
Ennerdale

Manchester Ship Canal

Lock Lane
Ash
Marine
Av
Sycamore

Wood La

Patterdale

Forest Gdns

Maple Rd

Primary
School

Myrtle
Road
Corse
Sq

Green
Road
Larch
Birch
PO

Walnut Rd
Plane
Tree
Road

Cedar
Rd

Carmichael Cl

Wood Lane

Willow
Rise
Blossom Rd
Redbrook Rd

Kent
Rd

Lancashire
Tulip

Cumberland Rd
Hampshire

Bro
Hi
Sc

Manchester Road A57

PO

Primary
School

Birch
Line
Glen Cl
Briar Av

Ortenbrook
School

Oak Road

Red Brook

Warrington Road A57

Trafford

Moss La

Bridge Road

Warburton
Park

Heathlands
Farm

Park Road

Jack Hey
Gate Farm

WARBURTON LANE

Church Green

Egerton Av

To

Lane

B5159

PADDOCK LANE

B5160
DUNHAM

The
Bent

Mossbrow

B5159
TOWNFIELD LA
BENT LANE

A   B   C

1 grid square represents 500 metres

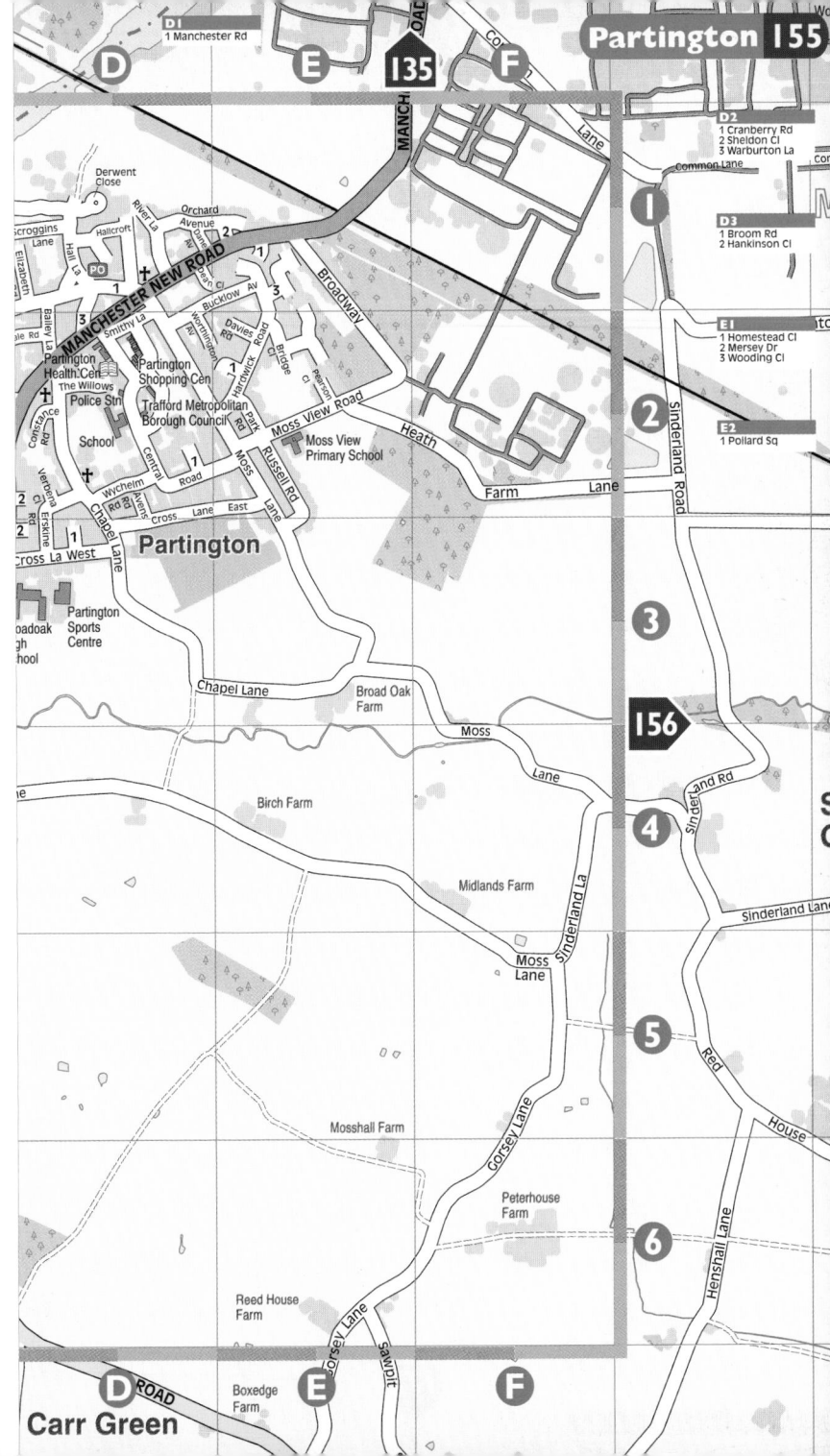

MANCHESTER

Common Lane

Works

A

B

C

1

Common Lane

Common Lane

M31

Dunham Road

North Road

Brookheys Road

Ashton Road

Heath

2

Farm Lane

Sinderland Road

Dunham Road

3

Oak

Moss

Lane

Brookheys Farm

LC

Brookheys Road

Sinderland Rd

4

Midlands Farm

Sinderland La

Sinderland Green

Moss Lane

Sinderland Lane

Sinderland Lane

5

Red

Lane

Lawn Cemetery

Whitehouse Farm

Gorsey Lane

House

Whitehouse

Peterhouse Farm

6

Lane

Henshall Lane

Black Moss Road

Black Brow Farm

A

B

C

1 grid square represents 500 metres

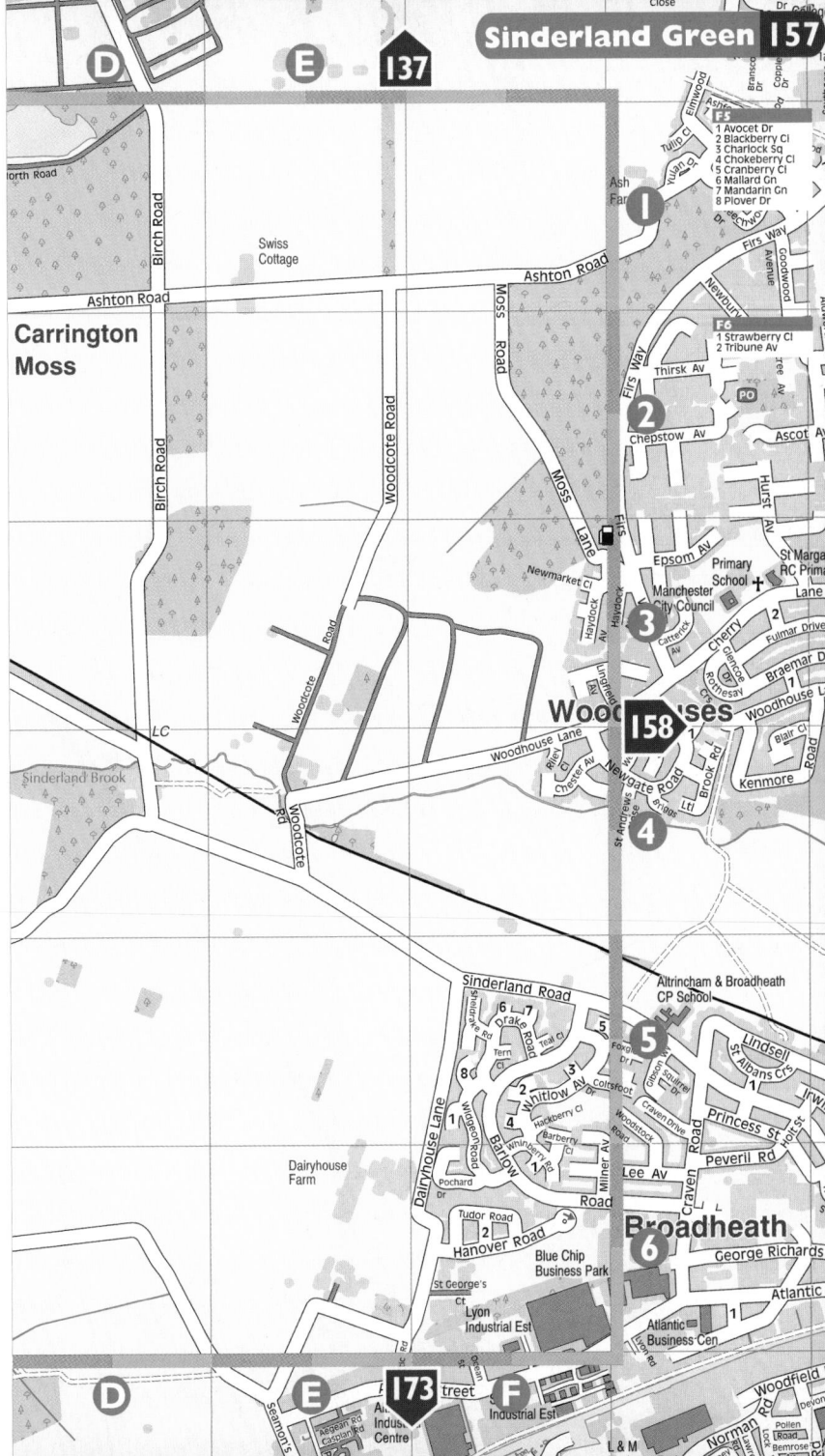

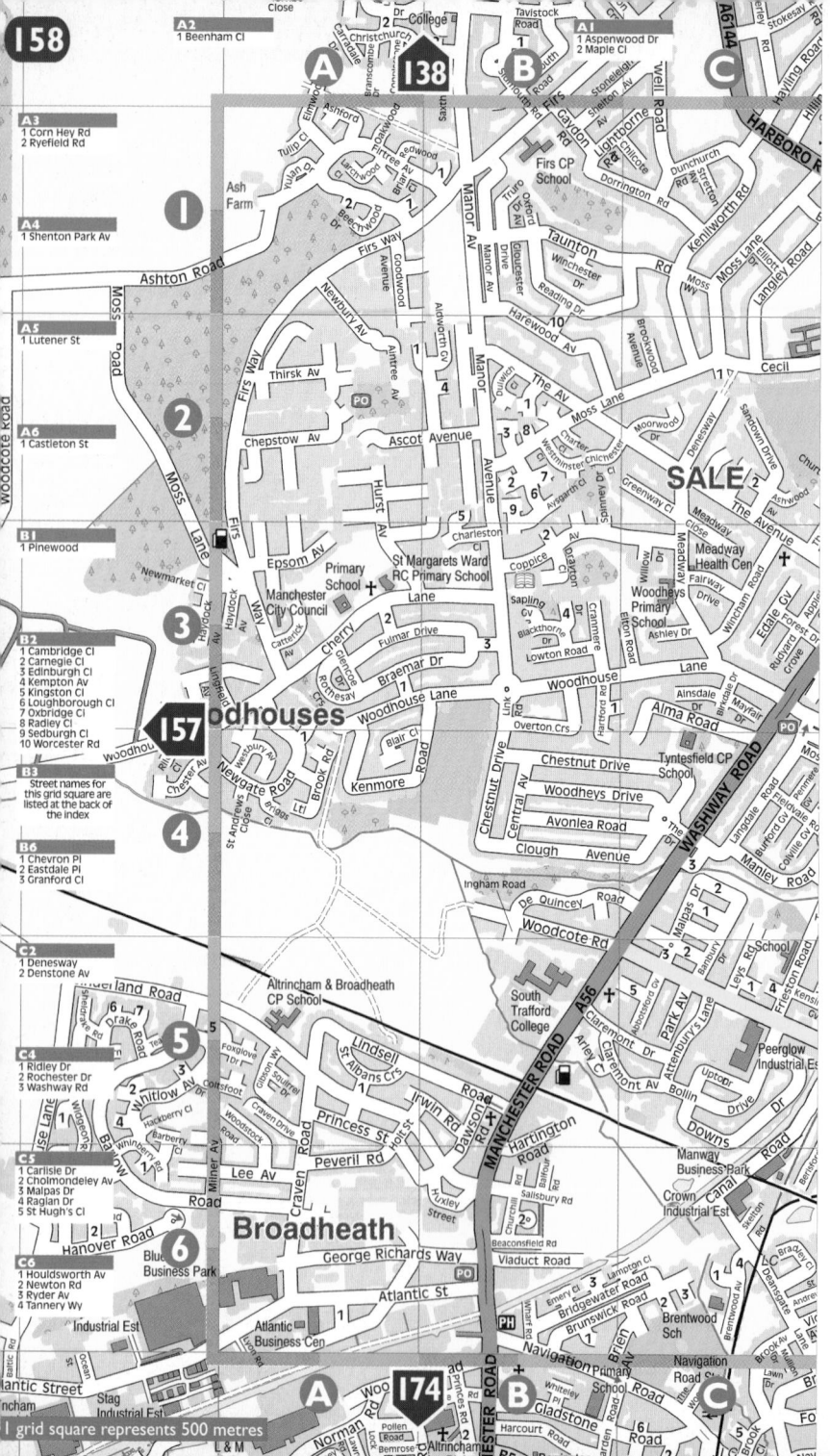

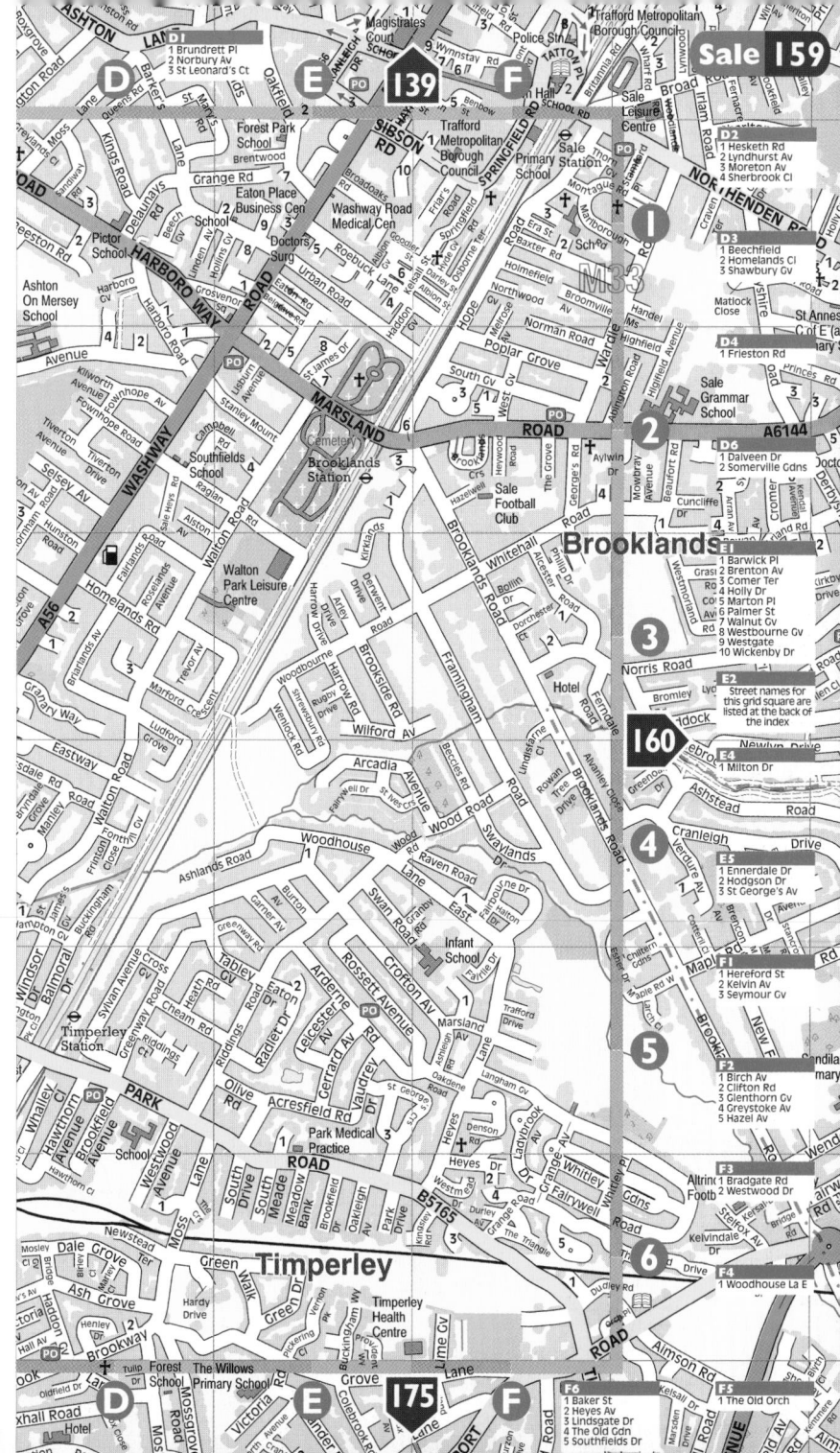

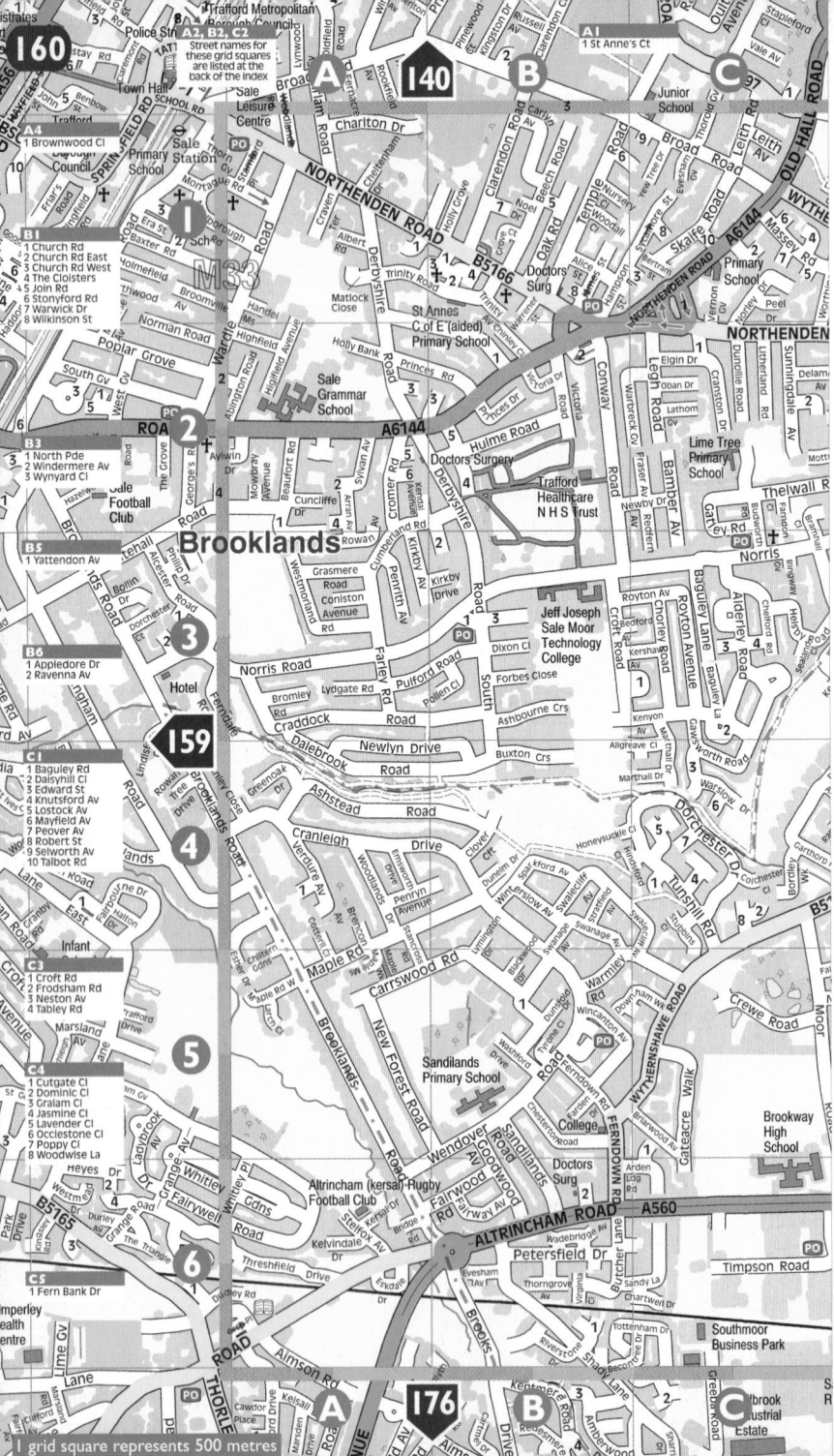

140

A   B   C

A1
1 St Anne's Ct

Brooklands

2

3

159

4

5

6

A   B   C

176

I grid square represents 500 metres

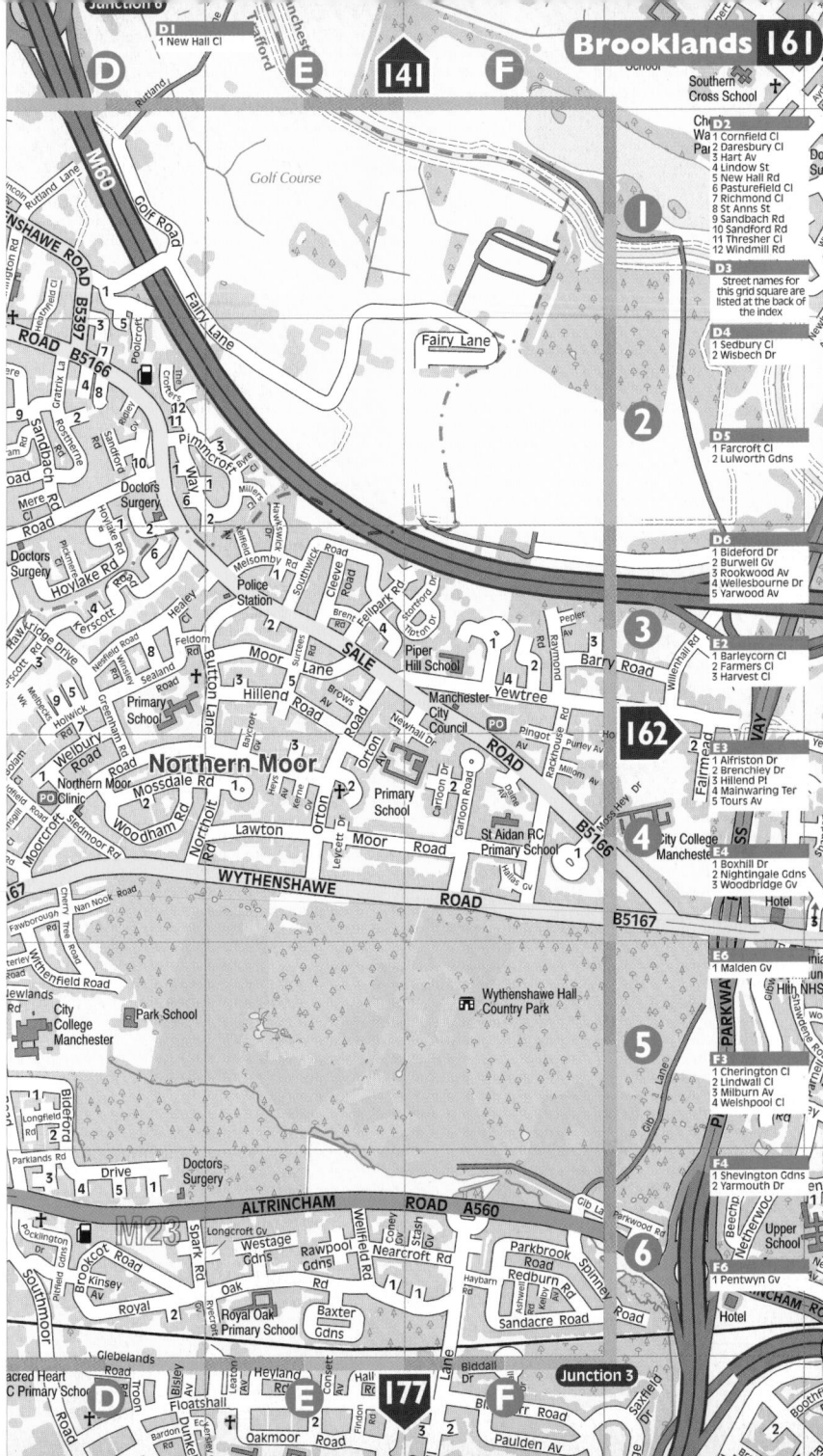

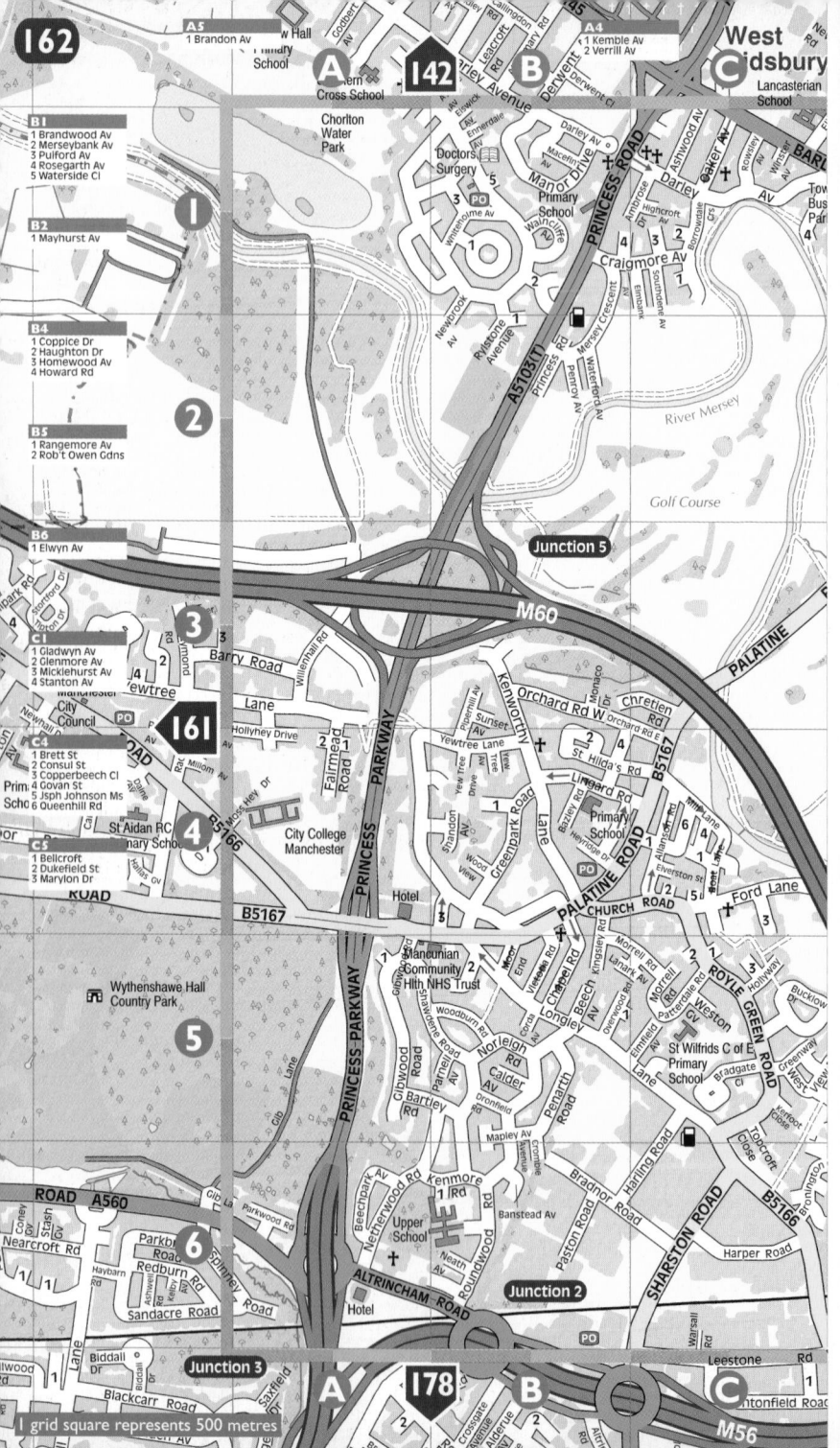

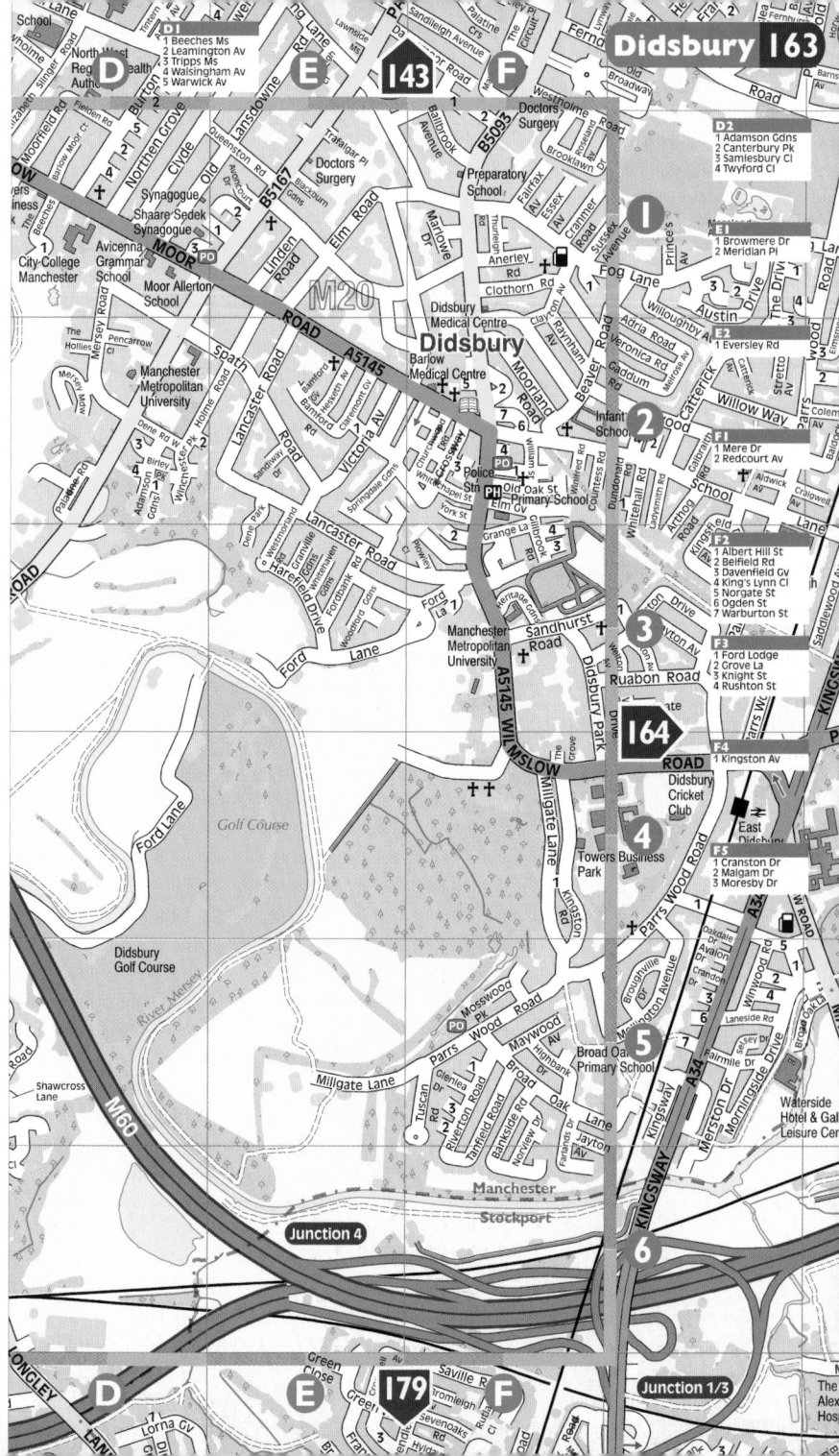

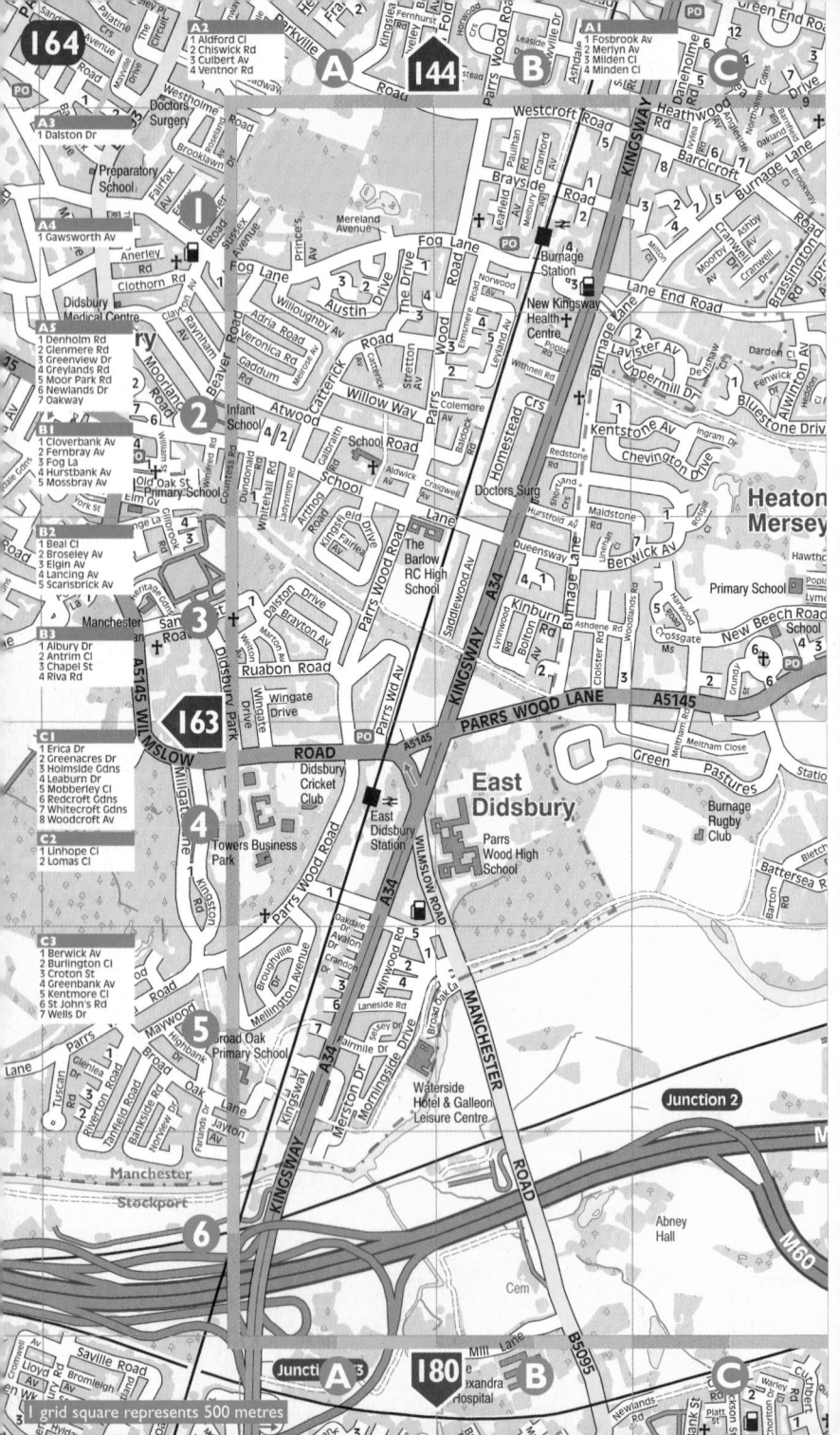

164

A2
1 Aldford Cl
2 Chiswick Rd
3 Culbert Av
4 Ventnor Rd

144

A1
1 Fosbrook Av
2 Merlyn Av
3 Milden Cl
4 Minden Cl

A3
1 Dalston Dr

A4
1 Gawsworth Av

A5
1 Denholm Rd
2 Glenmere Rd
3 Greenview Dr
4 Greylands Rd
5 Moor Park Rd
6 Newlands Dr
7 Oakway

B1
1 Cloverbank Av
2 Fernbray Av
3 Fog La
4 Hurstbank Av
5 Mossbray Av

B2
1 Beal Cl
2 Broseley Av
3 Elgin Av
4 Lancing Av
5 Scarisbrick Av

B3
1 Albury Dr
2 Antrim Cl
3 Chapel St
4 Riva Rd

163

C1
1 Erica Dr
2 Greenacres Dr
3 Holmside Gdns
4 Leaburn Dr
5 Mobberley Cl
6 Redcroft Gdns
7 Whitecroft Gdns
8 Woodcroft Av

1 Linhope Cl
2 Lomas Cl

C3
1 Berwick Av
2 Burlington Cl
3 Croton St
4 Greenbank Av
5 Kentmore Cl
6 St John's Rd
7 Wells Dr

1 grid square represents 500 metres

Juncti A 3

180

B C

East Didsbury

Heaton Mersey

Junction 2

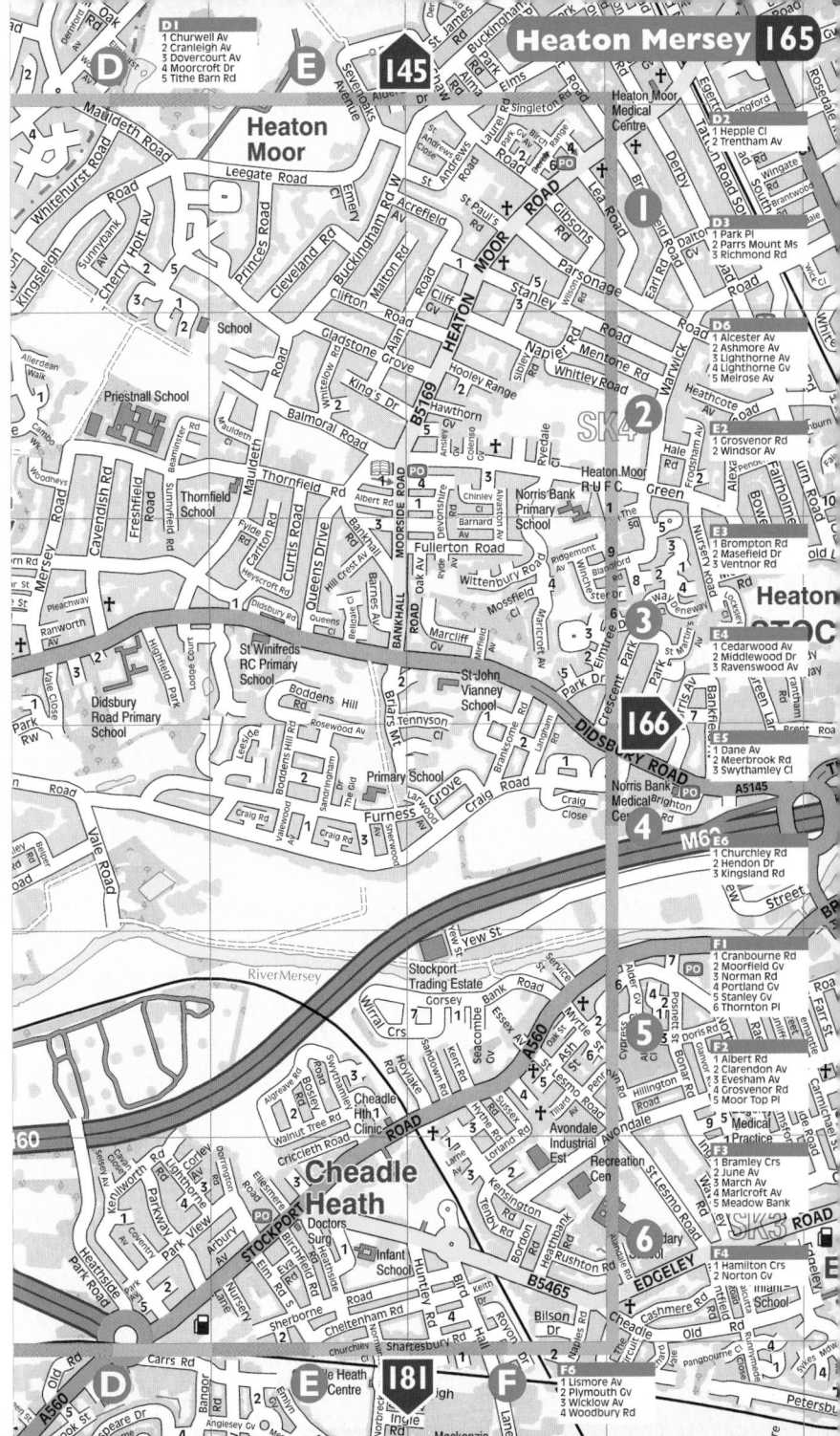

D1
1 Churwell Av
2 Cranleigh Av
3 Dovercourt Av
4 Moorcroft Dr
5 Tithe Barn Rd

D2
1 Hepple Cl
2 Trentham Av

D3
1 Park Pl
2 Parrs Mount Ms
3 Richmond Rd

D6
1 Alcester Av
2 Ashmore Av
3 Lighthorne Av
4 Lighthorne Gv
5 Melrose Av

E2
2 Grosvenor Rd
2 Windsor Av

E3
1 Brompton Rd
2 Masefield Dr
3 Ventnor Rd

E4
1 Cedarwood Av
2 Middlewood Dr
3 Ravenswood Av

E5
1 Dane Av
2 Meerbrook Rd
3 Swythamley Cl

E6
1 Churchley Rd
2 Hendon Dr
3 Kingsland Rd

F1
1 Cranbourne Rd
2 Moorfield Gv
3 Norman Rd
4 Portland Gv
5 Stanley Gv
6 Thornton Pl

F2
1 Albert Rd
2 Clarendon Av
3 Evesham Av
4 Grosvenor Rd
5 Moor Top Pl

F3
1 Bramley Crs
2 June Av
3 March Av
4 Marlcroft Av
5 Meadow Bank

F4
1 Hamilton Crs
2 Norton Gv

F6
1 Lismore Av
2 Plymouth Gv
3 Wicklow Av
4 Woodbury Rd

Heaton Moor

Heaton Moor Medical Centre

Priestnall School

Thornfield School

St Winifreds RC Primary School

Boddens Hill

Didsbury Road Primary School

St John Vianney School

Norris Bank Primary School

Heaton Moor R.U.F.C.

Heaton STOC

Heaton Moor Green

SK4

Norris Bank Medical Centre

River Mersey

Stockport Trading Estate

Cheadle Hth Clinic

Cheadle Heath

Doctors Surg

Infant School

Avondale Industrial Est

Recreation Cen

Medical Practice

Infant School

SK3

EDGELEY

ROAD

DIDSBURY ROAD

STOCKPORT ROAD

DIDSBURY ROAD

166

SK4

2

3

4

5

6

I

145

181

A5145

M60

B5169

A560

B5465

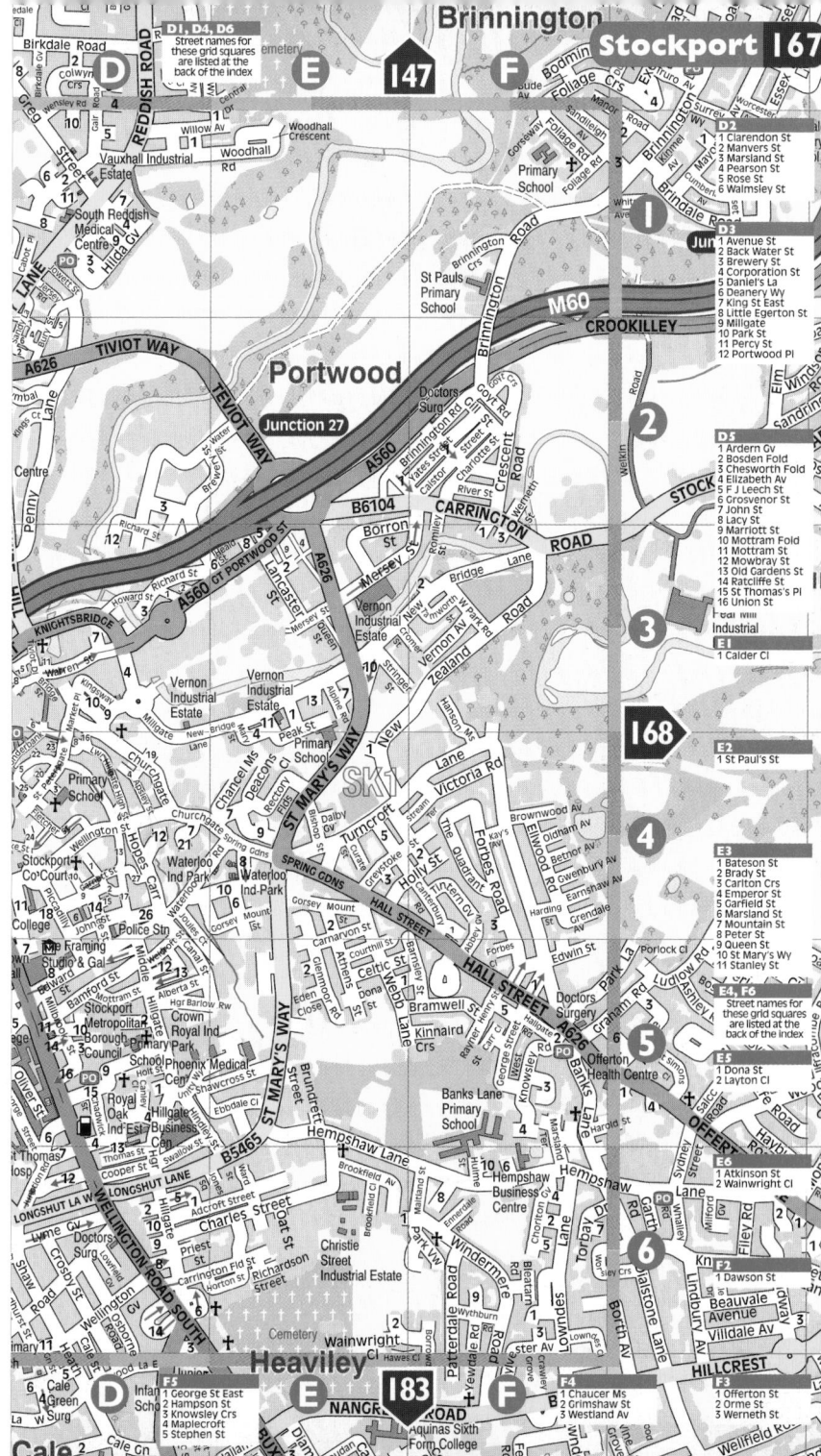

Birkdale Road
Colwyn
D
REDDISH ROAD
E
147
F
Bodmin
Follage Rd
Truro

Wensley Rd
Willow Av
Central
Woodhall Crescent
Woodhall Rd
Vauxhall Industrial Estate
South Reddish Medical Centre
Hilda Gv

LANE
Primary School

St Pauls Primary School

Brinnington Crs

M60
CROOKILLEY

TIVIOT WAY
A626
TEVIOT WAY

Portwood

Junction 27

A560
B6104
Brinnington Rd
Govt Rd
Cliff Rd
Charlotte St
River St
Castoor St
Crescent Road
Yates Street
Brewery St

I

2

CARRINGTON
Borron St
Mersey St
New Bridge
Lane
ROAD
Romiley

Vernon Industrial Estate

Zealand St
Vernon Industrial Estate
New Bridge Lane
Peak St
Primary School
SK1

168

KNIGHTSBRIDGE
Warren St
Millgate
Chancel Ms
Deacons
Churchgate
ST MARY'S WAY
Dalby St
Turncroft
Victoria Av
Brownwood Av
Oldham Av
Betnor Av
Gwenbury Av
Earnshaw Av
Grendale Av

3

Peal Mill
Industrial

4

Primary School
Wellington St
Churchgate
Spring Gdns
Waterloo Ind Park
Waterloo Ind Park
SPRING GDNS
Corsey Mount
HALL STREET
Holly St
Forbes Road
ELMWOOD
Kay's Row
Harding St
Edwin St
Park Rd
Porlock Cl
Ludlow
Ashley
Graham Rd

Stockport Co Court
College
John St
Police Stn
The Framing Studio & Gal
Boulevard
Banford St
Mottram St
Stockport Metropolitan Borough Council
Crown Royal Ind
Phoenix Medical Cen
Royal Oak Ind Est
Hillgate Business Cen
Thomas St
Cooper St
Middle Hillgate
ST MARY'S WAY
Brundrett Street
Hempshaw Lane
Carnarvon St
Courthill St
Celtic St
Leona Dr
Eden Close
Bramwell
Kinnaird Crs
Webb Lane
Rayner Henry St
George St
Hulme St
Knowsley
Banks Lane
Offerton Health Centre

5

Banks Lane Primary School

Harold St

OFFERTON

LONGSHUT LANE W
Lyme Gv
Doctors Surg
WELLINGTON ROAD SOUTH
Crosby Rd
St Thomas Hosp
Royal Oak Ind Est
Swallow St
LONGSHUT LANE
Adcroft Street
Charles Street
Priest St
Carrington Fld St
Horton St
Richardson St
B5465
Christie Street Industrial Estate
Brookfield Av
Maitland St
Hempshaw Business Centre
Hempshaw Lane
Chorlton Lane
Torbay Dr
Emerald St
Windermere Road
Patterdale Rd
Newtatale Rd
Wythburn
Bleasdale Rd
Borrowdale
Lowndes Lane
Crawley Grove
Sydney St
Milford Gv
Filey Rd
Havdn Rd
Calce
Kne

Beauvale Avenue
Villdale Av

6

Cale Green
La W Surg
Cale Gn
Cale

Doctors Surg
Lowfield Rd
Lyme Gv
Wellington Gv
Ophra Rd
Cemetery
Wainwright Cl
Hawes Cl

Infant Scho
D
Heavily
E
NANGR
183
F
ROAD
HILLCREST

Aquinas Sixth Form College

Welfield Grove

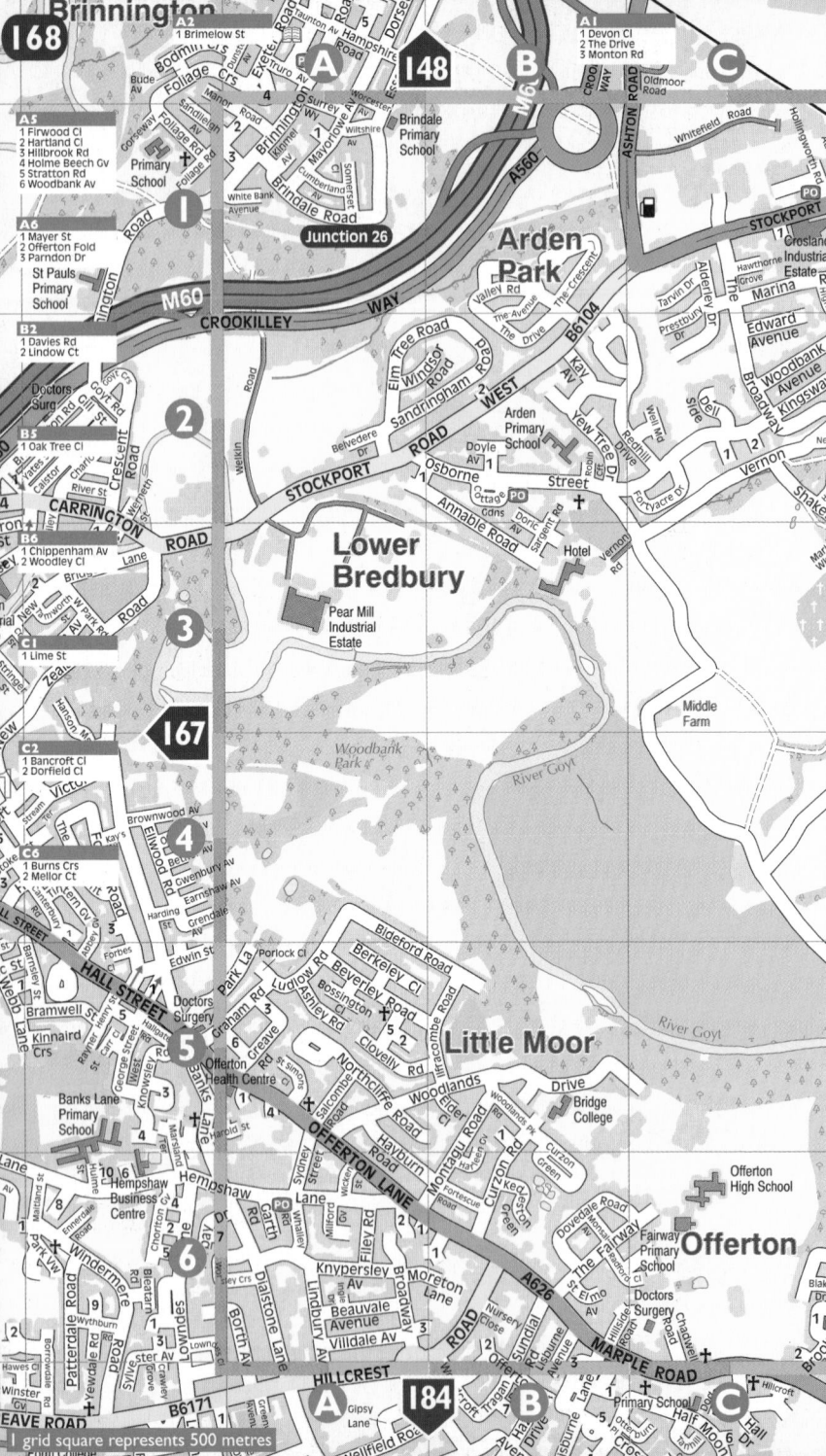

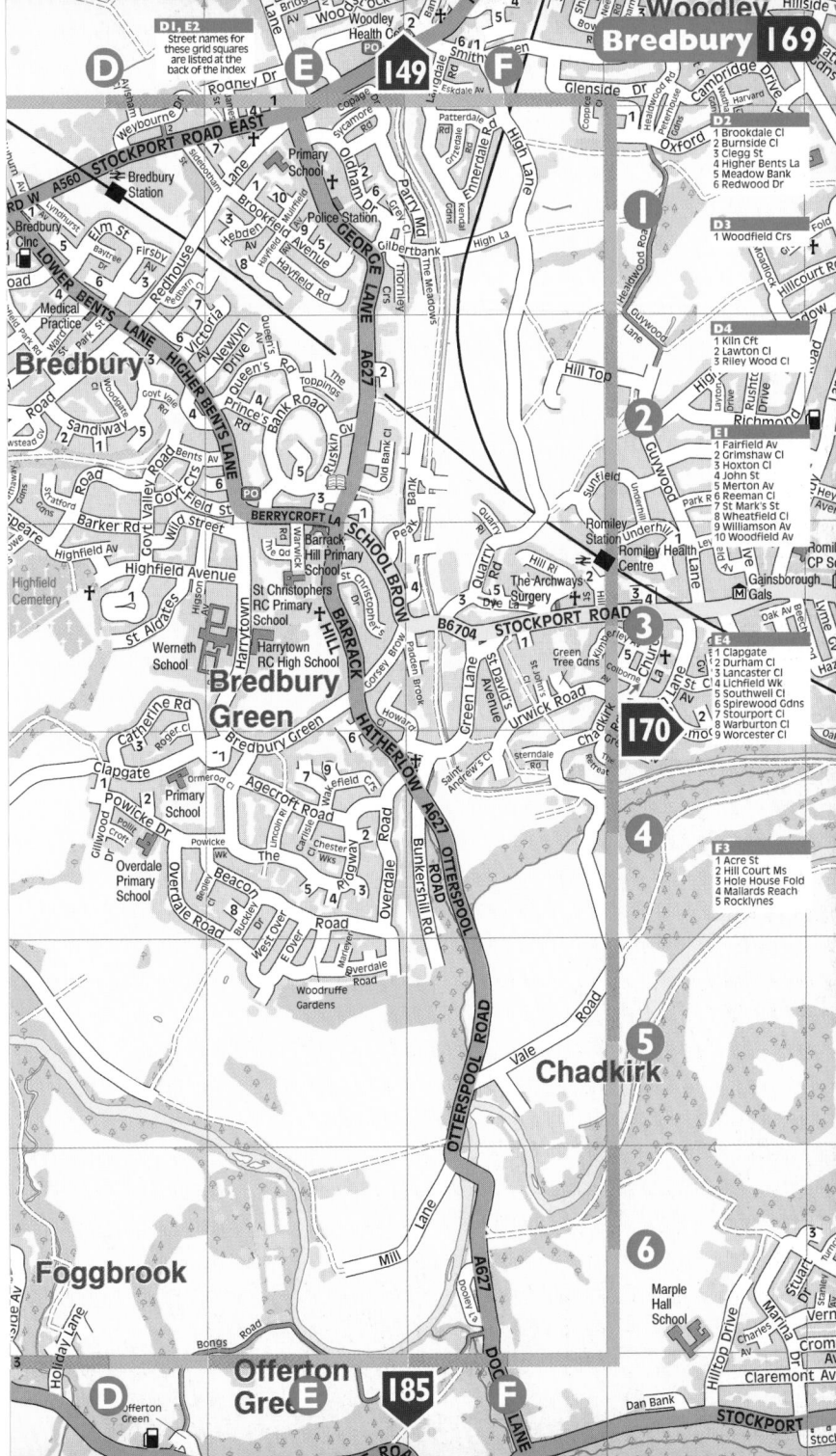

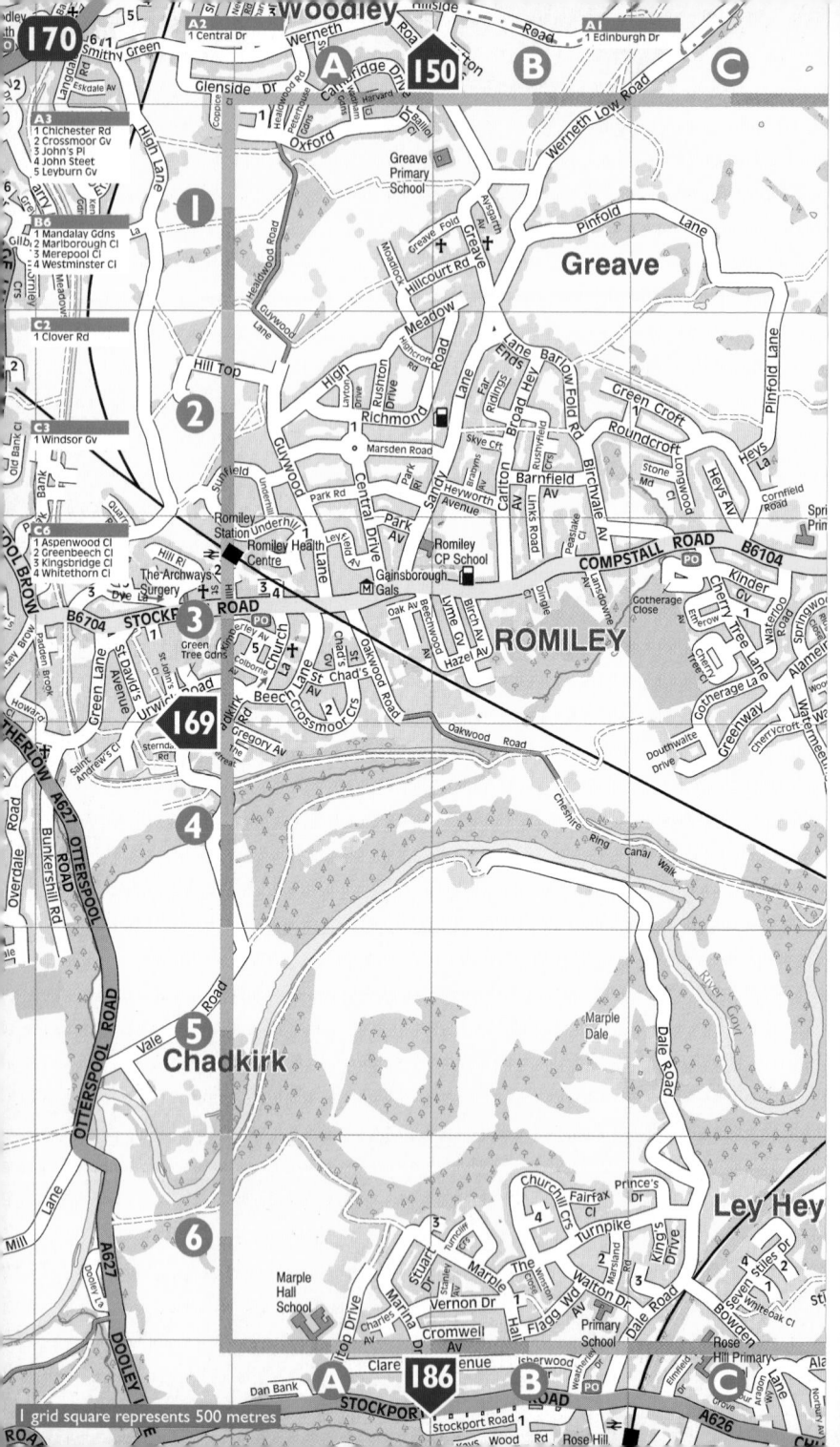

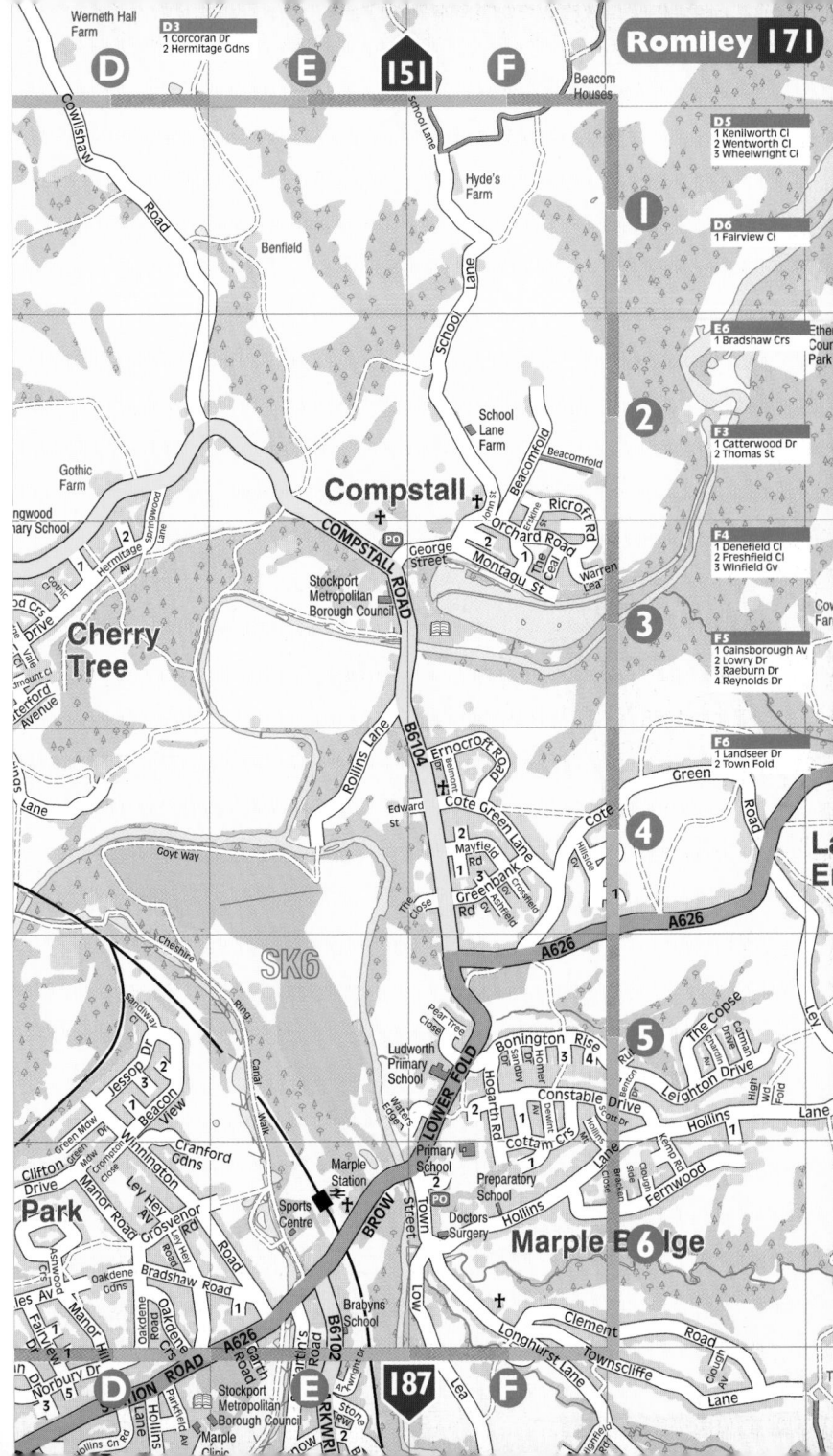

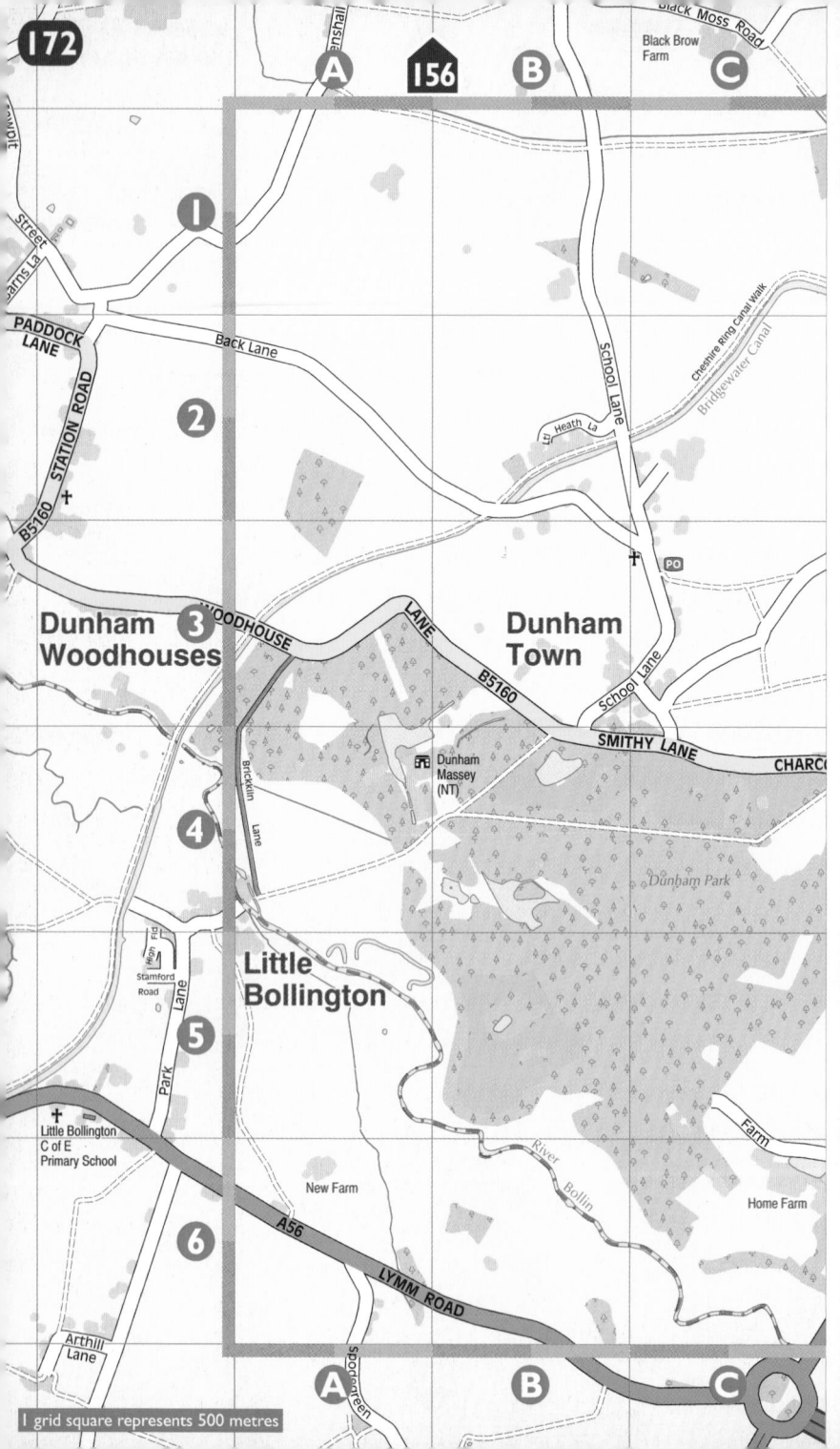

A

156

B

C

Black Moss Road

Black Brow
Farm

1

Street

Paddock Lane

Cams La

Back Lane

Station Road

B5160

School Lane

Cheshire Ring Canal Walk

Bridgewater Canal

2

Lt Heath La

PO

Dunham Woodhouses

3

Woodhouse

Lane

B5160

Dunham Town

School Lane

Smithy Lane

Charco

Bricklin Lane

Dunham Massey (NT)

Dunham Park

4

High Fld

Stamford Road

Little Bollington

5

Park Lane

Farm

River Bollin

Little Bollington
C of E
Primary School

New Farm

Home Farm

6

A56

Lymm Road

Arthill
Lane

Spoorateen

A

B

C

1 grid square represents 500 metres

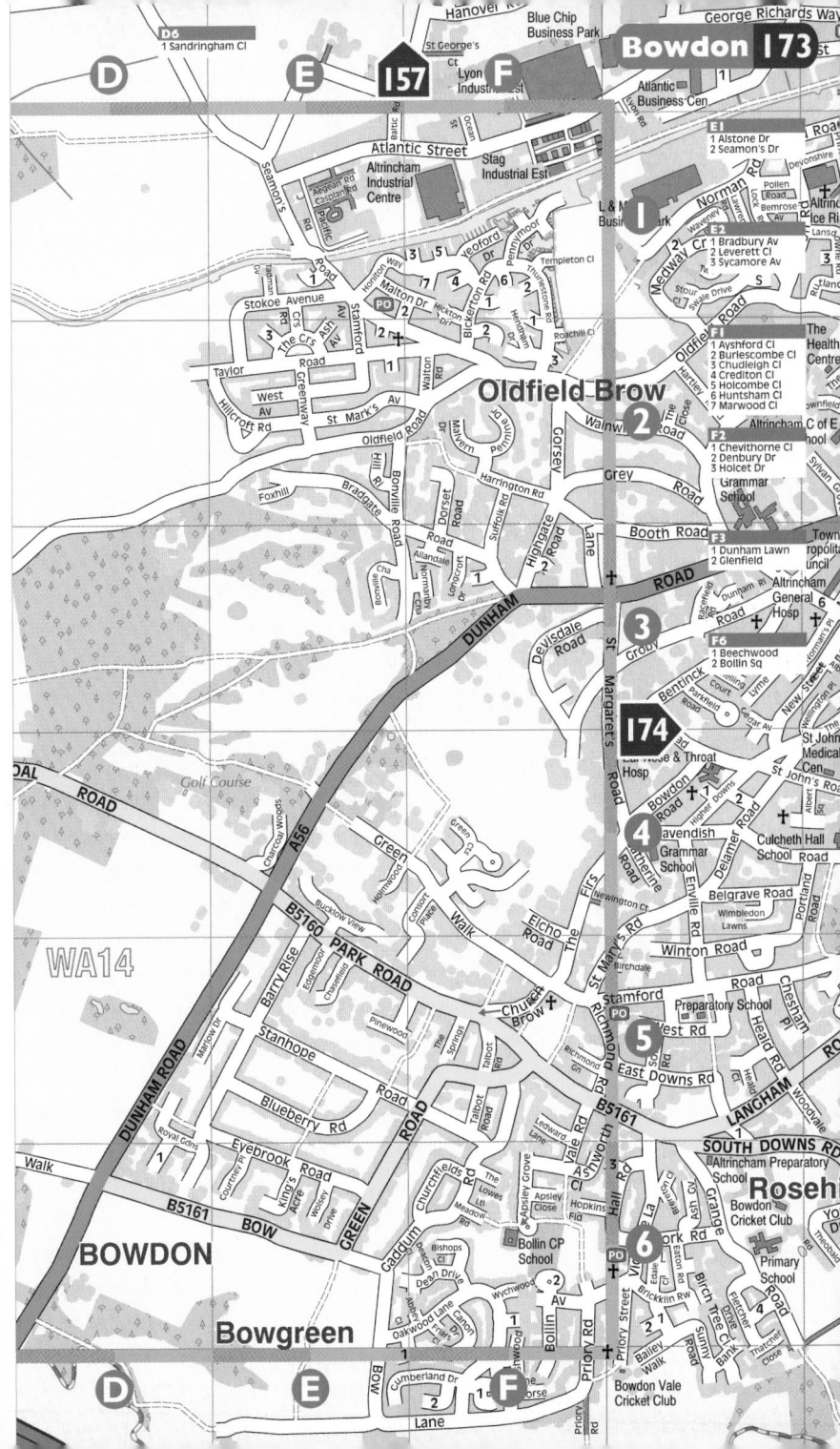

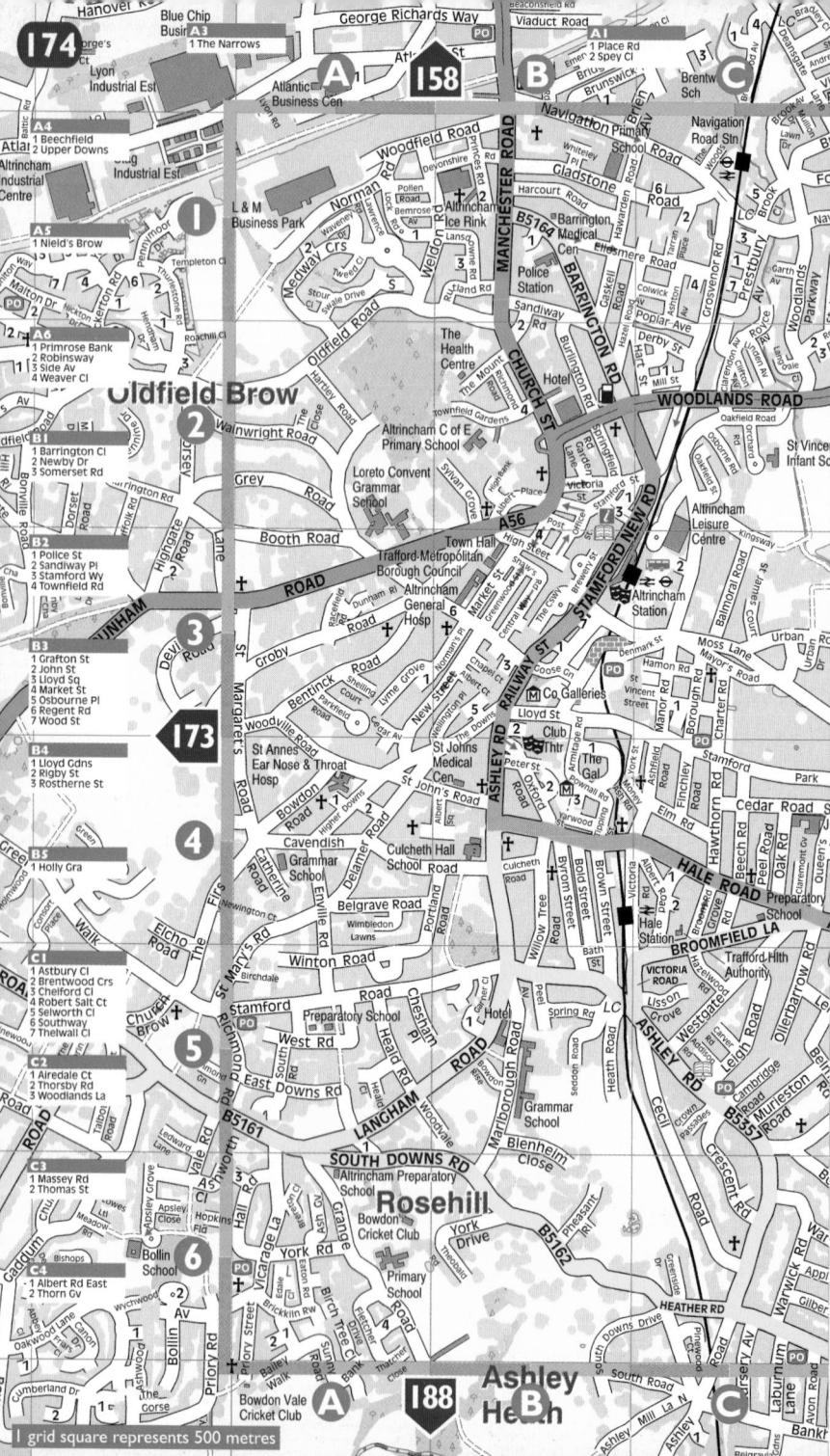

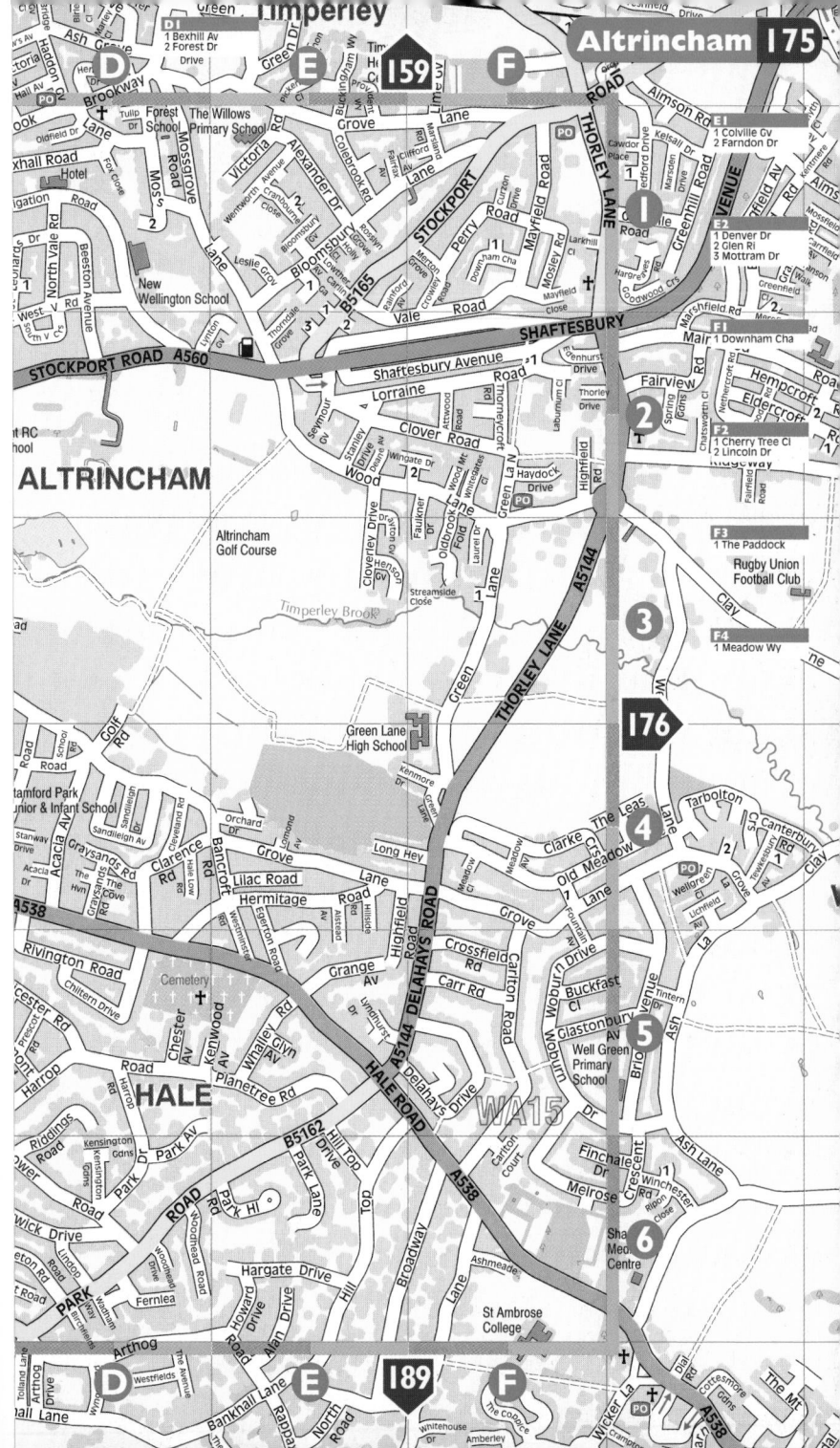

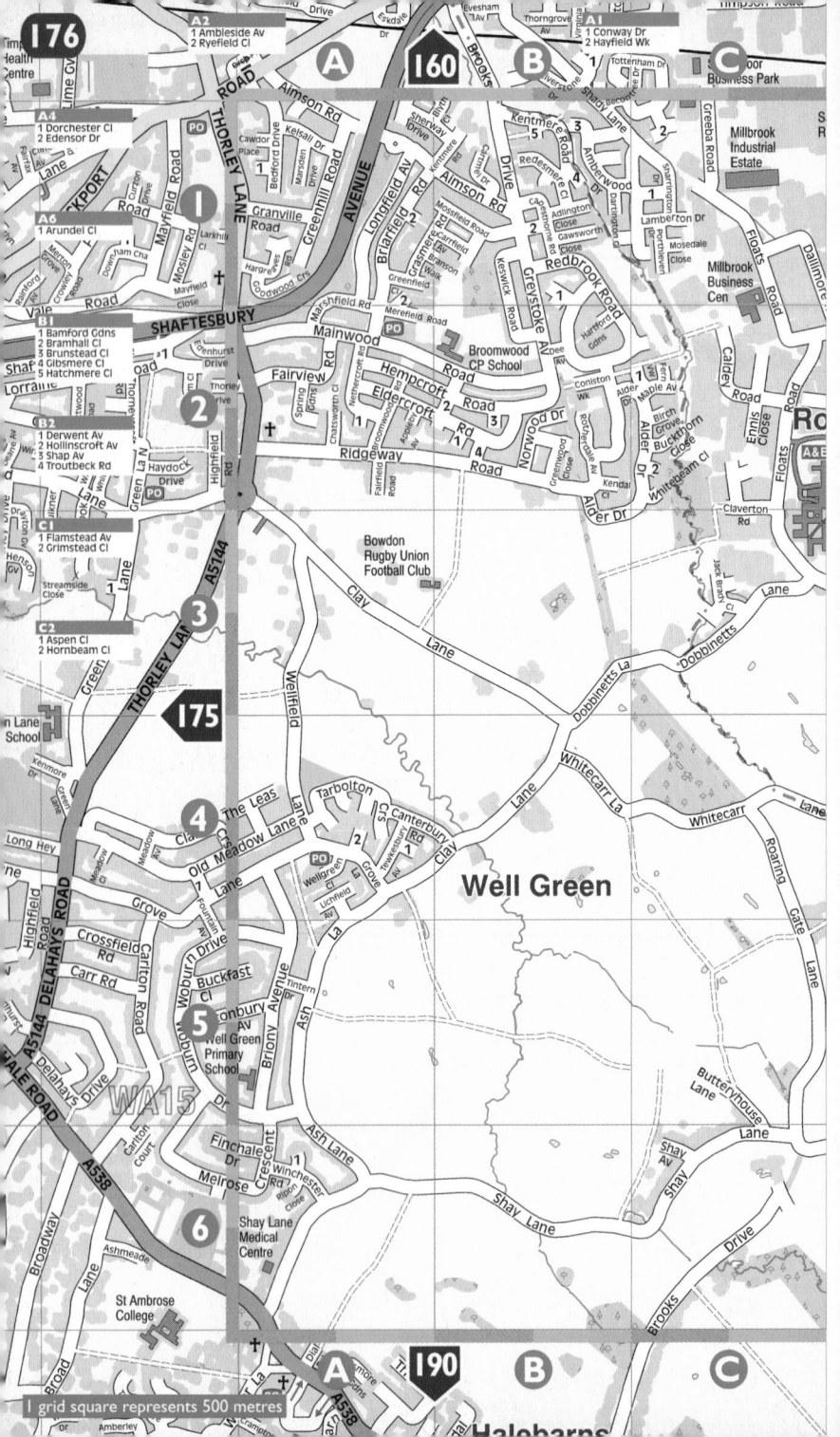

I grid square represents 500 metres

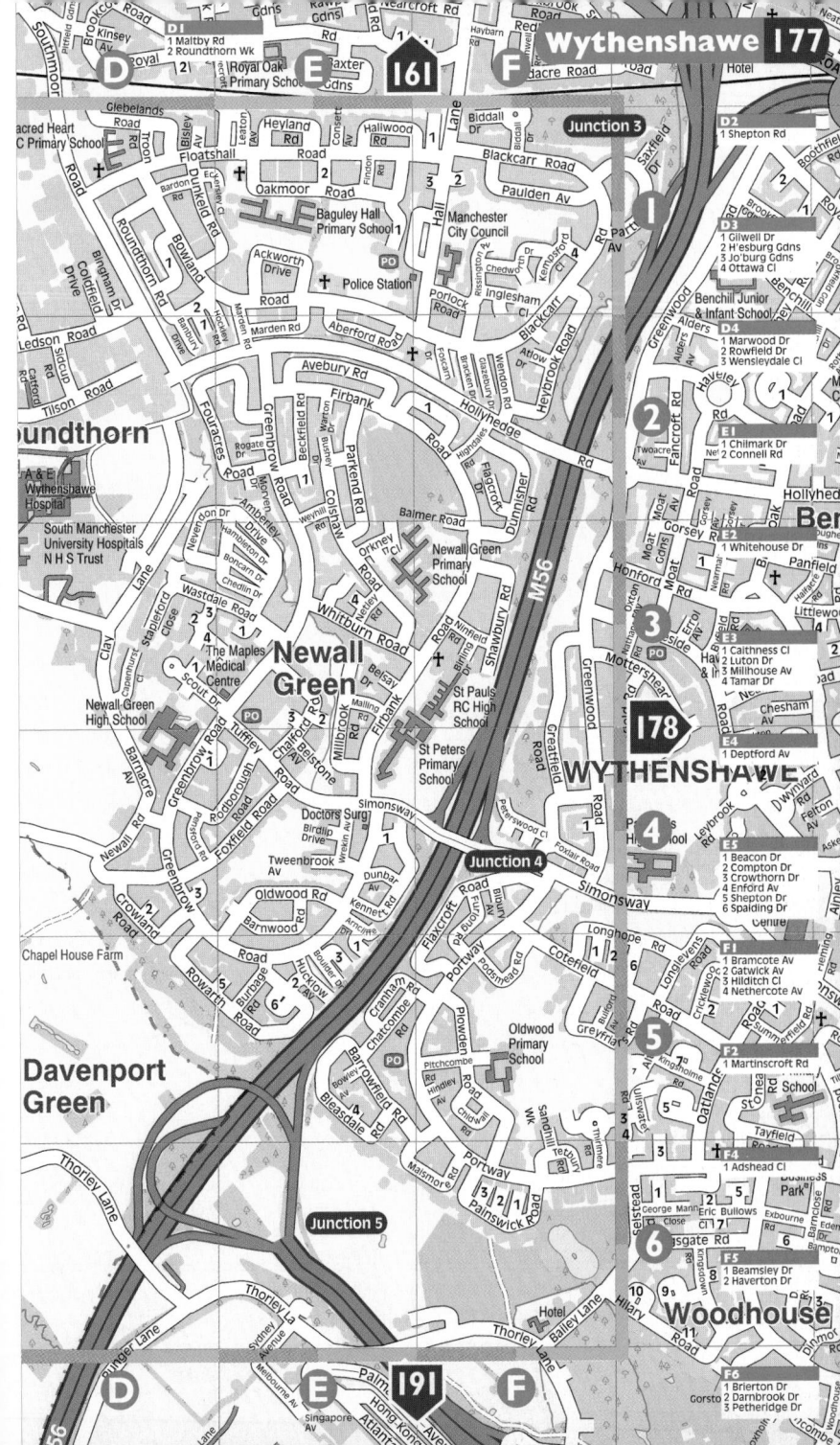

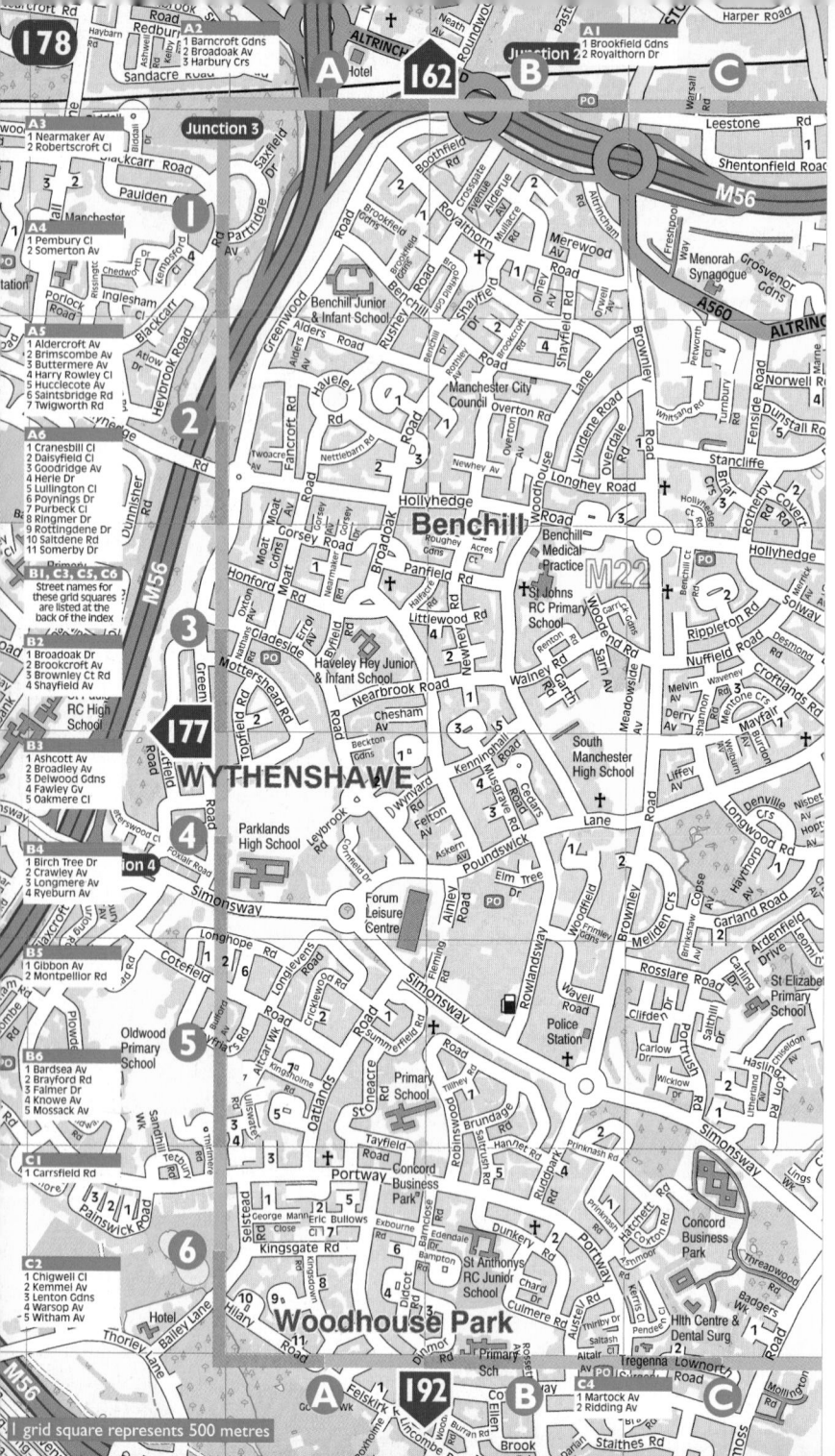

ALTRINCHAM

A2
1 Barncroft Gdns
2 Broadoak Av
3 Harbury Crs

A1
1 Brookfield Gdns
2 Royalthorn Dr

Junction 3

A3
1 Nearmaker Av
2 Robertscroft Cl

Leestone Rd

Shentonfield Road

M56

A4
1 Pembury Cl
2 Somerton Av

Menorah
Synagogue

A560

A5
1 Aldercroft Av
2 Brimscombe Av
3 Buttermere Av
4 Harry Rowley Cl
5 Hucclecote Av
6 Saintsbridge Rd
7 Twigworth Rd

Benchill Junior
& Infant School

Manchester City
Council

A6
1 Cranesbill Cl
2 Daisyfield Cl
3 Goodridge Av
4 Herle Dr
5 Lullington Cl
6 Poynings Dr
7 Purbeck Cl
8 Ringmer Dr
9 Rottingdene Dr
10 Saltdene Rd
11 Somerby Dr

Hollyhedge
Road

Benchill

B1, C3, C5, C6
street names for
these grid squares
are listed at the
back of the index

Benchill
Medical
Practice

M22

Hollyhedge

B2
1 Broadoak Dr
2 Brookcroft Av
3 Brownley Ct Rd
4 Shayfield Av

St Johns
RC Primary
School

Haveley Hey Junior
& Infant School

177

Nuffield Road

B3
1 Ashcott Av
2 Broadley Av
3 Delwood Gdns
4 Fawley Cv
5 Oakmere Cl

WYTHENSHAWE

South
Manchester
High School

B4
1 Birch Tree Dr
2 Crawley Av
3 Longmere Av
4 Ryeburn Av

Parklands
High School

B5
1 Gibbon Av
2 Montpellior Rd

Forum
Leisure
Centre

Longhope

Coterfield

St Elizabeth
Primary
School

Rosslare Road

B6
1 Bardsea Av
2 Brayford Rd
3 Falmer Dr
4 Knowe Av
5 Mossack Av

Oldwood
Primary
School

Simonsway

Police
Station

C1
1 Carrsfield Rd

Primary
School

Painswick Rd

Concord
Business
Park

C2
1 Chigwell Av
2 Kemmel Av
3 Lenton Gdns
4 Warsop Av
5 Witham Av

Tayfield
Road

Portway

Concord
Business
Park

Hotel

St Anthonys
RC Junior
School

Hlth Centre &
Dental Surg

Woodhouse Park

Kingsgate Rd

Eric Bullows
Close

M56

Thorley Lane

Bailey Lane

Primary
Sch

C4
1 Martock Av
2 Ridding Av

192

1 grid square represents 500 metres

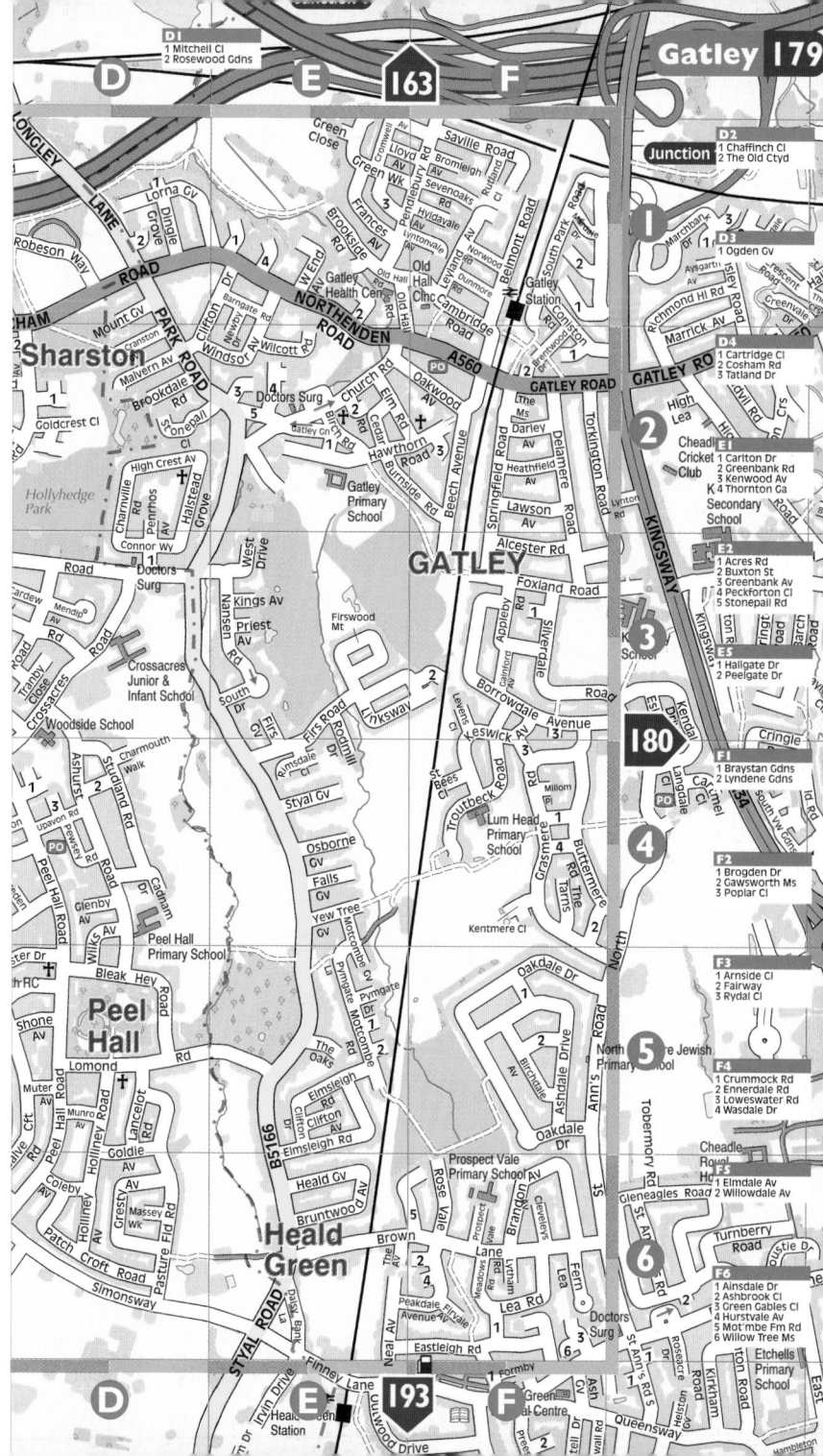

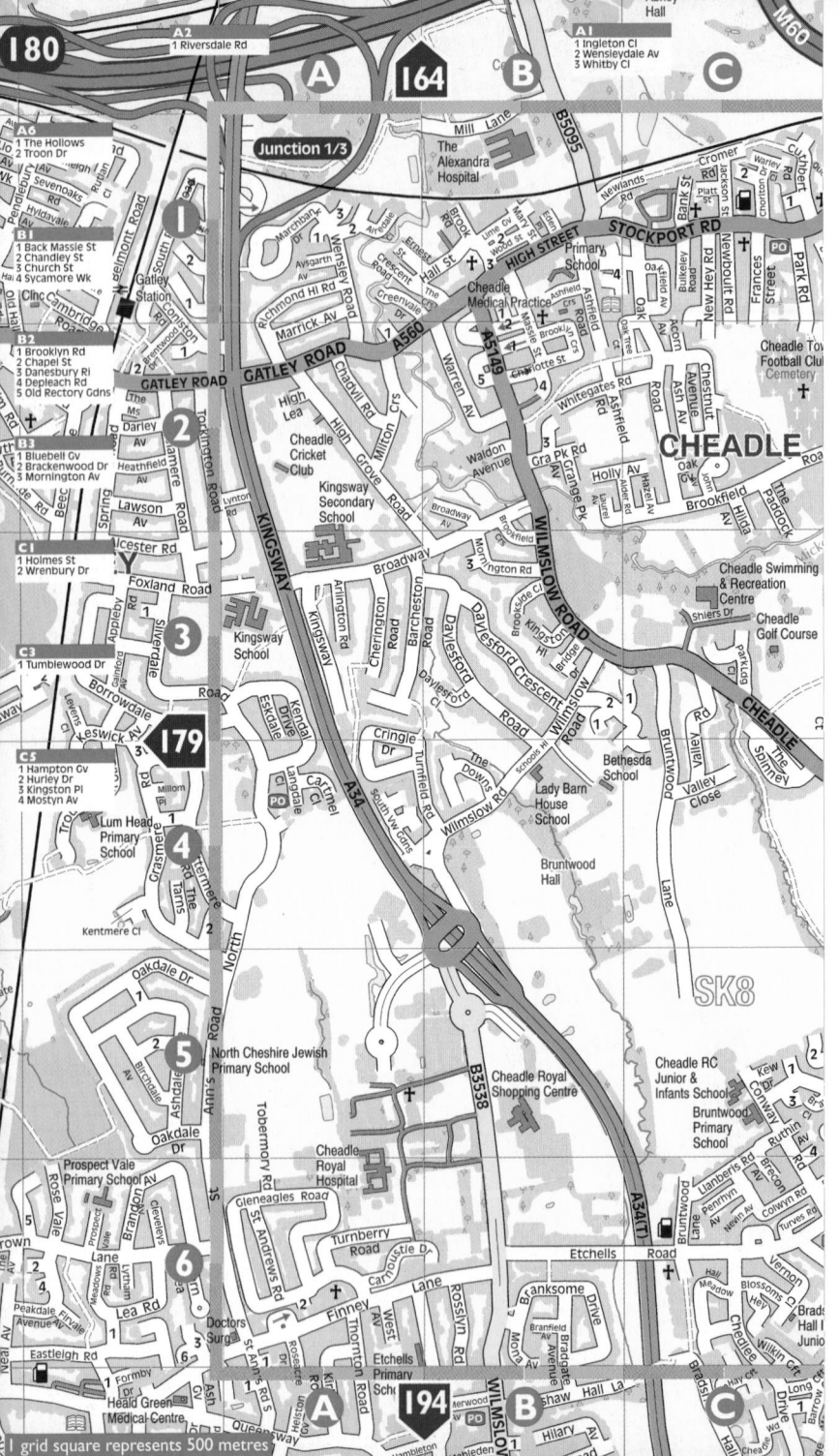

Junction 1/3

A2
1 Riversdale Rd

A1
1 Ingleton Cl
2 Wensleydale Av
3 Whitby Cl

A6
1 The Hollows
2 Troon Dr

B1
1 Back Massie St
2 Chandley St
3 Church St
4 Sycamore Wk

B2
1 Brooklyn Rd
2 Chapel St
3 Danesbury Rl
4 Deptach Rd
5 Old Rectory Gdns

B3
1 Bluebell Gv
2 Brackenwood Dr
3 Mornington Av

C1
1 Holmes St
2 Wrenbury Dr

C3
1 Tumblewood Dr

C5
1 Hampton Gv
2 Hurley Dr
3 Kingston Pl
4 Mostyn Av

1

2

179

3

4

5

6

The Alexandra Hospital

Mill Lane

STOCKPORT RD

Cromer

HIGH STREET

Cheadle Medical Practice

CHEADLE

Cheadle Town Football Club Cemetery

GATLEY ROAD

Cheadle Cricket Club

Kingsway Secondary School

Broadway

Cheadle Swimming & Recreation Centre

Cheadle Golf Course

CHEADLE

KINGSWAY

Kingsway School

Broadway

Davlesford Crescent

Wilmslow Rd

Bethesda School

Lady Barn House School

Lum Head Primary School

Kentmere Cl

Bruntwood Hall

SK8

Oakdale Dr

North Cheshire Jewish Primary School

Cheadle Royal Shopping Centre

Cheadle RC Junior & Infants School

Bruntwood Primary School

Oakdale Dr

Cheadle Royal Hospital

Prospect Vale Primary School

Gleneagles Road

Turnberry Road

Etchells Road

Doctors Surg

Eastleigh Rd

Finney Lane

Etchells Primary Sch

Heald Green Medical Centre

WILMSLOW RD

1 grid square represents 500 metres

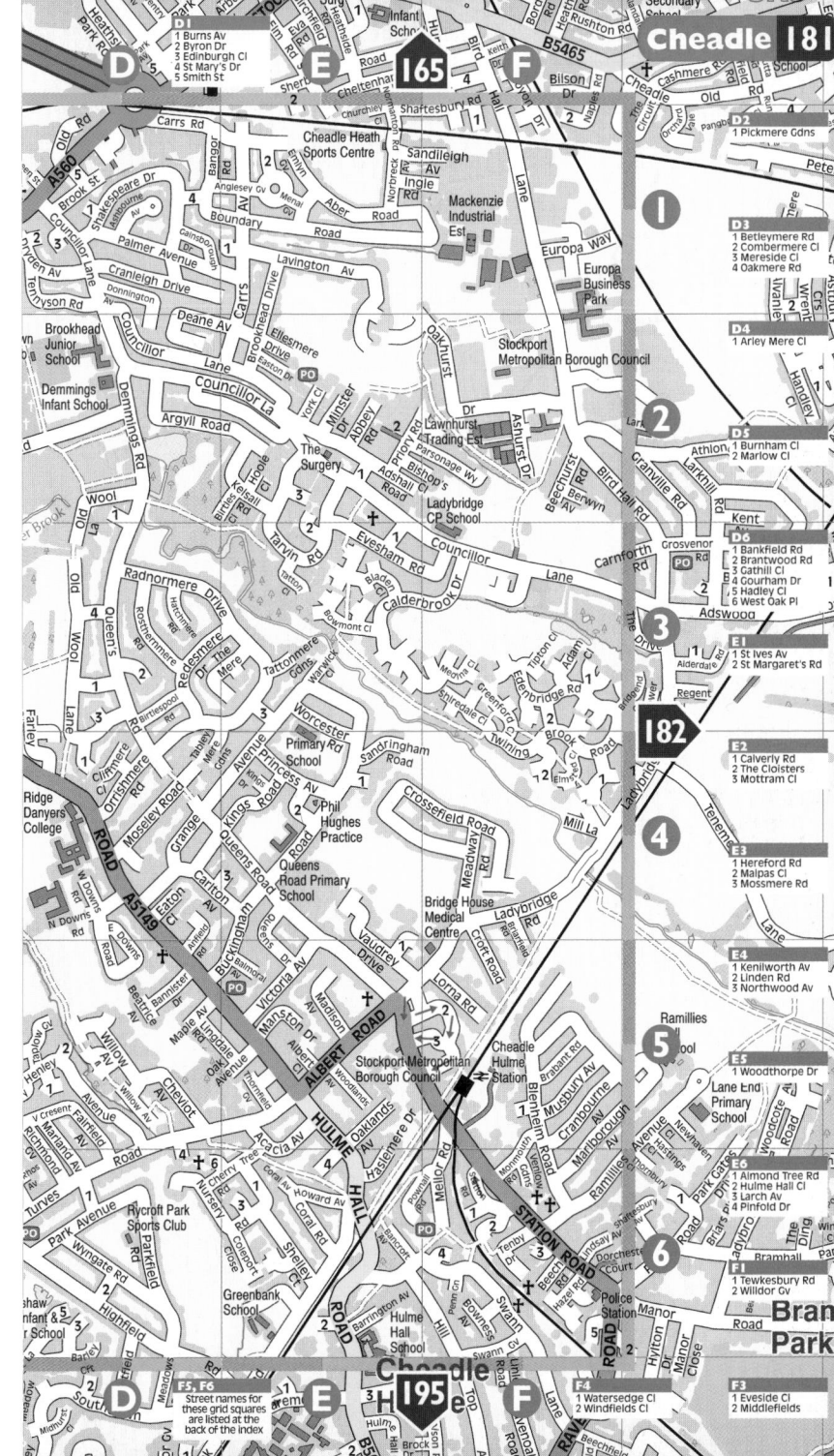

D
1 Burns Av
2 Byron Dr
3 Edinburgh Cl
4 St Mary's Dr
5 Smith St

165

D2
1 Pickmere Gdns

I

D3
1 Betleymere Rd
2 Combermere Cl
3 Mereside Cl
4 Oakmere Rd

D4
1 Arley Mere Cl

D5
1 Burnham Cl
2 Marlow Cl

D6
1 Bankfield Rd
2 Brantwood Rd
3 Gathill Cl
4 Gourham Dr
5 Hadley Cl
6 West Oak Pl

E1
1 St Ives Av
2 St Margaret's Rd

182

E2
1 Calverly Cl
2 The Cloisters
3 Mottram Cl

E3
1 Hereford Rd
2 Malpas Cl
3 Mossmere Rd

E4
1 Kenilworth Av
2 Linden Rd
3 Northwood Av

E5
1 Woodthorpe Dr

E6
1 Almond Tree Rd
2 Hulme Hall Cl
3 Larch Av
4 Pinfold Dr

F1
1 Tewkesbury Rd
2 Willdor Gv

Bram Park

F5, F6
Street names for
these grid squares
are listed at the
back of the index

F4
1 Watersedge Cl
2 Windfields Cl

F3
1 Eveside Cl
2 Middlefields

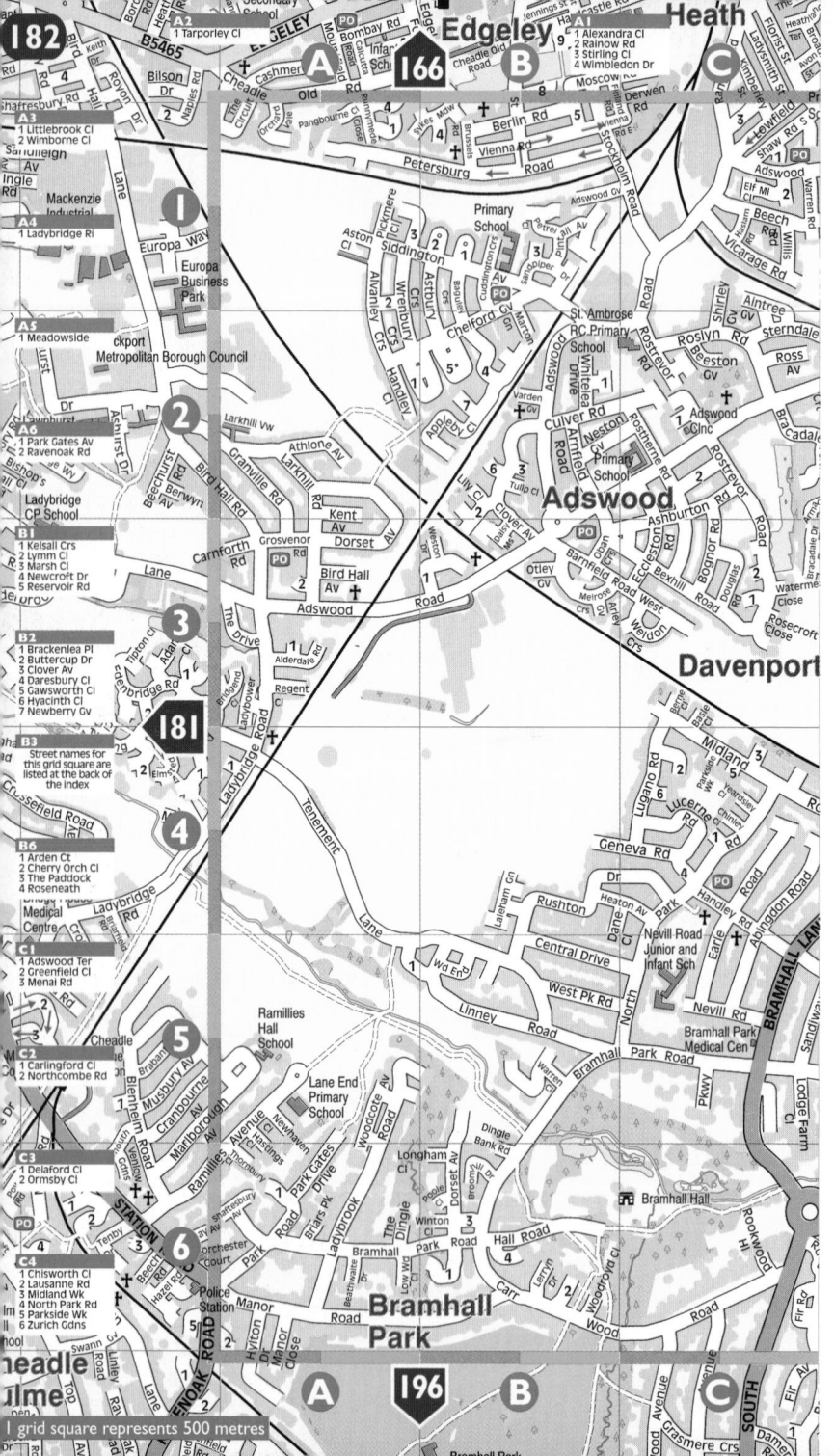

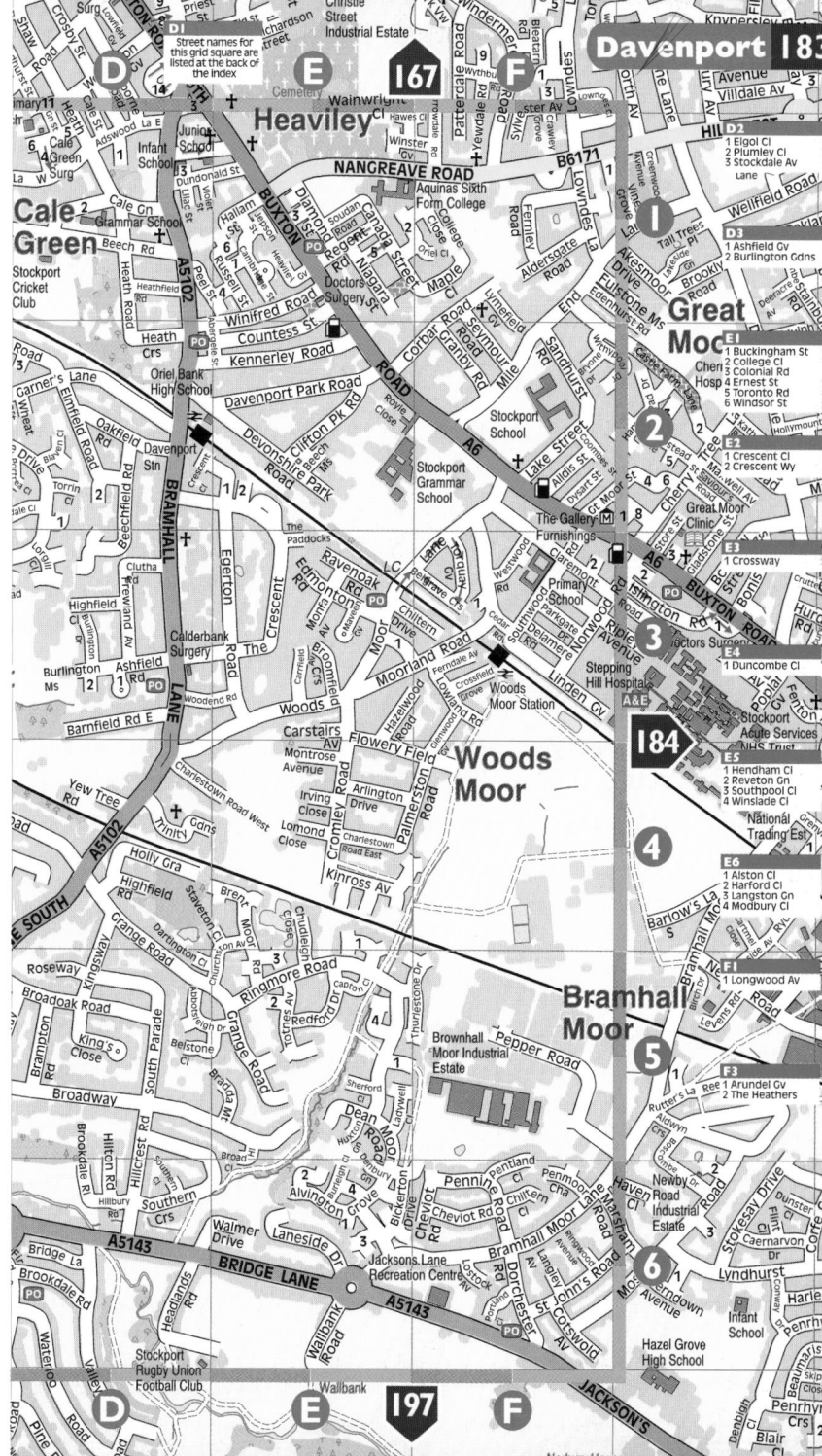

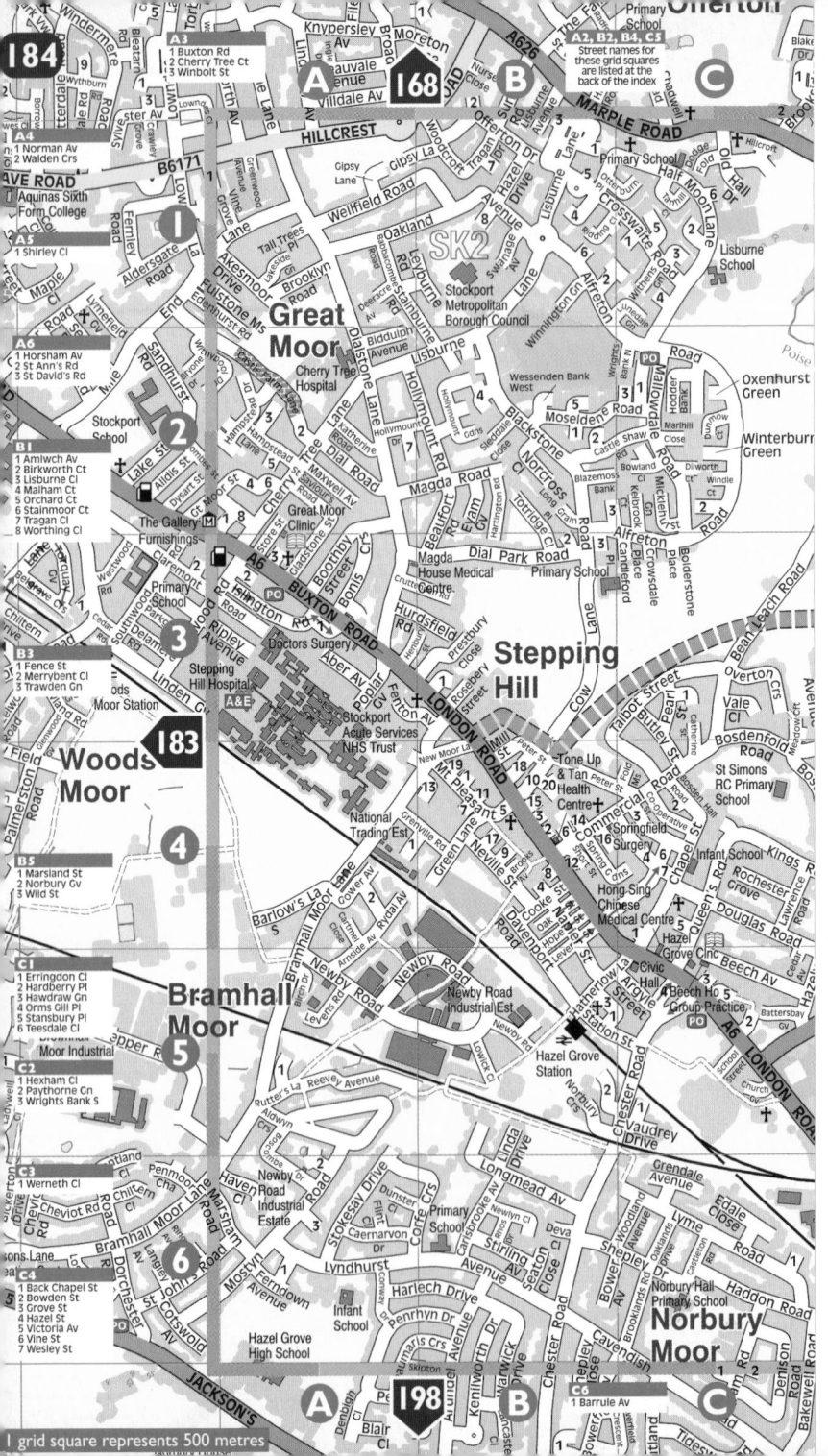

184

A3
1 Buxton Rd
2 Cherry Tree Ct
3 Winbolt St

168

A2, B2, B4, C5
Street names for these grid squares are listed at the back of the index

A4
1 Norman Av
2 Walden Crs

A5
1 Aquinas Sixth Form College

A6
1 Shirley Cl

HILLCREST

Gipsy Lane

Wellfield Road

Oakland

SK2

Stockport Metropolitan Borough Council

A6
1 Horsham Av
2 St Ann's Rd
3 St David's Rd

Stockport School

Cherry Tree Hospital

Wessenden Bank West

Oxenhurst Green

Moseldene Road

Winterburn Green

B1
1 Amiwch Av
2 Birkworth Ct
3 Lisburne Cl
4 Malham Ct
5 Orchard Ct
6 Stainmoor Ct
7 Tragan Cl
8 Worthing Cl

Lisburne School

Great Moor

The Gallery Furnishings

Great Moor Clinic

Magda Road

Dial Park Road

Magda House Medical Centre

Primary School

B3
1 Fence St
2 Merrybent Cl
3 Trawden Gn

183

Woods Moor

Stepping Hill Hospital

Doctors Surgery

Stepping Hill

Stockport Acute Services NHS Trust

National Trading Est

B5
1 Marsland St
2 Norbury Gv
3 Wild St

Tone Up & Tan

Health Centre

St Simons RC Primary School

Springfield Surgery

Infant School

C1
1 Errindon Cl
2 Hardberry Pl
3 Hawdraw Gn
4 Orms Gill Pl
5 Stansbury Pl
6 Teesdale Cl

Bramhall Moor

Bramhall Moor Industrial

Hong-Sing Chinese Medical Centre

Hazel Grove Clinic

Newby Road Industrial Est

Civic Hall

Beech Ho Group Practice

C2
1 Hexham Cl
2 Paythorne Gn
3 Wrights Bank S

Newby Road Industrial Estate

Hazel Grove Station

C3
1 Werneth Cl

Norbury Moor

Norbury Hall Primary School

C4
1 Back Chapel St
2 Bowden St
3 Grove St
4 Hazel St
5 Victoria Av
6 Vine St
7 Wesley St

Hazel Grove High School

Infant School

198

C6
1 Barrule Av

JACKSON'S

I grid square represents 500 metres

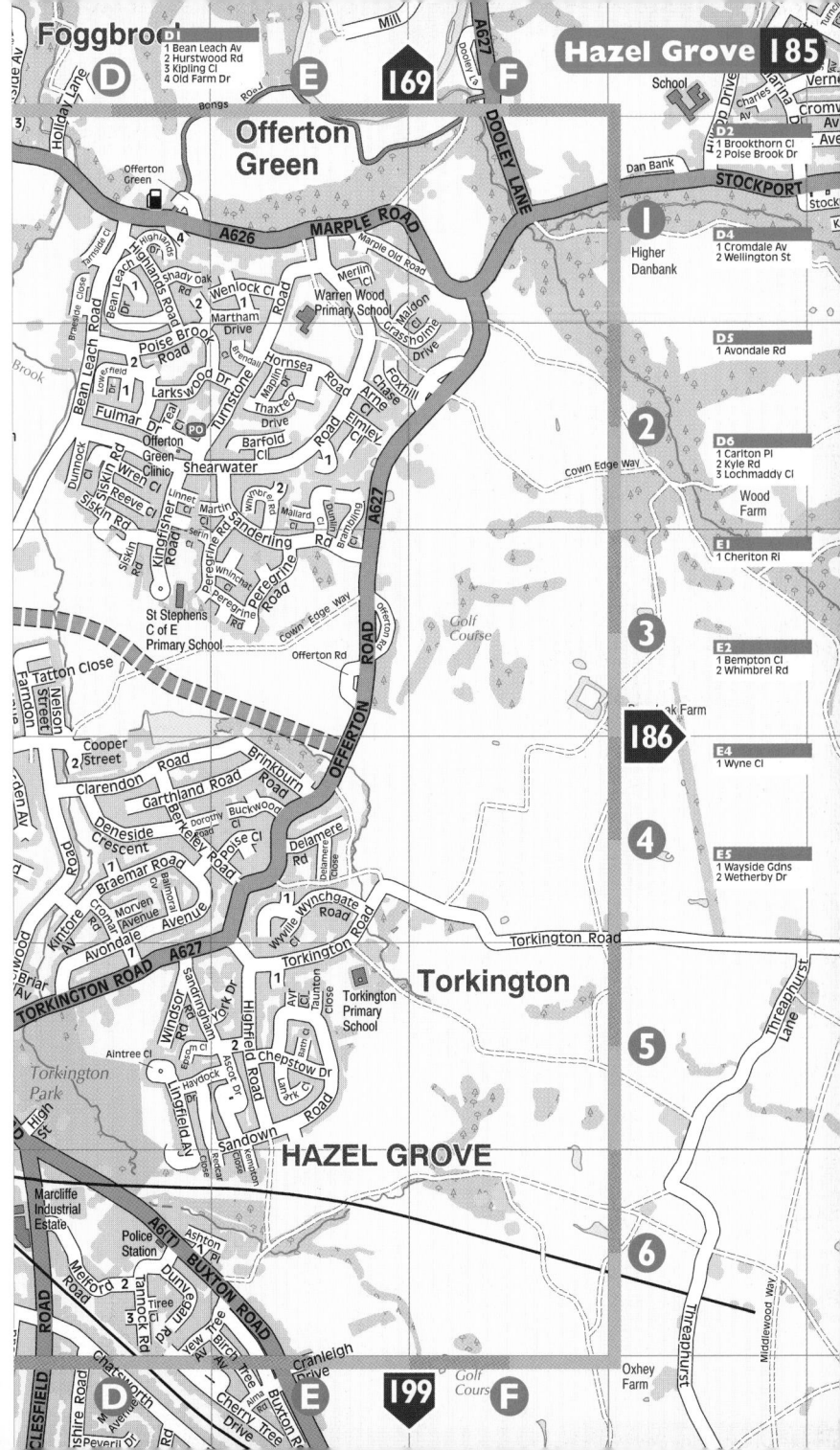

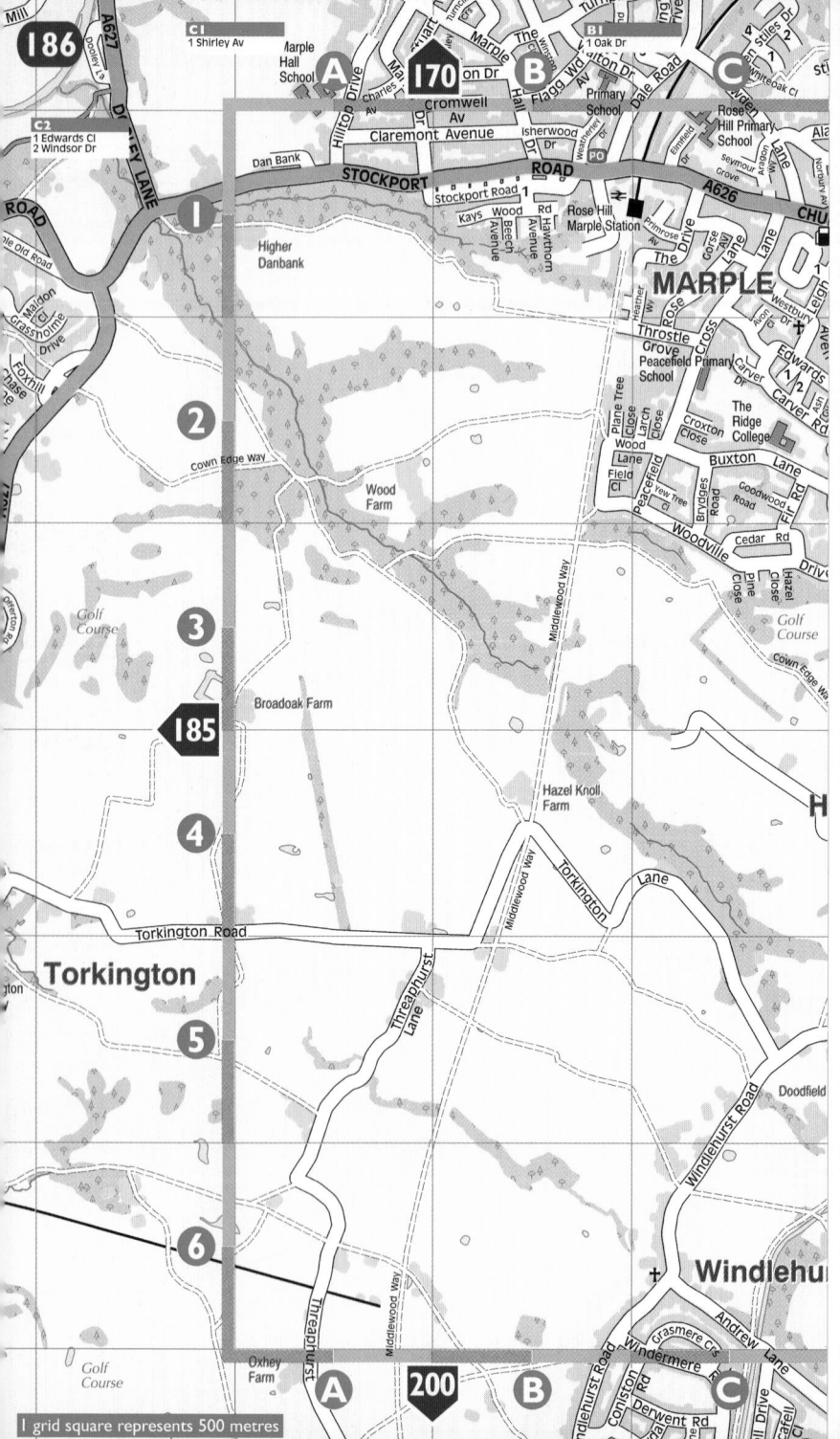

186

170

CI
1 Shirley Av

C2
1 Edwards Cl
2 Windsor Dr

B1
1 Oak Dr

Marple Hall School

A

Cromwell Av

Claremont Avenue

Primary School

Rose Hill Primary School

B

C

STOCKPORT

Dan Bank

Stockport Road

ROAD

Kays

A626

Rose Hill, Marple Station

Primrose

CHU

MARPLE

I

Higher Danbank

Wood

Beech Avenue

Hawthorn Avenue

Throstle Grove

Peacefield Primary School

Edwards

Carver Cl

2

Cown Edge Way

Wood Farm

Plane Tree Close

Larch Close

Wood Lane

Field Cl

Peacefield

Yew Tree Close

Croxton Close

The Ridge College

Buxton Lane

Bridges Close

Goodwood Cl

3

Golf Course

Broadoak Farm

Middlewood Way

Woodville

Cedar Rd

Pine Close

Golf Course

Cown Edge Wy

185

4

Hazel Knoll Farm

Torkington Lane

H

Torkington Road

New Broad Way

Torkington

Torkington

5

Threaphurst Lane

Middlewood Way

Windlehurst Road

Doodfield

6

Golf Course

Threaphurst Lane

Middlewood Way

Oxhey Farm

A

200

B

Windlehurst Road

Grasmere Crs

Windermere

Coniston Rd

Derwent Rd

Andrew Lane

Windlehu

C

I grid square represents 500 metres

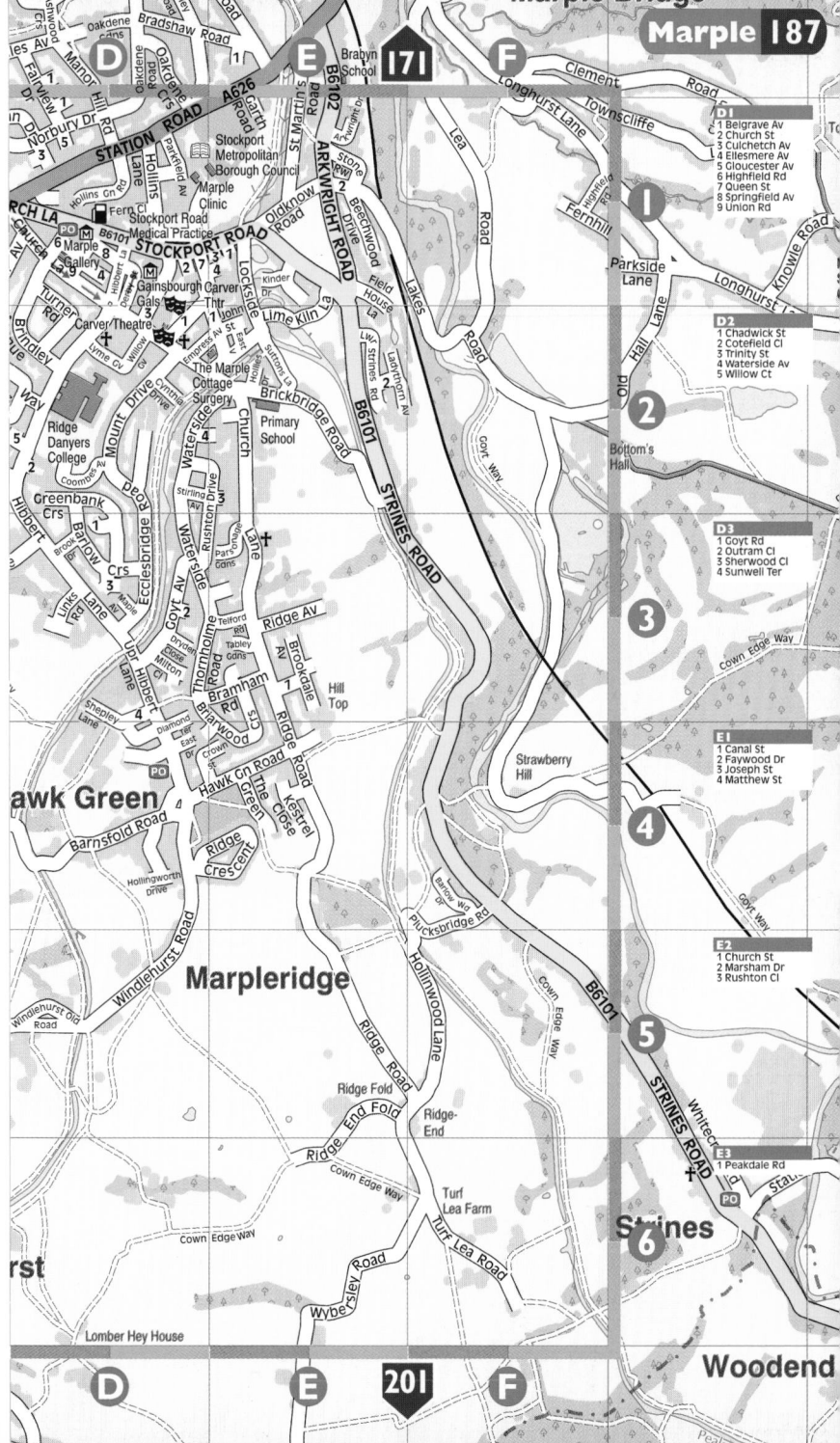

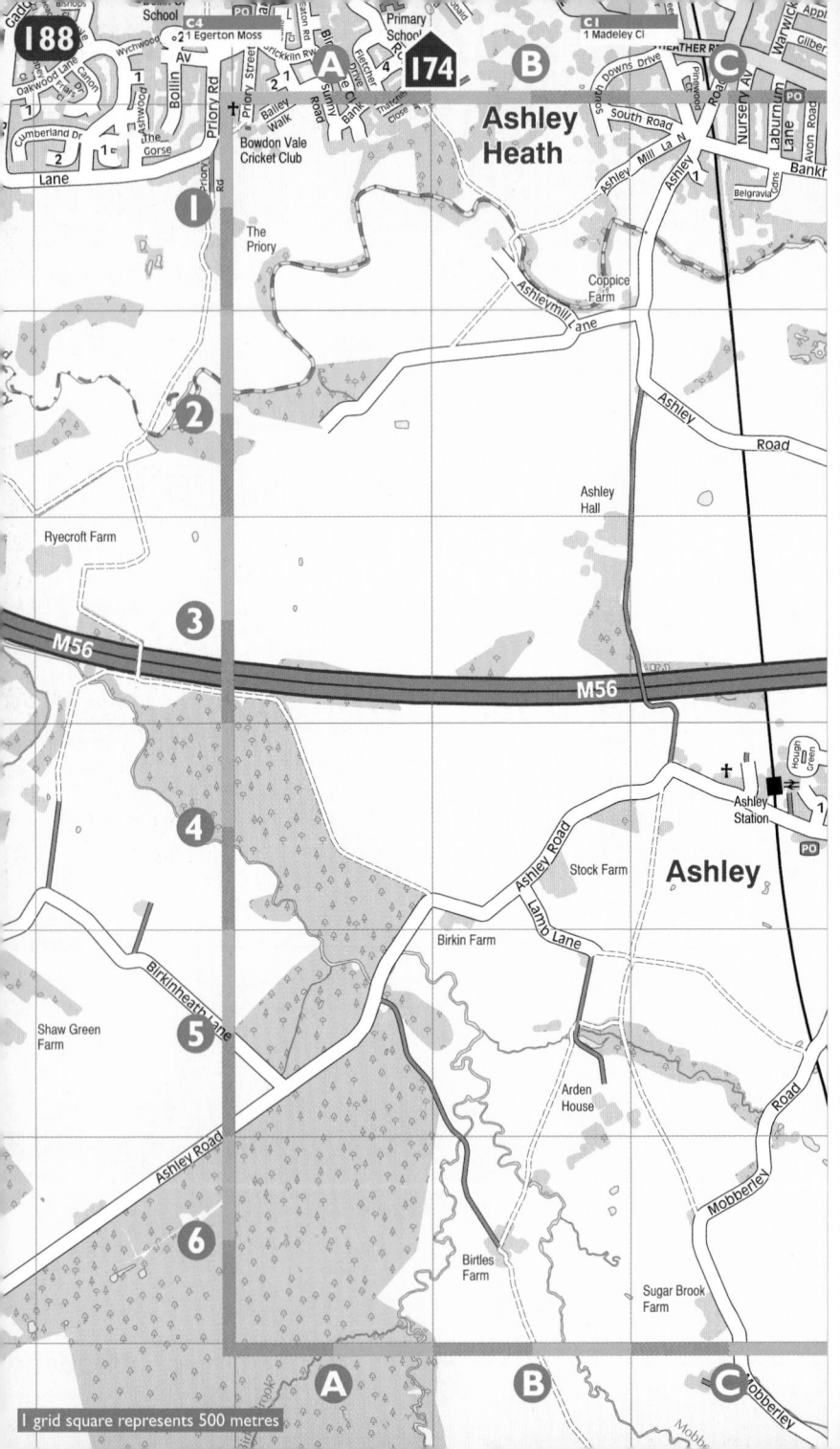

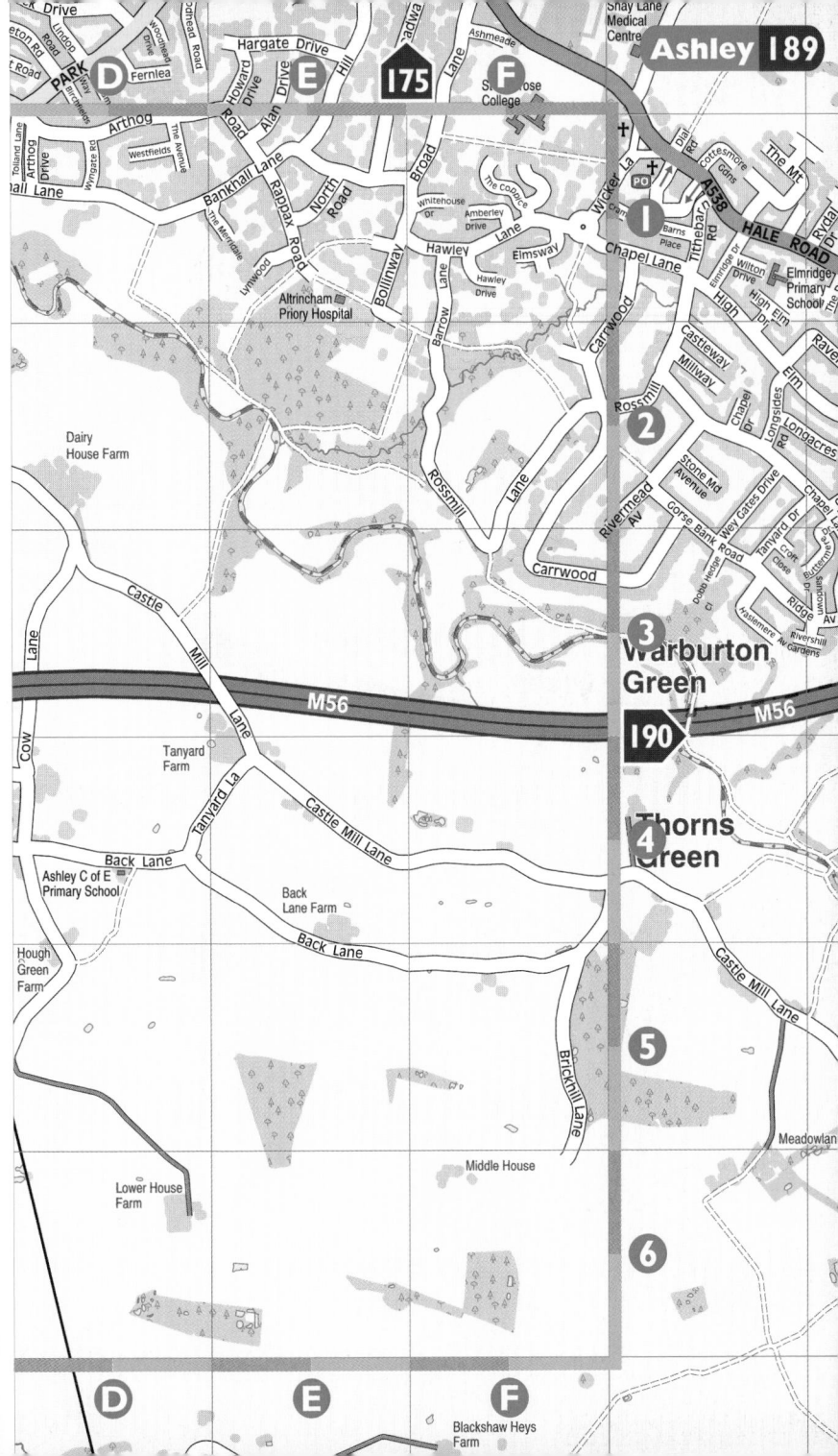

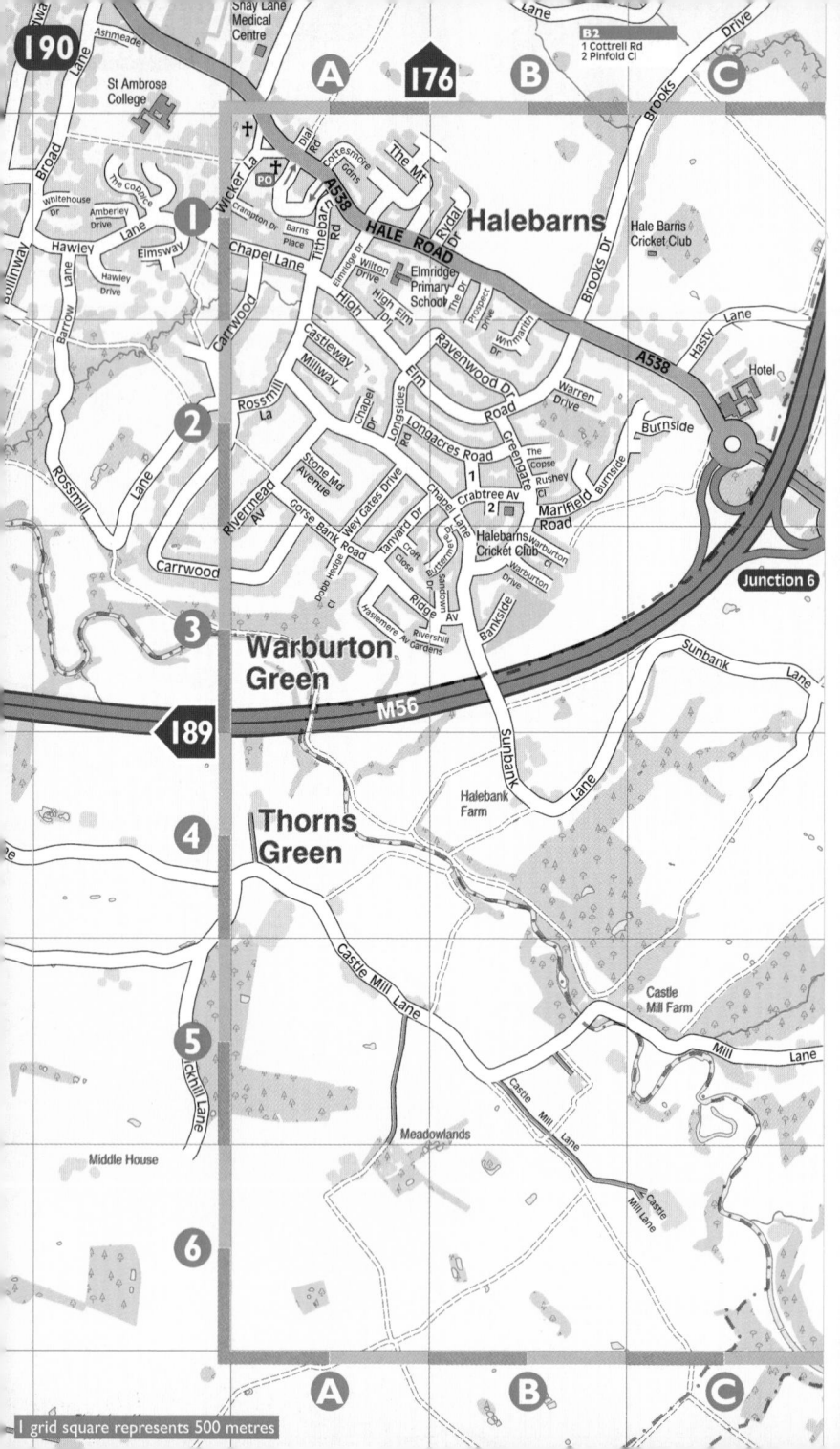

I grid square represents 500 metres

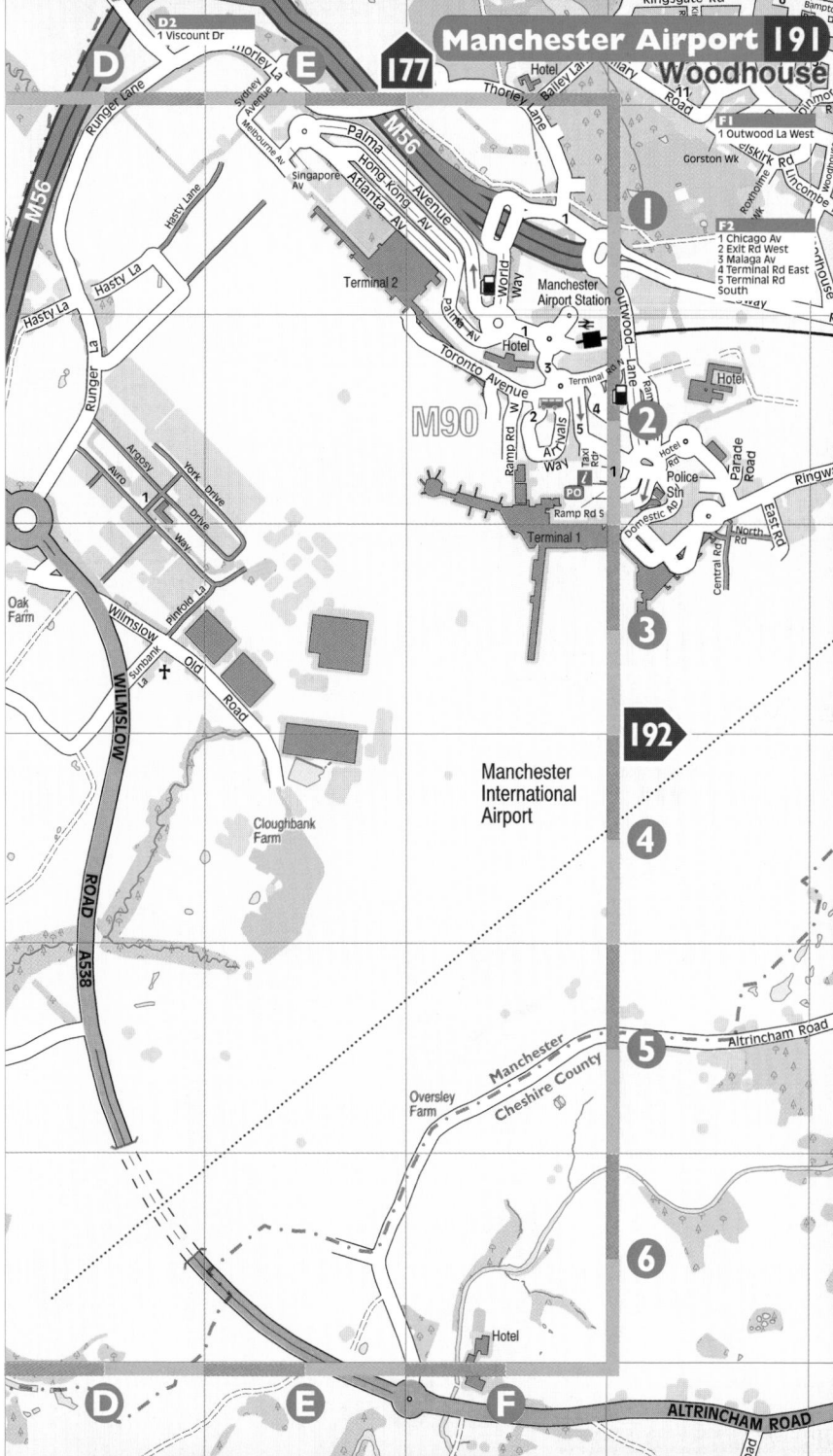

D2
1 Viscount Dr

177

F1
1 Outwood La West

F2
1 Chicago Av
2 Exit Rd West
3 Malaga Av
4 Terminal Rd East
5 Terminal Rd
South

Kingsgate Rd
Bampton
Hotel
Thorley Lane
Bailey Lane
11
Dinmor

M56
Palma Avenue
Hong Kong Av
Atlanta Av
Singapore Av
Sydney Avenue
Melbourne Av
Thorley La
Runger Lane

M56

Gorston Wk
Roxholme Rd
Lincombe
ciskirk Rd
Woodhouse

I

Terminal 2

Manchester
Airport Station

Hasty La
Hasty Lane
Hasty La
Runger La

M90

World Way
Palma Av
Hotel
Toronto Avenue

Ramp Rd W
Terminal
2
Arrivals
Way
Taxi
Rd
PO
Ramp Rd S
Terminal 1

Outwood Lane

Ramp

Hotel

Hotel
Parade Road
Ringwa

Police
Stn

Domestic Ap

East Rd

North
Rd

Central Rd

2

3

Oak
Farm
Argosy
Drive
Avro
York Drive
Way
Piatfold La
Wilmslow
Old
Road
Suncany
Way

WILMSLOW
ROAD
A538

Cloughbank
Farm

Manchester
International
Airport

192

4

5
Altrincham Road

Manchester
Cheshire County

Oversley
Farm

6

Hotel

D   E   F   ALTRINCHAM ROAD

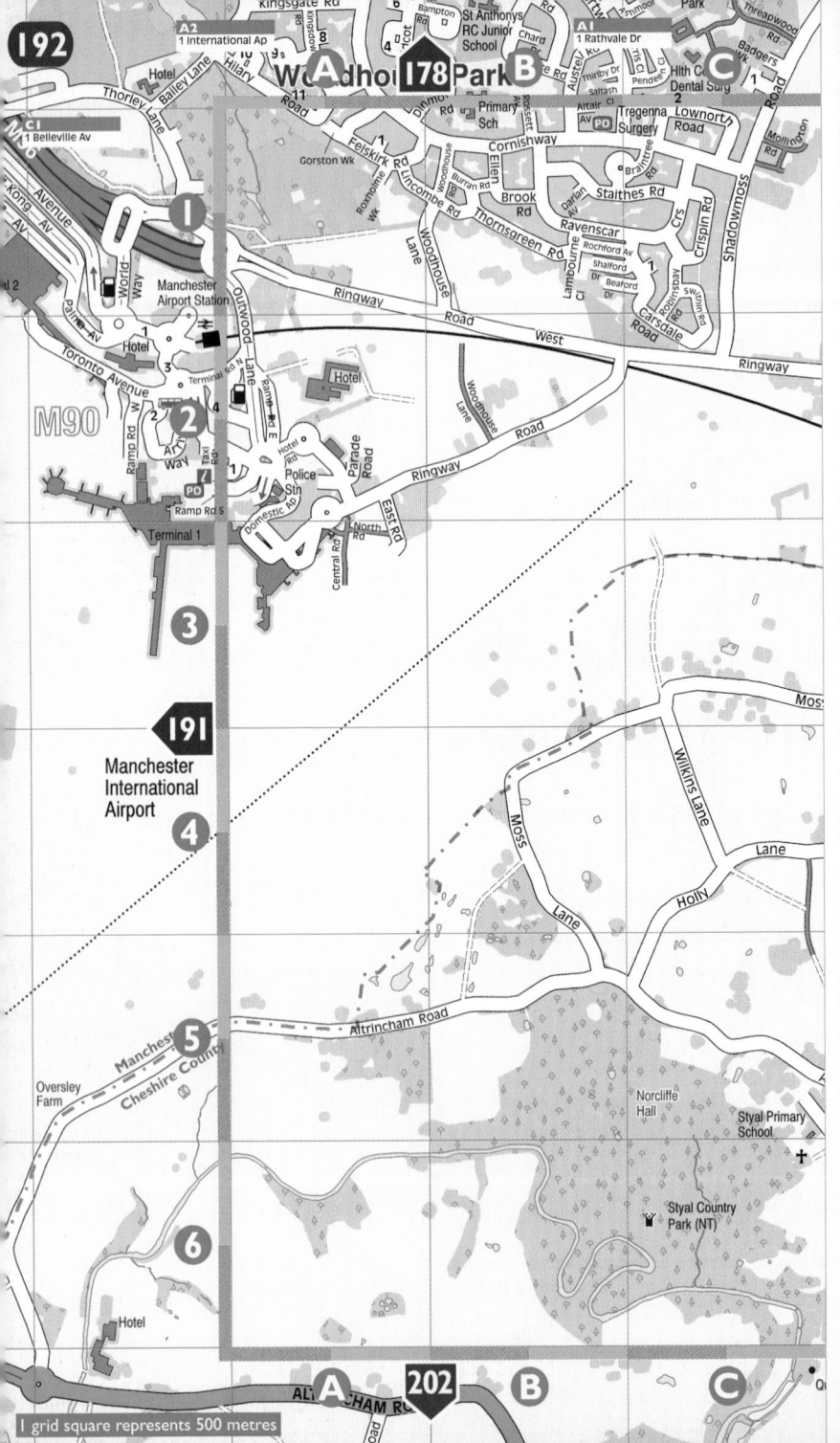

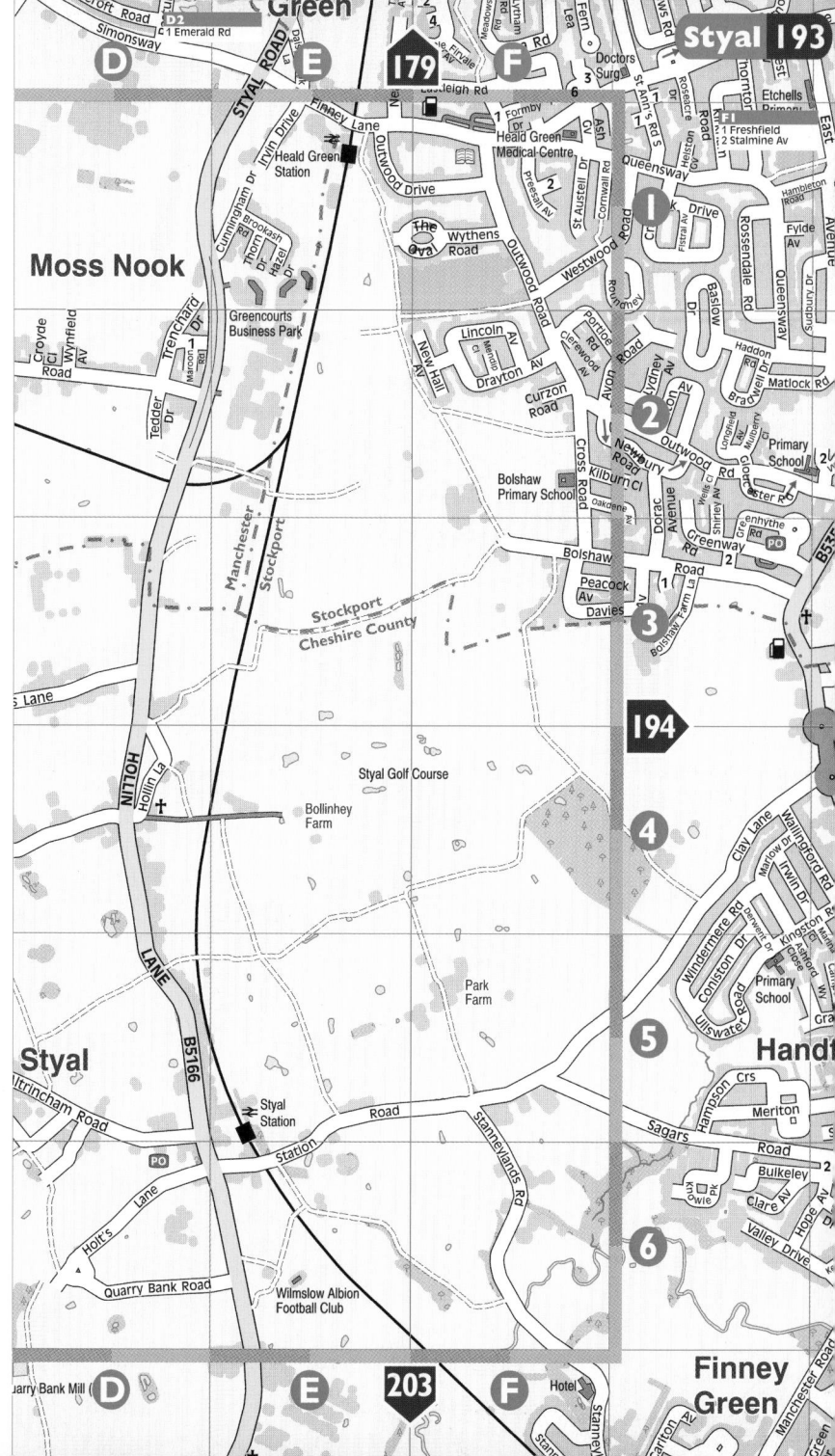

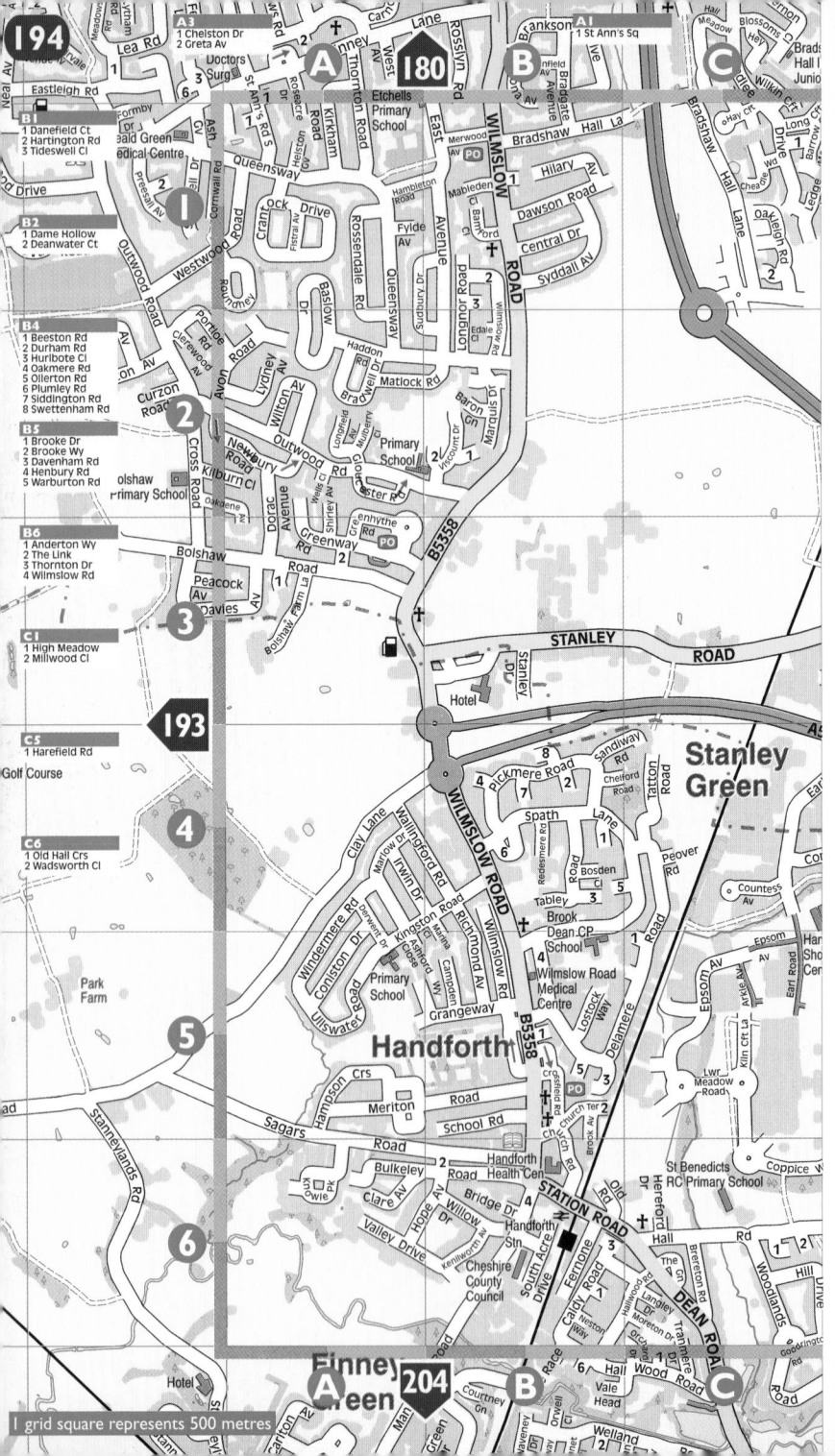

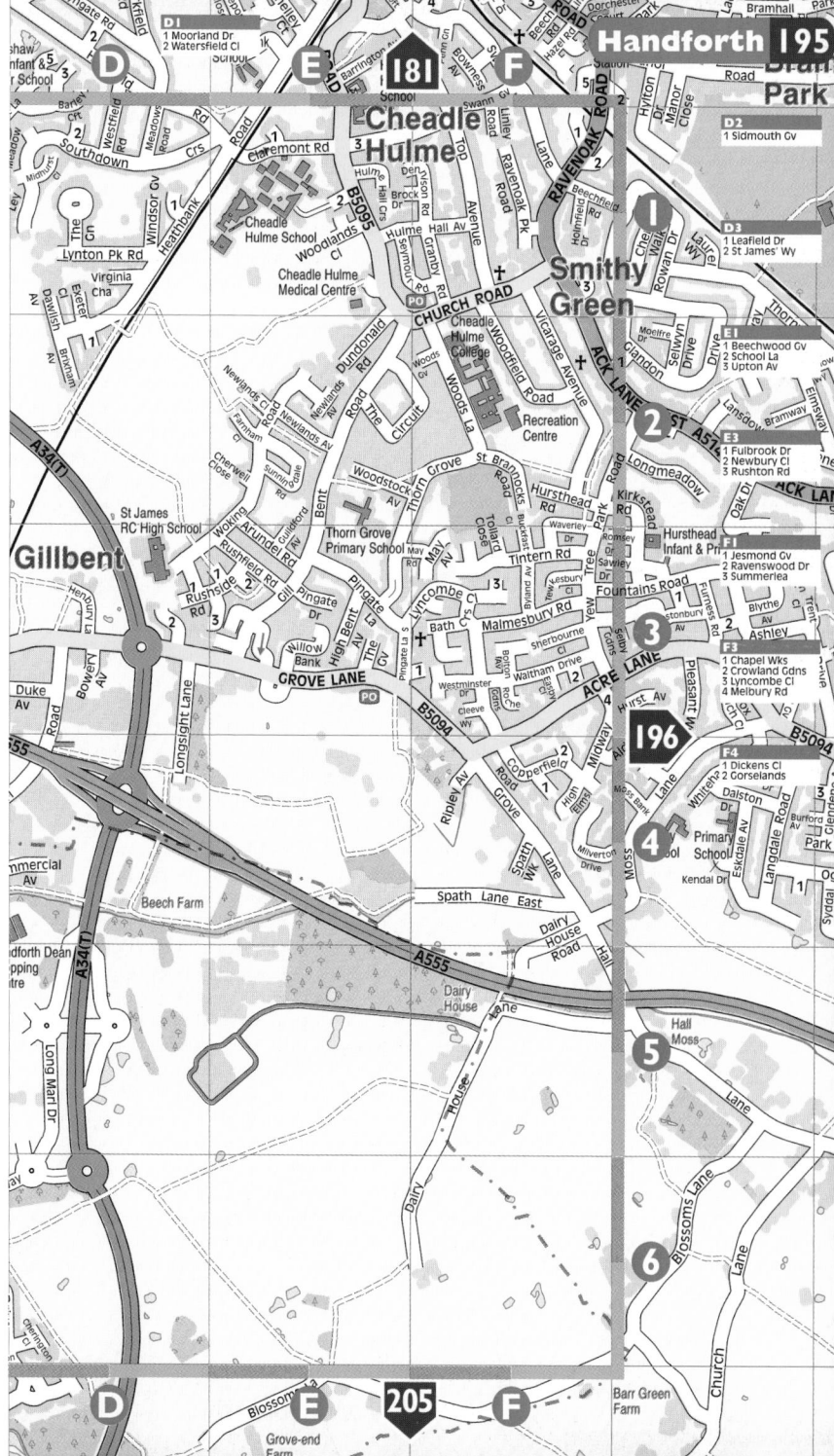

D1
1 Moorland Dr
2 Watersfield Cl

D **E** **181** **F**

Bram Park

D2
1 Sidmouth Gv

D3
1 Leafield Dr
2 St James' Wy

Cheadle Hulme

Cheadle Hulme School

Woodlands Cl

Cheadle Hulme Medical Centre

CHURCH ROAD

I

Smithy Green

E1
1 Beechwood Gv
2 School La
3 Upton Av

Cheadle Hulme College

2 **ST A5149**

E3
1 Fulbrook Dr
2 Newbury Cl
3 Rushton Rd

Dundonald Rd

The Circuit

Newlands Cl

Newlands Av

Recreation Centre

Woodstock Av

Bent

St Brannocks

Thorn Grove

Hursthead Rd

Waverley

Kirkstead Rd

Longmeadow

F1
1 Jesmond Gv
2 Ravenswood Dr
3 Summeriea

Hursthead Infant & Pri

Gillbent

St James RC High School

Woking Rd

Arundel Rd

Rushside Rd

Pingate Dr

Pingate La

Thorn Grove Primary School

May Av

Tintern Rd

Lyncombe Cl

Malmesbury Rd

Bath Cres

Fountains Rd

Sawley

Ashley

F2
1 Chapel Wks
2 Crowland Gdns
3 Lyncombe Cl
4 Melbury Rd

3 ACRE LANE

Willow Bank

High Bent Av

GROVE LANE

Waltham Drive

Westminster Dr

Cleeve Wy

B5094

Copperfield Rd

196

F4
1 Dickens Cl
2 Gorselands

Duke Av

Bower Av

Longsight Lane

Ripley Av

Grove

Spath Wk

Spath Lane

Moss Bank

Milverton Drive

Dalston Dr

Eskdale Av

Kendal Dr

Primary School

Langdale Road

Burford Av

Glendene Av

Park

4

B5094

mmercial Av

A34(T)

Beech Farm

Spath Lane East

Dairy House Road

A555

Dairy House Lane

Dairy House

ndforth Dean pping ntre

Long Marl Dr

Hall Moss

5

Lane

Dairy House

6

Blossoms Lane

Church Lane

D Blossom **E** **205** **F**

Grove-end Farm

Barr Green Farm

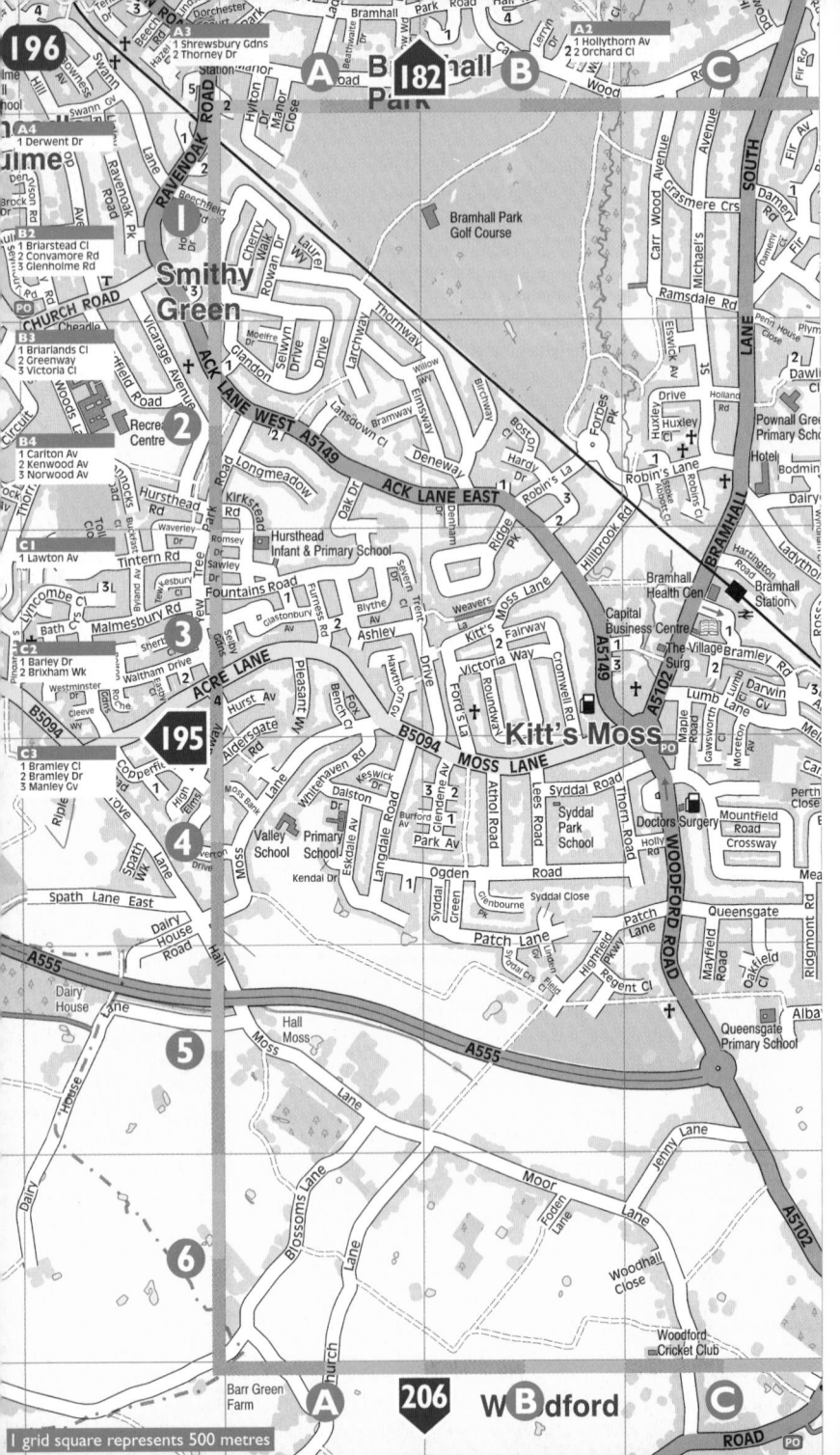

182

Bramhall Park

182

A B B C

A2
1 Hollythorn Av
2 2 Orchard Cl

A4
1 Derwent Dr

Smithy Green

Bramhall Park Golf Course

B2
1 Briarstead Cl
2 Convamore Rd
3 Glenholme Rd

CHURCH ROAD

B3
1 Briarlands Cl
2 Greenway
3 Victoria Cl

Recreation Centre

ACK LANE WEST A5149

Pownall Green Primary School

B4
1 Carlton Av
2 Kenwood Av
3 Norwood Av

Hurstead Rd

ACK LANE EAST

C1
1 Lawton Av

Tintern Rd

Hurstead Infant & Primary School

Fountains Road

Bramhall Health Cen

C2
1 Barley Dr
2 Brixham Wk

Malmesbury Rd

Waltham Drive

Bramhall Station

ACRE LANE

Capital Business Centre

The Village Surg

195

B5094

Kitt's Moss

C3
1 Bramley Cl
2 Bramley Dr
3 Manley Gv

MOSS LANE

Syddal Park School

Valley School

Primary School

Doctors Surgery

Mountfield Road Crossway

Spath Lane East

Syddal Close

WOODFORD ROAD

Dairy House Road

Ogden Road

Queensgate

Patch Lane

A555

Queensgate Primary School

Dairy House

Hall Moss

A555

Moss Lane

Moor Lane

Jenny Lane

A5102

Blossoms Lane

Foden Lane

Woodhall Close

Woodford Cricket Club

Church Road

Barr Green Farm

A **206** W**B**dford

C

ROAD

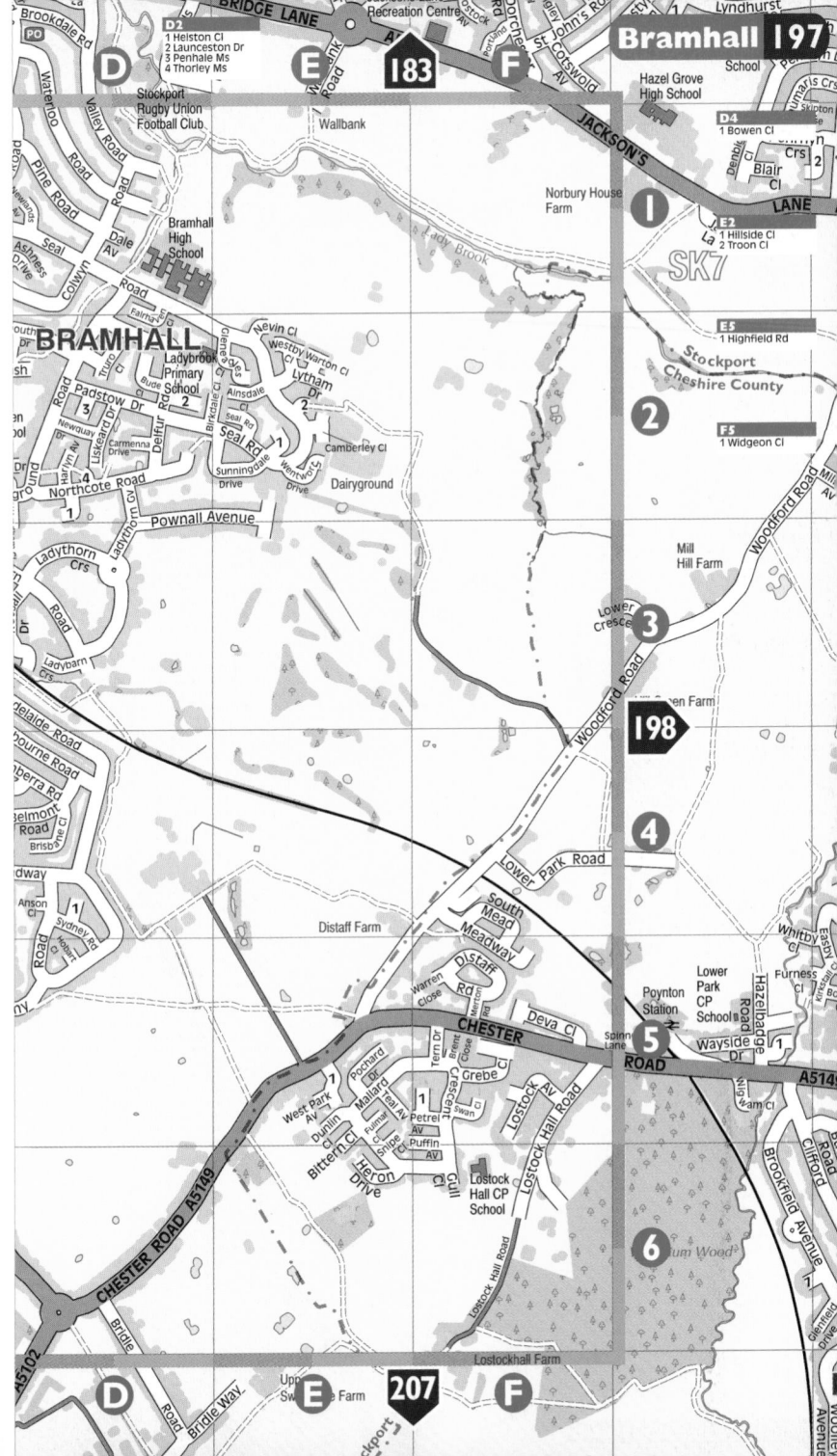

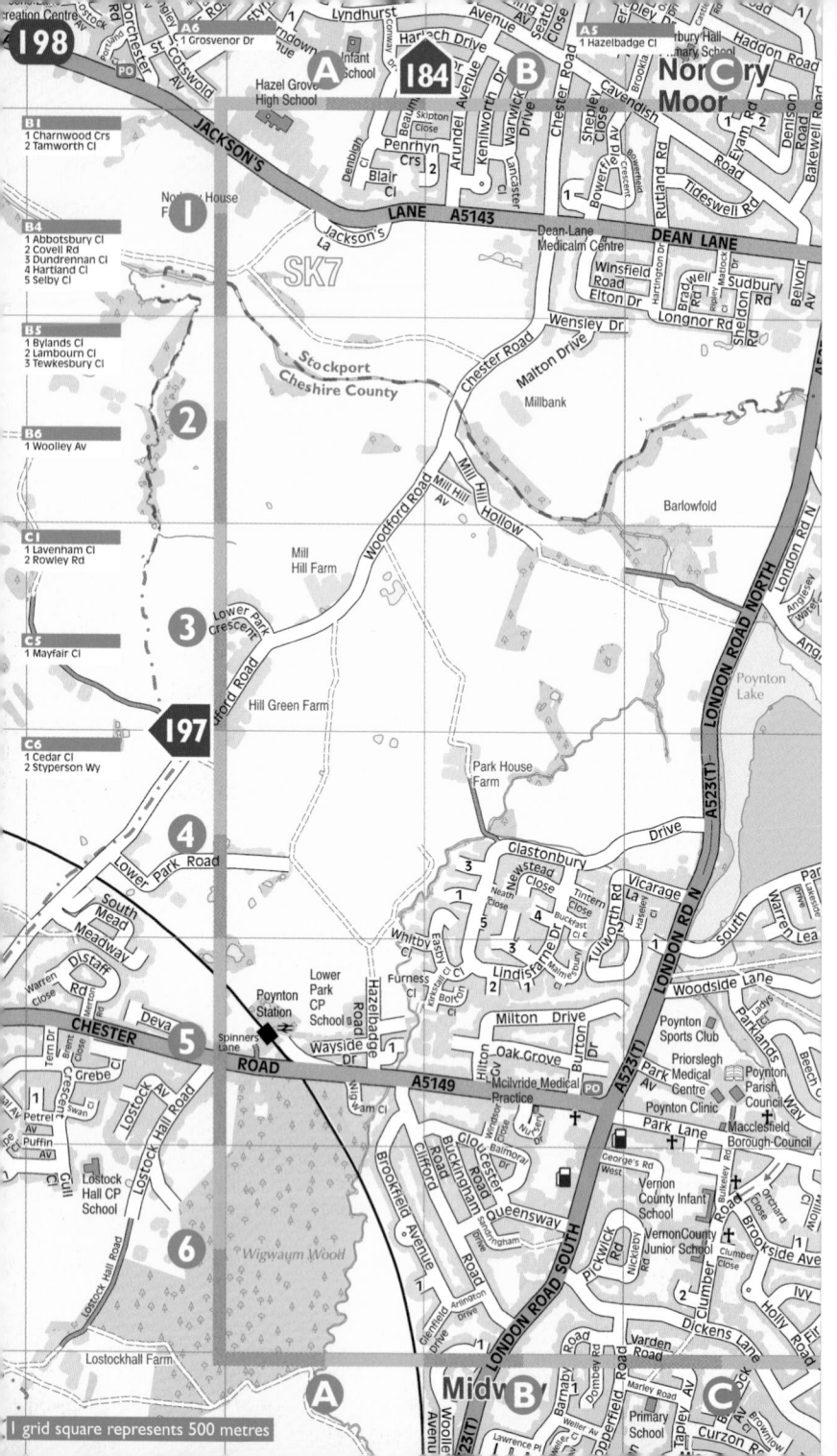

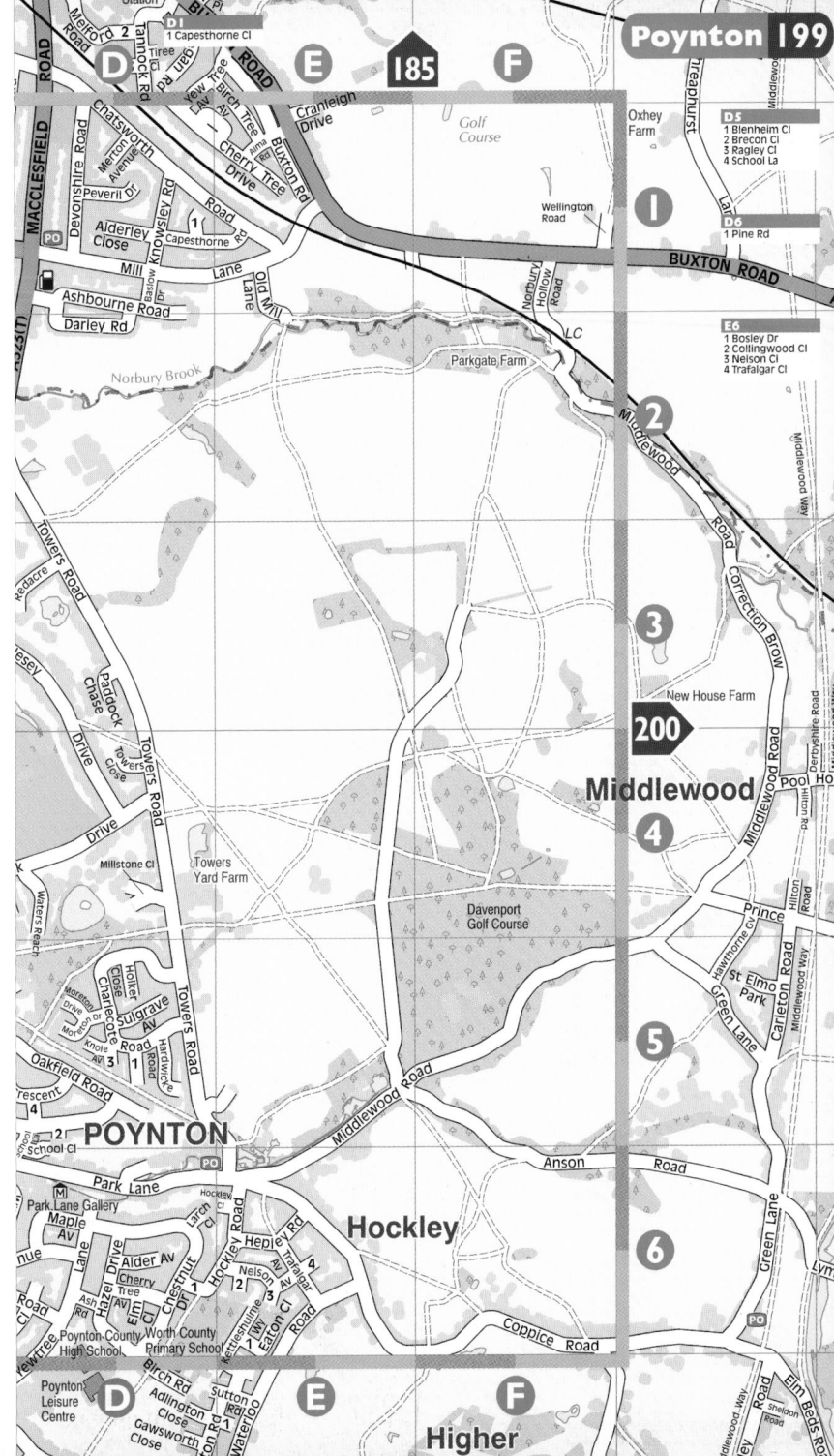

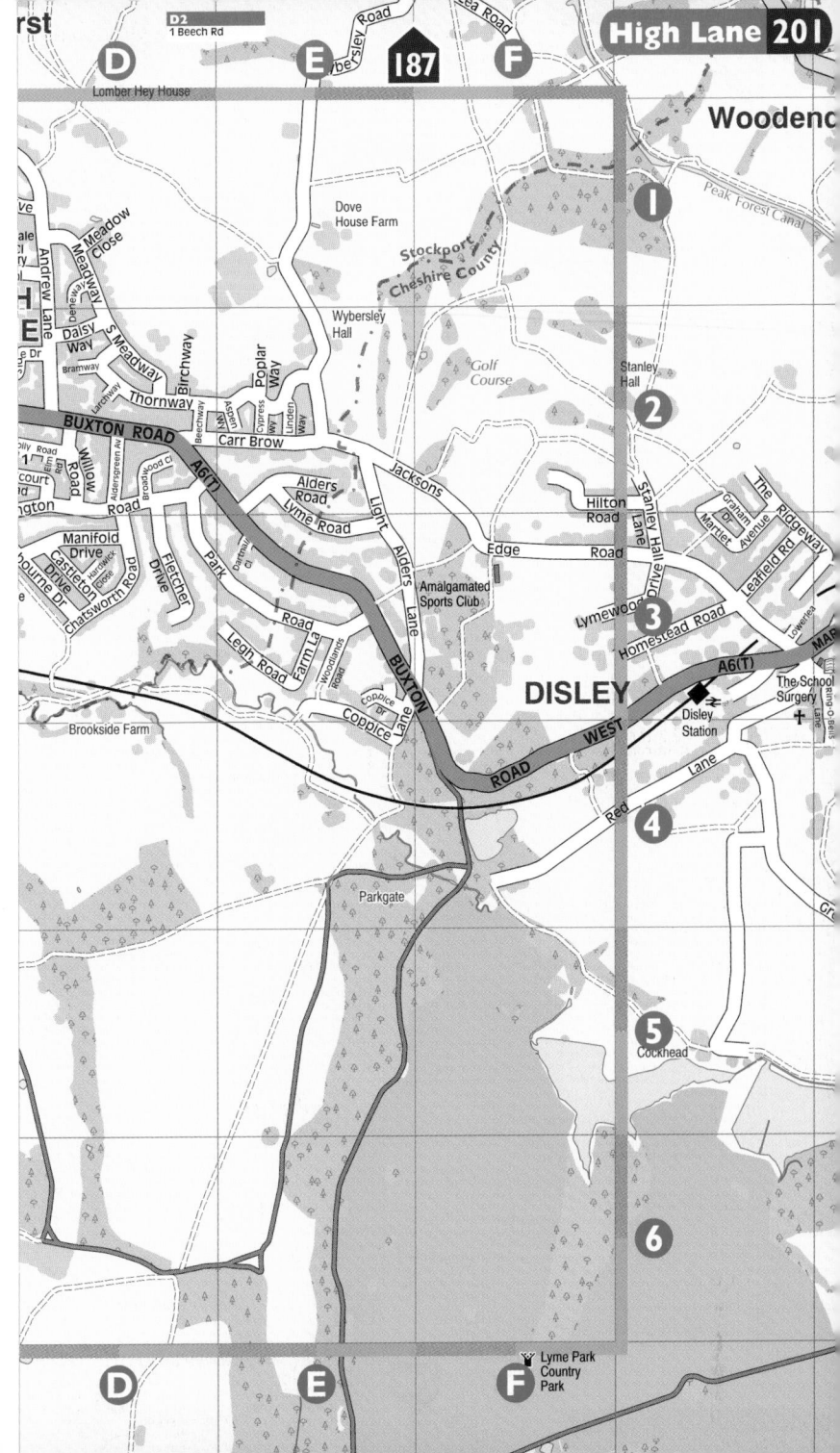

DISLEY

Woodend

Peak Forest Canal

Lomber Hey House

Dove House Farm

Stockport Cheshire County

Wybersley Hall

Golf Course

Stanley Hall

Meadow Close

Andrew Lane

Meadway

Daisy Way

Bramway

Birchway

Thornway

Poplar Way

Linden Way

Cypress

BUXTON ROAD

Carr Brow

Jacksons

Hilton Road

Stanley Hall Drive

Stanley Hall Lane

The Ridgeway

Graham Avenue

Martlet

Leafield Rd

Willow Road

Aldengreen Av

Brookfield

Alders Road

Lyme Road

Light Alders Lane

Edge Road

Lymewood

Homestead Road

Lowerfield

MAR

Manifold Drive

Castleton Drive

Chatsworth Road

Fletcher Drive

Park Road

Legh Road

Farm La

Woodlands Road

Coppice Lane

BUXTON ROAD

Amalgamated Sports Club

Edge Road

A6(T)

The School

Surgery

Brookside Farm

Coppice

ROAD WEST

Disley Station

DISLEY

Red Lane

Ring-O-Bells Lane

Parkgate

Cockhead

Gr

Lyme Park Country Park

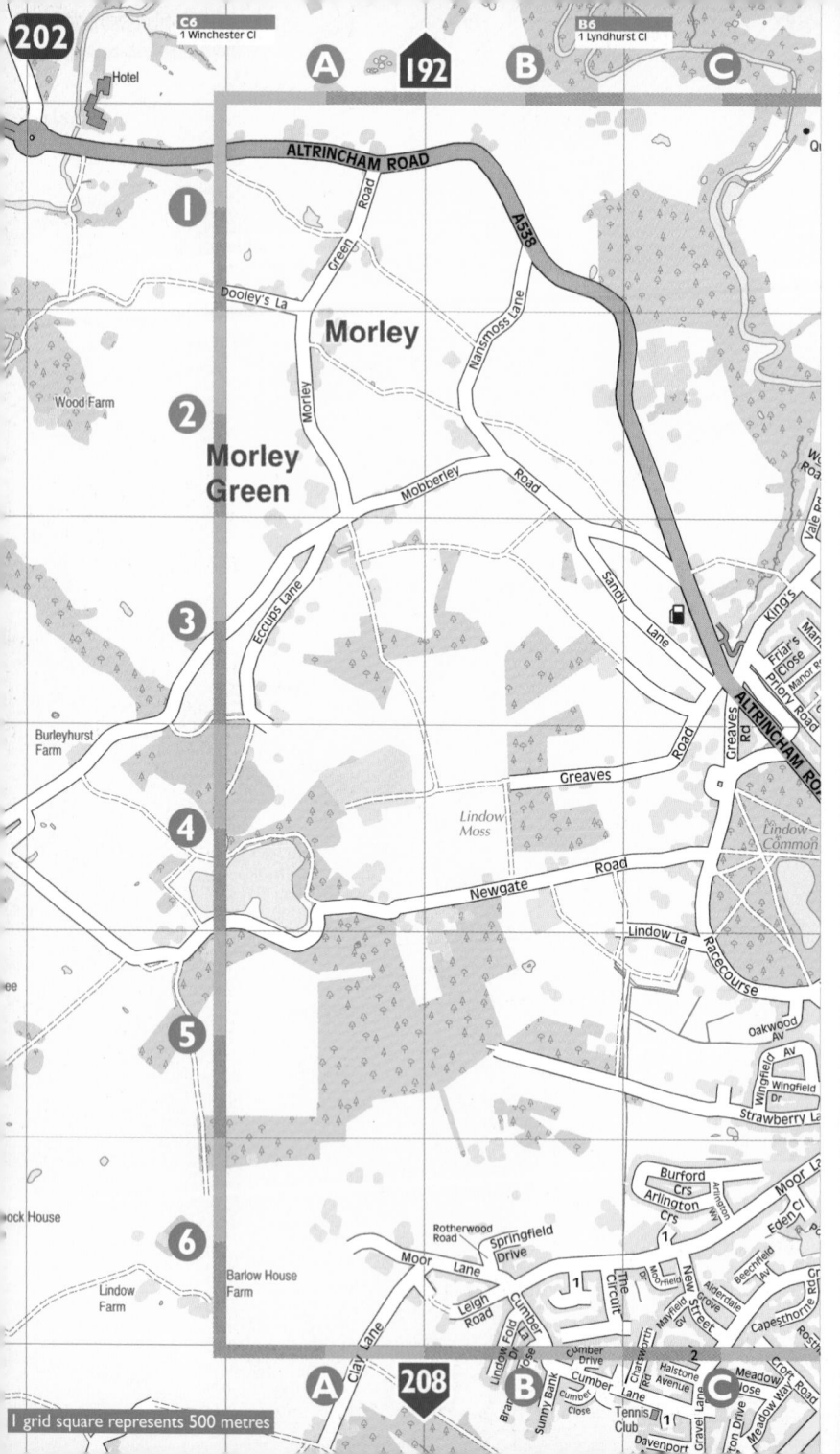

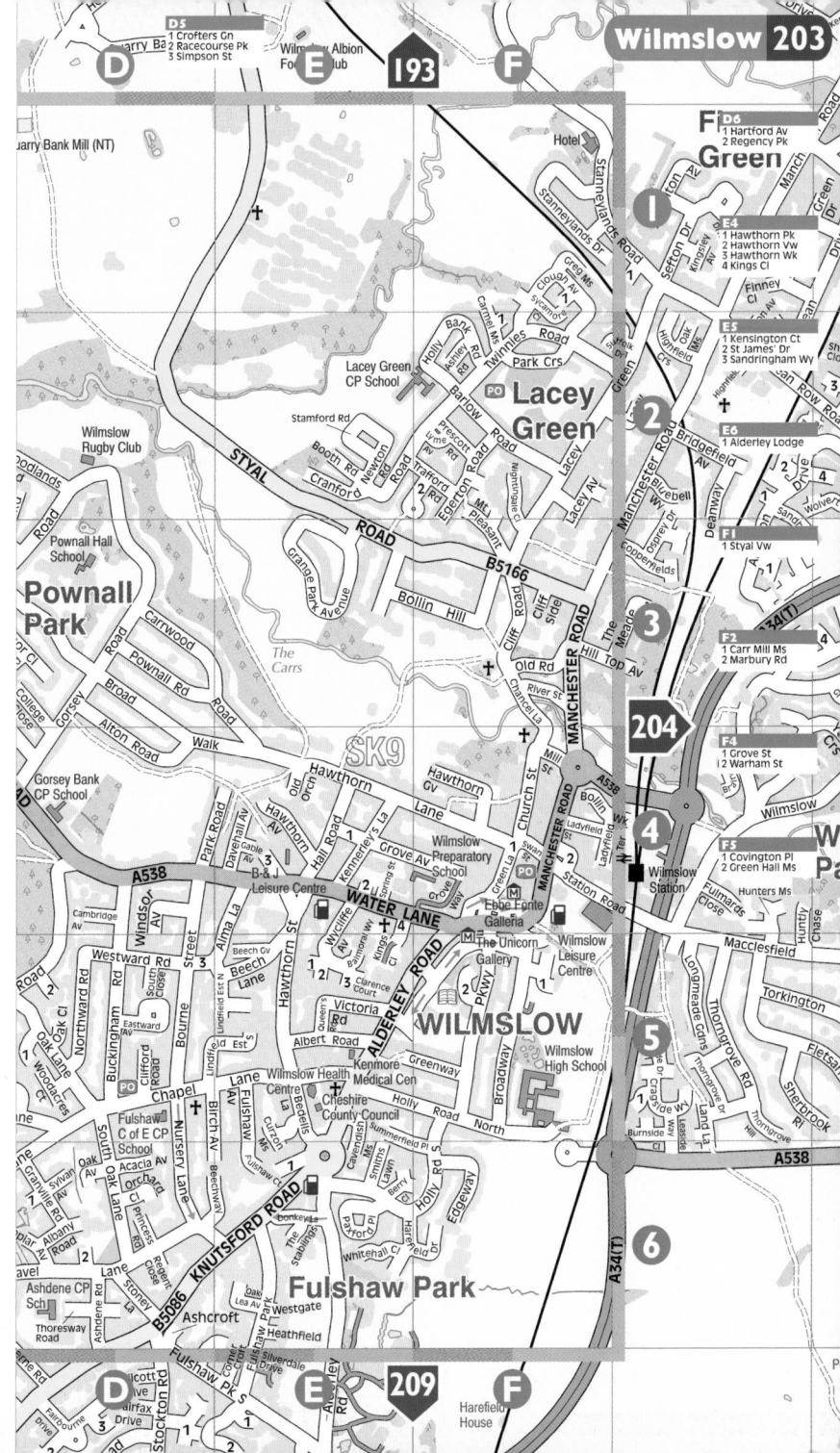

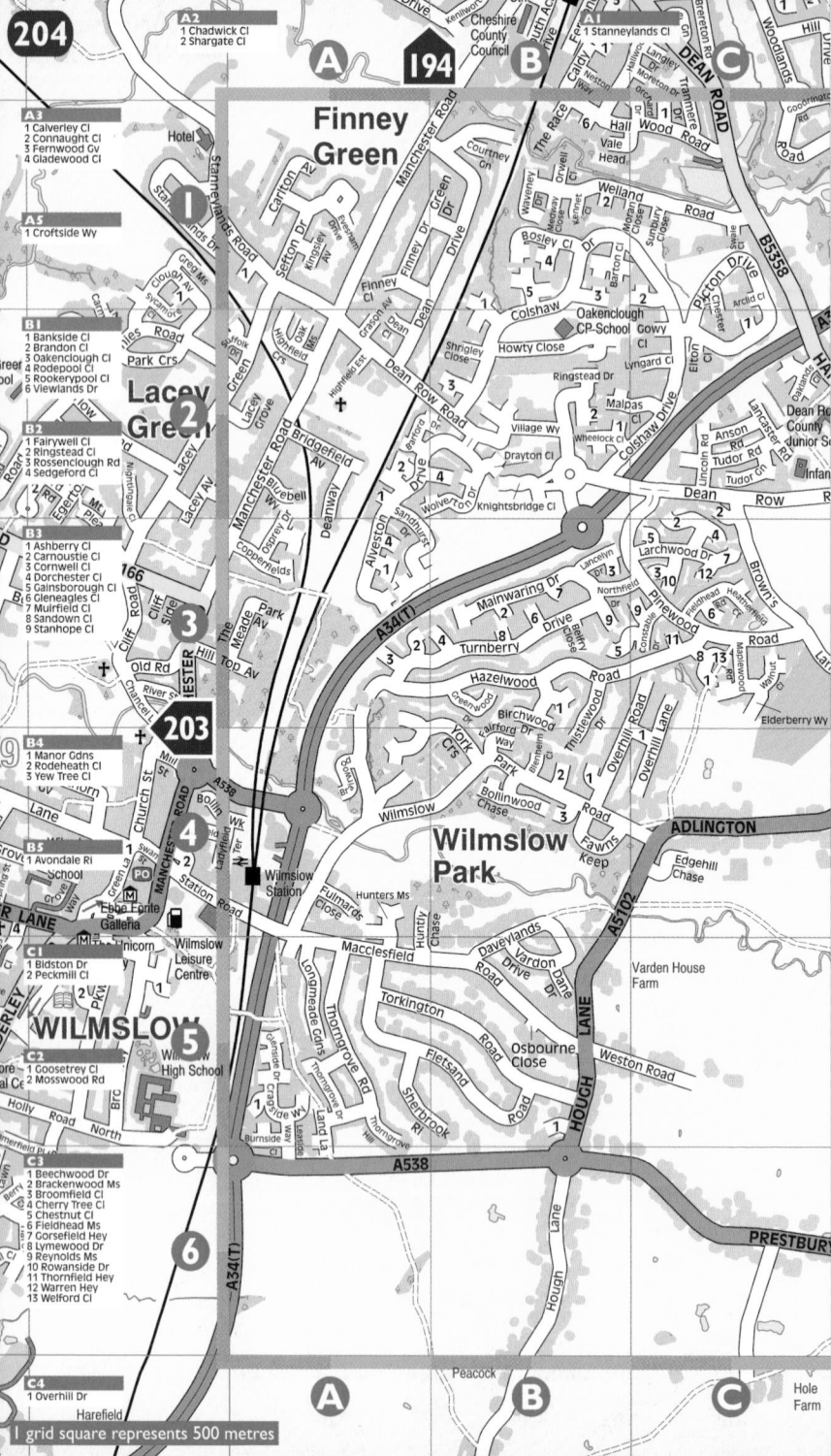

204

A2
1 Chadwick Cl
2 Shargate Cl

194

A3
1 Calverley Cl
2 Connaught Cl
3 Fernwood Gv
4 Gladewood Cl

A5
1 Croftside Wy

A1
1 Stanneylands Cl

Finney Green

Lacey Green

2

B1
1 Bankside Cl
2 Brandon Cl
3 Oakenclough Cl
4 Rodepool Cl
5 Rookerypool Cl
6 Viewlands Dr

B2
1 Fairywell Cl
2 Ringstead Cl
3 Rossenclough Rd
4 Sedgeford Cl

B3
1 Ashberry Cl
2 Carnoustie Cl
3 Cornwell Cl
4 Dorchester Cl
5 Gainsborough Cl
6 Gleneagles Cl
7 Muirfield Cl
8 Sandown Cl
9 Stanhope Cl

3

203

B4
1 Manor Gdns
2 Rodeheath Cl
3 Yew Tree Cl

B5
1 Avondale Ri

4

C1
1 Bidston Dr
2 Peckmill Cl

WILMSLOW

C2
1 Goosetrey Cl
2 Mosswood Rd

5

Wilmslow Park

C
1 Beechwood Dr
2 Brackenwood Ms
3 Broomfield Cl
4 Cherry Tree Cl
5 Chestnut Cl
6 Fieldhead Ms
7 Gorsefield Hey
8 Lymewood Dr
9 Reynolds Ms
10 Rowanside Dr
11 Thornfield Hey
12 Warren Hey
13 Welford Cl

6

PRESTBUR

C4
1 Overhill Dr
Harefield

I grid square represents 500 metres

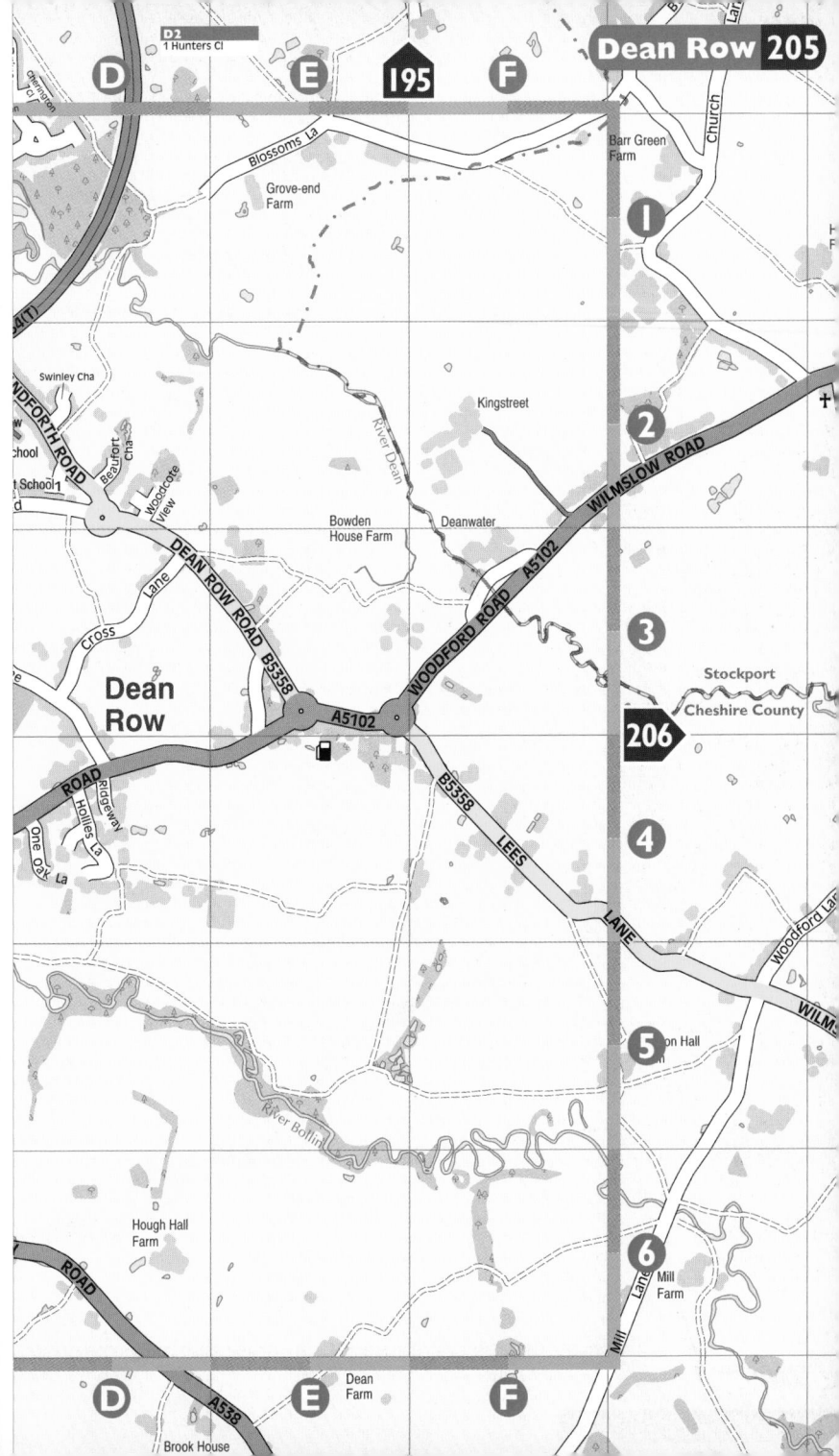

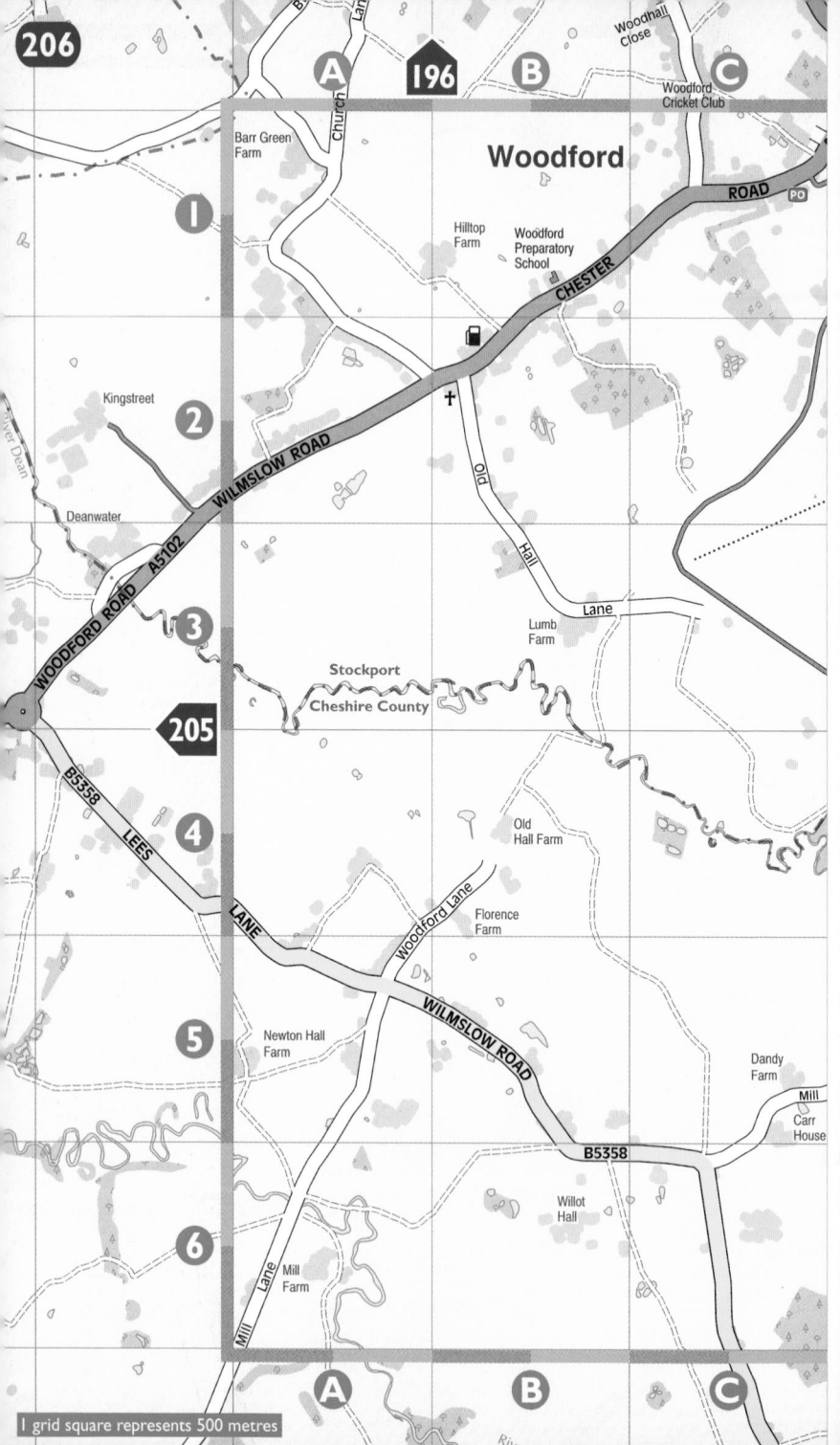

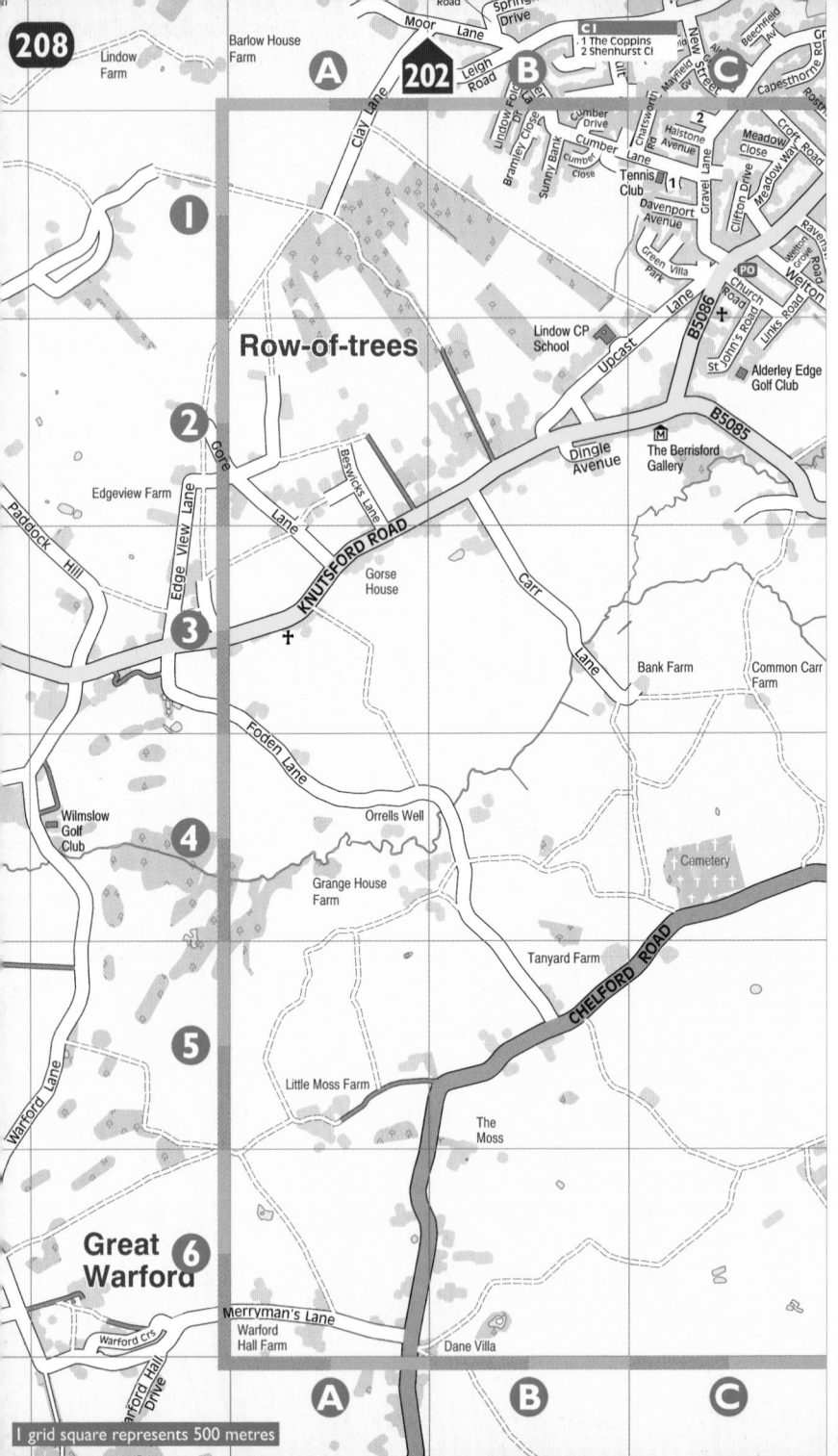

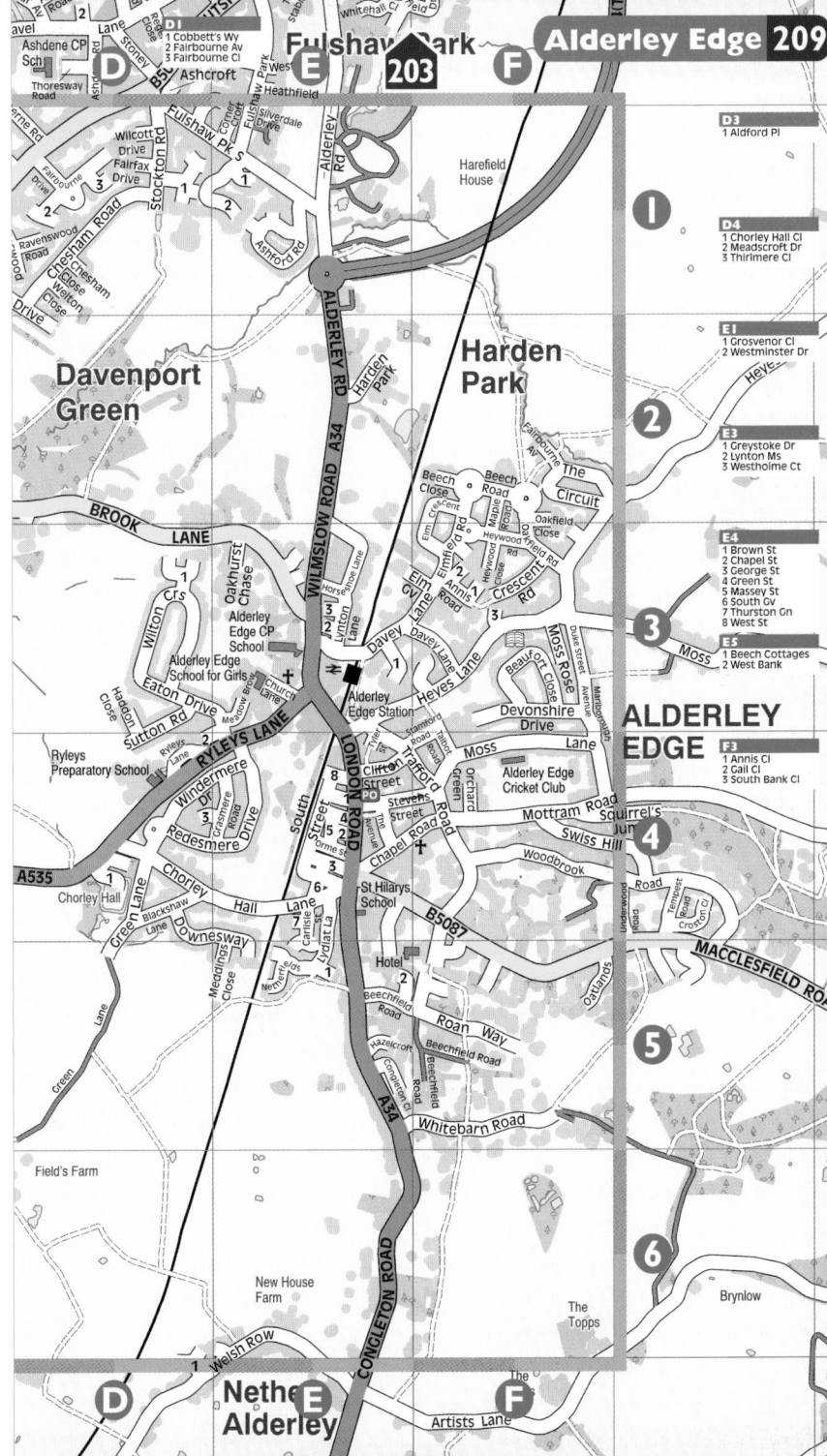

Abbey Hey	128 A4	
Acre	79 F3	
Adlington	207 F6	
Adswood	182 B2	
Affetside	16 C5	
Ainsworth	31 E6	
Alder Forest	100 A3	
Alkrington Garden Village	74 C6	
Alt	97 E2	
Alt Hill	97 D5	
Altrincham	175 D2	
Ancoats	107 D6	
Arden Park	168 B1	
Ardwick	125 D2	
Ashley	188 C4	
Ashley Heath	188 B1	
Ashton-under-Lyne	111 E5	
Ashton Upon Mersey	139 D5	
Astley Bridge	27 F3	
Audenshaw	129 F2	
Austerlands	81 F3	
Backbower	150 C3	
Bagslate Moor	21 D5	
Balderstone	40 C5	
Baldingstone	19 F4	
Bamford	20 B6	
Bank Lane	7 E4	
Bank Top	28 B2	
Bardsley	96 B4	
Barrow Bridge	26 B3	
Barton Upon Irwell	119 E1	
Belfield	24 B6	
Belgrave	4 A2	
Belle Vue	126 C4	
Benchill	178 A3	
Bentgate	42 B3	
Besses o' th' Barn	71 D4	
Beswick	108 A6	
Birch	56 A5	
Blackford Bridge	53 D5	
Black Lane	51 D3	
Blackley	91 F4	
Bolholt	32 B3	
Bolton	46 C1	
Bowdon	173 D6	
Bowgreen	173 E6	
Bowlee	73 E2	
Bradford	108 A5	
Bradley Fold	50 A2	
Bradshaw	29 D1	
Bramhall	197 D2	
Bramhall Moor	183 F5	
Bramhall Park	182 A6	
Bredbury	169 D2	
Bredbury Green	169 E3	
Breightmet	49 E1	
Brinnington	147 F6	
Britannia	5 D1	
Broadbottom	153 D3	
Broadfield	36 C6	
Broadhalgh	21 D6	
Broadheath	158 A6	
Broadley	9 D6	
Broadoak Park	101 D2	
Bromley Cross	28 B1	
Brook Bottom	98 B3	
Brooklands	159 F3	
Brooksbottoms	19 D2	
Broughton Park	89 F4	
Brownlow Fold	27 D6	
Brunswick	124 C3	
Brushes	115 F4	
Buckley	23 E2	
Buckton Vale	115 E1	
Buersil Head	41 D6	
Burnage	144 C6	
Burnden	47 E5	
Burnedge	41 F6	
Bury	33 F4	
Cadishead	154 A1	
Calderbrook	13 E2	
Caldermoor	12 B5	
Cale Green	183 D1	
Captain Fold	37 F4	
Carr	6 C4	
Carrbrook	115 F2	
Carrington	136 C5	
Carrington Moss	157 D2	
Castle Hill	148 C4	
Castleton	39 D5	
Catley Lane Head	21 E1	
Chadderton	76 C4	
Chadderton Fold	76 C1	
Chadkirk	169 F5	
Chapel Field	70 A2	
Chapeltown	15 E2	
Charlestown	92 B2	
Charlestown	104 C3	
Chatterton	6 C2	
Cheadle	180 C2	
Cheadle Heath	165 E6	
Cheadle Hulme	195 E1	
Cheetham Hill	106 C1	
Cherry Tree	171 D3	
Chesham	34 B2	
Chew Moor	44 A5	
Chisworth	153 F6	
Chorlton-cum-Hardy	142 B4	
Cinder Hill	68 B3	
Clarksfield	80 B4	
Clayton	109 D4	
Clifton	85 F2	
Clifton Green	86 C3	
Clifton Junction	87 D2	
Clough	12 B4	
Clough	62 B3	
Collyhurst	107 E1	
Compstall	171 E2	
Copley	115 D5	
Copster Hill	95 F2	
Cox Green	14 A4	
Crimble	38 A3	
Crofts Bank	119 D5	
Crompton Fold	43 D6	
Crowhill	112 A3	
Crumpsall	90 A4	
Cutgate	21 E5	
Daisy Nook	111 E2	
Dales Brow	101 E1	
Dane Bank	147 F1	
Darcy Lever	48 B4	
Darn Hill	36 A4	
Daubhill	46 A5	
Davenport	182 C3	
Davenport Green	177 D5	
Davenport Green	209 D2	
Davyhulme	118 C5	
Deane	45 F6	
Dean Row	205 D3	
Dearnley	25 D1	
Debdale	128 A5	
Denton	130 A4	
Didsbury	163 F2	
Disley	201 F3	
Doffcocker	26 B5	
Dog Hill	62 C2	
Droylsden	109 F6	
Dukinfield	131 D2	
Dumplington	119 D2	
Dunham Town	172 B3	
Durn	13 D6	
Eagley	14 A6	
East Didsbury	164 B4	
Eccles	102 B6	
Edge Fold	64 A2	
Edgeley	166 B6	
Ellenbrook	82 B5	
Ellesmere Park	101 F3	
Elton	32 C5	
Facit	9 F1	
Failsworth	93 F6	
Fairfield	35 E4	
Fairfield	128 B2	
Fallowfield	143 F3	
Farnworth	66 A3	
Fern Bank	114 C6	
Fernhill	33 F3	
Fernhill Gate	45 D5	
Finney Green	204 A1	
Firgrove	41 E1	
Firswood	122 C6	
Firwood Fold	29 D4	
Fishpool	52 B1	
Fitton Hill	96 B3	
Flixton	137 E2	
Flowery Field	131 E5	
Foggbrook	169 D6	
Fold Head	8 B3	
Four Lane Ends	31 E2	
Free Town	34 C4	
Fullwood	62 B4	
Fulshaw Park	203 E6	
Gale	13 D4	
Gatley	179 E3	
Gee Cross	150 B4	
Gigg	53 E2	
Gillbent	195 D3	
Gilnow	46 C3	
Glodwick	79 F6	
Godley	131 F6	
Godley Hill	132 C6	
Gorse Hill	121 F6	
Gorton	127 D5	
Grains Bar	63 E3	
Gravel Hole	60 B2	
Great Howarth	23 E1	
Great Lever	47 E6	
Great Moor	184 A1	
Greave	170 B1	
Greenacres	80 B4	
Greengate	24 B2	
Greenheys	64 B6	
Greenmount	17 F3	
Greenside	110 C4	
Grotton	81 F6	
Guide Bridge	111 F6	
Haggate	60 A6	
Hale	175 D5	
Halebarns	190 B1	
Halfway Houses	50 A2	
Hall i' th' Wood	28 B3	
Halliwell	27 F4	
Handforth	194 A5	
Harden Park	209 F2	
Harper Green	65 F2	
Harpurhey	91 F6	
Hartshead Green	98 C6	
Hartshead Pike	98 A4	
Harwood	30 B4	
Harwood Lee	29 F2	
Hathershaw	96 A2	
Hattersley	152 B1	
Haugh	43 D4	
Haughton Green	149 E3	
Hawk Green	186 C4	
Hawkshaw	17 D2	
Hazel Grove	185 E6	
Hazelhurst	18 A1	
Hazelhurst	100 C1	
Hazelhurst	114 B2	
Heady Hill	36 B5	
Heald Green	179 E6	
Healds Green	59 D6	
Healey	22 C1	
Heap Bridge	35 D6	
Heaton	45 E1	
Heaton Chapel	146 A5	
Heaton Mersey	164 C2	
Heaton Moor	165 E1	
Heaton Norris	166 A3	
Heaviley	183 E1	
Heyheads	99 E6	
Heyrod	114 C3	
Heyside	61 E5	
Heywood	37 D4	
Higginshaw	79 D1	
High Crompton	60 C2	
Higher Blackley	91 D1	
Higher Boarshaw	58 A6	
Higher Broughton	105 E1	
Higher Woodhill	33 E2	
Highfield	65 D4	
High Lane	200 C2	
Hill Top	83 E1	
Hilton Park	88 B3	
Hockley	199 E6	
Holcombe	6 B6	
Holcombe Brook	18 A2	
Holden Fold	60 B6	
Hollins	53 F4	
Hollins	64 B3	
Hollinwood	94 B4	
Holts	97 F1	
Honresfeld	13 E5	
Hooley Bridge	37 D2	
Hooley Brow	37 E3	
Hooley Hill	129 F2	
Hulme	123 F3	
Hunger Hill	44 B6	
Hurst	113 E2	
Hurstead	24 A1	
Hyde	131 F6	
Irlam	135 D2	
Irlams o' th' Height	103 D2	
Jericho	35 F3	
Jubilee	42 C5	
Kearsley	67 F5	
Kersal	88 C5	
Kingston	130 C6	
Kirkhams	71 F5	
Kirkholt	39 F4	
Kirklees	18 C6	
Kitt's Moss	196 B4	
Knott Lanes	96 A6	
Lacey Green	203 F2	
Lady House	41 F3	
Langley	56 A6	
Lees	80 C5	
Levenshulme	146 A3	
Lever-Edge	64 B1	
Ley Hey Park	170 C6	
Limefield	34 A1	
Limehurst	112 B1	
Lime Side	95 E4	
Linnyshaw	83 F2	
Little Bollington	172 A5	
Little Bolton	102 C5	

Littleborough	12 C6	Partington	155 D3	Stoneyfield	40 A3
Little Clegg	24 C3	Patricroft	101 D5	Strangeways	106 A3
Little Hulton	82 A1	Peel Green	118 A1	Stretford	139 F3
Little Lever	49 F5	Peel Hall	179 D5	Stubbins	7 D3
Little Moor	168 B5	Pendlebury	87 D6	Styal	193 D5
Littlemoss	111 D3	Pendleton	104 B4	Sudden	39 D3
Long Sight	79 D1	Pimhole	34 C5	Summerseat	18 C4
Longsight	126 A4	Pitses	97 E2	Summit	12 C2
Lostock Junction	44 B4	Portwood	167 E2	Summit	36 A5
Low Compton	60 C3	Pownall Park	203 D3	Summit	59 F2
Lower Bredbury	168 A3	Poynton	199 D5	Sun Green	115 F3
Lower Kersal	104 B1	Prestolee	67 F3	Sunny Bank	53 E5
Lower Place	41 D3	Prestwich	89 E1	Swinton	85 E5
Luzley	114 C1	Quick	99 D1	Swinton Park	102 C1
Luzley Brook	61 E4	Quick Edge	98 C2	Syke	23 D1
Manchester	125 F2	Radcliffe	51 E5	Taunton	111 F2
Markland Hill	44 C1	Rain Shore	20 A1	Thornham Fold	59 E2
Marland	38 C2	Rainsough	88 B4	Thorns Green	190 A4
Marple	186 C1	Ramsbottom	6 A5	Thorp	59 F5
Marple Bridge	171 F6	Reddish	146 B3	Timperley	159 C6
Marpleridge	187 D5	Redvales	52 C3	Tonge Fold	48 A1
Micklehurst	99 F4	Rhodes	73 F4	Tonge Moor	28 B5
Middleton	74 B2	Ridge Hill	114 A3	Top of Hebers	56 C5
Middlewood	199 F4	Ringley	68 B4	Top o' th' Meadows	81 D3
Miles Platting	107 E4	Roaches	99 E2	Toppings	14 C6
Millbrook	115 E3	Rochdale	22 C5	Torkington	185 F5
Millgate	5 D5	Roebuck Low	81 E1	Tottington	31 F1
Mill Hill	47 E1	Roe Green	84 B5	Trafford Park	120 B4
Milnrow	42 B1	Romiley	170 B3	Trough Gate	5 E1
Monton	101 E4	Rose Hill	47 E4	Trub	58 A2
Moorclose	76 A3	Rosehill	174 A6	Turf Hill	41 E3
Moorhey	79 F5	Rough Bank	43 E1	Unsworth	71 F1
Moorside	62 C6	Roundthorn	176 C2	Urmston	119 F5
Moorside	85 E6	Row-of-trees	208 A2	Walkden	83 E1
Morley	202 A2	Royton	60 C5	Wallbank	8 C4
Moses Gate	66 A1	Rusholme	125 E6	Walmersley	19 F6
Mosley Common	82 A6	Saint George's	123 D3	Walshaw	31 F3
Mossbrow	154 B6	Salford	104 A6	Warburton Green	190 A3
Mossley	99 E3	Sale	158 C2	Wardle	11 E5
Mossley Brow	99 D4	Scouthead	81 F3	Wardley	85 D4
Moss Nook	193 D1	Sedgley Park	89 D3	Waterloo	112 B2
Moss Side	124 A5	Seedley	103 F4	Watersheddings	80 B2
Moston	92 C4	Sharples	27 E3	Weaste	103 F6
Mottram Rise	133 F2	Sharston	179 D2	Well Green	176 B4
Mudd	153 E1	Shaw	61 E1	Werneth	78 A6
Mumps	78 C4	Shawclough	22 A3	Werneth Low	151 D6
Nangreaves	19 F2	Shawfield	21 D3	West Didsbury	142 C6
Newall Green	177 E3	Shawforth	5 E4	Westwood Park	100 B3
Newbold	23 F6	Shaw Heath	166 C6	Whalley Range	142 C1
New Bury	65 E4	Shaw Side	61 F4	Whitefield	70 C4
Newhey	42 A4	Sholver	62 B5	White Gate	94 A2
New Moston	93 D5	Shore	12 A5	Whitworth	9 E3
Newton	131 F4	Shuttleworth	7 F4	Willows	46 A4
Newton Heath	108 B2	Side of the Moor	29 F1	Wilmslow	203 F5
Newton Wood	130 B3	Simister	72 C3	Wilmslow Park	204 B4
Newtown	85 F4	Sinderland Green	156 B4	Windlehurst	186 C6
Nimble Nook	94 B1	Slackcote	63 F2	Winton	101 D4
Nob End	67 E1	Slattocks	58 A3	Wolstenholme	20 A2
Norbury Moor	184 C6	Smallbridge	24 B2	Woodford	206 B1
Norden	20 B4	Smallshaw	113 D1	Woodgate Hill	35 E3
Northern Moor	161 D4	Smithy Bridge	25 E2	Woodhey	18 B2
North Reddish	146 C2	Smithy Green	195 F1	Woodhouse Park	178 C4
Nuttall	18 C1	South Reddish	146 C6	Woodhouses	110 C1
Oak Bank	71 E4	Spotland Bridge	22 B5	Woodhouses	157 F3
Offerton	168 C6	Springhead	81 E5	Woodlands	133 D2
Offerton Green	185 E1	Spring Hill	80 B2	Woodley	150 A6
Oldfield Brow	173 F2	Stake Hill	58 C4	Wood Road	19 D4
Oldham	79 E5	Stalybridge	113 F6	Woodseats	153 E5
Oldham Edge	78 C2	Stand	70 A3	Woods End	117 F6
Old Tame	63 F1	Stanley Green	194 C4	Woods Moor	183 F6
Old Trafford	122 C4	Stancyliffe	57 F6	Woolfold	32 B3
Openshaw	127 D1	Starling	32 B5	Worsley	84 A6
Ordsall	122 C2	Stepping Hill	184 B3	Wythenshawe	177 F4
Outwood	69 E3	Stockport	166 A3	Yew Tree	131 F2
Park Bridge	97 D3	Stoneclough	67 F4		

USING THE STREET INDEX

Street names are listed alphabetically. Each street name is followed by its postal town or area locality, the Postcode District, the page number, and the reference to the square in which the name is found.

Example: **Abberley Dr** *NEWH/MOS* M40 ....**93** E3 **1**

Some entries are followed by a number in a blue box. This number indicates the location of the street within the referenced grid square. The full street name is listed at the side of the map page.

GENERAL ABBREVIATIONS

ACC	ACCESS
ALY	ALLEY
AP	APPROACH
AR	ARCADE
ASS	ASSOCIATION
AV	AVENUE
BCH	BEACH
BLDS	BUILDINGS
BND	BEND
BNK	BANK
BR	BRIDGE
BRK	BROOK
BTM	BOTTOM
BUS	BUSINESS
BVD	BOULEVARD
BY	BYPASS
CATH	CATHEDRAL
CEM	CEMETERY
CEN	CENTRE
CFT	CROFT
CH	CHURCH
CHA	CHASE
CHYD	CHURCHYARD
CIR	CIRCLE
CIRC	CIRCUS
CL	CLOSE
CLFS	CLIFFS
CMP	CAMP
CNR	CORNER
CO	COUNTY
COLL	COLLEGE
COM	COMMON
COMM	COMMISSION
CON	CONVENT
COT	COTTAGE
COTS	COTTAGES
CP	CAPE
CPS	COPSE
CR	CREEK
CREM	CREMATORIUM
CRS	CRESCENT
CSWY	CAUSEWAY
CT	COURT
CTRL	CENTRAL
CTS	COURTS
CTYD	COURTYARD
CUTT	CUTTINGS
CV	COVE
CYN	CANYON
DEPT	DEPARTMENT
DL	DALE
DM	DAM
DR	DRIVE
DRO	DROVE
DRY	DRIVEWAY
DWGS	DWELLINGS
E	EAST
EMB	EMBANKMENT
EMBY	EMBASSY
ESP	ESPLANADE
EST	ESTATE
EX	EXCHANGE
EXPY	EXPRESSWAY
EXT	EXTENSION
F/O	FLYOVER
FC	FOOTBALL CLUB
FK	FORK
FLD	FIELD
FLDS	FIELDS
FLS	FALLS
FLS	FLATS
FM	FARM
FT	FORT
FWY	FREEWAY
FY	FERRY
GA	GATE
GAL	GALLERY
GDN	GARDEN
GDNS	GARDENS
GLD	GLADE
GLN	GLEN
GN	GREEN
GND	GROUND
GRA	GRANGE
GRG	GARAGE
GT	GREAT
GTWY	GATEWAY
GV	GROVE
HGR	HIGHER
HL	HILL
HLS	HILLS
HO	HOUSE
HOL	HOLLOW
HOSP	HOSPITAL
HRB	HARBOUR
HTH	HEATH
HTS	HEIGHTS
HVN	HAVEN
HWY	HIGHWAY
IMP	IMPERIAL
IN	INLET
IND EST	INDUSTRIAL ESTATE
INF	INFIRMARY
INFO	INFORMATION
INT	INTERCHANGE
IS	ISLAND
JCT	JUNCTION
JTY	JETTY
KG	KING
KNL	KNOLL
L	LAKE
LA	LANE
LDG	LODGE
LGT	LIGHT
LK	LOCK
LKS	LAKES
LNDG	LANDING
LTL	LITTLE
LWR	LOWER
MAG	MAGISTRATE
MAN	MANSIONS
MD	MEAD
MDW	MEADOWS
MEM	MEMORIAL
MKT	MARKET
MKTS	MARKETS
ML	MALL
ML	MILL
MNR	MANOR
MS	MEWS
MSN	MISSION
MT	MOUNT
MTN	MOUNTAIN
MTS	MOUNTAINS
MUS	MUSEUM
MWY	MOTORWAY
N	NORTH
NE	NORTH EAST
NW	NORTH WEST
O/P	OVERPASS
OFF	OFFICE
ORCH	ORCHARD
OV	OVAL
PAL	PALACE
PAS	PASSAGE
PAV	PAVILION
PDE	PARADE
PH	PUBLIC HOUSE
PK	PARK
PKWY	PARKWAY
PL	PLACE
PLN	PLAIN
PLNS	PLAINS
PLZ	PLAZA
POL	POLICE STATION
PR	PRINCE
PREC	PRECINCT
PREP	PREPARATORY
PRIM	PRIMARY
PROM	PROMENADE
PRS	PRINCESS
PRT	PORT
PT	POINT
PTH	PATH
PZ	PIAZZA
QD	QUADRANT
QU	QUEEN
QY	QUAY
R	RIVER
RBT	ROUNDABOUT
RD	ROAD
RDG	RIDGE
REP	REPUBLIC
RES	RESERVOIR
RFC	RUGBY FOOTBALL CLUB
RI	RISE
RP	RAMP
RW	ROW
S	SOUTH
SCH	SCHOOL
SE	SOUTH EAST
SER	SERVICE AREA
SH	SHORE
SHOP	SHOPPING
SKWY	SKYWAY
SMT	SUMMIT
SOC	SOCIETY
SP	SPUR
SPR	SPRING
SQ	SQUARE
ST	STREET
STN	STATION
STR	STREAM
STRD	STRAND
SW	SOUTH WEST
TDG	TRADING
TER	TERRACE
THWY	THROUGHWAY
TNL	TUNNEL
TOLL	TOLLWAY
TPK	TURNPIKE
TR	TRACK
TRL	TRAIL
TWR	TOWER
U/P	UNDERPASS
UNI	UNIVERSITY
UPR	UPPER
V	VALE
VA	VALLEY
VIAD	VIADUCT
VIL	VILLA
VIS	VISTA
VLG	VILLAGE
VLS	VILLAS
VW	VIEW
W	WEST
WD	WOOD
WHF	WHARF
WK	WALK
WKS	WALKS
WLS	WELLS
WY	WAY
YD	YARD
YHA	YOUTH HOSTEL

POSTCODE TOWNS AND AREA ABBREVIATIONS

ALT	Altrincham
ANC	Ancoats
AUL	Ashton-under-Lyne
AULW	Ashton-under-Lyne west
BCUP	Bacup
BKLY	Blackley
BNG/LEV	Burnage/Levenshulme
BOL	Bolton
BOLE	Bolton east
BOLS/LL	Bolton south/Little Lever
BRAM/HZG	Bramhall/Hazel Grove
BRO	Broughton
BRUN/LGST	Brunswick/Longsight
BURY	Bury
CCHDY	Chorlton-cum-Hardy
CHAD	Chadderton
CHD/CHDH	Cheadle (Gtr. Man)/ Cheadle Hulme
CHH	Cheetham Hill
CMANE	Central Manchester east
CMANW	Central Manchester west
CSLFD	Central Salford
DID/WITH	Didsbury/Withington
DROY	Droylsden
DTN/ASHW	Denton/Audenshaw
DUK	Dukinfield
ECC	Eccles
EDGW/EG	Edgeworth/Egerton
EDGY/DAV	Edgeley/Davenport
FAIL	Failsworth
FWTH	Farnworth
GLSP	Glossop
GOL/RIS/CUL	Golborne/Risley/Culcheth
GTN	Gorton
HALE/TIMP	Hale/Timperley
HEY	Heywood

HOR/BR ....Horwich/Blackrod
HTNM ....Heaton Moor
HULME ....Hulme
HYDE ....Hyde
IRL ....Irlam
KNUT ....Knutsford
LHULT ....Little Hulton
LIT ....Littleborough
LYMM ....Lymm
MANAIR ....Manchester Airport
MCFLDN ....Macclesfield north
MDTN ....Middleton (Gtr. Man)
MILN ....Milnrow
MOSL ....Mossley
MPL/ROM ....Marple/Romiley
NEWH/MOS ....Newton Heath/Moston
NTHM/RTH ......Northern Moor/Roundthorn

OFTN ....Offerton
OLD ....Oldham
OLDE ....Oldham east
OLDS ....Oldham south
OLDTF/WHR ......Old Trafford/Whalley Range
OP/CLY ....Openshaw/Clayton
PART ....Partition
POY/DIS ....Poynton/Disley
PWCH ....Prestwich
RAD ....Radcliffe
RAMS ....Ramsbottom
RDSH ....Reddish
ROCH ....Rochdale
ROY/SHW ....Royton/Shaw
RUSH/FAL ....Rusholme/Fallowfield
SALE ....Sale
SALQ/ORD ....Salford Quays/Ordsall

SLFD ....Salford
STKP ....Stockport
STLY ....Stalybridge
STRET ....Stretford
SWIN ....Swinton
TOD ....Todmorden
TOT/BURYW ....Tottington/Bury west
TRPK ....Trafford Park
TYLD ....Tyldesley
URM ....Urmston
WALK ....Walkden
WGTN/LGST ....West Gorton/Longsight
WHIT ....Whitworth
WHTF ....Whitefield
WHTN ....Westhoughton
WILM/AE ....Wilmslow/Alderley Edge
WYTH/NTH ....Wythenshawe/Northenden

Abb - Ain

Index - streets

A

Abberley Dr NEWH/MOS M40 .... 93 E3 🖸
Abberton Rd DID/WITH M20 .... 143 E5
Abbey Cl ALT WA14 .... 173 E6
   RAD M26 .... 50 C4
   URM M41 .... 120 A6
Abbey Ct RAD M26 .... 50 C5
Abbey Crs HEY OL10 .... 36 C3
Abbeydale Cl AUL OL6 .... 113 F1
Abbey Dr LIT OL15 .... 25 D2
   SWIN M27 .... 85 F5
   TOT/BURYW BL8 .... 32 B6
Abbey Gv CHAD OL9 .... 94 B1
   ECC M30 .... 101 F5 🖸
   STKP SK1 .... 167 F5
Abbey Hey La GTN M18 .... 127 F3
Abbey Hills Rd OLDS OL8 .... 96 C1
Abbey Lawn OLDTF/WHR M16 ... 122 C6 🖸
Abbey Rd CHD/CHDH SK8 .... 181 E2
   DROY M43 .... 110 A4 🖸
   FAIL M35 .... 94 C5 🖸
   MDTN M24 .... 57 D5
   SALE M33 .... 139 E5
Abbeywood Av GTN M18 .... 127 F5 🖸
Abbotsbury Cl POY/DIS SK12 .... 198 B4 🖸
Abbots Cl SALE M33 .... 140 B6 🖸
Abbotsfield Cl URM M41 .... 117 E6 🖸
Abbot's Fold Rd WALK M28 .... 82 C6
Abbotsford Dr MDTN M24 .... 56 B5
Abbotsford Gv ALT WA14 .... 158 C5
Abbotsford Rd BOL BL1 .... 26 B6
   CCHDY M21 .... 141 F1
   CHAD OL9 .... 76 C5 🖸
   OLD OL1 .... 79 F2
Abbotside Cl OLDTF/WHR M16 ... 123 E6
Abbotsleigh Dr BRAM/HZG SK7 ... 183 D5
Abbott St BOLS/LL BL3 .... 46 C4 🖸
   ROCH OL11 .... 38 C4
Abden St RAD M26 .... 51 E6
Aber Av OFTN SK2 .... 184 A3
Abercarn Cl CHH M8 .... 90 B6
Abercorn Rd BOL BL1 .... 26 C4
Abercorn St OLDE OL4 .... 80 B5 🖸
Abercrombie Ct SALE M33 .... 140 B6 🖸
Aberdeen Crs EDGY/DAV SK3 ... 166 B5
Aberdeen Gdns WHIT OL12 .... 22 B1 🖸
Aberdeen Gv EDGY/DAV SK3 ... 166 B5 🖸
Aberdeen St HULME M15 .... 124 C4
Aberford Rd NTHM/RTH M23 ..... 177 E2
Abergele Rd RUSH/FAL M14 ..... 144 C3
Abergele St OFTN SK2 .... 183 D1
Abernant Cl OP/CLY M11 .... 108 A6 🖸
Aber Rd CHD/CHDH SK8 .... 181 E1
Abersoch Av RUSH/FAL M14 .... 144 C3 🖸
Abingdon Av WHTF M45 .... 71 D1
Abingdon Cl CHAD OL9 .... 94 C1 🖸
   ROCH OL11 .... 39 F3
   WHTF M45 .... 71 D1
Abingdon Rd BOLE BL2 .... 48 A1
   BRAM/HZG SK7 .... 182 C5
   RDSH SK5 .... 147 D4
   URM M41 .... 119 F6
Abingdon St AUL OL6 .... 113 E5
   CMANE M1 .... 3 E5
Abington Rd SALE M33 .... 160 A2
Abney Gra MOSL OL5 .... 99 F5
Abney Rd HTNM SK4 .... 146 A6
   MOSL OL5 .... 99 D5
Aboukir St MILN OL16 .... 23 F5 🖸
Abram Cl RUSH/FAL M14 .... 143 E2 🖸
Abram St SLFD M6 .... 104 A1
Absalom Dr CHH M8 .... 90 A5
Abson St OLD OL1 .... 78 A2 🖸
Acacia Av CHD/CHDH SK8 .... 181 E5
   DTN/ASHW M34 .... 130 B6
   HALE/TIMP WA15 .... 175 D4
   SWIN M27 .... 101 F1 🖸
   WILM/AE SK9 .... 203 D6
Acacia Dr HALE/TIMP WA15 .... 175 D4
   SLFD M6 .... 102 C4
Acacia Gv RDSH SK5 .... 167 D1 🖸
Acacia Rd OLDS OL8 .... 95 E4
Acer Cl HYDE SK14 .... 151 E1
   ROCH OL11 .... 20 B4
Acheson St GTN M18 .... 127 E4 🖸
Ackers La PART M31 .... 136 C5
Ack La East BRAM/HZG SK7 ..... 196 A2
Ack La West CHD/CHDH SK8 .... 195 F2
Ackroyd Av GTN M18 .... 128 B3
Ackroyd St OP/CLY M11 .... 127 F2
Ackworth Dr NTHM/RTH M23 ... 177 E1
Ackworth Rd SWIN M27 .... 85 F4
Acme Dr SWIN M27 .... 86 C5 🖸
Acomb St HULME M15 .... 124 C4
   RUSH/FAL M14 .... 124 C6
Acorn Av CHD/CHDH SK8 .... 180 C1
   HYDE SK14 .... 150 C3
Acorn Cl BNG/LEV M19 .... 145 D3
   WHTF M45 .... 71 D5
Acorn St OLDE OL4 .... 80 C5
Acre Barn ROY/SHW OL2 .... 60 C1 🖸
Acre Fld BOLE BL2 .... 29 E3
Acrefield SALE M33 .... 159 E2 🖸
Acrefield Av HTNM SK4 .... 165 E1
   URM M41 .... 139 D2
Acre La CHD/CHDH SK8 .... 195 F3
   OLD OL1 .... 79 E2
Acres Ct WYTH/NTH M22 .... 178 B3
Acresdale HOR/BR BL6 .... 44 A3
Acresfield Av DTN/ASHW M34 ... 110 C6
Acresfield Cl SWIN M27 .... 102 B1 🖸
Acresfield Rd HALE/TIMP WA15 . 159 E5
   HYDE SK14 .... 132 A4
   LHULT M38 .... 82 C1
   MDTN M24 .... 58 A6
   SLFD M6 .... 103 E2
Acres La STLY SK15 .... 114 C6
Acres Rd CCHDY M21 .... 141 E3
   CHD/CHDH SK8 .... 179 E2 🖸
Acres St TOT/BURYW BL8 .... 32 A2
Acre St CHAD OL9 .... 94 B3
   DTN/ASHW M34 .... 129 F6
   MPL/ROM SK6 .... 169 F3 🖸
   RAD M26 .... 50 C6 🖸
   WHIT OL12 .... 9 E2
Acre Top Rd BKLY M9 .... 73 F6
Acton Av NEWH/MOS M40 .... 108 C3
Acton St OLD OL1 .... 79 E5 🖸
   WHIT OL12 .... 23 E4 🖸
Adair St CMANE M1 .... 125 D1
Adam Cl CHD/CHDH SK8 .... 181 F3
Adams Av CCHDY M21 .... 141 F5
Adamson Gdns DID/WITH M20 ... 163 D2 🖸
Adamson Rd ECC M30 .... 119 D1 🖸
Adamson St DUK SK16 .... 131 D3 🖸
Adam St AUL OL6 .... 113 D4 🖸
   BOLS/LL BL3 .... 47 D4
   OLDS OL8 .... 96 A3
Ada St BKLY M9 .... 91 E4
   OLDE OL4 .... 79 E5
   RAMS BL0 .... 6 B6
   WHIT OL12 .... 23 E3
Adcroft St STKP SK1 .... 167 D6
Addington Rd BOLS/LL BL3 .... 45 D6
Addington St ANC M4 .... 3 G1
Addison Av AUL OL6 .... 113 E4 🖸
Addison Cl BRUN/LGST M13 ..... 125 D3
Addison Crs OLDTF/WHR M16 ... 122 C5
Addison Dr MDTN M24 .... 58 A6
Addison Rd HALE/TIMP WA15 ... 174 C5
   IRL M44 .... 117 D5
   PART M31 .... 136 B5 🖸
   STRET M32 .... 139 F1
   URM M41 .... 138 B2
Adelaide Rd BRAM/HZG SK7 .... 196 C3
   EDGY/DAV SK3 .... 166 A5
Adelaide St BOLS/LL BL3 .... 46 B5
   CHH M8 .... 106 A2
   ECC M30 .... 101 E6
   HEY OL10 .... 37 E5
   MDTN M24 .... 75 E3 🖸
   RAMS BL0 .... 18 B1 🖸
   SWIN M27 .... 85 E6
Adelaide St East HEY OL10 .... 37 F5 🖸
Adeline St ANC M4 .... 106 B4 🖸
Adelphi Dr LHULT M38 .... 65 F6 🖸
Adelphi Gv LHULT M38 .... 65 F6
Adelphi St RAD M26 .... 51 D4 🖸
Aden Cl WGTN/LGST M12 .... 125 E1
Aden St OLDE OL4 .... 80 B6
   WHIT OL12 .... 23 L4 🖸
Adisham Dr BOL BL1 .... 28 A6 🖸
Adlington Cl HALE/TIMP WA15 ... 176 B1
   TOT/BURYW BL8 .... 32 B6
Adlington Dr STRET M32 .... 122 A5 🖸
Adlington Rd WILM/AE SK9 ...... 204 C3
Adlington St BOLS/LL BL3 .... 46 B6
   OLDE OL4 .... 80 B2 🖸
Adrian Rd BOL BL1 .... 27 D5
Adrian St NEWH/MOS M40 .... 92 B6
Adrian Ter MILN OL16 .... 41 D1
Adria Rd DID/WITH M20 .... 164 A2
Adscombe St OLDTF/WHR M16... 123 F5
Adshall Rd CHD/CHDH SK8 .... 181 E2
Adshead Cl WYTH/NTH M22 ..... 177 F4 🖸
Adstone Cl ANC M4 .... 107 E6 🖸
Adswood Cl OLDE OL4 .... 80 B2 🖸
Adswood Gv EDGY/DAV SK3 .... 182 B1
Adswood La East OFTN SK2 ...... 183 D1
Adswood La West
   EDGY/DAV SK3 .... 182 C1
Adswood Old Hall Rd
   CHD/CHDH SK8 .... 182 B3 🖸
Adswood Rd CHD/CHDH SK8 .... 182 A3
   EDGY/DAV SK3 .... 182 B2
Adswood St NEWH/MOS M40 .... 107 F5 🖸
Adswood Ter EDGY/DAV SK3 .... 182 C1 🖸
Aegean Cl BRO M7 .... 105 D2 🖸
Aegean Rd ALT WA14 .... 173 E1
Affetside Dr TOT/BURYW BL8 ..... 31 F5
   BRO M7 .... 90 A6
Afghan St OLD OL1 .... 79 F3
Age Cft OLDS OL8 .... 97 D2
Agecroft Rd MPL/ROM SK6 ...... 169 E4
   SWIN M27 .... 87 D6
Agecroft Rd East PWCH M25 .... 88 B3
Agecroft Rd West PWCH M25 ...... 88 A3
Agincourt St HEY OL10 .... 36 C5 🖸
Agnes Cl CHAD OL9 .... 95 D1 🖸
Agnes St BNG/LEV M19 .... 145 E1
   BRO M7 .... 90 A6
   CHAD OL9 .... 77 F6
Agnew Pl SLFD M6 .... 104 B3 🖸
Agnew Rd GTN M18 .... 127 D4
Aigburth Gv RDSH SK5 .... 146 C1 🖸
Ailsa Cl NEWH/MOS M40 .... 107 E2 🖸
Aimson Rd HALE/TIMP WA15 .... 160 A6
Ainley Rd WYTH/NTH M22 .... 178 B4
Ainley Wd DUK SK16 .... 131 E2
Ainsdale Av PWCH M25 .... 89 E4
   TOT/BURYW BL8 .... 32 C5
Ainsdale Cl BRAM/HZG SK7 ..... 197 E2
   OLDS OL8 .... 95 E1 🖸
Ainsdale Crs ROY/SHW OL2 .... 78 C1
Ainsdale Dr CHD/CHDH SK8 .... 179 F6 🖸
   SALE M33 .... 158 C3
   WHIT OL12 .... 9 E4
Ainsdale Gv RDSH SK5 .... 147 D3
Ainsdale Rd BOLS/LL BL3 .... 46 C3
Ainsdale St WGTN/LGST M12 ... 126 A3
Ainsford Rd DID/WITH M20 ...... 144 B6
Ainsley Gv WALK M28 .... 83 E3
Ainslie Rd BOL BL1 .... 26 B6

Ainsty Rd *RUSH/FAL* M14 .... **124** B5
Ainsworth St *DTN/ASHW* M34 .... **128** C6
Ainsworth Hall Rd *BOLE* BL2 ...... **49** F2
Ainsworth La *BOLE* BL2 .... **28** C6
Ainsworth St *BOLS/LL* BL3 .... **49** E6
   RAD M26 .... **51** D4
   TOT/BURYW BL8 .... **32** B5
Ainsworth St *BOL* BL1 .... **27** D5 🔲
   MILN OL16 .... **40** B1
Aintree Av *SALE* M33 .... **158** A2
Aintree Cl *BRAM/HZG* SK7 .... **185** D5
Aintree Dr *ROCH* OL11 .... **20** C5 🔲
Aintree Gv *EDGY/DAV* SK3 .... **182** C1
Aintree Rd *BOLS/LL* BL3 .... **67** E1
Aintree St *OP/CLY* M11 .... **108** C6 🔲
Airedale Cl *CHAD/CHDH* SK8 ..... **180** A1
Airedale Ct *ALT* WA14 .... **174** C2 🔲
Aire Dr *BOLE* BL2 .... **28** C2
Air Hill Ter *WHIT* OL12 .... **22** A4 🔲
Airton Cl *NEWH/MOS* M40 .... **107** D4 🔲
Aitken Cl *RAMS* BL0 .... **6** C6
Aitken St *BNG/LEV* M19 .... **146** A2 🔲
Ajax Dr *BURY* BL9 .... **53** D6
Ajax St *RAMS* BL0 .... **6** C5
   ROCH OL11 .... **38** C4
Aked Cl *WGTN/LGST* M12 .... **125** E3
Akesmoor Dr *OFTN* SK2 .... **184** A1
Alamein Dr *MPL/ROM* SK6 .... **170** C5
Alan Av *FAIL* M35 .... **110** A2
Alandale Av *DTN/ASHW* M34 .... **129** F2 🔲
Alandale Rd *EDGY/DAV* SK3 ...... **166** A6
Alan Dr *HALE/TIMP* WA15 .... **189** E1
   MPL/ROM SK6 .... **186** C1
Alan Rd *DID/WITH* M20 .... **144** A5
   HTNM SK4 .... **165** E2
Alan St *BOL* BL1 .... **27** E4 🔲
Alan Turing Wy *NEWH/MOS* M40 ... **107** D4 🔲
   OP/CLY M11 .... **108** A5
Alasdair Cl *CHAD* OL9 .... **77** D3
Alba Cl *ECC* M30 .... **101** E6 🔲
Alban St *BRO* M7 .... **105** E2
Albany Cl *OP/CLY* M11 .... **124** A2
Albany Ct *URM* M41 .... **118** C6
Albany Dr *BURY* BL9 .... **53** D2
Albany Rd *BRAM/HZG* SK7 .... **196** C5
   CCHDY M21 .... **141** F2
   ECC M30 .... **100** C4 🔲
   WILM/AE SK9 .... **203** D6
Albany St *MDTN* M24 .... **75** H4
   OLDE OL4 .... **80** B2
   ROCH OL11 .... **40** B2 🔲
Alba Wy *STRET* M32 .... **120** B4
Albemarle Av *DID/WITH* M20 .... **143** E5
Albemarle Rd *CCHDY* M21 .... **141** E5
Albemarle St *AUL* OL6 .... **113** D4 🔲
   RUSH/FAL M14 .... **124** B5
Albemarle Ter *AUL* OL6 .... **113** D4 🔲
Alberta St *BOLS/LL* BL3 .... **46** A4
   STKP SK1 .... **167** D5
Albert Av *DUK* SK16 .... **131** D3
   GTN M18 .... **127** F5
   PWCH M25 .... **89** D4
   ROY/SHW OL2 .... **61** E4
   URM M41 .... **138** C1
   WALK M28 .... **66** A6
Albert Cl *CHD/CHDH* SK8 .... **181** E5
   WHTF M45 .... **71** E3
Albert Ct *ALT* WA14 .... **174** B3
Albert Gdns *NEWH/MOS* M40 ... **109** C2
Albert Gv *FWTH* BL4 .... **66** D3 🔲
   WGTN/LGST M12 .... **126** B5 🔲
Albert Hill St *DID/WITH* M20 ... **163** F2 🔲
Albert Park Rd *BRO* M7 .... **105** D2
Albert Pl *ALT* WA14 .... **174** B2
   BRUN/LGST M13 .... **126** A6
Albert Rd *BOL* BL1 .... **45** E1
   CHD SK8 .... **181** E5
   ECC M30 .... **102** A5
   FWTH BL4 .... **66** B3 🔲
   HALE/TIMP WA15 .... **174** C4
   HTNM SK4 .... **165** F2 🔲
   HYDE SK14 .... **150** B1
   SALE M33 .... **160** A1
   WHTF M45 .... **71** E3
   WILM/AE SK9 .... **203** E5
Albert Rd East
   HALE/TIMP WA15 .... **174** C4 🔲
Albert Rd West *BOL* BL1 .... **45** D1
Albert Royds St *MILN* OL16 .... **23** F3
Albert Sq *ALT* WA14 .... **174** B4
   STLY SK15 .... **114** A6
Albert St *BOLS/LL* BL3 .... **49** F6 🔲
   BRAM/HZG SK7 .... **184** B4 🔲
   BURY BL9 .... **34** B5
   CHAD OL9 .... **94** C2
   DROY M43 .... **110** C6
   DTN/ASHW M34 .... **130** A6 🔲
   EDGY/DAV SK3 .... **166** B4
   FWTH BL4 .... **66** B4 🔲
   FWTH BL4 .... **66** C3
   HEY OL10 .... **36** C5
   HYDE SK14 .... **132** A6
   IRL M44 .... **134** C5 🔲
   LIT OL15 .... **12** B6

MDTN M24 .... **75** F4
MILN OL16 .... **42** A2
OLDE OL4 .... **80** C6 🔲
OLDS OL8 .... **94** C4
OLDTF/WHR M16 .... **123** D3 🔲
OP/CLY M11 .... **108** A6
PWCH M25 .... **89** D1 🔲
RAMS BL0 .... **6** C5
ROY/SHW OL2 .... **60** B5
ROY/SHW OL2 .... **61** E2 🔲
WHIT OL12 .... **9** D3
Albert St West *FAIL* M35 .... **109** E4 🔲
Albine St *NEWH/MOS* M40 .... **92** A5
Albion Cl *HTNM* SK4 .... **166** C2
Albion Close Gdns *ROY/SHW* OL2 ... **61** D5
Albion Dr *DROY* M43 .... **110** B5
Albion Fold *DROY* M43 .... **110** B5
Albion Gdns *STLY* SK15 .... **114** C5
Albion Gv *SALE* M33 .... **159** E1
Albion Pl *BRAM/HZG* SK7 .... **184** B4 🔲
   BRO M7 .... **105** D2 🔲
   PWCH M25 .... **88** B1 🔲
   SALO/ORD M5 .... **105** D5 🔲
Albion Rd *ROCH* OL11 .... **39** E1
   RUSH/FAL M14 .... **144** A2
Albion St *AUL* OL6 .... **113** D4 🔲
   BOLS/LL BL3 .... **47** D4 🔲
   CHAD OL9 .... **77** E5
   CMANE M1 .... **2** C6
   FAIL M35 .... **106** A6
   FWTH BL4 .... **67** E4 🔲
   HYDE SK14 .... **150** B1 🔲
   LIT OL15 .... **12** B6 🔲
   OLD OL1 .... **79** D4
   OLDTF/WHR M16 .... **123** E5
   RAD M26 .... **67** E3
   ROCH OL11 .... **39** E6
   SALE M33 .... **160** B2 🔲
   STLY SK15 .... **114** C5
   SWIN M27 .... **86** B5
   TOT/BURYW BL8 .... **33** E5
Albion Wy *SALO/ORD* M5 .... **104** C6
   WHIT OL12 .... **21** D3
Albyns Av *CHH* M8 .... **90** B6 🔲
Alcester Av *EDGY/DAV* SK3 ...... **165** D6 🔲
Alcester Cl *MDTN* M24 .... **75** F5
   TOT/BURYW BL8 .... **37** E4
Alcester Rd *CHD/CHDH* SK8 ...... **179** F5
   SALE M33 .... **159** F5
Alcester St *CHAD* OL9 .... **94** B2
Aldborough Cl *DID/WITH* M20 ... **143** F5
Aldbourne Cl *NEWH/MOS* M40 ... **107** E2 🔲
Aldcroft St *GTN* M18 .... **128** A3 🔲
Alden Cl *WHTF* M45 .... **71** E3
Alder Av *BURY* BL9 .... **35** D4
   POY/DIS SK12 .... **199** D6
Alderbank *WHIT* OL12 .... **11** D4
Alderbank Cl *FWTH* BL4 .... **67** D5
Alder Cl *AUL* OL6 .... **96** C6
Alder Ct *CHH* M8 .... **90** A4 🔲
Aldercroft Av *BOLE* BL2 .... **29** E6
   WYTH/NTH M22 .... **178** A5 🔲
Alderdale Dr *DROY* M43 .... **109** D6
   HTNM SK4 .... **145** E6
   MPL/ROM SK6 .... **200** C2
Alderdale Gv *WILM/AE* SK9 ...... **202** C6
Alderdale Rd *CHD/CHDH* SK8 ... **182** A3
Alder Dr *HALE/TIMP* WA15 .... **176** B2
   SWIN M27 .... **85** D4
Alderfield Rd *CCHDY* M21 .... **141** D2
Alder Forest Av *ECC* M30 .... **100** B3
Aldergate Gv *AUL* OL6 .... **114** A2
Alderglen Rd *CHH* M8 .... **106** A1
Alder Gv *BOLE* BL2 .... **29** D1
   DTN/ASHW M34 .... **130** B6 🔲
   EDGY/DAV SK3 .... **166** A5 🔲
   STRET M32 .... **140** C1 🔲
Alder La *OLDS* OL8 .... **95** E3
Alderley Av *BOL* BL1 .... **27** E2 🔲
Alderley Cl *BRAM/HZG* SK7 ...... **199** D1
Alderley Dr *MPL/ROM* SK6 .... **168** C1
Alderley Ldg *WILM/AE* SK9 ...... **203** E6 🔲
Alderley Rd *RDSH* SK5 .... **147** D6
   SALE M33 .... **160** C3 🔲
   URM M41 .... **137** E1
   WILM/AE SK9 .... **203** E5
Alderley St *AUL* OL6 .... **113** E2 🔲
Alderman Foley Dr *WHIT* OL12 ... **21** E3 🔲
Alderman Sq *WGTN/LGST* M12 ... **125** F1 🔲
Aldermary Rd *CCHDY* M21 .... **142** B6
Aldermaston Gv *BKLY* M9 .... **73** F5
Alder Meadow Cl *WHIT* OL12 ... **21** E4 🔲
Aldermere Crs *URM* M41 .... **136** C3
Alderminster Av *LHULT* M38 ...... **65** E6 🔲
Aldermoor Cl *OP/CLY* M11 .... **127** E1 🔲
Alder Rd *CHD/CHDH* SK8 .... **180** B2
   FAIL M35 .... **110** A2
   MDTN M24 .... **76** A1 🔲
   ROCH OL11 .... **39** E5
Alders Av *WYTH/NTH* M22 ...... **178** A2
Alders Ct *OLDS* OL8 .... **96** B5
Aldersgate Rd *CHD/CHDH* SK8 ... **196** A4
   OFTN SK2 .... **183** F1
Aldersgreen Av *MPL/ROM* SK6 ... **201** D2

Alderside Rd *BKLY* M9 .... **91** E5
Aldersley Av *BKLY* M9 .... **90** C1
Alderson St *CHAD* OL9 .... **78** C4
   SLFD M6 .... **104** B3 🔲
Alders Rd *POY/DIS* SK12 .... **201** E2
   WYTH/NTH M22 .... **178** A2
Alder St *BOLS/LL* BL3 .... **47** D6 🔲
   ECC M30 .... **100** B3 🔲
   SLFD M6 .... **104** A5
Aldersyde St *BOLS/LL* BL3 .... **46** B6
Alderue Av *WYTH/NTH* M22 ..... **178** B1
Alderwood Fold *OLDE* OL4 .... **98** A1
Aldfield Rd *NTHM/RTH* M23 ..... **160** C4
Aldford Cl *DID/WITH* M20 .... **164** A2 🔲
Aldford Gv *BOLS/LL* BL3 .... **49** F4 🔲
Aldford Pl *WILM/AE* SK9 .... **209** D3 🔲
Aldham Av *NEWH/MOS* M40 ... **109** D3 🔲
Aldred Cl *CHH* M8 .... **106** C1 🔲
Aldred St *BOLS/LL* BL3 .... **45** F6
   ECC M30 .... **101** D6
   FAIL M35 .... **93** F6
   SALO/ORD M5 .... **104** C5 🔲
Aldsworth Dr *BOLS/LL* BL3 .... **46** C5
   NEWH/MOS M40 .... **107** F2 🔲
Aldwick Av *DID/WITH* M20 ...... **164** A2
Aldwinians Cl *DTN/ASHW* M34 ... **129** F4 🔲
Aldwinter Cv *SALE* M33 .... **158** B1 🔲
Aldwych *ROCH* OL11 .... **40** A4
Aldwych Av *RUSH/FAL* M14 ..... **124** C5 🔲
Aldwyn Cl *DTN/ASHW* M34 ...... **129** F4 🔲
Aldwyn Crs *BRAM/HZG* SK7 .... **184** A5
Aldwyn Park Rd *DTN/ASHW* M34 ... **129** D2
Alexander Av *FAIL* M35 .... **94** B5
Alexander Dr *BURY* BL9 .... **71** E2
   HALE/TIMP WA15 .... **175** E1
   MILN OL16 .... **41** F1
Alexander Gdns *BRO* M7 .... **105** E3 🔲
Alexander Rd *BOLE* BL2 .... **29** D6 🔲
Alexander St *ROCH* OL11 .... **38** C5
   SLFD M6 .... **103** F5 🔲
Alexandra Av *HYDE* SK14 .... **150** A1 🔲
   RUSH/FAL M14 .... **143** D1
   WHTF M45 .... **71** E3 🔲
Alexandra Cl *EDGY/DAV* SK3 ... **182** A1 🔲
Alexandra Ct *URM* M41 .... **136** C2 🔲
Alexandra Crs *OLD* OL1 .... **79** F3 🔲
Alexandra Dr *BNG/LEV* M19 ..... **145** D4 🔲
Alexandra Gv *IRL* M44 .... **135** D3 🔲
Alexandra Rd *AUL* OL6 .... **112** C3
   DTN/ASHW M34 .... **130** B5
   ECC M30 .... **100** C6
   FWTH BL4 .... **67** E4
   HTNM SK4 .... **166** A2 🔲
   OLDS OL8 .... **96** B1
   OLDTF/WHR M16 .... **123** F5
   RAD M26 .... **67** E3
   SALE M33 .... **160** B2 🔲
   WALK M28 .... **66** A6
Alexandra Rd South
   OLDTF/WHR M16 .... **123** F6
Alexandra St *AUL* OL6 .... **113** E3 🔲
   BOLS/LL BL3 .... **46** B5 🔲
   BRO M7 .... **105** E4 🔲
   FWTH BL4 .... **66** B4 🔲
   HEY OL10 .... **56** C1
   HYDE SK14 .... **150** A2
   OLDS OL8 .... **9** E6
Alexandra Ter *BNG/LEV* M19 ... **145** E2 🔲
Alford Av *DID/WITH* M20 .... **143** E3
Alford Cl *BOLE* BL2 .... **49** D3
Alford Rd *HTNM* SK4 .... **145** F5
Alford St *CHAD* OL9 .... **94** C3 🔲
Alfred Av *WALK* M28 .... **84** B6
Alfred James Cl
   NEWH/MOS M40 .... **107** E4 🔲
Alfred St *AUL* OL6 .... **113** E3 🔲
   BKLY M9 .... **91** E5
   BOLS/LL BL3 .... **47** F5 🔲
   BURY BL9 .... **34** B6
   CHAD OL9 .... **78** A5
   ECC M30 .... **101** E4
   FWTH BL4 .... **66** B1
   HYDE SK14 .... **131** D6
   IRL M44 .... **134** C5 🔲
   LIT OL15 .... **12** B5
   RAMS BL0 .... **6** C6
   ROY/SHW OL2 .... **61** E2
   WALK M28 .... **83** E2 🔲
   WHIT OL12 .... **9** E1 🔲
Alfreton Av *DTN/ASHW* M34 .... **149** E3
Alfreton Rd *OFTN* SK2 .... **184** B1
Alfriston Dr *NTHM/RTH* M23 ... **161** E3 🔲
Algernon Rd *WALK* M28 .... **83** D1
Algernon St *ECC* M30 .... **101** E4
   SWIN M27 .... **85** E5 🔲
Alger St *AUL* OL6 .... **113** E2 🔲
Algreave Rd *EDGY/DAV* SK3 .... **165** E5
Alice St *BOLS/LL* BL3 .... **46** A4 🔲
   HYDE SK14 .... **150** C4 🔲
   SALE M33 .... **160** B1 🔲
   SWIN M27 .... **86** C1 🔲
   WHIT OL12 .... **23** F4
Alicia Dr *WHIT* OL12 .... **22** C3
Alison St *ROY/SHW* OL2 .... **61** E1
   RUSH/FAL M14 .... **124** A6

Alker Rd *NEWH/MOS* M40 .... **107** E4 🔲
Alkrington Cl *BURY* BL9 .... **71** E1 🔲
Alkrington Gn *MDTN* M24 .... **75** D5
Alkrington Hall Rd North
   MDTN M24 .... **75** D4
Alkrington Hall Rd South
   MDTN M24 .... **74** C5
Alkrington Park Rd *MDTN* M24 .... **74** C4
Allandale *ALT* WA14 .... **173** F3
Allandale Dr *ROY/SHW* OL2 .... **60** A4
Allandale *BNG/LEV* M19 ..... **145** D2 🔲
Allan Roberts Cl *BKLY* M9 .... **91** E4
Allanson Rd *WYTH/NTH* M22 ...... **162** C4
Alldis Cl *OFTN* SK2 .... **183** F2
Allen Av *HYDE* SK14 .... **151** D3
Allenby Rd *IRL* M44 .... **154** B1
   SWIN M27 .... **101** D1
Allenby St *ROY/SHW* OL2 .... **61** E2 🔲
Allen Cl *ROY/SHW* OL2 .... **61** E3
Allendale Dr *BURY* BL9 .... **53** E6
Allen Rd *URM* M41 .... **139** D2
Allen St *BOLS/LL* BL3 .... **49** E6 🔲
   MILN OL16 .... **40** B2
   OLDS OL8 .... **78** B5 🔲
   RAD M26 .... **50** C6 🔲
   TOT/BURYW BL8 .... **33** D4 🔲
   TOT/BURYW BL8 .... **33** D4 🔲
Allerdean Wk *HTNM* SK4 .... **165** D2
Allesley Dr *CHH* M8 .... **106** A2
Allgreave Cl *SALE* M33 .... **160** B4
Alligin Cl *CHAD* OL9 .... **77** E3
Allingham St *BRUN/LGST* M13 ... **125** F5 🔲
Allington Dr *ECC* M30 .... **101** F3
Allison Gv *ECC* M30 .... **100** C6
Allison St *CHH* M8 .... **106** A2
Allotment Rd *IRL* M44 .... **134** B5
All Saint's Cl *ROY/SHW* OL2 ...... **60** B4
Allsaint's Rd *HTNM* SK4 .... **166** B2
All Saints' St *BOL* BL1 .... **47** D1
   NEWH/MOS M40 .... **109** D2 🔲
All Saints Ter *WHIT* OL12 .... **23** F3
Alma La *WILM/AE* SK9 .... **203** E5
Alma Rd *BNG/LEV* M19 .... **145** E3
   BRAM/HZG SK7 .... **199** E1
   HTNM SK4 .... **145** F6
   SALE M33 .... **158** C3
Alma St *BOLS/LL* BL3 .... **46** A5 🔲
   BOLS/LL BL3 .... **49** F6 🔲
   ECC M30 .... **102** A6
   FWTH BL4 .... **67** F6 🔲
   RAD M26 .... **51** D4
   STLY SK15 .... **114** C5
   WHIT OL12 .... **23** D4 🔲
Alminstone Cl
   NEWH/MOS M40 .... **109** E3 🔲
Almond Av *BURY* BL9 .... **35** D4 🔲
Almond Cl *EDGY/DAV* SK3 .... **166** A5
   FAIL M35 .... **110** A1
   LIT OL15 .... **12** A5
   SLFD M6 .... **104** B5 🔲
Almond Dr *SALE* M33 .... **139** D5
Almond Gv *BOL* BL1 .... **28** A4 🔲
Almond Rd *OLDE* OL4 .... **80** D2 🔲
Almond St *BOL* BL1 .... **28** A3
   FWTH BL4 .... **66** A3
   NEWH/MOS M40 .... **106** C3 🔲
Almond Tree Rd *CHD/CHDH* SK8 .. **181** E6 🔲
Almond Wy *HYDE* SK14 .... **151** E1
Alms Hill Rd *CHH* M8 .... **90** B6
Alness Rd *OLDTF/WHR* M16 ...... **142** C1
Alnwick Dr *BURY* BL9 .... **53** D4
Alnwick Rd *BKLY* M9 .... **74** B6
Alpha Ct *DTN/ASHW* M34 .... **129** D6
Alphagate Dr *DTN/ASHW* M34 ... **129** D6
Alpha Pl *HULME* M15 .... **123** F2 🔲
Alpha Rd *STRET* M32 .... **140** A2 🔲
Alpha St *OP/CLY* M11 .... **127** F2 🔲
   SLFD M6 .... **104** A4
Alpha St West *SLFD* M6 .... **103** F4
Alphin Cl *MOSL* OL5 .... **99** F2
Alphin Sq *MOSL* OL5 .... **99** E4
Alphonsus St *OLDTF/WHR* M16 .. **123** D5
Alpine Dr *MILN* OL16 .... **25** E6
   ROY/SHW OL2 .... **60** A6
   WHIT OL12 .... **11** D5
Alpine Rd *STKP* SK1 .... **167** E4 🔲
Alpine St *OP/CLY* M11 .... **108** C5 🔲
Alport Av *OLDTF/WHR* M16 ...... **142** A1 🔲
Alresford Rd *MDTN* M24 .... **75** D6
   SLFD M6 .... **103** E2
Alsager Cl *CCHDY* M21 .... **141** F5
Alsop Av *BRO* M7 .... **88** C6 🔲
Alstead Av *HALE/TIMP* WA15 .... **175** E4
Alston Av *ROY/SHW* OL2 .... **61** F1
   SALE M33 .... **159** D2
   STRET M32 .... **120** C6
Alston Cl *BRAM/HZG* SK7 .... **183** E6 🔲
Alstone Dr *ALT* WA14 .... **173** E1 🔲
Alstone Rd *HTNM* SK4 .... **146** A5
Alston Gdns *BNG/LEV* M19 .... **145** D6
Alston Rd *GTN* M18 .... **127** F4 🔲
Alston St *BOLS/LL* BL3 .... **46** C6 🔲
   TOT/BURYW BL8 .... **33** D3 🔲
Altair Av *WYTH/NTH* M22 .... **192** B1
Altair Pl *BRO* M7 .... **105** D3

Altcar Gv *RDSH* SK5 .... **146** C1
Altcar Wk *WYTH/NTH* M22 .... **178** A5
Alt Fold Dr *OLDS* OL8 .... **97** D2
Alt Gv *AUL* OL6 .... **112** C1
Altham Cl *BURY* BL9 .... **52** B2 🔲
Alt Hill La *AUL* OL6 .... **96** C5
Alt Hill Rd *AUL* OL6 .... **97** D4
Alt La *AUL* OL6 .... **97** D3
   OLDS OL8 .... **97** E2
Alton Av *URM* M41 .... **136** B1
Alton Cl *AUL* OL6 .... **97** D6
   BURY BL9 .... **53** E4 🔲
Alton Rd *WILM/AE* SK9 .... **203** D3
Alton Sq *OP/CLY* M11 .... **127** F2 🔲
Alton St *OLDS* OL8 .... **96** A2
Altrincham Rd *NTHM/RTH* M23 .. **160** B6
   WILM/AE SK9 .... **192** A5
   WYTH/NTH M22 .... **162** A6
Altrincham St *CMANE* M1 .... **3** G6
Alum Crs *BURY* BL9 .... **53** E6
Alvanley Cl *SALE* M33 .... **159** F4
Alvanley Crs *EDGY/DAV* SK3 .... **182** A1
Alvan Sq *OP/CLY* M11 .... **127** F2 🔲
Alva Rd *OLDE* OL4 .... **80** B1
Alvaston Av *HTNM* SK4 .... **165** F2
Alvaston Rd *GTN* M18 .... **127** F5
Alveley Av *DID/WITH* M20 .... **144** A6
Alverstone Rd *DID/WITH* M20 ... **144** A5 🔲
Alveston Dr *WILM/AE* SK9 .... **204** A3
Alvington Gv *BRAM/HZG* SK7 ... **183** E6
Alwin Rd *ROY/SHW* OL2 .... **61** E1
Alwinton Av *HTNM* SK4 .... **164** C2
Alworth Rd *BKLY* M9 .... **74** B6
Alwyn Dr *BRUN/LGST* M13 .... **125** F5
Ambergate St *OP/CLY* M11 .... **108** A5 🔲
Amberley Cl *BOLS/LL* BL3 .... **45** D4
Amberley Dr *HALE/TIMP* WA15 .. **189** F1
   IRL M44 .... **135** E2
   NTHM/RTH M23 .... **177** E2
Amberley Rd *SALE* M33 .... **138** C6
Amber St *ANC* M4 .... **3** F1
Amberwood *CHAD* OL9 .... **76** C5 🔲
Amberwood Dr *NTHM/RTH* M23 .. **176** B1
Amblecote Dr East *LHULT* M38 .. **65** C5
Amblecote Dr West *LHULT* M38 .. **65** E5
Ambleside *STLY* SK15 .... **114** B4
Ambleside Av *AULW* OL7 .... **112** A3
   HALE/TIMP WA15 .... **176** A2 🔲
Ambleside Cl *BOLE* BL2 .... **30** A3 🔲
   MDTN M24 .... **74** C2
Ambleside Rd *RDSH* SK5 .... **147** D5
   URM M41 .... **136** C2
Ambrose Dr *DID/WITH* M20 .... **162** B1
Ambrose St *ROCH* OL11 .... **40** A1
   WGTN/LGST M12 .... **126** B2
Ambush St *OP/CLY* M11 .... **128** A2
Amelia St *DTN/ASHW* M34 .... **130** A5
   HYDE SK14 .... **150** C1 🔲
Amersham Cl *URM* M41 .... **118** C4
Amersham Pl *BNG/LEV* M19 ...... **145** E5
Amersham St *SALQ/ORD* M5 ..... **104** A6
Amesbury Gv *RDSH* SK5 .... **147** D6 🔲
Amesbury Rd *BKLY* M9 .... **91** F1
Amherst Rd *DID/WITH* M20 .... **144** A3
Amlwch Av *OFTN* SK2 .... **184** B1 🔲
Amory St *WGTN/LGST* M12 .... **125** D1 🔲
Amos Av *NEWH/MOS* M40 .... **109** D3
Amos Sq *BKLY* M9 .... **92** A6
   SLFD M6 .... **103** F5
Ampney Cl *ECC* M30 .... **100** C6
Amwell St *CHH* M8 .... **90** C6
Amy St *MDTN* M24 .... **75** F2
   WHIT OL12 .... **21** F4
Anaconda Dr *CSLFD* M3 .... **105** F4
Anchorage Quay *SALQ/ORD* M5 . **122** B2
Anchorage Rd *URM* M41 .... **139** E2
Anchor Cl *BNG/LEV* M19 .... **146** A2
Anchor La *FWTH* BL4 .... **65** D4
Anchorside Cl *CCHDY* M21 .... **141** F4 🔲
Anchor St *OLD* OL1 .... **79** D3 🔲
Ancoats Gv *ANC* M4 .... **107** E6
Ancoats Gv North *ANC* M4 .... **107** E6
Ancoats St *OLDE* OL4 .... **80** C5 🔲
Anderton Cl *TOT/BURYW* BL8 .... **32** A6
Anderton Gv *AUL* OL6 .... **113** F2
Anderton Wy *WILM/AE* SK9 ...... **194** B6 🔲
Andoc Av *ECC* M30 .... **102** B6
Andover Av *MDTN* M24 .... **75** F6
Andover St *ECC* M30 .... **101** D6
Andre St *OP/CLY* M11 .... **109** D5 🔲
Andrew Cl *RAD* M26 .... **70** A2
   TOT/BURYW BL8 .... **18** A4
Andrew La *BOL* BL1 .... **28** A1
   MPL/ROM SK6 .... **186** C2
Andrew Rd *BKLY* M9 .... **91** E4
Andrews Av *URM* M41 .... **117** F6
Andrew St *AUL* OL6 .... **113** E2 🔲
   BURY BL9 .... **34** B5
   CHAD OL9 .... **77** E3
   DROY M43 .... **111** D3
   FAIL M35 .... **93** F5 🔲
   HTNM SK4 .... **166** B3 🔲
   HYDE SK14 .... **132** A6
   MDTN M24 .... **76** A4
   MOSL OL5 .... **99** D5

Anerley Rd *DID/WITH* M20 .... **163** F1
Anfield Cl *BURY* BL9 .... **53** F6
Anfield Rd *BOLS/LL* BL3 .... **64** C1
   CHD/CHDH SK8 .... **181** D5
   NEWH/MOS M40 .... **93** E4
   SALE M33 .... **140** A6 🔲
Angela Av *ROY/SHW* OL2 .... **78** C1
Angela St *HULME* M15 .... **123** E2
Angel Cl *DUK* SK16 .... **130** C2
Angelko Ri *OLD* OL1 .... **62** B6
Angelo St *BOL* BL1 .... **27** E4
Angel St *ANC* M4 .... **106** B4
   BRAM/HZG SK7 .... **184** B3 🔲
   DTN/ASHW M34 .... **130** B5
Anglers Rest *IRL* M44 .... **134** C6
Anglesea Av *OFTN* SK2 .... **183** D1 🔲
Anglesey Cl *AULW* OL7 .... **112** A1 🔲
Anglesey Dr *POY/DIS* SK12 ...... **198** C3
Anglesey Gv *CHD/CHDH* SK8 .... **181** D1
Anglesey Rd *AULW* OL7 .... **112** A1
Anglesey Water *POY/DIS* SK12 .. **198** C3
Angleside Av *BNG/LEV* M19 ...... **164** C1
Angle St *BOLE* BL2 .... **28** C6
Anglia Gv *BOLS/LL* BL3 .... **46** A5
Angora Cl *CSLFD* M3 .... **105** E4
Angouleme Wy *BURY* BL9 .... **33** F6
Angus Av *HEY* OL10 .... **36** B6
Annable Rd *DROY* M43 .... **127** F3 🔲
   GTN M18 .... **127** F3 🔲
   IRL M44 .... **135** D3
   MPL/ROM SK6 .... **168** B2
Annald Sq *DROY* M43 .... **128** B1 🔲
Annan St *DTN/ASHW* M34 .... **130** A5 🔲
Annecy Cl *TOT/BURYW* BL8 ...... **32** C3
Anne Nuttall Rd *HULME* M15 ..... **123** E2 🔲
Annersley Av *ROY/SHW* OL2 ..... **61** E3
Annesley Rd *NEWH/MOS* M40 ... **93** E4
Anne St *DUK* SK16 .... **131** E1
Annie St *RAMS* BL0 .... **18** B1 🔲
   SALQ/ORD M5 .... **103** F5
Annis Cl *WILM/AE* SK9 .... **209** F3 🔲
Annisdale Cl *ECC* M30 .... **100** C5 🔲
Annis Rd *BOLS/LL* BL3 .... **45** F5 🔲
   WILM/AE SK9 .... **209** F3
Ann Sq *AULW* OL7 .... **130** A1
   DTN/ASHW M34 .... **129** F6
   FWTH BL4 .... **66** C4
   HEY OL10 .... **37** E4
   HYDE SK14 .... **131** D6
   RDSH SK5 .... **166** C1
   ROCH OL11 .... **40** A1 🔲
Anscombe Cl *NEWH/MOS* M40 .. **107** E4 🔲
Ansdell Av *CCHDY* M21 .... **141** F3 🔲
Ansdell Dr *DROY* M43 .... **109** F5
Ansdell Rd *MILN* OL16 .... **40** C3
   RDSH SK5 .... **147** E2
Ansdell St *CHH* M8 .... **90** B6
Ansell Cl *GTN* M18 .... **127** E3 🔲
Anselms Ct *OLDS* OL8 .... **95** D1
Ansleigh Av *CHH* M8 .... **90** B4
Ansley Gv *HTNM* SK4 .... **165** F2
Anslow Cl *NEWH/MOS* M40 ...... **107** E2 🔲
Anson Av *SWIN* M27 .... **101** F1 🔲
Anson Cl *BRAM/HZG* SK7 .... **197** D4
Anson Rd *DTN/ASHW* M34 .... **147** E1
   POY/DIS SK12 .... **199** F6
   RUSH/FAL M14 .... **125** E5
   SWIN M27 .... **101** F1 🔲
   WILM/AE SK9 .... **204** C2
Anson St *BOL* BL1 .... **28** A4 🔲
   ECC M30 .... **100** C4
Answell Av *CHH* M8 .... **90** B3
Antares Av *BRO* M7 .... **105** E4 🔲
Anthony Cl *WGTN/LGST* M12 .... **125** F2
Anthony St *MOSL* OL5 .... **98** C4
Antrim Cl *BNG/LEV* M19 .... **164** B3 🔲
Apethorn La *HYDE* SK14 .... **150** A3
Apfel La *CHAD* OL9 .... **77** F4
Apollo Av *BURY* BL9 .... **53** D6
Apperley Gra *ECC* M30 .... **101** F3
Appian Wy *BRO* M7 .... **105** F2
Appleby Av *HALE/TIMP* WA15 ... **176** A2
   HYDE SK14 .... **131** D4 🔲
Appleby Cl *EDGY/DAV* SK3 .... **182** B2
   TOT/BURYW BL8 .... **32** A5
Appleby Rd *CHD/CHDH* SK8 ...... **179** F3
Apple Cl *OLDS* OL8 .... **97** D1
Appledore Dr *BOLE* BL2 .... **30** A5
   NTHM/RTH M23 .... **160** B6 🔲
Appleford Dr *CHH* M8 .... **106** C1
Apple St *HYDE* SK14 .... **152** A4
Appleton Gv *SALE* M33 .... **158** C3
Appleton Rd *HALE/TIMP* WA15 .. **174** C6
   HTNM SK4 .... **146** B5
Apple Tree Wk *SALE* M33 .... **138** A6 🔲
Apple Wy *MDTN* M24 .... **75** F5 🔲
Applewood *CHAD* OL9 .... **76** B4
April Cl *OLDS* OL8 .... **97** D1
Apsley Cl *ALT* WA14 .... **173** F6
Apsley Gv *ALT* WA14 .... **173** F6
   WGTN/LGST M12 .... **125** D3
Apsley Rd *DTN/ASHW* M34 ..... **130** A5 🔲
Apsley St *STKP* SK1 .... **167** D4 🔲
Aquarius La *SLFD* M6 .... **105** D3 🔲

Aquarius St HULME M15 .... 124 B4
Aqueduct Rd BOLS/LL BL3 .... 48 A5
Aragon Dr HEY OL10 .... 37 D5 🔢
Aragon Wy MPL/ROM SK6 .... 186 C1
Arbor Av BNG/LEV M19 .... 145 E4
Arbor Dr BNG/LEV M19 .... 145 D4
Arbor Gv DROY M43 .... 110 A4
Arbory Av NEWH/MOS M40 .... 82 C5
Arbour Cl BURY BL9 .... 33 F1 🔢
   SLFD M6 .... 104 A4 🔢
Arbour Rd OLDE OL4 .... 97 F1
Arbroath St OP/CLY M11 .... 109 E6
Arbury Av EDGY/DAV SK3 .... 165 D6
Arcadia Av SALE M33 .... 159 E4
Archer Av BOLE BL2 .... 48 A1
Archer Gv BOLE BL2 .... 48 A1 🔢
Archer Pk MDTN M24 .... 74 C3
Archer Pl URM M41 .... 120 A6 🔢
Archer St MOSL OL5 .... 99 D3
   OFTN SK2 .... 184 A2 🔢
   OP/CLY M11 .... 130 B2
Archie St SALQ/ORD M5 .... 122 B2 🔢
Arch St BOL BL1 .... 47 E1
Arclid Cl WILM/AE SK9 .... 204 C1
Arcon Cl MILN OL16 .... 41 F1
Arcon Dr OLDTF/WHR M16 .... 125 F6
Ardale Av NEWH/MOS M40 .... 93 D3
Ardcombe Av BKLY M9 .... 74 A6 🔢
Arden Av MDTN M24 .... 75 F6
Arden Cl AUL OL6 .... 114 A1
   BURY BL9 .... 52 C1 🔢
Arden Ct BRAM/HZG SK7 .... 182 B6 🔢
Ardent Wy BRO M7 .... 88 C4
Ardenfield DTN/ASHW M34 .... 149 E4
Ardenfield Dr WYTH/NTH M22 ...... 178 C5
Arden Gv NEWH/MOS M40 .... 93 D4
Arden Lodge Rd NTHM/RTH M23 .. 160 B6
Arden Rd HALE/TIMP WA15 .... 159 E5
Ardens Cl SWIN M27 .... 85 E3 🔢
Arden St CHAD OL9 .... 94 B2
Arderne Rd HALE/TIMP WA15 .... 159 E5
Ardern Gv STKP SK1 .... 167 D5 🔢
Ardern Rd CHH M8 .... 90 A4
Ardwick Gn North
   WGTN/LGST M12 .... 125 D2
Ardwick Gn South CMANE M1 ..... 124 C2
Argo St BOLS/LL BL3 .... 46 B5
Argosy Dr ECC M30 .... 118 A2
   MANAIR M90 .... 191 D2
Argus St OLDS OL8 .... 95 D3
Argyle Av RUSH/FAL M14 .... 125 F5 🔢
   WALK M28 .... 66 A6
   WHTF M45 .... 71 E3
Argyle Crs HEY OL10 .... 36 C6 🔢
Argyle St BRAM/HZG SK7 .... 184 C5
   BURY BL9 .... 34 A3
   DROY M43 .... 110 B6
   GTN M18 .... 127 E4 🔢
   HEY OL10 .... 36 B3 🔢
   MILN OL16 .... 40 B3 🔢
   OLD OL1 .... 79 F3
   SWIN M27 .... 85 F6
Argyll Av STRET M32 .... 139 F1
Argyll Cl FAIL M35 .... 94 C6 🔢
Argyll Park Rd FAIL M35 .... 94 C6
Argyll Rd CHAD OL9 .... 94 A2
   CHD/CHDH SK8 .... 181 D2
Argyll St AUL OL6 .... 115 F4
   MOSL OL5 .... 99 D4
Arkendale Cl FAIL M35 .... 95 D6 🔢
Arkholme WALK M28 .... 82 B5
Arkle Av WILM/AE SK9 .... 194 C5
Arkle Dr CHAD OL9 .... 77 D3
Ark St BNG/LEV M19 .... 145 E1 🔢
Arkwright Cl BOL BL1 .... 27 D6 🔢
Arkwright Dr MPL/ROM SK6 .... 187 E1
Arkwright Rd MPL/ROM SK6 .... 187 E1
Arkwright St CHAD OL9 .... 78 A5
Arlen Rd BOLE BL2 .... 47 F4
Arlen Wy HEY OL10 .... 36 C5 🔢
Arley Av BURY BL9 .... 33 F2
   DID/WITH M20 .... 143 D6
Arley Cl ALT WA14 .... 158 B5
   DUK SK16 .... 131 E3
Arley Dr ROY/SHW OL2 .... 62 A1
   SALE M33 .... 159 E3
Arley Gv EDGY/DAV SK3 .... 182 B5
Arley Mere Cl CHD/CHDH SK8 ..... 181 D4 🔢
Arley St RAD M26 .... 68 C2
Arlies Cl STLY SK15 .... 114 B3
Arlies La STLY SK15 .... 114 C2
Arlies St AUL OL6 .... 115 E3
Arlington Av DTN/ASHW M34 ...... 149 E1
   PWCH M25 .... 88 C3 🔢
   SWIN M27 .... 101 E1
Arlington Cl BURY BL9 .... 19 D3
Arlington Crs WILM/AE SK9 .... 202 C6
Arlington Dr OFTN SK2 .... 183 E4
   POY/DIS SK12 .... 198 B6
Arlington Rd CHD/CHDH SK8 .... 180 A3
   STRET M32 .... 139 F2
Arlington St AUL OL6 .... 113 D4 🔢
   BOLS/LL BL3 .... 47 D6
   CHH M8 .... 90 A4
   CSLFD M3 .... 105 E5

Arlington Wy WILM/AE SK9 .... 202 C6
Arliss Av BNG/LEV M19 .... 145 E3
Armadale Av BKLY M9 .... 92 B1 🔢
Armadale Cl EDGY/DAV SK3 .... 182 C3
Armadale Rd BOLS/LL BL3 .... 44 C5
   DUK SK16 .... 131 D1
Armdale Ri OLDE OL4 .... 80 C2
Armentieres Cl STLY SK15 .... 114 B6
Armitage Av LHULT M38 .... 82 B1 🔢
Armitage Cl HYDE SK14 .... 150 C3
   MDTN M24 .... 74 B4
   OLDS OL8 .... 95 D2
Armitage Gv LHULT M38 .... 82 A1 🔢
Armitage Rd ALT WA14 .... 174 B4
Armitage St ECC M30 .... 101 D6
Armit Rd OLDE OL4 .... 99 F1
Armour Pl BKLY M9 .... 91 D3 🔢
Armoury St EDGY/DAV SK3 .... 166 C5 🔢
Arm Rd WHIT OL12 .... 11 F6
Armstrong Hurst Cl WHIT OL12 ... 23 F2 🔢
Arncliffe Dr NTHM/RTH M23 .... 177 E4
Arncliffe Ri OLDE OL4 .... 65 E5
Arncot Rd BOL BL1 .... 28 A2
Arncott Cl ROY/SHW OL2 .... 61 E5 🔢
Arne Cl OFTN SK2 .... 185 E2
Arnesby Av SALE M33 .... 140 C5
Arne St CHAD OL9 .... 77 E6 🔢
Arnfield Rd DID/WITH M20 .... 144 A5
   EDGY/DAV SK3 .... 182 B2
Arnold Av HEY OL10 .... 56 C2
   HYDE SK14 .... 151 D4
Arnold Cl DUK SK16 .... 132 B2 🔢
Arnold Dr DROY M43 .... 110 B6
   MDTN M24 .... 58 A6
Arnold Rd EDGW/EG BL7 .... 14 A5
   HYDE SK14 .... 151 D4
   OLDTF/WHR M16 .... 142 C2
Arnold St AUL OL6 .... 113 D3
   BOL BL1 .... 27 D5
   EDGY/DAV SK3 .... 166 C6 🔢
   OLD OL1 .... 79 E3
Arnott Crs HULME M15 .... 124 A4
Arnside Av BRAM/HZG SK7 .... 184 A5
   CHAD OL9 .... 77 E6
   HTNM SK4 .... 146 B5
Arnside Cl CHD/CHDH SK8 .... 179 F3 🔢
   MPL/ROM SK6 .... 200 C1 🔢
   ROY/SHW OL2 .... 62 D2
Arnside Dr HYDE SK14 .... 131 D5
   ROCH OL11 .... 37 F2
Arnside Gv BOLE BL2 .... 48 C1
   SALE M33 .... 139 F6
Arnside St RUSH/FAL M14 .... 143 F1
Arran Av OLDS OL8 .... 96 A2
   SALE M33 .... 160 A2
   STRET M32 .... 139 E1
Arran Cl BOLS/LL BL3 .... 44 C3
Arran Gdns URM M41 .... 119 D4 🔢
   URM M41 .... 119 E4 🔢
Arran Gv RAD M26 .... 50 C4
Arran Rd DUK SK16 .... 131 D2 🔢
Arran St BRO M7 .... 105 E1
   NEWH/MOS M40 .... 92 A5 🔢
Arras Gv DTN/ASHW M34 .... 128 A6 🔢
Arrivals Wy MANAIR M90 .... 191 F2
Arrowfield Rd CCHDY M21 .... 142 B5
Arrowhill Rd RAD M26 .... 51 D1 🔢
Arrow St BOL BL1 .... 46 C1
   BRO M7 .... 105 E2
Arthington St MILN OL16 .... 23 F5
Arthog Dr HALE/TIMP WA15 .... 189 D1
Arthog Rd DID/WITH M20 .... 164 A3
   HALE/TIMP WA15 .... 189 D1
Arthur Av WALK M28 .... 66 A6
Arthur La BOLE BL2 .... 30 B4
Arthur Rd OLDTF/WHR M16 .... 126 D6 🔢
Arthur St BOLS/LL BL3 .... 49 E6
   ECC M30 .... 101 D6
   FWTH BL4 .... 66 B3 🔢
   HEY OL10 .... 37 E5 🔢
   HYDE SK14 .... 150 A2 🔢
   PWCH M25 .... 88 A1 🔢
   RDSH SK5 .... 146 C4 🔢
   ROY/SHW OL2 .... 61 E3 🔢
   SWIN M27 .... 85 E6
   TOT/BURYW BL8 .... 33 D5 🔢
   WALK M28 .... 83 F4 🔢
   WALK M28 .... 84 A3 🔢
   WHIT OL12 .... 22 B5
Artillery St BOLS/LL BL3 .... 47 D4
   CSLFD M3 .... 2 B5
Arundale Av OLDTF/WHR M16 ..... 142 C2
Arundel Av BRAM/HZG SK7 .... 198 B1
   ROCH OL11 .... 39 F3
   URM M41 .... 136 A2
   WHTF M45 .... 71 F4 🔢
Arundel Cl HALE/TIMP WA15 .... 176 A6 🔢
   TOT/BURYW BL8 .... 33 D1 🔢
Arundel Gv OFTN SK2 .... 183 F3 🔢
Arundel Rd CHD/CHDH SK8 .... 195 E3
Arundel St AUL OL6 .... 113 F4
   BOL BL1 .... 27 F2
   HULME M15 .... 123 E2
   MOSL OL5 .... 98 C4

OLDE OL4 .... 80 A4
ROCH OL11 .... 39 F3
SWIN M27 .... 85 D3 🔢
Asby Cl MDTN M24 .... 74 B1
Ascension Rd BRO M7 .... 105 E2
Ascot Av SALE M33 .... 158 A2
   STRET M32 .... 122 A6
Ascot Cl CHAD OL9 .... 78 A4
   ROCH OL11 .... 20 C5
Ascot Dr BRAM/HZG SK7 .... 185 E5
   URM M41 .... 136 A1
Ascot Mdw BURY BL9 .... 52 C3 🔢
Ascot Pde BNG/LEV M19 .... 145 D5 🔢
Ascot Rd BOLS/LL BL3 .... 49 D6
   NEWH/MOS M40 .... 108 C3
Ascroft St OLD OL1 .... 79 D5
Asgard Dr SALQ/ORD M5 .... 123 D1
Asgard Gv SALQ/ORD M5 .... 123 D1 🔢
Ash Av ALT WA14 .... 173 E2
   CHD/CHDH SK8 .... 180 C2
   IRL M44 .... 134 B6
Ashawe Gv LHULT M38 .... 82 A2 🔢
Ashbank Av BOLS/LL BL3 .... 44 C3
Ashbee St BOL BL1 .... 27 F4 🔢
Ashberry Cl WILM/AE SK9 .... 204 B3 🔢
Ashbourne Dr BURY BL9 .... 19 E3
Ashbourne Av BOLE BL2 .... 47 F3
   CHD/CHDH SK8 .... 181 D1
   MDTN M24 .... 58 A6
   URM M41 .... 136 C1 🔢
Ashbourne Cl WHIT OL12 .... 11 E5 🔢
Ashbourne Crs SALE M33 .... 160 B3
Ashbourne Dr AUL OL6 .... 114 A1
   MPL/ROM SK6 .... 200 C3
Ashbourne Gv BRO M7 .... 89 F6
   WALK M28 .... 83 F5
   WHTF M45 .... 70 C2
Ashbourne Rd BRAM/HZG SK7 .... 199 D1
   DTN/ASHW M34 .... 148 C3
   ECC M30 .... 101 F6
   SLFD M6 .... 103 D2 🔢
   STRET M32 .... 120 B5
Ashbourne St ROCH OL11 .... 20 C4
Ashbridge TRPK M17 .... 120 C3
Ashbridge Rd FAIL M35 .... 110 C1
Ashbrook Av DTN/ASHW M34 ...... 128 C6
Ashbrook Cl CHD/CHDH SK8 .... 179 F6 🔢
   DTN/ASHW M34 .... 128 C6 🔢
Ashbrook Crs WHIT OL12 .... 24 A1
Ashbrook Farm Cl RDSH SK5 ...... 147 D1 🔢
Ashbrook Hey La WHIT OL12 .... 24 A1
Ashbrook La RDSH SK5 .... 147 D1 🔢
Ashbrook St OP/CLY M11 .... 128 B2
Ashburner St BOL BL1 .... 46 C3
Ashburn Gv HTNM SK4 .... 166 A2
Ashburn Rd HTNM SK4 .... 166 A2
Ashburton Cl HYDE SK14 .... 152 C1
Ashburton Rd EDGY/DAV SK3 ..... 182 C3
Ashburton Rd West URM M41 ...... 119 E2
Ashbury Cl BOLS/LL BL3 .... 46 C4
Ashby Av BNG/LEV M19 .... 164 C1
Ashby Cl BOLS/LL BL3 .... 47 F6
Ashby Gv WHTF M45 .... 71 E4
Ash Cl AUL OL6 .... 113 E2
   WHIT OL12 .... 24 A1
Ashcombe Dr BOLE BL2 .... 49 E3
   RAD M26 .... 50 B4 🔢
Ascott Av WYTH/NTH M22 .... 178 B3 🔢
Ashcott Cl HOR/BR BL6 .... 44 B4
Ashcroft WILM/AE SK9 .... 203 D6
Ashcroft Av SLFD M6 .... 103 F3 🔢
Ashdale Av BOLS/LL BL3 .... 44 C3
Ashdale Cl RDSH SK5 .... 147 D6
Ashdale Dr CHD/CHDH SK8 .... 179 F5
   DID/WITH M20 .... 144 B6
Ashdene AUL OL6 .... 113 D5
Ashdene Cl CHAD OL9 .... 78 A2
Ashdene Crs BOLE BL2 .... 29 E3
Ashdene Ri OLD OL1 .... 62 B5
Ashdene Rd DID/WITH M20 .... 144 B5
   HTNM SK4 .... 164 B3
   WILM/AE SK9 .... 203 D6
Ashdown Av BKLY M9 .... 91 E1
   MPL/ROM SK6 .... 150 A6 🔢
Ashdown Dr BOLE BL2 .... 29 D4
   SWIN M27 .... 102 B1
   WALK M28 .... 82 A6
Ashdown Gv BKLY M9 .... 91 E1 🔢
Ashdown Rd HTNM SK4 .... 166 A2
Ashdown Ter BKLY M9 .... 91 E1 🔢
Ashdown Wy ROY/SHW OL2 .... 60 C1
Ash Dr SWIN M27 .... 85 D3
Asher St BOLS/LL BL3 .... 46 A6
Ashes Cl STLY SK15 .... 133 D1 🔢
Ashes Dr BOLE BL2 .... 49 D1
Ashes La MILN OL16 .... 24 C6
   OLDE OL4 .... 81 D5
   STLY SK15 .... 133 D1
Ashfield DTN/ASHW M34 .... 130 B4
Ashfield Av ROCH OL11 .... 40 A2
Ashfield Cl SLFD M6 .... 103 F4 🔢
Ashfield Crs CHD/CHDH SK8 .... 180 B1
   OLDE OL4 .... 81 D5

Ashfield Dr NEWH/MOS M40 .... 109 E3
Ashfield Gv BOL BL1 .... 28 B1 🔲
  EDGY/DAV SK3 .... 183 D3 🔲
  GTN M18 .... 128 A6 🔲
  IRL M44 .... 134 C5
  MPL/ROM SK6 .... 171 F4
Ashfield La MILN OL16 .... 42 A3
Ashfield Rd BRUN/LGST M13 .... 125 F6
  CHD/CHDH SK8 .... 180 B1
  EDGY/DAV SK3 .... 183 D3
  HALE/TIMP WA15 .... 174 C4
  ROCH OL11 .... 40 A2
  SALE M33 .... 139 F6
  URM M41 .... 138 B1
Ashfield Sq DROY M43 .... 110 A6 🔲
Ashfield St OLDS OL8 .... 95 D2
  OP/CLY M11 .... 108 A5
Ashford SALE M33 .... 158 A1
Ashford Av ECC M30 .... 119 D1 🔲
  RDSH SK5 .... 147 D1 🔲
  SWIN M27 .... 101 D1
Ashford Cl BOLE BL2 .... 29 F3 🔲
  OLDE OL4 .... 80 B2 🔲
  TOT/BURYW BL8 .... 32 C6
  WILM/AE SK9 .... 194 A5
Ashford Rd DID/WITH M20 .... 143 E4
  HTNM SK4 .... 146 B5
  WILM/AE SK9 .... 209 E1
Ashford St HEY OL10 .... 36 A5 🔲
Ashgate Av WYTH/NTH M22 .... 178 C3 🔲
Ash Gv ALT WA14 .... 174 A6
  BOL BL1 .... 45 F1
  BOLE BL2 .... 30 A4
  CHD/CHDH SK8 .... 193 F1
  DROY M43 .... 128 B1
  HALE/TIMP WA15 .... 159 D6
  HTNM SK4 .... 146 B6
  LIT OL15 .... 12 A6
Ash Hill Dr MOSL OL5 .... 99 F5
Ashgrove MILN OL16 .... 40 C6 🔲
  MPL/ROM SK6 .... 186 C2
  OLDE OL4 .... 81 E4
  PWCH M25 .... 71 E5
  ROY/SHW OL2 .... 60 B3
  RUSH/FAL M14 .... 125 F5
  STLY SK15 .... 114 A5
  STRET M32 .... 140 A3
  SWIN M27 .... 101 E2
  TOT/BURYW BL8 .... 18 A2
  TOT/BURYW BL8 .... 32 B2
  WALK M28 .... 83 F4
Ashia Cl MILN OL16 .... 40 B1
Ashington Cl BOL BL1 .... 26 C4 🔲
Ashington Dr TOT/BURYW BL8 .... 32 A6 🔲
  TOT/BURYW BL8 .... 32 A6 🔲
Ashkirk St GTN M18 .... 127 E4 🔲
Ashlands SALE M33 .... 139 E6
  SWIN M27 .... 101 D1
  WALK M28 .... 82 D6 🔲
Ashlands Av DTN/ASHW M34 .... 129 F3 🔲
Ashlands Rd HALE/TIMP WA15 ...... 159 D4
Ash La HALE/TIMP WA15 .... 176 A6
Ashlar Dr WGTN/LGST M12 .... 125 E1
Ashlea Gv OLDE OL4 .... 81 F5
Ashleigh Cl ROY/SHW OL2 .... 78 C1 🔲
Ash Leigh Dr BOL BL1 .... 44 C1
Ashleigh Rd HALE/TIMP WA15 .... 159 F5
Ashley Av BOLE BL2 .... 48 B1
  OLDTF/WHR M16 .... 123 E5
  SWIN M27 .... 101 E1
  URM M41 .... 136 C1
Ashley Cl ROCH OL11 .... 39 D3
Ashley Court Dr NEWH/MOS M40 .... 94 A4
Ashley Crs SWIN M27 .... 85 E6
Ashley Dr BRAM/HZG SK7 .... 196 A3
  SALE M33 .... 158 C3
  SWIN M27 .... 101 E1
Ashley Gdns HYDE SK14 .... 150 C2 🔲
  MPL/ROM SK6 .... 200 B1 🔲
Ashley La BKLY M9 .... 92 A5
Ashley Ms WHTF M45 .... 71 F4 🔲
Ashleymill La ALT WA14 .... 188 B1
Ashley Mill La North ALT WA14 ...... 188 B1 🔲
Ashley Rd ALT WA14 .... 174 B4
  DROY M43 .... 109 F5
  HALE/TIMP WA15 .... 174 C5
  OFTN SK2 .... 168 A5
  WILM/AE SK9 .... 203 F2
Ashley St CHAD OL9 .... 78 A3
  HYDE SK14 .... 131 F5
  SLFD M6 .... 103 F5
Ashlor St BURY BL9 .... 33 F6
Ashlyn Gv RUSH/FAL M14 .... 144 B3
Ashlynne AUL OL6 .... 113 D4 🔲
Ashmeade HALE/TIMP WA15 .... 175 F6
Ashmond Rd OLDE OL4 .... 81 D5
Ashmoor Rd WYTH/NTH M22 .... 178 B6
Ashmore Av EDGY/DAV SK3 .... 165 D6 🔲
Ashmount Dr WHIT OL12 .... 23 D3
Ashness Dr BOLE BL2 .... 29 F6
  BRAM/HZG SK7 .... 197 D1
  MDTN M24 .... 56 B6
Ashover Av WGTN/LGST M12 .... 126 A3 🔲

Ashover Cl EDGW/EG BL7 .... 28 A1
Ashover St STRET M32 .... 121 F6
Ashridge Cl HOR/BR BL6 .... 44 A3 🔲
Ashridge Dr DUK SK16 .... 130 C2
  ECC M30 .... 119 D1
Ash Rd DROY M43 .... 110 A5
  DTN/ASHW M34 .... 128 B5
  FWTH BL4 .... 67 D6
  PART M31 .... 154 B2
  POY/DIS SK12 .... 199 D6
Ash Sq OLDE OL4 .... 80 B3
Ashstead Rd SALE M33 .... 160 A4
Ash St BKLY M9 .... 91 E6
  BRAM/HZG SK7 .... 184 B4 🔲
  BURY BL9 .... 34 B5 🔲
  DTN/ASHW M34 .... 129 E2
  EDGY/DAV SK3 .... 165 F5
  FAIL M35 .... 93 F5
  HEY OL10 .... 36 C4
  MDTN M24 .... 76 A2
  OLDE OL4 .... 79 F5
  ROCH OL11 .... 39 D5 🔲
  SLFD M6 .... 104 A5
Ashton Av ALT WA14 .... 174 C1
Ashton Crs CHAD OL9 .... 94 B2
Ashton Field Dr LHULT M38 .... 83 D1
Ashton Gdns ROCH OL11 .... 39 F2
Ashton Hill La DROY M43 .... 128 B1
Ashton La MDTN M24 .... 75 E3
  SALE M33 .... 139 D6
Ashton New Rd OP/CLY M11 .... 108 A6
Ashton Old Rd OP/CLY M11 .... 125 E1
  OP/CLY M11 .... 128 A2
  WGTN/LGST M12 .... 125 E1
Ashton Pl BRAM/HZG SK7 .... 185 D6
Ashton Rd BKLY M9 .... 74 B5 🔲
  DROY M43 .... 110 B6
  DTN/ASHW M34 .... 129 F4
  FAIL M35 .... 111 D1
  HYDE SK14 .... 131 E3
  MPL/ROM SK6 .... 148 C5
  OLDS OL8 .... 96 A1
  PART M31 .... 156 A2
Ashton Rd East FAIL M35 .... 94 A5
Ashton Rd West FAIL M35 .... 93 F6
Ashton St BKLY M9 .... 92 A5
  BOLS/LL BL3 .... 49 F6 🔲
  CHAD OL9 .... 94 A2
  DUK SK16 .... 130 B3
  HEY OL10 .... 37 D5 🔲
  MPL/ROM SK6 .... 150 A5
  ROCH OL11 .... 39 F2 🔲
Ash Tree Av DROY M43 .... 110 A5
Ash Tree Dr DUK SK16 .... 132 A2
Ash Tree Rd CHH M8 .... 90 B4
  HYDE SK14 .... 132 C4
Ashurst Cl BOLE BL2 .... 30 A4 🔲
  HYDE SK14 .... 151 E2 🔲
Ashurst Dr EDGY/DAV SK3 .... 181 F2
Ashurst Rd WYTH/NTH M22 .... 179 D4
Ashville Ter NEWH/MOS M40 .... 92 A4
Ash Wk MDTN M24 .... 75 D5
Ashway Clough North
  OFTN SK2 .... 184 B2 🔲
Ashway Clough South
  OFTN SK2 .... 184 B2 🔲
Ashwell Rd NTHM/RTH M23 .... 161 F6
Ashwell St BOLE BL2 .... 28 C4 🔲
Ashwood CHAD OL9 .... 76 C4
  RAD M26 .... 67 F4
Ashwood Av DID/WITH M20 .... 162 C1
  DTN/ASHW M34 .... 128 B6
  RAMS BL0 .... 7 E4
  SALE M33 .... 158 C2
  WALK M28 .... 66 A6
Ashwood Crs MPL/ROM SK6 .... 171 D6
Ashwood Dr LIT OL15 .... 12 A6
  ROY/SHW OL2 .... 60 A4 🔲
  TOT/BURYW BL8 .... 32 C1 🔲
Ashworth Av BOLS/LL BL3 .... 50 A6 🔲
  DTN/ASHW M34 .... 130 A2 🔲
  URM M41 .... 136 C1 🔲
Ashworth Cl ALT WA14 .... 94 C1 🔲
  CHAD OL9 .... 94 C1 🔲
  LIT OL15 .... 12 B6 🔲
Ashworth La BOL BL1 .... 28 A2
Ashworth Ms HEY OL10 .... 36 B5 🔲
Ashworth St CHH M8 .... 105 F2 🔲
  DTN/ASHW M34 .... 129 F5
  FAIL M35 .... 109 E1
  FWTH BL4 .... 66 A3 🔲
  HEY OL10 .... 56 B1
  OLD OL1 .... 79 D5
  RAD M26 .... 52 A5
  TOT/BURYW BL8 .... 33 D4
  WHIT OL12 .... 22 C5 🔲
Asia St BOLS/LL BL3 .... 47 E5
Askern Av WYTH/NTH M22 .... 178 B4
Askett Cl NEWH/MOS M40 .... 109 E1
Aspen Cl HALE/TIMP WA15 .... 176 C2 🔲
Aspen Gdns WHIT OL12 .... 21 E4 🔲
Aspen Gn DTN/ASHW M34 .... 149 E1
Aspen Wy MPL/ROM SK6 .... 201 E2 🔲
Aspen Wd HYDE SK14 .... 132 A6
Aspenwood Cl MPL/ROM SK6 .... 170 C6 🔲

Aspen Wood Dr CHAD OL9 .... 76 C4
Aspenwood Dr SALE M33 .... 158 A1 🔲
Aspinall Cl WALK M28 .... 82 A2
Aspinall Crs WALK M28 .... 82 A3
Aspinall St HEY OL10 .... 37 F5
  MDTN M24 .... 76 A4
  RUSH/FAL M14 .... 125 D6 🔲
Aspin La ANC M4 .... 106 B4
Aspland Rd HYDE SK14 .... 151 E4
Aspull St OLDE OL4 .... 80 A6
Asquith Av DUK SK16 .... 131 D3 🔲
  RDSH SK5 .... 147 D2
Assheton Av DTN/ASHW M34 .... 111 D6
Assheton Cl AUL OL6 .... 112 C4 🔲
Assheton Crs NEWH/MOS M40 ...... 109 E3 🔲
Assheton Rd NEWH/MOS M40 ...... 109 E3
  ROY/SHW OL2 .... 61 D2
Assheton St MDTN M24 .... 75 E1 🔲
Assumption Rd MDTN M24 .... 56 B6 🔲
Astan Av DROY M43 .... 109 E4
Astbury Av DTN/ASHW M34 .... 111 E6
Astbury Cl HALE/TIMP WA15 .... 174 C1 🔲
  OLDE OL4 .... 81 D5
Astbury Crs EDGY/DAV SK3 .... 182 B1
Astbury St RAD M26 .... 69 F2
Aster St OLD OL1 .... 78 C2
Astley Cl ROY/SHW OL2 .... 61 D2 🔲
Astley Ct IRL M44 .... 134 C3 🔲
Astley Gdns DUK SK16 .... 130 C1
Astley Gv STLY SK15 .... 114 A4
Astley Hall Dr RAMS BL0 .... 19 D1 🔲
Astley La BOL BL1 .... 27 F4
  STLY SK15 .... 114 A5
Astley St BOL BL1 .... 27 F5
  DUK SK16 .... 130 B2
  EDGY/DAV SK3 .... 166 C4 🔲
  OP/CLY M11 .... 109 D6
  STLY SK15 .... 132 B1
Aston Av RUSH/FAL M14 .... 143 E2 🔲
Aston Cl EDGY/DAV SK3 .... 182 A1
Astor Rd BNG/LEV M19 .... 144 C4
  SALQ/ORD M5 .... 103 D2
Atcham Gv BKLY M9 .... 73 F5
Athenian Gdns BRO M7 .... 105 D2 🔲
Athens Dr WALK M28 .... 83 D3
Athens St STKP SK1 .... 167 E4 🔲
Athens Wy OLDE OL4 .... 80 C5
Atherfield BOLE BL2 .... 29 F3 🔲
Atherley Gv NEWH/MOS M40 .... 94 A3
Atherstone Av CHH M8 .... 90 A3
Atherstone Cl TOT/BURYW BL8 ...... 33 D3 🔲
Atherton Cl FAIL M35 .... 110 C2
Atherton La IRL M44 .... 134 C6
Atherton St CSLFD M3 .... 2 A5
  ECC M30 .... 100 C6
  EDGY/DAV SK3 .... 166 B5 🔲
  OLDE OL4 .... 80 C6
Athlone Av BOL BL1 .... 27 E2
  BURY BL9 .... 34 A3
  CHD/CHDH SK8 .... 182 A2
  NEWH/MOS M40 .... 92 B5
Athole St SALQ/ORD M5 .... 104 A6
Atholl Av STRET M32 .... 139 E1
Atholl Cl BOLS/LL BL3 .... 45 D3
Atholl Dr HEY OL10 .... 55 F1
Athol Rd BRAM/HZG SK7 .... 196 B6
  OLDTF/WHR M16 .... 142 C2
Athol St AUL OL6 .... 113 D4 🔲
  ECC M30 .... 100 C6
  GTN M18 .... 127 F6
  HTNM SK4 .... 166 B2 🔲
  RAMS BL0 .... 7 D4
  WHIT OL12 .... 23 F4
Atkinson Av BOLS/LL BL3 .... 47 F6 🔲
Atkinson Rd SALE M33 .... 139 E5
  URM M41 .... 138 B1 🔲
Atkinson St CHAD OL9 .... 78 B3 🔲
  CSLFD M3 .... 2 B4
  ROCH OL11 .... 39 D5 🔲
  STKP SK1 .... 167 E6 🔲
Atkin St WALK M28 .... 83 E5
Atlanta Av MANAIR M90 .... 191 E1
Atlantic St ALT WA14 .... 173 E1
Atlas Dr AULW OL7 .... 112 B3
  DUK SK16 .... 131 E1 🔲
Atlow Dr NTHM/RTH M23 .... 177 F2
Attenbury's La ALT WA14 .... 158 C5
Attercliffe Rd CCHDY M21 .... 141 E4
Attewell St OP/CLY M11 .... 126 B1 🔲
Attleboro Rd NEWH/MOS M40 .... 92 B6
Attwood Rd HALE/TIMP WA15 ...... 175 F2
Attwood St WGTN/LGST M12 .... 126 B6
Atwood Rd DID/WITH M20 .... 164 A2
Atwood St CMANE M1 .... 3 E6
Auberson Rd BOLS/LL BL3 .... 46 B6 🔲
Aubrey Rd DID/WITH M20 .... 144 C4 🔲
Aubrey St ROCH OL11 .... 40 A2 🔲
  SALQ/ORD M5 .... 122 B2 🔲
Auburn Av HYDE SK14 .... 150 C3
  MPL/ROM SK6 .... 168 C1
Auburn Dr URM M41 .... 138 C2
Auburn Rd DTN/ASHW M34 .... 148 B1

OLDTF/WHR M16 .... 122 C5
Auburn St BOLS/LL BL3 .... 46 B5
  CMANE M1 .... 3 G5 ⬦
Auckland Dr SLFD M6 .... 104 B2
Auckland Rd BNG/LEV M19 .... 145 D3 ⬦
Auden Cl OP/CLY M11 .... 109 E6 ⬦
Audenshaw Hall Gv
  DTN/ASHW M34 .... 128 C2
Audenshaw Rd DTN/ASHW M34... 128 C2
Audlem Cl NEWH/MOS M40 ...... 107 E5 ⬦
Audley Av STRET M32 .... 120 A5
Audley Rd BNG/LEV M19 .... 145 F1 ⬦
Audley St AUL OL6 .... 113 F5
  MOSL OL5 .... 99 E5
Audlum Ct BURY BL9 .... 34 B5 ⬦
Audrey Av GTN M18 .... 127 F4
Audrey St BKLY M9 .... 92 A5
Augusta Cl WHIT OL12 .... 22 C4
Augusta St WHIT OL12 .... 22 C4 ⬦
Augustine Webster Cl BKLY M9 .. 91 F5 ⬦
Augustus St BOLS/LL BL3 .... 47 E5 ⬦
  CSLFD M3 .... 106 B3 ⬦
Augustus Wy OLDTF/WHR M16 .. 123 E5 ⬦
Austell Rd WYTH/NTH M22 .... 178 B6
Austen Av BURY BL9 .... 53 D3
Austen Dr DID/WITH M20 .... 164 A1
Austin Av BURY BL9 .... 53 D3
Austin Dr DID/WITH M20 .... 164 A1
Austin Gv BNG/LEV M19 .... 145 D3
Autumn St BRUN/LGST M13 ..... 125 D5 ⬦
Avallon Cl TOT/BURYW BL8 .... 18 A6
Avalon Dr DID/WITH M20 .... 164 A5
Avebury Cl CHH M8 .... 106 A1 ⬦
Avebury Rd NEWH/RTH M23 ..... 177 E2
Avens Rd PART M31 .... 155 D2
Avenue St BOL BL1 .... 27 E6
  STKP SK1 .... 167 D3 ⬦
The Avenue BRO M7 .... 105 D2 ⬦
  BURY BL9 .... 34 A2
  CHD/CHDH SK8 .... 179 E6
  ECC M30 .... 101 E6
  HALE/TIMP WA15 .... 189 D1
  MPL/ROM SK6 .... 168 B2
  ROY/SHW OL2 .... 61 E3
  SALE M33 .... 158 B2 ⬦
  URM M41 .... 136 C1
  WALK M28 .... 83 E5
  WILM/AE SK9 .... 209 E4
Averhill WALK M28 .... 82 C5 ⬦
Averill Av NEWH/MOS M40 .... 109 E2
Averon Ri OLD OL1 .... 62 B5
Aveson Av CCHDY M21 .... 141 F5
Avian Dr RUSH/FAL M14 .... 143 F3
Avis St ROY/SHW OL2 .... 61 G2 ⬦
Avocet Dr ALT WA14 .... 157 F5 ⬦
  IRL M44 .... 116 B6
Avonbrook Dr NEWH/MOS M40 .. 94 A3 ⬦
Avoncliff Cl BOL BL1 .... 27 E4
Avon Cl MILN OL16 .... 42 B1
  MPL/ROM SK6 .... 186 C2
  WALK M28 .... 82 B3
Avoncourt Dr DID/WITH M20 ..... 163 E1
Avondale Av BRAM/HZG SK7 ..... 185 D5
  BURY BL9 .... 33 F3
Avondale Crs URM M41 .... 119 D6
Avondale Dr SLFD M6 .... 102 C2
  TOT/BURYW BL8 .... 18 A3
Avondale Ri WILM/AE SK9 .... 204 B5 ⬦
Avondale Rd BRAM/HZG SK7 .... 185 D5 ⬦
  EDGY/DAV SK3 .... 165 F6
  FWTH BL4 .... 65 D3
  STRET M32 .... 121 F5
  WHTF M45 .... 70 C2
Avondale St BOL BL1 .... 27 D6
  CHH M8 .... 90 B6
Avonlea Dr BNG/LEV M19 .... 144 C5
Avonlea Rd DROY M43 .... 109 F5
  SALE M33 .... 158 B4
Avon Rd BNG/LEV M19 .... 145 D3 ⬦
  CHAD OL9 .... 77 D3
  CHD/CHDH SK8 .... 193 F2
  FWTH BL4 .... 67 F6
  HALE/TIMP WA15 .... 188 C1
  HEY OL10 .... 56 B5
  ROY/SHW OL2 .... 61 F1
Avon St BOL BL1 .... 26 C6
  EDGY/DAV SK3 .... 166 C6
  OLDS OL8 .... 96 A1
Avril Cl RDSH SK5 .... 147 D3
Avro Cl RUSH/FAL M14 .... 143 F2
Avroe Rd ECC M30 .... 118 A2 ⬦
Avro Wy MANAIR M90 .... 191 D2
Awburn Rd HYDE SK14 .... 152 C2
Axford Cl BRO M7 .... 106 A1 ⬦
Axon Sq OLDTF/WHR M16 .... 124 C5
Aycliffe Av CCHDY M21 .... 142 B6
Aycliffe Gv BRUN/LGST M13 ..... 125 F6 ⬦
Aylesbury Av DTN/ASHW M34 ... 149 D2
  URM M41 .... 119 F5
Aylesbury Cl SALG/ORD M5 ...... 104 B6
Aylesbury Gv MDTN M24 .... 76 A1
Aylesby Av GTN M18 .... 126 C5
Aylesford Rd RUSH/FAL M14 .... 125 E6 ⬦
Aylsham Cl MPL/ROM SK6 .... 149 D6
Aylsham Ms SWIN M27 .... 101 E2 ⬦

Aylwin Dr SALE M33 .... 159 F2
Ayr Av OLDS OL8 .... 96 A2
Ayr Cl BRAM/HZG SK7 .... 185 E5
Ayres Rd OLDTF/WHR M16 .... 122 C5
Ayr Gv HEY OL10 .... 55 E1
Ayrshire Rd BRO M7 .... 104 B1
Ayr St BOLE BL2 .... 28 C3 ⬦
  BOLE BL2 .... 29 D3 ⬦
Ayrton Gv LHULT M38 .... 65 E6 ⬦
Aysgarth Av CHD/CHDH SK8 ..... 180 A1
  GTN M18 .... 127 F3 ⬦
  MPL/ROM SK6 .... 170 B1
Aysgarth Cl SALE M33 .... 158 B2
Ayshford Cl ALT WA14 .... 173 F1 ⬦
Ayton Gv RUSH/FAL M14 .... 125 F5
Aytoun St CMANE M1 .... 3 G5 ⬦
Azalea Av GTN M18 .... 127 E3 ⬦

B

Babbacombe Gv BKLY M9 .... 73 F6 ⬦
Babbacombe Rd OFTN SK2 .... 184 A1
Back Abingdon Rd BOLE BL2 ..... 29 D6 ⬦
Back Acton St CMANE M1 .... 3 G5 ⬦
Back Adcroft St STKP SK1 .... 167 D6 ⬦
Back Adrian Rd BOL BL1 .... 27 D5
Back Adrian Rd East BOL BL1 .... 27 D5 ⬦
Back Ainscow St BOL BL1 .... 46 C1 ⬦
Back Ainsworth La BOLE BL2 ..... 28 C6
Back Ainsworth La East
  BOLE BL2 .... 48 A1 ⬦
Back Ainsworth Rd North
  TOT/BURYW BL8 .... 32 C5 ⬦
  TOT/BURYW BL8 .... 33 D5 ⬦
Back Ainsworth Rd South
  TOT/BURYW BL8 .... 33 D5
Back Ainsworth St BOL BL1 .... 27 D4 ⬦
  BOL BL1 .... 27 E5 ⬦
Back Albert St BURY BL9 .... 34 B5 ⬦
Back Albion Pl BURY BL9 .... 34 A3 ⬦
Back Alder St BOLS/LL BL3 .... 47 D6 ⬦
Back Alexander Rd BOLE BL2 ..... 29 D6 ⬦
Back Alexandra St BOLS/LL BL3 .. 46 A5 ⬦
Back Alfred St BOLS/LL BL3 ...... 47 F5 ⬦
Back Alice St BOLS/LL BL3 .... 46 A4 ⬦
  BOLS/LL BL3 .... 49 F6 ⬦
Back Alicia St BOLS/LL BL3 .... 48 B5 ⬦
Back All Saints' St BOL BL1 .... 47 D1 ⬦
Back Alston St BOLS/LL BL3 ...... 46 C6 ⬦
Back Andrew St BURY BL9 .... 34 B5 ⬦
Back Andrew St North
  BURY BL9 .... 34 B5 ⬦
Back Anglia Gv BOLS/LL BL3 ..... 46 A5 ⬦
Back Annis Rd BOLS/LL BL3 ...... 45 F5 ⬦
Back Anson St BOL BL1 .... 28 A4 ⬦
Back Apple Ter BOL BL1 .... 27 E5 ⬦
Back Argo St BOLS/LL BL3 .... 46 B5 ⬦
Back Argyle St BURY BL9 .... 34 A2 ⬦
Back Arlington St BOLS/LL BL3 ... 47 D6 ⬦
Back Arnold St BOL BL1 .... 27 D5 ⬦
Back Arnold Ter BOL BL1 .... 26 A6 ⬦
Back Ashbee St BOL BL1 .... 27 F4 ⬦
Back Ashford Wk BOL BL1 .... 27 F6 ⬦
Back Ashley St ANC M4 .... 106 C4 ⬦
Back Ash St BURY BL9 .... 34 B5 ⬦
Back Ashton St BOLS/LL BL3 ..... 45 F5 ⬦
Back Ashworth La BOL BL1 .... 28 A2 ⬦
Back Ashworth St
  TOT/BURYW BL8 .... 33 D4 ⬦
Back Astley St BOL BL1 .... 27 F5 ⬦
Back Augustus St BOLS/LL BL3 .. 47 E5 ⬦
Back Augustus St West
  BOLS/LL BL3 .... 47 E5 ⬦
Back Avenue St BOL BL1 .... 46 B1 ⬦
Back Avondale St BOL BL1 .... 27 D6 ⬦
Back Baldwin St BOLS/LL BL3 .... 46 C4 ⬦
Back Baldwin St North
  BOLS/LL BL3 .... 46 C4 ⬦
Back Balloon St ANC M4 .... 3 E1 ⬦
Back Banbury St BOLE BL2 .... 29 D6 ⬦
Back Bankfield St BOLS/LL BL3 .. 46 A4 ⬦
Back Bantry St BOLS/LL BL3 ..... 46 C4 ⬦
Back Barbara St BOLS/LL BL3 .... 46 B5 ⬦
Back Bark St BOL BL1 .... 46 C2 ⬦
Back Bashall St BOL BL1 .... 46 A1 ⬦
Back Battenberg Rd BOL BL1 ..... 46 A1 ⬦
Back Baxendale St BOL BL1 .... 27 F3 ⬦
Back Bayley St BOL BL1 .... 46 B1 ⬦
Back Baythorpe St BOL BL1 ...... 28 A5 ⬦
Back Baytorpe St North BOL BL1 . 28 A4 ⬦
Back Beaconsfield St
  BOLS/LL BL3 .... 46 B3 ⬦
Back Beaconsfield Ter
  BOLE BL2 .... 28 C6 ⬦
Back Bedford St BOL BL1 .... 46 B1 ⬦
Back Beech St BOL BL1 .... 28 A5 ⬦
Back Beechwood St
  BOLS/LL BL3 .... 47 D6 ⬦
Back Belbeck St
  TOT/BURYW BL8 .... 33 D5 ⬦
Back Bell La BURY BL9 .... 34 B4 ⬦
Back Belmont Rd BOL BL1 .... 27 F2 ⬦

Back Belmont Rd East BOL BL1 .. 27 F2 ⬦
Back Bennett's La BOL BL1 .... 27 D5 ⬦
Back Bennett's La East
  BOL BL1 .... 27 D5 ⬦
Back Benson St BURY BL9 .... 34 B6
Back Bentinck St BOL BL1 .... 26 C6 ⬦
Back Bentley St BOLE BL2 .... 48 A4
Back Bertrand Rd BOL BL1 .... 46 A2 ⬦
  BOL BL1 .... 46 A3 ⬦
Back Beverley St BOL BL1 .... 46 A1 ⬦
Back Birch St BURY BL9 .... 34 A4 ⬦
  BURY BL9 .... 34 A4 ⬦
Back Birley St BOL BL1 .... 27 F3 ⬦
Back Blackbank St BOL BL1 .... 28 A6 ⬦
Back Blackburn Rd BOL BL1 ...... 28 A6 ⬦
Back Blackburn Rd West BOL BL1 . 27 F2 ⬦
  BOL BL1 .... 27 F3 ⬦
  BOL BL1 .... 27 F3 ⬦
  BOL BL1 .... 27 F4 ⬦
  BOL BL1 .... 27 F4 ⬦
Back Blackburn St BOL BL1 .... 28 A4 ⬦
Back Blackwood St BOLS/LL BL3 . 47 E5 ⬦
Back Bolton Rd North
  TOT/BURYW BL8 .... 33 D6 ⬦
Back Bolton Rd South
  TOT/BURYW BL8 .... 33 D6
Back Bolton St BOL BL1 .... 28 A5 ⬦
Back Bolton St South BURY BL9 .. 33 F5 ⬦
Back Bond St West BURY BL9 .... 34 B5 ⬦
Back Boundary St BOL BL1 .... 27 E5 ⬦
Back Bowen St BOL BL1 .... 26 C6 ⬦
Backbower La HYDE SK14 .... 151 D3 ⬦
Back Bowness Rd BOLS/LL BL3 .. 46 B5 ⬦
Back Bradford Rd BOLS/LL BL3 .. 47 E5 ⬦
Back Bradford Rd West
  BOLS/LL BL3 .... 47 E6 ⬦
Back Bradford St BOLE BL2 .... 47 F2 ⬦
Back Bradshaw BOLE BL2 .... 29 D3 ⬦
Back Bradshaw Brow West
  BOLE BL2 .... 29 D3 ⬦
Back Bradshawgate BOL BL1 ..... 47 D3 ⬦
Back Bradshaw Rd East
  BOLE BL2 .... 29 E2 ⬦
Back Bradshaw St MILN OL16 .... 23 E5
Back Brandon St BOLS/LL BL3 ... 46 B5 ⬦
Back Brandon St North
  BOLS/LL BL3 .... 46 B5 ⬦
Back Brandon St West
  BOLS/LL BL3 .... 46 B5 ⬦
Back Brandwood St BOLS/LL BL3 . 46 A5 ⬦
Back Bridgeman St
  BOLS/LL BL3 .... 46 B5 ⬦
  BOLS/LL BL3 .... 46 C5 ⬦
Back Bridge St BOL BL1 .... 47 D1 ⬦
  CSLFD M3 .... 2 C3
  RAMS BL0 .... 7 D5 ⬦
Back Brierley St BURY BL9 .... 52 C1
Back Brierley St South
  BURY BL9 .... 52 C1 ⬦
Back Brindley St BOL BL1 .... 28 A3 ⬦
Back Brink's Pl BOL BL1 .... 46 C2 ⬦
Back Bristol Av BOLE BL2 .... 29 D6 ⬦
Back Bristol St BOLS/LL BL3 ..... 46 B4 ⬦
Back Broach St BOLS/LL BL3 ..... 46 C5 ⬦
Back Broad O' Th' La BOL BL1 ... 27 F2 ⬦
Back Broad St BURY BL9 .... 33 F5 ⬦
Back Bromwich St BOLE BL2 ..... 47 F3 ⬦
Back Brookfield St BOLE BL2 ..... 47 F1 ⬦
Back Brook St North BURY BL9 ... 34 B3 ⬦
Back Broom St BOLE BL2 .... 47 E2 ⬦
Back Bryce St BOLS/LL BL3 ...... 46 C4 ⬦
Back Burnaby St BOLS/LL BL3 ... 46 B4 ⬦
Back Burnham Av BOL BL1 .... 26 B6 ⬦
Back Bury New Rd BOLE BL2 ..... 47 E2 ⬦
Back Bury Rd BOLE BL2 .... 48 C2 ⬦
Back Bury Rd East BOLE BL2 ..... 48 A2 ⬦
Back Bury Rd South BOLE BL2 ... 48 B2 ⬦
Back Bushell St BOLS/LL BL3 .... 45 F5 ⬦
Back Byrom St BOLS/LL BL3 ..... 46 A4 ⬦
Back Byrom St TOT/BURYW BL8 . 32 C3 ⬦
Back Byrom St South
  TOT/BURYW BL8 .... 32 C3 ⬦
Back Calder Rd BOLS/LL BL3 ..... 46 C6 ⬦
Back Caledonia St BOLS/LL BL3 .. 46 A4 ⬦
Back Calvert Rd BOLS/LL BL3 .... 47 D6 ⬦
Back Cambridge St AULW OL7 ... 112 A6 ⬦
Back Camp St BRO M7 .... 105 E2 ⬦
Back Canada St BOL BL1 .... 27 D5 ⬦
Back Canada St South BOL BL1 .. 27 D5 ⬦
Back Canning St BURY BL9 .... 34 A3 ⬦
Back Carter St BOLS/LL BL3 ...... 47 E5 ⬦
Back Castle St BOLE BL2 .... 47 E2 ⬦
Back Cateaton St BURY BL9 ...... 34 A3 ⬦
  BURY BL9 .... 34 A4 ⬦
Back Cecilia St BOLS/LL BL3 ..... 47 E5 ⬦
Back Cedar St BURY BL9 .... 34 B4 ⬦
Back Cedar St North BURY BL9 ... 34 C4 ⬦
Back Cemetery Rd East
  BOLE BL2 .... 47 F2 ⬦
Back Cestrian St BOLS/LL BL3 ... 47 D6 ⬦
Back Chalfont St BOL BL1 .... 28 A5 ⬦
Back Chapel St BNG/LEV M19 ... 145 E2 ⬦
  BRAM/HZG SK7 .... 184 C4 ⬦
  TOT/BURYW BL8 .... 18 A6 ⬦
  WHIT OL12 .... 11 D4 ⬦

Back Chapman St *BOL* BL1 .... 26 C6 ④
Back Charles Holden St
  BOL BL1 .... 46 B3 ①
Back Chaucer St *BOL* BL1 .... 27 E5 ④
Back Cheapside *BOL* BL1 .... 47 D2 ①
Back Chesham Rd North
  BURY BL9 .... 34 B2 ①
Back Chesham Rd South
  BURY BL9 .... 34 B3
Back Chester St *BURY* BL9 .... 34 B3 ②
Back China La *CMANE* M1 .... 3 G4
Back Chorley New Rd *BOL* BL1 ... 46 A2 ③
  BOL BL1 .... 46 B1 ④
Back Chorley New Rd North
  BOL BL1 .... 45 F2 ①
  BOL BL1 .... 46 A2 ②
Back Chorley Old Rd *BOL* BL1 .. 26 B6 ②
Back Chorley Old Rd North
  BOL BL1 .... 26 B6 ③
  BOL BL1 .... 46 A1 ⑤
Back Chorley Old Rd South
  BOL BL1 .... 46 A1 ⑥
Back Chorley St *BOL* BL1 .... 46 C2 ③
Back Chorley St East *BOL* BL1 ... 46 C1 ④
Back Church La *BOLS/LL* BL3 ...... 46 A5
Back Church Rd *BOL* BL1 .... 27 D5 ⑦
Back Church Rd North *BOL* BL1 .. 27 D5 ⑧
Back Church St *BOL* BL1 .... 46 C1 ③
  BOLS/LL BL3 .... 49 E6
Back Clarendon Rd *BOLE* BL2 .... 48 A2 ③
Back Clarke St *BOL* BL1 .... 46 A1 ④
Back Clay St East *EDGW/EG* BL7 .. 14 B6 ①
Back Clay St West
  EDGW/EG BL7 .... 14 B6 ②
Back Clegg St *BOLE* BL2 .... 48 A2
Back Clifton St *BURY* BL9 .... 34 A3 ⑤
Back Cloister St *BOL* BL1 .... 27 D5 ⑨
Back Clyde St *BOL* BL1 .... 27 F5
Back Cobden St *BOL* BL1 .... 27 E4 ②
Back Colenso Rd *BOLE* BL2 .... 48 B2 ②
Back College Land *CSLFD* M3 ...... 2 C3 ①
Back College Wy *BOLS/LL* BL3 .... 46 B3 ①
Back Columbia Rd *BOL* BL1 .... 46 A1 ⑦
Back Coniston St *BOL* BL1 .... 28 A4 ①
Back Coop St *BOL* BL1 .... 27 F3
Back Cornall St *TOT/BURYW* BL8 .. 33 D4
Back Corson St *FWTH* BL4 .... 66 B1 ①
Back Cottam St *TOT/BURYW* BL8 .. 33 D4 ②
Back Cotton St *BOL* BL1 .... 27 E5 ⑤
Back Cowm La *WHIT* OL12 .... 4 C6
Back Cox Green Rd North
  EDGW/EG BL7 .... 14 A5 ①
Back Crawford Av *BOLE* BL2 ...... 47 F3 ①
Back Crescent Av *BOL* BL1 .... 46 B1 ③
Back Crescent Rd *BOLS/LL* BL3 .. 47 E5
Back Crescent Rd West
  BOLS/LL BL3 .... 47 E6
Back Croft La *BOLS/LL* BL3 .... 47 F5
Back Cromer Av *BOLE* BL2 .... 29 D6 ③
Back Crostons Rd *TOT/BURYW* BL8 .. 33 E4
Back Croston St *BOLS/LL* BL3 .... 46 A5
Back Crumpsall St North
  BOL BL1 .... 27 F4 ①
Back Cundey St *BOL* BL1 .... 27 D6 ③
Back Curzon Rd *BOL* BL1 .... 46 A2 ②
Back Cyril St *BOLS/LL* BL3 .... 47 E4 ①
Back Daisy St *BOLS/LL* BL3 .... 46 A5
Back Darley St *FWTH* BL4 .... 66 C3
Back Darwen Rd North
  EDGW/EG BL7 .... 14 A5 ②
  EDGW/EG BL7 .... 14 A5 ③
  EDGW/EG BL7 .... 14 B5 ①
  EDGW/EG BL7 .... 14 C6 ①
Back Darwen Rd South
  EDGW/EG BL7 .... 14 B6
Back Darwin St *BOL* BL1 .... 27 E5 ⑥
Back Deal St *BOLS/LL* BL3 .... 47 D6 ③
  BURY BL9 .... 34 C5 ①
Back Deane Church La
  BOLS/LL BL3 .... 45 F5 ③
Back Deane Church La West
  BOLS/LL BL3 .... 45 F5 ④
Back Deane Rd *BOLS/LL* BL3 ...... 46 A4 ③
Back Deane Rd North
  BOLS/LL BL3 .... 46 A3 ②
  BOLS/LL BL3 .... 46 B3 ③
Back Delamere St South
  BURY BL9 .... 34 B2 ②
Back Denton St *BURY* BL9 .... 34 A3 ⑤
Back Derby St *BOLS/LL* BL3 .... 46 B5 ①
  BOLS/LL BL3 .... 46 C4 ③
  BURY BL9 .... 34 A5 ①
Back Design St *BOLS/LL* BL3 ...... 45 F5 ⑦
Back Devonshire Rd *BOL* BL1 .... 26 B6 ④
Back Devon St North *BURY* BL9 .. 52 C1 ①
Back Devon St South *BURY* BL9 .. 53 D1 ①
Back Dijon St *BOLS/LL* BL3 .... 46 A5
Back Dijon St North *BOLS/LL* BL3 .. 46 A5
Back Dobie St *BOLS/LL* BL3 .... 47 E5 ①
Back Doffcocker Brow *BOL* BL1 .. 26 B6 ①
Back Dorset St *BOLE* BL2 .... 47 E6
Back Dougill St *BOL* BL1 .... 26 C6 ①
Back Dougill St South *BOL* BL1 .. 26 C6 ②
Back Drake St *MILN* OL16 .... 40 A1
Back Drummond St *BOL* BL1 ...... 27 F3 ④

Back Ducie Av *BOL* BL1 .... 46 A2 ⑥
Back Duckworth St *BURY* BL9 .. 34 B3 ①
Back Duncan St *BRO* M7 .... 89 D6
Back Dunstan St *BOLE* BL2 .... 48 A2
Back Durham St *ROCH* OL11 ...... 40 B2 ②
Back Duxbury St *BOL* BL1 .... 27 E4 ①
Back Earnshaw St *BOLS/LL* BL3 .. 46 A6 ①
Back Eastbank St *BOL* BL1 .... 28 A5 ①
Back East St *BURY* BL9 .... 34 A6
Back Eckersley St *BOL* BL1 .... 27 F4 ①
Back Edditch Gv *BOLE* BL2 .... 48 A2 ①
Back Eden St *BOL* BL1 .... 27 F4 ①
Back Edgmont Av *BOLS/LL* BL3 .. 46 B5 ①
Back Eldon St *BURY* BL9 .... 34 A3
Back Elgin St *BOL* BL1 .... 27 E5 ①
Back Ellesmere Rd *BOLS/LL* BL3 .. 46 A6 ②
Back Ellesmere St *BOLS/LL* BL3 .. 46 B5 ①
Back Elm St *BURY* BL9 .... 34 C5 ③
Back Elmwood Gv *BOL* BL1 .... 46 A1 ②
Back Elmwood Gv West
  BOL BL1 .... 46 A1 ①
Back Elsworth St *CSLFD* M3 ...... 106 B3 ②
Back Empire Rd *BOLE* BL2 .... 48 B2 ③
Back Empress St *BOL* BL1 .... 26 C6 ⑦
Back Ena St *BOLS/LL* BL3 .... 47 E6 ②
Back Ernest St *BOL* BL1 .... 46 A3 ②
Back Eskrick St *BOL* BL1 .... 27 E5 ③
Back Eskrick St East *BOL* BL1 .... 27 E5 ②
Back Eskrick St South *BOL* BL1 .. 27 E5 ⑩
Back Eskrick St West *BOL* BL1 .... 27 E5
Back Essingdon St *BOLS/LL* BL3 .. 46 B5
Back Essingdon St South
  BOLS/LL BL3 .... 46 B5 ③
Back Eustace St *BOLS/LL* BL3 .... 47 E6 ③
Back Euxton St *BOLS/LL* BL3 ...... 46 B5 ⑩
Back Everton St North *BOL* BL1 .. 28 A5 ③
Back Ewart St *BOL* BL1 .... 27 F5 ②
Back Fairhaven Rd *BOL* BL1 ...... 28 A4 ②
Back Fair St *BOLS/LL* BL3 .... 46 A1 ④
Back Fenton St *TOT/BURYW* BL8 .. 33 D4 ①
Back Fern St East *BOLS/LL* BL3 .. 46 A3 ①
Back Fir St *BURY* BL9 .... 34 C5 ③
Back Fletcher St *BURY* BL9 .... 34 B5 ⑦
  RAD M26 .... 67 F4 ①
Back Fletcher St South
  BOLS/LL BL3 .... 47 D4
Back Flora St *BOLS/LL* BL3 .... 46 C5 ③
Back Florence Av *BOL* BL1 .... 28 A2 ①
Back Fortune St *BOLS/LL* BL3 .... 47 F4 ①
Back Foundry St *BURY* BL9 .... 34 A5 ②
Back Frances St *BOL* BL1 .... 27 E5 ⑪
Back Frank St *BOL* BL1 .... 27 E5 ⑫
  BURY BL9 .... 34 A6 ①
Back Fylde St *FWTH* BL4 .... 66 B1 ②
Back Gainsborough Av
  BOLS/LL BL3 .... 46 A5 ③
Back Garside Gv *BOL* BL1 .... 27 D5 ⑩
Back Garston St *BURY* BL9 .... 34 B5 ③
Back Gaskell St *BOL* BL1 .... 46 B1 ③
Back Gaskell St East *BOL* BL1 .... 46 B1 ②
Back Gaythorne St *BOL* BL1 ...... 28 A4 ③
Back George Barton St *BOLE* BL2 .. 28 C6 ③
Back George St *BOLS/LL* BL3 ...... 47 E5 ②
  CMANE M1 .... 3 E4 ①
  CMANE M1 .... 3 E5 ②
Back Georgiana St West
  BURY BL9 .... 34 A6 ②
Back Gibralter St *BOLS/LL* BL3 .. 46 B3 ③
Back Gibraltar St South
  BOLS/LL BL3 .... 46 B3 ⑥
Back Gigg La *BURY* BL9 .... 53 D1 ①
Back Gilmour St *MDTN* M24 .... 75 E3 ②
Back Gilnow Gv *BOL* BL1 .... 46 B3 ⑦
Back Gilnow La *BOLS/LL* BL3 ...... 46 B3 ⑧
Back Gilnow La West *BOLS/LL* BL3 .. 46 A3 ⑨
Back Gilnow Rd *BOL* BL1 .... 46 A2 ④
Back Glen Av *BOLS/LL* BL3 .... 46 C5 ⑥
Back Glenboro Av *TOT/BURYW* BL8 .. 32 C5
Back Glen Bott St *BOL* BL1 .... 27 E5 ⑬
Back Gloster St *BOLE* BL2 .... 47 E2 ③
Back Goldsmith St *BOLS/LL* BL3 .. 46 B5 ⑪
Back Goodlad St
  TOT/BURYW BL8 .... 32 C3 ①
Back Gordon Av *BOLS/LL* BL3 .... 46 A4 ④
Back Gorses Mt *BOLE* BL2 .... 48 A4 ①
Back Grafton St *BOL* BL1 .... 46 B1 ①
Back Grantham Cl *BOL* BL1 .... 27 F6 ①
Back Grasmere St *BOL* BL1 .... 28 A5
Back Greaves St *OLD* OL1 .... 79 D5 ①
Back Greenhalgh St *BOLS/LL* BL3 .. 49 E6 ②
Back Greenland Rd *BOLS/LL* BL3 .. 65 D1 ①
Back Green La *BOLS/LL* BL3.......... 65 F1
Back Green La South *BOLS/LL* BL3 .. 47 D6
Back Green St *MDTN* M24 .... 75 F2 ①
Back Gregory Av *BOLE* BL2 .... 48 C1 ①
Back Grendon St *BOLS/LL* BL3 .. 46 A6 ①
Back Gresham St *BOL* BL1 .... 28 A4 ④
Back Grosvenor St *STLY* SK15 .... 114 B6 ①
Back Grove St *BOL* BL1 .... 27 E5 ⑭
Back Hadwin St *BOL* BL1 .... 28 A6 ①
Back Halliwell La *CHH* M8 .... 90 A6 ①
Back Halliwell Rd *BOL* BL1 .... 27 E5 ⑮
Back Halliwell Rd South
  BOL BL1 .... 27 E5 ⑯
  BOL BL1 .... 27 E5 ⑯

Back Halstead St *BURY* BL9 ...... 34 B3 ⑤
Back Hamilton St *BRO* M7 .... 89 E6 ①
  BURY BL9 .... 34 A3 ①
Back Hampson St
  NEWH/MOS M40 .... 107 E3 ①
Back Hanson St *BURY* BL9 .... 34 A3 ②
Back Hargreaves St *BOL* BL1 ...... 27 F5 ③
Back Harper's La South *BOL* BL1 .. 26 C5 ①
Back Hartington Rd *BOL* BL1 ...... 46 A1 ⑩
Back Harvey St *TOT/BURYW* BL8 .. 33 D4 ③
Back Haslam St *BURY* BL9 .... 34 B5 ③
Back Hatfield Rd *BOL* BL1 .... 27 D6 ②
Back Hawthorne Rd *BOLS/LL* BL3 .. 45 F5 ③
Back Hawthorne Rd East
  BOLS/LL BL3 .... 45 F4 ②
Back Hawthorn Rd West
  BOLS/LL BL3 .... 45 F4 ③
Back Haydn St *BOL* BL1 .... 27 E5 ⑰
Back Haydock St *BOL* BL1 .... 47 D1 ③
Back Hayward St
  TOT/BURYW BL8 .... 33 D4 ④
Back Hengist St *BOLE* BL2 .... 48 A2 ③
Back Hennon St *BOL* BL1 .... 27 E6 ①
Back Henrietta St *BOLS/LL* BL3 .. 45 F5 ⑤
Back Henry Lee St *BOLS/LL* BL3 .. 46 A6 ③
Back Heywood St East *BURY* BL9 .. 34 B6
Back Heywood St West
  BURY BL9 .... 34 B6 ①
Back High Bank St *BOLE* BL2 ...... 48 A2 ②
Back Higher Darcy St
  BOLS/LL BL3 .... 48 A4 ②
Back Higher Shady La West
  EDGW/EG BL7 .... 14 C6 ②
Back Higher Swan La *BOLS/LL* BL3 .. 46 B6
Back Higher Swan La West
  BOLS/LL BL3 .... 46 B6 ③
Back High St *BOLS/LL* BL3 .... 46 B5 ⑫
  BOLS/LL BL3 .... 46 C5 ⑬
  EDGW/EG BL7 .... 15 D1 ①
Back High St South *BOLS/LL* BL3 .. 46 C5 ⑨
Back High St West *BOLS/LL* BL3 .. 46 C5 ⑩
Back Hilden St *BOLE* BL2 .... 47 E3 ①
Back Hilden St West *BOLE* BL2 .. 47 E3 ②
Back Hilton St *BRO* M7 .... 89 E6
  BURY BL9 .... 34 A3 ③
Back Hind St *BOLE* BL2 .... 48 A2 ③
Back Holland St *BOL* BL1 .... 27 F3 ⑤
  BOL BL1 .... 28 A3 ②
Back Holland St East *BOL* BL1 .... 28 A3 ③
Back Holly Pl *BOL* BL1 .... 27 F3 ⑤
Back Holly St *BOL* BL1 .... 28 A3 ④
  BURY BL9 .... 34 B5
Back Holly St South *BURY* BL9 .. 34 B5 ①
Back Hopefield St *BOLS/LL* BL3 .. 46 B5 ⑬
Back Hope St *SLFD* M6 .... 89 E6
Back Horbury St
  TOT/BURYW BL8 .... 33 D5 ⑦
Back Horeb St East *BOLS/LL* BL3 .. 46 B4 ⑥
Back Hornby St *BURY* BL9 .... 34 A2
Back Hornby St East *BURY* BL9 .. 34 A3
Back Hornby St West *BURY* BL9 .. 34 A4 ⑧
Back Horne St North *BURY* BL9 .. 52 C1 ③
Back Horne St South *BURY* BL9 .. 52 C1
Back Horsa St *BOLE* BL2.............. 28 C6
Back Horsa St North *BOLE* BL2 .. 28 C6 ③
Back Hough La East *EDGW/EG* BL7 .. 14 B6 ③
Back Howarden St *BOL* BL1 .... 27 F2 ③
Back Howcroft St *BOLS/LL* BL3 .. 46 B5 ⑭
Back Howe St *BRO* M7 .... 89 D6
Back Hughes St *BOL* BL1 .... 27 E5 ①
Back Hulbert St *TOT/BURYW* BL8 .. 33 D6 ②
Back Hulme St *SALQ/ORD* M5 .... 105 D6 ①
  TOT/BURYW BL8 .... 33 E4 ①
Back Hulton La *BOLS/LL* BL3 ...... 45 E5 ①
  BOLS/LL BL3 .... 45 E6 ①
Back Hulton La West
  BOLS/LL BL3 .... 45 E5 ②
Back Huntley Mount Rd
  BURY BL9 .... 34 C4 ②
Back Hurst St *BOLS/LL* BL3 .... 46 A6 ⑤
  BURY BL9 .... 34 B6
Back Huxley St *BOL* BL1 .... 27 D5 ⑪
Back Ingham St *BURY* BL9.......... 34 B6
Back Ingham St East *BURY* BL9 .. 34 B6 ①
Back Irlam St *BOL* BL1 .... 27 F4 ⑦
Back Irlam St North *BOL* BL1 .... 27 F4 ①
Back Ivy Bank Rd *BOL* BL1.......... 27 F2
Back Ivy Rd *BOL* BL1 .... 27 D5 ⑫
  BOL BL1 .... 27 D5 ⑬
  BOL BL1 .... 27 D6 ③
Back Ivy Rd West *BOL* BL1 .... 27 D5 ⑬
Back James St *BOLS/LL* BL3........ 49 F6
Back Jauncey St *BOLS/LL* BL3 .... 46 A4 ②
Back John Brown St *BOL* BL1 .... 46 B1 ③
Back John Cross St *BOLS/LL* BL3 .. 46 C5 ⑦
Back Johnson St *BOL* BL1 .... 47 D3 ②
Back John St *BOLS/LL* BL3 .... 46 C5 ②
Back Junction St *CMANE* M1........ 3 H3
Back Keighley St *BOL* BL1 .... 27 D5 ①
Back Kendal Rd *BOL* BL1 .... 46 A1 ⑱
Back Kershaw St *BURY* BL9 .... 34 B5 ①
Back Kingholm Gdns *BOL* BL1 .... 27 E6 ②
Back Kingsley St *BOL* BL1 .... 27 E5 ⑱
Back King St *BOL* BL1 .... 46 C2 ①
  OLD OL1 .... 78 C5 ①

Back King St North
EDGW/EG BL7 .... 14 A5 5
Back King St South *BOLE* BL2 .... 29 E2
Back Knight St *TOT/BURYW* BL8 .... 33 D5 3
Back Knowl St *STLY* SK15 .... 114 C5
Back Knowsley Rd *BOL* BL1 .... 26 C5 2
Back Knowsley St *BOL* BL1 .... 47 D2 2
BURY BL9 .... 33 F5 5
Back Kylemore Av *BOLS/LL* BL3 ..... 45 F4 4
Back La *AUL* OL6 .... 98 B3
AULW OL7 .... 111 E2
BOL BL1 .... 46 C1 4
HALE/TIMP WA15 .... 189 D4
WHIT OL12 .... 9 D1
Back Lark St *BOL* BL1 .... 47 D1 2
Back Latham St *BOL* BL1 .... 28 A5 9
Back Lathom St *BURY* BL9 .... 34 B3 4
Back Laurel St *BURY* BL9 .... 34 C5 4
Back Lawn St *BOL* BL1 .... 27 D6
Back Leachfield St *BOL* BL1 .... 27 E4 1
Back Leach St *BOLS/LL* BL3 .... 46 C4
Back Lee Av *BOLS/LL* BL3 .... 46 B6
Back Lena St *BOL* BL1 .... 28 A5
Back Lenora St *BOLS/LL* BL3 .... 45 F5 10
Back Lever Edge La *BOLS/LL* BL3 .. 46 C6 4
Back Lever Edge La South
BOLS/LL BL3 .... 46 C6 5
BOLS/LL BL3 .... 47 D4 2
Back Lever St North
BOLS/LL BL3 .... 49 E5 3
Back Lever St South
BOLS/LL BL3 .... 46 C5 4
Back Lightburne Av *BOL* BL1 .... 45 F2 4
Back Lilly St *BOL* BL1 .... 46 B1 10
Back Lincoln Rd *BOL* BL1 .... 46 A1 12
Back Lindley St *BOLS/LL* BL3 .... 49 F6 3
Back Linton Av *BURY* BL9 .... 34 A2 2
Back Longden St *BOL* BL1 .... 46 A1 13
Back Longfield Rd *BOLS/LL* BL3 .... 45 F6 6
Back Long La *BOLE* BL2 .... 48 C2 2
Back Longsight North *BOLE* BL2 ... 29 F2
Back Longsight South *BOLE* BL2 ... 29 E2 2
Back Lonsdale St *TOT/BURYW* BL8.. 33 D5
Back Lord St *BOLS/LL* BL3 .... 49 F6 5
BURY BL9 .... 34 A6 3
Back Loxham St *BOLS/LL* BL3 .... 66 B1
Back Lumsden St *BOLS/LL* BL3 ..... 46 C4
Back Luton St *BOLS/LL* BL3 .... 47 E5 10
Back Lytton St *BOL* BL1 .... 27 E5 19
Back Mackenzie St *BOL* BL1 .... 27 E3
Back Malvern Av *BOL* BL1 .... 26 B6 4
BURY BL9 .... 34 A2 3
Back Manchester Old Rd
BURY BL9 .... 33 F6 1
Back Manchester Rd
BOLS/LL BL3 .... 66 A1 1
BURY BL9 .... 33 F5 4
Back Manchester Rd South
BOLS/LL BL3 .... 47 E5 11
Back Manchester Rd West
BOLS/LL BL3 .... 47 F5 3
Back Manchester Rd West *HEY* OL10 .. 37 F6 6
Back Manor St *BURY* BL9 .... 34 B5 10
Back Maple St *BOLS/LL* BL3 .... 46 B4 4
Back Marion St South
BOLS/LL BL3 .... 66 A1 2
BURY BL9 .... 33 F5 3
RAD M26 .... 67 F4 2
Back Market St West *BURY* BL9 ..... 33 F5 6
Back Markland Hill La *BOL* BL1 ..... 26 A6 1
Back Markland Hill La East
BOL BL1 .... 26 A6 2
Back Markland Hill La West
BOL BL1 .... 26 A6 3
Back Marlborough St *BOL* BL1 ..... 46 B1 10
Back Mary St *BOLS/LL* BL3 .... 46 B4 5
Back Massie St *BURY* BL9 .... 34 B5 10
Back Massie St *CHD/CHDH* SK8 .. 180 B1 1
Back Mawdsley St *BOL* BL1 .... 47 D2 3
Back Maxwell St *BOL* BL1 .... 27 F5 7
Back Maybank St *BOLS/LL* BL3 ..... 46 B4 6
Back Mayfield Av *BOLS/LL* BL3 ..... 47 F6 2
Back Mayor St *BOLS/LL* BL3 .... 46 B3 10
TOT/BURYW BL8 .... 33 D4 3
Back Mayor St North *BOL* BL1 ...... 46 B3 10
Back Maze St *BOLS/LL* BL3 .... 48 A4
Back Mcdonna St *BOL* BL1 .... 27 D4 2
Back Mckean St *BOLS/LL* BL3 ..... 47 E5 12
Back Mckean St North
BOLS/LL BL3 .... 47 E5 13
Back Melbourne Rd *BOLS/LL* BL3 .. 46 A5 4
Back Melbourne St *STLY* SK15 .... 114 B6 2
Back Mellor Gv *BOL* BL1 .... 26 C6 5
Back Mellor Gv West *BOL* BL1 ...... 26 C6 6
Back Melrose Av *BOL* BL1 .... 26 B6 7
Back Melville St *BOLS/LL* BL3 ...... 47 F6 5
Back Mercia St *BOLS/LL* BL3 .... 46 A4 3
Back Meredith St *BOLS/LL* BL3 .... 47 D6 3
Back Mere Gdns *BOL* BL1 .... 46 C1 3
Back Merlin Gv *BOL* BL1 .... 26 C6 10
Back Merton St *TOT/BURYW* BL8 .. 33 E4
Back Methwold St *BOLS/LL* BL3 .... 46 A5 5

Back Milford Rd *BOLS/LL* BL3 ...... 46 C6 6
Back Miller St *BOL* BL1 .... 27 F3 5
Back Millet St *BURY* BL9 .... 33 E5 1
Back Mill St North *EDGW/EG* BL7 .. 14 A5 3
Back Mill St South *EDGW/EG* BL7 .. 14 A5 3
Back Milner Av *BURY* BL9 .... 34 A2 5
Back Minorca St *BOLS/LL* BL3 ..... 46 C5 10
Back Monmouth Av *BURY* BL9 ..... 34 A2 3
Back Moorfield Gv *BOLE* BL2 .... 28 C6
Back Moorgate *BURY* BL9 .... 34 A4 10
Back Mornington Rd East
BOL BL1 .... 46 A1 13
Back Morris Green La
BOL BL1 .... 64 A1 3
Back Morris Green La East
BOLS/LL BL3 .... 46 A6 7
BOLS/LL BL3 .... 64 A1 3
Back Moss Ter *BOL* BL1 .... 47 D1 6
Back Mostyn Av *BURY* BL9 .... 34 A2 6
Back Mowbray St *BOL* BL1 .... 26 C6 11
Back Murton Ter *BOL* BL1 .... 28 A3 3
Back Musgrave Rd *BOL* BL1 .... 46 A1 16
Back Musgrave Rd North
BOL BL1 .... 46 A1 17
Back Myrtle St *BURY* BL9 .... 34 C5 5
Back Myrtle St South *BURY* BL9 ... 34 C5 5
Back Nebo St *BOLS/LL* BL3 .... 46 B5 13
Back Nelson St South *BURY* BL9 .. 53 D1 2
Back Nevada St *BOL* BL1 .... 27 F6 2
Back Newbold St *TOT/BURYW* BL8 .. 33 D5
Back New George St
TOT/BURYW BL8 .... 33 D4 3
Back Newhall La *BOL* BL1 .... 26 B6 8
Back Newport Rd *BOLS/LL* BL3 .... 47 E5 14
Back Newton St *BOL* BL1 .... 27 F5 6
Back Nixon Rd *BOLS/LL* BL3 .... 46 A6 8
Back Norris St *BOLS/LL* BL3 .... 49 E6 5
Back Northern Gv *BOL* BL1 .... 27 D6 5
Back Norwood Gv *BOL* BL1 .... 46 B1 12
Back Nunnery Rd *BOLS/LL* BL3 .... 45 F5 11
Back Nut St *BOL* BL1 .... 27 E5 20
Back Oak St *RAD* M26 .... 70 A2
Back Olaf St *BOLE* BL2 .... 28 C6 1
Back Oldham Rd *MILN* OL16 .... 40 B1 2
Back Oldham St *BOLS/LL* BL3 ...... 46 B3 11
Back Olga St *BOL* BL1 .... 27 E5
Back Olga St North *BOL* BL1 .... 27 E5 21
Back Olive Bank
TOT/BURYW BL8 .... 32 C3 4
Back Oram St *BURY* BL9 .... 34 B3 3
Back Oriel St *BOLS/LL* BL3 .... 46 A4 3
Back Ormrod St *BURY* BL9 .... 34 B5 12
Back Osborne Gv *BOL* BL1 .... 27 D6 3
BOL BL1 .... 27 D6 3
Back O' Th' Low Rd *OLDE* OL4 ...... 81 D3
Back Oxford Gv North *BOL* BL1 .... 27 D6 2
BOL BL1 .... 46 B1 13
Back Oxford St *BURY* BL9 .... 34 B6 3
Back Packer St *BOL* BL1 .... 27 D5 15
Back Palace St *BOL* BL1 .... 47 D1 7
Back Palm St *BOL* BL1 .... 27 F4 6
Back Parkdale La *BOLE* BL2 .... 29 D6
Back Parkfield Rd *BOLS/LL* BL3 .... 47 E6
Back Parkhills Rd North
BURY BL9 .... 53 D1 3
Back Parkinson St *BOLS/LL* BL3 .. 46 A4 10
Back Park Rd *BOL* BL1 .... 46 A2 8
Back Park St *BOL* BL1 .... 46 B2 1
Back Park St *BOL* BL1 .... 46 B1 14
Back Park Vw *EDGW/EG* BL7 ...... 28 A1
Back Park View Rd *BOLS/LL* BL3 .. 46 A5 6
Back Parsonage St *BURY* BL9 ..... 34 B4 2
Back Parsons La *BURY* BL9 .... 34 A4 3
Back Partington St *BOLS/LL* BL3 .. 64 A1 3
Back Patience St *WHIT* OL12 .... 22 A4 2
Back Patterson St *BOLS/LL* BL3 .. 45 E5 3
Back Peabody St *BOLS/LL* BL3 .... 46 C5 4
Back Peace St *BOLS/LL* BL3 .... 46 B4 7
Back Pedder St *BOL* BL1 .... 27 D6 3
Back Peers St *TOT/BURYW* BL8 .... 33 D5
Back Penarth Rd *BOLS/LL* BL3 .... 45 F5 12
BOLS/LL BL3 .... 46 A4 11
Back Pennington Rd
BOLS/LL BL3 .... 47 D6 3
Back Percy St *BURY* BL9 .... 34 C4 3
Back Peter St *BURY* BL9 .... 34 B4 3
Back Peveril St *BOLS/LL* BL3 .... 45 F6 2
BOLS/LL BL3 .... 46 A6 3
Back Phoenix St *BURY* BL9 .... 33 F5 7
Back Piccadilly *CMANE* M1 .... 3 G3 10
Back Pikes La West
BOLS/LL BL3 .... 46 A4 12
Back Pine St *BOL* BL1 .... 28 A5 3
BURY BL9 .... 34 C5 2
Back Pleasant St *BOL* BL1 .... 46 C1 10
Back Pool Fold *CMANW* M2 .... 2 D3 10
Back Poplar Av *BOL* BL1 .... 28 A2 8
Back Porter St *BURY* BL9 .... 33 A3 10
Back Portland St *AUL* OL6 .... 112 B5
Back Preston St *BOLS/LL* BL3 ...... 47 F5 10
Back Primrose St *BOL* BL1 .... 28 A3 3
Back Primula St *BOL* BL1 .... 28 A2 3
Back Proctor St *TOT/BURYW* BL8 .. 33 D6 3
Back Progress St *BOL* BL1 .... 28 A6 5
Back Quay St *CSLFD* M3 .... 2 A4 3

Back Quebec St *BOLS/LL* BL3 ...... 46 B4 8
Back Queensgate *BOL* BL1 .... 46 A1
Back Queen St *BOL* BL1 .... 46 C2 3
Back Raimond St *BOL* BL1 .... 27 D4 3
Back Rainshaw St *BOL* BL1 .... 28 A3
Back Rake St *BURY* BL9 .... 34 A3 10
Back Randal St *BOLS/LL* BL3 ...... 46 A5 7
Back Range St *BOLS/LL* BL3 .... 46 B5 10
Back Raphael St *BOL* BL1 .... 27 E6 3
Back Raven St *BURY* BL9 .... 34 A3 11
Back Rawson Rd *BOL* BL1 .... 27 D6 3
Back Rawson Rd North
BOL BL1 .... 27 D6 10
Back Raymond Av *BURY* BL9 .... 34 A2 3
Back Red Bank *ANC* M4 .... 106 B4 2
Back Redhill Gv *BOL* BL1 .... 46 C1 7
Back Regent St *BURY* BL9 .... 34 A3 12
Back Ribblesdale Rd
BOLS/LL BL3 .... 46 B5 17
Back Richard Burch St *BURY* BL9 .. 34 A4 3
Back Richelieu St *BOLS/LL* BL3 .... 47 E5 13
Back Rigby La North *BOLE* BL2 .... 29 D1 3
Back Rigby La South *BOLE* BL2 .... 29 D1 2
Back Rishton La *BOLS/LL* BL3 ...... 47 D5 3
Back Rishton La East
BOLS/LL BL3 .... 47 D6 10
Back Rochdale Old North Rd
BURY BL9 .... 35 D4 2
Back Rochdale Old Rd South
BURY BL9 .... 34 C4 4
Back Rochdale Old South Rd
BURY BL9 .... 35 D4 3
BURY BL9 .... 35 E4 3
Back Rochdale Rd *BURY* BL9 .... 34 B5 13
BURY BL9 .... 34 B5 13
BURY BL9 .... 34 B5 13
Back Rochdale Rd South
BURY BL9 .... 34 B5 13
Back Rock Av *BOL* BL1 .... 27 D4 3
Back Roland Rd *BOLS/LL* BL3 ...... 46 A5 3
Back Roman Rd *BRO* M7 .... 105 F1 3
Back Romer St *BOLE* BL2 .... 48 A2 3
Back Rosamond St *BOLS/LL* BL3 .. 46 A5 3
Back Roscow Av *BOLE* BL2 .... 48 C1 2
Back Rose Bank *BURY* BL9 .... 34 A3 13
Back Roseberry St *BOLS/LL* BL3 .. 46 A5 10
Back Rossini St *BOL* BL1 .... 27 E4 3
Back Rowena St *BOLS/LL* BL3 ..... 66 A1 3
Back Rowland St *BOLS/LL* BL3 .... 45 F6 3
Back Roxalina St *BOLS/LL* BL3 .... 46 C5 12
Back Royal Av *BURY* BL9 .... 34 A2 3
Back Royds St *MILN* OL16 .... 40 B2 2
Back Rudolph St *BOLS/LL* BL3 .... 47 E5 11
Back Rumworth St
BOLS/LL BL3 .... 46 B5 13
Back Rushton Rd *BOL* BL1 .... 26 C6 12
Back Russell Cl *BOL* BL1 .... 46 A1 13
Back Russell St *BOL* BL1 .... 46 A1
Back Rutland Gv *BOL* BL1 .... 27 D6 11
Back Ryefield St *BOL* BL1 .... 28 B6 3
Back St Anne's St *BURY* BL9 .... 34 A3 14
Back St Ann St *BOL* BL1 .... 27 F6 3
Back St Augustine St *BOL* BL1 .... 27 E5 22
Back St George's Rd *ANC* M4 ...... 106 C4 3
BOL BL1 .... 46 C1 3
Back St George's Rd North
BOL BL1 .... 46 C1 3
Back St Helens Rd *BOLS/LL* BL3 .. 46 B5 21
Back St Helens Rd South
BOLS/LL BL3 .... 45 F6 3
BOLS/LL BL3 .... 46 A6 10
Back St James's St *OLD* OL1 .... 79 F4 3
Back St Mark's La *CHH* M8 .... 90 A5 3
Back St Mary's Pl *BURY* BL9 .... 33 F5 3
Back St Philip's Av *BOLS/LL* BL3 .. 46 B5
Back St Thomas St East
BOL BL1 .... 27 E5 23
Back Salford St *BURY* BL9 .... 34 B3
Back Salisbury St *BOLS/LL* BL3 ... 46 B3 12
Back Salisbury Ter *BOLE* BL2 ...... 48 B2 10
Back Sandon St *BOLS/LL* BL3 ..... 46 B5 13
Back Sandon St West
BOLS/LL BL3 .... 46 B5 20
Back Sankey St *BURY* BL9 .... 33 F5 2
Back Sapling Rd South
BOLS/LL BL3 .... 64 A1 3
Back Scholes St *TOT/BURYW* BL8 .. 33 D4 7
Back Scott St *OLDS* OL8 .... 79 D6 1
Back Scowcroft St *BOLE* BL2 ...... 28 C6 3
Back Settle St *BOLS/LL* BL3 .... 46 C6 3
BOLS/LL BL3 .... 47 D6 13
Back Settle St North
BOLS/LL BL3 .... 46 C6 3
Back Seymour Rd *BOL* BL1 .... 28 A4 10
BOL BL1 .... 28 A4 10
Back Sharman St *BOLS/LL* BL3 .... 47 F4 3
Back Shaw-street *BURY* BL9 .... 34 C4 3
Back Shepherd St *BURY* BL9 .... 34 A6 3
Back Sherwood St *BOL* BL1 .... 28 A4 11
Back Shipton St *BOL* BL1 .... 26 C6 13
Back Shuttle St *BOLS/LL* BL3 ...... 46 C3 3
Back Silverdale Rd *BOL* BL1 .... 46 C6 3
Back Silver St *BURY* BL9 .... 33 F5 3
Back Skipton St *BOLE* BL2 .... 48 A1 3
Back Sofa St *BOL* BL1 .... 26 C6 14

Back Soho St *BOL* BL1 .... 47 D3
Back Somerville St *BOL* BL1 .... 27 D4 5
Back South Cross St East
　BURY BL9 .... 34 B6 4
Back Southfield St *BOLS/LL* BL3 ...... 47 F5 5
Back South Pde *CSLFD* M3 .... 2 C3
Back South View St *BOLE* BL2 .... 48 A2 7
Back Spa Rd *BOLS/LL* BL3 .... 46 C6 6
Back Spa Rd North *BOL* BL1 .... 46 B5 13
Back Spa Rd West *BOL* BL1 .... 46 A3 6
Back Spear St *CMANE* M1 .... 3 G2 1
Back Springfield St *BOLS/LL* BL3 ..... 47 F5 6
Back Spring Gdns *MDTN* M24 .... 75 E1 8
Back Spring St East *BURY* BL9 .... 34 A6 3
Back Spring St West *BURY* BL9 .... 34 A6 9
Back Square St *RAMS* BL0 .... 7 D5
Back Stainsbury St
　BOLS/LL BL3 .... 46 A5 11
Back Stanley St *RAMS* BL0 .... 6 C6 2
Back Stephen St
　TOT/BURYW BL8 .... 33 D5 9
Back Stewart St *BOL* BL1 .... 27 F5 3
Back Stone St *BOLE* BL2 .... 28 C6 9
Back Sunlight Rd *BOL* BL1 .... 46 A2 10
Back Sunning Hill St
　BOLS/LL BL3 .... 46 B5 22
Back Sunnyside Rd *BOL* BL1 .... 27 D5 18
Back Swan La *BOLS/LL* BL3 .... 46 B5 23
Back Talbot St *BOL* BL1 .... 28 A3 7
Back Tavistock St *BOL* BL1 .... 46 B5 19
Back Teak St *BURY* BL9 .... 34 C5 10
Back Tenterden St *BURY* BL9 .... 33 E5 4
Back Tenterdon St *BURY* BL9 .... 33 E5 5
Back Thicketford Rd *BOLE* BL2 ...... 28 D6 2
Back Thicketford Rd West
　BOLE BL2 .... 28 C6 2
Back Thomasson Cl *BOL* BL1 .... 27 F6 6
Back Thomas St *ANC* M4 .... 3 F2 1
Back Thorns Rd *BOL* BL1 .... 27 F4
Back Thorn St *BOL* BL1 .... 28 A5 10
Back Thorpe St *BOL* BL1 .... 27 E5
Back Thurnham St *BOLS/LL* BL3 .... 46 A6 11
Back Tinline St *BURY* BL9 .... 34 B5 15
Back Tonge Moor Rd *BOLE* BL2 ...... 28 C4
Back Tonge Moor Rd East
　BOLE BL2 .... 28 C6 3
Back Tonge Old Rd *BOLE* BL2 .... 48 A2 8
Back Tottington Rd
　TOT/BURYW BL8 .... 32 C3 9
Back Tottington Rd East
　BOLE BL2 .... 29 F2 1
Back Tottington Rd North
　TOT/BURYW BL8 .... 33 D3 3
　TOT/BURYW BL8 .... 33 D4 5
Back Tottington Rd South
　TOT/BURYW BL8 .... 33 D3
Back Tudor St *BOLS/LL* BL3 .... 46 A5 12
Back Turner St *ANC* M4 .... 3 F2 5
Back Turton Rd East *BOLE* BL2 .... 29 D2
Back Turton Rd West *BOLE* BL2 ...... 29 D2 1
　BOLE BL2 .... 29 D2 3
　BOLE BL2 .... 29 D3 4
Back Uganda St *BOLS/LL* BL3 .... 64 A1 6
Back Ulleswater St *BOL* BL1 .... 28 A5 10
Back Union Rd *BOLE* BL2 .... 28 B6
Back Unsworth St South
　BOLS/LL BL3 .... 46 B4 6
Back Uttley St *BOL* BL1 .... 27 E5 24
Back Venice St *BOLS/LL* BL3 .... 46 A5 13
Back Vernon St *BOL* BL1 .... 46 C1 10
　BURY BL9 .... 34 A3
Back Vernon St South *BOL* BL1 ...... 46 C1 10
Back Vickerman St *BOL* BL1 .... 27 E5 25
Back Victoria Gv *BOL* BL1 .... 27 D6 12
Back Victoria St East *BOL* BL1 .... 46 A1 10
Back Victor St *BOLS/LL* BL3 .... 46 B4 10
Back Viking St North *BOLS/LL* BL3 .. 47 E5
Back Vincent St *BOL* BL1 .... 46 B3 10
Back Vine St *BOLS/LL* BL3 .... 46 A3 7
Back Viola St *BOL* BL1 .... 27 F4
Back Waldeck St *BOL* BL1 .... 46 A1 10
Back Walmersley Rd East
　BURY BL9 .... 34 A1 5
　BURY BL9 .... 34 A2 8
　BURY BL9 .... 34 A3 15
Back Walmersley Rd West
　BURY BL9 .... 34 A2 10
　BURY BL9 .... 34 A3 16
Back Walnut St *BOL* BL1 .... 28 A5 11
Back Walshaw Rd North
　TOT/BURYW BL8 .... 33 D4 3
　TOT/BURYW BL8 .... 33 D4 5
Back Walshaw Rd South
　TOT/BURYW BL8 .... 33 D4 10
Back Wapping St *BOL* BL1 .... 27 E5 10
Back Wardle St *BOLE* BL2 .... 48 A4 1
Back Wash La *BURY* BL9 .... 34 B5
Back Wash La South *BURY* BL9 ..... 34 B5 10
Back Water St *STKP* SK1 .... 167 D3 2
Back Waverley Rd *BOL* BL1 .... 27 F4 10
Back Webster St *BOLS/LL* BL3 ...... 47 F4 3
Back Wellington Rd South
　BURY BL9 .... 52 C1

Back Wells St *BURY* BL9 .... 33 F6 2
Back Westbourne Av
　BOLS/LL BL3 .... 47 E6 5
Back Weston St North
　BOLS/LL BL3 .... 47 E5 16
Back Weston St South
　BOLS/LL BL3 .... 47 E5 17
Back Westwood Rd *BOL* BL1 .... 46 A1 23
Back Whittle Gv *BOL* BL1 .... 26 C6 15
Back Whittle St
　TOT/BURYW BL8 .... 33 D4 11
Back Wigan Rd *BOLS/LL* BL3 .... 45 E5 6
　BOLS/LL BL3 .... 45 F4 6
Back Wigan Rd North
　BOLS/LL BL3 .... 45 F4 6
Back Wigan Rd South
　BOLS/LL BL3 .... 45 F4 6
Back Willows *BOLS/LL* BL3 .... 45 F5
Back Willows La *BOLS/LL* BL3 ...... 46 B5 24
Back Willows La North
　BOLS/LL BL3 .... 45 F5 13
　BOLS/LL BL3 .... 46 A5 14
Back Willows La South
　BOLS/LL BL3 .... 45 F5 14
Back Wilmot St *BOL* BL1 .... 27 D4 6
Back Wilton St *BOL* BL1 .... 28 A4 12
Back Windermere St *BOL* BL1 .... 28 A5 12
Back Windsor Gv *BOL* BL1 .... 27 D6 14
Back Wolfenden St *BOL* BL1 .... 27 F5 10
Back Woodbine Rd
　BOLS/LL BL3 .... 46 A6 12
Back Woodfield St *BOLS/LL* BL3 ... 47 E6 6
Back Woodgate St *BOLS/LL* BL3 ... 47 E6
Back Wood St *TOT/BURYW* BL8 .... 33 D4
Back Worcester St *BOL* BL1 .... 27 F6 6
Back Wordsworth St *BOL* BL1 .... 27 E5 20 7
Back Worsel St *BOLS/LL* BL3 .... 46 A5 15
Back Worsel St North
　BOLS/LL BL3 .... 46 A5 16
Back Wynne St *BOL* BL1 .... 27 F5 27
Bacon Av *DTN/ASHW* M34 .... 149 E4 1
Bacup St *NEWH/MOS* M40 .... 92 B5
Badby Cl *ANC* M4 .... 107 E6
Badder St *BOL* BL1 .... 47 D1 2
Baden St *OP/CLY* M11 .... 125 F1
Bader Dr *HEY* OL10 .... 56 B2
Badger Cl *ANC* M4 .... 41 D4
Badger La *MILN* OL16 .... 40 C5
Badger St *BURY* BL9 .... 34 A4 2
Badgers Wk *WYTH/NTH* M22 .... 178 C6
Bagnall Cl *WHIT* OL12 .... 21 D5
Bagot St *OP/CLY* M11 .... 109 D5 3
　SWIN M27 .... 85 D4 2
Bagshaw St *HYDE* SK14 .... 131 E4
Bagslate Moor La *ROCH* OL11 .... 21 D5 1
Bagslate Moor Rd *ROCH* OL11 .... 21 D6
Baguley Crs *EDGY/DAV* SK3 .... 182 B1
　MDTN M24 .... 73 E5
Baguley Dr *SALE* M33 .... 160 C2 3
Baguley La *SALE* M33 .... 160 C1 10
Baguley Rd *DROY* M43 .... 110 C6
Baildon Rd *NEWH/MOS* M40 .... 92 B4
Baildon St *NEWH/MOS* M40 .... 92 B4
Bailey La *BOLE* BL2 .... 29 F6
　MANAIR M90 .... 177 F6
　PART M31 .... 155 D1
Bailey Rd *TRPK* M17 .... 120 B2
Bailey St *OLD* OL1 .... 79 E4 1
　OP/CLY M11 .... 109 E6
　PWCH M25 .... 72 A6 1
Bailey Wk *ALT* WA14 .... 188 A1 1
Baillie St *MILN* OL16 .... 30 C6 3
　RAD M26 .... 52 C4 1
Baillie St East *MILN* OL16 .... 23 E5
The Bails *BRO* M7 .... 105 D1
Bainbridge Cl *WGTN/LGST* M12 .. 125 E3 1
Bainbridge Rd *OLDE* OL4 .... 80 B2 3
Bainburgh Clough *OLDS* OL8 .... 97 D1
Baines Av *IRL* M44 .... 135 D2
Baines St *BOL* BL1 .... 45 F1 1
Bain St *SWIN* M27 .... 86 A6
Baird St *CMANE* M1 .... 125 D1
Baker St *FWTH* BL4 .... 67 F5
　HALE/TIMP WA15 .... 159 F6 1
　HEY OL10 .... 56 C1 1
　HTNM SK4 .... 166 C2
　MDTN M24 .... 75 F3
　RAMS BL0 .... 6 C6
　STLY SK15 .... 114 C6
Bakewell Av *AUL* OL6 .... 114 A1
　DTN/ASHW M34 .... 118 E3
Bakewell Rd *BRAM/HZG* SK7 .... 198 C1 5
　DROY M43 .... 109 F5
　ECC M30 .... 118 C1
　STRET M32 .... 120 B6
Bakewell St *EDGY/DAV* SK3 .... 166 B5
　GTN M18 .... 127 D5 1
Bala Cl *SALQ/ORD* M5 .... 104 B5
Balcary Gv *BOL* BL1 .... 45 F1
Balcombe Cl *TOT/BURYW* BL8 ...... 18 C6
Balderstone Rd *ROCH* OL11 .... 40 A5
Baldock Rd *DID/WITH* M20 .... 164 B2
Baldwin Rd *BNG/LEV* M19 .... 145 D5 3

Bale St *CMANW* M2 .... 2 D5
Balfour Gv *RDSH* SK5 .... 147 D2
Balfour Rd *ALT* WA14 .... 158 B6
　URM M41 .... 137 F1
　WHIT OL12 .... 22 A4 8
Balfour St *CHH* M8 .... 90 B5 1
　OLDE OL4 .... 80 A4
　ROY/SHW OL2 .... 61 F1
　SLFD M6 .... 104 A1
Ballantine St *NEWH/MOS* M40 ...... 109 D3
Ballard Cl *LIT* OL15 .... 12 C4
Ballard Wy *ROY/SHW* OL2 .... 62 A2
Ballater Av *URM* M41 .... 137 E2
Ballater Cl *HEY* OL10 .... 36 B6
Ballbrook Av *DID/WITH* M20 .... 143 F6
Balleratt St *BNG/LEV* M19 .... 145 E2 1
Balliol Cl *MPL/ROM* SK6 .... 170 A1
Balliol St *CHH* M8 .... 90 B5
　SWIN M27 .... 85 F5 3
Ball St *MILN* OL16 .... 23 E5
Ball Wk *HYDE* SK14 .... 153 D2
Balmain Av *GTN* M18 .... 127 D6
Balmain Rd *URM* M41 .... 118 C6
Balmer Rd *NTHM/RTH* M23 .... 177 E2
Balmfield St *CHH* M8 .... 106 B2
Balmforth St *HULME* M15 .... 123 E2 1
Balmoral Av *BOLS/LL* BL3 .... 49 E6 6
　CHD/CHDH SK8 .... 181 E5
　DTN/ASHW M34 .... 129 E2
　HYDE SK14 .... 150 C3
　ROCH OL11 .... 61 F5 1
　ROY/SHW OL2 .... 61 D5
　STRET M32 .... 121 E6 1
　URM M41 .... 137 F2
　WHTF M45 .... 71 E4
Balmoral Cl *BURY* BL9 .... 53 E4
　MILN OL16 .... 42 B1
　TOT/BURYW BL8 .... 18 B4 1
Balmoral Dr *ALT* WA14 .... 159 D5
　DTN/ASHW M34 .... 128 B5
　HEY OL10 .... 36 B6
　MPL/ROM SK6 .... 200 C2
　POY/DIS SK12 .... 198 B6
　STLY SK15 .... 114 B4
Balmoral Gra *PWCH* M25 .... 89 F2 1
Balmoral Gv *BRAM/HZG* SK7 .... 185 D4
Balmoral Rd *FWTH* BL4 .... 66 A4
　HALE/TIMP WA15 .... 174 C5
　HTNM SK4 .... 165 E2
　RUSH/FAL M14 .... 144 C3 1
　SWIN M27 .... 86 B3
　URM M41 .... 137 E2
Balmoral St *GTN* M18 .... 127 D5 2
Balmoral Wy *WILM/AE* SK9 .... 203 E5 5
Balmore Cl *BOLS/LL* BL3 .... 45 E6
Balm St *RAMS* BL0 .... 18 B1 3
Balsam Cl *BRUN/LGST* M13 .... 125 D2 1
Balshaw Av *IRL* M44 .... 135 D1
Balshaw Cl *BOLS/LL* BL3 .... 46 A4 13
Balshaw Ct *IRL* M44 .... 135 E1 1
Baltic Rd *ALT* WA14 .... 173 E1
Baltic St *SALQ/ORD* M5 .... 103 F5 3
Baltimore St *NEWH/MOS* M40 ...... 108 A2
Bamber Av *SALE* M33 .... 160 C2
Bamber St *BKLY* M9 .... 74 B6 2
Bamburgh Cl *RAD* M26 .... 50 A4 1
Bamburgh Dr *AULW* OL7 .... 111 F2 1
Bambury St *BURY* BL9 .... 34 A4
　MDTN M24 .... 75 E1
Bamford Av *DTN/ASHW* M34 .... 149 D5
　MDTN M24 .... 75 F1
Bamford Cl *BURY* BL9 .... 35 F3
　CHD/CHDH SK8 .... 194 B1
Bamford Gdns
　HALE/TIMP WA15 .... 176 B1 1
Bamford Gv *AUL* OL6 .... 114 A1
　DID/WITH M20 .... 163 E2
Bamford Ms *ROCH* OL11 .... 20 C6
Bamford Rd *DID/WITH* M20 .... 163 E2
　HEY OL10 .... 37 D3
　RAMS BL0 .... 7 F3
Bamford St *CHAD* OL9 .... 78 A3
　LIT OL15 .... 12 A6 1
　OP/CLY M11 .... 108 C5
　ROY/SHW OL2 .... 60 C5
　STKP SK1 .... 167 D5
Bamford Wy *ROCH* OL11 .... 38 A1
Bampton Cl *STKP* SK1 .... 167 F6 1
Bampton Rd *WYTH/NTH* M22 .... 178 A6
Banbury Ms *SWIN* M27 .... 85 E4 3
Banbury Rd *FAIL* M35 .... 109 F3 1
　MDTN M24 .... 75 D6
　NTHM/RTH M23 .... 177 D2
Banbury St *BOLE* BL2 .... 29 D6 8
　STKP SK1 .... 167 D4 8
Bancroft Av *CHD/CHDH* SK8 .... 181 E6
Bancroft Cl *MPL/ROM* SK6 .... 168 C2 1
Bancroft Fold *HYDE* SK14 .... 132 C4 1
Bancroft Rd *HALE/TIMP* WA15 .... 175 E4
　SWIN M27 .... 85 E4 1
Banff Gv *HEY* OL10 .... 36 B6
Banff Rd *RUSH/FAL* M14 .... 125 D5
Bangor Rd *CHD/CHDH* SK8 .... 181 D1
Bangor St *AUL* OL6 .... 113 F5 1
　BOL BL1 .... 46 C1 12 3

MILN OL16 .... 40 C1 🔢
RDSH SK5 .... 167 D1 🔢
Bank Barn La WHIT OL12 .... 11 E4
Bank Bridge Rd OP/CLY M11 .... 108 B4
Bank CI LIT OL15 .... 25 E2
Banker St BOLS/LL BL3 .... 48 A4
Bankfield Av BRUN/LGST M13 .... 125 F6
DROY M43 .... 110 B5 🔢
HTNM SK4 .... 166 A3
IRL M44 .... 134 B6 🔢
Bankfield CI BOLE BL2 .... 31 D6
Bankfield Dr OLDS OL8 .... 96 C3
Bankfield La ROCH OL11 .... 20 C5
Bankfield Rd CHD/CHDH SK8 .... 181 D6 🔢
FWTH BL4 .... 66 B4
MPL/ROM SK6 .... 149 F6
SALE M33 .... 138 C5
Bankfield St BKLY M9 .... 91 E4
BOLS/LL BL3 .... 46 A5 🔢
HTNM SK4 .... 166 C1
Bank Field St RAD M26 .... 68 B4
Bank Gv LHULT M38 .... 65 D5
Bank Hall TOT/BURYW BL8 .... 32 B5
Bankhall La HALE/TIMP WA15 .... 188 C1 🔢
Bankhall Rd HTNM SK4 .... 165 E3
Bank Hill St OLDE OL4 .... 79 F4
Bankhirst CI CHH M8 .... 90 B4 🔢
Bank House Rd BKLY M9 .... 91 D1
Banklands CI IRL M44 .... 134 B6 🔢
Bank La LHULT M38 .... 65 D5
SLFD M6 .... 103 E1
WHIT OL12 .... 11 D4
Bankley St BNG/LEV M19 .... 145 E2 🔢
Bank Mere CI WALK M28 .... 83 D2
Bankmill CI BRUN/LGST M13 .... 124 C2 🔢
Bank PI CSLFD M3 .... 105 E5
Bank Rd CHH M8 .... 90 B3
MPL/ROM SK6 .... 169 E2
STLY SK15 .... 115 F2
Banks Cft HEY OL10 .... 56 B2
Bankside HALE/TIMP WA15 .... 190 B3
HYDE SK14 .... 131 F4
Bankside Av RAD M26 .... 52 B5
Bankside CI CHAD OL9 .... 78 B5
WILM/AE SK9 .... 204 B1 🔢
Bankside Rd DID/WITH M20 .... 163 F6
Banks La STKP SK1 .... 167 F5
Bank Stanway Av BOLS/LL BL3 .. 46 B3 🔢
Bank St AULW OL7 .... 112 C5
BOL BL1 .... 47 D2
BRO M7 .... 90 A5 🔢
BURY BL9 .... 33 F5 🔢
CHD/CHDH SK8 .... 180 C1
CSLFD M3 .... 105 E5
DROY M43 .... 128 A1
DTN/ASHW M34 .... 130 A3
DTN/ASHW M34 .... 149 F3 🔢
EDGW/EG BL7 .... 15 D1
FWTH BL4 .... 66 B3
HEY OL10 .... 36 C5 🔢
HYDE SK14 .... 131 E4
MPL/ROM SK6 .... 149 F6 🔢
OLDE OL4 .... 80 B5 🔢
OP/CLY M11 .... 108 B5
RAD M26 .... 69 F1
RAMS BL0 .... 7 F4 🔢
ROCH OL11 .... 40 B3
SALE M33 .... 140 A6 🔢
TOT/BURYW BL8 .... 32 A3
WHTF M45 .... 70 C2
Bank Top AUL OL6 .... 113 D5
HEY OL10 .... 36 C4 🔢
Bank Top Gv BOL BL1 .... 26 A3
Bank Top Pk OLDE OL4 .... 80 B5 🔢
Bank Top St HEY OL10 .... 36 C4
Bank Wd BOL BL1 .... 45 D2
Banky La SALE M33 .... 138 A5
Bannatyne CI NEWH/MOS M40 .. 93 F4 🔢
Banner Dale CI BRUN/LGST M13 .. 126 A5 🔢
Banner Rd DROY M43 .... 110 C6 🔢
Bannerman Av PWCH M25 .... 88 C2
Bannerman Sq OLDTF/WHR M16 .. 124 A5
Bannerman St OLDTF/WHR M16 .. 124 A5
Bannerman St BOLE BL2 .... 48 C1
STKP SK1 .... 167 D5 🔢
Bannister Dr CHD/CHDH SK8 .... 181 D5
Bannister St BOLE BL2 .... 48 C1
STKP SK1 .... 167 D5 🔢
Bann St EDGY/DAV SK3 .... 166 B5
Banstead Av WYTH/NTH M22 ... 162 B6
Bantry Av BKLY M9 .... 90 C2
Bantry St BOLS/LL BL3 .... 64 C4
Baptist St ANC M4 .... 106 C2
Barathea CI ROCH OL11 .... 38 B4
Barbara St BOLS/LL BL3 .... 46 B5
Barbeck CI NEWH/MOS M40 .... 107 F4 🔢
Barberry CI ALT WA14 .... 157 F5
Barber St OP/CLY M11 .... 127 F2 🔢
Barbican St DID/WITH M20 ...... 143 F4
DID/WITH M20 .... 143 F4 🔢
Barchester Av BOLE BL2 .... 29 F6 🔢
Barcheston Rd CHD/CHDH SK8 .. 180 A3
Barcicroft Rd BNG/LEV M19 .... 164 C5
Barcliffe Av NEWH/MOS M40 ..... 93 D3
Barclyde St ROCH OL11 .... 39 F2 🔢
Barcombe CI OLDE OL4 .... 80 B1 🔢
URM M41 .... 120 A6 🔢
Barcroft Rd BOL BL1 .... 26 C5
Barcroft St BURY BL9 .... 34 A4
Bardon Rd NTHM/RTH M23 ..... 177 D1
Bardsea Av WYTH/NTH M22 .... 178 B6 🔢
Bardsley Av FAIL M35 .... 94 A6
Bardsley CI BOLE BL2 .... 29 E2
HYDE SK14 .... 152 C1 🔢
Bardsley Gate Av STLY SK15 ..... 133 F3
Bardsley St CHAD OL9 .... 94 A2
HTNM SK4 .... 166 B2
MDTN M24 .... 75 E2 🔢
NEWH/MOS M40 .... 109 E2 🔢
OLDE OL4 .... 80 C6 🔢
Barehill St LIT OL15 .... 12 C5
Bare St BOL BL1 .... 47 D1
Barff Rd SALQ/ORD M5 .... 103 D5
Barfold CI OFTN SK2 .... 185 E2
Barfoot Br SALE M33 .... 140 A4
Barford Dr WILM/AE SK9 .... 204 A2
Bar Gap Rd OLD OL1 .... 79 D3
Barham St CMANE M1 .... 3 H6
Barkan Wy SWIN M27 .... 98 B5
Barker Rd MPL/ROM SK6 .... 169 D2
Barker's La SALE M33 .... 139 D6
Barker St BURY BL9 .... 33 F6 🔢
CSLFD M3 .... 106 A3
HEY OL10 .... 36 C6
Barke St MILN OL16 .... 24 C2
Barking St NEWH/MOS M40 .... 107 F4 🔢
Bark St BOL BL1 .... 46 C2
FWTH BL4 .... 67 F6
Bark St East BOL BL1 .... 47 D1 🔢
Bark Wk HULME M15 .... 124 A3 🔢
Barkway Rd STRET M32 .... 139 E2
Barkwell La MOSL OL5 .... 98 C4
Bar La BOL BL1 .... 27 F2
Barlea Av NEWH/MOS M40 .... 93 E4
Barley Brook Meadow BOL BL1 .. 28 A1
Barleycorn CI SALE M33 .... 161 E2 🔢
Barley Cft CHD/CHDH SK8 .... 195 D1
Barley Croft Rd HYDE SK14 ..... 131 F3
Barley Dr BRAM/HZG SK7 .... 196 C2 🔢
Barleyfield Wk MDTN M24 .... 74 C2
Barley Hall St HEY OL10 .... 37 F4
Barlow Crs MPL/ROM SK6 .... 187 D3
Barlow Fold BURY BL9 .... 53 D4 🔢
Barlow Fold CI BURY BL9 .... 52 C4
Barlow Fold Rd MPL/ROM SK6 .. 187 D3
RDSH SK5 .... 147 E3 🔢
Barlow La ECC M30 .... 101 D5
Barlow La North RDSH SK5 ...... 147 D3
Barlow Moor CI WHIT OL12 .... 20 C3 🔢
Barlow Moor Ct DID/WITH M20 .. 163 D1
Barlow Moor Rd CCHDY M21 .... 141 F3
Barlow Park Av BOL BL1 .... 27 E4
Barlow PI BRUN/LGST M13 ...... 125 D2 🔢
Barlow Rd ALT WA14 .... 157 F5
BNG/LEV M19 .... 145 F2
DUK SK16 .... 131 E4
SALQ/ORD M5 .... 105 D6 🔢
STRET M32 .... 122 A5
WILM/AE SK9 .... 203 F2
Barlow's Cft CSLFD M3 .... 2 B2
Barlow's La South BRAM/HZG SK7 .. 184 A4
Barlow St BURY BL9 .... 34 A4
ECC M30 .... 101 E6
HEY OL10 .... 56 C1
MILN OL16 .... 23 E6
OLDE OL4 .... 79 E5
RAD M26 .... 51 F6
WALK M28 .... 83 E1
Barlow Wood Dr MPL/ROM SK6 .. 187 F4
Barmhouse CI HYDE SK14 .... 132 B6
Barmhouse La HYDE SK14 .... 132 B6
Barmhouse Ms HYDE SK14 ..... 132 B6 🔢
Barmouth St OP/CLY M11 .... 126 A1
Barmouth Wk OLDS OL8 .... 94 C5 🔢
Barnacre Av BOLE BL2 .... 49 D2
NTHM/RTH M23 .... 177 D4
Barnard Av HTNM SK4 .... 165 F3
WHTF M45 .... 71 F4
Barnard CI AULW OL7 .... 112 A3
Barnard Rd DTN M18 .... 126 C6
Barnbrook St BURY BL9 .... 34 B4 🔢
Barnby St WGTN/LGST M12 .... 126 B6
Barn CI URM M41 .... 136 A1
Barnclose Rd WYTH/NTH M22 .. 178 B6
Barncroft Gdns
WYTH/NTH M22 .... 178 A2 🔢
Barncroft Rd FWTH BL4 .... 66 B3
Barnes Av HTNM SK4 .... 165 E3
Barnes CI FWTH BL4 .... 66 B3 🔢
RAMS BL0 .... 18 B2
Barnes Mdw LIT OL15 .... 13 D2
Barnes St FWTH BL4 .... 65 F2
Barnes Ter FWTH BL4 .... 67 E4 🔢
Barneswell St NEWH/MOS M40 .. 109 D2 🔢
Barnet Rd BOL BL1 .... 27 D5 🔢
Barnett Dr CSLFD M3 .... 105 E5 🔢
Barnfield URM M41 .... 137 F3
Barnfield Av MPL/ROM SK6 ..... 170 B2
Barnfield CI RAD M26 .... 50 C6 🔢
Barnfield Crs SALE M33 .... 139 D6 🔢
Barn Field La WHIT OL12 .... 10 B4
Barnfield Ri ROY/SHW OL2 .... 42 B6
Barnfield Rd BNG/LEV M19 ..... 164 C1
HYDE SK14 .... 132 C4
SWIN M27 .... 85 E3
Barnfield Rd East EDGY/DAV SK3 .. 183 D5
Barnfield Rd West EDGY/DAV SK3 .. 182 B3
HEY OL10 .... 37 F5 🔢
WHIT OL12 .... 23 D3 🔢
Barn Fold OLDE OL4 .... 80 C6
Barngate Dr MOSL OL5 .... 99 D5
Barngate Rd CHD/CHDH SK8 .. 179 E1
Barn Gv DTN/ASHW M34 .... 129 E2
Barnhill Av PWCH M25 .... 88 C3
Barnhill Dr PWCH M25 .... 88 C3
Barnhill Rd PWCH M25 .... 88 B2
Barnhill St RUSH/FAL M14 ...... 124 A5
Barnley CI IRL M44 .... 116 C6
Barnsdale CI BOLE BL2 .... 31 D6 🔢
Barnsdale Dr CHH M8 .... 106 B1
Barnsfold Av RUSH/FAL M14 .... 144 A3 🔢
Barnsfold Rd MPL/ROM SK6 ... 187 D4
Barnside Av WALK M28 .... 83 F3
Barnside CI BURY BL9 .... 19 F5
Barnside Wy FAIL M35 .... 111 D1
Barnsley St STKP SK1 .... 167 E5
Barns PI HALE/TIMP WA15 ...... 190 A1
Barnstable Dr NEWH/MOS M40 .. 107 D1
Barnstead Av DID/WITH M20 ... 144 B6
Barnston Av RUSH/FAL M14 .... 143 F1
Barnston CI BOL BL1 .... 28 A3
Barn St BOL BL1 .... 46 C2 🔢
OLD OL1 .... 78 C5
WHTF M45 .... 71 D4
Barnwell CI DTN/ASHW M34 ... 129 F4 🔢
Barnwood Dr BOL BL1 .... 27 F6 🔢
Barnwood Rd NTHM/RTH M23 .. 177 E4
Baroness Gv BRO M7 .... 105 D3 🔢
Baron Fold Crs LHULT M38 .... 65 D6
Baron Fold Gv LHULT M38 .... 65 D6 🔢
Baron Fold Rd LHULT M38 .... 65 D6 🔢
Baron Gn CHD/CHDH SK8 .... 194 B2
Baron Rd HYDE SK14 .... 151 D4
Barons Ct FAIL M35 .... 109 E1
Baron St BURY BL9 .... 33 E6
MILN OL16 .... 23 D6
Baron Wk BOLS/LL BL3 .... 50 A6
Barrack HI MPL/ROM SK6 .... 169 E3
Barrack Hill CI MPL/ROM SK6 .. 169 E2 🔢
Barrack St HULME M15 .... 123 E2
Barra Dr URM M41 .... 119 E4
Barrass St OP/CLY M11 .... 127 E3 🔢
Barratt Gdns MDTN M24 .... 56 B5 🔢
Barrett Av FWTH BL4 .... 67 D4
Barrett Ct BURY BL9 .... 34 B5 🔢
Barrett St OLDE OL4 .... 79 F6
Barrfield Rd SLFD M6 .... 105 F3
Barr Hill Av SLFD M6 .... 105 F2
Barrhill CI HULME M15 .... 123 F3 🔢
Barrie Wy BOL BL1 .... 28 C3
Barrington Av CHD/CHDH SK8 .. 181 E6
DROY M43 .... 110 A6 🔢
Barrington CI ALT WA14 .... 174 B1 🔢
Barrington Rd ALT WA14 .... 174 B1
Barrington St OP/CLY M11 ...... 109 D5
Barrisdale CI BOLS/LL BL3 .... 45 D4 🔢
Barrow Bridge Rd BOL BL1 .... 26 A3
Barrowfield Rd WYTH/NTH M22 .. 177 E5
Barrow Hill Rd CHH M8 .... 106 A2
Barrow La HALE/TIMP WA15 ... 189 F2
Barrow Meadow CHD/CHDH SK8 .. 194 C1
Barrows Ct BOL BL1 .... 47 D3 🔢
Barrowshaw CI WALK M28 .... 83 D3 🔢
Barrow St CSLFD M3 .... 105 E6 🔢
Barrule Av BRAM/HZG SK7 ..... 184 C6 🔢
Barry Crs WALK M28 .... 82 B2
Barry Lawson CI CHH M8 .... 90 A6 🔢
Barry Ri ALT WA14 .... 173 E5
Barry Rd NTHM/RTH M23 .... 161 F3
RDSH SK5 .... 147 D6 🔢
Barry St OLD OL1 .... 79 F3
Barsham Dr BOLS/LL BL3 .... 46 B4 🔢
Bar Ter WHIT OL12 .... 9 D4
Bartlam PI OLD OL1 .... 79 D4 🔢
Bartlemore St OLD OL1 .... 79 E2
Bartlett Rd ROY/SHW OL2 .... 61 E3
Bartlett St OP/CLY M11 .... 126 C2
Bartley Rd WYTH/NTH M22 ..... 162 A5
Barton Av URM M41 .... 137 F1
Barton CI WILM/AE SK9 .... 204 B1
Barton Dock Rd STRET M32 ..... 120 B5
URM M41 .... 119 E2
Barton Fold HYDE SK14 .... 150 B2
Barton Hall Av ECC M30 .... 100 B6
Barton La ECC M30 .... 119 E1
Barton Moss Rd ECC M30 .... 117 D1
Barton Rd ECC M30 .... 119 D1
FWTH BL4 .... 65 F4
HTNM SK4 .... 164 C4
HYDE SK14 .... 131 D4
MDTN M24 .... 75 D3 🔢

STRET M32 .... 120 A5
STRET M32 .... 140 A3 🔲
SWIN M27 .... 86 B6
URM M41 .... 119 D5
WALK M28 .... 100 A2
Barton Ct CSLFD M3 .... 2 B6
FWTH BL4 .... 66 C4 🔲
OLD OL1 .... 78 B3
Barway Rd CCHDY M21 .... 141 D2
Barwell Cl RDSH SK5 .... 147 E5
Barwell Rd SALE M33 .... 138 C6
Barwell Sq FWTH BL4 .... 65 F1 🔲
Barwick Pl SALE M33 .... 159 E1 🔲
Basford Rd OLDTF/WHR M16 .... 122 C6
Bashall St BOL BL1 .... 46 A1 🔲
Basildon Cl BRUN/LGST M13 .... 125 E4 🔲
Basil St BOLS/LL BL3 .... 46 C4 🔲
HTNM SK4 .... 166 B2
MILN OL16 .... 40 C1
RUSH/FAL M14 .... 125 D6 🔲
Basle Cl CSLFD M3 .... 182 C4
Baslow Av BNG/LEV M19 .... 145 F1
Baslow Dr BRAM/HZG SK7 .... 199 D3
CHD/CHDH SK8 .... 194 A1
Baslow Gv RDSH SK5 .... 147 D6
Baslow Rd DROY M43 .... 109 F4
DTN/ASHW M34 .... 149 D3
STRET M32 .... 120 B6 🔲
Baslow St OP/CLY M11 .... 107 F6 🔲
Basset Av SLFD M6 .... 105 D2
Bassett Wy WHIT OL12 .... 22 C3 🔲
Bass La BURY BL9 .... 19 F2
Bass St DUK SK16 .... 130 C1 🔲
Basten Dr BRO M7 .... 105 E1
Batchelor Cl CCHDY M21 .... 142 C4 🔲
Bates Cl ROCH OL11 .... 39 E6 🔲
Bateson Dr OLDE OL4 .... 81 D5
Bateson St STKP SK1 .... 167 E3 🔲
Bates St BRUN/LGST M13 .... 126 A5
DUK SK16 .... 131 D1 🔲
Bath Cl BRAM/HZG SK7 .... 185 E5
Bath Crs CHD/CHDH SK8 .... 195 F3
OLDTF/WHR M16 .... 123 D4 🔲
Bath St ALT WA14 .... 174 B5
BOL BL1 .... 47 D1
CHAD OL9 .... 78 A6
WHIT OL12 .... 23 F4 🔲
Batley St BKLY M9 .... 91 F5
Battenberg Rd BOL BL1 .... 46 A3 🔲
Battersbay Gv BRAM/HZG SK7 .... 184 C5
Battersby St BURY BL9 .... 35 E5
OP/CLY M11 .... 127 F2 🔲
ROCH OL11 .... 38 C1
Battersea Rd HTNM SK4 .... 164 C4
Batty St CHH M8 .... 107 D2
Baxendale St BOL BL1 .... 27 F3 🔲
Baxter Gdns NTHM/RTH M23 .... 161 E6
Baxter Rd SALE M33 .... 159 F1
Baxter St OLDS OL8 .... 94 C3
Baybutt St RAD M26 .... 52 A6 🔲
Baycroft Gv NTHM/RTH M23 .... 161 E4
Baydon Av CHH M8 .... 106 A1
Bayfield Gv NEWH/MOS M40 .... 92 B4 🔲
Bayley Ct BOL BL1 .... 46 B1 🔲🔲
Bayley St STLY SK15 .... 113 F5
Baysdale Av BOLS/LL BL3 .... 45 D5
Bay St CHAD OL9 .... 78 B4 🔲
HEY OL10 .... 36 C4
WHIT OL12 .... 23 E4
Bayswater Av NEWH/MOS M40 .... 108 C3
Bayswater St BOLS/LL BL3 .... 64 A1
Baythorpe St BOL BL1 .... 28 A4
Baytree Av CHAD OL9 .... 76 C3
DTN/ASHW M34 .... 130 B5
Bay Tree Av WALK M28 .... 100 B2 🔲
Baytree Dr MPL/ROM SK6 .... 169 D1
Baytree Gv TOT/BURYW BL8 .... 18 C3 🔲
Baytree La MDTN M24 .... 76 B3
Baytree Wk WHIT OL12 .... 9 D2 🔲
Baywood St BKLY M9 .... 91 E5 🔲
Bazaar St SLFD M6 .... 104 B3 🔲
Bazley Rd WYTH/NTH M22 .... 162 B4
Bazley St BOL BL1 .... 26 A4
Beacomfold MPL/ROM SK6 .... 171 F2
Beacon Dr NTHM/RTH M23 .... 177 E5 🔲
Beacon Rd MPL/ROM SK6 .... 169 E4
TRPK M17 .... 119 F2
Beaconsfield RUSH/FAL M14 .... 144 A4 🔲
Beaconsfield Rd ALT WA14 .... 158 B6
Beaconsfield St BOLS/LL BL3 .... 46 B3
Beacon Vw MPL/ROM SK6 .... 171 D5
Beadham Dr BKLY M9 .... 73 E6 🔲
Beaford Dr WYTH/NTH M22 .... 192 B1
Bealbank Cl MILN OL16 .... 42 B4
Beal Cl HTNM SK4 .... 164 B2 🔲
Beal Crs MILN OL16 .... 24 A4
Bealcroft Cl MILN OL16 .... 24 C6
Bealey Av RAD M26 .... 52 C4
Bealey Cl GTN M18 .... 126 C3
RAD M26 .... 52 B5
Bealey Dr BURY BL9 .... 52 B2 🔲
Beal La ROY/SHW OL2 .... 62 A3
Beaminster Rd HTNM SK4 .... 165 D2
Beamish Cl BRUN/LGST M13 .... 125 D3

Beamsley Dr WYTH/NTH M22 .... 177 F5 🔲
Beanfields WALK M28 .... 100 A2
Bean Leach Av OFTN SK2 .... 185 D1 🔲
Bean Leach Dr OFTN SK2 .... 185 D1
Bean Leach Rd BRAM/HZG SK7 .... 184 C3
Beard Rd GTN M18 .... 127 D5 🔲
Beard St DROY M43 .... 110 A6 🔲
ROY/SHW OL2 .... 60 C6 🔲
Beardwood Rd BKLY M9 .... 88 B4
Bearswood Cl HYDE SK14 .... 151 D2 🔲
Beathwaite Dr BRAM/HZG SK7 .... 182 A6
Beatrice Av CHD/CHDH SK8 .... 181 D5
GTN M18 .... 128 A5 🔲
Beatrice Rd BOL BL1 .... 46 A1 🔲🔲
WALK M28 .... 84 C6
Beatrice St DTN/ASHW M34 .... 129 F6 🔲
FWTH BL4 .... 65 F3
ROCH OL11 .... 22 B6 🔲
SWIN M27 .... 85 E4
Beatrice Wignall St DROY M43 .... 128 B3 🔲
DROY M43 .... 128 B3 🔲
Beattock St HULME M15 .... 123 E3 🔲
Beauchamp St AUL OL6 .... 113 D3 🔲
Beaufort Av DID/WITH M20 .... 143 E6 🔲
SALE M33 .... 160 A2 🔲
SWIN M27 .... 85 E6
Beaufort Cha WILM/AE SK9 .... 205 D2
Beaufort Cl HYDE SK14. .... 152 C1
WILM/AE SK9 .... 209 F3
Beaufort Rd AUL OL6 .... 113 E4
HYDE SK14 .... 152 C1
OFTN SK2 .... 184 B3
SALE M33 .... 160 A2
Beaufort St CSLFD M3 .... 2 A6 🔲
ECC M30 .... 100 C4 🔲
PWCH M25 .... 89 D1
WHIT OL12 .... 22 B4 🔲
Beauly Cl TOT/BURYW BL8 .... 18 B3
Beaumaris Crs BRAM/HZG SK7 .... 198 A1
Beaumonds Wy ROCH OL11 .... 38 A1
Beaumont Cha BOLS/LL BL3 .... 45 D6
Beaumont Cl LIT OL15 .... 12 A2 🔲
Beaumont Dr BOLS/LL BL3 .... 44 C4
HOR/BR BL6 .... 44 C3
Beaumont Rd CCHDY M21 .... 141 F4
Beaumont St AUL OL6 .... 113 D4
Beauvale Av OFTN SK2 .... 168 A6
Beaver Dr BURY BL9 .... 53 F5
Beaver Rd DID/WITH M20 .... 163 F2
Beaver St CMANE M1 .... 3 E6
Bebbington Cl SALE M33 .... 161 D3 🔲
Bebbington St OP/CLY M11 .... 109 D6 🔲
Beccles Rd SALE M33 .... 159 F4
Beckenham Cl TOT/BURYW BL8 .... 32 C6 🔲
Beckenham Rd CHH M8 .... 90 B3 🔲
Becket Av BRO M7 .... 105 F1 🔲
Becket Meadow St OLDE OL4 .... 79 F5
Beckett St GTN M18 .... 127 D5 🔲
OLDE OL4 .... 80 C4
Beckfield Rd NTHM/RTH M23 .... 177 E2
Beckfoot Dr BRUN/LGST M13 .... 125 F6 🔲
Beckford St NEWH/MOS M40 .... 107 F2
Beck Gv ROY/SHW OL2 .... 62 B1
WALK M28 .... 83 F4
Beckhampton Cl BRUN/LGST M13 .... 125 D4
Beckley Av PWCH M25 .... 88 B3
Beckley Cl ROY/SHW OL2 .... 61 E5
Beckside RDSH SK5 .... 147 E2
Beck St CSLFD M3 .... 8 A2
OP/CLY M11 .... 127 F2 🔲
Beckton Gdns WYTH/NTH M22 .... 178 A4
Becontree Av DTN/ASHW M34 .... 130 B5
Becontree Dr NTHM/RTH M23 .... 176 B1
Bedells La WILM/AE SK9 .... 203 E5 🔲
Bede St BOL BL1 .... 27 D5 🔲🔲
Bedford Av HYDE SK14 .... 131 F6
OLDTF/WHR M16 .... 142 B1
ROY/SHW OL2 .... 61 D2
SALE M33 .... 160 B3
SWIN M27 .... 85 F6 🔲
WALK M28 .... 83 D4
Bedford Dr HALE/TIMP WA15 .... 176 A1
Bedford Gn IRL M44 .... 134 A5
Bedford Rd ECC M30 .... 101 F4
OLDTF/WHR M16 .... 141 E1
URM M41 .... 119 D5
Bedford St BOL BL1 .... 46 B1 🔲
HEY OL10 .... 37 F5
PWCH M25 .... 72 A6 🔲
RDSH SK5 .... 148 C4
Bedford Ter BURY BL9 .... 34 B3 🔲
Bedlam Gn BURY BL9 .... 34 A5 🔲
Bednal Av NEWH/MOS M40 .... 107 E3
Bedwell Cl OLDTF/WHR M16 .... 124 A6
Bedworth St RAMS BL0 .... 7 E6 🔲
Beechacre RAMS BL0 .... 7 E6 🔲
Beech Av BOLS/LL BL3 .... 67 F1
BRAM/HZG SK7 .... 184 C5
CHAD OL9 .... 77 E1
CHD/CHDH SK8 .... 179 F2
DROY M43 .... 110 A6
DTN/ASHW M34 .... 129 E5
EDGY/DAV SK3 .... 183 D1 🔲
FWTH BL4 .... 65 E3

FWTH BL4 .... 67 F6
IRL M44 .... 117 D6
MPL/ROM SK6 .... 186 B1
OLDE OL4 .... 80 B3
RAD M26 .... 69 D3
SLFD M6 .... 103 F3 🔲
URM M41 .... 138 A2
WHTF M45 .... 71 D4
WYTH/NTH M22 .... 162 B5
Beech Cl BOLE BL2 .... 29 D1
PWCH M25 .... 89 D2
WHIT OL12 .... 9 D2
WILM/AE SK9 .... 209 F2
Beech Cottages WILM/AE SK9 .... 209 E5 🔲
Beech Crs POY/DIS SK12 .... 198 C5
Beechcroft PWCH M25 .... 89 D3
Beechcroft Av BOLE BL2 .... 48 C3
Beechcroft Cl NEWH/MOS M40 .... 107 E4 🔲
Beechcroft Gv BOLE BL2 .... 48 C3
Beechdale Cl NEWH/MOS M40 .... 93 D5
Beeches Ms DID/WITH M20 .... 163 D1 🔲
The Beeches BOL BL1 .... 27 E1
DID/WITH M20 .... 163 D1
MOSL OL5 .... 99 F3
Beechfield ALT WA14 .... 174 A4 🔲
SALE M33 .... 159 D3 🔲
Beechfield Av LHULT M38 .... 65 E6
RAD M26 .... 70 A2 🔲
URM M41 .... 118 B6 🔲
WILM/AE SK9 .... 202 C6
Beechfield Cl OLDE OL4 .... 81 D5 🔲
ROCH OL11 .... 37 F1
Beechfield Dr BURY BL9. .... 52 C2
Beechfield Ms HYDE SK14 .... 132 B6 🔲
Beechfield Rd BOL BL1 .... 26 C5
CHD/CHDH SK8 .... 195 F1
EDGY/DAV SK3 .... 183 D3
MILN OL16 .... 41 F2
SWIN M27 .... 101 F2
WILM/AE SK9 .... 209 F5
Beechfield St CHH M8 .... 106 B1
Beech Gv AULW OL7 .... 112 A6
LHULT M38 .... 64 C6
RUSH/FAL M14 .... 144 B3
SALE M33 .... 159 D1
SLFD M6 .... 103 F3 🔲
STLY SK15 .... 132 A1
TOT/BURYW BL8 .... 18 Ba
WILM/AE SK9 .... 203 E5
Beech Grove Cl BURY BL9 .... 34 C3 🔲
Beech Hurst Cl
OLDTF/WHR M16 .... 142 B1 🔲
WILM/AE SK9 .... 203 E5
Beech Ms CCHDY M21 .... 141 E3 🔲
OFTN SK2 .... 183 E2
Beech Mt AULW OL7 .... 112 B1
BKLY M9 .... 91 F5
Beechpark Av WYTH/NTH M22 .... 162 A6
Beech Rd CCHDY M21 .... 141 F3
CHD/CHDH SK8 .... 181 F6
EDGY/DAV SK3 .... 182 C1
HALE/TIMP WA15 .... 174 C4
MPL/ROM SK6 .... 201 D2 🔲
SALE M33 .... 160 B1
WILM/AE SK9 .... 209 F2
Beech St BOL BL1 .... 28 A5 🔲🔲
BURY BL9 .... 34 C5
ECC M30 .... 100 C6
FAIL M35 .... 93 F5
HYDE SK14 .... 131 E6
MDTN M24 .... 75 D3 🔲
MILN OL16 .... 42 B3 🔲
OLD OL1 .... 79 E4
RAD M26 .... 70 A2
RAMS BL0 .... 19 D2
ROCH OL11 .... 39 E1
SWIN M27 .... 86 A6
Beechurst Rd CHD/CHDH SK8 .... 181 F2
Beech Vw HYDE SK14 .... 151 E1
Beech Wk MDTN M24 .... 75 D5
STRET M32 .... 140 A3
Beechway MPL/ROM SK6 .... 201 D2
WILM/AE SK9 .... 203 D6
Beechwood ALT WA14 .... 173 F6 🔲
ROY/SHW OL2 .... 62 B1
Beechwood Av CCHDY M21 .... 142 C3 🔲
LIT OL15 .... 25 E2
MPL/ROM SK6 .... 170 A3
RAMS BL0 .... 7 E5 🔲
STLY SK15 .... 115 D3
URM M41 .... 117 F6 🔲
Beechwood Ct TOT/BURYW BL8.. .... 32 B2
Beechwood Dr HYDE SK14 .... 151 D2
MOSL OL5 .... 99 D3
MPL/ROM SK6 .... 187 E1
ROY/SHW OL2 .... 60 A3
SALE M33 .... 158 A1
WALK M28 .... 100 C1
WILM/AE SK9 .... 204 C3 🔲
Beechwood Gv BKLY M9 .... 91 F6 🔲
CHD/CHDH SK8 .... 195 E1 🔲
Beechwood Rd OLDS OL8 .... 96 A3
PWCH M25 .... 89 E2 🔲
Beechwood St BOLS/LL BL3 .... 47 D6 🔲🔲

Beede St OP/CLY M11 .... 126 B1 🅱
Beedon Av BOLS/LL BL3 .... 49 E5
Beehive St OLDS OL8 .... 96 A2
Beeley St HYDE SK14 .... 150 C1 🅱
  SLFD M6 .... 104 C2
Beenham Cl SALE M33 .... 158 A2 🅱
Beeston Av BRO M7 .... 104 C1
  HALE/TIMP WA15 .... 175 D1
Beeston Cl EDGW/EG BL7 .... 28 B1
Beeston Gv EDGY/DAV SK3 .... 182 C2
  WHTF M45 .... 71 F4
Beeston Rd SALE M33 .... 158 C1
  WILM/AE SK9 .... 194 B4 🅱
Beeston St M9 .... 91 F6
Beeth St OP/CLY M11 .... 127 E3 🅱
Beeton Gv BRUN/LGST M13 .... 125 F5 🅱
Beever St OLD OL1 .... 79 E4
  OLDTF/WHR M16 .... 123 D4
Begley Cl MPL/ROM SK6 .... 169 D4
Begonia Av FWTH BL4 .... 65 E2
Belbeck St TOT/BURYW BL8 .... 33 D5
Belbeck St South
  TOT/BURYW BL8 .... 33 D5 🅱
Belcroft Dr LHULT M38 .... 64 C5
Belcroft Gv LHULT M38 .... 64 C6 🅱
Belding Av NEWH/MOS M40 .... 94 A4 🅱
Beldon Rd BKLY M9 .... 90 C1
Belfairs Cl AULW OL7 .... 112 C1
Belfield Cl MILN OL16 .... 24 A5 🅱
Belfield La MILN OL16 .... 24 B6 🅱
Belfield Mill La MILN OL16 .... 24 A5
Belfield Old Rd MILN OL16 .... 24 A5
Belfield Rd DID/WITH M20 .... 163 F2 🅱
  MILN OL16 .... 23 F5
  PWCH M25 .... 89 F2
Belford Av DTN/ASHW M34 .... 128 B6
Belford Dr BOLS/LL BL3 .... 46 C5
Belford Rd STRET M32 .... 121 E6
Belfort Dr SALQ/ORD M5 .... 122 C1 🅱
Belfry Cl WILM/AE SK9 .... 204 B3
Belgate Cl WYTH/NTH M22 .... 126 B5
Belgium St ROCH OL11 .... 20 C6 🅱
Belgrave Av FAIL M35 .... 94 C5 🅱
  MPL/ROM SK6 .... 187 D1 🅱
  OLDS OL8 .... 96 B1
  URM M41 .... 117 F6
Belgrave Crs ECC M30 .... 102 A4
  OFTN SK2 .... 183 E3
Belgrave Dr RAD M26 .... 51 E5
Belgrave Rd ALT WA14 .... 174 A4
  IRL M44 .... 134 B6
  NEWH/MOS M40 .... 93 F4
  OLDS OL8 .... 96 A1 🅱
  SALE M33 .... 159 E1
Belgrave St BOL BL1 .... 27 F5 🅱
  HEY OL10 .... 37 D6
  RAD M26 .... 51 E5
  WHIT OL12 .... 22 A4
Belgrave St South BOL BL1 .... 27 F6
Belgravia Gdns HALE/TIMP WA15 .... 188 C1
Belgravia Ms ROY/SHW OL2 .... 62 A2 🅱
Belhaven Rd CHH M8 .... 90 A5
Bellairs St BOLS/LL BL3 .... 46 A6 🅱
Bella St BOLS/LL BL3 .... 46 A5
Bell Clough Rd DROY M43 .... 110 C4
Bell Crs OP/CLY M11 .... 126 A1
Bellcroft WYTH/NTH M22 .... 162 C5 🅱
Belldale Cl HTNM SK4 .... 165 E3
Belle Isle Av WHIT OL12 .... 9 D5
Bellerby Cl WHTF M45 .... 70 C3 🅱
Belleville Av WYTH/NTH M22 .... 192 C1 🅱
Belle Vue Av WGTN/LGST M12 .... 126 A4
Belle Vue St WGTN/LGST M12 .... 126 B3
Belle Vue Ter BURY BL9 .... 33 F6 🅱
Bellew St OP/CLY M11 .... 125 F1 🅱
Bellfield Av CHD/CHDH SK8 .... 181 F6 🅱
  OLDS OL8 .... 96 A3
Bellingham Cl ROY/SHW OL2 .... 61 F1 🅱
  TOT/BURYW BL8 .... 32 A5 🅱
Bellis Cl WGTN/LGST M12 .... 107 F6 🅱
  WGTN/LGST M12 .... 107 F6 🅱
Bell La BURY BL9 .... 54 B4
  MILN OL16 .... 25 F6
Bell Meadow Dr ROCH OL11 .... 38 A2
Bellott St WALK M28 .... 106 B1
Bellpit Cl WALK M28 .... 83 D6
Bells Croft La NEWH/MOS M40 .... 92 C6 🅱
Bellshill Crs MILN OL16 .... 24 A4
Bell St DROY M43 .... 110 C5
  MILN OL16 .... 23 D5 🅱
  OLD OL1 .... 79 E4
Bell Ter ECC M30 .... 119 D1
Belmont Av DTN/ASHW M34 .... 129 E5
  FWTH BL4 .... 68 B6
  OLDE OL4 .... 81 D4
  SLFD M6 .... 102 B4 🅱
Belmont Cl HTNM SK4 .... 166 C2 🅱
Belmont Dr MPL/ROM SK6 .... 171 F4
  TOT/BURYW BL8 .... 32 B6
Belmont Rd BOL BL1 .... 27 E1
  BRAM/HZG SK7 .... 196 C4
  CHD/CHDH SK8 .... 179 F1
  HALE/TIMP WA15 .... 174 C5
  RAD M26 .... 69 E2
  SALE M33 .... 139 E5

Belmont St ECC M30 .... 101 E4
  HTNM SK4 .... 166 B2 🅱
  OLD OL1 .... 78 C3
  OLDE OL4 .... 80 C6 🅱
  SALQ/ORD M5 .... 103 E6 🅱
Belmont Vw BOLE BL2 .... 30 A3
Belmont Wy CHAD OL9 .... 78 A3
  HTNM SK4 .... 166 C2
  WHIT OL12 .... 22 C3
Belper Rd ECC M30 .... 118 C1
  HTNM SK4 .... 165 D4
Belsay Cl AULW OL7 .... 112 A2 🅱
Belsay Dr NTHM/RTH M23 .... 177 E3
Belstone Av NTHM/RTH M23 .... 177 E4
Belstone Cl BRAM/HZG SK7 .... 183 D5
Belthorne Av BKLY M9 .... 92 C5 🅱
Belton Av MILN OL16 .... 24 A4
Beltone Cl STRET M32 .... 139 F2
Belvedere Av RDSH SK5 .... 147 D1
  TOT/BURYW BL8 .... 48 B4
Belvedere Dr DUK SK16 .... 131 F1
  MPL/ROM SK6 .... 168 A2
Belvedere Rd BOL OL1 .... 62 B6 🅱
  RUSH/FAL M14 .... 144 C3 🅱
  SLFD M6 .... 104 C4 🅱
Belvedere St SLFD M6 .... 104 C4 🅱
Belvoir Av BNG/LEV M19 .... 145 E1 🅱
  BRAM/HZG SK7 .... 198 C1
Belvoir Mdw MILN OL16 .... 24 C1 🅱
Belvoir St BOLE BL2 .... 48 A2 🅱
  WHIT OL12 .... 22 B4 🅱
Belvor Av DTN/ASHW M34 .... 129 F2
Belwood Rd CCHDY M21 .... 141 E4
Bembridge Cl RUSH/FAL M14 .... 125 D6 🅱
Bembridge Dr BOLS/LL BL3 .... 48 B4
Bembridge Rd DTN/ASHW M34 .... 149 F3
Bempton Cl OFTN SK2 .... 185 E2 🅱
Bemrose Av ALT WA14 .... 174 A1
Bemsley Pl SALQ/ORD M5 .... 122 B1 🅱
Benbecula Wy URM M41 .... 119 E4
Benbow Av WGTN/LGST M12 .... 126 A4
Benbow St SALE M33 .... 139 F6
Bench Carr WHIT OL12 .... 22 C4
Benchill Court Rd WYTH/NTH M22.. 178 C3
Benchill Dr WYTH/NTH M22 .... 178 B2
Benchill Rd WYTH/NTH M22 .... 178 A1
Bendall St OP/CLY M11 .... 127 F1
Bendemeer URM M41 .... 119 D6 🅱
Bendix St ANC M4 .... 3 G1
Benedict Cl BRO M7 .... 105 D2 🅱
Benedict Dr DUK SK16 .... 132 C3
Benfield Av NEWH/MOS M40 .... 93 D5 🅱
Benfield St HEY OL10 .... 37 E6 🅱
Benfleet Cl WGTN/LGST M12 .... 126 B3
Bengal La AUL OL6 .... 113 D3
Bengal St ANC M4 .... 3 H1
  EDGY/DAV SK3 .... 166 C5
Benmore Cl HEY OL10 .... 36 B5
Benmore Rd BKLY M9 .... 92 A1
Bennet St RAD M26 .... 50 B5
Bennett Cl EDGY/DAV SK3 .... 166 A5 🅱
Bennett Dr BRO M7 .... 105 F1
Bennett Rd CHH M8 .... 90 A4
Bennett's La BOL BL1 .... 27 D5
Bennett St AULW OL7 .... 112 A6
  EDGY/DAV SK3 .... 166 A5 🅱
  HYDE SK14 .... 131 D4
  STLY SK15 .... 114 B6 🅱
  STRET M32 .... 140 A2 🅱
  WGTN/LGST M12 .... 125 F3
Benny La DROY M43 .... 111 E4
Benson Cl BRO M7 .... 105 F2 🅱
Benson Rd BURY BL9 .... 34 B6
Ben St OP/CLY M11 .... 108 C5
Bentcliffe Wy ECC M30 .... 102 A6 🅱
Bentfield Crs MILN OL16 .... 42 B5 🅱
Bent Fold Dr BURY BL9 .... 71 E2 🅱
Bentgate Cl MILN OL16 .... 42 B3
Bentgate St MILN OL16 .... 42 B4
Bentham Cl TOT/BURYW BL8 .... 31 F4 🅱
Bent Hill St BOLS/LL BL3 .... 48 B5 🅱
Bentinck Rd ALT WA14 .... 174 A3
Bentinck St AUL OL6 .... 112 B5
  AULW OL7 .... 112 C5
  BOL BL1 .... 26 C6
  FWTH BL4 .... 66 A2 🅱
  HULME M15 .... 123 E2 🅱
  WHIT OL12 .... 22 A4 🅱
Bent La CHH M8 .... 90 A6
  PWCH M25 .... 89 D1
  URM M41 .... 118 A4
Bentley Av MDTN M24 .... 58 B4
Bentley Cl RAD M26 .... 52 A5
Bentley Ct FWTH BL4 .... 66 B2 🅱
Bentley Hall Rd TOT/BURYW BL8 .... 31 E3
Bentley Rd BRO M7 .... 89 F5
  CCHDY M21 .... 141 E2
  DTN/ASHW M34 .... 130 A6
Bentley St CHAD OL9 .... 77 F4
  FWTH BL4 .... 66 B2
  OLD OL1 .... 9 E2
  WHIT OL12 .... 22 C4
Bentmeadows WHIT OL12 .... 22 C4
Benton St BKLY M9 .... 92 A6 🅱

Bents Av MPL/ROM SK6 .... 169 D2
  URM M41 .... 136 C2
Bents Farm Cl LIT OL15 .... 12 A6 🅱
Bent Spur Rd FWTH BL4 .... 67 E6
Bent St CHH M8 .... 106 B2 🅱
  FWTH BL4 .... 66 C4
Beresford Av BOLS/LL BL3 .... 46 A4 🅱
Beresford Crs OLDE OL4 .... 80 B3 🅱
  RDSH SK5 .... 127 F6 🅱
Beresford Rd BRUN/LGST M13 .... 126 A6
  STRET M32 .... 121 F5 🅱
Beresford St FAIL M35 .... 93 F6
  MILN OL16 .... 42 C3 🅱
  OLDE OL4 .... 80 B3
  RUSH/FAL M14 .... 124 C4 🅱
Berigan Cl WGTN/LGST M12 .... 125 F4
Berisford Cl HALE/TIMP WA15 .... 158 C6
Berkeley Av CHAD OL9 .... 94 A2
  RUSH/FAL M14 .... 125 F5 🅱
  STRET M32 .... 120 B5 🅱
Berkeley Cl HYDE SK14 .... 150 B2 🅱
  OFTN SK2 .... 168 A5
Berkeley Crs HYDE SK14 .... 150 B2
  RAD M26 .... 50 A3 🅱
Berkeley Dr MILN OL16 .... 40 C3
  ROY/SHW OL2 .... 78 B1
Berkeley Rd BOL BL1 .... 27 F3
  BRAM/HZG SK7 .... 185 D4
Berkeley St AUL OL6 .... 112 B4 🅱
  BNG/LEV M19 .... 145 E1
Berkley St ROY/SHW OL2 .... 60 B4 🅱
Berkley Wk LIT OL15 .... 12 A6
Berkshire Cl CHAD OL9 .... 77 F6
Berkshire Dr IRL M44 .... 134 A6
Berkshire Rd NEWH/MOS M40 .... 107 E4
Berlin Rd EDGY/DAV SK3 .... 182 B1
Berlin St BOLS/LL BL3 .... 2 B4
Bermondsay St SALQ/ORD M5 .... 122 C1 🅱
Bernard Gv BOL BL1 .... 27 D5
Bernard St BKLY M9 .... 91 E5 🅱
  WHIT OL12 .... 22 C2
Berne Cl BRAM/HZG SK7 .... 182 C3
  CHAD OL9 .... 78 A5 🅱
Bernice Av CHAD OL9 .... 77 F5
Bernice St BOL BL1 .... 27 D5
Berrie Gv BNG/LEV M19 .... 145 F3 🅱
Berry Brow NEWH/MOS M40 .... 109 E3
Berry Cl WILM/AE SK9 .... 203 E6
Berrycroft La MPL/ROM SK6 .... 169 E2
Berry St CMANE M1 .... 3 H6
  ECC M30 .... 118 C1
  STLY SK15 .... 133 D1
  SWIN M27 .... 86 A3
Bertha Rd MILN OL16 .... 24 A6
Bertha St BOL BL1 .... 27 E5
  OP/CLY M11 .... 126 C2 🅱
  ROY/SHW OL2 .... 61 F4
Bertie St ROCH OL11 .... 39 E3 🅱
Bertram St SALE M33 .... 140 C1 🅱
  WGTN/LGST M12 .... 126 B3 🅱
Bertrand Rd BOL BL1 .... 46 A2
Bert St BOLS/LL BL3 .... 45 F6
Berwick Av HTNM SK4 .... 164 C3 🅱
  URM M41 .... 139 E1 🅱
  WHTF M45 .... 71 E4 🅱
Berwick Cl HEY OL10 .... 36 B6 🅱
  WALK M28 .... 82 A6
Berwick St MILN OL16 .... 40 C1
Berwyn Av BKLY M9 .... 74 A6
  CHD/CHDH SK8 .... 181 F2
  MDTN M24 .... 76 A3
Beryl Av TOT/BURYW BL8 .... 18 A6
Beryl St BOL BL1 .... 28 A4 🅱
Besom La STLY SK15 .... 115 F4 🅱
Bessemer Rd IRL M44 .... 135 D5
Bessemer St OP/CLY M11 .... 127 D2
Bessybrook Cl HOR/BR BL6 .... 44 A3
Beswick Dr FAIL M35 .... 110 B1
Beswicke Royds St MILN OL16 .... 23 F4
Beswicke St LIT OL15 .... 13 D6 🅱
  WHIT OL12 .... 22 C5 🅱
Beswick Rw ANC M4 .... 3 E1
Beswicks La WILM/AE SK9 .... 208 A2
Beswick St ANC M4 .... 107 E5
  DROY M43 .... 110 C6 🅱
Beta Av STRET M32 .... 140 A2
Beta St BOL BL1 .... 47 D1
Bethany La MILN OL16 .... 43 D3
Bethel Av FAIL M35 .... 93 F6 🅱
Bethel St HEY OL10 .... 37 D5 🅱
Bethesda St OLDS OL8 .... 96 A1
Bethnal Dr RUSH/FAL M14 .... 143 E3
Betjeman Pl ROY/SHW OL2 .... 62 A2 🅱
Betleymere Rd CHD/CHDH SK8 .. 181 D3 🅱
Betley Rd RDSH SK5 .... 147 D2
Betley St CMANE M1 .... 125 D1 🅱
  HEY OL10 .... 37 D6 🅱
  RAD M26 .... 52 A5 🅱
Betnor Av STKP SK1 .... 167 F4
Betony Cl WHIT OL12 .... 22 B2 🅱
Bettwood Dr CHH M8 .... 90 A5 🅱
Betula Gv BRO M7 .... 89 E6 🅱
Betula Ms ROCH OL11 .... 20 B4 🅱
Bevan Cl WGTN/LGST M12 .... 107 F6

Bevendon Sq BRO M7 105 F1 4
Beveridge St RUSH/FAL M14 124 B6 1
Beverley Av DTN/ASHW M34 149 E1
URM M41 119 F5
Beverley Cl WHTF M45 71 F2
Beverley Pl MILN OL16 23 E5 1
Beverley Rd BOL BL1 46 A1
BOLS/LL BL3 49 D6
OFTN SK2 168 A5
SWIN M27 87 D6
Beverley St BKLY M9 91 F4
Beverly Cl AUL OL6 112 C1
Beverly Rd RUSH/FAL M14 144 B4
Beverston Dr BRO M7 105 F1
Bewick St BOLE BL2 28 C4
Bewley St OLDS OL8 95 E2
Bexhill Av HALE/TIMP WA15 175 D1 1
Bexhill Cl BOLS/LL BL3 50 A6
Bexhill Dr BRUN/LGST M13 125 F6
Bexhill Rd EDGY/DAV SK3 182 C3
Bexley Cl URM M41 118 C5
Bexley Dr LHULT M38 83 D2
TOT/BURYW BL8 32 C6
Bexley Sq CSLFD M3 105 E5 2
CSLFD M3 105 E5 2
Bexley St CHAD OL9 78 A6 1
Beyer Cl GTN M18 127 D4
Bibby La BNG/LEV M19 145 D5 4
Bibby St BURY BL9 53 D4 2
HYDE SK14 131 E4 1
Bibury Av WYTH/NTH M22 177 F4
Bickerdike Av WGTN/LGST M12 126 C6
Bickershaw Dr WALK M28 83 D3 2
Bickerstaffe Cl ROY/SHW OL2 61 E4 1
Bickerton Dr BRAM/HZG SK7 183 E6
Bickerton Rd ALT WA14 173 F2
Biddall Dr NTHM/RTH M23 177 F1
Biddulph Av OFTN SK2 184 A2
Bideford Dr BOLE BL2 49 E3 1
NTHM/RTH M23 161 D6 1
Bideford Rd OFTN SK2 168 A4
ROCH OL11 38 C4
Bidston Cl ROY/SHW OL2 62 B3
TOT/BURYW BL8 32 B5 1
Bidston Dr WILM/AE SK9 204 C1 1
Bignor St CHH M8 106 B1
Bilbao St BOL BL1 46 A1
Bilberry St MILN OL16 40 B1
Bilbrook St ANC M4 106 C4
Billberry Cl WHTF M45 71 F3
Billing Av WGTN/LGST M12 125 D2
Billington Rd SWIN M27 87 F5
Bill Williams Cl OP/CLY M11 127 D1
Billy La SWIN M27 86 A3
Bilson Dr EDGY/DAV SK3 165 F6
Bindloss Av ECC M30 102 B4
Bingham Dr NTHM/RTH M23 177 D1
Bingham St SWIN M27 86 A5
Bingley Cl OP/CLY M11 126 A1 1
Bingley Dr URM M41 118 A5
Bingley Rd MILN OL16 24 A6
Bingley Sq MILN OL16 24 A6
Bingley Ter MILN OL16 24 A6
Binns Nook Rd WHIT OL12 23 E3
Binns Pl CMANE M1 3 H3
Binns St STLY SK15 113 F6
Binsley Cl IRL M44 135 E2
Birchacre Gv RUSH/FAL M14 144 B4 1
Birchall Cl DUK SK16 131 E3 1
Birchall Gn MPL/ROM SK6 149 D6
Birch Av FAIL M35 110 A1
HTNM SK4 165 F1
IRL M44 134 B6
MDTN M24 75 E4
MPL/ROM SK6 170 B3
OLD OL1 77 E1
OLDS OL8 95 E3
OLDTF/WHR M16 122 B5
SALE M33 159 F2 1
SLFD M6 103 F3
TOT/BURYW BL8 32 B2
WHIT OL12 24 B1
WHTF M45 71 D5
WILM/AE SK9 203 D5
Birch Cl WHIT OL12 9 D6
Birch Crs MILN OL16 42 B4
Birchdale ALT WA14 174 A5
Birchdale Av CHD/CHDH SK8 179 F5
Birch Dr BRAM/HZG SK7 184 A5
OLDE OL4 80 C6
SWIN M27 86 C5
Birchenall St NEWH/MOS M40 92 A5 2
Birchenlea St CHAD OL9 94 B2 1
Birches Rd EDGW/EG BL7 15 F2
The Birches SALE M33 138 C6 1
Birchfield BOLE BL2 29 F1
Birchfield Av HEY OL10 35 F6
Birchfield Dr ROCH OL11 39 D2
WALK M28 82 B6
Birchfield Gv BOLS/LL BL3 44 C5
Birchfield Ms HYDE SK14 150 B1 2
Birchfield Rd EDGY/DAV SK3 165 E6
Birchfields HALE/TIMP WA15 175 D6
Birchfields Av BRUN/LGST M13 125 F6
Birchfields Rd BRUN/LGST M13 125 F6
Birchfold Cl LHULT M38 82 C1 1
Birchgate Wk BOLS/LL BL3 47 D4 3
Birch Gv DTN/ASHW M34 129 F6
DTN/ASHW M34 130 A3
HALE/TIMP WA15 176 C2
PWCH M25 71 E5
RUSH/FAL M14 125 E6
TOT/BURYW BL8 18 B2 1
Birch Hall Cl OLDE OL4 97 F1
Birch Hall La BRUN/LGST M13 144 C1
Birch Hey Cl WHIT OL12 24 A1 1
Birch Hill Crs WHIT OL12 24 C1
Birch Hill La WHIT OL12 11 E5
Birchington Rd DID/WITH M20 143 E3
Birchinlee Av ROY/SHW OL2 59 F6
Birchin Pl ANC M4 3 F3 1
Birch La BRUN/LGST M13 125 F5
DUK SK16 131 E1
Birch-lea Cl BURY BL9 53 D2
Birchleaf Gv SALQ/ORD M5 103 D5 1
Birch Mt WHIT OL12 24 C1
Birch Polygon RUSH/FAL M14 125 E6
Birch Rd CHD/CHDH SK8 179 E2
CHH M8 90 C4
FWTH BL4 67 D5
MDTN M24 76 A1 2
PART M31 154 B2
PART M31 157 D2
SWIN M27 101 E2
WALK M28 83 F4
Birch St AULW OL7 112 A6
BURY BL9 34 A4
DROY M43 128 C1 1
HEY OL10 37 E6
RAD M26 52 C4 2
STLY SK15 115 D2
WGTN/LGST M12 126 B3
WHIT OL12 11 D5 1
Birch Tree Av BRAM/HZG SK7 185 E6
Birch Tree Cl ALT WA14 174 A6
Birch Tree Dr WYTH/NTH M22 178 B4 1
Birchvale Av MPL/ROM SK6 170 B2
Birchvale Cl HULME M15 123 F3
Birchway BRAM/HZG SK7 196 B2
MPL/ROM SK6 201 D2
Birchwood CHAD OL9 76 C4
Birchwood Dr WILM/AE SK9 204 B3
Birchwood Rd MDTN M24 76 A3
Birchwood Wy DUK SK16 131 E3 2
Bird Hall Av CHD/CHDH SK8 182 A3
Birdhall Gv BNG/LEV M19 145 E3
Bird Hall La CHD/CHDH SK8 165 F6
Bird Hall Rd CHD/CHDH SK8 181 F2
Birdlip Dr NTHM/RTH M23 177 E4
Birkby Dr MDTN M24 74 C1
Birkdale Av ROY/SHW OL2 78 C1
WHTF M45 70 B5 1
Birkdale Cl BRAM/HZG SK7 197 E2
HEY OL10 56 B1 1
HYDE SK14 131 F4
Birkdale Dr SALE M33 158 C3
TOT/BURYW BL8 32 C5
Birkdale Gdns BOLS/LL BL3 46 B4 12
Birkdale Gv ECC M30 102 A5 1
RDSH SK5 147 D6
Birkdale Rd MILN OL16 41 D3 1
RDSH SK5 147 D6
Birkdale St CHH M8 90 B6
Birkenhills Dr BOLS/LL BL3 44 C4 1
Birkett Cl BOL BL1 27 E1
Birkett Dr BOL BL1 27 E1
Birkinbrook Cl WHTF M45 71 E2 2
Birks Av OLDE OL4 81 D3
Birks Dr TOT/BURYW BL8 32 C1
Birkworth Ct OFTN SK2 184 B1 2
Birley Cl HALE/TIMP WA15 159 D6
Birley Pk DID/WITH M20 163 D2
Birley St BURY BL9 34 A2
WHIT OL12 23 E4 3
Birling Dr NTHM/RTH M23 177 F3
Birnham Gv HEY OL10 36 B6
Birshaw Cl ROY/SHW OL2 61 F4 1
Birtenshaw Crs EDGW/EG BL7 14 C6
Birtles Av RDSH SK5 128 A6 3
Birtles Cl CHD/CHDH SK8 181 D2
DUK SK16 131 E3
Birtlespool Rd CHD/CHDH SK8 181 D3
Birt St NEWH/MOS M40 107 E3 2
Birwood Rd CHH M8 90 C3
Biscay Cl OP/CLY M11 108 A6 2
Bishopbridge Cl BOLS/LL BL3 47 D5 2
Bishop Cl OLDTF/WHR M16 123 F5 1
Bishopdale Cl ROY/SHW OL2 60 B4 2
Bishopgate St CHAD OL9 77 E6 2
Bishop Marshall Cl
NEWH/MOS M40 107 E2 4
Bishop Marshall Wy MDTN M24 56 B5 2
Bishop Rd SLFD M6 102 C3
URM M41 136 B1
Bishops Cl ALT WA14 173 F6
AULW OL7 112 B2
BOLS/LL BL3 65 E1 1
CHD/CHDH SK8 181 E2
Bishopsgate CMANW M2 2 D5
Bishopsgate Wk MILN OL16 41 D3 2
Bishops Meadow MDTN M24 56 B6
Bishops Ms SALE M33 138 C5 1
Bishop's Rd BOLS/LL BL3 65 E1
PWCH M25 89 D2
Bishop St MDTN M24 76 B4
MILN OL16 23 F4
STKP SK1 167 E4
Bishopton Cl BNG/LEV M19 146 A2
Bisley Av NTHM/RTH M23 177 D1
Bisley St OLDS OL8 78 B5 2
Bismarck St OLDS OL8 79 E6
Bispham Av BOLE BL2 49 D2 1
RDSH SK5 128 A6 4
Bispham Cl TOT/BURYW BL8 32 A6
Bispham Gv BRO M7 89 F6 1
Bispham St BOLE BL2 48 A1 4
Bittern Cl POY/DIS SK12 197 E6
ROCH OL11 21 D6
Bittern Dr DROY M43 111 D4
Bk Clegg's Bldgs BOL BL1 46 C1 13
Blackbank St BOL BL1 28 A5
Blackberry Cl ALT WA14 157 F5 2
Blackberry La RDSH SK5 147 F4
Black Brock Rd HTNM SK4 146 B4
Blackburn Gdns DID/WITH M20 163 E1
Blackburn Pl SALQ/ORD M5 105 D6 3
Blackburn Rd BOL BL1 27 F4
Blackburn St CSLFD M3 105 E4
OLDTF/WHR M16 123 D4
PWCH M25 89 D1
RAD M26 69 F1 1
Blackcap Cl WALK M28 82 C6 1
Blackcarr Rd NTHM/RTH M23 177 F2
Blackchapel Dr MILN OL16 40 C4
Blackcroft Cl SWIN M27 85 F5
Blackfield La BRO M7 89 D5
Blackford Av BURY BL9 53 D5
Blackford Rd BNG/LEV M19 145 F4
Blackfriars Rd CSLFD M3 105 E4
Blackhill Cl BRUN/LGST M13 124 C2 2
Black Horse St BOL BL1 46 C2
FWTH BL4 66 C4 2
Blackledge St BOLS/LL BL3 46 A5
Blackley Cl BURY BL9 71 E1
Blackley New Rd BKLY M9 90 A2
Blackley Park Rd BKLY M9 91 E4 1
Blackley St MDTN M24 73 F4 1
OLDTF/WHR M16 123 D4 2
Blacklock St CSLFD M3 106 A3
Black Moss Cl RAD M26 50 B6 1
Black Moss Rd ALT WA14 156 C6
Blackpits Rd ROCH OL11 20 B4
Blackpool St OP/CLY M11 109 D5 3
Blackrock STLY SK15 115 D1
Blackrock St OP/CLY M11 108 A6
Blackrod Dr TOT/BURYW BL8 32 A6
Blackshaw La BOLS/LL BL3 46 A3
ROY/SHW OL2 61 D5
WILM/AE SK9 209 D4
Blackshaw St EDGY/DAV SK3 166 C5 2
Blacksmith La ROCH OL11 38 C3 1
Blackstock St BRUN/LGST M13 125 D5 2
Blackstone Av MILN OL16 24 A5
Blackstone Edge Old Rd LIT OL15 13 E5
Blackstone Rd OFTN SK2 184 B2
Blackthorn Cl WHIT OL12 22 C3 2
Blackthorne Cl BOL BL1 26 B6 9
Blackthorne Dr SALE M33 158 B3
Blackthorne Rd HYDE SK14 150 C5
Blackthorn Rd OLDS OL8 95 D5
Blackwin St WGTN/LGST M12 126 B3
Blackwood Dr NTHM/RTH M23 160 B5
Blackwood St BOLS/LL BL3 47 E5 18
Bladen Cl CHD/CHDH SK8 181 E3
Bladon St CMANE M1 3 G5 4
Blair Av LHULT M38 82 C1 2
URM M41 136 C1
Blair Cl BRAM/HZG SK7 198 A1
ROY/SHW OL2 61 F2
SALE M33 158 A4
Blairhall Av NEWH/MOS M40 92 B6
Blair La BOLE BL2 29 E6
Blairmore Dr BOLS/LL BL3 44 C5
Blair Rd OLDTF/WHR M16 142 C2
Blair St EDGW/EG BL7 14 A5
FWTH BL4 67 E5
OLDTF/WHR M16 123 E4
WHIT OL12 22 B4
Blake Dr OFTN SK2 168 C6
Blakefield Dr WALK M28 83 F4
Blake Gdns BOL BL1 27 E5 28
Blakelock St ROY/SHW OL2 61 E2
Blakemere Av SALE M33 160 C2 2
Blake St BOL BL1 27 E5 29
EDGW/EG BL7 14 B6 3
MILN OL16 23 E5
Blakeswell Cl URM M41 117 E6 2
Blakey Cl BOLS/LL BL3 45 D5
Blakey St WGTN/LGST M12 126 B5
Blanchard St HULME M15 123 F4 1
Blanche St WHIT OL12 23 E3
Bland Cl FAIL M35 93 F6
Blandford Av WALK M28 84 A5
Blandford Cl TOT/BURYW BL8 33 E2 1
Blandford Ct STLY SK15 114 B5 1

Blandford Dr NEWH/MOS M40 .... 93 D3
Blandford Rd ECC M30 .... 100 C5
HTNM SK4 .... 165 F3
SLFD M6 .... 104 C2 🔲
Blandford St AUL OL6 .... 112 B4
STLY SK15 .... 114 B5 🔲
Bland Rd PWCH M25 .... 88 C3
Blanefield Cl CCHDY M21 .... 142 C4
Blantyre Av WALK M28 .... 83 F3
Blantyre Rd SWIN M27 .... 102 C1
Blantyre St ECC M30 .... 100 B4
HULME M15 .... 123 E2
SWIN M27 .... 85 E5
Blanwood Dr CHH M8 .... 90 C6 🔲
Blaven Cl EDGY/DAV SK3 .... 183 C2 🔲
Blazemoss Bank OFTN SK2 .... 184 B2
Bleackley St TOT/BURYW BL8 .... 33 D3
Bleak Hey Rd WYTH/NTH M22 .... 179 D5
Bleakley St WHTF M45 .... 70 C2
Bleak St BOLE BL2 .... 28 C5 🔲
Bleasdale Rd BOL BL1 .... 80 A4
Bleasdale Rd BOL BL1 .... 26 A5
WYTH/NTH M22 .... 177 E5
Bleasdale St ROY/SHW OL2 .... 60 B4
Bleatarn Rd STKP SK1 .... 167 F6
Bledlow Cl ECC M30 .... 101 F4
Blenheim Av OLDTF/WHR M16 .... 142 B1
Blenheim Cl ALT WA14 .... 174 B5
BURY BL9 .... 53 D4
HEY OL10 .... 37 F5 🔲
POY/DIS SK12 .... 199 D5 🔲
WILM/AE SK9 .... 204 B3
Blenheim Rd BOLE BL2 .... 48 C2
CHD/CHDH SK8 .... 181 F5
OLDTF/WHR M16 .... 122 B6
Blenheim St WHIT OL12 .... 22 A4 🔲
Blenhiem Av OLD OL1 .... 62 B6 🔲
Blenmar Cl RAD M26 .... 52 A4
Bletchley Cl BRUN/LGST M13 .... 125 E4
Bletchley Rd HTNM SK4 .... 164 C4
Blinco Rd URM M41 .... 139 D2
Blind La WGTN/LGST M12 .... 125 E2
Blindsill Rd FWTH BL4 .... 65 F4
Blisworth Av ECC M30 .... 119 F1 🔲
Blisworth Cl ANC M4 .... 107 E6 🔲
Block La CHAD OL9 .... 77 F6
Blodwell St SLFD M6 .... 104 A5
Blomley St ROCH OL11 .... 39 D5
Bloomfield Dr BURY BL9 .... 53 F6
WALK M28 .... 82 B6 🔲
Bloomfield Rd FWTH BL4 .... 66 B5
Bloomfield St BOL BL1 .... 2 F4 🔲
Bloomsbury Gv HALE/TIMP WA15 .. 175 F3
Bloomsbury La HALE/TIMP WA15 .... 175 E1
Bloom St CMANE M1 .... 3 E6
CSLFD M3 .... 2 A2
EDGY/DAV SK3 .... 166 A5
RAMS BL0 .... 18 B1 🔲
Blossom Pl MILN OL16 .... 23 D5 🔲
Blossom Rd PART M31 .... 154 C3
Blossoms Hey CHD/CHDH SK8 .... 180 C6
Blossoms La BRAM/HZG SK7 .... 205 E1
Blossoms St OFTN SK2 .... 167 D6 🔲
Blossom St ANC M4 .... 3 H2
CSLFD M3 .... 2 B1 🔲
Blucher St AULW OL7 .... 112 A1
SALQ/ORD M5 .... 105 D6
WGTN/LGST M12 .... 125 F3
Blue Bell Av NEWH/MOS M40 .... 92 B4
Bluebell Cl HYDE SK14 .... 132 A4
Bluebell Dr ROCH OL11 .... 38 C4
Bluebell Gv CHD/CHDH SK8 .... 180 B3 🔲
Bluebell Wy WILM/AE SK9 .... 204 A2
Blueberry Dr ROY/SHW OL2 .... 62 B2 🔲
Blueberry Rd ALT WA14 .... 173 E5
Bluefields ROY/SHW OL2 .... 62 B1 🔲
Blue Ribbon Wk SWIN M27 .... 86 B4
Bluestone Dr HTNM SK4 .... 164 C2
Bluestone Rd DTN/ASHW M34 .... 147 E1
NEWH/MOS M40 .... 92 B5
Blundell Cl BURY BL9 .... 53 F6 🔲
Blundell St BOL BL1 .... 46 C2 🔲
Blundering La STLY SK15 .... 133 E3
Blunn St OLDS OL8 .... 96 A1 🔲
Blyborough Cl SLFD M6 .... 103 F3
Blyth Av LIT OL15 .... 25 D2 🔲
Blyth Cl HALE/TIMP WA15 .... 176 B1
Blythe Av BRAM/HZG SK7 .... 196 A3
Board St CMANE M1 .... 3 H5
Boardale Dr MDTN M24 .... 74 C2 🔲
Boardman Cl BOL BL1 .... 27 F5 🔲
Boardman Fold Cl MDTN M24 .... 75 E6
Boardman Fold Rd MDTN M24 .... 75 D6
Boardman La MDTN M24 .... 74 A3
Boardman Rd CHH M8 .... 90 A3
Boardman St BOL BL1 .... 27 F5
ECC M30 .... 101 F6
HYDE SK14 .... 150 B1 🔲
Board St AUL OL6 .... 113 C3
BOLS/LL BL3 .... 46 B3
Boar Green Cl NEWH/MOS M40 .... 93 D6
Boarshaw Clough MDTN M24 .... 75 F1
Boarshaw Clough Wy MDTN M24 .... 76 A1
Boarshaw Crs MDTN M24 .... 76 A1
Boarshaw La MDTN M24 .... 58 B6

Boarshaw Rd MDTN M24 .... 75 E2
Boat La IRL M44 .... 135 F1
WYTH/NTH M22 .... 162 C4
Bob Brook Cl FAIL M35 .... 109 D1
Bob Massey Cl OP/CLY M11 .... 127 D1
Bob's La IRL M44 .... 154 B1
Boddens Hill Rd HTNM SK4 .... 165 E4
Boddington Rd ECC M30 .... 100 A6
Bodiam Rd TOT/BURYW BL8 .... 18 A4
Bodley St OP/CLY M11 .... 109 D5
Bodmin Cl ROY/SHW OL2 .... 61 E6
Bodmin Crs RDSH SK5 .... 147 F6
Bodmin Dr BRAM/HZG SK7 .... 196 C2
Bodmin Rd SALE M33 .... 138 B6
Bognor Rd EDGY/DAV SK3 .... 182 C5
Bolam Cl NTHM/RTH M23 .... 161 D4
Boland Dr RUSH/FAL M14 .... 144 B3
Bolderod Pl OLD OL1 .... 79 E3 🔲
Bolderstone Pl OFTN SK2 .... 184 C3
Bold St ALT WA14 .... 174 B4
BOL BL1 .... 47 D3
BURY BL9 .... 34 B4
HULME M15 .... 123 F4
OLDTF/WHR M16 .... 123 F5
SWIN M27 .... 86 A3
Bolesworth Cl CCHDY M21 .... 141 D3 🔲
Boleyn Ct HEY OL10 .... 37 D6
Bolivia St SALQ/ORD M5 .... 103 D5 🔲
Bollin Cl FWTH BL4 .... 67 E5
Bollin Dr ALT WA14 .... 158 C5
SALE M33 .... 159 F3
Bollings Yd BOL BL1 .... 47 D3
Bollington Rd HTNM SK4 .... 146 B6
NEWH/MOS M40 .... 107 F3
Bollington St AULW OL7 .... 112 B6
Bollin Hl WILM/AE SK9 .... 203 F6 🔲
Bollin Sq ALT WA14 .... 173 F6 🔲
Bollin Wk WHTF M45 .... 72 A1
WILM/AE SK9 .... 203 F4
Bollinway HALE/TIMP WA15 .... 189 E1
Bollinwood Cha WILM/AE SK9 .... 204 B4
Bolshaw Farm La CHD/CHDH SK8 .. 194 A3
Bolshaw Rd CHD/CHDH SK8 .... 193 F5
Bolton Av BNG/LEV M19 .... 164 B3
CHD/CHDH SK8 .... 195 F3
Bolton Cl POY/DIS SK12 .... 198 B5 🔲
PWCH M25 .... 88 A3 🔲
Bolton Rd BOLE BL2 .... 29 D2
EDGW/EG BL7 .... 15 E1 🔲
FWTH BL4 .... 64 B3
RAD M26 .... 50 B5
ROCH OL11 .... 38 D3
SWIN M27 .... 86 B4
TOT/BURYW BL8 .... 17 D3
TOT/BURYW BL8 .... 33 D6
WALK M28 .... 83 E1
Bolton Rd North RAMS BL0 .... 7 E1
Bolton Rd West RAMS BL0 .... 18 B1
Bolton St BURY BL9 .... 33 E5
CSLFD M3 .... 2 A2
OLDE OL4 .... 79 F5
RAD M26 .... 51 D6
RAMS BL0 .... 6 C6
RDSH SK5 .... 146 C4
Bombay Rd EDGY/DAV SK3 .... 166 A6
Bombay St AUL OL6 .... 113 G3 🔲
CMANE M1 .... 3 F6 🔲
Bonar Cl EDGY/DAV SK3 .... 166 A5 🔲
Bonar Rd EDGY/DAV SK3 .... 166 A5
Boncarn Dr NTHM/RTH M23 .... 177 E3
Bonchurch Wk
WGTN/LGST M12 .... 126 C3 🔲
Bondmark Rd GTN M18 .... 127 D3
Bond Sq BRO M7 .... 105 F1 🔲
Bond St BURY BL9 .... 34 B5
DTN/ASHW M34 .... 130 A6
RAMS BL0 .... 7 F1
STLY SK15 .... 114 B3
WGTN/LGST M12 .... 125 D1
WHIT OL12 .... 23 E3
Bongs Rd OFTN SK2 .... 169 D6
Bonington Ri MPL/ROM SK6 .... 171 F5
Bonis Crs OFTN SK2 .... 184 A3
Bonny Brow St MDTN M24 .... 73 F4
Bonsall St HULME M15 .... 124 A3
Bonscale Crs MDTN M24 .... 56 C6
Bonville Cha ALT WA14 .... 173 E2
Bonville Rd ALT WA14 .... 173 E2
Boode Rd AUL OL6 .... 112 C3
AULW OL7 .... 112 C4
Boond St ANC M4 .... 107 E6 🔲
CSLFD M3 .... 2 C4
Boonfields EDGW/EG BL7 .... 14 B5
Booth Av RUSH/FAL M14 .... 144 B4
Booth Bridge Cl MDTN M24 .... 74 A1 🔲
Boothby Rd SWIN M27 .... 85 F4 🔲
Boothby St OFTN SK2 .... 184 A3
Booth Cl STLY SK15 .... 114 A6 🔲
Boothcote DTN/ASHW M34 .... 129 E3
Booth Dr URM M41 .... 118 A4
Boothfield ECC M30 .... 100 B4
Boothfield Rd WYTH/NTH M22 .... 178 A1
Booth Hall Dr TOT/BURYW BL8 ...... 32 A2 🔲
Booth Hall Rd BKLY M9 .... 92 B2
Booth Hill La OLD OL1 .... 78 C2

Booth Rd ALT WA14 .... 174 A3
BOLS/LL BL3 .... 67 F1
DTN/ASHW M34 .... 128 B2
OLDTF/WHR M16 .... 123 D8 🔲
SALE M33 .... 139 F5
WILM/AE SK9 .... 203 E2
Boothroyden Rd MDTN M24 .... 74 A4
Boothroyden Ter BKLY M9 .... 73 F5
Booth St AUL OL6 .... 112 C5 🔲
BOL BL1 .... 27 D4 🔲
CHAD OL9 .... 78 C4
CMANW M2 .... 2 D4
CSLFD M3 .... 2 C3
DTN/ASHW M34 .... 130 A4
EDGY/DAV SK3 .... 166 C6 🔲
FAIL M35 .... 93 F6
HYDE SK14 .... 150 C2 🔲
MDTN M24 .... 76 B5
OLDE OL4 .... 80 C5 🔲
STLY SK15 .... 132 A1 🔲
TOT/BURYW BL8 .... 32 A1 🔲
Booth St East BRUN/LGST M13 ...... 124 B3
Booth St West HULME M15 .... 124 B3
Booth Wy TOT/BURYW BL8 .... 32 A2 🔲
Bootle St CSLFD M3 .... 2 C4
Bordale Av BKLY M9 .... 92 A6
Bordan St OP/CLY M11 .... 126 A1
Border Brook La WALK M28 .... 82 B6
Bordley Wk NTHM/RTH M23 .... 160 C4
Bordon Rd EDGY/DAV SK3 .... 165 F6
Boringdon Cl NEWH/MOS M40 .... 108 C1 🔲
Borland Av NEWH/MOS M40 .... 93 D4
Borough Av RAD M26 .... 52 B4
SWIN M27 .... 86 B4
Borough Rd HALE/TIMP WA15 .... 174 C3
SALQ/ORD M5 .... 103 E6
Borough St STLY SK15 .... 114 B6 🔲
Borron St STKP SK1 .... 167 E3
Borrowdale Av BOL BL1 .... 45 E1 🔲
CHD/CHDH SK8 .... 179 F3
Borrowdale Cl ROY/SHW OL2 .... 60 B3
Borrowdale Crs AULW OL7 .... 112 A3
DID/WITH M20 .... 162 C1
Borrowdale Dr BURY BL9 .... 53 E6 🔲
BURY BL9 .... 53 E6 🔲
ROCH OL11 .... 38 C3
Borrowdale Rd MDTN M24 .... 74 C1
OFTN SK2 .... 167 F6
Borsden St SWIN M27 .... 85 E4
Borth Av OFTN SK2 .... 168 A6
Borwell St GTN M18 .... 127 E3
Boscobel Rd BOLS/LL BL3 .... 65 F1
Boscombe Av ECC M30 .... 119 D1
Boscombe Dr BRAM/HZG SK7 .... 184 A5
Boscombe St RDSH SK5 .... 147 D1
RUSH/FAL M14 .... 143 F1
Boscow Rd BOLS/LL BL3 .... 67 E1
Bosden Av BRAM/HZG SK7 .... 184 C4
Bosden Cl WILM/AE SK9 .... 194 B4
Bosden Fold STKP SK1 .... 167 D5 🔲
Bosdenfold Rd BRAM/HZG SK7 ...... 184 C4
Bosden Hall Rd BRAM/HZG SK7 .... 184 C4
Bosdin Rd East URM M41 .... 136 C2 🔲
Bosdin Rd West URM M41 .... 136 C2 🔲
Bosley Av DID/WITH M20 .... 143 E5
Bosley Cl WILM/AE SK9 .... 204 B1
Bosley Dr POY/DIS SK12 .... 199 E5 🔲
Bosley Rd EDGY/DAV SK3 .... 165 E5
Bossall Av BKLY M9 .... 91 F1 🔲
Bossington Cl OFTN SK2 .... 168 A5
Bostock Rd HYDE SK14 .... 153 E3
Boston Cl BRAM/HZG SK7 .... 196 B2
FAIL M35 .... 94 A4
Boston Ct SALQ/ORD M5 .... 121 F1
Boston St HYDE SK14 .... 131 F6
OLDS OL8 .... 96 A1
Boswell Av DTN/ASHW M34 .... 111 E6
Boswell Wy MDTN M24 .... 58 C4
Bosworth Cl WHTF M45 .... 72 A3
Bosworth St OP/CLY M11 .... 126 B1
ROCH OL11 .... 39 E2
Botanical Av OLDTF/WHR M16 ...... 122 B4 🔲
Botany Cl HEY OL10 .... 36 C4 🔲
Botany La AUL OL6 .... 113 D3
Botany Rd ECC M30 .... 100 B3
MPL/ROM SK6 .... 149 E5
Botham Cl HULME M15 .... 124 B4 🔲
Bothwell Rd NEWH/MOS M40 .... 107 D4 🔲
Bottesford Av DID/WITH M20 .... 143 D6 🔲
Bottomfield Cl OLD OL1 .... 79 E2
Bottomley Side BKLY M9 .... 91 D3
Bottom o' Th' Knotts Brow
EDGW/EG BL7 .... 16 A2
Bottom o'thmoor BOLE BL2 .... 29 E5
Bottom O' Th' Moor OLDE OL4 .... 79 E4
Bottom St HYDE SK14 .... 132 A6
Boulden Dr TOT/BURYW BL8 .... 33 D2
Boulder Dr NTHM/RTH M23 .... 177 E5
Boulderstone Rd STLY SK15 .... 114 B3
The Boulevard BRAM/HZG SK7 ...... 184 C5 🔲
Boundary Cl MPL/ROM SK6 .... 150 A6 🔲
STLY SK15 .... 115 D1
Boundary Dr BOLS/LL BL3 .... 49 E4
Boundary Gdns OLD OL1 .... 78 C2 🔲
Boundary Gv SALE M33 .... 161 D3 🔲

Boundary La HULME M15 ...... 124 B3
Boundary Park Rd OLD OL1 ...... 78 A2
Boundary Rd CHD/CHDH SK8 ...... 181 D1
  IRL M44 ...... 117 D6
  SWIN M27 ...... 86 A5
Boundary St BOL BL1 ...... 27 E5
  BOLS/LL BL3 ...... 49 F4
  LIT OL15 ...... 12 B5
  ROCH OL11 ...... 39 F2
  WGTN/LGST M12 ...... 126 B3
  WGTN/LGST M12 ...... 126 B4
Boundary St West HULME M15 ...... 124 B3
The Boundary SWIN M27 ...... 85 E1
Boundary Wk ROCH OL11 ...... 40 A2
Boundry Gn DTN/ASHW M34 ...... 129 F4
Bourdon St NEWH/MOS M40 ...... 107 E4
Bourget St CHH M8 ...... 90 A5
Bournbrook Av LHULT M38 ...... 65 E5
Bourne Av SWIN M27 ...... 86 A6
Bourne Dr NEWH/MOS M40 ...... 92 C4
Bournelea Av BNG/LEV M19 ...... 145 D5
Bourne Rd ROY/SHW OL2 ...... 61 E1
Bourne St CHAD OL9 ...... 94 C3
  HTNM SK4 ...... 166 C1
  WILM/AE SK9 ...... 203 D5
Bourneville Dr TOT/BURYW BL8 ...... 32 B5
Bournville Av HTNM SK4 ...... 166 C1
Bournville Gv BNG/LEV M19 ...... 145 F2
Bourton Cl TOT/BURYW BL8 ...... 32 C4
Bourton Dr GTN M18 ...... 126 C5
Bowden Cl HALE/TIMP WA15 ...... 152 C2
  ROCH OL11 ...... 58 B1
Bowden La MPL/ROM SK6 ...... 170 C6
Bowden Rd SWIN M27 ...... 86 B6
Bowden St BOLS/LL BL3 ...... 46 B3
  BRAM/HZG SK7 ...... 184 C4
  DTN/ASHW M34 ...... 129 F6
Bowdon Av RUSH/FAL M14 ...... 143 D2
Bowdon Ri ALT WA14 ...... 174 B5
Bowdon Rd ALT WA14 ...... 174 A4
Bowdon St EDGY/DAV SK3 ...... 166 C5
Bowen St BOL BL1 ...... 26 C5
Bower Av BRAM/HZG SK7 ...... 184 B6
  HTNM SK4 ...... 166 A2
  WHIT OL12 ...... 24 B1
Bower Ct HYDE SK14 ...... 132 B4
Bowerfield Av BRAM/HZG SK7 ...... 198 B1
Bowerfield Crs BRAM/HZG SK7 ...... 198 C1
Bowerfold La HTNM SK4 ...... 166 A3
Bower Gdns STLY SK15 ...... 133 E1
Bower Gv STLY SK15 ...... 115 D5
Bower Rd HALE/TIMP WA15 ...... 174 C6
Bowers Av URM M41 ...... 118 C5
Bower St BRO M7 ...... 89 F6
  NEWH/MOS M40 ...... 108 A2
  OLD OL1 ...... 79 F4
  RDSH SK5 ...... 147 D1
Bower Ter DROY M43 ...... 111 D4
Bowery Av CHD/CHDH SK8 ...... 195 D3
Bowes Cl TOT/BURYW BL8 ...... 32 C2
Bowes St RUSH/FAL M14 ...... 124 A6
Bowfell Dr MPL/ROM SK6 ...... 200 C1
Bowfell Gv BKLY M9 ...... 90 C2
Bowfell Rd URM M41 ...... 137 F1
Bowgreave Av BOLE BL2 ...... 49 D2
Bow Green Rd ALT WA14 ...... 173 E6
Bowker Av DTN/ASHW M34 ...... 149 E3
Bowker Bank Av CHH M8 ...... 90 A3
Bowker Cl ROCH OL11 ...... 20 C4
Bowker St BRO M7 ...... 105 E1
  HYDE SK14 ...... 131 F6
  RAD M26 ...... 51 E6
  WALK M28 ...... 82 C2
Bowlacre Rd HYDE SK14 ...... 150 B5
Bowland Av GTN M18 ...... 128 B5
Bowland Cl AUL OL6 ...... 97 D6
  OFTN SK2 ...... 184 C2
  ROY/SHW OL2 ...... 60 C2
  TOT/BURYW BL8 ...... 31 F4
Bowland Gv MILN OL16 ...... 42 A3
Bowland Rd DTN/ASHW M34 ...... 128 C6
  MPL/ROM SK6 ...... 149 F6
  NTHM/RTH M23 ...... 177 D1
Bow La CMANW M2 ...... 2 D4
  HEY OL10 ...... 37 D5
Bowlee Cl WHTF M45 ...... 71 E2
Bowler St BNG/LEV M19 ...... 145 E3
  ROY/SHW OL2 ...... 61 F2
Bowlers Wk WHIT OL12 ...... 23 D3
Bowley Av WYTH/NTH M22 ...... 177 E5
Bowling Green Wy ROCH OL11 ...... 37 E5
  HYDE SK14 ...... 150 A1
Bowling Rd GTN M18 ...... 127 F6
Bowling St CHAD OL9 ...... 94 C3
Bowman Crs AUL OL6 ...... 113 E4
Bowmont Cl CHD/CHDH SK8 ...... 181 E3
Bowness Av CHD/CHDH SK8 ...... 181 F6
  HTNM SK4 ...... 146 C5
  IRL M44 ...... 154 B1
  WHIT OL12 ...... 22 A4
Bowness Dr SALE M33 ...... 139 D6
Bowness Rd AULW OL7 ...... 112 A3
  BOLS/LL BL3 ...... 46 B5
  BOLS/LL BL3 ...... 49 D5
  MDTN M24 ...... 74 B2
Bowness St OP/CLY M11 ...... 128 A2
  STRET M32 ...... 121 E6
Bowring St BRO M7 ...... 105 D2
Bowscale Rd BRUN/LGST M13 ...... 126 A5
Bowstone Hill Rd BOLE BL2 ...... 30 C2
Bow St BOL BL1 ...... 47 D2
  CMANW M2 ...... 2 C4
  DUK SK16 ...... 113 D5
  EDGY/DAV SK3 ...... 166 A5
  OLD OL1 ...... 79 D5
  ROCH OL11 ...... 39 E4
Boxgrove Rd SALE M33 ...... 138 C6
Boxhill Dr NTHM/RTH M23 ...... 161 E4
Box St LIT OL15 ...... 12 B6
  RAMS BL0 ...... 7 E5
Boxtree Av GTN M18 ...... 127 E6
Boyd St WGTN/LGST M12 ...... 126 B2
Boyd's Wk DUK SK16 ...... 131 D2
Boyer St OLDTF/WHR M16 ...... 122 C4
Boyle St BOL BL1 ...... 26 B6
  CHH M8 ...... 106 C1
Brabant Rd CHD/CHDH SK8 ...... 181 F5
Brabham Cl CCHDY M21 ...... 141 F3
Brabham Ms SWIN M27 ...... 85 D6
Brabyns Av MPL/ROM SK6 ...... 170 B2
Brabyns Brow MPL/ROM SK6 ...... 171 E6
Brabyns Rd HYDE SK14 ...... 150 C4
Bracadale Dr EDGY/DAV SK3 ...... 182 C2
Bracken Cl BOL BL1 ...... 27 E1
  DROY M43 ...... 111 D5
  HEY OL10 ...... 56 B1
  OLDE OL4 ...... 81 D5
  SALE M33 ...... 138 A6
Bracken Dr NTHM/RTH M23 ...... 177 F2
Brackenhurst Av MOSL OL5 ...... 99 F4
Bracken Lea Fold WHIT OL12 ...... 21 F3
Brackenlea Pl EDGY/DAV SK3 ...... 182 B2
Brackenside SK5 ...... 147 E3
Brackenwood Cl BOLD OL1 ...... 78 A1
Brackenwood Dr
  CHD/CHDH SK8 ...... 180 B3
Brackenwood Ms WILM/AE SK9 ...... 204 C3
Brackley Av HULME M15 ...... 123 E2
  IRL M44 ...... 134 B5
Brackley Dr MDTN M24 ...... 75 E6
Brackley Rd ECC M30 ...... 101 E3
  HTNM SK4 ...... 146 B6
Brackley St FWTH BL4 ...... 66 B3
  OLD OL1 ...... 79 E3
  WALK M28 ...... 83 D1
Bracondale Av BOL BL1 ...... 26 C5
Bradbourne Cl BOLS/LL BL3 ...... 47 D4
Bradburn Cl ECC M30 ...... 101 E6
Bradburn Rd IRL M44 ...... 134 C4
Bradburn St ECC M30 ...... 101 E6
Bradbury Av ALT WA14 ...... 173 E2
Bradbury St AULW OL7 ...... 112 B3
  HYDE SK14 ...... 150 C2
  RAD M26 ...... 69 E1
Bradda Mt BRAM/HZG SK7 ...... 183 D5
Braddan Av SALE M33 ...... 160 A2
Bradden Cl SALQ/ORD M5 ...... 104 B6
Braddocks Cl WHIT OL12 ...... 24 B1
Braddon Av URM M41 ...... 138 B1
Braddon Rd MPL/ROM SK6 ...... 149 E6
Braddon St OP/CLY M11 ...... 109 D6
Brade Cl OP/CLY M11 ...... 127 D1
Bradfield Av SLFD M6 ...... 103 D5
Bradfield Cl RDSH SK5 ...... 146 C1
Bradfield Rd STRET M32 ...... 139 F1
  URM M41 ...... 139 D1
Bradford Av BOLS/LL BL3 ...... 47 F6
Bradford Park Dr BOLE BL2 ...... 47 F3
Bradford Rd BOLS/LL BL3 ...... 65 E1
  ECC M30 ...... 101 F3
  NEWH/MOS M40 ...... 107 F4
Bradford St BOLE BL2 ...... 47 F2
  FWTH BL4 ...... 66 B4
  OLD OL1 ...... 78 C3
Bradgate Av CHD/CHDH SK8 ...... 180 B6
Bradgate Cl WYTH/NTH M22 ...... 162 C5
Bradgate Rd ALT WA14 ...... 173 E2
  SALE M33 ...... 159 F3
Bradgate St AULW OL7 ...... 112 B6
Bradgreen Rd ECC M30 ...... 101 D4
Bradley Av BRO M7 ...... 88 C4
Bradley Cl HALE/TIMP WA15 ...... 158 C6
Bradley Dr BURY BL9 ...... 71 F1
Bradley Fold STLY SK15 ...... 114 C5
Bradley Fold Rd BOLS/LL BL3 ...... 49 F3
Bradley Green Rd HYDE SK14 ...... 132 A3
Bradley La BOLS/LL BL3 ...... 49 F4
  MILN OL16 ...... 42 C3
  STRET M32 ...... 139 F4
Bradleys Count CMANE M1 ...... 3 G3
Bradley Smithy Cl WHIT OL12 ...... 22 C3
Bradley St CMANE M1 ...... 3 G2
  MILN OL16 ...... 42 C3
Bradney Cl BKLY M9 ...... 90 C1
Bradnor Rd WYTH/NTH M22 ...... 162 B6
Bradshaw Av DID/WITH M20 ...... 143 F4

NEWH/MOS M40 ...... 109 F2
WHTF M45 ...... 70 C1
Bradshaw Brow BOLE BL2 ...... 28 C4
Bradshaw Crs MPL/ROM SK6 ...... 171 E6
Bradshaw Fold Av
  NEWH/MOS M40 ...... 93 E2
Bradshawgate BOL BL1 ...... 47 D2
Bradshaw Hall Dr BOLE BL2 ...... 29 D1
Bradshaw Hall La CHD/CHDH SK8 ...... 180 C6
Bradshaw La STRET M32 ...... 140 B3
Bradshaw Mdw BOLE BL2 ...... 29 E1
Bradshaw Rd BOLE BL2 ...... 15 E6
  MPL/ROM SK6 ...... 171 D6
  TOT/BURYW BL8 ...... 31 D1
Bradshaw St ANC M4 ...... 3 E1
  BRO M7 ...... 105 F1
  FWTH BL4 ...... 66 B4
  HEY OL10 ...... 37 F5
  MILN OL16 ...... 23 E5
  OLD OL1 ...... 79 D4
  RAD M26 ...... 51 D6
Bradshaw St North BRO M7 ...... 89 E6
Bradstone Rd CHH M8 ...... 106 A2
Bradwall Av DID/WITH M20 ...... 143 D5
  STRET M32 ...... 120 B6
Bradwell Dr CHD/CHDH SK8 ...... 194 A3
Bradwell Rd BRAM/HZG SK7 ...... 198 C1
Bradwen Av CHH M8 ...... 90 B4
Bradwen Cl DTN/ASHW M34 ...... 149 E2
Brady St STKP SK1 ...... 167 E3
Braemar Dr SALE M33 ...... 158 A3
  URM M41 ...... 137 E2
Braemar Gv HEY OL10 ...... 36 B6
Braemar Rd BRAM/HZG SK7 ...... 185 D4
  RUSH/FAL M14 ...... 144 C3
Braemore Cl ROY/SHW OL2 ...... 60 C1
Braemore Dr BURY BL9 ...... 35 E5
  HYDE SK14 ...... 153 D2
Brae Side OLDS OL8 ...... 95 F3
Braeside Cl OFTN SK2 ...... 185 D2
Braeside Gv BOLS/LL BL3 ...... 44 C4
Braewood Cl BURY BL9 ...... 35 D4
Bragenham St GTN M18 ...... 127 D4
Brailsford Rd BOLE BL2 ...... 29 D4
  RUSH/FAL M14 ...... 144 C3
Braintree Rd WYTH/NTH M22 ...... 192 C1
Braithwaite Rd MDTN M24 ...... 56 B5
Brakehouse Cl MILN OL16 ...... 41 F1
Brakenhurst Dr BRO M7 ...... 106 A1
Brakesmere Gv LHULT M38 ...... 82 A1
Braley St CMANE M1 ...... 124 C2
Bramall Cl BURY BL9 ...... 71 F1
Bramall St HYDE SK14 ...... 131 E5
Bramble Av OLDE OL4 ...... 80 B2
  SALQ/ORD M5 ...... 123 D2
Bramble Cl LIT OL15 ...... 12 A6
Brambling Cl DTN/ASHW M34 ...... 111 D5
  OFTN SK2 ...... 185 E3
Bramcote Av BOLE BL2 ...... 47 F4
  NTHM/RTH M23 ...... 177 F1
Bramdean Av BOLE BL2 ...... 29 F2
Bramhall Av BOLE BL2 ...... 30 B3
Bramhall Cl DUK SK16 ...... 131 E5
  HALE/TIMP WA15 ...... 176 B1
  MILN OL16 ...... 41 F1
  SALE M33 ...... 160 C2
Bramhall La South
  BRAM/HZG SK7 ...... 182 C5
  OFTN SK2 ...... 183 D1
Bramhall Moor La BRAM/HZG SK7 .. 183 F6
Bramhall Park Rd BRAM/HZG SK7 .. 182 A6
Bramhall St BOLS/LL BL3 ...... 47 F6
  GTN M18 ...... 127 F4
Bramham Rd MPL/ROM SK6 ...... 187 D3
Bramley Av BNG/LEV M19 ...... 145 E3
  STRET M32 ...... 139 F1
Bramley Cl BRAM/HZG SK7 ...... 196 C5
  SWIN M27 ...... 101 D1
  WILM/AE SK9 ...... 208 B1
Bramley Crs HTNM SK4 ...... 165 F5
Bramley Dr BRAM/HZG SK7 ...... 196 C5
  TOT/BURYW BL8 ...... 19 D6
Bramley Meade BRO M7 ...... 89 F6
Bramley Rd BRAM/HZG SK7 ...... 196 C5
  EDGW/EG BL7 ...... 28 A1
  ROCH OL11 ...... 20 C5
Brammay Dr TOT/BURYW BL8 ...... 31 F2
Brampton Rd BOLS/LL BL3 ...... 45 E6
  BRAM/HZG SK7 ...... 183 D5
Bramway BRAM/HZG SK7 ...... 196 A2
  MPL/ROM SK6 ...... 201 D2
Bramwell Dr BRUN/LGST M13 ...... 125 D3
Bramwell St STKP SK1 ...... 167 F5
Bramworth Av RAMS BL0 ...... 6 C5
Brancaster Rd CMANE M1 ...... 124 B2
Branch Cl TOT/BURYW BL8 ...... 33 E4
Branch Rd LIT OL15 ...... 24 C4
Brandish Cl BRUN/LGST M13 ...... 125 E5
Brandle Av TOT/BURYW BL8 ...... 33 D3
Brandlehow Dr MDTN M24 ...... 74 A1
Brandlesholme Rd
  TOT/BURYW BL8 ...... 33 E3
Brandon Av CHD/CHDH SK8 ...... 179 F6

DTN/ASHW M34 .... 128 A6
ECC M30 .... 102 B3
WYTH/NTH M22 .... 162 A5 ◰
Brandon Cl TOT/BURYW BL8 ...... 33 E2
 WILM/AE SK9 .... 204 B3 ◱
Brandon Crs ROY/SHW OL2 ...... 61 E1
Brandon Rd SLFD M6 .... 102 C2
Brandon St BOLS/LL BL3 .... 46 B5 ◰
Brandram Rd PWCH M25 .... 89 D1 ◰
Brandsby Gdns SALQ/ORD M5 .. 122 E2 ◰
Brandwood OLD OL1 .... 76 C2 ◰
Brandwood Av CCHDY M21 .... 162 B1 ◰
Brandwood Cl WALK M28 .... 82 B5 ◰
Brandwood St BOLS/LL BL3 .. 46 A5 ◰
Branfield Av CHD/CHDH SK8 .... 180 B6
Branksome Av PWCH M25 .... 88 B1
Branksome Dr BKLY M9 .... 73 F6 ◱
 CHD/CHDH SK8 .... 180 B6
 SLFD M6 .... 102 B2
Branksome Rd HTNM SK4 ...... 165 F4
Bransby Av BKLY M9 .... 91 F1
Branscombe Dr SALE M33 ...... 138 A6
Bransdale Av ROY/SHW OL2 .... 60 A5
Bransdale Cl BOLS/LL BL3 .... 65 D5
Bransford Rd OP/CLY M11 ...... 127 E1
 URM M41 .... 119 D6 ◱
Branson St NEWH/MOS M40 .... 107 E5
Branson Wk HALE/TIMP WA15 .. 176 A1
Branston Rd NEWH/MOS M40 ... 93 E3
Brantfell Gv BOLE BL2 .... 49 D1
Brantingham Rd CCHDY M21 .. 141 F2
 OLDTF/WHR M16 .... 142 C2
Brantwood Cl ROY/SHW OL2 .. 60 A5 ◱
Brantwood Dr BOLE BL2 .... 49 D1
Brantwood Rd BRO M7 .... 89 E5
 CHD/CHDH SK8 .... 181 D6 ◱
 HTNM SK4 .... 166 A1
Brantwood Ter BKLY M9 .... 92 A6 ◱
Brassey St AUL OL6 .... 112 C3
 MDTN M24 .... 75 E2
Brassington Av CCHDY M21 .... 141 F4
 SALQ/ORD M5 .... 122 C1 ◱
Brassington Rd HTNM SK4 .... 164 C1
Brathay Cl BOLE BL2 .... 30 A5 ◰
Brattray Dr MDTN M24 .... 56 C6
Braunston Cl ECC M30 .... 119 F1 ◰
Bray Av ECC M30 .... 100 C4
Braybrook Dr BOL BL1 .... 44 B2
Bray Cl CHD/CHDH SK8 .... 180 C5
Brayford Wy WYTH/NTH M22 .. 178 B6 ◰
Brayshaw Cl HEY OL10 .... 36 C6
Brayside Rd DID/WITH M20 .... 164 B1
Braystan Gdns CHD/CHDH SK8 .. 179 F1 ◰
Brayton Av DID/WITH M20 ...... 164 A3
 SALE M33 .... 138 B6
Brazennose St CSLFD M3 .... 2 C4
Brazil St CMANE M1 .... 3 F6
Brazley Av BOLS/LL BL3 .... 47 F6 ◱
Bread St GTN M18 .... 127 F3
Breckland Cl STLY SK15 .... 115 E5
Breckland Dr BOL BL1 .... 44 B1
Breckles Pl BOLS/LL BL3 .... 46 B4 ◱3
Breck Rd ECC M30 .... 100 C5
Brecon Av BNG/LEV M19 .... 145 D4 ◱
 CHD/CHDH SK8 .... 180 C6
 DTN/ASHW M34 .... 149 D2
 URM M41 .... 117 E6
Brecon Cl POY/DIS SK12 .... 199 D5 ◱
 ROY/SHW OL2 .... 60 A3
Brecon Crs AUL OL6 .... 112 C1
Brecon Dr BURY BL9 .... 53 D3
Brecon Wk OLDS OL8 .... 94 C3 ◰
Bredbury Dr FWTH BL4 .... 66 C3
Bredbury Gn MPL/ROM SK6 ... 169 E4
Bredbury Park Wy MPL/ROM SK6 .. 148 C6
Bredbury Rd RUSH/FAL M14 .. 143 F1
Bredbury St CHAD OL9 .... 77 F6
 HYDE SK14 .... 131 E4 ◰
Breeze Hill Rd OLDE OL4 .... 80 B6
Breeze Mt PWCH M25 .... 88 C3
Breightmet Dr BOLE BL2 .... 48 C2
Breightmet Fold La BOLE BL2 .. 30 A5 ◱
Breightmet St BOL BL1 .... 47 D3
Brellafield Dr ROY/SHW OL2 .... 42 A6
Brenbar Crs WHIT OL12 .... 9 E2 ◰
Brenchley Dr NTHM/RTH M23 .. 161 E3 ◱
Brencon Av SALE M33 .... 160 A4
Brendall Cl OFTN SK2 .... 185 E2
Brendon Av NEWH/MOS M40 .. 92 B6
 RDSH SK5 .... 147 D5 ◱
Brendon Dr DTN/ASHW M34 .. 111 E6
Brendon Hills ROY/SHW OL2 .. 60 A6
Brennan Cl HULME M15 .... 124 B4 ◱
Brennan Ct OLDS OL8 .... 95 D3 ◰
Brennock Cl OP/CLY M11 .... 126 A1
Brentbridge Rd RUSH/FAL M14 .. 143 F3
Brent Cl BOLS/LL BL3 .... 49 F4
 POY/DIS SK12 .... 197 F5
Brentford Av CHH M8 .... 106 A1
Brentford Av BOL BL1 .... 26 C5
Brentford Rd RDSH SK5 .... 147 D5
Brentford St BKLY M9 .... 91 F6
Brent Moor Rd BRAM/HZG SK7 .. 183 E4
Brentnall St STKP SK1 .... 167 D6 ◰
Brentnor Rd NEWH/MOS M40 .. 93 D3

Brenton Av SALE M33 .... 159 E1 ◰
Brent Rd HTNM SK4 .... 166 A4
 NTHM/RTH M23 .... 161 E3
Brentwood SALE M33 .... 159 E1
 SLFD M6 .... 103 F4
Brentwood Av ALT WA14 .... 158 C6
 IRL M44 .... 134 B5
 URM M41 .... 138 B3 ◰
 WALK M28 .... 100 C1 ◰
Brentwood Cl LIT OL15 .... 25 D2 ◱
 OLDTF/WHR M16 .... 124 A6
 RDSH SK5 .... 148 B6 ◰
 STLY SK15 .... 115 D5
Brentwood Ct PWCH M25 .... 88 A2
Brentwood Crs ALT WA14 ...... 174 C1 ◱
Brentwood Dr CHD/CHDH SK8 .. 179 F2
 ECC M30 .... 101 E3 ◰
 FWTH BL4 .... 66 A1 ◰
Brentwood Rd SWIN M27 .... 101 E1
Brereton Cl ALT WA14 .... 174 A6
Brereton Dr WALK M28 .... 84 A6
Brereton Gv IRL M44 .... 134 C5
Brereton Rd ECC M30 .... 100 A6
 WILM/AE SK9 .... 194 C6
Breslyn St CSLFD M3 .... 106 A4 ◰
Brethren's Ct DROY M43 .... 128 B3 ◱
Bretland Gdns HYDE SK14 ..... 152 C2 ◰
Brettargh St SLFD M6 .... 104 B3 ◰
Brett St WYTH/NTH M22 .... 162 C4 ◰
 WYTH/NTH M22 .... 162 C4 ◰
Brewer's Gn BRAM/HZG SK7 .. 184 B3 ◰
Brewer St CMANE M1 .... 3 G3
Brewerton Rd OLDE OL4 .... 80 A6
Brewery St ALT WA14 .... 174 B3
 STKP SK1 .... 167 D3 ◱
Brewster St BKLY M9 .... 91 E5 ◰
 MDTN M24 .... 75 E1
Brian Av DROY M43 .... 111 D4 ◰
Brian Rd FWTH BL4 .... 65 E1
Brian St ROCH OL11 .... 38 C5 ◰
Briar Av BRAM/HZG SK7 .... 185 D5 ◱
 OLDE OL4 .... 80 B2
Briar Cl SALE M33 .... 158 A1 ◱
 URM M41 .... 118 B6 ◰
 WHIT OL12 .... 21 E4 ◱
Briar Crs WYTH/NTH M22 ...... 178 C2 ◱
Briardene DTN/ASHW M34 ..... 130 B5 ◰
Briardene Gdns
 WYTH/NTH M22 .... 178 C3 ◱
Briarfield Rd BNG/LEV M19 .... 144 C5 ◱
 CHD/CHDH SK8 .... 181 F4
 DID/WITH M20 .... 144 B5 ◱
 FWTH BL4 .... 65 E2 ◱
 HALE/TIMP WA15 .... 176 A1
 HTNM SK4 .... 146 C5
 WALK M28 .... 84 A6
Briar Gv CHAD OL9 .... 77 F2
 MPL/ROM SK6 .... 149 E6
Briarlands Av SALE M33 .... 159 D3
Briarlands Cl BRAM/HZG SK7 .. 196 B5 ◱
Briarlea Gdns BNG/LEV M19 .. 144 C6 ◱
Briarley Gdns MPL/ROM SK6 .. 150 A5 ◱
Briarmere Wk CHAD OL9 .... 78 A4 ◰
Briars Mt HTNM SK4 .... 165 E3 ◱
Briars Pk CHD/CHDH SK8 ...... 182 A6 ◰
Briarstead Cl BRAM/HZG SK7 .. 196 B2 ◱
Briar St BOLE BL2 .... 48 B2 ◰
 ROCH OL11 .... 39 E1 ◰
Briarwood WILM/AE SK9 .... 204 A4
Briarwood Av DROY M43 .... 109 F4
 NTHM/RTH M23 .... 160 B5
Briarwood Crs MPL/ROM SK6 .. 187 D3 ◱
Brice St DUK SK16 .... 130 C1
Brickbridge Rd MPL/ROM SK6 .. 187 E2 ◱
Brickfield St MILN OL16 .... 23 F3 ◰
Brickhill La HALE/TIMP WA15 .. 189 F5 ◱
Brickkiln La ALT WA14 .... 172 A4
Brickkiln Rw ALT WA14 .... 174 A6
Brickley St ANC M4 .... 106 B4 ◰
Brick St ANC M4 .... 3 F2 ◰
 BURY BL9 .... 34 B4 ◰
Bridcam St CHH M8 .... 106 B2
Briddon St CSLFD M3 .... 106 A4 ◰
Brideoake St OLDE OL4 .... 80 C3
Brideoak St CHH M8 .... 106 B1 ◰
Bridestowe Av HYDE SK14 .... 133 D6
Bride St BOL BL1 .... 27 F5 ◰◰
Bridge Av MPL/ROM SK6 .... 149 E6
Bridge Bank Rd LIT OL15 .... 25 D2
Bridge Cl PART M31 .... 155 E2
 RAD M26 .... 69 F1 ◱
Bridge Dr CHD/CHDH SK8 ..... 180 B3 ◰
 WILM/AE SK9 .... 194 B6
Bridgefield Av WILM/AE SK9 .. 204 A2
Bridgefield Crs OLDE OL4 .... 81 D5 ◱
Bridgefield Dr BURY BL9 .... 35 D5
Bridgefield St RAD M26 .... 51 F6
 ROCH OL11 .... 21 D1 ◱
 STKP SK1 .... 166 C3
Bridgefold Rd ROCH OL11 .... 22 A6
Bridge Gv HALE/TIMP WA15 .. 159 D6
Bridge Hall Dr BURY BL9 .... 35 D5 ◰
Bridge Hall Fold BURY BL9 .. 35 D5 ◰
Bridge Hall La BURY BL9 .... 35 D5
Bridge La BRAM/HZG SK7 ..... 183 D6

Bridgelea Ms DID/WITH M20 .. 143 F5 ◰
Bridgelea Rd DID/WITH M20 .. 143 F5 ◰
Bridgeman Pl BOLE BL2 .... 47 E3
Bridgeman St BOLS/LL BL3 .... 46 C5
 FWTH BL4 .... 66 B2 ◰
Bridgemere Cl RAD M26 .... 51 D4
Bridgend Cl CHD/CHDH SK8 .. 181 F3
 WGTN/LGST M12 .... 126 B3
Bridgenorth Av URM M41 ...... 139 D1
Bridgenorth Dr LIT OL15 .... 25 D2 ◰
Bridge Rd BURY BL9 .... 33 E6
 HALE/TIMP WA15 .... 160 A6
Bridges Av BURY BL9 .... 53 D3
Bridges Ct BOL BL1 .... 47 D3 ◰
Bridge St BOL BL1 .... 47 D2
 BURY BL9 .... 34 B4
 CSLFD M3 .... 2 B3
 DROY M43 .... 127 F1 ◰
 DTN/ASHW M34 .... 130 A2
 DUK SK16 .... 130 B3
 FWTH BL4 .... 66 C2
 HEY OL10 .... 36 C5
 MDTN M24 .... 75 E3 ◰
 MILN OL16 .... 42 A1
 OLD OL1 .... 79 E5
 OLDE OL4 .... 81 D5
 RAD M26 .... 67 F3
 RAMS BL0 .... 7 D5
 ROCH OL11 .... 39 D6 ◰
 ROY/SHW OL2 .... 62 A1 ◰
 STKP SK1 .... 167 D3
 STLY SK15 .... 114 A6
 SWIN M27 .... 86 B5
 WHIT OL12 .... 9 D2 ◰
 WHIT OL12 .... 24 A2
Bridgewater Pl ANC M4 .... 3 E3
Bridgewater Rd ALT WA14 .... 158 B6
 SWIN M27 .... 86 C6 ◰
 WALK M28 .... 82 B6
Bridgewater St BOL BL1 .... 46 B5 ◰◰
 CSLFD M3 .... 2 A6 ◰
 ECC M30 .... 100 C5
 FWTH BL4 .... 66 C3 ◰
 LHULT M38 .... 82 C1
 OLD OL1 .... 79 E3 ◰
 SALE M33 .... 139 F6 ◰
 STRET M32 .... 140 C1 ◰
Bridgewater Wy HULME M15 .. 123 D3 ◱
 OLDTF/WHR M16 .... 122 C4
Bridgfield Cl MPL/ROM SK6 ... 200 C2 ◱
Bridgnorth Rd BKLY M9 .... 90 B2
Bridle Cl DROY M43 .... 111 D4
 URM M41 .... 136 C1
Bridle Fold RAD M26 .... 51 E5 ◰
Bridle Rd BRAM/HZG SK7 ...... 197 D6
 PWCH M25 .... 72 B4
Bridle Wy BRAM/HZG SK7 ..... 207 D1
Bridlington Av SLFD M6 .... 103 D4 ◰
Bridlington Cl NEWH/MOS M40 .. 109 D1 ◰
Bridport Av NEWH/MOS M40 .. 93 E5
Bridson La BOLE BL2 .... 29 E6 ◰
Bridson St OLDE OL4 .... 80 A4 ◰
 SALQ/ORD M5 .... 103 F6
Brief St BOLE BL2 .... 29 D6
Brien Av ALT WA14 .... 174 B1
Briercliffe Cl GTN M18 .... 127 D3 ◰
Briercliffe Rd BOLS/LL BL3 ..... 46 A4
Brierfield Dr BURY BL9 .... 19 F5
Brierley Av FAIL M35 .... 94 A6
 WHTF M45 .... 70 C1
Brierley Cl AUL OL6 .... 114 B1 ◰
 DTN/ASHW M34 .... 148 C1
Brierley Dr MDTN M24 .... 75 E4
Brierley Rd West SWIN M27 .... 85 F4
Brierley St BURY BL9 .... 52 C1 ◰
 CHAD OL9 .... 78 A3
 DUK SK16 .... 113 E6 ◰
 HEY OL10 .... 37 E5
 OLDS OL8 .... 96 A2
Brierton Dr WYTH/NTH M22 .. 177 F6 ◰
Brierwood Cl OLD OL1 .... 78 C2 ◰
Briery Av BOLE BL2 .... 29 E1
Brigade St BOL BL1 .... 46 A2 ◰◰
Brigadier Cl DID/WITH M20 .... 143 F5
Brigantine Cl SALQ/ORD M5 .. 122 B1 ◰
Briggs Cl SALE M33 .... 158 A4 ◰
Briggs Rd STRET M32 .... 122 A5 ◱
Briggs St CSLFD M3 .... 105 E4 ◰
Brigham St OP/CLY M11 .... 127 D1
Brightman St BOLE BL1 .... 127 E3
Brighton Av BNG/LEV M19 .... 145 D4 ◰
 BOL BL1 .... 26 B6 ◰
 BRO M7 .... 105 F1 ◰
 RDSH SK5 .... 147 D1
 URM M41 .... 117 D6 ◰
Brighton Gv HYDE SK14 .... 150 C2 ◱
 RUSH/FAL M14 .... 144 B1
 SALE M33 .... 139 E6 ◰
 URM M41 .... 117 D6
Brighton Pl BRUN/LGST M13 .. 124 C4 ◱
Brighton Range GTN M18 ...... 128 A5 ◱
Brighton Rd HTNM SK4 .... 166 A4
 OLDE OL4 .... 81 E2
Brighton St ANC M4 .... 106 B4 ◰
 BURY BL9 .... 34 C4 ◰

Bright Rd *ECC* M30 .... 101 F5
Bright St *AUL* OL6 .... 113 E5 🔟
 BURY BL9 .... 34 B4
 CHAD OL9 .... 94 B2
 DROY M43 .... 110 C6 🔟
 MILN OL16 .... 40 B2 🔟
 OLDS OL8 .... 78 B6 🔟
 RAD M26 .... 52 A5
Brightwater Cl *WHTF* M45 .... 71 E3 🔟
Brigstock Av *GTN* M18 .... 127 D4 🔟
Briksdal Wy *HOR/BR* BL6 .... 44 A2
Brimelow St *MPL/ROM* SK6 .... 168 A2 🔟
Brimrod La *ROCH* OL11 .... 39 E2
Brimscombe Av
 WYTH/NTH M22 .... 178 A5 🔟
Brindale Rd *RDSH* SK5 .... 168 A1
Brindle Cl *SLFD* M6 .... 104 A3
Brindle Heath Rd *SLFD* M6 .... 104 A3
Brindley Av *BKLY* M9 .... 73 F6
 MPL/ROM SK6 .... 187 D2
 SALE M33 .... 140 A5 🔟
Brinell Dr *IRL* M44 .... 135 D6
Brinkburn Rd *BRAM/HZG* SK7 .... 185 E4
Brinklow Cl *OP/CLY* M11 .... 127 F2
Brinkshaw Av *WYTH/NTH* M22 .... 178 C5
Brinks La *BOLE* BL2 .... 49 E2
Brinksway *EDGY/DAV* SK3 .... 166 B4
 HOR/BR BL6 .... 44 A2
Brinnington Crs *RDSH* SK5 .... 167 F1
Brinnington Rd *RDSH* SK5 .... 168 A1
 STKP SK1 .... 167 E2
Brinsop Sq *GTN* M18 .... 126 C3
Brinsworth Dr *SLFD* M8 .... 106 B1 🔟
Briony Av *HALE/TIMP* WA15 .... 176 A5
Briony Cl *ROY/SHW* OL2 .... 78 C1
Brisbane Cl *BRAM/HZG* SK7 .... 197 D4
Brisbane St *HULME* M15 .... 124 C4 🔟
Briscoe La *NEWH/MOS* M40 .... 108 C3
Briscoe St *OLD* OL1 .... 79 D3 🔟
Bristol Av *AUL* OL6 .... 96 C6
 BNG/LEV M19 .... 145 F3
 BOLE BL2 .... 29 D6
Bristol St *BRO* M7 .... 89 F6
Bristowe St *OP/CLY* M11 .... 109 E4
Britain St *BURY* BL9 .... 52 C3
Britannia Av *ROY/SHW* OL2 .... 62 A3
Britannia Rd *SALE* M33 .... 139 F6
Britannia St *AULW* OL7 .... 130 A1
 HEY OL10 .... 36 C5 🔟
 OLD OL1 .... 79 E4
 SLFD M6 .... 104 B1
Britannia Wy *BOL* BL1 .... 28 B5
Britnall Av *WGTN/LGST* M12 .... 125 F4
Briton St *MILN* OL16 .... 23 E5 🔟
 ROY/SHW OL2 .... 78 C1
Brixham Av *CHD/CHDH* SK8 .... 195 D2
Brixham Dr *SALE* M33 .... 138 B5
Brixham Rd *OLDTF/WHR* M16 .... 122 C5
Brixham Wk *BRAM/HZG* SK7 .... 196 C2 🔟
Brixton Av *DID/WITH* M20 .... 143 E5 🔟
Brierley Rd East *SWIN* M27 .... 85 F4 🔟
Broach St *BOLS/LL* BL3 .... 46 C5 🔟🔟
Broadacre *STLY* SK15 .... 133 F3
Broad Acre *WHIT* OL12 .... 20 C3
Broadbent Av *AUL* OL6 .... 113 D1
 DUK SK16 .... 131 E1
Broadbent Cl *ROY/SHW* OL2 .... 61 D4
 STLY SK15 .... 115 F1
Broadbent Dr *BURY* BL9 .... 35 F3
Broadbent Gv *HYDE* SK14 .... 152 C1 🔟
Broadbent Rd *OLD* OL1 .... 80 A1
Broadbent St *HYDE* SK14 .... 131 E5
 SWIN M27 .... 85 E6
Broadbottom Rd *HYDE* SK14 .... 153 D1
Broadcarr La *MOSL* OL5 .... 98 B4
Broadfield Dr *DTN/ASHW* M34 .... 149 E1
Broadfield Dr *LIT* OL15 .... 25 D2
Broadfield Gv *RDSH* SK5 .... 127 F6
Broadfield Rd *GTN* M18 .... 127 F6
 RUSH/FAL M14 .... 124 B6
Broadfield Stile *MILN* OL16 .... 39 F1 🔟
Broadfield St *HEY* OL10 .... 36 C2 🔟
 MILN OL16 .... 40 A1 🔟
Broadford Rd *BOLS/LL* BL3 .... 45 D4
Broadgate *MDTN* M24 .... 76 B5
Broadgreen Gdns *FWTH* BL4 .... 66 B1 🔟
Broadhalgh Av *ROCH* OL11 .... 21 E6
Broadhalgh Rd *ROCH* OL11 .... 38 B1
Broad Hey *MPL/ROM* SK6 .... 170 B2
Broad Hill Cl *BRAM/HZG* SK7 .... 183 E5
Broadhill Rd *BNG/LEV* M19 .... 144 C5
 STLY SK15 .... 114 B2
Broadhurst *DTN/ASHW* M34 .... 130 B4
Broadhurst Av *SWIN* M27 .... 86 A2
Broadhurst Ct *BOLS/LL* BL3 .... 46 B5 🔟🔟
Broadhurst Gv *AUL* OL6 .... 113 D1 🔟
Broadhurst St *BOLS/LL* BL3 .... 46 B5 🔟🔟
 EDGY/DAV SK3 .... 166 C6
Broad Ing *WHIT* OL12 .... 21 F4 🔟
Broadlands Rd *SWIN* M27 .... 101 D1

Broad La *HALE/TIMP* WA15 .... 189 F1
 MILN OL16 .... 40 C4
Broad Lea *URM* M41 .... 119 D6 🔟
Broadlea Av *WHIT* OL12 .... 22 A3
Broadlea Rd *BNG/LEV* M19 .... 144 C6 🔟
Broadley Av *WYTH/NTH* M22 .... 178 B3 🔟
Broadmeadow *EDGW/EG* BL7 .... 14 C5
Broadmeadow Av
 OLDTF/WHR M16 .... 143 D2 🔟
Broadmoss Dr *BKLY* M9 .... 92 B2
Broadmoss Rd *BKLY* M9 .... 92 B2 🔟
Broadoak Av *WALK* M28 .... 82 A6 🔟
 WYTH/NTH M22 .... 178 A2 🔟
Broadoak Crs *AUL* OL6 .... 112 C2
Broad Oak Crs *OLDS* OL8 .... 96 B3
Broadoak Dr *WYTH/NTH* M22 .... 178 B2 🔟
Broad Oak La *BURY* BL9 .... 35 D4
 DID/WITH M20 .... 163 F5
 WALK M28 .... 100 C1
Broadoak Rd *AUL* OL6 .... 112 C2
 BRAM/HZG SK7 .... 183 D5
Broad Oak Rd *FWTH* BL4 .... 65 E1
Broadoak Rd *ROCH* OL11 .... 37 F1
 WYTH/NTH M22 .... 178 A3
Broadoaks *BURY* BL9 .... 35 E4
Broadoaks *SALE* M33 .... 159 E1
 URM M41 .... 137 F2
Broad Oak Ter *BURY* BL9 .... 35 F4
Broad Rd *SALE* M33 .... 140 A6
Broad Shaw La *MILN* OL16 .... 41 F5
Broadstone Av *OLDE* OL4 .... 63 D5
Broadstone Cl *PWCH* M25 .... 88 B2
 WHIT OL12 .... 21 E4 🔟
Broadstone Hall Rd North
 HTNM SK4 .... 146 B5
Broadstone Hall Rd South
 HTNM SK4 .... 146 A5
Broadstone Rd *BOLE* BL2 .... 29 E2
 HTNM SK4 .... 146 B4
Broad St *BURY* BL9 .... 33 F5
 MDTN M24 .... 74 A4
 SLFD M6 .... 103 F2
 SWIN M27 .... 103 E1
Broad Wk *WILM/AE* SK9 .... 203 D3 🔟
Broadway *BRAM/HZG* SK7 .... 183 D5
 CHAD OL9 .... 77 D6
 CHD/CHDH SK8 .... 180 A3
 DROY M43 .... 128 B1
 FAIL M35 .... 93 E5
 FWTH BL4 .... 65 E1
 HALE/TIMP WA15 .... 175 E6
 HYDE SK14 .... 130 C4
 IRL M44 .... 135 E2
 OFTN SK2 .... 168 A6
 OLD OL1 .... 78 B1
 PART M31 .... 155 E1
 ROY/SHW OL2 .... 60 C6
 SALE M33 .... 139 E6
 SALQ/ORD M5 .... 121 E1
 URM M41 .... 118 B5
 WALK M28 .... 83 E4
 WILM/AE SK9 .... 203 F5
Broadway *CHD/CHDH* SK8 .... 180 B2
Broadway Cl *URM* M41 .... 119 D4 🔟
Broadway North *DROY* M43 .... 128 B1
Broadway St *OLDS* OL8 .... 96 A1
The Broadway *MPL/ROM* SK6 .... 168 C1
Broadwell Dr *BKLY* M9 .... 91 F6
Broadwood *HOR/BR* BL6 .... 44 A2
Broadwood Cl *MPL/ROM* SK6 .... 201 D2
Brocade Cl *CSLFD* M3 .... 105 E4 🔟
Broche Cl *ROCH* OL11 .... 38 C4 🔟
Brock Av *BOLE* BL2 .... 49 D2
Brock Cl *OP/CLY* M11 .... 127 E2
Brock Dr *CHD/CHDH* SK8 .... 195 E1
Brockenhurst Dr *BOLE* BL2 .... 30 A4 🔟
Brockford Dr *BKLY* M9 .... 74 C6
Brocklebank Rd *MILN* OL16 .... 24 B6 🔟
 RUSH/FAL M14 .... 144 A3
Brocklehurst Av *BURY* BL9 .... 34 A6 🔟
Brocklehurst St *BKLY* M9 .... 92 B1 🔟
Brockley Av *RUSH/FAL* M14 .... 143 F1 🔟
Brock St *CMANE* M1 .... 3 H3 🔟
Brockway *MILN* OL16 .... 41 D4 🔟
Brodick Dr *BOLE* BL2 .... 49 D3
Brodick St *NEWH/MOS* M40 .... 92 A5
Brodie Cl *ECC* M30 .... 100 C5 🔟
Brogan St *GTN* M18 .... 127 E4 🔟
Brogden Dr *CHD/CHDH* SK8 .... 179 F1
Brogden Gv *SALE* M33 .... 159 E2 🔟
Bromborough Av
 DID/WITH M20 .... 143 E5 🔟
Bromfield Av *BKLY* M9 .... 91 E4
Broming St *OP/CLY* M11 .... 108 A5
Bromleigh Av *CHD/CHDH* SK8 .... 179 F1
Bromley Av *ROY/SHW* OL2 .... 59 F3
 URM M41 .... 136 C2
Bromley Crs *AUL* OL6 .... 112 C1
Bromley Cross Rd *EDGW/EG* BL7 .... 14 C6
Bromley Rd *SALE* M33 .... 160 A3
Bromley St *ANC* M4 .... 90 C4
 CHAD OL9 .... 8 B3
 DTN/ASHW M34 .... 130 A6 🔟

Bromlow St *OP/CLY* M11 .... 109 D6
Brompton Av *FAIL* M35 .... 94 C5 🔟
Brompton Rd *HTNM* SK4 .... 165 E3 🔟
 RUSH/FAL M14 .... 143 F1
 STRET M32 .... 120 A6
Brompton St *OLDE* OL4 .... 79 E6
Bromsgrove Av *ECC* M30 .... 100 C5 🔟
Bromshill Dr *BRO* M7 .... 105 F1
Bromwich St *BOLE* BL2 .... 47 F3
Brondgate Meadow *SWIN* M27 .. 102 A1 🔟
Bronington Cl *WYTH/NTH* M22 .... 162 C6
Bronte Av *BURY* BL9 .... 53 D3
Bronte Cl *BOL* BL1 .... 27 E6 🔟
 OLD OL1 .... 62 B5
 WHIT OL12 .... 21 E3
Bronte St *HULME* M15 .... 124 B4
Bronville Cl *OLD* OL1 .... 78 A2
Brookash Rd *WYTH/NTH* M22 .... 193 E1
Brook Av *BNG/LEV* M19 .... 145 F1
 DROY M43 .... 109 F6 🔟
 HALE/TIMP WA15 .... 174 C1
 HTNM SK4 .... 146 B6
 ROY/SHW OL2 .... 61 F1
 SWIN M27 .... 86 A6 🔟
 WILM/AE SK9 .... 194 B6
Brookbank Cl *MDTN* M24 .... 75 F4 🔟
Brook Bottom Rd *RAD* M26 .... 51 D3
Brookburn Rd *CCHDY* M21 .... 141 E4
Brook Cl *HALE/TIMP* WA15 .... 174 C1
 WHTF M45 .... 71 F3
Brookcot Rd *NTHM/RTH* M23 .... 161 D6
Brookcroft Av *WYTH/NTH* M22 .... 178 B2 🔟
Brookcroft Rd *WYTH/NTH* M22 .... 178 B2
Brookdale *WHIT* OL12 .... 22 C2
Brookdale Av *DTN/ASHW* M34 .... 129 F2 🔟
 MPL/ROM SK6 .... 187 E3
 NEWH/MOS M40 .... 109 E3
Brookdale Cl *BOL* BL1 .... 28 A5 🔟
 MPL/ROM SK6 .... 169 D2 🔟
Brookdale Ri *BRAM/HZG* SK7 .... 183 D5
Brookdale Rd *BRAM/HZG* SK7 .... 183 D6
 CHD/CHDH SK8 .... 179 D2
Brookdale St *FAIL* M35 .... 93 E6
Brookdean Cl *BOL* BL1 .... 27 D4
Brookdene Rd *BNG/LEV* M19 .... 144 C5
 BURY BL9 .... 71 E2
Brook Dr *MPL/ROM* SK6 .... 187 D3
 WHTF M45 .... 71 F3
Brooke Dr *WILM/AE* SK9 .... 194 B5 🔟
Brookes St *MDTN* M24 .... 75 F1 🔟
Brooke Wy *WILM/AE* SK9 .... 194 B5 🔟
Brook Farm Cl *PART* M31 .... 154 C3 🔟
Brookfield *PWCH* M25 .... 88 C1
 ROY/SHW OL2 .... 42 B6
Brookfield Av *BOLE* BL2 .... 31 D6 🔟
 CCHDY M21 .... 142 A4
 HALE/TIMP WA15 .... 159 D6
 MPL/ROM SK6 .... 169 E1
 POY/DIS SK12 .... 198 A6
 ROY/SHW OL2 .... 60 B6
 SLFD M6 .... 103 D4
 STKP SK1 .... 167 E6
 URM M41 .... 137 E1 🔟
Brookfield Cl *OFTN* SK2 .... 167 E6
Brookfield Crs *CHD/CHDH* SK8 .... 180 B2
Brookfield Dr *HALE/TIMP* WA15 .... 159 E6
 LIT OL15 .... 11 F5
 SWIN M27 .... 85 F4
Brookfield Gdns
 WYTH/NTH M22 .... 178 A1 🔟
Brookfield Gv *AUL* OL6 .... 113 E5
Brookfield Rd *BURY* BL9 .... 19 F5
 CHD/CHDH SK8 .... 180 C2
 CHH M8 .... 90 B4 🔟
 ECC M30 .... 100 C3 🔟
Brookfield St *OLDS* OL8 .... 79 D6
Brookfold La *BOLE* BL2 .... 30 A3
Brook Fold La *HYDE* SK14 .... 151 E2
Brookfold Rd *HTNM* SK4 .... 146 B5
Brook Gdns *BOLE* BL2 .... 29 F3
 HEY OL10 .... 37 D5 🔟
Brook Green La *GTN* M18 .... 128 A6 🔟
Brook Gv *IRL* M44 .... 135 E1
Brookhead Av *DID/WITH* M20 .... 143 D4 🔟
Brookhead Dr *CHD/CHDH* SK8 .... 181 E2
Brookhey Av *BOLS/LL* BL3 .... 47 D6
Brook Hey Cl *WHIT* OL12 .... 24 B1 🔟
Brookheys Rd *PART* M31 .... 156 C1
Brookhill St *NEWH/MOS* M40 .... 107 F4 🔟
Brookhouse Av *ECC* M30 .... 100 B6
 FWTH BL4 .... 66 A5
Brook House Cl *BOLE* BL2 .... 29 F4 🔟
 TOT/BURYW BL8 .... 17 F5 🔟
Brookhurst La *LHULT* M38 .... 64 C5
Brookhurst Rd *GTN* M18 .... 127 E5
Brookland Av *DTN/ASHW* M34 .... 148 B1 🔟
 FWTH BL4 .... 66 A4
Brookland Gv *BOL* BL1 .... 26 B5
Brooklands Av *CHAD* OL9 .... 77 F6 🔟
 DID/WITH M20 .... 143 E5 🔟
Brooklands Cl *HTNM* SK4 .... 146 B6 🔟
 IRL M44 .... 135 D1
 MOSL OL5 .... 98 C3 🔟
Brooklands Ct *ROCH* OL11 .... 39 D1

Brooklands Crs SALE M33 .... 159 F2
Brooklands Dr DROY M43 .... 111 D4
 OLDE OL4 .... 81 F5
Brooklands Pde OLDE OL4 .... 81 F5 🔢
Brooklands Rd BRAM/HZG SK7 ... 184 C6
 NTHM/RTH M23 .... 160 A5
 PWCH M25 .... 89 F5
 RDSH SK5 .... 146 C1
 SALE M33 .... 159 F2
 SWIN M27 .... 101 E1 🔢
 TOT/BURYW BL8 .... 18 A3
Brooklands Station Ap
 SALE M33 .... 159 E2 🔢
Brooklands St ROY/SHW OL2 .... 60 B4 🔢
The Brooklands HEY OL10 .... 37 D5 🔢
Brookland St MILN OL16 .... 40 C4 🔢
Brook La BURY BL9 .... 53 E4
 HALE/TIMP WA15 .... 174 C1
 MILN OL16 .... 40 C4 🔢
 OLDE OL4 .... 80 B5
 OLDS OL8 .... 96 B1
 WILM/AE SK9 .... 209 D2
Brooklawn Dr DID/WITH M20 ..... 163 F1
 PWCH M25 .... 72 A5
Brookleigh Rd DID/WITH M20 ..... 144 B5
Brooklet Cl OLDE OL4 .... 81 D6
Brooklyn Av LIT OL15 .... 12 B4 🔢
 MILN OL16 .... 24 B1
 OLDTF/WHR M16 .... 141 F1
 URM M41 .... 136 C1
Brooklyn Crs CHD/CHDH SK8 ..... 180 B2
Brooklyn Rd CHD/CHDH SK8 ...... 180 B2 🔢
 OFTN SK2 .... 184 A1
Brooklyn St BOL BL1 .... 27 F5 🔢
 OLD OL1 .... 80 A2 🔢
Brook Rd CHD/CHDH SK8 .... 180 B1
 HTNM SK4 .... 146 A6
 RUSH/FAL M14 .... 144 A4
 URM M41 .... 118 B6
Brooks Av BRAM/HZG SK7 .... 184 B4
 HYDE SK14 .... 150 C2
 RAD M26 .... 51 D3 🔢
Brooksbottom Cl RAMS BL0 .... 19 D1
Brooks Dr FAIL M35 .... 109 F1
 HALE/TIMP WA15 .... 190 B1
 NTHM/RTH M23 .... 160 B6
Brooks End ROCH OL11 .... 20 C4
Brookshaw St BURY BL9 .... 34 B3 🔢
 BURY BL9 .... 34 B3 🔢
 OP/CLY M11 .... 108 B6 🔢
Brookside OLDE OL4 .... 80 B5 🔢
Brookside Av DROY M43 .... 111 D4 🔢
 FWTH BL4 .... 66 A4 🔢
 OFTN SK2 .... 184 C1
 OLDE OL4 .... 81 F5
 POY/DIS SK12 .... 198 C6
Brookside Cl BOLE BL2 .... 29 E2
 CHD/CHDH SK8 .... 180 B3
 HYDE SK14 .... 132 B6
 TOT/BURYW BL8 .... 18 B2
Brookside Crs MDTN M24 .... 76 A5
 TOT/BURYW BL8 .... 18 B2 🔢
 WALK M28 .... 83 F2
Brookside Dr HYDE SK14 .... 132 B6 🔢
 PWCH M25 .... 89 E4
Brookside La MPL/ROM SK6 .... 200 C2
Brookside Rd BOLE BL2 .... 48 B1 🔢
 CHD/CHDH SK8 .... 179 E1
 NEWH/MOS M40 .... 92 B4
 SALE M33 .... 159 E3
Brooksmouth TOT/BURYW BL8 ... 35 E5 🔢
Brook's Pl WHIT OL12 .... 22 C5 🔢
Brook's Rd OLDTF/WHR M16 .... 123 D4
Brooks St STKP SK1 .... 167 D6 🔢
Brookstone Cl CCHDY M21 .... 142 B5 🔢
Brook St BOL BL1 .... 47 D2 🔢
 BRAM/HZG SK7 .... 184 C5 🔢
 BURY BL9 .... 34 B3
 CHAD OL9 .... 77 F3
 CHD/CHDH SK8 .... 181 D1
 FAIL M35 .... 109 F2 🔢
 FWTH BL4 .... 66 C2
 HYDE SK14 .... 131 F6
 LIT OL15 .... 13 D6 🔢
 OLD OL1 .... 79 E3
 RAD M26 .... 51 F6
 RAD M26 .... 67 E4
 ROY/SHW OL2 .... 60 B6
 SALE M33 .... 140 A6 🔢
 SLFD M6 .... 104 C3 🔢
 SWIN M27 .... 85 E5
 WHIT OL12 .... 11 D5 🔢
Brook St East AUL OL6 .... 112 B5
Brook St West AUL OL6 .... 112 B5 🔢
The Brook LIT OL15 .... 13 D2
Brookthorn Cl OFTN SK2 .... 185 D2 🔢
Brookthorpe Av BNG/LEV M19 ... 144 A3
Brookthorpe Rd TOT/BURYW BL8 ... 32 B4
Brookwater Cl TOT/BURYW BL8 .. 32 A1
Brookway HALE/TIMP WA15 ...... 175 D1
 OLDE OL4 .... 80 C6
Brookway Cl BNG/LEV M19 .... 164 C1
Brookwood Av CHH M8 .... 91 D5 🔢
 SALE M33 .... 158 C2
Brookwood Cl DTN/ASHW M34... 149 E4

Broom Av BNG/LEV M19 .... 145 F3
 BRO M7 .... 89 F5
 RDSH SK5 .... 147 D5 🔢
Broome Gv FAIL M35 .... 110 A1
Broomehouse Av IRL M44 .... 134 C3
Broome St CHAD OL9 .... 78 B5
Broomfield SWIN M27 .... 103 E1
Broomfield Cl BOLE BL2 .... 50 A1
 RDSH SK5 .... 147 D5 🔢
 WILM/AE SK9 .... 204 C3 🔢
Broomfield Crs EDGY/DAV SK3 ... 183 E5 🔢
 MDTN M24 .... 74 B2
Broomfield Dr CHH M8 .... 90 A6 🔢
 RDSH SK5 .... 147 D5
Broomfield La HALE/TIMP WA15 ... 174 C5
Broomfield Rd BOLS/LL BL3 .... 46 A4 🔢
 HTNM SK4 .... 166 A1
Broomfields DTN/ASHW M34 .... 130 B4
Broomfield Sq ROCH OL11 .... 40 A2 🔢
Broomfield Ter MILN OL16 .... 42 C3 🔢
Broomgrove La DTN/ASHW M34 ... 130 B5
Broomhall Rd BKLY M9 .... 73 E6 🔢
 SWIN M27 .... 103 E1
Broomhill Dr BRAM/HZG SK7 .... 182 B6
Broomhurst Av OLDS OL8 .... 95 E1
Broom La BNG/LEV M19 .... 145 F3
 BRO M7 .... 89 E5
Broom Rd HALE/TIMP WA15 ...... 174 C4
 PART M31 .... 155 D3 🔢
Broomstair Rd DTN/ASHW M34 ... 130 A3
Broom St MILN OL16 .... 42 C3
 SWIN M27 .... 86 A6
 TOT/BURYW BL8 .... 18 A3
Broomville Av SALE M33 .... 159 F1
Broomwood Rd
 HALE/TIMP WA15 .... 176 A2
Broseley Av DID/WITH M20 .... 164 B2 🔢
Broseley Rd OLDTF/WHR M16 ... 141 E1
Brotherdale Cl ROY/SHW OL2 .... 60 B4 🔢
Brotherton Cl HULME M15 .... 123 E3 🔢
Brotherton Dr CSLFD M3 .... 105 E5
Brougham St SLFD SK15 .... 114 A6 🔢
 WALK M28 .... 83 D2
Broughton Av LHULT M38 .... 82 C1 🔢
Broughton Cl MDTN M24 .... 74 B1
Broughton La BRO M7 .... 105 E3
Broughton Rd RDSH SK5 .... 167 D3 🔢
 SLFD M6 .... 104 B4
Broughton Rd East SLFD M6 ...... 104 C3
 CHH M8 .... 106 B3
Broughville Dr DID/WITH M20 ... 164 A5
Brow Av MDTN M24 .... 75 F5
Brow East BOLE BL2 .... 29 D3
Browfield Av SALQ/ORD M5 .... 122 C2
Browfield Wy OLD OL1 .... 78 C2
Browmere Dr DID/WITH M20 ..... 163 E1 🔢
Brownacre St DID/WITH M20 ..... 143 F5 🔢
Brown Bank Rd LIT OL15 .... 25 D2 🔢
Browncross St CSLFD M3 .... 2 A3
Brown Edge Rd OLDE OL4 .... 97 F1
Brownhill Dr OLDE OL4 .... 81 E4 🔢
Brownhill St OP/CLY M11 .... 126 B1 🔢
Browning Av DROY M43 .... 110 B6 🔢
Browning Cl BOL BL1 .... 27 E6 🔢
 OLD OL1 .... 79 F2
 RDSH SK5 .... 146 B2
 SWIN M27 .... 85 F5
Browning St CSLFD M3 .... 105 E5 🔢
 HULME M15 .... 123 E3 🔢
Brown La CHD/CHDH SK8 .... 170 B5
Brownlea Av DUK SK16 .... 131 D2
Brownley Court Rd
 WYTH/NTH M22 .... 178 B2 🔢
Brownley Rd WYTH/NTH M22 ... 178 C2
Brown Lodge St LIT OL15 .... 25 D2
Brownlow Av ROY/SHW OL2 ..... 61 E6
Brownlow Wy BOL BL1 .... 27 F6
Brownside Cl MILN OL16 .... 24 B2 🔢
Browns La WILM/AE SK9 .... 204 C3
Browns Rd BOLE BL2 .... 49 F3
Brown St ALT WA14 .... 174 B4
 BOL BL1 .... 47 D2
 CHAD OL9 .... 77 E4
 CMANW M2 .... 3 E3
 CSLFD M3 .... 2 B2
 FAIL M35 .... 93 F6
 HEY OL10 .... 37 E4 🔢
 LIT OL15 .... 12 B6
 MDTN M24 .... 75 E1 🔢
 OLD OL1 .... 79 E4
 RAD M26 .... 50 D3
 RAMS BL0 .... 6 C6 🔢
 SLFD M6 .... 104 A6
 STKP SK1 .... 166 C4 🔢
 WILM/AE SK9 .... 209 E4 🔢
Brownsville Rd HTNM SK4 .... 145 F6
Brownville Gv DUK SK16 .... 131 F2 🔢
Brownwood Av STKP SK1 .... 167 F4
Brownwood Cl SALE M33 .... 160 A4 🔢
Brows Av NTHM/RTH M23 .... 161 E3
Brow St ROCH OL11 .... 40 B3 🔢
Broxton Av BOLS/LL BL3 .... 45 F6

Broxton St NEWH/MOS M40 ...... 108 A4 🔢
Broxwood Cl GTN M18 .... 127 E4 🔢
Bruce St ROCH OL11 .... 39 D3 🔢
Brundage Rd WYTH/NTH M22 ... 178 B5
Brundrett Pl SALE M33 .... 159 D1 🔢
Brundrett's Rd CCHDY M21 .... 141 F3
Brundrett St STKP SK1 .... 167 E5
Brunel Av SALQ/ORD M5 .... 104 C6
Brunel Cl STRET M32 .... 140 C1
Brunel St BOL BL1 .... 27 E4 🔢
Brunstead Cl NTHM/RTH M23 ... 176 B1 🔢
Brunswick Ct BOL BL1 .... 46 C1 🔢
 DID/WITH M20 .... 144 A5
Brunswick Rd ALT WA14 .... 158 A6 🔢
 DID/WITH M20 .... 144 A5
Brunswick St BRUN/LGST M13 ... 124 C3
 BURY BL9 .... 34 A4 🔢
 DUK SK16 .... 131 D1
 HEY OL10 .... 37 D5
 MILN OL16 .... 23 E5
 MOSL OL5 .... 99 E5
 OLD OL1 .... 78 C5
 ROY/SHW OL2 .... 61 F2
 STRET M32 .... 140 D5 🔢
Brunton Rd RDSH SK5 .... 147 D5 🔢
Brunt St RUSH/FAL M14 .... 124 C6
Bruntwood Av CHD/CHDH SK8 ... 179 E6
Bruntwood La CHD/CHDH SK8 ... 180 C6
Brushes Av STLY SK15 .... 115 E4
Brushes Rd STLY SK15 .... 115 E4
Brussels Rd EDGY/DAV SK3 .... 182 B1
Bruton Av STRET M32 .... 139 F2
Bryan Rd CCHDY M21 .... 141 F1 🔢
Bryan St OLDE OL4 .... 80 A2
Bryant Cl BRUN/LGST M13 .... 125 D4 🔢
Bryantsfield BOL BL1 .... 44 B3 🔢
Bryce St HYDE SK14 .... 131 E5
Brydges Rd MPL/ROM SK6 .... 186 C2
Brydon Av WGTN/LGST M12 ..... 125 D2 🔢
Brydon Cl SLFD M6 .... 104 A5
Bryndale Gv SALE M33 .... 159 D4
Brynden Av DID/WITH M20 .... 144 A6
Bryn Dr RDSH SK5 .... 147 D6
Brynford Av BKLY M9 .... 73 E6 🔢
Bryngs Dr BOLE BL2 .... 30 A3
Brynhall Cl RAD M26 .... 50 C4
Brynheys Cl LHULT M38 .... 65 E6 🔢
Bryn Lea Ter BOL BL1 .... 26 A3
Brynorme Rd CHH M8 .... 90 B3
Brynton Rd BRUN/LGST M13 ..... 125 F6 🔢
Bryone Dr OFTN SK2 .... 183 F2 🔢
Buchanan St RAMS BL0 .... 6 C5
 SWIN M27 .... 86 A4 🔢
Buchan St OP/CLY M11 .... 108 C5 🔢
Buckden Rd HTNM SK4 .... 146 B4
Buckfast Av OLDS OL8 .... 97 D1
Buckfast Cl CCHDY M21 .... 141 F2
 CHD/CHDH SK8 .... 195 F2
 HALE/TIMP WA15 .... 175 F5
 POY/DIS SK12 .... 198 B4
Buckfast Rd MDTN M24 .... 57 D5
 SALE M33 .... 138 B5
Buckfield Av SALQ/ORD M5 .... 122 C2 🔢
Buckhurst Rd BNG/LEV M19 ..... 145 E2
Buckingham Av SLFD M6 .... 103 E5 🔢
 WHTF M45 .... 71 F4 🔢
Buckingham Dr DUK SK16 .... 132 A2
 TOT/BURYW BL8 .... 51 F1
Buckingham Park Cl
 ROY/SHW OL2 .... 61 F1 🔢
Buckingham Rd ALT WA14 .... 159 D4
 CCHDY M21 .... 141 F2 🔢
 CHD/CHDH SK8 .... 181 D5
 DROY M43 .... 109 F6
 HTNM SK4 .... 145 F2
 IRL M44 .... 134 A5
 POY/DIS SK12 .... 198 D5
 PWCH M25 .... 89 D3 🔢
 STLY SK15 .... 114 A4
 STRET M32 .... 122 A4
 SWIN M27 .... 86 B3
 WILM/AE SK9 .... 203 D5
Buckingham Rd West HTNM SK4 ... 165 E1
Buckingham St MILN OL16 .... 23 E5
 OFTN SK2 .... 183 E1 🔢
 SALQ/ORD M5 .... 104 A6 🔢
Buckingham Wy
 HALE/TIMP WA15 .... 175 D1
Buckland Av BKLY M9 .... 90 B2
Buckland Gv HYDE SK14 .... 151 E3
Buckland Rd SLFD M6 .... 103 E3
Buck La SALE M33 .... 138 C5
Buckley Av GTN M18 .... 127 D5
Buckley Brook St WHIT OL12 ..... 23 F3 🔢
Buckley Cha MILN OL16 .... 41 F2
Buckley Cl HYDE SK14 .... 150 C4
Buckley Dr MPL/ROM SK6 .... 169 E4
Buckley Farm La WHIT OL12 ..... 23 F2
Buckley Flds WHIT OL12 .... 23 F2
Buckley Hill La MILN OL16 .... 41 F2
Buckley La FWTH BL4 .... 66 A4
 PWCH M25 .... 87 F2
 WHIT OL12 .... 23 F2
Buckley Rd GTN M18 .... 126 C5
 OLDE OL4 .... 80 B3
 WHIT OL12 .... 23 F3

Buckley Sq *FWTH* BL4 .... 66 A5 🔢
Buckley St *BRO* M7 .... 105 E3
BURY BL9... 34 A4
CHAD OL9 .... 77 E4
DROY M43 .... 128 B1
DTN/ASHW M34 .... 129 F2
HEY OL10... 37 F4
MILN OL16 .... 23 E5
OLDE OL4 .... 80 C6 🔢
OP/CLY M11 .... 127 F2
RDSH SK5.. 146 C1
ROY/SHW OL2 .... 62 A2 🔢
STLY SK15 .... 132 A1 🔢
Buckley Vw *WHIT* OL12 .... 23 F2
Bucklow Av *PART* M31 .... 155 D1
RUSH/FAL M14 .... 143 F2
Bucklow Cl *HYDE* SK14 .... 153 D2
OLDE OL4 .... 62 C5 🔢
Bucklow Dr *WYTH/NTH* M22 .... 162 C5
Bucklow Vw *ALT* WA14 .... 173 E4
Buckstones Rd *OLD* OL1 .... 62 C3
ROY/SHW OL2 .... 43 D6
Buckthorn Cl *CCHDY* M21 .... 142 B5 🔢
HALE/TIMP WA15 .... 176 C2
Buckthorn La *ECC* M30................. 100 A6
Buckton Dr *STLY* SK15 .... 115 F2
Buckton Vale Rd *STLY* SK15 .... 115 F1
Buckwood Cl *BRAM/HZG* SK7 .... 185 E4
Buddleia Dr *BRO* M7 .... 105 E1 🔢
Bude Av *RDSH* SK5 .... 147 F6
URM M41 .... 137 F3
Bude Cl *BRAM/HZG* SK7 .... 197 D2
Budsworth Av *DID/WITH* M20 .... 143 F4 🔢
Budworth Rd *SALE* M33 .... 160 C2
Buersil Av *MILN* OL16 .... 40 C3
Buersil St *MILN* OL16 .... 40 C4
Buerton Av *BKLY* M9 .... 73 E6
Bugle St *HULME* M15 .... 2 B6 🔢
Buile Hill Av *WHTF/NTH* M22 .... 177 F5
Buile Hill Dr *SALQ/ORD* M5............ 103 E3
Buile Hill Gv *LHULT* M38 .... 65 F6 🔢
Buile St *BRO* M7............................ 89 F6
Bulford Av *WYTH/NTH* M22 .... 177 F5
Bulkeley Rd *CHD/CHDH* SK8 .... 180 C1
POY/DIS SK12 .... 198 C6
WILM/AE SK9 .... 194 A6
Bulkeley St *EDGY/DAV* SK3 .... 166 C5 🔢
Bullcote Gn *ROY/SHW* OL2 .... 61 E5
Bullcote La *ROY/SHW* OL2 .... 61 F5
Buller Ms *TOT/BURYW* BL8............ 32 C6
Buller Rd *BRUN/LGST* M13 .... 145 D1
Buller St *BOLS/LL* BL3 .... 66 A1
DROY M43 .... 128 C1
OLDE OL4 .... 80 B3
TOT/BURYW BL8............................ 33 D6
Bullfinch Dr *BURY* BL9 .... 34 C2
Bull Hill Crs *RAD* M26 .... 69 F3
Bullock St *OFTN* SK2 .... 167 D6 🔢
Bullows Rd *LHULT* M38 .... 65 D5 🔢
Bulteel St *BOLS/LL* BL3 .... 64 A1 🔢
ECC M30 .... 100 C4
Bulwer St *MILN* OL16 .... 23 E5
Bunkers Hl *PWCH* M25 .... 87 F2
Bunkers Hill Rd *HYDE* SK14 .... 152 C2
Bunkershill Rd *MPL/ROM* SK6 ...... 169 F4
Bunsen St *CMANE* M1 .... 3 G3 🔢
Bunting Ms *WALK* M28 .... 82 C5 🔢
Bunyan Cl *OLD* OL1 .... 62 B5
Bunyan St *WHIT* OL12 .... 23 D4 🔢
Bunyard St *CHH* M8 .... 106 C1
Burbage Rd *NTHM/RTH* M23 .... 177 E5
Burbridge Cl *OP/CLY* M11 .... 125 F1
Burchall Fld *MILN* OL16 .... 23 H6
Burdale Dr *SLFD* M6 .... 102 C3 🔢
Burder St *OLDS* OL8 .... 95 D3 🔢
Burdett Av *ROCH* OL11 .... 21 D4
Burdith Av *RUSH/FAL* M14 .... 143 E1
Burdon Av *WYTH/NTH* M22 .... 178 C3
Burford Av *BRAM/HZG* SK7 .... 196 A4
OLDTF/WHR M16 .... 142 B1
URM M41 .... 119 F5
Burford Crs *WILM/AE* SK9 .... 202 C6
Burford Dr *BOLS/LL* BL3 .... 46 C4 🔢
OLDTF/WHR M16 .... 142 B1
SWIN M27 .... 85 F3
Burford Gv *SALE* M33 .... 158 C3
Burford Rd *OLDTF/WHR* M16 ...... 142 B1 🔢
Burgess Av *AUL* OL6 .... 113 D2
Burgess Dr *FAIL* M35 .... 94 A6
Brighley Cl *BOLS/LL* BL3 .... 49 F4
STLY SK15 .... 114 B5
Burghley Dr *BOLS/LL* BL3 .... 49 F4
Burgundy Dr *TOT/BURYW* BL8 ..... 18 A6
Burke St *BOL* BL1........................ 27 E5
Burkitt St *HYDE* SK14 .... 150 C1 🔢
Burland St *BRO* M7 .... 105 E2 🔢
Burleigh Cl *BRAM/HZG* SK7 .... 183 E6
Burleigh Ms *CCHDY* M21 .... 141 F5 🔢
Burleigh Rd *STRET* M32 .... 121 F3
Burleigh St *HULME* M15 .... 124 C4
Burlescombe Cl *ALT* WA14 .... 173 F2 🔢
Burley Ct *NTHM* SK4 .... 166 A3 🔢
Burlington Av *OLDS* OL8 .... 95 F1
Burlington Cl *NTHM* SK4 .... 164 C3 🔢
Burlington Dr *EDGY/DAV* SK3 ..... 183 D3

Burlington Gdns *EDGY/DAV* SK3 .. 183 D3 🔢
Burlington Ms *EDGY/DAV* SK3..... 183 D3
Burlington Rd *ALT* WA14 .... 174 B2
DID/WITH M20 .... 144 A4
ECC M30 .... 101 F3
Burlington St *AUL* OL6 .... 112 B4 🔢
AULW OL7 .... 112 A5
HULME M15 .... 124 B4
ROCH OL11 .... 40 B3 🔢
Burman St *OP/CLY* M11 .... 128 A2
Burnaby St *BOLS/LL* BL3 .... 46 B4
OLDS OL8 .... 78 B6 🔢
Burnage Av *BNG/LEV* M19 .... 145 D3
Burnage Hall Rd *BNG/LEV* M19..... 144 C4
Burnage La *BNG/LEV* M19 .... 145 D6
HTNM SK4 .... 164 B3
Burnage Range *BNG/LEV* M19 ..... 145 E2 🔢
Burnbray Av *BNG/LEV* M19 .... 144 C5
Burndale Dr *BURY* BL9 .... 53 E6
Burden Rd *BOLS/LL* BL3 .... 47 F4
Burnell Cl *NEWH/MOS* M40 .... 107 D4
Burneside Crs *MDTN* M24 .... 56 C6
Burnet Cl *MILN* OL16 .... 41 D3 🔢
Burnett Av *SALQ/ORD* M5 .... 122 C1
Burnett Cl *NEWH/MOS* M40 .... 107 E2 🔢
Burnfield Rd *GTN* M18 .... 127 E6 🔢
RDSH SK5 .... 128 A6 🔢
Burnham Av *BOL* BL1 .... 26 B6
RDSH SK5 .... 147 D2 🔢
Burnham Cl *CHD/CHDH* SK8 ...... 181 D5 🔢
Burnham Dr *BNG/LEV* M19 .... 145 D4
URM M41 .... 119 D6 🔢
Burnham Dr *DTN/ASHW* M34 ...... 128 B6 🔢
Burnley La *CHAD* OL9 .... 77 F1
OLD OL1 .... 77 F2
Burnley Rd *BURY* BL9 .... 19 F5
Burnley St *CHAD* OL9 .... 77 F4
FAIL M35 .... 94 B5 🔢
Burnmoor Rd *BOLE* BL2 .... 49 D1 🔢
Burnsall Av *WHTF* M45 .... 70 C3 🔢
Burnsall Gv *ROY/SHW* OL2 .... 60 B5
Burns Av *BURY* BL9 .... 53 D3
CHD/CHDH SK8 .... 181 D1 🔢
SWIN M27 .... 85 E4
Burns Cl *OLD* OL1 .... 62 C4
OP/CLY M11 .... 108 A6
Burns Crs *OFTN* SK2 .... 168 C6 🔢
Burns Fold *DUK* SK16 .... 132 B2 🔢
Burns Gdns *PWCH* M25 .... 88 A2 🔢
Burns Gv *DROY* M43 .... 110 B5
Burnside *HALE/TIMP* WA15 .... 190 B2
RAMS BL0 .... 7 E1
ROY/SHW OL2 .... 62 B3 🔢
STLY SK15 .... 133 C2
Burnside Av *HTNM* SK4 .... 146 C5
SLFD M6 .... 102 C2
Burnside Cl *HEY* OL10 .... 37 E6
MPL/ROM SK6 .... 169 D2 🔢
RAD M26 .... 51 D2
STLY SK15 .... 133 C2
WILM/AE SK9 .... 204 A5
Burnside Dr *BNG/LEV* M19 .... 144 C4
Burnside Rd *BOL* BL1 .... 26 C5 🔢
CHD/CHDH SK8 .... 179 E2
MILN OL16 .... 41 D1 🔢
Burns Rd *DTN/ASHW* M34 .... 149 E4
LHULT M38 .... 65 F6
Burns St *BOLS/LL* BL3 .... 47 D3
HEY OL10 .... 37 E6
Burnthorp Av *BKLY* M9 .... 90 C2 🔢
Burnthorpe Cl *ROCH* OL11 .... 37 F1 🔢
Burran Rd *WYTH/NTH* M22 .... 192 B1
Burrows Av *CCHDY* M21 .... 141 F5
Burrs Lea Cl *BURY* BL9 .... 33 H1
Burrswood Av *BURY* BL9 .... 33 F1
Burrswood Dr *BURY* BL9 .... 33 F1 🔢
Burslem Av *DID/WITH* M20 .... 143 E3
Burstead St *GTN* M18 .... 127 F3
Burstock St *ANC* M4 .... 106 C4 🔢
Burston St *GTN* M18 .... 127 D3 🔢
Burton Av *HALE/TIMP* WA15 ...... 159 E4
TOT/BURYW BL8............................ 32 A3
POY/DIS SK12 .... 198 B5 🔢
Burton Gv *WALK* M28 .... 85 D5
Burton Rd *DID/WITH* M20 .... 143 E5
Burton St *HTNM* SK4 .... 166 C2
MDTN M24 .... 75 D3 🔢
NEWH/MOS M40 .... 106 C3
OLDE OL4 .... 80 C5
Burton Wk *CSLFD* M3 .... 105 E5 🔢
Burtonwood Ct *MDTN* M24 .... 75 D2 🔢
Burtree St *WGTN/LGST* M12 ..... 126 B3 🔢
Burwell Cl *WHIT* OL12 .... 22 B2
Burwell Gv *NTHM/RTH* M23 .... 161 D6 🔢
Bury And Bolton Rd *RAD* M26 ..... 50 D2 🔢
Bury And Rochdale Old Rd
HEY OL10 .... 37 E2
Bury Av *OLDTF/WHR* M16 .... 142 A1 🔢
Bury New Rd *BOL* BL1 .... 47 D2
BOLE BL2 .... 48 C2
BOLE BL2 .... 49 F2
BRO M7 .... 89 E6
HEY OL10 .... 35 E5
PWCH M25 .... 71 E6
RAMS BL0 .... 7 F5 🔢

WHTF M45 .... 70 C2
Bury Old Rd *BOLE* BL2 .... 30 C6
BOLE BL2 .... 47 F2
HEY OL10 .... 35 F6
PWCH M25 .... 71 E5
Bury Pl *OP/CLY* M11 .... 109 D5 🔢
Bury Rd *BOLE* BL7 .... 18 A2
EDGW/EG BL7 .... 16 A2
RAD M26 .... 51 F5
RAMS BL0 .... 7 E1
ROCH OL11 .... 38 A1
TOT/BURYW BL8............................ 32 A1
Bury St *CSLFD* M3 .... 2 B1
HEY OL10 .... 36 C5
MOSL OL5 .... 99 D5
RAD M26 .... 52 A5
RDSH SK5 .... 167 D2
Bushell St *BOLS/LL* BL3 .... 45 F5
Bushey Dr *NTHM/RTH* M23 .... 177 E2
Busheyfield Cl *HYDE* SK14 .... 131 E4
Bush St *NEWH/MOS* M40 .... 107 E2
Busk Rd *CHAD* OL9 .... 78 A3
Butcher La *BURY* BL9 .... 34 A5
NTHM/RTH M23 .... 160 B6
ROY/SHW OL2 .... 60 A4
Bute Av *OLDS* OL8 .... 96 A2
Bute St *BOL* BL1 .... 26 C6
NEWH/MOS M40 .... 92 A4
SALQ/ORD M5 .... 103 E6
Butler Gn *CHAD* OL9 .... 94 B1
Butler La *NEWH/MOS* M40 .... 107 D4 🔢
Butler St *ANC* M4 .... 107 E5
RAMS BL0 .... 18 B1 🔢
Butley St *BRAM/HZG* SK7 .... 184 C3
Butman St *GTN* M18 .... 128 A3
Buttercup Av *WALK* M28 .... 82 A2 🔢
Buttercup Dr *EDGY/DAV* SK3 ..... 182 B2 🔢
ROCH OL11 .... 38 C4
Butterfield Cl *CHD/CHDH* SK8 ... 181 F6 🔢
Butter La *CSLFD* M3 .... 2 C3 🔢
Butterley Cl *DUK* SK16 .... 132 A2 🔢
Buttermere Av *HEY* OL10 .... 56 B1 🔢
SWIN M27 .... 102 A1 🔢
WYTH/NTH M22 .... 178 A5 🔢
Buttermere Cl *BOLS/LL* BL3 .... 49 D5 🔢
STRET M32 .... 121 D6 🔢
Buttermere Dr *HALE/TIMP* WA15 . 190 A3
MDTN M24 .... 74 C1
RAMS BL0 .... 6 C4 🔢
Buttermere Gv *ROY/SHW* OL2 ..... 60 B2 🔢
Buttermere Rd *AULW* OL7 .... 112 A3
CHD/CHDH SK8 .... 179 F4
FWTH BL4 .... 64 C4
OLDE OL4 .... 80 B3
PART M31 .... 154 C2
Butterstile La *PWCH* M25 .... 88 A3
Butterwick Cl *WGTN/LGST* M12 .. 126 C6
Butterworth Hall *MILN* OL16 ...... 42 B2 🔢
Butterworth La *CHAD* OL9 .... 93 F2
Butterworth St *CHAD* OL9 .... 77 F3 🔢
LIT OL15 .... 12 B6 🔢
MDTN M24 .... 76 A4 🔢
OLDE OL4 .... 80 A4 🔢
OP/CLY M11 .... 126 B1 🔢
Butteryhouse La
HALE/TIMP WA15 .... 176 C5
Butt Hill Av *PWCH* M25 .... 88 C2 🔢
Butt Hill Dr *PWCH* M25 .... 88 C2 🔢
Butt Hill Rd *PWCH* M25 .... 88 C2 🔢
Butt La *OLDE* OL4 .... 98 C1
Button Hole *ROY/SHW* OL2 .... 62 B2
Button La *NTHM/RTH* M23 .... 161 D3
Buttress St *GTN* M18 .... 127 D3
The Butts Av *MILN* OL16 .... 23 D6 🔢
Buxted Rd *OLD* OL1 .... 79 F2
Buxton Av *AUL* OL6 .... 114 A1
DID/WITH M20 .... 143 D5
Buxton Crs *MILN* OL16 .... 40 C3
SALE M33 .... 160 B4
Buxton La *DROY* M43 .... 127 F1
MPL/ROM SK6 .... 186 C2
Buxton Rd *BRAM/HZG* SK7 .... 185 D6
OFTN SK2 .... 183 E1 🔢
OFTN SK2 .... 184 A3 🔢
STRET M32 .... 120 B6
Buxton Rd West *POY/DIS* SK12 .. 201 E3
Buxton St *BRAM/HZG* SK7 .... 184 D4 🔢
CHD/CHDH SK8 .... 179 E2 🔢
CMANE M1 .... 3 H6
HEY OL10 .... 37 F6
TOT/BURYW BL8............................ 33 D5
WHIT OL12 .... 5 E6
Bye Rd *RAMS* BL0 .... 7 F4
Byfield Rd *WYTH/NTH* M22 .... 178 A3
Byland Av *CHD/CHDH* SK8 .... 195 F3
OLDE OL4 .... 97 F1
Byland Cl *BOL* BL1 .... 27 F5 🔢🔢
Bylands Cl *POY/DIS* SK12 .... 198 B5 🔢
Bylands Fold *DUK* SK16 .... 131 E3
Byng Av *IRL* M44 .... 154 A1
Byng St *FWTH* BL4 .... 66 B3 🔢
OLDE OL4 .... 80 B3 🔢
ROCH OL11 .... 56 C1
Byrcland Cl *WGTN/LGST* M12 ..... 125 F1 🔢
Byre Cl *SALE* M33 .... 161 E2
Byrom Av *BNG/LEV* M19 .... 146 A2

Byrom St ALT WA14 .... 174 B4
CSLFD M3 .... 2 B4
OLDTF/WHR M16 .... 123 E5
SALO/ORD M5 .... 122 B1 ⑩
TOT/BURYW BL8 .... 32 C3 ③
Byron Av DROY M43 .... 110 B5
PWCH M25 .... 88 A2
RAD M26 .... 50 B5
SWIN M27 .... 85 F5
Byron Dr CHD/CHDH SK8 ...... 181 D1 ⑨
Byron Gv RDSH SK5 .... 146 C2
Byron Rd DTN/ASHW M34 ..... 149 D3
MDTN M24 .... 75 F1
STRET M32 .... 121 F6
TOT/BURYW BL8 .... 18 A3
Byron St ECC M30 .... 101 E5
OLDS OL8 .... 94 C3
ROY/SHW OL2 .... 60 B5
Byron Wk FWTH BL4 .... 65 F5 ⑥
Byrth Rd OLDS OL8 .... 96 A5

C

Cabin La OLDE OL4 .... 63 E6
Cable St ANC M4 .... 3 F1
BOL BL1 .... 47 D1 ⑩
CSLFD M3 .... 2 B1
Cabot PI RDSH SK5 .... 167 D1
Cabot St BRUN/LGST M13 ..... 124 C3 ⑩
Cadishead Wy IRL M44 .... 135 E4
Cadnam Dr WYTH/NTH M22 ... 179 D4
Cadogan St RUSH/FAL M14 ... 124 B5
Caen Av NEWH/MOS M40 .... 93 D2
Caernarvon Cl TOT/BURYW BL8 . 18 A4 ⑪
Caernarvon Dr BRAM/HZG SK7 . 184 A6
Caesar St ROCH OL11 .... 40 B5
Cairn Dr ROCH OL11 .... 37 F2
SLFD M6 .... 105 D2
Cairngorm Dr BOLS/LL BL3 ..... 44 C5 ⑨
Cairns PI AUL OL6 .... 113 E2 ⑩
Cairnwell Rd CHAD OL9 .... 77 D3
Caister Av URM M41 .... 136 A2
Caister Cl URM M41 .... 136 A2
Caister Cl OLDTF/WHR M16 ... 142 C3
Caistor St STKP SK1 .... 167 F2
Caithness Av NTHM/RTH M23 . 177 E3 ⑪
Caithness Dr BOLS/LL BL3 .... 44 C4
Caithness Rd HEY OL10 .... 37 F2
Cakebread St WGTN/LGST M12 . 125 D2 ⑥
Calbourne Crs WGTN/LGST M12 . 126 C6 ⑨
Calcutta Rd EDGY/DAV SK3 ... 166 A6
Caldbeck Av BOL BL1 .... 26 A6
SALE M33 .... 140 C6
Caldbeck Dr FWTH BL4 .... 64 C4
MDTN M24 .... 74 C2
Caldecott Rd BKLY M9 .... 73 E6
Calder Av IRL M44 .... 135 D2
LIT OL15 .... 12 B4
WYTH/NTH M22 .... 162 B5
Calderbank Av URM M41 .... 117 F6
Calderbrook Dr CHD/CHDH SK8 . 181 E3
Calderbrook Rd LIT OL15 .... 12 C3
Calderbrook Wy OLDE OL4 ...... 79 F6 ⑩
Calder Cl BRSH SK5 .... 167 E1 ⑪
Calder Ct URM M41 .... 117 F5 ⑪
Calder Crs WHTF M45 .... 71 F1
Calder Dr FWTH BL4 .... 67 F6
SWIN M27 .... 85 F4
WALK M28 .... 82 B3
Calder Gv ROY/SHW OL2 .... 61 E1
Calder Rd BOLS/LL BL3 .... 46 C6 ⑩
Caldershaw La WHIT OL12 .... 21 E3
Caldershaw Rd WHIT OL12 .... 21 E5 ②
Calder St MILN OL16 .... 23 F3
Calderwood Cl TOT/BURYW BL8 . 32 A1 ⑪
Caldey Rd NTHM/RTH M23 ...... 176 C2
Caldon Cl ECC M30 .... 119 E1 ⑪
Caldy Dr TOT/BURYW BL8 .... 18 B2
Caldy Rd SLFD M6 .... 103 E3
WILM/AE SK9 .... 194 B6
Caledon Av NEWH/MOS M40 ... 92 B5
Caledonia Dr ECC M30 .... 119 F1
Caledonia St BOLS/LL BL3 ...... 46 A4
RAD M26 .... 52 A5 ③
Caledonia Wy STRET M32 ...... 120 B4
Cale Gn EDGY/DAV SK3 .... 183 D1
Cale St OFTN SK2 .... 167 D6
Caley St BOL BL1 .... 26 A5 ⑪
CMANE M1 .... 124 B2 ⑪
Calf Hey LIT OL15 .... 12 C5 ⑪
Calf Hey Cl RAD M26 .... 50 B6
Calf Hey North ROCH OL11 ..... 40 B3 ⑩
Calf Hey Rd ROY/SHW OL2 ...... 62 B1
Calf Hey South ROCH OL11 ..... 40 B3 ⑨
Calf La OLDE OL4 .... 99 F1
Calgarth Dr MDTN M24 .... 56 B6
Calgary St GTN M18 .... 127 D4
Calico Cl CSLFD M3 .... 105 E4 ⑥
Callaghan Wk HEY OL10 .... 37 D6
Calland Av HYDE SK14 .... 132 A6
Callender St RAMS BL0 .... 6 C5
Calliards Rd MILN OL16 .... 24 C1

Callingdon Rd CCHDY M21 ..... 142 B6
Callington Cl HYDE SK14 .... 152 C1 ⑧
Callington Dr HYDE SK14 .... 152 C1
Callis Rd BOLS/LL BL3 .... 46 A3
Caltha St RAMS BL0 .... 6 C5 ⑪
Calthorpe Av BKLY M9 .... 91 D6
Calton Av BRO M7 .... 88 B6
Calve Croft Rd WYTH/NTH M22 . 178 C6
Calver Av ECC M30 .... 119 D1 ⑧
Calver Cl URM M41 .... 117 E6
Calverley Av BNG/LEV M19 ..... 145 D4
Calverley Cl WILM/AE SK9 ..... 204 A3 ⑪
Calverley Wy WHIT OL12 .... 22 C1 ⑪
Calverly Rd CHD/CHDH SK8 ... 181 E2 ⑪
Calverton Dr NEWH/MOS M40 ... 93 D6
Calvert Rd BOLS/LL BL3 .... 47 D6 ⑯
Calvert St SALO/ORD M5 .... 103 E5 ②
Calvin St BOL BL1 .... 28 A6
Cambeck Cl WHTF M45 .... 71 F2
Cambell Rd ECC M30 .... 100 C5
Camberley Cl BRAM/HZG SK7 . 197 D3
Camberly Dr ROCH OL11 .... 38 A1
Cambert La GTN M18 .... 127 E4
Camberwell Dr AULW OL7 .... 96 B6
Camberwell St CHH M8 .... 106 B3 ⑪
OLDS OL8 .... 95 F1 ⑪
Camberwell Wy ROY/SHW OL2 . 60 A5
Camborne Av HYDE SK14 .... 133 F6
Camborne Rd RUSH/FAL M14 . 143 F1 ⑬
Cambourne Dr BOLS/LL BL3 ... 45 E4
Cambo Wk HTNM SK4 .... 165 D2
Cambrai Crs ECC M30 .... 100 B3
Cambrian Dr MILN OL16 .... 42 B1 ⑪
ROY/SHW OL2 .... 60 A6
Cambrian Rd EDGY/DAV SK3 . 166 A5 ③
Cambrian St NEWH/MOS M40 . 107 F5
Cambria St BOLS/LL BL3 .... 46 A4
OLDE OL4 .... 80 B4
Cambridge Av OLDTF/WHR M16 . 142 A1 ③
ROCH OL11 .... 38 B1
WILM/AE SK9 .... 203 D4
Cambridge Cl FWTH BL4 .... 65 D2
SALE M33 .... 158 B2 ⑪
Cambridge Dr BOLS/LL BL3 ..... 49 F5 ⑪
DTN/ASHW M34 .... 128 B6
MPL/ROM SK6 .... 150 A6
Cambridge Gv ECC M30 .... 102 A5 ⑪
WHTF M45 .... 71 E4 ③
Cambridge Rd BKLY M9 .... 91 E4 ②
CHD/CHDH SK8 .... 179 F1
DROY M43 .... 110 A4
FAIL M35 .... 107 F5
HALE/TIMP WA15 .... 178 C3
HTNM SK4 .... 146 A6 ⑪
URM M41 .... 137 F2
Cambridge St AULW OL7 .... 112 A4 ⑥
BRO M7 .... 105 F3
CHAD OL9 .... 95 D1
CMANE M1 .... 124 A2
DUK SK16 .... 113 D6
HULME M15 .... 124 B2
OFTN SK2 .... 183 E1
STLY SK15 .... 114 B5
Camden Av NEWH/MOS M40 ... 109 D3 ②
Camden Cl BOLE BL2 .... 31 D6 ⑧
Camden St MOSL OL5 .... 99 E2
Camelia Rd BKLY M9 .... 91 D6
Camellia Cl BOL BL1 .... 45 E2
Cameron Ct ROY/SHW OL2 ..... 60 B3 ⑪
Cameron St BOL BL1 .... 27 E2
CMANE M1 .... 2 C6 ⑪
TOT/BURYW BL8 .... 33 D5
Campania St ROY/SHW OL2 ... 78 C1
Campbell Cl TOT/BURYW BL8 ... 31 F3
Campbell Ct FWTH BL4 .... 66 A1 ③
RDSH SK5 .... 147 D2 ②
WHIT OL12 .... 22 C3 ⑪
Campbell Wy LHULT M38 .... 83 D2 ⑪
WALK M28 .... 83 D2
Campden Wy WILM/AE SK9 ... 194 B5
Campion Wy WHIT OL12 .... 22 A2
Camp St AUL OL6 .... 112 C4
BRO M7 .... 105 D3
CSLFD M3 .... 2 B5
TOT/BURYW BL8 .... 33 D4 ⑯
Cams Acre Cl RAD M26 .... 50 C6 ②
Cams La RAD M26 .... 68 C1
Canada St BOL BL1 .... 27 D5
NEWH/MOS M40 .... 88 A5
OFTN SK2 .... 183 E1
Canal Bank ECC M30 .... 101 D4
Canal Bridge La OP/CLY M11 . 109 F6
Canal Rd ALT WA14 .... 158 C6
Canal Side ECC M30 .... 101 D4 ②
Canal St CHAD OL9 .... 94 C2
CMANE M1 .... 3 F5
DROY M43 .... 110 B6
HEY OL10 .... 56 C1
HYDE SK14 .... 131 D6 ⑪
LIT OL15 .... 12 C6
MPL/ROM SK6 .... 187 E1 ⑪

ROCH OL11 .... 40 B2
SALO/ORD M5 .... 105 D6 ④
STKP SK1 .... 167 D5
STLY SK15 .... 114 B6 ③
Canberra Rd BRAM/HZG SK7 . 196 C4
Canberra St OP/CLY M11 .... 109 D5
Candahar St BOLS/LL BL3 .... 47 E6 ②
Candleford Pl OFTN SK2 .... 184 C3
Candleford Rd DID/WITH M20 . 143 F5 ③
Candlestick Pk BURY BL9 .... 35 E3 ⑪
Canisp Cl CHAD OL9 .... 77 E2
Canley Cl STKP SK1 .... 167 D5
Canmore Cl BOLS/LL BL3 .... 45 E6 ②
Cannel Fold WALK M28 .... 82 C6 ②
Canning Dr BOL BL1 .... 27 F5 ⑬
Canning St BOL BL1 .... 27 F5 ⑭
BURY BL9 .... 34 A3
HTNM SK4 .... 166 C3 ⑪
Cannon Ct CSLFD M3 .... 2 D2
Cannon Gv BOLS/LL BL3 .... 46 B3 ⑳
BOLS/LL BL3 .... 46 B4 ⑭
Cannon St ANC M4 .... 2 D2
BOLS/LL BL3 .... 46 B3 ⑳
CHAD OL9 .... 78 C5 ③
CSLFD M3 .... 105 E5
ECC M30 .... 101 F6
RAD M26 .... 51 D4 ②
RAMS BL0 .... 18 B1 ③
Cannon St North BOLS/LL BL3 . 46 B3 ㉒
Cann St TOT/BURYW BL8 .... 17 E5
Canon Dr ALT WA14 .... 173 F6
Canon Flynn Ct MILN OL16 ..... 24 A6 ⑪
Canons Gv NEWH/MOS M40 ... 107 F2
Canonsleigh Cl CHH M8 .... 105 F2 ③
Canon St BURY BL9 .... 34 B3 ⑪
MILN OL16 .... 23 F3
Canonsway SWIN M27 .... 85 F6
Canterbury Cl BOLS/LL BL3 ..... 21 E6
Canterbury Crs MDTN M24 ...... 76 B1
Canterbury Dr PWCH M25 .... 89 D3 ②
TOT/BURYW BL8 .... 33 E3
Canterbury Gdns SALO/ORD M5 . 102 C5 ⑪
Canterbury Gv BOLS/LL BL3 .... 46 B6 ⑪
Canterbury Pk DID/WITH M20 . 163 D2 ③
Canterbury Rd HALE/TIMP WA15 . 176 A4
STKP SK1 .... 167 F4
URM M41 .... 118 C6
Canterbury St AUL OL6 .... 112 C3
Canterfield Cl DROY M43 .... 111 E5 ⑪
Cantrell St OP/CLY M11 .... 108 C6 ②
Canute Rd STRET M32 .... 121 F6
Canute St BOLE BL2 .... 29 D6 ②
RAD M26 .... 50 C6 ③
SLFD M6 .... 104 C5 ②
Capenhurst Cl NTHM/RTH M23 . 177 D3
Capesthorne Cl BRAM/HZG SK7 . 199 D1 ⑪
Capesthorne Dr ROY/SHW OL2 . 61 D2
Capesthorne Rd BRAM/HZG SK7 . 199 D1
DUK SK16 .... 131 E3 ②
HALE/TIMP WA15 .... 176 B1
MPL/ROM SK6 .... 200 C2
WILM/AE SK9 .... 202 C6
Cape St DID/WITH M20 .... 144 A4
Capital Rd OP/CLY M11 .... 128 A2
Capricorn Wy SLFD M6 .... 105 D3 ⑧
Capstan St BKLY M9 .... 91 F5
Captain Clarke Rd HYDE SK14 . 130 C4
Captain Fold Rd LHULT M38 ... 65 D6
Captain's Clough Rd BOL BL1 .. 26 B5
Capton Cl BRAM/HZG SK7 ..... 183 E5
Carberry Rd GTN M18 .... 127 F4
Carden Av SWIN M27 .... 85 E6 ③
URM M41 .... 136 C1
Carder Cl SWIN M27 .... 86 A6 ③
Cardew Av WYTH/NTH M22 ... 178 C3
Cardiff Cl OLDS OL8 .... 94 C4
Cardiff St BRO M7 .... 89 F6
Cardigan Dr BURY BL9 .... 52 C2
Cardigan Rd OLDS OL8 .... 94 C3
Cardigan St ROY/SHW OL2 ...... 60 C5
SLFD M6 .... 103 F6 ⑪
WHIT OL12 .... 22 C2 ⑪
Cardinal Ms MDTN M24 .... 74 B1
Cardinal St CHH M8 .... 106 C1
OLD OL1 .... 79 D4
Carding Gv CSLFD M3 .... 105 F4 ⑧
Cardroom Rd ANC M4 .... 107 E1
Cardus St BNG/LEV M19 .... 145 E2
Cardwell Gdns BOL BL1 .... 27 F5 ⑬
BOL BL1 .... 27 F5 ⑬
Cardwell Rd ECC M30 .... 100 B6 ⑪
Cardwell St OLDS OL8 .... 96 A2
Carey Cl BRO M7 .... 105 E3 ②
Carfax Fold WHIT OL12 .... 21 F3 ②
Carfax St GTN M18 .... 127 E4
Carill Av NEWH/MOS M40 .... 92 B4
Carill Dr RUSH/FAL M14 .... 144 B3
Carisbrook Av URM M41 .... 138 A2 ⑪
WHTF M45 .... 71 E5 ⑪
Carisbrook Dr SWIN M27 .... 102 B3
Carisbrooke Av BRAM/HZG SK7 . 184 B6
Carisbrooke Dr BOL BL1 .... 28 A4 ⑪
Carisbrook St BKLY M9 .... 91 E6
Carlburn St OP/CLY M11 .... 109 E5
Carleton Rd POY/DIS SK12 ... 200 A5

Carley Gv *BKLY* M9 .... 90 C1
Carlford Gv *PWCH* M25 .... 88 A2
Carlile St *EDGY/DAV* SK3 .... 166 C5
Carlin Ga *HALE/TIMP* WA15 .... 175 E1
Carling Dr *WYTH/NTH* M22 .... 178 C5
Carlingford Cl *EDGY/DAV* SK3 .... 182 C2 🔢
Carl St *BOL* BL1 .... 27 E5 🔢
Carlton Av *BOLS/LL* BL3 .... 45 E5 🔢
   BRAM/HZG SK7 .... 196 B4 🔢
   CHD/CHDH SK8 .... 181 D4
   MPL/ROM SK6 .... 170 B2
   OLDE OL4 .... 80 B2
   PWCH M25 .... 89 F3 🔢
   WHTF M45 .... 70 B2
   WILM/AE SK9 .... 204 A1
Carlton Cl *BOLE* BL2 .... 29 F4 🔢
   WALK M28 .... 83 D4
Carlton Ct *HALE/TIMP* WA15 .... 175 F6
Carlton Crs *STKP* SK1 .... 167 E3 🔢
Carlton Dr *CHD/CHDH* SK8 .... 179 E1 🔢
   PWCH M25 .... 89 F3
Carlton Pl *BRAM/HZG* SK7 .... 185 D6 🔢
   FWTH BL4 .... 66 B2 🔢
Carlton Range *CTN* M18 .... 128 A5 🔢
Carlton Rd *AUL* OL6 .... 113 D2
   BOL BL1 ....
   HALE/TIMP WA15 .... 175 F5
   HTNM SK4 .... 165 E3
   HYDE SK14 .... 132 B6
   OLDTF/WHR M16 .... 123 E6
   SALE M33 .... 139 D5
   SLFD M6 .... 103 F3
   URM M41 .... 138 A2
   WALK M28 .... 83 D4
Carlton St *BOLE* BL2 .... 47 E3
   BURY BL9 .... 53 D1 🔢
   ECC M30 .... 101 F4
   FWTH BL4 .... 66 B2
   OLDTF/WHR M16 .... 123 D5
Carlton Wy *GOL/RIS/CU* WA3 .... 134 A3
   OLD OL1 .... 78 B1
Carlyle Cl *CHH* M8 .... 106 B1
Carlyle St *BURY* BL9 .... 33 F5
Carlyn Av *SALE* M33 .... 140 B6
Carmel Av *SALQ/ORD* M5 .... 123 D1 🔢
Carmel Cl *SALQ/ORD* M5 .... 123 D1 🔢
Carmel Ms *WILM/AE* SK9 .... 203 F1
Carmenna Dr *BRAM/HZG* SK7 .... 197 D2
Carmichael Cl *PART* M31 .... 154 C2
Carmichael St *EDGY/DAV* SK3 .... 166 B5
Carmine Fold *MDTN* M24 .... 75 D1
Carmoor Rd *BRUN/LGST* M13 .... 125 D2
Carnaby St *BKLY* M9 .... 92 A4 🔢
Carna Rd *RDSH* SK5 .... 146 C1
Carnarvon St *BRO* M7 .... 89 F6 🔢
   CSLFD M3 ....
   OLDS OL8 .... 94 C3
   STKP SK1 .... 167 E5 🔢
Carnation Rd *FWTH* BL4 .... 65 E2
   OLDE OL4 .... 97 F1
Carnegie Av *BNG/LEV* M19 .... 145 F1
Carnegie Cl *SALE* M33 .... 158 B2 🔢
Carnforth Av *CHAD* OL9 .... 77 E5
   ROCH OL11 .... 158 E2
   TOT/BURYW BL8 .... 18 B3 🔢
Carnforth Dr *SALE* M33 .... 139 E1 🔢
Carnforth Rd *CHD/CHDH* SK8 .... 181 F3
   HTNM SK4 .... 146 B5
Carnforth Sq *ROCH* OL11 .... 58 B2
Carnforth St *RUSH/FAL* M14 .... 124 C6
Carnoustie Cl *NEWH/MOS* M40 .... 93 D6
   WILM/AE SK9 .... 204 B3 🔢
Carnoustie Dr *CHD/CHDH* SK8 .... 180 A6
   RAMS BL0 .... 6 B6
Carnwood Cl *NEWH/MOS* M40 .... 109 E4
Caroline Dr *ANC* M4 .... 107 D6 🔢
Caroline St *AUL* OL6 .... 113 E4 🔢
   AUL OL6 .... 113 E4 🔢
   BOLS/LL BL3 .... 46 B5
   BRO M7 .... 105 F3 🔢
   EDGY/DAV SK3 .... 166 B5 🔢
   IRL M44 .... 134 C3
   STLY SK15 .... 114 B6
Carpenters La *ANC* M4 .... 3 F2
Carpenters Wk *DROY* M43 .... 128 A1
Carpenters Wy *MILN* OL16 .... 40 C5 🔢
Carradale Dr *SALE* M33 .... 138 A6
Carr Av *PWCH* M25 .... 88 A3
Carr Bank Av *CHH* M8 .... 90 A2
   RAMS BL0 .... 6 C4

Carr Bank Dr *RAMS* BL0 .... 6 C4
Carr Bank Rd *RAMS* BL0 .... 6 C4 🔢
Carrbrook Cl *STLY* SK15 .... 115 F1
Carrbrook Crs *STLY* SK15 .... 115 F1
Carrbrook Dr *OLD* OL1 .... 78 C2
Carrbrook Ter *RAD* M26 .... 52 A5 🔢
Carr Brow *MPL/ROM* SK6 .... 201 E3
Carr Cl *STKP* SK1 .... 167 F5
Carrfield Av *EDGY/DAV* SK3 .... 183 E3
   HALE/TIMP WA15 .... 176 B1
Carr Fold *RAMS* BL0 .... 6 C4 🔢
Carrgate Rd *DTN/ASHW* M34 .... 149 F2
Carrgreen Cl *BNG/LEV* M19 .... 145 D6 🔢
Carrhill Quarry Cl *MOSL* OL5 .... 99 D3 🔢
Carrhill Rd *MOSL* OL5 .... 99 D3
Carr House Rd *OLDE* OL4 .... 81 D4
Carriage Dr *LIT* OL15 .... 12 C4
Carriage St *OLDTF/WHR* M16 .... 123 E4
Carrick Gdns *MDTN* M24 .... 57 D5 🔢
Carrie St *BOL* BL1 .... 45 F1 🔢
Carrigart *PWCH* M25 .... 88 B2
Carrill Gv East *BNG/LEV* M19 .... 145 E2
Carrington Cl *MILN* OL16 .... 24 B2 🔢
Carrington Dr *BOLS/LL* BL3 .... 47 D4 🔢
Carrington Field St *OFTN* SK2 .... 167 D6
Carrington La *SALE* M33 .... 138 C6
Carrington Rd *RUSH/FAL* M14 .... 144 A3
   STKP SK1 .... 167 F3
   URM M41 .... 136 C3
Carrington St *CHAD* OL9 .... 94 C2 🔢
   SWIN M27 .... 86 C4
Carr La *MILN* OL16 .... 43 D1
   WILM/AE SK9 .... 208 B3
Carr Mill Ms *WILM/AE* SK9 .... 203 F2 🔢
Carron Av *BKLY* M9 .... 91 F4
Carron Gv *BOLE* BL2 .... 49 D2
Carr Rd *HALE/TIMP* WA15 .... 175 F5
   IRL M44 .... 135 F1
Carrs Av *CHD/CHDH* SK8 .... 181 E5
Carrsfield Rd *WYTH/NTH* M22 .... 178 C1 🔢
Carrslea Cl *RAD* M26 .... 50 A4 🔢
Carrs Rd *CHD/CHDH* SK8 .... 181 D1
Carr St *AUL* OL6 .... 113 E2
   RAMS BL0 .... 6 C4
   SWIN M27 .... 85 E6
Carrsvale Av *URM* M41 .... 118 C6
Carrswood Rd *NTHM/RTH* M23 .... 160 A5
Carruthers Cl *HEY* OL10 .... 38 A4 🔢
Carruthers St *ANC* M4 .... 107 E6
Carrwood *HALE/TIMP* WA15 .... 189 F2
Carr Wood Av *BRAM/HZG* SK7 .... 196 C1
Carrwood Hey *RAMS* BL0 .... 18 B1
Carr Wood Rd *BRAM/HZG* SK7 .... 182 B6
Carrwood Rd *WILM/AE* SK9 .... 203 D3
Carsdale Rd *WYTH/NTH* M22 .... 192 C2
Carslake Av *BOL* BL1 .... 46 A1
Carslake Rd *NEWH/MOS* M40 .... 107 E2
Carson Rd *BNG/LEV* M19 .... 145 E3
Carstairs Av *EDGY/DAV* SK3 .... 183 E3
Carstairs Cl *CHH* M8 .... 90 A6 🔢
Carter Cl *DTN/ASHW* M34 .... 149 D1 🔢
Carter Pl *HYDE* SK14 .... 131 E4 🔢
Carter St *BOLS/LL* BL3 .... 47 E5
   BRO M7 .... 105 E2 🔢
   FWTH BL4 .... 66 C4 🔢
   HYDE SK14 .... 131 E4
   MOSL OL5 .... 99 D5 🔢
   SALQ/ORD M5 .... 103 D6
   STLY SK15 .... 114 C5 🔢
Carthage St *OLDS* OL8 .... 96 A1
Cartleach Gv *WALK* M28 .... 82 B3 🔢
Cartleach La *WALK* M28 .... 82 A3
Cartmel Av *HTNM* SK4 .... 146 B5
   MILN OL16 .... 42 A3 🔢
Cartmel Cl *BRAM/HZG* SK7 .... 184 A4
   BURY BL9 .... 53 E6
   CHD/CHDH SK8 .... 180 A4
   OLDS OL8 .... 95 E2 🔢
Cartmel Crs *BOLE* BL2 .... 29 D5
   CHAD OL9 .... 94 A3
Cartmel Dr *HALE/TIMP* WA15 .... 176 B1
Cartmel Gv *WALK* M28 .... 84 C6
Cartridge Cl *WYTH/NTH* M22 .... 179 D4 🔢
Cartridge St *HEY* OL10 .... 37 D5
Cartwright Rd *CCHDY* M21 .... 141 D3
Cartwright St *DTN/ASHW* M34 .... 130 A3 🔢
   DTN/ASHW M34 .... 130 A3 🔢
   HYDE SK14 .... 132 B4
Carver Av *PWCH* M25 .... 72 A6
Carver Cl *OLDTF/WHR* M16 .... 122 C4 🔢
Carver Dr *MPL/ROM* SK6 .... 186 C2
Carver Rd *HALE/TIMP* WA15 .... 174 C5
   MPL/ROM SK6 .... 186 C2
Carver St *OLDTF/WHR* M16 .... 122 C4
Cascade Dr *CHH* M8 .... 105 F2 🔢
Cashmere Rd *EDGY/DAV* SK3 .... 166 A6
Caspian Rd *ALT* WA14 .... 173 E1
Cass Av *SALQ/ORD* M5 .... 122 D1 🔢
Cassidy Cl *ANC* M4 .... 3 H1
Cassidy Gdns *MDTN* M24 .... 56 B5 🔢
Casson Ga *WHIT* OL12 .... 29 E4
Casson St *FAIL* M35 .... 94 A6 🔢
Castle Av *DTN/ASHW* M34 .... 148 C1 🔢
   ROCH OL11 .... 39 F1
Castlebrook Cl *BURY* BL9 .... 53 F5 🔢

Castle Cl *DROY* M43 .... 110 C5 🔢
Castle Ct *AUL* OL6 .... 96 C6 🔢
Castle Cft *BOLE* BL2 .... 29 E4 🔢
Castlecroft Rd *BURY* BL9 .... 33 F4
Castledene Av *SLFD* M6 .... 103 F4 🔢
Castle Farm La *OFTN* SK2 .... 184 A2 🔢
Castlefield Av *BRO* M7 .... 89 F5 🔢
Castleford St *OLD* OL1 .... 78 A2 🔢
Castle Gv *TOT/BURYW* BL8 .... 18 B3
Castle Hall Cl *STLY* SK15 .... 114 C6
Castle Hall Ct *STLY* SK15 .... 114 B6 🔢
Castle Hall Vw *STLY* SK15 .... 114 B6
Castle Hill Crs *ROCH* OL11 .... 39 F1 🔢
Castle Hill Rd *BURY* BL9 .... 35 D1
   PWCH M25 .... 89 E3
Castle Hill St *BOLE* BL2 .... 28 C5 🔢
   BOLE BL2 .... 28 C5 🔢
Castlemere Dr *ROY/SHW* OL2 .... 62 B1
Castlemere Rd *BKLY* M9 .... 91 D2
Castlemere St *ROCH* OL11 .... 39 F1
Castlemere Ter *ROCH* OL11 .... 39 F1 🔢
Castle Mill La *HALE/TIMP* WA15 .... 189 D3
Castlemill St *OLD* OL1 .... 79 E4
Castlemoor Av *BRO* M7 .... 88 C5 🔢
Castlerea Cl *ECC* M30 .... 119 E3 🔢
Castlerigg Dr *MDTN* M24 .... 74 A1
   ROY/SHW OL2 .... 60 A3 🔢
Castle Rd *BURY* BL9 .... 54 A5
Castle Shaw Rd *OFTN* SK2 .... 184 B2
Castle St *BOLE* BL2 .... 47 E2
   BURY BL9 .... 19 E5 🔢
   BURY BL9 .... 33 F5 🔢
   CSLFD M3 ....
   ECC M30 .... 102 A5 🔢
   EDGY/DAV SK3 .... 166 C5
   FWTH BL4 .... 66 B4 🔢
   HYDE SK14 .... 132 A6 🔢
   MDTN M24 .... 76 B4 🔢
   STLY SK15 .... 114 B6
Castleton Av *STRET* M32 .... 120 C6
Castleton Dr *MPL/ROM* SK6 .... 201 D3
Castleton Gv *AUL* OL6 .... 114 A1
Castleton Rd *BRAM/HZG* SK7 .... 184 C6
   BRO M7 .... 89 F4
   ROY/SHW OL2 .... 60 A1
   STRET M32 .... 120 B5
Castleton Rd South *ROCH* OL11 .... 39 E4 🔢
Castleton St *ALT* WA14 .... 158 A6 🔢
   BOLE BL2 .... 28 C5
   CHAD OL9 .... 78 A5 🔢
Castleway *HALE/TIMP* WA15 .... 190 A2
   ROCH OL11 .... 38 C5
   SLFD M6 .... 103 F3
Castle Wy *SWIN* M27 .... 86 B3
Castlewood Gdns *OFTN* SK2 .... 184 A2 🔢
Castlewood Rd *BRO* M7 .... 88 A5
Castlewood Sq *BOLE* BL2 .... 29 D6 🔢🔢
Catchdale Cl *BKLY* M9 .... 74 A6 🔢
Catches Cl *ROCH* OL11 .... 21 F5 🔢
Catches La *ROCH* OL11 .... 21 F5 🔢
Cateaton St *BURY* BL9 .... 34 A4
   CSLFD M3 .... 2 D2
Caterham St *ANC* M4 .... 107 E6 🔢
Catford Rd *NTHM/RTH* M23 .... 177 D2
Cathedral Ap *CSLFD* M3 .... 2 D1
Cathedral Cl *DUK* SK16 .... 131 E3 🔢
Cathedral Gates *CSLFD* M3 .... 2 D2 🔢
Cathedral Rd *CHAD* OL9 .... 77 D2
Cathedral St *ANC* M4 .... 2 D2
Catherine Rd *ALT* WA14 .... 174 A4
   CHH M8 .... 89 F4
   MPL/ROM SK6 .... 169 D4
   SWIN M27 .... 85 D6
Catherine St *BRAM/HZG* SK7 .... 184 C5
   BURY BL9 .... 52 C3
   ECC M30 .... 100 B4
   HYDE SK14 .... 131 E6 🔢
   OLDE OL4 .... 80 C5
   OP/CLY M11 .... 127 F2
Catherston Cl *OLDTF/WHR* M16 .... 123 F6 🔢
Cathrine St East *DTN/ASHW* M34 .. 129 F6
Cathrine St West *DTN/ASHW* M34 .. 129 E6
Catlow La *ANC* M4 .... 3 F2 🔢
Catlow St *BRO* M7 .... 105 F3 🔢
Caton Cl *BURY* BL9 .... 52 C1
Caton St *MILN* OL16 .... 40 A1 🔢
Cato St *RAMS* BL0 .... 18 B1 🔢
Catterall Crs *BOLE* BL2 .... 29 E1
Catterick Av *DID/WITH* M20 .... 164 A2
   SALE M33 .... 158 A3
Catterick Dr *BOLS/LL* BL3 .... 49 E6 🔢
Catterick Rd *DID/WITH* M20 .... 164 A2
Catterwood Dr *MPL/ROM* SK6 .... 171 F3 🔢
Cattlin Wy *OLDS* OL8 .... 95 D3
The Causeway *ALT* WA14 .... 174 B3 🔢
   CHAD OL9 .... 76 B6
Causewood Cl *OLDE* OL4 .... 62 C5 🔢
Causey Dr *MDTN* M24 .... 56 B6
Cavanagh Cl *BRUN/LGST* M13 .... 125 E3
Cavan Cl *EDGY/DAV* SK3 .... 165 D6
Cavell St *CMANE* M1 .... 3 G3 🔢
Cavell Wy *SALQ/ORD* M5 .... 104 B6
   SLFD M6 .... 104 B5
Cavendish Av *DID/WITH* M20 .... 143 D5 🔢
   SWIN M27 .... 87 D2

Cavendish Gdns *BOLS/LL* BL3 .... 46 A6
Cavendish Gv *ECC* M30 .... 101 F4 🔟
Cavendish Ms *WILM/AE* SK9 .... 203 E6
Cavendish Pl *OP/CLY* M11 .... 108 B5
Cavendish Rd *ALT* WA14 .... 174 AA
 BRAM/HZG SK7 .... 184 B6
 BRO M7 .... 89 E4
 DID/WITH M20 .... 143 D5
 ECC M30 .... 101 F4
 HTNM SK4 .... 165 D3
 ROCH OL11 .... 39 F4
 STRET M32 .... 121 F5
 URM M41 .... 119 F6 🔟
 WALK M28 .... 100 C1
Cavendish St *AUL* OL6 .... 112 C5
 AULW OL7 .... 112 B4
 CHAD OL9 .... 78 C5 🔟
 HULME M15 .... 124 B2 🔟
 HULME M15 .... 124 B3 🔟
Cavendish Wy *OLD* OL1 .... 78 A1
Cavenham Gv *BOL* BL1 .... 46 A1 🔟
Caversham Dr *BKLY* M9 .... 91 F5 🔟
Cawdor Av *FWTH* BL4 .... 65 F1
Cawdor Ct *FWTH* BL4 .... 66 A1
Cawdor Pl *HALE/TIMP* WA15 .... 176 A1
Cawdor Rd *RUSH/FAL* M14 .... 144 A2
Cawdor St *ECC* M30 .... 101 D6
 FWTH BL4 .... 65 F1
 HULME M15 .... 123 E2 🔟
 SWIN M27 .... 85 E5 🔟
 WALK M28 .... 83 F5 🔟
Cawley Av *PWCH* M25 .... 88 A3
Cawood Sq *RDSH* SK5 .... 148 A5
Caxton Rd *RUSH/FAL* M14 .... 143 F2
Caxton St *CSLFD* M3 .... 2 B2 🔟
 HEY OL10 .... 37 E5 🔟
 ROCH OL11 .... 39 D5 🔟
Caxton Wy *SALQ/ORD* M5 .... 104 C5 🔟
 SALQ/ORD M5 .... 104 C6 🔟
Caygill St *CSLFD* M3 .... 2 B1
Cayley St *ROCH* OL11 .... 23 F6 🔟
Caythorpe St *RUSH/FAL* M14 .... 124 B6
Cayton St *WGTN/LGST* M12 .... 126 B6 🔟
The Ceal *MPL/ROM* SK6 .... 171 F3
Cecil Av *SALE* M33 .... 158 C2
Cecil Dr *URM* M41 .... 136 C1
Cecil Gv *GTN* M18 .... 127 E5 🔟
Cecilia St *BOLS/LL* BL3 .... 47 E5 🔟🔟
Cecil Rd *BKLY* M9 .... 91 E1
 ECC M30 .... 101 F6
 HALE/TIMP WA15 .... 174 C5
 STRET M32 .... 140 A2
Cecil St *AULW* OL7 .... 112 B6 🔟
 BURY BL9 .... 34 A6
 DUK SK16 .... 130 C1
 HULME M15 .... 124 C4
 LIT OL15 .... 12 A6
 MOSL OL5 .... 99 D5
 ROCH OL11 .... 40 A2
 ROY/SHW OL2 .... 60 A5
 STLY SK15 .... 114 C6
 WALK M28 .... 83 E2
Cedar Av *ALT* WA14 .... 174 A3
 AUL OL6 .... 113 E2
 BOLS/LL BL3 .... 67 F1
 BRAM/HZG SK7 .... 184 C5
 HEY OL10 .... 37 D4
 WHTF M45 .... 71 D5
Cedar Dr *POY/DIS* SK12 .... 198 C6 🔟🔟
 RAMS BLO .... 7 D4 🔟
Cedar Crs *CHAD* OL9 .... 77 F5
 RAMS BLO .... 7 D4 🔟
Cedar Dr *DROY* M43 .... 111 D5
 SWIN M27 .... 85 E1
 URM M41 .... 138 A2
Cedar Gv *DTN/ASHW* M34 .... 129 F6
 DUK SK16 .... 132 A1
 FWTH BL4 .... 65 F3
 HTNM SK4 .... 146 A6
 PWCH M25 .... 71 E5
 ROY/SHW OL2 .... 61 F3 🔟
 RUSH/FAL M14 .... 144 B3
Cedar La *MILN* OL16 .... 42 B4
Cedar Ms *AULW* OL7 .... 112 C2 🔟
Cedar Pl *BRO* M7 .... 105 D3
Cedar Rd *CHD/CHDH* SK8 .... 179 E2
 FAIL M35 .... 110 A1
 HALE/TIMP WA15 .... 174 C4
 MDTN M24 .... 76 A3
 MPL/ROM SK6 .... 186 C3
 OFTN SK2 .... 183 F5
 PART M31 .... 154 C2
 SALE M33 .... 158 B5
Cedars Rd *WYTH/NTH* M22 .... 178 B4
Cedar St *AUL* OL6 .... 113 E3
 BURY BL9 .... 34 B4
 HYDE SK14 .... 131 F4 🔟
 OLDE OL4 .... 80 A4
 WHIT OL12 .... 23 D4 🔟
Cedarwood Av *HTNM* SK4 .... 165 E4 🔟
Cedric Rd *CHH* M8 .... 89 F3
 OLDE OL4 .... 80 A4
Cedric St *SALQ/ORD* M5 .... 104 B6 🔟
Celandine Cl *LIT* OL15 .... 12 A5
Celia St *CHH* M8 .... 91 D5
Cellini Sq *BOL* BL1 .... 27 E6 🔟

Celtic St *STKP* SK1 .... 167 E5
Cemetery La *BURY* BL9 .... 53 D1
Cemetery Rd *BOLE* BL2 .... 47 F2
 DROY M43 .... 110 A6
 DTN/ASHW M34 .... 130 A3
 DTN/ASHW M34 .... 149 D2
 FAIL M35 .... 110 A1
 FWTH BL4 .... 67 D2
 MOSL OL5 .... 99 E6
 RAD M26 .... 68 B1
 ROY/SHW OL2 .... 60 A4
 SALQ/ORD M5 .... 103 F6
 SWIN M27 .... 85 F4
Cemetery Rd North *SWIN* M27 .... 85 F3 🔟
Cemetery St *MDTN* M24 .... 75 E2 🔟
Cennick Cl *OLDE* OL4 .... 80 A5
Ceno St *OLD* OL1 .... 79 E2
Centaur Cl *SWIN* M27 .... 86 A3 🔟
Centenary Cl *BOLS/LL* BL3 .... 47 D5
Centenary Wy *SALQ/ORD* M5 .... 102 B6
Central Av *BNG/LEV* M19 .... 145 E1
 BURY BL9 .... 52 B2
 FWTH BL4 .... 65 E3
 LIT OL15 .... 12 C5
 RAMS BLO 7 E1
 SALE M33 .... 158 B4
 SLFD M6 .... 103 F1
 SWIN M27 .... 87 E3
 WALK M28 .... 66 A6 🔟
Central Dr *BRAM/HZG* SK7 .... 182 B5
 CHD/CHDH SK8 .... 194 D1
 MPL/ROM SK6 .... 170 A2 🔟
 RDSH SK5 .... 147 E6
 SWIN M27 .... 86 C6 🔟
 URM M41 .... 138 B1
Central Rd *DID/WITH* M20 .... 143 E6
 MANAIR M90 .... 192 A3
 PART M31 .... 155 D2
Central St *BOL* BL1 .... 46 C2
 CMANW M2 .... 2 D4
 RAMS BLO 6 C5
Central Wy *ALT* WA14 .... 174 B3
Centre Park Rd *BOL* BL1 .... 27 E6
Centre Vale *LIT* OL15 .... 13 D4 🔟
Centurion Gv *BRO* M7 .... 105 F1 🔟
Century Ldg *FWTH* BL4 .... 66 A3
Century St *CSLFD* M3 .... 2 B6
Cestrian St *BOLS/LL* BL3 .... 47 D6 🔟🔟
Ceylon St *NEWH/MOS* M40 .... 108 B1
 OLDE OL4 .... 80 B6 🔟
Chadderton Dr *BURY* BL9 .... 71 E1
Chadderton Hall Rd *CHAD* OL9 .... 77 D2
Chadderton Park Rd *CHAD* OL9 .... 77 D2
 ANC M4 .... 3 C1
Chadderton Wy *CHAD* OL9 .... 78 B3
 OLD OL1 .... 78 A2
Chadkirk Rd *MPL/ROM* SK6 .... 169 F4
Chadvil Rd *CHD/CHDH* SK8 .... 180 A2
Chadwell Rd *OFTN* SK2 .... 168 C6
Chadwick Cl *MILN* OL16 .... 42 B2
 WILM/AE SK9 .... 204 A2 🔟
Chadwick Hall Rd *ROCH* OL11 .... 38 C1 🔟
Chadwick La *HEY* OL10 .... 38 B5
 MILN OL16 .... 41 D5
Chadwick Rd *ECC* M30 .... 101 F5
 URM M41 .... 139 D1
Chadwick St *AUL* OL6 .... 113 F5
 BOLE BL2 .... 47 E3
 BOLS/LL BL3 .... 49 F6
 BURY BL9 .... 35 F3
 MILN OL16 .... 24 B6 🔟
 MPL/ROM SK6 .... 187 D2 🔟
 ROCH OL11 .... 22 B6
 STKP SK1 .... 167 D5
 SWIN M27 .... 86 A5 🔟
Chaffinch Cl *DROY* M43 .... 111 D4 🔟
 OLDE OL4 .... 97 E1
 WYTH/NTH M22 .... 179 D2 🔟
Chaffinch Dr *BURY* BL9 .... 35 D3
Chain Bar La *HYDE* SK14 .... 153 D1
Chain Rd *BKLY* M9 .... 74 B6
Chain St *CMANE* M1 .... 3 E4
Chale Dr *MDTN* M24 .... 76 A5
Chale Gn *BOLE* BL2 .... 29 F4
Chalfont Av *URM* M41 .... 138 C1 🔟
Chalfont Dr *CHH* M8 .... 90 B6 🔟
 WALK M28 .... 83 F5
Chalfont St *BOL* BL1 .... 28 A5 🔟
Chalford Rd *NTHM/RTH* M23 .... 177 E4
Chalium Dr *CHAD* OL9 .... 77 E3
Chamber Hall Cl *OLDS* OL8 .... 95 E1 🔟
Chamberhall St *BURY* BL9 .... 33 F4
Chamber House Dr *ROCH* OL11 .... 38 C3 🔟
Chamberlain Rd *STLY* SK15 .... 115 D2
Chamberlain St *BOLS/LL* BL3 .... 46 B3 🔟
Chamber St *OLDS* OL8 .... 95 D2
 ROY/SHW OL2 .... 61 E2
Chambers Field Ct
 SALQ/ORD M5 .... 104 B6 🔟
Chancel Av *SALQ/ORD* M5 .... 123 D1 🔟
Chancel Cl *DUK* SK16 .... 131 D3 🔟
Chancel La *WILM/AE* SK9 .... 203 F3
Chancellor La *WGTN/LGST* M12 .... 125 E1
Chancel Ms *STKP* SK1 .... 167 E4

Chancel Pl *MILN* OL16 .... 23 D6 🔟
Chancery La *CMANW* M2 .... 2 D4
 ROY/SHW OL2 .... 62 A2 🔟
Chancery St *CHAD* OL9 .... 78 A3
 OLDE OL4 .... 80 A5 🔟
Chandley St *CHD/CHDH* SK8 .... 180 B1 🔟
Chandos Gv *SALQ/ORD* M5 .... 103 E5
Chandos Rd *CCHDY* M21 .... 142 A2
 HTNM SK4 .... 145 F5
 PWCH M25 .... 88 C3 🔟
Chandos Rd South *CCHDY* M21 .... 142 A2
Chandos St *ROY/SHW* OL2 .... 62 A2
Change Wy *CSLFD* M3 .... 105 F4
Channing Sq *MILN* OL16 .... 40 C1 🔟
Channing St *MILN* OL16 .... 40 C1 🔟
The Chanters *WALK* M28 .... 83 D6 🔟
Chantlers Av *TOT/BURYW* BL8 .... 32 B6
Chantry Cl *RDSH* SK5 .... 146 C4 🔟
Chapel Aly *BOL* BL1 .... 47 D2 🔟
Chapel Cl *BURY* BL9 .... 53 F5
 DUK SK16 .... 131 D1
Chapel Ct *ALT* WA14 .... 174 B3
Chapel Cft *ROY/SHW* OL2 .... 60 B5 🔟
Chapel Dr *HALE/TIMP* WA15 .... 190 A2
Chapelfield *RAD* M26 .... 70 A2
Chapelfield Cl *STLY* SK15 .... 115 E3 🔟
Chapelfield Dr *WALK* M28 .... 82 C2
Chapel Field Rd *DTN/ASHW* M34 .... 130 A6
Chapelfield Rd
 WGTN/LGST M12 .... 125 D1 🔟
Chapel Flds *EDGW/EG* BL7 .... 15 D1 🔟
Chapelfield St *BOL* BL1 .... 27 F4
Chapel Ga *MILN* OL16 .... 42 A1
Chapel Gra *EDGW/EG* BL7 .... 15 D1
Chapel Gn *DTN/ASHW* M34 .... 130 A6
Chapel Gv *URM* M41 .... 138 C1
Chapel Hl *LIT* OL15 .... 12 C6 🔟
Chapelhill Dr *BKLY* M9 .... 91 D2
Chapel La *BKLY* M9 .... 90 C2
 HALE/TIMP WA15 .... 189 F1
 PART M31 .... 155 D2
 ROY/SHW OL2 .... 60 B5 🔟
 SALE M33 .... 138 C5
 TOT/BURYW BL8 .... 6 B5
 WILM/AE SK9 .... 203 D5
Chapel Meadow *WALK* M28 .... 82 C6 🔟
Chapel Pl *BOLS/LL* BL3 .... 48 A4
 URM M41 .... 119 E1
Chapel Rd *IRL* M44 .... 135 E1
 OLDS OL8 .... 95 D2
 PWCH M25 .... 88 A4
 SALE M33 .... 139 F6 🔟
 SWIN M27 .... 85 D6
 WILM/AE SK9 .... 209 E4
 WYTH/NTH M22 .... 162 B5
Chapel St *AUL* OL6 .... 113 D4
 BNG/LEV M19 .... 145 E2
 BOL BL1 .... 47 D1 🔟🔟
 BOLS/LL BL3 .... 49 F6 🔟
 BRAM/HZG SK7 .... 184 C4
 BURY BL9 .... 34 A5
 CHD/CHDH SK8 .... 180 B2 🔟
 CSLFD M3 .... 2 A2
 DROY M43 .... 110 C6 🔟
 DUK SK16 .... 130 C1
 ECC M30 .... 101 D6 🔟
 FWTH BL4 .... 66 C3 🔟
 HEY OL10 .... 37 E5 🔟
 HTNM SK4 .... 164 B3 🔟
 HYDE SK14 .... 150 B2
 LIT OL15 .... 13 E1
 MDTN M24 .... 74 A4 🔟
 MOSL OL5 .... 99 D4
 MPL/ROM SK6 .... 149 F6 🔟
 OLDE OL4 .... 80 C5 🔟
 PWCH M25 .... 88 B3 🔟
 ROCH OL11 .... 40 B3 🔟
 ROY/SHW OL2 .... 60 B5
 ROY/SHW OL2 .... 61 F2 🔟
 STLY SK15 .... 114 B5
 SWIN M27 .... 86 B4
 TOT/BURYW BL8 .... 18 A6
 WHIT OL12 .... 11 D4
 WILM/AE SK9 .... 209 E4 🔟
Chapeltown Rd *EDGW/EG* BL7 .... 14 C5
 RAD M26 .... 69 E2
Chapeltown St *CMANE* M1 .... 107 D6
Chapel Vw *DUK* SK16 .... 131 D1
Chapel Wks *CHD/CHDH* SK8 .... 195 F3 🔟
 CMANW M2 .... 2 D5 🔟
Chapelway Gdns *ROY/SHW* OL2 .... 60 B3 🔟
Chaplin Cl *SLFD* M6 .... 103 F3
Chapman Ms *GTN* M18 .... 127 E4 🔟
Chapman Rd *HYDE* SK14 .... 152 C2
Chapman St *BOL* BL1 .... 27 E6 🔟
 GTN M18 .... 127 E3
Chappell Rd *DROY* M43 .... 110 B5
Chappeltown Rd *RAD* M26 .... 69 E2 🔟
Chapter St *NEWH/MOS* M40 .... 108 A3
Charcoal Rd *ALT* WA14 .... 172 C4
Charcoal Woods *ALT* WA14 .... 173 E4 🔟
Chard Dr *WYTH/NTH* M22 .... 178 B6
Chard St *RAD* M26 .... 51 E6
Charfield St *NEWH/MOS* M40 .... 109 E2 🔟
Charges St *AULW* OL7 .... 112 A6 🔟

Chariot St *OP/CLY* M11 127 E1
Charlbury Av *PWCH* M25 89 E2
RDSH SK5 147 D5
Charlbury Wy *ROY/SHW* OL2 61 E4
Charlecote Rd *POY/DIS* SK12 199 D5
Charles Av *DTN/ASHW* M34 128 B2
MPL/ROM SK6 170 A6
Charles Barry Crs *HULME* M15 123 F3 2
Charles Halle Rd *HULME* M15 124 B4
Charles Holden St *BOL* BL1 46 B3 24
Charles La *MILN* OL16 42 B2
Charles Morris Cl *FAIL* M35 94 C5 4
Charles Shaw Cl *OLDE* OL4 80 C2 1
Charles St *AULW* OL7 112 C5 2
BOL BL1 47 D1 11
BRAM/HZG SK7 184 B4 7
BURY BL9 34 A4 9
CHAD OL9 78 A5 3
CMANE M1 3 F6
DROY M43 109 F6 2
DTN/ASHW M34 130 A4
DUK SK16 112 C6
FWTH BL4 66 C2 1
FWTH BL4 66 C4 4
HEY OL10 56 C1 2
IRL M44 134 C5 2
LIT OL15 12 B6
ROY/SHW OL2 60 B5
SLFD M6 104 A3
STKP SK1 167 D6
SWIN M27 85 E4
WHIT OL12 9 E1 2
WHTF M45 71 D4
Charleston Cl *SALE* M33 158 B3
Charleston Sq *URM* M41 118 C6 1
Charleston St *OLDS* OL8 96 A1
Charlestown Rd *BKLY* M9 91 E3
Charlestown Rd East *OFTN* SK2 183 E4
Charlestown Rd West
EDGY/DAV SK3 183 D4
Charles Whittaker St *WHIT* OL12 21 D4 1
Charlesworth Av *BOLS/LL* BL3 65 F1
DTN/ASHW M34 149 D3 1
Charlesworth St *OP/CLY* M11 126 A1
STKP SK1 167 D6 7
Charley Av *BRO* M7 105 E3 3
Charlock Sq *ALT* WA14 157 F5 3
Charlotte St *BOL* BL1 27 F5 16
CHD/CHDH SK8 180 B2
CMANW M2 3 E4 2
EDGW/EG BL7 15 D1
RAMS BL0 6 C6 4
ROCH OL11 40 B3
STKP SK1 167 F2
Charlton Av *ECC* M30 101 E6
HYDE SK14 132 B5
PWCH M25 88 C2
Charlton Dr *SALE* M33 160 A1
SWIN M27 85 E3 2
Charlton Pl *CMANE* M1 124 C2 4
Charlton Rd *BNG/LEV* M19 145 F1 2
Charminster Dr *CHH* M8 90 C5
Charmouth Wk *WYTH/NTH* M22 179 D4
Charnley Cl *NEWH/MOS* M40 107 F5 2
Charnley St *WHTF* M45 71 D3
Charnock Dr *BOL* BL1 27 F6
Charnville Rd *CHD/CHDH* SK8 179 D3
Charnwood Av *DTN/ASHW* M34 128 C6
Charnwood Cl *AUL* OL6 97 D6
ROY/SHW OL2 60 C1
WALK M28 83 D3
Charnwood Crs *BRAM/HZG* SK7 198 B1 1
Charnwood Rd *BKLY* M9 74 B6
MPL/ROM SK6 150 A6
Charter Av *RAD* M26 70 A1
Charter Cl *SALE* M33 158 B2
Charter Rd *HALE/TIMP* WA15 174 C3
Charter St *CSLFD* M3 106 A4
MILN OL16 40 C3
OLD OL1 79 E3
Chartwell Cl *SALQ/ORD* M5 104 A5
Chartwell Dr *NTHM/RTH* M23 160 B6
Chase Briar Wd *CHD/CHDH* SK8 181 F6 3
Chasefield *ALT* WA14 173 E5
Chaseley Rd *SLFD* M6 103 F3
WHIT OL12 22 C5
The Chase *WALK* M28 100 B2 2
Chassen Av *URM* M41 137 F1 1
Chassen Rd *BOL* BL1 45 F2
URM M41 137 F2
Chataway Rd *CHH* M8 90 C5
Chatburn Av *ROCH* OL11 58 B1
Chatburn Gdns *HEY* OL10 36 A5 2
Chatburn Rd *BOL* BL1 26 A4 1
CCHDY M21 142 A3
Chatburn Sq *ROCH* OL11 58 B2
Chatcombe Rd *WYTH/NTH* M22 177 E5
Chatfield Rd *CCHDY* M21 141 F3
Chatford Cl *BRO* M7 105 F3 2
Chatham Gdns *BOLS/LL* BL3 46 B4 15
Chatham Gv *DID/WITH* M20 143 E5
Chatham Rd *GTN* M18 127 F6 2
OLDTF/WHR M16 122 C6
Chatham St *CMANE* M1 3 G4
EDGY/DAV SK3 166 B5
HYDE SK14 150 B4 1
Chatley Rd *ECC* M30 100 A6
Chatley St *CSLFD* M3 106 A3
Chatswood Av *OFTN* SK2 183 D1 3
Chatsworth Av *PWCH* M25 88 C1 1
Chatsworth Cl *BURY* BL9 53 E4 2
DROY M43 109 E4 1
HALE/TIMP WA15 176 A2
ROY/SHW OL2 62 A1
URM M41 138 C1 2
Chatsworth Gv
OLDTF/WHR M16 142 B1 2
Chatsworth Rd *BRAM/HZG* SK7 185 D6
DROY M43 109 F4
ECC M30 102 A3
GTN M18 127 D4 3
MPL/ROM SK6 201 D3
RAD M26 50 C4
STRET M32 120 A6
SWIN M27 100 C2
WILM/AE SK9 208 C1
Chatsworth St *OLDE* OL4 80 A6 1
WHIT OL12 22 C2 2
Chatterton Cl *DID/WITH* M20 144 A5 2
Chatterton Old La *RAMS* BL0 7 D1
Chatterton Rd *RAMS* BL0 7 D1
Chattock Cl *OLDTF/WHR* M16 123 F6 2
Chatton Cl *TOT/BURYW* BL8 32 A5
Chatwood Rd *NEWH/MOS* M40 93 E3
Chaucer Av *DROY* M43 110 B6 2
DTN/ASHW M34 149 E4
RDSH SK5 146 B3
Chaucer Ms *STKP* SK1 167 F4 1
Chaucer Ri *DUK* SK16 132 B2 3
Chaucer Rd *MDTN* M24 75 F1 3
Chaucer St *BOL* BL1 27 E5 33
OLD OL1 78 C5
ROCH OL11 39 D5 4
ROY/SHW OL2 60 C4
Chauncy Rd *NEWH/MOS* M40 93 F5
Chaytor Av *NEWH/MOS* M40 92 C6 2
Cheadle Av *BRO* M7 88 B6 1
Cheadle Old Rd *EDGY/DAV* SK3 166 B6
Cheadle Rd *CHD/CHDH* SK8 180 C3
Cheadle Sq *BOL* BL1 46 C2 8
Cheadle St *OP/CLY* M11 127 E1
Cheadle Wd *CHD/CHDH* SK8 194 C1
Cheam Rd *HALE/TIMP* WA15 159 D5
Cheapside *CMANW* M2 2 D3
HYDE SK14 131 F6 2
Cheap Side *MDTN* M24 75 E1
Cheapside *OLD* OL1 78 C4
Cheddar St *GTN* M18 127 E4 7
Chedlee Dr *CHD/CHDH* SK8 180 C6
Chedlin Dr *NTHM/RTH* M23 177 E3
Chedworth Crs *LHULT* M38 65 E5
Chedworth Dr *NTHM/RTH* M23 177 F1
Cheeryble St *DROY* M43 128 A1 1
OP/CLY M11 128 A2
Cheetham Fold Rd *HYDE* SK14 150 B3 1
Cheetham Hl *ROY/SHW* OL2 61 F3 2
Cheetham Hill Rd *ANC* M4 106 B4 6
CHH M8 106 B1
DUK SK16 131 E3
Cheetham Pl *MPL/ROM* SK6 169 D1 1
Cheetham Rd *SWIN* M27 86 B6
Cheetham St *FAIL* M35 94 B5
MDTN M24 75 D3
MILN OL16 23 D5 3
NEWH/MOS M40 107 F2 2
OLD OL1 79 F4 2
RAD M26 52 A5
ROY/SHW OL2 62 A3
Cheetwood Rd *CHH* M8 106 A2
Cheetwood St *CHH* M8 105 F3 3
Chelbourne Dr *OLDS* OL8 94 C3 4
Chelburn Vw *LIT* OL15 13 D2 1
Chelford Av *BOL* BL1 27 F2
Chelford Cl *HALE/TIMP* WA15 174 C1 3
MDTN M24 76 A1
Chelford Dr *SWIN* M27 85 F3
Chelford Gv *EDGY/DAV* SK3 182 B2
Chelford Rd *OLDTF/WHR* M16 142 A1 4
SALE M33 160 C3
WILM/AE SK9 194 B4
Chellow Dene *MOSL* OL5 98 C4
Chell St *WGTN/LGST* M12 126 A5
Chelmer Gv *HEY* OL10 36 B4
Chelmsford Av
NEWH/MOS M40 108 C3 1
Chelmsford Rd *EDGY/DAV* SK3 166 A5
Chelmsford St *OLDS* OL8 78 C6
Chelsea Av *RAD* M26 50 B5
Chelsea Cl *ROY/SHW* OL2 61 F2
Chelsea Rd *BOLS/LL* BL3 46 A6
NEWH/MOS M40 109 D2
URM M41 136 A2 1
Chelsea St *BURY* BL9 53 D5 1
ROCH OL11 39 E2 1
Chelsfield Gv *CCHDY* M21 142 B3
Chelston Av *NEWH/MOS* M40 93 E3 2
Chelston Dr *CHD/CHDH* SK8 194 A3 1
Cheltenham Crs *BRO* M7 89 F5
Cheltenham Dr *SALE* M33 160 A1
Cheltenham Gn *MDTN* M24 75 E5
Cheltenham Rd *CCHDY* M21 141 F1
EDGY/DAV SK3 165 E6
MDTN M24 75 E5
Cheltenham St *OLD* OL1 79 F2
ROCH OL11 39 E3
SLFD M6 104 B3
Chelwood Dr *DROY* M43 110 A5
Chemist St *BOL* BL1 28 A6
Cheney Cl *OP/CLY* M11 127 E2 1
Chepstow Av *SALE* M33 158 A2
Chepstow Cl *ROCH* OL11 21 D5 2
Chepstow Dr *BRAM/HZG* SK7 185 E5
Chepstow Rd *CCHDY* M21 141 E2 1
SWIN M27 86 B3
Chepstow St *CMANE* M1 2 D6
Chepstow St South *CMANE* M1 2 D6 1
Chequers Rd *CCHDY* M21 141 F3
Cherington Cl *NTHM/RTH* M23 161 F3 1
WILM/AE SK9 195 D6
Cherington Rd *CHD/CHDH* SK8 180 A3
Cheriton Av *SALE* M33 140 A6
Cheriton Cl *HYDE* SK14 152 B1
Cheriton Dr *BOLE* BL2 48 C3
Cheriton Ri *OFTN* SK2 185 E1 1
Cheriton Rd *URM* M41 136 B1
Cherrington Dr *ROCH* OL11 58 B1
Cherry Av *AUL* OL6 112 C1
BURY BL9 35 D4
OLDS OL8 97 D2
Cherry Cl *BURY* BL9 53 E2
Cherrycroft *MPL/ROM* SK6 170 C4
Cherry Dr *SWIN* M27 86 B5
Cherry Gv *ROCH* OL11 21 E5
ROY/SHW OL2 60 A3
STLY SK15 132 B1
Cherry Hall Dr *ROY/SHW* OL2 60 C2 2
Cherry Holt Av *HTNM* SK4 165 D1
Cherry La *SALE* M33 158 A3
Cherry Orchard Cl
BRAM/HZG SK7 182 B6 2
Cherry St *PWCH* M25 72 A6 3
Cherryton Wk *BRUN/LGST* M13 125 D3 1
Cherry Tree Av *FWTH* BL4 65 E3 1
POY/DIS SK12 199 D6
Cherry Tree Cl *HALE/TIMP* WA15 175 F2 1
MPL/ROM SK6 170 C3
WILM/AE SK9 204 C3 4
Cherry Tree Ct *OFTN* SK2 184 A3 2
Cherry Tree Dr *BRAM/HZG* SK7 199 E1
Cherry Tree La *MPL/ROM* SK6 170 C3
OFTN SK2 184 A2
TOT/BURYW BL8 33 D6
Cherry Tree Rd *CHD/CHDH* SK8 181 D6
NTHM/RTH M23 161 D4
Cherry Tree Wk *STRET* M32 139 F2
Cherry Tree Wy *BOLE* BL2 28 C3
Cherry Wk *CHD/CHDH* SK8 196 A1
Cherrywood *CHAD* OL9 76 B4 2
Cherrywood Cl *WALK* M28 82 C5 3
Chertsey Cl *GTN* M18 127 F4 3
ROY/SHW OL2 61 F1 3
Cherwell Av *HEY* OL10 36 B4
Cherwell Cl *CHD/CHDH* SK8 195 E2
OLDS OL8 95 D4
WHTF M45 71 E3 3
Chesham Av *BOL* BL1 27 F5 17
ROCH OL11 58 B2
URM M41 117 F6
WYTH/NTH M22 178 A3
Chesham Cl *WILM/AE* SK9 209 D1
Chesham Crs *BURY* BL9 34 B4 6
BURY BL9 34 B4 6
Chesham Fold Rd *BURY* BL9 34 C4
Chesham Pl *ALT* WA14 174 A5
Chesham Rd *BURY* BL9 34 C2
ECC M30 119 D1 4
OLDE OL4 80 A5 2
WILM/AE SK9 209 D1
Cheshire Cl *STRET* M32 139 F2
Cheshire Ct *RAMS* BL0 7 E5
Cheshire Ring Canal Wk
ALT WA14 172 C2
MPL/ROM SK6 149 F5
MPL/ROM SK6 171 D5
Cheshire Rd *PART* M31 154 B3 1
STLY SK15 115 E2
Cheshire Sq *STLY* SK15 115 F2
The Cheshires *MOSL* OL5 99 E4
Cheshire St *MOSL* OL5 99 E5
Chesney Av *CHAD* OL9 93 F3
Chesshyre Av *ANC* M4 107 E6 5
Chessington Ri *SWIN* M27 86 B2
Chester Av *BOLS/LL* BL3 49 F5
DUK SK16 131 F2
HALE/TIMP WA15 175 D5
ROCH OL11 38 B1
SALE M33 157 F4
STLY SK15 115 E4
URM M41 119 F6 2
WHTF M45 71 E4
Chester Cl *BOLS/LL* BL3 49 F5 2
IRL M44 134 B6 3
WILM/AE SK9 204 C1
Chester Dr *RAMS* BL0 18 B1
Chesterfield Gv *AUL* OL6 113 E4

Chesterfield St *OLDE* OL4 .... **79** F5 🔟
Chestergate *EDGY/DAV* SK3 ..... **166** C4 🔟
  STKP SK1 .... **166** C4
Chester Rd *BRAM/HZG* SK7 .... **197** D6
  HULME M15 .... **123** F2
  OLDTF/WHR M16 .... **122** B4
  POY/DIS SK12 .... **197** F5
  STRET M32 .... **121** F5
Chester St *BURY* BL9 .... **34** B3 🔟🔟
  CHAD OL9 .... **78** A6
  DTN/ASHW M34 .... **149** D1
  EDGY/DAV SK3 .... **166** B4 🔟
  HULME M15 .... **124** A2
  PWCH M25 .... **71** E6
  SWIN M27 .... **85** F6
Chesterton Dr *BOLS/LL* BL3 .... **44** C4
Chesterton Gv *DROY* M43 .... **110** B5
Chesterton Rd *NTHM/RTH* M23 .. **160** B5
Chester Wks *MPL/ROM* SK6 ...... **169** E4
Chestnut Av *BURY* BL9 .... **34** C5
  CCHDY M21 .... **141** E5 🔟
  CHD/CHDH SK8 .... **180** C2
  DROY M43 .... **109** F4
  IRL M44 .... **134** B6
  TOT/BURYW BL8 .... **32** B2
  WALK M28 .... **83** E3
  WHTF M45 .... **71** D4 🔟
Chestnut Cl *BOLS/LL* BL3 ...... **45** F5 🔟🔟
  OLDE OL4 .... **80** B3
  STLY SK15 .... **132** B1
  WILM/AE SK9 .... **204** C3 🔟
Chestnut Crs *OLDS* OL8 .... **96** B3
Chestnut Dr *POY/DIS* SK12 ...... **199** D6
  SALE M33 .... **158** B4
Chestnut Fold *RAD* M26 .... **51** E5
  RAD M26 .... **69** D3 🔟
Chestnut Gdns *DTN/ASHW* M34 .. **148** C1
Chestnut Gv *FAIL* M35 .... **110** A1 🔟
Chestnut Rd *ECC* M30 .... **100** B3
Chestnut St *CHAD* OL9 .... **94** A2
Chestnut Wy *LIT* OL15 .... **11** F6
Chesworth Fold *STKP* SK1 ...... **167** D5 🔟
Chetham St *SALO/ORD* M5 ...... **122** C2 🔟
Chetwyn Av *EDGW/EG* BL7 ...... **14** B6
  ROY/SHW OL2 .... **60** A5
Chetwynd Av *URM* M41 .... **138** A2 🔟
Chetwynd Cl *SALE* M33 .... **138** C5 🔟
Chevassut St *HULME* M15 .... **123** F3
Chevington Dr *BKLY* M9 .... **107** E1
  HTNM SK4 .... **164** B2
Cheviot Av *CHD/CHDH* SK8 ...... **181** D5
  OLDS OL8 .... **95** F2
  ROY/SHW OL2 .... **60** A6 🔟
Cheviot Cl *BOL* BL1 .... **27** E2
  CHAD OL9 .... **77** E6 🔟
  HTNM SK4 .... **166** B2 🔟
  MDTN M24 .... **76** B3
  MILN OL16 .... **25** E6
  RAMS BL0 .... **19** D1
  SLFD M6 .... **103** F4 🔟
  TOT/BURYW BL8 .... **32** B4
Cheviot Rd *BRAM/HZG* SK7 ...... **183** F6
Cheviots Rd *ROY/SHW* OL2 .... **61** E1
Cheviot St *CSLFD* M3 .... **106** A4
Chevithorne Cl *ALT* WA14 .... **173** F2 🔟
Chevril Cl *HULME* M15 .... **124** B3 🔟
Chevron Cl *ROCH* OL11 .... **38** C4
  SALO/ORD M5 .... **104** C5 🔟
Chevron Pl *ALT* WA14 .... **158** B6 🔟
Chew V *DUK* SK16 .... **132** A2
Chicago Av *MANAIR* M90 .... **191** F2 🔟
Chichester Cl *LIT* OL15 .... **25** D2
  SALE M33 .... **158** B2
Chichester Crs *CHAD* OL9 .... **77** D2 🔟
Chichester Rd *HULME* M15 .... **123** F4
  MPL/ROM SK6 .... **170** A3 🔟
Chichester St *MILN* OL16 .... **23** E6
Chidwall Rd *WYTH/NTH* M22 .... **177** F5
Chief St *OLDE* OL4 .... **79** E5
Chiffon Wy *CSLFD* M3 .... **105** E4
Chigwell Cl *WYTH/NTH* M22 .. **178** C2 🔟
Chilcote Av *SALE* M33 .... **158** B1
Childwall Cl *BOLS/LL* BL3 ...... **64** C1 🔟
Chilham Rd *ECC* M30 .... **102** A3
  WALK M28 .... **83** F3
Chilham St *SWIN* M27 .... **101** F1 🔟
Chilmark Dr *NTHM/RTH* M23 .. **177** F1 🔟
Chiltern Av *URM* M41 .... **118** A6 🔟
Chiltern Cl *BRAM/HZG* SK7 ...... **183** F6
  RAMS BL0 .... **19** D1 🔟
  ROY/SHW OL2 .... **61** D1 🔟
  WALK M28 .... **83** F5
Chiltern Dr *BOLE* BL2 .... **48** A2
  HALE/TIMP WA15 .... **175** D5
  OFTN SK2 .... **183** E3
  ROY/SHW OL2 .... **60** A5 🔟
  SWIN M27 .... **102** A1
  TOT/BURYW BL8 .... **32** C3
Chiltern Gdns *SALE* M33 .... **160** A5
Chiltern Rd *RAMS* BL0 .... **19** D1
Chilton Av *CHAD* OL9 .... **77** E5
Chilton Dr *MDTN* M24 .... **76** A4
Chilworth St *RUSH/FAL* M14 .. **143** F1 🔟
Chime Bank *CHH* M8 .... **107** D1
China La *CMANE* M1 .... **3** G4 🔟

Chinley Av *NEWH/MOS* M40 ...... **92** B5 🔟
  STRET M32 .... **120** B5 🔟
Chinley Cl *BRAM/HZG* SK7 ...... **182** C4
  HTNM SK4 .... **165** F2
  SALE M33 .... **160** B2
Chinley St *SLFD* M6 .... **104** C2
Chinwell Vw *BNG/LEV* M19 .... **145** E2 🔟
Chip Hill Rd *BOLS/LL* BL3 .... **45** E5
Chippendale Pl *AUL* OL6 .... **113** F2 🔟
Chippenham Av *OFTN* SK2 ...... **168** B6 🔟
Chippenham Rd *ANC* M4 .... **107** D5
Chipping Fold *MILN* OL16 .... **42** A2 🔟
Chipping Fold *BOL* BL1 .... **26** A5
Chipstead Av *WGTN/LGST* M12 .. **125** F4 🔟
Chirmside St *TOT/BURYW* BL8 .. **32** C6 🔟
Chiseldon Av *WTH/NTH* M22 .. **178** C5
Chiselhurst St *CHH* M8 .... **90** B6
Chisholme Cl *TOT/BURYW* BL8 .. **18** A3 🔟
Chisholm St *OP/CLY* M11 .... **127** E2
Chisledon Av *CHH* M8 .... **106** A1 🔟
Chislehurst Av *URM* M41 .... **119** D6
Chislehurst Cl *TOT/BURYW* BL8 .. **32** C6 🔟
Chiswick Dr *BOLS/LL* BL3 .... **49** F4
Chiswick Rd *DID/WITH* M20 .. **164** A2 🔟
Chisworth Cl *BRAM/HZG* SK7 .. **182** C4 🔟
Chisworth St *BOLE* BL2 .... **28** C4 🔟
Choir St *BRO* M7 .... **105** F3
Chokeberry Cl *ALT* WA14 ...... **157** F5 🔟
Cholmondeley Av *ALT* WA14 .. **158** C5 🔟
Cholmondeley Rd *SLFD* M6 .... **102** C3
Choral Gv *BRO* M7 .... **105** E2
Chorley Cl *TOT/BURYW* BL8 .... **32** A6 🔟
Chorley Hall Cl *WILM/AE* SK9 .. **209** D4 🔟
Chorley Hall La *WILM/AE* SK9 .. **209** D4
Chorley New Rd *BOL* BL1 .... **44** C2
Chorley Old Rd *BOL* BL1 .... **26** B6
Chorley Rd *SALE* M33 .... **160** C3
  SWIN M27 .... **85** F4
Chorley St *BOL* BL1 .... **46** C1
  STRET M32 .... **122** A5
Chorley Wood Av *BNG/LEV* M19 .. **145** D5 🔟
Choriton Dr *CHD/CHDH* SK8 .... **180** D2
Choriton Fold *ECC* M30 .... **101** E2
Choriton Gv *STKP* SK1 .... **167** F6
Choriton Rd *HULME* M15 .... **123** E3
  OLDTF/WHR M16 .... **123** E4
Choriton St *CMANE* M1 .... **3** F4
  OLDTF/WHR M16 .... **123** D4
Chretien Rd *WYTH/NTH* M22 .. **162** B3
Christchurch Av *SALO/ORD* M5 .. **104** C5 🔟
Christ Church Cl *BOLE* BL2 ...... **30** A5 🔟
Christ Church La *BOLE* BL2 ...... **30** A4
Christchurch Rd *SALE* M33 .... **138** A6
Christie Rd *STRET* M32 .... **121** F6
Christine St *ROY/SHW* OL2 ...... **61** F2
Christleton Av *HTNM* SK4 ...... **146** B6
Christopher Acre *ROCH* OL11 .... **20** C4 🔟
Christopher St *NEWH/MOS* M40 .. **109** E3 🔟
  SALO/ORD M5 .... **104** C6 🔟
Chronnell Dr *BOLE* BL2 .... **48** C1
Chudleigh Cl *ALT* WA14 .... **173** F1 🔟
  BRAM/HZG SK7 .... **183** E4
Chudleigh Rd *CHH* M8 .... **90** B3
Chulsey St *BOLS/LL* BL3 .... **45** F5 🔟
Church Av *BOLS/LL* BL3 .... **46** A5
  DTN/ASHW M34 .... **149** E3
  HYDE SK14 .... **151** D3
  MDTN M24 .... **58** B3
  NEWH/MOS M40 .... **109** D2 🔟
  SLFD M6 .... **105** E5
Church Bank *BOL* BL1 .... **47** D2
Churchbank *STLY* SK15 .... **115** E5 🔟
Church Brow *ALT* WA14 .... **150** B2
  HYDE SK14 .... **150** D2
Church Cl *RAD* M26 .... **67** F3 🔟
  RAMS BL0 .... **6** C6 🔟
Church Ct *DUK* SK16 .... **112** C6 🔟
Church Cft *BURY* BL9 .... **53** F5
Church Dr *PWCH* M25 .... **88** A1
Churchfield Rd *SLFD* M6 .... **103** E2 🔟
Churchfields *ALT* WA14 .... **173** F6
  DTN/ASHW M34 .... **129** F2
  SALE M33 .... **138** B5
Churchgate *BOL* BL1 .... **47** D2
  STKP SK1 .... **167** D4
  URM M41 .... **138** C2
Churchgate Buildings
  CMANE M1 .... **125** D1 🔟
Church Gn *RAD* M26 .... **52** B5 🔟
Church Gv *BRAM/HZG* SK7 .... **184** C5
Churchill Av *BOLE* BL2 .... **31** E6 🔟
Churchill Cl *HEY* OL10 .... **56** C1 🔟
Churchill Crs *MPL/ROM* SK6 .... **170** B6
  RDSH SK5 .... **146** C2
Churchill Dr *BOLS/LL* BL3 .... **50** A6
Churchill Rd *ALT* WA14 .... **158** B6
Churchill St *BOLE* BL2 .... **48** A2 🔟🔟
  HTNM SK4 .... **166** B2
  OLDE OL4 .... **79** E5
  WHIT OL12 .... **22** A4
Churchill St East *OLDE* OL4 .... **79** E5
Churchill Wy *SLFD* M6 .... **105** B5
  TRPK M17 .... **121** D2
Church La *BKLY* M9 .... **91** E5

Churchley Cl *EDGY/DAV* SK3 .. **181** E1
Churchley Rd *EDGY/DAV* SK3 .. **165** E6 🔟
Church Meadow *BURY* BL9 ...... **54** A5 🔟
  HYDE SK14 .... **131** D6
Church Mdw *BOLE* BL2 .... **30** A4
Church Ms *DTN/ASHW* M34 .... **129** F6 🔟
Church Rd *BOL* BL1 .... **26** C5
  CHD/CHDH SK8 .... **179** E2
  CHD/CHDH SK8 .... **195** F2
  ECC M30 .... **102** A5
  FWTH BL4 .... **66** C3
  HTNM SK4 .... **166** C3
  MDTN M24 .... **76** B3 🔟
  MILN OL16 .... **40** C1
  RAD M26 .... **67** E3
  RAMS BL0 .... **7** F5
  ROY/SHW OL2 .... **61** F3
  SALE M33 .... **160** B1 🔟
  URM M41 .... **137** C2
  URM M41 .... **138** B2 🔟
  WALK M28 .... **83** E2
  WILM/AE SK9 .... **194** B6
  WILM/AE SK9 .... **208** C1
  WYTH/NTH M22 .... **162** B4
Church Rd East *SALE* M33 ...... **160** B1 🔟
Church Rd West *SALE* M33 .... **160** B1 🔟
Churchside *FWTH* BL4 .... **65** F4 🔟
Churchside Cl *BKLY* M9 .... **91** E3 🔟
Church Stile *MILN* OL16 .... **23** D6
Churchston Av *BRAM/HZG* SK7 .. **185** E5
Church St *ALT* WA14 .... **174** B2 🔟
  ANC M4 .... **3** F2
  AUL OL6 .... **112** C5
  BOLE BL2 .... **29** E2
  BOLE BL2 .... **31** D6
  BOLS/LL BL3 .... **49** D6
  BURY BL9 .... **34** B4
  CHD/CHDH SK8 .... **180** B1 🔟
  CSLFD M3 .... **105** E5 🔟
  DROY M43 .... **110** B6
  DTN/ASHW M34 .... **130** A2
  DUK SK16 .... **120** C6
  ECC M30 .... **101** F5
  FAIL M35 .... **94** A5
  FWTH BL4 .... **66** C4 🔟
  HEY OL10 .... **37** E5
  HTNM SK4 .... **166** C2 🔟
  HYDE SK14 .... **133** F5
  LIT OL15 .... **12** C6
  MDTN M24 .... **75** E1 🔟
  MILN OL16 .... **11** G6
  MILN OL16 .... **42** C3
  MPL/ROM SK6 .... **149** E6 🔟
  MPL/ROM SK6 .... **187** D1 🔟
  MPL/ROM SK6 .... **187** E2 🔟
  OLD OL1 .... **79** D4
  OLDE OL4 .... **80** C3
  RAMS BL0 .... **7** D5 🔟
  ROCH OL11 .... **22** C6
  ROY/SHW OL2 .... **60** B5
  STLY SK15 .... **114** B5
  STRET M32 .... **140** A2
  SWIN M27 .... **85** F5 🔟
  SWIN M27 .... **86** C5 🔟
  TOT/BURYW BL8 .... **32** A2
  WHIT OL12 .... **9** D3 🔟
  WILM/AE SK9 .... **203** F4
Church St East *OLDE* OL4 .... **80** C3
  RAD M26 .... **52** A6
Church Ter West *RAD* M26 ...... **51** F6
Church Ter *MILN* OL16 .... **42** B2 🔟
  WILM/AE SK9 .... **194** B5
Churchtown Av *BOLE* BL2 ...... **49** D2 🔟
Church Vw *HYDE* SK14 .... **150** B2 🔟
  IRL M44 .... **135** E1 🔟
  WHIT OL12 .... **20** C3 🔟
Church Wk *FWTH* BL4 .... **66** A3 🔟
  STLY SK15 .... **114** B4
  SWIN M27 .... **86** A1
Churchwood Rd *DID/WITH* M20 .. **163** F2 🔟
Churnet St *NEWH/MOS* M40 .. **107** E2
Churston Av *BKLY* M9 .... **91** F1
Churton Av *SALE* M33 .... **158** C3
Churton Rd *GTN* M18 .... **127** D6
Churwell Av *HTNM* SK4 .... **165** D1 🔟
Cicero St *BKLY* M9 .... **91** F5 🔟
  OLD OL1 .... **79** D2
Cinamon St *WHIT* OL12 .... **22** B5 🔟
Cinder Hill La *OLD* OL1 .... **59** E6
Cinder St *ANC* M4 .... **107** D5 🔟
Cinnabar Dr *MDTN* M24 .... **75** D1
Cipher St *ANC* M4 .... **107** D4 🔟
Circle South *TRPK* M17 .... **121** F3

The Circuit CHD/CDH SK8 .... 195 E2
  DID/WITH M20 .... 143 F6
  EDGY/DAV SK3 .... 182 A1
  WILM/AE SK9 .... 202 B6
Circus St CMANE M1 .... 3 G4 🔟
Cirencester Cl LHULT M38 .... 65 E5 🔽
Ciss La URM M41 .... 138 C1
Citrus Wy SLFD M6 .... 104 B5
City Av DTN/ASHW M34 .... 148 C1
City Rd HULME M15 .... 123 E3
  WALK M28 .... 82 B5
City Rd East HULME M15 .... 124 A2
City Wk SWIN M27 .... 86 C5
Clague St OP/CLY M11 .... 108 B5
Claife Av NEWH/MOS M40 .... 92 C3 🔟
Clammerclough Rd FWTH BL4 .... 67 D3 🔟
Clandon Av ECC M30 .... 100 C5
Clapgate MPL/ROM SK6 .... 169 E4 🔟
Clapgate Rd ROCH OL11 .... 20 C4 🔽
Clapham St NEWH/MOS M40 .... 93 D5
Clara St CHAD OL9 .... 95 D1
  ROCH OL11 .... 40 A2
  WHIT OL12 .... 9 E2
Clare Av WILM/AE SK9 .... 194 A6
Clare Cl TOT/BURYW BL8 .... 33 E1
Claremont Av ALT WA14 .... 158 B5
  DID/WITH M20 .... 143 E6 🔽
  HTNM SK4 .... 146 A6
  MPL/ROM SK6 .... 186 A1
Claremont Dr ALT WA15 .... 158 B5
  LHULT M38 .... 65 F6
Claremont Gv DID/WITH M20 .... 165 E2
  HALE/TIMP WA15 .... 174 C4
Claremont Range GTN M18 .... 128 A5 🔟
Claremont Rd CHD/CHDH SK8 .... 195 E1
  MILN OL16 .... 41 F2
  OFTN SK2 .... 183 F3
  OLDTF/WHR M16 .... 124 A6
  ROCH OL11 .... 22 A6 🔟
  RUSH/FAL M14 .... 124 A6
  SALE M33 .... 139 F6
  SLFD M6 .... 103 D2
Claremont St AUL OL6 .... 113 E3 🔟
  CHAD OL9 .... 78 A2 🔽
  FAIL M35 .... 94 A5 🔟
  OLDS OL8 .... 96 A3
Clarence Av OLDS OL8 .... 95 E1
  TRPK M17 .... 120 A3
  WHTF M45 .... 71 E4 🔽
Clarence Ct BOL BL1 .... 46 C1 🔟
  WILM/AE SK9 .... 203 E5
Clarence Rd AUL OL6 .... 113 D3
  BRUN/LGST M13 .... 125 F6
  HALE/TIMP WA15 .... 175 D4
  HTNM SK4 .... 145 F6
  SWIN M27 .... 85 D6 🔽
Clarence St BOL BL1 .... 47 D1
  BRO M7 .... 105 E3
  CMANW M2 .... 2 D4 🔟
  FWTH BL4 .... 66 C2
  HYDE SK14 .... 131 F5
  ROY/SHW OL2 .... 61 E6
  STLY SK15 .... 113 F6
  WHIT OL12 .... 22 B5 🔟
Clarendon Av HALE/TIMP WA15 .... 174 C2
  HTNM SK4 .... 165 F2 🔽
Clarendon Crs ECC M30 .... 102 A4
  SALE M33 .... 140 B6
Clarendon Gv BOLE BL2 .... 47 F3
Clarendon Pl HYDE SK14 .... 150 B1
Clarendon Rd BOLE BL2 .... 48 A2 🔟
  BRAM/HZG SK7 .... 185 D4
  DTN/ASHW M34 .... 128 B2
  ECC M30 .... 102 A5 🔟
  HYDE SK14 .... 131 E6
  IRL M44 .... 134 C4
  OLDTF/WHR M16 .... 142 A1
  SALE M33 .... 160 B1
  SWIN M27 .... 86 A5
  URM M41 .... 117 F6 🔽
Clarendon Rd West CCHDY M21 .... 141 F1
Clarendon St BOLS/LL BL3 .... 46 C5
  BURY BL9 .... 34 B3
  DUK SK16 .... 130 B1
  HULME M15 .... 124 A3
  HYDE SK14 .... 131 E6
  HYDE SK14 .... 150 B1 🔟
  MILN OL16 .... 40 C3
  MOSL OL5 .... 99 E5 🔟
  RDSH SK5 .... 167 D2 🔟
  WHTF M45 .... 71 D3 🔟
Clare Rd BNG/LEV M19 .... 143 E1
  RDSH SK5 .... 167 D1 🔟
Clare St CMANE M1 .... 124 C2 🔽
  DTN/ASHW M34 .... 129 F5
  SALQ/ORD M5 .... 105 D6 🔟
Claribel St OP/CLY M11 .... 125 F1
Claridge Rd CCHDY M21 .... 141 E2
Clarion St ANC M4 .... 107 D4
Clark Av GTN M18 .... 127 F4
Clarke Av SALQ/ORD M5 .... 122 C2 🔟
Clarke Brow MDTN M24 .... 75 E2

Clarke Crs HALE/TIMP WA15 .... 175 F4
  LHULT M38 .... 64 D5 🔟
Clarkes Cft BURY BL9 .... 35 D4
Clarke's La WHIT OL12 .... 22 B5
Clarke St AULW OL7 .... 130 A1 🔟
  BOL BL1 .... 46 A1 🔢
  HEY OL10 .... 37 E5 🔽
  MILN OL16 .... 23 F3
Clarksfield Rd OLDE OL4 .... 80 A5
Clarksfield St OLDE OL4 .... 80 B5 🔟
Clarkson Cl DTN/ASHW M34 .... 148 B1
Clark Wy HYDE SK14 .... 131 E6
Clarkwell Cl CHAD OL9 .... 78 C3 🔟
Class St OP/CLY M11 .... 108 A6 🔟
Claude Av SWIN M27 .... 85 F5
Claude Rd CCHDY M21 .... 141 E4
Claude St CHH M8 .... 90 B4
  ECC M30 .... 100 C3
  SWIN M27 .... 85 F5 🔟
Claudia Sq STLY SK15 .... 115 F2 🔟
Claughton Av BOLE BL2 .... 49 D2
  WALK M28 .... 83 D5
Claughton Rd TOT/BURYW BL8 .... 32 A2
Claverton Rd NTHM/RTH M23 .... 176 C3
Claxton Av BKLY M9 .... 91 E2
Clay Bank DROY M43 .... 109 F6 🔟
Claybank Dr TOT/BURYW BL8 .... 17 F6
Clay Bank St HEY OL10 .... 37 D4
Claybar Dr ECC M30 .... 101 F4 🔽
Claycourt Av ECC M30 .... 100 C3 🔟
Claydon Dr BOLS/LL BL3 .... 49 F4
Clayfield Dr ROCH OL11 .... 21 D5
Claygate Dr BKLY M9 .... 74 B6
Clay La HALE/TIMP WA15 .... 176 A3
  NTHM/RTH M23 .... 177 D3
  ROCH OL11 .... 20 C5
  WILM/AE SK9 .... 194 A4
Claymere Av ROCH OL11 .... 20 C5
Claymore St BOLS/LL BL3 .... 47 D6 🔢
  GTN M18 .... 127 F5
Clay St EDGW/EG BL7 .... 14 B6 🔟
  EDGW/EG BL7 .... 14 B6 🔽
  LIT OL15 .... 12 A6 🔟
  OLDS OL8 .... 95 F1
Clayton Av BOLS/LL BL3 .... 47 F4
  DID/WITH M20 .... 163 F2
Claytonbrook Rd OP/CLY M11 .... 109 D6
Clayton Cl HULME M15 .... 123 F4
  TOT/BURYW BL8 .... 32 A6 🔟
Clayton Hall Rd OP/CLY M11 .... 109 D5 🔽
Clayton La OP/CLY M11 .... 126 C1
Clayton La South OP/CLY M11 .... 126 B2
Claytons Cl OLDE OL4 .... 81 D4
Clayton St BOLS/LL BL3 .... 47 F4
  CHAD OL9 .... 94 B2 🔽
  DTN/ASHW M34 .... 149 D1 🔽
  DUK SK16 .... 131 E1 🔽
  FAIL M35 .... 94 A6 🔽
  OP/CLY M11 .... 108 C4
  WHIT OL12 .... 23 F3 🔟
Cleadon Av GTN M18 .... 127 D5
Cleadon Dr South
  TOT/BURYW BL8 .... 33 D2 🔟
Cleavley St ECC M30 .... 100 C5 🔟
Clee Av BRUN/LGST M13 .... 145 D1
Cleethorpes Av BKLY M9 .... 90 C2 🔟
Cleeve Rd NTHM/RTH M23 .... 161 E3
  OLDE OL4 .... 80 A5
Cleeve Wy CHD/CHDH SK8 .... 195 E5
Clegg Hall Rd MILN OL16 .... 24 B3
Clegg Pl AUL OL6 .... 113 E5
Clegg's Buildings BOL BL1 .... 46 C1 🔟🔟
Clegg's La LHULT M38 .... 65 F5
Clegg St BOLE BL2 .... 48 A2
  DROY M43 .... 110 A6 🔟
  LIT OL15 .... 12 A4
  MILN OL16 .... 42 B2 🔽
  MPL/ROM SK6 .... 169 E2 🔽
  OLD OL1 .... 79 D5
  OLDE OL4 .... 79 D5
  OLDE OL4 .... 81 E5 🔟
  ROY/SHW OL2 .... 61 D1
  WHIT OL12 .... 9 D1 🔟
  WHTF M45 .... 71 D4
Cleggswood Av LIT OL15 .... 25 E2
Cleiland St FWTH BL4 .... 66 C4 🔟
Clementina St WHIT OL12 .... 23 D4 🔟
  WHIT OL12 .... 23 D4 🔟
Clementine Cl SLFD M6 .... 104 C5 🔽
Clement Rd MPL/ROM SK6 .... 171 F6
Clement Royds St WHIT OL12 .... 22 C5 🔟
Clement Scott Cl BKLY M9 .... 92 A1 🔟
Clement St BRO M7 .... 106 C2 🔟
  HTNM SK4 .... 166 C2 🔟
Clemnson St CSLFD M3 .... 105 E5 🔟
Clemshaw Cl HEY OL10 .... 37 D6
Clerewood Av CHD/CHDH SK8 .... 193 F2 🔟
Clerke St BURY BL9 .... 34 A5 🔟
Clevedon Av URM M41 .... 139 E1
Clevedon Rd CHAD OL9 .... 77 E2
Clevedon St BKLY M9 .... 91 F6
Cleveland Av BNG/LEV M19 .... 145 F1 🔟
  HYDE SK14 .... 150 A1 🔽
  SLFD M6 .... 102 C4

Cleveland Cl RAMS BL0 .... 19 D2 🔟
Cleveland Dr MILN OL16 .... 42 C1
Cleveland Gdns BOLS/LL BL3 .... 45 F5 🔢
Cleveland Gv ROY/SHW OL2 .... 60 A6 🔽
Cleveland Rd CHH M8 .... 90 C2
  HALE/TIMP WA15 .... 175 D4
  HTNM SK4 .... 165 E1
Cleveland St BOLS/LL BL3 .... 45 F5 🔢
Cleveleys Av BOLE BL2 .... 48 A1
  BURY BL9 .... 52 C1 🔟
  CCHDY M21 .... 142 A4 🔟
  CHD/CHDH SK8 .... 179 F6
  MILN OL16 .... 43 E2
Cleveleys Gv BRO M7 .... 89 F6 🔟
Cleves Ct HEY OL10 .... 37 D6 🔽
Clevlands Cl ROY/SHW OL2 .... 61 E1 🔽
Cleworth Rd MDTN M24 .... 75 D1
Cleworth St HULME M15 .... 123 E4 🔟
Cliburn St CHH M8 .... 106 C1
Clifden Dr WYTH/NTH M22 .... 178 C5
Cliff Av BRO M7 .... 105 D1
  BURY BL9 .... 19 E3
  TOT/BURYW BL8 .... 17 F6
Cliff Crs BRO M7 .... 89 E6
Cliff Dl STLY SK15 .... 132 A1
Cliffdale Dr CHH M8 .... 90 B4 🔟
Cliffe St LIT OL15 .... 13 E1
Cliff Gv HTNM SK4 .... 165 F1
Cliff Hill Rd ROY/SHW OL2 .... 43 D6
Cliffmere Cl CHD/CHDH SK8 .... 181 D4
Clifford Av DTN/ASHW M34 .... 129 F4
  HALE/TIMP WA15 .... 175 E1
Clifford Rd ROY/DIS SK12 .... 198 A5 🔟
  WILM/AE SK9 .... 203 D5
Clifford St ECC M30 .... 118 C1
  ROCH OL11 .... 40 A2
  SWIN M27 .... 86 C5 🔟
Cliff Rd WILM/AE SK9 .... 203 F3
Cliff Side WILM/AE SK9 .... 203 F3
Cliff St MILN OL16 .... 23 F4
Clifton Av CHD/CHDH SK8 .... 179 E5
  ECC M30 .... 101 E4 🔟
  HALE/TIMP WA15 .... 174 C2
  OLDE OL4 .... 79 F6 🔽
  RUSH/FAL M14 .... 144 B3
Clifton Cl HEY OL10 .... 37 D6 🔽
  OLDE OL4 .... 79 F6
  OLDTF/WHR M16 .... 123 E4
Clifton Ct FWTH BL4 .... 65 F1
Clifton Crs ROY/SHW OL2 .... 61 E6 🔟
Clifton Dr CHD/CHDH SK8 .... 179 E5
  MPL/ROM SK6 .... 171 D6
  SWIN M27 .... 85 E3
  WILM/AE SK9 .... 208 C1 🔟
Clifton Gv SWIN M27 .... 85 D3
Clifton House Rd SWIN M27 .... 85 F1 🔟
Clifton Park Rd OFTN SK2 .... 183 E2
Clifton Pl PWCH M25 .... 71 E6 🔟
Clifton Rd CCHDY M21 .... 142 A3
  ECC M30 .... 101 E4
  HTNM SK4 .... 165 E1
  MDTN M24 .... 58 B3
  PWCH M25 .... 87 F1
  SALE M33 .... 159 F2 🔽
  URM M41 .... 137 E1
Clifton St AUL OL6 .... 112 B4 🔟
  BOL BL1 .... 46 C1
  BURY BL9 .... 34 B4
  FAIL M35 .... 94 B4
  FWTH BL4 .... 67 D4
  MILN OL16 .... 42 A1 🔟
  NEWH/MOS M40 .... 108 A4
  OLDTF/WHR M16 .... 123 E4
  ROCH OL11 .... 40 B2 🔟
  WILM/AE SK9 .... 209 E4 🔟
Clifton Vw SWIN M27 .... 85 F1
Cliftonville Dr SLFD M6 .... 102 C1
Cliftonville Rd MILN OL16 .... 60 A1
Clinton Av RUSH/FAL M14 .... 143 D1
Clinton Gdns RUSH/FAL M14 .... 143 E1 🔟
Clinton St AUL OL6 .... 113 E3 🔟
Clippers Quay SALQ/ORD M5 .... 122 B3
Clipsley Crs OLDE OL4 .... 63 D5
Clitheroe Cl HEY OL10 .... 37 E4
Clitheroe Dr TOT/BURYW BL8 .... 32 A5
Clitheroe Rd BRUN/LGST M13 .... 126 A6
Clito St BKLY M9 .... 92 A5 🔟
Clive Av WHTF M45 .... 70 C2
Clively Av SWIN M27 .... 86 C4
Clive Rd FAIL M35 .... 93 F4
Clive St ANC M4 .... 106 C4 🔟
  AULW OL7 .... 112 B2
  BOLE BL2 .... 47 D2
  OLDS OL8 .... 95 E3
Clivia Gv BRO M7 .... 105 E1 🔟
Clock House Av DROY M43 .... 109 F4
Clock St CHAD OL9 .... 94 C3
Clock Tower Cl WALK M28 .... 82 A3 🔽
Cloister Cl DUK SK16 .... 131 D3 🔟
Cloister Rd HTNM SK4 .... 164 B3
The Cloisters CHD/CHDH SK8 .... 181 E2 🔽
  MILN OL16 .... 23 F4 🔟
  SALE M33 .... 160 B1 🔟
Cloister St BOL BL1 .... 27 D5
The Close ALT WA14 .... 174 A2

BOLE BL2 .... 28 C4 ⬛
MDTN M24 .... 57 F6
MPL/ROM SK6 .... 171 E4
STLY SK15 .... 114 A3
TOT/BURYW BL8 .... 33 D1
Clothorn Rd *DID/WITH* M20 .... 165 F1
Cloudstock Gv *LHULT* M38 .... 64 C6
Clough Av *SALE* M33 .... 158 B4
WILM/AE SK9 .... 205 F1
Cloughbank *RAD* M26 .... 68 A4 ⬛
Clough Dr *PWCH* M25 .... 88 A1
Clough End Rd *HYDE* SK14 .... 152 C2
Cloughfield Av *SALQ/ORD* M5 .... 122 C1 ⬛
Cloughfold *RAD* M26 .... 67 F4
Clough Fold Rd *HYDE* SK14 .... 150 A2
Clough Ga *HYDE* SK14 .... 151 D3 ⬛
OLDS OL8 .... 95 E3 ⬛
Clough Gv *WHTF* M45 .... 70 B1 ⬛
Clough House La *WHIT* OL12 .... 10 C5
Clough La *HEY* OL10 .... 37 D3
PWCH M25 .... 88 A1
Clough Meadow *BOL* BL1 .... 44 B3
MPL/ROM SK6 .... 150 A6
Clough Meadow Rd *RAD* M26 .... 50 C6 ⬛
Clough Rd *BKLY* M9 .... 92 A5
DROY M43 .... 110 C5
FAIL M35 .... 94 B6
LIT OL15 .... 12 B3
MDTN M24 .... 75 E1
ROY/SHW OL2 .... 62 B3
Cloughs Av *CHAD* OL9 .... 76 B3 ⬛
Clough St *FWTH* BL4 .... 67 D4
MDTN M24 .... 75 F1 ⬛
NEWH/MOS M40 .... 109 D3 ⬛
RAD M26 .... 70 A2 ⬛
WHIT OL12 .... 11 D5
The Clough *RDSH* SK5 .... 147 F5
Clough Top Rd *BKLY* M9 .... 92 B3
Clovelly Av *OLDS* OL8 .... 95 D3
Clovelly Rd *CCHDY* M21 .... 142 A3
OFTN SK2 .... 168 A5
SWIN M27 .... 85 D6
Clovelly St *NEWH/MOS* M40 .... 109 E2 ⬛
ROCH OL11 .... 38 C4
Cloverbank Av *BNG/LEV* M19 .... 144 B1
Cloverbank Av *BNC/LEV* M19 .... 164 B1 ⬛
Clover Crs *OLDS* OL8 .... 97 D2
Clover Cft *SALE* M33 .... 160 B4
Cloverdale Sq *BOL* BL1 .... 26 B6 ⬛
Clover Hall Crs *MILN* OL16 .... 24 A4
Cloverley Dr *HALE/TIMP* WA15 ...... 175 E3
Clover Rd *HALE/TIMP* WA15 .... 175 E2
MPL/ROM SK6 .... 170 C2 ⬛
Clover St *WHIT* OL12 .... 22 C5
Clowes St *CHAD* OL9 .... 94 B3
CSLFD M3 .... 2 B2
WGTN/LGST M12 .... 126 B3 ⬛
Club St *OP/CLY* M11 .... 128 A2
Clumber Cl *POY/DIS* SK12 .... 198 C6
Clumber Rd *GTN* M18 .... 128 A5
POY/DIS SK12 .... 198 C6
Clunton Av *BOLS/LL* BL3 .... 45 F5 ⬛
Clutha Rd *EDGY/DAV* SK3 .... 183 D3
Clwyd Av *EDGY/DAV* SK3 .... 166 B6 ⬛
Clyde Av *WHTF* M45 .... 71 D5
Clyde Ct *MILN* OL16 .... 40 C1
Clyde Rd *DID/WITH* M20 .... 163 D1
EDGY/DAV SK3 .... 166 A6
RAD M26 .... 51 D4
Clydesdale St *OLDS* OL8 .... 95 F1 ⬛
Clyde St *AULW* OL7 .... 130 A1 ⬛
OLD OL1 .... 80 A2
Clyde Ter *RAD* M26 .... 51 D4 ⬛
Clyne St *STRET* M32 .... 122 A4
Coach La *ROCH* OL11 .... 37 F2 ⬛
Coal Pit La *OLDS* OL8 .... 95 E6
Coalshaw Green Rd *CHAD* OL9 ...... 94 B2
Coatbridge St *OP/CLY* M11 .... 109 D6
Cobalt Av *URM* M41 .... 120 A3
Cobb Cl *CHH* M8 .... 89 F2
Coberley Av *URM* M41 .... 118 A3
Cob Hall Rd *STRET* M32 .... 140 A2 ⬛
Cobham Av *BOLS/LL* BL3 .... 46 B6
NEWH/MOS M40 .... 93 D3 ⬛
Cobourg St *CMANE* M1 .... 3 G5
Coburg Av *BRO* M7 .... 105 E3
Cochrane Av *WGTN/LGST* M12 ...... 125 F4
Cochrane St *BOLS/LL* BL3 .... 47 D4
Cock Brow *HYDE* SK14 .... 152 A4
Cock Clod St *RAD* M26 .... 52 A6 ⬛
Cockcroft St *BKLY* M9 .... 91 E4
Cocker Hl *STLY* SK15 .... 114 C5

Cocker Mill La *ROY/SHW* OL2 .... 61 D4
Cockers La *STLY* SK15 .... 133 E1
Cocker St *LHULT* M38 .... 82 B1 ⬛
Cockey Moor Rd *BOLE* BL2 .... 31 E6
Cock Hall La *WHIT* OL12 .... 8 C2
Cockhall La *WHIT* OL12 .... 9 D2
Coconut Gv *SLFD* M6 .... 104 C5 ⬛
Codale Dr *BOLE* BL2 .... 30 A6 ⬛
Coddington Av *OP/CLY* M11 .... 127 F1 ⬛
Coe St *BOLS/LL* BL3 .... 47 D4
Coghlan Cl *OP/CLY* M11 .... 100 C5
Colborne Av *ECC* M30 .... 100 C5
MPL/ROM SK6 .... 169 F3
RDSH SK5 .... 128 A6 ⬛
Colbourne Av *CHH* M8 .... 90 A4 ⬛
Colbourne Gv *HYDE* SK14 .... 133 F6
Colchester Av *BOLE* BL2 .... 48 C1
Colchester Dr *NTHM/RTH* M23 .... 160 C4
Colchester Dr *FWTH* BL4 .... 65 E2
Colchester Pl *HTNM* SK4 .... 166 A2 ⬛
Colclough Cl *NEWH/MOS* M40 .... 108 C2 ⬛
Coldfield Dr *NTHM/RTH* M23 .... 177 D1
Cold Greave Cl *MILN* OL16 .... 43 D3
Coldhurst St *OLD* OL1 .... 78 C3
Coldstream Av *BKLY* M9 .... 91 E1 ⬛
Colebrook Dr *NEWH/MOS* M40 ...... 108 B1
Colebrook Rd *HALE/TIMP* WA15 .... 175 E1
Coleby Av *OLDTF/WHR* M16 .... 125 D5
WYTH/NTH M22 .... 179 D6
Coledale Dr *MDTN* M24 .... 74 A1 ⬛
Coleford Gv *BOL* BL1 .... 46 C3 ⬛
Colemore Av *DID/WITH* M20 .... 164 B2
Colenso Ct *BOLE* BL2 .... 48 A2 ⬛
Colenso Gv *HTNM* SK4 .... 165 F2
Colenso St *OLDS* OL8 .... 95 E2
Coleport Cl *CHD/CHDH* SK8 .... 181 E6
Coleridge Av *MDTN* M24 .... 58 A6 ⬛
RAD M26 .... 50 C6
Coleridge Cl *RDSH* SK5 .... 146 C2
Coleridge Rd *LIT* OL15 .... 25 D3
OLD OL1 .... 62 C5
OLDTF/WHR M16 .... 123 D6
RDSH SK5 .... 146 C2
TOT/BURYW BL8 .... 18 A3 ⬛
Colesbourne Dr *LHULT* M38 .... 65 E5 ⬛
Coleshill St *NEWH/MOS* M40 .... 107 H4
Cole St *NEWH/MOS* M40 .... 92 A5
Colgate Crs *RUSH/FAL* M14 .... 143 F3
Colgate La *SALQ/ORD* M5 .... 122 B3
Colgrove Av *NEWH/MOS* M40 ...... 93 D3
Colina Dr *CHH* M8 .... 105 F2 ⬛
Colindale Av *BKLY* M9 .... 91 F1
Colin Rd *HTNM* SK4 .... 166 C1
Colinton Cl *BOL* BL1 .... 27 E6 ⬛
Colinwood Cl *BURY* BL9 .... 53 D6
Coll Dr *URM* M41 .... 119 E4
College Av *OLDS* OL8 .... 95 E2
College Cl *BOLS/LL* BL3 .... 46 C3
OFTN SK2 .... 183 E1 ⬛
WILM/AE SK9 .... 202 C3
College Cft *ECC* M30 .... 102 A5 ⬛
College Dr *OLDTF/WHR* M16 .... 142 A1
OLDS OL8 .... 95 E1
OLDTF/WHR M16 .... 142 B1
WHIT OL12 .... 22 B6
College Wy *BOLS/LL* BL3 .... 46 B5
Collen Crs *TOT/BURYW* BL8 .... 32 C1
Collett St *OLD* OL1 .... 80 A3
Colley St *MILN* OL16 .... 23 E4
STRET M32 .... 122 A4
Collie Av *SLFD* M6 .... 105 D2
Collier Av *MILN* OL16 .... 25 D6
Collier Cl *HYDE* SK14 .... 152 C2
Collier Hl *OLDS* OL8 .... 95 D2
Collier Hill Av *OLDS* OL8 .... 95 D2
Collier St *CSLFD* M3 .... 2 A6
CSLFD M3 .... 2 B1
SLFD M6 .... 104 A1
SWIN M27 .... 85 F6 ⬛
Colliery St *OP/CLY* M11 .... 108 B6
Collin Av *GTN* M18 .... 127 D5
Collingburn Av *SALQ/ORD* M5 ...... 122 C2
Colling Cl *IRL* M44 .... 135 E2
Collinge Av *MDTN* M24 .... 76 A3 ⬛
Collinge St *HEY* OL10 .... 37 D5 ⬛
MDTN M24 .... 76 B4
ROY/SHW OL2 .... 61 F2 ⬛
TOT/BURYW BL8 .... 32 C3 ⬛
Collingham St *CHH* M8 .... 106 B3
Colling St *RAMS* BL0 .... 6 C6 ⬛
Collington Cl *WGTN/LGST* M12 .... 126 B4
Collingwood Av *DROY* M43 .... 109 F4 ⬛
Collingwood Cl *POY/DIS* SK12 ..... 199 E6 ⬛
Collingwood Dr *SWIN* M27 .... 86 B6
Collingwood Rd *BNG/LEV* M19 .... 145 D2
Collingwood St *ROCH* OL11 .... 58 A1
Collins St *TOT/BURYW* BL8 .... 32 A3
Collop Dr *HEY* OL10 .... 56 C2
Collyhurst Av *WALK* M28 .... 83 F3 ⬛
Collyhurst Rd *NEWH/MOS* M40 .... 106 C3
Collyhurst St *NEWH/MOS* M40 .... 107 D2
Colman Gdns *SALQ/ORD* M5 ...... 122 C2 ⬛
Colmore Dr *BKLY* M9 .... 92 B1
Colmore Gv *BOLE* BL2 .... 28 C3 ⬛

Colmore St *BOLE* BL2 .... 28 C4
Colne St *ROCH* OL11 .... 39 E6
Colonial Rd *OFTN* SK2 .... 183 E1 ⬛
Colshaw Dr *WILM/AE* SK9 .... 204 B6
Colshaw Rd *NTHM/RTH* M23 .... 177 E2
Colson Dr *MDTN* M24 .... 75 D4 ⬛
Colsterdale Cl *ROY/SHW* OL2 ..... 60 C4
Coltsfoot Dr *ALT* WA14 .... 157 F5
Columbia Av *GTN* M18 .... 128 C3
Columbia Rd *BOL* BL1 .... 46 A1 ⬛⬛
Columbia St *OLDS* OL8 .... 96 A1 ⬛
Columbine Cl *WHIT* OL12 .... 22 A2 ⬛
Columbine St *OP/CLY* M11 .... 127 E2
Colville Dr *TOT/BURYW* BL8 .... 32 C6
Colville Gv *HALE/TIMP* WA15 ...... 175 E1 ⬛
SALE M33 .... 158 C4
Colville Rd *OLD* OL1 .... 78 B2
Colwell Av *STRET* M32 .... 139 F2
Colwick Av *ALT* WA14 .... 174 C1
Colwith Av *BOLE* BL2 .... 29 F6 ⬛
Colwyn Av *MDTN* M24 .... 75 E5
RUSH/FAL M14 .... 144 C3
Colwyn Crs *RDSH* SK5 .... 147 D6
Colwyn Rd *BRAM/HZG* SK7 .... 197 D1
CHD/CHDH SK8 .... 180 C6
Colwyn St *AULW* OL7 .... 101 D1 ⬛
CHAD OL9 .... 78 B4
ROCH OL11 .... 38 C5 ⬛
SLFD M6 .... 104 A4 ⬛
Combe Cl *OP/CLY* M11 .... 108 C4
Combermere Av *DID/WITH* M20 ... 143 E3 ⬛
Combermere Cl *CHD/CHDH* SK8 .. 181 D3 ⬛
Combermere St *DUK* SK16 .... 113 D6
Comer Ter *SALE* M33 .... 159 E1 ⬛
Comet St *CMANE* M1 .... 3 H4 ⬛
CMANE M1 .... 107 D6 ⬛
Commercial Av *CHD/CHDH* SK8 ... 194 C4
Commercial Brow *HYDE* SK14 ..... 131 F5
Commercial Rd *BRAM/HZG* SK7 .. 184 B4
OLD OL1 .... 79 D5 ⬛
Commercial St *CHAD* OL9 .... 78 A5 ⬛
HULME M15 .... 123 F2 ⬛
HYDE SK14 .... 131 F6
Common La *PART* M31 .... 156 B1
Common Side Rd *WALK* M28 ...... 82 A6
Como St *BOLS/LL* BL3 .... 46 A5 ⬛
Compass St *OP/CLY* M11 .... 127 D2 ⬛
Compstall Av *RUSH/FAL* M14 ..... 143 F2
Compstall Gv *GTN* M18 .... 127 F3 ⬛
Compstall Rd *MPL/ROM* SK6 ...... 170 B3
Compton Cl *URM* M41 .... 136 A2
Compton Dr *NTHM/RTH* M23 ...... 177 E5 ⬛
Compton Wy *MDTN* M24 .... 76 A4
ROY/SHW OL2 .... 61 F3
Comus St *SALQ/ORD* M5 .... 123 D1
Concert La *CMANW* M2 .... 3 E4
Concord Pl *SLFD* M6 .... 104 B2
Condor Cl *DROY* M43 .... 111 D4 ⬛
Condor Pl *SLFD* M6 .... 104 B2 ⬛
Conduit St *AUL* OL6 .... 113 D5
OLD OL1 .... 62 B6
Coney Gv *NTHM/RTH* M23 .... 161 E6
Coneymead *STLY* SK15 .... 114 B3
Congleton Cl *WILM/AE* SK9 .... 209 E5
Congou St *CMANE* M1 .... 125 D1 ⬛
Congreave St *OLD* OL1 .... 78 C3
Coningsby Dr *BKLY* M9 .... 91 E5
Conisborough Pl *WHTF* M45 .... 71 F4 ⬛
Coniston *BOL* BL1 .... 28 A4 ⬛⬛
Coniston Av *BKLY* M9 .... 91 E5 ⬛
FWTH BL4 .... 64 C4
HYDE SK14 .... 131 D5 ⬛
LHULT M38 .... 82 B1
OLDS OL8 .... 95 E2
SALE M33 .... 160 A3
WHTF M45 .... 71 D3
Coniston Cl *BOLS/LL* BL3 .... 49 E5 ⬛
CHAD OL9 .... 77 E4
DTN/ASHW M34 .... 147 F1
RAMS BL0 .... 7 D4 ⬛
Coniston Dr *BURY* BL9 .... 52 C2
MDTN M24 .... 74 C1
STLY SK15 .... 114 B4
WILM/AE SK9 .... 194 A5
Coniston Gv *AULW* OL7 .... 112 B5
HEY OL10 .... 56 B1
LHULT M38 .... 82 B1
ROY/SHW OL2 .... 60 B3
Coniston Rd *CHD/CHDH* SK8 ..... 179 F1
MPL/ROM SK6 .... 200 B1
PART M31 .... 154 C1
RDSH SK5 .... 147 D5 ⬛
STRET M32 .... 122 A4
SWIN M27 .... 102 A1
URM M41 .... 136 C3
Coniston St *NEWH/MOS* M40 ..... 109 D2 ⬛
SLFD M6 .... 104 C3
Coniston Wk *HALE/TIMP* WA15 .. 176 B2
Connaught Av *BNG/LEV* M19 ...... 145 D4
MILN OL16 .... 40 C4 ⬛
WHTF M45 .... 71 D3
Connaught Cl *WILM/AE* SK9 ...... 204 A3 ⬛
Connaught Sq *BOLE* BL2 .... 28 C5
Connaught St *CHAD* OL9 .... 78 C5 ⬛

TOT/BURYW BL8 .... 32 C6
Connel Cl BOLE BL2 .... 49 D3
Connell Rd NTHM/RTH M23 ... 177 E1 🔢
Connell Wy OL10 .... 38 A4 🔢
Connery Crs AUL OL6 .... 113 E1
Connie St OP/CLY M11 .... 127 D1
Conningsby Cl EDGW/EG BL7 ...... 14 A5
Connington Av BKLY M9 .... 91 E4
Connington Cl ROY/SHW OL2 .... 60 A1
Connor Wy CHD/CHDH SK8 .... 179 D3
Conrad Cl OLD OL1 .... 62 C5
Conran St BKLY M9 .... 91 F6 🔢
Consett Av NTHM/RTH M23 .... 177 E1
Consort Av ROY/SHW OL2 .... 60 B1
Consort Cl DUK SK16 .... 131 D3 🔢
Consort Pl ALT WA14 .... 173 F4
Constable Cl BOL BL1 .... 27 E6 🔢
Constable Dr MPL/ROM SK6 ...... 171 F5
  WILM/AE SK9 .... 204 C3
Constable St GTN M18 .... 127 F3
Constance Rd BOLS/LL BL3 .... 46 A5 🔢🔢
  PART M31 .... 155 D2
Constantine Rd MILN OL16 .... 23 D6 🔢
Constantine St OLDE OL4 .... 80 B5
Consul St WYTH/NTH M22 .... 162 C4 🔢
Convamore Rd BRAM/HZG SK7 . 196 B2 🔢
Convent St OLDS OL8 .... 97 D1
Conway Av BOL BL1 .... 26 B6
  IRL M44 .... 135 D3
  SWIN M27 .... 86 C2
  WHTF M45 .... 71 D4
Conway Cl HEY OL10 .... 36 B4
  MDTN M24 .... 72 B6 🔢
  OLDTF/WHR M16 .... 122 B6 🔢
  RAMS BL0 .... 6 C5 🔢
Conway Crs TOT/BURYW BL8 .... 18 A3 🔢
Conway Dr BRAM/HZG SK7 .... 184 A6
  BURY BL9 .... 35 E5 🔢
  HALE/TIMP WA15 .... 176 A1 🔢
  STLY SK15 .... 114 B4
Conway Gv CHAD OL9 .... 77 D3
Conway Rd CHD/CHDH SK8 .... 180 C5
  SALE M33 .... 160 B2
  URM M41 .... 119 E5
Conway St FWTH BL4 .... 66 B4
  RDSH SK5 .... 166 C1
Conyngham Rd RUSH/FAL M14 .. 125 E5
Cooke St BRAM/HZG SK7 .... 184 B4
  DTN/ASHW M34 .... 130 A6
  FAIL M35 .... 94 A5
  FWTH BL4 .... 66 C4
  HYDE SK14 .... 132 A4 🔢
Cook St BURY BL9 .... 34 A5
  CSLFD M3 .... 2 A1 🔢
  DTN/ASHW M34 .... 130 A3
  ECC M30 .... 101 D5 🔢
  EDGY/DAV SK3 .... 166 C4 🔢
  MILN OL16 .... 23 F4
  OLDE OL4 .... 80 A4
Cook Ter MILN OL16 .... 23 F4 🔢
Coomassie St HEY OL10 .... 37 D5
  RAD M26 .... 51 E6
  SLFD M6 .... 104 A4 🔢
Coombes Av HYDE SK14 .... 151 D2
  MPL/ROM SK6 .... 187 D2
Coombes St OFTN SK2 .... 183 F2
Coombes Vw HYDE SK14 .... 153 D3
Co-operation St FAIL M35 .... 94 A4
Co-operative St BRAM/HZG SK7 . 184 C4
  LHULT M38 .... 64 C6 🔢
  OLDE OL4 .... 81 D5
  ROY/SHW OL2 .... 61 F2 🔢
Cooper Fold MDTN M24 .... 57 E5
  MDTN M24 .... 57 D6 🔢
Cooper La BKLY M9 .... 74 B6
  MDTN M24 .... 57 D6 🔢
Cooper St BRAM/HZG SK7 .... 185 D4
  BURY BL9 .... 33 F5 🔢🔢
  CMANW M2 .... 2 D4
  DROY M43 .... 109 F6 🔢
  DUK SK16 .... 112 C6
  MILN OL16 .... 24 B1 🔢
  OLDE OL4 .... 80 B3
  STKP SK1 .... 167 D6
  STRET M32 .... 140 B2
Coopers Wk MILN OL16 .... 24 A3
Cooper Ter MILN OL16 .... 23 F5 🔢
Coop St ANC M4 .... 3 G1 🔢
  BOL BL1 .... 27 F3
Copage Dr MPL/ROM SK6 .... 169 E1
Cope Bank West BOL BL1 .... 26 C5 🔢
Cope Cl OP/CLY M11 .... 127 F2 🔢
Copeland Av SWIN M27 .... 87 D4
Copeland Cl MDTN M24 .... 74 A2 🔢
Copeland Ms BOL BL1 .... 45 E2 🔢
Copeland St HYDE SK14 .... 131 E4
Copeman Cl BRUN/LGST M13 .... 125 D3 🔢
Copenhagen Sq MILN OL16 .... 23 E5 🔢
Copenhagen St MILN OL16 .... 23 E5 🔢
  NEWH/MOS M40 .... 108 D1 🔢
Copgrove Rd CCHDY M21 .... 141 F4 🔢
Copley St STLY SK15 .... 115 D5
Copley Park Ms STLY SK15 .... 115 D5
Copley Rd CCHDY M21 .... 141 E1
Copley St ROY/SHW OL2 .... 62 A1 🔢
Copperas La DROY M43 .... 127 F1

Copperbeech Cl
  WYTH/NTH M22 .... 162 C4 🔢
Copperfield Rd CHD/CHDH SK8 . 195 F4
Copperfields WILM/AE SK9 .... 204 A6
Copper La WHTF M45 .... 69 F4
Coppice Av SALE M33 .... 158 B3
Coppice Cl MPL/ROM SK6 .... 169 F1
Coppice Dr POY/DIS SK12 .... 201 E3
  WHIT OL12 .... 9 D4
  WYTH/NTH M22 .... 162 B4 🔢
Coppice La POY/DIS SK12 .... 201 E3
Coppice Rd POY/DIS SK12 .... 199 F6
Coppice St BURY BL9 .... 34 C4
  OLDS OL8 .... 78 B6
The Coppice BOLE BL2 .... 29 E2
  HALE/TIMP WA15 .... 189 F1
  PWCH M25 .... 88 B1
  RAMS BL0 .... 18 B1 🔢
  SWIN M27 .... 101 D2
  WALK M28 .... 84 A5
Coppice V RAMS BL0 .... 19 D2
Coppice Wk DTN/ASHW M34 ...... 148 B1
Coppice Wy WILM/AE SK9 .... 194 C6
Copping St WGTN/LGST M12 ...... 126 A3
The Coppins WILM/AE SK9 .... 208 C1 🔢
Coppleridge Dr CHH M8 .... 90 B3
Copplestone Dr SALE M33 .... 138 A6
Cop Rd ROY/SHW OL2 .... 62 A5
Copse Av WYTH/NTH M22 .... 178 C4
Copse Dr BURY BL9 .... 34 A1
The Copse EDGW/EG BL7 .... 15 D3
  HALE/TIMP WA15 .... 190 B2
Copson St DID/WITH M20 .... 143 F4
Copster Av OLDS OL8 .... 95 F2
Copster Hill Rd OLDS OL8 .... 95 F2
Copster Pl OLDS OL8 .... 95 F2
Copthall La CHH M8 .... 90 A5
Copthorne Cl HEY OL10 .... 56 B1
Copthorne Crs BRUN/LGST M13 . 144 C1
Copthorne Dr BOLE BL2 .... 48 C3
Coptrod Head Cl WHIT OL12 ...... 22 C1 🔢
Coral Av CHD/CHDH SK8 .... 181 E6
Coral Rd CHD/CHDH SK8 .... 181 E6
Coral St BRUN/LGST M13 .... 125 D2
Coram St GTN M18 .... 128 A3
Corbar Rd OFTN SK2 .... 183 E2
Corbett St MILN OL16 .... 23 E5
  OP/CLY M11 .... 108 B5
Corbrook Rd CHAD OL9 .... 76 C2 🔢
Corby St WGTN/LGST M12 .... 126 B3 🔢
Corcoran Dr MPL/ROM SK6 .... 171 D3 🔢
Corda Av WYTH/NTH M22 .... 162 B5
Cordingley Av DROY M43 .... 128 A1 🔢
Cordova Av DTN/ASHW M34 ...... 128 A6
Corelli St NEWH/MOS M40 .... 108 A3
Corfe Cl URM M41 .... 136 A2
Corfe Crs BRAM/HZG SK7 .... 184 B6
Corinthian Av BRO M7 .... 105 D2
Corkland Cl AUL OL6 .... 113 E5
Corkland Rd CCHDY M21 .... 141 F3
Corkland St AUL OL6 .... 113 F5
Cork St BURY BL9 .... 34 B5
  WGTN/LGST M12 .... 125 E1 🔢
Corley Av EDGY/DAV SK3 .... 165 D6
Cormallen Gv FAIL M35 .... 94 B6 🔢
Cornall St TOT/BURYW BL8 .... 33 D4
Cornbrook Cl WHIT OL12 .... 11 D5
Cornbrook Gv OLDTF/WHR M16 . 123 E4
Cornbrook St OLDTF/WHR M16 . 123 E4
Corn Cl BRUN/LGST M13 .... 125 D4
Cornell St ANC M4 .... 3 H1
Corner Cft WILM/AE SK9 .... 205 E1
Cornet St BRO M7 .... 105 E1 🔢
Cornfield STLY SK15 .... 133 F2 🔢
Cornfield Cl SALE M33 .... 161 D2 🔢
Cornfield Dr WYTH/NTH M22 .... 178 A4
Cornfield Rd MPL/ROM SK6 .... 170 C2
Cornfield St MILN OL16 .... 42 A2 🔢
Cornford Av GTN M18 .... 126 C6 🔢
Corn Hey Rd SALE M33 .... 158 A3 🔢
Cornhill Av URM M41 .... 118 C6
Corn Hill La DTN/ASHW M34 ...... 128 B4
Cornhill Rd URM M41 .... 118 C6
Cornhill St OLD OL1 .... 80 A1
Cornish Wy ROY/SHW OL2 .... 61 D6
Cornishway WYTH/NTH M22 ...... 192 B1
Cornlea Dr WALK M28 .... 83 D6
Corn Mill Cl WHIT OL12 .... 24 A1 🔢
Corn St FAIL M35 .... 109 E1 🔢
Cornwall Av BNG/LEV M19 .... 145 F3 🔢
Cornwall Cl MPL/ROM SK6 .... 200 C2 🔢
Cornwall Crs RDSH SK5 .... 148 A5
Cornwall Dr BURY BL9 .... 53 E1 🔢
Cornwall Rd CHD/CHDH SK8 .... 193 F1
  DROY M43 .... 110 B4
  IRL M44 .... 134 B6
Cornwall St CHAD OL9 .... 77 F6
  ECC M30 .... 101 D6 🔢
  OP/CLY M11 .... 127 E2
Cornwell St OLDTF/WHR M16 .... 204 B3 🔢
Corona Av HYDE SK14 .... 131 F6
  OLDS OL8 .... 95 E2
Coronation Av DUK SK16 .... 132 A2
  HEY OL10 .... 56 C1

Coronation Gdns RAD M26 .... 50 C5
Coronation Rd AUL OL6 .... 113 D1
  DROY M43 .... 110 A4
  FAIL M35 .... 109 F1 🔢
  RAD M26 .... 50 C5
Coronation Sq WGTN/LGST M12 . 125 D3 🔢
Coronation St BOL BL1 .... 47 D2
  DTN/ASHW M34 .... 129 D6
  OP/CLY M11 .... 127 D1 🔢
  RDSH SK5 .... 166 C1
  SALQ/ORD M5 .... 122 C1
  SWIN M27 .... 86 B4
Corporation Rd DTN/ASHW M34 . 129 E4
  ROCH OL11 .... 39 F1
Corporation St ANC M4 .... 106 B4
  CMANE M1 .... 2 D3
  CMANW M2 .... 2 D3
  HYDE SK14 .... 150 B1 🔢
  MDTN M24 .... 75 E3 🔢
  STKP SK1 .... 167 D3 🔢
  STLY SK15 .... 114 B6
Corran Cl ECC M30 .... 100 C5 🔢
Correction Brow POY/DIS SK12 .. 200 A3
Corrie Cl DTN/ASHW M34 .... 149 D2
Corrie Crs FWTH BL4 .... 85 E1
Corrie Dr FWTH BL4 .... 85 E1
Corrie Rd SWIN M27 .... 86 B2 🔢
Corrie St LHULT M38 .... 82 B1
Corrie Wy MPL/ROM SK6 .... 148 C6
Corrigan St GTN M18 .... 127 F3 🔢
Corringham Rd BNG/LEV M19 .... 146 A4
Corring Wy BOL BL1 .... 28 C5 🔢
Corrin Rd BOLE BL2 .... 47 F3
Corriss Av BKLY M9 .... 73 E6
Corry St HEY OL10 .... 37 F5
Corson St FWTH BL4 .... 66 B1 🔢
Corwen Av BKLY M9 .... 91 F5
Corwen Cl OLDS OL8 .... 94 C3
Cosgrove Crs FAIL M35 .... 109 F2
Cosgrove Rd FAIL M35 .... 109 F2
Cosham Rd WYTH/NTH M22 .... 179 D4 🔢
Cotaline Cl ROCH OL11 .... 38 C4 🔢
Cotefield Av BOLS/LL BL3 .... 47 D6 🔢
Cotefield Cl MPL/ROM SK6 .... 187 D2 🔢
Cotefield Rd WYTH/NTH M22 .... 177 F5
Cote Green La MPL/ROM SK6 .... 171 F4
Cote Green Rd MPL/ROM SK6 .... 171 F4
Cote La LIT OL15 .... 12 A5
  MOSL OL5 .... 99 F2
Cotford Rd BOL BL1 .... 28 A5
Cotham St CSLFD M3 .... 106 A4
Cotswold Av BRAM/HZG SK7 .... 183 F6
  CHAD OL9 .... 77 E6
  ROY/SHW OL2 .... 61 D1
  URM M41 .... 118 A6 🔢
Cotswold Cl PWCH M25 .... 72 A6 🔢
  RAMS BL0 .... 19 D1 🔢
Cotswold Crs MILN OL16 .... 25 E6
  TOT/BURYW BL8 .... 32 C4
Cotswold Dr ROY/SHW OL2 .... 59 F6
  SLFD M6 .... 104 A2 🔢
Cotswold Rd HTNM SK4 .... 166 B2 🔢
Cottage Cft BOLE BL2 .... 29 E2 🔢
Cottage Gdns MPL/ROM SK6 .... 168 B2
Cottam Crs MPL/ROM SK6 .... 171 F6
Cottam Gv SWIN M27 .... 86 B6 🔢
Cottam St OLD OL1 .... 78 B3
  TOT/BURYW BL8 .... 33 D4 🔢
  TOT/BURYW BL8 .... 33 D4 🔢🔢
Cottenham La BRO M7 .... 105 F3
Cottenham St BRUN/LGST M13 . 124 C3 🔢
Cotterdale Cl OLDTF/WHR M16 . 142 B1 🔢
Cotteril Cl SALE M33 .... 160 A4
Cotterill St SLFD M6 .... 104 B5
Cotter St WGTN/LGST M12 .... 125 D2
Cottesmore Dr CHH M8 .... 91 D3 🔢
Cottesmore Gdns
  HALE/TIMP WA15 .... 190 A1
Cottingham Dr AUL OL6 .... 113 D3
Cottingham Rd
  WGTN/LGST M12 .... 125 F3 🔢
Cottonfield Rd DID/WITH M20 .... 144 A5 🔢
Cotton Fold MILN OL16 .... 41 D1 🔢
Cotton Hl DID/WITH M20 .... 144 A6
Cotton La DID/WITH M20 .... 144 A5
Cotton St ANC M4 .... 3 H2
  BOL BL1 .... 27 E5
Cotton St East AUL OL6 .... 112 B5 🔢
  AUL OL6 .... 112 C4 🔢
Cotton St West AULW OL7 .... 112 B5
Cotton Tree Cl OLDE OL4 .... 80 B3
Cotton Tree St EDGY/DAV SK3 .. 166 C4 🔢
Cottonwood Dr SALE M33 .... 138 A6 🔢
Cottrell La HALE/TIMP WA15 .... 190 B2 🔢
Coucill Sq FWTH BL4 .... 66 C3 🔢
Coulsden Dr BKLY M9 .... 91 E2
Coulthart St AUL OL6 .... 112 C5 🔢
Coulthurst St RAMS BL0 .... 6 C5 🔢
Councillor La CHD/CHDH SK8 .... 181 D1
Councillor St OP/CLY M11 .... 107 F6
Countess Av CHD/CHDH SK8 .... 194 C4
Countess Gv BRO M7 .... 105 E2 🔢
Countess La RAD M26 .... 50 B4
Countess Pl PWCH M25 .... 89 D1 🔢

Countess Rd DID/WITH M20 .... 163 F2
Countess St AUL OL6 .... 113 E5
  OFTN SK2 .... 183 E2
Counthill Dr CHH M8 .... 89 F3 🔢
Counthill Rd OLDE OL4 .... 80 B1
Count St MILN OL16 .... 40 B3
County Av AUL OL6 .... 113 F3
County Rd WALK M28 .... 82 B1 🔢
County St CMANW M2 .... 2 D4 🔢
  OLDS OL8 .... 95 D3
Coupland Cl OLDE OL4 .... 63 D5
Coupland St WHIT OL12 .... 9 D3 🔢
Courier St GTN M18 .... 127 F3 🔢
Course Vw OLDE OL4 .... 97 F2
Court Dr NEWH/MOS M40 .... 109 F3
Courtfield Av BKLY M9 .... 91 E1 🔢
Counthill St STKP SK1 .... 167 E5
Courtney Gn WILM/AE SK9 .... 204 B1
Courtney Pl ALT WA14 .... 173 E6
Court St BOLE BL2 .... 47 E2
Courtyard Dr WALK M28 .... 82 A2
Cousin Flds BOLE BL2 .... 15 D6 🔢
Covell Rd POY/DIS SK12 .... 198 B4 🔢
Covent Gdn STKP SK1 .... 167 E5
Coventry Av EDGY/DAV SK3 .... 165 D6
Coventry Gv CHAD OL9 .... 77 E2
Coventry Rd RAD M26 .... 51 E4 🔢
Coventry St ROCH OL11 .... 40 A1 🔢
Coverdale Av BOL BL1 .... 45 E1
  ROY/SHW OL2 .... 60 A4 🔢
Coverdale Cl HEY OL10 .... 37 D6 🔢
Coverdale Crs WGTN/LGST M12 .... 125 E3
Coverham Av OLDE OL4 .... 97 E1
Coverhill Rd OLDE OL4 .... 81 F6
Covert Rd OLDE OL4 .... 97 F2
  WYTH/NTH M22 .... 178 C2
The Cove HALE/TIMP WA15 .... 175 D4
Covington Pl WILM/AE SK9 .... 203 F5 🔢
Cowan St NEWH/MOS M40 .... 107 E5 🔢
Cowburn St CSLFD M3 .... 106 A4
  HEY OL10 .... 37 F6
Cowesby St RUSH/FAL M14 .... 124 B6 🔢
Cowhill La AUL OL6 .... 113 D4
Cowie St ROY/SHW OL2 .... 61 F1
Cow La BRAM/HZG M19 .... 184 B3
  FAIL M35 .... 93 F6
  HALE/TIMP WA15 .... 189 D4
  OLDE OL4 .... 80 A4
  SALE M33 .... 140 C5
  SALQ/ORD M5 .... 105 D6
Cowley Rd BOL BL1 .... 28 A2 🔢
Cowley St NEWH/MOS M40 .... 109 D1 🔢
Cowling Dr BRO M7 .... 88 A5
Cowlishaw ROY/SHW OL2 .... 61 E4
Cowlishaw La ROY/SHW OL2 .... 61 E4
Cowlishaw Rd HYDE SK14 .... 151 D6
Cowm Park Wy North WHIT OL12 .. 9 E1 🔢
Cowm Park Wy South WHIT OL12 .. 9 D5
Cowm St WHIT OL12 .... 5 F4
Cowm Top La ROCH OL11 .... 39 F5
Cown Edge Wy HYDE SK14 .... 150 B5
  HYDE SK14 .... 152 C4
  OFTN SK2 .... 185 E3
Cowper St AUL OL6 .... 113 D4
  MDTN M24 .... 76 B4
Coxton Rd WYTH/NTH M22 .... 178 C6
Crabbe St ANC M4 .... 106 B4 🔢
Crab La BKLY M9 .... 90 C1
Crabtree Av HALE/TIMP WA15 ..... 190 B2
Crabtree La OP/CLY M11 .... 109 E6
Crabtree Rd OLD OL1 .... 79 F3
Crabtree St BURY BL9 .... 34 C4 🔢
Craddock Rd SALE M33 .... 160 A3
Craddock St MOSL OL5 .... 99 D4 🔢
Cradley Av OP/CLY M11 .... 127 E1
Crag Av BURY BL9 .... 19 E5
Cragg Rd OLD OL1 .... 77 D1
Cragie St CHH M8 .... 106 A2
Crag La BURY BL9 .... 19 E5
Cragside Wy WILM/AE SK9 .... 204 A5 🔢
Craig Av TOT/BURYW BL8 .... 32 C6
  URM M41 .... 118 B6
Craig Cl HTNM SK4 .... 165 E4
Craighall Av BNG/LEV M19 .... 145 D3 🔢
Craighall Rd BOL BL1 .... 27 F1
Craiglands MILN OL16 .... 40 C5
Craigmore Av DID/WITH M20 .... 162 B3
Craig Rd GTN M18 .... 127 D5
  HTNM SK4 .... 165 F4
Craigslands Av NEWH/MOS M40 .. 108 C3 🔢
Craigweil Av DID/WITH M20 .... 164 A3
Craigwell Rd PWCH M25 .... 89 E3
Cramer St NEWH/MOS M40 .... 108 A2 🔢
Crammond Cl NEWH/MOS M40 .... 109 E1
Cramond Cl BOL BL1 .... 27 E6 🔢
Crampton Dr HALE/TIMP WA15 ... 190 A1
Crampton La PART M31 .... 136 B5
Cranage Rd BNG/LEV M19 .... 145 F5 🔢
Cranark Cl BOL BL1 .... 45 E2 🔢
Cranberry Cl ALT WA14 .... 157 F5 🔢
Cranberry Rd PART M31 .... 155 D2 🔢
Cranberry St OLDE OL4 .... 79 F6 🔢
Cranbourne Av CHD/CHDH SK8 ... 181 F5
Cranbourne Cl HALE/TIMP WA15 . 175 E1
Cranbourne Rd AULW OL7 .... 112 C2

CCHDY M21 .... 141 F3 🔢
HTNM SK4 .... 165 F1 🔢
OLDTF/WHR M16 .... 125 D3
ROCH OL11 .... 38 C3
Cranbourne Ter AUL OL6 .... 112 C2
Cranbrook Dr PWCH M25 .... 89 D3
Cranbrook Gdns AULW OL7 .... 112 C3 🔢
Cranbrook Rd ECC M30 .... 100 B3
  GTN M18 .... 128 A6 🔢
Cranbrook St AULW OL7 .... 112 B3
  OLDE OL4 .... 80 A5
  RAD M26 .... 52 A4
Crandon Dr DID/WITH M20 .... 164 A5
Cranesbill Cl WYTH/NTH M22 ..... 178 A6 🔢
Crane St BOLS/LL BL3 .... 45 F6 🔢
  WGTN/LGST M12 .... 125 D1 🔢
Cranfield Cl NEWH/MOS M40 ...... 107 F5 🔢
Cranford Av DID/WITH M20 .... 164 B1
  SALE M33 .... 140 A5
  STRET M32 .... 122 A6
  WHTF M45 .... 70 C1
Cranford Cl SLFD M6 .... 102 C1 🔢
  WHTF M45 .... 70 C1 🔢
Cranford Dr IRL M44 .... 116 A6
Cranford Gdns MPL/ROM SK6 ..... 171 D5
  URM M41 .... 117 F6 🔢
Cranford Rd URM M41 .... 117 F6
  WILM/AE SK9 .... 203 E2 🔢
Cranford St BOLS/LL BL3 .... 64 A1 🔢
Cranham Cl TOT/BURYW BL8 .... 32 C4
Cranham Close Crs LHULT M38 ... 65 E5 🔢
Cranham Rd WYTH/NTH M22 ..... 177 E5
Cranleigh Av HTNM SK4 .... 165 D1 🔢
Cranleigh Cl OLDE OL4 .... 80 C2 🔢
Cranleigh Dr BRAM/HZG SK7 ..... 199 E1 🔢
  CHD/CHDH SK8 .... 181 D1
  SALE M33 .... 139 E6
  SALE M33 .... 160 A4
  WALK M28 .... 83 F5
Cranlington Dr CHH M8 .... 106 A1 🔢
Cranmer Ct HEY OL10 .... 37 D6 🔢
Cranmere Av BNG/LEV M19 .... 146 A5
Cranmere Dr SALE M33 .... 158 B3
Cranmer Rd DID/WITH M20 .... 163 F1
Cranston Dr DID/WITH M20 .... 163 F5 🔢
  SALE M33 .... 160 C2
Cranston Gv CHD/CHDH SK8 ...... 179 D2
Cranswick St RUSH/FAL M14 ..... 124 B6
Crantock Dr CHD/CHDH SK8 ...... 194 A1
  STLY SK15 .... 115 F2
Crantock St WGTN/LGST M12 .... 126 C6
Cranwell Dr BNG/LEV M19 .... 164 C1
Cranworth St STLY SK15 .... 114 C6 🔢
Craston Rd BRUN/LGST M13 ...... 144 C1
Craven Av SALQ/ORD M5 .... 122 C1
Craven Dr ALT WA14 .... 158 A5
  RDSH SK5 .... 147 D5 🔢
Craven Pl OP/CLY M11 .... 109 E6
Craven Rd ALT WA14 .... 158 A6
  RDSH SK5 .... 147 D5 🔢
Craven St AUL OL6 .... 113 E2 🔢
  BURY BL9 .... 34 C3
  OLD OL1 .... 78 C3
  SALQ/ORD M5 .... 105 D6 🔢
Craven Ter SALE M33 .... 160 A1
Cravenwood Rd CHH M8 .... 90 B5
Crawford Av BOLE BL2 .... 47 F3
  WALK M28 .... 84 A5
Crawford St AUL OL6 .... 113 E5 🔢
  ECC M30 .... 101 E4
  MILN OL16 .... 40 E2
  NEWH/MOS M40 .... 109 D2 🔢
Crawley Av ECC M30 .... 102 B4 🔢
  WYTH/NTH M22 .... 178 B4 🔢
Crawley Gv OFTN SK2 .... 183 F1
Craydon St OP/CLY M11 .... 127 D1 🔢
Crayfield Rd BNG/LEV M19 .... 145 F3
Crayford Rd NEWH/MOS M40 ..... 108 C3
The Cray MILN OL16 .... 41 F1
Creaton Wy MDTN M24 .... 56 B5 🔢
Creden Av WYTH/NTH M22 .... 178 C6
Crediton Cl ALT WA14 .... 173 F1 🔢
  HULME M15 .... 124 A3
Crediton Dr BOLE BL2 .... 49 E2
Cresbury St WGTN/LGST M12 .... 125 E1 🔢
Crescent SALQ/ORD M5 .... 105 D5
Crescent Av BOL BL1 .... 46 B1 🔢
  CHH M8 .... 90 B5
  FWTH BL4 .... 66 A5
  PWCH M25 .... 88 C3
  SWIN M27 .... 86 C5
Crescent Cl DUK SK16 .... 113 D6
  EDGY/DAV SK3 .... 183 E2 🔢
Crescent Dr LHULT M38 .... 65 F6
Crescent Gv BNG/LEV M19 .... 145 E2 🔢
  PWCH M25 .... 88 C3 🔢
Crescent Pk HTNM SK4 .... 165 F4
Crescent Range RUSH/FAL M14 .. 125 D6 🔢
Crescent Rd ALT WA14 .... 173 E1
  BOLS/LL BL3 .... 47 F6
  CHAD OL9 .... 93 F3

CHD/CHDH SK8 .... 180 A1
CHH M8 .... 90 B5
DUK SK16 .... 113 D6
FWTH BL4 .... 67 D5
HALE/TIMP WA15 .... 174 C5
ROCH OL11 .... 38 C3
STKP SK1 .... 167 F2
WILM/AE SK9 .... 209 F3
Crescent St CHH M8 .... 91 D5
The Crescent ALT WA14 .... 173 E2
  BNG/LEV M19 .... 145 E2
  BOLE BL2 .... 30 A3
  BOLS/LL BL3 .... 67 F1
  BURY BL9 .... 34 B4 🔢
  CHD/CHDH SK8 .... 180 B1
  DROY M43 .... 110 A6
  EDGW/EG BL7 .... 14 B5
  EDGY/DAV SK3 .... 183 E3
  HALE/TIMP WA15 .... 159 D6
  IRL M44 .... 116 C6
  MDTN M24 .... 74 C3
  MOSL OL5 .... 98 C4
  MPL/ROM SK6 .... 168 B1
  PWCH M25 .... 88 C1 🔢
  RAD M26 .... 50 B4
  ROY/SHW OL2 .... 61 E3
  STLY SK15 .... 133 E3
  URM M41 .... 118 A6
Crescent Wy EDGY/DAV SK3 ...... 183 E2 🔢
Cressfield Wy CCHDY M21 .... 142 B4
Cressingham Rd BOLS/LL BL3 ..... 45 D6
  STRET M32 .... 139 F2
Cressington Cl SALQ/ORD M5 .... 105 F5 🔢
Cresswell Gv DID/WITH M20 ...... 143 E6
Crestfold WALK M28 .... 82 B1 🔢
Crest St CSLFD M3 .... 106 B4 🔢
The Crest DROY M43 .... 128 B2
Crete St OLDS OL8 .... 96 A1
Crewe Rd NTHM/RTH M23 .... 160 C5
Criccieth Rd EDGY/DAV SK3 .... 165 E6
Cricketfield La WALK M28 .... 83 D2 🔢
Cricket's La AUL OL6 .... 113 D4 🔢
Cricket St BOLS/LL BL3 .... 46 B4 🔢🔢
  DTN/ASHW M34 .... 130 B5 🔢
Cricket Vw MILN OL16 .... 42 A3
Cricklewood Rd WYTH/NTH M22 . 178 A5
Crimble La HEY OL10 .... 37 F2
Crimble St OLDE OL4 .... 80 C3 🔢
Crimbles St WHIT OL12 .... 22 B5
Crime La OLDS OL8 .... 95 E6
Crimsworth Av
  OLDTF/WHR M16 .... 141 F5 🔢
Cringle Cl BOLS/LL BL3 .... 44 C5
Cringle Dr CHD/CHDH SK8 .... 180 A3
Cringleford Wk
  WGTN/LGST M12 .... 126 A4 🔢
Cringle Hall Rd BNG/LEV M19 .... 145 D3
Cringle Rd BNG/LEV M19 .... 145 F5
Cripple Gate La ROCH OL11 .... 39 F6
Crispin Rd WYTH/NTH M22 .... 192 C1
Critchley Cl HYDE SK14 .... 151 D2
Criterion St RDSH SK5 .... 147 D1
Croal St BOL BL1 .... 46 B3
Croasdale Dr ROY/SHW OL2 ...... 60 C4
Croasdale St BOL BL1 .... 28 A6
Crocus Dr ROY/SHW OL2 .... 61 E4
Croft Acres RAMS BL0 .... 7 E1
Croft Av PWCH M25 .... 73 D3
Croft Bank GTN M18 .... 127 F4 🔢
Croft Cl HALE/TIMP WA15 .... 190 A3
Croft Dr TOT/BURYW BL8 .... 31 F1
Crofters Brook Rd RAD M26 .... 52 A5
Crofters Gn WILM/AE SK9 .... 203 D5 🔢
The Crofters SALE M33 .... 161 D2
Crofters Wk BOLE BL2 .... 29 D1
Croft Ga BOLE BL2 .... 29 F3
Croft Gates Rd MDTN M24 .... 74 B4
Croft Head ROY/SHW OL2 .... 60 B5 🔢
Croft Head Dr MILN OL16 .... 25 D6
Croft Hill Rd NEWH/MOS M40 ... 92 B4
Croftlands RAMS BL0 .... 18 B2 🔢
Croftlands Rd WYTH/NTH M22 ... 178 C3
Croft La BOLS/LL BL3 .... 47 F4
  BURY BL9 .... 53 E4
  RAD M26 .... 52 A5
Croftleigh Cl WHTF M45 .... 70 C1 🔢
Crofton Av HALE/TIMP WA15 ..... 159 E5
Crofton St OLDS OL8 .... 95 F2 🔢
  OLDTF/WHR M16 .... 123 E5
  RUSH/FAL M14 .... 124 C6
Croft Rd CHD/CHDH SK8 .... 181 F4
  SALE M33 .... 160 C3 🔢
  WILM/AE SK9 .... 208 C1
Crofts Bank Rd URM M41 .... 119 D5
Croftside Av WALK M28 .... 83 F2
Croftside Cl WALK M28 .... 83 F2 🔢
Croftside Wy WILM/AE SK9 .... 204 A5 🔢
Croft St BOLS/LL BL3 .... 47 F5
  BRO M7 .... 105 D2
  BURY BL9 .... 34 B5
  FAIL M35 .... 94 B4
  HYDE SK14 .... 150 B1

LHULT M38 .... 65 D6 🔲
OP/CLY M11 .... 108 C6
STLY SK15 .... 114 C5
WHIT OL12 .... 24 A2
The Croft BURY BL9 .... 53 E3
OLDS OL8 .... 95 F3
Croichbank TOT/BURYW BL8 .... 16 C3
Cromar Rd BRAM/HZG SK7 .... 185 D4
Cromarty Av CHAD OL9 .... 94 A2 🔟
Crombie Av WYTH/NTH M22 .... 162 B5
Crombouke Fold WALK M28 .... 82 C6 🔟
Cromdale Av BOL BL1 .... 45 F1 🔟
BRAM/HZG SK7 .... 185 D4 🔟
Cromer Av BOLE BL2 .... 29 D6
DID/WITH M20 .... 143 F5
DTN/ASHW M34 .... 128 B6 🔟
Cromer Rd CHD/CHDH SK8 .... 180 C1
SALE M33 .... 160 A2
TOT/BURYW BL8 .... 33 E2
Cromer St MDTN M24 .... 75 F2 🔟
OP/CLY M11 .... 109 E6 🔟
ROY/SHW OL2 .... 61 F2 🔟
STKP SK1 .... 167 E3
WHIT OL12 .... 22 C5 🔟
Cromford Av STRET M32 .... 120 C6
Cromford Cl BOL BL1 .... 27 F6 🔟
Cromford Gdns BOL BL1 .... 28 A5 🔟🔟
Cromford St OLD OL1 .... 79 E3
Cromhurst St CHH M8 .... 90 B5 🔟
Cromley Rd MPL/ROM SK6 .... 200 C2
OFTN SK2 .... 183 E4
Crompton Av BOLE BL2 .... 48 C1
ROCH OL11 .... 40 C4
Crompton Cl BOL BL1 .... 28 B3
MPL/ROM SK6 .... 171 D6
RAD M26 .... 69 F3
Crompton Pl RAD M26 .... 51 F6
RAD M26 .... 67 F3
Crompton Rd BNG/LEV M19 .... 145 E4
Crompton St AUL OL6 .... 113 F3
BOL BL1 .... 47 E1 🔟
BURY BL9 .... 33 F5 🔟🔟
CHAD OL9 .... 78 A4
FWTH BL4 .... 66 C4
OLD OL1 .... 78 C3
ROY/SHW OL2 .... 60 C6 🔟
ROY/SHW OL2 .... 61 F2 🔟
SWIN M27 .... 85 F5 🔟
WALK M28 .... 84 A3
Crompton V BOLE BL2 .... 48 B1
Crompton Wy BOLE BL2 .... 29 D4
Cromwell Av CHD/CHDH SK8 .... 179 E1
MPL/ROM SK6 .... 170 A6
OLDTF/WHR M16 .... 142 A1
Cromwell Gv BNG/LEV M19 .... 145 E2
BRO M7 .... 105 D2 🔟
Cromwell Range
RUSH/FAL M14 .... 144 B1 🔟
Cromwell Rd BRAM/HZG SK7 .... 196 B3
ECC M30 .... 101 D5 🔟
IRL M44 .... 134 C4
MPL/ROM SK6 .... 148 B5
PWCH M25 .... 89 D1
ROY/SHW OL2 .... 60 A3
SLFD M6 .... 104 B3
STRET M32 .... 140 C2
SWIN M27 .... 85 F4
WHTF M45 .... 70 B1
Cromwell St BOL BL1 .... 46 C2 🔟
HEY OL10 .... 37 E6
HTNM SK4 .... 166 B2 🔟
OLD OL1 .... 79 D5
Crondall St RUSH/FAL M14 .... 124 B6
Cronkeyshaw Rd WHIT OL12 .... 22 C4
Cronshaw St BNG/LEV M19 .... 145 F3 🔟
Crookhill Dr CHH M8 .... 90 A6 🔟
Crookilley Wy MPL/ROM SK6 .... 148 B6
STKP SK1 .... 167 F2
Crook St BOLS/LL BL3 .... 47 D3
HYDE SK14 .... 150 B1
MILN OL16 .... 23 D5
Crosby Av WALK M28 .... 84 A3 🔟
Crosby Rd BOL BL1 .... 45 F1
NEWH/MOS M40 .... 109 E2
RAD M26 .... 50 C2
SLFD M6 .... 103 E2 🔟
Crosby St OFTN SK2 .... 167 D6
WHIT OL12 .... 23 D3
Crosfield Av BURY BL9 .... 19 D3
Crosfield Gv GTN M18 .... 127 E5 🔟
Crossacres Rd WYTH/NTH M22 .... 179 D3
Cross Av PWCH M25 .... 71 E5
Crossbank St OLDE OL4 .... 81 D4
Crossbank Cl BRUN/LGST M13 .... 125 E4 🔟
Crossbank St CHAD OL9 .... 78 C5 🔟
OLDS OL8 .... 78 C3
Crossbridge Rd HYDE SK14 .... 151 E1
Crossby Cl MDTN M24 .... 75 D6
Crosscliffe Cl OLDTF/WHR M16 ... 124 A5 🔟
Crossdale Rd BKLY M9 .... 91 F1
BOLE BL2 .... 49 D1
Crossefield Rd CHD/CHDH SK8 .... 181 E4
Crossen St BOLS/LL BL3 .... 48 A4
Crossfell Av BKLY M9 .... 73 F6
Crossfield Cl DTN/ASHW M34 ...... 149 E1 🔟

Cross Field Cl ROY/SHW OL2 .... 43 D6 🔟
Crossfield Cl STLY SK15 .... 114 B6
WHIT OL12 .... 11 D4 🔟
Crossfield Dr RAD M26 .... 50 C6
SWIN M27 .... 85 F4
WALK M28 .... 84 A6
Crossfield Gv MPL/ROM SK6 .... 171 F4
OFTN SK2 .... 183 F3
Crossfield Pl ROCH OL11 .... 40 B2 🔟
Crossfield Rd ECC M30 .... 117 D5
HALE/TIMP WA15 .... 175 D5
WHIT OL12 .... 11 D5
WILM/AE SK9 .... 194 B5
Crossfield St BURY BL9 .... 53 D5
Crossford Br SALE M33 .... 140 A4
Crossford Dr BOLS/LL BL3 .... 44 C4
Crossford St STRET M32 .... 140 B2
Crossgate Av WYTH/NTH M22 ..... 178 B1
Crossgate Ms HTNM SK4 .... 164 C3
Crossgates Rd MILN OL16 .... 25 D6
Cross Glebe St AUL OL6 .... 113 D4 🔟
Cross Gv HALE/TIMP WA15 .... 159 D5
Crosshill Cl OLDTF/WHR M16 ...... 124 A5
Cross Keys St ANC M4 .... 3 G1
Cross Knowle Vw URM M41 .... 118 A5
Crossland Rd DROY M43 .... 141 E3
DROY M43 .... 110 B5
Crosslands PWCH M25 .... 88 B2 🔟
Crosslands Rd WALK M28 .... 82 A6 🔟
Cross La DROY M43 .... 111 E3
GTN M18 .... 127 E4
MPL/ROM SK6 .... 186 C2
RAD M26 .... 52 A5
SALE/ORD M5 .... 104 C5
TOT/BURYW BL8 .... 8 B6
WILM/AE SK9 .... 205 D3
Cross La East PART M31 .... 155 D3
Cross La West PART M31 .... 154 C3
Cross Lees WHIT OL12 .... 23 E2
Crossley Ct ANC M4 .... 107 E6 🔟
Crossley Crs AUL OL6 .... 113 C6
Crossley Rd BNG/LEV M19 .... 145 E4
SALE M33 .... 139 E5
Crossley St BOLS/LL BL3 .... 49 E6 🔟
GTN M18 .... 126 C3
MILN OL16 .... 41 F1
ROY/SHW OL2 .... 62 A3
ROY/SHW OL2 .... 78 C1
STLY SK15 .... 114 A5 🔟
Crossmead Dr BKLY M9 .... 74 C6 🔟
Crossmoor Crs MPL/ROM SK6 ..... 170 A3
Crossmoor Gv MPL/ROM SK6 ...... 170 A3 🔟
Cross Ormrod St BOLS/LL BL3 ..... 46 B3 🔟🔟
Cross Rd CCHDY M21 .... 141 F4
CHD/CHDH SK8 .... 182 B2
Cross St AUL OL6 .... 112 B5
AUL OL6 .... 113 E2
BOL BL1 .... 47 D1
BOLS/LL BL3 .... 49 F6
BURY BL9 .... 34 A5
CMANW M2 .... 2 D3
CSLFD M3 .... 2 B2
DTN/ASHW M34 .... 129 F4
EDGW/EG BL7 .... 14 A6
FWTH BL4 .... 66 B2
FWTH BL4 .... 67 F5 🔟
HEY OL10 .... 37 F6
HYDE SK14 .... 150 B1
MDTN M24 .... 75 D2
MILN OL16 .... 24 B6 🔟
MOSL OL5 .... 99 D3 🔟
OLDE OL4 .... 79 F4
OLDE OL4 .... 80 C5 🔟
OLDE OL4 .... 81 E5
OLDTF/WHR M16 .... 123 E4
RAMS BL0 .... 7 D5
ROCH OL11 .... 39 E5 🔟
SALE M33 .... 139 F5
STLY SK15 .... 115 E3 🔟
STRET M32 .... 140 B3
SWIN M27 .... 87 E3
URM M41 .... 138 A2
WALK M28 .... 85 D6
WHTF M45 .... 70 C1
Crosswaite Rd OFTN SK2 .... 184 B1
Crossway BRAM/HZG SK7 .... 196 C4
DID/WITH M20 .... 163 F2
OFTN SK2 .... 183 E3 🔟
Crossways OLDS OL8 .... 96 B4 🔟
Croston St BOLS/LL BL3 .... 46 A5 🔟🔟
Croton St HTNM SK4 .... 164 C3 🔟
Croughton Cl OP/CLY M11 .... 127 E2 🔟
Crowcroft Rd BRUN/LGST M13 ... 126 B6
Crowden Rd NEWH/MOS M40 ..... 92 C3
Crow Hl STLY SK15 .... 115 F2
Crow Hl North MDTN M24 .... 75 D5
Crowhill Rd AULW OL7 .... 112 A3
Crow Hl South MDTN M24 .... 75 D5
Crow Hill Vw OLDE OL4 .... 98 A1
Crowland Gdns CHD/CHDH SK8 ... 195 F3 🔟
Crowland Rd BOLE BL2 .... 29 D5
NTHM/RTH M23 .... 177 D4
Crow La RAMS BL0 .... 7 D5
Crowley La OLDE OL4 .... 80 B2
Crowley Rd BKLY M9 .... 92 A5

HALE/TIMP WA15 .... 175 F1
Crown Ct BRAM/HZG SK7 .... 184 B4 🔟
Crowneast St ROCH OL11 .... 22 A6 🔟
Crown Gdns MILN OL16 .... 40 C2 🔟
Crown Hl MOSL OL5 .... 99 E5
Crownhill Dr DROY M43 .... 110 B5
Crown La ANC M4 .... 106 B4 🔟
Crown Passages
HALE/TIMP WA15 .... 174 C5
Crown Point Av
NEWH/MOS M40 .... 109 D2 🔟
Crown Rd HEY OL10 .... 36 C5
Crown Sq CSLFD M3 .... 2 B4
Crown St AUL OL6 .... 112 C5
BOL BL1 .... 47 D2
CSLFD M3 .... 2 B1
DTN/ASHW M34 .... 129 F5 🔟
FAIL M35 .... 94 A5
HULME M15 .... 123 F2 🔟
MILN OL16 .... 40 B2
MPL/ROM SK6 .... 169 D1 🔟
MPL/ROM SK6 .... 187 D4
NEWH/MOS M40 .... 109 D2 🔟
ROY/SHW OL2 .... 61 D2 🔟
Crowsdale Pl OFTN SK2 .... 184 C3
Crowshaw Dr WHIT OL12 .... 22 C2
Crow's Nest BOLS/LL BL3 .... 49 D4
Crowswood Dr STLY SK15 .... 115 E2
Crowther Av SALQ/ORD M5 .... 122 B1
Crowther St GTN M18 .... 127 E4 🔟
LIT OL15 .... 24 C1 🔟
MILN OL16 .... 40 B3
Crowthorn Dr NTHM/RTH M23 .... 177 E5 🔟
Crowthorn Rd AULW OL7 .... 112 A6
HTNM SK4 .... 146 B4
Crowton Av SALE M33 .... 158 B3 🔟
Croxdale Cl AULW OL7 .... 111 F2
Croxton Av MILN OL16 .... 24 A5
Croxton Cl MPL/ROM SK6 .... 186 C2
SALE M33 .... 158 B3 🔟
Croyde Cl BOLE BL2 .... 30 A4
WYTH/NTH M22 .... 193 D2
Croydon Av ROCH OL11 .... 58 B2
ROY/SHW OL2 .... 60 A3
Croydon Dr NEWH/MOS M40 ...... 109 D3
Croydon Sq ROCH OL11 .... 58 B1 🔟
Crummock Cl BOLS/LL BL3 .... 49 D6 🔟
Crummock Dr MDTN M24 .... 56 C6
Crummock Rd CHD/CHDH SK8 ... 179 F4 🔟
FWTH BL4 .... 64 C4 🔟
Crumpall La CHH M8 .... 90 A4
Crumpall St BOL BL1 .... 27 F5
Crumpall V BKLY M9 .... 91 D3
Crumpsall Wy CHH M8 .... 90 C4 🔟
Crundale Rd EDGW/EG BL7 .... 28 B1 🔟
Cruttenden Rd OFTN SK2 .... 184 A3
Cryer St DROY M43 .... 111 D3
Cuba St MDTN M24 .... 76 A3 🔟
Cubley Rd BRO M7 .... 89 F5
Cuckoo Gv PWCH M25 .... 71 F5 🔟
Cuckoo La BURY BL9 .... 35 D4 🔟
PWCH M25 .... 71 F5
Cuddington Av DID/WITH M20 ..... 143 E3 🔟
Cuddington Crs EDGY/DAV SK3 ... 182 B1
Cudworth Rd BKLY M9 .... 73 E6
Culand St WGTN/LGST M12 .... 125 F3 🔟
Culbert Av DID/WITH M20 .... 164 A2 🔟
Culcheth Av MPL/ROM SK6 .... 187 D1 🔟
Culcheth La NEWH/MOS M40 ..... 109 D2
Culcheth Rd ALT WA14 .... 174 B4
Culford Cl WGTN/LGST M12 .... 125 F4 🔟
Cullen Gv BKLY M9 .... 91 F2
Culmere Rd WYTH/NTH M22 ...... 178 B6
Culross Av BOLS/LL BL3 .... 44 C3
NEWH/MOS M40 .... 93 H4 🔟
Culver Rd EDGY/DAV SK3 .... 182 B2
Culvert St MILN OL16 .... 40 C5
OLDE OL4 .... 80 C2
Culverwell Dr SALQ/ORD M5 .... 104 C5
Cumber Cl WILM/AE SK9 .... 208 B1
Cumber Dr WILM/AE SK9 .... 208 B1
Cumberland Av DUK SK16 .... 131 F1
HEY OL10 .... 36 B6 🔟
IRL M44 .... 134 A6
RDSH SK5. .... 168 A1
SWIN M27 .... 86 A3
Cumberland Cl BURY BL9 .... 52 C3 🔟
Cumberland Dr OLD OL1 .... 78 B2
Cumberland Gv AULW OL7 .... 112 C3
Cumberland Rd BKLY M9 .... 91 E4 🔟
PART M31 .... 154 B3
ROCH OL11 .... 40 A5
SALE M33 .... 160 A3
URM M41 .... 138 A2
Cumberland St BRO M7 .... 105 E3
STLY SK15 .... 114 A5 🔟
Cumber La WILM/AE SK9 .... 208 B1
Cumbrae Gdns SALQ/ORD M5 .... 103 F6 🔟
Cumbrae Rd BNG/LEV M19 .... 146 A2 🔟
Cumbrian Cl BRUN/LGST M13 .... 125 D3 🔟
ROY/SHW OL2 .... 61 D1
Cummings St OLDS OL8 .... 95 D3 🔟
Cunard Cl BRUN/LGST M13 .... 125 D3 🔟
Cuncliffe Dr ROY/SHW OL2 .... 62 B2 🔟
SALE M33 .... 160 A2

Cundey St BOL BL1 .... 27 D6 15
Cundiff Rd CCHDY M21 .... 141 F5
Cundy St HYDE SK14 .... 131 F5
Cunliffe Av RAMS BL0 .... 18 B1
Cunliffe Brow BOL BL1 .... 26 C5
Cunliffe St EDGY/DAV SK3 .... 166 A5
 HYDE SK14 .... 131 D5 2
 RAMS BL0 .... 7 D4
Cunningham Dr BURY BL9 ..... 71 F2
 WYTH/NTH M22 .... 193 E1
Curate St STKP SK1 .... 167 E4
Curlew Cl ROCH OL11 .... 21 D6
Curlew Dr IRL M44 .... 116 B5
Curlew Rd OLDE OL4 .... 97 F1
Currier La AUL OL6 .... 113 D5
Curtels St WALK M28 .... 85 D6
Curtis Rd BNG/LEV M19 ...... 146 A2
 HTNM SK4 .... 165 E5
Curtis St BOLS/LL BL3 .... 64 A1 3
Curzon Av RUSH/FAL M14 .... 125 F5 8
Curzon Dr HALE/TIMP WA15 .. 175 F1
Curzon Dr IRL M44 .... 168 B5
Curzon Ms WILM/AE SK9 ...... 203 E5
Curzon St AUL OL6 .... 113 D6
 BOL BL1 .... 46 A2 13
 BRO M7 .... 89 E6
 CHD/CHDH SK8 .... 193 F2
 OFTN SK2 .... 168 B6
 ROCH OL11 .... 42 C6
 SALE M33 .... 139 F6 8
 STRET M32 .... 120 B6
Curzon St MOSL OL5 .... 99 D4
 OLD OL1 .... 79 D4
Cutgate Cl NTHM/RTH M23 .. 160 C4 8
Cutgate Rd WHIT OL12 .... 21 F4
Cuthbert Av BNG/LEV M19 ... 145 F1
Cuthbert Rd CHD/CHDH SK8 .. 180 C1
Cutland St NEWH/MOS M40 .. 108 B1
Cut La WHIT OL12 .... 21 D4
Cutler Hill Rd FAIL M35 .... 95 D6
Cutnook La IRL M44 .... 116 A4
Cycle St OP/CLY M11 .... 126 C1
Cyclone St OP/CLY M11 .... 126 A1 2
Cygnus Av BRO M7 .... 105 D4 1
Cymbal St RDSH SK5 .... 166 C2
Cynthia Dr MPL/ROM SK6 .... 187 D2
Cypress Av CHAD OL9 .... 77 F3
Cypress Cl EDGY/DAV SK3 .... 166 A5
Cypress Gv DTN/ASHW M34.. 130 B6
 FWTH BL4 .... 67 D4 1
Cypress Rd DROY M43 .... 110 B4
 ECC M30 .... 100 B3
 OLDE OL4 .... 80 B3
Cyprus Cl OLDE OL4 .... 80 B6 8
 SALO/ORD M5 .... 104 A6
Cyprus St STRET M32 .... 140 B1
Cyril St BOLS/LL BL3 .... 47 E4 2
 ROY/SHW OL2 .... 62 A2 11
Cyrus St NEWH/MOS M40 ... 107 E5

D

Daccamill Dr SWIN M27 .... 102 A1
Dacre Av OLDTF/WHR M16 ... 141 F1 8
Dacre Cl MDTN M24 .... 73 F2
Dacre Rd ROCH OL11 .... 40 A3
Daffodil Cl WHIT OL12 .... 22 C2 8
Daffodil Rd FWTH BL4 .... 65 E2
Daffodil St BOL BL1 .... 28 A2 8
Dagenham Rd RUSH/FAL M14 125 D6 8
Dagmar St WALK M28 .... 83 D1
Dagnall Av CCHDY M21 .... 141 F5
Dahlia Cl WHIT OL12 .... 22 B2
Daimler St CHH M8 .... 106 B1
Dain Cl DUK SK16 .... 131 E1
Daine Av NTHM/RTH M23 .... 161 F4
Dainton St WGTN/LGST M12 . 125 E2 8
Daintry Rd CHAD OL9 .... 78 A4
Dairyground Rd BRAM/HZG SK7.. 196 C3
Dairyhouse La ALT WA14 ...... 157 F6
Dairy House La BRAM/HZG SK7. 195 F6
Dairy House Rd CHD/CHDH SK8 .. 195 F4
Dairy St CHAD OL9 .... 77 F4
Daisy Av BRUN/LGST M13 .... 125 F5
 FWTH BL4 .... 65 E2
Daisy Bank NEWH/MOS M40 . 109 D3
Daisy Bank Av SLFD M6 .... 103 D1
Daisy Bank La WYTH/NTH M22 179 E6
Daisy Bank Rd RUSH/FAL M14 . 125 E6
Daisyfield Cl WYTH/NTH M22 178 A6 8
Daisyhill Cl SALE M33 .... 160 C1 2
Daisy Ms EDGY/DAV SK3....... 182 B3
Daisy St BOLS/LL BL3 .... 46 A5
 CHAD OL9 .... 91 F1
 OFTN SK2 .... 167 D6 8
 WHIT OL12 .... 22 C5 8
Daisy Wy MPL/ROM SK6 ...... 201 D2
Dakerwood Cl NEWH/MOS M40 .. 109 D2 8

Dakley St OP/CLY M11 .... 127 D2 8
Dakota Av SALQ/ORD M5........ 121 F1
Dakota South SALQ/ORD M5... 122 A1
Dalbeattie St BKLY M9 .... 91 F4
Dalberg St WGTN/LGST M12 . 125 E2
Dalbury Dr NEWH/MOS M40 . 107 D2
Dalby Av SWIN M27 .... 85 F6 8
Dalby Gv STKP SK1 .... 167 E4
Dale Av BRAM/HZG SK7 .... 197 D1
 ECC M30 .... 101 D4
 MOSL OL5 .... 99 F3
Dalebeck Cl WHTF M45 .... 71 F3
Dale Brook Av DUK SK16 ...... 131 E3 8
Dalebrook Rd SALE M33....... 160 A4
Dalegarth Av HOR/BR BL6....... 44 A2
Dale Gv AULW OL7 .... 112 B2
 HALE/TIMP WA15 .... 159 D6
 IRL M44 .... 134 C5
Dalehead Dr ROY/SHW OL2 .... 62 B2
Dale Rd MDTN M24 .... 75 F1
 MPL/ROM SK6 .... 170 C6
Dales Av CHH M8 .... 90 A3
 WHTF M45 .... 70 B2
Dales Brow EDGW/EG BL7 ..... 28 A1
 SWIN M27 .... 101 F1 8
Dales Brow Av AULW OL7 .... 112 B2 8
Dalesfield Crs MOSL OL5 .... 99 F4
Dales Gv WALK M28 .... 84 A4
Dales La WHTF M45 .... 70 C2
Dalesman Dr OLD OL1 .... 62 B6
Dales Park Dr SWIN M27 ..... 101 E1 8
Dale St CMANE M1 .... 3 C3
 EDGY/DAV SK3 .... 166 B6
 FWTH BL4 .... 66 C2 8
 MDTN M24 .... 75 F4 8
 MILN OL16 .... 24 A6
 MILN OL16 .... 42 A1
 RAD M26 .... 69 E1
 RAMS BL0 .... 7 D3
 ROY/SHW OL2 .... 61 F3
 STLY SK15 .... 114 A6
 SWIN M27 .... 101 F1 8
 TOT/BURYW BL8 .... 33 D3 8
Dale St West AULW OL7 .... 112 B5
Daleswood Av WHTF M45 ...... 70 B2
Dale Vw DTN/ASHW M34 ..... 149 E4
 HYDE SK14....................... 150 B3
 LIT OL15 .... 25 D3
Dalham Av BKLY M9 .... 92 B3
Dalkeith Gv BOLS/LL BL3 ...... 45 D4 2
Dalkeith Rd RDSH SK5 .... 147 D6
Dalkeith St GTN M18 .... 126 C3
Dallas Ct SALQ/ORD M5........ 121 F1
Dalley Av BRO M7 .... 105 E3
Dallimore Rd NTHM/RTH M23.. 167 F4
Dalmahoy Cl NEWH/MOS M40.. 93 D5
Dalmain Cl CHH M8 .... 106 A1 8
Dalmeny Ter ROCH OL11 .... 40 A3
Dalmorton Rd CCHDY M21 ... 142 B3
Dalny St BNG/LEV M19 .... 145 F2
Dalston Av FAIL M35 .... 94 C5
Dalston Dr BRAM/HZG SK7.. 196 A4
 DID/WITH M20 .... 164 A3 8
Dalton Av MILN OL16 .... 24 B6 8
 RUSH/FAL M14 .... 143 E1
 STRET M32 .... 120 A5
 WHTF M45 .... 71 E4
Dalton Cl MILN OL16 .... 24 B6
 RAMS BL0 .... 18 B1 8
Dalton Dr SWIN M27 .... 87 E6
Dalton Gdns URM M41 .... 118 C6 8
Dalton Rd BKLY M9 .... 74 B6 8
Dalton St ANC M4 .... 106 C4
 CHAD OL9 .... 77 F4
 ECC M30 .... 101 E4
 FAIL M35 .... 93 F5
 OLD OL1 .... 79 F4 8
 SALE M33 .... 140 A5 8
 TOT/BURYW BL8 .... 32 C5 8
Daltry St OLD OL1 .... 79 E3
Dalveen Av URM M41 .... 119 D5
Dalveen Dr HALE/TIMP WA15 .. 159 D2 8
Damask Av CSLFD M3 .... 105 E3 8
Dame Hollow CHD/CHDH SK8.. 194 B2 8
Dameral Cl CHH M8 .... 106 B1 8
Damery Rd BRAM/HZG SK7.. 196 C1
Dame St CHAD OL9 .... 78 B3
Dam Head Dr BKLY M9 .... 91 F2
Damien St BNG/LEV M19 ..... 145 F1
Dan Bank MPL/ROM SK6 ..... 186 A5
Danby Cl HYDE SK14 .... 132 A5
Danby Pl HYDE SK14 .... 132 A5
Danby Rd BOLS/LL BL3 .... 46 C6 8
 HYDE SK14....................... 132 A5
Dane Av EDGY/DAV SK3....... 165 E5 8
 PART M31 .... 155 D1
Dane Bank MDTN M24 .... 75 F3
Danebank Ms DTN/ASHW M34 .. 147 F1
Danebank Wk BRUN/LGST M13 124 C2 8
Danebridge Cl FWTH BL4 .... 66 C3 8
Dane Cl BRAM/HZG SK7....... 182 B5
Danecroft Cl BRUN/LGST M13.. 125 E4

Dane Dr WILM/AE SK9 .... 204 B5
Danefield Ct CHD/CHDH SK8 .. 194 B3 8
Danefield Rd SALE M33 .... 140 A5
Daneholme Rd BNG/LEV M19.. 144 C6
Dane Rd DTN/ASHW M34 ..... 147 E1
 SALE M33 .... 140 A5
Danesbury Ri CHD/CHDH SK8.. 180 C5 8
Danesbury Rd BOL BL1 .... 28 C3
Daneshill PWCH M25 .... 71 F5
Danesmoor Dr BURY BL9........ 34 B3
Danesmoor Rd DID/WITH M20 .. 143 E6
Danes Rd RUSH/FAL M14 ..... 144 B1
Dane St BOLS/LL BL3 .... 46 A5 23B
 OLDE OL4 .... 80 A4
 OP/CLY M11 .... 127 F2
 ROCH OL11 .... 22 C6
Danesway PWCH M25 .... 89 E3
 SWIN M27 .... 103 D1
Daneswood Av BKLY M9 .... 92 A1 8
 WHIT OL12 .... 9 D4
Daneswood Cl WHIT OL12 .... 9 D3 8
Danett Cl WGTN/LGST M12 .. 126 C3 8
Dan Fold OLD OL1 .... 78 C4 8
Danforth Gv BNG/LEV M19 .. 145 F3 8
Daniel Adamson Av PART M31.. 154 B2 8
Daniel Adamson Rd
 SALO/ORD M5................. 121 E1
Daniel Fold WHIT OL12 .... 21 F3
Daniel's La STKP SK1 .... 167 E3 8
Daniel St BRAM/HZG SK7..... 184 C5 8
 HEY OL10 .... 36 C5 8
 OLD OL1 .... 79 F3
 ROY/SHW OL2 .... 61 E6 8
 WHIT OL12 .... 22 B3
Danisher La OLDS OL8 .... 96 A5
Dannywood Cl HYDE SK14 .... 150 A3 8
Danson St NEWH/MOS M40 . 107 F4 8
Dantall Av BKLY M9 .... 92 B2
Dante Cl SLFD M6 .... 102 B3
Danty St DUK SK16 .... 112 C6 8
Dantzic St ANC M4 .... 106 B4
Dantzic St ANC M4 .... 106 C4
Danwood Cl HYDE SK14 .... 149 F2 8
Darbishire St BOL BL1 .... 28 B6
Darby Rd IRL M44 .... 135 E5
Darbyshire Cl BOL BL1 .... 46 A1 23B
Darbyshire St RAD M26 .... 51 E6
Darcy St BOLE BL2................. 48 A4
Darden Cl HTNM SK4............ 164 C2
Daresbury Av URM M41 .... 117 E5
Daresbury Cl EDGY/DAV SK3 . 182 B2 8
 SALE M33 .... 161 D2 8
Daresbury Rd CCHDY M21 ... 141 D2
Daresbury St CHH M8 .... 90 B3
Dargai St OP/CLY M11 .... 109 E6
Dargle Rd SALE M33 .... 139 F5
Darian Av WYTH/NTH M22 .. 192 B1
Dark La MOSL OL5 .... 99 E3
 WGTN/LGST M12 .... 125 E1
Darley Av CCHDY M21 .... 142 A5
 CHD/CHDH SK8 .... 179 F2
 DID/WITH M20 .... 162 C1
 ECC M30 .... 119 D3 8
 FWTH BL4 .... 66 C2
Darley Gv FWTH BL4 .... 66 C2
Darley Rd BRAM/HZG SK7.... 199 D2
 OLDTF/WHR M16 .... 123 D6
 ROCH OL11 .... 40 A3
Darley St BOL BL1 .... 27 E6
 FWTH BL4 .... 66 C3
 OP/CLY M11 .... 107 F6
 SALE M33 .... 159 F1
 STRET M32 .... 121 E5
Darlington Cl TOT/BURYW BL8.. 32 C5 8
Darlington Rd DID/WITH M20 . 143 E5
 ROCH OL11 .... 40 A4
Darliston Av BKLY M9 .... 73 E6 8
Darnall Av DID/WITH M20 .... 143 E3
Darnbrook Dr WYTH/NTH M22.. 177 F6 8
Darncombe Cl OLDTF/WHR M16.. 124 A4 8
Darnley Av WALK M28 .... 83 D4 8
Darnley St OLDTF/WHR M16 . 123 E5
Darnton Gdns AUL OL6 .... 113 F4
Darnton Rd AUL OL6 .... 113 F4
Darras Rd GTN M18 .... 127 D6
Dart Cl CHAD OL9 .... 77 D3
Dartford Av ECC M30 .... 100 C5
 RDSH SK5........................ 147 F5
Dartford Cl WGTN/LGST M12 125 E3
Dartford Rd URM M41 .... 138 A2
Dartington Cl BRAM/HZG SK7 183 D4
 NTHM/RTH M23 .... 176 B3
Dartmouth Cl OLDS OL8 .... 96 A1 8
Dartmouth Crs RDSH SK5 .... 148 A6 8
Dartmouth Rd CCHDY M21 .. 142 A5
 WHTF M45 .... 71 E4 8
Dartnall Cl POY/DIS SK12 .... 201 E5
Darton Av NEWH/MOS M40 . 107 E4
Darvel Cl BOLE BL2................. 49 D3
Darwell Av ECC M30 .... 119 D1
Darwen Rd EDGW/EG BL7 .... 14 A5
Darwen St OLDTF/WHR M16 . 123 D6 8
Darwin Gv BRAM/HZG SK7... 196 C3
Darwin St BOL BL1 .... 27 E5
 HYDE SK14....................... 132 B4

OLDE OL4 .... 80 A6 🔲
Dashwood Rd *PWCH* M25 .... 71 E6 🔲
Datchett Ter *ROCH* OL11 .... 40 A3
Dauntesy Av *SWIN* M27 .... 87 E6 🔲
Davehall Av *WILM/AE* SK9 .... 203 E4
Davenfield Gv *DID/WITH* M20 ..... 163 F2 🔲
Davenham Rd *RDSH* SK5 .... 147 D1
 SALE M33 .... 138 C5
 WILM/AE SK9 .... 194 B5 🔲
Davenhill Rd *BNG/LEV* M19 .... 145 E3
 WILM/AE SK9 .... 208 C1
Davenport Dr *MPL/ROM* SK6 .... 149 F5
Davenport Fold Rd *BOLE* BL2 .... 30 B3 🔲
 BOLE BL2 .... 30 B4 🔲
Davenport Gdns *BOL* BL1 .... 46 C1 🔳
Davenport Park Rd *OFTN* SK2...... 183 E2
Davenport Rd *BRAM/HZG* SK7 ..... 184 B4
Davenport St *BOL* BL1 .... 46 C1
 DROY M43 .... 109 F6 🔲
 DTN/ASHW M34 .... 129 F1 🔲
Daventry Rd *CCHDY* M21 .... 142 B3
 ROCH OL11 .... 40 A4
Daveyhulme St *WHIT* OL12 .... 23 E4
Daveylands *URM* M41 .... 118 A4
 WILM/AE SK9 .... 204 B5
Davey La *WILM/AE* SK9 .... 209 E3
David Lewis Cl *MILN* OL16 .... 41 D1
David's Farm Cl *MDTN* M24 .... 75 F4
Davids La *OLDE* OL4 .... 81 D4
Davidson Dr *MDTN* M24 .... 75 F5
David's Rd *DROY* M43 .... 109 F5
David St *DTN/ASHW* M34 .... 149 E2
 RDSH SK5 .... 146 C3
 TOT/BURYW BL8 .... 33 D3 🔲
 WHIT OL12 .... 23 D4
David St North *WHIT* OL12 .... 23 D4 🔲
Davies Av *ROY/SHW* OL2 .... 61 F3 🔲
Davies La *BOL* BL1 .... 46 C1
Davies Rd *ALT* WA14 .... 58 B6
 CHD/CHDH SK8 .... 194 B1
Davies St *AULW* OL7 .... 112 A6
 FWTH BL4 .... 67 E4 🔲
 OLD OL1 .... 78 B3
Davis St *ECC* M30 .... 101 F6
Davy Av *SWIN* M27 .... 87 E3
Davyhulme Rd *STRET* M32 .... 121 D6
 URM M41 .... 117 F5
Davyhulme Rd East *STRET* M32 ... 121 E4
Davy St *NEWH/MOS* M40 .... 106 C3 🔲
Dawes St *BOL* BL1 .... 47 D3
Dawlish Av *CHAD* OL9 .... 77 D2
 CHD/CHDH SK8 .... 195 D1
 DROY M43 .... 109 F5
 RDSH SK5 .... 147 F6
Dawlish Cl *BRAM/HZG* SK7 .... 196 C2
 HYDE SK14 .... 133 F6
Dawlish Rd *CCHDY* M21 .... 142 A3
 SALE M33 .... 138 C6
Dawnay St *OP/CLY* M11 .... 126 C2 🔲
Dawn St *ROY/SHW* OL2 .... 61 F3 🔲
Dawson La *BOL* BL1 .... 46 C1
Dawson Rd *ALT* WA14 .... 173 E6
 CHD/CHDH SK8 .... 194 B1
Dawson St *BURY* BL9 .... 34 B3
 CSLFD M3 .... 2 C1 🔲
 CSLFD M3 .... 123 E1
 HEY OL10 .... 37 D5
 HYDE SK14 .... 150 C2
 OLDE OL4 .... 80 B5 🔲
 OLDE OL4 .... 80 C6 🔲
 STKP SK1 .... 167 F2 🔲
 SWIN M27 .... 86 C5 🔲
Day Dr *FAIL* M35 .... 110 A4
Daylesford Cl *CHD/CHDH* SK8 ...... 180 A3
Daylesford Crs *CHD/CHDH* SK8 .... 180 B3
Daylesford Rd *CHD/CHDH* SK8 ..... 180 B3
Deacon Cl *ALT* WA14 .... 173 F6
Deacons Cl *STKP* SK1 .... 167 F6
Deacons Crs *TOT/BURYW* BL8 ..... 32 B2 🔲
Deacons Dr *SLFD* M6 .... 103 E1
Deacon St *MILN* OL16 .... 23 I4 🔲
Deal Av *RDSH* SK5 .... 147 F5
Deal Cl *NEWH/MOS* M40 .... 108 E2 🔲
Dealey Rd *BOLS/LL* BL3 .... 64 A5
Deal St *BOLS/LL* BL3 .... 47 D6 🔳🔳
 BURY BL9 .... 34 C4
 CSLFD M3 .... 2 B2 🔲
 HYDE SK14 .... 150 C1
Dean Av *NEWH/MOS* M40 .... 108 C1
 OLDTF/WHR M16 .... 122 C6
Deanbank Av *BNG/LEV* M19 .... 145 D3 🔲
Dean Bank Dr *MILN* OL16 .... 40 C6
Dean Brook Cl *NEWH/MOS* M40 ... 92 C6 🔲
Dean Cl *FWTH* BL4 .... 65 D3
 PART M31 .... 155 D1
 WHTF M45 .... 70 B4
 WILM/AE SK9 .... 204 A2
Dean Ct *BOL* BL1 .... 47 D1
Deancourt *ROCH* OL11 .... 39 F5
Dean Dr *ALT* WA14 .... 173 F6
 WILM/AE SK9 .... 204 A2
Deane Av *BOLS/LL* BL3 .... 45 F4
 CHD/CHDH SK8............................... 181 D2
 HALE/TIMP WA15 .... 175 E2
Deane Church La *BOLS/LL* BL3 ..... 45 F5

Deane Rd *BOLS/LL* BL3 .... 46 A4
Deanery Wy *STKP* SK1 .... 167 D5 🔲
Dean La *BRAM/HZG* SK7 .... 198 C1
 NEWH/MOS M40 .... 108 C1
Dean Moor Rd *BRAM/HZG* SK7 ... 183 E5
Dean Rd *CSLFD* M3 .... 105 F4
 GTN M18 .... 127 F5
 IRL M44 .... 134 C5
 WILM/AE SK9 .... 194 C6
Dean Row Rd *WILM/AE* SK9 .... 204 A2
Deanscourt Av *SWIN* M27 .... 85 F6
Deansgate *BOL* BL1 .... 46 C2
 CSLFD M3 .... 2 B5
 HULME M15 .... 123 F2
Deansgate La *HALE/TIMP* WA15 .. 158 C6
Deansgreave Rd *BCUP* OL13 .... 4 C2
Deanshut Rd *OLDS* OL8 .... 96 B3
Deans Rd *SWIN* M27 .... 85 F6
Dean St *AUL* OL6 .... 112 B4
 CMANE M1 .... 3 H3
 FAIL M35 .... 93 F6
 MILN OL16 .... 23 F4
 MOSL OL5 .... 98 C4
 RAD M26 .... 51 D6
 STLY SK15 .... 114 B6
Deansway *SWIN* M27 .... 85 F6
Deanswood Dr *BKLY* M9 .... 73 E6
Deanwater Cl *BRUN/LGST* M13 ... 124 C2 🔲
Deanwater Ct *CHD/CHDH* SK8 ..... 194 B2 🔲
Deanway *NEWH/MOS* M40 .... 92 B5
 URM M41.. 136 B1
 WILM/AE SK9 .... 204 A3
Dearden Av *LHULT* M38 .... 65 E6
Dearden Clough *RAMS* BL0 .... 7 F1
Dearden Fold *RAMS* BL0 .... 7 F1
Deardens St *TOT/BURYW* BL8 ...... 33 D6
Dearden St *BOLS/LL* BL3 .... 49 E5
 LIT OL15 .... 12 C5
 STLY SK15 .... 114 B5 🔲
Dearmans Pl *CSLFD* M3 .... 2 B2
Dearne Dr *STRET* M32..................... 140 C1
Dearnley Cl *LIT* OL15 .... 25 D1
Debdale La *GTN* M18 .... 128 A5
Debenham Av *NEWH/MOS* M40 ... 109 D3
Debenham Ct *FWTH* BL4 .... 66 B4 🔲
Debenham Rd *STRET* M32 .... 139 E2
Dee Av *HALE/TIMP* WA15 .... 176 B2
Dee Dr *FWTH* BL4 .... 67 E6
Deepcar St *BNG/LEV* M19 .... 145 E1
Deepdale *OLDE* OL4 .... 80 B5
Deepdale Av *DID/WITH* M20 .... 143 E3
 MILN OL16 .... 41 D1
 ROY/SHW OL2 .... 60 A1
Deepdale Dr *SWIN* M27 .... 87 E6
Deepdale Rd *BOLE* BL2 .... 48 C1
Deeplish Rd *ROCH* OL11 .... 40 B2 🔳
Deeplish St *ROCH* OL11 .... 40 A2 🔲
Deeracre Av *OFTN* SK2 .... 184 A1
Deerfold Cl *GTN* M18 .... 127 E4 🔲
Deerhurst Dr *CHH* M8...................... 106 A1
Deeroak Cl *GTN* M18 .... 128 C3
Deerpark Rd *OLDTF/WHR* M16 .... 123 F6
Deer St *CMANE* M1 .... 125 D1 🔲
Defence St *BOLS/LL* BL3 .... 46 B3 🔲
Deganwy Gv *RDSH* SK5 .... 147 D6 🔲
Deighton Av *DID/WITH* M20 .... 143 E3 🔲
Delacourt Rd *RUSH/FAL* M14 .... 143 E3
De Lacy Dr *BOLE* BL2 .... 28 C6
Delafield Av *WGTN/LGST* M12 ..... 145 E1
Delaford Cl *EDGY/DAV* SK3 .... 182 C3 🔲
Delahays Dr *HALE/TIMP* WA15 ..... 175 F5
Delahays Range *GTN* M18 .... 128 A5 🔲
Delahays Rd *HALE/TIMP* WA15 ..... 175 F5
Delaine Rd *DID/WITH* M20 .... 144 A5
Delamere Av *ROY/SHW* OL2 .... 62 B1
 SALE M33 .... 160 C2
 SLFD M6 .... 103 D1
 STRET M32 .... 140 B1
 WHTF M45 .... 86 C3
Delamere Cl *BRAM/HZG* SK7 .... 185 E4
 MPL/ROM SK6 .... 150 A6 🔲
 STLY SK15 .... 115 F1 🔲
Delamere Dr *AUL* OL6 .... 112 C5 🔳
 BURY BL9 .... 34 B2
 OLDS OL8 .... 79 F6 🔲
 OP/CLY M11 .... 128 A2 🔲
Delamer Rd *ALT* WA14 .... 174 A4
Delaunays Rd *CHH* M8 .... 90 C3
 SALE M33 .... 159 D1
Delibooth Av *URM* M41................. 117 F5
Delfur Rd *BRAM/HZG* SK7 .... 197 D2
Delhi Rd *IRL* M44 .... 135 D3
Dellar St *WHIT* OL12 .... 22 A4 🔲

Dell Av *SWIN* M27 .... 87 E6
Dell Cl *OLDE* OL4 .... 81 D6
Dellcot Cl *PWCH* M25 .... 89 E3 🔲
 SLFD M6.. 102 C2
Dell Gdns *WHIT* OL12 .... 21 F3
Dellhide Cl *OLDE* OL4 .... 81 E5
Dell Meadow *WHIT* OL12 .... 9 D6 🔲
Dell Rd *WHIT* OL12 .... 21 F1
Dell Side *MPL/ROM* SK6 .... 168 C2
Dellside Gv *WALK* M28 .... 83 F2 🔲
Dell Side Wy *WHIT* OL12 .... 22 A3
Dell St *BOLE* BL2 .... 29 D2
Delph Av *WALK* M28 .... 83 E3 🔲
Delph La *BOLE* BL2 .... 31 D6
Delph St *BOLS/LL* BL3 .... 46 B4
 MILN OL16 .... 42 A1
Delside Av *NEWH/MOS* M40 .... 92 B5 🔲
Delta Cl *ROY/SHW* OL2 .... 78 B1
Delta Rd *DTN/ASHW* M34 .... 129 F2
Delwood Gdns *WYTH/NTH* M22 .. 178 B3 🔲
De-massey Cl *MPL/ROM* SK6 .... 149 F5 🔲
Demesne Cl *STLY* SK15 .... 115 D6 🔲
Demesne Crs *STLY* SK15 .... 115 D6
Demesne Dr *STLY* SK15 .... 115 D6
Demesne Rd *OLDTF/WHR* M16 .... 142 C1
Demmings Rd *CHD/CHDH* SK8 ..... 181 D2
Dempsey Dr *BURY* BL9 .... 71 F1 🔲
Denbigh Cl *BRAM/HZG* SK7 .... 198 A1
Denbigh Dr *ROY/SHW* OL2 .... 61 D3
Denbigh Pl *SALQ/ORD* M5 .... 104 B6
Denbigh Rd *BOLE* BL2 .... 47 F4 🔲
 DTN/ASHW M34 .... 149 D2
 SWIN M27 .... 86 B3
Denbigh St *HTNM* SK4 .... 166 B2 🔲
 MOSL OL5 .... 99 E5
 OLDS OL8 .... 96 A2 🔲
Denbury Dr *ALT* WA14 .... 173 F2 🔲
Denbury Gn *BRAM/HZG* SK7 .... 185 E5
Denbydale Wy *ROY/SHW* OL2 .... 60 A4
Denby La *HTNM* SK4 .... 166 B1
Denby Rd *DUK* SK16 .... 131 D2
Dencombe St *BRUN/LGST* M13 .... 126 A5 🔲
Dene Bank *BOLE* BL2 .... 29 D2 🔲
Dene Brow *DTN/ASHW* M34 .... 149 F3
Dene Ct *HTNM* SK4 .... 166 A3 🔲
Dene Dr *MDTN* M24 .... 75 D4
Denefield Cl *MPL/ROM* SK6 .... 171 F4 🔲
Dene Hollow *RDSH* SK5 .... 147 F6
Denehurst Rd *ROCH* OL11 .... 21 F5
Denehurst St *WGTN/LGST* M12 ... 126 A3 🔲
Dene Pk *DID/WITH* M20 .... 163 E3
Dene Rd West *DID/WITH* M20 ..... 163 D3
Deneside Crs *BRAM/HZG* SK7 ...... 185 D4
Dene St *BOLE* BL2 .... 29 D2 🔲
Deneway *BRAM/HZG* SK7 .... 196 A2
 HTNM SK4 .... 166 A3
 MPL/ROM SK6 .... 201 D2
Deneway Cl *HTNM* SK4 .... 166 A3 🔲
Deneway Ms *HTNM* SK4 .... 166 A3 🔲
Denewell Cl *BRUN/LGST* M13 ...... 125 E4 🔲
Denham Cl *BOL* BL1 .... 28 B2 🔲
Denham Dr *BRAM/HZG* SK7 .... 196 B2
 IRL M44 .... 135 F2
Denham St *BRUN/LGST* M13 .... 125 E5 🔲
Den Hill Dr *OLDE* OL4 .... 81 D5
Denhill Rd *HULME* M15 .... 124 A5
Denholme Rd *ROCH* OL11 .... 40 A3
Denholm Rd *DID/WITH* M20 .... 164 A5 🔲
Denhurst Rd *LIT* OL15 .... 12 E5
Denis Av *OLDTF/WHR* M16 .... 142 C1
Denison Rd *BRAM/HZG* SK7 .... 198 C1
 RUSH/FAL M14 .... 125 E6
Denison St *RUSH/FAL* M14 .... 125 D6 🔲
Deniston Rd *HTNM* SK4 .... 145 F6
Den La *OLDE* OL4 .... 81 D4
Denmark Rd *RUSH/FAL* M14 .... 124 B5
 SALE M33 .... 139 F5 🔲
Denmark St *CHAD* OL9 .... 78 A3
 HALE/TIMP WA15 .... 174 B3
 MILN OL16 .... 23 E5 🔲
 OLDE OL4 .... 79 F4 🔲
Denmark Wy *CHAD* OL9 .... 78 A3
Dennmore Rd *NEWH/MOS* M40 ..... 93 D2
Dennington Dr *URM* M41 .... 119 D5
Dennison Av *DID/WITH* M20 .... 143 F4
Dennison Rd *CHD/CHDH* SK8 .... 195 E1
Denshaw Av *DTN/ASHW* M34 ...... 129 E1
Denshaw Cl *BNG/LEV* M19 .... 164 C2
Densmore St *FAIL* M35 .... 93 F6 🔲
Denson Rd *HALE/TIMP* WA15 .... 159 F5
Denstone Av *ECC* M30 .... 101 F4
 SALE M33 .... 158 C2 🔲
 URM M41 .... 119 D6
Denstone Crs *BOLE* BL2 .... 29 E5
Denstone Rd *RDSH* SK5 .... 147 D2 🔲
 SLFD M6.. 103 E2
 URM M41 .... 119 D6
Dentdale Cl *BOL* BL1 .... 44 B3
Denton La *CHAD* OL9 .... 77 E6
Denton Rd *BOLS/LL* BL3 .... 49 F3
 DTN/ASHW M34 .... 129 F4
Denton St *BURY* BL9........................ 34 A3
 HEY OL10 .... 37 D6 🔲

WHIT OL12 .... 23 D4 🗄
Denver Av NEWH/MOS M40 ..... 107 E4
Denver Dr HALE/TIMP WA15 .... 175 E2 🗄
Denver Rd ROCH OL11 .... 40 A3
Denville Crs WYTH/NTH M22 ..... 178 C4
Depleach Rd CHD/CHDH SK8 .... 180 B2 🗄
Deptford Av NTHM/RTH M23 ..... 177 E4 🗄
De Quincey Rd ALT WA14 .... 158 B4
Deramore Cl AUL OL6 .... 113 F4
Deramore St RUSH/FAL M14 ..... 124 C6 🗄
Derby Av SLFD M6 .... 103 F5 🗄
Derby Cl IRL M44 .... 134 A6
Derby Ct CHAD OL9 .... 78 A6 🗄
    SALE M33 .... 160 A2 🗄
Derby Gv BNG/LEV M19 .... 145 F2 🗄
Derby Range HTNM SK4 .... 165 F1
Derby Rd AUL OL6 .... 113 E4
    HTNM SK4 .... 166 A1
    RAD M26 .... 67 E3 🗄
    RUSH/FAL M14 .... 144 A4
    SALE M33 .... 138 C5 🗄
    SLFD M6 .... 103 F5
    URM M41 .... 119 E6
    WHTF M45 .... 71 E5
Derbyshire Av STRET M32 .... 120 C6
Derbyshire Crs STRET M32 .... 120 C6
Derbyshire Gv STRET M32 .... 120 C6 🗄
Derbyshire La STRET M32 .... 140 A1
Derbyshire La West URM M41 .... 120 B6
Derbyshire Rd NEWH/MOS M40 . 109 E3
    PART M31 .... 154 C3 🗄
    POY/DIS SK12 .... 200 B4
    SALE M33 .... 160 A1
Derbyshire Rd South SALE M33 . 160 B2
Derbyshire Rw BOL BL1 .... 27 F4 🗄🗄
Derbyshire St OP/CLY M11 .... 127 D2 🗄
Derby St ALT WA14 .... 174 C2
    AULW OL7 .... 112 B2 🗄
    BOLS/LL BL3 .... 48 B6
    BURY BL9 .... 34 A5
    CHAD OL9 .... 78 A6
    DTN/ASHW M34 .... 129 E5
    EDGY/DAV SK3 .... 166 B5
    FAIL M35 .... 94 A4 🗄
    HEY OL10 .... 36 C5
    MOSL OL5 .... 99 E5 🗄
    MPL/ROM SK6 .... 187 D2
    PWCH M25 .... 88 B1
    RAMS BL0 .... 7 E5
    ROCH OL11 .... 40 B2
Dereham Cl TOT/BURYW BL8 .... 33 E2
Derg St SLFD M6 .... 104 A5
Derker St OLD OL1 .... 79 E3
Dermott Murphy Cl
    DID/WITH M20 .... 143 D5 🗄
Dernford Av BNG/LEV M19 .... 145 D6
Derry Av WYTH/NTH M22 .... 178 C3
Derwen Rd EDGY/DAV SK3 ...... 166 C6
Derwent Av AULW OL7 .... 112 B3
    CCHDY M21 .... 142 B6
    DROY M43 .... 109 F6
    HALE/TIMP WA15 .... 176 B2 🗄
    HEY OL10 .... 56 B1
    MILN OL16 .... 42 C1
    WHTF M45 .... 71 F3
Derwent Cl BOLS/LL BL3 .... 49 D6
    CCHDY M21 .... 142 B6
    DTN/ASHW M34 .... 147 F1
    PART M31 .... 155 D1
    WALK M28 .... 82 C3
    WHTF M45 .... 71 F4
Derwent Dr BRAM/HZG SK7 ..... 196 A4 🗄
    BURY BL9 .... 52 B2
    CHAD OL9 .... 77 E4 🗄
    FWTH BL4 .... 67 F6
    LIT OL15 .... 25 D3
    ROY/SHW OL2 .... 61 E1
    SALE M33 .... 159 E3
    WILM/AE SK9 .... 194 A4
Derwent Rd FWTH BL4 .... 65 D3
    MDTN M24 .... 66 C6
    MPL/ROM SK6 .... 200 C1
    STRET M32 .... 121 E6 🗄
    URM M41 .... 136 C1
Derwent St CHH M8 .... 107 D1 🗄
    OP/CLY M11 .... 109 E6 🗄
    WHIT OL12 .... 23 D4 🗄
Design St BOLS/LL BL3 .... 45 F6
Desmond Rd WYTH/NTH M22 ... 178 C3
The Dettingens IRL M44 .... 116 B6
Dettingen St SLFD M6 .... 103 F1
Deva Cl BRAM/HZG SK7 .... 184 B6
    POY/DIS SK12 .... 197 F5
Devas St HULME M15 .... 124 C4 🗄
Deverill Av GTN M18 .... 128 A5 🗄
Devine Cl CSLFD M3 .... 105 E5
    ROY/SHW OL2 .... 60 B3 🗄
Devisdale Rd ALT WA14 .... 173 F3
Devoke Av WALK M28 .... 83 F3
Devoke Gv FWTH BL4 .... 64 C3
Devon Av BNG/LEV M19 .... 145 D5
    WHTF M45 .... 70 C2 🗄
Devon Cl BOLS/LL BL3 .... 49 F5 🗄
    RDSH SK5 .... 168 A1 🗄
    ROY/SHW OL2 .... 61 D2

SLFD M6 .... 102 B4
Devon Dr BOLE BL2 .... 31 D6
Devonport Crs ROY/SHW OL2 .... 61 D5
Devon Rd DROY M43 .... 110 B4
    FAIL M35 .... 109 F1
    IRL M44 .... 134 B6
    PART M31 .... 154 C3 🗄
    URM M41 .... 136 C2
Devonshire Cl HEY OL10 .... 36 B5
    URM M41 .... 138 C1 🗄
Devonshire Dr WILM/AE SK9 .... 209 F3
Devonshire Park Rd OFTN SK2 .. 183 E2
Devonshire Pl PWCH M25 .... 71 E6 🗄
Devonshire Rd ALT WA14 .... 174 A1
    BOL BL1 .... 45 F1
    BRAM/HZG SK7 .... 199 D1
    CCHDY M21 .... 142 A3
    ECC M30 .... 101 F5 🗄
    HTNM SK4 .... 165 F3
    ROCH OL11 .... 40 A5
    SLFD M6 .... 102 B4
    WALK M28 .... 66 A5
Devonshire St BRO M7 .... 105 F1
    WGTN/LGST M12 .... 125 E1
Devonshire St East FAIL M35 ..... 109 E2 🗄
Devonshire St North
    WGTN/LGST M12 .... 125 D2
Devonshire St South
    BRUN/LGST M13 .... 125 E4
Devon St BURY BL9 .... 53 D1 🗄
    CHAD OL9 .... 94 C1
    FWTH BL4 .... 66 B1
    ROCH OL11 .... 40 A1 🗄
    SWIN M27 .... 86 A3
Devon Wy OLDS OL8 .... 95 D3
Dewar Cl OP/CLY M11 .... 108 B6 🗄
Dewes Av SWIN M27 .... 86 C5 🗄
Dewey St OP/CLY M11 .... 127 E2
Dewhirst Rd WHIT OL12 .... 10 A6
Dewhirst Wy WHIT OL12 .... 23 D1 🗄
Dewhurst La BOLE BL2 .... 29 F4
Dewhurst St CHH M8 .... 106 A3
    HEY OL10 .... 37 F5 🗄
Dewint Av MPL/ROM SK6 .... 171 F5
Dew Meadow Cl WHIT OL12 ...... 22 C3 🗄
Dewsnap Cl DUK SK16 .... 131 D3 🗄
Dewsnap La DUK SK16 .... 131 D3
Dew Wy CHAD OL9 .... 78 B4
Dexter Rd BKLY M9 .... 73 E6
Deyne Av PWCH M25 .... 88 C1
    RUSH/FAL M14 .... 125 D5
Deyne St SALQ/ORD M5 .... 103 F5
Dial Ct FWTH BL4 .... 66 B3 🗄
Dial Park Rd OFTN SK2 .... 184 B3
Dial Rd HALE/TIMP WA15 .... 190 A1
    OFTN SK2 .... 184 A2
Dialstone La OFTN SK2 .... 168 A6
Diamond St AUL OL6 .... 113 E3
    OFTN SK2 .... 183 E1
Diamond Ter MPL/ROM SK6 ..... 187 D4
Dicken Gn ROCH OL11 .... 40 A3
Dicken Green La ROCH OL11 ...... 40 A3
Dickens Cl CHD/CHDH SK8 ..... 195 F4 🗄
Dickens La POY/DIS SK12 .... 198 C6
Dickenson Rd RUSH/FAL M14 .... 125 E6
Dickens Rd ECC M30 .... 101 E6 🗄
Dickens St HEY OL10 .... 36 C5 🗄
    OLD OL1 .... 62 C5 🗄
Dickinson St BOL BL1 .... 27 F6
    CMANE M1 .... 3 E5
    CMANW M1 .... 2 D5 🗄
    OLDE OL4 .... 79 F4
Didcot Av WYTH/NTH M22 .... 178 A6
Didley Sq WGTN/LGST M12 ...... 126 B2 🗄
Didsbury Pk DID/WITH M20 ..... 163 F3
Didsbury Rd HTNM SK4 .... 164 C3
Digby Rd ROCH OL11 .... 40 A3
Dig Gate La MILN OL16 .... 41 F4
Diggles La ROCH OL11 .... 37 F1
Diggle St ROY/SHW OL2 .... 61 F3 🗄
Dijon St BOLS/LL BL3 .... 46 A5
Dilham Ct BOL BL1 .... 46 A1 🗄
Dillon Dr WGTN/LGST M12 ...... 125 F4
Dilston Cl BRUN/LGST M13 ...... 125 E4
Dilworth Cl HEY OL10 .... 36 B5 🗄
Dilworth St OFTN SK2 .... 184 C2
Dilworth St HULME M15 .... 124 C4
Dingle Av ROY/SHW OL2 .... 43 D6
    WILM/AE SK9 .... 208 B2
Dingle Bank Rd BRAM/HZG SK7 . 182 B5
Dingle La MPL/ROM SK6 .... 170 B3
Dingle Dr DROY M43 .... 110 C4
Dingle Gv CHD/CHDH SK8 ...... 179 D1
Dingle Rd MDTN M24 .... 74 C5
Dingle Ter AUL OL6 .... 96 C3
The Dingle BRAM/HZG SK7 ...... 182 A6
    HYDE SK14 .... 150 C5
Dinmor Rd WYTH/NTH M22 ..... 192 A1
Dinnington Dr CHH M8 .... 106 B1 🗄
Dinorwic Cl CHH M8 .... 90 B3
Dinsdale Dr BOLS/LL BL3 .... 46 B4 🗄
Dinting Av DID/WITH M20 .... 143 E4 🗄
Dinton St HULME M15 .... 123 D2
Dirty La OLDE OL4 .... 81 F2
Dirty Leech WHIT OL12 .... 10 A5

Disley Av DID/WITH M20 .... 143 D5
Disley St ROCH OL11 .... 39 D3
Distaff Rd POY/DIS SK12 .... 197 F5
Ditton Mead Cl WHIT OL12 .... 23 F3
Division St BOLS/LL BL3 .... 47 D6
    WHIT OL12 .... 23 F3
Dixon Av BRO M7 .... 105 E1
Dixon Cl SALE M33 .... 160 B3
Dixon Closes ROCH OL11 .... 20 C6
Dixon Dr SWIN M27 .... 85 F1
Dixon Green Dr FWTH BL4 .... 66 A3
Dixon Rd DTN/ASHW M34 .... 149 F2
Dixon St AUL OL6 .... 113 E3
    IRL M44 .... 134 C3
    MDTN M24 .... 75 E1 🗄
    NEWH/MOS M40 .... 108 C1 🗄
    OLDE OL4 .... 80 C3 🗄
    ROCH OL11 .... 39 D3
    SLFD M6 .... 100 A1
Dobb Hedge Cl HALE/TIMP WA15 . 190 A3
Dobbin Dr ROCH OL11 .... 40 A4
Dobbinetts La HALE/TIMP WA15 . 176 B3
    NTHM/RTH M23 .... 176 C3
Dobhill St FWTH BL4 .... 66 B3 🗄
Dobroyd St CHH M8 .... 90 B5
Dobson Cl BRUN/LGST M13 ..... 125 E3
Dobson Rd BOL BL1 .... 46 A2
Dobson St BOL BL1 .... 27 E5 🗄🗄
Doctor Fold La HEY OL10 .... 55 F3
Doctors La BURY BL9 .... 33 E5 🗄
Dodd Cft MILN OL16 .... 40 C5
Doddington Cl OLDTF/WHR M16 . 124 A5
Doddington La SALQ/ORD M5 .... 122 B1 🗄
Doddington Wk
    DTN/ASHW M34 .... 148 C2 🗄
Dodd St SALQ/ORD M5 .... 103 E5
Dodge Fold OFTN SK2 .... 184 C1
Dodge Hl HTNM SK4 .... 166 C3
Dodgson St MILN OL16 .... 40 B1
Dodworth Cl HULME M15 .... 124 A3 🗄
Doe Brow SWIN M27 .... 85 F1 🗄
Doefield Av WALK M28 .... 83 D5
Doe Hey Gv FWTH BL4 .... 65 F1 🗄
Doe Hey Rd BOLS/LL BL3 .... 65 F1
Doffcocker Brow BOL BL1 .... 26 A6
Doffcocker La BOL BL1 .... 26 A6
Dogford Rd ROY/SHW OL2 .... 60 B4
Dolbey St SALQ/ORD M5 .... 103 F6 🗄
Dolefield CSLFD M3 .... 2 B4
D'olivera Ct MDTN M24 .... 74 C1 🗄
Dollond St BKLY M9 .... 91 F4
Dolphin Pl WGTN/LGST M12 .... 125 D2
Dolphin St WGTN/LGST M12 .... 125 D2
Doman St BOLS/LL BL3 .... 47 D4 🗄
Domestic Ap MANAIR M90 .... 192 A3
Domett St BKLY M9 .... 91 D3
Dominic Cl NTHM/RTH M23 ..... 160 C4 🗄
Donald Av HYDE SK14 .... 151 D2
Donald St CMANE M1 .... 3 F6 🗄
Dona St STKP SK1 .... 167 E5 🗄
Don Av SLFD M6 .... 103 D5
Doncaster Av DID/WITH M20 .... 143 E4
Doncaster Cl BOLS/LL BL3 .... 49 D6 🗄
Donkey La WILM/AE SK9 .... 203 E6
Donleigh St NEWH/MOS M40 ... 109 E1
Donnington Av CHD/CHDH SK8 . 181 D1
Donnington Rd GTN M18 .... 127 F4 🗄
    RAD M26 .... 50 A4
Donnison St WGTN/LGST M12 .. 126 A3 🗄
    WGTN/LGST M12 .... 126 B3 🗄
Donovan Av NEWH/MOS M40 ... 107 D3 🗄
Don St BOLS/LL BL3 .... 46 B6 🗄
    MDTN M24 .... 76 A2
Doodson Av IRL M44 .... 135 D1
Doodson Sq FWTH BL4 .... 66 B3 🗄
Dooley La MPL/ROM SK6 .... 169 F6
Dorac Av CHD/CHDH SK8 .... 194 A3
Dora St RAMS BL0 .... 18 B1 🗄
Dorchester Av BOLE BL2 .... 29 F6
    DTN/ASHW M34 .... 149 D2 🗄
    PWCH M25 .... 89 D3
    URM M41 .... 138 C1
Dorchester Cl HALE/TIMP WA15 . 176 A4 🗄
    WILM/AE SK9 .... 204 B3 🗄
Dorchester Ct CHD/CHDH SK8 . 181 F6
    SALE M33 .... 159 F3
Dorchester Dr NTHM/RTH M23 . 160 C4
    ROY/SHW OL2 .... 78 C1 🗄
Dorchester Gv HEY OL10 .... 56 A1 🗄
Dorchester Rd BRAM/HZG SK7 . 183 F6
    SWIN M27 .... 102 A1 🗄
Dorclyn Av URM M41 .... 138 C1 🗄
Dorfield Cl MPL/ROM SK6 .... 168 C2 🗄
Doric Av MPL/ROM SK6 .... 168 B2
Doric Cl OP/CLY M11 .... 108 A6
Doris Av BOLE BL2 .... 48 B2
Doris Rd EDGY/DAV SK3 .... 166 A5
Doris St MDTN M24 .... 75 E1 🗄
Dorking Cl BOL BL1 .... 28 A5
    STKP SK1 .... 167 F6 🗄
Dorlan Av GTN M18 .... 128 A5
Dorland Gv OFTN SK2 .... 167 F6 🗄
Dorman St OP/CLY M11 .... 127 E2 🗄
Dormer St BOL BL1 .... 28 A4 🗄🗄
Dorney St GTN M18 .... 127 E4

Dorning Rd *SWIN* M27 .... **86** B6
Dorning St *ECC* M30 .... **101** E6 4
  FWTH BL4 .... **67** D3 2
  TOT/BURYW BL8 .... **32** C3 3
Dorothy Rd *BRAM/HZG* SK7 .... **185** D4
Dorothy St *BRO* M7 .... **90** A6 3
  RAMS BL0 .... **6** C6
Dorrington Rd *EDGY/DAV* SK3 .... **165** E6
  SALE M33 .... **158** B1
Dorris St *BNG/LEV* M19 .... **145** F5
  BOLS/LL BL3 .... **46** A6 8
Dorset Av *BRAM/HZG* SK7 .... **182** B6
  CHD/CHDH SK8 .... **182** A3
  DTN/ASHW M34 .... **129** D1
  FWTH BL4 .... **66** A3
  RDSH SK5 .... **148** A6
  ROY/SHW OL2 .... **61** D2
  RUSH/FAL M14 .... **143** E1
Dorset Cl *FWTH* BL4 .... **66** A3 3
  HEY OL10 .... **36** B6
Dorset Dr *BURY* BL9 .... **53** E1
Dorset Rd *ALT* WA14 .... **173** F3
  BNG/LEV M19 .... **146** A2
  DROY M43 .... **110** A4 2
  FAIL M35 .... **110** A2
  IRL M44 .... **134** B5
Dorset St *AUL* OL6 .... **113** E5
  BOLE BL2 .... **47** E2
  CHAD OL9 .... **78** A6
  ROCH OL11 .... **40** B1 1
  STRET M32 .... **140** B2 8
  SWIN M27 .... **86** A3
Dorsey St *ANC* M4 .... **3** G2 3
Dorstone Cl *NEWH/MOS* M40 .... **109** D3
Dorwood Av *BKLY* M9 .... **74** A6
Doughty Av *ECC* M30 .... **102** A4 1
Dougill St *BOL* BL1 .... **26** C5 13
Douglas Av *STRET* M32 .... **121** E6 2
  TOT/BURYW BL8 .... **32** C5 3
Douglas Cl *WHTF* M45 .... **72** A2 1
Douglas Gn *SLFD* M6 .... **104** B2
Douglas Rd *BRAM/HZG* SK7 .... **184** C4
  EDGY/DAV SK3 .... **182** C3
  SWIN M27 .... **85** D6
Douglas St *AUL* OL6 .... **113** E4
  BOL BL1 .... **27** F2
  BRO M7 .... **105** E1
  FAIL M35 .... **94** B6
  HYDE SK14 .... **150** C3
  NEWH/MOS M40 .... **92** B6
  OLD OL1 .... **79** E3 8
  RAMS BL0 .... **6** C5 3
  SWIN M27 .... **86** B6
Doulton St *NEWH/MOS* M40 .... **93** D5 1
Dounby Av *ECC* M30 .... **100** C4 3
Douro St *NEWH/MOS* M40 .... **108** A2
Douthwaite Dr *MPL/ROM* SK6 .... **179** F4
Dove Bank Rd *BOLS/LL* BL3 .... **49** D5
Dovebrook Cl *STLY* SK15 .... **99** F6 1
Dovecote Cl *EDGW/EG* BL7 .... **14** C5 1
Dovecote Ms *CCHDY* M21 .... **141** E3 2
Dovedale Av *DID/WITH* M20 .... **143** E4
  DROY M43 .... **109** F5 1
  ECC M30 .... **101** F4
  PWCH M25 .... **89** E2
  URM M41 .... **138** B1 8
Dovedale Cl *MPL/ROM* SK6 .... **200** C2
Dovedale Dr *WHIT* OL12 .... **11** E5
Dovedale Rd *BOLE* BL2 .... **30** A5
  OFTN SK2 .... **168** B6
Dovedale St *FAIL* M35 .... **93** F6
Dove Dr *BURY* BL9 .... **34** C3 8
  IRL M44 .... **116** B6
Dovehouse Cl *WHTF* M45 .... **70** B5
Doveleys Rd *SLFD* M6 .... **103** F2 1
Dover Cl *TOT/BURYW* BL8 .... **18** B4 2
Dovercourt Av *HTNM* SK4 .... **165** D1 3
Dover Gv *BOLS/LL* BL3 .... **46** A5
Doveridge Gdns *SLFD* M6 .... **104** A4 3
Dover Pk *URM* M41 .... **119** E5
Dover Rd *SWIN* M27 .... **86** B3
Dover St *BRUN/LGST* M13 .... **124** C3
  CHAD OL9 .... **78** A6 8
  ECC M30 .... **100** C5
  FWTH BL4 .... **66** A1 8
  MILN OL16 .... **23** F3 8
  RDSH SK5 .... **146** C4 8
Dovestone Crs *DUK* SK16 .... **132** A2 8
Dovestone Wk *NEWH/MOS* M40 .... **93** F4 8
Doveston Rd *SALE* M33 .... **139** F5
Dove St *BOL* BL1 .... **27** F5
  OLDE OL4 .... **80** A5
  ROCH OL11 .... **22** B6
Dow Fold *TOT/BURYW* BL8 .... **32** A4 1
Dowland Cl *NTHM/RTH* M23 .... **161** D3 8
Dow La *TOT/BURYW* BL8 .... **32** A4
Dowling St *ROCH* OL11 .... **40** A1
Downesway *WILM/AE* SK9 .... **209** D4
Downfield Cl *TOT/BURYW* BL8 .... **6** B5
Downfields *RDSH* SK5 .... **147** E2 8
Downgreen Rd *BOLE* BL2 .... **29** F4
Downhall Gn *BOL* BL1 .... **46** C1 18

Downham Av *BOLE* BL2 .... **48** A1
Downham Cha
  HALE/TIMP WA15 .... **175** F1 1
Downham Cl *OLD* OL1 .... **78** A1
Downham Crs *PWCH* M25 .... **89** E2
Downham Gdns *PWCH* M25 .... **89** F2
Downham Rd *HEY* OL10 .... **36** B5 8
  HTNM SK4 .... **146** B6
Downham Wk *NTHM/RTH* M23 .... **160** B5
Downhill Cl *OLD* OL1 .... **78** C2
Downing Cl *AULW* OL7 .... **112** A1 8
Downing St *AULW* OL7 .... **112** A1
  CMANE M1 .... **124** C2
Downley Cl *WHIT* OL12 .... **21** F3 8
Downley Dr *ANC* M4 .... **107** D5 8
Downs Dr *ALT* WA14 .... **158** C5
Downshaw Rd *AULW* OL7 .... **112** B1
The Downs *ALT* WA14 .... **174** B4
  CHD/CHDH SK8 .... **180** B4
  MDTN M24 .... **75** F5
  PWCH M25 .... **88** B2
Dowry Rd *OLDE* OL4 .... **80** C4
Dowry St *OLDS* OL8 .... **96** A2
Dowson Rd *HYDE* SK14 .... **150** C3
Dow St *HYDE* SK14 .... **131** E4
Doyle Av *MPL/ROM* SK6 .... **168** B2
Doyle Rd *BOLS/LL* BL3 .... **44** C6
Drake Av *FWTH* BL4 .... **66** B4 8
  IRL M44 .... **134** C5
Drake Cl *OLD* OL1 .... **78** C3
Drake Ct *RDSH* SK5 .... **166** C1 8
Drake Rd *ALT* WA14 .... **157** F5
  LIT OL15 .... **13** D2
Drake St *MILN* OL16 .... **23** D6
  ROCH OL11 .... **40** A1
Draycott St *BOL* BL1 .... **27** F5
Draycott St East *BOL* BL1 .... **28** A5 17
Drayfields *DROY* M43 .... **111** E5
Drayford Cl *NTHM/RTH* M23 .... **161** D3 8
Drayton Av *CHD/CHDH* SK8 .... **193** F2
Drayton Cl *BOL* BL1 .... **27** E5
  SALE M33 .... **158** B3
  WILM/AE SK9 .... **204** B2
Drayton Gv *HALE/TIMP* WA15 .... **175** E3
Dresden St *NEWH/MOS* M40 .... **93** D5
Drewett St *NEWH/MOS* M40 .... **107** F3
Dreyfus Av *OP/CLY* M11 .... **109** D5
Driffield St *ECC* M30 .... **119** D1 8
  RUSH/FAL M14 .... **124** C3 8
Drinkwater Rd *PWCH* M25 .... **88** A4 8
Driscoll St *BRUN/LGST* M13 .... **126** A6 8
The Drive *BRO* M7 .... **89** D4
  BURY BL9 .... **34** A2
  CHD/CHDH SK8 .... **182** A3
  DID/WITH M20 .... **164** A2
  HALE/TIMP WA15 .... **190** B1
  MPL/ROM SK6 .... **168** B2
  MPL/ROM SK6 .... **186** C1
  PWCH M25 .... **88** C1
  RDSH SK5 .... **168** A2 8
  SALE M33 .... **158** C4
Droitwich Rd *NEWH/MOS* M40 .... **107** E3
Dronfield Rd *SLFD* M6 .... **103** F2 8
  WYTH/NTH M22 .... **162** B5
Droughts La *PWCH* M25 .... **72** B3
Droylsden Rd *DTN/ASHW* M34 .... **110** C6
  NEWH/MOS M40 .... **109** E2
Drummond St *BOL* BL1 .... **27** F3 10
Drury La *CHAD* OL9 .... **94** B2
Drury St *BNG/LEV* M19 .... **145** E2 8
Dryad St *SWIN* M27 .... **86** A3 8
Drybrook Cl *BRUN/LGST* M13 .... **125** F4 8
Drybrugh Av *BOL* BL1 .... **27** E5 8
Dryden Av *CHD/CHDH* SK8 .... **180** C1
  SWIN M27 .... **85** E6
Dryden Cl *DUK* SK16 .... **132** C2 8
  MPL/ROM SK6 .... **187** D3
Dryden Rd *OLDTF/WHR* M16 .... **123** D6 8
Dryden St *BRUN/LGST* M13 .... **125** D3
Dryhurst Wk *HULME* M15 .... **124** B3 8
Drymoss *OLDS* OL8 .... **96** A4 8
Drywood Av *WALK* M28 .... **100** B2
Ducal St *ANC* M4 .... **106** C4
Duchess Park Cl *ROY/SHW* OL2 .... **61** F1
Duchess Rd *CHH* M8 .... **90** C5
Duchess St *ROY/SHW* OL2 .... **61** E1
Duchy Av *WALK* M28 .... **83** E5
Duchy Bank *SLFD* M6 .... **103** E1
Duchy Rd *SLFD* M6 .... **103** E1
Duchy St *EDGY/DAV* SK3 .... **166** B6
  SLFD M6 .... **104** A4
Ducie Av *BOL* BL1 .... **46** A2 13
Ducie Gv *HULME* M15 .... **124** C4 8
Ducie St *CMANE* M1 .... **3** H4
  RAD M26 .... **66** A5 8
  RAD M26 .... **51** D4 8
  WHTF M45 .... **71** D3
Duckshaw La *FWTH* BL4 .... **66** B3 8
Duckworth Rd *PWCH* M25 .... **88** A2
Duckworth St *BURY* BL9 .... **34** B3
  ROY/SHW OL2 .... **62** A2
Duddon Av *BOLE* BL2 .... **30** A6
Duddon Cl *WHTF* M45 .... **71** F3 8
Dudley Av *BOLE* BL2 .... **29** D6
  WHTF M45 .... **71** D3

Dudley Cl *HULME* M15 .... **123** F4
Dudley Rd *HALE/TIMP* WA15 .... **159** F6
  IRL M44 .... **154** B1
  OLDTF/WHR M16 .... **123** E6
  SALE M33 .... **140** A5
  SWIN M27 .... **86** A4
Dudley St *CHH* M8 .... **106** A1
  DTN/ASHW M34 .... **129** F5
  ECC M30 .... **101** D6 8
  OLDE OL4 .... **80** B5
Dudwell Cl *BOL* BL1 .... **27** D5 19
Duffield Gdns *MDTN* M24 .... **75** D6 8
Duffield Rd *MDTN* M24 .... **75** D6
  SLFD M6 .... **105** E2
Duffins Cl *WHIT* OL12 .... **22** B2
Dugdale Av *BKLY* M9 .... **91** F1 2
Dugie St *RAMS* BL0 .... **6** C4
Duice Pl *SALQ/ORD* M5 .... **105** D4
Duke Av *CHD/CHDH* SK8 .... **195** D3
Dukefield St *WYTH/NTH* M22 .... **162** C5 2
Duke Pl *CSLFD* M3 .... **2** A6
Duke Rd *BOLE* BL2 .... **31** D6
  HYDE SK14 .... **132** A4
Dukes Platting *AUL* OL6 .... **114** A2 8
Duke St *AUL* OL6 .... **112** C5 8
  BOL BL1 .... **46** C1 19
  BOL BL1 .... **46** C2 10
  BRO M7 .... **105** E2
  CSLFD M3 .... **2** A6
  CSLFD M3 .... **2** C1
  DTN/ASHW M34 .... **129** F6
  ECC M30 .... **101** D3 8
  FAIL M35 .... **94** B5
  HEY OL10 .... **36** C5
  LHULT M38 .... **65** E6 8
  LIT OL15 .... **12** B6
  MOSL OL5 .... **99** F4
  RAD M26 .... **69** F1
  RAMS BL0 .... **18** B1
  ROY/SHW OL2 .... **62** A3
  STKP SK1 .... **166** C2
  STLY SK15 .... **114** A6
  WALK M28 .... **84** B3
  WHIT OL12 .... **23** D4
  WILM/AE SK9 .... **209** F3
Duke St North *BOL* BL1 .... **46** C1 20
Dukinfield Rd *HYDE* SK14 .... **131** D4
Dulgar St *OP/CLY* M11 .... **126** C1 8
Dulverton St *NEWH/MOS* M40 .... **108** C1 4
Dulwich Cl *SALE* M33 .... **158** B2
Dulwich St *ANC* M4 .... **106** C4 8
Dumbarton Cl *RDSH* SK5 .... **147** D5 7
Dumbarton Dr *HEY* OL10 .... **36** B6 8
Dumbarton Rd *RDSH* SK5 .... **147** D5
Dumbell St *SWIN* M27 .... **86** A5 8
Dumber La *SALE* M33 .... **139** D5
Dumers La *RAD* M26 .... **52** B5
Dumfries Hollow *HEY* OL10 .... **38** A4
Dunbar Av *NTHM/RTH* M23 .... **177** E4
Dunbar Dr *BOLS/LL* BL3 .... **46** C5 14
Dunbar Gv *HEY* OL10 .... **55** D1
Dunbar St *OLD* OL1 .... **78** B3
Dunblane Av *BOLS/LL* BL3 .... **44** C4
  HTNM SK4 .... **166** B2
Dunblane Gv *HEY* OL10 .... **55** E1
Duncan Cl *HOR/BR* BL6 .... **44** B3 8
Dunchurch Rd *SALE* M33 .... **158** C1
Dun Cl *CSLFD* M3 .... **105** E5 8
Duncombe Cl *BRAM/HZG* SK7 .... **183** E4 8
Duncombe Rd *BOLS/LL* BL3 .... **64** C1 8
Duncombe St *BRO* M7 .... **105** F1 8
Duncote Gv *ROY/SHW* OL2 .... **61** E4 8
Dundee Cl *HEY* OL10 .... **36** A6 8
Dundee La *RAMS* BL0 .... **6** C5
Dundonald Rd *CHD/CHDH* SK8 .... **195** E2 2
  DID/WITH M20 .... **164** A2
Dundonald St *OFTN* SK2 .... **183** D1
Dundraw Cl *MDTN* M24 .... **73** F2
Dundrennan Cl *POY/DIS* SK12 .... **198** B4 8
Dunecroft *DTN/ASHW* M34 .... **130** B5 8
Dunedin Dr *SLFD* M6 .... **104** A2
Dunedin Rd *TOT/BURYW* BL8 .... **18** A3 8
Dunelm Dr *NTHM/RTH* M23 .... **160** B4
Dunham Lawn *ALT* WA14 .... **173** F3
Dunham Ri *ALT* WA14 .... **174** A3
Dunham Rd *ALT* WA14 .... **173** F3
  DUK SK16 .... **131** E3
  LYMM WA13 .... **154** C6
  PART M31 .... **156** B2
Dunham St *OLDE* OL4 .... **80** C3
Dunkeld Rd *NTHM/RTH* M23 .... **177** D1
Dunkerley Av *FAIL* M35 .... **94** A6
Dunkerley St *AULW* OL7 .... **112** B2 8
  OLDE OL4 .... **80** A3
  ROY/SHW OL2 .... **60** B5 8
Dunkery Rd *WYTH/NTH* M22 .... **178** B6
Dunkirk Cl *DTN/ASHW* M34 .... **147** E1
Dunkirk La *HYDE* SK14 .... **130** C5
Dunkirk Rd *WHTF* M45 .... **71** D2
Dunkirk St *DROY* M43 .... **110** C3

Dunley Cl *WGTN/LGST* M12 ...... 126 B4 2
Dunlin Cl *OFTN* SK2 ...... 185 E2
 POY/DIS SK12 ...... 197 E5
 ROCH OL11 ...... 21 D6 1
Dunlop Av *ROCH* OL11 ...... 39 F4
Dunlop St *CSLFD* M3 ...... 2 C3 3
Dunmail Rd *MDTN* M24 ...... 56 C6
Dunmore Rd *CHD/CHDH* SK8... 179 F1
Dunmow St *OFTN* SK2 ...... 184 C2
Dunnisher Rd *NTHM/RTH* M23 ... 177 F3
Dunnock Cl *OFTN* SK2 ...... 185 D2
Dunollie Rd *SALE* M33 ...... 160 C2
Dunoon Cl *HEY* OL10 ...... 36 B6
Dunoon Dr *BOL* BL1 ...... 27 D2
Dunoon Rd *RDSH* SK5 ...... 147 D4
Dunrobin Cl *HEY* OL10 ...... 55 E1
Dunscar Cl *WHTF* M45 ...... 70 B4 8
Dunsfold Dr *NTHM/RTH* M23 ...... 160 B5
Dunsley Av *NEWH/MOS* M40... 93 E3
Dunsmore Cl *OLDTF/WHR* M16 ... 123 C5 2
Dunsop Dr *BOL* BL1 ...... 26 A4
Dunstable *BNG/LEV* M19... 145 F2
Dunstall Rd *WYTH/NTH* M22 ...... 178 C2
Dunstan St *BOLE* BL2 ...... 48 A2
Dunstar Av *DTN/ASHW* M34 ...... 129 F2 3
Dunster Av *BKLY* M9 ...... 91 F1 3
 RDSH SK5 ...... 148 A6
 ROCH OL11 ...... 39 F2
 SWIN M27 ...... 86 C3
Dunster Cl *BRAM/HZG* SK7 ...... 184 A6
Dunster Dr *URM* M41 ...... 136 A2
Dunster Pl *WALK* M28 ...... 82 A6 3
Dunster Rd *WALK* M28 ...... 82 A6
Dunsters Av *TOT/BURYW* BL8 ...... 33 D2
Dunsterville Ter *ROCH* OL11 ...... 39 F2 4
Dunston St *OP/CLY* M11 ...... 127 D1
Dunton Gn *RDSH* SK5 ...... 147 F5 6
Dunwegan Rd *BRAM/HZG* SK7... 185 D6
Dunwood Av *ROY/SHW* OL2 ...... 62 A1 1
Dunwoods Park Cts
 ROY/SHW OL2 ...... 43 D6
Dunworth St *RUSH/FAL* M14 ...... 124 C6 3
Durant St *ANC* M4 ...... 106 C4 7
Durban Cl *ROY/SHW* OL2 ...... 61 E3
Durban Rd *BOL* BL1 ...... 27 F2 2
Durban St *AULW* OL7 ...... 111 F6 1
 OLDS OL8 ...... 95 D2
 ROCH OL11 ...... 39 D5 2
Durden Ms *ROY/SHW* OL2 ...... 61 F3 3
Durham Av *URM* M41 ...... 119 F6 3
Durham Cl *BOLS/LL* BL3 ...... 49 F5
 DUK SK16 ...... 131 E3
 MPL/ROM SK6 ...... 169 E4 2
Durham Crs *FAIL* M35 ...... 110 B1
Durham Dr *AUL* OL6 ...... 97 E5
 BURY BL9 ...... 53 E1 3
 RAMS BL0 ...... 18 B2
Durham Gv *IRL* M44 ...... 134 A5
Durham Rd *SLFD* M6 ...... 103 D2
 WILM/AE SK9 ...... 194 B4 2
Durham St *BKLY* M9 ...... 91 F6 3
 BOL BL1 ...... 28 A5 15
 CHAD OL9 ...... 95 D1 2
 DROY M43 ...... 128 B1 1
 RAD M26 ...... 52 A4
 RDSH SK5 ...... 146 C1
 ROCH OL11 ...... 40 B2
Durley Av *CHH* M8 ...... 90 C6
 HALE/TIMP WA15 ...... 159 F6
Durling St *WGTN/LGST* M12 ...... 125 D2
Durnford Av *URM* M41 ...... 139 E1
Durnford Cl *WHIT* OL12 ...... 20 B3
Durnford St *MDTN* M24 ...... 75 D2
Durn St *LIT* OL15 ...... 13 D5
Dutton St *CSLFD* M3 ...... 106 A4
Duty St *BOL* BL1 ...... 27 F4 13
Duxbury Av *BOLE* BL2 ...... 29 F2
 BOLS/LL BL3 ...... 49 E4
Duxbury Dr *BURY* BL9 ...... 35 D5
Duxbury St *BOL* BL1 ...... 27 E5 18
Dyche St *ANC* M4 ...... 3 F1
Dye House La *MILN* OL16 ...... 24 A2
Dye La *MPL/ROM* SK6... 169 F3
Dyers St *LIT* OL15 ...... 12 B5 1
Dyer St *OP/CLY* M11 ...... 126 B1 3
 SALQ/ORD M5 ...... 123 D2
Dymchurch Av *RAD* M26 ...... 68 A2 3
Dymchurch St
 NEWH/MOS M40 ...... 109 D3 3
Dysarts Cl *MOSL* OL5 ...... 99 F2
Dysart St *AUL* OL6 ...... 113 E5
 OFTN SK2 ...... 183 F2 7
Dyserth Gv *RDSH* SK5 ...... 147 D6 6
Dyson Cl *FWTH* BL4 ...... 66 B3
Dyson Gv *OLDE* OL4 ...... 81 D3 1
Dyson St *FWTH* BL4 ...... 66 B4 7
 MOSL OL5 ...... 98 C3 2
 OLD OL1 ...... 79 D5

E

Eades St *SLFD* M6 ...... 104 B4 1
Eadington St *CHH* M8 ...... 90 B2 3
Eafield Av *MILN* OL16 ...... 25 D6
Eafield Cl *MILN* OL16 ...... 25 D6
Eafield Rd *MILN* OL16 ...... 24 C2
Eagar St *NEWH/MOS* M40 ...... 109 D1
Eagle Dr *SLFD* M6 ...... 104 B2
Eagle St *BOLE* BL2 ...... 47 E2
 CHAD OL9 ...... 78 C5
Eagley Brook Wy *BOL* BL1 ...... 28 A4 17
Eagley Brow *EDGW/EG* BL7 ...... 28 A1
Eagley Dr *TOT/BURYW* BL8 ...... 32 B6
Eagley Wy *EDGW/EG* BL7 ...... 28 A1
Ealees Rd *LIT* OL15 ...... 13 D6
Ealing Av *RUSH/FAL* M14 ...... 143 F1
Ealing Pl *BNG/LEV* M19 ...... 145 E5 3
Eames Av *RAD* M26 ...... 67 E3
Earby Gv *BKLY* M9 ...... 92 A2
Earle Rd *BRAM/HZG* SK7 ...... 182 C5
Earle St *AULW* OL7 ...... 112 A6
Earl Rd *CHD/CHDH* SK8 ...... 194 C4
 HTNM SK4 ...... 166 A1
 RAMS BL0 ...... 6 C5
 WILM/AE SK9 ...... 194 C5
Earlston Av *DTN/ASHW* M34 ...... 128 B6
Earl St *BRO* M7 ...... 105 E3
 BURY BL9 ...... 34 A5 8
 DTN/ASHW M34 ...... 128 B5
 EDGY/DAV SK3 ...... 166 B5
 HEY OL10 ...... 37 D5 7
 MOSL OL5 ...... 98 C4
 PWCH M25 ...... 89 D1
 RAMS BL0 ...... 7 E5
 ROCH OL11 ...... 58 A1
Earls Wy *FAIL* M35 ...... 109 E1
Earl Wk *WGTN/LGST* M12 ...... 126 A4 3
Early Bank *STLY* SK15 ...... 133 D2
Early Bank Rd *STLY* SK14 ...... 132 C3
Earnshaw Av *STKP* SK1 ...... 167 F4
 WHIT OL12 ...... 22 C2 2
Earnshaw Cl *AULW* OL7 ...... 112 A2 2
Earnshaw St *BOLS/LL* BL3 ...... 46 A6 15
 POY/DIS SK12 ...... 198 B4
Easby Cl *CHD/CHDH* SK8... 195 F3
 POY/DIS SK12 ...... 199 E6
Easby Rd *MDTN* M24 ...... 57 D6
Easedale Cl *URM* M41 ...... 118 A6 3
Easedale Rd *BOL* BL1 ...... 45 E1
East Aisle Rd *TRPK* M17 ...... 121 D5
East Av *BNG/LEV* M19 ...... 145 D4
 CHD/CHDH SK8 ...... 194 B1
 STLY SK15 ...... 114 B4
 WHTF M45 ...... 70 C1
Eastbank St *BOL* BL1 ...... 28 A5 16
Eastbourne Gv *BOL* BL1 ...... 45 E1
Eastbourne St *OLDS* OL8 ...... 79 F6
 ROCH OL11 ...... 40 A2 7
Eastbrook Av *RAD* M26 ...... 52 A5 5
Eastburn Av *NEWH/MOS* M40 ...... 107 D4
East Central Dr *SWIN* M27 ...... 86 C6 3
Eastchurch Cl *FWTH* BL4 ...... 66 B4 8
Eastcombe Av *BRO* M7 ...... 88 C6
Eastcote Rd *RDSH* SK5 ...... 147 D6
Eastdale Pl *ALT* WA14 ...... 158 B6 2
East Downs Rd *ALT* WA14 ...... 174 A5
 CHD/CHDH SK8 ...... 181 D5
East Dr *BURY* BL9 ...... 53 F5
 MPL/ROM SK6 ...... 187 D4
 SLFD M6 ...... 103 F2
 SWIN M27 ...... 86 C6
Easterdale *OLDE* OL4 ...... 80 A5 8
Eastern Av *SWIN* M27 ...... 87 E2
Eastern By-pass *OP/CLY* M11 ...... 109 D5
Eastern Cir *BNG/LEV* M19 ...... 145 E5
Eastfield *SLFD* M6 ...... 103 F3
Eastfield Av *MDTN* M24 ...... 75 E4
 NEWH/MOS M40 ...... 107 F4 13
Eastfields *RAD* M26 ...... 50 C4
Eastgate *WHIT* OL12 ...... 9 D4
Eastgate St *AULW* OL7 ...... 112 B6 8
East Gate St *WHIT* OL12 ...... 23 D5 1
East Gra *OP/CLY* M11 ...... 109 D4 1
East Gv *BRUN/LGST* M13 ...... 125 D4
Eastgrove Av *BOL* BL1 ...... 27 F1
Eastham Av *BURY* BL9 ...... 33 F1
 RUSH/FAL M14 ...... 143 F2 1
Eastham Wy *LHULT* M38 ...... 65 F6
Easthaven Av *OP/CLY* M11 ...... 109 D5 7
East Hill St *OLDE* OL4 ...... 79 E5 10
Eastholme Av *BNG/LEV* M19 ...... 145 F4
Easthope Cl *DID/WITH* M20 ...... 143 F4 2
East Lancashire Rd *WALK* M28 ...... 82 A6 1
Eastlands Rd *BKLY* M9 ...... 74 B6
East Lea *DTN/ASHW* M34 ...... 130 B6
Eastleigh Av *BRO* M7 ...... 89 F5
Eastleigh Dr *NEWH/MOS* M40 ...... 107 F4 15
Eastleigh Rd *CHD/CHDH* SK8 ...... 179 F6
 PWCH M25 ...... 89 F2
East Lynn Dr *WALK* M28 ...... 84 B3
East Market St *CSLFD* M3 ...... 105 E5 15
East Meade *BOLS/LL* BL3 ...... 64 C1
 CCHDY M21 ...... 141 F4

 PWCH M25 ...... 89 E3
 SWIN M27 ...... 101 F1
East Moor *WALK* M28 ...... 82 B6
Eastmoor Dr *NEWH/MOS* M40 ...... 109 E3
East Newton St *ANC* M4 ...... 107 D4 8
Easton Cl *MDTN* M24 ...... 76 A4 2
Easton Dr *CHD/CHDH* SK8 ...... 181 E2
Easton Rd *DROY* M43 ...... 109 F5
East Ordsall La *CSLFD* M3 ...... 105 E6
East Over *MPL/ROM* SK6 ...... 169 E5
East Park Cl *BRUN/LGST* M13 ...... 125 D3 3
 BRUN/LGST M13 ...... 125 D3 3
Eastpark Cl *BRUN/LGST* M13 ...... 125 D3
East Philip St *CSLFD* M3 ...... 105 F4
East Rd *BOL* BL1 ...... 27 F3 13
 GTN M18 ...... 126 C6
 MANAIR M90 ...... 192 A2
 STLY SK15 ...... 115 F1
 STRET M32 ...... 120 C5
 WGTN/LGST M12 ...... 126 B6
Eastry Av *RDSH* SK5 ...... 147 F5 2
East St *AUL* OL6 ...... 113 E3
 BURY BL9 ...... 34 A6
 DTN/ASHW M34 ...... 130 A3
 LIT OL15 ...... 13 D6 3
 MILN OL16 ...... 24 B6 2
 RAD M26 ...... 51 F6
 WHIT OL12 ...... 11 D5
East V *MPL/ROM* SK6 ...... 187 E2
East Vw *MDTN* M24 ...... 75 D3
 RAMS BL0 ...... 6 C2
 RAMS BL0 ...... 19 D2 2
Eastville Gdns *BNG/LEV* M19 ...... 144 C6 5
Eastward Av *WILM/AE* SK9 ...... 203 D5
East Wy *BOL* BL1 ...... 28 C4
Eastway *MDTN* M24 ...... 75 D2
 ROY/SHW OL2 ...... 61 F3
 SALE M33 ...... 159 D4
 URM M41 ...... 117 F6
Eastwood Av *DROY* M43 ...... 109 F6
 NEWH/MOS M40 ...... 94 A4 3
 URM M41 ...... 138 B1
 WALK M28 ...... 82 B2
Eastwood Cl *BURY* BL9 ...... 34 C5 3
Eastwood Dr *BOLS/LL* BL3 ...... 45 E6
Eastwood Rd *NEWH/MOS* M40... 94 A4
Eastwood St *DTN/ASHW* M34 ...... 129 E2 1
 LIT OL15 ...... 12 C6 2
Eastwood Ter *BOL* BL1 ...... 45 D1
Eaton Cl *CHD/CHDH* SK8... 181 D4
 DUK SK16 ...... 131 D3
 POY/DIS SK12 ...... 199 E6
Eaton Dr *AULW* OL7 ...... 112 A3 1
 HALE/TIMP WA15 ...... 159 E5
 WILM/AE SK9 ...... 209 D3
Eaton Rd *ALT* WA14 ...... 174 A6
 CHH M8 ...... 90 A4
 SALE M33 ...... 159 F1
Eaves La *CHAD* OL9 ...... 77 E6
Ebbdale Cl *STKP* SK1 ...... 167 E5
Ebberstone St *RUSH/FAL* M14 ...... 143 E1 3
Ebden St *CMANE* M1 ...... 3 G6 1
Ebor Cl *ROY/SHW* OL2 ...... 61 E1
Ebor Rd *WYTH/NTH* M22 ...... 178 C3 3
Ebor St *LIT* OL15 ...... 13 D6
Ebsworth St *NEWH/MOS* M40 ...... 92 A5
Ebury St *RAD* M26 ...... 51 D5
Ecclesbridge Rd *MPL/ROM* SK6 ...... 187 D3
Eccles Cl *OP/CLY* M11 ...... 127 D1
Eccleshall St *OP/CLY* M11 ...... 108 C6
Eccles New Rd *SALQ/ORD* M5 ...... 102 C5
Eccles Old Rd *SLFD* M6 ...... 102 C4
Eccles Rd *SWIN* M27 ...... 102 A1
Eccles St *RAMS* BL0 ...... 6 C5
Eccleston Av *BOLE* BL2 ...... 28 C6 2
 SWIN M27 ...... 85 E6 2
Eccleston Cl *TOT/BURYW* BL8 ...... 32 B6 1
Eccleston Dr *EDGY/DAV* SK3 ...... 182 C5
Eccleston St *FAIL* M35 ...... 94 B5 8
Eccups La *WILM/AE* SK9 ...... 202 A3
Echo St *CMANE* M1 ...... 3 G6
Eckersley La *NTHM/RTH* M23... 177 D1
Eckersley Rd *BOL* BL1... 27 F4
Eckersley St *BOLS/LL* BL3 ...... 46 A5 16
Eckford St *CHH* M8 ...... 106 C1
Eclipse Cl *MILN* OL16... 23 F6
Edale Av *DTN/ASHW* M34... 129 E2
 DTN/ASHW M34 ...... 149 D3
 NEWH/MOS M40 ...... 92 B5
 RDSH SK5 ...... 147 E2
 URM M41 ...... 137 F2
Edale Cl *ALT* WA14 ...... 174 A6
 BRAM/HZG SK7 ...... 184 C6
 CHD/CHDH SK8 ...... 194 B2
 IRL M44 ...... 135 E2
Edale Gv *AUL* OL6 ...... 114 B1
 SALE M33 ...... 158 C3
Edale Rd *BOLS/LL* BL3 ...... 45 E5 7
 FWTH BL4 ...... 66 A4 2
 STRET M32 ...... 120 C6
Edale St *SLFD* M6 ...... 104 C2 2
Eddie Colman Cl
 NEWH/MOS M40 ...... 108 C2 3
Eddisbury Av *DID/WITH* M20... 143 D3
 URM M41 ...... 117 E5

Edditch Gv *BOLE* BL2 .... 48 A2 🔢
Eden Av *BOL* BL1 .... 27 F4 🔢
  MPL/ROM SK6 .... 200 C2
  RAMS BL0 .... 7 E1
Edenbridge Dr *RAD* M26 .... 67 F4
Edenbridge Rd *CHD/CHDH* SK8 .. 181 F3
  NEWH/MOS M40 .... 108 C3
Eden Cl *HEY* OL10 .... 36 B4
  HULME M15 .... 124 A3
  STKP SK1 .... 167 E5
  WILM/AE SK9 .... 202 C6
Eden Ct *RAMS* BL0 .... 7 E1
Edendale Dr *WYTH/NTH* M22 .... 178 B6
Edenfield La *WALK* M28 .... 100 A3
Edenfield Rd *PWCH* M25 .... 89 F2
  ROCH OL11 .... 20 B3 🔢
Edenfield St *WHIT* OL12 .... 22 A4
Eden Gv *BOL* BL1 .... 27 F4 🔢
Edenhall Av *BNG/LEV* M19 .... 145 D3 🔢
Edenhurst Dr *HALE/TIMP* WA15 .. 175 F2
Edenhurst Rd *OFTN* SK2 .... 183 F1
Edensor Dr *HALE/TIMP* WA15 .. 176 A4 🔢
Eden St *BOL* BL1 .... 27 F4
  BURY BL9 .... 34 A5 🔢
  OLD OL1 .... 78 C4
  RAMS BL0 .... 7 E2
  WHIT OL12 .... 22 B5 🔢
Edenvale *WALK* M28 .... 82 B5
Eden Wy *ROY/SHW* OL2 .... 61 E1
Edgar St *BOLS/LL* BL3 .... 46 C3
  MILN OL16 .... 24 A3
  RAMS BL0 .... 6 C6
Edgar St West *RAMS* BL0 .... 6 C6 🔢
Edgbaston Dr *OLDTF/WHR* M16 .. 122 B6
Edgedale Av *BNG/LEV* M19 ..... 144 C6 🔢
Edgefield Av *BKLY* M9 .... 91 F1
Edge Fold Crs *WALK* M28 .... 83 E5
Edge Fold Rd *WALK* M28 .... 83 E4
Edge Gn *WALK* M28 .... 83 D5 🔢
Edge Hill Av *ROY/SHW* OL2 .... 78 C1
Edgehill Cha *WILM/AE* SK9 .... 204 C4
Edge Hill Rd *BOLS/LL* BL3 .... 45 F6
  ROY/SHW OL2 .... 60 C6 🔢
Edgehill Rd *SLFD* M6 .... 103 D4
Edgehill St *ANC* M4 .... 3 F2 🔢
Edge La *BCUP* OL13 .... 5 D1
  HYDE SK14 .... 133 F5
  OP/CLY M11 .... 109 F6
  STRET M32 .... 140 B2
Edge Lane Rd *OLD* OL1 .... 79 D3
Edge Lane St *ROY/SHW* OL2 .... 60 C5
Edgeley Fold *EDGY/DAV* SK3 .... 166 A6
Edgeley Rd *EDGY/DAV* SK3 ...... 166 A6
  URM M41 .... 137 F3
Edgemoor *ALT* WA14 .... 175 E5
Edgemoor Cl *OLDE* OL4 .... 80 B2
  RAD M26 .... 50 C4 🔢
Edgemoor Dr *ROCH* OL11 .... 38 A2
Edge St *ANC* M4 .... 3 F2
Edge Vw *OLD* OL1 .... 76 C2
Edgeware Av *PWCH* M25 .... 90 A1
Edgeware Rd *CHAD* OL9 .... 93 F2 🔢
  ECC M30 .... 100 B3 🔢
Edgewater *SALQ/ORD* M5 .... 103 E5 🔢
Edgeway *WILM/AE* SK9 .... 203 F6
Edgeworth Av *BOLE* BL2 .... 31 E6
Edgeworth Dr *RUSH/FAL* M14 .. 144 C4
  TOT/BURYW BL8 .... 32 B6
Edgmont Av *BOLS/LL* BL3 .... 46 B5 🔢
Edgware Rd *NEWH/MOS* M40 .... 108 C3
Edgworth Cl *HEY* OL10 .... 36 B5
Edilom Rd *CHH* M8 .... 89 F3
Edinburgh Cl *CHD/CHDH* SK8 .. 181 D1 🔢
Edinburgh Dr *MPL/ROM* SK6 .... 170 A1 🔢
Edinburgh Rd *BOLS/LL* BL3 .... 67 E3
Edinburgh Wy *ROCH* OL11 .... 39 E3
Edison Rd *ECC* M30 .... 119 D1
Edison St *OP/CLY* M11 .... 127 F2
Edith Av *RUSH/FAL* M14 .... 143 E1
Edith Cavell Cl *OP/CLY* M11 ..... 109 D6
Edith St *BOL* BL1 .... 46 A3
  FWTH BL4 .... 66 B4
  OLDS OL8 .... 96 A2
Edlin Cl *WGTN/LGST* M12 .... 125 F4 🔢
Edlington Cl *SALE* M33 .... 158 B2 🔢
Edmonds St *MDTN* M24 .... 76 A2 🔢
Edmonton Rd *EDGY/DAV* SK3 .. 183 E3
  NEWH/MOS M40 .... 108 B3
Edmund Cl *HTNM* SK4 .... 166 C2 🔢
Edmunds Ct *BOLS/LL* BL3 .... 46 B3 🔢
Edmunds Fold *LIT* OL15 .... 12 A5
Edmund St *CSLFD* M3 .... 2 A2 🔢
  DROY M43 .... 128 B1
  FAIL M35 .... 94 A5 🔢
  RAD M26 .... 52 A5 🔢
  ROY/SHW OL2 .... 62 A2 🔢
  SLFD M6 .... 103 F4
  WHIT OL12 .... 22 B5
Edna Rd *HYDE* SK14 .... 150 B1
Edson Rd *CHH* M8 .... 90 A2 🔢
Edward Av *CCHDY* M21 .... 141 D4
  LIT OL15 .... 25 D2 🔢
  MPL/ROM SK6 .... 168 C2

Edward Charlton Rd
  OLDTF/WHR M16 .... 141 F1
Edward Rd *BKLY* M9 .... 74 B6
  ROY/SHW OL2 .... 61 E3
Edwards Cl *MPL/ROM* SK6 .... 186 C2 🔢
Edwards Dr *WHTF* M45 .... 71 F3 🔢
Edward St *AUL* OL6 .... 113 F5
  BKLY M9 .... 91 F5
  BOLS/LL BL3 .... 46 B4 🔢
  BRO M7 .... 105 F3
  BURY BL9 .... 34 A6
  CHAD OL9 .... 77 E4
  CHAD OL9 .... 78 A5
  DROY M43 .... 128 B1 🔢
  DTN/ASHW M34 .... 129 E2
  DTN/ASHW M34 .... 130 A5
  DUK SK16 .... 131 D3
  FWTH BL4 .... 65 F1 🔢
  HYDE SK14 .... 131 D6 🔢
  MDTN M24 .... 75 E1
  MILN OL16 .... 23 E5
  MPL/ROM SK6 .... 171 E4
  PWCH M25 .... 71 E6 🔢
  RAD M26 .... 67 F3
  RAD M26 .... 69 F1
  SALE M33 .... 160 C1 🔢
  STKP SK1 .... 167 D5
  WHIT OL12 .... 9 E1
  WHIT OL12 .... 24 B1 🔢
Edwards Wy *MPL/ROM* SK6 ..... 186 C2
Edwin Rd *OP/CLY* M11 .... 107 F6
Edwin St *BURY* BL9 .... 33 F5 🔢
  STKP SK1 .... 167 F5
Eeasbrook *URM* M41 .... 138 B2
Egbert St *NEWH/MOS* M40 .... 92 C6
Egerton Av *DID/WITH* M20 .... 143 F4 🔢
Egerton Dr *SALE* M33 .... 139 F6 🔢
Egerton Gv *WALK* M28 .... 83 E2
Egerton Crs *DID/WITH* M20 ...... 143 F4 🔢
Egerton Ms *RUSH/FAL* M14 ..... 144 B3 🔢
Egerton Moss *HALE/TIMP* WA15 .. 188 C4 🔢
Egerton Pk *WALK* M28 .... 84 C6
Egerton Pl *ROY/SHW* OL2 .... 61 E3 🔢
Egerton Rd *ECC* M30 .... 101 E3
  EDGY/DAV SK3 .... 183 E3
  HALE/TIMP WA15 .... 175 E4
  RUSH/FAL M14 .... 144 B3
  WALK M28 .... 83 E2 🔢
  WHTF M45 .... 71 D4
  WILM/AE SK9 .... 203 F3
Egerton Rd North *CCHDY* M21 .. 142 A1
  HTNM SK4 .... 146 A3
Egerton Rd South *CCHDY* M21 .. 142 A3
  HTNM SK4 .... 146 A4
Egerton St *AUL* OL6 .... 113 D4
  CSLFD M3 .... 105 E6 🔢
  DROY M43 .... 110 C3
  DTN/ASHW M34 .... 129 E4
  ECC M30 .... 100 C5 🔢
  FWTH BL4 .... 66 A2
  HEY OL10 .... 37 D6
  LIT OL15 .... 13 D6
  MDTN M24 .... 74 A4 🔢
  MOSL OL5 .... 99 D3
  OLD OL1 .... 79 E3 🔢
  PWCH M25 .... 89 D1 🔢
Egerton Ter *RUSH/FAL* M14 ..... 144 B4 🔢
Eggington St *NEWH/MOS* M40 . 107 D2
Egmont St *CHH* M8 .... 90 B5
  MOSL OL5 .... 99 D5
  SLFD M6 .... 103 F1
Egremont Cl *WHTF* M45 .... 71 E2
Egremont Gv *EDGY/DAV* SK3 .. 165 F5 🔢
Egremont Rd *MILN* OL16 .... 41 F3
Egret Dr *IRL* M44 .... 116 B6 🔢
Egyptian St *BOL* BL1 .... 28 A6
Egypt La *PWCH* M25 .... 72 B2
Eida Wy *TRPK* M17 .... 121 D1
Eight Acre *WHTF* M45 .... 70 A4
Eighth Av *OLDS* OL8 .... 95 D4
Eighth St *TRPK* M17 .... 121 E3 🔢
Eileen Gv *RUSH/FAL* M14 .... 144 A1
Eileen Gv West *RUSH/FAL* M14 . 143 F1
Elaine Av *BKLY* M9 .... 92 C3 🔢
Elbe St *WGTN/LGST* M12 .... 125 D1
Elbow St *BNG/LEV* M19 .... 145 E1
Elbut La *BURY* BL9 .... 36 A2
Elcho Rd *ALT* WA14 .... 173 F4
Elcot Cl *NEWH/MOS* M40 .... 107 D2 🔢
Elderberry Wy *WILM/AE* SK9 ... 204 B4
Elder Cl *OFTN* SK2 .... 168 B5
Eldercot Gv *BOLS/LL* BL3 .... 45 E5 🔢
Eldercot Rd *BOLS/LL* BL3 .... 45 E5
Eldercroft Rd *HALE/TIMP* WA15 . 176 A2
Elderfield Dr *MPL/ROM* SK6 .... 169 D1 🔢
Elder Gv *NEWH/MOS* M40 .... 94 A3 🔢
Eldermount Rd *BKLY* M9 .... 91 E3
Elder Rd *OLDE* OL4 .... 80 C5
Elder St *MILN* OL16 .... 40 C2
Elderwood *CHAD* OL9 .... 76 C4 🔢
Eldon Cl *DTN/ASHW* M34 .... 129 D3
Eldon Pl *ECC* M30 .... 101 D6
Eldon Rd *EDGY/DAV* SK3 .... 166 A6
  IRL M44 .... 135 E1

Eldon St *BOLE* BL2 .... 28 C3
  BURY BL9 .... 34 A3
  OLDS OL8 .... 79 D6
Eldridge Dr *NEWH/MOS* M40 .. 108 B2
Eleanor Rd *CCHDY* M21 .... 141 E3 🔢
  ROY/SHW OL2 .... 78 C1
Eleanor St *BOL* BL1 .... 28 B2 🔢
  OLD OL1 .... 78 B3
Electo St *OP/CLY* M11 .... 127 F2 🔢
Elevator Rd *TRPK* M17 .... 121 F3
Eleventh St *TRPK* M17 .... 121 E3
Elf Mill Cl *EDGY/DAV* SK3 .... 182 C1
Elford Cv *GTN* M18 .... 128 B5
Elgar St *WGTN/LGST* M12 .... 126 B6
Elgin Av *DID/WITH* M20 .... 164 B2 🔢
Elgin Rd *DUK* SK16 .... 131 D3
  OLDE OL4 .... 79 F5
Elgin St *AULW* OL7 .... 112 B3
  BOL BL1 .... 27 D5
  STLY SK15 .... 114 C6
Elgol Cl *EDGY/DAV* SK3 .... 183 D2 🔢
Elgol Dr *BOLS/LL* BL3 .... 44 C4
Elham Cl *RAD* M26 .... 68 A4
Elim St *LIT* OL15 .... 13 D4
Eliot Rd *ECC* M30 .... 101 E6 🔢
Eli St *CHAD* OL9 .... 94 B2 🔢
Eliza Ann St *ECC* M30 .... 101 D6 🔢
  NEWH/MOS M40 .... 107 D3
Elizabethan Wy *MILN* OL16 .... 41 F1
Elizabeth Av *CHAD* OL9 .... 94 B2 🔢
  DTN/ASHW M34 .... 129 F4
  ROY/SHW OL2 .... 60 A2 🔢
  STKP SK1 .... 167 D5 🔢
Elizabeth Ct *HTNM* SK4 .... 146 A5 🔢
  RUSH/FAL M14 .... 144 B4 🔢
Elizabeth Gv *ROY/SHW* OL2 ..... 61 F2 🔢
Elizabeth Rd *PART* M31 .... 155 D1

Elizabeth Slinger Rd
  DID/WITH M20 .... 162 C1
Elizabeth St *AUL* OL6 .... 112 C3
  CHH M8 .... 106 A1
  DTN/ASHW M34 .... 129 E6
  HEY OL10 .... 37 D5 🔢
  HYDE SK14 .... 131 E6 🔢
  RAD M26 .... 51 E6 🔢
  ROCH OL11 .... 39 D4 🔢
  SWIN M27 .... 86 A4
  WHTF M45 .... 71 D4 🔢
Eliza St *HULME* M15 .... 123 F3 🔢
  RAMS BL0 .... 7 E5
Elkanagh Gdns *SLFD* M6 .... 104 A4 🔢
Elkstone Av *LHULT* M38 .... 65 E3 🔢
Ellanby Cl *RUSH/FAL* M14 .... 124 C6
Elland Cl *BURY* BL9 .... 71 F1
Ellaston Dr *URM* M41 .... 138 B1 🔢
Ellastone Rd *SLFD* M6 .... 103 D3
Ellbourne Rd *BKLY* M9 .... 90 B2
Ellenbrook Cl *WGTN/LGST* M12 . 126 C3
Ellenbrook Rd *WALK* M28 .... 82 C5 🔢
Ellen Brook Rd *WYTH/NTH* M22 . 192 B1
Ellendale Gra *WALK* M28 .... 82 C5 🔢
Ellen Gv *FWTH* BL4 .... 85 D1
Ellenhall Cl *BKLY* M9 .... 91 E5
Ellenroad Ap *MILN* OL16 .... 42 B3
Ellenroad St *MILN* OL16 .... 42 B3
Ellenrod Dr *WHIT* OL12 .... 21 E3
Ellenrod La *WHIT* OL12 .... 21 E3
Ellenshaw Cl *WHIT* OL12 .... 21 F3 🔢
Ellen St *BOL* BL1 .... 27 D4 🔢
  CHAD OL9 .... 78 B3
  DROY M43 .... 128 C1
  HTNM SK4 .... 166 B2

Ellen Wilkinson Crs
  WGTN/LGST M12 .... 126 B4
Elleray Cl *BOLS/LL* BL3 .... 50 A6
Elleray Rd *MDTN* M24 .... 75 D6
  SLFD M6 .... 103 E2
Ellerbeck Cl *BOLE* BL2 .... 28 C2
Ellerbeck Crs *WALK* M28 .... 83 D6
Ellerby Av *SWIN* M27 .... 86 B2
Ellesmere Av *AUL* OL6 .... 97 D6
  ECC M30 .... 101 F5 🔢
  MPL/ROM SK6 .... 187 D1 🔢
  WALK M28 .... 83 D2 🔢
Ellesmere Cl *DUK* SK16 .... 131 F2
Ellesmere Dr *CHD/CHDH* SK8 .. 181 E2
Ellesmere Gdns *BOLS/LL* BL3 .... 46 B6 🔢
Ellesmere Rd *ALT* WA14 .... 174 B1
  BOLS/LL BL3 .... 46 B6 🔢
  CCHDY M21 .... 142 A5
  ECC M30 .... 101 F3
  EDGY/DAV SK3 .... 165 E6
Ellesmere Rd North *HTNM* M24 . 146 A6
Ellesmere Rd South *CCHDY* M21 . 142 A3
Ellesmere St *BOLS/LL* BL3 .... 46 B5
  ECC M30 .... 101 E6 🔢
  FAIL M35 .... 94 A5 🔢
  FWTH BL4 .... 66 B3
  HULME M15 .... 123 F2
  LHULT M38 .... 83 D2
  ROCH OL11 .... 40 A2 🔢
  SWIN M27 .... 86 B4 🔢
Ellesmere Ter *RUSH/FAL* M14 .. 144 B4 🔢
Elliot St *BOL* BL1 .... 27 D4 🔢

OLDE OL4....................................80 C5
Elliott Av HYDE SK14...............131 E4
Elliott Dr SALE M33..................158 C1
Elliott St FWTH BL4....................66 A4
    WHIT OL15................................23 E5
Ellis Crs WALK M28....................82 C2 3
Ellis Fold WHIT OL12..................20 C3
Ellis La MDTN M24......................73 F3
Ellis St BOLS/LL BL3....................46 B4
    BRO M7....................................105 F3
    HULME M15..............................123 F3
    HYDE SK14...............................151 D1
    TOT/BURYW BL8.......................32 C5 6
Ellor St SLFD M6........................104 A4 7
    SLFD M6..................................104 C5 7
Ellwood Rd STKP SK1...............167 F4
Elm Av RAD M26..........................69 D5
Elmbank Av DID/WITH M20.......162 C1
Elmbank Rd MDTN M24...............76 A3
Elmbridge Wk BOLS/LL BL3.......46 B4 6
Elm Cl POY/DIS SK12.................199 D6
Elm Crs WALK M28.....................84 B6
    WILM/AE SK9...........................209 F3
Elmdale Av CHD/CHDH SK8.......179 F5 1
Elm Dr DTN/ASHW M34..............129 E4
    STRET M32...............................139 F2
Elmfield Av WYTH/NTH M22.......162 C5
Elmfield Dr MPL/ROM SK6.........186 C1
Elmfield Rd DTN/ASHW M34......129 D1
    EDGY/DAV SK3..........................183 D2
    WILM/AE SK9............................209 F3
Elmfield St BOL BL1....................28 A5 6
    BOL BL1...................................28 A5 6
    CHH M8...................................106 B1
Elmgate Gv BNG/LEV M19.........145 E2
Elm Gv AUL OL6.........................113 D2
    DID/WITH M20..........................163 F2
    DROY M43................................109 E5
    EDGW/EG BL7............................14 B5
    FWTH BL4..................................65 F3
    HYDE SK14...............................151 D1
    MILN OL16.................................42 B4
    OLDE OL4...................................81 F5
    PWCH M25..................................71 E5
    ROCH OL11.................................39 F2 3
    SALE M33..................................137 D3
    URM M41..................................138 C1
    WALK M28...................................84 C4
    WHIT OL12...................................11 D6
    WILM/AE SK9..............................209 E3
Elmhurst Dr BNG/LEV M19........145 D6
Elmley Cl OFTN SK2..................185 E2
Elmore Wd LIT OL15.....................11 F5
Elmpark Ga WHIT OL12...............21 F2
Elmpark Gv WHIT OL12................21 F2
Elmpark V WHIT OL12.................21 F2 3
Elmpark Vw WHIT OL12...............21 F2
Elmpark Wy WHIT OL12...............21 F2
Elmridge Dr HALE/TIMP WA15...190 A1
Elm Rd BOLS/LL BL3.....................67 F1
    CHD/CHDH SK8........................179 E2
    DID/WITH M20..........................163 E1
    FWTH BL4...................................67 D6
    HALE/TIMP WA15.......................174 C4
    MPL/ROM SK6............................201 D2
    OLDS OL8....................................95 E4
Elm Rd South EDGY/DAV SK3....165 E6
Elms Cl WHTF M45........................71 D1
Elmsdale Av BKLY M9...................74 B6
Elmsfield Av ROCH OL11..............20 C4
Elmsleigh Rd CHD/CHDH SK8....179 E5
Elmsmere Rd DID/WITH M20......164 B2
Elms Rd HTNM SK4.....................145 F6
    STLY SK15.................................115 E4
    WHTF M45...................................71 D2
Elms St WHTF M45........................70 C2
Elmstead Av DID/WITH M20.......143 E5
Elmsted Cl CHD/CHDH SK8........181 F4
The Elms LIT OL15........................24 C1
    MOSL OL5...................................98 C4 1
Elm St BURY BL9..........................34 C5 10
    ECC M30...................................101 E6 2
    FAIL M35....................................94 A5
    FWTH BL4...................................66 C2 3
    HEY OL10....................................37 E5
    MDTN M24...................................76 A3
    MPL/ROM SK6............................169 D1
    RAMS BL0.....................................7 E5
    SWIN M27....................................85 F4 6
    WHIT OL12.....................................9 E1
    WHIT OL12...................................23 D4 8
Elmsway BRAM/HZG SK7...........196 A2
    HALE/TIMP WA15.......................189 F1
    MPL/ROM SK6............................200 C3
Elmswood Av RUSH/FAL M14.....143 D1 3
Elmswood Dr HYDE SK14...........132 B6 3
Elmsworth Av BNG/LEV M19......145 F2
Elmton Rd BKLY M9.....................91 F2 1
Elm Tree Cl FAIL M35...................94 C6
Elm Tree Dr DUK SK16...............132 A2
Elmtree Dr HTNM SK4................165 F3
Elm Tree Dr WYTH/NTH M22.....178 B4
Elm Tree Rd MPL/ROM SK6.......168 A2
Elmwood SALE M33.....................158 A1
Elmwood Dr ROY/SHW OL2.........60 A4

Elmwood Gv BKLY M9...................92 A6 3
    BOL BL1......................................46 A1 3
    FWTH BL4....................................66 A5 2
Elsa Rd BNG/LEV M19................146 A2 3
Elsdon Dr GTN M18.....................127 E3
Elsdon Rd BRUN/LGST M13.......145 D1
Elsham Dr WALK M28...................82 C2
Elsham Gdns GTN M18...............126 C5
Elsie St BKLY M9...........................91 F5 6
    FWTH BL4....................................66 A3
    RAMS BL0....................................18 B1 11
Elsinore Av IRL M44....................135 D2
Elsinore Cl FAIL M35....................94 C6 2
Elsinore Rd OLDTF/WHR M16....122 B5
Elsinore St BOLE BL2....................28 C4 3
Elsma Rd NEWH/MOS M40.........109 F3 1
Elsmore Rd RUSH/FAL M14.......143 E2
Elson St TOT/BURYW BL8............32 C3
Elstree Av NEWH/MOS M40.......108 C3
Elstree Gv EDGY/DAV SK3.........166 B5 3
Elswick Av BOLS/LL BL3...............45 F4
    BRAM/HZG SK7.........................196 C2
    CCHDY M21..............................162 B1
Elsworth Dr BOL BL1....................28 A3
Elsworth St CSLFD M3................106 B4
Elterwater Cl TOT/BURYW BL8....32 C3
Elterwater Rd FWTH BL4..............64 C4 2
Eltham Av OFTN SK2..................184 A2 4
Eltham Dr URM M41....................119 D5
Eltham St BNG/LEV M19.............145 E1 3
Elton Av BNG/LEV M19...............145 E3
    FWTH BL4....................................65 D3
Elton Brook Cl TOT/BURYW BL8...32 C4
Elton Cl WHTF M45.......................71 E3
    WILM/AE SK9............................204 C2
Elton Dr BRAM/HZG SK7............198 B1
Elton Rd SALE M33.....................158 B3
Elton St BRO M7.........................105 F4
    ROCH OL11.................................39 D6
    STRET M32...............................122 A4
Elton's Yd BRO M7.....................105 E4 3
Elton Vale Rd TOT/BURYW BL8....32 C4
Elvate Crs CHH M8......................106 A2 1
Elverdon Cl HULME M15.............123 F4 2
Elverston St WYTH/NTH M22.....162 C4
Elvey St NEWH/MOS M40..........108 A2
Elvington Crs WALK M28..............83 D5 2
Elwick Cl OLDTF/WHR M16.........124 A6
Elwyn Av WYTH/NTH M22...........162 B6 1
Ely Av STRET M32......................120 A6
Ely Cl WALK M28..........................82 C5
Ely Crs FAIL M35........................110 A2
Ely Dr TOT/BURYW BL8...............33 E5 1
Elysian St OP/CLY M11................127 D1
Ely St CHAD OL9..........................77 F6 2
Emaline Gra SLFD M6.................103 F5 3
Ember St OP/CLY M11................109 E5 1
Embden St BOLS/LL BL3...............46 B4
Embleton Cl BOLE BL2..................29 F6
Embsay Cl BOL BL1......................27 E2
Emerald Rd WYTH/NTH M22......193 D2 3
Emerald St BOL BL1.....................28 A4 10
    DTN/ASHW M34.......................129 F6 5
Emerson Av ECC M30..................102 B4 3
Emerson Dr MDTN M24................75 D2
Emerson St SALQ/ORD M5.........103 E5
Emery Av CCHDY M21.................142 A5
Emery Cl ALT WA14....................158 B6
    HTNM SK4................................165 E1
Emily Beavan Cl OP/CLY M11.....108 C6
Emily Pl DROY M43.....................110 A6 3
Emley St BNG/LEV M19..............145 F2
Emlyn Gv CHD/CHDH SK8..........181 E1
Emlyn St FWTH BL4......................66 A2
    SWIN M27...................................85 E5 6
    WALK M28....................................83 E2
Emma St OLDS OL8......................95 E4 3
    WHIT OL12...................................22 C5
Emmett St East NEWH/MOS M40...107 F2
Emmott Cl HEY OL10....................37 D5 3
Emmott St OLD OL1......................79 D5 3
Emperor St STKP SK1................167 E5 3
Empire Rd BOLE BL2.....................48 B1 2
    DUK SK16.................................131 D3
Empire St CSLFD M3...................106 A3
Empress Av MPL/ROM SK6........187 D2
Empress Dr HTNM SK4...............166 B1
Empress St BOL BL1.....................26 C6 3
    CHH M8......................................90 A5 1
    OLDTF/WHR M16.......................123 D3
Emsworth Dr SALE M33..............160 A4
Ena St BOLS/LL BL3......................47 E6
    OLD OL1.....................................80 A2 2
Enbridge St SALQ/ORD M5.........122 B3 7
Encombe Pl CSLFD M3................105 E5 10
Endcott Cl GTN M18....................126 C3
Enderby Rd NEWH/MOS M40.......93 D4
Ending Rake WHIT OL12...............22 A1
Endon Dr CCHDY M21................143 D3
Endon St BOL BL1.........................26 C6
Endsleigh Rd DID/WITH M20......144 A5
Endsley Av WALK M28...................83 D4
Endsor Cl OLDTF/WHR M16.......124 A6 1
Enfield Av BNG/LEV M19............145 E5
    OLDS OL8....................................95 F2

Enfield Cl BOL BL1........................27 F6
    BURY BL9...................................53 D4
    ECC M30...................................119 E1
    ROCH OL11................................20 C5 2
Enfield Dr OP/CLY M11...............109 D5 3
Enfield Rd ECC M30....................101 E3
    SWIN M27.................................101 F1
Enfield St HYDE SK14................150 C4 3
    WALK M28....................................66 B6 1
Enford Av WYTH/NTH M22.........177 E5 2
Engell Cl GTN M18......................127 D4
Engine Fold Rd WALK M28............82 B2 1
Engine St CHAD OL9....................94 C1 3
Engledene BOL BL1.......................27 E1 2
Enid Cl BRO M7...........................105 F2 3
Ennerdale Av BOLE BL2................30 A6 3
    BOLE BL2..................................162 B1
    CCHDY M21..............................162 B1
    ROY/SHW OL2.............................60 A2 1
    SWIN M27.................................102 A1 3
Ennerdale Cl BOLS/LL BL3...........49 D6 3
Ennerdale Dr BURY BL9...............71 E1
    HALE/TIMP WA15.....................159 E5 1
    SALE M33.................................138 C6 2
Ennerdale Gv AULW OL7.............112 A2
    FWTH BL4....................................64 C3 1
Ennerdale Rd CHD/CHDH SK8...179 F4 2
    MDTN M24...................................74 C1
    MPL/ROM SK6...........................169 F1
    PART M31..................................154 C2
    ROCH OL11..................................38 C3
    STKP SK1..................................167 F6
    STRET M32...............................121 D6 3
Ennerdale Ter STLY SK15............114 B4
Ennis Cl DTN/ASHW M34............176 C2
Ennismore Av ECC M30...............102 B5
Enstone Dr NEWH/MOS M40.......93 E3 3
Enticott Rd IRL M44...................134 A6
Entwisle Av URM M41.................118 C5
Entwisle Rd MILN OL16................23 E6
Entwisle Rw FWTH BL4................66 B3 10
Entwisle St FWTH BL4.................66 B2 4
    MILN OL16...................................41 F1 2
    SWIN M27...................................85 E4
Entwistle St BOLE BL2.................47 F1
Enver Rd CHH M8..........................90 C5
Enville Rd ALT WA14...................174 A4
    NEWH/MOS M40.........................92 C4
    SLFD M6....................................103 F1
Enville St AUL OL6......................113 D4 10
    BKLY M9......................................91 E2 2
    DTN/ASHW M34........................130 A2 2
Epping Av AUL OL6.......................97 D6
    CHAD OL9....................................76 C3
Epping Dr SALE M33...................138 A6
Epping Rd DTN/ASHW M34........147 F1 3
Epping St HULME M15................123 F4
Epsleworth Ri SWIN M27..............86 B2 3
Epsley Cl HULME M15................124 B3 3
Epsom Av CHD/CHDH SK8.........194 C5
    SALE M33.................................158 A3
    WILM/AE SK9............................194 A3
Epsom Cl BRAM/HZG SK7..........185 D5
Epson Cl ROCH OL11....................20 C5
Epworth St CMANE M1...............107 D6 3
Equitable St MILN OL16................42 A2
    OLDE OL4....................................80 B3
Era St BOLE BL2...........................48 B2 3
    SALE M33.................................159 F1
Ercall Av WGTN/LGST M12.........125 F3
Erica Av OLDE OL4........................63 D5
Erica Cl RDSH SK5.....................147 D3
Erica Dr BNG/LEV M19...............164 C1 1
Eric Bullows Cl WYTH/NTH M22...178 A6
Eric St LIT OL15.............................12 B5
    OLDE OL4....................................80 A5
Erith St OP/CLY M11...................127 F2 3
Erith Cl RDSH SK5......................147 F5
Erith Rd OLDE OL4........................79 F5
Erlesmere Av DTN/ASHW M34....130 B5
Erlesmere Cl OLDE OL4................63 D5
Erlington Av OLDTF/WHR M16....122 C6
Ermen Rd ECC M30....................119 D1
Ermington Dr CHH M8.................106 A1 7
Erneley Cl WGTN/LGST M12......126 C6
Ernest St BCUP OL13.....................5 D1
    BOL BL1......................................46 A3 2
    BOL BL1......................................46 B2 2
    CHD/CHDH SK8.........................180 A1
    OFTN SK2..................................183 E1 4
    PWCH M25...................................88 A1
Ernest Ter WHIT OL12..................23 F4 3
Ernlouen Av BOL BL1....................45 E1
Ernocroft Gv GTN M18...............127 F3 3
Ernocroft Rd MPL/ROM SK6.......171 F4
Erringdon Cl OFTN SK2..............184 C1 3
Errington Cl BOLS/LL BL3.............45 D4
Errington Dr BRO M7..................105 E3
Errol Av BKLY M9..........................73 E6
    WYTH/NTH M22........................178 A3
Errwood Crs BNG/LEV M19........145 E3 3
Errwood Rd BNG/LEV M19.........145 E4
Erskine Cl BOLS/LL BL3................44 C4
Erskine Rd BKLY M9.....................74 C6
    PART M31..................................155 D2

Erskine St HULME M15 .... 123 E3
MPL/ROM SK6 .... 171 F3
Erwin St NEWH/MOS M40 .... 108 C1 🄰
Erwood Rd HTNM SK4 .... 145 D6
Eryngo St STKP SK1 .... 167 E4 🄱
Esher Dr SALE M33 .... 159 F5
Esk Cl URM M41 .... 118 B5
Eskdale Av BOLE BL2 .... 30 A5
BRAM/HZG SK7 .... 196 A4
DID/WITH M20 .... 143 E4 🄱
MPL/ROM SK6 .... 149 F6
OLDS OL8 .... 95 E1
ROCH OL11 .... 38 C3
ROY/SHW OL2 .... 60 B2
Eskdale Cl BURY BL9 .... 53 E6 🄱
Eskdale Dr HALE/TIMP WA15 ... 160 A6
MDTN M24 .... 57 D6
Eskdale Gv FWTH BL4 .... 65 D3
Eskrick St BOL BL1 .... 27 E5
Eskrigge Cl BRO M7 .... 90 A5 🄱
Esmond Rd CHH M8 .... 90 B6 🄱
Esmont Dr BOLS/LL BL3 .... 56 C6
The Esplanade MILN OL16 .... 22 C6
Essex Av DID/WITH M20 .... 163 F1
DROY M43 .... 110 B4
EDGY/DAV SK3 .... 165 F5
HEY OL10 .... 35 F6
Essex Cl FAIL M35 .... 110 A2
ROY/SHW OL2 .... 61 D2
Essex Dr BURY BL9 .... 53 D1
Essex Gdns IRL M44 .... 154 A1
Essex Rd GTN M18 .... 128 A5 🄱
RDSH SK5 .... 148 A6 🄱
Essex St CMANW M2 .... 2 D3 🄱
ROCH OL11 .... 40 A1 🄱
Essex Wy HULME M15 .... 123 E4
Essingdon St BOLS/LL BL3 .... 46 B5 🄱🄱
Estate St OLDS OL8 .... 96 A1
Estate St South OLDS OL8 .... 96 A1 🄱
Est Bank Rd RAMS BL0 .... 18 B2 🄱
RAMS BL0 .... 18 B2 🄱
Esther St OLDE OL4 .... 80 A4
Estonfield Dr URM M41 .... 139 D1
Eston St BRUN/LGST M13 .... 125 E5
Eswick St OP/CLY M11 .... 109 D6 🄱
Etchells Rd CHD/CDH SK8 .... 180 B6
Etchells St STKP SK1 .... 167 D4 🄱
Etchell St NEWH/MOS M40 .... 107 D2 🄱
Ethel Av BKLY M9 .... 74 B6
SWIN M27 .... 86 C5 🄱
Ethel St BOLS/LL BL3 .... 46 B5 🄱
OLDS OL8 .... 96 A2
WHIT OL12 .... 9 E1
Ethel Ter BNG/LEV M19 .... 145 E2 🄱
Etherley Cl IRL M44 .... 135 E1 🄱
Etherow Av MPL/ROM SK6 .... 170 C3
NEWH/MOS M40 .... 94 A3 🄱
Etherow Brow HYDE SK14 .... 153 F3 🄱
Etherstone St CHH M8 .... 91 D5
Eton Av OLDS OL8 .... 95 F2
Eton Cl OLDTF/WHR M16 .... 123 E4
ROCH OL11 .... 38 C1
Eton Hill Rd RAD M26 .... 52 A4
Eton Wy North RAD M26 .... 52 A4
Eton Wy South RAD M26 .... 52 A4
Etruria Cl BRUN/LGST M13 .... 125 F4 🄱
Ettington Cl TOT/BURYW BL8 ...... 32 B4
Ettrick Cl OP/CLY M11 .... 127 E2
Euclid Cl OP/CLY M11 .... 107 F6 🄱
Europa Ga TRPK M17 .... 121 E4
Europa Wy EDGY/DAV SK3 .... 181 F1
RAD M26 .... 67 E4
TRPK M17 .... 121 E4
Eustace St BOLS/LL BL3 .... 47 E6
CHAD OL9 .... 77 F2
Euston Av BKLY M9 .... 92 B2
Euxton Cl TOT/BURYW BL8 .... 32 B6
Evans Rd ECC M30 .... 100 B6 🄱
Evans St AUL OL6 .... 113 E3
CSLFD M3 .... 105 F2 🄱
MDTN M24 .... 75 F3
OLD OL1 .... 79 D3 🄱
Evan St NEWH/MOS M40 .... 107 F2 🄱
Eva Rd EDGY/DAV SK3 .... 165 E6
Eva St RUSH/FAL M14 .... 125 D6 🄱
WHIT OL12 .... 23 E1 🄱
Evelyn St OLD OL1 .... 79 F2
RUSH/FAL M14 .... 144 B3
Evening St FAIL M35 .... 94 A5
Evenley Cl GTN M18 .... 127 F3 🄱
Everard Cl WALK M28 .... 83 D5
Everard St SALQ/ORD M5 .... 123 D2
Everest Av AULW OL7 .... 112 C2
Everest Cl HYDE SK14 .... 132 B5 🄱
Everest Rd ROCH OL11 .... 40 B5
Everglade OLDS OL8 .... 96 B4
Everleigh Cl BOLE BL2 .... 29 F2 🄱
Everleigh Dr BRO M7 .... 106 A1 🄱
Eversley Rd DID/WITH M20 ...... 163 E2 🄱
Everton Rd OLDS OL8 .... 95 E1
RDSH SK5 .... 147 D1 🄱
Everton St SWIN M27 .... 85 F5 🄱
Every St ANC M4 .... 107 E6

Bury BL9 .... 34 A3
RAMS BL0 .... 7 E5 🄱
Evesham Av HTNM SK4 .... 165 F2 🄱
NTHM/RTH M23 .... 160 B6
Evesham Cl MDTN M24 .... 75 F6
Evesham Dr FWTH BL4 .... 65 C1 🄱
Evesham Drive WILM/AE SK9 .... 204 A1
Evesham Gv AUL OL6 .... 97 D6
SALE M33 .... 160 C1
Evesham Rd BKLY M9 .... 92 B3
CHD/CDH SK8 .... 181 E3
MDTN M24 .... 75 E6
Eveside Cl CHD/CDH SK8 .... 181 F3 🄱
Eve St OLDS OL8 .... 96 A3 🄱
Ewan St GTN M18 .... 127 E3
Ewart Av SALQ/ORD M5 .... 104 B6
Ewart St BOL BL1 .... 27 F5
Ewhurst Av SWIN M27 .... 101 E1 🄱
Ewing Cl CHH M8 .... 90 B4
Ewood OLDS OL8 .... 96 B5
Ewood Dr TOT/BURYW BL8 .... 51 E1 🄱
Exbourne Rd WYTH/NTH M22 .... 178 A6
Exbury St RUSH/FAL M14 .... 144 B4
Excalibur Wy IRL M44 .... 135 D4
Excelsior Ter MILN OL16 .... 25 D2 🄱
Exchange Quay SALQ/ORD M5 .. 122 B3
Exchange St EDGY/DAV SK3 ...... 166 C4
Exeter Av BOLE BL2 .... 28 C5
DTN/ASHW M34 .... 149 D2
ECC M30 .... 102 B3
FWTH BL4 .... 50 B4
RAD M26 .... 50 A4
Exeter Cl CHD/CDH SK8 .... 195 D1
DUK SK16 .... 131 E3
Exeter Dr AUL OL6 .... 97 E6
IRL M44 .... 135 F1
Exeter Rd RDSH SK5 .... 148 A6
URM M41 .... 119 C5
Exeter St ROCH OL11 .... 40 A2
SLFD M6 .... 103 F5
Exford Cl NEWH/MOS M40 .... 107 E4 🄱
RDSH SK5 .... 147 D5 🄱
Exford Dr BOLE BL2 .... 49 D3
Exit Rd West MANAIR M90 .... 191 F2 🄱
Exmoor Cl AUL OL6 .... 97 D6
Exmouth Av RDSH SK5 .... 148 A6 🄱
Exmouth Pl ROCH OL11 .... 40 B4 🄱
Exmouth Rd SALE M33 .... 138 B6
Exmouth Sq ROCH OL11 .... 40 B3 🄱
Exmouth St ROCH OL11 .... 40 B4 🄱
Eyam Gv OFTN SK2 .... 184 B5
Eyam Rd BRAM/HZG SK7 .... 198 C1 🄱
Eyebrook Rd ALT WA14 .... 173 E6
Eynford Av RDSH SK5 .... 147 F5
Eyre St HULME M15 .... 124 B4

Faber St ANC M4 .... 106 B4
Factory Brow MDTN M24 .... 74 A4
Factory La BKLY M9 .... 91 E4
SALQ/ORD M5 .... 105 E3 🄱
Factory St MDTN M24 .... 75 D3
RAD M26 .... 51 F6 🄱
RAMS BL0 .... 7 D4
Failsworth Rd FAIL M35 .... 94 C6
Fair Acres BOLE BL2 .... 29 F4 🄱
Fairacres Rd MPL/ROM SK6 ...... 200 C1 🄱
Fairbairn St OP/CLY M11 .... 108 A6 🄱
Fairbank Dr MDTN M24 .... 74 B1
Fairbottom St OLD OL1 .... 79 D4 🄱
Fairbourne Cl WILM/AE SK9 ..... 209 D1 🄱
Fairbourne Cl WILM/AE SK9 ..... 209 D1 🄱
Fairbourne Dr HALE/TIMP WA15 . 159 F4
WILM/AE SK9 .... 209 D1
Fairbourne Rd BNG/LEV M19 .... 146 A2
DTN/ASHW M34 .... 148 C1 🄱
Fairbrook Dr SLFD M6 .... 103 F5
Fairbrother St SALQ/ORD M5 ... 123 D2
Fairclough St BOLS/LL BL3 .... 47 D5
OP/CLY M11 .... 108 B5
Fairfax Av DID/WITH M20 .... 163 F1
HALE/TIMP WA15 .... 175 F1
Fairfax Cl MPL/ROM SK6 .... 170 B6
Fairfax Dr LIT OL15 .... 25 D2
WILM/AE SK9 .... 209 D1
Fairfax Rd PWCH M25 .... 71 E6
Fairfield Av CHD/CDH SK8 .... 181 D5
DROY M43 .... 128 B3
MPL/ROM SK6 .... 169 E1 🄱
Fairfield Dr BURY BL9 .... 35 E4
Fairfield Rd DROY M43 .... 128 A1
FWTH BL4 .... 66 A4
HALE/TIMP WA15 .... 176 A2
IRL M44 .... 134 A6
MDTN M24 .... 74 C2
OP/CLY M11 .... 127 F2
Fairfields EDGW/EG BL7 .... 14 A5
OLDS OL8 .... 95 F3
Fairfield Sq DROY M43 .... 128 B1
Fairfield St CMANE M1 .... 3 H6
SLFD M6 .... 103 E2
Fairford Rd RDSH SK5 .... 147 D6

Fairford Dr BOLS/LL BL3 .... 46 C4 🄱
Fairford Wy RDSH SK5 .... 147 D6 🄱
WILM/AE SK9 .... 204 B4 🄱
Fairhaven Av CCHDY M21 .... 141 F3 🄱
WHTF M45 .... 70 B4
Fairhaven Cl BRAM/HZG SK7 .... 197 D1
Fairhaven Rd BOL BL1 .... 28 A4
Fairhaven St WGTN/LGST M12 . 126 A3
Fairhills Rd IRL M44 .... 135 E3
Fairholme Av URM M41 .... 138 A2 🄱
Fairholme Rd DID/WITH M20 .... 144 A5
HTNM SK4 .... 166 A2
Fairhope Av SLFD M6 .... 102 C3
Fairhurst Dr WALK M28 .... 82 A3
Fairisle Cl OP/CLY M11 .... 108 A6 🄱
Fairlands Rd SALE M33 .... 159 D3
Fairlands St ROCH OL11 .... 40 C5 🄱
Fairlawn HTNM SK4 .... 166 B2
Fairlawn Cl RUSH/FAL M14 .... 124 B5 🄱
Fairlea DTN/ASHW M34 .... 149 E1
Fairlea Av DID/WITH M20 .... 164 A3
Fairlee Av DROY M43 .... 111 D6
Fairleigh Av SLFD M6 .... 103 D4
Fairless Rd ECC M30 .... 101 E6
Fairlie Av BOLS/LL BL3 .... 45 D4
Fairlie Dr HALE/TIMP WA15 ...... 159 F5
Fairman St OLDTF/WHR M16 .... 124 A6 🄱
Fairmead Rd NTHM/RTH M23 .... 162 A4
Fairmile Dr DID/WITH M20 .... 164 A5
Fairmount Av BOLE BL2 .... 48 C1
Fairmount Rd SWIN M27 .... 100 C1
Fairoak Ct BOLS/LL BL3 .... 46 B4 🄱🄱
Fair Oak Rd BNG/LEV M19 .... 145 D6
Fairstead Wk OP/CLY M11 .... 128 A2
Fair St BOLS/LL BL3 .... 64 A1 🄱🄱
CMANE M1 .... 107 D6 🄱
SWIN M27 .... 86 B4
Fairview Av BNG/LEV M19 .... 145 D1
DTN/ASHW M34 .... 147 E2
Fairview Cl CHAD OL9 .... 76 C3
MPL/ROM SK6 .... 171 D6 🄱
WHIT OL12 .... 20 A3
Fairview Dr MPL/ROM SK6 .... 171 D6
Fairview Rd DTN/ASHW M34 ..... 147 E1
HALE/TIMP WA15 .... 176 A2
Fairway BRAM/HZG SK7 .... 196 B3
CHD/CDH SK8 .... 179 F3 🄱
DROY M43 .... 128 B3
PWCH M25 .... 89 E3
Fair Wy ROCH OL11 .... 38 C6
Fairway SWIN M27 .... 87 D6
WHIT OL12 .... 9 D4
Fairway Av BOLE BL2 .... 30 B3
NTHM/RTH M23 .... 160 B6
Fairway Crs ROY/SHW OL2 .... 60 B3
Fairway Dr SALE M33 .... 158 C3
Fairway Rd BURY BL9 .... 53 E6
OLDE OL4 .... 97 F1
The Fairways WHTF M45 .... 71 D5 🄱
The Fairway NEWH/MOS M40 .... 93 E5
OFTN SK2 .... 168 B6
Fairwood Rd NTHM/RTH M23 .... 160 B6
Fairy La CHH M8 .... 105 F2
SALE M33 .... 161 F2
Fairy St TOT/BURYW BL8 .... 33 D5
Fairywell Cl WILM/AE SK9 .... 204 B2 🄱
Fairywell Dr SALE M33 .... 159 E4
Fairywell Dr HALE/TIMP WA15 .. 159 F6
Faith St BOL BL1 .... 26 A6
Falcon Av URM M41 .... 138 C1
Falcon Cl BURY BL9 .... 34 B3
WHIT OL12 .... 20 B3
Falcon Crs SWIN M27 .... 86 C3 🄱
Falcon Dr CHAD OL9 .... 78 A3
IRL M44 .... 116 C5
LHULT M38 .... 65 C6
MDTN M24 .... 56 C6
Falcon St OLDS OL8 .... 78 C6
Falfield Dr CHH M8 .... 106 C2
Falinge Fold WHIT OL12 .... 22 B4
Falinge Ms WHIT OL12 .... 22 C5 🄱
Falinge Rd WHIT OL12 .... 22 B4
Falkirk Dr BOLE BL2 .... 49 D3
Falkirk St OLDE OL4 .... 80 A4 🄱
Falkland Av NEWH/MOS M40 .... 107 E3 🄱
Falkland Cl OLDE OL4 .... 62 C5 🄱
Falkland Rd BOLE BL2 .... 49 E2
Fallowfield Av SALQ/ORD M5 ... 122 C2 🄱
Fallowfield Dr WHIT OL12 .... 22 B3
Fallow Fields Dr RDSH SK5 .... 147 F2
The Fallows CHAD OL9 .... 77 E6 🄱
Falls Gv CHD/CDH SK8 .... 179 E5
Falmer Cl TOT/BURYW BL8 .... 33 D1
Falmer Dr WYTH/NTH M22 .... 178 B6 🄱
Falmer St GTN M18 .... 117 F6
Falmouth Av SALE M33 .... 138 B6 🄱
URM M41 .... 137 F6
Falmouth Crs RDSH SK5 .... 148 A6
Falmouth Rd IRL M44 .... 135 F1
Falmouth St NEWH/MOS M40 .. 108 A3 🄱
OLDS OL8 .... 96 A1
ROCH OL11 .... 40 B2
Falsgrave Cl NEWH/MOS M40 .. 108 B2 🄱
Falshaw Dr BURY BL9 .... 19 F4
Falston Av NEWH/MOS M40 .... 93 E3

Entry	Ref
Falstone Av *RAMS* BL0	19 D1
Falterley Rd *NTHM/RTH* M23	160 C5
Fancroft Rd *WYTH/NTH* M22	178 A2
Faraday Av *CHH* M8	106 B1
SWIN M27	87 E3
Faraday Dr *BOL* BL1	27 F6
Faraday St *CMANE* M1	3 G2
CMANE M1	3 G3
Farcroft Av *RAD* M26	52 A4
Farcroft Cl *NTHM/RTH* M23	161 D5
Fardale *ROY/SHW* OL2	61 F3
Farden Dr *NTHM/RTH* M23	160 B5
Farewell Cl *ROCH* OL11	39 D5
Far Hey Cl *RAD* M26	50 C6
Farholme *OLD* OL1	78 A1
Faringdon Wk *BOLS/LL* BL3	46 C4
Farland Pl *BOLS/LL* BL3	45 D4
Farlands Dr *DID/WITH* M20	163 F6
Farlands Ri *MILN* OL16	41 D4
Far La *GTN* M18	127 E5
Farley Av *GTN* M18	128 B5
Farley Ct *CHD/CHDH* SK8	181 D3
Farley Rd *SALE* M33	160 A3
Farley Wy *ROCH* SK5	146 C2
Farman St *BOLS/LL* BL3	46 B6
Farm Av *STRET* M32	120 B5
Farm Cl *HTNM* SK4	146 A5
TOT/BURYW BL8	32 A1
Farmers Cl *HTNM* SK4	161 E2
Farmer St *HTNM* SK4	166 B2
Farmfield *SALE* M33	138 C5
Farmlands Wk *OLD* OL1	62 A5
Farm La *HYDE* SK14	150 B3
POY/DIS SK12	201 E3
PWCH M25	72 C3
WALK M28	100 A2
Farm Rd *OLDS* OL8	95 D5
Farmside Av *IRL* M44	116 B6
Farmstead Cl *FAIL* M35	111 D1
Farm St *CHAD* OL9	77 F2
FAIL M35	109 E1
HEY OL10	56 C1
Farm Wk *ALT* WA14	172 C5
LIT OL15	12 A6
MILN OL16	24 A4
Farmway *MDTN* M24	75 D4
Farm Yd *BNG/LEV* M19	145 E2
Farn Av *BNG/LEV* M19	146 C1
Famborough Av *OLDE* OL4	80 B5
Farnborough Rd *BOL* BL1	27 F1
NEWH/MOS M40	107 E4
Farndale Sq *LHULT* M38	83 D2
Farndon Av *BRAM/HZG* SK7	185 D3
Farndon Cl *SALE* M33	160 C2
Farndon Dr *HALE/TIMP* WA15	175 E1
Farndon Rd *RDSH* SK5	146 C1
Farnham Av *BKLY* M9	74 B6
Farnham Cl *CHD/CHDH* SK8	195 E2
Farnham Dr *IRL* M44	135 C2
Farnley Cl *WHIT* OL12	21 D3
Farnley St *WGTN/LGST* M12	126 B3
Farnsworth Cl *AULW* OL7	112 C2
Farnworth Dr *RUSH/FAL* M14	144 A1
Farnworth St *BOLS/LL* BL3	46 A5
HEY OL10	37 D5
Farrand Rd *OLDS* OL8	94 C3
Farrant Rd *WGTN/LGST* M12	126 B6
Farrar Rd *DROY* M43	128 A1
Farrell St *CSLFD* M3	105 F4
Farrer Rd *BRUN/LGST* M13	126 A6
Far Ridings *MPL/ROM* SK6	170 B2
Farriers La *ROCH* OL11	38 C3
Farringdon Dr *SLFD* M6	103 F4
Farrowdale Av *ROY/SHW* OL2	61 F3
Farrow St *ROY/SHW* OL2	61 F3
Farrow St East *ROY/SHW* OL2	61 F3
Farr St *EDGY/DAV* SK3	166 B5
Farwood Cl *OLDTF/WHR* M16	123 D4
Far Woodseats La *GLSP* SK13	153 D5
Fastnet St *OP/CLY* M11	126 B1
Faulkenhurst St *CHAD* OL9	78 A3
Fawborough Rd *NTHM/RTH* M23	161 D4
Fawcett St *BOLE* BL2	47 F2
Fawley Av *HYDE* SK14	150 B2
Fawley Gv *WYTH/NTH* M22	178 B3
Fawns Keep *STLY* SK15	133 F3
WILM/AE SK9	204 B4
Fay Av *BKLY* M9	92 C3
Faywood Dr *MPL/ROM* SK6	187 E1
Fearney Side *BOLS/LL* BL3	49 D6
Fearnhead St *BOLS/LL* BL3	46 A5
Fearn St *HEY* OL10	37 D5
Featherstall Rd *LIT* OL15	12 A6
Featherstall Rd North *CHAD* OL9	78 B4
OLD OL1	78 B3
Federation St *ANC* M4	3 E1
PWCH M25	71 D6
Feldom Rd *NTHM/RTH* M23	161 D3
Fellbrigg Cl *GTN* M18	127 D6
Fellpark Rd *NTHM/RTH* M23	161 E3
Fells Gv *WALK* M28	84 A4
Fellside *BOLE* BL2	30 B4
Fellside Cl *TOT/BURYW* BL8	18 A4
Fellside Gn *STLY* SK15	114 B4
Fell St *TOT/BURYW* BL8	33 D5
Felltop Dr *RDSH* SK5	147 E3
Felskirk Rd *WYTH/NTH* M22	192 A1
Felsted *BOL* BL1	44 C1
Felthorpe Dr *CHH* M8	106 A1
Felton Av *WYTH/NTH* M22	178 A4
Felton Cl *BURY* BL9	53 E4
Fencegate Av *HTNM* SK4	146 B6
Fence St *OFTN* SK2	184 B5
Fenchurch Av *NEWH/MOS* M40	109 D3
Fencot Dr *WGTN/LGST* M12	126 B5
Fenella St *BRUN/LGST* M13	125 F5
Fenham Cl *NEWH/MOS* M40	107 D2
Fenmore Av *GTN* M18	126 C6
Fennel St *ANC* M4	2 D1
Fenners Cl *BOLS/LL* BL3	46 B6
Fenney St *BRO* M7	105 F1
Fenney St East *BRO* M7	105 F1
Fenn St *HULME* M15	123 F3
Fenside Rd *WYTH/NTH* M22	178 C2
Fenton Av *OFTN* SK2	184 A3
Fenton Ms *ROCH* OL11	39 F2
Fenton St *OLDE* OL4	79 F5
ROCH OL11	39 F2
ROY/SHW OL2	61 F4
TOT/BURYW BL8	33 D4
Fenwick Dr *HTNM* SK4	164 C2
Fenwick St *HULME* M15	124 B3
ROCH OL11	22 C6
Ferdinand St *NEWH/MOS* M40	107 E3
Fereday St *WALK* M28	83 D1
Fernacre *SALE* M33	140 A6
Fernally St *HYDE* SK14	150 C1
Fern Av *URM* M41	137 E1
Fernbank *RAD* M26	69 E3
Fern Bank *STLY* SK15	133 D1
Fern Bank *STLY* SK15	133 D1
Fern Bank Dr *NTHM/RTH* M23	160 C5
Fern Bank St *HYDE* SK14	150 C3
Fernbray Av *BNG/LEV* M19	164 B3
Fernbrook Cl *BRUN/LGST* M13	125 E4
Fern Cl *MDTN* M24	76 B3
MPL/ROM SK6	187 D1
OLDE OL4	81 D5
Fern Clough *BOL* BL1	45 D2
Fernclough Rd *BKLY* M9	107 E1
Fern Crs *STLY* SK15	133 D1
Ferndale Av *MILN* OL16	41 D6
OFTN SK2	183 F5
WHTF M45	70 A4
Ferndale Cl *OLDE* OL4	97 E1
Ferndale Gdns *BNG/LEV* M19	144 C5
Ferndale Rd *SALE* M33	159 F3
Fern Dene *WHIT* OL12	21 F3
Ferndene Rd *DID/WITH* M20	143 F6
WHTF M45	72 A4
Ferndown Av *BRAM/HZG* SK7	184 A6
CHAD OL9	76 B4
Ferndown Dr *IRL* M44	116 B6
NTHM/RTH M23	160 B5
Ferndown Rd *BOLE* BL2	29 F4
NTHM/RTH M23	160 B5
Ferney Field Rd *CHAD* OL9	77 D4
Ferngate Dr *DID/WITH* M20	143 F5
Ferngrove *BURY* BL9	34 C3
Fernhill *MPL/ROM* SK6	187 F1
Fernhill Av *BOLS/LL* BL3	45 E5
Fernhill Dr *GTN* M18	126 C5
Fern Hill La *WHIT* OL12	21 E1
Fernhill St *BURY* BL9	34 A1
Fernholme Ct *OLDS* OL8	95 D1
Fernhurst Rd *DID/WITH* M20	144 A6
Fernhurst St *CHAD* OL9	78 A2
Fernie St *ANC* M4	106 B4
Fern Isle Cl *WHIT* OL12	8 C5
Fern Lea *CHD/CHDH* SK8	179 F6
Fernlea *HALE/TIMP* WA15	175 D6
Fernlea Av *OLD* OL1	78 A2
Fernlea Cl *WHIT* OL12	21 F3
Fernlea Crs *SWIN* M27	85 F6
Fern Lea Gv *LHULT* M38	82 A1
Fernleigh Av *BNG/LEV* M19	146 A2
Fernleigh Dr *OLDTF/WHR* M16	123 E4
Fernley Av *DTN/ASHW* M34	149 E1
Fernley Rd *OFTN* SK2	183 F1
Fernone *WILM/AE* SK9	194 B6
Ferns Gv *BOL* BL1	45 F2
Fernside *RAD* M26	67 F5
Fernside Av *DID/WITH* M20	144 B6
Fernside Gv *WALK* M28	83 F1
Fernside Wy *WHIT* OL12	21 E4
Fern St *BOLS/LL* BL3	46 A3
BURY BL9	34 A4
CHAD OL9	77 E3
CHH M8	106 B3
FWTH BL4	66 C2
OLDS OL8	78 B6
RAMS BL0	7 E5
ROCH OL11	39 E1
WHIT OL12	11 D5
Fern Vw *HALE/TIMP* WA15	176 C2
Fernview Dr *TOT/BURYW* BL8	18 B4
Fernwood Av *GTN* M18	127 E6
Fernwood Gv *WILM/AE* SK9	204 A3
Ferrand Ldg *LIT* OL15	13 D4
Ferrand Rd *LIT* OL15	12 C5
Ferris St *OP/CLY* M11	127 E1
Ferrous Wy *IRL* M44	135 D5
Ferryhill Rd *IRL* M44	135 F1
Ferry Rd *IRL* M44	135 F1
Ferry St *OP/CLY* M11	125 F1
Fettler Cl *SWIN* M27	85 F6
Fewston Cl *BOL* BL1	27 E2
Fiddlers La *IRL* M44	116 C6
Field Bank Gv *BNG/LEV* M19	145 E2
Field Cl *BRAM/HZG* SK7	196 B5
MPL/ROM SK6	186 B2
Fieldcroft *ROCH* OL11	21 F6
Fielden Av *CCHDY* M21	141 F2
Field End Cl *STLY* SK15	133 E1
Fielden Rd *DID/WITH* M20	143 D6
Fielders Wy *SWIN* M27	85 F1
Fieldfare Av *NEWH/MOS* M40	108 C3
Fieldfare Wy *AULW* OL7	96 B6
Fieldhead Av *ROCH* OL11	21 E6
TOT/BURYW BL8	32 B6
Fieldhead Ms *WILM/AE* SK9	204 C3
Fieldhead Rd *WILM/AE* SK9	204 C3
Field House La *MPL/ROM* SK6	187 E1
Fieldhouse Rd *WHIT* OL12	23 D3
Fielding St *ECC* M30	101 D6
MDTN M24	75 E1
Field La *AUL* OL6	113 E2
Field Rd *MILN* OL16	24 B6
SALE M33	138 C5
Fields End Fold *ECC* M30	117 D5
Fields Farm Cl *HYDE* SK14	152 B2
Fields Farm Rd *HYDE* SK14	152 B1
Fields New Rd *CHAD* OL9	77 E6
Field St *DROY* M43	128 A1
FAIL M35	93 F6
GTN M18	127 F3
HYDE SK14	131 E4
MPL/ROM SK6	169 D2
ROCH OL11	40 B3
SLFD M6	104 A5
Fieldsway *OLDS* OL8	95 F3
Field Vale Dr *RDSH* SK5	147 E2
Fieldvale Rd *SALE* M33	158 C4
Fieldway *MILN* OL16	40 C4
Fife Av *CHAD* OL9	94 A1
Fifield Cl *OLDS* OL8	96 B2
Fifth Av *BOL* BL1	45 F2
BURY BL9	35 E3
OLDS OL8	95 D3
OP/CLY M11	109 D5
TRPK M17	121 D4
Fifth St *BOL* BL1	26 A3
TRPK M17	121 D4
Filbert St *OLD* OL1	80 A2
Filby Wk *NEWH/MOS* M40	107 F3
Fildes St *MDTN* M24	76 B4
Filey Av *OLDTF/WHR* M16	142 B1
URM M41	118 B5
Filey Dr *SLFD* M6	103 E1
Filey Rd *OFTN* SK2	168 A6
RUSH/FAL M14	144 B3
Filey St *MILN* OL16	24 A3
Finance St *LIT* OL15	25 D1
Finborough Cl *OLDTF/WHR* M16	125 E3
Finchale Dr *HALE/TIMP* WA15	175 F6
Finch Av *FWTH* BL4	65 D4
Finchley Av *NEWH/MOS* M40	109 D3
Finchley Gv *NEWH/MOS* M40	92 B4
Finchley Rd *HALE/TIMP* WA15	174 C4
RUSH/FAL M14	143 F3
Findon Rd *NTHM/RTH* M23	177 E1
Finghall Rd *URM* M41	137 E1
Finland Rd *EDGY/DAV* SK3	166 B6
Finlan Rd *MDTN* M24	58 B4
Finlay St *FWTH* BL4	66 B3
Finney Cl *WILM/AE* SK9	204 A1
Finney Dr *CCHDY* M21	141 E4
WILM/AE SK9	204 A1
Finney La *CHD/CHDH* SK8	180 A6
WYTH/NTH M22	193 E1
Finney St *BOLS/LL* BL3	47 D5
Finningley Rd *BKLY* M9	73 F5
Finny Bank Rd *SALE* M33	139 E5
Finsbury Av *NEWH/MOS* M40	109 D3
Finsbury Rd *RDSH* SK5	146 C3
Finsbury St *ROCH* OL11	39 E2
Finstock Cl *ECC* M30	100 C6
Fintry Gv *ECC* M30	101 E6
Fir Av *BRAM/HZG* SK7	196 C1
Firbank Rd *NTHM/RTH* M23	177 E4
Fir Bank Rd *ROY/SHW* OL2	60 B3
Firbarn Cl *MILN* OL16	24 B6
Firbeck Dr *ANC* M4	107 E5
Fir Cl *POY/DIS* SK12	198 C6
Fircroft Rd *OLDS* OL8	94 B3
Firdale Av *NEWH/MOS* M40	93 F4
Firdale Wk *CHAD* OL9	78 A4
Firecrest Cl *WALK* M28	82 C5
Firefly Cl *CSLFD* M3	105 E6

Fire Station Sq SALQ/ORD M5 ...... 105 D5 2
Firethorn Av BNG/LEV M19 ...... 145 D5 7
Firethorn Dr HYDE SK14 ...... 151 E1
Firfield Gv WALK M28 ...... 84 A2
Fir Gv BNG/LEV M19 ...... 145 E2
  CHAD OL9 ...... 77 F3
Firgrove Av MILN OL16 ...... 24 B5
Firgrove Gdns MILN OL16 ...... 24 B5
Fir La ROY/SHW OL2 ...... 60 B3
Fir Rd BRAM/HZG SK7 ...... 182 C6
  DTN/ASHW M34 ...... 130 B6
  FWTH BL4 ...... 65 F3 1
  MPL/ROM SK6 ...... 186 C3
  SWIN M27 ...... 101 F1
Firs Av AUL OL6 ...... 112 C3
  FAIL M35 ...... 93 F6 6
  OLDTF/WHR M16 ...... 141 F1
Firsby Av MPL/ROM SK6 ...... 169 D1
Firsby St BNG/LEV M19 ...... 145 E2 10
Firs Gv CHD/CHDH SK8 ...... 179 E3
Firs Rd CHD/CHDH SK8 ...... 179 E4
  SALE M33 ...... 138 C6 3
First Av OLDS OL8 ...... 95 E3
  OP/CLY M11 ...... 109 E5
  STLY SK15 ...... 115 F2
  SWIN M27 ...... 101 E2
  TOT/BURYW BL8 ...... 32 A1
  TRPK M17 ...... 121 E4
The Firs ALT WA14 ...... 173 F5
Fir St BOL BL1 ...... 28 A5
  BURY BL9 ...... 34 B5
  ECC M30 ...... 101 E6
  FAIL M35 ...... 93 F6 8
  HEY OL10 ...... 37 F6
  HTNM SK4 ...... 166 C3
  IRL M44 ...... 134 A5
  NEWH/MOS M40 ...... 107 E3
  OLDTF/WHR M16 ...... 123 D5 1
  RAD M26 ...... 69 F1
  RAMS BL0 ...... 7 E4
  ROY/SHW OL2 ...... 60 B4
  SLFD M6 ...... 104 A5
First St BOL BL1 ...... 26 A3
Firs Wy SALE M33 ...... 158 A2
Firswood Dr HYDE SK14 ...... 132 B6 8
  ROY/SHW OL2 ...... 60 A4
  SWIN M27 ...... 101 F1
Firswood Mt CHD/CHDH SK8 ...... 179 E3
Firth St OLD OL1 ...... 79 D5
Fir Tree Av OLDS OL8 ...... 96 B3
Fir Tree Av SALE M33 ...... 158 A1
Fir Tree Cl DUK SK16 ...... 132 A1 8
Fir Tree Crs DUK SK16 ...... 132 A1
Fir Tree Dr HYDE SK14 ...... 131 F3 8
Fir Tree La DUK SK16 ...... 132 A2
Firvale Av CHD/CHDH SK8 ...... 179 F6
Firwood Av FWTH BL4 ...... 66 A5
  URM M41 ...... 139 E2
Firwood Cl OFTN SK2 ...... 168 A5 8
Firwood Crs RAD M26 ...... 69 F2
Firwood Gv BOLE BL2 ...... 28 C5
Firwood La BOLE BL2 ...... 28 C4
Firwood Pk CHAD OL9 ...... 76 C4
Fisherfield WHIT OL12 ...... 21 D4
Fishermore Rd URM M41 ...... 136 C1 3
Fisher St OLD OL1 ...... 79 D3 4
Fishwick St MILN OL16 ...... 40 B1
Fistral Av CHD/CHDH SK8 ...... 194 A1
Fistral Crs STLY SK15 ...... 115 E4
Fitton Av CCHDY M21 ...... 141 F5
Fitton Av SWIN M27 ...... 86 A2
Fitton Hill Rd OLDS OL8 ...... 96 B1
Fitton St MILN OL16 ...... 23 E5
  ROY/SHW OL2 ...... 61 D2
Fitzgerald Cl PWCH M25 ...... 88 A3 2
Fitzhugh St BOL BL1 ...... 28 B2 8
Fitzroy St AULW OL7 ...... 112 A6
  DROY M43 ...... 128 C1
  STLY SK15 ...... 115 E4
Fitzwarren St SLFD M6 ...... 104 A4
Fitzwilliam St BRO M7 ...... 105 E3 6
Five Quarters RAD M26 ...... 50 C4 2
Flagcroft Dr NTHM/RTH M23 ...... 177 F1
Flagg Wood Av MPL/ROM SK6 ...... 170 B6
Flag Rw ANC M4 ...... 106 C4 8
Flagship Av SALQ/ORD M5 ...... 122 C1 8
Flake La ROY/SHW OL2 ...... 60 B5
Flamingo Cl WGTN/LGST M12 ...... 126 B3 8
Flamstead Av NTHM/RTH M23 ...... 176 C1 1
Flannel St WHIT OL12 ...... 23 E5 3
Flashfields PWCH M25 ...... 88 A4 8
Flash St NEWH/MOS M40 ...... 109 D1
Flatley Cl HULME M15 ...... 124 B4 8
Flaxcroft Rd WYTH/NTH M22 ...... 177 F5
Flaxfield Av STLY SK15 ...... 115 E5
Flaxman Ri OLD OL1 ...... 62 A5
Flaxpool Cl OLDTF/WHR M16 ...... 123 F5
Flax St CSLFD M3 ...... 105 E3 6
  RAMS BL0 ...... 18 B1 12
Fleece St MILN OL16 ...... 23 D6 7
  OLDE OL4 ...... 79 F4 8
Fleeson St RUSH/FAL M14 ...... 125 D6
Fleet St AUL OL6 ...... 112 B5
  GTN M18 ...... 128 A3
  HYDE SK14 ...... 131 F5

OLDE OL4 ...... 80 A4 4
Fleetwood Rd WALK M28 ...... 82 B2 8
Fleming Rd WYTH/NTH M22 ...... 178 B5
Flemish Rd HYDE SK14 ...... 149 F1
Fletcher Av SWIN M27 ...... 86 B2
Fletcher Cl CHAD OL9 ...... 78 B5 8
  HEY OL10 ...... 37 E6
Fletcher Dr ALT WA14 ...... 174 A6
  POY/DIS SK12 ...... 201 D3
Fletcher Fold Rd BURY BL9 ...... 53 D3 8
Fletcher Sq CMANE M1 ...... 125 D1 8
Fletcher St BOLS/LL BL3 ...... 49 C4
  BOLS/LL BL3 ...... 2 A6
  BURY BL9 ...... 34 B5 13
  FWTH BL4 ...... 66 B3 12
  NEWH/MOS M40 ...... 108 A2 8
  RAD M26 ...... 52 A5
  ROCH OL11 ...... 40 B2 8
  STKP SK1 ...... 167 D4
Fletsand Rd WILM/AE SK9 ...... 204 A5
Flint Cl BRAM/HZG SK7 ...... 184 A6
  OP/CLY M11 ...... 108 C5 2
Flint Gv IRL M44 ...... 134 A5
Flint St DROY M43 ...... 110 C5
  EDGY/DAV SK3 ...... 166 C6
  OLD OL1 ...... 80 A3 8
Flitcroft Ct BOLS/LL BL3 ...... 47 D5 8
Flixton Rd PART M31 ...... 136 C3
  URM M41 ...... 137 E1
Floatshall Rd NTHM/RTH M23 ...... 177 D1
Floats Rd NTHM/RTH M23 ...... 176 C1
Flora St BKLY M9 ...... 91 D2
  OLD OL1 ...... 78 C4
Florence Av BOL BL1 ...... 28 A3
Florence Steet MILN OL16 ...... 40 C1
Florence St BOLS/LL BL3 ...... 46 B5 31
  DROY M43 ...... 128 C1 8
  ECC M30 ...... 100 C6
  FAIL M35 ...... 94 A5 4
  HTNM SK4 ...... 166 C3 8
  SALE M33 ...... 139 F5
Florida St OLDS OL8 ...... 78 C6
Florist St EDGY/DAV SK3 ...... 166 C6
Flowery Bank OLDS OL8 ...... 96 C1 8
Flowery Fld OFTN SK2 ...... 183 F6
Flowery Field Gn HYDE SK14 ...... 131 D5
Floyd Av CCHDY M21 ...... 142 A5
Floyer Rd BKLY M9 ...... 91 F1
Foden La BRAM/HZG SK7 ...... 196 B6
  WILM/AE SK9 ...... 208 A3
Fog La BNG/LEV M19 ...... 164 B1 8
  DID/WITH M20 ...... 165 F1
Fold Av DROY M43 ...... 110 C5
Fold Gn CHAD OL9 ...... 77 E5
Fold Ms BRAM/HZG SK7 ...... 184 C4
Fold Rd RAD M26 ...... 68 A4
Folds Rd BOL BL1 ...... 47 E1
  BOLE BL2 ...... 47 E1
Fold St BURY BL9 ...... 33 E5 8
  HEY OL10 ...... 37 F4
  NEWH/MOS M40 ...... 92 B5
The Fold BKLY M9 ...... 91 E2 8
  URM M41 ...... 118 B6
Fold Vw OLDS OL8 ...... 96 B3 8
Foleshill Av BKLY M9 ...... 91 E6
Foley Gdns HEY OL10 ...... 56 C2
Foliage Crs RDSH SK5 ...... 147 F6
Foliage Gdns RDSH SK5 ...... 148 A6 4
Foliage Rd RDSH SK5 ...... 167 F1
Folkestone Rd OP/CLY M11 ...... 109 E5
Folkestone Rd East OP/CLY M11 ...... 109 E5
Folkestone Rd West OP/CLY M11 ...... 109 D5
Follows St GTN M18 ...... 127 E3 8
Folly La SWIN M27 ...... 101 E2
Folly Wk WHIT OL12 ...... 23 D4
Fonthill Gv SALE M33 ...... 159 D4
Fontwell Cl OLDTF/WHR M16 ...... 123 D6
Fontwell La OLD OL1 ...... 79 E2
Fontwell Rd BOLS/LL BL3 ...... 67 E1
Fooley Cl DROY M43 ...... 127 F1
Foot Mill Crs WHIT OL12 ...... 22 B3
Foot Wood Crs WHIT OL12 ...... 22 B3
Forber Crs GTN M18 ...... 127 D6
Forbes Cl SALE M33 ...... 160 B3
  STKP SK1 ...... 167 D5
Forbes Pk BRAM/HZG SK7 ...... 196 B2
Forbes Rd STKP SK1 ...... 167 F4
Forbes St MPL/ROM SK6 ...... 169 D1 8
Fordbank Rd DID/WITH M20 ...... 163 E3
Fordham Gv BOL BL1 ...... 46 A1 31
Ford La DID/WITH M20 ...... 163 E3
  SLFD M6 ...... 104 B3
  WYTH/NTH M22 ...... 162 C4
Ford Ldg DID/WITH M20 ...... 163 F3 8
Fordoe La WHIT OL12 ...... 20 A1
Ford's La BRAM/HZG SK7 ...... 196 B5
Ford St CSLFD M3 ...... 105 E5
  DUK SK16 ...... 131 F5 8
  EDGY/DAV SK3 ...... 166 B4
  RAD M26 ...... 67 E3 8
  WGTN/LGST M12 ...... 125 E3
Foreland Cl NEWH/MOS M40 ...... 107 E2 8
Forest Cl DUK SK16 ...... 131 D3 8
Forest Dr HALE/TIMP WA15 ...... 175 D1 8
  SALE M33 ...... 158 C3

Forester Dr STLY SK15 ...... 114 B6
Forester Hill Av BOLS/LL BL3 ...... 47 E6
Forester Hill Cl BOLS/LL BL3 ...... 47 D6 19
Forest Gdns PART M31 ...... 154 B2
Forest Range BNG/LEV M19 ...... 145 E2
Forest Rd BOL BL1 ...... 26 C4
Forest St AUL OL6 ...... 113 D3
  ECC M30 ...... 100 B3 8
  OLDS OL8 ...... 96 A2
Forest Vw WHIT OL12 ...... 22 B3
Forest Wy BOLE BL2 ...... 29 D1
Forfar St BOL BL1 ...... 27 F2
Forge La OP/CLY M11 ...... 108 A5
Forge St OLDE OL4 ...... 79 F4
Formby Av CCHDY M21 ...... 142 B4
Formby Dr CHD/CHDH SK8 ...... 193 F1
Formby Rd SLFD M6 ...... 103 F2
Forrester Dr ROY/SHW OL2 ...... 62 B1 8
Forrester St WALK M28 ...... 84 B5
Forrest Rd DTN/ASHW M34 ...... 149 F2
Forshaw Av GTN M18 ...... 128 A3
Forshaw St DTN/ASHW M34 ...... 129 E5 8
Forsyth St WHIT OL12 ...... 20 C3
Fortescue Rd OFTN SK2 ...... 168 B6
Forth Pl RAD M26 ...... 51 D4
Forth Rd RAD M26 ...... 51 D4
Forton Av BOLE BL2 ...... 48 C2
Fortran Cl SALQ/ORD M5 ...... 104 B6 2
Fort Rd PWCH M25 ...... 89 E3
Fortrose Av BKLY M9 ...... 90 C2
Fortuna Gv BNG/LEV M19 ...... 145 D5
Fortune St BOLS/LL BL3 ...... 47 F4 8
Fortyacre Dr MPL/ROM SK6 ...... 168 C2
Forum Gv BRO M7 ...... 105 F2 8
Fosbrook Av DID/WITH M20 ...... 164 A1 1
Foscarn Dr NTHM/RTH M23 ...... 177 F2
Fossgill Av BOLE BL2 ...... 29 D2
Foster La BOLE BL2 ...... 30 A6
Foster St DTN/ASHW M34 ...... 130 A6
  OLDE OL4 ...... 80 A5
  RAD M26 ...... 51 D6 8
  SALQ/ORD M5 ...... 103 E6 2
Fotherby Dr BKLY M9 ...... 91 E2
Foulds Av TOT/BURYW BL8 ...... 32 B5
Foundry La ANC M4 ...... 3 G2
Foundry St BOLS/LL BL3 ...... 47 D4 7
  BOLS/LL BL3 ...... 49 E6 8
  BURY BL9 ...... 34 A5
  CHAD OL9 ...... 78 C5
  DUK SK16 ...... 131 D1
  HEY OL10 ...... 37 D5 13
  RAD M26 ...... 51 E6 8
Fountain Av HALE/TIMP WA15 ...... 175 F4
Fountain Pl WHTF M45 ...... 71 D4
Fountains Av BOLE BL2 ...... 29 D6
Fountains Rd CHD/CHDH SK8 ...... 195 F3
  STRET M32 ...... 120 A6
Fountain St AUL OL6 ...... 113 F4
  BURY BL9 ...... 34 B5
  CMANW M2 ...... 3 E4
  ECC M30 ...... 119 E1 8
  HYDE SK14 ...... 132 A6
  MDTN M24 ...... 75 D3
  OLD OL1 ...... 78 C4 8
  TOT/BURYW BL8 ...... 33 D6 4
Fountain St North BURY BL9 ...... 34 B5
Fountains Wk DUK SK16 ...... 131 D3
Fouracres Rd NTHM/RTH M23 ...... 177 D2
Four Lanes Wy ROCH OL11 ...... 20 A3
Fourth Av BOL BL1 ...... 45 F2
  BURY BL9 ...... 35 D3
  CHAD OL9 ...... 77 E6
  OLDS OL8 ...... 95 D4
  OP/CLY M11 ...... 109 D4
  STLY SK15 ...... 115 F1
  SWIN M27 ...... 101 E2 2
Fourth St BOL BL1 ...... 26 A3
  TRPK M17 ...... 121 D4
Fourways TRPK M17 ...... 120 B3
Four Yards CMANW M2 ...... 2 D4 3
Fovant Crs RDSH SK5 ...... 146 C2
Fowler Av GTN M18 ...... 128 A2 3
Fowler St OLDS OL8 ...... 95 D2
Fownhope Av SALE M33 ...... 159 D2
Fownhope Rd SALE M33 ...... 159 D2
Foxall Cl MDTN M24 ...... 74 A4
Foxall St MDTN M24 ...... 74 A4
Foxbank St BRUN/LGST M13 ...... 125 F5 8
Fox Bench Cl CHD/CHDH SK8 ...... 196 A3
Foxbench Wk CCHDY M21 ...... 142 B5
Fox Cl HALE/TIMP WA15 ...... 175 D1
Foxcroft St LIT OL15 ...... 11 D2
Foxdale St OP/CLY M11 ...... 109 D6 8
Foxdenton Cl URM M41 ...... 120 A6
Foxdenton La MDTN M24 ...... 76 C5
Foxfield Cl TOT/BURYW BL8 ...... 32 C2
Foxfield Dr OLDS OL8 ...... 95 D4
Foxfield Rd NTHM/RTH M23 ...... 177 E4
Foxglove Ct WHIT OL12 ...... 22 B2
Foxglove Dr ALT WA14 ...... 158 A5
  BURY BL9 ...... 35 E4
Foxglove La STLY SK15 ...... 114 A4
Foxhall Rd DTN/ASHW M34 ...... 129 E5
  HALE/TIMP WA15 ...... 174 C1
Foxhill ALT WA14 ...... 173 E2

Fox Hl *ROY/SHW* OL2 .... 60 C1
Foxhill Cha *OFTN* SK2 .... 185 E2
Foxhill Dr *STLY* SK15 .... 133 D1
Foxhill Rd *ECC* M30 .... 100 A6
Fox Hill Rd *ROCH* OL11 .... 58 B1
Foxholes Cl *WHIT* OL12 .... 23 E4
Foxholes Rd *HYDE* SK14 .... 150 B3
   WHIT OL12 .... 23 E4
Foxlair Rd *WYTH/NTH* M22 .... 177 F4
Foxland Rd *CHD/CHDH* SK8 .... 179 F3
Foxley Gv *BOLS/LL* BL3 .... 46 B3
Fox Park Rd *OLDS* OL8 .... 95 D3
Fox Platt Rd *MOSL* OL5 .... 98 C4
Fox Platt Ter *MOSL* OL5 .... 99 D5
Fox St *BURY* BL9 .... 34 A4
   ECC M30 .... 102 A5
   EDGY/DAV SK3 .... 166 B5
   HEY OL10 .... 37 D5
   MILN OL16 .... 23 F5
   MILN OL16 .... 41 F1
   OLDS OL8 .... 95 D3
Foxton St *MDTN* M24 .... 74 A4
Foxwood Dr *MOSL* OL5 .... 99 E5
Foxwood Gdns *BNG/LEV* M19 .... 144 C6
Foynes Cl *NEWH/MOS* M40 .... 107 E2
Framingham Rd *SALE* M33 .... 159 F3
Framley Rd *CCHDY* M21 .... 143 D4
Frampton Cl *MDTN* M24 .... 75 F4
Fram St *BKLY* M9 .... 92 A5
   SLFD M6 .... 103 F5
Frances Av *CHD/CHDH* SK8 ...... 179 E1
Frances James Leech St
   EDGY/DAV SK3 .... 167 D5
Frances St *BOL* BL1 .... 27 E5
   BRUN/LGST M13 .... 124 C3
   CHD/CHDH SK8 .... 180 C1
   DTN/ASHW M34 .... 149 F3
   HYDE SK14 .... 131 D6
   IRL M44 .... 134 C6
   MILN OL16 .... 24 B2
   OLD OL1 .... 79 E2
Frances St West *HYDE* SK14 .... 130 C6
Francis Av *ECC* M30 .... 101 F5
   WALK M28 .... 84 A3
Francis Rd *DID/WITH* M20 .... 144 A6
   IRL M44 .... 135 D3
Francis St *CSLFD* M3 .... 106 A4
   ECC M30 .... 101 E4
   FAIL M35 .... 94 A6
   FWTH BL4 .... 66 A2
Frankby Cl *SWIN* M27 .... 87 D6
Frankford Av *BOL* BL1 .... 27 D5
Frankford Sq *BOL* BL1 .... 27 D5
Frankland Cl *OP/CLY* M11 .... 108 C5
Franklin Cl *DTN/ASHW* M34 ..... 147 E1
Franklin Rd *DROY* M43 .... 110 B6
Franklin St *ECC* M30 .... 101 E5
   MILN OL16 .... 40 C2
   OLD OL1 .... 78 C3
Franklyn Av *URM* M41 .... 136 C1
Franklyn Rd *GTN* M18 .... 127 F3
Frank Perkins Wy *IRL* M44 ...... 135 D4
Frank St *BOL* BL1 .... 27 E5
   BURY BL9 .... 34 A6
   FAIL M35 .... 93 F6
   HYDE SK14 .... 150 C1
   SLFD M6 .... 104 A3
Frankton Rd *WHTF* M45 .... 71 D4
Franton Rd *OP/CLY* M11 .... 108 C5
Fraser Av *SALE* M33 .... 160 C2
Fraser Pl *TRPK* M17 .... 121 E4
Fraser Rd *CHH* M8 .... 90 A4
Fraser St *AUL* OL6 .... 113 D4
   MILN OL16 .... 40 C3
   ROY/SHW OL2 .... 61 E1
   SWIN M27 .... 86 B4
Freckleton Dr *TOT/BURYW* BL8 ... 31 D1
Frederick Av *ROY/SHW* OL2 ...... 61 F4
Frederick Rd *SLFD* M6 .... 104 C3
Frederick St *AUL* OL6 .... 113 F5
   CHAD OL9 .... 77 F5
   CSLFD M3 .... 2 A2
   DTN/ASHW M34 .... 130 A4
   FWTH BL4 .... 66 B3
   LIT OL15 .... 12 B5
   OLDS OL8 .... 95 E1
   RAMS BL0 .... 6 C6
Fred Tilson Cl *RUSH/FAL* M14 .. 124 B6
Freeholds Rd *WHIT* OL12 .... 5 F3
Freehold St *ROCH* OL11 .... 39 F2
Freeman Av *AUL* OL6 .... 113 E4
Freeman Rd *DUK* SK16 .... 131 D5
Freeman Sq *HULME* M15 .... 124 B5
Freemantle St *EDGY/DAV* SK3 .. 166 A5
Freesia Av *WALK* M28 .... 82 A2
Freestone Cl *TOT/BURYW* BL8 .. 33 E3
Freetown Cl *RUSH/FAL* M14 ... 124 B5
Freetrade St *ROCH* OL11 .... 39 F2
Fremantle Av *GTN* M18 .... 127 E6
French Av *OLD* OL1 .... 80 A2
   STLY SK15 .... 115 D6
French Barn La *BKLY* M9 .... 91 D2
French Gv *BOLS/LL* BL3 .... 48 B4
French St *AUL* OL6 .... 113 E3
   STLY SK15 .... 115 D6

Fresca Rd *OLD* OL1 .... 62 B5
Freshfield *CHD/CHDH* SK8 ...... 193 F1
Freshfield Av *BOLS/LL* BL3 .... 64 B1
   HYDE SK14 .... 150 B2
   PWCH M25 .... 72 A5
Freshfield Cl *FAIL* M35 .... 110 B1
   MPL/ROM SK6 .... 171 F4
Freshfield Gv *BOLS/LL* BL3 ...... 65 D1
Freshfield Rd *HTNM* SK4 .... 165 D3
Freshfields *RAD* M26 .... 50 B4
Freshpool Wy *WYTH/NTH* M22 .. 178 C1
Freshville St *CMANE* M1 .... 3 H5
Freshwater Dr *DTN/ASHW* M34 .. 149 F3
Freshwater St *GTN* M18 .... 127 F3
Fresnel Cl *HYDE* SK14 .... 132 C3
Frewland Av *EDGY/DAV* SK3 .... 183 D5
Freya Gv *SALO/ORD* M5 .... 123 D1
Friars Cl *ALT* WA14 .... 173 F6
   WILM/AE SK9 .... 202 C3
Friars Crs *ROCH* OL11 .... 40 A5
Friar's Rd *SALE* M33 .... 159 F1
Friendship Av *GTN* M18 .... 127 F5
Frieston Rd *ALT* WA14 .... 159 D4
Friezland Cl *STLY* SK15 .... 115 F2
Frimley Gdns *WYTH/NTH* M22 .. 178 B4
Frinton Av *NEWH/MOS* M40 ...... 93 E2
Frinton Cl *SALE* M33 .... 159 D4
Frinton Rd *BOLS/LL* BL3 .... 45 F6
Frith Rd *DID/WITH* M20 .... 144 A6
Frobisher Cl *BRUN/LGST* M13 .. 125 E4
Frobisher Pl *RDSH* SK5 .... 166 C1
Frobisher Rd *LIT* OL15 .... 13 D2
Frodsham Av *HTNM* SK4 .... 166 A2
Frodsham Rd *SALE* M33 .... 160 C3
Frodsham St *RUSH/FAL* M14 ... 124 C6
Frogley St *BOLE* BL2 .... 28 C4
Frogmore Av *HYDE* SK14 .... 150 C4
Frome Av *OFTN* SK2 .... 184 A2
   URM M41 .... 137 F3
Frome Dr *CHH* M8 .... 90 C6
Frome St *OLDE* OL4 .... 80 A5
Frostlands St *OLDTF/WHR* M16 .. 123 F6
Frost St *ANC* M4 .... 107 E6
   OLDS OL8 .... 95 F1
Froxmer St *GTN* M18 .... 127 D3
Fulbrook Dr *CHD/CHDH* SK8 ... 195 E3
Fulham Av *NEWH/MOS* M40 .... 108 C2
Fulham St *OLDE* OL4 .... 80 A5
Fullerton Rd *HTNM* SK4 .... 165 F3
Full Pot La *ROCH* OL11 .... 20 C5
Fulmar Cl *POY/DIS* SK12 .... 197 E5
Fulmar Dr *OFTN* SK2 .... 185 D2
   SALE M33 .... 158 A3
Fulmards Cl *WILM/AE* SK9 ...... 204 A4
Fulmar Gdns *ROCH* OL11 .... 21 D6
Fulmer Dr *ANC* M4 .... 107 D5
Fulmere Ct *SWIN* M27 .... 101 E1
Fulneck Sq *DROY* M43 .... 128 B1
Fulshaw Av *WILM/AE* SK9 ...... 203 E5
Fulshaw Ct *WILM/AE* SK9 ...... 203 E6
Fulshaw Pk *WILM/AE* SK9 ...... 209 E1
Fulshaw Pk South *WILM/AE* SK9 .. 209 D1
Fulstone Ms *OFTN* SK2 .... 183 F1
Fulwood Av *BKLY* M9 .... 92 A1
Fulwood Cl *TOT/BURYW* BL8 ... 32 A6
Furball St *HYDE* SK14 .... 131 D5
Furbarn La *ROCH* OL11 .... 20 B5
Furbarn Rd *ROCH* OL11 .... 20 B5
Furlong Rd *WYTH/NTH* M22 .... 177 F4
Furnace St *DUK* SK16 .... 112 C6
   HYDE SK14 .... 131 D5
Furness Av *AULW* OL7 .... 112 A2
   BOLE BL2 .... 28 C5
   HEY OL10 .... 37 D3
   LIT OL15 .... 12 B5
   OLDS OL8 .... 91 F4
   WHTF M45 .... 71 E3
Furness Cl *MILN* OL16 .... 41 F1
   POY/DIS SK12 .... 198 A5
Furness Gv *HTNM* SK4 .... 165 E4
Furness Quay *SALO/ORD* M5 ... 122 B2
Furness Rd *BOL* BL1 .... 45 F2
   CHD/CHDH SK8 .... 196 A3
   MDTN M24 .... 57 D6
   RUSH/FAL M14 .... 144 A2
   URM M41 .... 119 E6
Furnival Cl *DTN/ASHW* M34 .... 147 E1
Furnival Rd *GTN* M18 .... 127 D3
Furnival St *RDSH* SK5 .... 146 C1
Furrow Dr *ECC* M30 .... 100 C3
Further Fld *ROCH* OL11 .... 20 B4
Further Heights Rd *WHIT* OL12 .. 22 C3
Further Hey Cl *OLDE* OL4 .... 80 C4
Further La *HYDE* SK14 .... 133 F6
Further Pits *ROCH* OL11 .... 22 A6
Furzegate *MILN* OL16 .... 41 D4
Furze La *OLDE* OL4 .... 80 B2
Fushia Gv *BRO* M7 .... 105 E1
Fylde Av *BOLE* BL2 .... 48 C2
   CHD/CHDH SK8 .... 194 A1
Fylde Rd *HTNM* SK4 .... 165 E3
Fylde St *FWTH* BL4 .... 66 B1
Fylde St East *FWTH* BL4 .... 66 B1

G

Gable Av *WILM/AE* SK9 .... 203 E4
Gable Dr *MDTN* M24 .... 74 C2
Gable St *BOLE* BL2 .... 29 E2
   OP/CLY M11 .... 126 A1
Gabriels Ter *MDTN* M24 .... 76 A4
The Gabriels *ROY/SHW* OL2 .... 61 D2
Gaddum Rd *ALT* WA14 .... 173 E6
   DID/WITH M20 .... 164 A2
   HTNM SK4 .... 166 B3
Gail Av *HTNM* SK4 .... 166 B3
Gail Cl *FAIL* M35 .... 109 F2
   WILM/AE SK9 .... 209 F3
Gainford Av *CHD/CHDH* SK8 ... 179 F3
Gainford Gdns *NEWH/MOS* M40 .. 92 C4
Gainford Rd *RDSH* SK5 .... 147 D2
Gainsborough Av *BOLS/LL* BL3 .. 46 A6
   DID/WITH M20 .... 144 A6
   MPL/ROM SK6 .... 171 F5
   OLDS OL8 .... 95 F1
   STRET M32 .... 139 F1
Gainsborough Cl *WILM/AE* SK9 .. 204 B3
Gainsborough Dr *CHD/CHDH* SK8 .. 181 D1
   ROCH OL11 .... 39 F4
Gainsborough Rd *CHAD* OL9 .... 76 C2
   DTN/ASHW M34 .... 111 E6
   TOT/BURYW BL8 .... 18 B4
Gainsborough St *BRO* M7 .... 89 F6
Gairloch Av *STRET* M32 .... 139 F1
Gair Rd *RDSH* SK5 .... 167 D1
Gair St *HYDE* SK14 .... 131 E5
Gaitskell Cl *WGTN/LGST* M12 .. 107 H6
Galbraith Rd *DID/WITH* M20 .... 164 A2
Galbraith St *CMANE* M1 .... 3 F6
Galbraith Wy *ROCH* OL11 .... 20 C5
Gale Dr *MDTN* M24 .... 74 B1
Gale Rd *PWCH* M25 .... 88 A2
Gales Ter *ROCH* OL11 .... 39 F2
Gale St *HEY* OL10 .... 36 C5
   WHIT OL12 .... 23 D2
Galgate Cl *HULME* M15 .... 123 F2
   TOT/BURYW BL8 .... 32 A6
Galindo St *BOLE* BL2 .... 29 D5
Galland St *OLDE* OL4 .... 80 B4
Galloway Cl *BOLS/LL* BL3 .... 44 C4
   HEY OL10 .... 36 A6
Galloway Dr *SWIN* M27 .... 86 A1
Galloway Rd *SWIN* M27 .... 101 E1
Gallowsclough Rd *STLY* SK15 .. 133 F3
Galston St *OP/CLY* M11 .... 126 B1
Galsworthy Av *CHH* M8 .... 106 B2
Galvin Rd *BKLY* M9 .... 90 C2
Galway St *OLD* OL1 .... 79 E5
Gambleside Cl *WALK* M28 .... 82 C5
Gambrel Bank Rd *AUL* OL6 .... 112 C1
Gambrel Gv *AUL* OL6 .... 112 C1
Game St *OLDE* OL4 .... 80 A6
Gandy La *WHIT* OL12 .... 22 A1
Ganton Av *WHTF* M45 .... 70 B4
Garbrook Av *BKLY* M9 .... 74 A6
Garden Av *DROY* M43 .... 110 C5
   STRET M32 .... 140 B1
Garden City *TOT/BURYW* BL8 ... 18 B3
Garden Cl *LIT* OL15 .... 25 D3
Garden La *ALT* WA14 .... 174 B2
   CSLFD M3 .... 2 C3
   MILN OL16 .... 23 E5
Garden Rw *HEY* OL10 .... 36 C3
The Gardens *EDGW/EG* BL7 .... 15 F1
   EDGW/EG BL7 .... 28 A1
Garden St *ANC* M4 .... 3 F2
   DTN/ASHW M34 .... 130 A3
   ECC M30 .... 101 F6
   FWTH BL4 .... 66 C3
   HEY OL10 .... 37 D4
   HYDE SK14 .... 131 F5
   MILN OL16 .... 42 C3
   OFTN SK2 .... 184 A2
   OLD OL1 .... 79 E4
   RAMS BL0 .... 7 D5
Garden Ter *ROY/SHW* OL2 .... 60 B1
Garden Wk *AUL* OL6 .... 113 D2
Garden Wall Cl *SALO/ORD* M5 .. 123 D1
Garden Wy *LIT* OL15 .... 25 D3
Gardner Rd *PWCH* M25 .... 88 A1
Gardner St *SLFD* M6 .... 104 B3
   WGTN/LGST M12 .... 126 C3
Garfield Av *BNG/LEV* M19 ...... 145 F2
Garfield Cl *ROCH* OL11 .... 20 C5
Garfield Gv *BOLS/LL* BL3 .... 46 A6
Garfield St *BOLS/LL* BL3 .... 46 A6
   STKP SK1 .... 167 E3
Garforth Av *ANC* M4 .... 107 D5
Garforth St *CHAD* OL9 .... 78 A4
Gargrave Av *BOL* BL1 .... 26 A5
Gargrave St *BRO* M7 .... 88 A5
   OLDE OL4 .... 79 F5
Garland Rd *WYTH/NTH* M22 ... 178 C4
Garlick St *CHAD* OL9 .... 78 C5
   GTN M18 .... 127 E1
   HYDE SK14 .... 132 A6
Garnant Cl *BKLY* M9 .... 92 A5
Garner Av *HALE/TIMP* WA15 ... 159 E4

Garner Cl ALT WA14......... 174 B5
Garner Dr ECC M30 .... 101 D4 ⑧
  SLFD M6............................. 103 E4
Garner's La EDGY/DAV SK3 ..... 183 D2
Garnet St OLD OL4............. 79 F3 ⑧
Garnett St BOL BL1 .... 27 F4
  RAMS BL0 .... 6 C5
  STKP SK1 .... 167 D4
Garratt Wy GTN M18........... 127 D4
Garret Gv ROY/SHW OL2 .... 62 A2
Garrett Wk EDGY/DAV SK3 ..... 166 A5 ⑧
Garrick Gdns WYTH/NTH M22 .. 178 B3
Garsdale La HOR/BR BL6 .... 44 B2
Garside Gv BOL BL1 .... 27 D5 ⑧
Garside Hey Rd TOT/BURYW BL8 .. 32 C1
Garside St BOL BL1 .... 46 C2
  DTN/ASHW M34 .... 149 D1 ⑧
  HYDE SK14............................ 150 C2
Garstang Av BOLE BL2 .... 48 C5
Garstang Dr TOT/BURYW BL8 .... 32 A6
Garston Cl HTNM SK4 .... 166 A2 ⑧
Garston Dr BURY BL9 .... 34 B5 ⑧
  RUSH/FAL M14 .... 143 D1
Garswood Dr TOT/BURYW BL8 ... 32 C1 ②
Garswood Rd BOLS/LL BL3 .... 64 C1
  ECC M30 .... 101 E6
Garth Av HALE/TIMP WA15 ...... 174 B1
Garthland Rd BRAM/HZG SK7 ... 185 D4
Garthorne Cl OLDTF/WHR M16 .. 123 E5 ⑧
  OLDTF/WHR M16 .... 123 E5 ⑧
Garthorp Rd NTHM/RTH M23 ... 160 C4
Garth Rd MPL/ROM SK6........ 187 E1 ⑧
  OFTN SK2 .... 168 A6
  WYTH/NTH M22 .... 178 B3
The Garth SALQ/ORD M5 .... 103 E5
Garthwaite Av OLDS OL8 .... 95 F2
Gartside St AULW OL7 .... 111 F6 ②
  CSLFD M3............................. 2 B4
  OLDE OL4 .... 79 F6
Garwick Rd BOL BL1 .... 26 C4
Gaskell Cl LIT OL15 .... 12 B5 ⑧
Gaskell Ri OLD OL1 .... 62 C4
Gaskell Rd ALT WA14 .... 174 B1
  ECC M30 .... 101 E6
Gaskell St BOL BL1 .... 46 B1 ⑧
  DUK SK16 .... 112 C6 ⑧
  NEWH/MOS M40 .... 109 E1 ⑧
  SWIN M27 .... 86 A3 ⑧
Gaskill St HEY OL10 .... 36 B5 ⑧
Gas St AUL OL6 .... 112 C4
  BOL BL1............................... 46 C2
  FWTH BL4 .... 66 B2
  HEY OL10 .... 37 E5 ⑧
  HTNM SK4 .... 166 C5 ⑧
  ROCH OL11 .... 22 C6
Gateacre Wk NTHM/RTH M23 .. 160 C6
Gate Field Cl RAD M26 .... 50 C6
Gatehouse Rd WALK M28......... 82 B1 ⑧
Gate Keeper Fold AULW OL7 ...... 96 B6 ⑧
Gatesgarth Rd MDTN M24 .... 74 A1
Gateshead Cl RUSH/FAL M14 .. 124 C5 ⑧
Gate St DUK SK16 .... 130 B3
  OP/CLY M11 .... 127 D1
  ROCH OL11 .... 40 A2
Gateway Crs CHAD OL9 .... 93 F1
Gateway Rd GTN M18 .... 127 D3 ②
The Gateways SWIN M27 .... 86 A4 ⑧
Gathill Cl CHD/CHDH SK8 ...... 181 D6 ⑧
Gathurst St GTN M18 .... 127 F3 ⑧
Gatley Av RUSH/FAL M14 ...... 143 E2
Gatley Gn CHD/CHDH SK8 ..... 179 E2
Gatley Rd CHD/CHDH SK8 ..... 179 F2
  SALE M33 .... 160 C2
Gatling Av WGTN/LGST M12 ... 145 E1
Gatwick Av NTHM/RTH M23 ... 177 F1 ②
Gavin Av SALQ/ORD M5 .... 104 B6
Gawsworth Av DID/WITH M20 .. 164 A4 ⑧
Gawsworth Cl BRAM/HZG SK7 . 196 C4
  EDGY/DAV SK3 .... 182 B2 ⑧
  HALE/TIMP WA15 .... 176 B1
  ROY/SHW OL2 .... 61 D2
Gawsworth Ms CHD/CHDH SK8 179 F2 ⑧
Gawsworth Rd SALE M33 .... 160 C3
Gawthorpe Cl BURY BL9 .... 53 E4 ⑧
Gaydon Rd SALE M33 .... 158 B1
Gaythorne St BOL BL1 .... 28 A4 ⑧
Gee Cross Fold HYDE SK14 ..... 150 C4 ⑧
Gee La ECC M30 .... 100 C4
Gee St EDGY/DAV SK3 .... 166 B6
Geinsbury Cl OLDS OL8 .... 96 C1 ②
Gemini Rd SLFD M6............. 105 D3
Gencoyne Dr BOL BL1 .... 27 E1 ②
Geneva Rd BRAM/HZG SK7 .... 182 B4
Genista Gv BRO M7 .... 105 E3
Geoffrey St BURY BL9 .... 34 B3 ⑭
  RAMS BL0 .... 18 B1
George Barton St BOLE BL2 ..... 28 C6 ⑩
George La MPL/ROM SK6....... 169 D4
George Leigh St ANC M4 .... 3 C2
George Mann Cl WYTH/NTH M22 178 A6
George Richards Wy ALT WA14... 158 A6
George Rd RAMS BL0 .... 6 C6
George's Rd HTNM SK4 .... 166 B5
  SALE M33 .... 159 F2
George's Rd West POY/DIS SK12 .. 198 B6
George St AUL OL6 .... 112 C4

  BURY BL9 .... 34 A5
  CHAD OL9 .... 77 E4
  CMANE M1 .... 3 E4
  DTN/ASHW M34 .... 130 B6 ⑧
  ECC M30 .... 101 D6
  FAIL M35 .... 94 A5
  FWTH BL4 .... 65 F4
  HEY OL10 .... 36 C4
  IRL M44 .... 116 C6 ⑧
  LIT OL15 .... 12 C6 ⑧
  MILN OL16 .... 23 E5
  MOSL OL5 .... 99 D4
  MPL/ROM SK6 .... 171 F3
  OLD OL1 .... 78 C5 ⑦
  PWCH M25 .... 88 C4
  RAD M26 .... 51 D6 ⑧
  ROY/SHW OL2 .... 43 D6
  STKP SK1 .... 167 E4 ⑧
  STLY SK15 .... 114 A5
  URM M41 .... 138 C1
  WHIT OL12 .... 9 D5 ⑧
  WHTF M45 .... 70 C2
  WILM/AE SK9 .... 209 E4 ⑧
George St East STKP SK1 ...... 167 F5 ⑧
George St North BRO M7 .... 90 A5
George St South BRO M7 .... 89 F5
George St West STKP SK1 ...... 167 F5
Georgiana St BURY BL9 .... 34 A6 ⑧
  FWTH BL4 .... 65 F1 ⑧
Gerald Av CHH M8 .... 90 B5
Gerald Rd SLFD M6 .... 104 B2
Germain Cl BKLY M9 .... 74 A6
Gerrard Av HALE/TIMP WA15 .. 159 E5
Gerrards Cl IRL M44 .... 135 E1
Gerrards Gdns HYDE SK14 .... 150 C4 ⑧
Gerrards Hollow HYDE SK14 ... 150 B4 ⑧
Gerrard St FWTH BL4 .... 66 C3
  ROCH OL11 .... 40 B6
  SLFD M6............................. 104 B4
  STLY SK15 .... 114 C6
Gertrude St SALQ/ORD M5..... 122 B1
Gervis Cl NEWH/MOS M40 ..... 107 F2 ⑧
Ghyll Gv WALK M28 .... 83 F3
Gibbon Av WYTH/NTH M22 .... 178 B5 ⑧
Gibbon St BOLS/LL BL3.......... 46 B4
  OP/CLY M11 .... 108 B5
Gibb Rd WALK M28 .... 84 C6
Gibbs St CSLFD M3 .... 105 E6 ⑧
Gib La NTHM/RTH M23 .... 161 F6 ⑧
Gibraltar La DTN/ASHW M34 .. 149 F3
Gibraltar St BOLS/LL BL3 .... 46 B3
  OLDE OL4 .... 80 B6
Gibsmere Cl HALE/TIMP WA15 . 176 B1 ⑧
Gibson Av GTN M18 .... 128 A2 ⑧
Gibson Gv WALK M28 .... 82 B2 ⑧
Gibson La WALK M28.............. 82 B2 ⑧
Gibson Pl CSLFD M3 .... 106 B4 ⑪
Gibsons Rd HTNM SK4 .... 165 F1
Gibson St BOLE BL2 .... 29 D6 ⑩
  MILN OL16 .... 24 A5
  OLDE OL4 .... 80 B6
Gibson Wy ALT WA14 .... 158 A5
Gibwood Rd WYTH/NTH M22 . 162 A5
Gidlow St GTN M18 .... 127 F3 ⑧
Gifford Av BKLY M9 .... 92 A1
Gigg La BURY BL9 .... 53 D1
Gilbertbank MPL/ROM SK6 .... 169 E1
Gilbert Rd HALE/TIMP WA15 .. 174 C6
Gilbert St ECC M30 .... 118 C1
  HULME M15 .... 123 F2 ⑧
  RAMS BL0 .... 7 D2
  SLFD M6............................. 104 A6 ②
  WALK M28 .... 83 E4 ⑧
Gilbrook Wy MILN OL16 .... 40 C5
Gilchrist Rd IRL M44 .... 134 C5
Gilda Brook Rd ECC M30 .... 102 B5
Gilda Crs ECC M30 .... 102 B4
Gildenhall FAIL M35 .... 94 B6
Gilderdale Cl ROY/SHW OL2 ..... 61 F1 ⑧
Gilderdale St BOLS/LL BL3 .... 47 E4
Gilderdale Dr BKLY M9 .... 73 E5
Gildridge Rd OLDTF/WHR M16 . 142 C2
Giles St WGTN/LGST M12 ..... 126 B5 ⑧
Gill Bent Rd CHD/CHDH SK8 .. 195 E3
Gillbrook Rd DID/WITH M20 ... 163 F2
Gillemere Gv ROY/SHW OL2 .... 62 A2 ⑧
Gillers Gn WALK M28 .... 83 D2 ⑧
Gillford Av BKLY M9 .... 92 A5 ⑧
Gillingham Rd ECC M30 .... 100 C5
Gill St BKLY M9 .... 92 A4
  STKP SK1 .... 167 F2
Gillwood Dr MPL/ROM SK6 .... 169 D4
Gilman Cl BKLY M9 .... 91 D3 ②
Gilman St BKLY M9 .... 91 D3 ⑧
Gilmerton Dr NEWH/MOS M40 109 D2 ⑧
Gilmore Dr PWCH M25 .... 71 F6
Gilmore St EDGY/DAV SK3 ..... 166 C6 ⑧
Gilmour St MDTN M24 .... 75 E3
Gilmour Ter BKLY M9 .... 92 A4
Gilnow Gdns BOL BL1 .... 46 A3
Gilnow Gv BOL BL1 .... 46 B5 ⑧
Gilnow La BOLS/LL BL3 .... 46 A3
Gilnow Rd BOL BL1 .... 46 A3
Gilpin Rd URM M41 .... 139 D2
Giltbrook Av NEWH/MOS M40 .. 107 E3

Gilwell Dr NTHM/RTH M23 .... 177 D3 ①
Gilwood Gv MDTN M24 .... 57 D5
Gingham Pk RAD M26 .... 50 C4
Gipsy La OFTN SK2 .... 184 A1
Girton St BRO M7 .... 105 F3
Girvan Av NEWH/MOS M40 ...... 93 E3
Girvan Cl BOLS/LL BL3 .... 46 A6 ⑱
Gisborn Dr SLFD M6 .... 104 A2 ⑧
Gisburn Dr TOT/BURYW BL8 .... 31 F4
Gisburne Av NEWH/MOS M40 ... 93 E3 ⑧
Gisburn Rd ROCH OL11 .... 40 B4
Givendale Dr CHH M8 .... 90 B3
Glade Brow OLDE OL4 .... 81 E5 ②
Gladeside Rd WYTH/NTH M22 . 178 A3
Glade St BOL BL1 .... 46 A2
The Glade BOL BL1 .... 27 E6
  HTNM SK4 .... 165 F4
Gladewood Cl WILM/AE SK9 .. 204 A3 ⑧
Gladstone Ct HULME M15 ..... 123 F5 ⑧
Gladstone Crs ROCH OL11 ...... 40 B4
Gladstone Gv HTNM SK4 ...... 165 E2
Gladstone Pl FWTH BL4 .... 66 A2
  ECC M30 .... 101 F5
  FWTH BL4 .... 66 A2
  URM M41 .... 138 C1
Gladstone St BOL BL1 .... 27 F5
  BURY BL9 .... 34 C4
  OFTN SK2 .... 184 A3
  OLDE OL4 .... 79 F5
  SWIN M27 .... 86 B5
Gladwyn Av DID/WITH M20 ... 162 C1 ⑧
Gladys St FWTH BL4 .... 66 B1 ⑦
Glaisdale OLDE OL4 .... 80 B5 ⑦
Glaisdale Cl BOLE BL2 .... 28 C5
Glaisdale St BOLE BL2 .... 28 C5 ⑧
Glaister La BOLE BL2 .... 29 E6
Glamis Av HEY OL10 .... 56 C2
  OP/CLY M11 .... 108 C4
  STRET M32 .... 139 E1 ⑧
Glandon Dr CHD/CHDH SK8 ... 196 A2
Glanford Av BKLY M9 .... 90 B2 ⑧
Glanvor Rd EDGY/DAV SK3 .... 166 A5
Glasshouse St ANC M4 .... 107 D4 ⑧
Glass St FWTH BL4 .... 66 C4 ⑦
Glastonbury Av CHD/CHDH SK8 196 A3
  HALE/TIMP WA15 .... 175 F3
Glastonbury Dr POY/DIS SK12 . 198 B4
Glastonbury Rd STRET M32 ... 120 A6
Glaswen Gv RDSH SK5 .... 167 D1 ⑧
Glazebrook Cl HEY OL10.......... 37 D6
Glazebury Dr NTHM/RTH M23 . 177 F2
Glazedale Av ROY/SHW OL2 ..... 60 A5 ②
Glaze Wk WHTF M45 .... 72 A1
Gleaves Av BOLE BL2 .... 30 B3
Gleaves Rd ECC M30 .... 101 E3
Gleave St BOL BL1 .... 47 D1 ⑫
  SALE M33 .... 139 F5 ⑧
Glebelands Rd NTHM/RTH M23 177 D1
  PWCH M25 .... 71 E6
  SALE M33 .... 139 D5
Glebe La OLD OL1 .... 62 C6
Glebe Rd URM M41 .... 138 B1 ⑧
Glebe St BOLE BL2 .... 47 E3
  CHAD OL9 .... 93 B2
  RAD M26 .... 51 F6 ②
  ROY/SHW OL2 .... 61 F2
  STKP SK1 .... 167 E4 ⑧
Gleden St NEWH/MOS M40 .... 107 F5
Gledhall St STLY SK15 .... 114 A5
Gledhill Av SALQ/ORD M5....... 122 B2
Gledhill Cl ROY/SHW OL2 .... 42 B6
Gledhill St DID/WITH M20 ..... 143 F4 ⑧
Gledhill Wy EDCW/EG BL7 ...... 14 B4
Glemsford Cl NEWH/MOS M40 108 C1 ⑧
Glenacre Gdns GTN M18 .... 127 F6 ⑧
Glenart ECC M30 .... 101 F4 ⑧
Glen Av BKLY M9 .... 91 F4
  BOLS/LL BL3 .... 45 F4
  FWTH BL4 .... 67 F5
  SALE M33 .... 139 E5
  SWIN M27 .... 85 E5
  WALK M28 .... 84 B5
Glenavon Dr ROY/SHW OL2 .... 61 D1 ⑧
  WHIT OL12 .... 22 B2
Glenbarry Cl BRUN/LGST M13 124 C3 ⑧
Glenbarry St WGTN/LGST M12.. 125 E1 ⑧
Glenbeck Rd WHTF M45 .... 70 C2
Glenboro Av TOT/BURYW BL8... 32 C5
Glen Bott St BOL BL1 .... 27 E5 ⑱
Glenbourne Pk BRAM/HZG SK7.. 196 A5
Glenbrook Gdns FWTH BL4 ...... 66 B1 ⑧
Glenbrook Rd BKLY M9 .... 73 E6
Glenburn St BOLS/LL BL3 .... 46 B6
Glenby Av WYTH/NTH M22 .... 179 D4
Glencastle Rd GTN M18 .... 127 D4 ⑧
  GTN M18 .... 127 E5 ⑧
Glencoe Cl HEY OL10.............. 35 F6
Glencoe Dr BOLE BL2 .... 49 D3
  SALE M33 .... 158 A3
Glencoe Pl ROCH OL11 .... 22 B6
Glencoe St OLDS OL8 .... 95 D3 ⑧
Glencross Av CCHDY M21 ...... 141 E1
Glendale SWIN M27 .... 86 C3 ⑧
Glendale Av BNG/LEV M19 .... 145 D5

BURY BL9 .... 53 D6
Glendale Ct OLDS OL8 .... 96 A1
Glendale Dr BOLS/LL BL3 .... 45 D3
Glendale Rd ECC M30 .... 102 B4
  WALK M28 .... 82 A6
Glendene Av BRAM/HZG SK7 .... 196 B4
  DROY M43 .... 111 D3
Glenden Foot WHIT OL12 .... 22 B3
Glendevon Cl BOLS/LL BL3 .... 45 D4
Glendevon Pl WHTF M45 .... 71 F4
Glendinning St SLFD M6 .... 103 F5
Glendon Ct OLD OL1 .... 62 C5
Glendon Crs AUL OL6 .... 96 C6
Glendore SALQ/ORD M5 .... 103 D5
Glendower Dr NEWH/MOS M40 .... 107 D2
Gleneagles BOLS/LL BL3 .... 45 D6
Gleneagles Av HEY OL10 .... 56 B1
Gleneagles Cl BRAM/HZG SK7 .... 197 E2
  WILM/AE SK9 .... 204 B3
Gleneagles Rd CHD/CHDH SK8 .... 180 A6
  URM M41 .... 117 F5
Gleneagles Wy RAMS BL0 .... 6 C6
Glenfield ALT WA14 .... 173 F3
Glenfield Cl OLDE OL4 .... 80 B5
Glenfield Dr POY/DIS SK12 .... 198 B6
Glenfield Rd HTNM SK4 .... 166 B1
Glenfield Sq FWTH BL4 .... 65 F1
Glenfyne Dr SLFD M6 .... 103 E2
Glen Gdns WHIT OL12 .... 23 D2
Glengarth Dr HOR/BR BL6 .... 44 A3
Glen Gv MDTN M24 .... 76 A5
  ROY/SHW OL2 .... 60 B4
Glenhaven Av URM M41 .... 138 A1
Glenholme Rd BRAM/HZG SK7 .... 196 B2
Glenhurst Rd BNG/LEV M19 .... 144 C6
Glenilla Av M28 .... 83 F6
Glenlea Dr DID/WITH M20 .... 163 F5
Glenmere Rd STKP SK1 .... 167 E5
Glenmore Av DID/WITH M20 .... 162 C1
  FWTH BL4 .... 65 E1
Glenmore Cl BOLS/LL BL3 .... 44 C4
  ROCH OL11 .... 37 F2
Glenmore Dr CHH M8 .... 90 C6
  FAIL M35 .... 94 C5
Glenmore Gv DUK SK16 .... 131 D1
Glenmore Rd TOT/BURYW BL8 .... 18 A3
Glenmore St BURY BL9 .... 33 F6
Glenolden St OP/CLY M11 .... 109 E5
Glenridding Cl OLD OL1 .... 79 E2
Glenridge Cl BOL BL1 .... 28 A5
Glen Ri HALE/TIMP WA15 .... 175 E2
Glen Rd OLDE OL4 .... 80 A5
Glensdale Dr NEWH/MOS M40 .... 93 F4
Glenshee Dr BOLS/LL BL3 .... 45 D4
Glenside Av GTN M18 .... 127 E6
Glenside Dr BOLS/LL BL3 .... 65 D1
  MPL/ROM SK6 .... 149 F6
  WILM/AE SK9 .... 204 A5
Glenside Gdns FAIL M35 .... 94 B6
Glenside Gv WALK M28 .... 83 F1
Glent St RAMS BL0 .... 6 C4
  SALQ/ORD M5 .... 122 B2
The Glen BOL BL1 .... 44 C2
  MDTN M24 .... 75 F5
Glenthorne Av BOL BL1 .... 27 F6
Glenthorn Gv SALE M33 .... 159 F2
Glenthorn Rd BKLY M9 .... 74 B5
Glentrool Ms BOL BL1 .... 45 E2
Glent Vw STLY SK15 .... 114 B3
Glenvale Cl RAD M26 .... 51 F6
Glen Vw ROY/SHW OL2 .... 60 B4
Glenville Wy DTN/ASHW M34 .... 149 E1
Glenwood Av HYDE SK14 .... 131 E4
Glenwood Dr BKLY M9 .... 91 F6
  MDTN M24 .... 76 B1
Glenwood Gv OFTN SK2 .... 183 F4
Glenwyn Av BKLY M9 .... 91 F1
Globe Cl OLDTF/WHR M16 .... 123 E4
Globe La DUK SK16 .... 130 C2
Globe Sq DUK SK16 .... 130 B2
Glodwick Rd OLDE OL4 .... 79 F5
Gloucester Av BNG/LEV M19 .... 143 F3
  HEY OL10 .... 56 A2
  MPL/ROM SK6 .... 187 D1
  WHIT OL12 .... 24 B1
  WHTF M45 .... 71 E3
Gloucester Cl AUL OL6 .... 97 E5
Gloucester Dr SALE M33 .... 158 B1
Gloucester Pl SLFD M6 .... 104 B4
Gloucester Ri DUK SK16 .... 132 B2
Gloucester Rd CHD/CHDH SK8 .... 194 A2
  DROY M43 .... 110 B4
  DTN/ASHW M34 .... 147 E1
  HYDE SK14 .... 150 C3
  MDTN M24 .... 75 E5
  POY/DIS SK12 .... 198 B5
  SLFD M6 .... 103 D3
  URM M41 .... 138 B2
Gloucester St CMANE M1 .... 124 A2
  EDGY/DAV SK3 .... 166 B6
  SALQ/ORD M5 .... 123 D1
  SLFD M6 .... 104 B3
Gloucester St North CHAD OL9 .... 78 A6
Glyn Av HALE/TIMP WA15 .... 175 E5

Glynne St FWTH BL4 .... 66 A3
Glynrene Dr SWIN M27 .... 85 D3
Glynwood Pk FWTH BL4 .... 66 A2
Godbert Av CCHDY M21 .... 142 A6
Goddard St OLDS OL8 .... 96 A1
Godfrey Av DROY M43 .... 109 E4
Godfrey Range GTN M18 .... 128 A5
Godfrey Rd SLFD M6 .... 103 D2
Godlee Dr SWIN M27 .... 85 F6
Godley Cl OP/CLY M11 .... 127 D2
Godley Hill Rd HYDE SK14 .... 132 C6
Godley St HYDE SK14 .... 132 A5
Godson St OLD OL1 .... 78 C2
Godwin St GTN M18 .... 127 F3
Golborne Av DID/WITH M20 .... 143 D4
Goldbourne Dr ROY/SHW OL2 .... 61 F1
Goldbrook Cl HEY OL10 .... 37 F6
Goldcrest Cl WALK M28 .... 82 C6
  WYTH/NTH M22 .... 179 D2
Goldenhill Av OP/CLY M11 .... 109 D4
Golden St ECC M30 .... 101 E6
  ROY/SHW OL2 .... 62 C1
Goldfinch Dr BURY BL9 .... 35 D2
Goldfinch Wy DROY M43 .... 111 D4
Goldie Av WYTH/NTH M22 .... 179 D6
Goldrill Av BOLE BL2 .... 49 D1
Goldrill Gdns BOLE BL2 .... 49 D1
Goldsmith Av OLD OL1 .... 62 C5
  SALQ/ORD M5 .... 103 E5
Goldsmith Rd RDSH SK5 .... 146 C2
Goldsmith St BOLS/LL BL3 .... 46 B5
Gold St CMANE M1 .... 3 F4
Goldsworthy Rd URM M41 .... 136 C1
Goldsworthy Rd URM M41 .... 117 F6
Golf Rd HALE/TIMP WA15 .... 175 D4
  SALE M33 .... 161 D1
Golfview Dr ECC M30 .... 101 E3
Goodacre HYDE SK14 .... 132 C3
Gooden St HEY OL10 .... 37 F6
Goodiers Dr SALQ/ORD M5 .... 122 C1
Goodier St NEWH/MOS M40 .... 107 F2
  SALE M33 .... 159 E1
Godier Vw HYDE SK14 .... 132 A4
Goodison Cl BURY BL9 .... 53 F6
Goodlad St TOT/BURYW BL8 .... 32 C3
Goodman St BKLY M9 .... 91 F4
Goodridge Av WYTH/NTH M22 .... 178 A6
Goodrington Rd WILM/AE SK9 .... 204 C1
Goodshaw Rd WALK M28 .... 83 D5
Goodwill Cl SWIN M27 .... 86 A6
Goodwin Sq BKLY M9 .... 91 E6
Goodwin St BOL BL1 .... 47 E1
Goodwood Av NTHM/RTH M23 .... 160 B5
  SALE M33 .... 158 A1
Goodwood Cl BOLS/LL BL3 .... 49 D6
Goodwood Crs HALE/TIMP WA15 .... 176 A1
Goodwood Dr OLD OL1 .... 79 F2
  SWIN M27 .... 86 C6
Goodwood Rd MPL/ROM SK6 .... 186 C2
Goole St OP/CLY M11 .... 126 B1
Goose Gn ALT WA14 .... 174 B3
Goose La WHIT OL12 .... 23 D5
Goostrey Cl WILM/AE SK9 .... 204 C2
Goostrey Av DID/WITH M20 .... 143 E3
Gordon Av BNG/LEV M19 .... 145 F2
  BOLS/LL BL3 .... 46 A4
  BRAM/HZG SK7 .... 184 B4
  CHAD OL9 .... 92 B2
  OLDE OL4 .... 80 C1
Gordon Ct LIT OL15 .... 12 C5
Gordon Pl DID/WITH M20 .... 143 F6
Gordon Rd ECC M30 .... 101 E4
  SALE M33 .... 139 F5
  SWIN M27 .... 101 D1
Gordon St AUL OL6 .... 113 E3
  BRO M7 .... 105 E3
  BURY BL9 .... 33 F3
  CHAD OL9 .... 94 A1
  GTN M18 .... 127 F3
  HTNM SK4 .... 166 C3
  HYDE SK14 .... 150 C1
  MILN OL16 .... 42 C4
  OLDE OL4 .... 81 E5
  OLDTF/WHR M16 .... 123 E4
  ROCH OL11 .... 40 B2
  ROY/SHW OL2 .... 62 A2
  STLY SK15 .... 114 C6
Gordon Wy HEY OL10 .... 36 A4
Gore Av FAIL M35 .... 94 C6
  SALQ/ORD M5 .... 103 E5
Gorebrook Ct WGTN/LGST M12 ...... 126 B3
Gore Crs SALQ/ORD M5 .... 103 E4
Goredale Av GTN M18 .... 127 F6
Gore Dr SLFD M6 .... 103 E4
Gorelan Rd GTN M18 .... 127 E4
Gore St BURY BL9 .... 35 D6
  CMANE M1 .... 3 G4
  CSLFD M3 .... 2 A3
  SLFD M6 .... 104 B4
Goring Av GTN M18 .... 127 E3
Gorrells Wy ROCH OL11 .... 39 E4
Gorrells Cl ROCH OL11 .... 39 E4
Gorrel St ROCH OL11 .... 40 B2
Gorse Av DROY M43 .... 111 D5
  MOSL OL5 .... 99 F4

MPL/ROM SK6 .... 186 C1
  OLDS OL8 .... 97 D2
  STRET M32 .... 122 A6
Gorse Bank BURY BL9 .... 35 D4
Gorse Bank Rd HALE/TIMP WA15 .... 190 B3
Gorse Crs STRET M32 .... 122 A6
Gorse Dr LHULT M38 .... 65 D5
  STRET M32 .... 122 A6
Gorsefield Dr SWIN M27 .... 86 A6
Gorsefield Hey WILM/AE SK9 .... 204 C3
Gorse Hall Dr STLY SK15 .... 114 A6
Gorse Hall Rd DUK SK16 .... 132 A2
Gorselands CHD/CHDH SK8 .... 195 F4
Gorse La STRET M32 .... 122 A6
Gorse Rd MILN OL16 .... 42 A1
  SWIN M27 .... 101 F1
  WALK M28 .... 83 F3
Gorses Mt BOLE BL2 .... 48 A4
Gorse Sq PART M31 .... 154 B2
Gorses Rd BOLS/LL BL3 .... 48 B4
Gorse St CHAD OL9 .... 94 A1
  STRET M32 .... 121 F6
Gorseway RDSH SK5 .... 167 F1
Gorsey Av WYTH/NTH M22 .... 178 A3
Gorsey Bank Rd EDGY/DAV SK3 ..... 165 F5
Gorsey Brow HYDE SK14 .... 153 E2
  MPL/ROM SK6 .... 169 E3
  STKP SK1 .... 167 E4
Gorsey Dr WYTH/NTH M22 .... 178 A3
Gorseyfields DROY M43 .... 128 B1
Gorsey Hill St HEY OL10 .... 37 E6
Gorsey Intakes HYDE SK14 .... 153 E3
Gorsey La ALT WA14 .... 173 F2
  AUL OL6 .... 114 A1
Gorsey Mount St STKP SK1 .... 167 E4
Gorsey Rd WILM/AE SK9 .... 203 D4
  WYTH/NTH M22 .... 178 A3
Gorsey Wy AUL OL6 .... 113 F1
Gorslev Bank LIT OL15 .... 13 D4
Gorston Wk WYTH/NTH M22 .... 192 A1
Gort Cl BURY BL9 .... 71 E2
Gorton Crs DTN/ASHW M34 .... 148 A1
Gorton Gv WALK M28 .... 66 A6
Gorton La WGTN/LGST M12 .... 126 B3
Gorton Rd OP/CLY M11 .... 126 A2
  RDSH SK5 .... 147 D3
  WGTN/LGST M12 .... 126 B2
Gorton St AULW OL7 .... 112 A6
  BOLE BL2 .... 47 E3
  CHAD OL9 .... 77 F5
  CSLFD M3 .... 2 C1
  ECC M30 .... 100 B6
  FWTH BL4 .... 65 F4
  HEY OL10 .... 37 F5
  NEWH/MOS M40 .... 107 D3
Gosforth Cl OLD OL1 .... 79 E2
  TOT/BURYW BL8 .... 33 D2
Goshen La BURY BL9 .... 53 D3
Gosport Sq BRO M7 .... 105 E2
Goss Hall St OLDE OL4 .... 80 A5
Gotherage Cl MPL/ROM SK6 .... 170 C3
Gotherage La MPL/ROM SK6 .... 170 C3
Gothic Cl MPL/ROM SK6 .... 171 D3
Gough St EDGY/DAV SK3 .... 166 B4
  HEY OL10 .... 37 F5
Goulden Rd DID/WITH M20 .... 143 E6
Goulden St ANC M4 .... 3 G1
  SLFD M6 .... 103 F5
Goulder Rd GTN M18 .... 127 F6
Gould St ANC M4 .... 106 C4
  DTN/ASHW M34 .... 129 F6
  OLD OL1 .... 79 F3
Gourham Dr CHD/CHDH SK8 .... 181 D6
Govan St WYTH/NTH M22 .... 162 C4
Gowan Dr MDTN M24 .... 74 B1
Gowanlock's St BOL BL1 .... 27 F5
Gowan Rd OLDTF/WHR M16 .... 142 C2
Gower Av BRAM/HZG SK7 .... 184 A4
Gowerdale Rd RDSH SK5 .... 148 A6
Gower Rd HTNM SK4 .... 166 B1
  HYDE SK14 .... 150 B2
Gowers St MILN OL16 .... 23 F5
Gower St AUL OL6 .... 113 D4
  BOL BL1 .... 46 B1
  FWTH BL4 .... 66 A2
  OLD OL1 .... 79 E4
  SWIN M27 .... 86 B4
Gowran Pk OLDE OL4 .... 80 B5
Gowy Cl WILM/AE SK9 .... 204 C2
Goyt Crs MPL/ROM SK6 .... 187 D3
Goyt Crs MPL/ROM SK6 .... 187 F2
  STKP SK1 .... 167 F2
Goyt Rd MPL/ROM SK6 .... 187 D3
  STKP SK1 .... 167 F2
Goyt Valley Rd MPL/ROM SK6 .... 169 D2
Goyt Wy MPL/ROM SK6 .... 171 D4
Grace St WHIT OL12 .... 23 E3
Gracie Av OLD OL1 .... 79 F2
Gradwell St EDGY/DAV SK3 .... 166 B5
Grafton Av ECC M30 .... 102 B3
Grafton St ALT WA14 .... 174 B3
  AUL OL6 .... 113 E4
  BOL BL1 .... 46 B1
  BRUN/LGST M13 .... 125 D4

BURY BL9 .... 53 D1
FAIL M35 .... 94 A5
HTNM SK4 .... 166 C2
MILN OL16 .... 40 C1
OLD OL1 .... 62 C5
STLY SK15 .... 115 E4
Graham Crs IRL M44 .... 154 A1
Graham Rd SLFD M6 .... 103 D3
STKP SK1 .... 167 F5
Graham St AULW OL7 .... 112 A6 [4]
BOL BL1 .... 47 D1 [13]
OP/CLY M11 .... 126 B1
Grainger Av WCTN/LGST M12 .... 126 B6
Grains Rd ROY/SHW OL2 .... 62 A2
UPML OL3 .... 63 F4
Grain Vw SALQ/ORD M5 .... 122 B1 [8]
Gralam Cl SALE M33 .... 160 C4 [8]
Grammar School Rd OLDS OL8 .... 94 C2
Grampian Cl CHAD OL9 .... 77 E6
Grampian Wy ROY/SHW OL2 .... 61 E1
Granada Rd DTN/ASHW M34 .... 128 D6
Granary La WALK M28 .... 100 A3
Granary Wy SALE M33 .... 159 D3
Granby Rd CHD/CHDH SK8 .... 195 F1
HALE/TIMP WA15 .... 159 E4
OFTN SK2 .... 183 F2
STRET M32 .... 140 C2
SWIN M27 .... 85 D6
Granby Rw CMANE M1 .... 3 G6
Granby St CHAD OL9 .... 94 B3
TOT/BURYW BL8 .... 32 A3
Grandale St RUSH/FAL M14 .... 125 D6 [8]
Grandidge St ROCH OL11 .... 39 F2 [8]
Grand Union Wy ECC M30 .... 119 E1
Granford Cl ALT WA14 .... 158 B6 [8]
Grange Av BNG/LEV M19 .... 145 D3
BOLS/LL BL3 .... 50 A6
CHD/CHDH SK8 .... 181 D4
ECC M30 .... 101 E3 [8]
HALE/TIMP WA15 .... 159 F6
HALE/TIMP WA15 .... 175 E5
HTNM SK4 .... 146 A6
MILN OL16 .... 42 A3 [8]
OLDS OL8 .... 95 D1
SWIN M27 .... 85 E3 [8]
URM M41 .... 136 C1
Grange Cl HYDE SK14 .... 151 D2
Grange Crs URM M41 .... 138 A2
Grange Dr BKLY M9 .... 92 A2
ECC M30 .... 101 E3
Grangeforth Rd CHH M8 .... 90 A5
Grange Gv WHTF M45 .... 71 D3 [8]
Grange La DID/WITH M20 .... 163 F3
CHD/CHDH SK8 .... 180 B2
Grange Pl IRL M44 .... 134 B6
Grange Rd ALT WA14 .... 174 A6
BOLE BL2 .... 15 D6
BOLS/LL BL3 .... 45 F4
BRAM/HZG SK7 .... 183 D4
CCHDY M21 .... 141 E1
ECC M30 .... 100 A3
FWTH BL4 .... 65 E2 [8]
HALE/TIMP WA15 .... 159 F6
HYDE SK14 .... 151 D2
MDTN M24 .... 58 B3
SALE M33 .... 159 D1
TOT/BURYW BL8 .... 32 C5
URM M41 .... 138 A2
WHIT OL12 .... 9 E1
Grange Rd North HYDE SK14 .... 151 D1
Grange Rd South HYDE SK14 .... 151 D2
The Grange HYDE SK14 .... 151 D2
RUSH/FAL M14 .... 125 D6
Grangethorpe Dr BNG/LEV M19 .... 144 C4
Grangethorpe Rd URM M41 .... 138 A2
Grangeway WILM/AE SK9 .... 194 B5
Grangewood BOLE BL2 .... 15 D6 [8]
Grangewood Dr BKLY M9 .... 91 E6
Granite St OLD OL1 .... 79 F3 [8]
Gransden Dr CHH M8 .... 107 D3 [8]
Granshaw St NEWH/MOS M40 .... 107 F4 [8]
Gransmoor Av OP/CLY M11 .... 128 A3
Gransmoor Rd OP/CLY M11 .... 128 A2
Grantchester Pl FWTH BL4 .... 65 D3 [8]
Grantchester Wy BOLE BL2 .... 29 F6
Grant Cl BKLY M9 .... 91 E3
Grantham Dr TOT/BURYW BL8 .... 33 E2
Grantham Rd HTNM SK4 .... 166 A3
Grantham St OLDE OL4 .... 79 E6 [8]
Grants La RAMS BL0 .... 7 D5
Grant St FWTH BL4 .... 65 F1
ROCH OL11 .... 39 E5
Granville Av BRO M7 .... 89 F5 [8]
Granville Cl CHAD OL9 .... 78 A4 [8]
Granville Ct MILN OL16 .... 42 C4 [8]
Granville Gdns DID/WITH M20 .... 163 E3

Granville Rd BOLS/LL BL3 .... 46 A6 [10]
CHD/CHDH SK8 .... 182 A2
DTN/ASHW M34 .... 110 C6
HALE/TIMP WA15 .... 176 A1
RUSH/FAL M14 .... 144 A3
URM M41 .... 119 F6
WILM/AE SK9 .... 203 D6
Granville St AUL OL6 .... 113 C5
CHAD OL9 .... 78 A3 [8]
ECC M30 .... 101 E4
FWTH BL4 .... 66 B1 [8]
OLD OL1 .... 78 C2
WALK M28 .... 83 D2
Grasmere Av BOLS/LL BL3 .... 49 E5 [8]
FWTH BL4 .... 65 D4
HEY OL10 .... 56 B1
HTNM SK4 .... 146 C5
SWIN M27 .... 85 D3
URM M41 .... 136 C2 [8]
WHTF M45 .... 70 A4 [8]
Grasmere Cl STLY SK15 .... 114 B3
Grasmere Crs BRAM/HZG SK7 .... 196 C1
ECC M30 .... 100 C3
MPL/ROM SK6 .... 186 C6
Grasmere Gv AULW OL7 .... 112 A3
Grasmere Rd CHD/CHDH SK8 .... 179 F4
HALE/TIMP WA15 .... 176 A1
OLDE OL4 .... 80 A5
PART M31 .... 154 C2
ROY/SHW OL2 .... 60 B3
SALE M33 .... 160 A3
STRET M32 .... 121 E6
SWIN M27 .... 102 A1
WILM/AE SK9 .... 209 E4
Grasmere St BOL BL1 .... 28 A5 [21]
WGTN/LGST M12 .... 126 C6
WHIT OL12 .... 23 D4 [8]
Grasmere Wk MDTN M24 .... 75 D1 [8]
Grason Av WILM/AE SK9 .... 204 A2
Grasscroft RDSH SK5 .... 148 A5
Grasscroft Cl RUSH/FAL M14 .... 143 E1 [8]
Grasscroft Rd STLY SK15 .... 114 B6
Grassfield Av BRO M7 .... 105 D1 [8]
Grassholme Dr OFTN SK2 .... 185 E2
Grassington Gdns SLFD M6 .... 104 A4 [8]
Grassington Av NEWH/MOS M40 .... 92 B4 [8]
Grassington Ct TOT/BURYW BL8 .... 31 F3
Grassington Dr HEY OL10 .... 35 E6
Grass Md DTN/ASHW M34 .... 149 E3
Gratrix Av SALQ/ORD M5 .... 122 C2
Gratrix La SALE M33 .... 161 D2
Gratrix St GTN M18 .... 127 F5 [8]
Gratten Cl WALK M28 .... 83 D1 [8]
Gravel Bank Rd MPL/ROM SK6 .... 149 F5
Gravel La CSLFD M3 .... 2 C1
WILM/AE SK9 .... 202 C6
Gravel Wks OLDE OL4 .... 79 E4 [8]
Gravenmoor Dr BRO M7 .... 105 F1
Graver La NEWH/MOS M40 .... 109 E2 [8]
Graymar Rd LHULT M38 .... 82 B1
Graysands Rd HALE/TIMP WA15 .... 175 D4
Grayson Av WHTF M45 .... 71 E4
Grayson Rd LHULT M38 .... 82 C1
Gray St BOL BL1 .... 46 C1
Gray St North BOL BL1 .... 46 C1 [21]
Graythwaite Rd BOL BL1 .... 26 A5 [8]
Grazing Dr IRL M44 .... 116 C6
Greame St RUSH/FAL M14 .... 124 A6
Great Ancoats St ANC M4 .... 3 G2
Great Bent Cl WHIT OL12 .... 24 B1 [8]
Great Bridgewater St CMANW M2 .... 2 C6
Great Cheetham St East BRO M7 .... 89 E6
Great Cheetham St West BRO M7 .... 105 D2
Great Clowes St BRO M7 .... 89 E6
CSLFD M3 .... 105 E4
Great Ducie St CHH M8 .... 106 A3
Great Eaves Rd RAMS BL0 .... 7 D4 [8]
Great Egerton St STKP SK1 .... 166 B4
Greatfield Rd WYTH/NTH M22 .... 177 F3
Great Flatt WHIT OL12 .... 21 F4
Great Gable Cl OLD OL1 .... 79 E5
Great Gates Cl ROCH OL11 .... 40 B3
Great Gates Rd ROCH OL11 .... 40 B5
Great George St CSLFD M3 .... 105 E5 [8]
MILN OL16 .... 23 D6 [8]
Great Heaton Cl MDTN M24 .... 74 A4 [8]
Great Holme BOLS/LL BL3 .... 47 D6
Great Howarth WHIT OL12 .... 23 F1
Great Jackson St HULME M15 .... 123 F1
Great John St CSLFD M3 .... 2 A5
Great Jones St WGTN/LGST M12 .... 126 B3
Great Lee WHIT OL12 .... 22 B2 [8]
Great Marld Cl BOL BL1 .... 26 A5
Great Meadow ROY/SHW OL2 .... 42 A6
Great Moor St BOL BL1 .... 46 C3
OFTN SK2 .... 183 F2
Great Newton St NEWH/MOS M40 .... 109 D4
Great Norbury St HYDE SK14 .... 150 A1
Great Portwood St STKP SK1 .... 167 D3
Great Southern St RUSH/FAL M14 .... 124 C6
Great Stone Cl RAD M26 .... 50 B6 [8]
Great Stone Rd STRET M32 .... 122 A5
Great St CMANE M1 .... 125 D1
Great Western St RUSH/FAL M14 .... 124 B5
Greave MPL/ROM SK6 .... 170 B1

Greave Av ROCH OL11 .... 21 F5
Greave Fold MPL/ROM SK6 .... 170 A1
Greave Rd STKP SK1 .... 168 A5
Greaves Av FAIL M35 .... 109 F1 [8]
Greaves Rd WILM/AE SK9 .... 202 B4
Greaves St MOSL OL5 .... 98 C3
OLD OL1 .... 79 D5
OLDE OL4 .... 81 D5 [8]
ROY/SHW OL2 .... 62 A2 [8]
Grebe Cl POY/DIS SK12 .... 197 F5
Grecian Crs BOLS/LL BL3 .... 47 D5
Grecian St BRO M7 .... 105 D2
Grecian St North BRO M7 .... 105 D1
Gredle Cl URM M41 .... 139 D1 [8]
Greeba Rd NTHM/RTH M23 .... 176 C1
Greek St CMANE M1 .... 124 C2 [8]
EDGY/DAV SK3 .... 166 C5
Greenacre Cl RAMS BL0 .... 7 F4
Greenacre La WALK M28 .... 100 A3
Greenacres Dr BNG/LEV M19 .... 164 C1 [8]
Greenacres Rd OLDE OL4 .... 80 A4
Green Av BOLS/LL BL3 .... 47 F6
LHULT M38 .... 64 C6
SWIN M27 .... 86 A6
Green Bank BOLE BL2 .... 29 F4
HTNM SK4 .... 164 C1 [8]
SWIN M27 .... 101 E1 [8]
Greenbank Crs MPL/ROM SK6 .... 187 D2
Greenbank Dr LIT OL15 .... 25 D2 [8]
Greenbank Rd BOLS/LL BL3 .... 45 F4 [8]
BOLS/LL BL3 .... 45 F5 [20]
CHD/CHDH SK8 .... 179 E1 [8]
MPL/ROM SK6 .... 171 F4
RAD M26 .... 51 D4
SALE M33 .... 138 C6
SLFD M6 .... 103 F4
WHIT OL12 .... 23 D3
Greenbank Ter MDTN M24 .... 76 A2
Green Booth Cl DUK SK16 .... 132 A2
Greenbooth Rd WHIT OL12 .... 20 B2
Green Bridge Cl ROCH OL11 .... 40 A3 [8]
Green Brook Cl BURY BL9 .... 34 B3 [15]
Greenbrook St BURY BL9 .... 34 B3 [8]
Greenbrow Rd NTHM/RTH M23 .... 177 D4
Greenburn Dr BOLE BL2 .... 29 F5
Green Cl CHD/CHDH SK8 .... 179 E1
Greencourt Dr LHULT M38 .... 82 A1
Green Cts ALT WA14 .... 173 F4
Green Cft MPL/ROM SK6 .... 170 B2
Greencroft Meadow ROY/SHW OL2 .... 61 D4
Greencroft Rd ECC M30 .... 100 C3
Greendale Dr BKLY M9 .... 91 F2
Greendale Gv DTN/ASHW M34 .... 149 F3 [8]
Green Dr BNG/LEV M19 .... 145 D2 [8]
HALE/TIMP WA15 .... 159 E6
HOR/BR BL6 .... 44 A2
WILM/AE SK9 .... 204 B1
Green End DTN/ASHW M34 .... 149 F3
Green End Rd BNG/LEV M19 .... 144 C6
Greenfield Av ECC M30 .... 118 B1 [8]
URM M41 .... 138 B1
Greenfield Cl EDGY/DAV SK3 .... 182 C1 [8]
HALE/TIMP WA15 .... 159 E6
TOT/BURYW BL8 .... 32 B6 [8]
Greenfield Ct HEY OL10 .... 37 E6 [8]
Greenfield La MILN OL16 .... 24 B2
ROCH OL11 .... 40 B3
ROY/SHW OL2 .... 61 F3
Greenfield St DTN/ASHW M34 .... 129 E2
HYDE SK14 .... 150 B1 [8]
ROCH OL11 .... 40 B3
Green Fold GTN M18 .... 128 A3
Greenfold Av FWTH BL4 .... 65 F4
Greenford Cl CHD/CHDH SK8 .... 181 F3
Greenford Rd CHH M8 .... 90 B6
Green Gables Cl CHD/CHDH SK8 .... 179 F6 [8]
Greengate CSLFD M3 .... 2 C1
HALE/TIMP WA15 .... 190 B2
HYDE SK14 .... 150 B3 [8]
MDTN M24 .... 76 B6
Greengate Cl WHIT OL12 .... 24 B1
Greengate East NEWH/MOS M40 .... 93 D2
Greengate La BOLE BL2 .... 49 D1 [8]
PWCH M25 .... 86 B3
Greengate Rd DTN/ASHW M34 .... 130 B5 [8]
Greengate St OLDE OL4 .... 79 E6
Greengate West CSLFD M3 .... 105 F4
Green Grove Bank MILN OL16 .... 24 B2 [8]
Greenhalgh Moss La
    TOT/BURYW BL8 .... 32 C2 [8]
Greenhalgh St FAIL M35 .... 109 D1 [8]
HTNM SK4 .... 166 C3 [8]
Green Hall Ms WILM/AE SK9 .... 203 F5 [8]
Greenham Rd NTHM/RTH M23 .... 161 D3
Greenheys BOLE BL2 .... 29 F4 [8]
DROY M43 .... 110 B5
Greenheys Crs TOT/BURYW BL8 .... 17 F4
Greenheys La HULME M15 .... 124 A4
Greenheys La West HULME M15 .... 124 A4
Greenheys Rd LHULT M38 .... 64 C5
Greenhill PWCH M25 .... 88 B1 [8]
Greenhill Av BOLS/LL BL3 .... 45 F4
FWTH BL4 .... 66 A4

ROY/SHW OL2 .... 41 F6
SALE M33 .... 139 E5
WHIT OL12 .... 22 C5 1
Greenhill Pas OLD OL1 .... 79 C5 2
Greenhill Rd CHH M8 .... 90 B5 1
HALE/TIMP WA15 .... 176 A1
Green Hill Rd HYDE SK14 .... 132 A6
Greenhill Rd MDTN M24 .... 76 A4
TOT/BURYW BL8 .... 32 B6
Green Hill St EDGY/DAV SK3 ..... 166 B6 5
Green Hill Ter EDGY/DAV SK3 .... 166 B6 3
Greenholm Cl NEWH/MOS M40 ... 93 E4 1
Greenhow St DROY M43 .... 128 A1
Greenhurst Crs OLDS OL8 .... 96 B3 2
Greenhurst La AUL OL6 .... 113 F1
Greenhurst Rd AUL OL6 .... 97 F6
Greenhythe Rd CHD/CHDH SK8 .. 194 A3
Greening Rd BNG/LEV M19 .... 145 F1 1
Greenland Rd BOLS/LL BL3 .... 65 D1
Greenland St CHH M8 .... 90 A6
SLFD M6 .... 103 F5 5
Green La AUL OL6 .... 112 C2
BOLS/LL BL3 .... 47 D6
BRAM/HZG SK7 .... 184 B4
ECC M30 .... 101 D5
FAIL M35 .... 109 F3
FWTH BL4 .... 67 E4
GTN M18 .... 127 E3
HALE/TIMP WA15 .... 175 F3
HEY OL10 .... 37 F5
HEY OL10 .... 56 C1 1
HTNM SK4 .... 166 B3 2
HYDE SK14 .... 151 E2
IRL M44 .... 134 B6
MDTN M24 .... 75 F2
MPL/ROM SK6 .... 169 F4
OLDE OL4 .... 81 E1
OLDS OL8 .... 95 F3
POY/DIS SK12 .... 200 A5
SALE M33 .... 138 C5
WHIT OL12 .... 22 C5 3
WHTF M45 .... 71 D2
WILM/AE SK9 .... 203 F4
WILM/AE SK9 .... 209 D5
Green La North HALE/TIMP WA15 175 F3
Greenlea Av GTN M18 .... 127 E6 3
Greenleach La WALK M28 .... 84 A5
Greenleas HOR/BR BL6 .... 44 A3
Greenlees St WHIT OL12 .... 23 D5 2
Green Meadow WHIT OL12 .... 24 B1
Green Mdw MPL/ROM SK6 .... 171 D6
Green Meadows Dr
MPL/ROM SK6 .... 171 D6
Green Meadows Wk
WYTH/NTH M22 .... 178 C6 1
Greenmount Cl TOT/BURYW BL8 . 18 A3 4
Greenmount Ct BOL BL1 .... 45 E1 2
Greenmount Dr HEY OL10 .... 57 D2
TOT/BURYW BL8 .... 18 A2
Greenmount La BOL BL1 .... 45 D1
Greenmount Pk FWTH BL4 .... 67 E5
Greenoak RAD M26 .... 68 A5 5
Greenoak Dr SALE M33 .... 160 A4
WALK M28 .... 66 A6 2
Greenock Cl BOLS/LL BL3 .... 44 C4 8
Greenpark Cl TOT/BURYW BL8 ... 17 F4
Greenpark Rd WYTH/NTH M22 ... 162 B4
Green Pastures HTNM SK4 .... 164 C4
Green Rd PART M31 .... 154 C2
Greenroyd Av BOLE BL2 .... 29 F5
Greenshank Cl ROCH OL11 .... 21 D6 3
Greenside WALK M28 .... 100 B3
Greenside Av FWTH BL4 .... 67 D5
OLDE OL4 .... 80 B1
Greenside Cl DUK SK16 .... 132 B1
TOT/BURYW BL8 .... 16 C2
Greenside Crs DROY M43 .... 110 A5 5
Greenside Dr ALT WA14 .... 174 C6
IRL M44 .... 135 D2
TOT/BURYW BL8 .... 17 F5
Greenside La DROY M43 .... 109 F4
Greenside Pl DTN/ASHW M34 .... 149 E3 4
Greenside St BOLE BL2 .... 31 D6
OP/CLY M11 .... 108 C6
Greenside Wy MDTN M24 .... 76 A6
Greenson Dr MDTN M24 .... 90 B5
Greenstead Av CHH M8 .... 90 B5
The Greens WHIT OL12 .... 9 D2
Greenstone Dr SLFD M6 .... 104 A2 2
Green St BOL BL1 .... 47 D2
ECC M30 .... 118 C1
EDGY/DAV SK3 .... 183 D1
FWTH BL4 .... 66 A2
HYDE SK14 .... 150 C2
MDTN M24 .... 75 F2
OLDS OL8 .... 78 B5
RAD M26 .... 51 E6
RUSH/FAL M14 .... 144 C4
STRET M32 .... 140 A5 3
TOT/BURYW BL8 .... 32 C3
WILM/AE SK9 .... 209 E4 1
The Green CHD/CHDH SK8 .... 195 D1
HTNM SK4 .... 166 A3 4
MPL/ROM SK6 .... 187 E4
OLDS OL8 .... 96 B2 1

ROCH OL11 .... 39 D4
SWIN M27 .... 86 C3
TOT/BURYW BL8 .... 18 A4
WALK M28 .... 100 A2
WILM/AE SK9 .... 194 C6
Greenthorne Av HTNM SK4 .... 146 B4
Green Tree Gdns MPL/ROM SK6 . 169 F3
Greenvale ROCH OL11 .... 20 B5
Greenvale Dr CHD/CHDH SK8 ... 180 A1
Greenview Dr DID/WITH M20 .... 164 A5 3
Green Villa Pk WILM/AE SK9 ..... 208 C1
Green Wk ALT WA14 .... 173 E4
CHD/CHDH SK8 .... 179 E1
HALE/TIMP WA15 .... 159 D6
OLDTF/WHR M16 .... 142 A1
STRET M32 .... 139 F1
Greenwatch Cl ECC M30 .... 101 D6 3
Greenway ALT WA14 .... 173 E2
Green Wy BOL BL1 .... 28 C4
Greenway BRAM/HZG SK7 .... 196 B3 2
HYDE SK14 .... 150 B2 3
MDTN M24 .... 74 C6
MPL/ROM SK6 .... 170 C4
Green Wy ROCH OL11 .... 38 C6
Greenway ROY/SHW OL2 .... 42 A6 1
WILM/AE SK9 .... 203 E5
WYTH/NTH M22 .... 162 C5
Greenway Av BNG/LEV M19 ..... 145 F3
Green Way Cl BOL BL1 .... 28 B3 1
Greenway Cl SALE M33 .... 158 B2
TOT/BURYW BL8 .... 32 C4 1
Greenway Dr MOSL OL5 .... 99 D3
Greenway Rd CHD/CHDH SK8 ... 194 A3
HALE/TIMP WA15 .... 159 E4
Greenways AULW OL7 .... 112 A1
NEWH/MOS M40 .... 93 E4 2
Greenwich Cl NEWH/MOS M40 . 109 E3
ROCH OL11 .... 38 A1
Greenwood Av AUL OL6 .... 113 D1
LHULT M38 .... 65 D2
OFTN SK2 .... 184 A1
SWIN M27 .... 86 C4 1
Greenwood Cl HALE/TIMP WA15 . 176 B2
Greenwood Dr WILM/AE SK9 .... 204 B3
Greenwood Rd WYTH/NTH M22 . 177 F3
Greenwoods La BOLE BL2 .... 30 A3
Greenwood St ALT WA14 .... 174 B3
FWTH BL4 .... 66 B3 13
LIT OL15 .... 12 C6 4
MILN OL16 .... 23 H2 8
OLDE OL4 .... 80 A3
OLDS OL8 .... 96 A4 1
SLFD M6 .... 104 A3
Greenwood V BOL BL1 .... 27 F4 16
Greenwood V South BOL BL1 .... 28 A4 20
Greer St HEY OL10 .... 37 F6
Gregge St HEY OL10 .... 37 F6
Greg Ms WILM/AE SK9 .... 203 F1
Gregory Av BOLE BL2 .... 48 C1
MPL/ROM SK6 .... 169 F4
Gregory St OLDS OL8 .... 95 D2
WGTN/LGST M12 .... 126 A3
Gregory Wy RDSH SK5 .... 147 D5
Gregson Fld BOLS/LL BL3 .... 46 C4 13
BOLS/LL BL3 .... 46 C5 11
Gregson Rd RDSH SK5 .... 146 C5 1
Greg St RDSH SK5 .... 146 C5
Grendale Av BRAM/HZG SK7 .... 184 C6
STKP SK1 .... 167 F4
Grendon Av OLDS OL8 .... 95 F2
Grendon St BOLS/LL BL3 .... 46 A6 20
Grenham Av HULME M15 .... 123 E3
Grenville Rd BRAM/HZG SK7 .... 184 A4
Grenville St DUK SK16 .... 131 D1
EDGY/DAV SK3 .... 166 B5
STLY SK15 .... 115 E3
Gresford Cl CCHDY M21 .... 141 E3 4
Gresham Cl WHTF M45 .... 70 B4 2
Gresham Dr CHAD OL9 .... 78 A4 3
Gresham St BOL BL1 .... 28 A4
DTN/ASHW M34 .... 130 A5 13
Gresty Av WYTH/NTH M22 .... 179 D6
Greswell St DTN/ASHW M34 ..... 129 F5
Greta Av CHD/CHDH SK8 .... 194 A3 2
Greton Cl BRUN/LGST M13 ...... 125 F5 7
Gretton Cl ROY/SHW OL2 .... 61 D5
Greville St BRUN/LGST M13 ..... 125 F6
Grey Cl MPL/ROM SK6 .... 169 E1
Greyfriars Rd WYTH/NTH M22 .. 177 F5
Greyhound Dr SLFD M6 .... 105 D2 3
Greylag Crs WALK M28 .... 83 E5
Greylands Cl SALE M33 .... 158 C1
Greylands Rd DID/WITH M20 .... 164 A5 5
Grey Mare La OP/CLY M11 .... 126 B1 3
Greymont Rd BURY BL9 .... 34 A1
Grey Rd ALT WA14 .... 174 A2
Greystoke Av BNG/LEV M19 ..... 146 A2
HALE/TIMP WA15 .... 176 B1
SALE M33 .... 159 F2 2
Greystoke Crs WHTF M45 .... 70 C1 3
Greystoke Dr BOL BL1 .... 27 E1
MDTN M24 .... 74 B1
WILM/AE SK9 .... 209 E3 1
Greystoke La FAIL M35 .... 109 E1

Greystoke St STKP SK1 .... 167 E4
Greystone Av OLDTF/WHR M16 . 143 D3
Grey St AUL OL6 .... 113 D5 1
DTN/ASHW M34 .... 129 E6
MDTN M24 .... 75 D2
PWCH M25 .... 89 D1 3
STLY SK15 .... 115 D6
WGTN/LGST M12 .... 125 F3
Greyswood Av CHH M8 .... 106 A1 5
Greytown Cl SLFD M6 .... 104 A2 3
Greywood Av BURY BL9 .... 34 C5 11
Grierson St BOL BL1 .... 27 F4 17
Griffe La BURY BL9 .... 54 A5
Griffin Cl BURY BL9 .... 34 B5
Griffin Ct CSLFD M3 .... 2 A2 2
Griffin Gv BNG/LEV M19 .... 145 E3
Griffin Rd FAIL M35 .... 93 E6
Griffin St BRO M7 .... 105 D1
Griffiths Cl BRO M7 .... 105 E3 5
Griffiths St NEWH/MOS M40 .... 109 D2 10
Grimes St WHIT OL12 .... 21 D4 2
Grime St RAMS BL0 .... 18 B1 13
Grimscott Cl BKLY M9 .... 92 A4 2
Grimshaw Av FAIL M35 .... 94 B5
Grimshaw Cl MPL/ROM SK6 ..... 169 E1 2
Grimshaw La MDTN M24 .... 75 F4
NEWH/MOS M40 .... 108 A2
Grimshaw St FAIL M35 .... 93 F5 2
STKP SK1 .... 167 F4 2
Grimstead Cl NTHM/RTH M23 .. 176 C1 2
Grindall Av BKLY M9 .... 92 C3
Grindley Av CCHDY M21 .... 142 B6
Grindlow St BRUN/LGST M13 ... 125 F4
Grindon Av BRO M7 .... 88 B6
Grindrod St RAD M26 .... 51 D5 3
RAD M26 .... 51 E5 2
Grindsbrook Rd RAD M26 .... 51 D2
Grinton Av BRUN/LGST M13 .... 144 C1
Grisdale Dr MDTN M24 .... 74 C1
Grisdale Rd BOLS/LL BL3 .... 46 A4
Grisedale Av ROY/SHW OL2 ..... 60 A1 1
Grisedale Rd ROCH OL11 .... 38 C5 1
Gristlehurst La BURY BL9 .... 36 A2
Grizebeck Cl GTN M18 .... 127 D3
Grizedale Cl BOL BL1 .... 26 A5
STLY SK15 .... 99 F6
Grizedale Rd MPL/ROM SK6 ..... 169 F4
Groby Rd ALT WA14 .... 174 A3
CCHDY M21 .... 141 E3 6
DTN/ASHW M34 .... 129 F2
Groby Rd North DTN/ASHW M34 129 E1
Groby St OLDS OL8 .... 96 A2
STLY SK15 .... 115 D6
Groom St CMANE M1 .... 124 C2 2
Grosvenor Av WHTF M45 .... 70 C3
Grosvenor Cl WALK M28 .... 66 A6 3
WILM/AE SK9 .... 209 E1 1
Grosvenor Ct AULW OL7 .... 112 B6 1
Grosvenor Crs HYDE SK14 .... 150 A2
Grosvenor Dr POY/DIS SK12 .... 198 A6 1
WALK M28 .... 66 A6
Grosvenor Gdns BRO M7 .... 105 E3 3
WYTH/NTH M22 .... 178 C1
Grosvenor Pl AULW OL7 .... 112 B6 3
Grosvenor Rd ALT WA14 .... 174 C1
CHD/CHDH SK8 .... 182 A3
ECC M30 .... 100 B4 1
HTNM SK4 .... 165 E2 1
HTNM SK4 .... 165 F2 3
HYDE SK14 .... 150 B2
MPL/ROM SK6 .... 171 D6
OLDTF/WHR M16 .... 142 B1
SALE M33 .... 139 D6
SWIN M27 .... 86 C6
URM M41 .... 138 A1
WALK M28 .... 66 A6
WHTF M45 .... 70 C2
Grosvenor Sq BRO M7 .... 105 E3 2
SALE M33 .... 159 D1
Grosvenor St AULW OL7 .... 112 B6
BOLE BL2 .... 47 E3
BOLS/LL BL3 .... 49 E5
BRAM/HZG SK7 .... 184 B4 10
BURY BL9 .... 53 D1 2
CMANE M1 .... 124 C2
DTN/ASHW M34 .... 129 E5
FWTH BL4 .... 67 D3
HEY OL10 .... 36 C6
PWCH M25 .... 89 D1
RAD M26 .... 51 D6 2
ROCH OL11 .... 39 D6 2
STKP SK1 .... 167 D5 5
STLY SK15 .... 114 B6 7
STRET M32 .... 140 B1 1
SWIN M27 .... 86 A3 1
Grosvenor Wy OLD OL1 .... 78 B1
Grotton Hollow OLDE OL4 .... 81 F3
Grotton Mdw OLDE OL4 .... 81 F6
Grouse St WHIT OL12 .... 23 D4
Grove Av FAIL M35 .... 109 F2
WILM/AE SK9 .... 203 E4
Grove Cl RUSH/FAL M14 .... 125 D6
Grove Ct SALE M33 .... 160 B1
Grovehurst SWIN M27 .... 100 C1 2
Grove La CHD/CHDH SK8 .... 195 F4

DID/WITH M20 .... 163 F3 🖫
HALE/TIMP WA15 .... 175 C4
Grove Rd HALE/TIMP WA15 .... 174 C4
MDTN M24 .... 75 F1
STLY SK15 .... 115 E3
Grove Spring WHTF M45 .... 70 C1
Grove St AULW OL7 .... 111 F2
BOL BL1 .... 27 E5
BRAM/HZG SK7 .... 184 C4 🖫
BRO M7 .... 105 F2
BURY BL9 .... 35 D3
DROY M43 .... 128 A1
DUK SK16 .... 113 E6
FWTH BL4 .... 66 C3
HEY OL10 .... 37 F5 🖫
OLD OL1 .... 79 E4
ROCH OL11 .... 39 F2 🖫
WILM/AE SK9 .... 203 F4 🖫
Grove Wy WILM/AE SK9 .... 203 F4
Grovewood Cl AULW OL7 .... 111 F2 🖫
Grundey St BRAM/HZG SK7 .... 184 C5 🖫
Grundy Av PWCH M25 .... 87 F3
Grundy Rd FWTH BL4 .... 66 C4
Grundy St BOLS/LL BL3 .... 46 B5 🖫
HEY OL10 .... 56 C1
HTNM SK4 .... 164 C3
WALK M28 .... 84 A3 🖫
Guest Rd PWCH M25 .... 71 E5
Guide La DTN/ASHW M34 .... 129 F1
Guide Post Sq BRUN/LGST M13 .. 125 E3 🖫
Guide St SALQ/ORD M5 .... 103 D6
Guido St BOL BL1 .... 27 E5
FAIL M35 .... 95 F6
Guild Av WALK M28 .... 83 E5
Guildford Av CHD/CHDH SK8 .... 195 E3
Guildford Cl STKP SK1 .... 167 F6 🖫
Guildford Dr AUL OL6 .... 97 D6
Guildford Gv MDTN M24 .... 58 A6
Guildford Rd BNG/LEV M19 .... 145 F1
BOL BL1 .... 26 C5 🖫
DUK SK16 .... 132 B2
SLFD M6 .... 102 C3
URM M41 .... 119 F5
Guildford St MILN OL16 .... 23 E6 🖫
Guildhall Cl HULME M15 .... 124 B4 🖫
Guild St EDGW/EG BL7 .... 28 C1
Guilford Rd ECC M30 .... 100 C6
Guiseley Cl BURY BL9 .... 19 F5
Gullane Cl NEWH/MOS M40 .... 93 D6
Gull Cl POY/DIS SK12 .... 197 F6
Gulvain Pl CHAD OL9 .... 77 D3 🖫
Gunson St NEWH/MOS M40 .... 107 D4
Gun St ANC M4 .... 3 H2 🖫
Gurner Av SALQ/ORD M5 .... 122 C2 🖫
Gurney St ANC M4 .... 107 E6
Gutter La RAMS BL0 .... 6 C4
Guy Fawkes St SALQ/ORD M5 .... 122 C2 🖫
Guy St BRO M7 .... 90 A6 🖫
Guywood La NEWH/ROM SK6 ...... 170 A2
Gwelo St OP/CLY M11 .... 108 B5 🖫
Gwenbury Av STKP SK1 .... 167 F4
Gwendor Av CHH M8 .... 90 A2
Gwladys St STKS SK15 .... 115 F1
Gylden Cl HYDE SK14 .... 132 C3
Gypsy La ROCH OL11 .... 39 D4
Gyte's La BNG/LEV M19 .... 146 A1

H

Habergham Cl WALK M28 .... 83 D6 🖫
Hackberry Cl ALT WA14 .... 157 F3
Hacken Bridge Rd BOLS/LL BL3 .. 48 B5
Hacken La BOLS/LL BL3 .... 48 A5
Hackford Cl BOL BL1 .... 46 A1 🖫
TOT/BURYW BL8 .... 33 E2
Hacking St BRO M7 .... 105 F1
BURY BL9 .... 34 B5
PWCH M25 .... 88 B1 🖫
Hackle St OP/CLY M11 .... 109 D5
Hackleton Cl ANC M4 .... 107 E6 🖫
Hackness Rd CCHDY M21 .... 141 D3
Hackney Av NEWH/MOS M40 ...... 109 D3 🖫
Hackney Cl RAD M26 .... 51 E4 🖫
Haddington Dr BKLY M9 .... 91 F2
Haddon Av NEWH/MOS M40 .... 93 F4
Haddon Cl BURY BL9 .... 53 E4
MPL/ROM SK6 .... 200 C5 🖫
WILM/AE SK9 .... 209 D3
Haddon Gv HALE/TIMP WA15 ...... 159 D6
RDSH SK5 .... 146 C4 🖫
SALE M33 .... 159 E2
Haddon Hall Rd DROY M43 .... 109 F5 🖫
Haddon Rd BRAM/HZG SK7 .... 184 C6

CCHDY M21 .... 142 B6 🖫
CHD/CHDH SK8 .... 194 A2
ECC M30 .... 119 D1
SWIN M27 .... 101 D2
Haddon St ROCH OL11 .... 39 F3 🖫
SLFD M6 .... 104 C2
STRET M32 .... 121 E5 🖫
Haddon Wy ROY/SHW OL2 .... 62 A1
Hadfield Av CHAD OL9 .... 77 F6
Hadfield Crs AUL OL6 .... 113 F2
Hadfield St BRO M7 .... 105 F1 🖫🖫
DUK SK16 .... 130 B2
OLDS OL8 .... 95 F2
OLDTF/WHR M16 .... 123 D3
Hadleigh Cl BOL BL1 .... 28 B1
Hadley Av BRUN/LGST M13 .... 144 C1
Hadley Cl CHD/CHDH SK8 .... 181 D6 🖫
Hadley St SLFD M6 .... 104 C2 🖫
Hadlow Gn RDSH SK5 .... 147 F5 🖫
Hadwin St BOL BL1 .... 28 A6 🖫
Hafton Rd BRO M7 .... 104 C1
Haggate ROY/SHW OL2 .... 60 A6 🖫
Haggate Crs ROY/SHW OL2 .... 60 A6
Hagley Rd SALQ/ORD M5 .... 122 B3
The Hags BURY BL9 .... 53 E4
Hague Rd DID/WITH M20 .... 143 E6
HYDE SK14 .... 153 F2
Hague St AUL OL6 .... 113 D3
NEWH/MOS M40 .... 108 A2 🖫
OLDE OL4 .... 80 C3
Haig Av IRL M44 .... 154 A1
Haigh Av HTNM SK4 .... 166 C1
Haigh Hall Cl RAMS BL0 .... 18 C1
Haigh La CHAD OL9 .... 76 C2
Haigh Pk HTNM SK4 .... 146 C6
Haigh St BOL BL1 .... 47 D1
ROCH OL11 .... 40 B1 🖫
Haig Rd STRET M32 .... 121 E6
TOT/BURYW BL8 .... 32 C5
Hailsham Cl TOT/BURYW BL8 ...... 19 D6
Hailsham St OP/CLY M11 .... 108 A5 🖫
Hail St RAMS BL0 .... 18 B1 🖫🖫
Haldon Rd DID/WITH M20 .... 144 B6
Hale La FAIL M35 .... 93 F5
Hale Low Rd HALE/TIMP WA15 .. 175 D4
Hale Rd HALE/TIMP WA15 .... 174 C4
HTNM SK4 .... 166 A2
Hales Cl DROY M43 .... 110 A4
Halesden Rd HTNM SK4 .... 146 B6
Haley Cl RDSH SK5 .... 147 D3
Haley St CHH M8 .... 90 B6
Half Acre RAD M26 .... 51 D3
Half Acre Dr ROCH OL11 .... 39 D1
Half Acre La ROCH OL11 .... 38 C3 🖫
Half Acre Ms ROCH OL11 .... 38 C1 🖫
Half Acre Rd ROCH OL11 .... 38 C1
Halfacre Rd WYTH/NTH M22 ...... 178 A3
Half Edge La ECC M30 .... 102 A4
Half Moon La OFTN SK2 .... 184 C1
Halford Dr NEWH/MOS M40 .... 92 C5
Half St CSLFD M3 .... 105 F4 🖫
MDTN M24 .... 75 D2
Halifax Rd MILN OL16 .... 23 F4
Halifax St AUL OL6 .... 112 C3 🖫
Haliwell St LIT OL15 .... 13 D6 🖫
Hallam Rd NEWH/MOS M40 .... 108 C2
Hallam St OFTN SK2 .... 183 E1
RAD M26 .... 52 B5
Hallas Gv NTHM/RTH M23 .... 161 F4
Hall Av HALE/TIMP WA15 .... 159 D6
RUSH/FAL M14 .... 125 E6 🖫
SALE M33 .... 138 C5
STLY SK15 .... 115 D2
Hall Bank ECC M30 .... 101 D5
Hallbottom St HYDE SK14 .... 132 A4
Hallcroft PART M31 .... 155 D1
Hallcroft Gdns MILN OL16 .... 41 F1 🖫
Hall Dr MDTN M24 .... 75 D5 🖫
Hall Farm Av URM M41 .... 118 C6
Hall Fold WHIT OL12 .... 9 D3
Hall Gdns WHIT OL12 .... 22 A3
Hallgate Dr CHD/CHDH SK8 ...... 179 E5 🖫
Hallgate Rd STKP SK1 .... 167 F5
Hall Green Cl DUK SK16 .... 113 D6 🖫
Hall Green Rd DUK SK16 .... 113 D6
Hall Gv RUSH/FAL M14 .... 125 E6 🖫
Halliday Rd NEWH/MOS M40 ...... 108 A1
Hallford Rd NEWH/MOS M40 ...... 108 B1
Hallington Cl BOLS/LL BL3 .... 47 D4 🖫
Hall I' Th' Wood La BOL BL1 .... 28 C4
Halliwell Av OLDS OL8 .... 95 F2
Halliwell La CHH M8 .... 90 A6
Halliwell Rd BOL BL1 .... 27 D4
PWCH M25 .... 88 A4
Halliwell St BOL BL1 .... 27 E5 🖫🖫
CHAD OL9 .... 94 B3 🖫
MILN OL16 .... 24 C6
WHIT OL12 .... 22 C5 🖫
Halliwell St West CHH M8 .... 90 A6 🖫
Hall La BOLS/LL BL3 .... 48 C6
FWTH BL4 .... 66 B1
MPL/ROM SK6 .... 149 F5
NTHM/RTH M23 .... 177 F1
PART M31 .... 155 D1
Hall Meadow CHD/CHDH SK8 .... 180 C6

Hall Moss La BRAM/HZG SK7 ...... 195 F5
Hall Moss Rd BKLY M9 .... 92 B2
Hallows Farm Av WHIT OL12 .... 22 B3 🖫
Hall Rd ALT WA14 .... 174 A6
AUL OL6 .... 113 D2
BRAM/HZG SK7 .... 182 B6
RUSH/FAL M14 .... 125 E6
WILM/AE SK9 .... 194 C6
WILM/AE SK9 .... 203 E4
Hall St AUL OL6 .... 113 F5
CHD/CHDH SK8 .... 180 B1
CMANW M2 .... 2 D5
FAIL M35 .... 109 E1 🖫
FWTH BL4 .... 66 B1 🖫🖫
HEY OL10 .... 37 E6
HYDE SK14 .... 130 C6
MDTN M24 .... 75 E3
OLDE OL4 .... 79 F4 🖫
RAD M26 .... 51 D3 🖫
ROY/SHW OL2 .... 60 B5
STKP SK1 .... 167 F5
SWIN M27 .... 86 A3 🖫
TOT/BURYW BL8 .... 19 D3
TOT/BURYW BL8 .... 31 F2
TOT/BURYW BL8 .... 33 D3
WHIT OL12 .... 8 C3
Hallsville Rd BNG/LEV M19 .... 146 A2
Hallsworth Rd ECC M30 .... 100 C6 🖫
Hallwood Av SLFD M6 .... 103 D3
Hallwood Rd NTHM/RTH M23 .... 177 E1
WILM/AE SK9 .... 194 C6
Hall Wood Rd WILM/AE SK9 .... 204 B1
Hallworth Av DTN/ASHW M34 ... 110 C6
Hallworth Rd CHH M8 .... 90 C5 🖫
Halmore Rd NEWH/MOS M40 .... 107 E5 🖫
Halsall Cl BURY BL9 .... 34 A1
Halsall Dr BOLS/LL BL3 .... 46 C6
Halsbury Cl WGTN/LGST M12 .... 125 F3
Halsey Cl CHAD OL9 .... 93 F2
Halshaw La FWTH BL4 .... 67 D4
Halsmere Dr BKLY M9 .... 91 F2 🖫
Halstead Av CCHDY M21 .... 141 E4
SLFD M6 .... 103 F2 🖫
Halstead Dr IRL M44 .... 135 F1 🖫
Halstead Gv CHD/CHDH SK8 ...... 179 D2
Halstead St BOLE BL2 .... 47 E2 🖫
BURY BL9 .... 34 B2
Halstead Wk BURY BL9 .... 34 B2 🖫
Halston St RDSH SK5 .... 167 D1 🖫
Halstone Av WILM/AE SK9 .... 208 C1
Halter Cl RAD M26 .... 51 E4
Halton Bank SLFD M6 .... 104 A3
Halton Dr HALE/TIMP WA15 .... 159 F4
Halton Rd OP/CLY M11 .... 109 D5
Halton St BOLE BL2 .... 47 F2
HYDE SK14 .... 132 A6
Halvard Av BURY BL9 .... 34 A1 🖫
Halvard Ct BURY BL9 .... 34 A1 🖫
Halvis Cv OLDTF/WHR M16 .... 122 C6
Hambleden Cl BOLS/LL BL3 .... 45 D4 🖫
Hambleton Cl TOT/BURYW BL8 .. 32 A6 🖫
SALE M33 .... 138 B6 🖫
Hambleton Rd CHD/CHDH SK8 .. 194 A1
Hambridge Cl CHH M8 .... 90 B6 🖫
Hamel St BOLS/LL BL3 .... 46 B6
HYDE SK14 .... 132 A4
Hamer Dr OLDTF/WHR M16 .... 123 E4
Hamer Hall Crs WHIT OL12 .... 23 F3 🖫
Hamer Hl BKLY M9 .... 91 D2 🖫
Hamer La MILN OL16 .... 24 C6
Hamer St BOLE BL2 .... 28 C6 🖫🖫
HEY OL10 .... 36 C5 🖫
RAD M26 .... 52 A5
TOT/BURYW BL8 .... 18 C3 🖫
Hamerton Rd NEWH/MOS M40 . 107 D3
Hamilcar Av ECC M30 .... 101 F5
Hamilton Av IRL M44 .... 59 F6
ROY/SHW OL2 .... 59 F6
Hamilton Cl PWCH M25 .... 88 B2 🖫
TOT/BURYW BL8 .... 32 C4 🖫
Hamilton Crs HTNM SK4 .... 165 F4 🖫
Hamilton Sq HTNM SK4 .... 166 C2 🖫
Hamilton St AULW OL7 .... 112 A6 🖫
BOL BL1 .... 27 F2 🖫
BRO M7 .... 89 E6 🖫
BURY BL9 .... 35 F4 🖫
CHAD OL9 .... 77 E4
ECC M30 .... 100 C4 🖫
OLDE OL4 .... 79 F5
OLDTF/WHR M16 .... 123 E4
STLY SK15 .... 114 A5
SWIN M27 .... 85 E4
Hamilton Wy HEY OL10 .... 35 F5 🖫
Hamlet Dr SALE M33 .... 138 C5 🖫
Hammerstone Rd GTN M18 .... 127 D3
Hammett Rd CCHDY M21 .... 141 E3 🖫
Hammond Av HTNM SK4 .... 146 C6
Hamnet Cl BOL BL1 .... 28 B2 🖫
Hamnett St HYDE SK14 .... 131 E6 🖫
OP/CLY M11 .... 109 E6
Hamon Rd HALE/TIMP WA15 ..... 174 C3

Hampden Crs *GTN* M18 .... 127 D4
Hampden Gv *ECC* M30 .... 101 E5
Hampden Rd *PWCH* M25 .... 88 C1
  ROY/SHW OL2 .... 62 B3
  SALE M33 .... 159 E2 ▣
Hampden St *HEY* OL10 .... 37 E6 ▣
Hampshire Cl *BURY* BL9 .... 53 E1
Hampshire Rd *CHAD* OL9 .... 77 F6 ▣
  DROY M43 .... 110 B4
  PART M31 .... 154 B3
  RDSH SK5 .... 148 A6
Hampshire St *BRO* M7 .... 105 E1
Hampson Crs *WILM/AE* SK9 .... 194 A5
Hampson Fold *RAD* M26 .... 51 D5 ▣
Hampson Rd *AUL* OL6 .... 113 F1
  STRET M32 .... 140 A1
Hampson St *DROY* M43 .... 110 B5
  ECC M30 .... 100 C6
  NEWH/MOS M40 .... 107 E3 ▣
  RAD M26 .... 51 E6
  SALE M33 .... 160 B1
  SALQ/ORD M5 .... 105 D6
  STKP SK1 .... 167 F5 ▣
  SWIN M27 .... 86 B4 ▣
Hampstead Av *URM* M41 .... 136 C2 ▣
Hampstead Dr *OFTN* SK2 .... 184 A2
Hampstead La *OFTN* SK2 .... 184 A2
Hampton Gv *ALT* WA14 .... 158 C4
  BURY BL9 .... 34 A1
  CHD/CHDH SK8 .... 180 C5 ▣
Hampton Rd *BOLS/LL* BL3 .... 47 E5
  CCHDY M21 .... 141 D2
  FAIL M35 .... 94 B5
  IRL M44 .... 154 B1
  URM M41 .... 138 B2
Hampton St *OLDS* OL8 .... 95 E1
Hamsell Rd *BRUN/LGST* M13 .... 125 D2 ▣
Hancock Cl *RUSH/FAL* M14 .... 124 C6 ▣
Hancock St *STRET* M32 .... 140 B3
Handel Av *URM* M41 .... 137 E1 ▣
Handel Ms *SALE* M33 .... 160 A1
Handel St *BOL* BL1 .... 27 E4
Handforth Gv *BRUN/LGST* M13 .... 144 C1
Handforth Rd *RDSH* SK5 .... 147 D6
  WILM/AE SK9 .... 204 C2
Handley Av *RUSH/FAL* M14 .... 143 F2
Handley Cl *EDGY/DAV* SK3 .... 182 A2
Handley Rd *BRAM/HZG* SK7 .... 182 C4
Handley St *BURY* BL9 .... 53 D1
  WHIT OL12 .... 22 B5 ▣
Hands La *ROCH* OL11 .... 21 E6
Handsworth St *WGTN/LGST* M12 .... 125 E2
Hanging Chadder La *ROY/SHW* OL2 .. 60 A2
Hanging Ditch *ANC* M4 .... 2 D2
Hankinson Cl *PART* M31 .... 155 D3 ▣
Hankinson Wy *SLFD* M6 .... 104 B4 ▣
Hanley Cl *MDTN* M24 .... 75 E6
Hanlith Ms *BNG/LEV* M19 .... 145 D3
Hanlon St *CHH* M8 .... 90 A5
Hannah Baldwin Cl
  OP/CLY M11 .... 126 A1 ▣
Hannah St *WGTN/LGST* M12 .... 145 E1
Hannerton Rd *ROY/SHW* OL2 .... 62 B1
Hannesburg Gdns
  NTHM/RTH M23 .... 177 D3 ▣
Hannet Rd *WYTH/NTH* M22 .... 178 B6
Hanover Ct *BRO* M7 .... 89 E6
Hanover Crs *RUSH/FAL* M14 .... 125 E5 ▣
Hanover Rd *ALT* WA14 .... 157 F6
Hanover St *ANC* M4 .... 3 E1
  BOL BL1 .... 46 C2
  LIT OL15 .... 12 B6 ▣
  MOSL OL5 .... 99 D3
  ROCH OL11 .... 39 D5
  STLY SK15 .... 114 A5
Hanover St North
  DTN/ASHW M34 .... 129 F1
Hanover St South
  DTN/ASHW M34 .... 129 F1 ▣
Hansdon Cl *CHH* M8 .... 106 B1 ▣
Hanson Cl *MDTN* M24 .... 75 E2
Hanson Ms *STKP* SK1 .... 167 F3
Hanson Rd *NEWH/MOS* M40 .... 92 B6
Hanson St *BURY* BL9 .... 34 A3
  MDTN M24 .... 75 F3 ▣
  OLDE OL4 .... 80 A4
Hanworth Cl *BRUN/LGST* M13 .... 124 C2
Hapton Av *STRET* M32 .... 140 B2
Hapton Pl *HTNM* SK4 .... 166 C2 ▣
Hapton St *BNG/LEV* M19 .... 145 E2
Harbern Cl *ECC* M30 .... 101 E3
Harbord St *MDTN* M24 .... 75 E3
Harboro Gv *SALE* M33 .... 159 D1
Harboro Rd *SALE* M33 .... 158 C1
Harboro Wy *SALE* M33 .... 159 D1
Harbour Farm Rd *HYDE* SK14 .... 131 F4
Harbour La *MILN* OL16 .... 42 A2
Harbour La North *MILN* OL16 .... 42 A2
Harbourne Av *WALK* M28 .... 83 D5
Harbourne Cl *WALK* M28 .... 83 D5 ▣
Harbury Crs *WYTH/NTH* M22 .... 178 A2 ▣
Harcles Dr *TOT/BURYW* BL8 .... 18 C3
Harcombe Rd *DID/WITH* M20 .... 144 A5

Harcourt Av *URM* M41 .... 139 D2
Harcourt Cl *URM* M41 .... 139 D2
Harcourt Rd *ALT* WA14 .... 174 B1
  SALE M33 .... 139 E5
Harcourt St *OLD* OL1 .... 79 F3
  RDSH SK5 .... 147 D3
  STRET M32 .... 121 F6 ▣
  WALK M28 .... 66 B6
Hardberry Pl *OFTN* SK2 .... 184 C1 ▣
Hardcastle Av *CCHDY* M21 .... 142 A5
Hardcastle Cl *BOLE* BL2 .... 29 D1 ▣
Hardcastle Gdns *BOLE* BL2 .... 29 D1
Hardcastle Rd *EDGY/DAV* SK3 .... 166 B6
Hardcastle St *BOL* BL1 .... 28 A5
  OLD OL1 .... 79 E4 ▣
Harden Dr *BOLE* BL2 .... 29 E5
Harden Hills *ROY/SHW* OL2 .... 62 B1
Harden Pk *WILM/AE* SK9 .... 209 E2
Hardfield Rd *MDTN* M24 .... 75 E6
Hardfield St *HEY* OL10 .... 37 E5
Hardicker St *BNG/LEV* M19 .... 145 F4
Hardie Av *FWTH* BL4 .... 65 F4
Harding Av *ANC* M4 .... 107 E6 ▣
  CSLFD M3 .... 2 C1 ▣
  HYDE SK14 .... 131 E4
  SLFD M6 .... 104 B3 ▣
  STKP SK1 .... 167 F4
Hard La *WHIT* OL12 .... 10 B3
Hardman Av *MPL/ROM* SK6 .... 169 E2 ▣
  PWCH M25 .... 89 E3
Hardman Cl *RAD* M26 .... 51 D3 ▣
Hardman La *FAIL* M35 .... 93 F5
Hardman Rd *RDSH* SK5 .... 147 D3
Hardmans *EDGW/EG* BL7 .... 14 A5
Hardman's La *EDGW/EG* BL7 .... 14 A5
Hardman's Rd *WHTF* M45 .... 71 D5
Hardman St *BURY* BL9 .... 34 A3
  CHAD OL9 .... 94 C2
  CSLFD M3 .... 2 B4
  EDGY/DAV SK3 .... 166 B4
  FAIL M35 .... 93 E6
  FWTH BL4 .... 65 F3
  HEY OL10 .... 37 E5 ▣
  RAD M26 .... 51 D3
Hardon Gv *BRUN/LGST* M13 .... 145 D1
Hardrush Fold *FAIL* M35 .... 110 B1
Hardshaw Cl *BRUN/LGST* M13 .... 124 C3 ▣
Hardwick Cl *BOLS/LL* BL3 .... 49 F4 ▣
  MPL/ROM SK6 .... 201 D3
Hardwicke Rd *MPL/DIS* SK12 .... 199 D5
Hardwick Rd *PART* M31 .... 155 E2
Hardwick St *AULW* OL7 .... 112 A5
Hardy Av *CCHDY* M21 .... 141 E3 ▣
Hardy Cl *ROCH* OL11 .... 40 A4
Hardy Dr *BRAM/HZG* SK7 .... 196 B2
  HALE/TIMP WA15 .... 159 D6
Hardy Gv *SWIN* M27 .... 101 E2
  WALK M28 .... 84 A5
Hardy La *CCHDY* M21 .... 141 F5
Hardy Mill Rd *BOLE* BL2 .... 30 A4
Hardy St *ECC* M30 .... 100 C6
  OLDE OL4 .... 79 E6
Hardywood Rd *DTN/ASHW* M34 .... 149 E4
Harebell Av *WALK* M28 .... 82 A2 ▣
Harebell Cl *WHIT* OL12 .... 22 B2
Haredale Dr *CHH* M8 .... 106 C1 ▣
Hare Dr *BURY* BL9 .... 53 F5
Harefield Av *ROCH* OL11 .... 40 A2
Harefield Dr *DID/WITH* M20 .... 163 E3
  HEY OL10 .... 38 A5
  WILM/AE SK9 .... 203 E6
Harefield Rd *WILM/AE* SK9 .... 194 C5 ▣
Harehill Cl *BRUN/LGST* M13 .... 124 C2 ▣▣
Hare Hill Rd *HYDE* SK14 .... 133 D6
  LIT OL15 .... 12 B5
Hareshill Rd *HEY* OL10 .... 55 F2
Hare St *ANC* M4 .... 3 F2 ▣
  ROCH OL11 .... 40 A2
Harewood Av *ROCH* OL11 .... 20 B3 ▣
  SALE M33 .... 158 B1
Harewood Cl *ROCH* OL11 .... 20 A4
Harewood Dr *ROCH* OL11 .... 20 A3
  ROY/SHW OL2 .... 60 A4
Harewood Gv *RDSH* SK5 .... 146 C3 ▣
Harewood Rd *IRL* M44 .... 135 F1
  ROCH OL11 .... 20 A3
  ROY/SHW OL2 .... 62 A1
Harewood Wy *ROCH* OL11 .... 20 A4
  SWIN M27 .... 86 A3
Harford Cl *BRAM/HZG* SK7 .... 183 E6 ▣
Hargate Av *WHIT* OL12 .... 21 E3
Hargate Cl *BURY* BL9 .... 19 D3 ▣
Hargate Dr *HALE/TIMP* WA15 .... 175 E6
  IRL M44 .... 116 B6 ▣
Hargrave Cl *BKLY* M9 .... 72 C3
Hargreaves Rd *HALE/TIMP* WA15 ... 176 A1
Hargreaves St *BOL* BL1 .... 27 F5 ▣▣
  CHAD OL9 .... 78 A3
  OLD OL1 .... 79 D4 ▣
  ROCH OL11 .... 39 D3 ▣
Harkness St *WGTN/LGST* M12 .... 125 D2
Harland Dr *CHH* M8 .... 90 C6 ▣
Harland Wy *WHIT* OL12 .... 21 E3
Harlech Av *WHTF* M45 .... 71 F5

Harlech Dr *BRAM/HZG* SK7 .... 184 A6
Harleen Gv *OFTN* SK2 .... 168 B6
Harley Av *BOLE* BL2 .... 29 F4
  BOLE BL2 .... 31 E6
  RUSH/FAL M14 .... 125 F6 ▣
Harley Ct *MDTN* M24 .... 75 D2 ▣
Harley Rd *MDTN* M24 .... 75 D2
  SALE M33 .... 140 A6
Harley St *AUL* OL6 .... 112 C4 ▣
  OP/CLY M11 .... 127 C1
Harling Rd *WYTH/NTH* M22 .... 162 B6
Harlow Dr *GTN* M18 .... 127 E6 ▣
Harlyn Av *BRAM/HZG* SK7 .... 197 D2
Harmer Cl *NEWH/MOS* M40 .... 108 B2
Harmol Gv *AULW* OL7 .... 112 A1
Harmony St *OLDE* OL4 .... 79 E5
Harmsworth Dr *HTNM* SK4 .... 145 F6
Harmsworth St *SLFD* M6 .... 103 F5
Harold Av *DUK* SK16 .... 113 E6
  GTN M18 .... 128 A5 ▣
Haroldene St *BOLE* BL2 .... 28 C5
Harold Lees Rd *HEY* OL10 .... 38 A4
Harold Priestnall Cl
  NEWH/MOS M40 .... 108 C1 ▣
Harold St *BOL* BL1 .... 27 E5 ▣▣
  CHAD OL9 .... 78 B4 ▣
  FAIL M35 .... 93 F6 ▣
  MDTN M24 .... 74 C2
  MILN OL16 .... 24 A3 ▣
  OLDTF/WHR M16 .... 123 D3
  PWCH M25 .... 88 A1
  STKP SK1 .... 167 F5
Harper Fold Rd *RAD* M26 .... 50 B6
Harper Green Rd *FWTH* BL4 .... 65 F2
Harper Pl *AUL* OL6 .... 113 D4 ▣▣
Harper Rd *WYTH/NTH* M22 .... 162 C6
Harper's La *BOL* BL1 .... 26 C5
Harper Sq *ROY/SHW* OL2 .... 62 A2
Harper St *EDGY/DAV* SK3 .... 166 C6 ▣
  FWTH BL4 .... 65 F1
  OLDS OL8 .... 95 F1
Harpford Cl *BOLE* BL2 .... 49 E4
Harpford Dr *BOLE* BL2 .... 49 E4
Harp Rd *TRPK* M17 .... 120 B1
Harp St *OP/CLY* M11 .... 127 E3
Harpurhey Rd *CHH* M8 .... 91 D5
Harridge Av *STLY* SK15 .... 115 E5
  WHIT OL12 .... 22 A2
Harridge St *WHIT* OL12 .... 22 A2
The Harridge *WHIT* OL12 .... 22 A2 ▣
Harrier Cl *WALK* M28 .... 83 E5 ▣
Harriet St *IRL* M44 .... 134 C6
  WALK M28 .... 83 E2 ▣
Harriett St *ANC* M4 .... 107 D5
  MILN OL16 .... 23 E6
Harringay Rd *NEWH/MOS* M40 .... 108 C2
Harrington Rd *ALT* WA14 .... 173 F2
Harrington St *GTN* M18 .... 127 F4
Harris Av *DTN/ASHW* M34 .... 128 C6
  URM M41 .... 119 E4
Harris Cl *DTN/ASHW* M34 .... 128 C6
  HEY OL10 .... 35 F6
Harris Dr *BURY* BL9 .... 71 F1
  HYDE SK14 .... 132 B5
Harrison Av *BNG/LEV* M19 .... 145 F1
Harrison Cl *WHIT* OL12 .... 21 D4 ▣
Harrison's Dr *MPL/ROM* SK6 .... 150 A6
Harrison St *ANC* M4 .... 107 E6
  BCUP OL13 .... 4 C1 ▣
  BRO M7 .... 105 E3
  ECC M30 .... 118 B1
  HYDE SK14 .... 151 D3 ▣
  HYDE SK14 .... 151 D3 ▣
  LHULT M38 .... 82 B1 ▣
  OFTN SK2 .... 167 D6 ▣
  OLD OL1 .... 79 D5 ▣
  RAMS BL0 .... 7 D4
  STLY SK15 .... 114 B5
Harris St *BOLS/LL* BL3 .... 46 C3 ▣
  CHH M8 .... 105 F3
Harrogate Av *PWCH* M25 .... 89 E3
Harrogate Cl *OP/CLY* M11 .... 127 F2 ▣
Harrogate Dr *RDSH* SK5 .... 146 C3
Harrogate Rd *RDSH* SK5 .... 146 C2
Harrop Edge Rd *HYDE* SK14 .... 133 F5
Harrop Fold *OLDS* OL8 .... 96 B4
Harrop Rd *HALE/TIMP* WA15 .... 175 D5
Harrop St *BOLS/LL* BL3 .... 45 E5 ▣
  GTN M18 .... 128 A3
  STLY SK15 .... 114 A5 ▣
  WALK M28 .... 82 C2
Harrow Av *BNG/LEV* M19 .... 145 E5
  OLDS OL8 .... 95 E2
  ROCH OL11 .... 38 B1
Harrowby Dr *NEWH/MOS* M40 .... 107 E2
Harrowby Fold *FWTH* BL4 .... 66 A3 ▣
Harrowby La *FWTH* BL4 .... 66 A3
Harrowby Rd *BOL* BL1 .... 26 A5 ▣
  BOLS/LL BL3 .... 45 E6 ▣
  SWIN M27 .... 85 F6
Harrowby St *FWTH* BL4 .... 65 F3
Harrow Cl *BURY* BL9 .... 53 D4
Harrow Dr *SALE* M33 .... 158 D3
Harrow Ms *ROY/SHW* OL2 .... 61 F2 ▣
Harrow Rd *BOL* BL1 .... 46 A1 ▣▣

SALE M33 .... 159 E3
Harrow St CHH M8 .... 90 C4
ROCH OL11 .... 40 C5 2
Harrycroft Rd MPL/ROM SK6 .. 149 F6 5
Harry Rd RDSH SK5 .... 147 D3 1
Harry Rowley Cl
  WYTH/NTH M22 .... 178 A5 1
Harry St CHAD OL9 .... 78 A5
ROCH OL11 .... 38 C4
ROY/SHW OL2 .... 78 C1
Harrytown MPL/ROM SK6 .... 169 E3
Hart Av DROY M43 .... 110 C6
SALE M33 .... 161 D2 1
Hart Ct MOSL OL5 .... 98 C3
Hart Dr BURY BL9 .... 53 F5
Harter St CMANE M1 .... 3 E5
Hatfield Cl BRUN/LGST M13 .. 125 D3 2
Hartford Av HEY OL10 .... 36 C5
HTNM SK4 .... 146 B5
WILM/AE SK9 .... 203 D6 1
Hartford Cl HEY OL10 .... 36 C4 2
Hartford Gdns HALE/TIMP WA15 .. 176 B2
Hartford Rd SALE M33 .... 158 B4
URM M41 .... 119 F5
Hart St DTN/ASHW M34 .... 129 F4 2
Hart Hill Dr SALQ/ORD M5 .... 103 F4
Harthill St CHH M8 .... 106 A2
Hartington Cl URM M41 .... 138 C1 2
Hartington Dr BRAM/HZG SK7 .. 198 C1
OP/CLY M11 .... 108 C4
Hartington Rd ALT WA14 .... 158 B6
BOL BL1 .... 46 A1 11
BRAM/HZG SK7 .... 196 C3
CCHDY M21 .... 141 F3
CHD/CHDH SK8 .... 194 B1 1
ECC M30 .... 100 B4 2
MPL/ROM SK6 .... 200 C3
OFTN SK2 .... 184 B3
Hartington St RUSH/FAL M14 .. 124 A6
Hartis Av BRO M7 .... 105 F1
Hartland Cl OFTN SK2 .... 168 A5 2
POY/DIS SK12 .... 198 B4 2
Hartland St HEY OL10 .... 37 E5 2
Hartlepool Cl RUSH/FAL M14 .. 124 C6 2
Hartley Av PWCH M25 .... 89 D2
Hartley Gv IRL M44 .... 116 C5
Hartley La ROCH OL11 .... 39 F4
Hartley Rd ALT WA14 .... 174 A2
CCHDY M21 .... 141 E2
Hartley St EDGY/DAV SK3 .... 166 B5 2
HEY OL10 .... 37 E5 4
LIT OL15 .... 12 B6
MILN OL16 .... 24 B6 2
NEWH/MOS M40 .... 92 A5 7
STLY SK15 .... 115 E4 1
WHIT OL12 .... 11 D5 3
WHIT OL12 .... 21 F4
Hart Mill Cl MOSL OL5 .... 98 C3
Harton Av AUL OL6 .... 113 D1
Harton Cl ROY/SHW OL2 .... 61 E3
Hart Rd RUSH/FAL M14 .... 143 F2
Hartshead Av AUL OL6 .... 114 B2 1
Hartshead Cl OP/CLY M11 ..... 128 B2 1
Hartshead Crs FAIL M35 .... 111 D1
Hartshead Rd AUL OL6 .... 113 D1 2
Hartshead St OLDE OL4 .... 81 D6
Hartshead Vw HYDE SK14 .... 151 D2
Hartsop Dr MDTN M24 .... 74 A1
Hart St ALT WA14 .... 174 B2
CMANE M1 .... 3 F5 1
DROY M43 .... 110 B5
Hartswood Cl DTN/ASHW M34 .. 130 B5 3
Hartswood Rd DID/WITH M20 .. 144 A5
Hartwell Cl BOLE BL2 .... 29 D4 1
OP/CLY M11 .... 126 A1
Harvard Cl MPL/ROM SK6 .... 150 A6
Harvard St ROCH OL11 .... 40 B5 3
Harvest Cl SALE M33 .... 161 E2 3
SLFD M6 .... 103 F2 1
Harvey St BOL BL1 .... 27 E4
STKP SK1 .... 167 D4 2
TOT/BURYW BL8 .... 33 D3
WHIT OL12 .... 23 F4 3
Harvin Gv BNG/LEV M19 .... 145 E2 1
Harwich Cl BNG/LEV M19 .... 145 F2 2
RDSH SK5 .... 148 A5 1
Harwin Cl WHIT OL12 .... 22 B2
Harwood Crs TOT/BURYW BL8 ... 17 F6
Harwood Dr TOT/BURYW BL8 ... 32 B6
Harwood Gv BOLE BL2 .... 28 C6 1
Harwood Meadow BOLE BL2 ... 30 A4 3
Harwood Rd BNG/LEV M19 ..... 144 C5 2
BOLE BL2 .... 30 C3
HTNM SK4 .... 164 C3
Harwood St HTNM SK4 .... 166 C2 2
LIT OL15 .... 12 A6
Harwood V BOLE BL2 .... 29 F4
Haseley Cl BOLS/LL BL3 .... 49 F4
POY/DIS SK12 .... 198 C4
Haselhurst Wk NTHM/RTH M23 .. 161 D3 3
Hasguard Cl BOL BL1 .... 45 D1 1
Haslam Brow BURY BL9 .... 52 C1
Haslam Hey Cl BOLE BL2 .... 31 D6 4

TOT/BURYW BL8 .... 32 A5
Haslam Rd EDGY/DAV SK3 ..... 182 C1
Haslam St BOLS/LL BL3 .... 46 B4 23
BURY BL9 .... 34 B3 17
MDTN M24 .... 76 A4 4
WHIT OL12 .... 22 C5
Haslemere Av HALE/TIMP WA15 .. 190 A3
Haslemere Dr CHD/CHDH SK8 .. 181 E6
Haslemere Rd DID/WITH M20 .. 144 B5 1
URM M41 .... 137 F2
Haslington Rd WYTH/NTH M22 .. 178 C5
Hasper Av DID/WITH M20 .... 143 E4
Hassall Av DID/WITH M20 .... 143 D3
Hassall St STLY SK15 .... 114 C6 5
Hassop Av BRO M7 .... 88 B6
Hassop Cl OP/CLY M11 .... 107 F6 3
Hassop Rd RDSH SK5 .... 147 E2
Hastings Av CCHDY M21 .... 141 E3
WHIT M45 .... 71 F4
Hastings Cl CHD/CHDH SK8 ..... 182 A5
STKP SK1 .... 167 F6 5
WHTF M45 .... 71 F4
Hastings Dr URM M41 .... 117 F6
Hastings Rd BOL BL1 .... 45 F1 6
ECC M30 .... 100 B3
PWCH M25 .... 72 A6
Hastings St ROCH OL11 .... 40 A2 5
MANAIR M90 .... 191 D1
Hatchett Rd WYTH/NTH M22 ... 178 C6
Hatchmere Cl HALE/TIMP WA15 .. 178 D2
Hatchmere Rd CHD/CHDH SK8 .. 181 D3
Hatfield Rd BOL BL1 .... 27 D6
Hathaway Dr BOL BL1 .... 28 B2
Hathaway Gdns MPL/ROM SK6 .. 168 C1
Hathaway Rd BURY BL9 .... 53 E6 8
Hatherley Rd DID/WITH M20 ... 144 B5
Hatherlow MPL/ROM SK6 .... 169 E3
Hatherlow La BRAM/HZG SK7 .. 184 B5
Hatherop Cl ECC M30 .... 100 C6
Hathersage Av BRUN/LGST M13 .. 125 D3
Hathersage Rd CHAD OL9 .... 78 A5
Hathersage St CHAD OL9 .... 78 A5
Hathershaw La OLDS OL8 .... 96 A2
Hatro Ct URM M41 .... 139 E2
Hattersley Rd East HYDE SK14 .. 152 B2
Hattersley Rd West HYDE SK14 .. 152 A1
Hatter St ANC M4 .... 3 G1
Hatton Av BRO M7 .... 105 E3 5
Hatton Gv BOL BL1 .... 28 B2 4
Hattons Ct STRET M32 .... 121 D6
Hattons Rd TRPK M17 .... 120 C3
Hatton St STKP SK1 .... 166 C3 2
Haugh Hill Rd OLDE OL4 .... 62 C6
Haugh La MILN OL16 .... 43 D3
Haughton Cl MPL/ROM SK6 ..... 149 E5
Haughton Dr WYTH/NTH M22 .. 162 B4 3
Haughton Green Rd
  DTN/ASHW M34 .... 149 E3
Haughton Hall Rd
  DTN/ASHW M34 .... 130 B6
Haughton St DTN/ASHW M34 .. 130 A4
  HYDE SK14 .... 150 C2
Havana Cl OP/CLY M11 .... 108 A6
Haveley Rd WYTH/NTH M22 ..... 178 A2
Havelock Dr BRO M7 .... 105 E3
Havelock St OLDS OL8 .... 79 D6 2
Havenbrook Gv TOT/BURYW BL8 .. 18 B2 2
  RAD M26 .... 50 B4
Haven Av DROY M43 .... 109 F5
Haven Dr DROY M43 .... 109 F5
Haven La OLDE OL4 .... 62 C6
Havenscroft Av ECC M30 .... 119 E1
Haven St SLFD M6 .... 103 F6 4
The Haven HALE/TIMP WA15 ... 175 D4
Haverfield Rd BKLY M9 .... 91 F2
Haverford St WGTN/LGST M12 .. 126 A3 2
Haversham Rd CHH M8 .... 89 F3
Havers Rd GTN M18 .... 127 F4
Haverton Dr WYTH/NTH M22 ... 177 F5 2
Hawarden Av OLDTF/WHR M16 .. 142 A1 3
Hawarden Rd ALT WA14 .... 174 B1
Hawarden St BOL BL1 .... 27 F2 10
Hawdraw Gn OFTN SK2 .... 184 C1 3
Hawes Av FWTH BL4 .... 64 C3
  RUSH/FAL M14 .... 144 C4 5
  SWIN M27 .... 102 A1 2
Hawes Cl OFTN SK2 .... 183 E1
  TOT/BURYW BL8 .... 32 A5
Haweswater Cl DTN/ASHW M34 .. 147 E1 1
Haweswater Crs BURY BL9 ..... 53 F4 1
Haweswater Dr MDTN M24 .... 74 C2
Hawfinch Gv WALK M28 .... 83 E5 2
Hawk Cl BURY BL9 .... 34 C3
Hawker Av BOLS/LL BL3 .... 46 B6
Hawkeshead Rd CHH M8 .... 106 C1 3
Hawke St STLY SK15 .... 115 D6
Hawk Green Rd MPL/ROM SK6 .. 187 D4
Hawkhurst Rd BRUN/LGST M13 .. 126 A6 5
Hawkins St RDSH SK5 .... 166 C1
Hawkins Wy LIT OL15 .... 13 D2 4
Hawkridge Dr NTHM/RTH M23 .. 161 D3
Hawk Rd IRL M44 .... 116 B6
Hawkshaw Ct SALQ/ORD M5 ... 104 B6 4
Hawkshaw La TOT/BURYW BL8 .. 17 D2
Hawkshead Dr BOLS/LL BL3 ...... 45 E6

MDTN M24 .... 74 C2
ROY/SHW OL2 .... 60 B3
Hawkshead Rd ROY/SHW OL2 .. 61 E1 8
Hawksley St OLDS OL8 .... 95 D2
Hawksmoor Dr ROY/SHW OL2 .. 61 F1
Hawkstone Av DROY M43 ...... 109 F4 2
  WHTF M45 .... 70 B4
Hawkstone Cl BOLE BL2 .... 29 F4
Hawkswick Dr NTHM/RTH M23 .. 161 E2
Hawley Dr HALE/TIMP WA15 .... 189 F1
Hawley Gn WHIT OL12 .... 22 B3 4
Hawley La HALE/TIMP WA15 .... 189 F1
Hawley St BNG/LEV M19 .... 145 F3 6
Haworth Av TOT/BURYW BL8 ..... 18 C3
Haworth Cl BURY BL9 .... 53 D3
Haworth Dr STRET M32 .... 120 A6
Haworth Rd GTN M18 .... 127 D5
Haworth St OLD OL1 .... 78 C2
  RAD M26 .... 51 F6
  TOT/BURYW BL8 .... 31 F3
Hawthorn Av ECC M30 .... 101 E4
  HALE/TIMP WA15 .... 159 D6
  MPL/ROM SK6 .... 186 B1
  RAD M26 .... 69 F2
  TOT/BURYW BL8 .... 18 B3
  TOT/BURYW BL8 .... 33 D3
  URM M41 .... 139 D2 1
  WALK M28 .... 83 F4
  WILM/AE SK9 .... 203 E4
Hawthorn Cl HALE/TIMP WA15 .. 159 D6
Hawthorn Crs ROY/SHW OL2 .. 61 F3 7
  TOT/BURYW BL8 .... 18 A6
Hawthorn Dr IRL M44 .... 134 B6 4
  SLFD M6 .... 102 B3
  STLY SK15 .... 132 A1
  SWIN M27 .... 87 D6
Hawthorne Av FWTH BL4 .... 65 F3
Hawthorne Crs OLDS OL8 ...... 96 A3 8
Hawthorne Dr WALK M28 .... 84 B6
Hawthorne Gv AULW OL7 ...... 112 A6 2
  CHAD OL9 .... 77 F3
  MPL/ROM SK6 .... 168 C1
  POY/DIS SK12 .... 200 A5
Hawthorne La MILN OL16 .... 42 B3
Hawthorne Rd BOLS/LL BL3 ..... 45 F5
Hawthorne St BOLS/LL BL3 ... 46 A4 17
Hawthorn Gv BRAM/HZG SK7 .. 196 A3
  HTNM SK4 .... 165 F2
  HYDE SK14 .... 150 B2 4
  WILM/AE SK9 .... 203 F4
Hawthorn La CCHDY M21 .... 141 D3 2
  SALE M33 .... 138 B5
  WILM/AE SK9 .... 203 E4
Hawthorn Pk WILM/AE SK9 ... 203 E4 1
Hawthorn Rd CHD/CHDH SK8 .. 179 E2
  DROY M43 .... 111 D5
  DTN/ASHW M34 .... 128 C5
  FWTH BL4 .... 67 F6
  HALE/TIMP WA15 .... 174 C4
  HTNM SK4 .... 164 C3
  NEWH/MOS M40 .... 93 F4
  OLDS OL8 .... 94 C3
  ROCH OL11 .... 37 F1
  STRET M32 .... 140 C3
Hawthorn Rd South DROY M43 .. 111 D5
The Hawthorns DTN/ASHW M34 .. 129 F3
Hawthorn St DTN/ASHW M34 .. 129 F3
  GTN M18 .... 127 E3
  WILM/AE SK9 .... 203 E5
Hawthorn Vw WILM/AE SK9 ... 203 E4 2
Hawthorn Wk LIT OL15 .... 12 A6 9
  WILM/AE SK9 .... 203 E4 3
Haxby Rd GTN M18 .... 127 E6
Haybarn Rd NTHM/RTH M23 .... 161 F6
Hayburn Rd OFTN SK2 .... 168 A5
Haycock Cl STLY SK15 .... 133 E2 8
  STLY SK15 .... 133 F2 8
Hay Cft CHD/CHDH SK8 .... 194 C1
Haydn Av RUSH/FAL M14 .... 124 C5
Haydock Av SALE M33 .... 157 F3
Haydock Dr BRAM/HZG SK7 ... 185 D5
  HALE/TIMP WA15 .... 175 F2
Haydock La EDGW/EG BL7 ...... 14 C5
Haydock St BOL BL1 .... 47 D1 14
Haye's Rd IRL M44 .... 134 C6
Hayeswater Rd URM M41 .... 119 D6
Hayfield Av MPL/ROM SK6 ...... 169 E1
Hayfield Cl MDTN M24 .... 58 A6 2
  OLDE OL4 .... 63 D5
  TOT/BURYW BL8 .... 18 A4
  WGTN/LGST M12 .... 125 F3
Hayfield Rd MPL/ROM SK6 ..... 169 E1
  SLFD M6 .... 102 C3
Hayfield St SALE M33 .... 159 E1
Hayfield Wk HALE/TIMP WA15 .. 176 A1 6
Hayle Rd OLD OL1 .... 62 B5
Hayley St BRUN/LGST M13 .... 125 F5 13
Hayling Rd SALE M33 .... 138 C6
Haymaker Ri WHIT OL12 .... 11 D5
Haymarket Cl BRUN/LGST M13 .. 125 D4 3
Haymarket St BURY BL9 .... 33 F6
The Haymarket BURY BL9 ...... 34 A3 3
Haymill Av LHULT M38 .... 65 E5 3
Haymond Cl SLFD M6 .... 104 B1
Haynes St BOLS/LL BL3 .... 45 F6

WHIT OL12 .... 23 D5
Haysbrook Av *LHULT* M38 .... 82 B1 🔢
Haysbrook Cl *AULW* OL7 .... 96 B6 🔢
Haythorp Av *WYTH/NTH* M22 ..... 178 C4
Hayward Av *BOLS/LL* BL3 .... 50 A6
Hayward St *TOT/BURYW* BL8 ...... 33 D4 🔢
Hazel Av *AUL* OL6 .... 113 F1
  BURY BL9 .... 34 C5
  CHD/CHDH SK8 .... 180 C2
  LHULT M38 .... 64 C6
  MILN OL16 .... 42 B4
  MPL/ROM SK6 .... 170 B3
  OLDTF/WHR M16 .... 142 B1
  RAD M26 .... 67 E3
  SALE M33 .... 159 F2 🔢
  SWIN M27 .... 86 B6
  TOT/BURYW BL8 .... 18 C4
  TOT/BURYW BL8 .... 32 A2
Hazelbadge Cl *POY/DIS* SK12 .... 198 A5 🔢
Hazelbadge Rd *POY/DIS* SK12 .... 198 A5
Hazelbank Av *DID/WITH* M20 ..... 143 F4
Hazelbottom Rd *CHH* M8 .... 90 C6
Hazel Cl *DROY* M43 .... 111 D5 🔢
  MPL/ROM SK6 .... 186 C3
Hazelcroft *WILM/AE* SK9 .... 209 E5
Hazel-dene Cl *BURY* BL9 .... 53 D2 🔢
Hazeldene Rd *NEWH/MOS* M40 ..... 93 F4
Hazel Dr *OFTN* SK2 .... 184 B1
  POY/DIS SK12 .... 199 D6
  WYTH/NTH M22 .... 193 E1
Hazelfields *WALK* M28 .... 84 C6
Hazel Gv *CHAD* OL9 .... 77 F3
  FWTH BL4 .... 65 F3
  RAD M26 .... 69 D3
  URM M41 .... 138 C1
Hazel Hall La *TOT/BURYW* BL8 ..... 18 C4
Hazelhurst Cl *BOL* BL1 .... 27 F5 🔢
  RAMS BL0 .... 18 C1
Hazelhurst Dr *MDTN* M24 .... 57 D5
Hazelhurst Fold *WALK* M28 .... 85 D6
Hazelhurst Rd *AUL* OL6 .... 114 A1
  STLY SK15 .... 114 B3
  WALK M28 .... 84 C6
Hazel La *OLDS* OL8 .... 95 E3
Hazelmere Av *ECC* M30 .... 101 D3 🔢
Hazelmere Cl *ECC* M30 .... 119 F1 🔢
Hazel Rd *ALT* WA14 .... 174 B2
  CHD/CHDH SK8 .... 181 F6
  MDTN M24 .... 75 F1
  WHTF M45 .... 71 F3
Hazel St *BRAM/HZG* SK7 .... 184 C4 🔢
  DTN/ASHW M34 .... 129 F3
  RAMS BL0 .... 18 B1
Hazelwell *SALE* M33 .... 159 F2
Hazelwood *CHAD* OL9 .... 76 C4 🔢
Hazelwood Av *BOLE* BL2 .... 29 F4 🔢
Hazelwood Cl *HYDE* SK14 .... 151 E1
Hazelwood Dr *DTN/ASHW* M34 .. 130 A3 🔢
Hazelwood Rd *BOL* BL1 .... 26 C5
  BRAM/HZG SK7 .... 184 C5
  HALE/TIMP WA15 .... 174 C5
  OFTN SK2 .... 183 E3
  WILM/AE SK9 .... 204 B3
Hazlemere *FWTH* BL4 .... 67 E4
Headingley Dr *OLDTF/WHR* M16.. 122 B6
Headingley Rd *RUSH/FAL* M14 ... 144 C4 🔢
Headingley Wy *BOLS/LL* BL3 .... 46 B6
Headlands Dr *PWCH* M25 .... 88 B4
Headlands Rd *BRAM/HZG* SK7 .. 183 D6
Headlands St *WHIT* OL12 .... 22 C4 🔢
Heady Hill Rd *HEY* OL10 .... 36 B5
Heald Av *RUSH/FAL* M14 .... 124 C5
Heald Cl *ALT* WA14 .... 174 A5
  LIT OL15 .... 25 E2
  WHIT OL12 .... 22 A2
Heald Dr *WHIT* OL12 .... 22 A2
Heald Gv *CHD/CHDH* SK8 .... 179 E6
  RUSH/FAL M14 .... 124 C5
Heald Pl *RUSH/FAL* M14 .... 124 C6
Heald Rd *ALT* WA14 .... 174 A5
Healds Gn *OLD* OL1 .... 59 D6
Healdwood Rd *MPL/ROM* SK6 ... 170 A1
Healey Av *HEY* OL10 .... 37 F4 🔢
  WHIT OL12 .... 22 B1
Healey Cl *BRO* M7 .... 89 D5
  NTHM/RTH M23 .... 161 D3
Healey La *WHIT* OL12 .... 9 D6 🔢
Healey St *WHIT* OL12 .... 22 C2
  MILN OL16 .... 22 C6
Healing St *ROCH* OL11 .... 40 B2 🔢 🔢
Heanor Av *DTN/ASHW* M34 ...... 149 F3
Heap Brow *BURY* BL9 .... 35 E6
Heape St *ROCH* OL11 .... 39 D6
Heapfold *WHIT* OL12 .... 21 F3
Heaplands *TOT/BURYW* BL8 ...... 18 A4 🔢
Heaps Farm Ct *STLY* SK15 .... 133 E1
Heap St *BOLS/LL* BL3 .... 46 C5 🔢 🔢
  HEY OL10 .... 35 E6
  OLDE OL4 .... 80 A4
  WHTF M45 .... 71 D4 🔢
Heapworth Av *RAMS* BL0 .... 6 C5
Heapy Cl *TOT/BURYW* BL8 .... 32 A5
Heath Av *BRO* M7 .... 105 D3
  TOT/BURYW BL8 .... 18 C4

CHD/CHDH SK8 .... 195 D1
  EDGY/DAV SK3 .... 165 F6
Heathcote Av *SALE* M33 .... 166 A2
Heathcote Rd *GTN* M18 .... 127 D5
Heath Crs *EDGY/DAV* SK3 .... 183 D2
Heather Av *DROY* M43 .... 111 D5
  IRL M44 .... 134 B5
  ROY/SHW OL2 .... 62 B1
Heather Bank *TOT/BURYW* BL8 . 17 F6 🔢
Heather Brow *STLY* SK15 .... 133 F2
Heather Cl *OLDE* OL4 .... 80 C2 🔢
Heatherdale Dr *CHH* M8 .... 106 B1
Heatherfield *BOL* BL1 .... 27 E2 🔢
Heatherfield Ct *WILM/AE* SK9 .. 204 C3
Heather Gv *DROY* M43 .... 128 C1
Heatherlands *WHIT* OL12 .... 5 E5
Heather Lea *DTN/ASHW* M34 .... 149 E1
Heather Rd *ALT* WA14 .... 174 C6
Heatherside *RDSH* SK5 .... 147 E2 🔢
  STLY SK15 .... 115 E5
Heatherside Av *MOSL* OL5 .... 99 F4 🔢
Heatherside Rd *RAMS* BL0 .... 6 C4
The Heathers *OFTN* SK2 .... 183 F3 🔢
Heather St *OP/CLY* M11 .... 108 C5
Heather Wy *MPL/ROM* SK6 ...... 186 C2
Heatherway *SALE* M33 .... 138 B6
Heath Farm La *PART* M31 .... 155 E2
Heathfield *BOLE* BL2 .... 30 A3
  FWTH BL4 .... 66 C2
  WALK M28 .... 100 A2 🔢
  WILM/AE SK9 .... 205 E6
Heathfield Av *CHD/CHDH* SK8 ... 179 F2
  DTN/ASHW M34 .... 148 B1 🔢
  HTNM SK4 .... 146 A6
Heathfield Cl *SALE* M33 .... 161 D2
Heathfield Dr *SWIN* M27 .... 86 B6
Heathfield Rd *BURY* BL9 .... 53 D6
  OFTN SK2 .... 183 D1
Heathfield St *NEWH/MOS* M40 .. 109 D2 🔢
Heathland Rd *BRO* M7 .... 88 C5
Heathlands Dr *PWCH* M25 .... 88 B4
Heathland Ter *EDGY/DAV* SK3 .. 166 C6
Heath Rd *ALT* WA14 .... 174 B5
  EDGY/DAV SK3 .... 183 D1
  HALE/TIMP WA15 .... 159 D5
  WHIT OL12 .... 11 D5
Heathside Gv *WALK* M28 .... 83 E2
Heathside Park Rd *EDGY/DAV* SK3 .. 165 D6
Heathside Rd *DID/WITH* M20 .... 144 B6
  EDGY/DAV SK3 .... 165 E6
Heath St *CHH* M8 .... 90 A6
  ROCH OL11 .... 39 E1
The Heath *AULW* OL7 .... 96 B6
  MDTN M24 .... 75 F5
Heathwood Rd *BNG/LEV* M19 .. 164 C1
Heatley Cl *DTN/ASHW* M34 ...... 147 F1
Heatley Rd *MILN* OL16 .... 41 E1
Heaton Av *BOL* BL1 .... 26 A6
  BOLE BL2 .... 29 F2
  BOLS/LL BL3 .... 49 E5
  BRAM/HZG SK7 .... 182 B4
  FWTH BL4 .... 66 A3
Heaton Cl *BURY* BL9 .... 53 E4 🔢
Heaton Dr *BURY* BL9 .... 53 E4
Heaton Fold *BURY* BL9 .... 52 C1
Heaton Grange Dr *BOL* BL1 ...... 45 E2 🔢
Heaton Gv *BURY* BL9 .... 52 C2
Heaton La *HTNM* SK4 .... 166 B4 🔢
Heaton Moor Rd *HTNM* SK4 ..... 165 F2
Heaton Mt *BOL* BL1 .... 26 A6 🔢
Heaton Park Rd *BKLY* M9 .... 73 E6
Heaton Park Rd West *BKLY* M9 ... 73 E6 🔢
Heaton Rd *BOLS/LL* BL3 .... 49 F4
  DID/WITH M20 .... 144 A4
  HOR/BR BL6 .... 44 B3 🔢
  HTNM SK4 .... 166 B2
Heaton St *BRO* M7 .... 89 F6
  DTN/ASHW M34 .... 129 E6
  MILN OL16 .... 42 B2
  PWCH M25 .... 89 D1
Heaviley Gv *OFTN* SK2 .... 183 E3
Hebble Butt Cl *MILN* OL16 .... 41 F1 🔢
Hebble Cl *BOLE* BL2 .... 28 C2
Hebburn Dr *TOT/BURYW* BL8 .... 33 D2
Hebden Av *MPL/ROM* SK6 .... 169 E1
  SLFD M6 .... 103 D4
Heber Pl *LIT* OL15 .... 12 C6 🔢
Heber St *RAD* M26 .... 51 E6
Hebron St *ROY/SHW* OL2 .... 61 E5
Hector Av *MILN* OL16 .... 23 E5
Heddon Cl *HTNM* SK4 .... 164 C2
Hedge Rows *WHIT* OL12 .... 9 D1
The Hedgerows *HYDE* SK14 .... 132 B6
Hedges St *FAIL* M35 .... 94 B5
Hedley St *BOL* BL1 .... 27 D5
Heginbottom Crs *AUL* OL6 ...... 113 D2
Height Barn La *BCUP* OL13 .... 4 A1
Heights Av *WHIT* OL12 .... 22 C4
Heights Cl *WHIT* OL12 .... 22 C3 🔢
Heights La *OLD* OL1 .... 77 D1
  WHIT OL12 .... 22 C4
Helena St *SLFD* M6 .... 103 D2 🔢
Helen St *BRO* M7 .... 105 D2
  ECC M30 .... 118 C1

FWTH BL4 .... 66 B3
Helensville Av *SLFD* M6 .... 104 B2 🔢
Helga St *NEWH/MOS* M40 .... 107 E3 🔢
Helias Cl *LHULT* M38 .... 82 A2 🔢
Helmclough Wy *WALK* M28 .... 83 D5 🔢
Helmet St *CMANE* M1 .... 125 D1
Helmsdale *WALK* M28 .... 83 E3 🔢
Helmsdale Av *BOLS/LL* BL3 ...... 45 D3 🔢
Helmsdale Cl *RAMS* BL0 .... 18 B2
Helmshore Av *OLDE* OL4 .... 62 B6
Helmshore Rd *RAMS* BL0 .... 6 B3
Helmshore Wy *ROY/SHW* OL2 ... 61 F1 🔢
Helsby Cl *OLDE* OL4 .... 81 E5 🔢
Helsby Gdns *BOL* BL1 .... 28 A3 🔢
Helsby Rd *SALE* M33 .... 160 C3
Helston Cl *BRAM/HZG* SK7 ...... 197 D2 🔢
  IRL M44 .... 135 F1
Helston Dr *ROY/SHW* OL2 .... 61 D5
Helston Gv *CHD/CHDH* SK8 ..... 194 A1
Helston St *NEWH/MOS* M40 .... 108 A3 🔢
Helvellyn Dr *MDTN* M24 .... 56 A3
Hembury Av *BNG/LEV* M19 ...... 145 D5
Hembury Cl *MDTN* M24 .... 75 F1
Hemlock Av *OLDS* OL8 .... 95 F2 🔢
Hemming Dr *ECC* M30 .... 101 F6 🔢
Hemmington Dr *BKLY* M9 .... 91 E6
Hemmons Rd *WGTN/LGST* M12.. 145 F1
Hempcroft Rd *HALE/TIMP* WA15 .. 176 A2
Hempshaw La *STKP* SK1 .... 167 E5
Hemsley St *BKLY* M9 .... 91 F4
Hemsley St South *BKLY* M9 .... 91 F5
Hemswell Cl *SLFD* M6 .... 103 F3 🔢
Hemsworth Rd *BOL* BL1 .... 46 B1 🔢
  GTN M18 .... 127 E6
Henbury Dr *MPL/ROM* SK6 ...... 149 F5
Henbury La *CHD/CHDH* SK8 .... 195 D3
Henbury Rd *WILM/AE* SK9 .... 194 B5 🔢
Henbury St *OFTN* SK2 .... 184 A3
  RUSH/FAL M14 .... 124 B6
Henderson Av *SWIN* M27 .... 86 A4 🔢
Henderson St *BNG/LEV* M19 .... 145 F3
  LIT OL15 .... 12 B6
  WHIT OL12 .... 23 F3
Henderville St *LIT* OL15 .... 12 B5 🔢
Hendham Cl *BRAM/HZG* SK7 ... 185 E5 🔢
Hendham Dr *ALT* WA14 .... 173 F1
Hendham V *BKLY* M9 .... 91 D6
Hendon Dr *BURY* BL9 .... 53 D4
  EDGY/DAV SK3 .... 165 E6 🔢
Hendon Rd *BKLY* M9 .... 91 D1 🔢
Hendrift Pl *WHIT* OL12 .... 23 D4 🔢
Hengist St *BOLE* BL2 .... 48 A2 🔢
  GTN M18 .... 127 E5
Henley Av *CHD/CHDH* SK8 ...... 181 D5
  IRL M44 .... 134 C5
  OLDTF/WHR M16 .... 122 C6
Henley Cl *TOT/BURYW* BL8 .... 51 E1
Henley Dr *AULW* OL7 .... 112 A3 🔢
  HALE/TIMP WA15 .... 159 D6
Henley Gv *BOLS/LL* BL3 .... 46 A6
Henley Pl *BNG/LEV* M19 .... 145 F5
Henley St *CHAD* OL9 .... 94 B2
  OLD OL1 .... 78 B3 🔢
  WHIT OL12 .... 22 C4 🔢
Henley Ter *ROCH* OL11 .... 39 F2 🔢
Henniker St *SWIN* M27 .... 101 F1
  WALK M28 .... 83 E4
Hennon St *BOL* BL1 .... 27 E6 🔢
Henrietta St *AUL* OL6 .... 112 C2
  BOLS/LL BL3 .... 45 F5
  OLDTF/WHR M16 .... 123 D4
Henry Herman St *BOLS/LL* BL3 .. 45 E6 🔢
Henry Lee St *BOLS/LL* BL3 ...... 46 A2 🔢 🔢
Henry St *ANC* M4 .... 3 G2
  BOLE BL2 .... 47 E3
  DROY M43 .... 110 B6 🔢
  DTN/ASHW M34 .... 149 F3 🔢
  ECC M30 .... 101 D6 🔢
  FAIL M35 .... 94 A6 🔢
  HYDE SK14 .... 150 B1 🔢
  LIT OL15 .... 25 D2
  MDTN M24 .... 75 D3 🔢
  OLDTF/WHR M16 .... 123 D4
  PWCH M25 .... 72 A6
  RAMS BL0 .... 7 E4 🔢
  ROCH OL11 .... 40 A1
  STKP SK1 .... 167 F5
Henshall La *ALT* WA14 .... 156 A6
Henshaw La *CHAD* OL9 .... 94 A3
Henshaw St *OLD* OL1 .... 78 C4
  STRET M32 .... 140 B1
Henson Gv *HALE/TIMP* WA15 ... 175 E3
Henthorn St *ROY/SHW* OL2 .... 61 F3 🔢
Henwick Hall Av *RAMS* BL0 .... 18 C1
Henwood Rd *DID/WITH* M20 .... 144 A6
Hepley Rd *POY/DIS* SK12 .... 199 E6
Hepple Cl *HTNM* SK4 .... 165 D2 🔢
Heppleton Rd *NEWH/MOS* M40 .. 93 E3
Hepple Wk *AULW* OL7 .... 111 F2 🔢
Hepton St *OLD* OL1 .... 78 C5
Hepworth St *HYDE* SK14 .... 150 C4 🔢
Herbert St *BOLS/LL* BL3 .... 77 F4 🔢
  CHAD OL9 .... 77 F4 🔢
  CHH M8 .... 106 A2 🔢
  DROY M43 .... 110 A6

DTN/ASHW M34 .... 130 B5
EDGY/DAV SK3 .... 166 B6
OLDE OL4 .... 80 A2
PWCH M25 .... 88 A1
RAD M26 .... 51 D4
STRET M32 .... 140 B1
Hereford Cl AUL OL6 .... 97 E6
ROY/SHW OL2 .... 61 D2
Hereford Dr BURY BL9 .... 53 D1
PWCH M25 .... 89 D3
SWIN M27 .... 102 A1
WILM/AE SK9 .... 194 C6
Hereford Gv URM M41 .... 138 A1
Hereford Rd BOL BL1 .... 45 F1
CHD/CHDH SK8 .... 181 E3
ECC M30 .... 102 B2
RDSH SK5 .... 148 A6
Hereford St BOL BL1 .... 28 A5
CHAD OL9 .... 77 F6
ROCH OL11 .... 40 B2
SALE M33 .... 139 F6
SALE M33 .... 159 F1
Hereford Wy MDTN M24 .... 76 A2
STLY SK15 .... 133 E2
Herevale Gra WALK M28 .... 82 C6
Herevale Hall Dr RAMS BL0 .... 18 C1
Heristone Av DTN/ASHW M34 .... 129 F6
Heritage Gdns DID/WITH M20 .... 163 F3
Herle Dr WYTH/NTH M22 .... 178 A6
Hermitage Av MPL/ROM SK6 .... 171 D3
Hermitage Gdns MPL/ROM SK6 .... 171 D3
Hermitage Rd CHH M8 .... 90 B4
HALE/TIMP WA15 .... 175 E4
Hermon Av OLDS OL8 .... 95 F2
Herne St OP/CLY M11 .... 126 B1
Heron Av DUK SK16 .... 131 F2
FWTH BL4 .... 65 D3
Heron Ct SLFD M6 .... 102 C4
Herondale Cl NEWH/MOS M40 .... 108 C2
Heron Dr DTN/ASHW M34 .... 111 D6
IRL M44 .... 116 B6
POY/DIS SK12 .... 197 E6
Heron St EDGY/DAV SK3 .... 166 B5
HULME M15 .... 123 F4
OLDS OL8 .... 95 D2
SWIN M27 .... 86 B4
Herries St AUL OL6 .... 113 E3
Herristone Rd CHH M8 .... 90 B3
Herrod Av HTNM SK4 .... 146 C6
Herschel St NEWH/MOS M40 .... 92 B5
Hersey St SLFD M6 .... 103 F5
Hertford Gv IRL M44 .... 134 A3
Hertford Rd BKLY M9 .... 91 E4
Hertfordshire Park Cl
ROY/SHW OL2 .... 61 F1
Hertford St AULW OL7 .... 112 B6
Hesford Av BKLY M9 .... 92 A6
Hesketh Av BOL BL1 .... 28 A2
DID/WITH M20 .... 163 E2
ROY/SHW OL2 .... 61 E4
Hesketh Rd MILN OL16 .... 24 A6
SALE M33 .... 159 D2
Hesketh St HTNM SK4 .... 166 C2
HTNM SK4 .... 166 C2
Hessel St SALQ/ORD M5 .... 103 E6
Heston Av URM M41 .... 119 D6
Heston Dr URM M41 .... 119 D6
Heswall Av DID/WITH M20 .... 143 F4
Heswall Dr TOT/BURYW BL8 .... 31 F2
Heswall Rd RDSH SK5 .... 147 D2
Hethorn St NEWH/MOS M40 .... 109 D2
Hetton Av BRUN/LGST M13 .... 144 C1
Heversham St NEWH/MOS M40 .... 107 D3
Hewart Dr BURY BL9 .... 35 D5
Hewitt Av DTN/ASHW M34 .... 128 A6
Hewitt St HULME M15 .... 124 A2
Hewlett Rd CCHDY M21 .... 141 E2
Hexham Av BOL BL1 .... 26 A6
Hexham Cl CHAD OL9 .... 78 A4
OFTN SK2 .... 184 C2
Hexham Rd GTN M18 .... 126 C5
Hey Bottom La WHIT OL12 .... 10 A5
Heybrook Cl WHTF M45 .... 72 A3
Heybrook Rd NTHM/RTH M23 .... 177 F2
Heybrook St MILN OL16 .... 23 F5
Heybury Cl OP/CLY M11 .... 126 A1
Hey Crs OLDE OL4 .... 81 D4
Heyes Av HALE/TIMP WA15 .... 159 F6
Heyes Dr HALE/TIMP WA15 .... 159 F6
Heyes La HALE/TIMP WA15 .... 159 F5
WILM/AE SK9 .... 209 F3
Heyford Av NEWH/MOS M40 .... 93 E3
Hey Head La LIT OL15 .... 12 C2
Heyheads New Rd MOSL OL5 .... 99 F6
Hey Hill Cl ROY/SHW OL2 .... 61 E4
Heyland Rd NTHM/RTH M23 .... 177 E1
Heyridge Dr WYTH/NTH M22 .... 162 B4
Heyrod St CMANE M1 .... 125 D1
STLY SK15 .... 115 E2
Heys Av MPL/ROM SK6 .... 170 C2
NTHM/RTH M23 .... 161 E4
SWIN M27 .... 85 D3
Heys Cl North SWIN M27 .... 85 D3

Heyscroft Rd DID/WITH M20 .... 144 A5
HTNM SK4 .... 165 E3
Heysham Av DID/WITH M20 .... 143 D4
Heyside ROY/SHW OL2 .... 61 E5
Heyside Av ROY/SHW OL2 .... 61 E6
Heyside Cl STLY SK15 .... 115 F1
Heys La HEY OL10 .... 36 B5
MPL/ROM SK6 .... 170 C2
Heys Rd AUL OL6 .... 113 E4
PWCH M25 .... 71 F6
Heys St TOT/BURYW BL8 .... 33 E5
The Heys PWCH M25 .... 71 F6
RDSH SK5 .... 147 E2
Hey St MILN OL16 .... 23 F5
Heys Vw PWCH M25 .... 88 C1
Hey Willow BOLE BL2 .... 15 D6
Heywood Av OLDE OL4 .... 81 E3
SWIN M27 .... 86 C3
Heywood Cl WILM/AE SK9 .... 209 F3
Heywood Fold Rd OLDE OL4 .... 81 D4
Heywood Gdns PWCH M25 .... 88 C1
Heywood Gv SALE M33 .... 139 E5
Heywood Hall Rd HEY OL10 .... 37 E4
Heywood La OLDE OL4 .... 81 E4
Heywood Old Rd MDTN M24 .... 56 A5
SALE M33 .... 159 F2
WILM/AE SK9 .... 209 F3
Heywood's Hollow BOL BL1 .... 47 D1
Heywood St BOL BL1 .... 28 A1
BOLS/LL BL3 .... 49 F6
BURY BL9 .... 34 B6
CHH M8 .... 106 B1
FAIL M35 .... 93 E6
OLDE OL4 .... 80 C3
SWIN M27 .... 85 F5
Heywood Wy SLFD M6 .... 104 A4
Heyworth Av MPL/ROM SK6 .... 170 B2
Heyworth St SALQ/ORD M5 .... 103 F6
Hibbert Av DTN/ASHW M34 .... 129 E4
HYDE SK14 .... 150 C2
Hibbert Crs FAIL M35 .... 94 B6
Hibbert La MPL/ROM SK6 .... 187 D2
Hibbert St BOL BL1 .... 28 A5
HTNM SK4 .... 146 C6
OLDE OL4 .... 81 D4
RUSH/FAL M14 .... 125 D6
Hibernia St BOLS/LL BL3 .... 46 A4
Hibernia Wy STRET M32 .... 120 B4
Hibson Av WHIT OL12 .... 20 C3
Hibson Cl WHIT OL12 .... 11 D5
Hickenfield Rd HYDE SK14 .... 132 A4
Hicken Pl HYDE SK14 .... 132 A4
Hickton Dr ALT WA14 .... 173 F1
Higginshaw La OLD OL1 .... 79 E1
Higginshaw Rd OLD OL1 .... 79 D2
Higginson Rd RDSH SK5 .... 146 C4
Higgs Cl OLDE OL4 .... 80 B4
Higham Cl ROY/SHW OL2 .... 61 E4
Higham La HYDE SK14 .... 151 D3
Higham Vw SLFD M6 .... 104 B4
High Ash Gv DTN/ASHW M34 .... 129 E2
High Av BOLE BL2 .... 48 C2
High Bank ALT WA14 .... 174 B2
EDGW/EG BL7 .... 14 A4
GTN M18 .... 127 F4
High Bank Av STLY SK15 .... 133 E2
High Bank Cl IRL M44 .... 134 B5
High Bank Crs PWCH M25 .... 89 D2
Highbank Dr DID/WITH M20 .... 163 F5
High Bank Gv PWCH M25 .... 89 D2
Highbank Rd BURY BL9 .... 53 D6
High Bank Rd DROY M43 .... 128 A1
HYDE SK14 .... 132 A6
Highbank Rd MILN OL16 .... 43 D4
High Bank Rd SWIN M27 .... 86 C5
High Bank Side STKP SK1 .... 167 D4
High Bank St BOLE BL2 .... 48 A2
High Barn Cl ROCH OL11 .... 39 F2
High Barn La WHIT OL12 .... 5 D6
High Barn Rd MDTN M24 .... 75 D4
ROY/SHW OL2 .... 61 D5
High Barn St ROY/SHW OL2 .... 60 C5
High Beeches BOLS/LL BL3 .... 49 F4
High Bent Av CHD/CHDH SK8 .... 195 E3
Highbridge Cl BOLE BL2 .... 49 E3
Highbury Av IRL M44 .... 135 E2
URM M41 .... 136 C1
Highbury Rd HTNM SK4 .... 146 A5
OLDTF/WHR M16 .... 142 C2
Highbury Wy ROY/SHW OL2 .... 60 B3
Highclere Av CHH M8 .... 106 A1
Highclere Rd CHH M8 .... 90 A3
Highcliffe Rd BKLY M9 .... 90 B2
High Crest Av CHD/CHDH SK8 .... 179 D2
Highcroft HYDE SK14 .... 150 C4
Highcroft Av DID/WITH M20 .... 162 C1
High Croft Cl STLY SK15 .... 132 B1
Highcroft Rd MPL/ROM SK6 .... 170 A2
Highcroft Wy WHIT OL12 .... 23 D1
Highdales Rd NTHM/RTH M23 .... 177 F2
High Elm Dr HALE/TIMP WA15 .... 190 A1
High Elm Rd HALE/TIMP WA15 .... 190 A1
High Elms CHD/CHDH SK8 .... 195 F4
Higher Ainsworth Rd RAD M26 .... 50 C2

Higher Ardwick WGTN/LGST M12 .... 125 D2
Higher Bank Rd LIT OL15 .... 25 E2
Higher Barlow Rw STKP SK1 .... 167 D5
Higher Bents La MPL/ROM SK6 .... 169 D2
Higher Bridge St BOL BL1 .... 28 A6
Higher Bury St HTNM SK4 .... 166 B3
Higher Calderbrook Rd LIT OL15 .... 13 D2
Higher Cambridge St HULME M15 .... 124 B3
Higher Chatham St HULME M15 .... 124 B3
Higher Cleggswood Av LIT OL15 .... 25 E2
Higher Cft ECC M30 .... 119 D1
WHTF M45 .... 70 A5
Higher Crossbank OLDE OL4 .... 81 D3
Higher Darcy St BOLS/LL BL3 .... 48 A4
Higher Dean St RAD M26 .... 50 C6
Higher Downs ALT WA14 .... 174 A4
Higher Fold La RAMS BL0 .... 7 F4
Higher Fullwood OLD OL1 .... 62 B5
Higher Henry St HYDE SK14 .... 150 B3
Higher Hillgate STKP SK1 .... 167 D6
Higher House Cl CHAD OL9 .... 94 B1
Higher La WHTF M45 .... 70 C3
Higher Lime Rd OLDS OL8 .... 95 D5
Higher Ldg WHIT OL12 .... 20 A3
Higher Lomax La HEY OL10 .... 36 B4
Higher Market St FWTH BL4 .... 66 C3
Higher Ormond St HULME M15 .... 124 B3
Higher Ridings EDGW/EG BL7 .... 14 A6
Higher Ri ROY/SHW OL2 .... 42 B6
Higher Rd URM M41 .... 138 B1
Higher Rw BURY BL9 .... 34 C4
Higher Shady La EDGW/EG BL7 .... 15 D6
Higher Shore Rd WHIT OL12 .... 11 F4
Higher Summerseat
TOT/BURYW BL8 .... 18 C4
Higher Swan La BOLS/LL BL3 .... 46 B5
Higher Tame St STLY SK15 .... 114 C5
Higher Turf La OLDE OL4 .... 81 F3
Higher Turf Pk ROY/SHW OL2 .... 60 C6
Higher Wharf St AULW OL7 .... 112 C5
Higher Wheat La MILN OL16 .... 24 A5
Higher Wood St MDTN M24 .... 75 D1
Highfield SALE M33 .... 160 A2
Highfield Av BOLE BL2 .... 30 B4
HEY OL10 .... 36 B5
MPL/ROM SK6 .... 169 D3
RAD M26 .... 70 A2
WALK M28 .... 82 A6
Highfield Cl EDGY/DAV SK3 .... 183 D3
HYDE SK14 .... 132 A3
STRET M32 .... 140 A3
Highfield Crs WILM/AE SK9 .... 204 A2
Highfield Dr ECC M30 .... 101 E4
FWTH BL4 .... 65 E4
MDTN M24 .... 75 D4
MOSL OL5 .... 99 D5
ROY/SHW OL2 .... 78 C1
SWIN M27 .... 87 D6
URM M41 .... 119 D6
Highfield Est WILM/AE SK9 .... 204 A2
Highfield Gdns HYDE SK14 .... 132 A6
Highfield Gln ALT WA14 .... 114 A2
Highfield La WHTF M45 .... 71 D1
Highfield Pk HTNM SK4 .... 166 C3
Highfield Park Rd MPL/ROM SK6 .... 168 C1
Highfield Pkwy BRAM/HZG SK7 .... 196 B5
Highfield Pl GTN M18 .... 128 B5
Highfield Range GTN M18 .... 128 A5
Highfield Rd BNG/LEV M19 .... 145 F2
BOL BL1 .... 26 C5
BRAM/HZG SK7 .... 183 D4
BRAM/HZG SK7 .... 185 E5
CHD/CHDH SK8 .... 181 D6
ECC M30 .... 101 E3
FWTH BL4 .... 64 C3
HALE/TIMP WA15 .... 175 F2
HALE/TIMP WA15 .... 175 F2
HTNM SK4 .... 146 A3
LHULT M38 .... 65 D6
MILN OL16 .... 42 B1
MPL/ROM SK6 .... 187 D1
MPL/ROM SK6 .... 187 F1
POY/DIS SK12 .... 197 E5
PWCH M25 .... 71 E5
ROCH OL11 .... 20 C4
SLFD M6 .... 104 A4
STRET M32 .... 140 A3
Highfield St BRO M7 .... 90 A6
CHAD OL9 .... 78 B4
DTN/ASHW M34 .... 129 F4
DTN/ASHW M34 .... 130 A3
DUK SK16 .... 112 C6
EDGY/DAV SK3 .... 166 A5
FWTH BL4 .... 67 E5
MDTN M24 .... 75 F3
Highfield Ter BKLY M9 .... 91 E5
OLDE OL4 .... 80 B1
Highgate Av URM M41 .... 118 B5
Highgate Crs GTN M18 .... 127 E5
Highgate Dr LHULT M38 .... 64 C6
ROY/SHW OL2 .... 59 F2
Highgate La LHULT M38 .... 64 C6
WHIT OL12 .... 9 D5
Highgate Rd ALT WA14 .... 173 F3

Highgrove Cl *BOL* BL1.....................**28** A4
High Grove Rd *CHD/CHDH* SK8 ...**180** A2
High Hurst Rd *MDTN* M24 .... **74** A4 🔳
Highland Rd *EDGW/EG* BL7 .... **14** C5
Highlands *LIT* OL15 ....**25** E2
ROY/SHW OL2 .... **60** A6
Highlands Dr *OFTN* SK2 ....**185** D1
Highlands Rd *HEY* OL10 .... **37** E2
OFTN SK2 ....**185** D1
ROY/SHW OL2 .... **60** A6
ROY/SHW OL2 .... **61** D1
The Highlands *MOSL* OL5 .... **99** D4 🔳
High La *CCHDY* M21 ....**141** F3
MPL/ROM SK6 ....**169** F1
High Lea *CHD/CHDH* SK8 ....**180** A2
High Lee La *OLDE* OL4....................**63** F6
High Legh Rd *OP/CLY* M11 ....**127** E1
High Level Rd *ROCH* OL11 ....**40** B1
High Meadow *CHD/CHDH* SK8 ...**194** C1 🔳
Highmeadow *RAD* M26 ....**69** D2
High Mdw *EDGW/EG* BL7 .... **14** C5
MPL/ROM SK6 ....**170** A2
Highmead St *GTN* M18 ....**127** E4
Highmoor Crs *OLDE* OL4 ....**80** C2
Highmore Dr *BKLY* M9 .... **91** F2 🔳
High Mt *BOLE* BL2 ....**29** F4 🔳
High Peak Rd *AUL* OL6 ....**114** A1
WHIT OL12 ....**9** D5
High Peak St *NEWH/MOS* M40 ...**108** C1
Highshore Dr *CHH* M8 .... **90** A6 🔳
High Stile St *WHTF* BL4..................**66** C4
Highstone Dr *CHH* M8 ....**107** D1 🔳
High St *ALT* WA14 ....**174** B3
ANC M4 ....**3** E3
BOLS/LL BL3 ....**46** C5
BOLS/LL BL3 ....**49** F6
BRAM/HZG SK7 ....**185** D5
CHD/CHDH SK8 ....**180** B1
DROY M43 ....**110** B6
EDGW/EG BL7 .... **15** D1
HEY OL10...**36** C5
HYDE SK14 ....**132** A6
LIT OL15 ....**12** A6
MDTN M24 ....**75** E2
MOSL OL5 ....**99** E3 🔳
OLD OL1 ....**78** C4
OLDE OL4...**80** C5
ROY/SHW OL2 ....**60** B5 🔳
ROY/SHW OL2 ....**61** F3 🔳
STKP SK1 ....**167** D4
STLY SK15 ....**114** A6
TOT/BURYW BL8............................**32** A4
WALK M28 ....**83** D2
WHIT OL12 ....**23** D5
Highthorne Gn *ROY/SHW* OL2.....**60** A1
High View St *BOL* BL1......................**27** F2
BOLS/LL BL3 ....**46** A5 🔳
Highwood *ROCH* OL11 ....**30** C4
Highwood Cl *BOLE* BL2 ....**30** A6 🔳
Highworth Dr *NEWH/MOS* M40 ...**93** E5 🔳
Higifield Av *SALE* M33...................**160** A2
Higson Av *CCHDY* M21 ....**141** F4
ECC M30 ....**119** D1
MPL/ROM SK6 ....**169** D3
Hilary Av *CHD/CHDH* SK8 ....**194** B1
OLDS OL8...**96** A4
Hilary Cl *HTNM* SK4 ....**166** B3 🔳
Hilary Gv *FWTH* BL4.......................**66** B4 🔳
Hilary Rd *WYTH/NTH* M22 ....**177** F6
Hilary St *ROCH* OL11......................**39** E6 🔳
Hilbre Av *OLD* OL1 ....**78** B1
Hilbury Av *BKLY* M9 ....**91** F5
Hilda Av *CHD/CHDH* SK8 ....**180** C2
TOT/BURYW BL8............................**32** A1
Hilda Gv *RDSH* SK5 ....**167** D1
Hilda Rd *HYDE* SK14 ....**150** B4
Hilda St *BOLS/LL* BL3 ....**47** E5 🔳
CHAD OL9 ....**8** B4
HEY OL10...**37** E5 🔳
Hilden Ct *OLDTF/WHR* M16 .....**123** E5
Hilden St *BOLE* BL2 ....**47** E3
Hilditch Cl *NTHM/RTH* M23 .....**177** F1 🔳
Hiley Rd *ECC* M30 ....**118** A3
Hillam Cl *URM* M41 ....**139** D2
Hillary Av *AULW* OL7 ....**112** C2
Hillary Rd *HYDE* SK14 ....**132** B4
Hillbank Cl *BOL* BL1 ....**27** D4 🔳
Hillbank St *BOL* BL1 ....**58** B3
Hillbrook Av *NEWH/MOS* M40 ...**92** C3 🔳
Hillbrook Rd *BRAM/HZG* SK7 ....**196** B3
STKP SK1 ....**168** A5 🔳
Hillbury Rd *BRAM/HZG* SK7 ....**183** D6
Hill Cot Rd *BOL* BL1 ....**28** A2
Hill Court Ms *MPL/ROM* SK6 ....**169** F3 🔳
Hillcourt Rd *MPL/ROM* SK6 .....**170** A1
MPL/ROM SK6 ....**200** C2
Hill Crs *BKLY* M9 ....**90** B2
Hillcrest *HYDE* SK14 ....**151** D4
MDTN M24 ....**75** D6
Hillcrest Av *HEY* OL10 .... **36** B4
Hill Crest Av *HTNM* SK4 ....**165** E3
Hillcrest Crs *HEY* OL10 ....**36** B4 🔳
Hillcrest Dr *BNG/LEV* M19 ....**146** A4
DTN/ASHW M34 ....**149** F2 🔳
Hillcrest Rd *BRAM/HZG* SK7 ....**183** D6

OFTN SK2 ....**184** A1
PWCH M25 ....**88** A3
ROCH OL11 ....**39** D5
Hillcroft *OFTN* SK2 ....**184** C1
OLDS OL8...**96** B5
Hillcroft Cl *CHH* M8 ....**90** B5 🔳
Hillcroft Rd *ALT* WA14 ....**173** E2
Hilldale Av *BKLY* M9 .... **91** E1
Hill Dr *WILM/AE* SK9 ....**194** C6
Hillend La *HYDE* SK14 ....**153** D2
Hillend Pl *NTHM/RTH* M23 ......**161** E3 🔳
Hillend Rd *NTHM/RTH* M23 ......**161** E5
Hill Farm Cl *OLDS* OL8...................**96** C2
Hillfield *SALO/ORD* M5 ....**103** E5
Hillfield Cl *BRUN/LGST* M13 .....**125** E4
Hillfield Dr *BOLE* BL2 ....**28** C5
WALK M28 ....**82** B6
Hillgate Av *SALQ/ORD* M5 ......**122** C2 🔳
Hillgate St *AUL* OL6 ....**113** D3 🔳
Hillier St *BKLY* M9 .... **91** F5
Hillier St North *BKLY* M9 .... **91** F5
Hillingdon Cl *OLDS* OL8 ....**94** C4
Hillingdon Dr *NEWH/MOS* M40 ...**92** C3
Hillingdon Rd *STRET* M32 ....**140** C2
WHTF M45 ....**70** A4
Hillington Rd *EDGY/DAV* SK3 ...**166** A5
SALE M33 ....**158** C3
Hillkirk Dr *WHIT* OL12 .... **22** A2
Hillkirk St *OP/CLY* M11 ....**107** F6
Hill La *BKLY* M9................................ **91** E2
BOLE BL2 ....**47** E1
Hillman Cl *NEWH/MOS* M40 .....**107** E2 🔳
Hill Mt *STLY* SK15 ....**132** B1
Hill Ri *ALT* WA14 ....**173** E2
MPL/ROM SK6 ....**169** F3
RAMS BL0 ....**18** B1 🔳
Hillsborough Dr *BURY* BL9........... **71** F1
Hill's Ct *TOT/BURYW* BL8 ....**32** C3 🔳
Hillsdale Gv *BOLE* BL2 .... **29** F4 🔳
Hill Side *BOL* BL1 ....**45** D2
EDGW/EG BL7 .... **14** C6
FWTH BL4 ....**66** A4
HYDE SK14 ....**151** D5
OLDE OL4...**80** A4
OLDE OL4...**81** E6
ROY/SHW OL2 ....**60** C4
ROY/SHW OL2 ....**62** B3
WALK M28 ....**83** D1
WHTF M45 ....**70** C1
Hillside Cl *BOLE* BL2......................**29** F2
BRAM/HZG SK7 ....**197** E2 🔳
NEWH/MOS M40 ....**92** B4
Hillside Crs *AUL* OL6 ....**114** A2
BURY BL9..**34** A1
Hillside Dr *MDTN* M24 ....**75** E2
SWIN M27 ....**103** E1
Hillside Gv *MPL/ROM* SK6 ....**171** F4
Hillside Rd *HALE/TIMP* WA15 ....**175** E4
MPL/ROM SK6 ....**150** A6
OFTN SK2 ....**168** B6
RAMS BL0 ....**6** B6
Hillside St *BOLS/LL* BL3 ....**46** B4 🔳
Hillside Vw *DTN/ASHW* M34......**149** E4
Hillside Wk *WHIT* OL12 .... **22** B1
Hills La *BURY* BL9........................... **72** A1
Hillspring Rd *OLDE* OL4 ....**81** E5
Hillstone Av *WHIT* OL12 .... **22** A1
Hillstone Cl *TOT/BURYW* BL8 ....**18** A3
Hill St *AULW* OL7 ....**112** B5
BRO M7 ....**105** E1 🔳
BURY BL9..**19** D2
DID/WITH M20 ....**143** F4
HEY OL10...**37** D5
MDTN M24 ....**57** E6
MILN OL16 ....**23** E6 🔳
MPL/ROM SK6 ....**169** F3
OLDE OL4...**79** F4
RAD M26 ....**51** D5
ROY/SHW OL2 ....**62** A3
TOT/BURYW BL8............................**32** A3 🔳
Hill Top *BOLS/LL* BL3 ....**49** E5
HALE/TIMP WA15 ....**175** E6
MPL/ROM SK6 ....**169** F2
Hill Top Av *BKLY* M9....................... **91** E2
Hill Top Av *WILM/AE* SK9 ....**203** F3
Hill Top Cl *CHD/CHDH* SK8 .....**181** F6 🔳
Hill Top Dr *HALE/TIMP* WA15 ...**175** E5
Hilltop Dr *MPL/ROM* SK6 ....**186** A1
Hill Top Dr *ROCH* OL11 ....**40** A5
Hilltop Dr *ROY/SHW* OL2 ....**78** C1
TOT/BURYW BL8............................**31** F1
Hilltop Gv *WHTF* M45 ....**71** F5
Hill Top Rd *WALK* M28 ....**81** E3
Hill Vw *STLY* SK15.........................**133** E3
Hill View Cl *OLD* OL1 ....**80** A1
Hillview Rd *BOL* BL1 ....**27** F3 🔳
DTN/ASHW M34 ....**147** E2
Hillwood Av *CHH* M8 ....**90** A2
Hillyard St *TOT/BURYW* BL8 ....**33** D4 🔳
Hilly Cft *EDGW/EG* BL7 .... **14** A5

Hilmarton Cl *BOLE* BL2 ....**29** F2 🔳
Hilrose Av *URM* M41 ....**139** D1
Hilton Av *URM* M41 ....**138** B1 🔳
Hilton Crs *AUL* OL6 ....**113** D2
Hilton Dr *AULW* OL7 ....**112** A2
IRL M44 ....**134** A6
PWCH M25 ....**88** C3 🔳
Hilton Fold La *MDTN* M24 .... **75** F2
Hilton Gv *POY/DIS* SK12 ....**198** B5
WALK M28 ....**82** C2 🔳
Hilton La *PWCH* M25 ....**88** B3
WALK M28 ....**82** C3
Hilton Rd *BRAM/HZG* SK7 ....**183** D5
BURY BL9..**34** A5 🔳
POY/DIS SK12 ....**200** A4
POY/DIS SK12 ....**201** F2
Hiltons Farm Cl *DTN/ASHW* M34...**129** F3
Hilton Sq *SWIN* M27........................**86** B4
Hilton St *ANC* M4 ....**3** F2
BOLE BL2 ....**48** A2
BRO M7 ....**105** E1
BURY BL9..**34** A3
CMANE M1 ....**3** G3
EDGY/DAV SK3 ....**166** B5
HYDE SK14 ....**132** A4 🔳
LHULT M38 ....**82** B1
Hilton St North *BRO* M7 ....**105** E1
Himley Rd *OP/CLY* M11 ....**109** D4
Hinchcombe Cl *LHULT* M38 .... **65** E5 🔳
Hinckley St *OP/CLY* M11.............**126** A1
Hindburn Cl *WHTF* M45 .... **71** F2 🔳
Hindburn Dr *WALK* M28 ....**82** B5
Hinde St *NEWH/MOS* M40 ....**92** B5
Hind Hill St *HEY* OL10 .... **37** E6
Hindle Dr *ROY/SHW* OL2.............. **60** A6
Hindle St *RAD* M26 ....**51** E6
Hindley Av *WYTH/NTH* M22 ......**177** F5
Hindley St *AULW* OL7 ....**112** A6 🔳
AULW OL7 ....**112** A6 🔳
STKP SK1 ....**167** D5
Hindsford Cl *NTHM/RTH* M23 ...**160** B4
Hinds La *RAD* M26 ....**52** A3
TOT/BURYW BL8............................**33** D6
Hind St *BOLE* BL2............................**48** B2
Hinkler Av *BOLS/LL* BL3 ....**46** C5
Hinton Cl *ROCH* OL11 .... **37** F1
Hinton Gv *HYDE* SK14 ....**151** E3
Hinton St *ANC* M4 ....**106** C4 🔳
OLDS OL8...**79** D6 🔳
Hipley Cl *MPL/ROM* SK6 ....**149** E6 🔳
Hirons La *OLDE* OL4 ....**81** E6 🔳
Hirst Av *WALK* M28 ....**66** A6
Hitchen Cl *DUK* SK16 ....**132** A2 🔳
Hitchen Dr *DUK* SK16 ....**132** A2
Hive St *OLDS* OL8 ....**94** C3
Hobart Cl *BRAM/HZG* SK7 ....**197** D4
Hobart St *BOL* BL1 ....**27** E5
GTN M18 ....**127** E4
Hobson Ct *DTN/ASHW* M34 ....**129** F3
Hobson Crs *DTN/ASHW* M34 .....**129** F3
Hobson St *FAIL* M35 ....**109** E1
OLD OL1 ....**79** D5 🔳
OP/CLY M11 ....**128** B2
RDSH SK5.......................................**147** D1
Hockenhull Cl *WYTH/NTH* M22 ...**178** C5 🔳
Hockley Cl *POY/DIS* SK12 ....**199** D6
Hockley Rd *NTHM/RTH* M23 .....**177** D1
POY/DIS SK12 ....**199** D6
Hodder Av *LIT* OL15 .... **12** A5
Hodder Bank *OFTN* SK2 ....**184** C2
Hodder Wy *WHTF* M45 .... **72** A3 🔳
Hoddesdon St *CHH* M8 ....**90** C6
Hodge Clough Rd *OLD* OL1 ....**62** A5
Hodge La *HYDE* SK14 ....**153** D3
SLFD M6...**104** A6
Hodge Rd *OLD* OL1 ....**62** B6
WALK M28 ....**83** E5
Hodge St *BKLY* M9 ....**92** A4
Hodgson Dr *HALE/TIMP* WA15 ...**159** E5 🔳
Hodgson St *AUL* OL6 ....**112** B5 🔳
CHH M8 ....**106** A2
Hodnett Av *URM* M41 ....**136** C2 🔳
Hodson Fold *OLDS* OL8..................**96** B4
Hodson Rd *SWIN* M27.....................**85** F3 🔳
Hodson St *CSLFD* M3 ....**2** A1 🔳
Hogarth Ri *OLD* OL1........................**62** B5
Hogarth Rd *MPL/ROM* SK6 ....**171** F5
ROCH OL11 ....**40** A5
Holbeach Cl *TOT/BURYW* BL8 ....**33** E2
Holbeck *WHIT* OL12 .... **22** B1
Holbeck Gv *RUSH/FAL* M14 ......**125** F5 🔳
Holberton Cl *CHH* M8 ....**105** F2 🔳
Holborn Av *FAIL* M35 ....**94** C6 🔳
RAD M26 ....**50** B5
Holborn Dr *CHH* M8 ....**106** C2
Holborn Sq *ROCH* OL11 ....**39** E2
Holborn St *ROCH* OL11 ....**39** E2
STKP SK1 ....**167** D4 🔳
Holbrook Av *LHULT* M38 .... **65** E5
Holbrook St *CMANE* M1 ....**3** F6 🔳
Holcet Dr *ALT* WA14 ....**173** E2 🔳
Holcombe Av *TOT/BURYW* BL8 ...**32** C5
Holcombe Cl *ALT* WA14 ....**173** F1 🔳
FWTH BL4 ....**67** E5

OLDE OL4 .... 81 E4 🔟
SLFD M6 .... 104 B5

Holcombe Ct TOT/BURYW BL8 ..... 18 A3 🔟
Holcombe Crs FWTH BL4 .... 67 E5
Holcombe Lee RAMS BL0 .... 18 B2
Holcombe Old Rd TOT/BURYW BL8 .. 18 A2
Holcombe Rd BOLS/LL BL3 .... 49 D6 🔟
  RUSH/FAL M14 .... 144 C4 🔟
  TOT/BURYW BL8 .... 18 A5
Holcombe View Cl OLDE OL4 .... 80 B1
Holden Av BOL BL1 .... 28 A1 🔟
  BURY BL9 .... 35 F3
  RAMS BL0 .... 6 B6
Holden Clough Dr AULW OL7 .... 96 B6
Holden Fold La OLD OL1 .... 78 A1
Holden Rd BRO M7 .... 89 E4
Holden St AUL OL6 .... 113 E3 🔟
  OLDS OL8 .... 96 A2 🔟
  WHIT OL12 .... 23 E3
Holder Av BOLS/LL BL3 .... 49 E4 🔟
Holderness Dr OLD OL1 .... 78 A1
Holdgate Cl HULME M15 .... 123 F4
Holdsworth St SWIN M27 .... 85 E6
Holebottom AUL OL6 .... 113 D4 🔟
Hole House Fold MPL/ROM SK6 .. 169 F3 🔟
Holford Av RUSH/FAL M14 .... 143 F1
Holford St SLFD M6 .... 105 D3
Holford Wk MILN OL16 .... 24 B6
Holgate St OLDE OL4 .... 80 C2
Holhouse La TOT/BURYW BL8 ...... 17 F3
Holiday La OFTN SK2 .... 185 D1
Holker Cl BRUN/LGST M13 .... 125 E4
  POY/DIS SK12 .... 199 D5
Holkham Cl ANC M4 .... 107 D5 🔟
Holland Av STLY SK15 .... 114 B3
Holland Ct RAD M26 .... 52 A5
Holland Gv AUL OL6 .... 112 C1
Holland Rd BRAM/HZG SK7 .... 196 C3
  CHH M8 .... 90 A3 🔟
  HYDE SK14 .... 132 A4
Holland St BOL BL1 .... 28 A3
  DTN/ASHW M34 .... 129 E5
  HEY OL10 .... 37 E5 🔟
  MILN OL16 .... 24 B1 🔟
  NEWH/MOS M40 .... 107 E5
  RAD M26 .... 52 A5
  SLFD M6 .... 104 B2
  WHIT OL12 .... 22 C5
Holland St East DTN/ASHW M34 .. 129 E5
Holland St West
  DTN/ASHW M34 .... 129 E5 🔟
Hollies Dr MPL/ROM SK6 .... 187 E2
Hollies La WILM/AE SK9 .... 205 D4
The Hollies DID/WITH M20 .... 163 D2
Hollin Bank HTNM SK4 .... 146 B4 🔟
Hollin Crs OLDE OL4 .... 99 F1
Hollin Dr MDTN M24 .... 56 C5
Holliney Av WYTH/NTH M22 .... 179 D6
Holliney Rd WYTH/NTH M22 .... 179 D6
Hollingworth Av
  NEWH/MOS M40 .... 94 A3 🔟
Hollingworth Dr MPL/ROM SK6 .. 187 D4
Hollingworth Rd LIT OL15 .... 25 F1
  MPL/ROM SK6 .... 168 C1
Hollingworth St CHAD OL9 .... 94 C2 🔟
Hollinhall St OLDE OL4 .... 80 A4
Hollinhurst Dr HOR/BR BL6 .... 44 A2
Hollinhurst Rd RAD M26 .... 70 A1
Hollin La MDTN M24 .... 57 D5
  ROCH OL11 .... 37 F1 🔟
  WILM/AE SK9 .... 193 D4
Hollins Av HYDE SK14 .... 150 C4 🔟
  OLDE OL4 .... 81 D3
Hollins Brook Cl BURY BL9 .... 53 F4 🔟
Hollins Brow BURY BL9 .... 53 D5
Hollins Cl BURY BL9 .... 53 F5
Hollinscroft Av
  HALE/TIMP WA15 .... 176 B2 🔟
Hollins Gn MDTN M24 .... 57 E6
Hollins Green Rd MPL/ROM SK6 .. 187 D1
Hollins Gv SALE M33 .... 159 E1
  WGTN/LGST M12 .... 126 B6 🔟
Hollins La BURY BL9 .... 53 E4
  MOSL OL5 .... 99 E4
  MPL/ROM SK6 .... 171 F6
  RAMS BL0 .... 7 F2
Hollins Ms BURY BL9 .... 54 A5
Hollins Mt MPL/ROM SK6 .... 171 F5
Hollins Rd OLDE OL4 .... 81 D5
  OLDS OL8 .... 95 D3
Hollins St BOLE BL2 .... 47 F3
  OLDE OL4 .... 81 D5 🔟
  STLY SK15 .... 132 A1
Hollinswood Rd BOLE BL2 .... 47 F3
Hollinwood Av NEWH/MOS M40 .. 93 E3
Hollinwood La MPL/ROM SK6 .... 187 D5
Holloway Dr WALK M28 .... 85 D4
Hollowbrook Wy WHIT OL12 .... 22 B5 🔟
Hollow End RDSH SK5 .... 147 F4
Hollowfield ROCH OL11 .... 20 B4
Hollow Mdw RAD M26 .... 68 A5
Hollowspell WHIT OL12 .... 24 A2
The Hollows CHD/CHDH SK8 ..... 180 A6 🔟
Hollow Vale Dr RDSH SK5 .... 147 F4
Holly Av CHD/CHDH SK8 .... 180 B2

URM M41 .... 137 F1
  WALK M28 .... 83 F3
Holly Bank ROY/SHW OL2 .... 60 B4
  SALE M33 .... 160 A2
Hollybank Ri DUK SK16 .... 132 A1
Holly Bank Rd WILM/AE SK9 ..... 203 F2
Hollybush St RAD M26 .... 51 D6
Hollybush St GTN M18 .... 127 F3
Holly Cl HALE/TIMP WA15 .... 175 E1
Holly Ct HYDE SK14 .... 151 E1
Hollycroft Av BOLE BL2 .... 48 C4
  WYTH/NTH M22 .... 178 D1 🔟
Holly Dr SALE M33 .... 159 E1 🔟
Hollyedge Dr PWCH M25 .... 88 B3 🔟
Holly Fold WHTF M45 .... 71 D2 🔟
Holly Gra ALT WA14 .... 174 B5 🔟
  BRAM/HZG SK7 .... 183 D4
Holly Gv BOL BL1 .... 27 D6
  CHAD OL9 .... 77 F3
  DTN/ASHW M34 .... 130 B6
  DUK SK16 .... 131 F1
  FWTH BL4 .... 65 E3
  OLDE OL4 .... 80 C3
  SALE M33 .... 160 B1
Hollyedge Court Rd
  WYTH/NTH M22 .... 178 A2 🔟
Hollyhedge Rd NTHM/RTH M23 .. 177 F2
  WYTH/NTH M22 .... 178 A2
Hollyhey Dr NTHM/RTH M23 ...... 161 F4
Hollyhouse Dr MPL/ROM SK6 .... 149 E6 🔟
Holly House Dr URM M41 .... 137 D1 🔟
Hollyhurst WALK M28 .... 100 C1
Holly La OLDS OL8 .... 95 D3 🔟
  WILM/AE SK9 .... 192 C4
Holly Mill Crs BOL BL1 .... 28 A3
Hollymount Av OFTN SK2 .... 184 A2 🔟
Hollymount Dr OFTN SK2 .... 184 A2
  OLDE OL4 .... 62 C6 🔟
Hollymount Gdns OFTN SK2 ...... 184 B2 🔟
Hollymount Rd OFTN SK2 .... 184 A2
Holly Oak Gdns HEY OL10 .... 37 D5 🔟
Holly Rd BRAM/HZG SK7 .... 196 C4
  HTNM SK4 .... 146 A6
  MPL/ROM SK6 .... 200 C2
  POY/DIS SK12 .... 198 C6
  SWIN M27 .... 101 E1
Holly Rd North WILM/AE SK9 ... 203 E5
Holly Rd South WILM/AE SK9 .... 203 F6
Holly St BOL BL1 .... 28 A3
  BURY BL9 .... 34 B5
  DROY M43 .... 109 E5
  OP/CLY M11 .... 125 F1
  RAMS BL0 .... 19 D2
  STKP SK1 .... 167 E4
  TOT/BURYW BL8 .... 11 D5
Hollythorn Av CHD/CHDH SK8 .. 196 A2 🔟
Hollyway WYTH/NTH M22 .... 162 C5
Hollywood Rd BOL BL1 .... 26 C5
Holmbrook Wk CHH M8 .... 106 B1 🔟
Holmcroft Rd GTN M18 .... 146 B1
Holmdale Av BNG/LEV M19 ...... 144 C6 🔟
Holme Av TOT/BURYW BL8 .... 33 D2
Holme Beech Gv OFTN SK2 ...... 168 A5 🔟
Holme Crs OLD OL1 .... 78 A1 🔟
Holmefield SALE M33 .... 159 F1
Holme House St LIT OL15 .... 13 E2 🔟
Holme Park Wy FAIL M35 .... 94 C6
Holme Rd DID/WITH M20 .... 163 D2
Holmes St BOLS/LL BL3 .... 47 D5 🔟
  CHD/CHDH SK8 .... 180 C1 🔟
  EDGY/DAV SK3 .... 166 C6 🔟
  WHIT OL12 .... 22 B5
  WHIT OL12 .... 24 A2 🔟
Holme St HYDE SK14 .... 150 B1
Holmeswood Rd BOLS/LL BL3 .... 64 D1
Holme Ter LIT OL15 .... 13 E2 🔟
Holmfield Av BKLY M9 .... 92 A6
  PWCH M25 .... 89 D2
Holmfield Av West
  NEWH/MOS M40 .... 108 A1
Holmfield Cl HTNM SK4 .... 166 B2 🔟
Holmfield Dr CHD/CHDH SK8 .... 195 F1
Holmfield Gn BOLS/LL BL3 .... 45 D3
Holmfirth St BRUN/LGST M13 .... 126 A5
Holmleigh Av BKLY M9 .... 91 F4 🔟
Holmpark Rd OP/CLY M11 .... 128 A2 🔟
Holmside Gdns BNG/LEV M19 .. 164 C1 🔟
Holmwood ALT WA14 .... 173 E4
Holmwood Rd DID/WITH M20 .. 143 F6 🔟
Holroyd St MILN OL16 .... 23 E6
  OP/CLY M11 .... 126 B1 🔟
Holst Av CHH M8 .... 106 B1
Holstein Av WHIT OL12 .... 22 B1
Holtby St BKLY M9 .... 91 F4
Holthouse Rd TOT/BURYW BL8 .. 31 F2
Holt La FAIL M35 .... 94 C6
Holt Lane Ms FAIL M35 .... 94 B6
Holts La OLDE OL4 .... 97 E1
  WILM/AE SK9 .... 193 D6
Holt St ALT WA14 .... 158 A6 🔟
  BOLS/LL BL3 .... 46 A3 🔟
  DTN/ASHW M34 .... 129 F1

ECC M30 .... 119 D1
LIT OL15 .... 13 E1 🔟
MILN OL16 .... 42 B2 🔟
NEWH/MOS M40 .... 108 A2
OLDE OL4 .... 80 A3
RAMS BL0 .... 7 E5 🔟
STKP SK1 .... 167 D5
SWIN M27 .... 86 A3 🔟
WHIT OL12 .... 9 D2 🔟
Holt St West RAMS BL0 .... 6 C6
Holt Town NEWH/MOS M40 ...... 107 F5
Holwick Rd NTHM/RTH M23 ...... 161 D3
Holwood Dr OLDTF/WHR M16 .. 142 C5 🔟
Holy Harbour St BOL BL1 .... 27 D5 🔟
Holyoake Rd WALK M28 .... 85 E3
Holyoake St DROY M43 .... 111 D5
Holyrood Dr NEWH/MOS M40 .. 109 D1
Holyrood Dr PWCH M25 .... 72 A5 🔟
  SWIN M27 .... 85 D6
Holyrood Gv PWCH M25 .... 71 F5
Holyrood Rd NEWH/MOS M40 .. 72 A6
Holyrood St NEWH/MOS M40 .. 109 F3 🔟
  OLD OL1 .... 79 E2
Holy St ROCH OL11 .... 40 C5 🔟
Homebury Dr OP/CLY M11 .... 108 C5 🔟
Home Dr MDTN M24 .... 75 D4
Home Farm Av HYDE SK14 .... 153 D2
Homelands Cl SALE M33 .... 159 D3
Homelands Rd SALE M33 .... 159 D3
Homer Dr MPL/ROM SK6 .... 171 F5
Homerton Rd NEWH/MOS M40 .. 108 C3 🔟
Homestead Cl PART M31 .... 155 E1
Homestead Crs BNG/LEV M19 .. 164 B2
Homestead Gdns WHIT OL12 .. 11 E6 🔟
Hometel RUSH/FAL M14 .... 144 A2
Homewood Av WYTH/NTH M22 .. 162 B4 🔟
Honduras St OLDE OL4 .... 79 F4 🔟
Hondwith Cl BOLE BL2 .... 28 C2 🔟
Honeysuckle Cl MPL/ROM SK6 .. 149 E6 🔟
  NTHM/RTH M23 .... 160 B4
Honeysuckle Dr STLY SK15 .... 114 C5
Honeysuckle Wy WHIT OL12 ..... 22 B2
Honeywell La OLDS OL8 .... 96 A2
Honeywood Cl TOT/BURYW BL8 .. 18 B2 🔟
Honford Rd WYTH/NTH M22 .... 177 F3
Hong Kong Av MANAIR M90 ..... 191 E1
Honister Dr MDTN M24 .... 75 D1 🔟
Honister Rd BKLY M9 .... 92 A6
Honister Wy ROCH OL11 .... 38 C3 🔟
Honiton Av HYDE SK14 .... 152 A1
Honiton Cl CHAD OL9 .... 76 C2 🔟
  HEY OL10 .... 56 A1
Honiton Dr BOLE BL2 .... 49 E3
Honiton Gv RAD M26 .... 50 B5 🔟
Honiton Wy ALT WA14 .... 178 A1
Honor St BRUN/LGST M13 .... 125 F6
Hood Sq OLDE OL4 .... 81 E6
Hood St ANC M4 .... 3 H2
Hoole Cl CHD/CHDH SK8 .... 181 E2
Hooley Range HTNM SK4 .... 165 F2
Hooper St OLDE OL4 .... 79 E3 🔟
  STKP SK1 .... 166 C4 🔟
  WGTN/LGST M12 .... 125 E1
Hooton St BOLS/LL BL3 .... 46 A6
  NEWH/MOS M40 .... 107 F4
Hopcroft Cl SLFD M6 .... 103 E3 🔟
Hopedale Rd RDSH SK5 .... 147 D5
Hopefield St BOLS/LL BL3 .... 46 B5 🔟
Hopefold Dr WALK M28 .... 83 F3
Hope Hey La LHULT M38 .... 65 D6
Hopelea St DID/WITH M20 .... 143 F4 🔟
Hope Park Cl PWCH M25 .... 88 C2
Hope Park Rd PWCH M25 .... 88 C2
Hope Pl ROCH OL11 .... 39 D6 🔟
Hope Rd PWCH M25 .... 88 B3
  RUSH/FAL M14 .... 125 E5 🔟
  SALE M33 .... 159 E2 🔟
Hopes Carr STKP SK1 .... 167 D4
Hope St AUL OL6 .... 113 E2 🔟
  BRAM/HZG SK7 .... 184 B5
  BRO M7 .... 89 D6
  CMANE M1 .... 3 F4
  DTN/ASHW M34 .... 129 F4
  DUK SK16 .... 113 D6 🔟
  ECC M30 .... 102 A5 🔟
  HEY OL10 .... 57 D1
  HTNM SK4 .... 166 B4 🔟
  LHULT M38 .... 82 B1 🔟
  OLD OL1 .... 79 F4
  RAMS BL0 .... 6 C6
  ROY/SHW OL2 .... 61 F2
  SALO/ORD M5 .... 105 D6
  SWIN M27 .... 86 B5
  WHIT OL12 .... 23 D5
Hope Ter EDGY/DAV SK3 .... 166 C5 🔟
Hopkin Av OLD OL1 .... 79 F3
Hopkins Fld ALT WA14 .... 173 F6
Hopkinson Av DTN/ASHW M34 .. 129 F4
Hopkinson Rd BKLY M9 .... 74 B6

Hopkins St *HYDE* SK14 .... 131 F5 🔳
Hopkin St *OLD* OL1 .... 79 D4 🔳
Hoppet La *DROY* M43 .... 111 D5
Hopton Av *WYTH/NTH* M22 .... 178 C4
Hopwood Av *ECC* M30 .... 101 F4 🔳
  HEY OL10 .... 56 B1
Hopwood Cl *BURY* BL9 .... 53 D6 🔳
Hopwood Rd *MDTN* M24 .... 57 E5
Hopwood St *CSLFD* M3 .... 2 B1 🔳
  NEWH/MOS M40 .... 108 C1
  SWIN M27 .... 86 C5 🔳
Horace Barnes Cl
  RUSH/FAL M14 .... 124 B6 🔳
Horace Gv *HTNM* SK4 .... 166 C1
Horace St *BOL* BL1 .... 27 E5 🔳
Horatio St *GTN* M18 .... 128 A3 🔳
Horbury Av *GTN* M18 .... 127 E6
Horbury Dr *TOT/BURYW* BL8 ... 33 D5
Horeb St *BOLS/LL* BL3 .... 46 B4
Horest La *UPML* OL3 .... 63 F1
Horley Cl *TOT/BURYW* BL8 ...... 19 D6
Hornbeam Cl *HALE/TIMP* WA15 .. 176 C2 🔳
  SALE M33 .... 138 A6
Hornbeam Rd *BNG/LEV* M19 ... 145 F1
Hornby Av *BKLY* M9 .... 74 C6 🔳
Hornby Rd *STRET* M32 .... 122 A5
Hornby St *BURY* BL9 .... 34 A2
  CHH M8 .... 106 A3
  HEY OL10 .... 37 E6
  MDTN M24 .... 75 E3 🔳
  OLDS OL8 .... 78 B6 🔳
Horncastle Cl *TOT/BURYW* BL8 .. 33 E2 🔳
Horncastle Rd *NEWH/MOS* M40 .. 92 C4
Hornchurch St *HULME* M15 .... 123 F5 🔳
Horne Dr *ANC* M4 .... 7 J2
Horne St *BURY* BL9 .... 52 C1
Hornsea Cl *CHAD* OL9 .... 77 D2
  TOT/BURYW BL8 .... 32 A5
Hornsea Rd *OFTN* SK2 .... 185 E2
Horridge St *TOT/BURYW* BL8 .. 32 C3
Horrobin La *EDGW/EG* BL7 ..... 15 D3
Horrocks Fold Av *BOL* BL1 .... 27 E1
Horrocks St *RAD* M26 .... 52 A5 🔳
Horsa St *BOLE* BL2 .... 28 C6
Horsedge St *OLD* OL1 .... 79 D3
Horsefield Av *WHIT* OL12 .... 9 D5
Horsefield Cl *CCHDY* M21 ...... 142 C3 🔳
Horseshoe La *CHAD* OL9 .... 77 D5
  EDGW/EG BL7 .... 14 B5
  WILM/AE SK9 .... 209 E3
Horsfield St *BOLS/LL* BL3 .... 45 E5 🔳
Horsfield Wy *MPL/ROM* SK6 .. 149 D5
Horsham Av *BRAM/HZG* SK7 .. 184 A6 🔳
Horsham Cl *TOT/BURYW* BL8 .. 19 D6
Horsham St *SLFD* M6 .... 103 F5 🔳
Horton Av *BOL* BL1 .... 27 F1
Horton Rd *RUSH/FAL* M14 ...... 143 E1
Horton St *OFTN* SK2 .... 167 D6
Hortree Rd *STRET* M32 .... 140 C1
Horwood Crs *DID/WITH* M20 .. 144 B6
Hoscar Dr *BNG/LEV* M19 .... 144 C4
Hoskins Cl *WGTN/LGST* M12 .. 126 B4 🔳
Hospital Rd *EDGW/EG* BL7 ...... 14 B5
  SWIN M27 .... 86 C6
Hotel Rd *MANAIR* M90 .... 192 A2
Hotel St *BOL* BL1 .... 47 D2 🔳
Hothersall Rd *RDSH* SK5 .... 147 D4 🔳
Hothersall St *BRO* M7 .... 105 F4 🔳
Hough Cl *OLDS* OL8 .... 96 B3
Hough End Av *CCHDY* M21 ..... 142 A6
Houghend Crs *CCHDY* M21 ..... 142 C3 🔳
Hough Fold Wy *BOLE* BL2 .... 29 E3
Hough Gn *HALE/TIMP* WA15 .. 188 C4
Hough Hall Rd *NEWH/MOS* M40 .. 92 A5
Hough Hill Rd *STLY* SK15 .... 114 B6
Hough La *EDGW/EG* BL7 .... 14 A6
  HYDE SK14 .... 132 A4
  MDTN M24 .... 59 D4
  WILM/AE SK9 .... 204 B6
Hough St *BOLS/LL* BL3 .... 45 E4
Houghton Av *OLDS* OL8 .... 95 E3 🔳
Houghton Cl *MILN* OL16 .... 41 D1
Houghton La *SWIN* M27 .... 101 D2
Houghton Rd *CHH* M8 .... 90 B4
Houghton St *BOLS/LL* BL3 .... 46 C4
  BURY BL9 .... 53 G6
  ROY/SHW OL2 .... 78 C1 🔳
  SWIN M27 .... 103 E1 🔳
Houldsworth Av *ALT* WA14 .... 158 C6 🔳
Houldsworth St *CMANE* M1 .... 3 G3 🔳
  RAD M26 .... 51 D4 🔳
  RDSH SK5 .... 146 C4
Houseley Av *CHAD* OL9 .... 94 B2
Houson St *OLDS* OL8 .... 79 D6
Houston Pk *SALQ/ORD* M5 .... 104 A6
Hove Cl *TOT/BURYW* BL8 .... 18 A4
Hoveden St *CHH* M8 .... 106 A3 🔳
Hove Dr *RUSH/FAL* M14 .... 144 C4
Hove St *BOLS/LL* BL3 .... 46 A4 🔳
Hove St North *BOLS/LL* BL3 .... 46 A4 🔳
Hovey Cl *CHH* M8 .... 90 A6 🔳
Hovingham St *MILN* OL16 .... 23 F5
Hovis St *OP/CLY* M11 .... 127 D1
Howard Av *BOLS/LL* BL3 .... 45 E5
  CHD/CHDH SK8 .... 181 E6

  ECC M30 .... 101 E4 🔳
  FWTH BL4 .... 67 D4
  HTNM SK4 .... 146 A5
Howard Cl *MPL/ROM* SK6 ...... 169 E3
Howard Ct *AUL* OL6 .... 112 C4
Howard Dr *HALE/TIMP* WA15 .. 175 E6
Howard La *DTN/ASHW* M34 .... 130 A5
Howard Pl *MILN* OL16 .... 23 D5 🔳
Howard Rd *WYTH/NTH* M22 ... 162 B4 🔳
Howard St *AULW* OL7 .... 112 B3 🔳
  BOL BL1 .... 28 A6
  CHH M8 .... 106 A3 🔳
  DTN/ASHW M34 .... 129 F4
  OLDE OL4 .... 80 C3
  RAD M26 .... 51 F6
  ROY/SHW OL2 .... 61 E2
  SALQ/ORD M5 .... 122 B1
  STKP SK1 .... 167 D3
  STLY SK15 .... 115 E3
  STRET M32 .... 140 B1
  WHIT OL12 .... 23 D5
Howard Wy *LIT* OL15 .... 13 D2
Howarth Av *SWIN* M27 .... 85 D6 🔳
Howarth Cross St *MILN* OL16 ... 23 F3
Howarth Dr *IRL* M44 .... 135 D2 🔳
Howarth Farm Wy *WHIT* OL12 .. 24 A2 🔳
Howarth Sq *MILN* OL16 .... 23 E5
Howarth St *FWTH* BL4 .... 66 B4 🔳
  LIT OL15 .... 12 C5
  OLDTF/WHR M16 .... 123 D5
Howbridge Cl *WALK* M28 .... 83 D5 🔳
Howbro Dr *AULW* OL7 .... 111 F2
How Clough Cl *WALK* M28 .... 84 A5 🔳
How Clough Dr *WALK* M28 ...... 84 A5
Howcroft Cl *BOL* BL1 .... 46 C1 🔳
Howcroft St *BOLS/LL* BL3 .... 46 B4 🔳
Howden Cl *RDSH* SK5 .... 146 C1
Howden Rd *BKLY* M9 .... 74 A6
Howe Dr *TOT/BURYW* BL8 ...... 18 C3 🔳
Howell Cft North *BOL* BL1 .... 47 D2 🔳
Howells Av *SALE* M33 .... 139 E6
Howe St *AULW* OL7 .... 129 F1
  BRO M7 .... 89 D6
Howgill St *OP/CLY* M11 .... 109 E6
How Lea Dr *BURY* BL9 .... 34 A1
Howsin Av *BOLE* BL2 .... 28 C3
Howty Cl *WILM/AE* SK9 .... 204 B2
Hoxton Cl *MPL/ROM* SK6 ...... 169 E1 🔳
Hoy Dr *URM* M41 .... 119 C4
Hoylake Cl *NEWH/MOS* M40 ... 93 E5 🔳
Hoylake Rd *EDGY/DAV* SK3 .... 165 E5
  SALE M33 .... 161 D3
Hoyland Cl *WGTN/LGST* M12 .. 126 A3 🔳
Hoyle Av *OLDS* OL8 .... 78 C6
Hoyle's Ter *MILN* OL16 .... 41 F1 🔳
Hoyle St *RAD* M26 .... 69 F2
  WGTN/LGST M12 .... 125 D1
  WHIT OL12 .... 5 E6
Hucclecote Av *WYTH/NTH* M22 .. 178 A3 🔳
Hucklow Av *NTHM/RTH* M23 .. 177 E5
Hudcar La *BURY* BL9 .... 34 B3
Huddart Cl *SALQ/ORD* M5 ...... 122 C1 🔳
Huddersfield Rd *MILN* OL16 .... 43 D3
  OLDE OL4 .... 79 F4
  STLY SK15 .... 115 F1
Hudson Rd *BOLS/LL* BL3 .... 45 F6
  HYDE SK14 .... 150 C4
Hudson St *CHAD* OL9 .... 94 B3
Hudsons Wk *ROCH* OL11 .... 21 F6
Hudswell St *WHTF* M45 .... 70 C3
Hughes St *BOL* BL1 .... 27 D5
  OP/CLY M11 .... 125 F1 🔳
Hughley Cl *ROY/SHW* OL2 .... 61 D5 🔳
Hugh Lupus St *BOL* BL1 .... 28 B2
Hugh Oldham Dr *BRO* M7 ...... 105 D1
Hugh St *MILN* OL16 .... 23 E5 🔳
Hughtrede St *MILN* OL16 .... 40 C4 🔳
Hugo St *FWTH* BL4 .... 65 F1
  NEWH/MOS M40 .... 92 B6
  ROCH OL11 .... 39 E5
Hulbert St *MDTN* M24 .... 73 D6 🔳
  TOT/BURYW BL8 .... 33 D6 🔳
Hull Sq *CSLFD* M3 .... 105 E5 🔳
Hully St *STLY* SK15 .... 114 A5 🔳
Hulme Hall Av *CHD/CHDH* SK8 .. 195 E1
Hulme Hall Cl *CHD/CHDH* SK8 .. 181 E6 🔳
Hulme Hall Crs *CHD/CHDH* SK8 .. 195 E1
Hulme Hall Rd *CHD/CHDH* SK8 .. 181 E5
  HULME M15 .... 123 E2
Hulme Pl *SALQ/ORD* M5 .... 105 D6 🔳
Hulme Rd *BOLE* BL2 .... 29 F1
  DTN/ASHW M34 .... 128 C6
  FWTH BL4 .... 68 A5
  HTNM SK4 .... 146 B6
  RAD M26 .... 68 A4
  SALE M33 .... 160 B2
Hulmes Rd *NEWH/MOS* M40 .. 109 F2
Hulme St *AUL* OL6 .... 113 E3
  BOL BL1 .... 47 D1 🔳
  HULME M15 .... 123 F2
  OLDS OL8 .... 95 F1
  STKP SK1 .... 167 F6
  TOT/BURYW BL8 .... 33 E4
Hulme Wk *HULME* M15 .... 124 A3

Hulton Av *WALK* M28 .... 82 C2
Hulton Dr *BOLS/LL* BL3 .... 45 E6
  OLDTF/WHR M16 .... 123 F5
Hulton La *BOLS/LL* BL3 .... 45 E6
Hulton St *FAIL* M35 .... 93 E6
  SALQ/ORD M5 .... 122 B2
Humber Rd *MILN* OL16 .... 42 B1
Humberstone Av *HULME* M15 .. 124 A3 🔳
Humber St *CHH* M8 .... 90 C6 🔳
  SALQ/ORD M5 .... 103 E6
Hume St *BNG/LEV* M19 .... 145 F3 🔳
  MILN OL16 .... 40 B2 🔳🔳
Humphrey Crs *URM* M41 .... 139 E1 🔳
Humphrey La *URM* M41 .... 139 E1
Humphrey Pk *URM* M41 .... 139 E2
Humphrey Rd *OLDTF/WHR* M16 .. 122 C4
Humphrey St *CHH* M8 .... 90 A5 🔳
Huncoat Av *HTNM* SK4 .... 146 B5
Huncote Dr *BKLY* M9 .... 91 F4 🔳
Hunmanby Av *HULME* M15 .... 124 A3 🔳
Hunstanton Dr *TOT/BURYW* BL8 .. 33 E2
Hunston Rd *SALE* M33 .... 159 D2
Hunt Av *AULW* OL7 .... 112 C2
Hunter Dr *RAD* M26 .... 51 E4
Hunters Cl *WILM/AE* SK9 ...... 205 D2 🔳
Hunters Ct *STLY* SK15 .... 133 E1
Hunters Gn *TOT/BURYW* BL8 .. 18 A2 🔳
Hunter's La *MILN* OL16 .... 23 D5 🔳
  OLD OL1 .... 79 D5 🔳
Hunters Ms *SALE* M33 .... 139 E6 🔳
  WILM/AE SK9 .... 204 A4
Hunterston Av *ECC* M30 .... 102 B6 🔳
Hunt Fold Dr *TOT/BURYW* BL8 .. 18 A4
Huntingdon Av *CHAD* OL9 .... 77 F6 🔳
Huntingdon Crs *RDSH* SK5 .... 148 A6 🔳
Hunt La *CHAD* OL9 .... 77 D3
Huntley Mount Rd *BURY* BL9 .. 34 C2 🔳
Huntley Rd *CHH* M8 .... 89 F3
  EDGY/DAV SK3 .... 165 F6
Huntley St *BURY* BL9 .... 34 C4 🔳🔳
Huntly Cha *WILM/AE* SK9 ...... 204 A5
Hunt Rd *HYDE* SK14 .... 132 B4
Huntroyde Av *BOLE* BL2 .... 29 D6 🔳
Huntsham Cl *ALT* WA14 .... 173 F1 🔳
Huntsman Dr *IRL* M44 .... 135 D4
Hunts Rd *SLFD* M6 .... 103 E2 🔳
Hunt St *BKLY* M9 .... 91 E4
Hurdlow Av *BRO* M7 .... 88 B6
Hurdsfield Rd *OFTN* SK2 .... 184 A3
Hurford Av *GTN* M18 .... 127 E3 🔳
Hurlbote Cl *WILM/AE* SK9 ..... 194 B4 🔳
Hurley Dr *CHD/CHDH* SK8 .... 180 C5 🔳
Hurlston Rd *BOLS/LL* BL3 .... 64 B1 🔳
Hurst Av *CHD/CHDH* SK8 ...... 196 A3
  SALE M33 .... 158 A2
Hurstbank Av *BNG/LEV* M19 .. 164 B1 🔳
Hurst Bank Rd *AUL* OL6 .... 113 F3
Hurstbourne Av *OP/CLY* M11 .. 108 C5 🔳
Hurstbrook Dr *URM* M41 .... 120 A6 🔳
Hurstead Gn *WHIT* OL12 .... 24 B1 🔳
Hurstead Rd *MILN* OL16 .... 42 A1
Hurstfield Rd *WALK* M28 .... 82 C5
Hurstfold Av *BNG/LEV* M19 ... 164 B2 🔳
Hurst Green Cl *RAD* M26 .... 51 D1
Hurst Gv *AUL* OL6 .... 113 F2
Hurst Hall Dr *AUL* OL6 .... 113 E2
Hursthead Rd *CHD/CHDH* SK8 .. 195 F2 🔳
Hurst Meadow *MILN* OL16 ..... 40 C5
Hurst St *BOLS/LL* BL3 .... 46 A6
  BURY BL9 .... 34 B6
  CHAD OL9 .... 78 B4 🔳
  DUK SK16 .... 130 B3
  RDSH SK5 .... 146 C4
  ROCH OL11 .... 40 B2
  WALK M28 .... 66 C5
Hurstvale Av *CHD/CHDH* SK8 .. 179 F6 🔳
Hurstville Rd *CCHDY* M21 ...... 141 F5
Hurstway Dr *BKLY* M9 .... 91 F2 🔳
Hurstwood *BOL* BL1 .... 27 F2
Hurstwood Ct *BOLS/LL* BL3 ..... 47 F5
Hurstwood Rd *OFTN* SK2 ...... 185 D1 🔳
Hus St *DROY* M43 .... 128 A1
Hutchins La *OLDE* OL4 .... 80 B2
Hutchinson Rd *ROCH* OL11 ..... 20 B4
Hutchinson St *ROCH* OL11 ...... 38 C1 🔳
Hutchinson Wy *RAD* M26 .... 51 E6 🔳
Hutton Av *AUL* OL6 .... 113 F5
Huxley Av *CHH* M8 .... 106 B1 🔳
Huxley Cl *BRAM/HZG* SK7 ..... 196 C2
Huxley Dr *BRAM/HZG* SK7 .... 196 C2
Huxley St *ALT* WA14 .... 158 B6
  BOL BL1 .... 27 D5
  OLDE OL4 .... 80 A6
Huxton Gn *BRAM/HZG* SK7 ... 183 E5
Hyacinth Cl *EDGY/DAV* SK3 ... 182 B2 🔳
Hyde Dr *WALK* M28 .... 83 D3
Hyde Fold Cl *BNG/LEV* M19 ... 145 D5
Hyde Gv *BRUN/LGST* M13 ..... 125 D4
  SALE M33 .... 159 F1
  WALK M28 .... 83 D3
Hyde Pl *BRUN/LGST* M13 ...... 125 D4
Hyde Rd *DTN/ASHW* M34 ...... 130 A6
  GTN M18 .... 128 A5
  MDTN M24 .... 76 C5

MPL/ROM SK6 .... **149** F6
WALK M28 .... **83** D3
WGTN/LGST M12 .... **125** E3
Hyde Sq *MDTN* M24 .... **74** C3
Hyde St *BOLS/LL* BL3 .... **46** A6 🔢
DROY M43 .... **111** D3
DUK SK16 .... **131** E1 🔢
Hydrangea Cl *SALE* M33 .... **138** A6 🔢
Hyldavale Av *CHD/CHDH* SK8 ...... **179** F1
Hylton Dr *CHD/CHDH* SK8 .... **196** A1
Hythe Cl *RUSH/FAL* M14 .... **125** D6 🔢
Hythe Rd *EDGY/DAV* SK3 .... **165** F5
Hythe St *BOLS/LL* BL3 .... **45** E5 🔢

I

Ice House Cl *WALK* M28 .... **82** A2 🔢
Iceland St *SLFD* M6 .... **104** A5 🔢
Idonia St *BOL* BL1 .... **27** E4
Ilex Gv *BRO* M7 .... **105** E1 🔢
Ilford St *OP/CLY* M11 .... **108** C5
Ilfracombe Rd *OFTN* SK2 .... **168** B5
Ilfracombe St *NEWH/MOS* M40 ... **109** E1 🔢
Ilkley Cl *CHAD* OL9 .... **77** F5
Ilkley Crs *RDSH* SK5 .... **146** C3
Ilkley Dr *URM* M41 .... **118** F3
Ilkley St *NEWH/MOS* M40 .... **92** B4
Ilk St *OP/CLY* M11 .... **108** C5
Illingworth Av *STLY* SK15 .... **115** D6
Illona Dr *BRO* M7 .... **88** B5
Ina Av *BOL* BL1 .... **26** A6
Ince Cl *DID/WITH* M20 .... **143** F4 🔢
HTNM SK4 .... **166** C2
Ince St *HTNM* SK4 .... **166** C2 🔢
Inchcape Dr *BKLY* M9 .... **90** C1 🔢
Inchfield Cl *ROCH* OL11 .... **20** C4 🔢
Inchfield Rd *NEWH/MOS* M40 .... **92** B4
Inchley Rd *BRUN/LGST* M13 .... **124** C2 🔢
Inchwood Ms *OLDE* OL4 .... **62** C5 🔢
Incline Cl *OLDS* OL8 .... **94** C3
Independent St *BOLS/LL* BL3 .... **49** E6
Indigo St *SLFD* M6 .... **104** A2
Industrial St *RAMS* BL0 .... **7** D2 🔢
Industry Rd *WHIT* OL12 .... **23** D4 🔢
Industry St *CHAD* OL9 .... **94** B1
LIT OL15 .... **12** C6
ROCH OL11 .... **20** C4 🔢
WHIT OL12 .... **9** E1 🔢
Infant St *PWCH* M25 .... **89** D1 🔢
Ingham Rd *ALT* WA14 .... **158** B5
Inghams La *LIT* OL15 .... **12** C6
Ingham St *BURY* BL9 .... **5** H5 🔢
NEWH/MOS M40 .... **109** F3 🔢
Inghamwood Cl *BRO* M7 .... **90** A6 🔢
Ingleby Av *BKLY* M9 .... **92** A1 🔢
Ingleby Cl *ROY/SHW* OL2 .... **61** E1 🔢
Ingleby Wy *ROY/SHW* OL2 .... **61** E1 🔢
Ingledene Av *BRO* M7 .... **89** F4 🔢
Ingledene Gv *BOL* BL1 .... **26** B5 🔢
Ingle Dr *OFTN* SK2 .... **168** A6
Inglefield *ROCH* OL11 .... **20** C4
Inglehead Cl *DTN/ASHW* M34 ..... **149** E1 🔢
Ingle Rd *CHD/CHDH* SK8 .... **181** E1
Ingles Fold *WALK* M28 .... **82** C6 🔢
Inglesham Cl *NTHM/RTH* M23 ...... **177** F1
Ingleton Av *CHH* M8 .... **90** C3
Ingleton Cl *BOLE* BL2 .... **29** E3
CHD/CHDH SK8 .... **180** A1 🔢
ROY/SHW OL2 .... **60** B3 🔢
Ingleton Ms *TOT/BURYW* BL8 ..... **32** C3 🔢
Ingleton Rd *EDGY/DAV* SK3 .... **166** A6
Inglewhite Cl *BURY* BL9 .... **52** B2
Inglewood Cl *AULW* OL7 .... **112** A2 🔢
BURY BL9 .... **35** D3
Inglewood Hollow *STLY* SK15 ..... **133** D1 🔢
Inglewood Rd *CHAD* OL9 .... **76** B2 🔢
Inglis St *LIT* OL15 .... **12** C5
Ingoe Cl *HEY* OL10 .... **38** A4 🔢
Ingoldsby Av *BRUN/LGST* M13 .... **125** E5 🔢
Ingram St *HTNM* SK4 .... **164** C2
Ings Av *WHIT* OL12 .... **21** F3
Ings La *WHIT* OL12 .... **21** F3
Inkerman St *HYDE* SK14 .... **131** E5 🔢
WHIT OL12 .... **23** D4 🔢
Ink St *MILN* OL16 .... **23** D6 🔢
Inman St *BURY* BL9 .... **52** C1
DTN/ASHW M34 .... **130** A6 🔢
Innes Av *WGTN/LGST* M12 .... **126** C6
Innis Av *NEWH/MOS* M40 .... **109** D2
Instow Cl *BRUN/LGST* M13 .... **125** E4 🔢
CHAD OL9 .... **77** D2 🔢
International Ap *MANAIR* M90 ...... **192** A2 🔢
Invar Rd *WALK* M28 .... **85** E4
Inverbeg Dr *BOLE* BL2 .... **49** E2 🔢
Inverlael Av *BOL* BL1 .... **45** F1
Inverness Av *BKLY* M9 .... **92** B1 🔢
Inverness Rd *DUK* SK16 .... **131** D2
Iona Pl *BOLE* BL2 .... **29** D5
Iona Wy *URM* M41 .... **119** E4
Ionian Gdns *BRO* M7 .... **105** D2 🔢
Ipswich St *ROCH* OL11 .... **40** A2 🔢
Iqbal Cl *WGTN/LGST* M12 .... **126** B4

Ireby Cl *MDTN* M24 .... **74** A1
Iredine St *OP/CLY* M11 .... **109** D6 🔢
Irene Av *HYDE* SK14 .... **131** F5
Iris Av *FWTH* BL4 .... **65** C2
FWTH BL4 .... **67** D6
Iris St *OLDS* OL8 .... **96** A3
RAMS BL0 .... **6** C5
Irkdale St *CHH* M8 .... **107** D1
Irk Vale Dr *CHAD* OL9 .... **76** C2
Irlam Av *ECC* M30 .... **101** E6
Irlam Rd *SALE* M33 .... **140** A6
URM M41 .... **135** F2
Irlam Sq *SLFD* M6 .... **103** E2
Irlam St *BOL* BL1 .... **27** F4 🔢
Irlam Wharf Rd *IRL* M44 .... **135** E5
Irma St *BOL* BL1 .... **28** A4
Ironmonger La *OLD* OL1 .... **79** D5 🔢
Iron St *DTN/ASHW* M34 .... **130** A6 🔢
NEWH/MOS M40 .... **107** F4
Irvin Dr *WYTH/NTH* M22 .... **193** E1
Irving Cl *OFTN* SK2 .... **183** E4
Irving St *BOL* BL1 .... **27** F5 🔢
OLDS OL8 .... **94** C3 🔢
Irvin St *NEWH/MOS* M40 .... **109** D1
Irwell Av *ECC* M30 .... **102** A6
LHULT M38 .... **82** C1
Irwell Gv *ECC* M30 .... **102** A6 🔢
SALO/ORD M5 .... **105** D5
Irwell Pl *ECC* M30 .... **102** A6 🔢
SALO/ORD M5 .... **105** D5
Irwell St *BURY* BL9 .... **33** F5
CHH M8 .... **105** F3
RAD M26 .... **67** E4
RAD M26 .... **69** F1
RAMS BL0 .... **7** D5
SLFD M6 .... **104** B1
Irwell Valley Wy *RAMS* BL0 .... **19** D1
Irwin Dr *WILM/AE* SK9 .... **194** A4
Irwin Rd *ALT* WA14 .... **158** A5
Irwin St *DTN/ASHW* M34 .... **129** F6 🔢
Isaac Cl *SALO/ORD* M5 .... **122** B1 🔢
Isaac St *BOL* BL1 .... **46** A1 🔢
Isabella Cl *OLDTF/WHR* M16 .... **123** D5 🔢
Isabella St *WHIT* OL12 .... **23** D3 🔢
Isaiah St *OLDS* OL8 .... **96** A1 🔢
Isa St *RAMS* BL0 .... **18** B1 🔢
Isca St *OP/CLY* M11 .... **108** A6 🔢
Isherwood Dr *MPL/ROM* SK6 .... **186** B1
Isherwood Rd *PART* M31 .... **137** D5
Isherwood St *HEY* OL10 .... **37** F5
ROCH OL11 .... **40** B2
Isis Cl *BRO* M7 .... **88** B5
Islington Rd *OFTN* SK2 .... **184** A3
Islington St *CSLFD* M3 .... **105** E5 🔢
Islington Wy *CSLFD* M3 .... **105** E6 🔢
Isobel Cl *ECC* M30 .... **100** C2 🔢
Ivanhoe Ct *BOLS/LL* BL3 .... **66** A1 🔢
Ivanhoe St *BOLS/LL* BL3 .... **48** A6
OLD OL1 .... **80** A2 🔢
Ivor St *ROCH* OL11 .... **38** C4
Ivy Bank Rd *BOL* BL1 .... **27** F1
Ivybridge Cl *BRUN/LGST* M13 .... **125** E4
Ivy Cl *DROY* M43 .... **110** A4
ROY/SHW OL2 .... **61** F2
Ivy Dr *MDTN* M24 .... **75** D5
Ivy Gv *FWTH* BL4 .... **65** F3 🔢
FWTH BL4 .... **67** D4 🔢
LHULT M38 .... **82** A1
Ivyleaf Sq *BRO* M7 .... **105** F1 🔢
Ivylea Rd *BNG/LEV* M19 .... **164** C1
Ivy Rd *BOL* BL1 .... **27** D6
POY/DIS SK12 .... **198** C6
TOT/BURYW BL8 .... **32** C5
Ivy St *BOLS/LL* BL3 .... **46** A5 🔢
ECC M30 .... **101** E6 🔢
NEWH/MOS M40 .... **92** B5

J

Jack Brady Cl *NTHM/RTH* M23 ..... **176** D3 🔢
Jackdaw Rd *TOT/BURYW* BL8 ...... **18** A3 🔢
Jack La *DROY* M43 .... **110** C5
URM M41 .... **138** C1
Jackman Av *HEY* OL10 .... **56** B2
Jackroom Dr *ANC* M4 .... **107** D6 🔢
Jackson Av *DUK* SK16 .... **131** E1 🔢
Jackson Cl *OLDS* OL8 .... **78** C6 🔢
Jackson Ct *URM* M41 .... **118** D6
Jackson Crs *HULME* M15 .... **123** F3
Jackson Gdns *DTN/ASHW* M34 ... **148** B1
Jacksons Edge Rd *POY/DIS* SK12 .. **201** E2
Jackson's La *BRAM/HZG* SK7 ...... **197** F1
Jackson's Rw *CSLFD* M3 .... **2** C4
Jackson St *CHD/CHDH* SK8 .... **180** C1
FAIL M35 .... **109** E1
FWTH BL4 .... **66** B3
FWTH BL4 .... **67** D4 🔢
HYDE SK14 .... **150** B1 🔢
MDTN M24 .... **75** F3 🔢
MILN OL16 .... **40** C1
OLDE OL4 .... **79** F4
OLDE OL4 .... **81** D5 🔢

RAD M26 .... **69** F1
SALE M33 .... **140** B6 🔢
STRET M32 .... **140** A2
WALK M28 .... **83** D1
WHIT OL12 .... **11** D5 🔢
WHTF M45 .... **71** D4
Jack St *BOLE* BL2 .... **29** D6 🔢
Jacobsen Av *HYDE* SK14 .... **132** A5
James Andrew St *MDTN* M24 ...... **75** F2 🔢
James Butterworth St *MILN* OL16 .. **23** F6
James Cl *DUK* SK16 .... **131** F1
James Corbett Rd *SALO/ORD* M5 .. **103** D6
James Henry Av *SALO/ORD* M5 .... **122** C1 🔢
James Hill St *LIT* OL15 .... **12** C6 🔢
Jameson St *ROCH* OL11 .... **38** C5 🔢
James Rd *ROY/SHW* OL2 .... **61** F1
James's St *OLDE* OL4 .... **80** B2
James St *BOLS/LL* BL3 .... **49** F6
BURY BL9 .... **34** B6
DROY M43 .... **110** C5
DTN/ASHW M34 .... **130** B2 🔢
DUK SK16 .... **131** F1 🔢
EDGY/DAV SK3 .... **166** C6
FAIL M35 .... **94** B5
FWTH BL4 .... **67** D3
HEY OL10 .... **37** E5 🔢
LIT OL15 .... **12** A6
MPL/ROM SK6 .... **149** E6
NEWH/MOS M40 .... **107** E4
PWCH M25 .... **71** E6 🔢
RAD M26 .... **69** E2
ROY/SHW OL2 .... **61** E4 🔢
SALE M33 .... **160** B1
SALO/ORD M5 .... **105** E6
WHIT OL12 .... **9** E1 🔢
WHIT OL12 .... **9** E1 🔢
WHIT OL12 .... **23** E5 🔢
James St South *CHAD* OL9 .... **77** F4 🔢
Jammy La *CHAD* OL9 .... **78** A5
Jane St *CHAD* OL9 .... **77** F5
WHIT OL12 .... **5** F3
WHIT OL12 .... **22** C5 🔢
Japan St *BRO* M7 .... **90** A6
Jarvis St *OLDE* OL4 .... **79** E5 🔢
WHIT OL12 .... **23** D4
Jasmine Av *DROY* M43 .... **111** D3 🔢
Jasmine Cl *NTHM/RTH* M23 .... **160** C4 🔢
Jason St *ANC* M4 .... **106** C4 🔢
Jauncey St *BOLS/LL* BL3 .... **46** A4 🔢
Jayton Av *DID/WITH* M20 .... **163** F5
Jean Cl *BNG/LEV* M19 .... **145** E1 🔢
Jedburgh Av *BOL* BL1 .... **45** F1
Jefferson Wy *WHIT* OL12 .... **23** D2
Jeffreys Dr *DUK* SK16 .... **131** E1
Jehlum Cl *CHH* M8 .... **90** C6
Jellicoe Av *IRL* M44 .... **134** C5 🔢
Jenner Cl *HULME* M15 .... **123** F3 🔢
Jennings Av *SALO/ORD* M5 .... **122** B1 🔢
Jennings Cl *HYDE* SK14 .... **132** C4
Jennings St *EDGY/DAV* SK3 .... **166** B6
Jennison Cl *WGTN/LGST* M12 ...... **126** C3
Jenny La *BRAM/HZG* SK7 .... **196** C6
Jenny St *OLDS* OL8 .... **95** D3
Jepheys Pl *WHIT* OL12 .... **23** D4 🔢
Jepheys St *WHIT* OL12 .... **23** D4
Jepson St *OFTN* SK2 .... **183** E1
Jericho Rd *BURY* BL9 .... **35** F4
Jermyn St *WHIT* OL12 .... **22** C5
Jerrold St *LIT* OL15 .... **12** C6 🔢
Jersey Rd *RDSH* SK5 .... **167** D1
Jersey St *ANC* M4 .... **3** H2
AUL OL6 .... **112** C3
Jerusalem Pl *CMANW* M2 .... **2** C5 🔢
Jesmond Av *PWCH* M25 .... **88** C3 🔢
Jesmond Dr *TOT/BURYW* BL8 ..... **33** D2
Jesmond Gv *CHD/CHDH* SK8 .... **195** F1 🔢
Jesmond Rd *BOL* BL1 .... **26** C3
Jespersen St *OLD* OL1 .... **79** D4
Jessamine Av *BRO* M7 .... **105** E3 🔢
Jessel Cl *BRUN/LGST* M13 .... **125** D3 🔢
Jessie St *BOLS/LL* BL3 .... **46** A2 🔢
NEWH/MOS M40 .... **108** B1 🔢
Jessop Dr *MPL/ROM* SK6 .... **171** D5
Jessop St *GTN* M18 .... **127** E4
Jethro St *BOLE* BL2 .... **29** D3 🔢
BOLE BL2 .... **48** A1
Jetson St *GTN* M18 .... **128** A3
Jinnah Cl *OP/CLY* M11 .... **127** D1
Joan St *NEWH/MOS* M40 .... **92** B6 🔢
Jobling St *OP/CLY* M11 .... **126** A1
Jocelyn St *NEWH/MOS* M40 .... **107** F1
Joddrell St *CSLFD* M3 .... **2** B4 🔢
Joel La *HYDE* SK14 .... **151** D4
Johannesburg Gdns
NTHM/RTH M23 .... **177** D3 🔢
John Ashworth St *WHIT* OL12 ..... **23** F4 🔢
John Atkinson Ct *SALO/ORD* M5 .. **103** E6 🔢
John Av *CHD/CHDH* SK8 .... **180** C2
John Beeley Av *OP/CLY* M11 .... **127** E1 🔢
John Booth St *OLDE* OL4 .... **81** D6 🔢
John Brown St *BOL* BL1 .... **46** C1 🔢
John Clynes Av
NEWH/MOS M40 .... **107** D4 🔢
John Cross St *BOLS/LL* BL3 .... **46** C5

John Dalton St CSLFD M3 ...... 2 C3
John Foran Cl NEWH/MOS M40 .... 108 C1 [8]
John Gilbert Wy TRPK M17 ...... 121 F3
John Heywood St OP/CLY M11.... 108 C5
John Knott Fold OLDE OL4 ...... 81 D5
John Lee Fold MDTN M24 ...... 75 E2
John Nash Crs HULME M15 ...... 123 F3
Johnny King Cl
  NEWH/MOS M40 ...... 107 E2 [10]
John Roberts Cl ROCH OL11 .... 39 F2 [11]
Johns Cl CCHDY M21 ...... 141 F3 [7]
John Shepley St HYDE SK14 .... 150 C1 [8]
Johnson Av OLD OL1 ...... 62 C3
Johnsonbrook Rd HYDE SK14.... 131 E4
Johnson Gv MDTN M24 ...... 74 C2
Johnson's Sq NEWH/MOS M40 .... 107 E3 [7]
Johnson St BOL BL1 ...... 47 D3
  CSLFD M3 ...... 2 B2 [8]
  RAD M26 ...... 69 F1
  SLFD M6 ...... 103 E1 [8]
John's Pl MPL/ROM SK6 ...... 170 A3 [8]
John Steet MPL/ROM SK6 ...... 170 A3 [8]
Johnston Av LIT OL15 ...... 25 D2 [8]
John St ALT WA14 ...... 178 B3 [2]
  ANC M4 ...... 3 F2
  BOLS/LL BL3 ...... 49 F6 [8]
  BRAM/HZG SK7 ...... 184 B4 [11]
  BRO M7 ...... 105 E3 [10]
  BURY BL9 ...... 34 A4 [3]
  CHAD OL9 ...... 78 C5
  CSLFD M3 ...... 2 B1
  DROY M43 ...... 128 A1
  DTN/ASHW M34 ...... 130 A6 [3]
  ECC M30 ...... 100 C6 [3]
  EDGW/EG BL7 ...... 14 B6
  FAIL M35 ...... 94 A4
  FWTH BL4 ...... 66 C3 [3]
  HEY OL10 ...... 37 E5
  HYDE SK14 ...... 131 E6 [8]
  IRL M44 ...... 134 C6
  LIT OL15 ...... 12 B6
  MILN OL16 ...... 24 A2
  MPL/ROM SK6 ...... 169 E1 [4]
  MPL/ROM SK6 ...... 171 F3
  MPL/ROM SK6 ...... 187 E2 [8]
  PWCH M25 ...... 72 C3
  ROY/SHW OL2 ...... 60 B5
  ROY/SHW OL2 ...... 61 E4 [8]
  SALE M33 ...... 139 F6
  STKP SK1 ...... 167 D5 [8]
  STLY SK15 ...... 115 D2 [8]
  SWIN M27 ...... 86 B5
  WALK M28 ...... 83 E1
  WHIT OL12 ...... 9 E1 [3]
John St East AULW OL7 ...... 112 A6 [8]
  AULW OL7 ...... 112 B6 [8]
John St West AULW OL7 ...... 130 A1
John William St ECC M30 ...... 102 A5
  OP/CLY M11 ...... 109 D6 [3]
Joiner St ANC M4 ...... 3 F3
  SALQ/ORD M5 ...... 105 D6 [2]
Join Rd SALE M33 ...... 160 B1 [8]
Jolly Brows BOLE BL2 ...... 29 E4 [2]
Jonas St BKLY M9 ...... 91 F5 [3]
Jones Sq STKP SK1 ...... 167 D6
Jones St MILN OL16 ...... 40 B1
  OLD OL1 ...... 79 E3
  RAD M26 ...... 51 F5 [3]
  ROY/SHW OL2 ...... 78 B1
  SLFD M6 ...... 104 A4
Jonquil Dr LHULT M38 ...... 82 A3
Jopson St MDTN M24 ...... 75 F2
Jordan Av ROY/SHW OL2 ...... 43 D6 [3]
Jordan St HULME M15 ...... 123 F2
Josephine Dr SWIN M27 ...... 86 B6 [3]
Joseph Johnson Ms
  WYTH/NTH M22 ...... 162 C4 [8]
Joseph St ECC M30 ...... 100 C6 [3]
  FAIL M35 ...... 94 A5 [8]
  FWTH BL4 ...... 66 B2 [8]
  LIT OL15 ...... 12 C5
  MDTN M24 ...... 75 D2
  MPL/ROM SK6 ...... 187 E1 [8]
  RAD M26 ...... 69 F1 [8]
  WHIT OL12 ...... 22 B3 [8]
Joshua La MDTN M24 ...... 76 B4
Josslyn Rd SALQ/ORD M5.... 103 E4
Jo St SALQ/ORD M5 ...... 104 B6 [8]
Joules Ct STKP SK1 ...... 167 D4
Joule St BKLY M9 ...... 91 F4
Jowett St OLD OL1 ...... 80 A2
  RDSH SK5 ...... 167 D1
Jowett's Wk AULW OL7 ...... 112 A5
Jowkin La ROCH OL11 ...... 20 B6
Joyce St NEWH/MOS M40 ...... 92 C5
Joynson Av BRO M7 ...... 105 E3 [11]
Joynson St SALE M33 ...... 139 F6
Joy St RAMS BL0 ...... 6 C5
  WHIT OL12 ...... 23 D5
Jubilee Av DUK SK16 ...... 113 F6
  RAD M26 ...... 70 A2
Jubilee Rd MDTN M24 ...... 75 F2
Jubilee St ROY/SHW OL2 ...... 62 A2
  SLFD M6 ...... 104 A5
Jubilee Ter MDTN M24 ...... 75 F1

Jubilee Wy BURY BL9 ...... 33 F5
Judith St WHIT OL12 ...... 22 A2
Judson Av CCHDY M21 ...... 142 A6
Judy St NEWH/MOS M40 ...... 92 A5 [3]
Julia St CSLFD M3 ...... 106 A4
  WHIT OL12 ...... 22 C5
Julius St BNG/LEV M19 ...... 145 F3
Junction Aly MILN OL16 ...... 23 D6 [11]
Junction Dr BOLS/LL BL3 ...... 45 D4
  HYDE SK14 ...... 131 D4
  OFTN SK2 ...... 167 D6
Junction Rd West HOR/BR BL6.... 44 A4
Junction St MDTN M24 ...... 76 B5
  OLDS OL8 ...... 95 F1 [8]
June Av HTNM SK4 ...... 165 F3 [8]
June St AULW OL7 ...... 112 B5
Juniper Bank RDSH SK5 ...... 147 E3
Juniper Cl OLDE OL4 ...... 63 D5
  SALE M33 ...... 139 D5
Juniper Dr MILN OL16 ...... 41 E1
Juno St OLD OL1 ...... 79 E2
Jura Cl DUK SK16 ...... 131 E1 [8]
Jura Dr URM M41 ...... 119 F4
Jura Gv HEY OL10 ...... 36 C6
Jurby Av BKLY M9 ...... 91 D1
Jury St CHH M8 ...... 106 A3
Justin Cl BRUN/LGST M13 ...... 124 C2 [11]
Jutland St CMANE M1 ...... 3 H4

K

Kale St BRUN/LGST M13 ...... 124 C2
Kalima Gv BRO M7 ...... 105 E1 [3]
Kansas Av SALQ/ORD M5 ...... 121 F1
Kara St SLFD M6 ...... 103 F5
Kate St RAMS BL0 ...... 6 C5 [3]
Kathan Cl MILN OL16 ...... 23 F6
Katherine Rd OFTN SK2 ...... 184 A3 [2]
Katherine St AUL OL6 ...... 112 C4
  AULW OL7 ...... 112 A5
Kathkin Av CHH M8 ...... 90 C3
Kathleen Gv RUSH/FAL M14.... 144 A3 [3]
Kathleen St WHIT OL12 ...... 22 B5
Kay Av MPL/ROM SK6 ...... 188 B2 [8]
Kay Brow HEY OL10 ...... 37 D5
  RAMS BL0 ...... 7 D5
Kayfields BOLE BL2 ...... 29 F3 [8]
Kay's Av STKP SK1 ...... 167 F4 [8]
Kays Gdns CSLFD M3 ...... 105 E5 [14]
Kay St BOL BL1 ...... 28 A6
  BOLS/LL BL3 ...... 49 E6 [8]
  BURY BL9 ...... 19 D2 [3]
  BURY BL9 ...... 34 B4 [3]
  EDGW/EG BL7 ...... 15 D1
  HEY OL10 ...... 37 E5 [13]
  OP/CLY M11 ...... 126 A2 [3]
  ROCH OL11 ...... 39 F2 [3]
  SLFD M6 ...... 104 A1 [8]
  STLY SK15 ...... 114 B6 [8]
Kays Gdns MPL/ROM SK6 ...... 186 B1 [8]
Keadby Cl ECC M30 ...... 119 E1 [4]
Keal Dr IRL M44 ...... 116 B5
Kearsley Dr BOLS/LL BL3 ...... 47 F6
Kearsley Hall Rd RAD M26 ...... 68 A4
Kearsley Rd CHH M8 ...... 90 B3
  RAD M26 ...... 68 A3
Kearsley St ECC M30 ...... 100 C5 [7]
Kearsley V RAD M26 ...... 67 F3 [3]
Kearton Dr ECC M30 ...... 102 B6
Keary Cl GTN M18 ...... 127 E3
Keaton Cl SLFD M6 ...... 103 F3 [8]
Keats Av DROY M43 ...... 110 B6 [3]
  DTN/ASHW M34 ...... 149 F3 [3]
  WHIT OL12 ...... 21 E4
Keats Crs RAD M26 ...... 50 C5
Keats Fold DUK SK16 ...... 132 C2 [8]
Keats Rd ECC M30 ...... 101 E6
  OLD OL1 ...... 79 F2 [3]
  TOT/BURYW BL8 ...... 18 A3
Keb La OLDS OL8 ...... 96 B5
Keble Av OLDS OL8 ...... 95 F2
Kedleston Av RUSH/FAL M14.... 125 F5 [10]
Kedleston Gn OFTN SK2 ...... 168 B6
Keele Wk NEWH/MOS M40 ...... 107 D4 [8]
Keepers Dr WHIT OL12 ...... 20 C3 [8]
Keighley Av DROY M43 ...... 110 B4 [8]
Keighley Cl TOT/BURYW BL8 .... 32 A5 [8]
Keighley St BOL BL1 ...... 27 D5
Keilder Ms BOL BL1 ...... 45 E1
Keith Dr EDGY/DAV SK3 ...... 165 F6
Kelboro Av DTN/ASHW M34 .... 129 E2
Kelbrook Ct OFTN SK2 ...... 184 C2
Kelbrook Rd OP/CLY M11 ...... 126 C1
Kelby Av NTHM/RTH M23 ...... 161 F6
Keld Cl TOT/BURYW BL8 ...... 32 C2
Kelfield Av NTHM/RTH M23 .... 161 E3
Kellbank Rd BRO M7 ...... 88 B5 [2]
Kellbrook Crs BRO M7 ...... 88 B5 [2]
Kellett Cl EDGW/EG BL7 ...... 28 A1 [3]
  MILN OL16 ...... 23 F5
Kelmarsh Cl OP/CLY M11 ...... 127 E2 [4]
Kelsall Crs EDGY/DAV SK3 ...... 182 B1 [1]
Kelsall Dr DROY M43 ...... 110 A4

HALE/TIMP WA15 ...... 176 A1
Kelsall Rd CHD/CHDH SK8 ...... 181 E2 [2]
Kelsall St CHAD OL9 ...... 78 B5
  MILN OL16 ...... 23 D5
  SALE M33 ...... 159 E1
  WGTN/LGST M12 ...... 126 A3 [8]
Kelso Cl OLDS OL8 ...... 96 A4
Kelson Av AULW OL7 ...... 112 B2
Kelstern Av BRUN/LGST M13.... 125 F6 [8]
Kelstern Sq BRUN/LGST M13.... 125 F6
Kelverlow St OLDE OL4 ...... 80 A4
Kelvin Av MDTN M24 ...... 73 F4
  SALE M33 ...... 159 F1 [8]
Kelvin Gv CHH M8 ...... 106 B1
Kelvington Dr BKLY M9 ...... 107 E1
Kelvin St ANC M4 ...... 3 F2
  AULW OL7 ...... 130 A1
Kemble Av NTHM/RTH M23 .... 162 A4 [8]
Kemmel Av WYTH/NTH M22 .... 178 C2 [8]
Kempnough Hall Rd WALK M28 .... 83 F6
Kempsey Ct CHAD OL9 ...... 77 E4
Kempsey St CHAD OL9 ...... 77 F4 [8]
Kempsford Cl NTHM/RTH M23 .... 177 F1
Kempster St BRO M7 ...... 105 E3
Kemp St HYDE SK14 ...... 131 F5 [8]
  MDTN M24 ...... 75 D3
Kempton Av BOLS/LL BL3 ...... 67 E1 [8]
  SALE M33 ...... 158 B2 [8]
Kempton Cl BRAM/HZG SK7 .... 185 E5
  DROY M43 ...... 111 D5 [8]
Kempton Wy CHAD OL9 ...... 78 A4 [8]
Kenchester Av OP/CLY M11 .... 127 E1 [8]
Kendal Av AULW OL7 ...... 112 A3
  DTN/ASHW M34 ...... 149 E2
  HYDE SK14 ...... 131 D4 [8]
  SALE M33 ...... 160 A2
  URM M41 ...... 117 F5
  WHIT OL12 ...... 20 C3
Kendal Cl HALE/TIMP WA15 .... 176 B2
  HEY OL10 ...... 56 C1
Kendal Dr BRAM/HZG SK7 ...... 196 A4
  BURY BL9 ...... 52 B2
  CHD/CHDH SK8 ...... 180 A3
  ROY/SHW OL2 ...... 62 B2
Kendal Gdns MPL/ROM SK6 .... 169 F1 [8]
Kendal Gv WALK M28 ...... 84 A3 [8]
  WHTF M45 ...... 71 D3 [8]
Kendall Rd CHH M8 ...... 90 A2
Kendal Rd BOL BL1 ...... 46 A1 [16]
  SLFD M6 ...... 103 D2 [8]
  STRET M32 ...... 121 F6
  TOT/BURYW BL8 ...... 18 A3
Kendal Rd West TOT/BURYW BL8.... 18 A3
Kendon Gv DTN/ASHW M34 .... 129 F6
Kendrew Rd BOLS/LL BL3 ...... 45 E5
Kenilworth Av CHAD OL9 ...... 76 C2 [8]
  CHD/CHDH SK8 ...... 181 E4 [8]
  DID/WITH M20 ...... 143 D6 [8]
  SWIN M27 ...... 86 C2
  WHTF M45 ...... 71 E5
  WILM/AE SK9 ...... 194 B6
Kenilworth Cl MPL/ROM SK6 .... 171 D5 [8]
  OLDE OL4 ...... 81 D6
  RAD M26 ...... 51 D3
Kenilworth Dr BRAM/HZG SK7 .... 198 B1
Kenilworth Gv DTN/ASHW M34 .... 129 D1
Kenilworth Rd EDGY/DAV SK3 .... 165 D6
  MILN OL16 ...... 60 A1
  SALE M33 ...... 158 C1
  URM M41 ...... 136 A2
Kenilworth Sq BOL BL1 ...... 26 C6 [20]
Kenion Rd ROCH OL11 ...... 38 D1
Kenion St MILN OL16 ...... 23 D6 [8]
Kenmay Av BOLS/LL BL3 ...... 45 D5
Kenmere Gv NEWH/MOS M40.... 92 C4
Kenmor Av TOT/BURYW BL8 .... 51 E1
Kenmore Cl WHTF M45 ...... 71 F3 [8]
Kenmore Dr HALE/TIMP WA15 .... 175 E4
Kenmore Gv IRL M44 ...... 134 B5
Kenmore Rd SALE M33 ...... 158 A4
  WHTF M45 ...... 71 F3
  WYTH/NTH M22 ...... 162 A6
Kenmore Wy WHTF M45 ...... 71 F3
Kennard Cl BKLY M9 ...... 92 A4 [8]
Kennedy Dr BOLS/LL BL3 ...... 50 A5
  BURY BL9 ...... 71 F1
Kennedy Rd SALQ/ORD M5 .... 103 D5
Kennedy St CMANW M2 ...... 2 D4
  OLDS OL8 ...... 78 C6 [8]
Kennedy Wy DTN/ASHW M34 .... 148 B1
  HTNM SK4 ...... 166 A3
Kennerley Rd OFTN SK2 ...... 183 E2
Kennerey's La WILM/AE SK9 .... 203 E4
Kennet Cl WILM/AE SK9 ...... 204 B1
Kenneth Sq BRO M7 ...... 105 F1 [13]
Kennett Rd NTHM/RTH M23 .... 177 E4
Kenninghall Rd WYTH/NTH M22 .... 178 B4
Kennington Av
  NEWH/MOS M40 ...... 108 C3 [3]
Kennington Fold BOLS/LL BL3 .... 46 B6 [3]
Kenny Cl OLDE OL4 ...... 80 B6
Kensington Av AUL OL6 ...... 113 F3 [8]
  CHAD OL9 ...... 76 C5
  HYDE SK14 ...... 150 C2 [8]

RAD M26 .... **50** B5
ROY/SHW OL2 .... **60** A3
RUSH/FAL M14 .... **125** E5
Kensington CI MILN OL16.......................... **42** B1
TOT/BURYW BL8 .... **18** B4
Kensington Ct HYDE SK14 .... **150** C2
WILM/AE SK9 .... **203** E5
Kensington Dr SALQ/ORD M5 .... **103** E4
TOT/BURYW SL8.................................. **51** E1
Kensington Gdns
HALE/TIMP WA15 .... **175** D6
Kensington Gv ALT WA14........................ **158** C5
DTN/ASHW M34 .... **128** C5
STLY SK15 .... **114** B6
Kensington Rd CCHDY M21................... **141** E1
EDGY/DAV SK3 .... **165** F6
FAIL M35 .... **94** C4
OLDS OL8 .... **95** F1
Kensington St BOL BL1 .... **46** C2
HYDE SK14... **150** C2
ROCH OL11 .... **39** F3
RUSH/FAL M14 .... **126** B6
Kenslow Av CHH M8 .... **90** A3
Kensworth Dr BOL BL1 .... **27** E6
Kent Av CHAD OL9 .... **77** E5
CHD/CHDH SK8 .... **182** A3
DROY M43 .... **109** F6
Kent CI WALK M28 .... **82** B3
Kent Dr BURY BL9 .... **53** D1
FWTH BL4 .... **67** F5
Kentford Dr NEWH/MOS M40 .... **107** D3
Kentford Rd BOL BL1 .... **27** F6
Kentmere Av WHIT OL12 .... **23** F2
Kentmere CI CHD/CHDH SK8 .... **179** F4
Kentmere Dr MDTN M24 .... **56** C6
Kentmere Gv FWTH BL4......................... **65** D4
Kentmere Rd BOLE BL2 .... **30** A6
HALE/TIMP WA15............................... **176** A1
Kentmore CI HTNM SK4 .... **164** C3
Kenton Av GTN M18 .... **127** D6
Kenton CI BOL BL1 .... **27** E6
DTN/ASHW M34 .... **129** E2
Kenton Rd ROY/SHW OL2 .... **61** E2
Kenton St OLDS OL8 .... **79** F6
Kent Rd DTN/ASHW M34 .... **147** E1
EDGY/DAV SK3 .... **165** F5
FAIL M35 .... **109** F1
IRL M44 .... **134** A6
PART M31 .... **154** C3
Kent Rd East RUSH/FAL M14............... **125** E6
Kent Rd West RUSH/FAL M14.............. **125** D6
Kentsford Dr BOLS/LL BL3................... **49** F4
Kentstone Av HTNM SK4 .... **164** B2
Kent St BOL BL1 .... **46** C1
BRO M7 .... **105** E3
CMANW M2 .... **2** D3
OLDS OL8 .... **96** A1
ROCH OL11 .... **40** A1
SWIN M27 .... **86** A3
Kentucky St OLDE OL4 .... **80** A5
Kentwell CI DUK SK16......................... **130** C2
Kenwick Dr NEWH/MOS M40 .... **93** F3
Kenwood Av BNG/LEV M19 .... **145** D5
BRAM/HZG SK7 .... **196** B6
CHD/CHDH SK8 .... **179** E3
HALE/TIMP WA15 .... **175** D5
Kenwood Ct STRET M32 .... **140** C1
Kenwood La WALK M28 .... **100** A3
Kenwood Rd BOL BL1 .... **26** C4
OLD OL1 .... **78** A3
RDSH SK5 .... **146** C1
STRET M32 .... **140** C2
Kenworthy Av AUL OL6 .... **113** E2
Kenworthy CI HYDE SK14 .... **152** A1
Kenworthy La WYTH/NTH M22........... **162** B3
Kenworthy St MILN OL16 .... **24** A6
STLY SK15 .... **114** B6
STLY SK15 .... **114** B6
Kenworthy Ter MILN OL16 .... **24** A6
Kenwright St ANC M4............................. **3** F1
Kenwyn St NEWH/MOS M40 .... **74** F7
OLDS OL8 .... **96** A2
SALE M33 .... **160** C3
Kenyon Av DUK SK16 .... **131** F2
OLDS OL8 .... **96** A2
Kenyon Fold ROCH OL11 .... **37** F2
Kenyon La MDTN M24 .... **76** A3
NEWH/MOS M40 .... **92** B5
PWCH M25 .... **89** D1
Kenyon Rd BOLS/LL BL3 .... **49** F4
BCUP OL13 .... **4** C1
BURY BL9 .... **34** B4
DUK SK16 .... **130** C1
GTN M18 .... **128** A3
HEY OL10 .... **37** D5
RAMS BL0 .... **7** D4
Kenyon Wy TOT/BURYW BL8 .... **32** A2
Keppel Rd CCHDY M21 .... **141** F2
Keppel St AUL OL6................................. **113** D4
Kepwick Dr WYTH/NTH M22 .... **178** C6
Kerenhappuch St RAMS BL0 .... **6** C5
Kerfoot CI WYTH/NTH M22 .... **162** C5
Kermoor Av BOL BL1 .... **27** F1
Kerne Gv NTHM/RTH M23 .... **161** E4

Kerrera Dr SALQ/ORD M5 .... **103** E6
Kerridge Dr MPL/ROM SK6 .... **169** D1
Kerris CI WYTH/NTH M22 .... **178** C6
Kerr St BKLY M9 .... **91** E2
SWIN M27 .... **87** D5
Kersal Av LHULT M38 .... **82** C1
SWIN M27 .... **87** D5
Kersal Bank BRO M7 .... **89** D5
Kersal CI PWCH M25 .... **88** B4
Kersal Crag BRO M7 .... **89** D4
Kersal Dr HALE/TIMP WA15 .... **160** A6
Kersal Hall Av BRO M7 .... **88** B5
Kersal Rd PWCH M25 .... **88** B4
Kersal Vale Rd SWIN M27 .... **88** A4
Kersal Wy BRO M7 .... **88** C6
Kersh Av BNG/LEV M19 .... **145** F3
Kershaw Av BOLS/LL BL3 .... **49** E5
PWCH M25 .... **88** A3
SALE M33 .... **155** E4
Kershaw Dr CHAD OL9 .... **93** E2
Kershaw Gv DTN/ASHW M34 .... **128** C1
Kershaw La DTN/ASHW M34 .... **111** D6
Kershaw Rd FAIL M35 .... **94** A5
Kershaw St AULW OL7 .... **130** A1
BOLE BL2 .... **29** D2
BOLS/LL BL3 .... **46** B4
BURY BL9 .... **34** B5
DROY M43 .... **110** A6
HEY OL10 .... **36** C5
ROY/SHW OL2 .... **60** A3
ROY/SHW OL2 .... **61** F2
Kershaw St East ROY/SHW OL2 .... **61** F2
Kershope Gv SALQ/ORD M5 .... **122** B1
Kersley St OLDE OL4 .... **79** F5
Kerwood Dr ROY/SHW OL2 .... **60** C6
Kesteven Rd BKLY M9 .... **91** E6
Keston Av BKLY M9 .... **92** B2
DROY M43 .... **109** F6
Keston Crs RDSH SK5 .... **147** F5
Kestor Rd OLD OL1 .... **80** A2
Kestor St BOLE BL2 .... **47** F2
Kestrel Av DTN/ASHW M34 .... **111** D6
FWTH BL4 .... **65** D4
LHULT M38 .... **65** E6
OLDE OL4 .... **80** A6
SWIN M27 .... **86** C3
Kestrel CI MPL/ROM SK6 .... **187** E4
PWCH M25 .... **71** E5
Kestrel Dr BURY BL9 .... **34** C3
IRL M44 .... **116** B6
Kestrel Rd TRPK M17 .... **120** A1
Kestrel St BOLE BL2 .... **47** E1
Keswick Av AULW OL7 .... **112** A2
CHAD OL9 .... **77** E4
CHD/CHDH SK8 .... **179** F4
DTN/ASHW M34 .... **129** E5
HYDE SK14... **131** D5
OLDS OL8 .... **96** B1
URM M41 .... **136** C2
Keswick CI BRUN/LGST M13 .... **125** E5
IRL M44 .... **154** B1
MDTN M24 .... **74** B1
STLY SK15 .... **114** B3
Keswick Dr BRAM/HZG SK7 .... **196** A4
BURY BL9 .... **52** B2
Keswick Gv SLFD M6 .... **104** A4
Keswick Rd HALE/TIMP WA15 .... **176** B1
HTNM SK4 .... **146** B4
MPL/ROM SK6 .... **200** C1
STRET M32 .... **121** D6
WALK M28 .... **84** A3
Keswick St BOL BL1 .... **28** A5
ROCH OL11 .... **38** C5
Kettering Rd BNG/LEV M19 .... **145** F1
Ketton CI OP/CLY M11 .... **127** F2
Kevin Av ROY/SHW OL2 .... **78** C1
Kevin St BNG/LEV M19 .... **145** F3
Kew Av HYDE SK14 .... **150** C2
Kew Dr CHD/CHDH SK8 .... **180** C5
URM M41 .... **118** B5
Kew Gdns NEWH/MOS M40 .... **92** B4
Kew Rd FAIL M35 .... **94** B5
OLDE OL4 .... **79** F5
ROCH OL11 .... **40** B4
Key Ct DTN/ASHW M34 .... **149** E3
Keymer St OP/CLY M11 .... **107** F5
Keynsham Rd OP/CLY M11 .... **108** C4
Keystone CI SLFD M6 .... **103** F3
Key West CI OP/CLY M11 .... **108** A6
Khartoum St OLDTF/WHR M16........... **125** E5
OP/CLY M11 .... **109** D1
Kibbles Brow EDGW/EG BL7 .... **14** C5
Kibboth Crew RAMS BL0 .... **6** C4
Kibworth CI WHTF M45 .... **70** B3
Kid St MDTN M24 .... **75** D2
Kiel CI ECC M30 .... **119** F1
Kielder HI MDTN M24 .... **57** D5
Kilbride Av BOLE BL2 .... **49** D3
Kilburn Av BKLY M9 .... **74** B6
Kilburn CI CHD/CHDH SK8 .... **193** F2
Kilburn Rd EDGY/DAV SK3 .... **166** A6
RAD M26 .... **50** B5
Kilburn St OLD OL1 .... **80** A2
Kildale CI BOLS/LL BL3 .... **44** C5
Kildare Crs ROCH OL11 .... **40** A5

Kildare Rd CCHDY M21........................ **142** B3
SWIN M27 .... **85** F6
Kildare St FWTH BL4.............................. **66** A4
Kildonan Dr BOLS/LL BL3 .... **45** D3
Killer St RAMS BL0 .... **7** D5
Killon St BURY BL9 .... **34** B6
Kilmaine Dr BOLS/LL BL3 .... **44** C4
Kilmington Dr CHH M8 .... **106** A1
Kilmory Dr BOLE BL2 .... **49** D3
Kiln Bank La WHIT OL12 .... **9** D1
Kiln Brow EDGW/EG BL7 .... **15** D5
Kiln Cft MPL/ROM SK6 .... **169** D4
Kiln Croft La WILM/AE SK9 .... **194** C5
Kilner CI BURY BL9 .... **53** F5
Kiln Fld EDGW/EG BL7 .... **14** C5
Kiln Hill CI OLD OL1 .... **77** D1
Kiln Hill La OLD OL1 .... **77** D1
Kiln La MILN OL16 .... **42** A1
Kilnside Dr BKLY M9 .... **91** E6
Kiln St RAMS BL0 .... **6** C6
Kiln Wk WHIT OL12 .... **22** C3
Kilnwick CI GTN M18 .... **126** C6
Kilrush Av ECC M30 .... **119** E1
Kilsby CI FWTH BL4 .... **65** F1
HOR/BR BL6 .... **44** A3
Kilvert Dr SALE M33 .... **139** D6
Kilvert St TRPK M17 .... **122** A4
Kilworth Av SALE M33 .... **159** D2
Kilworth Dr HOR/BR BL6 .... **44** B3
Kilworth St ROCH OL11 .... **39** E2
Kimberley Av MPL/ROM SK6.............. **169** F3
Kimberley Rd BOL BL1 .... **27** F1
Kimberley St BRO M7 .... **89** F6
EDGY/DAV SK3 .... **166** C6
OLDS OL8 .... **95** D2
Kimble CI TOT/BURYW BL8.................... **18** A3
Kimbolton CI WGTN/LGST M12 .... **126** B2
Kinburn Rd BNG/LEV M19 .... **164** B3
Kincardine Rd BRUN/LGST M13 .... **124** C3
Kincraig CI BOLS/LL BL3 .... **44** C5
OP/CLY M11 .... **109** D6
Kinder Av AUL OL6 .... **114** B1
OLDE OL4 .... **80** B6
Kinder Dr MPL/ROM SK6 .... **187** E1
Kinder Fold STLY SK15 .... **133** E3
Kinder Gv MPL/ROM SK6 .... **170** C3
Kinders Fold LIT OL15............................ **12** A4
Kinder St EDGY/DAV SK3 .... **166** C6
STLY SK15 .... **114** B5
Kinder Wy MDTN M24 .... **75** D1
King Albert St ROY/SHW OL2 .... **61** F2
King Edward Rd HYDE SK14 .... **150** C4
King Edward St BNG/LEV M19 .... **145** F2
ECC M30 .... **101** D5
SALQ/ORD M5 .... **122** C1
Kingfisher Av DTN/ASHW M34 .... **111** D6
Kingfisher CI WGTN/LGST M12 .... **125** F5
Kingfisher Dr BURY BL9 .... **34** C3
FWTH BL4 .... **65** D4
Kingfisher Rd OFTN SK2 .... **185** D5
King George Rd HYDE SK14 .... **150** C2
Kingham Dr ANC M4 .... **107** D5
King La BOL BL1 .... **62** C4
Kingmoor Av RAD M26 .... **51** F5
King's Acre ALT WA14 .... **173** E6
Kings CI CHD/CHDH SK8 .... **179** E3
CHH M8 .... **90** B5
WHTF M45 .... **70** C1
Kingsbridge Av BOLE BL2 .... **31** E6
HYDE SK14... **152** A1
Kingsbridge CI MPL/ROM SK6 .... **170** C6
Kingsbridge Dr DUK SK16 .... **130** C2
OLDS OL8 .... **79** F6
Kingsbrook Rd OLDTF/WHR M16 ...... **142** C3
Kingsbury Av BOL BL1 .... **26** A6
Kingsbury Rd OP/CLY M11 .... **109** D5
Kingscliffe St BKLY M9 .... **91** F6
King's CI BRAM/HZG SK7 .... **183** D5
GTN M18 .... **128** A3
PWCH M25 .... **72** A6
WILM/AE SK9 .... **203** E4
Kings Ct RDSH SK5 .... **167** D2
Kingscourt Av BOL BL1 .... **27** D5
Kingsdale Rd DTN/ASHW M34........... **128** B5
Kingsdown Dr BOL BL1 .... **28** A6
Kingsdown Rd WYTH/NTH M22 .... **178** A6
Kings Dr CHD/CHDH SK8 .... **181** E4
HTNM SK4 .... **165** E2
MDTN M24 .... **74** B3
MPL/ROM SK6 .... **170** C6
Kingsfield Dr DID/WITH M20 .... **164** A3
Kingsfold Av NEWH/MOS M40 .... **107** D3
Kingsford St SALQ/ORD M5 .... **103** E5
Kingsgate BOL BL1 .... **46** C2
Kings Ga WYTH/NTH M22 .... **178** A6
Kings Gv STRET M32 .... **122** A6
WHIT OL12 .... **24** A1
Kingshill Rd CCHDY M21...................... **141** E2
Kingsholme Rd WYTH/NTH M22 .... **178** A5
Kingsland CI NEWH/MOS M40 .... **107** E4
Kingsland Rd EDGY/DAV SK3 .... **165** E6
FWTH BL4 .... **65** D2
ROCH OL11 .... **38** C4

Kings La *STRET* M32 .... **122** A6
Kingslea Rd *DID/WITH* M20 .... **144** A6
Kingsleigh Rd *HTNM* SK4 .... **165** D1
Kingsley Av *BKLY* M9 .... **92** A6
  BRO M7 .... **88** B6
  HTNM SK4 .... **166** C1 ▣
  STRET M32 .... **122** A6
  URM M41 .... **137** F1 ▣
  WHTF M45 .... **71** E4
  WILM/AE SK9 .... **204** A1
Kingsley Cl *AUL* OL6 .... **114** B2
  DTN/ASHW M34 .... **148** B2
Kingsley Dr *OLDE* OL4 .... **80** C4
Kingsley Gv *DTN/ASHW* M34 .... **129** D1
Kingsley Rd *HALE/TIMP* WA15 ... **159** F6
  MDTN M24 .... **75** F1
  OLDE OL4 .... **80** A5
  SWIN M27 .... **85** E4
  WALK M28 .... **84** C4
  WYTH/NTH M22 .... **162** B5
Kingsley St *BOL* BL1 .... **27** E5
  TOT/BURYW BL8 .... **32** C5
King's Lynn Cl *DID/WITH* M20 .. **163** F2 ▣
Kingsmead Ms *BKLY* M9 .... **74** A3
Kingsmere Av *BNG/LEV* M19 .... **145** D2 ▣
Kingsmill Av *BNG/LEV* M19 .... **145** F3 ▥
Kingsnorth Rd *URM* M41 .... **117** E6
King's Rd *AUL* OL6 .... **113** C2
  BRAM/HZG SK7 .... **184** C4
  CCHDY M21 .... **142** B3
  CHAD OL9 .... **93** F2
  CHD/CHDH SK8 .... **181** E6
  DTN/ASHW M34 .... **128** B4
  IRL M44 .... **134** C5
  MILN OL16 .... **40** C2
  MPL/ROM SK6 .... **169** E2 ▣
  OLDS OL8 .... **79** D6
  OLDTF/WHR M16 .... **122** B6
  PWCH M25 .... **89** D3
  ROY/SHW OL2 .... **61** E5
  SALE M33 .... **159** D1
  STRET M32 .... **140** C1
  WILM/AE SK9 .... **202** C3
Kings Ter *STRET* M32 .... **122** A6 ▣
Kingston Av *BOLE* BL2 .... **29** D6 ▤
  CHAD OL9 .... **94** B1 ▣
  DID/WITH M20 .... **163** F4 ▣
  OLD OL1 .... **79** F2 ▣
Kingston Cl *BRO* M7 .... **89** E5 ▣
  HYDE SK14 .... **148** B6
  ROY/SHW OL2 .... **61** F1 ▣
  SALE M33 .... **158** B2 ▣
Kingston Dr *ROY/SHW* OL2 ...... **60** A3 ▣
  SALE M33 .... **140** B6
  URM M41 .... **137** F3
Kingston Gdns *HYDE* SK14 ...... **130** C6 ▣
Kingston Gv *BKLY* M9 .... **92** A1 ▣
Kingston Hl *CHD/CHDH* SK8 ..... **180** B3
Kingston Pl *CHD/CHDH* SK8 ..... **180** C5 ▣
Kingston Rd *DID/WITH* M20 ..... **163** F4 ▣
  FAIL M35 .... **94** C6
  RAD M26 .... **52** A3
  WILM/AE SK9 .... **194** A5
Kingston St *EDGY/DAV* SK3 ..... **166** B4
King St *BOL* BL1 .... **46** C2
  BOLE BL2 .... **29** E2
  BRO M7 .... **78** C4 ▣
  CHAD OL9 .... **8** C5
  CMANW M2 .... **2** D3
  CSLFD M3 .... **2** B1
  DROY M43 .... **128** B1
  DTN/ASHW M34 .... **130** A6
  DUK SK16 .... **130** C1
  ECC M30 .... **102** A6 ▣
  EDGW/EG BL7 .... **14** A5 ▣
  FAIL M35 .... **109** E1
  FWTH BL4 .... **66** B3
  HEY OL10 .... **37** E6
  HYDE SK14 .... **131** E6
  HYDE SK14 .... **133** E3
  MDTN M24 .... **75** E2 ▣
  MILN OL16 .... **23** D6
  MOSL OL5 .... **99** E4
  RAD M26 .... **69** F1
  RAMS BL0 .... **7** D5
  SLFD M6 .... **105** E2
  STLY SK15 .... **114** B5
  WHIT OL12 .... **5** E6
King St East *ROCH* OL11 .... **39** F2
  STKP SK1 .... **167** D3 ▧
King St South *ROCH* OL11 ...... **39** F2
King St West *CSLFD* M3 .... **2** C3
  EDGY/DAV SK3 .... **166** C5
  HTNM SK4 .... **166** B4
Kingsway *BNG/LEV* M19 .... **145** D2
  BRAM/HZG SK7 .... **183** D5
  CHD/CHDH SK8 .... **180** A3
  DUK SK16 .... **131** F2
  FWTH BL4 .... **67** D5
  HALE/TIMP WA15 .... **174** C3
  MDTN M24 .... **76** B6
  MILN OL16 .... **41** D1
  MPL/ROM SK6 .... **168** C2
  STKP SK1 .... **167** D3
  STRET M32 .... **140** A2

SWIN M27 .... **103** D1
WALK M28 .... **83** E5
Kingsway Av *BNG/LEV* M19 ...... **145** D2 ▣
Kingsway Cl *OLDS* OL8 .... **78** C6
Kingsway Crs *BNG/LEV* M19 ..... **144** C6 ▣
Kingsway Pk *URM* M41 .... **119** E5
Kingswear Dr *BOL* BL1 .... **27** D6 ▧
Kingswood Gv *RDSH* SK5 .... **147** D2 ▣
Kingswood Rd *ECC* M30 .... **100** C3
  MDTN M24 .... **57** D6
  PWCH M25 .... **71** D6
  RUSH/FAL M14 .... **144** C4
King William St *ECC* M30 ...... **100** B4 ▣
  SALQ/ORD M5 .... **122** B1
Kingwood Av *BOL* BL1 .... **45** D1
Kinloch Dr *BOL* BL1 .... **45** F2
Kinloch St *OLDS* OL8 .... **96** B1 ▣
  OP/CLY M11 .... **108** B5
Kinmel Av *RDSH* SK5 .... **168** A1
Kinnaird Crs *STKP* SK1 .... **167** F5
Kinnaird Rd *DID/WITH* M20 ..... **143** F6
Kinnerly Gv *WALK* M28 .... **82** B4
Kinross Av *OFTN* SK2 .... **183** E4
Kinross Dr *BOLS/LL* BL3 .... **45** D4
Kinross Rd *RUSH/FAL* M14 ...... **125** F6
Kinsey Av *NTHM/RTH* M23 .... **161** D5
Kinsley Dr *WALK* M28 .... **83** D3
Kintore Av *BRAM/HZG* SK7 ...... **185** D5
Kintyre Av *SALQ/ORD* M5 .... **103** E6
Kintyre Cl *OP/CLY* M11 .... **109** D6 ▣
Kintyre Dr *BOLS/LL* BL3 .... **44** C4
Kinver Rd *NEWH/MOS* M40 .... **93** D3
Kipling Av *DROY* M43 .... **110** B4
  DTN/ASHW M34 .... **149** E4
Kipling Cl *OFTN* SK2 .... **185** D1 ▣
Kipling Rd *OLD* OL1 .... **79** F1
Kipling St *BRO* M7 .... **105** E1
Kippax St *RUSH/FAL* M14 .... **124** C6
Kirby Av *CHAD* OL9 .... **93** E2
  SWIN M27 .... **101** E2 ▣
Kirkbank St *CHAD* OL9 .... **78** B3 ▣
Kirkburn Vw *TOT/BURYW* BL8 .... **33** D2 ▣
Kirkby Av *NEWH/MOS* M40 .... **92** C6
  SALE M33 .... **160** A3
Kirkby Dr *BURY* BL9 .... **52** C2
Kirkby Dr *SALE* M33 .... **160** B3
Kirkby Rd *BOL* BL1 .... **45** D1
Kirkdale Av *NEWH/MOS* M40 ..... **93** E3 ▣
Kirkdale Dr *ROY/SHW* OL2 ...... **60** A4
Kirkebrok Rd *BOLS/LL* BL3 ..... **45** E5
Kirkfell Dr *MPL/ROM* SK6 ...... **200** C1 ▣
Kirkgate Cl *NEWH/MOS* M40 ..... **107** D4 ▣
Kirkhall La *BOL* BL1 .... **46** A1
Kirkham Av *GTN* M18 .... **127** E3
Kirkham Cl *DTN/ASHW* M34 ...... **130** A6
Kirkham Rd *CHD/CHDH* SK8 ...... **194** A1
Kirkham St *BOLE* BL2 .... **29** D6 ▣
  CHAD OL9 .... **78** C4 ▣
  LHULT M38 .... **65** E6
  SALQ/ORD M5 .... **103** F6
Kirkhaven Sq *NEWH/MOS* M40 .... **107** F3 ▣
Kirkhope Dr *BOL* BL1 .... **27** E6
Kirklands *BOLE* BL2 .... **29** E5
  SALE M33 .... **159** E3
Kirklee Av *CHAD* OL9 .... **77** E2
Kirklee Rd *ROCH* OL11 .... **39** E5
Kirklees St *TOT/BURYW* BL8 .... **18** A6
Kirkley St *HYDE* SK14 .... **150** B3
Kirklinton Dr *BKLY* M9 .... **107** E1 ▧
Kirkman Av *ECC* M30 .... **119** D1
Kirkman Cl *GTN* M18 .... **127** E5
Kirkmanshulme La *GTN* M18 ..... **126** C4 ▣
  WGTN/LGST M12 .... **126** B5
Kirkman St *BURY* BL9 .... **53** D6
Kirk Rd *BNG/LEV* M19 .... **145** F4
Kirkstall Av *HEY* OL10 .... **37** D4
  LIT OL15 .... **12** B5
Kirkstall Cl *POY/DIS* SK12 .... **195** F5
Kirkstall Rd *MDTN* M24 .... **57** D6
  URM M41 .... **119** D6
Kirkstall Sq *BRUN/LGST* M13 ... **125** D3 ▣
Kirkstead Cl *OP/CLY* M11 ...... **126** B3 ▥
Kirkstead Rd *CHD/CHDH* SK8 .... **196** A2
Kirkstile Pl *SWIN* M27 .... **85** F1
Kirkstone Av *WALK* M28 .... **84** A4
Kirkstone Cl *OLD* OL1 .... **79** D2
Kirkstone Dr *MDTN* M24 .... **74** C1
  ROY/SHW OL2 .... **60** A3
Kirkstone Rd *HYDE* SK14 .... **131** D4 ▣
  NEWH/MOS M40 .... **93** D3
Kirk St *GTN* M18 .... **127** E4
Kirkwall Dr *BOLE* BL2 .... **47** F4
Kirkway *BKLY* M9 .... **92** B1
  MDTN M24 .... **75** E5
  ROCH OL11 .... **40** A5
Kirkwood Dr *NEWH/MOS* M40 ..... **107** D3
Kirtley Av *ECC* M30 .... **101** E4
Kirtlington Cl *ROY/SHW* OL2 ... **61** E4
Kitchener St *IRL* M44 .... **137** F6 ▧
Kitchener St *BOLS/LL* BL3 ..... **47** F6 ▣
  TOT/BURYW BL8 .... **32** C5
Kitchen St *MILN* OL16 .... **23** E5 ▣
Kitepool St *ECC* M30 .... **100** B4 ▣
Kitter St *WHIT* OL12 .... **23** F2 ▣
Kitt's Moss La *BRAM/HZG* SK7 .. **196** B3

Kiveton Cl *WALK* M28 .... **83** D3 ▣
Knacks La *WHIT* OL12 .... **8** B6
Knaresborough Cl *RDSH* SK5 .... **146** C2 ▣
Knight Crs *MDTN* M24 .... **56** B6
Knightsbridge *STKP* SK1 .... **167** D3 ▣
Knightsbridge Cl *BRO* M7 ...... **89** E5 ▧
  WILM/AE SK9 .... **204** B2
Knight's Cl *PWCH* M25 .... **71** F6
Knight St *AULW* OL7 .... **112** A5
  BOL BL1 .... **47** D1 ▧
  DID/WITH M20 .... **163** F3 ▣
  HYDE SK14 .... **150** C2
  TOT/BURYW BL8 .... **33** D5 ▣
Knightswood *BOLS/LL* BL3 ...... **45** D6
Kniveton Rd *WGTN/LGST* M12 .... **126** A3
Knivton St *HYDE* SK14 .... **132** A6 ▣
Knole Av *POY/DIS* SK12 .... **199** D5
Knoll St *BRO* M7 .... **89** E6
  ROCH OL11 .... **38** C4
The Knoll *MOSL* OL5 .... **98** C4
  ROY/SHW OL2 .... **62** A3 ▣
Knott Fold *HYDE* SK14 .... **150** B3
Knott Hill St *WHIT* OL12 ...... **5** F3
Knott La *BOL* BL1 .... **26** A5
  HYDE SK14 .... **150** B3
  OLDS OL8 .... **95** F6
Knotts Brow *EDGW/EG* BL7 ...... **16** A1
Knott St *SALQ/ORD* M5 .... **103** E6
Knowe Av *WYTH/NTH* M22 .... **178** B5 ▣
Knowl Cl *DTN/ASHW* M34 .... **147** E1
  RAMS BL0 .... **19** D1
Knowle Av *AULW* OL7 .... **112** A3
Knowle Dr *PWCH* M25 .... **88** B3
Knowle Pk *WILM/AE* SK9 .... **194** A6
Knowles Edge St *BOL* BL1 ...... **27** D5 ▣▣
Knowles St *BOL* BL1 .... **28** B6 ▣
  RAD M26 .... **51** E5
The Knowles *OLDS* OL8 .... **94** C4
Knowl Hill Dr *WHIT* OL12 ...... **20** C5 ▣
Knowl Rd *MILN* OL16 .... **41** E1 ▣
  ROY/SHW OL2 .... **62** A3
Knowls La *OLDE* OL4 .... **81** D6
Knowl St *OLDS* OL8 .... **95** D3
  STLY SK15 .... **114** C5
Knowl Syke St *WHIT* OL12 ...... **11** D4
Knowl Vw *LIT* OL15 .... **25** D3
  TOT/BURYW BL8 .... **32** B1
Knowsley Av *OLDE* OL4 .... **81** E4
  SALQ/ORD M5 .... **122** C1 ▣
  URM M41 .... **119** D5
Knowsley Crs *STKP* SK1 .... **167** F5 ▣
  WHIT OL12 .... **5** F3
Knowsley Dr *OLDE* OL4 .... **81** E4 ▣
  SWIN M27 .... **101** E1
Knowsley Gn *OLDE* OL4 .... **81** E4 ▣
Knowsley Rd *BOL* BL1 .... **26** C5
  BOLE BL2 .... **31** D6
  BRAM/HZG SK7 .... **199** D1
  STKP SK1 .... **167** F5
  WHTF M45 .... **71** D3
Knowsley St *BOL* BL1 .... **47** D2
  BURY BL9 .... **33** F6
  CHH M8 .... **106** B3 ▣
  WHIT OL12 .... **22** C5 ▣▣
Knowsley Ter *OLDE* OL4 .... **81** E4 ▣
Knutsford Av *HTNM* SK4 .... **146** B4
  SALE M33 .... **160** C1 ▣
Knutsford Rd *GTN* M18 .... **127** D5
  WILM/AE SK9 .... **203** D6
Knutsford St *SLFD* M6 .... **103** F5
Knypersley Av *OFTN* SK2 .... **168** A6
Kranj Wy *OLD* OL1 .... **79** D4
Kylemore Av *BOLS/LL* BL3 ...... **45** F4 ▣
Kyle Rd *BRAM/HZG* SK7 .... **185** D6 ▣
Kynder St *DTN/ASHW* M34 .... **130** A6 ▣

L

Labtec St *SWIN* M27 .... **86** C4
Laburnum Av *AUL* OL6 .... **113** D1
  CHAD OL9 .... **77** F2
  DTN/ASHW M34 .... **111** D6
  ECC M30 .... **118** B1 ▣
  FAIL M35 .... **110** A1
  HYDE SK14 .... **150** B3
  ROY/SHW OL2 .... **61** F3
  STLY SK15 .... **132** A1
  SWIN M27 .... **101** E1 ▣
  TOT/BURYW BL8 .... **18** A6
  WHTF M45 .... **71** D3
Laburnum Cl *HALE/TIMP* WA15 ... **175** E2
Laburnum Dr *WHTF* M45 .... **71** E2
Laburnum Gv *PWCH* M25 .... **71** E6 ▣
Laburnum La *HALE/TIMP* WA15 ... **188** C1
  MILN OL16 .... **42** B4
Laburnum Pk *BOLE* BL2 .... **28** C2
Laburnum Rd *DTN/ASHW* M34 ..... **128** A5
  FWTH BL4 .... **65** F3
  GTN M18 .... **127** E5
  IRL M44 .... **134** B6
  MDTN M24 .... **76** A3 ▣
  OLDS OL8 .... **95** D5
  URM M41 .... **118** C5

WALK M28 .... 83 F3
Laburnum St *BOL* BL1 .... 46 B1 🔳
SLFD M6 .... 104 A5
Laburnum Ter *ROCH* OL11 .... 39 F3 🔳
Laburnum Wy *EDGY/DAV* SK3 .... 165 F5 🔳
LIT OL15 .... 12 A6
Lacey Av *WILM/AE* SK9 .... 203 F3
Lacey Gn *WILM/AE* SK9 .... 203 F2
Lacey Gv *WILM/AE* SK9 .... 204 A2
Lackford Dr *NEWH/MOS* M40 .... 107 D3 🔳
Lacrosse Av *OLDS* OL8 .... 95 D1
Lacy Gv *STRET* M32 .... 140 B2
Lacy St *STKP* SK1 .... 167 D5 🔳
STRET M32 .... 140 B2
Ladbrooke Cl *AUL* OL6 .... 113 D3 🔳
Ladbrooke Rd *AUL* OL6 .... 113 D2
Ladybarn Crs *BRAM/HZG* SK7 .... 197 D3
RUSH/FAL M14 .... 144 B4 🔳
Ladybarn La *RUSH/FAL* M14 ...... 144 B3
Ladybarn Rd *RUSH/FAL* M14 ...... 144 B3
Ladybower *CHD/CHDH* SK8 .... 182 A4
Lady Bridge La *BOL* BL1 .... 45 D2
Ladybridge Av *WALK* M28 .... 83 D5
Ladybridge Ri *CHD/CHDH* SK8 .... 182 A4 🔳
Ladybridge Rd *CHD/CHDH* SK8 .... 181 F4
Ladybrook Av *HALE/TIMP* WA15 .. 159 F6
Ladybrook Rd *BRAM/HZG* SK7 .... 182 A6
Ladyfield St *WILM/AE* SK9 .... 203 F4
Ladyfield Ter *WILM/AE* SK9 ...... 203 F4
Ladyhill Vw *WALK* M28 .... 83 D5 🔳
Ladyhouse Cl *MILN* OL16 .... 42 B3
Ladyhouse La *MILN* OL16 .... 42 A2
Ladymere Dr *WALK* M28 .... 82 C5
Lady Rd *OLDE* OL4 .... 80 C5
Ladys Cl *POY/DIS* SK12 .... 198 C5
Ladyshore Rd *BOLS/LL* BL3 ...... 68 A1
Ladysmith Av *BURY* BL9 .... 34 A5
Ladysmith Dr *AUL* OL6 .... 114 A2 🔳
Ladysmith Rd *AUL* OL6 .... 114 A2
DID/WITH M20 .... 164 A3
STLY SK15 .... 114 A3
Ladysmith St *EDGY/DAV* SK3 .... 166 C6
OLDS OL8 .... 95 D2 🔳
The Ladysmith *AUL* OL6 .... 114 A2
Ladythorn Av *MPL/ROM* SK6 ...... 187 E2
Ladythorn Crt *PWCH* M25 .... 88 B3 🔳
Ladythorn Crs *BRAM/HZG* SK7 .... 197 D3
Ladythorne Av *PWCH* M25 .... 88 B3 🔳
Ladythorne Dr *PWCH* M25 .... 88 B3 🔳
Ladythorn Gv *BRAM/HZG* SK7 .... 197 D3
Ladythorn Rd *BRAM/HZG* SK7 .... 196 C3
Ladywell Av *LHULT* M38 .... 82 B1
Ladywell Cl *BRAM/HZG* SK7 ...... 183 E5
Ladywell Gv *LHULT* M38 .... 65 E6 🔳
Lagos Cl *RUSH/FAL* M14 .... 124 B5
Laindon Rd *RUSH/FAL* M14 .... 125 F5
Lake Bank *LIT* OL15 .... 25 E3
Lake Dr *MDTN* M24 .... 75 D4
Lakeland Crs *BURY* BL9 .... 52 C3
Lakeland Dr *ROY/SHW* OL2 .... 60 A1 🔳
Lakelands Dr *BOLS/LL* BL3 ...... 45 D4
Lakenheath Cl *BOL* BL1 .... 28 A1 🔳
Lakenheath Dr *BOL* BL1 .... 28 A1
Lake Rd *DTN/ASHW* M34 .... 130 A5
STLY SK15 .... 114 A3
TRPK M17 .... 121 D2
Lakeside *LIT* OL15 .... 25 E3
Lakeside Av *AULW* OL7 .... 112 A3
BOLS/LL BL3 .... 65 E1
WALK M28 .... 66 B6
Lakeside Cl *GTN* M18 .... 128 A3
Lakeside Dr *POY/DIS* SK12 .... 198 C4
Lakeside Gn *OFTN* SK2 .... 184 A1
Lakes Rd *DUK* SK16 .... 131 D1
MPL/ROM SK6 .... 187 E1
Lake St *BOLS/LL* BL3 .... 47 D4 🔳
OFTN SK2 .... 183 F2
Lake Vw *BKLY* M9 .... 92 B3
Lakin St *NEWH/MOS* M40 .... 92 B6
Laleham Gn *BRAM/HZG* SK7 ...... 182 A4
Lamb Cl *WGTN/LGST* M12 .... 126 A4 🔳
Lamb Ct *CSLFD* M3 .... 2 A2 🔳
Lambert Dr *SALE* M33 .... 138 B5
Lamberton Dr *NTHM/RTH* M23 .... 176 C1
Lambert St *AULW* OL7 .... 112 A6
Lambeth Av *FAIL* M35 .... 94 B5
Lambeth Gv *MPL/ROM* SK6 .... 149 E6
Lambeth Rd *NEWH/MOS* M40 ...... 109 D3 🔳
RDSH SK5 .... 147 D4 🔳
Lambeth Ter *ROCH* OL11 .... 39 E2 🔳
Lamb La *ALT* WA14 .... 188 B4
CSLFD M3 .... 2 A2
Lambourn Cl *POY/DIS* SK12 ...... 198 B5 🔳
Lambourne Cl *WYTH/NTH* M22 .... 192 B1
Lambourne Gv *MILN* OL16 .... 42 A2 🔳
Lambourn Rd *URM* M41 .... 117 E6 🔳
Lambs Fold *HTNM* SK4 .... 146 B6 🔳
Lambton Rd *WALK* M28 .... 101 D1 🔳
Lambton St *BOLS/LL* BL3 .... 64 A1 🔳
ECC M30 .... 100 C3
Lamburn Av *NEWH/MOS* M40 ...... 93 D3 🔳
Lamorna Cl *BRO* M7 .... 102 A2
Lamport Cl *CMANE* M1 .... 124 C2 🔳
Lampson St *CHH* M8 .... 105 F3 🔳

Lampton Cl *ALT* WA14 .... 158 B6
Lamsholme Cl *BNG/LEV* M19 ...... 145 E1 🔳
Lanark Av *WYTH/NTH* M22 .... 162 B5
Lanark Cl *BRAM/HZG* SK7 .... 185 E5
HEY OL10 .... 36 A6
Lanbury Dr *CHH* M8 .... 90 A6 🔳
Lancashire Hl *RDSH* SK5 .... 166 C2
Lancashire Rd *PART* M31 .... 154 C2
Lancashire St *NEWH/MOS* M40 .... 108 A2 🔳
Lancaster Av *FAIL* M35 .... 93 F6
FWTH BL4 .... 65 D3
MDTN M24 .... 76 A4
RAMS BL0 .... 18 B1
STLY SK15 .... 114 B3
URM M41 .... 119 F6 🔳
WHTF M45 .... 71 E4
Lancaster Cl *BRAM/HZG* SK7 .... 198 B1
MPL/ROM SK6 .... 169 E4 🔳
PWCH M25 .... 89 D3
Lancaster Dr *BOLS/LL* BL3 ...... 49 F5
PWCH M25 .... 89 D3
Lancaster Rd *DID/WITH* M20 ...... 163 E2
DROY M43 .... 110 A2
DTN/ASHW M34 .... 149 D2
IRL M44 .... 134 A6
SLFD M6 .... 102 C2
WILM/AE SK9 .... 204 C2
Lancaster St *CHAD* OL9 .... 94 B1 🔳
MOSL OL5 .... 98 C4 🔳
RAD M26 .... 50 C6 🔳
STKP SK1 .... 167 E5
Lancelot Cl *BRAM/HZG* SK7 ...... 198 B1
Lancelyn Dr *WILM/AE* SK9 .... 204 B3
Lanchester Dr *BOLS/LL* BL3 ...... 46 B4
Lanchester St *NEWH/MOS* M40 .... 107 F4 🔳
Lancing Av *DID/WITH* M20 .... 164 B2 🔳
Landcross Rd *RUSH/FAL* M14 ...... 144 A2
Lander Gv *BKLY* M9 .... 92 A2
Land Ga *WHIT* OL12 .... 5 F4
Landkey Cl *NTHM/RTH* M23 .... 161 D3 🔳
Land La *WILM/AE* SK9 .... 204 A5
Landos Rd *NEWH/MOS* M40 .... 107 D4
Landsberg Rd *FAIL* M35 .... 94 C5
Landseer Dr *MPL/ROM* SK6 .... 171 F5 🔳
Landseer St *OLDS* OL8 .... 79 E6
Lands End Rd *MDTN* M24 .... 73 F4
Lane Brow *OLDE* OL4 .... 81 F6
Lane Dr *OLDE* OL4 .... 81 F6
Lane End *ECC* M30 .... 102 A6
HEY OL10 .... 57 D1
Lane End Rd *BCUP* OL13 .... 4 B1
BNG/LEV M19 .... 164 B1
Lane Ends *MPL/ROM* SK6 .... 170 B1
Lanegate *HYDE* SK14 .... 150 B3
Lane Head Av *OLDE* OL4 .... 98 C3
Lane North *BOLS/LL* BL3 .... 45 F5 🔳
Laneside Av *ROY/SHW* OL2 .... 62 B2
Laneside Cl *LIT* OL15 .... 12 B5
Laneside Dr *BRAM/HZG* SK7 ...... 183 E6
Laneside Rd *DID/WITH* M20 ...... 164 A5
The Lane *BOL* BL1 .... 44 B2
Lanfield Dr *CHH* M8 .... 90 A6 🔳
Langcroft Dr *NEWH/MOS* M40 .... 109 D2 🔳
Langdale Av *BNG/LEV* M19 .... 145 F3
MILN OL16 .... 60 A1 🔳
OLDS OL8 .... 95 E1
Langdale Cl *CHD/CHDH* SK8 ...... 180 A4
DTN/ASHW M34 .... 148 C2
HALE/TIMP WA15 .... 174 C2
MPL/ROM SK6 .... 200 C1
Langdale Dr *BURY* BL9 .... 53 E6
MDTN M24 .... 56 C6
WALK M28 .... 84 A4
Langdale Rd *BRAM/HZG* SK7 ...... 196 A4
HTNM SK4 .... 146 A5
MPL/ROM SK6 .... 149 E5
PART M31 .... 154 C2
RUSH/FAL M14 .... 125 E5
SALE M33 .... 158 C4
STRET M32 .... 121 D6 🔳
Langdale St *BOLS/LL* BL3 .... 46 C6
FWTH BL4 .... 66 A4 🔳
Langden Cl *ROY/SHW* OL2 .... 61 E1
Langdon Cl *BOL* BL1 .... 46 B1 🔳
Langfield Crs *DROY* M43 .... 111 D5 🔳
Langford Cl *IRL* M44 .... 135 D2
Langford Rd *DID/WITH* M20 ...... 143 E5 🔳
HTNM SK4 .... 166 A1
Langford St *DTN/ASHW* M34 ...... 130 A6 🔳
Langham Cl *BOL* BL1 .... 28 B1
Langham Ct *STRET* M32 .... 120 B5
Langham Gv *HALE/TIMP* WA15 .... 159 F5
Langham Rd *ALT* WA14 .... 174 A5
HTNM SK4 .... 165 F4
OLDS OL8 .... 95 F1
SLFD M6 .... 104 A5 🔳
Langham St *AULW* OL7 .... 112 A2
Langholm Dr *BOLE* BL2 .... 49 D3
Langholme Cl *HULME* M15 .... 123 D2 🔳
Langholme Pl *ECC* M30 .... 100 C5 🔳
Langholme Wy *HEY* OL10 .... 36 A6
Langland Cl *RDSH* SK5 .... 146 B1
Langland Dr *ECC* M30 .... 119 D2
Langley Av *BRAM/HZG* SK7 .... 183 F6
MDTN M24 .... 56 C5
OLDE OL4 .... 81 F6

Langley Dr *URM* M41 .... 138 C1
Langley Dr *WILM/AE* SK9 .... 194 C6
Langley Hall Rd *PWCH* M25 ...... 71 F5
Langley La *MDTN* M24 .... 56 A5
Langley Rd *PWCH* M25 .... 71 E6
RUSH/FAL M14 .... 144 A2
SALE M33 .... 158 C1
SWIN M27 .... 88 A5
Langley Rd South *SLFD* M6 ...... 104 A2
Langness St *OP/CLY* M11 .... 109 D6 🔳
Lango St *OLDTF/WHR* M16 .... 123 D4 🔳
OLDTF/WHR M16 .... 123 D5 🔳
Langport Av *WGTN/LGST* M12 .... 125 F3
Langsett Av *SLFD* M6 .... 103 D4
Langshaw Rd *BOLS/LL* BL3 ...... 46 A4 🔳
Langshaw St *SLFD* M6 .... 104 A6
OLDTF/WHR M16 .... 91 F1 🔳
Langside Av *BKLY* M9 .... 91 F1 🔳
Langside Dr *BOLS/LL* BL3 .... 44 C5
Langston Gn *BRAM/HZG* SK7 ...... 183 E6 🔳
Langston St *CSLFD* M3 .... 106 A4 🔳
Langthorne St *BNG/LEV* M19 ...... 158 B3 🔳
Langton Cl *FAIL* M35 .... 94 C5
Langton St *HEY* OL10 .... 37 D3
MDTN M24 .... 75 E3 🔳
SLFD M6 .... 103 F5
Langton Ter *ROCH* OL11 .... 39 F3 🔳
Langtree Cl *WALK* M28 .... 82 C5 🔳
Langworthy Av *LHULT* M38 .... 82 C1
Langworthy Rd *NEWH/MOS* M40 .. 92 B6
SLFD M6 .... 104 A4
Lanhill Dr *CHH* M8 .... 107 D1 🔳
Lankro Wy *ECC* M30 .... 102 A6
Lansdale Gdns *BNG/LEV* M19 ...... 144 C6 🔳
Lansdale St *ECC* M30 .... 118 B3 🔳
Lansdown Cl *BRAM/HZG* SK7 ...... 196 A2
Lansdowne Av *DTN/ASHW* M34 .... 111 D6
MPL/ROM SK6 .... 170 B3
Lansdowne Dr *WALK* M28 .... 83 D5
Lansdowne Rd *ALT* WA14 .... 174 B1
BOLE BL2 .... 28 C6 🔳
CHAD OL9 .... 78 A5
CHH M8 .... 90 B5
ECC M30 .... 101 E4
SALE M33 .... 139 E5
URM M41 .... 136 C3
Lansdowne Rd North *URM* M41 .. 136 C2
Lansdowne St *ROCH* OL11 .... 22 A6 🔳
Lanstead Dr *NEWH/MOS* M40 .... 107 F5 🔳
Lapwing Cl *ROCH* OL11 .... 20 C6 🔳
STLY SK15 .... 114 B3
Lapwing La *DID/WITH* M20 .... 143 E6
RDSH SK5 .... 148 A5
Larch Av *CHD/CHDH* SK8 .... 181 E6 🔳
RAD M26 .... 69 F2
STRET M32 .... 140 B3
SWIN M27 .... 101 D1 🔳
Larch Cl *FAIL* M35 .... 110 A1 🔳
MPL/ROM SK6 .... 186 C2
NTHM/RTH M23 .... 160 A5
POY/DIS SK12 .... 199 D6
The Larches *MOSL* OL5 .... 99 E4
Larch Gv *CHAD* OL9 .... 77 F3 🔳
SWIN M27 .... 84 C3
Larch Rd *DTN/ASHW* M34 .... 130 B6
ECC M30 .... 100 B3
PART M31 .... 154 C2
Larch St *BURY* BL9 .... 34 C5 🔳
OLDS OL8 .... 76 B5
Larchview Rd *MDTN* M24 .... 57 D4
Larchway *BRAM/HZG* SK7 .... 196 A2
MILN OL16 .... 24 B6
MPL/ROM SK6 .... 201 D2
Larchwood *CHAD* OL9 .... 76 C4
Larchwood Av *BKLY* M9 .... 92 A6 🔳
Larchwood Cl *SALE* M33 .... 158 A1
Larchwood Dr *WILM/AE* SK9 ...... 204 C3
Larchwood St *BOL* BL1 .... 28 A5 🔳
Larkfield Av *LHULT* M38 .... 65 D6
Larkfield Cl *AULW* OL7 .... 96 C6
TOT/BURYW BL8 .... 17 F3
Larkfield Gv *BOLE* BL2 .... 47 F1
Lark Hl *FWTH* BL4 .... 66 B4
STLY SK15 .... 114 B3
Larkhill Cl *HALE/TIMP* WA15 ...... 175 F1
Larkhill Rd *CHD/CHDH* SK8 ...... 182 A2
Lark Hill Rd *EDGY/DAV* SK3 ...... 166 A5
Larkhill Vw *EDGY/DAV* SK3 ...... 182 A2
Larkside Av *WALK* M28 .... 83 E4
Larks Ri *DROY* M43 .... 111 E4
Lark St *BOL* BL1 .... 47 D1 🔳
FWTH BL4 .... 66 B4 🔳
OLD OL1 .... 62 B6 🔳
Larkswood Dr *OFTN* SK2 .... 185 D2
Larkwood Cl *STLY* SK15 .... 99 F6 🔳
Larmuth Av *CCHDY* M21 .... 142 A5
Larne Av *EDGY/DAV* SK3 .... 165 F6
STRET M32 .... 140 A1
Larne St *OP/CLY* M11 .... 126 B1
Larwood Av *HTNM* SK4 .... 165 E4
Lascar Av *SALQ/ORD* M5 .... 122 B1 🔳
Lashbrook Cl *NEWH/MOS* M40 .... 107 D4
Lassell Fold *NEWH/MOS* M40 .... 132 C3
Lassell St *OP/CLY* M11 .... 128 A2 🔳
Lastingham St *NEWH/MOS* M40 .. 109 D1 🔳

Latchford St *AULW* OL7 .... 112 B3 🄫
Latchmere Rd *RUSH/FAL* M14 .... 144 A3 🄫
Latham St *BOL* BL1 .... 28 A5 🄫
  OP/CLY M11 .... 128 A2
Lathbury Rd *BKLY* M9 .... 107 E1
Lathom Gv *SALE* M33 .... 160 C2
Lathom Hall Av *OLDE* OL4 .... 81 E4 🄫
Lathom Rd *DID/WITH* M20 .... 144 B4
  IRL M44 .... 135 D3 🄫
Latimer St *OLDE* OL4 .... 79 E5
Latrigg Crs *MDTN* M24 .... 74 A1
Latrobe St *DROY* M43 .... 128 D1
Lauderdale Crs *BRUN/LGST* M13 .. 125 E2
Launceston Dr *BRAM/HZG* SK7 .. 197 D2 🄫
Launceston Rd *RAD* M26 .... 50 B4 🄫
Laundry St *SLFD* M6 .... 104 A3
Laurel Av *CHAD* OL9 .... 76 B3
  CHD/CHDH SK8 .... 180 B2
  RUSH/FAL M14 .... 143 E1 🄫
Laurel Bank *HYDE* SK14 .... 150 A3
  STLY SK15 .... 132 C1
Laurel Bank Gdns *BKLY* M9 .... 91 E1
Laurel Dr *HALE/TIMP* WA15 .... 175 F3
  LHULT M38 .... 82 B1
Laurel Gn *DTN/ASHW* M34 .... 149 E1
Laurel Gv *SALQ/ORD* M5 .... 103 D5 🄫
Laurel Rd *HTNM* SK4 .... 165 F1
Laurels Dr *LIT* OL15 .... 25 D3
The Laurels *MOSL* OL5 .... 99 E4
Laurel St *BOL* BL1 .... 46 A2
  BURY BL9 .... 34 C5
  HTNM SK4 .... 166 C3 🄫
  MDTN M24 .... 76 B3 🄫
  TOT/BURYW BL8 .... 32 A1
Laurel Wk *PART* M31 .... 154 C3
Laurel Wy *CHD/CHDH* SK8 .... 196 A1
Laurence La *WGTN/LGST* M12 ... 126 B3
Lauria Ter *BOLE* BL2 .... 31 E6 🄫
Laurie Pl *WHIT* OL12 .... 23 D4 🄫
Lausanne Rd *BRAM/HZG* SK7 .... 182 C4 🄫
  DID/WITH M20 .... 143 F4
Lavender Cl *NTHM/RTH* M23 ...... 160 C4 🄫
  SALE M33 .... 138 A6
Lavender Rd *FWTH* BL4 .... 65 E2
  OLDE OL4 .... 97 F1 🄫
Lavenders Brow *STKP* SK1 .... 167 G4 🄫
Lavender St *RAD* M26 .... 50 B6
Lavenham Av *OP/CLY* M11 .... 109 E6 🄫
Lavenham Cl *BRAM/HZG* SK7 .... 198 C1 🄫
  BURY BL9 .... 53 D6 🄫
Laverton Cl *HEY* OL10 .... 35 E6
Lavington Av *CHD/CHDH* SK8 .... 181 E1
Lavington Gv *GTN* M18 .... 127 E5 🄫
Lavinia St *ECC* M30 .... 100 C5 🄫
Lavister Av *BNG/LEV* M19 .... 164 B2
Lawefield Crs *SWIN* M27 .... 68 B6
Lawers Av *CHAD* OL9 .... 77 E3
Lawflat *WHIT* OL12 .... 11 D6
Lawler Av *SALQ/ORD* M5 .... 122 C3
Lawnbank Cl *MDTN* M24 .... 74 C2
Lawn Cl *OLDS* OL8 .... 97 D2
Lawn Dr *HALE/TIMP* WA15 .... 174 C1
  SWIN M27 .... 85 F6
Lawngreen Av *CCHDY* M21 .... 141 E4
Lawnside Ms *DID/WITH* M20 ..... 143 E6
Lawn St *BOL* BL1 .... 27 D6
Lawnswood *OLDE* OL4 .... 39 D5
Lawnswood Dr *SWIN* M27 .... 102 C1 🄫
Lawnswood Park Rd *SWIN* M27 .. 102 B1
Lawrence Cl *WHIT* OL12 .... 21 E4 🄫
Lawrence Rd *ALT* WA14 .... 174 A1
  BRAM/HZG SK7 .... 184 C4
  URM M41 .... 117 F6
Lawrence La *BURY* BL9 .... 53 D5
  STKP SK1 .... 166 C4 🄫
Lawrie Av *RAMS* BL0 .... 6 C4
Lawson Av *CHD/CHDH* SK8 .... 179 F2
Lawson Cl *MDTN* M24 .... 57 E5
  WALK M28 .... 85 D6
Lawson Gv *SALE* M33 .... 139 E5
Lawson Rd *BOL* BL1 .... 27 D5 🄫
Lawson St *BKLY* M9 .... 91 D3
  BOL BL1 .... 27 F3 🄫
Law St *ROCH* OL11 .... 39 D2
Lawton Av *BRAM/HZG* SK7 .... 196 C1 🄫
Lawton Cl *MPL/ROM* SK6 .... 169 D4 🄫
Lawton Moor Rd *NTHM/RTH* M23 .. 161 E4
Lawton Rd *HTNM* SK4 .... 166 A1
Lawton St *DROY* M43 .... 110 C5 🄫
  HYDE SK14 .... 131 F6 🄫
  OP/CLY M11 .... 112 C2 🄫
  STLY SK15 .... 119 F3
  WHIT OL12 .... 23 E4
Laxey Av *NEWH/MOS* M40 .... 92 C6 🄫
Laxfield Dr *URM* M41 .... 117 E5
Laxford Gv *BOLS/LL* BL3 .... 44 C3
Layard St *AUL* OL6 .... 112 B4
Laycock Av *BOLE* BL2 .... 28 C4
  STLY SK15 .... 115 F3
Laycock Crs *FAIL* M35 .... 110 A1
Laycock Dr *DUK* SK16 .... 132 B2
Laycock Gv *FAIL* M35 .... 94 A6 🄫
Laycock St *MILN* OL16 .... 24 B2 🄫
Layfield Cl *TOT/BURYW* BL8 ..... 17 E6 🄫
Laystall St *CMANE* M1 .... 3 H3

Laythe Barn Cl *MILN* OL16 .... 41 F1 🄫
Layton Av *HYDE* SK14 .... 130 C6
Layton Cl *STKP* SK1 .... 167 E5 🄫
Layton Dr *FWTH* BL4 .... 65 E2 🄫
  MPL/ROM SK6 .... 170 A2
Layton St *NEWH/MOS* M40 .... 107 E5 🄫
Leabank St *BNG/LEV* M19 .... 145 E2 🄫🄫
Leabrook Dr *NEWH/MOS* M40 ... 93 F5
Leaburn Dr *BNG/LEV* M19 .... 164 C1 🄫
Leach Cl *MILN* OL16 .... 24 A3
Leaches Rd *RAMS* BL0 .... 7 E1
Leach St *BOLS/LL* BL3 .... 46 C4 🄫🄫
  FWTH BL4 .... 66 C2 🄫
  GTN M18 .... 126 C4
  MILN OL16 .... 40 C1
  MILN OL16 .... 42 A3 🄫
  PWCH M25 .... 88 A1
  ROY/SHW OL2 .... 62 A3
Leaconfield Dr *WALK* M28 .... 84 A6
Lea Ct *FAIL* M35 .... 93 F6 🄫
Leacroft Av *BOLE* BL2 .... 49 E3
Leacroft Rd *CCHDY* M21 .... 142 B6
Leadale Ri *OLDE* OL4 .... 81 E5 🄫
Leader Williams Rd *IRL* M44 ..... 135 D2 🄫
Lea Dr *BKLY* M9 .... 92 A2
Leafield Av *DID/WITH* M20 .... 164 B1
Leafield Cl *RAD* M26 .... 50 C6 🄫
Leafield Dr *CHD/CHDH* SK8 ...... 195 D3 🄫
Leaford Av *DTN/ASHW* M34 ...... 129 E5
Leaford Cl *DTN/ASHW* M34 .... 129 E5
Leaf St *HULME* M15 .... 124 A3 🄫
  RDSH SK5 .... 146 C4
Leagate *URM* M41 .... 138 C2
Lea Gate Cl *BOLE* BL2 .... 29 E2
Leaholme Cl *NEWH/MOS* M40 .. 109 E2 🄫
Leah St *LIT* OL15 .... 12 C6 🄫
Leak St *OLDTF/WHR* M16 .... 123 D3 🄫
Leamington Av *BURY* BL9 .... 19 F5 🄫
  DID/WITH M20 .... 163 D1 🄫
Leamington Rd *ECC* M30 .... 100 C4
  RDSH SK5 .... 146 C4 🄫
  URM M41 .... 118 C6
Leamington St *OLDE* OL4 .... 80 A3
  OP/CLY M11 .... 127 E2 🄫
  WHIT OL12 .... 22 C5 🄫🄫
Leam St *AUL* OL6 .... 113 E3
Leander Cl *BKLY* M9 .... 91 F3
Leander Dr *ROCH* OL11 .... 39 E6
Lea Rd *CHD/CHDH* SK8 .... 179 F4
  HTNM SK4 .... 165 F1
Leaside Av *OLD* OL1 .... 77 F2
Leaside Cl *WHIT* OL12 .... 22 B5 🄫
Leaside Dr *DID/WITH* M20 .... 144 B6
Leaside Gv *WALK* M28 .... 83 F2
Leaside Wy *WILM/AE* SK9 .... 204 A5 🄫
The Leas *HALE/TIMP* WA15 .... 175 F4
Lea Thorn *BOLE* BL2 .... 29 E3
Leaton Av *NTHM/RTH* M23 .... 177 E1
Lea Vw *ROY/SHW* OL2 .... 60 A6
Lecester Rd *CHH* M8 .... 106 C1
Leconfield Dr *BKLY* M9 .... 91 F2
Leconfield Rd *ECC* M30 .... 100 A3
Lecturers Cl *BOLS/LL* BL3 .... 47 D4
Ledbrooke Cl *SALQ/ORD* M5 .... 122 C1 🄫🄫
Ledburn St *HULME* M15 .... 123 E3 🄫
Ledbury Av *URM* M41 .... 119 D6
Ledbury Cl *MDTN* M24 .... 75 E5 🄫
Ledbury Rd *FAIL* M35 .... 109 E3 🄫
Ledge Ley *CHD/CHDH* SK8 .... 194 C1
Ledsham Av *BKLY* M9 .... 73 E6
Ledson Rd *NTHM/RTH* M23 .... 177 D2
Ledward La *ALT* WA14 .... 173 F5
Lee Av *ALT* WA14 .... 158 A6
  BOLS/LL BL3 .... 46 B6
Leech Av *AUL* OL6 .... 113 F2
Leech Brook Av *DTN/ASHW* M34 .. 129 F3
Leech St *HYDE* SK14 .... 132 A6 🄫
  STLY SK15 .... 114 B6
Lee Cl *IRL* M44 .... 135 D2
Lee Dale Cl *DTN/ASHW* M34 ..... 149 E1
Leeds Cl *BURY* BL9 .... 53 F6
Lee Ga *BOLE* BL2 .... 29 E2
Leegate Rd *HTNM* SK4 .... 165 E1
Leegrange Rd *BKLY* M9 .... 91 F4
Lee Gv *FWTH* BL4 .... 65 D3
Leek St *RAD* M26 .... 50 C6 🄫🄫
Leemans Hill St *TOT/BURYW* BL8 .. 32 B2
Lees Av *DTN/ASHW* M34 .... 148 C1
Lees Brook Pk *OLDE* OL4 .... 80 B5
Lees Gv *OLDE* OL4 .... 80 B6
Lees Hall Crs *RUSH/FAL* M14 .... 144 B5
Leeside *HTNM* SK4 .... 165 E4
Lees La *MCFLDN* SK10 .... 205 F4
  OLDE OL4 .... 98 A1
Lees Rd *AUL* OL6 .... 97 E6
  BRAM/HZG SK7 .... 196 B4
  OLDE OL4 .... 79 E4
Lees St *AUL* OL6 .... 112 C3
  BCUP OL13 .... 5 D1
  DROY M43 .... 110 C5
  GTN M18 .... 127 F3
  MDTN M24 .... 76 B4
  MOSL OL5 .... 99 D3 🄫

OLDS OL8 .... 96 A5
  ROY/SHW OL2 .... 61 F2
  STLY SK15 .... 114 B5 🄫
  SWIN M27 .... 86 A4
Leestone Rd *WYTH/NTH* M22 ... 178 C1
Lee St *LIT* OL15 .... 12 C5
  MDTN M24 .... 57 D6 🄫
  OLDS OL8 .... 78 B5
  STKP SK1 .... 167 D4
Leesway *OLDE* OL4 .... 80 C6
Leesway Dr *DTN/ASHW* M34 .... 149 E1
Leeswood Av *CCHDY* M21 .... 142 A5 🄫
Leewood *SWIN* M27 .... 85 E1
Left Bank *CSLFD* M3 .... 2 B3 🄫
Le Gendre St *BOLE* BL2 .... 28 C6 🄫🄫
Legh Dr *DTN/ASHW* M34 .... 110 C6
  MPL/ROM SK6 .... 149 F5
Legh Rd *BRO* M7 .... 89 E5
  POY/DIS SK12 .... 201 E3
  SALE M33 .... 160 C2
Legh St *BRO* M7 .... 89 E5
  ECC M30 .... 101 D6
Legion Gv *BRO* M7 .... 105 F1 🄫🄫
Legwood Ct *URM* M41 .... 138 A1 🄫
Leicester Av *BRO* M7 .... 90 A4 🄫
  DROY M43 .... 110 A4
  DTN/ASHW M34 .... 149 D2
  HALE/TIMP WA15 .... 159 E5
Leicester Rd *BRO* M7 .... 89 F6
  FAIL M35 .... 110 B2
  HALE/TIMP WA15 .... 174 C5
  SALE M33 .... 139 F6
  WHTF M45 .... 70 B2
Leicester St *AULW* OL7 .... 112 C3 🄫
  OLDE OL4 .... 79 F5
  RDSH SK5 .... 146 C1
  ROCH OL11 .... 40 B2 🄫🄫
Leigh Av *MPL/ROM* SK6 .... 186 C1
  SWIN M27 .... 101 E2 🄫
Leighbrook Rd *RUSH/FAL* M14 .. 143 F3
Leigh Cl *TOT/BURYW* BL8 .... 17 F6
Leigh Fold *HYDE* SK14 .... 131 F4
Leigh La *TOT/BURYW* BL8 .... 32 B4
Leigh Rd *HALE/TIMP* WA15 ...... 174 C5
  WILM/AE SK9 .... 202 B6
Leigh St *BRO* M7 .... 89 E6
  FWTH BL4 .... 66 B3 🄫🄫
  HEY OL10 .... 36 C5 🄫
  HYDE SK14 .... 150 C1
  MILN OL16 .... 24 B6 🄫
  TOT/BURYW BL8 .... 32 A3 🄫
Leighton Av *BOL* BL1 .... 45 F1
  LIT OL15 .... 25 D3
Leighton Rd *OLDTF/WHR* M16 .. 123 D5
Leighton St *NEWH/MOS* M40 ... 92 B5
Leinster Rd *SWIN* M27 .... 85 F6 🄫
Leinster St *FWTH* BL4 .... 66 A3
Leith Av *SALE* M33 .... 160 C1
Leith Rd *SALE* M33 .... 160 C1
Le Mans Crs *BOL* BL1 .... 47 D2 🄫
Lemnos St *OLD* OL1 .... 79 E4
Lena St *BOL* BL1 .... 28 A5
  CMANE M1 .... 3 G4
Leng Rd *NEWH/MOS* M40 .... 109 D2
Lenham Cl *RDSH* SK5 .... 147 F5
Lenham Gdns *BOLE* BL2 .... 48 C3
Lennox Gdns *BOLS/LL* BL3 .... 45 D4
Lennox St *AUL* OL6 .... 113 D4
Lenora St *BOLS/LL* BL3 .... 45 F4
Lennox Gv *HEY* OL10 .... 56 C2
Lentmead Dr *NEWH/MOS* M40 .. 92 B4 🄫
Lenton Gdns *WYTH/NTH* M22 ... 178 C2 🄫
Leominster Dr *WYTH/NTH* M22 .. 178 C4
Leominster Rd *MDTN* M24 .... 75 F5 🄫
Leonardin Cl *ROY/SHW* OL2 ..... 61 D1 🄫
Leonard St *BOLS/LL* BL3 .... 46 C6
  ROCH OL11 .... 39 D6 🄫
Leopold Av *DID/WITH* M20 .... 143 E6 🄫
Leopold St *ROCH* OL11 .... 22 B6 🄫
Lepp Crs *TOT/BURYW* BL8 .... 33 D1
Leroy Dr *BKLY* M9 .... 91 E3
Lerryn Dr *BRAM/HZG* SK7 .... 182 B6
Lesley Rd *STRET* M32 .... 139 E2
Leslie Av *BURY* BL9 .... 53 D6 🄫
  CHAD OL9 .... 94 C2
Leslie Gv *HALE/TIMP* WA15 ..... 175 E1
Leslie Hough Wy *SLFD* M6 .... 104 C3
Leslie St *BOLE* BL2 .... 28 C6
  RUSH/FAL M14 .... 124 C6 🄫
Lester Rd *LHULT* M38 .... 64 C6
Lester St *STRET* M32 .... 140 B1
Letchworth Av *ROCH* OL11 .... 40 A2
Letchworth St *RUSH/FAL* M14 .. 124 C6 🄫
Letham St *OLDS* OL8 .... 96 A3 🄫
Levedale Rd *BKLY* M9 .... 91 F1
Leven Cl *FWTH* BL4 .... 67 F6
Levenhurst Rd *CHH* M8 .... 90 A6
Levens Cl *CHD/CHDH* SK8 .... 179 F3
Levens Dr *BOLE* BL2 .... 29 F6
Levenshulme Rd *GTN* M18 .... 127 E5
Levenshulme Ter
  BNG/LEV M19 .... 145 E2 🄫🄫
Levens Rd *BRAM/HZG* SK7 .... 184 A5
Levens St *NEWH/MOS* M40 ...... 92 B6
  SLFD M6 .... 104 C2

Lever Av *SWIN* M27 .... 86 C3
Lever Bridge Pl *BOLS/LL* BL3 ..... 48 B4
Lever Dr *BOLS/LL* BL3 .... 46 C4
Lever Edge La *BOLS/LL* BL3 .... 64 C1 🔟
Lever Gv *BOLE* BL2 .... 47 E4
Lever Hall Rd *BOLE* BL2 .... 48 B2 🔟
Leverhulme Av *BOLS/LL* BL3 .... 47 E6
Lever St *BOLS/LL* BL3 .... 46 C5
  BOLS/LL BL3 .... 49 E5
  BRAM/HZG SK7 .... 184 B5
  CMANE M1 .... 3 F3 🔟
  HEY OL10 .... 37 E4
  MDTN M24 .... 75 E2
  RAD M26 .... 51 D4 🔟
  RAMS BL0 .... 7 D5 🔟
Lever Wk *MDTN* M24 .... 75 D4
Levington Dr *OLDS* OL8 .... 96 B5
Levi St *BOL* BL1 .... 26 A6 🔟
Lewes Av *BKLY* M9 .... 91 F4
  URM M41 .... 119 E4
Lewis Dr *HEY* OL10 .... 36 A6
Lewisham Av *NEWH/MOS* M40 ..... 108 C3 🔟
Lewisham St *ROY/SHW* OL2 .... 60 A3 🔟
Lewis Rd *DROY* M43 .... 109 F5
  RDSH SK5 .... 147 D2
Lewis St *ECC* M30 .... 101 E6
  HEY OL10 .... 37 F4 🔟
  NEWH/MOS M40 .... 107 E4
  ROY/SHW OL2 .... 61 F4 🔟
Lewtas St *ECC* M30 .... 101 F6
Lexton Av *CHH* M8 .... 90 C3
Leybourne Av *BNG/LEV* M19 ... 145 F1 🔟
Leybourne St *BOL* BL1 .... 27 F5
Leybrook Rd *WYTH/NTH* M22 ..... 178 A4
Leyburn Av *ROY/SHW* OL2 .... 60 B5 🔟
  STRET M32 .... 139 F1
  URM M41 .... 137 E2
Leyburn Cl *WHTF* M45 .... 70 C3
Leyburn Rd *OFTN* SK2 .... 184 A1
Leyburn Gv *MPL/ROM* SK6 ..... 170 A3 🔟
Leyburn Rd *NTHM/RTH* M23 ..... 161 E4
Leycett Dr *NTHM/RTH* M23 .... 161 E4
Leycroft St *CMANE* M1 .... 3 H4 🔟
  CMANE M1 .... 3 H5 🔟
Ley Dr *HEY* OL10 .... 56 C2
Leyfield Av *MPL/ROM* SK6 ..... 170 A3
Leyfield Rd *MILN* OL16 .... 41 E1
Ley Hey Av *MPL/ROM* SK6 ...... 171 D6
Ley Hey Rd *MPL/ROM* SK6 ...... 171 D6
Leyland Av *CHD/CHDH* SK8 ...... 179 E5
  DID/WITH M20 .... 164 B2
  IRL M44 .... 116 C5
Leylands La *HYDE* SK14 .... 152 C5
Leyland St *BURY* BL9 .... 53 D5
  STKP SK1 .... 166 C4 🔟
  STKP SK1 .... 166 C4 🔟
Leys Rd *ALT* WA14 .... 158 C5
Leyton Av *NEWH/MOS* M40 ...... 92 C6 🔟
Leyton Cl *FWTH* BL4 .... 65 D2
Leyton Dr *BURY* BL9 .... 53 D4
Leyton St *WHIT* OL12 .... 23 D3 🔟
Leywell Dr *OLD* OL1 .... 62 B6
Library La *CHAD* OL9 .... 78 B3 🔟
Libra St *BOL* BL1 .... 27 E5 🔟🔟
Lichens Crs *OLDS* OL8 .... 96 B2
Lichfield Av *AUL* OL6 .... 97 E6
  BOLE BL2 .... 28 C5
  HALE/TIMP WA15 ..... 176 A4
  RDSH SK5 .... 146 C4
Lichfield Cl *FWTH* BL4 .... 65 E2
Lichfield Dr *CHAD* OL9 .... 77 E2
  CHH M8 .... 90 C6 🔟
  PWCH M25 .... 89 D3
  SWIN M27 .... 102 A1 🔟
  TOT/BURYW BL8 ...... 33 E3
Lichfield Rd *ECC* M30 .... 102 A3 🔟
  RAD M26 .... 50 B4
  URM M41 .... 119 E5
Lichfield St *SLFD* M6 .... 104 B2
Lichfield Ter *MILN* OL16 .... 41 D3
Lichfield Wk *MPL/ROM* SK6 .... 169 E4 🔟
Lidbrook Wk *WGTN/LGST* M12 ... 125 F3
Liddington Hall Dr *RAMS* BL0 .... 18 C1
Lidgett Cl *WALK* M28 .... 66 A6
Lidiard St *CHH* M8 .... 90 B4 🔟
Liffey Av *WYTH/NTH* M22 .... 178 C4
Lifton Av *NEWH/MOS* M40 ...... 107 F3 🔟
Light Alders La *POY/DIS* SK12 ... 201 E2
Lightborne Rd *SALE* M33 .... 158 B1
Lightbounds Rd *BOL* BL1 .... 26 A4
Lightbourne Av *SWIN* M27 .... 86 A6
Lightbowne Rd *NEWH/MOS* M40 .. 92 C5
Lightburn Av *LIT* OL15 .... 24 C1
Lighthorne Av *EDGY/DAV* SK3 .. 165 D6 🔟
Lighthorne Gv *EDGY/DAV* SK3 .. 165 D6 🔟
Lighthorne Rd *EDGY/DAV* SK3 ... 165 D6
Light Oaks Rd *SLFD* M6 .... 102 C3
Lightowlers La *LIT* OL15 .... 13 E4
Lightwood *WALK* M28 .... 82 C5 🔟
Lightwood Cl *FWTH* BL4 .... 66 C2 🔟
Lignum Av *CHAD* OL9 .... 77 F3
Lilac Av *BURY* BL9 .... 52 B2
  HYDE SK14 .... 150 B3

Lilac Cl *MILN* OL16 .... 42 B4
  SWIN M27 .... 86 B5
Lilac Gv *CHAD* OL9 .... 77 F3
  NEWH/MOS M40 ...... 92 B4 🔟
  PWCH M25 .... 71 E5
Lilac La *OLDS* OL8 .... 95 E3
Lilac Rd *HALE/TIMP* WA15 ..... 175 E4
  ROCH OL11 .... 40 A5 🔟
Lilac St *OFTN* SK2 .... 183 D1
Lilac View Cl *ROY/SHW* OL2 ..... 62 B3
Lila St *BKLY* M9 .... 92 A6 🔟
Lilburn Cl *RAMS* BL0 .... 19 D1 🔟
Liley St *MILN* OL16 .... 23 E6
Lilford Cl *WGTN/LGST* M12 .... 126 B3 🔟
Lilian St *OLDTF/WHR* M16 ...... 123 D5
Lillian Gv *RDSH* SK5 .... 147 D3 🔟
Lilly St *BOL* BL1 .... 46 B1 🔟🔟
  HYDE SK14 .... 151 D3
Lilmore Av *NEWH/MOS* M40 .... 109 D1
Lily Av *FWTH* BL4 .... 65 F2
Lily Cl *EDGY/DAV* SK3 .... 182 B2
Lily Hill St *WHTF* M45 .... 70 C1
Lily La *BKLY* M9 .... 92 A6
  AUL OL6 .... 97 F5
Lily St *ECC* M30 .... 100 C6
  MDTN M24 .... 76 A3
  MILN OL16 .... 11 D1 🔟
  OLD OL1 .... 78 C2
  ROY/SHW OL2 .... 61 D5
Lima St *BURY* BL9 .... 34 C4
Limbert Cir *CHH* M8 .... 91 D4 🔟
Lime Av *SWIN* M27 .... 101 D1 🔟
  URM M41 .... 137 F1
  WHTF M45 .... 71 D4
Lime Bank St *WGTN/LGST* M12 .. 125 E1
Limebrook Cl *OP/CLY* M11 .... 127 F2 🔟🔟
Lime Cl *DUK* SK16 .... 131 E3
  SLFD M6 .... 104 B4
Lime Crs *OLDTF/WHR* M16 .... 122 C5
Limeditch Rd *FAIL* M35 .... 94 B4
Limefield *MDTN* M24 .... 74 C4
  MOSL OL5 .... 98 C3
Limefield Av *FWTH* BL4 .... 66 B2 🔟
Limefield Cl *BOL* BL1 .... 26 B3
Limefield Rd *BOL* BL1 .... 26 C3
  BRO M7 .... 89 E4
  RAD M26 .... 50 B6
Limefield Ter *BNG/LEV* M19 ... 145 E2 🔟🔟
Lime Gdns *DUK* SK16 .... 130 C3 🔟
  MDTN M24 .... 74 C3
Lime Ga *OLDS* OL8 .... 95 D3
Lime Gn *OLDS* OL8 .... 95 E4
Lime Green Rd *OLDS* OL8 .... 95 D5
Lime Gv *AUL* OL6 .... 113 D2
  CHD/CHDH SK8 ..... 180 B1
  DTN/ASHW M34 ..... 130 A5
  HALE/TIMP WA15 ... 175 F1
  HEY OL10 .... 37 D4
  LIT OL15 .... 12 A6
  OLDTF/WHR M16 ... 122 C5
  PWCH M25 .... 71 E5
  RAMS BL0 .... 7 E4
  ROY/SHW OL2 ...... 60 B3
  STLY SK15 .... 131 F1
  WALK M28 .... 83 E4
Limehurst Av *AULW* OL7 ...... 112 B1 🔟
  DID/WITH M20 ...... 143 D3
Limehurst Rd *AULW* OL7 ...... 112 B1 🔟
Lime Kiln La *MPL/ROM* SK6 .... 187 E2
Limekiln La *WGTN/LGST* M12 ... 125 E1
Lime La *OLDS* OL8 .... 95 D4
Lime Rd *STRET* M32 .... 140 B2
Limers Ga *WHIT* OL12 .... 10 A6
Limerston Av *NEWH/MOS* M40 .. 108 A2
Limesdale Cl *BOLS/LL* BL3 ...... 49 F4 🔟
Limeside Rd *OLDS* OL8 .... 95 D3
Limestead Av *CHH* M8 .... 90 B5 🔟
The Limes *MOSL* OL5 .... 98 C4
  MOSL OL5 .... 99 F4
Lime St *BURY* BL9 .... 34 A1 🔟
  DUK SK16 .... 130 C1 🔟
  ECC M30 .... 101 E6
  FWTH BL4 .... 66 C3
  MPL/ROM SK6 ..... 168 C1 🔟
  NEWH/MOS M40 .... 107 E4
  OLD OL1 .... 78 A2
  ROCH OL11 .... 39 D3
Lime Tree Cl *URM* M41 .... 138 C2
Lime Tree Gv *FAIL* M35 .... 94 C6 🔟
Limetrees Rd *MDTN* M24 .... 75 D3
Limley Gv *CCHDY* M21 .... 142 A4
Linacre Av *BOLS/LL* BL3 .... 64 C1
Linby St *HULME* M15 .... 123 F2
Lincoln Av *BNG/LEV* M19 .... 145 F2
  BOLS/LL BL3 .... 49 E6
  CHD/CHDH SK8 .... 193 F1
  DROY M43 .... 110 B4
  DTN/ASHW M34 .... 149 D2 🔟
  IRL M44 .... 154 A1
  STRET M32 .... 120 A6
Lincoln Cl *AUL* OL6 .... 97 E5
  ROCH OL11 .... 40 B1 🔟
Lincoln Dr *BURY* BL9 .... 53 D1 🔟
  HALE/TIMP WA15 .. 175 F2 🔟
  LIT OL15 .... 25 E2

Lincoln Gv *BOLE* BL2 .... 30 A3
  BRUN/LGST M13 .... 125 D4
  SALE M33 .... 160 C1
Lincoln Leach Ct *ROCH* OL11 ... 40 A2 🔟
Lincoln Mnr *MPL/ROM* SK6 ..... 169 E4
Lincoln Rd *BOL* BL1 .... 46 A1 🔟🔟
  FAIL M35 .... 110 B1 🔟
  MDTN M24 .... 76 A6
  WILM/AE SK9 ..... 204 C2
Lincoln St *BRUN/LGST* M13 .... 126 A5
  CHAD OL9 .... 77 F6
  ECC M30 .... 101 D6 🔟
  ROCH OL11 .... 40 B1
Lincombe Rd *WYTH/NTH* M22 ... 192 A1
Linda Dr *BRAM/HZG* SK7 .... 184 B6
Lindale *HYDE* SK14 .... 131 D4
Lindale Av *BOL* BL1 .... 45 D1
  BURY BL9 .... 53 E6
  CHAD OL9 .... 77 E5
  NEWH/MOS M40 .... 93 E3 🔟
  ROY/SHW OL2 ...... 60 A2
  URM M41 .... 118 A6
Lindale Dr *MDTN* M24 .... 56 C6
Lindale Ri *ROY/SHW* OL2 .... 62 B2
Lindbury Av *OFTN* SK2 .... 168 A6
Linden Av *BOLS/LL* BL3 .... 49 E4
  DTN/ASHW M34 ... 130 A6
  HALE/TIMP WA15 .. 174 C2
  OLDE OL4 .... 80 B3
  RAMS BL0 .... 7 E5 🔟
  SALE M33 .... 159 D1
  SLFD M6 .... 103 F1
  SWIN M27 .... 85 E6 🔟
Linden Cl *DTN/ASHW* M34 ..... 130 B6
  RAMS BL0 .... 7 E1 🔟
Linden Dr *SALQ/ORD* M5 .... 122 B1 🔟🔟
Linden Gv *BRAM/HZG* SK7 ..... 196 B5
  OFTN SK2 .... 183 F3
  RUSH/FAL M14 .... 144 B3 🔟
Linden Pk *BNG/LEV* M19 .... 145 D3
Linden Rd *CHD/CHDH* SK8 .... 181 E4 🔟
  DID/WITH M20 ..... 163 E1
  DTN/ASHW M34 .... 130 B6
  STLY SK15 .... 133 E2
Linden Wk *BOLE* BL2 .... 28 C2
Linden Wy *MPL/ROM* SK6 ..... 201 E2
Lindenwood *CHAD* OL9 .... 76 C5 🔟
Lindeth Av *OP/CLY* M11 ...... 117 E5 🔟
Lindfield Dr *BOL* BL1 .... 27 F6
Lindfield Est North *WILM/AE* SK9 .. 203 E5
Lindfield Est South *WILM/AE* SK9 .. 203 D5
Lindfield Rd *RDSH* SK5 .... 147 D2 🔟
Lindinis Av *SALQ/ORD* M5 ..... 104 B5
Lindisfarne *SALE* M33 .... 159 F4
Lindisfarne Dr *POY/DIS* SK12 ... 198 B5
Lindisfarne Pl *BOLE* BL2 .... 29 D5 🔟
Lindisfarne Rd *AULW* OL7 ...... 107 F5
Lindley St *BOLS/LL* BL3 .... 49 F6 🔟🔟
  FWTH BL4 .... 67 F5
Lindleywood Rd *RUSH/FAL* M14 .. 144 C3
Lindon Wy *DROY* M43 .... 127 F1
Lindop Rd *HALE/TIMP* WA15 ... 175 D6
Lindow Cl *TOT/BURYW* BL8 ..... 32 C1
Lindow Ct *MPL/ROM* SK6 ..... 168 B2 🔟
Lindow Fold Dr *WILM/AE* SK9 .. 208 B1
Lindow La *WILM/AE* SK9 .... 202 C5
Lindow Rd *OLDTF/WHR* M16 ... 141 F1
Lindow St *SALE* M33 .... 161 D2 🔟
Lindrick Av *WHTF* M45 .... 70 B5
Lindrick Cl *NEWH/MOS* M40 .... 93 D6
Lindsay Av *BNG/LEV* M19 ...... 145 D2
  CHD/CHDH SK8 ... 181 F6
  SWIN M27 .... 85 F6 🔟
Lindsay Cl *OLDE* OL4 .... 80 B1 🔟
Lindsay Rd *BNG/LEV* M19 ...... 145 D3
Lindsay St *STLY* SK15 .... 114 C5
Lindsell Rd *ALT* WA14 .... 158 A5
Lindsgate Dr *HALE/TIMP* WA15 .. 159 F6 🔟
Lind St *NEWH/MOS* M40 .... 107 F5 🔟
Lindum Av *OLDTF/WHR* M16 ... 123 D5
Lindum St *RUSH/FAL* M14 ...... 124 C6
Lindwall Cl *NTHM/RTH* M23 ... 161 F3 🔟
Linehan Cl *HTNM* SK4 .... 164 B3
Lineholme *OLD* OL1 .... 78 A1 🔟
Linen Ct *CSLFD* M3 .... 105 E4 🔟
Lines Rd *DROY* M43 .... 110 C6
  IRL M44 .... 135 E5
Linfield Cl *BOLE* BL2 .... 29 E3
Linfield St *OP/CLY* M11 .... 108 C6
Linford Av *NEWH/MOS* M40 .... 93 D3
Lingard La *MPL/ROM* SK6 ..... 148 B6
Lingard Rd *WYTH/NTH* M22 .... 162 B4
Lingard St *RDSH* SK5 .... 147 D3
Lingcrest Rd *BNG/LEV* M19 .... 146 A4
Lingdale Rd *CHD/CHDH* SK8 ... 181 D5
Lingfield Av *BRAM/HZG* SK7 ... 185 D5
  SALE M33 .... 157 F3
Lingfield Cl *FWTH* BL4 .... 66 A4
  TOT/BURYW BL8 ... 19 D6 🔟
Lingfield Rd *OP/CLY* M11 ...... 109 D3
Lingholme Dr *MDTN* M24 .... 74 A1
Lingmell Cl *BOL* BL1 .... 45 D1
  MDTN M24 .... 74 B1 🔟
  URM M41 .... 118 A5 🔟
Lingmoor Cl *MDTN* M24 .... 74 A1

Lingmoor Rd BOL BL1............26 A6
Lings Wk WYTH/NTH M22 ......178 C6
Linhope CI HTNM SK4.........164 C2 ⓫
Link Av URM M41................139 E2
Link La OLDS OL8................95 F3
Link Rd OLDE OL4................81 D4
SALE M33.........................158 B3
Links Av FAIL M35...............110 A2
Links Crs PWCH M25........89 F3 ⓷
Linksfield DTN/ASHW M34......130 A4
Linkside Av ROY/SHW OL2.......60 B4
Links PI AUL OL6................113 F1
Links Ri URM M41..............118 B5
Links Rd BOLE BL2...............30 B3
HEY OL10...........................56 B1
MPL/ROM SK6..................170 B2
MPL/ROM SK6..................187 D3
WILM/AE SK9.....................208 C2
The Links NEWH/MOS M40.......93 D6
Links Vw PWCH M25..............88 B4
ROCH OL11..........................38 C1
Linksway CHD/CHDH SK8.......179 E3
PWCH M25..........................89 E3
SWIN M27........................102 B3 ⓫
Linksway Ct HTNM SK4..........145 E6
Linksway Dr BURY BL9...........53 E6
The Links RDSH SK5.............148 A5
ROY/SHW OL2.....................42 A6
WILM/AE SK9....................194 B6 ⓷
Linley Av RAD M26.................52 C4 ⓷
Linley Dr OLDE OL4................9 F1
Linley Gv TOT/BURYW BL8.......18 B3
Linley Rd CHD/CHDH SK8.......195 F1
SALE M33.........................139 F6
Linnell Dr ROCH OL11............20 C5
Linnet CI DTN/ASHW M34.......111 D5
OFTN SK2.........................185 D2
WGTN/LGST M12...............126 A5 ⓷
Linnet Dr BURY BL9................34 C3
IRL M44............................116 B6 ⓷
Linnet HI ROCH OL11.............39 D1
Linnet's Wood Ms WALK M28.....83 F2
Linney La ROY/SHW OL2...........62 A2
Linney Rd BRAM/HZG SK7......182 B5
Linn St CHH M8.....................90 B4
Linsley St CSLFD M3................2 B1 ⓷
Linstead Dr CHH M8..........106 A1 ⓫ ⓷
Linton Av BURY BL9................34 A2
DTN/ASHW M34...................128 B6
Linton Ct WGTN/LGST M12...125 E1 ⓷
Linton Rd SALE M33...............140 A5
Linwood CI WGTN/LGST M12...145 E1 ⓷
Linwood St FAIL M35.............109 D1 ⓷
Lion Brow BKLY M9.................91 E3
Lion Fold La BKLY M9...........91 E2 ⓷
Lions Dr SWIN M27.................86 B6
Lion St BKLY M9....................91 E3
Lisbon St ROCH OL11..............21 F5
Lisburn Av CCHDY M21...........142 A2
SALE M33.........................159 E2
Lisburne Av OFTN SK2............184 B1
Lisburne CI OFTN SK2............184 B1 ⓷
Lisburne La OFTN SK2............184 A2
Lisburn Rd NEWH/MOS M40......92 B5
Liscard Av RUSH/FAL M14.......143 F2
Liskeard Av ROY/SHW OL2.......61 D6
Liskeard Dr BRAM/HZG SK7....197 D2
Lisle St WHIT OL12.................23 E5
Lismore Av BOLS/LL BL3...........45 D4 ⓷
EDGY/DAV SK3..................165 F6 ⓫
Lismore Rd DUK SK16............131 E2
Lismore Wy URM M41.............119 E4
Lissadel St SLFD M6..............104 C4
Lisson Gv HALE/TIMP WA15....174 C5
Lister Rd MDTN M24................73 F5
Lister St BOLS/LL BL3.............45 F6 ⓷
Liston St DUK SK16...............132 A1 ⓷
Litcham CI CMANE M1.........124 C2 ⓫ ⓷
Litchfield Gv WALK M28............84 C6 ⓷
Litherland Av WYTH/NTH M22...178 C5
Litherland Rd BOLS/LL BL3.......64 C1
SALE M33.........................160 C2
Little Ancoats St CMANE M1......3 G2 ⓷
Little Bank Rd OLDE OL4..........79 F5
Littlebourne Wk EDGW/EG BL7...28 B3 ⓷
Littlebrook CI CHD/CHDH SK8..182 A3 ⓫
Little Brook Rd SALE M33........158 A4
Little Brow EDGW/EG BL7.........14 B6
Little Clegg Rd LIT OL15...........25 D3
Littledale St WHIT OL12........22 C5 ⓫
Little David St CMANE M1.........3 F1
Little Ees La SALE M33...........139 D4
Little Egerton St STKP SK1......167 D3 ⓫
Little Flatt WHIT OL12............21 F4 ⓷
Littlegreen SLFD M6..............104 A4 ⓷
Little Harwood Lee BOLE BL2.....29 E4
Littlehaven CI WGTN/LGST M12..125 F4
Little Heath La ALT WA14.........172 B2
Little Hey St ROY/SHW OL2.......61 F5
Littlehills CI MDTN M24............74 C2
Little Holme St ANC M4.........107 E6 ⓫
Little Howarth Wy WHIT OL12...24 A1 ⓷
Little John St CSLFD M3...........2 A5
Little Lever St CMANE M1......3 G3 ⓷
Little Meadow Rd ALT WA14....173 F6

Little Mdw EDGW/EG BL7........14 A6 ⓫
Little Moor La OLDE OL4..........80 A3
Littlemoor Rd HYDE SK14.......153 E1
Little Moss La SWIN M27...........86 A3
Little Nelson St ANC M4.......106 B4 ⓷
Little Oak CI OLDE OL4.............80 C5
Little Peter St HULME M15.....124 A2 ⓷
Little Pitt St CMANE M1...........3 H3 ⓫
Little Quay St CSLFD M3............2 C4
Littleton Rd BRO M7.................88 B5
Little Underbank STKP SK1.....167 D4 ⓫
Littlewood Av BURY BL9...........34 A2 ⓫
Littlewood Rd WYTH/NTH M22...178 A3
Littlewood St SLFD M6..........103 F5 ⓫ ⓷
Littondale CI ROY/SHW OL2.......60 C4
Liverpool CI RDSH SK5...........146 C4 ⓷
Liverpool Rd CSLFD M3...........123 E1
ECC M30...........................100 C6
IRL M44............................135 D3
Liverpool St RDSH SK5..........146 C4 ⓷
SALO/ORD M5....................104 B6
SLFD M6...........................103 F5
Liverstudd Av RDSH SK5.........147 D3 ⓷
Livesey Av ANC M4...............107 D4
BNG/LEV M19.....................145 F3
OLD OL1............................80 A3 ⓷
Livingstone Av MOSL OL5.........98 C4
Livingstone St OLDE OL4..........80 C6 ⓷
Livsey La HEY OL10.................36 B5
Livsey St BURY BL9.................23 E6
WHIT OL12..........................71 D3
Lizard St CMANE M1.................3 G3
Lizmar Ter NEWH/MOS M40......92 A5
Llanberis Rd CHD/CHDH SK8...180 C6
Llanfair Rd EDGY/DAV SK3....166 A5 ⓷
Lloyd Av CHD/CHDH SK8.........179 E1
Lloyd Gdns ALT WA14..........174 B4 ⓫
Lloyd Rd BNG/LEV M19..........145 F4
Lloyd Sq ALT WA14..............174 B3 ⓷
Lloyd St ALT WA14...............174 B3
CMANW M2..........................2 C4
HEY OL10............................37 E6
HTNM SK4.........................166 B3
ROCH OL11..........................39 E3
WHIT OL12...........................9 D2
Lloyd St South RUSH/FAL M14...143 D2
Lobden Crs WHIT OL12............12 A4
Lobelia Av FWTH BL4...............65 E2
Lobley CI WHIT OL12...............23 E3
Lochawe CI HEY OL10..............36 B6
Lochinver Gv HEY OL10...........36 B6 ⓫
Lochmaddy CI BRAM/HZG SK7..185 D6 ⓷
Lock CI HEY OL10..................56 C1
Lockett Gdns CSLFD M3.......105 E5 ⓫ ⓷
Lockett St CHH M8................104 B2 ⓷
SLFD M6...........................104 B2 ⓷
Lockhart CI WGTN/LGST M12..126 B4 ⓷
Lockhart St MILN OL16............40 C2 ⓷
Lockingate St AUL OL6...........112 C1
Locking Gate Ri OLDE OL4.......80 C2
Locklands La IRL M44............135 E1
Lock La HOR/BR BL6................44 A5
PART M31..........................154 B2
Lock Rd ALT WA14................174 A1
Lockside MPL/ROM SK6.........187 E1
Lockside Vw MOSL OL5.........99 F1 ⓫
Locksley CI HTNM SK4...........166 A3
Lockton CI RDSH SK5............146 C5
Lockwood St WGTN/LGST M12..126 C6 ⓷
Lodge Av URM M41................138 C1
Lodge Bank Rd LIT OL15.........25 D2 ⓫
Lodge Brow RAD M26..............69 F1
Lodge CI DUK SK16...............131 F2
Lodge Ct HTNM SK4.............165 D3
Lodge Farm CI BRAM/HZG SK7.182 C5
Lodge Fold DROY M43...........110 C5
Lodge Gn DUK SK16...........131 F2 ⓷
Lodge La DUK SK16...............131 E1
HYDE SK14........................131 E5
Lodgepole CI ECC M30...........118 A1
Lodge Ri DROY M43..............110 C5
Lodge Rd RAD M26.................69 F1
Lodgeside CI DROY M43........110 C5 ⓷
Lodge St AULW OL7..............112 A6
HYDE SK14........................131 E5
LIT OL15............................12 C5
MDTN M24...........................75 E2
NEWH/MOS M40................107 F2 ⓫
RAMS BL0............................7 D5
WHIT OL12..........................11 D5 ⓷
Loen Crs BOL BL1..................27 D4
Loganberry Av SLFD M6........104 B4 ⓫
Logan St BOL BL1...............27 F2 ⓫
Logwood Av TOT/BURYW BL8...33 E4 ⓷
Loisine CI ROCH OL11.............38 B4
Lois St CHAD OL9....................94 B3
Lomas CI BNG/LEV M19........164 C2 ⓷
Lomas St EDGY/DAV SK3......166 B6
FAIL M35.............................94 B4
MDTN M24...........................75 F2 ⓷

WHIT OL12..........................23 D4 ⓭
WHTF M45............................70 C1 ⓫
Lombard CI MPL/ROM SK6.....169 D1 ⓫
Lombard Gv RUSH/FAL M14....144 A3
Lombard St OLD OL1................78 C4
WHIT OL12..........................22 B5 ⓫
Lomond Av HALE/TIMP WA15...175 E4
STRET M32.........................121 E6
Lomond CI OFTN SK2.............183 E4
Lomond Dr TOT/BURYW BL8.....32 C3
Lomond PI BOLS/LL BL3......44 C3 ⓫
Lomond Rd WYTH/NTH M22....179 D5
Lomond Ter MILN OL16............30 A1
London PI STKP SK1.............167 D4 ⓫
London Rd CMANE M1..............3 G5
OFTN SK2.........................184 B3
OLD OL1.............................79 F2 ⓫
WILM/AE SK9.....................209 E4
London Rd North POY/DIS SK12.198 C5
London Sq STKP SK1...........167 D4 ⓫
London St BOLS/LL BL3...........46 C5
SLFD M6...........................104 C3
WHTF M45............................71 D4
Long Acres Dr WHIT OL12..........9 E2
Longacres La WHIT OL12............9 E1 ⓫
Longacres Rd HALE/TIMP WA15..190 A2
Longacre St CMANE M1.........125 D1
Longbow Ct BRO M7............105 E5 ⓫
Longbridge Rd TRPK M17.......120 B3
Long Cswy FWTH BL4..............66 B4
Longcroft Dr ALT WA14.........173 F3
Longcroft Gv DTN/ASHW M34...128 C1 ⓷
NTHM/RTH M23..................161 E6
Long Croft La CHD/CHDH SK8...194 C1
Longdale CI ROY/SHW OL2.......60 A5
Longden Av OLDE OL4.........62 C6 ⓷
Longden Rd WGTN/LGST M12...145 E1
Longden St BOL BL1..........46 A1 ⓭ ⓷
Longfellow Av BOLS/LL BL3......45 F6
Longfellow Crs OLD OL1...........62 B5
Longfellow St SLFD M6.........105 D3 ⓷
Longfield Av CHD/CHDH SK8....194 A2
HALE/TIMP WA15................176 A1
URM M41............................137 F1
Longfield CI HYDE SK14.........131 F3
Longfield Crs OLDE OL4...........80 A2
Longfield Dr URM M41..........137 F1 ⓫
Longfield La OLDE OL4.........80 B2 ⓷
Longfield Pk ROY/SHW OL2......61 E4
Longfield Rd NTHM/RTH M23...161 D5
ROCH OL11..........................22 A5
ROY/SHW OL2.....................61 E3
Longford Av BOL BL1..........27 D5 ⓫ ⓷
STRET M32.........................140 A3
Longford CI STRET M32.........121 F6 ⓷
Longford PI RUSH/FAL M14.....125 F5
Longford Rd CCHDY M21........141 E2
RDSH SK5.........................147 D2
STRET M32.........................121 F6
Longford Rd West RDSH SK5...146 B2
Longford St GTN M18...........127 E3 ⓫
HEY OL10............................37 D5
Long Grain PI OFTN SK2........184 B2
Longham CI BRAM/HZG SK7....182 A6
OP/CLY M11.....................107 F6 ⓫
Long Hey HALE/TIMP WA15.....175 E4
Longhey Rd WYTH/NTH M22....178 B2
Long HI ROCH OL11.................39 E3
Longhirst CI BOL BL1..........26 C4 ⓫
Longhope Rd WYTH/NTH M22..177 F4
Longhurst La MPL/ROM SK6....171 F6
Longhurst Rd BKLY M9............90 C1
Longla CI BOLE BL2.................48 B4
BURY BL9............................19 F6
CHAD OL9............................94 B3
Longlevens Rd WYTH/NTH M22..178 A5
Longley Dr WALK M28...........100 C3
Longley La WYTH/NTH M22.....162 B5
Longley St OLD OL1...............79 D5 ⓫
ROY/SHW OL2.....................61 F4
WALK M28...........................83 E3 ⓫
Long Marl Dr WILM/AE SK9.....195 D5
Longmead Av BRAM/HZG SK7..184 B6
Longmeade Gdns WILM/AE SK9.204 A5
Long Meadow BOLE BL2...........15 D6
Longmeadow CHD/CHDH SK8..196 A2
Long Meadow HYDE SK14......132 A3
Longmeadow Gv
DTN/ASHW M34.................148 C2
Long Meadow Pas HYDE SK14..131 E6 ⓫
Longmead Rd SLFD M6..........103 E2
Longmead Wy MDTN M24........75 E2
Longmere Av WYTH/NTH M22..178 B4 ⓫
Long Millgate ANC M4...............2 D1
Longnor Rd BRAM/HZG SK7....198 C2
CHD/CHDH SK8..................194 B2
Longport Av DID/WITH M20....154 A1
Longridge EDGW/EG BL7.........15 D5
Longridge Av STLY SK15........114 B3
Longridge Crs BOL BL1...........26 A5
Longridge Dr HEY OL10...........51 D1
TOT/BURYW BL8...................51 D1
Longridge Pl CSLFD M3.............2 D2
Long Rushes ROY/SHW OL2......61 D1
Longshaw Av SWIN M27.......86 A4 ⓫

Longshaw Dr WALK M28 ...... 82 B1
Longshaw Ford Rd BOL BL1 ...... 26 A2
Longsight La STKP SK1 ...... 167 D6
Longshut La West OFTN SK2 ...... 167 D6
Longsides Rd HALE/TIMP WA15 ...... 199 H2
Longsight BOLE BL2 ...... 29 E2
Longsight La BOLE BL2 ...... 29 E3
  CHD/CHDH SK8 ...... 195 D4
Longsight Rd GTN M18 ...... 126 C6
  TOT/BURYW BL8 ...... 18 B4
Longsight St HTNM SK4 ...... 166 B3
Longson St BOL BL1 ...... 28 B6
Long St GTN M18 ...... 127 F3
  MDTN M24 ...... 75 E2
  SWIN M27 ...... 86 A6
Longton Av DID/WITH M20 ...... 143 E6
Longton Rd BKLY M9 ...... 91 D1
  SLFD M6 ...... 103 D2
Longton St BURY BL9 ...... 53 D5
Longview Dr SWIN M27 ...... 85 D4
Longwall Av WALK M28 ...... 83 D5
Longwood Av OFTN SK2 ...... 183 F1
Longwood Cl MPL/ROM SK6 ...... 170 C2
Longwood Rd TRPK M17 ...... 120 C3
  WYTH/NTH M22 ...... 178 C4
Longworth Cl URM M41 ...... 136 B2
Longworth St BOLE BL2 ...... 48 A2
  CSLFD M3 ...... 2 B5
Lonsdale Av MILN OL16 ...... 40 C2
  RDSH SK5 ...... 128 A6
  SWIN M27 ...... 101 E2
  URM M41 ...... 118 C5
Lonsdale Rd BNG/LEV M19 ...... 145 F1
  BOL BL1 ...... 45 F1
  OLDS OL8 ...... 94 C3
Lonsdale Rd NEWH/MOS M40 ...... 109 D1
  TOT/BURYW BL8 ...... 33 D5
Loom St ANC M4 ...... 3 H2
Lord Byron Sq SALQ/ORD M5 ...... 104 A6
Lord Derby Rd HYDE SK14 ...... 150 C5
Lord La FAIL M35 ...... 109 F3
Lord Napier Dr SALQ/ORD M5 ...... 122 B2
Lord North St NEWH/MOS M40 ...... 107 F3
Lord's Av SALQ/ORD M5 ...... 103 E5
Lordsfields Av AULW OL7 ...... 112 C3
Lordship Cl BKLY M9 ...... 92 A4
Lordsmead St HULME M15 ...... 123 E2
Lord's Stile La EDGW/EG BL7 ...... 14 C6
Lord's St IRL M44 ...... 134 A6
Lord St ANC M4 ...... 106 B4
  BOLS/LL BL3 ...... 49 F6
  BURY BL9 ...... 34 A5
  BURY BL9 ...... 35 D6
  CSLFD M3 ...... 106 A3
  DTN/ASHW M34 ...... 128 B5
  DUK SK16 ...... 132 A1
  FWTH BL4 ...... 66 C3
  MDTN M24 ...... 75 E2
  OLD OL1 ...... 79 D4
  RAD M26 ...... 51 E6
  STKP SK1 ...... 168 C4
  STKP SK1 ...... 167 D4
Loretto Rd URM M41 ...... 139 D2
Lorgill Cl EDGY/DAV SK3 ...... 183 D3
Loring St NEWH/MOS M40 ...... 109 D2
Lorland Rd EDGY/DAV SK3 ...... 165 F6
Lorna Gv CHD/CHDH SK8 ...... 179 D1
Lorna Rd CHD/CHDH SK8 ...... 181 F5
Lorne Av ROY/SHW OL2 ...... 59 F6
Lorne Gv URM M41 ...... 138 C1
Lorne Rd RUSH/FAL M14 ...... 144 A3
Lorne St ECC M30 ...... 118 C1
  FWTH BL4 ...... 66 A1
  HEY OL10 ...... 37 E6
  MOSL OL5 ...... 99 D4
  OLDS OL8 ...... 95 F1
  WHIT OL12 ...... 23 F2
Lorne Wy HEY OL10 ...... 36 A6
Lorraine Cl HEY OL10 ...... 56 C1
Lorraine Rd HALE/TIMP WA15 ...... 177 E5
Lorton Cl MDTN M24 ...... 74 A1
Lorton Gv BOLE BL2 ...... 49 D1
Lostock Av BNG/LEV M19 ...... 145 F2
  BRAM/HZG SK7 ...... 183 F6
  POY/DIS SK12 ...... 197 F5
  SALE M33 ...... 160 C3
  URM M41 ...... 118 C6
Lostock Cl HEY OL10 ...... 36 C4
Lostock Dr BURY BL9 ...... 34 A1
Lostock Gv STRET M32 ...... 120 C6
Lostock Hall Rd POY/DIS SK12 ...... 197 F6
Lostock Junction La HOR/BR BL6 ...... 44 A3
Lostock Rd SALQ/ORD M5 ...... 103 F5
  URM M41 ...... 119 E5
Lostock St NEWH/MOS M40 ...... 107 F3
Lostock Wy WILM/AE SK9 ...... 194 B5
Lothian Av ECC M30 ...... 100 C4
Lottery Rw BOL BL1 ...... 47 D2
Lottery St EDGY/DAV SK3 ...... 166 B4
Lottie St SWIN M27 ...... 86 B5
Loughborough Cl SALE M33 ...... 158 B2
Loughfield URM M41 ...... 137 E3
Loughrigg Av ROY/SHW OL2 ...... 60 A1
Louisa St BOL BL1 ...... 27 E5
  OP/CLY M11 ...... 127 E1

WALK M28 ...... 83 E1
Louis Av BURY BL9 ...... 34 A3
Louise Gdns WHIT OL12 ...... 23 F2
Louise St WHIT OL12 ...... 23 F2
Louvaine Av BOL BL1 ...... 26 A3
Louvain St FAIL M35 ...... 93 F6
Lovalle St BOL BL1 ...... 27 D6
Lovat Rd BOLE BL2 ...... 49 D2
Love La HTNM SK4 ...... 166 C3
Lovell Dr HYDE SK14 ...... 132 A5
Lowcock St BRO M7 ...... 105 F3
Lowcroft Crs CHAD OL9 ...... 77 D3
Lowcross Rd NEWH/MOS M40 ...... 108 B1
Lower Albion St CMANE M1 ...... 3 G6
Lower Alma St AULW OL7 ...... 112 C5
Lowerbank DTN/ASHW M34 ...... 130 A4
Lower Bank St BURY BL9 ...... 33 E5
Lower Bennett St HYDE SK14 ...... 131 D5
Lower Bents La MPL/ROM SK6 ...... 169 D1
Lower Bridgeman St BOLE BL2 ...... 47 E3
Lower Broadacre STLY SK15 ...... 133 F3
Lower Brook La WALK M28 ...... 100 B2
Lower Brook St CMANE M1 ...... 3 G5
Lower Broughton Rd BRO M7 ...... 105 D2
Lower Bury St HTNM SK4 ...... 166 B3
Lower Byrom St CSLFD M3 ...... 2 A5
Lower Carrs STKP SK1 ...... 167 D4
Lower Chatham St HULME M15 ...... 124 A2
Lower Crofts WHTF M45 ...... 32 A5
Lowercroft Rd TOT/BURYW BL8 ...... 32 A5
Lower Crossbank OLDE OL4 ...... 81 D3
Lower Darcy St BOLS/LL BL3 ...... 48 A4
Lower Dingle OLD OL1 ...... 62 A5
Lower Edge Av OLD OL1 ...... 78 C3
Lowerfield Dr OFTN SK2 ...... 185 D2
Lowerfields OLDS OL8 ...... 96 C1
Lowerfields Ri ROY/SHW OL2 ...... 61 F1
Lower Fold DTN/ASHW M34 ...... 149 E1
  MPL/ROM SK6 ...... 171 F6
Lowerfold Cl WHIT OL12 ...... 22 A1
Lowerfold Crs WHIT OL12 ...... 22 A1
Lowerfold Dr WHIT OL12 ...... 22 A1
Lowerfold Wy WHIT OL12 ...... 22 A1
Lowerford Av ROY/SHW OL2 ...... 61 E5
Lower Goodwin Cl BOLE BL2 ...... 29 F5
Lower Gn AUL OL6 ...... 113 D3
  MDTN M24 ...... 75 D2
  WHIT OL12 ...... 22 A4
Lower Hardman St CSLFD M3 ...... 2 A4
Lower Hey La MOSL OL5 ...... 99 F2
Lower Hillgate STKP SK1 ...... 167 D4
Lower House Dr HOR/BR BL6 ...... 44 A2
Lower House La WHIT OL12 ...... 10 C4
Lower House St OLD OL1 ...... 79 F3
Lower House Wk EDGW/EG BL7 ...... 14 B5
Lower Jowkin La ROCH OL11 ...... 20 B6
Lower La MILN OL16 ...... 41 E3
Lower Lime Rd OLDS OL8 ...... 95 D5
Lower Marlands EDGW/EG BL7 ...... 14 A5
Lower Md EDGW/EG BL7 ...... 14 A4
Lower Meadow Rd WILM/AE SK9 ...... 194 C5
Lower Moat Cl HTNM SK4 ...... 166 C2
Lower Monton Rd ECC M30 ...... 102 A5
Lower Mosley St CMANW M2 ...... 2 C6
Lower Moss La HULME M15 ...... 123 E2
  WHTF M45 ...... 71 D3
Lower New Rw WALK M28 ...... 82 B4
Lower Ormond St CMANE M1 ...... 124 B2
  HULME M15 ...... 124 B2
Lower Park Crs POY/DIS SK12 ...... 197 F3
Lower Park Rd POY/DIS SK12 ...... 197 F4
  RUSH/FAL M14 ...... 125 D5
Lower Rawson St FWTH BL4 ...... 66 C2
Lower Rd RAMS BL0 ...... 7 E3
Lower Seedley Rd SLFD M6 ...... 103 F4
Lower Sheriff St WHIT OL12 ...... 22 C5
Lower St FWTH BL4 ...... 66 A4
  MILN OL16 ...... 40 B3
Lower Strines Rd MPL/ROM SK6 ...... 187 E2
Lower Sutherland St SWIN M27 ...... 85 F5
Lower Tenterfield ROCH OL11 ...... 20 B3
Lower Tong EDGW/EG BL7 ...... 14 A6
Lower Turf La OLDE OL4 ...... 81 E4
Lower Tweedale St ROCH OL11 ...... 40 A1
Lower Vickers St NEWH/MOS M40 ...... 107 E4
Lower Victoria St CHAD OL9 ...... 77 F4
Lower Wharf St AUL OL6 ...... 112 C5
Lower Wheat End MILN OL16 ...... 23 F5
Lower Woodhill Rd
  TOT/BURYW BL8 ...... 33 E4
Lowerwood La BOLE BL2 ...... 28 C6
Lowes Rd BURY BL9 ...... 34 A1
Lowestead Rd OP/CLY M11 ...... 109 D5
The Lowes ALT WA14 ...... 173 F6
Lowestoft St RUSH/FAL M14 ...... 143 F1
Lowe St DTN/ASHW M34 ...... 130 C6
  RAD M26 ...... 51 D5
  STKP SK1 ...... 167 D4
Loweswater Rd CHD/CHDH SK8 ...... 179 F4
  FWTH BL4 ...... 64 C3
Lowfield Av AUL OL6 ...... 114 A2
  DROY M43 ...... 110 A4

Lowfield Gv OFTN SK2 ...... 167 D6
Lowfield Rd EDGY/DAV SK3 ...... 182 C1
Low HI WHIT OL12 ...... 24 A2
Lowhouse Cl MILN OL16 ...... 25 E6
Lowick Av BOLS/LL BL3 ...... 47 E6
Lowick Cl BRAM/HZG SK7 ...... 184 B5
Lowick Gn MPL/ROM SK6 ...... 149 D6
Lowland Gv AULW OL7 ...... 112 B3
Lowland Rd OFTN SK2 ...... 183 F3
Lowlands Cl MDTN M24 ...... 93 D1
Low Lea Rd MPL/ROM SK6 ...... 171 F6
Low Mdw ROY/SHW OL2 ...... 60 B3
Lowndes Cl OFTN SK2 ...... 167 F6
Lowndes La OFTN SK2 ...... 167 F6
Lowndes St BOL BL1 ...... 45 F1
Lowndes Wk BRUN/LGST M13 ...... 125 D3
Lownorth Rd WYTH/NTH M22 ...... 192 C1
Lowood Av URM M41 ...... 118 A5
Lowry Dr MPL/ROM SK6 ...... 171 F5
  SWIN M27 ...... 86 A4
Lowry Wk BOL BL1 ...... 27 G3
Lowside Av HOR/BR BL6 ...... 44 A5
  MPL/ROM SK6 ...... 150 A5
Lowside Dr OLDE OL4 ...... 79 F6
Low's Pl WHIT OL12 ...... 23 E3
The Lows OLDE OL4 ...... 79 F6
Lowther Av GTN M18 ...... 126 C6
  HALE/TIMP WA15 ...... 175 E1
  ROY/SHW OL2 ...... 60 A1
Lowther Cl PWCH M25 ...... 88 B2
Lowther Crs MDTN M24 ...... 74 C2
Lowther Gdns URM M41 ...... 117 E6
Lowther Rd CHH M8 ...... 90 B4
  PWCH M25 ...... 88 A2
  ROCH OL11 ...... 39 F3
Lowther St BOLS/LL BL3 ...... 65 E1
Lowthorpe St RUSH/FAL M14 ...... 143 E1
Lowton Av BKLY M9 ...... 92 A5
Lowton Rd SALE M33 ...... 158 B3
Lowton St RAD M26 ...... 51 E5
Low Wood Cl BRAM/HZG SK7 ...... 182 A6
Low Wood Rd DTN/ASHW M34 ...... 128 B5
Loxford St HULME M15 ...... 124 A3
Loxham St FWTH BL4 ...... 66 B1
Lubeck St BKLY M9 ...... 91 F5
Lucas Av FWTH BL4 ...... 65 F2
Lucas St BURY BL9 ...... 34 B4
  OLDE OL4 ...... 79 F4
Lucerne Cl CHAD OL9 ...... 78 A5
Lucerne Rd BRAM/HZG SK7 ...... 182 C4
Lucien Cl WGTN/LGST M12 ...... 125 F4
Lucknow St ROCH OL11 ...... 40 A2
Lucy St BOL BL1 ...... 26 B6
  BRO M7 ...... 105 E2
  EDGY/DAV SK3 ...... 166 C5
  HULME M15 ...... 123 E3
Ludford Cl NEWH/MOS M40 ...... 109 D3
Ludgate Hl ANC M4 ...... 106 C4
Ludgate Rd NEWH/MOS M40 ...... 109 D3
  ROCH OL11 ...... 40 B5
Ludgate St ANC M4 ...... 106 B4
Ludlow Av SWIN M27 ...... 86 B3
  WHTF M45 ...... 71 F5
Ludlow Pk OLDE OL4 ...... 80 B5
Ludlow Rd STKP SK1 ...... 168 A5
Lugano Rd BRAM/HZG SK7 ...... 182 C4
Luke Rd DROY M43 ...... 110 C6
Lullington Cl WYTH/NTH M22 ...... 178 A6
Lullington Rd SLFD M6 ...... 103 D3
Lulworth Av URM M41 ...... 137 D1
Lulworth Cl TOT/BURYW BL8 ...... 33 D1
Lulworth Crs FAIL M35 ...... 94 C5
Lulworth Gdns NTHM/RTH M23 ...... 161 D5
Lulworth Rd BOLS/LL BL3 ...... 45 E6
  ECC M30 ...... 101 D5
  MDTN M24 ...... 75 F1
Lumb Carr Av RAMS BL0 ...... 18 B1
Lumb Carr Rd RAMS BL0 ...... 18 B1
Lumb Cl BRAM/HZG SK7 ...... 196 C3
Lumber La WALK M28 ...... 83 F5
Lumb La BRAM/HZG SK7 ...... 196 C3
  DROY M43 ...... 111 E2
  DTN/ASHW M34 ...... 111 D6
Lumley Cl RUSH/FAL M14 ...... 124 C1
Lumn Hollow HYDE SK14 ...... 150 C1
  HYDE SK14 ...... 150 C1
Lumn Rd HYDE SK14 ...... 150 C1
Lumn's La SWIN M27 ...... 87 D3
Lumsden St BOLS/LL BL3 ...... 46 C4
Lum St BOL BL1 ...... 47 E1
Lumwood BOL BL1 ...... 46 C1
Luna St ANC M4 ...... 3 G2
Lund Av RAD M26 ...... 69 F3
Lund St OLDTF/WHR M16 ...... 123 D3
Lune Cl WHTF M45 ...... 71 E3
Lunedale Gn OFTN SK2 ...... 184 C1
Lune Dr WHTF M45 ...... 71 E3
Lune Gv HEY OL10 ...... 36 B4
Lune St OLDS OL8 ...... 95 F1
Lune Wy RDSH SK5 ...... 147 D6
Lunn Av GTN M18 ...... 128 A3
Lupin Av FWTH BL4 ...... 65 E2
Lupton St CSLFD M3 ...... 105 E5
  DTN/ASHW M34 ...... 130 A5
Lurgan Av SALE M33 ...... 160 A2

Lutener St *ALT* WA14 .... **158** A5 🔟
Luton Dr *NTHM/RTH* M23 .... **177** E3 🔁
Luton Rd *RDSH* SK5................ **147** D3
Luton St *TOT/BURYW* BL8 .... **32** C6 🔁
Luxor Gv *DTN/ASHW* M34 .... **128** A6
Luzley Brook Rd *ROY/SHW* OL2 .... **61** E4
Luzley Rd *AUL* OL6 .... **114** B1
STLY SK15 .... **114** C2
Lyceum Pas *MILN* OL16 .... **23** D6 🔢
Lyceum Pl *HULME* M15 .... **124** B2 🔁
Lychgate Cl *OLDE* OL4 .... **97** F2
Lydbrook Cl *BOLS/LL* BL3 .... **46** B3
Lydden Av *OP/CLY* M11 .... **109** E4 🔁
Lydford Gdns *BOLE* BL2 .... **49** D4
Lydford St *SLFD* M6 .... **104** C3 🔁
Lydgate Av *BOLE* BL2 .... **48** C1
Lydgate Cl *DTN/ASHW* M34 ...... **149** F2 🔁
STLY SK15 .... **115** F1
WHTF M45 .... **71** E3
Lydgate Dr *OLDE* OL4 .... **80** A6
Lydgate Rd *DROY* M43 .... **109** F4
SALE M33 .... **160** A3
Lydiate Cl *BOLS/LL* BL3 .... **47** E6
Lydiat La *WILM/AE* SK9 .... **209** E5
Lydney Av *CHD/CHDH* SK8 .... **194** A2
Lydney Rd *URM* M41 .... **117** E6
Lyme Av *WILM/AE* SK9 .... **203** F2
Lyme Clough Wy *MDTN* M24...... **57** D5
Lymefield Dr *WALK* M28 .... **82** B6
Lymefield Gv *OFTN* SK2 .... **183** F1
Lyme Gv *ALT* WA14 .... **174** A3
DROY M43 .... **128** A1
MPL/ROM SK6 .... **170** B3
MPL/ROM SK6 .... **187** D2
OFTN SK2 .... **167** D6
Lyme Rd *BRAM/HZG* SK7 .... **184** C6
POY/DIS SK12 .... **200** A6
POY/DIS SK12 .... **201** E2
Lyme St *BRAM/HZG* SK7 .. **184** B3 🔁
HTNM SK4 .... **164** C3
Lymewood Dr *POY/DIS* SK12...... **201** F3
WILM/AE SK9 .... **204** C3 🔁
Lymington Cl *MDTN* M24 .... **75** F6
Lymington Dr *NTHM/RTH* M23 .. **160** B5
Lymm Cl *EDGY/DAV* SK3 .... **182** B1 🔁
WALK M28 .... **82** B2
Lyncombe Cl *CHD/CHDH* SK8 .. **195** F3 🔁
Lyndale Av *RDSH* SK5 .... **128** A6
SWIN M27 .... **101** E1 🔟
Lyndale Dr *LIT* OL15................ **12** B5
Lyndene Av *WALK* M28 .... **84** B5 🔟
Lyndene Gdns *CHD/CHDH* SK8 .. **179** F1 🔁
Lyndene Rd *WYTH/NTH* M22 ...... **178** B2
Lyndhurst Av *AUL* OL6 .... **112** C2
BRAM/HZG SK7 .... **184** A6
CHAD OL9 .... **77** D6
DTN/ASHW M34 .... **129** F6 🔁
IRL M44 .... **116** B6
MPL/ROM SK6 .... **169** D1
PWCH M25 .... **89** F2 🔁
ROCH OL11 .... **58** B1
SALE M33 .... **159** D2 🔁
URM M41 .... **119** D5
Lyndhurst Cl *WILM/AE* SK9 .... **202** B6 🔟
Lyndhurst Dr *HALE/TIMP* WA15 .. **175** E5
Lyndhurst Rd *OLDS* OL8 .... **91** F3
RDSH SK5 .... **146** C1 🔁
STRET M32 .... **139** F1
Lyndhurst St *SALQ/ORD* M5 ...... **103** F5 🔁
Lyndhurst Vw *DUK* SK16 .... **113** D6 🔁
Lyndon Cl *OLDE* OL4 .... **81** F3
TOT/BURYW BL8 .... **32** A1
Lyndon Rd *IRL* M44 .... **135** D2
Lyne Edge Crs *DUK* SK16 .... **132** A2
Lyne Edge Rd *DUK* SK16 .... **132** B2
Lyne Vw *DUK* SK14 .... **132** A3
Lyngard Cl *WILM/AE* SK9 .... **204** B2
Lyn Gv *HEY* OL10 .... **36** B4
Lynham Dr *HEY* OL10 .... **56** B1
Lynmouth Av *DID/WITH* M20 .... **143** E5 🔁
OLDS OL8 .... **96** A2
RDSH SK5 .... **146** C4 🔁
ROY/SHW OL2 .... **60** A6
URM M41 .... **137** F3 🔁
Lynmouth Cl *CHAD* OL9 .... **76** C2 🔁
RAD M26 .... **52** A5
Lynmouth Gv *PWCH* M25 .... **88** A2
Lynn Av *SALE* M33 .... **140** B5
Lynn Dr *DROY* M43 .... **109** F5
Lynn St *CHAD* OL9 .... **95** D1
Lynnwood Dr *ROCH* OL11 .... **21** F5
Lynnwood Rd *BNG/LEV* M19 .... **164** B3
Lynroyle Wy *ROCH* OL11 .... **39** E4
Lynsted Av *BOLS/LL* BL3 .... **47** E6 🔁
Lynthorpe Av *IRL* M44 .... **134** B5
Lynthorpe Rd *NEWH/MOS* M40 .. **93** E3
Lynton Av *HYDE* SK14 .... **152** A1
IRL M44 .... **134** C5
OLDS OL8 .... **95** D3 🔁
ROCH OL11 .... **38** C4
SWIN M27 .... **86** A4
URM M41 .... **136** A1
Lynton Cl *CHAD* OL9 .... **77** D2
Lynton Crs *WALK* M28 .... **83** E5
Lynton Dr *BNG/LEV* M19 .... **145** D4

MPL/ROM SK6 .... **200** C1
PWCH M25 .... **72** A5 🔁
Lynton Gv *HALE/TIMP* WA15 .... **175** E2
Lynton La *WILM/AE* SK9 .... **209** E3
Lynton Lea *RAD* M26................ **52** A5
Lynton Ms *WILM/AE* SK9 .... **209** E3 🔁
Lynton Park Rd *CHD/CHDH* SK8 .. **195** D1
Lynton Rd *BOLS/LL* BL3 .... **64** A1
CCHDY M21 .... **141** F3
CHD/CHDH SK8 .... **180** A2
HTNM SK4 .... **145** F6
SWIN M27 .... **86** A4 🔁
Lynton St *RUSH/FAL* M14 .... **143** F1 🔁
Lyntonvale Av *CHD/CHDH* SK8 .. **179** E1
Lynway Dr *DID/WITH* M20 .... **143** F6
Lynway Gv *MDTN* M24 .... **75** F1
Lynwood *HALE/TIMP* WA15 ...... **189** E1
Lynwood Av *BOLS/LL* BL3 .... **47** F6
ECC M30 .... **101** E5 🔁
OLDTF/WHR M16 .... **142** A1 🔁
Lynwood Cl *AULW* OL7 .... **96** B6
Lynwood Dr *OLDE* OL4 .... **80** C3
Lynwood Gv *BOLE* BL2 .... **29** E3
DTN/ASHW M34 .... **111** D6
HTNM SK4 .... **146** A5 🔁
SALE M33 .... **140** A6
Lyon Gv *WALK* M28 .... **84** B5
Lyon Rd *FWTH* BL4 .... **66** C6
Lyons Dr *TOT/BURYW* BL8 ...... **32** B6
Lyons Fold *SALE* M33 .... **139** F5 🔁
Lyons Rd *TRPK* M17 .... **120** B2
Lyon St *ROY/SHW* OL2 .... **61** F2
SWIN M27 .... **85** F6 🔁
Lytham Av *CCHDY* M21 .... **142** A4 🔁
Lytham Cl *AUL* OL6 .... **113** F1
Lytham Dr *BRAM/HZG* SK7 ...... **197** E2
HEY OL10 .... **37** D6
Lytham Rd *CHD/CHDH* SK8 ...... **179** F6
RUSH/FAL M14 .... **145** D2
URM M41 .... **136** B1
Lytham St *EDGY/DAV* SK3 ...... **183** D1 🔁
WHIT OL12 .... **22** C2 🔁
Lytherton Av *IRL* M44.............. **154** B1
Lyth St *RUSH/FAL* M14 .... **144** B4
Lytton Av *CHH* M8 .... **106** B1
Lytton Rd *DROY* M43 .... **110** B5 🔁
Lytton St *BOL* BL1 .... **27** E5 🔢🔁

M

Mabel Av *BOLS/LL* BL3 .... **47** E6 🔁
WALK M28 .... **84** B6
Mabel Rd *FAIL* M35 .... **94** B4
Mabel's Brow *FWTH* BL4 .... **66** C4 🔁
Mabel St *BOL* BL1 .... **46** A1 🔢
NEWH/MOS M40 .... **109** E2 🔁
WHIT OL12 .... **22** B3 🔁
Mabfield Rd *RUSH/FAL* M14 ...... **144** A2
Mableden Cl *CHD/CHDH* SK8 .... **194** B1
Mabs Ct *AUL* OL6 .... **113** E5
Macaulay St *ROCH* OL11 .... **39** E5 🔁
ROY/SHW OL2 .... **60** C5 🔁
Macauley Cl *DUK* SK16 .... **132** B2
Macauley Rd *OLDTF/WHR* M16 .. **141** F1
RDSH SK5 .... **145** F5
Macclesfield Rd *BRAM/HZG* SK7 .. **199** D1
WILM/AE SK9 .... **204** A5
Macdonald Av *FWTH* BL4 .... **65** E4
Macdonald Rd *IRL* M44 .... **134** C4
Macdonald St *OLDS* OL8 .... **96** A1 🔁
Macefin Av *CCHDY* M21 .... **162** B1
Mackenzie Gv *BOL* BL1 .... **27** E2 🔁
Mackenzie Rd *BRO* M7 .... **104** C1 🔁
Mackenzie St *BOL* BL1 .... **27** E2 🔁
WGTN/LGST M12.................. **126** B6
Mackenzie Wk *OLD* OL1 .... **62** C4
Mackeson Dr *AUL* OL6 .... **113** F3
Mackeson Rd *AUL* OL6 .... **113** F3
Maclaren Dr *CHH* M8 .... **89** F3
Maclure Rd *ROCH* OL11 .... **40** A1 🔟
Madams Wood Rd *WALK* M28.... **82** A2
Maddison Rd *DROY* M43 .... **110** A6
Madeley Cl *ALT* WA14 .... **188** C1 🔟
Madeley Dr *CHAD* OL9 .... **77** F5 🔁
Madeley Gdns *WHIT* OL12 .... **22** B4 🔁
Maden's Sq *LIT* OL15 .... **12** C6 🔟
Madison Av *CHD/CHDH* SK8...... **181** E5
DTN/ASHW M34 .... **129** D1
Madison St *GTN* M18................ **127** F3
Madras Rd *EDGY/DAV* SK3 ...... **166** A6 🔁
Mafeking Av *BURY* BL9 .... **34** B2
Mafeking Rd *BOLE* BL2 .... **48** C2 🔁
Mafeking St *OLDS* OL8 .... **95** D2 🔁
Magdala St *HEY* OL10 .... **56** C1 🔁
OLD OL1 .... **78** C3
Magda Rd *OFTN* SK2 .... **184** A2
Magenta Av *IRL* M44................ **134** C5
Magnolia Cl *SALE* M33 .... **138** A6
Magnolia Dr *CHH* M8 .... **106** B1 🔁
Magpie Cl *DROY* M43 .... **111** D4
Magpie La *OLDE* OL4................ **97** E1
Maher Gdns *HULME* M15 .... **123** F5

Mahood St *EDGY/DAV* SK3 ...... **166** B6 🔁
Maida St *BNG/LEV* M19 .... **145** F1
Maidford Cl *ANC* M4 .... **107** E6 🔢
STRET M32 .... **140** C1 🔁
Maidstone Av *CCHDY* M21 ...... **141** E2
Maidstone Ms *CCHDY* M21 ...... **141** E2 🔁
Maidstone Rd *HTNM* SK4 .... **164** B2
Main Av *BNG/LEV* M19 .... **145** D4 🔁
TRPK M17 .... **121** D5
Maine Rd *RUSH/FAL* M14 .... **143** E1
Mainprice Cl *SLFD* M6 .... **104** A4 🔟
Main Rd *CHAD* OL9 .... **78** A4
SWIN M27 .... **87** E2
Main St *FAIL* M35 .... **94** A5
HYDE SK14.......................... **131** E5
Mainwaring Dr *WILM/AE* SK9 .. **204** B3
Mainwaring Ter
NTHM/RTH M23 .... **161** E3 🔁
Mainway *MDTN* M24 .... **75** D5
Mainway East *MDTN* M24 .... **76** A5
Maismore Rd *WYTH/NTH* M22.... **177** E6
Maitland Cl *WHIT* OL12 .... **24** A2 🔁
Maitland St *STKP* SK1 .... **167** F6
Major St *CMANE* M1 .... **3** F5
MILN OL16 .... **42** A1
RAMS BL0 .... **6** C5 🔁
Makin Cl *HEY* OL10 .... **37** E6
Makin St *CMANE* M1 .... **3** F6 🔁
CMANE M1 .... **124** B2 🔁
Makkah Cl *NEWH/MOS* M40 ...... **108** B2
Malaga Av *MANAIR* M90 .... **191** F2 🔁
Malakoff St *STLY* SK15 .... **131** F1
Malby St *OLD* OL1 .... **79** D3
Malcolm Av *SWIN* M27 .... **86** B2 🔁
Malcolm Dr *SWIN* M27 .... **86** B3 🔟
Malcolm St *ROCH* OL11 .... **39** E4 🔁
Malden Gv *NTHM/RTH* M23 ...... **161** E6 🔁
Maldon Cl *OFTN* SK2 .... **185** E2
Maldon Crs *SWIN* M27 .... **102** A1
Maldon Dr *ECC* M30 .... **101** F3 🔁
Maldon St *ROCH* OL11 .... **40** A2 🔟
Maldwyn Av *CHH* M8 .... **90** B3
Maleham St *BRO* M7 .... **105** F1 🔢
Malgam Dr *DID/WITH* M20 ...... **163** F5 🔁
Malham Cl *ROY/SHW* OL2 .... **60** B5 🔁
Malham Ct *OFTN* SK2 .... **184** B1 🔁
Malham Dr *WHTF* M45 .... **71** E3
Mallard Cl *DUK* SK16 .... **131** F2
OFTN SK2 .... **185** E2
OLDS OL8 .... **95** E3 🔁
Mallard Crs *POY/DIS* SK12 ...... **197** E5
Mallard Gn *ALT* WA14 .... **157** F5 🔁
Mallards Reach *MPL/ROM* SK6 .. **169** F3 🔁
Mallard St *CMANE* M1 .... **124** B2 🔁
Mallet Crs *BOL* BL1 .... **26** A5
Malling Rd *NTHM/RTH* M23 ...... **177** E3
Mallison St *BOL* BL1 .... **28** A4
Mallory Av *AULW* OL7 .... **112** C2
Mallory Rd *HYDE* SK14 .... **132** B5
Mallow Cft *MILN* OL16 .... **41** D3
Mallowdale *WALK* M28 .... **82** C5 🔟
Mallowdale Cl *BOL* BL1 .... **44** B2 🔟
Mallowdale Rd *OFTN* SK2 .... **184** C2
Mallow St *HULME* M15 .... **123** F5 🔁
The Mall *STLY* SK15 .... **133** F3
Malmesbury Cl *POY/DIS* SK12 .. **198** B5
Malmesbury Rd *CHD/CHDH* SK8 .. **195** F3
Malpas Cl *CHD/CHDH* SK8 ...... **181** E3 🔁
WILM/AE SK9 .... **204** B2
Malpas Dr *ALT* WA14 .... **158** C5 🔁
Malpas St *OLD* OL1 .... **79** D4
WGTN/LGST M12.................. **126** B3
Malsham Rd *NTHM/RTH* M23 .... **161** D3 🔁
Malta Cl *MDTN* M24.................. **76** B3
Malta St *ANC* M4 .... **107** E6
OLDE OL4 .... **80** B5 🔢
Maltby Cl *BOLS/LL* BL3 .... **64** A1
Maltby Rd *NTHM/RTH* M23 ...... **177** D1 🔟
Malton Av *BOLS/LL* BL3 .... **45** E5
CCHDY M21 .... **141** F3
WHTF M45 .... **71** D1
Malton Cl *CHAD* OL9 .... **77** D2
Malton Dr *ALT* WA14 .... **173** E1
BRAM/HZG SK7 .... **198** E2
Malton Rd *HTNM* SK4 .... **165** E1
Malton St *OLDS* OL8 .... **78** B6
Malvern Av *AUL* OL6 .... **97** D6
BOL BL1 .... **26** B6 🔢
BURY BL9 .... **34** A2
CHD/CHDH SK8 .... **179** D2
DROY M43 .... **111** D5
URM M41 .... **137** F1
Malvern Cl *FWTH* BL4 .... **65** D2
HTNM SK4 .... **166** B2 🔁
MILN OL16 .... **25** E6
PWCH M25 .... **72** A6
ROY/SHW OL2 .... **60** A6
ROY/SHW OL2 .... **61** D1
SWIN M27 .... **103** E1 🔁
Malvern Dr *ALT* WA14 .... **173** F2
SWIN M27 .... **103** E1 🔁
Malvern Gv *DID/WITH* M20 ...... **143** E5
SLFD M6 .... **103** D4 🔁
WALK M28 .... **83** E2 🔁

Malvern Rd *MDTN* M24 ...... 75 E6
Malvern St *OLDS* OL8 ...... 78 B6
Malvern St East *ROCH* OL11 .. 22 A6
Malvern St West *ROCH* OL11 .. 22 A6
Manby Rd *GTN* M18 ...... 126 C5
Manby Sq *GTN* M18 ...... 126 C5 🔟
Manchester New Rd *MDTN* M24 .. 75 D3
  PART M31 ...... 155 D2
Manchester Old Rd *BURY* BL9 .. 33 F6 🔟
  MDTN M24 ...... 74 A4
Manchester Rd *ALT* WA14 ...... 158 B6
  BOLS/LL BL3 ...... 47 E4
  BURY BL9 ...... 33 F5 🔟
  BURY BL9 ...... 52 C3
  CCHDY M21 ...... 141 F2 🔟
  CHD/CHDH SK8 ...... 164 B5
  DROY M43 ...... 109 F6
  DROY M43 ...... 110 B6 🔟
  DTN/ASHW M34 ...... 128 C2
  FWTH BL4 ...... 67 F5
  HEY OL10 ...... 56 B3
  HTNM SK4 ...... 146 B6
  HYDE SK14 ...... 130 C6
  MOSL OL5 ...... 99 D6
  OLDS OL8 ...... 95 D1
  PART M31 ...... 155 D1 🔟
  RAMS BL0 ...... 7 F6
  ROCH OL11 ...... 39 F1
  ROY/SHW OL2 ...... 61 E4
  SWIN M27 ...... 86 A3
  WALK M28 ...... 84 A3
  WILM/AE SK9 ...... 203 F4
Manchester Rd East *WALK* M28 .. 83 D2 🔟
Manchester Rd North
  DTN/ASHW M34 ...... 129 D5
Manchester Rd South
  DTN/ASHW M34 ...... 129 D6
Manchester Rd West *LHULT* M38 .. 64 C6
Manchester St *HEY* OL10 ...... 37 E5
  OLDTF/WHR M16 ...... 123 D4 🔟
Manchet St *ROCH* OL11 ...... 38 C6
Mancroft Av *BOLS/LL* BL3 .. 46 B5 🔟
Mancunian Rd *DTN/ASHW* M34 .. 149 E1
Mancunian Wy *WGTN/LGST* M12 .. 125 D2
Mandalay Gdns *MPL/ROM* SK6 .. 170 B6 🔟
Mandarin Gn *ALT* WA14 ...... 157 F5 🔟
Mandeville St *BNG/LEV* M19 .. 145 F3 🔟
Mandley Av *NEWH/MOS* M40 .. 93 E3 🔟
Mandley Cl *BOLS/LL* BL3 ...... 49 E4
Mandley Park Av *BRO* M7 ...... 89 F6
Mandon Cl *RAD* M26 ...... 50 C4
Manesty Cl *MDTN* M24 ...... 74 A1 🔟
Mangle St *CMANE* M1 ...... 3 G3
Mango Pl *SLFD* M6 ...... 104 B5
Manifold Dr *MPL/ROM* SK6 .. 201 D3
Manifold St *SLFD* M6 ...... 104 C2 🔟
Manipur St *OP/CLY* M11 ...... 126 A1
Manley Av *SWIN* M27 ...... 86 A1
Manley Cl *BURY* BL9 ...... 19 D3 🔟
Manley Gv *BRAM/HZG* SK7 .. 196 C3 🔟
Manley Rd *CCHDY* M21 ...... 142 A2
  OLDS OL8 ...... 95 F1
  OLDTF/WHR M16 ...... 142 B2
  ROCH OL11 ...... 39 D3
  SALE M33 ...... 158 C4
Manley St *BRO* M7 ...... 105 E1
Manley Ter *BRO* M7 ...... 27 F3 🔟
Manningham Rd *BOLS/LL* BL3.. 45 F4
Mannington Dr *BKLY* M9 ...... 107 D1
Mannock St *OLDS* OL8 ...... 78 B5 🔟
Manor Av *BOLS/LL* BL3 ...... 50 A6 🔟
  OLDTF/WHR M16 ...... 142 B1 🔟
  SALE M33 ...... 138 B6
  URM M41 ...... 138 B2
Manor Cl *CHAD* OL9 ...... 78 A3
  CHD/CHDH SK8 ...... 196 A1
  DTN/ASHW M34 ...... 149 F1 🔟
  WILM/AE SK9 ...... 202 C3
Manor Ct *STRET* M32 ...... 139 F2
Manor Dr *CCHDY* M21 ...... 162 B1
  ROY/SHW OL2 ...... 60 C6
Manor Farm Cl *AULW* OL7 .. 112 A1
Manor Farm Ri *OLDE* OL4 ...... 80 B4
Manorfield Cl *BOL* BL1 ...... 26 B6
Manor Gdns *WILM/AE* SK9 .. 204 B4 🔟
Manor Gate Rd *BOLE* BL2 ...... 49 E1
Manor Hill Rd *MPL/ROM* SK6.. 171 D6
Manorial Dr *LHULT* M38 ...... 64 C6 🔟
Manor Rd *BNG/LEV* M19 ...... 145 F1
  CHD/CHDH SK8 ...... 182 A6
  DROY M43 ...... 109 F6
  DTN/ASHW M34 ...... 149 F1
  DTN/ASHW M34 ...... 149 F2
  HALE/TIMP WA15 ...... 174 C3
  HYDE SK14 ...... 132 A4
  MDTN M24 ...... 75 D3
  MPL/ROM SK6 ...... 149 F6
  MPL/ROM SK6 ...... 171 D6
  OLDE OL4 ...... 97 D1
  RDSH SK5 ...... 147 F6
  ROY/SHW OL2 ...... 61 E2
  SALE M33 ...... 139 F6
  SLFD M6 ...... 103 E3
  STRET M32 ...... 139 F2
  SWIN M27 ...... 102 A1

Manor St *BOL* BL1 ...... 47 D2
  BURY BL9 ...... 34 B5
  DTN/ASHW M34 ...... 130 A2
  FWTH BL4 ...... 66 A4 🔟
  FWTH BL4 ...... 67 F6
  MDTN M24 ...... 75 E1 🔟
  MOSL OL5 ...... 99 D3
  OLD OL1 ...... 79 E1
  RAMS BL0 ...... 6 C4
  WGTN/LGST M12 ...... 125 D2 🔟
Manor Vw *MPL/ROM* SK6 ...... 149 F5
The Manse *MOSL* OL5 ...... 99 D5 🔟
Mansfield Av *BKLY* M9 ...... 91 E1
  DTN/ASHW M34 ...... 129 E4
  TOT/BURYW BL8 ...... 18 C3 🔟
Mansfield Cl *AULW* OL7 ...... 112 A6 🔟
  DTN/ASHW M34 ...... 129 E4 🔟
Mansfield Crs *DTN/ASHW* M34 .. 129 E5
Mansfield Dr *BKLY* M9 ...... 91 F1 🔟
Mansfield Gra *ROCH* OL11 .. 39 D1 🔟
Mansfield Gv *BOL* BL1 ...... 26 C6
Mansfield Rd *BKLY* M9 ...... 91 E1
  HYDE SK14 ...... 150 C3
  MOSL OL5 ...... 99 F4
  OLDS OL8 ...... 79 F6
  ROCH OL11 ...... 20 C6
  URM M41 ...... 137 E2
Mansfield St *AULW* OL7 ...... 129 F1
Mansford Dr *CHH* M8 ...... 90 A2 🔟
Manshaw Crs *OP/CLY* M11 ...... 128 B2
Manshaw Rd *OP/CLY* M11 ...... 128 B2
Mansion Av *WHTF* M45 ...... 52 C6
Manson Av *HULME* M15 ...... 123 E2
Manston Dr *CHD/CHDH* SK8 .. 181 E5
Manswood Dr *CHH* M8 ...... 90 B6
Mantley La *ROY/SHW* OL2 ...... 63 E2
Manton Av *BKLY* M9 ...... 92 C2
  DTN/ASHW M34 ...... 128 B6
Manton Cl *CHH* M8 ...... 106 A1
Manvers St *RDSH* SK5 ...... 167 D2 🔟
Manwaring St *FAIL* M35 ...... 95 F3 🔟
Maple Av *BOL* BL1 ...... 26 C6 🔟
  BURY BL9 ...... 34 C5 🔟
  CCHDY M21 ...... 141 F3
  CHD/CHDH SK8 ...... 181 D5
  DTN/ASHW M34 ...... 110 C6
  DTN/ASHW M34 ...... 129 F6
  ECC M30 ...... 100 B3
  HALE/TIMP WA15 ...... 176 C2
  MPL/ROM SK6 ...... 187 D3
  POY/DIS SK12 ...... 199 D6
  STLY SK15 ...... 132 A1
  STRET M32 ...... 140 B2
  WHTF M45 ...... 71 D4
Maple Cl *FWTH* BL4 ...... 67 D6 🔟
  MDTN M24 ...... 73 F1
  OFTN SK2 ...... 183 F1
  ROY/SHW OL2 ...... 61 D3 🔟
  SALE M33 ...... 158 A1 🔟
  SLFD M6 ...... 104 B5
Maplecroft *STKP* SK1 ...... 167 F5 🔟
Maplefield Dr *WALK* M28 ...... 82 C6
Maple Gv *BRAM/HZG* SK7 .. 196 C4
  CHAD OL9 ...... 77 F2
  FWTH BL4 ...... 65 E3
  NTHM/RTH M23 ...... 160 A5
  PART M31 ...... 154 C2
  SWIN M27 ...... 101 F1
  WILM/AE SK9 ...... 209 F3
Maple Rd West *NTHM/RTH* M23 .. 160 A5
Maple St *BOLE* BL2 ...... 29 D2 🔟
  BOLS/LL BL3 ...... 46 B4 🔟
  OLDS OL8 ...... 95 D2
  ROCH OL11 ...... 39 E1 🔟
Maple Wk *NTHM/RTH* M23 .. 160 A5
Maplewood Cl *OLD* OL1 ...... 78 A1 🔟
Maplewood Gdns *BOL* BL1 .. 27 F5 🔟
Maplewood Rd *WILM/AE* SK9 .. 204 C3
Mapley Av *WYTH/NTH* M22 .. 162 B5
Maplin Cl *BRUN/LGST* M13 .. 125 D2 🔟
Maplin Dr *OFTN* SK2 ...... 185 E2
Marble St *CMANW* M2 ...... 3 G3
  OLD OL1 ...... 79 F3 🔟
Marbury Cl *URM* M41 ...... 117 E6 🔟
Marbury Rd *HTNM* SK4 ...... 146 B4
  WILM/AE SK9 ...... 203 F2 🔟
Marcer Rd *NEWH/MOS* M40 .. 107 E5
March Av *HTNM* SK4 ...... 165 F3 🔟
Marchbank Dr *CHD/CHDH* SK8 .. 180 A1
March Dr *TOT/BURYW* BL8 .. 33 E2
Marchioness St *GTN* M18 .. 128 A3 🔟
Marchmont Cl *BRUN/LGST* M13 .. 125 E3 🔟
March St *MILN* OL16 ...... 23 E6
Marchwood Av *CCHDY* M21 .. 142 B2
Marcliffe Dr *BNG/LEV* M19.. 146 A2
  ROCH OL11 ...... 38 C1
Marcliff Gv *HTNM* SK4 ...... 165 F3

Marcroft Pl *ROCH* OL11 ...... 40 B3 🔟
Marcus Gv *RUSH/FAL* M14 .. 144 A1
Marcus St *BOL* BL1 ...... 26 C6 🔟
Mardale Av *DID/WITH* M20 .. 144 A6
  ROY/SHW OL2 ...... 60 A1
  SWIN M27 ...... 85 D3
  URM M41 ...... 118 A6
Mardale Cl *BOLE* BL2 ...... 30 A6
  PWCH M25 ...... 72 A4
  STLY SK15 ...... 114 B4
Mardale Dr *BOLE* BL2 ...... 30 A6 🔟
  CHD/CHDH SK8 ...... 179 F1
  MDTN M24 ...... 74 C2
Mardale Rd *SWIN* M27 ...... 101 E1
Marden Rd *NTHM/RTH* M23 .. 177 E2
Marfield *BKLY* M9 ...... 91 F4 🔟
Marfield Av *CHAD* OL9 ...... 77 E6
Marford Cl *WYTH/NTH* M22 .. 178 B1 🔟
Marford Crs *SALE* M33 ...... 159 D3
Margaret Ashton Cl *BKLY* M9 .. 92 A6 🔟
Margaret Av *MILN* OL16 ...... 42 A6
Margaret Rd *DROY* M43 ...... 109 F5 🔟
  DTN/ASHW M34 ...... 130 B5
Margaret St *AUL* OL6 ...... 112 B5
  AULW OL7 ...... 112 B5
  BURY BL9 ...... 34 A6 🔟
  HEY OL10 ...... 36 C5
  OLDS OL8 ...... 94 C3
  RDSH SK5 ...... 146 C4
  ROY/SHW OL2 ...... 61 F3 🔟
Margate Av *NEWH/MOS* M40 .. 108 C3
Margate Rd *RDSH* SK5 ...... 147 D4
Margrove Cl *FAIL* M35 ...... 95 D6 🔟
Margrove Rd *SLFD* M6 ...... 103 D3
Margroy Cl *WHIT* OL12 ...... 23 E3
Marguerita Rd *NEWH/MOS* M40 .. 109 E2 🔟
Marham Cl *CCHDY* M21 ...... 142 C5 🔟
  HYDE SK14 ...... 131 E3 🔟
Maria St *BOL* BL1 ...... 27 F5
Marie Cl *DTN/ASHW* M34 ...... 149 D1 🔟
Marie St *BRO* M7 ...... 89 F6 🔟
Marigold St *ROCH* OL11 ...... 40 A2
Mariman Dr *CHH* M8 ...... 90 B3
Marina Av *DTN/ASHW* M34 .. 149 E2
Marina Cl *WILM/AE* SK9 ...... 194 B3
Marina Crs *OP/CLY* M11 ...... 108 C4
Marina Dr *MPL/ROM* SK6 ...... 170 A6
Marina Rd *DROY* M43 ...... 110 C5
  MPL/ROM SK6 ...... 168 C1
Marine Av *PART* M31 ...... 154 B2
Marion St *BOLS/LL* BL3 ...... 66 A1 🔟
  OLDS OL8 ...... 96 A2 🔟
Marjorie Cl *GTN* M18 ...... 126 C3
Mark Av *SLFD* M6 ...... 104 C5
Markenfield Dr *ROY/SHW* OL2 .. 61 D2 🔟
Market Pde *BURY* BL9 ...... 34 A5
Market Pl *BURY* BL9 ...... 33 F5 🔟
  HYDE SK14 ...... 150 B1 🔟
  MDTN M24 ...... 75 E2
  RAMS BL0 ...... 7 D4 🔟
  STKP SK1 ...... 167 D4
Market Sq *ROY/SHW* OL2 ...... 60 B5
Market St *ALT* WA14 ...... 174 B3 🔟
  BCUP OL13 ...... 5 E2
  BOLS/LL BL3 ...... 49 E6
  BURY BL9 ...... 33 F5
  BURY BL9 ...... 53 D1
  CMANE M1 ...... 2 D3
  DROY M43 ...... 129 F6 🔟
  DTN/ASHW M34 ...... 129 F6 🔟
  DTN/ASHW M34 ...... 130 A6 🔟
  FWTH BL4 ...... 66 B2
  HEY OL10 ...... 37 D5
  HYDE SK14 ...... 131 E6
  MDTN M24 ...... 75 D2 🔟
  MOSL OL5 ...... 99 D4
  RAD M26 ...... 67 E4
  ROY/SHW OL2 ...... 61 F3
  STLY SK15 ...... 114 A5
  SWIN M27 ...... 86 B4 🔟
  TOT/BURYW BL8 ...... 32 A1
  WHIT OL12 ...... 9 D5
Market Wy *SLFD* M6 ...... 104 A4
Markfield Av *BRUN/LGST* M13.. 125 E4
Markham Cl *WGTN/LGST* M12.. 125 E1
Markham St *HYDE* SK14 ...... 131 E3
Markington St *RUSH/FAL* M14 .. 124 B6 🔟
Markland Hl *BOL* BL1 ...... 44 C1
Markland Hill La *BOL* BL1 ...... 26 A6
Markland St *HYDE* SK14 ...... 150 C2 🔟
  RAMS BL0 ...... 7 D5 🔟
Mark La *ROY/SHW* OL2 ...... 62 B3
Marks St *RAD* M26 ...... 51 E6 🔟
Mark St *CHAD* OL9 ...... 78 B4 🔟
  WALK M28 ...... 82 A6
  WHIT OL12 ...... 23 F4 🔟
Marland Av *CHD/CHDH* SK8 .. 181 D5
  OLDS OL8 ...... 96 B4
  ROCH OL11 ...... 38 C3
Marland Cl *ROCH* OL11 ...... 38 C2
Marland Crs *RDSH* SK5 ...... 147 D3
Marland Fold *ROCH* OL11 ...... 38 C3
Marland Fold La *OLDS* OL8 .. 96 A4 🔟
Marland Gn *ROCH* OL11 ...... 38 C3
Marland Hill Rd *ROCH* OL11 .. 39 D2

Marland Old Rd *ROCH* OL11 .... 38 C3
Marland St *CHAD* OL9 .... 94 B2 ⑤
Marlborough Av *CCHDY* M21 .... 142 A2
  CHD/CHDH SK8 .... 181 F6
  WILM/AE SK9 .... 209 F3
Marlborough Cl *AULW* OL7 .... 129 F1 ③
  DTN/ASHW M34 .... 130 A6
  MPL/ROM SK6 .... 170 B6 ②
  RAMS BL0 .... 19 D2 ⑧
Marlborough Dr *FAIL* M35 .... 109 F1
  HTNM SK4 .... 166 B1 ⑨
Marlborough Gdns *FWTH* BL4 .... 65 E3 ⑨
Marlborough Gv *DROY* M43 .... 111 D5 ⑨
Marlborough Rd *ALT* WA14 .... 174 B5
  BRO M7 .... 106 A1 ⑱
  ECC M30 .... 102 B3
  HYDE SK14 .... 150 C3
  IRL M44 .... 116 C6
  ROY/SHW OL2 .... 78 C1
  SALE M33 .... 159 F1
  STRET M32 .... 121 D6
  URM M41 .... 118 A6
  URM M41 .... 137 D1 ③
Marlborough St *AULW* OL7 .... 112 B6 ⑦
  BOL BL1 .... 46 A1
  HEY OL10 .... 56 C1 ⑦
  OLDE OL4 .... 79 E5
  WHIT OL12 .... 22 A4 ⑩
Marlcroft Av *HTNM* SK4 .... 165 F3 ④
Marld Crs *BOL* BL1 .... 26 A5
Marle Av *MOSL* OL5 .... 99 F4
Marle Cft *WHTF* M45 .... 70 A5
Marle Ri *MOSL* OL5 .... 99 F4
Marler Rd *HYDE* SK14 .... 131 F5
Marley Cl *HALE/TIMP* WA15 .... 159 D6
Marley Dr *SALE* M33 .... 139 E5 ①
Marleyer Cl *NEWH/MOS* M40 .... 93 D6 ①
Marleyer Ri *MPL/ROM* SK6 .... 169 E5
Marley Rd *BNG/LEV* M19 .... 145 F3
Marlfield Rd *HALE/TIMP* WA15 .... 190 B2
  ROY/SHW OL2 .... 60 C1
Marlhill Cl *OFTN* SK2 .... 184 C2
Marlinford Dr
  NEWH/MOS M40 .... 109 D2 ⑬
Marlor St *DTN/ASHW* M34 .... 129 F1
Marlow Cl *BOLE* BL2 .... 30 A6
  CHD/CHDH SK8 .... 181 D5 ②
  URM M41 .... 118 C5
Marlow Dr *ALT* WA14 .... 173 D5
  IRL M44 .... 116 B6
  SWIN M27 .... 101 F1 ⑦
  WILM/AE SK9 .... 194 A4
Marlowe Dr *DID/WITH* M20 .... 163 F1
Marlowe Wks *MPL/ROM* SK6 .... 168 C3
Marlow Rd *BKLY* M9 .... 92 A4
Marlwood Rd *BOL* BL1 .... 26 A5
Marmion Dr *CCHDY* M21 .... 141 E5 ⑦
Marne Av *AUL* OL6 .... 114 A2
  WYTH/NTH M22 .... 178 C2
Marne Crs *ROCH* OL11 .... 22 A6
Marnland Gv *BOLS/LL* BL3 .... 44 C5
Maroon Rd *WYTH/NTH* M22 .... 193 D2
Marple Av *BOL* BL1 .... 28 B3 ②
Marple Cl *OLDS* OL8 .... 95 E3 ④
Marple Crs *STRET* M32 .... 121 D6
Marple Hall Cl *MPL/ROM* SK6 .... 170 B6
Marple Old Rd *OFTN* SK2 .... 185 E1
Marple Rd *GLSP* SK13 .... 153 E6
  OFTN SK2 .... 168 B6
Marquis Av *BURY* BL9 .... 33 F3
Marquis Dr *CHD/CHDH* SK8 .... 194 B2
Marquis St *BNG/LEV* M19 .... 146 B2
Marrick Av *CHD/CHDH* SK8 .... 180 A2
Marriott St *DID/WITH* M20 .... 143 F5 ⑨
  STKP SK1 .... 167 D5 ②
Marron Pl *CMANW* M2 .... 2 C5 ⑫
Mars Av *BOLS/LL* BL3 .... 46 A6
Marsden Cl *AULW* OL7 .... 111 F3
  MILN OL16 .... 60 A1
Marsden Dr *HALE/TIMP* WA15 .... 176 A1
Marsden Rd *BOL* BL1 .... 46 C2
  MPL/ROM SK6 .... 170 A2
Marsden St *BURY* BL9 .... 34 A4 ⑱
  CMANW M2 .... 2 D3
  ECC M30 .... 101 D4 ②
Marsett Cl *WHIT* OL12 .... 21 E4 ③
Marshall Ct *AUL* OL6 .... 113 E5 ④
Marshall Rd *BNG/LEV* M19 .... 145 E2
Marshall Stevens Wy *TRPK* M17 .... 120 C4
Marshall St *ANC* M4 .... 3 G1
  DTN/ASHW M34 .... 129 F1
  MILN OL16 .... 24 A4
  WGTN/LGST M12 .... 125 D3
Marsham Cl *BRUN/LGST* M13 .... 125 F5 ⑯
  OLDE OL4 .... 61 F6
Marsham Dr *MPL/ROM* SK6 .... 187 E2 ②
Marsham Rd *BRAM/HZG* SK7 .... 183 F6
Marshbrook Rd *URM* M41 .... 119 D6 ③
Marsh Cl *EDGY/DAV* SK3 .... 182 B1 ③
Marshdale Rd *BOL* BL1 .... 45 D1
Marshfield Rd *HALE/TIMP* WA15 .... 176 A2
Marsh Fold La *BOL* BL1 .... 46 A1
Marsh La *FWTH* BL4 .... 65 E3
Marsh Rd *BOLS/LL* BL3 .... 49 E5
  LHULT M38 .... 82 C1

Marsh St *WALK* M28 .... 84 A3 ⑥
Marsland Av *HALE/TIMP* WA15 .... 159 F5
Marsland Cl *DTN/ASHW* M34 .... 128 C6
Marsland Rd *HALE/TIMP* WA15 .... 175 F1
  MPL/ROM SK6 .... 170 B6
  SALE M33 .... 160 B2 ②
Marsland St North *BRO* M7 .... 89 F6
Marsland St South *BRO* M7 .... 90 A6
Marsland Ter *STKP* SK1 .... 167 F5
Mars St *CHAD* OL9 .... 78 A4
Marston Cl *FAIL* M35 .... 110 C1
  WHTF M45 .... 72 A3
Marston Dr *IRL* M44 .... 135 F1
Marston Rd *BRO* M7 .... 89 F5
  STRET M32 .... 140 C1
Marsworth Dr *ANC* M4 .... 107 D5
Martens Rd *IRL* M44 .... 134 C2
Marthall Dr *SALE* M33 .... 160 C3
Martham Dr *OFTN* SK2 .... 185 E1
Martha's Ter *MILN* OL16 .... 24 A2 ③
Martha St *BOLS/LL* BL3 .... 46 B5 ⑯
  CHAD OL9 .... 78 B3
Martin Av *BOLS/LL* BL3 .... 50 A6 ③
  FWTH BL4 .... 65 D4
  OLDE OL4 .... 80 A5
Martin Cl *DTN/ASHW* M34 .... 130 A4
  OFTN SK2 .... 185 D2
Martindale Cl *ROY/SHW* OL2 .... 60 C4
Martindale Crs *MDTN* M24 .... 56 B6
  WGTN/LGST M12 .... 125 F5
Martin Dr *IRL* M44 .... 116 B5
Martingale Cl *RAD* M26 .... 51 E4 ③
Martingale Wy *DROY* M43 .... 111 E4
Martin Gv *FWTH* BL4 .... 67 D4
Martin La *WHIT* OL12 .... 29 F2
Martin Rd *SWIN* M27 .... 86 C3
Martinsclough *HOR/BR* BL6 .... 44 A3
Martinscroft Rd
  NTHM/RTH M23 .... 177 F2 ①
Martins Fld *WHIT* OL12 .... 21 D4 ⑭
Martin St *BURY* BL9 .... 35 E4 ②
  DTN/ASHW M34 .... 130 A3 ⑤
  EDGW/EG BL7 .... 15 E1
  HYDE SK14 .... 150 C1
  SALQ/ORD M5 .... 103 E5
Martlet Av *ROCH* OL11 .... 20 C6
Martock Av *WYTH/NTH* M22 .... 178 C4 ⑨
Marton Av *BOLE* BL2 .... 48 A1
  DID/WITH M20 .... 164 A3
Marton Gra *PWCH* M25 .... 89 E3
Marton Gn *EDGY/DAV* SK3 .... 182 B2
Marton Gv *HTNM* SK4 .... 146 C5
Marton Pl *SALE* M33 .... 159 E1 ③
Marwood Cl *ALT* WA14 .... 173 F1
  RAD M26 .... 67 E3
Marwood Dr *NTHM/RTH* M23 .... 177 D4 ③
Mary France St *HULME* M15 .... 123 F3
Maryland Av *BOLE* BL2 .... 48 B2
Marylon Dr *WYTH/NTH* M22 .... 162 C5 ③
Mary St *CHD/CHDH* SK8 .... 180 B1
  CSLFD M3 .... 106 A4
  DROY M43 .... 110 C6
  DTN/ASHW M34 .... 130 B5 ⑦
  DUK SK16 .... 130 C1
  FWTH BL4 .... 66 B4 ⑱
  HEY OL10 .... 37 D5
  HYDE SK14 .... 131 D6 ⑨
  MILN OL16 .... 24 B1
  RAMS BL0 .... 6 C6
  STKP SK1 .... 167 E3
Masboro St *CHH* M8 .... 90 A6 ⑮
Masefield Av *PWCH* M25 .... 88 A2
  RAD M26 .... 50 C5 ③
Masefield Cl *DUK* SK16 .... 132 C2
Masefield Crs *DROY* M43 .... 110 B6 ③
Masefield Dr *FWTH* BL4 .... 65 F4
  HTNM SK4 .... 165 E3 ②
Masefield Gv *RDSH* SK5 .... 146 C2 ③
Masefield Rd *BOLS/LL* BL3 .... 49 F5
  DROY M43 .... 110 B6
  OLD OL1 .... 79 F1
Mason Gdns *BOLS/LL* BL3 .... 46 C3 ③
Mason St *ANC* M4 .... 3 H3 ⑩
  BURY BL9 .... 34 B5 ⑩
  CSLFD M3 .... 105 E6 ②
  HEY OL10 .... 36 C5 ⑦
  MILN OL16 .... 23 D6 ⑩
Massey Av *AUL* OL6 .... 113 D1 ⑤
  FAIL M35 .... 94 C5
Massey Cft *WHIT* OL12 .... 9 D4
Massey Rd *HALE/TIMP* WA15 .... 174 C3 ③
  SALE M33 .... 160 C1
Massey St *BURY* BL9 .... 34 B4
  SALQ/ORD M5 .... 105 D6 ⑩
  STKP SK1 .... 167 D4 ⑤
  WILM/AE SK9 .... 209 E4 ③
Massey Wk *WYTH/NTH* M22 .... 179 D6
Massie St *CHD/CHDH* SK8 .... 181 D6 ③
Mather Av *ECC* M30 .... 101 F5 ⑤
  PWCH M25 .... 89 D4
  WHTF M45 .... 71 D1
Mather Cl *WHTF* M45 .... 71 D2

Mather Fold Rd *WALK* M28 .... 82 C4
Mather Rd *ECC* M30 .... 101 F5
  FAIL M35 .... 93 E6
  FWTH BL4 .... 66 C3
  RAD M26 .... 51 E6 ③
Matley Cl *HYDE* SK14 .... 132 C4
Matley Gn *RDSH* SK5 .... 148 A5
Matley La *STLY* SK15 .... 133 D3
Matlock Av *AUL* OL6 .... 114 A1
  BRO M7 .... 88 B6
  DID/WITH M20 .... 143 D5 ③
  DTN/ASHW M34 .... 149 E3 ③
  URM M41 .... 137 F3
Matlock Cl *FWTH* BL4 .... 66 C2 ⑥
  SALE M33 .... 160 A1
Matlock Dr *BRAM/HZG* SK7 .... 198 C3
Matlock Rd *CHD/CHDH* SK8 .... 194 A2
  RDSH SK5 .... 147 E2
  STRET M32 .... 120 B6
Matlock St *ECC* M30 .... 119 D1 ⑦
Matt Busby Cl *SWIN* M27 .... 86 C6
Matthew Moss La *ROCH* OL11 .... 38 C3
Matthews Av *FWTH* BL4 .... 67 D4
Matthews La *BNG/LEV* M19 .... 145 F1
Matthew's St *WGTN/LGST* M12 .... 126 A2
Matthew St *MPL/ROM* SK6 .... 187 E1 ①
Mattison St *OP/CLY* M11 .... 127 F2 ⑮
Maudsley St *BURY* BL9 .... 33 E6
Maud St *BOLE* BL2 .... 29 D2 ③
  WHIT OL12 .... 23 E3
Mauldeth Cl *HTNM* SK4 .... 165 E2
Mauldeth Rd *BNG/LEV* M19 .... 144 A4
  DID/WITH M20 .... 144 A4
  HTNM SK4 .... 165 E2
  RUSH/FAL M14 .... 144 A4
Mauldeth Rd West *CCHDY* M21 .... 142 C5
Maunby Gdns *LHULT* M38 .... 83 D2 ⑦
Maureen Av *CHH* M8 .... 90 B5 ⑦
Maureen St *WHIT* OL12 .... 23 E3 ⑤
Maurice Cl *DUK* SK16 .... 131 F2
Maurice Dr *SLFD* M6 .... 104 A3
Maurice St *SLFD* M6 .... 104 A3 ①
Maveen Gv *OFTN* SK2 .... 183 E3
Mavis Gv *MILN* OL16 .... 42 B1
Mavis St *WHIT* OL12 .... 39 D6 ③
Mawdsley Dr *CHH* M8 .... 91 D5
Mawdsley St *BOL* BL1 .... 47 D2
Maxwell Av *OFTN* SK2 .... 184 A2
Maxwell St *BOL* BL1 .... 27 F3 ⑬
  BOL BL1 .... 27 F1 ⑬
  BURY BL9 .... 34 C4
Mayall St *MOSL* OL5 .... 99 D4
Mayall St East *OLDE* OL4 .... 80 A4 ③
Mayan Av *CSLFD* M3 .... 105 E5
May Av *CHD/CHDH* SK8 .... 195 F3 ③
  HTNM SK4 .... 166 A3 ③
Maybank St *BOLS/LL* BL3 .... 46 B5
Mayberth Av *CHH* M8 .... 90 B3
Maybreck Cl *BOLS/LL* BL3 .... 46 A4
Mayburn Cl *MDTN* M24 .... 76 A6
Maybury St *GTN* M18 .... 127 E3
Maycroft Av *DID/WITH* M20 .... 144 A6
Mayer St *OFTN* SK2 .... 168 A6 ①
Mayes St *ANC* M4 .... 3 E1
Mayfair Av *RAD* M26 .... 50 B5 ②
  SLFD M6 .... 102 C4
  URM M41 .... 137 F1
  WHTF M45 .... 71 D4 ⑥
Mayfair Cl *DUK* SK16 .... 132 A1
  POY/DIS SK12 .... 198 C5 ⑤
Mayfair Crs *FAIL* M35 .... 94 C5 ③
Mayfair Dr *IRL* M44 .... 135 E1 ④
  ROY/SHW OL2 .... 78 B1
  SALE M33 .... 158 C3
Mayfair Gdns *ROCH* OL11 .... 39 E2 ③
Mayfair Rd *WYTH/NTH* M22 .... 178 C3
Mayfield *BOLE* BL2 .... 29 E2
Mayfield Av *BOLS/LL* BL3 .... 47 F6 ②
  DTN/ASHW M34 .... 149 E4 ③
  FWTH BL4 .... 66 A4
  OLDE OL4 .... 81 E4
  RDSH SK5 .... 147 D6
  SALE M33 .... 160 C1 ⑥
  STRET M32 .... 139 F2
  SWIN M27 .... 101 D1
  WALK M28 .... 83 E2 ⑤
Mayfield Cl *HALE/TIMP* WA15 .... 175 F1
  TOT/BURYW BL8 .... 18 B3 ③
Mayfield Gv *GTN* M18 .... 128 A6
  RDSH SK5 .... 147 D6
  WILM/AE SK9 .... 202 C6
Mayfield Rd *BRAM/HZG* SK7 .... 196 C5
  BRO M7 .... 88 C4
  HALE/TIMP WA15 .... 175 F1
  MPL/ROM SK6 .... 171 F4
  OLD OL1 .... 79 F2
  OLDTF/WHR M16 .... 125 F6
  TOT/BURYW BL8 .... 18 B3
Mayfield St *DTN/ASHW* M34 .... 129 F4 ③
  MILN OL16 .... 23 H4 ③
Mayflower Av *SALQ/ORD* M5 .... 122 B1
Mayford Rd *BNG/LEV* M19 .... 145 E1
Maygate *OLD* OL1 .... 78 B3
May Gv *BNG/LEV* M19 .... 145 F3 ⑬

Mayhill Dr *SLFD* M6 .... 102 B3 **1**
  WALK M28 .... 84 B5 **2**
Mayhurst Av *CCHDY* M21 .... 162 B2 **1**
Mayorlowe Av *RDSH* SK5 .... 168 A1
Mayor's Rd *HALE/TIMP* WA15 .... 174 C3
Mayor St *BOL* BL1 .... 46 B2
  BOLS/LL BL3 .... 46 B3 **5 1**
  CHAD OL9 .... 78 A4 **6**
  TOT/BURYW BL8 .... 33 D4 **16**
Mayo St *WGTN/LGST* M12 .... 125 E1 **4**
Maypool Dr *RDSH* SK5 .... 147 D5 **2**
May Rd *CHD/CHDH* SK8 .... 195 E3
  OLDTF/WHR M16 .... 123 E6
  SWIN M27 .... 102 C1
May St *ECC* M30 .... 101 D3
  HEY OL10 .... 56 C1 **8**
  NEWH/MOS M40 .... 109 D2
  OLDS OL8 .... 95 D1
  RAD M26 .... 51 E6
Mayton St *OP/CLY* M11 .... 116 B1 **11**
Mayville Dr *DID/WITH* M20 ...... 143 F6
Maywood Av *DID/WITH* M20 ..... 163 F5
Maze St *BOLS/LL* BL3 .... 48 B4
Mcconnell Rd *NEWH/MOS* M40.. 92 B6
Mccready Dr *SALQ/ORD* M5 ..... 122 C1 **11**
Mcdonna St *BOL* BL1 .... 27 D4 **11**
Mcdonough Cl *OLDS* OL8 .... 96 B2
Mcevoy St *BOL* BL1 .... 28 A5 **2 6**
Mckean St *BOLS/LL* BL3 .... 47 E5 **2 1**
Mckie Cl *OLDS* OL8 .... 96 B2
Mclaren Cl *CCHDY* M21 .... 141 E2
Mclean Dr *IRL* M44 .... 116 B5
Mc Naught St *MILN* OL16 .... 40 C1 **8**
Meachin Av *CCHDY* M21 .... 142 A5
Meade Cl *URM* M41 .... 138 A1 **2**
Meade Gv *BRUN/LGST* M13 .... 126 A6
Meade Hill Rd *PWCH* M25 .... 89 F2
The Meade *BOLS/LL* BL3 .... 64 C1
  WILM/AE SK9 .... 203 F3
Meadfoot Av *PWCH* M25 .... 89 D2
Meadfoot Rd *GTN* M18 .... 127 E3
Meadland Gv *BOL* BL1 .... 28 A3
Meadow Av *HALE/TIMP* WA15 .... 175 F4
  SWIN M27 .... 86 C4
Meadowbank *AULW* OL7 .... 112 B1
Meadow Bank *CCHDY* M21 .... 141 E4
  HALE/TIMP WA15 .... 159 E6
  HTNM SK4 .... 165 F3 **5**
  MPL/ROM SK6 .... 169 D2 **8**
Meadowbank Cl *FAIL* M35 .... 110 B1
Meadow Bank Cl *OLDE* OL4 ...... 97 F1 **2**
Meadow Bank Ct *STRET* M32 ... 139 F2
Meadowbrook *BURY* BL9 .... 35 D3 **1**
  HOR/BR BL6 .... 44 A6
Meadow Brow *WILM/AE* SK9 .... 209 E3
Meadow Cl *BOLS/LL* BL3 .... 67 F1
  DTN/ASHW M34 .... 149 E4 **8**
  HALE/TIMP WA15 .... 175 F4
  HEY OL10 .... 37 D5 **11**
  MOSL OL5 .... 99 F2
  MPL/ROM SK6 .... 149 E6 **8**
  MPL/ROM SK6 .... 201 D1
  STRET M32 .... 140 C2
  WILM/AE SK9 .... 208 C1
Meadow Ct *CCHDY* M21 .... 141 D3
Meadow Cft *BRAM/HZG* SK7 .... 184 C4
Meadowcroft *RAD* M26 .... 51 D4
Meadow Cft *WHTF* M45 .... 70 A5
Meadowcroft La *OLD* OL1 .... 79 F2 **2**
  ROCH OL11 .... 38 A1
Meadowfield *MILN* OL16 .... 40 C4
Meadowfield Ct *HYDE* SK14 ..... 131 E5 **3**
Meadowgate *URM* M41 .... 138 B2
  WALK M28 .... 84 A5
Meadowgate Rd *SLFD* M6 .... 102 C4
Meadow Head Av *WHIT* OL12 ... 9 E5
Meadow La *BOLE* BL2 .... 49 E2 **2**
  DTN/ASHW M34 .... 149 E4
  DUK SK16 .... 131 E1
  OLDS OL8 .... 95 F3
  ROY/SHW OL2 .... 61 E3
  WALK M28 .... 100 A2
Meadow Ri *ROY/SHW* OL2 .... 42 B6
Meadow Rd *BRO* M7 .... 105 D4
  MDTN M24 .... 74 C5
  URM M41 .... 138 B2
Meadowside *BRAM/HZG* SK7 ... 182 A5 **1**
  MILN OL16 .... 43 D3
Meadowside Av *BOLE* BL2 .... 48 A1
  IRL M44 .... 135 E1
  WALK M28 .... 83 F1 **2**
  WYTH/NTH M22 .... 178 C3
Meadowside Cl *RAD* M26 .... 51 E4 **8**
Meadowside Gv *WALK* M28 .... 83 F2 **6**
Meadows La *BOLE* BL2 .... 30 A4
Meadows Rd *CHD/CHDH* SK8 ... 179 F6
  CHD/CHDH SK8 .... 195 D1
  HTNM SK4 .... 146 A5
  SALE M33 .... 140 A5
The Meadows *IRL* M44 .... 134 B5
  MDTN M24 .... 74 C1
  MPL/ROM SK6 .... 169 F1
  OLDE OL4 .... 81 E5
  PWCH M25 .... 88 C1
  RAD M26 .... 50 C4

WHIT OL12 .... 9 D2 **4**
Meadow St *HYDE* SK14 .... 150 C2 **8**
  OFTN SK2 .... 184 A2 **8**
The Meadow *HOR/BR* BL6 .... 44 B2 **2**
Meadow Vw *WHIT* OL12 .... 21 E4
Meadow Wk *FWTH* BL4 .... 65 E3
  LIT OL15 .... 12 A6 **7**
Meadow Wy *HALE/TIMP* WA15 ... 175 F4 **1**
  NEWH/MOS M40 .... 92 B4
  TOT/BURYW BL8 .... 31 F1
  WILM/AE SK9 .... 208 C1
Meadscroft Dr *WILM/AE* SK9 ... 209 D4 **2**
Meads Gv *FWTH* BL4 .... 64 B3
The Meads *CHAD* OL9 .... 77 E5
The Mead *CCHDY* M21 .... 141 F4 **3**
  SALQ/ORD M5 .... 103 F5
Meadway *BRAM/HZG* SK7 .... 196 C4
  BURY BL9 .... 53 D3
  CHAD OL9 .... 93 F3
  DUK SK16 .... 131 F2 **8**
  MPL/ROM SK6 .... 201 D1
  POY/DIS SK12 .... 197 F4
  RAMS BL0 .... 7 D2 **2**
  ROCH OL11 .... 38 C3
  SALE M33 .... 158 C3
  STLY SK15 .... 133 F3
Meadway Cl *SALE* M33 .... 158 C2
Meadway Rd *CHD/CHDH* SK8 ... 181 F4
Mealhouse Brow *STKP* SK1 ..... 167 D4 **16**
Meal St *HTNM* SK4 .... 166 C2
Meanwood Brow *WHIT* OL12 ..... 22 B4
Measham Ms *CMANE* M1 .... 124 B2 **7**
Meddings Cl *WILM/AE* SK9 .... 209 E5
Medina Cl *CHD/CHDH* SK8 .... 181 F5
Medley St *WHIT* OL12 .... 23 D4 **16**
Medlock Cl *FWTH* BL4 .... 65 E3
Medlock Dr *OLDS* OL8 .... 96 B4
Medlock Rd *FAIL* M35 .... 110 B2
Medlock St *CMANE* M1 .... 124 A2
  DROY M43 .... 110 B5
  OLD OL1 .... 79 E4 **8**
Medlock Valley Wy *OLDE* OL4 ... 63 E4
Medlock Wy *OLDE* OL4 .... 80 C5
  WHTF M45 .... 72 A3
Medway Cl *OLDS* OL8 .... 95 D2
  SALQ/ORD M5 .... 103 F4 **2**
  WILM/AE SK9 .... 204 B1
Medway Crs *ALT* WA14 .... 174 A1
Medway Dr *FWTH* BL4 .... 67 F6
Medway Rd *OLDS* OL8 .... 95 D2
  ROY/SHW OL2 .... 61 E1
  WALK M28 .... 82 C5
The Medway *HEY* OL10 .... 36 C4
Meech St *OP/CLY* M11 .... 127 D1
Meek St *OLD* OL1 .... 79 E1
Meerbrook Rd *EDGY/DAV* SK3 .. 165 E5 **2**
Mee's Sq *ECC* M30 .... 119 E1 **8**
Melandra Crs *HYDE* SK14 .... 152 C1
Melanie Dr *RDSH* SK5 .... 147 D3
Melba St *OP/CLY* M11 .... 127 F1
Melbecks Wk *NTHM/RTH* M23 .. 161 D3
Melbourne Av *CHAD* OL9 .... 77 F4 **8**
  MANAIR M90 .... 191 F1
  STRET M32 .... 140 B1 **8**
Melbourne Cl *ROCH* OL11 .... 40 B5
Melbourne Gv *BOLS/LL* BL3 ...... 45 F4
  BRAM/HZG SK7 .... 196 C3
  ROCH OL11 .... 40 B5
Melbourne St *BKLY* M9 .... 91 F5
  BRO M7 .... 105 F2 **8**
  CHAD OL9 .... 77 F4
  DTN/ASHW M34 .... 148 C1
  HULME M15 .... 123 F2 **8**
  RDSH SK5 .... 147 D3
  STLY SK15 .... 114 B5
  SWIN M27 .... 86 C5 **8**
Melbourne St North *AUL* OL6 ... 113 D3 **8**
Melbourne St South *AUL* OL6 ... 113 D3 **2**
Melbury Av *DID/WITH* M20 .... 164 B1
Melbury Rd *CHD/CHDH* SK8 ..... 195 F3 **4**
Meldon Rd *BRUN/LGST* M13 ..... 144 C1
Meldrum St *OLDS* OL8 .... 96 A1
Melford Av *NEWH/MOS* M40 ..... 93 F4
Melford Gv *OLDE* OL4 .... 80 B5
Melford Rd *BRAM/HZG* SK7 ..... 185 D6
Melfort Av *STRET* M32 .... 140 C1
Meliden Crs *BOL* BL1 .... 26 C6 **23**
  WYTH/NTH M22 .... 178 C5
Melksham Cl *SALQ/ORD* M5 ..... 104 C5 **8**
Mellalieu St *MDTN* M24 .... 74 C2
  ROY/SHW OL2 .... 78 C1
Melland Av *CCHDY* M21 .... 142 A6
Melland Rd *GTN* M18 .... 127 D6
Melling Av *CHAD* OL9 .... 76 C2 **7**
  HTNM SK4 .... 146 C5
Melling Rd *OLDE* OL4 .... 80 A5
Melling St *WGTN/LGST* M12 ..... 126 B5
Mellington Av *DID/WITH* M20 ... 164 A5
Mellodew Dr *OLD* OL1 .... 62 B6
Mellor Brow *HEY* OL10 .... 36 C5 **10**
Mellor Cl *AUL* OL6 .... 113 F5
Mellor Ct *OFTN* SK2 .... 168 C6 **3**
Mellor Dr *BURY* BL9 .... 52 B2
  WALK M28 .... 83 D4
Mellor Gv *BOL* BL1 .... 26 C6

Mellor Rd *AUL* OL6 .... 113 F4
  CHD/CHDH SK8 .... 181 F6
Mellors Rd *TRPK* M17 .... 120 C2
Mellor St *DROY* M43 .... 110 A6
  ECC M30 .... 101 E6
  FAIL M35 .... 109 E1
  NEWH/MOS M40 .... 107 E4
  OLDE OL4 .... 80 C5
  PWCH M25 .... 88 A1
  RAD M26 .... 69 F1 **4**
  ROCH OL11 .... 22 B6
  ROY/SHW OL2 .... 60 B4
  STRET M32 .... 121 E5
Mellor Wy *CHAD* OL9 .... 94 C1
Mellowstone Dr
  OLDTF/WHR M16 .... 143 D3
Melloy Pl *CHH* M8 .... 106 B3 **8**
Melon Pl *SLFD* M6 .... 104 C5 **8**
Melrose Av *BOL* BL1 .... 26 B6
  DID/WITH M20 .... 164 A2
  ECC M30 .... 100 C3 **8**
  EDGY/DAV SK3 .... 165 D6 **8**
  HEY OL10 .... 37 D4
  LIT OL15 .... 12 B4
  SALE M33 .... 159 F2
  TOT/BURYW BL8 .... 33 D4 **17**
Melrose Cl *WHTF* M45 .... 71 D1
Melrose Crs *EDGY/DAV* SK3 ..... 182 B3
  HALE/TIMP WA15 .... 175 F6
  POY/DIS SK12 .... 200 B4
Melrose Gdns *RAD* M26 .... 50 C4 **8**
Melrose Rd *BOLS/LL* BL3 .... 49 D6
  RAD M26 .... 50 C4
Melrose St *NEWH/MOS* M40 .... 109 D2
  OLD OL1 .... 79 F2 **8**
  ROCH OL11 .... 22 B6 **4**
  TOT/BURYW BL8 .... 18 C3
Melsomby Rd *NTHM/RTH* M23 .. 161 E3
Meltham Av *DID/WITH* M20 ...... 143 E5
Meltham Cl *HTNM* SK4 .... 164 C4
Meltham Rd *HTNM* SK4 .... 164 C4
Melton Av *DTN/ASHW* M34 ...... 128 B6
  URM M41 .... 117 D6
Melton Cl *HEY* OL10 .... 36 C6 **8**
  WALK M28 .... 83 D3
Melton Dr *BURY* BL9 .... 53 F4
Melton Rd *CHH* M8 .... 89 F4
Melton St *BKLY* M9 .... 92 A4 **8**
  HEY OL10 .... 36 C6
  RAD M26 .... 51 D5 **8**
  RDSH SK5 .... 167 D1 **7**
Melverley Rd *BKLY* M9 .... 73 E6
Melville Cl *OP/CLY* M11 .... 127 F2
Melville Rd *FWTH* BL4 .... 67 D5
  IRL M44 .... 134 A6
  STRET M32 .... 120 C6
Melville St *AUL* OL6 .... 112 C4 **8**
  BOLS/LL BL3 .... 47 E5 **22**
  CSLFD M3 .... 105 E5 **17**
  OLDE OL4 .... 80 C6
  ROCH OL11 .... 39 E6
Melvin Av *WYTH/NTH* M22 .... 178 C3
Melyncourt Rd *HYDE* SK14 ...... 133 F6 **8**
Memorial Rd *WALK* M28 .... 85 E2
Menai Gv *CHD/CHDH* SK8 .... 181 E1
Menai Rd *EDGY/DAV* SK3 .... 182 C1 **8**
Menai St *BOLS/LL* BL3 .... 45 F5 **22**
Mendip Av *WYTH/NTH* M22 ...... 179 D3
Mendip Cl *BOLE* BL2 .... 49 E2
  CHAD OL9 .... 77 E6 **8**
  CHD/CHDH SK8 .... 193 F2
  HTNM SK4 .... 166 C2
  ROY/SHW OL2 .... 60 A6
Mendip Crs *TOT/BURYW* BL8 .... 32 B4
Mendip Dr *BOLE* BL2 .... 49 E3 **2**
  MILN OL16 .... 42 B1
Mendip Rd *OLDS* OL8 .... 95 E2 **8**
Menston Av *NEWH/MOS* M40 .... 93 F4
Mentmore Rd *MILN* OL16 .... 24 B6
Mentone Crs *WYTH/NTH* M22 ... 178 C3
Mentone Rd *HTNM* SK4 .... 165 F2
Mercer La *ROCH* OL11 .... 27 G5
Mercer Rd *GTN* M18 .... 127 E4
Mercer's Rd *HEY* OL10 .... 56 B2
Mercer St *BNG/LEV* M19 .... 145 F2 **8**
  DROY M43 .... 110 C5 **8**
Merchants Quay *SALQ/ORD* M5 .. 122 B3
Mercian Wy *EDGY/DAV* SK3 ..... 166 C6
Mercia St *BOLS/LL* BL3 .... 46 A4 **23**
Mercury Wy *URM* M41 .... 120 A4
Mere Av *DROY* M43 .... 127 F1
  MDTN M24 .... 75 E5
  SLFD M6 .... 103 F5 **13**
Merebank Cl *ROCH* OL11 .... 20 C5 **8**
Mere Cl *BURY* BL9 .... 53 F4
  DTN/ASHW M34 .... 147 F1
  SALE M33 .... 161 D2
Mereclough Av *WALK* M28 .... 84 A4
Meredew Av *SWIN* M27 .... 101 F1 **8**
Meredith St *BOLS/LL* BL3 .... 47 D6 **20**
  RUSH/FAL M14 .... 144 B4 **8**
Mere Dr *DID/WITH* M20 .... 163 F1 **8**
  SWIN M27 .... 86 B3
Merefield Av *ROCH* OL11 .... 39 F2 **12**

Merefield Rd *HALE/TIMP* WA15 .... 176 A2
Merefield St *ROCH* OL11 .... 39 F2
Mere Fold *WALK* M28 .... 82 C2
Merehall Dr *BOL* BL1 .... 46 C1
Merehall St *BOL* BL1 .... 27 E6
Mereland Av *DID/WITH* M20 .... 164 A1
Mere La *ROCH* OL11 .... 40 A1
Meremanor *WALK* M28 .... 84 A4
Merepool Cl *MPL/ROM* SK6 .... 170 B6
Mere Side *STLY* SK15 .... 114 A3
Mereside Cl *CHD/CHDH* SK8 .... 181 D3
Mereside Gv *WALK* M28 .... 83 F2
Mere St *ROCH* OL11 .... 40 A1
The Mere *AUL* OL6 .... 113 F1
  CHD/CHDH SK8 .... 181 D3
Merewood Av *WYTH/NTH* M22 .... 178 B1
Meriden Cl *RAD* M26 .... 51 D4
Meriden Gv *HOR/BR* BL6 .... 44 B3
Meridian Pl *DID/WITH* M20 .... 163 E1
Merinall Cl *MILN* OL16 .... 24 A6
Meriton Rd *WILM/AE* SK9 .... 194 A3
Merlewood Av *BNG/LEV* M19 .... 110 C6
  DTN/ASHW M34 .... 100 C1
Merlewood Dr *SWIN* M27 .... 101 D1
Merlin Cl *LIT* OL15 .... 25 E3
  OFTN SK2 .... 185 E1
  OLDS OL8 .... 96 B5
Merlin Gv *BOL* BL1 .... 26 C6
Merlin Rd *IRL* M44 .... 116 B5
  MILN OL16 .... 42 A1
Merlyn Av *DID/WITH* M20 .... 164 A1
  DTN/ASHW M34 .... 148 C1
  SALE M33 .... 140 A5
Merrick Av *WYTH/NTH* M22 .... 178 C3
Merrick St *HEY* OL10 .... 37 F6
The Merridale *HALE/TIMP* WA15 .... 189 D1
Merrill St *ANC* M4 .... 107 E6
Merriman St *OLDTF/WHR* M16 .... 123 F5
Merrion St *FWTH* BL4 .... 66 A1
Merrybent Cl *OFTN* SK2 .... 184 B3
Merrybower Rd *BRO* M7 .... 89 F5
Merrydale Av *ECC* M30 .... 101 F3
Merryman Hall *MILN* OL16 .... 23 F3
Merseybank Av *CHDY* M21 .... 162 B1
Mersey Cl *WHTF* M45 .... 71 F2
Mersey Dr *DID/WITH* M20 .... 162 B2
  PART M31 .... 155 F2
  WHTF M45 .... 71 F2
Mersey Mdw *DID/WITH* M20 .... 163 D2
Mersey Rd *DID/WITH* M20 .... 163 D2
  HTNM SK4 .... 165 D3
  SALE M33 .... 139 F5
Mersey Rd North *FAIL* M35 .... 94 B4
Mersey Sq *STKP* SK1 .... 166 C4
Mersey St *OP/CLY* M11 .... 127 F1
  OP/CLY M11 .... 127 F2
  STKP SK1 .... 167 E3
Merston Dr *DID/WITH* M20 .... 164 A1
Merton Av *BRAM/HZG* SK7 .... 199 D1
  MPL/ROM SK6 .... 169 E1
  OLDS OL8 .... 95 E2
Merton Dr *DROY* M43 .... 109 F6
Merton Gv *CHAD* OL9 .... 93 E2
  HALE/TIMP WA15 .... 175 F1
Merton Rd *EDGY/DAV* SK3 .... 165 F5
  POY/DIS SK12 .... 197 F5
  PWCH M25 .... 72 A6
  SALE M33 .... 139 E6
Merton St *TOT/BURYW* BL8 .... 33 E4
Merville Av *NEWH/MOS* M40 .... 92 A4
Mervyn Rd *BRO* M7 .... 104 B1
Merwell Rd *URM* M41 .... 136 C2
Merwood Av *CHD/CHDH* SK8 .... 194 B1
Merwood Dr *RUSH/FAL* M14 .... 125 F3
Mesnefield Rd *BRO* M7 .... 88 B5
Mesne Lea Gv *WALK* M28 .... 83 F5
Mesne Lea Rd *WALK* M28 .... 83 F5
Metfield Pl *BOL* BL1 .... 46 C1
Methuen St *WGTN/LGST* M12 .... 126 C6
Methwold St *BOLS/LL* BL3 .... 46 A5
The Mews *BOL* BL1 .... 45 F1
  CHD/CHDH SK8 .... 179 F2
  NEWH/MOS M40 .... 107 F4
  PWCH M25 .... 88 C2
Meyer St *EDGY/DAV* SK3 .... 183 D1
Meyrick Rd *SLFD* M6 .... 104 B4
Miall St *ROCH* OL11 .... 40 A1
Michael St *MDTN* M24 .... 75 D5
Michael Wife La *RAMS* BL0 .... 7 F1
Michigan Av *SALQ/ORD* M5 .... 122 A1
Micklehurst Av *DID/WITH* M20 .... 162 C1
Micklehurst Gn *OFTN* SK2 .... 184 A6
Micklehurst Rd *MOSL* OL5 .... 99 F4
Middlebourne St *SLFD* M6 .... 103 F5
Middlebrook Dr *HOR/BR* BL6 .... 44 A3
Middlefield *OLDS* OL8 .... 95 D3
Middlefields *CHD/CHDH* SK8 .... 181 F5
Middlegate *NEWH/MOS* M40 .... 93 D2
Middle Ga *OLDS* OL8 .... 95 F3
Middle Gn *AUL* OL6 .... 113 D3
Middleham St *RUSH/FAL* M14 .... 143 E1
Middle Hl *WHIT* OL12 .... 23 D1
Middle Hillgate *STKP* SK1 .... 167 D4
Middlesex Dr *BURY* BL9 .... 53 D1

Middlesex Rd *BKLY* M9 .... 91 E3
  RDSH M5 .... 148 A5
Middlestone Dr *BKLY* M9 .... 91 E6
Middle St *WHIT* OL12 .... 9 D2
Middleton Av *FAIL* M35 .... 94 A6
Middleton Dr *BURY* BL9 .... 53 D6
Middleton Old Rd *BKLY* M9 .... 91 E3
Middleton Rd *BKLY* M9 .... 73 D6
  CHAD OL9 .... 76 B2
  CHH M8 .... 90 A3
  HEY OL10 .... 56 C1
  MDTN M24 .... 73 E5
  RDSH SK5 .... 147 D1
  ROY/SHW OL2 .... 59 F6
Middleton Rd West *CHAD* OL9 .... 76 C3
Middleton Wy *MDTN* M24 .... 75 D3
Middleway *OLDE* OL4 .... 81 F6
Middlewood Dr *HTNM* SK4 .... 165 E4
Middle Wood La *WHIT* OL12 .... 11 F5
Middlewood Rd *MPL/ROM* SK6 .... 200 B2
  POY/DIS SK12 .... 199 D5
Midford Av *ECC* M30 .... 100 C5
Midford Dr *BOL* BL1 .... 27 F1
Midge Hall Dr *ROCH* OL11 .... 38 B1
Midgley Av *GTN* M18 .... 127 F3
Midgley Crs *AUL* OL6 .... 113 F3
Midgley Dr *SWIN* M27 .... 101 E1
Midhurst Av *NEWH/MOS* M40 .... 108 C3
Midhurst Cl *CHD/CHDH* SK8 .... 195 D1
Midhurst St *ROCH* OL11 .... 40 A1
Midland Rd *BRAM/HZG* SK7 .... 182 C4
  RDSH SK5 .... 147 D1
Midland St *WGTN/LGST* M12 .... 125 E2
Midland Wk *BRAM/HZG* SK7 .... 182 C4
Midlothian St *OP/CLY* M11 .... 108 C5
Midville Rd *OP/CLY* M11 .... 109 D4
Midway *CHD/CHDH* SK8 .... 195 D1
Midway St *BNG/LEV* M19 .... 145 E1
Milan St *BRO* M7 .... 105 F1
Milbourne Rd *BURY* BL9 .... 38 A1
Milburn Av *NTHM/RTH* M23 .... 161 F5
Milbury Dr *LIT* OL15 .... 25 E3
Milden Cl *DID/WITH* M20 .... 164 A1
Mildred Av *OLDE* OL4 .... 81 F6
  PWCH M25 .... 89 D3
  ROY/SHW OL2 .... 78 C1
Mildred St *BRO* M7 .... 105 D2
Mile End La *OFTN* SK2 .... 183 F2
Mile La *TOT/BURYW* BL8 .... 32 A6
Miles St *BOL* BL1 .... 27 E5
  HYDE SK14 .... 151 D1
  OLD OL1 .... 79 F3
  WGTN/LGST M12 .... 126 B2
Milford Av *OLDS* OL8 .... 95 D3
Milford Brow *OLDE* OL4 .... 80 C4
Milford Crs *LIT* OL15 .... 12 C5
Milford Dr *BNG/LEV* M19 .... 146 A4
Milford Gv *OFTN* SK2 .... 168 A6
Milford Rd *BOLE* BL2 .... 30 A3
  BOLS/LL BL3 .... 46 C6
Milford St *BKLY* M9 .... 103 F6
  SLFD M6 .... 104 B2
  WHIT OL12 .... 23 D4
Milkstone Pl *ROCH* OL11 .... 40 A1
Milkstone Rd *ROCH* OL11 .... 40 A1
Milk St *CMANW* M2 .... 3 E3
  HYDE SK14 .... 150 B1
  OLDE OL4 .... 80 A4
  RAMS BL0 .... 6 C6
  ROCH OL11 .... 40 A1
Milkwood Gv *GTN* M18 .... 127 E5
Millais St *NEWH/MOS* M40 .... 92 B4
Millard St *CHAD* OL9 .... 77 E4
Mill Bank *RAD* M26 .... 69 F1
Millbank St *CMANE* M1 .... 107 D6
  HEY OL10 .... 36 C5
Millbeck Rd *MDTN* M24 .... 74 B1
Millbeck St *HULME* M15 .... 124 B3
Millbrae Gdns *ROY/SHW* OL2 .... 61 D2
Millbrook Av *DTN/ASHW* M34 .... 148 B2
Millbrook Bank *ROCH* OL11 .... 20 B4
Millbrook Cl *ROY/SHW* OL2 .... 62 B3
Millbrook Rd *NTHM/RTH* M23 .... 177 E4
Millbrook St *STKP* SK1 .... 167 D5
Mill Brow *AUL* OL6 .... 97 D4
  BKLY M9 .... 91 D3
  HYDE SK14 .... 153 E3
  OLD OL1 .... 77 E1
  WALK M28 .... 100 A1
Mill Cft *BOL* BL1 .... 46 B1
Mill Croft Cl *ROCH* OL11 .... 20 A3
Miller Meadow Cl *ROY/SHW* OL2 .... 62 A1
Miller Rd *OLDS* OL8 .... 95 F2
Millers Brook Cl *HEY* OL10 .... 37 E4
Millers Cl *SALE* M33 .... 161 E2
Millers Ct *SALQ/ORD* M5 .... 102 B5
Millers St *ECC* M30 .... 101 D6
Miller St *ANC* M4 .... 3 F1
  AUL OL6 .... 113 D3
  BOL BL1 .... 27 F5
  BURY BL9 .... 19 D5
  HEY OL10 .... 37 E5
  RAD M26 .... 51 D3

Millett St *BURY* BL9 .... 33 E5
  RAMS BL0 .... 7 E4
Millfield Gv *MILN* OL16 .... 40 C1
Millfield Rd *BOLE* BL2 .... 49 E2
Millfold *WHIT* OL12 .... 9 E1
Mill Fold Rd *MDTN* M24 .... 75 D4
Millford Av *URM* M41 .... 136 C2
Mill Ga *MILN* OL16 .... 23 F3
  OLDS OL8 .... 95 E2
Millgate *STKP* SK1 .... 167 D3
Millgate La *DID/WITH* M20 .... 163 E5
Mill Green St *WGTN/LGST* M12 .... 125 E1
Millhall Cl *HULME* M15 .... 123 F4
Millhead Av *NEWH/MOS* M40 .... 107 F5
Mill HI *LHULT* M38 .... 64 C5
Mill Hill Av *POY/DIS* SK12 .... 198 B2
Mill Hill Gv *HYDE* SK14 .... 153 D1
Mill Hill Hollow *POY/DIS* SK12 .... 198 B2
Mill Hill St *BOLE* BL2 .... 47 E1
Millhouse Av *NTHM/RTH* M23 .... 177 E3
Mill House Cl *WHIT* OL12 .... 24 B1
Millhouse St *RAMS* BL0 .... 7 F3
Mill La *AUL* OL6 .... 112 C5
  BRAM/HZG SK7 .... 199 D1
  CHAD OL9 .... 95 D1
  CHD/CHDH SK8 .... 180 B1
  CHD/CHDH SK8 .... 181 F4
  DTN/ASHW M34 .... 149 F2
  FAIL M35 .... 109 E1
  HALE/TIMP WA15 .... 190 C5
  MCFLDN SK10 .... 206 C5
  MOSL OL5 .... 99 D3
  MPL/ROM SK6 .... 149 E6
  RDSH SK5 .... 147 E2
  ROY/SHW OL2 .... 60 A5
  TOT/BURYW BL8 .... 32 C5
  WYTH/NTH M22 .... 162 C4
Millom Av *NTHM/RTH* M23 .... 161 F4
Millom Dr *BURY* BL9 .... 71 E1
Millom Pl *CHD/CHDH* SK8 .... 179 F4
Millow St *ANC* M4 .... 106 B4
Mills Farm Cl *OLDS* OL8 .... 96 B4
Mills Hill Rd *CHAD* OL9 .... 76 B2
Mills St *HEY* OL10 .... 56 C2
  WHIT OL12 .... 9 E1
Millstone Cl *POY/DIS* SK12 .... 199 D4
Millstone Rd *BOL* BL1 .... 26 A6
Millstream La *DROY* M43 .... 109 F4
Mill St *ALT* WA14 .... 174 C2
  BOL BL1 .... 47 E2
  BRAM/HZG SK7 .... 184 B4
  EDGW/EG BL7 .... 14 A5
  FAIL M35 .... 93 D6
  FWTH BL4 .... 66 A3
  HYDE SK14 .... 131 F4
  MOSL OL5 .... 99 D5
  OP/CLY M11 .... 126 B1
  RAD M26 .... 69 F1
  RAMS BL0 .... 18 B1
  ROY/SHW OL2 .... 60 B5
  SLFD M6 .... 104 B3
  STLY SK15 .... 115 D6
  TOT/BURYW BL8 .... 18 A5
  WALK M28 .... 82 B6
  WILM/AE SK9 .... 203 F4
Milltown St *RAD* M26 .... 69 F1
Millwall Cl *GTN* M18 .... 127 E4
Millway *HALE/TIMP* WA15 .... 190 A2
Millwood Cl *CHD/CHDH* SK8 .... 194 C1
Millwood Ct *BURY* BL9 .... 53 D2
Millwood Ter *HYDE* SK14 .... 150 A1
Millwright St *NEWH/MOS* M40 .... 108 C2
Mill Yd *BURY* BL9 .... 34 B4
Milne Cl *WGTN/LGST* M12 .... 126 B3
Milner Av *ALT* WA14 .... 157 F6
  BURY BL9 .... 34 A2
Milner St *OLDTF/WHR* M16 .... 123 E5
  RAD M26 .... 50 C6
  SWIN M27 .... 86 B5
  WHIT OL12 .... 9 D3
Milne St *CHAD* OL9 .... 77 F4
  OLD OL1 .... 79 E1
  ROCH OL11 .... 39 D5
  ROY/SHW OL2 .... 61 F5
Milngate Cl *MILN* OL16 .... 41 D4
Milnholme *BOL* BL1 .... 26 C4
Milnrow Cl *BRUN/LGST* M13 .... 124 C2
Milnrow Rd *LIT* OL15 .... 25 D3
  MILN OL16 .... 23 F6
  ROY/SHW OL2 .... 43 D6
  ROY/SHW OL2 .... 61 F2
Milnthorpe Rd *BOLE* BL2 .... 48 C1
Milnthorpe St *SLFD* M6 .... 104 B2
Milnthorpe Wy
  WGTN/LGST M12 .... 125 F3
Milo St *BKLY* M9 .... 91 E2
Milsom Av *BOLS/LL* BL3 .... 46 A6
Milton Av *BOLS/LL* BL3 .... 45 F6
  BOLS/LL BL3 .... 49 F5
  DROY M43 .... 110 B6
  IRL M44 .... 136 C6
  SALQ/ORD M5 .... 103 E5
  STLY SK15 .... 115 F3
Milton Cl *DUK* SK16 .... 132 C2
  MPL/ROM SK6 .... 187 D3

Stret M32 .... 121 F6
Milton Ct BNG/LEV M19 .... 164 C1
Milton Crs CHD/CHDH SK8 .... 180 A2
FWTH BL4 .... 65 F5
Milton Dr CHAD OL9 .... 77 E5
HALE/TIMP WA15 .... 159 E4
POY/DIS SK12 .... 198 B5
SALE M33 .... 139 E5
Milton Gv OLDTF/WHR M16 .... 142 A1
SALE M33 .... 139 E5
Milton Pl SLFD M6 .... 104 B4
Milton Rd DTN/ASHW M34 .... 111 E6
PWCH M25 .... 72 A6
RAD M26 .... 50 B5
STRET M32 .... 121 F6
SWIN M27 .... 85 E4
Milton St BRO M7 .... 105 F5
DTN/ASHW M34 .... 129 F5
ECC M30 .... 101 E5
HYDE SK14 .... 131 E5
MDTN M24 .... 71 D2
MILN OL16 .... 23 D5
MOSL OL5 .... 99 D3
RAMS BL0 .... 6 C5
ROY/SHW OL2 .... 60 C4
Milton Vw MOSL OL5 .... 99 E3
Milverton Av HYDE SK14 .... 152 A1
Milverton Cl HOR/BR BL6 .... 44 B4
Milverton Dr CHD/CHDH SK8 .... 195 F4
Milverton Rd RUSH/FAL M14 .... 125 E6
Milverton Wk HYDE SK14 .... 152 A1
Milwain Dr HTNM SK4 .... 146 A5
Milwain Rd BNG/LEV M19 .... 145 D3
STRET M32 .... 140 A2
Mimosa Dr SWIN M27 .... 86 A3
Mincing St ANC M4 .... 106 B4
Minden Cl DID/WITH M20 .... 164 A1
TOT/BURYW BL8 .... 32 C5
Minden St SLFD M6 .... 103 F1
Minehead Av DID/WITH M20 .... 143 D4
URM M41 .... 137 F3
Minerva Rd DUK SK16 .... 113 D5
FWTH BL4 .... 65 D2
Mine St HEY OL10 .... 37 E3
Minnie St BOLS/LL BL3 .... 45 F6
WHIT OL12 .... 9 E1
Minoan Gdns BRO M7 .... 105 D3
Minorca Cl ROCH OL11 .... 20 C5
Minorca St BOLS/LL BL3 .... 46 C5
Minor St FAIL M35 .... 94 B4
OLDS OL8 .... 78 C6
ROCH OL11 .... 39 D6
Minshull St CMANE M1 .... 3 F4
Minshull St South CMANE M1 .... 3 C5
Minstead Cl HYDE SK14 .... 151 E2
Minster Cl BOLE BL2 .... 29 D5
DUK SK16 .... 131 E3
Minster Dr CHD/CHDH SK8 .... 181 E2
Minster Rd BOLE BL2 .... 29 D5
Minton St NEWH/MOS M40 .... 93 D5
OLDE OL4 ....
Minto St AULW OL7 .... 112 B3
Mint St RAMS BL0 .... 7 D1
Mirabel St CSLFD M3 .... 106 A4
Mirfield Av BKLY M9 .... 91 E1
HTNM SK4 .... 165 F5
OLDS OL8 .... 95 F1
Mirfield Dr ECC M30 .... 101 E3
MDTN M24 .... 75 D2
URM M41 .... 119 D5
Mirfield Rd BKLY M9 .... 91 E1
Miriam St BOLS/LL BL3 .... 48 F5
FAIL M35 .... 109 F2
NEWH/MOS M40 .... 109 E1
Mission St HEY OL10 .... 37 D5
Missouri Av SALQ/ORD M5 .... 103 F6
Mistletoe Gv CSLFD M3 .... 105 E4
Mitcham Av BKLY M9 .... 92 B2
Mitchell Cl CHD/CHDH SK8 .... 179 D1
Mitchells Quay FAIL M35 .... 93 F6
Mitchell St ECC M30 .... 101 D4
MDTN M24 .... 75 D2
MILN OL16 .... 24 A2
NEWH/MOS M40 .... 108 C2
OLD OL1 .... 78 B3
OP/CLY M11 .... 126 A1
TOT/BURYW BL8 .... 33 D3
WHIT OL12 .... 22 B5
Mitcheson Gdns SLFD M6 .... 104 A4
Mitford Rd RUSH/FAL M14 .... 144 A4
Mitford St STRET M32 .... 140 A2
Mitre Cl BRUN/LGST M13 .... 126 A3
Mitre St BOL BL1 .... 27 F3
FAIL M35 .... 94 A5
Mitton Cl HEY OL10 .... 36 A5
TOT/BURYW BL8 .... 31 F5
Mizpah Gv TOT/BURYW BL8 .... 32 C5
Mizzy Rd WHIT OL12 .... 22 C4
Moadlock MPL/ROM SK6 .... 170 A1
Moat Av WYTH/NTH M22 .... 178 A3
Moatfield Gdns BOL BL1 .... 46 B1
Moat Gdns WYTH/NTH M22 .... 178 A3
Moat Hall Av ECC M30 .... 118 B1
Moat Rd WYTH/NTH M22 .... 178 A3
Mobberley Cl BNG/LEV M19 .... 164 C1

Mobberley Rd BOLE BL2 .... 48 B1
WILM/AE SK9 .... 202 A2
Modbury Cl BRAM/HZG SK7 .... 183 E6
Mode Hill La WHTF M45 .... 72 A3
Mode Wheel Rd South
SALQ/ORD M5 .... 103 E6
Modwen Rd SALQ/ORD M5 .... 122 C3
Moelfre Dr CHD/CHDH SK8 .... 196 A2
Moffat Cl BOLE BL2 .... 49 D3
Moisant St BOLS/LL BL3 .... 46 B6
Mold St BOL BL1 .... 27 F4
OLD OL1 .... 78 C3
Molesworth St MILN OL16 .... 23 E6
Mollets Wd DTN/ASHW M34 .... 130 B4
Mollington Rd WYTH/NTH M22 .... 192 C1
Molyneux Rd BNG/LEV M19 .... 146 A2
Molyneux St WHIT OL12 .... 22 B5
Mona Av CHD/CHDH SK8 .... 180 B6
STRET M32 .... 121 D6
Monaco Dr WYTH/NTH M22 .... 162 B3
Monarch Cl IRL M44 .... 134 C5
ROY/SHW OL2 .... 78 C1
Monart Rd BKLY M9 .... 91 F4
Mona St HYDE SK14 .... 150 C1
SLFD M6 .... 104 B3
Moncrieffe St BOLS/LL BL3 .... 47 D3
Mond Rd IRL M44 .... 133 D6
Money Ash Rd HALE/TIMP WA15 .... 174 B4
Monfa Av EDGY/DAV SK3 .... 183 E3
Monica Av CHH M8 .... 90 A3
Monica Gv BNG/LEV M19 .... 145 D3
Monks Cl MILN OL16 .... 41 F1
Monksdale Av URM M41 .... 137 F1
Monks Hall Gv ECC M30 .... 102 A5
Monks La BOLE BL2 .... 29 E5
Monkton Av GTN M18 .... 127 D6
Monkwood Dr BKLY M9 .... 91 F5
SALE M33 .... 139 D6
Monmouth Av BURY BL9 .... 34 A2
Monmouth Rd CHD/CHDH SK8 .... 181 F6
Monmouth St CHAD OL9 .... 78 A6
GTN M18 .... 127 F3
MDTN M24 .... 76 A3
ROCH OL11 .... 40 A1
Monroe Cl SLFD M6 .... 103 F3
Monsal Av BRO M7 .... 88 B6
OFTN SK2 .... 168 B6
Monsall Cl BURY BL9 .... 71 E1
Monsall Rd NEWH/MOS M40 .... 107 F1
Monsall St NEWH/MOS M40 .... 107 E2
OLDS OL8 .... 95 F2
Mons Av ROCH OL11 .... 22 A5
Montague Rd AUL OL6 .... 113 E4
OLDTF/WHR M16 .... 122 B4
SALE M33 .... 159 F4
Montague St BOLS/LL BL3 .... 45 F6
Montague Wy STLY SK15 .... 114 B5
Montagu Rd OFTN SK2 .... 168 B6
Montagu St MPL/ROM SK6 .... 171 F3
Montana Sq OP/CLY M11 .... 127 F2
Montcliffe Crs OLDTF/WHR M16 .... 143 D2
Monteagle St BKLY M9 .... 90 C1
Montford St SALQ/ORD M5 .... 104 B5
Montgomery Dr BURY BL9 .... 71 F1
Montgomery Rd BRUN/LGST M13 .... 145 D1
Montgomery St OLDS OL8 .... 94 C3
ROCH OL11 .... 39 E3
Montgomery Wy RAD M26 .... 50 A4
Monton Av ECC M30 .... 101 F4
Montondale ECC M30 .... 101 D4
Montonfields Rd ECC M30 .... 101 D4
Monton Gn ECC M30 .... 101 E3
Monton La ECC M30 .... 101 F5
Monton Mill Gdns ECC M30 .... 101 D4
Monton Rd ECC M30 .... 101 E4
RDSH SK5 .... 168 A1
Monton St BOLS/LL BL3 .... 46 C5
RAD M26 .... 51 D6
RUSH/FAL M14 .... 124 B5
Montpellier Rd WYTH/NTH M22 .... 178 D5
Montreal St BNG/LEV M19 .... 145 F2
OLDS OL8 .... 96 A1
Montrose Av BOLE BL2 .... 29 D6
DID/WITH M20 .... 143 E6
DUK SK16 .... 131 D2
EDGY/DAV SK3 .... 183 E4
STRET M32 .... 139 F1
TOT/BURYW BL8 .... 18 B5
Montrose Dr EDGW/EG BL7 .... 14 C6
Montrose St ROCH OL11 .... 58 A1
Moon Gv RUSH/FAL M14 .... 125 E6
Moon St CHAD OL9 .... 78 A4
Moorbank La MILN OL16 .... 41 E3
Moorby Av BNG/LEV M19 .... 164 C1
Moor Cl RAD M26 .... 50 C4
Moorclose St MDTN M24 .... 76 A3
Moorcock Av SWIN M27 .... 86 C5
Moorcroft RAMS BL0 .... 7 E1
ROCH OL11 .... 40 A4
Moorcroft Rd DID/WITH M20 .... 165 D1
Moorcroft Rd NTHM/RTH M23 .... 161 D4
Moorcroft St DROY M43 .... 110 C6
OLDS OL8 .... 95 D3
Moordale Av OLDE OL4 .... 80 C2
Moordale St DID/WITH M20 .... 143 E6

Moordown Cl CHH M8 .... 106 C1
Mooredge Ter ROY/SHW OL2 .... 78 C1
Moor End Av WYTH/NTH M22 .... 162 B5
Moor End Av BRO M7 .... 89 D5
Moore's Ct BOL BL1 .... 46 A1
Moore St MILN OL16 .... 23 D6
Moorfield Av DTN/ASHW M34 .... 149 E1
LIT OL15 .... 12 B4
RUSH/FAL M14 .... 144 A2
STLY SK15 .... 133 E2
Moorfield Cha FWTH BL4 .... 66 B4
Moorfield Cl IRL M44 .... 116 C6
SWIN M27 .... 101 E1
Moorfield Dr HYDE SK14 .... 131 F4
WILM/AE SK9 .... 202 C6
Moorfield Gv BOLE BL2 .... 28 C6
HTNM SK4 .... 165 F1
SALE M33 .... 160 B2
Moorfield Hamlet ROY/SHW OL2 .... 61 D2
Moorfield Hts MOSL OL5 .... 99 F6
Moorfield Ms ROY/SHW OL2 .... 61 F2
Moorfield Pl WHIT OL12 .... 22 C4
Moorfield Rd DID/WITH M20 .... 163 D1
IRL M44 .... 116 B6
OLDS OL8 .... 94 C3
SLFD M6 .... 103 E2
SWIN M27 .... 101 D1
Moorfield St DID/WITH M20 .... 143 F4
DID/WITH M20 .... 143 F4
Moor Ga BOLE BL2 .... 29 E2
Moorgate Av DID/WITH M20 .... 143 D5
ROCH OL11 .... 21 E6
Moorgate Dr STLY SK15 .... 115 F1
Moor Gate La WHIT OL12 .... 11 F4
Moorgate Ms MOSL OL5 .... 99 F6
Moorgate Rd RAD M26 .... 50 C1
STLY SK15 .... 99 F6
Moorhead St ANC M4 .... 106 C4
Moorhey Rd LHULT M38 .... 65 D5
Moorhey St OLDE OL4 .... 79 F5
Moor Hi ROCH OL11 .... 20 C4
Moorhouse Farm MILN OL16 .... 41 F1
Moorings Rd TRPK M17 .... 120 C1
The Moorings MOSL OL5 .... 99 F2
WALK M28 .... 100 B2
Moorland Av CHH M8 .... 90 A3
DROY M43 .... 109 F6
MILN OL16 .... 42 A2
ROCH OL11 .... 21 D5
SALE M33 .... 160 A2
WHIT OL12 .... 9 D5
Moorland Crs WHIT OL12 .... 9 D4
Moorland Dr CHD/CHDH SK8 .... 195 D1
LHULT M38 .... 65 E5
Moorland Gv BOL BL1 .... 26 B5
Moorland Rd DID/WITH M20 .... 163 F2
OFTN SK2 .... 183 E5
STLY SK15 .... 115 F2
Moorlands Av URM M41 .... 118 C6
Moorlands Crs MOSL OL5 .... 99 E4
Moorlands Dr MOSL OL5 .... 99 F2
Moorlands St ROY/SHW OL2 .... 62 A2
Moorland St WHIT OL12 .... 22 C4
Moorland Ter WHIT OL12 .... 21 E4
Moor La BOL BL1 .... 46 C2
BOLS/LL BL3 .... 46 C3
BRAM/HZG SK7 .... 196 B6
BRO M7 .... 88 B5
NTHM/RTH M23 .... 161 E3
URM M41 .... 118 B6
WILM/AE SK9 .... 202 A6
Moor Nook SALE M33 .... 160 B2
Moor Park Av ROCH OL11 .... 38 C5
Moor Park Rd DID/WITH M20 .... 164 A5
Moor Rd LIT OL15 .... 13 D2
NTHM/RTH M23 .... 160 C5
TOT/BURYW BL8 .... 6 B5
Moorsholme Av
NEWH/MOS M40 .... 92 B6
Moorside ROCH OL11 .... 40 A4
Moorside Av BOL BL1 .... 26 B5
BOLE BL2 .... 31 E6
DROY M43 .... 111 D6
FWTH BL4 .... 65 F4
OLDE OL4 .... 63 D6
Moorside Cl DTN/ASHW M34 .... 130 A5
DROY M43 .... 111 D5
Moorside La DTN/ASHW M34 .... 130 B5
Moorside Rd BRO M7 .... 89 D4
CHH M8 .... 90 B4
HTNM SK4 .... 165 E3
MOSL OL5 .... 99 F4
SWIN M27 .... 85 E5
TOT/BURYW BL8 .... 31 F2
URM M41 .... 117 F6
Moorside St DROY M43 .... 110 C5
Moor St BURY BL9 .... 34 A4
ECC M30 .... 100 C6
HEY OL10 .... 36 C5
OLD OL1 .... 79 F4
ROY/SHW OL2 .... 61 E3
SWIN M27 .... 86 A6
Moorsview RAMS BL0 .... 6 C5

Moorton Av *BNG/LEV* M19 .... 145 D4
Moorton Pk *BNG/LEV* M19 .... 145 D4 🖪
Moortop Cl *BKLY* M9 .... 74 A5 🖪
Moor Top Pl *HTNM* SK4 .... 165 F2 🖪
Moor View Cl *WHIT* OL12 .... 21 D4
Moorville Rd *SLFD* M6 .... 103 D2
Moor Wy *TOT/BURYW* BL8 .... 16 C2
Moorway Dr *BKLY* M9 .... 92 B1
Moorwood Dr *OLDS* OL8 .... 97 D1
  SALE M33 .... 158 C2
Mora Av *CHAD* OL9 .... 77 F2
Moran Cl *WILM/AE* SK9 .... 204 B1
Morar Dr *BOLE* BL2 .... 49 E1
Morar Rd *DUK* SK16 .... 131 E2
Mora St *BKLY* M9 .... 92 A5
Moravian Cl *DUK* SK16 .... 113 D6
Moravian Fld *DROY* M43 .... 128 B1 🖪
Moray Cl *RAMS* BL0 .... 18 B1
Moray Rd *CHAD* OL9 .... 94 B1
Morbourne Cl *WGTN/LGST* M12 .... 125 F3
Morecambe Cl *NEWH/MOS* M40 .... 108 C1
Morely St *OLDE* OL4 .... 80 B2
Moresby Dr *DID/WITH* M20 .... 165 F5 🖪
Moreton Av *BRAM/HZG* SK7 .... 196 C4
  SALE M33 .... 159 D2 🖪
  STRET M32 .... 140 B1
  WHTF M45 .... 71 D2
Moreton Cl *DUK* SK16 .... 131 E3
Moreton Dr *POY/DIS* SK12 .... 199 D5
  TOT/BURYW BL8 .... 32 C4
  WILM/AE SK9 .... 194 C6
Moreton La *OFTN* SK2 .... 168 A6
Moreton St *CHAD* OL9 .... 77 D3
Morgan Pl *RDSH* SK5 .... 167 D1 🖪
Morgan St *LIT* OL15 .... 12 C6 🖪🖪
Morillon Rd *IRL* M44 .... 116 B1
Morland Rd *OLDTF/WHR* M16 .... 123 D5
Morley Av *RUSH/FAL* M14 .... 143 E2
  SWIN M27 .... 101 F1 🖪
Morley Green Rd *WILM/AE* SK9 .... 202 A2
Morley Rd *RAD* M26 .... 50 B5
Morley St *BOLS/LL* BL3 .... 46 B3 🖪🖪
  BURY BL9 .... 53 D1
  MILN OL16 .... 30 B4
  WHTF M45 .... 71 D3
Morningside Cl *DROY* M43 .... 128 A2
  MILN OL16 .... 40 C1 🖪
Morningside Dr *DID/WITH* M20 .... 164 A5
Mornington Av *CHD/CHDH* SK8 .... 180 B3
Mornington Crs *RUSH/FAL* M14 .... 143 E3
Mornington Rd *BOL* BL1 .... 27 D6
  CHD/CHDH SK8 .... 180 B3
  ROCH OL11 .... 40 A5 🖪
  SALE M33 .... 140 B6
Morpeth Cl *AULW* OL7 .... 111 F3
Morpeth St *SWIN* M27 .... 101 F1
Morrell Rd *WYTH/NTH* M22 .... 162 B5
Morris Fold Dr *HOR/BR* BL6 .... 44 A3
Morris Gn *BOLS/LL* BL3 .... 64 A1 🖪
Morris Green La *BOLS/LL* BL3 .... 46 A6
Morris Green St *BOLS/LL* BL3 .... 46 A6 🖪🖪
Morris Gv *URM* M41 .... 136 C3
Morrison St *BOLS/LL* BL3 .... 46 C6
Morton St *FAIL* M35 .... 47 E2 🖪
  HTNM SK4 .... 166 C1
  MDTN M24 .... 75 E2
  RAD M26 .... 69 F1
Mort St *FWTH* BL4 .... 65 F3 🖪
Morven Av *BRAM/HZG* SK7 .... 185 D4
Morven Dr *NTHM/RTH* M23 .... 177 E2
Morven Gv *BOLE* BL2 .... 49 D2
Morville Rd *CCHDY* M21 .... 142 B2
Morville St *CMANE* M1 .... 125 D1 🖪🖪
Moscow Cl *EDGY/DAV* SK3 .... 166 B6 🖪
Moscow Rd East *EDGY/DAV* SK3 .... 166 B6
Mosedale Cl *NTHM/RTH* M23 .... 176 C1
Mosedale Rd *MDTN* M24 .... 74 B1
Moseldene Rd *OFTN* SK2 .... 184 B2
Moseley Rd *BNG/LEV* M19 .... 145 D3
  CHD/CHDH SK8 .... 181 D4
  RUSH/FAL M14 .... 144 C3
Moseley St *EDGY/DAV* SK3 .... 166 C5 🖪
Mosley Av *BURY* BL9 .... 34 A2 🖪
  TOT/BURYW BL8 .... 18 C3
Mosley Cl *HALE/TIMP* WA15 .... 159 D6
Mosley Common Rd *WALK* M28 .... 82 A6
Mosley Rd *HALE/TIMP* WA15 .... 175 F1
  TRPK M17 .... 121 D5
Mosley Rd North *TRPK* M17 .... 121 D5
Mosley St *CMANW* M2 .... 2 D4 🖪
  RAD M26 .... 51 D5 🖪
Mossack Av *WYTH/NTH* M22 .... 178 B6 🖪

Moss Av *MILN* OL16 .... 41 D1
Moss Bank *CHD/CHDH* SK8 .... 196 A4
  CHH M8 .... 90 B5
Moss Bank Av *DROY* M43 .... 111 D5
Moss Bank Cl *BOL* BL1 .... 27 E3
Moss Bank Ct *DROY* M43 .... 111 D5 🖪
Mossbank Gv *HEY* OL10 .... 37 D4 🖪
Moss Bank Rd *SWIN* M27 .... 85 D3
Moss Bank Gv *SWIN* M27 .... 85 E3
Moss Bank Wy *BOL* BL1 .... 26 B5
Mossbray Av *BNG/LEV* M19 .... 164 B1 🖪
Moss Bridge Rd *MILN* OL16 .... 40 C1
Mossbrook Dr *LHULT* M38 .... 64 C5
Moss Brook Rd *BKLY* M9 .... 91 F6
Moss Cl *RAD* M26 .... 50 B4 🖪
Mossclough Ct *BKLY* M9 .... 91 F6 🖪
Moss Colliery Rd *SWIN* M27 .... 85 E2
Mosscot Wk *BRUN/LGST* M13 .... 124 C2 🖪🖪
Moss Croft Cl *URM* M41 .... 117 F6 🖪
Mossdale Av *BOL* BL1 .... 44 B2
Mossdale Rd *NTHM/RTH* M23 .... 168 D4
  SALE M33 .... 158 C4
Mossdown Rd *ROY/SHW* OL2 .... 61 E6
Mossfield Cl *BURY* BL9 .... 34 C3 🖪
  HTNM SK4 .... 165 F3
Mossfield Ct *BOL* BL1 .... 46 C1 🖪🖪
Mossfield Dr *BKLY* M9 .... 92 B1
Mossfield Rd *FWTH* BL4 .... 65 F3
  FWTH BL4 .... 67 D5 🖪
  HALE/TIMP WA15 .... 176 B1
  SWIN M27 .... 85 F3
Moss Gate Rd *ROY/SHW* OL2 .... 42 C6
Moss Grange Av
  OLDTF/WHR M16 .... 123 E6 🖪
Moss Gn *PART* M31 .... 137 D5
Moss Gv *ROY/SHW* OL2 .... 41 F6 🖪
Mossgrove Rd *HALE/TIMP* WA15 .... 175 D1
Mosshall Rd *HULME* M15 .... 123 E4 🖪
Moss Hall Rd *BURY* BL9 .... 35 E6
Moss Hey Dr *NTHM/RTH* M23 .... 161 F4
Moss Hey St *ROY/SHW* OL2 .... 61 F3
Mossland Cl *HEY* OL10 .... 56 B1 🖪
Moss La *AULW* OL7 .... 112 A5
  BOL BL1 .... 26 B4
  BRAM/HZG SK7 .... 196 A4
  FWTH BL4 .... 67 F6
  HALE/TIMP WA15 .... 159 D6
  HALE/TIMP WA15 .... 174 C3
  HYDE SK14 .... 153 D3
  IRL M44 .... 134 B6
  LYMM WA13 .... 154 C1
  LYMM WA13 .... 155 F5
  MDTN M24 .... 75 D6
  MILN OL16 .... 40 B1
  PART M31 .... 155 E2
  ROY/SHW OL2 .... 61 E6
  SALE M33 .... 157 D2
  SALE M33 .... 158 B2
  SALE M33 .... 159 D1
  SWIN M27 .... 85 E4
  URM M41 .... 119 E4
  WALK M28 .... 83 F1
  WHTF M45 .... 71 D3
  WILM/AE SK9 .... 192 B4
  WILM/AE SK9 .... 209 F4
Moss La West *HULME* M15 .... 123 F5
  RUSH/FAL M14 .... 124 B3
Moss Lea *BOL* BL1 .... 27 E3
Mosslee Av *CHH* M8 .... 90 A2 🖪
Mossley Rd *AUL* OL6 .... 113 D4
  OLDE OL4 .... 99 E1
Moss Lodge La *AULW* OL7 .... 111 E6
Moss Meadow Rd *SLFD* M6 .... 103 D3 🖪
Mossmere Rd *CHD/CHDH* SK8 .... 181 E3 🖪
Moss Park Rd *STRET* M32 .... 139 E1
Moss Rd *FWTH* BL4 .... 66 C4
  IRL M44 .... 134 A4
  PART M31 .... 157 F4
  STRET M32 .... 121 D6
Moss Rose *WILM/AE* SK9 .... 209 F3
Moss Shaw Wy *RAD* M26 .... 50 C4
Moss Side La *MILN* OL16 .... 41 D2
Moss Side Rd *IRL* M44 .... 134 B5
Moss Side St *WHIT* OL12 .... 10 C2
Moss St *BRO* M7 .... 105 E2
  BURY BL9 .... 5 J5
  BURY BL9 .... 33 F5
  DTN/ASHW M34 .... 110 C6
  FWTH BL4 .... 66 C2
  HEY OL10 .... 37 D5 🖪🖪
  MILN OL16 .... 40 C1
  OLDE OL4 .... 80 C3
Moss St West *AULW* OL7 .... 112 A5
Moss Ter *MILN* OL16 .... 40 C1
The Moss *MDTN* M24 .... 75 F5
Moss Vale Crs *STRET* M32 .... 120 A5 🖪
Moss Vale Rd *STRET* M32 .... 120 A6
  URM M41 .... 138 C1
Moss View Rd *BOLE* BL2 .... 48 C1 🖪
  PART M31 .... 155 E2
Mossway *MDTN* M24 .... 75 D6
Moss Wy *SALE* M33 .... 158 C1 🖪
Mosswood Pk *DID/WITH* M20 .... 163 F5
Mosswood Rd *WILM/AE* SK9 .... 204 C2 🖪
Moston Bank Av *BKLY* M9 .... 91 F6

Moston La *BKLY* M9 .... 91 F5
  NEWH/MOS M40 .... 92 B4
Moston La East *NEWH/MOS* M40 .... 93 E3
Moston Rd *MDTN* M24 .... 76 B6
Moston St *BRO* M7 .... 90 A6 🖪🖪
Mostyn Av *BURY* BL9 .... 34 A2
  CHD/CHDH SK8 .... 180 C5 🖪
  RUSH/FAL M14 .... 144 C3 🖪
Mostyn Rd *BRAM/HZG* SK7 .... 184 A6
Mostyn St *DUK* SK16 .... 132 A1
Motcombe Farm Rd
  CHD/CHDH SK8 .... 179 F6 🖪
Motcombe Gv *CHD/CHDH* SK8 .... 179 E4
Motcombe Rd *CHD/CHDH* SK8 .... 179 E5
Mottershead Av *BOLS/LL* BL3 .... 49 E5
Mottershead Rd *WYTH/NTH* M22 .... 177 F3
Mottram Cl *CHD/CHDH* SK8 .... 181 E2 🖪
Mottram Dr *HALE/TIMP* WA15 .... 175 D3 🖪
Mottram Fold *STKP* SK1 .... 167 D5 🖪🖪
Mottram Old Rd *HYDE* SK14 .... 151 E3
  STLY SK15 .... 115 D6
Mottram Rd *HYDE* SK14 .... 153 E3
  SALE M33 .... 160 C2
  STLY SK15 .... 115 D6
  WILM/AE SK9 .... 209 F4
Mottram St *STKP* SK1 .... 167 D5 🖪🖪
Mough La *CHAD* OL9 .... 93 E2
Mouldsworth Av *DID/WITH* M20 .... 143 E4
  HTNM SK4 .... 146 B5
Moulton St *CHH* M8 .... 105 F3
Mouncey St *CMANE* M1 .... 124 B2 🖪
Mountain Ash *WHIT* OL12 .... 21 F2
Mountain Ash Cl *SALE* M33 .... 138 A6 🖪
  WHIT OL12 .... 21 F2 🖪
Mountain Gv *WALK* M28 .... 99 D4
Mountain St *MOSL* OL5 .... 99 F1
  NEWH/MOS M40 .... 109 E3 🖪
  STKP SK1 .... 167 E3 🖪
  WALK M28 .... 83 D1
Mount Av *LIT* OL15 .... 12 B4
  WHIT OL12 .... 24 C1 🖪
Mountbatten Av *DUK* SK16 .... 132 A2
Mountbatten Cl *BURY* BL9 .... 71 F1
Mountbatten St *GTN* M18 .... 127 D4 🖪
Mount Carmel Crs
  SALQ/ORD M5 .... 123 D2 🖪
Mount Dr *MPL/ROM* SK6 .... 187 D2
  URM M41 .... 139 D1
Mountfield *PWCH* M25 .... 88 C1
Mountfield Rd *BRAM/HZG* SK7 .... 196 C4
  EDGY/DAV SK3 .... 166 A6
Mount Fold *MDTN* M24 .... 75 E4
Mountford Av *CHH* M8 .... 90 A3 🖪
Mount Gv *WYTH/NTH* M22 .... 179 D2
Mount Pleasant *BRAM/HZG* SK7 .... 184 B4
  MDTN M24 .... 74 A3
  PWCH M25 .... 72 C3
  WILM/AE SK9 .... 203 F2
Mount Pleasant Rd
  DTN/ASHW M34 .... 149 D1
  FWTH BL4 .... 65 D3 🖪
Mount Pleasant St *AUL* OL6 .... 113 D4 🖪🖪
  DTN/ASHW M34 .... 130 A2
  OLDE OL4 .... 79 F4 🖪🖪
Mount Pleasant Wk *RAD* M26 .... 51 E5
Mount Rd *GTN* M18 .... 127 D4 🖪
  HTNM SK4 .... 166 A3
  HYDE SK14 .... 151 E5
  MDTN M24 .... 75 D4
  PWCH M25 .... 72 A4
Mountroyal Cl *HYDE* SK14 .... 132 B4 🖪
Mount St Joseph's Rd
  BOLS/LL BL3 .... 45 F4
Mountside Cl *WHIT* OL12 .... 23 D3 🖪
Mountside Crs *PWCH* M25 .... 88 C1
Mount Sion Rd *RAD* M26 .... 68 C1
Mount Skip La *LHULT* M38 .... 82 B1
Mount St *BOL* BL1 .... 2 D5
  CMANW M2 .... 6 D5
  CSLFD M3 .... 105 E4
  ECC M30 .... 119 D1 🖪
  HEY OL10 .... 37 E6
  HYDE SK14 .... 150 C1 🖪
  RAMS BL0 .... 6 C5 🖪
  ROCH OL11 .... 39 D6
  ROY/SHW OL2 .... 60 C6 🖪
  SWIN M27 .... 86 A6
  WHIT OL12 .... 22 C5 🖪🖪
The Mount *ALT* WA14 .... 174 B2
  HALE/TIMP WA15 .... 190 A1
Mount View Rd *ROY/SHW* OL2 .... 62 A3
Mount Zion Rd *BURY* BL9 .... 53 D4
Mousell St *CHH* M8 .... 106 B3
Mowbray Av *PWCH* M25 .... 89 D3
  SALE M33 .... 160 A2
Mowbray St *AULW* OL7 .... 112 A5
  BOL BL1 .... 28 C6 🖪🖪
  OLD OL1 .... 79 D5 🖪🖪
  ROCH OL11 .... 38 C4 🖪
  STKP SK1 .... 167 D5 🖪🖪
Moxley Rd *CHH* M8 .... 89 F4
Moyse Av *TOT/BURYW* BL8 .... 32 A2
Mozart Cl *ANC* M4 .... 107 D5 🖪
Muirfield Av *MPL/ROM* SK6 .... 169 E1

Muirfield Cl BOLS/LL BL3 .... 45 D6
  HEY OL10 .... 37 F6
  NEWH/MOS M40 .... 93 D6
  WILM/AE SK9 .... 204 B3 🔟
Mulberry Cl CHD/CHDH SK8......... 194 A2
  ROCH OL11 .... 39 F2
Mulberry Ms HTNM SK4 .... 166 C5 🔟
Mulberry Mount St
  EDGY/DAV SK3 .... 166 C5
Mulberry Rd SLFD M6 .... 104 B4 🔟
Mulberry St AUL OL6 .... 113 D4 🔟🔟
  CMANW M2 .... 2 C4
Mulberry Wk DROY M43 .... 127 F1
  SALE M33 .... 138 B5 🔟
Mule St BOLE BL2 .... 47 F1
Mulgrave Rd WALK M28 .... 84 B5
Mulgrave St BOLS/LL BL3 .... 64 A1
  SWIN M27 .... 85 E4 🔟
Mullacre Rd WYTH/NTH M22 .... 178 B1
Mull Av WGTN/LGST M12 .... 126 A4 🔟
Mulliner St BOL BL1 .... 28 A6 🔟
Mullion Cl RDSH SK5 .... 146 B1
Mullion Dr HALE/TIMP WA15 .... 158 C6
Mulmount Cl OLDS OL8 .... 95 D2
Munday St ANC M4 .... 107 E6
Municipal Cl HEY OL10 .... 37 E5 🔟🔟
Munn Rd BKLY M9 .... 73 F6
Munro Av WYTH/NTH M22 .... 179 D5
Munster St ANC M4 .... 106 B4 🔟🔟
Muriel St BRO M7 .... 105 E2
  HEY OL10 .... 37 F5 🔟
  MILN OL16 .... 40 C2
Murieston Rd HALE/TIMP WA15 ... 174 C5
Murrayfield ROCH OL11 .... 37 F1 🔟
Murray Rd BURY BL9 .... 34 A5
Murray St BRO M7 .... 105 E1
Musbury Av CHD/CHDH SK8 .... 181 F5
Museum St CMANW M2 .... 2 C5 🔟
Musgrave Gdns BURY BL9 .... 34 C5 🔟🔟
Musgrave Rd BOL BL1 .... 46 A1
  WYTH/NTH M22 .... 178 B1
Muslin St SALQ/ORD M5 .... 105 D6 🔟🔟
Muter Av WYTH/NTH M22 .... 179 D5
Mutual St HEY OL10 .... 37 F1
Myerscroft Cl NEWH/MOS M40..... 93 E5
Myrrh St BOL BL1 .... 27 F4
Myrtle Bank PWCH M25 .... 88 B4
Myrtle Cl OLDS OL8 .... 78 C6
Myrtle Gdns BURY BL9 .... 34 C5 🔟🔟
Myrtle Gv DROY M43 .... 111 D5 🔟
  DTN/ASHW M34 .... 128 A6
  PWCH M25 .... 88 C3
  WHTF M45 .... 70 B1
Myrtleleaf Gv SALQ/ORD M5 .... 103 E5 🔟
Myrtle Pl BRO M7 .... 105 D3 🔟
Myrtle Rd MDTN M24 .... 76 A2
  PART M31 .... 154 B5
Myrtle St BOL BL1 .... 46 B1 🔟🔟
  EDGY/DAV SK3 .... 165 F5
  OLDTF/WHR M16 .... 123 D5 🔟
  OP/CLY M11 .... 125 F1
Myrtle St North BURY BL9 .... 34 C5 🔟🔟
My St SALQ/ORD M5 .... 103 F6
Mytham Gdns BOLS/LL BL3 .... 67 E1 🔟
Mytham Rd BOLS/LL BL3 .... 49 F6
Mythorne Av IRL M44 .... 154 A2 🔟
Mytton Rd BOL BL1 .... 26 C4

N

Nabbs Fold TOT/BURYW BL8 .... 18 A2 🔟
Nabbs Wy TOT/BURYW BL8 .... 18 B4
Naburn Cl RDSH SK5 .... 148 A3 🔟
Naburn St BRUN/LGST M13 .... 125 E5
Nada Rd CHH M8 .... 90 A4 🔟
Nadine St SLFD M6 .... 104 B4
Nadin St OLDS OL8 .... 95 F2
Nall St BNG/LEV M19 .... 145 F4
  MILN OL16 .... 41 F1
Nameplate Cl ECC M30 .... 100 C5 🔟🔟
Nancy St HULME M15 .... 123 E1
Nandywell BOLS/LL BL3 .... 49 F6
Nangreave Rd OFTN SK2 .... 183 E1
Nangreave St SALQ/ORD M5 .... 105 E6 🔟
Nan Nook Rd NTHM/RTH M23 ...... 161 D4
Nansen Av ECC M30 .... 101 D4 🔟
Nansen Cl STRET M32 .... 121 F5
Nansen Rd CHD/CHDH SK8 .... 179 E3
Nansen St OP/CLY M11.................. 125 F1
  SLFD M6 .... 103 F5
  STRET M32 .... 121 E6
Nansmoss La WILM/AE SK9 .... 202 B2
Nantwich Av ROCH OL11 .... 23 D2 🔟
Nantwich Rd RUSH/FAL M14 .... 143 E2
Napier Gn SALQ/ORD M5 .... 122 C2 🔟
Napier Rd CCHDY M21 .... 141 F3
  ECC M30 .... 101 D4
  HTNM SK4 .... 165 F2
Napier St BRAM/HZG SK7 .... 184 B4
  HYDE SK14 .... 150 C3 🔟
  ROY/SHW OL2 .... 61 F1
  SWIN M27 .... 85 E6
Napier St East OLDS OL8 .... 78 B6
Napier St West OLDS OL8 .... 78 A6

Naples Rd EDGY/DAV SK3 .... 181 F1
Narbonne Av ECC M30 .... 102 B3
Narbuth Dr CHH M8 .... 90 A6 🔟🔟
The Narrows ALT WA14 .... 174 A3 🔟
Naseby Av BKLY M9 .... 92 A1
Naseby Pl PWCH M25 .... 89 D1 🔟
Naseby Wk RDSH SK5 .... 146 C3
Naseby Wk WHTF M45 .... 72 A3 🔟
Nash Rd TRPK M17 .... 119 F1
Nash St HULME M15 .... 123 F3
Nasmyth Av DTN/ASHW M34 .... 130 B5
Nasmyth Rd ECC M30 .... 119 D1
Nasmyth St CHH M8 .... 107 D2 🔟
Nately Rd OLDTF/WHR M16 .... 141 E1 🔟
Nathan Dr CSLFD M3 .... 2 A1
Nathans Rd WYTH/NTH M22 .... 178 A3
Naunton Rd MDTN M24 .... 75 F4 🔟
Naval St ANC M4 .... 107 D5 🔟
Nave Ct SLFD M6 .... 104 A3
Navenby Rd OLDTF/WHR M16 ...... 123 D5 🔟
Navigation Rd ALT WA14 .... 158 B6
  HALE/TIMP WA15 .... 174 C1
Naylor St NEWH/MOS M40 .... 107 E4
  OLD OL1 .... 78 C4
Neal Av AUL OL6 .... 113 E4
  CHD/CHDH SK8 .... 193 E1
Neale Rd CCHDY M21 .... 141 E4
Near Birches Pde OLDE OL4 .... 97 F1
Nearbrook Rd WYTH/NTH M22 .... 178 A3
Nearcroft Rd NTHM/RTH M23 ..... 161 E6
Near Hey Cl RAD M26 .... 50 C6
Nearmaker Av WYTH/NTH M22 ... 178 A3 🔟
Nearmaker Rd WYTH/NTH M22 ... 178 A3
Neary Wy URM M41 .... 119 D4
Neath Av WYTH/NTH M22 .... 162 B6
Neath Cl POY/DIS SK12 .... 198 B4
  WHTF M45 .... 72 A1 🔟
Neath Fold BOLS/LL BL3 .... 46 B6
Neath St CHAD OL9 .... 78 A3 🔟
Nebo St BOLS/LL BL3 .... 46 B5
Nebraska St BOL BL1 .... 27 F6 🔟
Neden Cl OP/CLY M11 .... 126 C1 🔟
Needham Av CCHDY M21 .... 141 F3 🔟
Needwood Cl NEWH/MOS M40 ..... 107 E2 🔟🔟
Needwood Rd MPL/ROM SK6 .... 150 A6
Neenton Sq WGTN/LGST M12 ...... 126 B2 🔟
Neild St CMANE M1 .... 3 H6
  OLDS OL8 .... 95 F1
Neill St BRO M7 .... 105 F3 🔟
Neilson Cl MDTN M24 .... 76 A4
Nell Carrs RAMS BL0 .... 7 F4
Nellie St HEY OL10 .... 36 C5
Nell La CCHDY M21 .... 142 C5
Nell St BOL BL1 .... 28 A3
Nelson Av ECC M30 .... 101 E4 🔟
  POY/DIS SK12 .... 199 E6
Nelson Cl POY/DIS SK12 .... 199 E6 🔟
Nelson Dr DROY M43 .... 109 E5
  IRL M44 .... 134 C5
Nelson Fold SWIN M27 .... 86 B4
Nelson Rd BKLY M9 .... 74 B6
Nelson St BCUP OL13 .... 5 D1 🔟
  BOLS/LL BL3 .... 47 E4
  BOLS/LL BL3 .... 49 F6 🔟🔟
  BRAM/HZG SK7 .... 185 D3
  BRO M7 .... 105 E2 🔟
  BURY BL9 .... 53 D1
  DTN/ASHW M34 .... 130 A3 🔟
  DTN/ASHW M34 .... 130 A5 🔟
  ECC M30 .... 101 E5
  FWTH BL4 .... 66 C3
  HEY OL10 .... 37 E6 🔟
  HYDE SK14 .... 150 C1
  LIT OL15 .... 12 C6 🔟🔟
  MDTN M24 .... 76 A4
  MILN OL16 .... 23 D6 🔟
  NEWH/MOS M40 .... 107 D3
  OLDE OL4 .... 80 C5 🔟
  SALQ/ORD M5 .... 103 F6
  STRET M32 .... 140 B2
Nelson Wy CHAD OL9 .... 94 B1 🔟
Nelstrop Crs HTNM SK4 .... 146 B5 🔟
Nelstrop Rd HTNM SK4 .... 146 A5
Nelstrop Rd North RDSH SK5 .... 146 B3
Nepaul Rd BKLY M9 .... 91 F4
Neptune Gdns BRO M7 .... 105 D2 🔟🔟
Nesbit St BOLE BL2 .... 28 C4 🔟
Nesfield Rd NTHM/RTH M23 .... 161 D3
Neston Av BOL BL1 .... 28 A2
  SALE M33 .... 160 C3 🔟
Neston Cl ROY/SHW OL2 .... 62 B2
Neston Gv EDGY/DAV SK3 .... 182 B2
Neston Rd MILN OL16 .... 41 D3
  TOT/BURYW BL8 .... 18 A3
Neston St OP/CLY M11 .... 128 A2
Neston Wy WILM/AE SK9 .... 198 B6
Nethanon Gv CTN M18 .... 127 D6 🔟
Nethercote Av NTHM/RTH M23 ... 177 F1 🔟
Nethercroft Rd HALE/TIMP WA15 . 176 A2
Netherfield Cl OLDS OL8 .... 95 D1
Netherfield Rd BOLS/LL BL3 .... 64 C1
Netherfields WILM/AE SK9 .... 209 E5
Netherhey La OLD OL1 .... 78 A3 🔟
Nether Hey St OLDS OL8 .... 79 F6
Netherhouse Rd ROY/SHW OL2 ..... 61 E2

Netherland St SALQ/ORD M5 .... 104 A6
Netherlees OLDE OL4 .... 80 B6
Nether St HYDE SK14 .... 151 D3 🔟
  WGTN/LGST M12 .... 125 D1
Netherton Rd RUSH/FAL M14 ...... 143 E2 🔟
Nethervale Dr BKLY M9 .... 91 F6 🔟
Netherwood Rd WYTH/NTH M22 . 162 A6
Netley Av WHIT OL12 .... 23 D2
Netley Gv OLDS OL8 .... 97 D1 🔟
Netley Rd NTHM/RTH M23 .... 177 E3
Nettlebarn Rd WYTH/NTH M22 ... 178 A2
Nettleford Rd CCHDY M21 .... 142 C3
Nettleton Gv BKLY M9 .... 92 A4 🔟
Nevendon Dr NTHM/RTH M23 ..... 177 D5
Nevile Rd BRO M7 .... 88 C5
Nevill Cl BOL BL1 .... 64 C1 🔟🔟
Neville Dr IRL M44 .... 116 B5
Neville Rd BRAM/HZG SK7 .... 184 B4
  CHAD OL9 .... 78 A4
Nevill Rd BRAM/HZG SK7 .... 182 C5
Nevin Av CHD/CHDH SK8 .... 180 C6
Nevin Cl BRAM/HZG SK7 .... 197 E2
Nevin Rd NEWH/MOS M40 .... 93 E4
Nevis Gv BOL BL1 .... 27 F2 🔟
Nevis St ROCH OL11 .... 40 B5
New Allen St NEWH/MOS M40 ..... 107 D4
Newall Rd NTHM/RTH M23 .... 177 D4
Newall St CHAD OL9 .... 94 C3
  LIT OL15 .... 12 C5
Newark Av RAD M26 .... 50 A4 🔟
  RUSH/FAL M14 .... 124 C6 🔟
Newark Park Wy ROY/SHW OL2 ..... 60 A3
Newark Rd RDSH SK5 .... 147 D6
  SWIN M27 .... 86 C3
  WHIT OL12 .... 23 D2
Newark Sq WHIT OL12 .... 23 D2
New Bailey St CSLFD M3 .... 2 A3
Newbank Cha CHAD OL9 .... 77 E3
New Bank St WGTN/LGST M12 .... 125 F4
Newbarn Cl ROY/SHW OL2 .... 61 E2 🔟
New Barn La ROCH OL11 .... 39 E2
New Barn Rd OLDS OL8 .... 96 B3
New Barn St BOL BL1 .... 26 C6
  MILN OL16 .... 40 E2
  ROY/SHW OL2 .... 61 E2
New Barton St SLFD M6 .... 103 D2
Newbeck St ANC M4 .... 3 F1 🔟
New Beech Rd HTNM SK4 .... 164 C3
Newberry Gv EDGY/DAV SK3 .... 182 B2 🔟
Newbold Moss MILN OL16 .... 23 F6
Newbold St MILN OL16 .... 24 A5
  TOT/BURYW BL8 .... 33 D5
Newboult Rd CHD/CHDH SK8 ...... 180 C1
Newbourne Cl BRAM/HZG SK7 .... 184 B4 🔟🔟
Newbreak Cl OLDE OL4 .... 80 B3 🔟
Newbreak St OLDE OL4 .... 80 B3 🔟
Newbridge Gdns BOLE BL2 .... 29 F3 🔟
New Bridge La STKP SK1 .... 167 D4
New Bridge St CSLFD M3 .... 2 C1
Newbridge Vw MOSL OL5 .... 99 E5 🔟
New Broad La MILN OL16 .... 41 D4
Newbrook Av CCHDY M21 .... 162 B6
New Buildings Pl MILN OL16 .... 23 D5 🔟
Newburn Av BKLY M9 .... 92 A1 🔟
Newbury Av SALE M33 .... 158 A1
Newbury Cl CHD/CHDH SK8 .... 195 E3 🔟
Newbury Dr ECC M30 .... 100 C4 🔟
  URM M41 .... 119 D3
Newbury Gv HEY OL10 .... 56 A1
Newbury Rd BOLS/LL BL3 .... 49 D6
  CHD/CHDH SK8 .... 194 A2
Newby Dr ALT WA14 .... 174 B1 🔟
  CHD/CHDH SK8 .... 179 E2
  MDTN M24 .... 57 D6
  SALE M33 .... 160 B2
Newby Rd BOLE BL2 .... 29 F6
  BRAM/HZG SK7 .... 184 A5
  HTNM SK4 .... 166 A3 🔟
Newcastle St HULME M15 .... 124 A2 🔟
  HULME M15 .... 124 A2 🔟
Newchurch OLDS OL8 .... 96 B5 🔟
New Church Rd BOL BL1 .... 26 A5
Newchurch St OP/CLY M11 .... 126 A1 🔟
New Church St RAD M26 .... 51 E6
Newchurch St ROCH OL11 .... 39 D6
New City Rd WALK M28 .... 82 B5
Newcliffe Rd BKLY M9 .... 92 A1
New Coin St ROY/SHW OL2 .... 60 B6
Newcombe Cl OP/CLY M11 .... 108 A6
Newcombe Dr LHULT M38 .... 65 D5
Newcombe Rd TOT/BURYW BL8 ... 18 B4
Newcombe St CSLFD M3 .... 106 A4 🔟
Newcroft FAIL M35 .... 110 C1
Newcroft Crs URM M41 .... 139 D2
Newcroft Dr EDGY/DAV SK3 .... 182 B1 🔟
  URM M41 .... 139 D2
Newcroft Rd URM M41 .... 139 D2
New Cross St SLFD M6 .... 103 D5
  SWIN M27 .... 86 B6
Newdale Rd BNG/LEV M19 .... 145 F1 🔟
Newearth Rd WALK M28 .... 82 C5
New Earth St MOSL OL5 .... 99 E3
  OLDE OL4 .... 80 A6
New Elizabeth St CHH M8 .... 106 B2
New Ellesmere Ap WALK M28 ...... 83 E1 🔟

New Elm Rd *CSLFD* M3 .... 123 E1 🔟
  CSLFD M3 .... 123 E1 🔟
New Field Cl *MILN* OL16 .... 23 F5
  RAD M26 .... 50 C6 🔟
Newfield Head La *MILN* OL16 .... 42 C2
Newfield Vw *MILN* OL16 .... 42 B1
New Forest Rd *NTHM/RTH* M23 .... 160 A5
Newgate *BOLS/LL* M3 .... 22 C6
Newgate Dr *LHULT* M38 .... 65 D5
Newgate Rd *SALE* M33 .... 157 F4
  WILM/AE SK9 .... 202 B4
Newgate St *ANC* M4 .... 3 F2
New George St *TOT/BURYW* BL8 ... 33 D4
Newhall Av *BOLS/LL* BL3 .... 49 F3
  ECC M30 .... 118 B2
  WYTH/NTH M22 .... 193 F2
New Hall Av *SALE* M33 .... 161 D1 🔟
Newhall Dr *NTHM/RTH* M23 .... 161 E3
New Hall La *BOL* BL1 .... 45 E1
New Hall Pl *BOL* BL1 .... 45 E1
New Hall Rd *BRO* M7 .... 89 E5
  BURY BL9 .... 35 F3
Newhall Rd *RDSH* SK5 .... 147 E1
New Hall Rd *SALE* M33 .... 161 D2 🔟
Newhaven Av *OP/CLY* M11 .... 128 A2
Newhaven Cl *CHD/CHDH* SK8 ..... 182 A5
  TOT/BURYW BL8 .... 19 D6
New Herbert St *SLFD* M6 .... 103 D2 🔟
Newhey Av *WYTH/NTH* M22 .... 178 B2
New Hey Rd *CHD/CHDH* SK8 ...... 180 C2
Newhey Rd *MILN* OL16 .... 42 B2
  WYTH/NTH M22 .... 178 B3
New Heys Wy *BOLE* BL2 .... 29 E1
New Holder St *BOL* BL1 .... 46 C2
Newholme Gdns *LHULT* M38 .... 83 D2 🔟
Newholme Rd *DID/WITH* M20 ..... 142 C6
Newhouse Crs *ROCH* OL11 .... 20 C5
Newhouse Rd *HEY* OL10 .... 56 B1
Newington Av *CHH* M8 .... 90 A2
Newington Ct *ALT* WA14 .... 173 F4
Newington Dr *BOL* BL1 .... 28 A6 🔟
  TOT/BURYW BL8 .... 51 E1
New Islington *ANC* M4 .... 107 D5 🔟
New Kings Head Yd *CSLFD* M3 .... 2 C1 🔟
Newlands *FAIL* M35 .... 109 F3
Newlands Av *BOLE* BL2 .... 30 A6
  BRAM/HZG SK7 .... 196 C1
  CHD/CHDH SK8 .... 195 E2
  ECC M30 .... 118 A1
  IRL M44 .... 116 A6
  WHIT OL12 .... 23 D2
  WHTF M45 .... 70 C2 🔟
Newlands Cl *CHD/CHDH* SK8 ..... 195 E2
  WHIT OL12 .... 23 D2
Newlands Dr *DID/WITH* M20 ..... 164 A5 🔟
  PWCH M25 .... 71 E6
  SWIN M27 .... 103 D1 🔟
Newlands Rd *CHD/CHDH* SK8 .... 180 B1
  NTHM/RTH M23 .... 160 C5
Newland St *CHH* M8 .... 90 C4
New La *BOLE* BL2 .... 29 E6
  ECC M30 .... 100 C6
  MDTN M24 .... 75 E2
  ROY/SHW OL2 .... 60 B5 🔟
New Lane Ct *BOLE* BL2 .... 29 F5 🔟
New Lawns *RDSH* SK5 .... 147 E3 🔟
New Lees St *AUL* OL6 .... 113 E2 🔟
New Line *BCUP* OL13 .... 4 B1
Newlyn Av *STLY* SK15 .... 115 E4
New Lyn Cl *BRAM/HZG* SK7 ...... 184 B6
Newlyn Dr *MPL/ROM* SK6 .... 169 E2
  SALE M33 .... 160 A4
Newlyn St *RUSH/FAL* M14 .... 143 F1 🔟
Newman St *AUL* OL6 .... 112 B4
  HYDE SK14 .... 131 F6
  MILN OL16 .... 24 B1
New Market *CMANW* M2 .... 2 D3
Newmarket Cl *ALT* WA14 .... 157 F3
Newmarket Gv *AULW* OL7 .... 111 F2 🔟
New Market La *CMANW* M2 .... 2 D3
Newmarket Rd *AULW* OL7 .... 111 F2
  BOLS/LL BL3 .... 67 E1
New Meadow *HOR/BR* BL6 .... 44 A2
New Mill St *LIT* OL15 .... 12 B6
New Moor La *BRAM/HZG* SK7 .... 184 B6
New Moss Rd *IRL* M44 .... 134 B5
Newnham St *BOL* BL1 .... 27 F4
New Park Rd *SALQ/ORD* M5 ..... 122 C2 🔟
Newport Av *RDSH* SK5 .... 146 C4
Newport Rd *BOLS/LL* BL3 .... 47 E6
  CCHDY M21 .... 141 D5
  DTN/ASHW M34 .... 149 F3
Newport St *BOL* BL1 .... 47 D2
  FWTH BL4 .... 66 B4
  MDTN M24 .... 76 A2
  OLDS OL8 .... 78 B6
  RUSH/FAL M14 .... 124 C6 🔟
  SLFD M6 .... 103 F5
  TOT/BURYW BL8 .... 32 B2 🔟
Newquay Av *BOLE* BL2 .... 31 E6
  RDSH SK5 .... 146 C4
Newquay Dr *BRAM/HZG* SK7 ..... 197 D2
New Quay St *CSLFD* M3 .... 2 A3

New Raven Ct *BOLS/LL* BL3 .... 49 E6 🔟
New Ridd Ri *HYDE* SK14 .... 150 B3 🔟
New Rd *LIT* OL15 .... 24 C1
  OLDS OL8 .... 95 F1
  RAD M26 .... 69 F1
  WHIT OL12 .... 8 C2
New Royd Av *OLDE* OL4 .... 81 D2
Newry Rd *ECC* M30 .... 119 F1
Newry St *BOL* BL1 .... 27 E4 🔟
Newsham Cl *BOLS/LL* BL3 .... 46 B4 🔟
Newsholme St *CHH* M8 .... 90 A6
Newstead Av *AUL* OL6 .... 97 D6
  DID/WITH M20 .... 144 B6
Newstead Cl *POY/DIS* SK12 .... 198 B4
Newstead Gv *MPL/ROM* SK6 ..... 168 C2
Newstead Rd *URM* M41 .... 119 F6
Newstead Ter *HALE/TIMP* WA15 . 159 D6
New St *ALT* WA14 .... 174 A3
  BOL BL1 .... 46 C3
  DROY M43 .... 128 B1
  ECC M30 .... 101 D6
  HYDE SK14 .... 153 E3 🔟
  LIT OL15 .... 25 D1
  MILN OL16 .... 42 B3
  NEWH/MOS M40 .... 107 F3
  OLDE OL4 .... 80 C5
  RAD M26 .... 69 F1
  STLY SK15 .... 132 B1
  SWIN M27 .... 86 B4
  TOT/BURYW BL8 .... 32 A1
  WHIT OL12 .... 22 C3
  WILM/AE SK9 .... 202 C6
New Tempest Rd *HOR/BR* BL6 .... 44 A5
New Thomas St *SLFD* M6 .... 104 B3 🔟
Newton Av *DID/WITH* M20 .... 143 E5 🔟
  WGTN/LGST M12 .... 126 A5
Newton Crs *MDTN* M24 .... 56 B6
Newton Dr *TOT/BURYW* BL8 .... 18 B4
New Tong Fld *EDGW/EG* BL7 ...... 14 A6
Newton Hall Rd *HYDE* SK14 ...... 131 D4
Newton Rd *ALT* WA14 .... 158 C6 🔟
  FAIL M35 .... 109 F2 🔟
  MDTN M24 .... 73 F4 🔟
  URM M41 .... 138 A1
  WILM/AE SK9 .... 203 E2
Newton St *AUL* OL6 .... 113 D4 🔟
  BOL BL1 .... 27 F5 🔟
  BURY BL9 .... 34 A1 🔟
  CMANE M1 .... 3 G3
  DROY M43 .... 111 D4
  EDGY/DAV SK3 .... 166 C5 🔟
  FAIL M35 .... 109 D1 🔟
  HYDE SK14 .... 131 E6
  MILN OL16 .... 40 C2
  STLY SK15 .... 114 A3 🔟
  STRET M32 .... 140 B2
Newton Wk *BOL* BL1 .... 27 F5 🔟
Newton Wood Rd *DUK* SK16 ...... 130 C3
Newtown Av *DTN/ASHW* M34 ... 149 D1 🔟
Newtown Cl *OP/CLY* M11 .... 126 C1 🔟
  SWIN M27 .... 86 A3 🔟
Newtown St *PWCH* M25 .... 89 D1
  ROY/SHW OL2 .... 61 F3 🔟
New Union St *ANC* M4 .... 107 F5
New Vernon St *BURY* BL9 .... 34 A3 🔟
New Viaduct St *OP/CLY* M11 ..... 107 F5
Newville Dr *DID/WITH* M20 ...... 144 B6
New Wakefield St *CMANE* M1 ... 124 B2 🔟
New Wy *WHIT* OL12 .... 9 D2
New York St *BOLS/LL* BL3 .... 45 D5
New York St *HEY* OL10 .... 36 C5 🔟
New Zealand Rd *STKP* SK1 .... 167 E4
Neyland Cl *BOL* BL1 .... 45 D2
Ney St *AULW* OL7 .... 112 A1
Niagara St *OFTN* SK2 .... 183 E1
Nicholas Cft *ANC* M4 .... 3 E2
Nicholas Owen Cl *OP/CLY* M11 .. 127 D1
Nicholas St *BOLE* BL2 .... 47 E1
  CMANW M2 .... 3 E4
Nicholson Rd *HYDE* SK14 .... 131 D4
Nicholson Sq *DUK* SK16 .... 130 C2
Nicholson St *HTNM* SK4 .... 166 C5 🔟
  OLDE OL4 .... 80 C5
  ROCH OL11 .... 40 A2 🔟
Nichols St *SLFD* M6 .... 104 B4 🔟
Nickleby Rd *POY/DIS* SK12 .... 198 C6
Nicolas St *CCHDY* M21 .... 141 E2
Nield Rd *DTN/ASHW* M34 .... 130 A6
Nield's Brow *ALT* WA14 .... 174 A5 🔟
Nield St *MOSL* OL5 .... 98 C3
Nigel Rd *BKLY* M9 .... 92 B5
Nigher Moss Av *MILN* OL16 .... 41 D1 🔟
Nightingale Cl *WILM/AE* SK9 .... 203 F1 🔟
Nightingale Dr *DTN/ASHW* M34 . 111 D5
Nightingale Gdns
  NTHM/RTH M23 .... 161 E4 🔟
Nile St *AULW* OL7 .... 130 A1
  BOLS/LL BL3 .... 47 D4
  MILN OL16 .... 23 E5
  OLD OL1 .... 78 C3
Nile Ter *BRO* M7 .... 105 E2 🔟
Nimble Nook *CHAD* OL9 .... 77 E6
Nina Dr *NEWH/MOS* M40 .... 93 D2
Nine Acre Dr *SALQ/ORD* M5 ..... 122 C2 🔟
Ninfield Rd *NTHM/RTH* M23 ...... 177 F3

Ninth Av *OLDS* OL8 .... 95 E4
Nipper La *WHTF* M45 .... 70 C2
Nisbet Av *WYTH/NTH* M22 .... 178 C4
Niven St *WGTN/LGST* M12 .... 125 D2 🔟
Nixon Rd *BOLS/LL* BL3 .... 48 A6 🔟
Nixon Rd South *BOLS/LL* BL3 .... 46 A6 🔟
Nixon St *EDGY/DAV* SK3 .... 166 C5 🔟
  FAIL M35 .... 93 F6
  ROCH OL11 .... 38 C4
No 11 Pas *DID/WITH* M20 .... 143 D6 🔟
Noble Meadow *WHIT* OL12 .... 24 B1 🔟
Noble St *BOLS/LL* BL3 .... 46 C4 🔟
  OLDS OL8 .... 96 A1 🔟
Noel Dr *SALE* M33 .... 160 B1
Nolan St *BKLY* M9 .... 91 F6
Nona St *SLFD* M6 .... 103 F5 🔟
Nook Farm Av *WHIT* OL12 .... 23 D2 🔟
Nook Flds *BOLE* BL2 .... 29 F5
Nook La *AUL* OL6 .... 113 F1
The Nook *ECC* M30 .... 100 B4
Noon Sun St *WHIT* OL12 .... 23 D4 🔟
Norbet Wk *BKLY* M9 .... 91 F6 🔟
Norbreck Av *CCHDY* M21 .... 141 F4 🔟
  CHD/CHDH SK8 .... 181 E1
Norbreck St *BOLE* BL2 .... 47 F1
Norbury Av *MPL/ROM* SK6 .... 186 C5
  SALE M33 .... 159 F3 🔟
  SLFD M6 .... 103 E2 🔟
Norbury Crs *BRAM/HZG* SK7 .... 184 B5
Norbury Dr *MPL/ROM* SK6 .... 187 D1
Norbury Gv *BOL* BL1 .... 28 A3
  BRAM/HZG SK7 .... 184 B5 🔟
  SWIN M27 .... 86 A4
Norbury Hollow Rd
  BRAM/HZG SK7 .... 199 F1
Norbury La *OLDS* OL8 .... 97 E2
Norbury St *BRO* M7 .... 105 F1
  MILN OL16 .... 40 C3 🔟
  STKP SK1 .... 167 D4 🔟
Norcross Cl *OFTN* SK2 .... 184 B2
Nordale Pk *WHIT* OL12 .... 20 B3
Nordek Cl *ROY/SHW* OL2 .... 60 B4 🔟
Nordek Dr *ROY/SHW* OL2 .... 60 B4
Norden Av *DID/WITH* M20 .... 143 E5
Norden Cl *ROCH* OL11 .... 20 A3 🔟
Norden Rd *HEY* OL10 .... 37 E2
Nordens Dr *CHAD* OL9 .... 77 D2
Nordens Rd *CHAD* OL9 .... 77 D3 🔟
Nordens St *CHAD* OL9 .... 77 E3
Norden Wy *ROCH* OL11 .... 20 A3
Noreen Av *PWCH* M25 .... 72 A6
Norfield Cl *DUK* SK16 .... 131 D1
Norfolk Av *DROY* M43 .... 110 A4 🔟
  DTN/ASHW M34 .... 146 A5
  GTN M18 .... 127 D5 🔟
  HEY OL10 .... 36 A5
  HTNM SK4 .... 146 A5
  WHTF M45 .... 71 E3 🔟
Norfolk Cl *BOLS/LL* BL3 .... 49 F5 🔟
  IRL M44 .... 134 A6
  LIT OL15 .... 13 D5
  ROY/SHW OL2 .... 61 D2 🔟
Norfolk Crs *FAIL* M35 .... 109 F1
Norfolk Dr *FWTH* BL4 .... 66 B2
Norfolk Gdns *URM* M41 .... 117 E6
Norfolk Rd *GTN* M18 .... 127 D5
Norfolk St *CHAD* OL9 .... 95 D1 🔟
  CMANW M2 .... 2 D3
  HYDE SK14 .... 150 B1
  ROCH OL11 .... 39 F1
  SLFD M6 .... 104 B2
  WALK M28 .... 66 B5
Norfolk Wy *ROY/SHW* OL2 .... 78 B1
Norford Wy *ROCH* OL11 .... 20 C6
Norgate St *DID/WITH* M20 .... 163 F2 🔟
Norlan Av *DTN/ASHW* M34 ...... 129 F2 🔟
Norleigh Rd *WYTH/NTH* M22 .... 162 B5
Norley Av *STRET* M32 .... 122 A4
Norley Cl *OLD* OL1 .... 77 F1
Norley Dr *BNG/LEV* M19 .... 146 A1 🔟
  SALE M33 .... 160 C2
Norman Av *BRAM/HZG* SK7 ..... 184 A4 🔟
Normanby Cha *ALT* WA14 .... 173 F3
Normanby Gv *SWIN* M27 .... 85 F4 🔟
Normanby Rd *WALK* M28 .... 83 D4
Normanby St *RUSH/FAL* M14 .... 124 B5
  SWIN M27 .... 85 F4
Norman Cl *MDTN* M24 .... 76 A2 🔟
Normandale Av *BOL* BL1 .... 26 B6
Normandy Crs *RAD* M26 .... 51 D6 🔟
Norman Gv *RDSH* SK5 .... 146 C4 🔟
  WGTN/LGST M12 .... 126 B5 🔟
Norman Rd *ALT* WA14 .... 174 A1
  AUL OL6 .... 113 D1
  BRO M7 .... 89 F6 🔟
  HTNM SK4 .... 165 F1 🔟
  ROCH OL11 .... 39 E1
  RUSH/FAL M14 .... 144 B1
  SALE M33 .... 159 F1
  STLY SK15 .... 114 A5
Norman West *BKLY* M9 .... 92 A6 🔟
Norman's Pl *ALT* WA14 .... 174 B3
Norman St *BURY* BL9 .... 34 C3 🔟
  CHAD OL9 .... 78 B3 🔟
  FAIL M35 .... 94 B4

HYDE SK14.. **150** C1
MDTN M24 .... **75** F2
Normanton Av *SLFD* M6 .... **103** C4
Normanton Dr *BKLY* M9 .... **91** F2 🔢
Normanton Rd *EDGY/DAV* SK3 .... **165** E6
Normington St *OLDE* OL4 .... **80** A4 🔢
Norreys Av *URM* M41 .... **117** F6
Norreys St *MILN* OL16 .... **23** E5 🔢
Norris Av *HTNM* SK4 .... **166** A4
Norris Hill Dr *HTNM* SK4 .... **166** A3 🔢
Norris Rd *SALE* M33 .... **160** A3
Norris St *BOLS/LL* BL3 .... **46** C4 🔢
BOLS/LL BL3 .... **49** E6 🔢
FWTH BL4 .... **66** A4
Northallerton Rd *BRO* M7 .... **104** C1
Northampton Rd
NEWH/MOS M40 .... **108** A1
North Av *BNG/LEV* M19 .... **145** C4
BURY BL9 .... **53** F5
FWTH BL4 .... **65** E3
STLY SK15 .... **114** B4
TOT/BURYW BL8 .... **18** A4 🔢
URM M41 .... **119** F2
North Back Rock *BURY* BL9 .... **33** F5 🔢
Northbank Gdns *BNG/LEV* M19 .... **144** C5
North Blackfield La *BRO* M7 .... **89** D5 🔢
Northbourne St *SLFD* M6 .... **103** F5 🔢
Northbrook Av *CHH* M8 .... **90** A1
North Broughton St *CSLFD* M3 .... **2** A1 🔢
North Cir *WHTF* M45 .... **71** E5
North Clifden La *BRO* M7 .... **105** F1
Northcliffe Rd *OFTN* SK2 .... **168** A5
Northcombe Rd *EDGY/DAV* SK3 .... **182** C2 🔢
Northcote Rd *BRAM/HZG* SK7 .... **197** D2
North Crs *NEWH/MOS* M40 .... **93** E2
OP/CLY M11 .... **109** E4
North Cft *OLDS* OL8 .... **96** B2
Northdale Rd *BKLY* M9 .... **73** F6
North Dean St *SWIN* M27 .... **86** B4
Northdene Dr *ROCH* OL11 .... **38** A1
Northdown Av *HULME* M15 .... **123** E3
MPL/ROM SK6 .... **150** A6 🔢
North Downs *CHD/CHDH* SK8 .... **181** C6
Northdowns Rd *ROY/SHW* OL2 .... **61** D1
North Dr *DTN/ASHW* M34 .... **111** D6
SWIN M27 .... **86** C6
Northenden Rd *CHD/CHDH* SK8 .... **179** E1
SALE M33 .... **160** A1
Northend Rd *STLY* SK15 .... **114** C5
Northen Gv *OLDTF/WHR* M20 .... **163** D1
Northern Av *SWIN* M27 .... **87** D2
Northern Gv *BOL* BL1 .... **27** D6 🔢
Northfield Av *NEWH/MOS* M40 .... **94** A3 🔢
Northfield Dr *WILM/AE* SK9 .... **204** B3
Northfield Rd *BURY* BL9 .... **54** A1
NEWH/MOS M40 .... **94** A3
Northfield St *BOLS/LL* BL3 .... **46** A4
Northfleet Rd *ECC* M30 .... **118** A1
North Ga *OLDS* OL8 .... **95** F2
Northgate *WHIT* OL12 .... **9** D4
Northgate La *OLD* OL1 .... **62** C5
Northgate Rd *EDGY/DAV* SK3 .... **166** A5
North George St *CSLFD* M3 .... **105** E4
North Gv *BRUN/LGST* M13 .... **125** E7 🔢
URM M41 .... **138** A2
WALK M28 .... **83** D2
North Harvey St *STKP* SK1 .... **167** D4 🔢
North Hill St *CSLFD* M3 .... **105** E4
Northland Rd *BKLY* M9 .... **92** B2
BOL BL1 .... **28** A1 🔢
Northlands *RAD* M26 .... **50** C4
North La *WHIT* OL12 .... **23** D5
Northleach Cl *TOT/BURYW* BL8 .... **32** C4 🔢
Northleigh Dr *PWCH* M25 .... **89** E2 🔢
Northleigh Rd *OLDTF/WHR* M16 .... **122** C6
North Lonsdale St *STRET* M32 .... **121** F6
North Md *CCHDY* M21 .... **141** F4 🔢
Northmoor Rd *WGTN/LGST* M12 .... **126** B5
North Nook *OLDE* OL4 .... **81** D3
Northolme Gdns *BNG/LEV* M19 .... **164** C1
Northolt Dr *BOLS/LL* BL3 .... **47** D5
Northolt Rd *NTHM/RTH* M23 .... **161** D4
North Pde *MILN* OL16 .... **43** D3
SALE M33 .... **160** B3 🔢
North Park Rd *BRAM/HZG* SK7 .... **182** C4 🔢
North Phoebe St *SALO/ORD* M5 ..... **122** C1
North Pl *STKP* SK1 .... **167** D4 🔢
Northridge Rd *BKLY* M9 .... **74** B5
North Rd *DTN/ASHW* M34 .... **111** E6
HALE/TIMP WA15 .... **189** E1
MANAIR M90 .... **192** A3
OP/CLY M11 .... **125** E1
PART M31 .... **156** B1
PWCH M25 .... **71** D6
STRET M32 .... **120** C5
TRPK M17 .... **121** D4
Northside Av *URM* M41 .... **137** D2 🔢
North Star Dr *CSLFD* M3 .... **105** E6 🔢
Northstead Av *DTN/ASHW* M34 .... **149** F1
North St *AUL* OL6 .... **112** C4 🔢
CHH M8 .... **106** B2
HEY OL10 .... **36** C5 🔢
MDTN M24 .... **75** E1
MILN OL16 .... **23** E5
RAD M26 .... **52** A5

RAMS BL0 .... **7** D1
ROY/SHW OL2 .... **60** B6
WHIT OL12 .... **9** D2
Northumberland Av *AULW* OL7 .... **112** C3
Northumberland Cl
OLDTF/WHR M16 .... **123** D4 🔢
Northumberland Crs
OLDTF/WHR M16 .... **123** D4 🔢
Northumberland Rd
OLDTF/WHR M16 .... **123** D5
PART M31 .... **154** C3 🔢
RDSH SK5 .... **147** F5
Northumberland St *BRO* M7 .... **89** C6
Northumbria St *BOLS/LL* BL3 .... **46** A4 🔢
Northurst Dr *CHH* M8 .... **90** A2
North Vale Rd *HALE/TIMP* WA15 ...... **175** D1
North Veiw *WHTF* M45 .... **70** C1
Northward Rd *WILM/AE* SK9 .... **203** D5
North Wy *BOL* BL1 .... **28** C3
Northway *DROY* M43 .... **128** B1
North Wy *RDSH* SK5 .... **148** B5
North Western St *BNG/LEV* M19 ..... **145** E3 🔢
CMANE M1 .... **125** F1
Northwold Dr *BKLY* M9 .... **92** C2
BOL BL1 .... **44** C1
Northwood *BOLE* BL2 .... **29** E3
Northwood Av *CHD/CHDH* SK8 .... **181** E4 🔢
Northwood Gv *SALE* M33 .... **159** F1
Norton Av *DTN/ASHW* M34 .... **128** B6
SALE M33 .... **138** B6
URM M41 .... **119** E5
WGTN/LGST M12 .... **126** C6
Norton Gra *PWCH* M25 .... **89** E2
Norton Gv *HTNM* SK4 .... **165** F4 🔢
Norton Rd *WHIT* OL12 .... **23** D2
Norton St *BOL* BL1 .... **28** A4 🔢
BRO M7 .... **89** F6
CMANE M1 .... **107** D6 🔢
CSLFD M3 .... **2** C1
NEWH/MOS M40 .... **107** F3
Norview Dr *DID/WITH* M20 .... **163** F6
Norville Av *NEWH/MOS* M40 .... **93** E2
Norway Gv *RDSH* SK5 .... **167** D1 🔢
Norway St *BOL* BL1 .... **27** E5 🔢
OP/CLY M11 .... **125** F1
SLFD M6 .... **103** F5
STRET M32 .... **121** F6
Norwell Rd *WYTH/NTH* M22 .... **178** C2
Norwich Av *CHAD* OL9 .... **77** E2
DTN/ASHW M34 .... **149** D2
ROCH OL11 .... **21** E6
Norwich Cl *AUL* OL6 .... **97** E5
DUK SK16 .... **132** B2
Norwich Dr *TOT/BURYW* BL8 .... **33** E4 🔢
Norwich Rd *STRET* M32 .... **120** A6
Norwich St *ROCH* OL11 .... **42** A4
Norwick Cl *BOLS/LL* BL3 .... **44** C5
Norwood *PWCH* M25 .... **88** C3
Norwood Av *BRAM/HZG* SK7 .... **196** B4 🔢
BRO M7 .... **88** C5
DID/WITH M20 .... **164** B1
MPL/ROM SK6 .... **200** B2
Norwood Cl *ROY/SHW* OL2 .... **61** E5 🔢
WALK M28 .... **83** F5
Norwood Crs *ROY/SHW* OL2 .... **78** C1
Norwood Dr *HALE/TIMP* WA15 .... **176** B2
SWIN M27 .... **85** D6
Norwood Gv *BOL* BL1 .... **46** A1 🔢
OFTN SK2 .... **183** F5
STRET M32 .... **140** C2
Nottingham Av *RDSH* SK5 .... **148** A5
Nottingham Cl *RDSH* SK5 .... **148** A6 🔢
Nottingham Dr *AUL* OL6 .... **96** C6
BOL BL1 .... **27** F6 🔢
FAIL M35 .... **105** E2
RDSH SK5 .... **148** A5 🔢
Nowell Rd *MDTN* M24 .... **57** E6
Nuffield Rd *WYTH/NTH* M22 .... **178** C3
Nugent Rd *BOLS/LL* BL3 .... **46** C6
Nugget St *OLDE* OL4 .... **79** F5 🔢
Nuneaton Dr *NEWH/MOS* M40 ..... **107** E4 🔢
Nuneham Av *DID/WITH* M20 .... **144** A4
Nunfield Cl *NEWH/MOS* M40 .... **92** C3
Nunnery Rd *BOLS/LL* BL3 .... **45** F5
Nunthorpe Dr *CHH* M8 .... **91** D5 🔢
Nursery Av *HALE/TIMP* WA15 .... **188** C1
Nursery Cl *OFTN* SK2 .... **168** B6
SALE M33 .... **160** B1
Nursery Dr *POY/DIS* SK12 .... **198** B5
Nursery Gdns *MILN* OL16 .... **24** A5 🔢
Nursery La *EDGY/DAV* SK3 .... **165** E6
WILM/AE SK9 .... **203** D5
Nursery Rd *CHD/CHDH* SK8 .... **181** D6
FAIL M35 .... **110** B1
HTNM SK4 .... **166** A3
PWCH M25 .... **71** E5
URM M41 .... **118** C5
Nursery St *OLDTF/WHR* M16 .... **124** A6
SLFD M6 .... **104** A3
Nuthatch Av *WALK* M28 .... **83** E5 🔢
Nuthurst Rd *NEWH/MOS* M40 .... **93** D3
Nutsford V *WGTN/LGST* M12 .... **126** B5
Nuttall Av *BOLS/LL* BL3 .... **50** A6
WHTF M45 .... **71** D2

Nuttall Cl *RAMS* BL0 .... **7** D6
Nuttall Hall Rd *RAMS* BL0 .... **19** E1
Nuttall La *RAMS* BL0 .... **6** C6
Nuttall Ms *WHTF* M45 .... **71** D3
Nuttall Rd *RAMS* BL0 .... **19** E1
Nuttall Sq *BURY* BL9 .... **53** D4 🔢
Nuttall St *BURY* BL9 .... **34** B6
IRL M44 .... **134** C5
OLDS OL8 .... **96** C1 🔢
OLDTF/WHR M16 .... **123** D4 🔢
OP/CLY M11 .... **126** B2 🔢
Nutt La *PWCH* M25 .... **72** C3

O

Oadby Cl *WGTN/LGST* M12 .... **126** B5
Oak Av *BOLS/LL* BL3 .... **49** F6
CCHDY M21 .... **141** F3
CHD/CHDH SK8 .... **181** D5
GTN M18 .... **127** F5 🔢
HTNM SK4 .... **165** F3
IRL M44 .... **134** B6
MDTN M24 .... **75** E4
MPL/ROM SK6 .... **170** A3
ROY/SHW OL2 .... **60** B5
TOT/BURYW BL8 .... **18** B3 🔢
WHTF M45 .... **71** D4
WILM/AE SK9 .... **203** D6
Oak Bank *BKLY* M9 .... **91** E5
PWCH M25 .... **88** A4
Oak Bank Av *BKLY* M9 .... **92** A4
Oakbank Av *CHAD* OL9 .... **76** C3
Oak Bank Cl *WHTF* M45 .... **71** F5 🔢
Oakbank Dr *BOL* BL1 .... **27** E1 🔢
Oakbarton *HOR/BR* BL6 .... **44** A5
Oakcliffe Rd *WHIT* OL12 .... **24** A1
Oak Cl *WHIT* OL12 .... **5** E5
WILM/AE SK9 .... **203** D5
Oak Coppice *BOL* BL1 .... **45** E2
Oakcroft *STLY* SK15 .... **133** F2
Oakdale *BOLE* BL2 .... **29** E3
Oakdale Cl *WHTF* M45 .... **70** B5
Oakdale Dr *CHD/CHDH* SK8 .... **179** F5
DID/WITH M20 .... **164** A4
Oakdene *SWIN* M27 .... **100** C1 🔢
Oakdene Av *CHD/CHDH* SK8 .... **193** F2 🔢
HTNM SK4 .... **146** B6 🔢
Oakdene Crs *MPL/ROM* SK6 .... **171** D6
Oakdene Gdns *MPL/ROM* SK6 .... **171** D6
Oakdene Rd *HALE/TIMP* WA15 .... **159** F5
MDTN M24 .... **76** A3
MPL/ROM SK6 .... **171** D6
Oakdene St *BKLY* M9 .... **92** A5 🔢
Oak Dr *BRAM/HZG* SK7 .... **196** A2
DTN/ASHW M34 .... **128** B5
MPL/ROM SK6 .... **186** B1 🔢
RUSH/FAL M14 .... **144** B2
Oaken Bank Rd *MDTN* M24 .... **57** D3
Oakenbottom Rd *BOLE* BL2 .... **48** B3
Oaken Clough *AULW* OL7 .... **112** A1
Oakenclough Cl *WILM/AE* SK9 .... **204** B3 🔢
Oaken Clough Dr *AULW* OL7 .... **112** A1
Oakenclough Dr *BOL* BL1 .... **26** A5
Oakenrod Hl *ROCH* OL11 .... **22** A6
Oakenshaw Av *WHIT* OL12 .... **9** D5 🔢
Oakenshaw Vw *WHIT* OL12 .... **9** D5 🔢
Oaker Av *DID/WITH* M20 .... **162** C1
Oakes St *FWTH* BL4 .... **67** D4
Oakfield *DUK* SK16 .... **131** F3
PWCH M25 .... **89** E2
SALE M33 .... **139** E6
Oakfield Av *CHD/CHDH* SK8 .... **180** C1
DROY M43 .... **110** A6
OLDTF/WHR M16 .... **122** B6
OLDTF/WHR M16 .... **123** E6 🔢
STLY SK15 .... **115** F1 🔢
Oakfield Cl *BRAM/HZG* SK7 .... **196** C5
WILM/AE SK9 .... **209** F2
Oakfield Dr *LHULT* M38 .... **64** C6
Oakfield Gv *FWTH* BL4 .... **66** A5 🔢
GTN M18 .... **127** E5
Oakfield Rd *EDGY/DAV* SK3 .... **183** C2
HALE/TIMP WA15 .... **174** C2
HYDE SK14 .... **131** F4
POY/DIS SK12 .... **199** D5
WILM/AE SK9 .... **209** F3
Oakfield St *CHH* M8 .... **106** B1
HALE/TIMP WA15 .... **174** C2
Oakfield Ter *ROCH* OL11 .... **22** A5
Oakfold Av *AUL* OL6 .... **113** E1
Oakford Av *NEWH/MOS* M40 .... **107** D4 🔢
Oak Gv *AUL* OL6 .... **113** E1
CHD/CHDH SK8 .... **180** C2
ECC M30 .... **100** C6
POY/DIS SK12 .... **198** B5
URM M41 .... **138** C1
Oakham Cl *TOT/BURYW* BL8 .... **33** F2
Oakham Ms *BRO* M7 .... **89** D4 🔢
Oakham Rd *DTN/ASHW* M34 .... **149** E2 🔢
Oak Hl *LIT* OL15 .... **12** A6
Oakhill Cl *BOLE* BL2 .... **49** E2
Oakhill Wy *CHH* M8 .... **90** A6
Oakhouse Dr *CCHDY* M21 .... **141** F4

Oakhurst Cha WILM/AE SK9 ...... 209 E3
Oakhurst Dr CHD/CHDH SK8 ...... 181 F2
Oakland Av BNG/LEV M19 ...... 164 C1
　OFTN SK2 ...... 184 A1
　SLFD M6 ...... 102 B3
Oakland Gv BOL BL1 ...... 26 B5 ②
Oaklands BOL BL1 ...... 45 D2
Oaklands Av CHD/CHDH SK8 ...... 181 E5
Oaklands Cl WILM/AE SK9 ...... 204 C3
Oaklands Dene HYDE SK14 ...... 151 E1
　HYDE SK14 ...... 151 E1
　PWCH M25 ...... 71 F6
　SALE M33 ...... 139 E6 ⑤
Oaklands Rd BRO M7 ...... 88 B6
　RAMS BL0 ...... 7 E1
　ROY/SHW OL2 ...... 78 C1
　SWIN M27 ...... 101 D1
Oak La WHTF M45 ...... 71 F3
　WILM/AE SK9 ...... 203 D5
Oak Lea Av WILM/AE SK9 ...... 203 E6
Oaklea Rd SALE M33 ...... 138 C5
Oakleigh Av BNG/LEV M19 ...... 145 D4 ⑨
　BOLS/LL BL3 ...... 65 E1
　HALE/TIMP WA15 ...... 159 E6
Oakleigh Cl HEY OL10 ...... 56 C2
Oakleigh Rd CHD/CHDH SK8 ...... 194 C1
　RAD M26 ...... 69 E3
Oakley Cl NEWH/MOS M40 ...... 109 D2
　RAD M26 ...... 69 E3
Oakley Pk BOL BL1 ...... 45 D2
Oakley St SALQ/ORD M5 ...... 103 E6
Oakmere Av ECC M30 ...... 101 D3 ③
Oakmere Cl WYTH/NTH M22 ...... 178 B3 ⑤
Oakmere Rd CHD/CHDH SK8 ...... 181 D3 ⑥
　WILM/AE SK9 ...... 194 B4 ③
Oak Ms WILM/AE SK9 ...... 204 A2
Oakmoor Dr BRO M7 ...... 88 B5 ⑤
Oakmoor Rd NTHM/RTH M23 ...... 177 E1
Oak Rd BRO M7 ...... 105 D1
　CHD/CHDH SK8 ...... 180 C1
　DID/WITH M20 ...... 143 F6
　FAIL M35 ...... 110 A1
　HALE/TIMP WA15 ...... 174 C4
　OLDS OL8 ...... 95 D3
　PART M31 ...... 154 B3
　SALE M33 ...... 160 B1
Oaks Av BOLE BL2 ...... 29 D3
Oakshaw Dr WHIT OL12 ...... 21 E4
Oaks La BOLE BL2 ...... 28 C2
The Oaks CHD/CHDH SK8 ...... 179 E5
　HYDE SK14 ...... 132 B6
Oak St ANC M4 ...... 3 G2 ⑦
　BRAM/HZG SK7 ...... 184 B4
　DTN/ASHW M34 ......
　ECC M30 ...... 101 E6 ⑩
　EDGY/DAV SK3 ...... 165 F5
　HEY OL10 ...... 36 C4
　HYDE SK14 ...... 131 F5
　LIT OL15 ...... 13 E1
　MDTN M24 ...... 76 B4 ⑩
　MILN OL16 ...... 23 D6 ⑰
　MILN OL16 ...... 42 B4 ①
　RAMS BL0 ...... 6 C5 ⑩
　ROY/SHW OL2 ...... 62 A3
　SWIN M27 ...... 86 B4
　WHIT OL12 ...... 5 E5
Oak Ter OL15 ...... 13 E1
Oak Tree Cl OFTN SK2 ...... 168 B5 ⑤
Oak Tree Ct CHD/CHDH SK8 ...... 180 B1
Oak Tree Crs STLY SK15 ...... 132 B1
Oak Tree Dr DUK SK16 ...... 132 A2
Oak Vw WHIT OL12 ...... 5 E4
Oakville Dr SLFD M6 ...... 102 B3
Oakville Ter NEWH/MOS M40 ...... 92 A4
Oakway DID/WITH M20 ...... 164 A5 ⑦
　MDTN M24 ...... 57 D5
Oakwell Dr BRO M7 ...... 89 F4 ⑦
　BURY BL9 ...... 53 F6
Oakwell Man BRO M7 ...... 89 F4
Oakwood CHAD OL9 ...... 76 C4
　SALE M33 ...... 158 A1
Oakwood Av DTN/ASHW M34 ...... 129 F2
　NEWH/MOS M40 ...... 93 E4
　SWIN M27 ...... 85 F1
　WALK M28 ...... 84 A3 ⑦
　WILM/AE SK9 ...... 202 C5
Oakwood Cl TOT/BURYW BL8 ...... 32 C4 ⑥
Oakwood Dr BOL BL1 ...... 45 D1
　SLFD M6 ...... 102 C2
　WALK M28 ...... 84 A3
Oakwood La ALT WA14 ...... 173 E6
Oakwood Rd MPL/ROM SK6 ...... 170 A3
Oakworth Cft OLDE OL4 ...... 63 D5
Oakworth Dr BOL BL1 ...... 27 E2
Oakworth St BKLY M9 ...... 91 D2
Oatlands WILM/AE SK9 ...... 209 E5
Oatlands Rd WYTH/NTH M22 ...... 178 A5
Oat St STKP SK1 ...... 167 E6
Oban Av OLD OL1 ...... 79 F2
Oban Crs EDGY/DAV SK3 ...... 182 B3
Oban Dr SALE M33 ...... 160 C2
Oban Gv BOL BL1 ...... 27 F2
Oban St BOL BL1 ...... 27 E4 ⑨
Oberlin St OLDE OL4 ...... 80 B4

ROCH OL11 ...... 39 E2 ②
Occlestone Cl SALE M33 ...... 160 C4 ③
Ocean St ALT WA14 ...... 173 F1
Ockendon Dr BKLY M9 ...... 91 F6 ⑤
Octavia Dr NEWH/MOS M40 ...... 109 D3
Odell St OP/CLY M11 ...... 126 C2 ③
Odessa Av SLFD M6 ...... 102 C2
Odette St GTN M18 ...... 127 D5 ⑤
Offerton Dr OFTN SK2 ...... 168 B6
Offerton Fold OFTN SK2 ...... 168 A6 ②
Offerton Gn OFTN SK2 ...... 185 D1
Offerton La OFTN SK2 ...... 168 A5
Offerton Rd BRAM/HZG SK7 ...... 185 E4
　OFTN SK2 ...... 185 E3
Offerton St STKP SK1 ...... 167 F3 ①
Off Grove Rd STLY SK15 ...... 115 E3
Off Ridge Hill La STLY SK15 ...... 114 A5 ⑤
Off Stamford St STLY SK15 ...... 115 E3 ⑥
Ogden Cl HEY OL10 ...... 36 B5
　WHTF M45 ...... 71 E2
Ogden Gv CHD/CHDH SK8 ...... 179 D3 ⑥
Ogden La MILN OL16 ...... 43 E2 ⑥
　OP/CLY M11 ...... 127 E2
Ogden Rd BRAM/HZG SK7 ...... 196 B4
　FAIL M35 ...... 110 A1
Ogden Sq DUK SK16 ...... 130 C1 ③
Ogden St CHAD OL9 ...... 77 F3
　DID/WITH M20 ...... 163 F2 ⑥
　HYDE SK14 ...... 153 F3
　MDTN M24 ...... 75 E3 ⑤
　OLDE OL4 ...... 80 B5 ⑫
　PWCH M25 ...... 89 D1
　ROCH OL11 ...... 39 D5 ⑨
　SWIN M27 ...... 86 A6 ⑥
Ogwen Dr PWCH M25 ...... 71 F6
Ohio Av SALQ/ORD M5 ...... 122 A1
Okehampton Cl RAD M26 ...... 50 A4 ⑥
Okehampton Crs SALE M33 ...... 138 B6
Okeover Rd BRO M7 ...... 89 E5
Olaf St BOLE BL2 ...... 28 C6
Old Bank Cl MPL/ROM SK6 ...... 169 E2
Old Bank Vw OLD OL1 ...... 62 A5
Old Barn Pl EDGW/EG BL7 ...... 14 B5
Old Barton Rd URM M41 ...... 119 D2
Old Bent La WHIT OL12 ...... 10 B4
Old Birley St HULME M15 ...... 124 A3
Old Broadway DID/WITH M20 ...... 144 A6
Old Brook Cl ROY/SHW OL2 ...... 62 B1 ⑥
Oldbrook Fold HALE/TIMP WA15 ...... 175 F3
Old Brow MOSL OL5 ...... 99 D5
Old Brow La MILN OL16 ...... 24 A2 ⑦
Old Brown Ct MOSL OL5 ...... 99 D5 ③
Oldbury Cl HEY OL10 ...... 56 B2
　NEWH/MOS M40 ...... 107 E4 ⑪
Oldcastle Av DID/WITH M20 ...... 143 D4
Old Chapel St EDGY/DAV SK3 ...... 166 B6
Old Church St NEWH/MOS M40 ...... 108 C1
Old Clay Dr WHIT OL12 ...... 24 B1 ⑥
Old Clough La WALK M28 ...... 84 A4
The Old Ctyd WYTH/NTH M22 ...... 179 D2 ⑥
Oldcroft OLDE OL4 ...... 81 E5 ⑥
Old Croft Ms STKP SK1 ...... 167 F6 ⑥
Old Crofts Bank URM M41 ...... 111 E5
Old Cross St AUL OL6 ...... 113 D4 ⑱
Old Delph Rd ROCH OL11 ...... 21 D4 ⑥
Old Doctors St TOT/BURYW BL8 ...... 18 A6
Old Eagley Ms BOL BL1 ...... 28 B1 ⑥
Old Edge La ROY/SHW OL2 ...... 78 C1
Old Elm St BRUN/LGST M13 ...... 125 D3 ⑩
Oldershaw Dr BKLY M9 ...... 107 E3 ⑥
Old Farm Crs DROY M43 ...... 128 A1
Old Farm Dr OFTN SK2 ...... 185 D1 ⑥
Oldfield Dr HALE/TIMP WA15 ...... 175 D1
Oldfield Gv SALE M33 ...... 140 A6 ⑥
Oldfield Rd ALT WA14 ...... 173 E2 ⑥
　PWCH M25 ...... 72 A4
　SALE M33 ...... 140 A6
　SALQ/ORD M5 ...... 105 D6
Oldfield St OP/CLY M11 ...... 108 C5
Old Gardens St STKP SK1 ...... 167 D5 ⑬
The Old Gdn HALE/TIMP WA15 ...... 159 F6 ⑥
Old Gn BOLE BL2 ...... 29 F1
Old Ground St RAMS BL0 ...... 7 D5 ⑥
Old Hall Clough HOR/BR BL6 ...... 44 A2
Old Hall Crs WILM/AE SK9 ...... 194 C6 ①
Old Hall Dr GTN M18 ...... 127 E5
　OFTN SK2 ...... 184 C1
Old Hall La BRAM/HZG SK7 ...... 206 B2
　BRUN/LGST M13 ...... 144 C1
　PWCH M25 ...... 73 D4
　WALK M28 ...... 83 F6
　WHTF M45 ...... 70 A5
Old Hall Rd BRO M7 ...... 89 D5
　CHD/CHDH SK8 ...... 179 E1
　NEWH/MOS M40 ...... 92 C6
　SALE M33 ...... 160 C1
　STRET M32 ...... 120 B5
　WHTF M45 ...... 70 A4
Old Hall St DUK SK16 ...... 130 B2
　FWTH BL4 ...... 66 C4
　MDTN M24 ...... 75 E3
　OP/CLY M11 ...... 127 F2 ⑬
Old Hall St North BOL BL1 ...... 47 D2 ⑩
Oldham Av STKP SK1 ...... 167 F4
Oldham Dr MPL/ROM SK6 ...... 169 E1

Oldham Rd ANC M4 ...... 3 H1
　AULW OL7 ...... 112 B1
　FAIL M35 ...... 93 F6
　MDTN M24 ...... 75 D3
　MILN OL16 ...... 23 D6
　NEWH/MOS M40 ...... 107 D4
　OLDE OL4 ...... 81 E5
　ROCH OL11 ...... 40 B2
　ROY/SHW OL2 ...... 60 C1
　UPML OL3 ...... 63 E3
Oldhams La BOL BL1 ...... 27 E2
Oldham St CMANE M1 ...... 3 F3
　DROY M43 ...... 110 C5
　DTN/ASHW M34 ...... 148 A1
　HYDE SK14 ...... 150 B1
　RDSH SK5 ...... 146 C4 ⑩
　SALQ/ORD M5 ...... 105 E6 ⑥
Oldham Wy MILN OL16 ...... 42 A6
　OLD OL1 ...... 78 C5
Old Kiln La OLDE OL4 ...... 98 C1
Oldknow Rd MPL/ROM SK6 ...... 187 E1
Old La CHAD OL9 ...... 94 C1
　LHULT M38 ...... 65 D5
　OLDE OL4 ...... 81 D3
　OP/CLY M11 ...... 127 E2
　WHIT OL12 ...... 5 F3
Old Lansdowne Rd
　DID/WITH M20 ...... 163 D1
Old Lees St AUL OL6 ...... 113 C2 ⑥
Old Malt La DID/WITH M20 ...... 143 E4
Old Market St BKLY M9 ...... 91 D3
Old Meadow Dr DTN/ASHW M34 ...... 130 A4
Old Meadow La HALE/TIMP WA15 ...... 175 F4
Old Medlock St CSLFD M3 ...... 123 E1 ⑥
Old Mill Cl SWIN M27 ...... 86 C5
Old Mill La BRAM/HZG SK7 ...... 199 E1
　OLDE OL4 ...... 81 E5
Old Mills HI MDTN M24 ...... 76 B2
Old Mill St ANC M4 ...... 107 D2
Oldmill St WHIT OL12 ...... 23 D5 ⑩
Old Moat La DID/WITH M20 ...... 143 F4 ⑪
Oldmoor Rd MPL/ROM SK6 ...... 148 C6
Old Nans La BOLE BL2 ...... 30 A5
Old Nursery Fold BOLE BL2 ...... 29 F3 ⑥
Old Oak Cl BOLS/LL BL3 ...... 49 F4
Old Oak Dr DTN/ASHW M34 ...... 130 B6
Old Oake Cl WALK M28 ...... 83 F3 ⑥
Old Oak St DID/WITH M20 ...... 163 F2
Old Orch WILM/AE SK9 ...... 203 E4
The Old Orch HALE/TIMP WA15 ...... 159 F5 ①
Old Parrin La ECC M30 ...... 100 C4 ③
Old Quarry La EDGW/EG BL7 ...... 14 A4
Old Rectory Gdns
　CHD/CHDH SK8 ...... 180 B2 ⑥
Old River Cl IRL M44 ...... 135 E1
Old Rd AUL OL6 ...... 114 A2
　BKLY M9 ...... 91 E3
　BOL BL1 ...... 27 F4
　CHD/CHDH SK8 ...... 181 D1
　DUK SK16 ...... 113 D6
　FAIL M35 ...... 93 F6
　HTNM SK4 ...... 166 C2
　HYDE SK14 ...... 131 E5
　MILN OL16 ...... 24 C1
　STLY SK15 ...... 133 D1
　WILM/AE SK9 ...... 194 B6
Old School Dr BKLY M9 ...... 91 D3 ④
Old School Ms DUK SK16 ...... 131 F1 ②
Old Shaw St SALQ/ORD M5 ...... 122 C1 ②
Old Station St ECC M30 ...... 101 D6 ⑥
Oldstead Gv BOLS/LL BL3 ...... 45 D5
Old St AUL OL6 ...... 112 C5
　HYDE SK14 ...... 153 E3
　OLDE OL4 ...... 80 B6
　STLY SK15 ...... 114 B5
Old Towns Cl TOT/BURYW BL8 ...... 18 A6 ⑥
Old Vicarage Gdns WALK M28 ...... 83 E2 ⑥
Old Wellington Rd ECC M30 ...... 101 F5
Old Wells Cl LHULT M38 ...... 65 E5 ⑥
Oldwood Rd NTHM/RTH M23 ...... 177 E4
Old Wool La CHD/CHDH SK8 ...... 181 D5
Olebrook Cl WGTN/LGST M12 ...... 125 E3 ⑥
Olga St BOL BL1 ...... 27 E5
Olivant St BKLY M9 ...... 52 C1
Olive Bank TOT/BURYW BL8 ...... 32 C3
Oliver Cl LIT OL15 ...... 12 A6
Olive Rd HALE/TIMP WA15 ...... 159 E5
Oliver St EDGY/DAV SK3 ...... 167 D5
　OLD OL1 ...... 79 D5
　OP/CLY M11 ...... 126 A1 ⑥
Olive St BOLS/LL BL3 ...... 46 B5 ⑤⑦
　FAIL M35 ...... 93 F5 ④
　HEY OL10 ...... 37 F5 ⑥
　RAD M26 ...... 52 A6 ③
　ROCH OL11 ...... 39 D6 ⑦
　TOT/BURYW BL8 ...... 33 E5 ⑥
Olivia Gv RUSH/FAL M14 ...... 125 E6
Ollerbarrow Rd HALE/TIMP WA15 ...... 174 C5
Ollerbrook Ct BOL BL1 ...... 28 A5 ⑥
Ollerton Av SALE M33 ...... 138 B6
Ollerton Rd WILM/AE SK9 ...... 194 B4 ⑥
Ollerton St BOL BL1 ...... 28 A1 ⑥
Ollier Av WGTN/LGST M12 ...... 145 E1 ⑥
Olney Av WYTH/NTH M22 ...... 178 B1
Olney St BRUN/LGST M13 ...... 125 E5 ⑥

Olsberg Ct *RAD* M26 .... 52 A5
Olwen Crs *RDSH* SK5 .... 147 D3
Olympic Ct *SALQ/ORD* M5 .... 122 A1
Omer Av *BRUN/LGST* M13 .... 145 D1
Omer Dr *BNG/LEV* M19 .... 144 C4
Onchan Av *OLDE* OL4 .... 79 F5 ▣
One Ash Cl *WHIT* OL12 .... 23 D3
One Oak La *WILM/AE* SK9 .... 205 D4
Onslow Av *NEWH/MOS* M40 .... 93 F4
Onslow Cl *OLD* OL1 .... 78 C3 ▣
Onslow Rd *EDGY/DAV* SK3 .... 166 A5 ▣
Onslow St *ROCH* OL11 .... 39 D3
Onward St *HYDE* SK14 .... 150 B1 ▣
Opal St *BNG/LEV* M19 .... 145 F3 ▣

Openshaw Fold Rd *BURY* BL9 ..... 52 B2
Openshaw La *IRL* M44 .... 134 C5 ▣
Openshaw Pl *FWTH* BL4 .... 65 F3 ▣
Openshaw St *BURY* BL9 .... 34 B6 ▣
Orama Av *SLFD* M6 .... 102 B3
Oram St *BURY* BL9 .... 34 B3 ▣
Orange Hill Rd *PWCH* M25 .... 72 A6
Orange St *SLFD* M6 .... 100 B4
Orchard Av *BOL* BL1 .... 28 A4 ▣
  GTN M18 .... 127 F5 ▣
  PART M31 .... 155 D1
  WALK M28 .... 82 C6
Orchard Cl *CHD/CHDH* SK8 .... 196 A2 ▣
  OLD OL1 .... 78 B2
  POY/DIS SK12 .... 198 C6
  WILM/AE SK9 .... 203 D6
Orchard Ct *OFTN* SK2 .... 184 B1 ▣
Orchard Dr *HALE/TIMP* WA15 ..... 175 E4
  WILM/AE SK9 .... 194 C6
Orchard Gdns *BOLE* BL2 .... 30 A4
Orchard Gn *WILM/AE* SK9 .... 209 F4
Orchard Gv *DID/WITH* M20 .... 143 D6
  ROY/SHW OL2 .... 61 E2
Orchard Pl *HALE/TIMP* WA15 ...... 159 F6
  SALE M33 .... 139 F6 ▣
Orchard Ri *HYDE* SK14 .... 151 D3
Orchard Rd *FAIL* M35 .... 94 A6
  HALE/TIMP WA15 .... 174 C2
  MPL/ROM SK6 .... 171 F3
Orchard Rd East *WYTH/NTH* M22 . 162 B3
Orchard Rd West *WYTH/NTH* M22 . 162 B3
Orchard St *DID/WITH* M20 .... 143 D6 ▣
  HEY OL10 .... 37 F4
  HYDE SK14 .... 150 C1
  SLFD M6 .... 104 B3 ▣
  STKP SK1 .... 167 D4 ▣
Orchard V *EDGY/DAV* SK3 .... 182 A1
Orchid Av *FWTH* BL4 .... 65 F2
Orchid Cl *IRL* M44 .... 134 C3
Orchid Dr *BURY* BL9 .... 53 E1
Orchid St *BKLY* M9 .... 91 E6
Ordsall Av *LHULT* M38 .... 82 C1
Ordsall Dr *SALQ/ORD* M5 .... 122 C2
Ordsall La *SALQ/ORD* M5 .... 122 C2
Oregon Av *OLD* OL1 .... 78 C3 ▣
Oregon Cl *BRUN/LGST* M13 .... 125 D3 ▣
Orford Cl *MPL/ROM* SK6 .... 200 C3
Orford Rd *NEWH/MOS* M40 .... 109 D2
  PWCH M25 .... 71 E6
Oriel Av *OLDS* OL8 .... 95 F2
Oriel Cl *CHAD* OL9 .... 94 B1
  OFTN SK2 .... 183 F1
Oriel St *BOLS/LL* BL3 .... 46 A4 ▣
  ROCH OL11 .... 40 A2
Orient Rd *SLFD* M6 .... 102 B3
Orient St *BRO* M7 .... 90 A6
Oriole Cl *WALK* M28 .... 82 C5
Oriole Dr *WALK* M28 .... 82 C5
Orion Pl *BRO* M7 .... 105 D3
Orkney Cl *NTHM/RTH* M23 .... 177 E3
  RAD M26 .... 51 F5
Orkney Dr *URM* M41 .... 119 C3
Orlanda Av *SLFD* M6 .... 102 B3
Orlanda Dr *BRO* M7 .... 106 A1
Orlando St *BOLS/LL* BL3 .... 47 E4
Orley Wk *OLD* OL1 .... 62 B5
Orme Av *MDTN* M24 .... 75 E4
  SLFD M6 .... 102 C2
Orme Cl *OP/CLY* M11 .... 107 F6 ▣
  URM M41 .... 139 D1 ▣
Ormerod Av *ROY/SHW* OL2 .... 60 C6 ▣
Ormerod Cl *MPL/ROM* SK6 .... 169 D4
Ormerod St *HEY* OL10 .... 37 F6 ▣
Orme St *OLDE* OL4 .... 79 E6 ▣
  STKP SK1 .... 167 F3 ▣
  WILM/AE SK9 .... 209 E4
Ormonde Av *SLFD* M6 .... 102 B3
Ormonde Ct *AUL* OL6 .... 113 D3 ▣
Ormond St *BOLS/LL* BL3 .... 48 B4 ▣
  BURY BL9 .... 34 B4 ▣
Ormrod St *BOL* BL1 .... 46 C3
  BOLE BL2 .... 29 D3 ▣
  BURY BL9 .... 34 B5
  FWTH BL4 .... 66 A3 ▣
Ormsby Av *GTN* M18 .... 126 C5
Ormsby Cl *EDGY/DAV* SK3 .... 182 C3 ▣
Ormsgill St *HULME* M15 .... 124 A3 ▣
Orms Gill Pl *OFTN* SK2 .... 184 C1 ▣
Ormskirk Av *DID/WITH* M20 .... 143 D5
Ormskirk Cl *TOT/BURYW* BL8 ..... 51 D1

Ormskirk Rd *RDSH* SK5 .... 147 D5 ▣
Ornatus St *BOL* BL1 .... 28 A2 ▣
Oronsay Gv *SALQ/ORD* M5 .... 103 E6 ▣
Orphanage St *HTNM* SK4 .... 166 C2 ▣
Orpington Dr *TOT/BURYW* BL8 ... 32 C6
Orpington Rd *BKLY* M9 .... 91 F6 ▣
Orrell St *OP/CLY* M11 .... 127 E1 ▣
  TOT/BURYW BL8 .... 33 D4
Orrel St *SALQ/ORD* M5 .... 103 F5
Orrishmere Rd *CHD/CHDH* SK8 ... 181 D3
Orron St *LIT* OL15 .... 12 B6 ▣
Orsett Cl *NEWH/MOS* M40 .... 107 D3
Orthes Av *HTNM* SK4 .... 146 B6
Orton Av *NTHM/RTH* M23 .... 161 E4
Orton Rd *NTHM/RTH* M23 .... 161 E4
Orvietto Av *SLFD* M6 .... 102 B3
Orville Dr *BNG/LEV* M19 .... 145 D4
Orwell Av *DTN/ASHW* M34 .... 128 B6
  WYTH/NTH M22 .... 178 B1
Orwell Cl *TOT/BURYW* BL8 .... 33 E3
  WILM/AE SK9 .... 204 B1
Orwell Rd *BOL* BL1 .... 26 C5
Osborne Cl *TOT/BURYW* BL8 ..... 51 F1 ▣
Osborne Dr *SWIN* M27 .... 87 D6
Osborne Gv *BOL* BL1 .... 27 D6
  CHD/CHDH SK8 .... 179 F4
Osborne Rd *BKLY* M9 .... 91 F6 ▣
  BNG/LEV M19 .... 145 D2
  DTN/ASHW M34 .... 130 A5
  HALE/TIMP WA15 .... 174 C2
  HYDE SK14 .... 150 C2
  OFTN SK2 .... 167 D6
  OLDS OL8 .... 78 B6
  SLFD M6 .... 102 B4 ▣
Osborne St *CHAD* OL9 .... 78 A3
  HEY OL10 .... 37 E6 ▣
  MPL/ROM SK6 .... 168 C2
  NEWH/MOS M40 .... 107 D3
  ROCH OL11 .... 39 F2
  ROY/SHW OL2 .... 61 F3 ▣
  SLFD M6 .... 104 A4
Osborne Ter *SALE* M33 .... 159 F1
Osbourne Cl *FWTH* BL4 .... 66 B2 ▣
  WILM/AE SK9 .... 204 B5
Osbourne Pl *ALT* WA14 .... 174 C5 ▣
Oscar St *BOL* BL1 .... 27 D5 ▣
  NEWH/MOS M40 .... 105 E6 ▣
Oscott Av *LHULT* M38 .... 65 E5 ▣
Oscroft Cl *CHH* M8 .... 106 A1 ▣
Osmond St *OLDE* OL4 .... 80 A4 ▣
Osmund Av *BOLE* BL2 .... 48 B2
Osprey Cl *DUK* SK16 .... 131 F2
  HULME M15 .... 123 F4 ▣
Osprey Dr *DROY* M43 .... 111 D4
  IRL M44 .... 116 B6
  WILM/AE SK9 .... 204 A3
Ossory St *RUSH/FAL* M14 .... 124 C6
Osterley Rd *BKLY* M9 .... 92 A3
Ostlers Ga *DROY* M43 .... 111 E5
Ostrich La *PWCH* M25 .... 89 D3
Oswald Cl *SLFD* M6 .... 104 B2
Oswald La *CCHDY* M21 .... 141 E2 ▣
Oswald Rd *CCHDY* M21 .... 141 F1 ▣
Oswald St *ANC* M4 .... 106 B4 ▣
  ANC M4 .... 107 E6 ▣
  BOLS/LL BL3 .... 46 A5 ▣
  CHAD OL9 .... 78 B3
  MILN OL16 .... 23 E5
  RDSH SK5 .... 128 A6
  ROY/SHW OL2 .... 62 A1
Oswestry Cl *TOT/BURYW* BL8 .... 18 A5 ▣
Otago St *OLDE* OL4 .... 80 A2 ▣
Othello Dr *ECC* M30 .... 101 E1 ▣
Otley Av *SLFD* M6 .... 103 D4
Otley Cl *CHAD* OL9 .... 77 F5 ▣
Otley Gv *EDGY/DAV* SK3 .... 182 B3
Otmoor Wy *ROY/SHW* OL2 .... 61 E5
Otranto Av *SLFD* M6 .... 102 C3
Ottawa Cl *NTHM/RTH* M23 .... 177 D3 ▣
Otterburn Cl *HULME* M15 .... 124 A3 ▣
Otterburn Pl *OFTN* SK2 .... 184 B1
Otterbury Cl *TOT/BURYW* BL8 ... 32 A5 ▣
Otter Dr *BURY* BL9 .... 53 F5
  CHH M8 .... 105 F2 ▣
Otterspool Rd *MPL/ROM* SK6 .... 169 F6
Oulder Hi *ROCH* OL11 .... 21 E6
Oulder Hill Dr *ROCH* OL11 .... 21 F6
Ouldfield Cl *MILN* OL16 .... 40 C1 ▣
Oulton Av *SALE* M33 .... 140 C6
Oulton St *BOL* BL1 .... 28 B2
Oundle Cl *RUSH/FAL* M14 .... 125 D6 ▣
Ouse St *SALQ/ORD* M5 .... 103 D6
Outram Cl *MPL/ROM* SK6 .... 187 D3 ▣
Outram Rd *DUK* SK16 .... 130 C3
Outram Sq *DROY* M43 .... 128 A1 ▣
Outrington Dr *OP/CLY* M11 .... 126 B1 ▣
Outwood Av *SWIN* M27 .... 85 E1
Outwood Dr *CHD/CHDH* SK8 ..... 193 E1
Outwood Gv *BOL* BL1 .... 27 F2 ▣
Outwood La *MANAIR* M90 .... 192 A1
Outwood La West *MANAIR* M90 .. 191 F1 ▣
Outwood Rd *CHD/CHDH* SK8 ..... 193 F1
  RAD M26 .... 69 E2
Oval Dr *DUK* SK16 .... 130 C2
The Oval *CHD/CHDH* SK8 .... 193 F1

Overbridge Rd *BRO* M7 .... 105 F3
Overbrook Av
  NEWH/MOS M40 .... 107 E2 ▣
Overbrook Dr *PWCH* M25 .... 88 C2
Overdale *SWIN* M27 .... 102 B1
Overdale Cl *OLD* OL1 .... 78 C2 ▣
Overdale Crs *URM* M41 .... 137 D1
Overdale Dr *BOL* BL1 .... 45 E2
Overdale Rd *MPL/ROM* SK6 .... 169 E5
  WYTH/NTH M22 .... 178 B2
Overdell Dr *WHIT* OL12 .... 22 A2
Overens St *OLDE* OL4 .... 79 F4
Overfield Wy *WHIT* OL12 .... 23 D3 ▣
Overgreen *BOLE* BL2 .... 29 F4
Overhill Dr *WILM/AE* SK9 .... 204 C4 ▣
Overhill La *WILM/AE* SK9 .... 204 C4
Overhill Rd *CHAD* OL9 .... 77 D3
  WILM/AE SK9 .... 204 B4
Overlea Dr *BNG/LEV* M19 .... 144 C6
Overlinks Dr *SLFD* M6 .... 102 C2
Overstone Dr *CHH* M8 .... 90 A6 ▣
Overton Av *WYTH/NTH* M22 ...... 178 B2
Overton Crs *BRAM/HZG* SK7 ..... 184 C3
  SALE M33 .... 158 B5
Overton Rd *WYTH/NTH* M22 ...... 178 B2
Over Town La *WHIT* OL12 .... 20 A2
Overt St *ROCH* OL11 .... 40 A2 ▣
Overwood Rd *WYTH/NTH* M22 ... 162 B5
Owen Fold *OLDE* OL4 .... 80 B1
Owenington Gv *LHULT* M38 ...... 65 E6 ▣
Owens Cl *CHAD* OL9 .... 76 C3 ▣
Owen St *ECC* M30 .... 100 C6
  EDGY/DAV SK3 .... 166 B4
  OLD OL1 .... 62 C6
  SLFD M6 .... 104 B2
Owlerbarrow Rd *TOT/BURYW* BL8 . 32 B4
Owler La *CHAD* OL9 .... 93 E2
Oxbridge Cl *SALE* M33 .... 158 B2 ▣
Oxbrow Wy *WHTF* M45 .... 71 E3
Oxendale Dr *MDTN* M24 .... 74 A2
Oxenhurst Gn *OFTN* SK2 .... 184 C2
Oxford Av *DROY* M43 .... 110 A4
  ROCH OL11 .... 38 B1
  SALE M33 .... 158 B1
  WHTF M45 .... 71 E3
Oxford Cl *FWTH* BL4 .... 65 D5 ▣
Oxford Dr *MDTN* M24 .... 76 A1
  MPL/ROM SK6 .... 170 A1
Oxford Gv *BOL* BL1 .... 27 D6
  IRL M44 .... 134 A5
Oxford Pl *MILN* OL16 .... 40 D3
  RUSH/FAL M14 .... 125 D5
Oxford Rd *ALT* WA14 .... 174 B4
  BOLS/LL BL3 .... 49 D6
  BRUN/LGST M13 .... 124 C4
  CMANE M1 .... 124 B2
  DUK SK16 .... 131 E1
  SLFD M6 .... 102 B3
Oxford St *BURY* BL9 .... 34 B6
  CHAD OL9 .... 77 F6
  CMANE M1 .... 3 E6
  CMANW M2 .... 2 D5
  ECC M30 .... 101 E2
  ROY/SHW OL2 .... 61 F2
  STLY SK15 .... 115 D6
  STLY SK15 .... 115 E3 ▣
Oxford St East *AULW* OL7 .... 130 A1
Oxford St West *AULW* OL7 .... 130 A1
Oxford Wy *HTNM* SK4 .... 166 B2 ▣
  WHIT OL12 .... 22 C3
Ox Ga *BOLE* BL2 .... 29 E2
Oxley St *OP/CLY* M11 .... 108 B3
Oxney Rd *RUSH/FAL* M14 .... 125 D5
Ox St *RAMS* BL0 .... 6 C6 ▣
Oxton Av *WYTH/NTH* M22 .... 178 A3
Oxton St *OP/CLY* M11 .... 128 A2 ▣

P

Pacific Wy *SALQ/ORD* M5 .... 121 D1
Packer St *BOL* BL1 .... 27 D5 ▣
  MILN OL16 .... 23 D6 ▣
Packwood Cha *CHAD* OL9 .... 77 D3 ▣
Padbury Cl *URM* M41 .... 117 E6 ▣
Padbury Wy *BOLE* BL2 .... 29 F5
Padden Brook *MPL/ROM* SK6 ..... 169 F3
Paddington Av
  NEWH/MOS M40 .... 108 C2 ▣
Paddington Cl *SLFD* M6 .... 104 B5 ▣
Paddison St *SWIN* M27 .... 85 F6 ▣
Paddock Cha *POY/DIS* SK12 ...... 199 D3
Paddock La *FAIL* M35 .... 110 A2
  LYMM WA13 .... 154 C6
Paddock Rd *HYDE* SK14 .... 150 B5 ▣
Paddock St *WGTN/LGST* M12 .... 125 D2 ▣
The Paddocks *BRAM/HZG* SK7 ... 182 B6 ▣
  CHD/CHDH SK8 .... 180 C2
  HALE/TIMP WA15 .... 175 F3 ▣
  RAMS BL0 .... 6 C4
  WALK M28 .... 83 F6 ▣
The Paddock *BRAM/HZG* SK7 .... 182 B6
Padiham Cl *BURY* BL9 .... 52 B2

Padstow Cl *HYDE* SK14.................... **133** E6
Padstow Dr *BRAM/HZG* SK7 .... **197** D2
Padstow St *NEWH/MOS* M40 .... **107** F4 ⑩
Padstow Wk *HYDE* SK14 .... **133** E6 ⑪
Pagan St *WHIT* OL12 .... **23** D5
Paget St *NEWH/MOS* M40 .... **107** E2
Pagnall Ct *CHAD* OL9 .... **77** F6 ③
Paignton Av *BNG/LEV* M19 .... **145** D3 ⑤
HYDE SK14...................................... **152** A1
Paignton Dr *SALE* M33 .... **138** B6
Paignton Gv *HTNM* SK4 .... **146** C4
Pailin Dr *DROY* M43......................... **111** D5
Pailton Cl *HOR/BR* BL6 .... **44** B3
Painswick Rd *WYTH/NTH* M22 .... **177** F6
Paiton St *BOL* BL1 .... **46** A3 ⑱
Palace Gdns *OLD* OL1 .... **78** B1 ⑨
Palace Rd *AUL* OL6 .... **113** F2
SALE M33 .... **139** E6 ④
Palace St *BOL* BL1 .... **47** D1 ⑪
BURY BL9 .... **34** B5 ⑩
CHAD OL9 .... **78** A4 ③
Palatine Av
DID/WITH M20 .... **143** F5
ROCH OL11 .... **21** E5
Palatine Cl *IRL* M44 .... **135** D2
Palatine Crs *DID/WITH* M20 .... **143** F6
Palatine Rd *DID/WITH* M20 .... **143** E6
ROCH OL11 .... **21** E5 ⑩
WYTH/NTH M22 .... **162** B4
Palatine St *BOL* BL1 .... **47** D2 ⑱
DTN/ASHW M34 .... **129** E6
MILN OL16 .... **24** A6
RAMS BL0 .... **7** D5 ⑦
Palfrey Pl *WGTN/LGST* M12 ... **125** D2 ⑩
Pall Ml *CMANW* M2 .... **2** D3
Pallotine Wk *ROCH* OL11 .... **39** E2
Palma Av *MANAIR* M90 .... **191** E1
Palm Cl *SALE* M33 .... **138** A6
Palmer Av *CHD/CHDH* SK8 .... **181** D1
Palmer Cl *OLDS* OL8 .... **96** A1
Palmerston Av
OLDTF/WHR M16 .... **142** B1 ③
Palmerston Cl *DTN/ASHW* M34 ... **128** C6 ⑤
RAMS BL0 .... **18** C2
Palmerston Rd *DTN/ASHW* M34 ... **128** C6
OFTN SK2 .... **183** E4
Palmerston St *WGTN/LGST* M12 ... **125** E1
Palmer St *BRO* M7 .... **105** D2 ⑪
DUK SK16 .... **112** C6 ④
SALE M33 .... **159** E1 ⑱
Palm Gv *CHAD* OL9 .... **77** F3
Palm St *BOL* BL1 .... **28** A4 ⑭
DROY M43 .... **109** E5
OLDE OL4 .... **80** A3
Pandora St *DID/WITH* M20 .... **143** E6 ⑩
Panfield Rd *WYTH/NTH* M22 ...... **178** A3
Pangbourne Av *URM* M41 .... **119** F6 ⑧
Pangbourne Cl *EDGY/DAV* SK3 ... **182** A1
Panmure St *OLDS* OL8 .... **96** A1 ⑨
Pansy Rd *FWTH* BL4 .... **65** E3
Paper Mill Rd *EDGW/EG* BL7 .... **14** A6
Parade St *MANAIR* M90 .... **192** A2
Paradise St *DTN/ASHW* M34 .... **130** A2
RAMS BL0 .... **7** D5
Parbold Av *DID/WITH* M20........... **143** E4
Parcel Cl *OP/CLY* M11 .... **108** A5
Paris Av *SALQ/ORD* M5 .... **122** C1 ⑬
Paris St *BOLS/LL* BL3 .... **45** F5
Park Av *ALT* WA14 .... **158** C5
BNG/LEV M19 .... **145** D2
BOL BL1 .... **27** F5 ⑱
BRAM/HZG SK7 .... **196** A4
BRO M7 .... **90** A5
CHAD OL9 .... **77** F2
CHD/CHDH SK8 .... **181** D6
EDGY/DAV SK3 .... **165** D6
FAIL M35 .... **93** E5
HALE/TIMP WA15 .... **175** D6
HYDE SK14 .... **131** E5
MPL/ROM SK6 .... **170** A3
OLDTF/WHR M16 .... **123** D4
POY/DIS SK12 .... **198** C5
PWCH M25 .... **88** C1
RAD M26 .... **52** B5
RAMS BL0 .... **7** E5
SALE M33 .... **139** F5
URM M41 .... **138** A1 ⑧
WHTF M45 .... **70** B5
WILM/AE SK9 .... **204** A3
Parkbrook Rd *NTHM/RTH* M23 ... **161** F6
Park Brow *CII CCHDY* M21 .... **142** A4 ③
Park Cl *ALT* WA14 .... **159** D5
CHAD OL9 .... **77** E2
STLY SK15 .... **114** A4
WHTF M45 .... **71** D5 ③
Park Crs *AUL* OL6 .... **113** F5 ③
CHAD OL9 .... **77** D2
RUSH/FAL M14 .... **125** D6
WILM/AE SK9 .... **203** F2
Parkdale *CHAD* OL9 .... **77** F2 ②
Parkdale Av *DTN/ASHW* M34....... **129** E2
GTN M18 .... **127** D5 ⑦
Parkdale Rd *BOLE* BL2 .... **29** D6
Parkdene Cl *BOLE* BL2 .... **29** E3
Park Dr *ECC* M30 .... **101** E3

HALE/TIMP* WA15 .... **159** E6
HALE/TIMP WA15 .... **175** D6
HTNM SK4 .... **165** F3
HYDE SK14 .... **131** E5
OLDTF/WHR M16 .... **142** A1
Parkend Rd *NTHM/RTH* M23 ...... **177** E2
Parker St *BURY* BL9 .... **34** B5
CMANE M1 .... **3** F4
Parkfield *CHAD* OL9 .... **77** F2
SALQ/ORD M5 .... **103** E5 ⑱
Parkfield Av *FWTH* BL4 .... **66** A4
MPL/ROM SK6 .... **187** D1
OLDS OL8 .... **94** C3 ⑦
PWCH M25 .... **89** E2 ⑱
RUSH/FAL M14 .... **124** C6
URM M41 .... **137** F2 ⑩
Parkfield Dr *MDTN* M24 .... **74** C3
Parkfield Rd *ALT* WA14 .... **174** A3
BOLS/LL BL3 .... **47** D6
CHD/CHDH SK8 .... **181** D6
Parkfield Rd North
NEWH/MOS M40 .... **93** F3
Parkfields *STLY* SK15 .... **115** E4 ③
Parkfield St *ROCH* OL11 .... **40** C5 ④
RUSH/FAL M14 .... **124** C5 ②
Parkgate *CHAD* OL9 .... **77** F2
TOT/BURYW BL8 .... **31** F2
Parkgate Dr *BOL* BL1 .... **28** A2
OFTN SK2 .... **183** F3
SWIN M27 .... **86** C6 ⑩
Park Gates Av *CHD/CHDH* SK8 ... **182** A6 ⑤
Park Gates Dr *CHD/CHDH* SK8 ... **182** A6
Park Gv *BNG/LEV* M19 .... **145** E1
HTNM SK4 .... **165** F1
RAD M26 .... **51** D5
WALK M28 .... **83** E5
Parkhill Av *CHH* M8 .... **90** C3
Park Hill Dr *WHTF* M45 .... **70** C3
Park Hill Rd *HALE/TIMP* WA15 ... **175** E6
Parkhills Rd *BURY* BL9 .... **34** A6
Park Hill St *BOL* BL1 .... **46** B1
Park House Bridge Rd *SLFD* M6 ... **104** A1 ⑩
Parkhouse St *OP/CLY* M11 .... **126** C1
Parkhurst Av *NEWH/MOS* M40 ... **93** F4
Parkin Cl *DUK* SK16 .... **131** D1 ②
Parkinson St *BOLS/LL* BL3 .... **46** A4 ⑯
BURY BL9 .... **34** A2
Parkin St *WGTN/LGST* M12......... **126** B6
Parklake Av *BRO* M7 .... **89** E5
Parklands *ROY/SHW* OL2 .... **60** A3
ROY/SHW OL2 .... **62** B1
WHTF M45 .... **70** C3
Parklands Dr *SALE* M33 .... **158** B3 ⑱
Parklands Rd *NTHM/RTH* M23 ... **161** D6
The Parklands *HTNM* SK4 .... **166** C1
Parklands Wy *POY/DIS* SK12 ..... **198** C5
Park La *BRO* M7 .... **89** E5
DUK SK16 .... **131** D1
HALE/TIMP WA15 .... **175** E6
MILN OL16 .... **23** D5 ⑪
OLDS OL8 .... **96** A3
POY/DIS SK12 .... **198** C5
ROY/SHW OL2 .... **60** C4
SLFD M6 .... **103** D2
STKP SK1 .... **167** F5
WHTF M45 .... **70** C4
Park La West *SWIN* M27 .... **87** E6
Parkleigh Dr *NEWH/MOS* M40 ..... **93** F3
Park Lodge Cl *CHD/CHDH* SK8 ... **180** C3
Park Ms *OLDTF/WHR* M16 .... **142** A1 ⑦
Parkmount Rd *BKLY* M9 .... **91** F4
Park Pde *AULW* OL7 .... **112** B5
ROY/SHW OL2 .... **43** D6
Park Pl *ANC* M4 .... **106** B4
HTNM SK4 .... **165** D3 ⑩
PWCH M25 .... **72** A4
SLFD M6 .... **102** B4
Park Range *RUSH/FAL* M14 .... **125** E6
Park Ri *MPL/ROM* SK6 .... **170** A2
Park Rd *ALT* WA14 .... **173** E5
BOL BL1 .... **46** A2
BOLS/LL BL3 .... **49** D5
BURY BL9 .... **33** F3
CHD/CHDH SK8 .... **179** D1
CHD/CHDH SK8 .... **180** C1
CHD/CHDH SK8 .... **182** A6
DTN/ASHW M34 .... **129** E1
DTN/ASHW M34 .... **129** F6
DUK SK16 .... **113** E6
ECC M30 .... **101** E3
HALE/TIMP WA15 .... **159** D5
HALE/TIMP WA15 .... **175** D6
HTNM SK4 .... **145** F6
HYDE SK14 .... **131** E5
LYMM WA13 .... **154** A5
MDTN M24 .... **75** D3
MPL/ROM SK6 .... **170** A2
OLDS OL8 .... **79** D6
PART M31 .... **155** E2
POY/DIS SK12 .... **201** D3
PWCH M25 .... **89** E2
SALE M33 .... **139** E5
SLFD M6 .... **102** B3
STRET M32 .... **121** D6
TOT/BURYW BL8 .... **18** A2

WALK* M28 .... **83** D4
WHIT* OL12 .... **23** F4
WILM/AE* SK9 .... **203** D4
Park Rd North *URM* M41 .... **119** D6
Park Rd South *URM* M41 .... **138** A1
Park Rw *HTNM* SK4 .... **165** D4
Park Seventeen *WHTF* M45 .... **71** D2
Parkside Av *MDTN* M24 .... **74** C5
Parkside Av *BRO* M7 .... **89** F5
ECC M30 .... **109** D6 ⑩
FAIL M35 .... **109** F2
Park Side Av *ROY/SHW* OL2 .... **62** A1 ⑥
Parkside Av *WALK* M28 .... **83** E4 ②
Parkside Cl *MPL/ROM* SK6 .... **200** B1
RAD M26 .... **52** B5
Parkside Rd *RUSH/FAL* M14 ...... **143** D1
SALE M33 .... **160** B2 ⑨
Parkside St *BOLE* BL2 .... **29** D6 ⑰
WGTN/LGST M12 .... **125** D2 ⑪
Parkside Wk *BRAM/HZG* SK7 ... **182** C4 ③
Parks Nook *FWTH* BL4 .... **66** A4 ⑧
Park Sq *OLDTF/WHR* M16........... **141** E1
Parkstead Dr *BKLY* M9 .... **107** E1 ③
Parkstone Av *GTN* M18 .... **128** A3
WHTF M45 .... **70** B5
Parkstone Cl *TOT/BURYW* BL8 ... **32** A5
Parkstone Dr *SLFD* M6 .... **102** C1 ③
Parkstone La *WALK* M28 .... **100** A3
Parkstone Rd *IRL* M44 .... **116** B6
Park St *AULW* OL7 .... **112** C5
BOL BL1 .... **46** B1 ⑮
BOL BL1 .... **46** B1 ㉕
BRO M7 .... **89** D5
CSLFD M3 .... **105** E6
DROY M43 .... **111** D5 ⑧
DTN/ASHW M34 .... **129** E6
FWTH BL4 .... **66** B2
HEY OL10 .... **56** C1
MILN OL16 .... **40** A1 ⑬
MOSL OL5 .... **99** D5
MPL/ROM SK6 .... **169** D2
OLDS OL8 .... **78** C6
PWCH M25 .... **89** D1 ⑧
RAD M26 .... **52** A5
ROY/SHW OL2 .... **60** C5
ROY/SHW OL2 .... **61** F3
STKP SK1 .... **167** D3 ⑩
STLY SK15 .... **114** B6
SWIN M27 .... **86** B6
Parksway *BKLY* M9 .... **73** F5
PWCH M25 .... **89** D3
SWIN M27 .... **103** D1 ②
Parks Yd *BURY* BL9 .... **33** F5 ⑲
Park Ter *HEY* OL10 .... **37** E4
MOSL OL5 .... **99** D5 ④
Park Vw *BKLY* M9 .... **107** D1
CHAD OL9 .... **77** E2
DTN/ASHW M34 .... **129** E1 ⑩
EDGY/DAV SK3 .... **165** D6
FWTH BL4 .... **66** B2 ⑧
LIT OL15 .... **12** C5
RUSH/FAL M14 .... **144** C4 ⑧
STKP SK1 .... **167** F6
Park View Rd *BOLS/LL* BL3 .... **46** A5 ㉙
PWCH M25 .... **88** C2
Parkville Rd *DID/WITH* M20 .... **144** A6
PWCH M25 .... **72** A4
Parkway *BRAM/HZG* SK7 .... **182** C5
CHAD OL9 .... **77** E2
EDGY/DAV SK3 .... **165** D6
ROCH OL11 .... **21** F5
Park Wy *STRET* M32 .... **120** A5
Parkway *WILM/AE* SK9 .... **203** F5
Parkwood Rd *NTHM/RTH* M23 ... **162** A6
Parliament St *BURY* BL9 .... **33** F6
Parndon Dr *OFTN* SK2 .... **168** A6 ③
Parneet Av *DID/WITH* M20 .... **143** F5
Parnell Av *WYTH/NTH* M22 .... **162** B5
Parnham Cl *BOLS/LL* BL3 .... **49** F4 ⑧
Parrbrook Cl *WHTF* M45 .... **71** E2
Parr Cl *FWTH* BL4 .... **65** F3 ③
Parrenthorn Rd *PWCH* M25 .... **72** A3
Parrfield Rd *WALK* M28 .... **84** B6
Parr Fold *BURY* BL9 .... **71** F1
Parr Fold Av *WALK* M28 .... **83** D4
Parrin La *ECC* M30 .... **101** D4
Parr La *BURY* BL9 .... **71** E2
Parrot St *BOLS/LL* BL3 .... **46** C4
OP/CLY M11 .... **109** D6 ③
Parrs Mount Ms *HTNM* SK4 ..... **165** D3 ③
Parr St *ECC* M30 .... **101** E6
OP/CLY M11 .... **127** F2 ⑩
Parrs Wood Av *DID/WITH* M20 ... **164** A4
Parrs Wood La *DID/WITH* M20 ... **164** B4
Parrs Wood Rd *DID/WITH* M20 ... **163** F5
Parry Md *MPL/ROM* SK6 .... **169** E1
Parslow Av *CHH* M8 .... **90** B5 ③
Parsonage Cl *BURY* BL9 .... **34** B5 ㉑
SALQ/ORD M5 .... **123** D1 ⑦
Parsonage Dr *WALK* M28 .... **83** D3
Parsonage Gdns *MPL/ROM* SK6 ... **187** E3
Parsonage La *CSLFD* M3 .... **2** C2 ③
Parsonage Rd *DID/WITH* M20..... **144** A4
HTNM SK4 .... **165** F1
RAD M26 .... **68** A4 ③

URM M41 ... 136 C2 7
WALK M28 ... 83 D3
Parsonage St BURY BL9 ... 34 B5
  CHH M8 ... 90 A4 8
  HTNM SK4 ... 166 C3
  HULME M15 ... 123 F4
  HYDE SK14 ... 150 B1 10
Parsonage Wk MILN OL16 ... 25 D6 9
Parsons Dr MDTN M24 ... 75 D1
Parsons Fld SLFD M6 ... 104 B2 7
Parson's La BURY BL9 ... 34 A5
Parsons St CHAD OL9 ... 78 A5
Parth St HEY OL10 ... 35 E6
Partington Ct FWTH BL4 ... 66 A2
Partington La SWIN M27 ... 85 F6
Partington Pl BOLS/LL BL3 ... 64 A1 13
  ECC M30 ... 101 E4 1
  FAIL M35 ... 94 A6
  HEY OL10 ... 36 B5 8
  NEWH/MOS M40 ... 108 A2 3
  OLD OL1 ... 79 E4 7
  ROCH OL11 ... 38 C5
  WALK M28 ... 85 D5
Partridge Av NTHM/RTH M23 ... 177 F1
Partridge Cl ROCH OL11 ... 21 D6 4
Partridge Fld DROY M43 ... 111 E4
Partridge Rd FAIL M35 ... 111 F1
Partridge St STRET M32 ... 122 A4 2
Parvet Av DROY M43 ... 110 A4
Pascal St BNG/LEV M19 ... 145 E1
Passmonds Crs WHIT OL12 ... 21 F4 5
Passmonds Wy ROCH OL11 ... 21 F5 6
Pass St CHAD OL9 ... 78 B5
The Pass MILN OL16 ... 23 E5 11
Paston St WYTH/NTH M22 ... 162 B6
Pasture Cl HEY OL10 ... 36 C6
Pasturefield Cl SALE M33 ... 161 D2 8
Pasture Field Rd WYTH/NTH M22 ... 179 D6
Pasturegreen Wy IRL M44 ... 116 C6
Pastures La OLDE OL4 ... 81 F3
Patch Croft Rd WYTH/NTH M22 ... 179 D6
Patchett St WGTN/LGST M12 ... 126 A3 7
Patch La BRAM/HZG SK7 ... 196 B6
Patey St WGTN/LGST M12 ... 126 B5
Patience St WHIT OL12 ... 22 A4 10
Patmos St RAMS BL0 ... 7 E5 7
Paton Av BOLS/LL BL3 ... 47 E6
Paton Ct BRO M7 ... 105 D3 7
Paton St CMANE M1 ... 3 G4 4
  WHIT OL12 ... 22 B2
Patricia Dr WALK M28 ... 83 E5 8
Patten St DID/WITH M20 ... 143 F4 12
Patterdale Av AULW OL7 ... 112 A2 4
  URM M41 ... 118 C5
  ROCH OL11 ... 38 C7 4
Patterdale Cl OLD OL1 ...
  MDTN M24 ... 74 C1 2
Patterdale Dr BURY BL9 ... 52 C2 8
Patterdale Rd AULW OL7 ... 112 A2
  BOLE BL2 ... 29 F3
  MPL/ROM SK6 ... 169 F1
  OFTN SK2 ... 183 F1
  PART M31 ... 154 C2
  WYTH/NTH M22 ... 162 C5
Patterson Av CCHDY M21 ... 141 E2
Pattishall Cl ANC M4 ... 107 E6
Pattison Cl WHIT OL12 ... 22 A2
Patton Cl BURY BL9 ... 71 F1
Paulden Av NTHM/RTH M23 ... 177 F1
  OLDE OL4 ... 80 C2
Paulden Dr FAIL M35 ... 94 B6
Paulette St BOL BL1 ... 27 F5 6
Paulhan Rd DID/WITH M20 ... 164 B1
Paulhan St BOLS/LL BL3 ... 46 C6
Pavilion Cl WHIT OL12 ... 30 B3 7
Pavilion Dr AUL OL6 ... 113 C2
Pavilion Wk RAD M26 ... 51 D5
Paxford Pl WILM/AE SK9 ... 203 E6
Paythorne Gn OFTN SK2 ... 183 F1
Peabody St BOLS/LL BL3 ... 46 C5 13
Peacefield MPL/ROM SK6 ... 186 C3
Peace St BOLS/LL BL3 ... 46 B4
  FAIL M35 ... 94 B4 1
Peaceville Rd BNG/LEV M19 ... 145 D2 3
Peach Bank MDTN M24 ... 75 E3
Peachey Cl OLDTF/WHR M16 ... 124 A6 3
Peach Rd OLDE OL4 ... 80 B2
Peach St PWCH M25 ... 72 A6 8
Peach Tree Cl BRO M7 ... 106 A1 15
Peacock Av CHD/CHDH SK8 ... 183 F2 8
  SLFD M6 ... 103 F2 8
Peacock Cl GTN M18 ... 127 D3
Peacock Gv GTN M18 ... 127 E5
Peak Bank MPL/ROM SK6 ... 169 E3
Peak Cl OLDE OL4 ... 60 D5
Peakdale Av CHD/CHDH SK8 ... 179 E6
  CHH M8 ... 90 C5
Peakdale Rd DROY M43 ... 109 F4
  MPL/ROM SK6 ... 187 E3 1
Peaknaze Cl SWIN M27 ... 86 C5 10

Peak St BOL BL1 ... 27 E5 16
  CHAD OL9 ... 78 A5
  CMANE M1 ... 3 H4
  STKP SK1 ... 167 E4
Pear Av BURY BL9 ... 35 D4
Pear Cl MDTN M24 ... 75 F5
Pearl Av BRO M7 ... 89 F4
Pearl Mill Cl OLDS OL8 ... 96 C1
Pearl St BRAM/HZG SK7 ... 184 C3
  DTN/ASHW M34 ... 129 F6 9
  ROCH OL11 ... 22 A5
Pearly Bank OLD OL1 ... 62 B4
Pearn Rd BNG/LEV M19 ... 145 D6
Pearson Cl MILN OL16 ... 25 D6
  PART M31 ... 155 E2
Pearson Gv OLDE OL4 ... 80 C5 9
Pearson St BURY BL9 ... 34 C4 11
  DUK SK16 ... 131 D3
  RAD M26 ... 24 A5 3
  RDSH SK5 ... 167 D2 4
Peart Av MPL/ROM SK6 ... 150 A5
Pear Tree Dr STLY SK15 ... 114 C5
  SLFD M6 ... 104 B5
Pear Tree Gv MPL/ROM SK6 ... 171 F5
Peary St ANC M4 ... 106 C4
Peaslake Cl MPL/ROM SK6 ... 170 B3
Peatfield Av SWIN M27 ... 85 E3
Pebble Cl STLY SK15 ... 114 B3 11
Pebworth St MDTN M24 ... 75 D6
Peckford Dr NEWH/MOS M40 ... 108 B2 2
Peckforton Cl CHD/CHDH SK8 ... 179 E2 4
Peckmill St WILM/AE SK9 ... 204 C1 2
Pedder St BOL BL1 ... 27 D6
Pedler Brow La WHIT OL12 ... 11 F5
Peebles Dr NEWH/MOS M40 ... 109 E3
Peel Av ALT WA14 ... 174 B5
Peel Brow RAMS BL0 ... 7 E5
Peel Cross Rd SALQ/ORD M5 ... 104 B3 8
Peel Dr LHULT M38 ... 82 A1
  SALE M33 ... 160 C1
Peelgate Dr CHD/CHDH SK8 ... 179 E5 8
Peel Green Rd ECC M30 ... 118 C1
Peel Gv WALK M28 ... 83 F5
  WGTN/LGST M12 ... 126 B5
Peel Hall Rd TOT/BURYW BL8 ... 18 C3
  WYTH/NTH M22 ... 179 D4
Peel La HEY OL10 ... 36 C4
  LHULT M38 ... 82 A1
Peel Moat Rd HTNM SK4 ... 145 F6
Peel Mt RAMS BL0 ... 7 E5
  SLFD M6 ... 104 C4 3
Peel Park Crs LHULT M38 ... 82 A1
Peel Rd HALE/TIMP WA15 ... 174 C4
Peels Av OLDE OL4 ... 81 E4
Peel St AUL OL6 ... 112 C4
  CHAD OL9 ... 77 F4
  DROY M43 ... 128 A1
  DTN/ASHW M34 ... 129 F5 3
  DUK SK16 ... 113 D6
  ECC M30 ... 102 A5
  FAIL M35 ... 109 E1 8
  FWTH BL4 ... 66 C3
  HEY OL10 ... 36 C4
  HYDE SK14 ... 151 D2
  LIT OL15 ... 12 C6
  OFTN SK2 ... 183 D1
  RAD M26 ... 69 F1 3
  STLY SK15 ... 114 A6
  WHIT OL12 ... 22 C5
Peel Vw TOT/BURYW BL8 ... 32 B1
Peel Wk BURY BL9 ... 33 F1
  RAMS BL0 ... 18 C2
  TOT/BURYW BL8 ... 6 A6
  TOT/BURYW BL8 ... 33 F3
Peel Wy BURY BL9 ... 33 F5
Peelwood Av LHULT M38 ... 65 E6
Peers Cl URM M41 ... 117 E5
Peers St TOT/BURYW BL8 ... 33 F3
Pegamoid St BOLE BL2 ... 28 C4
Pegasus Sq BRO M7 ... 105 D4 8
Pegwell Dr BRO M7 ... 105 F2
Pekin St AUL OL6 ... 113 C3
Pelham Pl CHH M8 ... 90 C3
Pelham St AULW OL7 ... 129 F1
  BOLS/LL BL3 ... 46 A6
  OLDS OL8 ... 90 A3
Pellowe Rd OLDS OL8 ... 95 F1 8
Pelton Av SWIN M27 ... 85 E3 8
Pemberton St BOL BL1 ... 27 F3 18
  LHULT M38 ... 65 E6
  ROCH OL11 ... 39 D5
Pemberton Wy ROY/SHW OL2 ... 61 F1 9
Pembridge Fold MDTN M24 ... 76 A3 8
Pembridge Rd BKLY M9 ... 89 D1
Pembroke Av ECC M30 ... 101 E5 9
  SALE M33 ... 160 A3
Pembroke Cl BRUN/LGST M13 ... 125 E3 8
Pembroke Dr BURY BL9 ... 52 C2
  OLDE OL4 ... 62 C5 7
Pembroke Gv IRL M44 ... 134 A5
Pembroke St BOL BL1 ... 46 B1
  BRO M7 ... 105 F1 10
  LIT OL15 ... 12 C5
  OLDS OL8 ... 78 B5 8

SLFD M6 ... 103 F6 6
Pembry Cl RDSH SK5 ... 147 F5
Pembury Cl WYTH/NTH M22 ... 178 A4 1
Penarth Rd BOLS/LL BL3 ... 45 F5 22
  WYTH/NTH M22 ... 162 B5
Pencarrow Cl DID/WITH M20 ... 163 D2
Pencombe Cl WCTN/LGST M12 ... 126 B3 6
Pencroft Wy HULME M15 ... 124 B4
Pendeen Cl WYTH/NTH M22 ... 178 C6
Pendennis Av HOR/BR BL6 ... 44 B4
Pendennis Cl RAD M26 ... 50 A4 3
Pendennis Rd HTNM SK4 ... 166 A2
Pendlebury Cl PWCH M25 ... 88 A3 3
Pendlebury Rd CHD/CHDH SK8 ... 179 E1
  SWIN M27 ... 86 B5
Pendlebury St BOL BL1 ... 28 A4
Pendle Cl OLDE OL4 ... 80 B6
  TOT/BURYW BL8 ... 32 C3
Pendle Ct BOL BL1 ... 27 E4
Pendlecroft Av SWIN M27 ... 87 D6 2
Pendlegreen Cl OP/CLY M11 ... 126 A1
Pendle Gv ROY/SHW OL2 ... 60 A1
Pendle Rd DTN/ASHW M34 ... 149 D1 3
Pendleton Wy SLFD M6 ... 104 A4
Pendleway SWIN M27 ... 86 B4
Pendragon Pl FAIL M35 ... 94 B6
Penelope Rd SLFD M6 ... 103 E2 8
Penerly Dr BKLY M9 ... 107 E1 2
Penfield Cl CMANE M1 ... 124 C2 10
Pengwern Av BOLS/LL BL3 ... 45 F5 23
Penhale Ms BRAM/HZG SK7 ... 197 D2 3
Penistone Av BKLY M9 ... 92 B2 2
  MILN OL16 ... 41 D1
  SLFD M6 ... 103 D4 3
Penketh Av GTN M18 ... 126 C5
Penmere Gv SALE M33 ... 158 C4
Penmoor Cha BRAM/HZG SK7 ... 183 F6
Penmore Cl ROY/SHW OL2 ... 62 A2
Pennant Dr PWCH M25 ... 71 E6
Pennant St OLD OL1 ... 79 F3
Pennell St OP/CLY M11 ... 109 E6 8
Penn Gn CHD/CHDH SK8 ... 181 F6
Penn House Cl BRAM/HZG SK7 ... 196 C2
Pennine Av CHAD OL9 ... 77 E6
Pennine Cl BKLY M9 ... 92 A1
  TOT/BURYW BL8 ... 32 B4
Pennine Ct STLY SK15 ... 115 E4 3
Pennine Dr ALT WA14 ... 173 F2
  AUL OL6 ... 113 F3
  MILN OL16 ... 42 B1
  WHIT OL12 ... 11 D5
Pennine Gv AUL OL6 ... 113 F1
Pennine Rd BRAM/HZG SK7 ... 183 F6
  MPL/ROM SK6 ... 150 A5
Pennine V ROY/SHW OL2 ... 62 A1
Pennine Vw DTN/ASHW M34 ... 129 F4 7
  LIT OL15 ... 15 E4 1
  MOSL OL5 ... 99 E4 11
  ROY/SHW OL2 ... 60 C5
  STLY SK15 ... 115 D2
Pennington Cl BOLS/LL BL3 ... 47 D6
Pennington St CHAD OL9 ... 94 B3 7
  TOT/BURYW BL8 ... 31 F3
  WALK M28 ... 83 E2
  WGTN/LGST M12 ... 145 E1
Penn St FWTH BL4 ... 66 A3 3
  HEY OL10 ... 37 E6 8
  MILN OL16 ... 11 D6
  NEWH/MOS M40 ... 92 A5
  OLDS OL8 ... 78 B6
Penny Bridge La URM M41 ... 137 E1
Penny La RDSH SK5 ... 167 D3
Penny Meadow AUL OL6 ... 112 C4
Pennymoor Dr ALT WA14 ... 173 F1
Penrhos Av CHD/CHDH SK8 ... 179 D3
Penrhyn Av CHD/CHDH SK8 ... 180 C6
  MDTN M24 ... 75 E4
Penrhyn Crs BRAM/HZG SK7 ... 198 A1
Penrhyn Dr BRAM/HZG SK7 ... 184 A6
  PWCH M25 ... 88 C2
Penrhyn Rd EDGY/DAV SK3 ... 165 F5
Penrice Cl RAD M26 ... 50 A6
Penrice Fold WALK M28 ... 82 C6 8
Penrith Av AULW OL7 ... 112 A2
  BOL BL1 ... 26 B6
  OLDS OL8 ... 95 D2
  RDSH SK5 ... 147 D2
  SALE M33 ... 160 A3
  WALK M28 ... 84 A3
  WHTF M45 ... 71 F4
Penrith Cl PART M31 ... 154 C1
Penrith Ct ROCH OL11 ... 40 A2 14
Penrod Pl SLFD M6 ... 104 C3 3
Penrose Gdns MDTN M24 ... 75 D2
Penrose Wk MDTN M24 ... 57 D5
Penroy Av DID/WITH M20 ... 162 B2
Penry Av IRL M44 ... 134 C5
Penryn Av ROY/SHW OL2 ... 61 D5
  SALE M33 ... 160 A4
Pensarn Av RUSH/FAL M14 ... 144 C3
Pensarn Gv RDSH SK5 ... 167 D1 10
Pensby Cl SWIN M27 ... 87 D6
Pensford Ct BOLE BL2 ... 29 F1 1
Pensford Rd NTHM/RTH M23 ... 177 D4
Penshurst Rd RDSH SK5 ... 147 F5

Penthorpe Dr *ROY/SHW* OL2..... 61 D6
Pentland Av *NEWH/MOS* M40 ....93 D3
Pentland Cl *BRAM/HZG* SK7.... 185 F6
Pentlands Av *BRO* M7 .... 105 E1
Pentland Wy *HYDE* SK14 .... 132 C3
Pentwyn Gv *NTHM/RTH* M23 .. 161 F6 🗗

Penwortham St
NEWH/MOS M40 .... 108 A3 🗗
Penzance St *NEWH/MOS* M40 107 F4 🗗
Peover Av *SALE* M33 .... 160 C1 🗗
Peover Rd *ALT* WA14 .... 194 C4
Pepler Av *NTHM/RTH* M23....... 161 F3
Pepperhill Rd *OLDTF/WHR* M16 ... 124 A5
Peppermint Cl *MILN* OL16 .... 43 D3
Pepper Rd *BRAM/HZG* SK7...... 185 F5
Percival Cl *BRO* M7 .... 106 A1 🗗
Percival Rd *DROY* M43............ 110 C6 🗗
Percy Dr *SALQ/ORD* M5........... 122 C2 🗗
Percy Rd *DTN/ASHW* M34 .... 148 C1
Percy St *BOL* BL1................... 28 A5 🗗
  BURY BL9.............................. 34 C4
  FWTH BL4 .... 66 C4 🗗
  HULME M15 .... 123 E3 🗗
  MILN OL16............................. 40 C2
  OLDE OL4.............................. 80 A4
  RAMS BL0 .... 6 C6 🗗
  STKP SK1 .... 167 D3 🗗
  STLY SK15 .... 114 C5 🗗
  WHIT OL12 .... 5 F3
Peregrine Crs *DROY* M43 .... 111 D4
Peregrine Dr *IRL* M44 .... 116 B5 🗗
Peregrine Rd *OFTN* SK2 .... 185 E3
Perivale Dr *OLDS* OL8 .... 96 C1
Pernham St *OLDE* OL4 .... 80 A4
Perrin St *HYDE* SK14 .... 150 B1
Perry Av *HALE/TIMP* WA15 ...... 175 F1
Perrygate Av *DID/WITH* M20 ... 143 E5 🗗
Perry Rd *HALE/TIMP* WA15 ...... 175 F1
Pershore Rd *MDTN* M24 .... 57 E6
Perth Av *CHAD* OL9 .... 94 B1
Perth Cl *BRAM/HZG* SK7......... 196 C4
Perth Rd *ROCH* OL11 .... 40 C5
Perth St *BOLS/LL* BL3 .... 46 A6 🗗
  ROY/SHW OL2......................... 61 E6
  SWIN M27 .... 85 E6 🗗
Peru St *CSLFD* M3................... 105 E5
Peterborough Cl *AUL* OL6....... 112 C1
Peterborough St *BOL* BL1 .... 28 A6 🗗
Peterborough St *GTN* M18 .... 128 A3 🗗
Peterhead Cl *BOL* BL1 .... 27 E6
Peterhouse Gdns *MPL/ROM* SK6 ... 170 A1
Peter Moss Wy *BNG/LEV* M19 .. 146 A2
Petersburg Rd *EDGY/DAV* SK3 ..182 A1
Petersfield Dr *NTHM/RTH* M23 160 B6
Peter St *ALT* WA14.................. 174 B4
  BRAM/HZG SK7 .... 184 B4
  BURY BL9................................ 34 A4
  CMANW M2 .... 2 D5
  DTN/ASHW M34 .... 130 B6
  ECC M30 .... 101 E6
  OLD OL1 .... 79 D5
  STKP SK1 .... 167 E3 🗗
Peterswood Cl *WYTH/NTH* M22 177 F6 🗗
Petheridge Dr *WYTH/NTH* M22 177 F6 🗗
Petrel Av *POY/DIS* SK12 .... 197 E5
Petrel Cl *DROY* M43................ 111 D4 🗗
  EDGY/DAV SK3 .... 182 B1
  ROCH OL11 .... 21 D6
Petrie St *WHIT* OL12 .... 23 D5 🗗
Petrock Wk *NEWH/MOS* M40 .. 109 D1 🗗
Petts Crs *LIT* OL15 .... 12 B5
Petworth Cl *WYTH/NTH* M22 .. 178 C2
Petworth Rd *CHAD* OL9 .... 77 F5
Pevensey Av *SLFD* M6 .... 103 F2
Peveril Cl *WHTF* M45 .... 72 A4
Peveril Dr *BRAM/HZG* SK7 ...... 199 D1
Peveril Rd *ALT* WA14 .... 158 A6
  OLD OL1 .... 80 A2
  SALQ/ORD M5 .... 103 E5
Peveril St *BOLS/LL* BL3 .... 45 F6
Peveril Ter *HYDE* SK14 .... 151 D3
Pewsey Rd *WYTH/NTH* M22 .... 179 D4
Pexwood Rd *CHAD* OL9 .... 76 C2 🗗
Pheasant Cl *CCHDY* M21 .... 142 B4
Pheasant Ri *ALT* WA14............ 174 B6
Phelan Cl *NEWH/MOS* M40 ..... 107 D2
Phethean St *FWTH* BL4 .... 66 A2
Philip Av *DTN/ASHW* M34........ 129 E4
Philip Dr *SALE* M33 .... 159 F3
Philips Av *FWTH* BL4............... 66 B4
Philips Dr *WHTF* M45 .... 70 B5
Philips Park Rd *OP/CLY* M11 .. 107 F5
  WHTF M45.............................. 70 A4
Philip St *BOLS/LL* BL3 .... 46 B4 🗗
  ECC M30 .... 101 E6
  OLDE OL4.............................. 80 A3
  ROCH OL11 .... 40 A2
Phillimore St *OLDE* OL4 .... 80 C6
Phillips Park Rd *WHTF* M45 ..... 71 D5
Phipps St *WALK* M28 .... 83 D1 🗗
Phoebe St *BOLS/LL* BL3 .... 46 A5 🗗
  SALQ/ORD M5 .... 122 B1
Phoenix Cl *HEY* OL10 .... 38 A6
Phoenix St *BOL* BL1 .... 47 E1 🗗
  BURY BL9................................ 33 E5

CMANW M2 .... 3 E3 🗗
FWTH BL4 .... 66 B4
LIT OL15 .... 12 C5
OLD OL1 .... 78 C5
WHIT OL12 .... 22 A4
Phoenix Wy *RAD* M26.............. 69 E1
URM M41 .... 119 F3
Phyllis St *MDTN* M24 .... 76 A4
WHIT OL12 .... 21 F4
Piccadilly *CMANE* M1 .... 167 D4
STKP SK1 .... 167 D4
Pickering Cl *HALE/TIMP* WA15 159 E6
RAD M26 .... 67 E3 🗗
TOT/BURYW BL8 .... 32 C2
URM M41 .... 137 F1 🗗
Pickford Av *BOLS/LL* BL3 .... 50 A6
Pickford La *DUK* SK16............ 131 D1
Pickford's Brow *STKP* SK1 ..... 167 D4 🗗
Pickford St *ANC* M4 .... 3 H2
Pickmere Av *DID/WITH* M20 ... 143 F3
Pickmere Cl *DROY* M43.......... 110 C6 🗗
  EDGY/DAV SK3 .... 182 A1
  SALE M33.............................. 169 F6
Pickmere Gdns *CHD/CHDH* SK8 ... 181 D2 🗗
Pickmere Rd *WILM/AE* SK9.... 198 A4
Pickup St *MILN* OL16 .... 23 E6 🗗
Pickwick Rd *POY/DIS* SK12 ..... 198 B6
Picton Cl *CSLFD* M3................... 2 A1
Picton Dr *WILM/AE* SK9 .... 204 C2
Picton Sq *OLDE* OL4 .... 79 E5 🗗
Picton St *AULW* OL7 .... 112 B1
  CSLFD M3 .... 105 E4
Pierce St *OLD* OL1 .... 80 A2
Piercy Av *BRO* M7................. 105 E3
Piercy St *ANC* M4 .... 107 E6
  FAIL M35................................. 93 F6 🗗
Piethorne Cl *MILN* OL16 .... 43 D3
Pigeon St *CMANE* M1 .... 3 H5
Piggott St *FWTH* BL4 .... 66 A4
Pike Av *FAIL* M35................... 111 D1
Pike Fold La *BKLY* M9 .... 91 D2
Pike Rd *BOLS/LL* BL3 .... 46 B5
Pike St *ROCH* OL11 .... 40 A2 🗗
Pilgrim Dr *OP/CLY* M11 .... 108 A6 🗗
Pilkington Dr *WHTF* M45 .... 71 F1 🗗
Pilkington Rd *BKLY* M9............ 92 B3
  FWTH BL4 .... 67 D5
  RAD M26 .... 51 D4
Pilkington St *BOLS/LL* BL3 ...... 46 C4 🗗
  MDTN M24 .... 75 F2
  RAMS BL0 .... 6 C6 🗗
Pilkington Wy *RAD* M26 .... 69 E1
Pilling St *DTN/ASHW* M34 ...... 130 A6 🗗
  NEWH/MOS M40 .... 108 A2
  TOT/BURYW BL8 .... 33 D4 🗗
  WHIT OL12 .... 22 B5
Pilning St *BOLS/LL* BL3 .... 47 E5
Pilot St *BURY* BL9 .... 34 A6 🗗
Pilsworth Rd *BURY* BL9 .... 53 E3
  HEY OL10............................... 36 C6
Pilsworth Wy *BURY* BL9........... 53 E3
Pimblett St *CSLFD* M3............ 106 A4
Pimhole Rd *BURY* BL9 .... 34 B5
Pimlico *BRO* M7..................... 105 E1 🗗
Pimlott Gv *HYDE* SK14 .... 131 E4
  PWCH M25 .... 87 F3
Pimlott Rd *BOL* BL1................. 28 C4
Pimmcroft Wy *SALE* M33 .... 161 D2
Pine Av *WHTF* M45 .... 71 D4
Pine Cl *DTN/ASHW* M34 .... 129 F3 🗗
  MPL/ROM SK6 .... 186 C5
Pine Gv *DTN/ASHW* M34......... 130 B6
  DUK SK16 .... 132 A1
  ECC M30 .... 83 F3
  FWTH BL4 .... 65 F3 🗗
  PWCH M25 .... 71 E5
  ROY/SHW OL2 .... 60 B3
  RUSH/FAL M14 .... 125 F5
  SALE M33.............................. 138 B5
  SWIN M27 .... 85 E6
  WALK M28 .... 83 F5
Pinehurst Rd *NEWH/MOS* M40 .. 107 F2
Pine Meadow *RAD* M26 .... 68 A5 🗗
Pine Rd *BRAM/HZG* SK7 .... 197 D1
  DUK SK16............................. 131 F1
  POY/DIS SK12 .... 199 D6 🗗
Pine St *AUL* OL6 .... 112 C5 🗗
  BOL BL1 .... 28 A5
  BURY BL9................................ 34 C4
  CHAD OL9 .... 77 E3
  CMANE M1 .... 3 E4
  EDGY/DAV SK3 .... 166 B4
  HEY OL10............................... 37 E5 🗗
  HYDE SK14............................ 131 E4
  LIT OL15 .... 12 C5
  MDTN M24 .... 76 A4
  MILN OL16.............................. 23 F6 🗗
  MILN OL16.............................. 42 C4 🗗
  MPL/ROM SK6 .... 149 F6 🗗
Pinetop Cl *CCHDY* M21 .... 142 B4 🗗
Pine Tree Rd *OLDS* OL8 .... 95 E4
Pinetree St *GTN* M18............. 127 D4 🗗
Pineway *OLDE* OL4.................. 81 D5
Pinewood *ALT* WA14.............. 173 E5
  CHAD OL9 .... 76 C4

SALE M33 .... 158 B1 🗗
Pinewood Cl *BOL* BL1 .... 27 F5 🗗🗗
  DUK SK16.............................. 113 D6 🗗
Pinewood Ct *ALT* WA14 .... 174 C6
  HALE/TIMP WA15 .... 174 C6
  SALE M33.............................. 140 B6
Pinewood Rd *CCHDY* M21 ...... 141 E4 🗗
  WILM/AE SK9 .... 204 C3
The Pinewoods *MPL/ROM* SK6 149 F6 🗗
Pinfold Av *BKLY* M9 .... 92 B3
Pinfold Cl *HALE/TIMP* WA15 ... 190 B2 🗗
Pinfold Dr *CHD/CHDH* SK8 ..... 181 E6 🗗
  PWCH M25 .... 71 D6 🗗
Pinfold La *MANAIR* M90 .... 191 D3
  MPL/ROM SK6 .... 170 B1
  WHTF M45.............................. 70 C3
Pinfold Rd *WALK* M28 .... 83 D4 🗗
Pingate Dr *CHD/CHDH* SK8 .... 195 E3
Pingate La *CHD/CHDH* SK8 .... 195 E3
Pingate La South *CHD/CHDH* SK8 195 E3
Pingot Av *NTHM/RTH* M23 ...... 161 F3
Pingot La *HYDE* SK14 .... 153 F2
The Pingot *IRL* M44............... 116 C6 🗗
Pink Bank La *WGTN/LGST* M12 ... 126 B5
Pin Mill Brow *WGTN/LGST* M12 125 F5
Pinner Pl *BNG/LEV* M19 .... 145 E5
Pinners Cl *RAMS* BL0 .... 7 D4 🗗
Pinnington La *STRET* M32 ...... 140 B2 🗗
Pinnington Rd *GTN* M18 .... 127 D3
Pintail Av *EDGY/DAV* SK3 ...... 182 B1
Pioneer Rd *SWIN* M27 .... 87 E3 🗗
Pioneer St *LIT* OL15 .... 12 C5 🗗
  OP/CLY M11 .... 108 C4
Piperhill Av *WYTH/NTH* M22 ... 162 B4
Pipers Cl *ROCH* OL11 .... 20 B5 🗗
Pipewell Av *GTN* M18 .... 127 D3
Pipit Cl *DTN/ASHW* M34 .... 111 D5 🗗
Pitchcombe Rd *WYTH/NTH* M22 ... 177 F5
Pitfield Gdns *NTHM/RTH* M23 . 161 D6
Pitfield La *BOLE* BL2 .... 30 A4
Pit La *ROY/SHW* OL2................ 61 E6
Pitman Cl *OP/CLY* M11 .... 126 B1 🗗
Pits Farm Av *ROCH* OL11 .... 42 A6
Pitsford Rd *NEWH/MOS* M40 .. 107 F2
Pitshouse La *WHIT* OL12......... 20 C3 🗗
Pitt St East *OLDE* OL4 .... 79 F6
Pixmore Av *BOL* BL1 .... 28 C3
Place Rd *ALT* WA14................. 174 A3 🗗
Plain Pit St *HYDE* SK14 .... 131 D4
Plainsfield Cl *OLDTF/WHR* M16 124 A5
Plane Av *BOL* BL1 .... 110 A2
Plane St *OLDE* OL4................... 79 F4
Plane Tree Cl *MPL/ROM* SK6 . 186 B2
Planetree Rd *HALE/TIMP* WA15 175 E5
Plane Tree Rd *PART* M31 .... 154 B2
Planet Wy *DTN/ASHW* M34 .... 129 F4
Plantation Av *WALK* M28 .... 83 D1 🗗
Plantation St *DUK* SK16 .... 113 E6
  GTN M18............................... 127 F4 🗗
Plant Cl *SALE* M33 .... 139 E6
Plant Hill Rd *BKLY* M9 .... 74 A6
Plant St *CMANE* M1 .... 3 G4 🗗
Plate St *OLD* OL1 .... 79 D4 🗗
Plato St *CHAD* OL9 .... 78 B4
Platt Av *AUL* OL6 .... 113 D1
Plattbrook Cl *RUSH/FAL* M14 . 143 F2 🗗
Platt Cl *MILN* OL16 .... 42 B2
Platt Hill Av *BOLS/LL* BL3 .... 45 E5
Platting La *ROCH* OL11 .... 40 B3
Platt La *RUSH/FAL* M14 .... 143 D2
Platts Dr *IRL* M44 .... 135 E1
Platt St *CHD/CHDH* SK8 .... 180 C1
  DUK SK16.............................. 130 B2
Playfair St *HEY* OL10 .... 56 C2 🗗
Playfair St *EDGW/EG* BL7 .... 28 A1 🗗
  RUSH/FAL M14 .... 124 C5
Pleachway *HTNM* SK4 .... 165 D3
Pleasant Gdns *BOL* BL1 .... 46 C1 🗗
Pleasant Rd *ECC* M30 .... 101 F6
Pleasant St *BKLY* M9 .... 91 E6
  HEY OL10............................... 37 E5
  ROCH OL11 .... 39 D5 🗗
  TOT/BURYW BL8 .... 32 A3 🗗
Pleasant Wy *CHD/CHDH* SK8 . 196 A3
Pleasington Dr *NEWH/MOS* M40 93 D3
  TOT/BURYW BL8 .... 31 F5 🗗
Plodder La *FWTH* BL4.............. 64 B3
Ploughbank Dr *CCHDY* M21 ... 142 B4
Plough Cl *URM* M41 .... 136 A2
Plough St *DUK* SK16............... 131 E1 🗗
Plover Cl *ROCH* OL11 .... 20 C6
Plover Dr *ALT* WA14................ 157 F5 🗗
  BURY BL9................................ 34 C3
  IRL M44................................ 116 B5 🗗
Plowden Av *BOLS/LL* BL3 .... 46 A6 🗗🗗
Plowden Rd *WYTH/NTH* M22 .. 177 F5

Plowley Cl DID/WITH M20 .... 163 F3
Plucksbridge Rd MPL/ROM SK6 .... 187 E4
Plumbley Dr OLDTF/WHR M16 .... 123 D6 ⁶
Plumbley St OP/CLY M11 .... 127 F2 ⁵
Plumley Cl EDGY/DAV SK3 .... 183 D2 ²
Plumley Rd WILM/AE SK9 .... 194 B4 ⁶
Plummer Av CCHDY M21 .... 141 F5
Plumpton Cl AUL OL3 .... 78 C2 ⁶
Plumpton Dr BURY BL9 .... 33 F1
Plumpton Rd ROCH OL11 .... 59 F1
Plumpton Wk BRUN/LGST M13 .. 126 A5 ⁶
Pluto Cl SLFD M6 .... 105 D3 ²
Plymouth Av BRUN/LGST M13 .... 125 F4 ⁷
Plymouth Cl AUL OL6 .... 97 D6 ⁶
Plymouth Dr BRAM/HZG SK7 .... 196 C2 ⁷
   FWTH BL4 .... 65 D3 ⁴
Plymouth Gv BRUN/LGST M13 .... 125 F4
   EDGY/DAV SK3 .... 165 F6 ²
   RAD M26 .... 50 B4
Plymouth Gv West
   BRUN/LGST M13 .... 125 F4
Plymouth Rd SALE M33 .... 138 B6
Plymouth St OLDS OL8 .... 96 A1
Plymouth Vw BRUN/LGST M13.... 125 D3
Plymtree Cl CHH M8 .... 89 F3
Pochard Dr ALT WA14 .... 157 F6
   POY/DIS SK12 .... 197 E5
Pochin St NEWH/MOS M40 .... 107 F4 ¹¹
Pocklington Dr WYTH/NTH M23... 161 D6
Podsmead Rd WYTH/NTH M22 ... 177 F5
Poise Brook Dr OFTN SK2 .... 185 D2 ⁸
Poise Brook Rd OFTN SK2 .... 185 D2
Poise Cl BRAM/HZG SK7 .... 185 E4
Poland St ANC M4 .... 107 D5
   DTN/ASHW M34 .... 129 F1
Poleacre La MPL/ROM SK6 .... 150 A5
Polefield Ap PWCH M25 .... 71 F5
Polefield Cir PWCH M25 .... 71 F5
Polefield Gdns PWCH M25 .... 71 F5 ²
Polefield Gra PWCH M25 .... 71 F5
Polefield Gv PWCH M25 .... 71 F5 ³
Polefield Hall Rd PWCH M25 .... 71 F5
Polefield Rd BKLY M9 .... 91 E3
   PWCH M25 .... 71 F4
Pole La BURY BL9 .... 72 A1
   FAIL M35 .... 94 A5
   WHTF M45 .... 72 B2
Pole St BOLE BL2 .... 28 C6
Polesworth Cl
   WGTN/LGST M12 .... 126 B3 ⁸
Police St ALT WA14 .... 174 B2 ¹
   CMANW M2 .... 2 C3
   ECC M30 .... 101 D5
Pollards La BURY BL9 .... 19 D3 ⁵
Pollard Sq PART M31 .... 155 E2 ¹
Pollard St ANC M4 .... 107 E6
Pollard St East NEWH/MOS M40 . 107 E6
Pollen Cl SALE M33 .... 160 A3
Pollen Cl ALT WA14 .... 174 A1
Polletts Av RDSH SK5 .... 148 A5
Pollitt Av AUL OL6 .... 113 D2
Pollitt Cl WGTN/LGST M12 .... 126 A3 ⁸
Pollitts Cl ECC M30 .... 100 C5 ²
Polonia St OLDS OL8 .... 95 D2 ³
Polperro Cl ROY/SHW OL2 .... 61 E5 ²
Polruan Rd CCHDY M21 .... 141 E1
Polworth Rd BKLY M9 .... 91 F4 ⁵
Polygon Av BRUN/LGST M13 ..... 125 D3
Polygon Rd CHH M8 .... 90 A4
Polygon St BRUN/LGST M13 ..... 125 D3 ⁵
The Polygon BRO M7 .... 105 D1
   ECC M30 .... 102 B4 ⁸
Pomfret St SLFD M6 .... 103 D2 ⁸
Pomona Crs SALQ/ORD M5 .... 122 C2
Pomona Strd HULME M15 .... 123 D3
   TRPK M17 .... 122 B4
Pomona St ROCH OL11 .... 40 C5
Ponds Cl CCHDY M21 .... 141 F2 ⁶
Pondwater Cl LHULT M38 .... 82 A2
Ponsford Av BKLY M9 .... 92 B2 ³
Ponsonby Rd STRET M32 .... 121 E6
Pontefract Cl SWIN M27 .... 86 C6
Pool Bank St MDTN M24 .... 74 A4 ⁸
Poolcroft SALE M33 .... 161 D2
Poole Cl BRAM/HZG SK7 .... 182 B6
Pooley Cl MDTN M24 .... 73 F2
Poolfield Cl RAD M26 .... 50 B6 ⁸
Pool Fold FAIL M35 .... 110 B1 ²
Pool House Rd POY/DIS SK12 .... 200 A4
Pool St BOL BL1 .... 46 C1 ¹²
   OLDS OL8 .... 96 A1
Pool Ter BOL BL1 .... 26 B5 ⁸
Poolton Rd BKLY M9 .... 90 C1
Poorfield St OLDS OL8 .... 78 C6 ¹³
Poplar Av ALT WA14 .... 174 B1
   BNG/LEV M19 .... 145 E4
   BOL BL1 .... 28 A2 ⁷
   BOLE BL2 .... 29 D1
   BURY BL9 .... 34 C4
   OLDE OL4 .... 99 D1
   OLDS OL8 .... 95 E3
   WILM/AE SK9 .... 202 C6
Poplar Cl CHD/CHDH SK8 .... 179 F2 ³
Poplar Dr PWCH M25 .... 88 B3 ⁵
Poplar Gv AUL OL6 .... 113 D2
   GTN M18 .... 127 E5
   IRL M44 .... 134 B5
   OFTN SK2 .... 184 A3
   RAMS BL0 .... 7 E4
   SALE M33 .... 159 F2
   URM M41 .... 138 C1
Poplar Rd BNG/LEV M19 .... 164 B2
   DUK SK16 .... 132 A2
   ECC M30 .... 101 F3
   STRET M32 .... 140 A3
   SWIN M27 .... 85 E6
   WALK M28 .... 83 F5
Poplars Rd STLY SK15 .... 115 E4
The Poplars MOSL OL5 .... 99 F4
Poplar St DTN/ASHW M34 .... 130 A3
   FAIL M35 .... 109 E1
   HTNM SK4 .... 164 C3
   OP/CLY M11 .... 125 F1 ⁴
Poplar Wy MPL/ROM SK6 .... 201 C2
Poplin Dr CSLFD M3 .... 105 F4 ⁸
Poppy Cl MDTN M24 .... 76 B4
   NTHM/RTH M23 .... 160 C4 ⁷
Poppythorn La PWCH M25 .... 71 E6 ⁷
Porchester Dr RAD M26 .... 50 A4 ⁶
Porlock Av DTN/ASHW M34 .... 129 D1
   HYDE SK14 .... 152 A1
Porlock Cl STKP SK1 .... 168 A5
Porlock Rd NTHM/RTH M23 .... 177 F1
   URM M41 .... 137 F3
Porritt Cl ROCH OL11 .... 37 F1
Porritt St BURY BL9 .... 34 B4
Porritt Wy RAMS BL0 .... 7 D4
Portal Gv DTN/ASHW M34 .... 149 F2
Porter St BURY BL9 .... 34 A3 ⁱ¹
   CHAD OL9 .... 78 A6 ⁸
Porthleven Dr NTHM/RTH M23... 176 C1
Portinscale Cl TOT/BURYW BL8... 32 C4
Portland Cl BRAM/HZG SK7 .... 183 F6
Portland Crs BRUN/LGST M13 ... 125 E4
Portland Gv HTNM SK4 .... 165 F1 ⁴
Portland Pl AULW OL7 .... 112 B5 ⁴
Portland Rd ALT WA14 .... 174 A4
   BRUN/LGST M13 .... 126 A6
   ECC M30 .... 102 A4
   STRET M32 .... 121 F5
   SWIN M27 .... 86 B6
   WALK M28 .... 66 A6
Portland St BOL BL1 .... 27 F5
   BURY BL9 .... 34 B3
   CMANE M1 .... 3 E5
Portland St North AUL OL6 .... 112 B4
Portland St South AUL OL6 .... 112 B5 ⁸
   AULW OL7 .... 112 B5
Portloe Rd CHD/CHDH SK8 .... 193 F2
Portman Cl OLDTF/WHR M16 .... 123 F6 ⁸
Portman St MOSL OL5 .... 99 D4
Portrea Cl EDGY/DAV SK3 .... 182 C2
Portree Cl ECC M30 .... 100 C5 ¹⁵
Portrush Rd WYTH/NTH M22 .... 178 C5
Portsmouth Cl BRO M7 .... 105 E2
Portsmouth St BRUN/LGST M13 . 124 C4 ⁸
Port Soderick Av SALQ/ORD M5 . 104 B6 ⁸
Portstone Cl OLDTF/WHR M16 ... 123 F5 ⁶
Port St CMANE M1 .... 3 G3
   OLDS OL8 .... 95 D2 ⁸
   STKP SK1 .... 166 C4 ¹²
Portugal Rd PWCH M25 .... 88 C3 ⁸
Portugal St ANC M4 .... 107 D5 ⁸
   AULW OL7 .... 112 A6 ¹⁰
   BOLE BL2 .... 47 E2
   NEWH/MOS M40 .... 107 D4 ⁴⁸
Portugal St East CMANE M1 ...... 125 D1
Portville Rd BNG/LEV M19 .... 145 E2
Portway WYTH/NTH M22 .... 177 F5
Portwood Pl STKP SK1 .... 167 D3 ¹²
Posnett St EDGY/DAV SK3 .... 166 A5
Postal St CMANE M1 .... 3 G3 ⁷
Postbridge Cl BRUN/LGST M13 . 125 D3
Post Office St ALT WA14 .... 174 B2
Potato Whf CSLFD M3 .... 123 E1
Pot Hl AUL OL6 .... 113 D2
Pot Hill Sq AUL OL6 .... 113 D3 ⁸
Potters La BKLY M9 .... 91 F6
Potter St BURY BL9 .... 34 B4 ¹⁴
   RAD M26 .... 52 B5
Pottery La OP/CLY M11 .... 126 B1
Pottinger St AULW OL7 .... 112 A6
Pott St SWIN M27 .... 86 A3 ¹²
Poulton Av BOLE BL2 .... 48 C2
Poulton St OP/CLY M11 .... 127 F2 ¹⁶
Poundswick La WYTH/NTH M22.. 178 B4
Powell Av HYDE SK14 .... 131 F6
Powell St OLDTF/WHR M16 .... 123 D5
   OP/CLY M11 .... 109 E5
   TOT/BURYW BL8 .... 32 C6
Powicke Dr MPL/ROM SK6 .... 169 D4
Powicke Wk MPL/ROM SK6 ..... 169 D4
Powis Rd URM M41 .... 136 A2 ⁸
Pownall Av BRAM/HZG SK7 ...... 197 D3
Pownall Rd ALT WA14 .... 174 B4
   CHD/CHDH SK8 .... 181 E6
   WILM/AE SK9 .... 203 D5
Pownall St BRAM/HZG SK7 ...... 184 B4 ¹⁴

Poynings Dr WYTH/NTH M22 .... 178 A6 ⁶
Poynter St NEWH/MOS M40 .... 93 D4 ¹
Poynton St BURY BL9 .... 34 B6 ⁶
   HULME M15 .... 124 A3
Praed Rd TRPK M17 .... 121 D4
Preece Cl HYDE SK14 .... 132 B5
Preesall Av CHD/CHDH SK8 ...... 193 F1
Preesall Cl TOT/BURYW BL8 .... 51 D1
Premier Av CHH M8 .... 106 A3 ⁸
Premier St OLDTF/WHR M16 .... 123 E5
Prenton St OP/CLY M11 .... 127 F1
Prenton Wy TOT/BURYW BL8 ..... 32 A2
Presall St BOLE BL2 .... 48 A1 ⁸
Prescot Cl BURY BL9 .... 34 B6 ⁸
Prescot Rd BKLY M9 .... 91 E6 ⁸
   HALE/TIMP WA15 .... 175 D5
Prescott Rd WILM/AE SK9 .... 203 F2
Prescott St BOLS/LL BL3 .... 46 A5 ⁵¹
   MILN OL16 .... 24 A3 ²
   WALK M28 .... 82 C2
Press St OP/CLY M11 .... 127 E2
Prestage St OLDTF/WHR M16 ... 123 E5
   WGTN/LGST M12 .... 145 F1 ⁷
Prestbury Av HALE/TIMP WA15 . 174 C1
   RUSH/FAL M14 .... 143 D2
Prestbury Cl OFTN SK2 .... 184 B3
Prestbury Dr MPL/ROM SK6 ..... 168 C2
   OLD OL1 .... 78 B2
Prestbury Rd BOL BL1 .... 28 B2
   WILM/AE SK9 .... 204 C6
Prestfield Rd WHTF M45 .... 71 E4 ⁸
Presto Gdns BOLS/LL BL3 .... 45 F5 ²⁶
Prestolee Rd BOLS/LL BL3 .... 67 F2
   RAD M26 .... 68 A2
Preston Av ECC M30 .... 102 B4
   IRL M44 .... 135 D4
Preston Cl ECC M30 .... 102 B4 ⁶
Preston Rd BNG/LEV M19 .... 145 E3
Preston St GTN M18 .... 127 D3
   MDTN M24 .... 75 E3
   OLDE OL4 .... 79 E5
   WHIT OL12 .... 22 A4 ¹¹
Presto St BOLS/LL BL3 .... 45 F5
   FWTH BL4 .... 66 C2
Prestwich Cl OFTN SK2 .... 167 F6 ⁷
Prestwich Hills PWCH M25 .... 88 B3
Prestwich Park Rd South
   PWCH M25 .... 88 B2
Prestwood Dr BOL BL1 .... 27 E6 ¹³
Prestwood Rd FWTH BL4 .... 65 E2 ²
   SLFD M6 .... 103 D3
Pretoria Rd BOLE BL2 .... 48 C1 ⁸
   OLDS OL8 .... 95 D2 ⁸
Pretoria St WHIT OL12 .... 22 A4 ¹²
Price St ANC M4 .... 107 E6 ¹⁵
   BURY BL9 .... 34 B6
   DUK SK16 .... 131 D1 ⁸
   FWTH BL4 .... 66 B2
Prichard St STRET M32 .... 140 B1
Prickshaw La WHIT OL12 .... 8 C5
Pridmouth Rd DID/WITH M20 ... 144 A5
Priest Av CHD/CHDH SK8 .... 179 E3
Priestley Rd WALK M28 .... 85 D5
Priestley Wy ROY/SHW OL2 .... 62 B2
Priestnall Rd HTNM SK4 .... 164 C3
Priest St STKP SK1 .... 167 D6
Primley Wk BKLY M9 .... 96 A1
Primrose Av FWTH BL4 .... 65 E2
   HYDE SK14 .... 150 B4
   MPL/ROM SK6 .... 186 C1
   URM M41 .... 138 B1 ⁸
   WALK M28 .... 82 C3 ⁸
Primrose Bank ALT WA14 .... 174 C6
   OLDS OL8 .... 78 C6
   TOT/BURYW BL8 .... 17 F6
   WALK M28 .... 82 C3 ⁸
Primrose Cl BOLE BL2 .... 30 B3 ²
Primrose Crs HYDE SK14 .... 150 B3 ⁸
Primrose Dr BURY BL9 .... 35 E3
   DROY M43 .... 111 D4
Primrose St ANC M4 .... 3 H1 ⁸
   BOL BL1 .... 28 A2 ⁸
   FWTH BL4 .... 66 C4
   OLDS OL8 .... 78 C6
   WHIT OL12 .... 22 B5
Primula St BOL BL1 .... 27 F1
Prince Albert Av BNG/LEV M19 .. 145 E1 ⁸
   OLDE OL4 .... 80 A4 ⁷
Prince George St OLD OL1 .... 80 A2
Prince Rd POY/DIS SK12 .... 200 A4
Prince's Av BOLS/LL BL3 .... 49 E5
   DID/WITH M20 .... 164 A1
   IRL M44 .... 117 D6
   MPL/ROM SK6 .... 169 E2 ⁸
Prince's Br CSLFD M3 .... 123 E1 ⁸
Prince's Dr MPL/ROM SK6 .... 170 B6
   SALE M33 .... 160 B2
Princes Rd ALT WA14 .... 174 B1
   HTNM SK4 .... 165 E1
   MPL/ROM SK6 .... 169 E2
   SALE M33 .... 160 A2

Princess Av CHD/CHDH SK8 ..... **181** E4
DTN/ASHW M34 ..... **129** F6 🔟
FWTH BL4 ..... **67** D6
PWCH M25 ..... **89** D3
WHIT OL12 ..... **24** A1 🔟
Princess Cl DUK SK16 ..... **131** E1
HEY OL10 ..... **37** E6 🔟
MOSL OL5 ..... **99** F5
Princess Dr MDTN M24 ..... **74** C3
Princess Gv FWTH BL4 ..... **66** B3 🔟
Princess Pkwy WYTH/NTH M22 ..... **162** A6
Princess Rd CHAD OL9 ..... **93** F2
DID/WITH M20 ..... **162** B2
HULME M15 ..... **124** A3
MILN OL16 ..... **26** B6
PWCH M25 ..... **89** D1 🔟
ROY/SHW OL2 ..... **61** E3
RUSH/FAL M14 ..... **143** D3
URM M41 ..... **137** F1
WILM/AE SK9 ..... **203** D6
Princess St ALT WA14 ..... **158** A5
AUL OL6 ..... **113** E3
BOL BL1 ..... **47** D2
CMANE M1 ..... **3** E5
ECC M30 ..... **101** D5 🔟
FAIL M35 ..... **93** F6 🔟
HYDE SK14 ..... **150** C1 🔟
NEWH/MOS M40 ..... **107** F3 🔟
OLDE OL4 ..... **80** C5
OP/CLY M11 ..... **108** B5
RAD M26 ..... **50** C6 🔟
SLFD M6 ..... **104** B3 🔟
SWIN M27 ..... **86** B6
WHIT OL12 ..... **23** D4
Prince's La STKP SK1 ..... **166** C4
Prince St BCUP OL13 ..... **5** E2
BOL BL1 ..... **46** C1
HEY OL10 ..... **37** E5
MILN OL16 ..... **40** B2
OLD OL1 ..... **79** E4 🔟
RAMS BL0 ..... **7** D5
Princethorpe Cl HOR/BR BL6 ..... **44** B3 🔟
Prinknash Rd WYTH/NTH M22 ..... **178** A6
Printers La BOLE BL2 ..... **29** D5
Printer St OLD OL1 ..... **79** D5 🔟
OP/CLY M11 ..... **127** E1 🔟
Printon Av BKLY M9 ..... **90** C2
Printworks La BNG/LEV M19 ..... **146** A2
Printworks Rd STLY SK15 ..... **114** C4
Prior St OLDS OL8 ..... **96** C1
Priory Av BRO M7 ..... **105** D2 🔟
CCHDY M21 ..... **141** F3 🔟
Priory Cl DUK SK16 ..... **131** E3
OLDS OL8 ..... **95** E2
SALE M33 ..... **140** B5
Priory Ct RDSH SK5 ..... **146** C3 🔟
Priory Gv BRO M7 ..... **105** D1
CHAD OL9 ..... **94** B1 🔟
Priory La RDSH SK5 ..... **146** C3
Priory Pl BOLE BL2 ..... **29** D5
Priory Rd CHD/CHDH SK8 ..... **181** C2
SALE M33 ..... **140** B6
SWIN M27 ..... **85** F4
WILM/AE SK9 ..... **202** C3
Priory St ALT WA14 ..... **188** A1
The Priory BRO M7 ..... **105** D1
Pritchard St CMANE M1 ..... **3** F6 🔟
Privet St OLDE OL4 ..... **80** B2
Proctor Wy ECC M30 ..... **109** E4 🔟
Progress Av DTN/ASHW M34 ..... **130** A3
Progress St AUL OL6 ..... **112** B4
BOL BL1 ..... **28** A6 🔟
ROCH OL11 ..... **39** D6 🔟
Promenade St HEY OL10 ..... **37** F5 🔟
Propps Hall Dr FAIL M35 ..... **109** E1
Prospect Av FWTH BL4 ..... **66** D4 🔟
IRL M44 ..... **134** C5
Prospect Ct TOT/BURYW BL8 ..... **18** A6 🔟
Prospect Dr FAIL M35 ..... **110** A2
HALE/TIMP WA15 ..... **190** B2
Prospect Hl BOLE BL2 ..... **30** A3
Prospect Pl AUL OL6 ..... **113** E2
FWTH BL4 ..... **66** A4 🔟
HEY OL10 ..... **37** E4 🔟
Prospect Rd AUL OL6 ..... **113** F2
CHAD OL9 ..... **78** A4
DUK SK16 ..... **113** E6
IRL M44 ..... **134** C5
Prospect St BOL BL1 ..... **28** A6 🔟
HEY OL10 ..... **56** C1
LIT OL15 ..... **12** C5 🔟
ROCH OL11 ..... **39** F3 🔟
Prospect V CHD/CHDH SK8 ..... **179** F6
Prospect Vw SWIN M27 ..... **86** B6 🔟
Prout St WGTN/LGST M12 ..... **126** B6
Providence St ANC M4 ..... **107** E6 🔟
AUL OL6 ..... **113** E3 🔟
DTN/ASHW M34 ..... **130** A2 🔟
Provident Av BNG/LEV M19 ..... **146** A2 🔟
Provident St ROY/SHW OL2 ..... **61** F2 🔟
Provident Wy HALE/TIMP WA15 ..... **159** E6
Provis Rd CCHDY M21 ..... **141** F4
Prubella Av DTN/ASHW M34 ..... **129** F4
Pryce St BOL BL1 ..... **27** F3
Pryme St HULME M15 ..... **123** F2 🔟

Pudding La HYDE SK14 ..... **133** D6
Puffin Av POY/DIS SK12 ..... **197** E6
Pulborough Cl TOT/BURYW BL8 ..... **18** C6 🔟
Pulford Av CCHDY M21 ..... **162** B1 🔟
Pulford Rd SALE M33 ..... **160** A3
Pullman Cl BNG/LEV M19 ..... **145** F3
Pullman Dr URM M41 ..... **120** A6 🔟
Pullman St ROCH OL11 ..... **40** A2
Punch St BOLS/LL BL3 ..... **46** B3 🔟
Purbeck Cl WYTH/NTH M22 ..... **178** A6 🔟
Purbeck Dr TOT/BURYW BL8 ..... **33** D1
Purcell Cl BOL BL1 ..... **27** E6 🔟
Purcell St WGTN/LGST M12 ..... **126** B6 🔟
Purdon St BURY BL9 ..... **34** A1 🔟
Purley Av NTHM/RTH M23 ..... **161** F4
Purley Dr IRL M44 ..... **134** A6
Purslow Cl WGTN/LGST M12 ..... **107** F6
Putney St OLD OL1 ..... **78** C2
Pygmate Cl CHD/CHDH SK8 ..... **179** E5
Pygmate La CHD/CHDH SK8 ..... **179** E5
Pym St ECC M30 ..... **101** E5 🔟
HEY OL10 ..... **37** E6
NEWH/MOS M40 ..... **92** A5 🔟
Pyramid Ct BRO M7 ..... **105** E1 🔟
Pyrus Cl ECC M30 ..... **118** A1 🔟
Pytha Fold Rd DID/WITH M20 ..... **144** B6

Q

The Quadrant BKLY M9 ..... **92** B2
DROY M43 ..... **110** A6
MPL/ROM SK6 ..... **169** E3
STKP SK1 ..... **167** F4
Quail Dr IRL M44 ..... **116** B3
Quail St OLDE OL4 ..... **80** A6
Quakers Fld TOT/BURYW BL8 ..... **18** A5
Quantock Cl HTNM SK4 ..... **166** C3
Quarlton Dr TOT/BURYW BL8 ..... **16** C3
Quarmby Rd GTN M18 ..... **128** A3 🔟
Quarry Bank Rd WILM/AE SK9 ..... **193** D6
Quarry Clough STLY SK15 ..... **133** E1
Quarry Pond Rd WALK M28 ..... **82** A2
Quarry Ri MPL/ROM SK6 ..... **169** F2
STLY SK15 ..... **132** A1
Quarry Rd FWTH BL4 ..... **67** E4
MPL/ROM SK6 ..... **169** F2
Quarry St MPL/ROM SK6 ..... **149** F6 🔟
RAD M26 ..... **51** F6
RAMS BL0 ..... **7** E5 🔟
STLY SK15 ..... **114** A6
WHIT OL12 ..... **5** F4
WHIT OL12 ..... **22** C4
The Quays SALQ/ORD M5 ..... **122** A2
Quay St CSLFD M3 ..... **2** B2
HEY OL10 ..... **37** F6 🔟
Quay Vw SALQ/ORD M5 ..... **122** B1 🔟
Quebec Pl BOLS/LL BL3 ..... **46** A3
Quebec St BOLS/LL BL3 ..... **46** B4
CHAD OL9 ..... **78** A3
DTN/ASHW M34 ..... **129** F4
Queen Ann Dr WALK M28 ..... **82** B6
Queenhill Dr HYDE SK14 ..... **132** A4
Queenhill Rd WYTH/NTH M22 ..... **162** B6
Queen's Av EDGW/EG BL7 ..... **14** B6
MPL/ROM SK6 ..... **169** E2
WHIT OL12 ..... **24** A1
Queensbrook BOL BL1 ..... **46** C2
Queensbury Cl BOL BL1 ..... **27** E4 🔟
Queens Cl HTNM SK4 ..... **150** C4 🔟
WALK M28 ..... **82** A6
Queens Dr CHD/CHDH SK8 ..... **181** E4
HTNM SK4 ..... **165** E3
HYDE SK14 ..... **151** D4
PWCH M25 ..... **89** D3
ROCH OL11 ..... **39** F4
Queens Gdns NEWH/MOS M40 ..... **107** E2
Queens Gv CHD/CHDH SK8 ..... **181** E4
HTNM SK4 ..... **165** E3
HYDE SK14 ..... **151** D4
PWCH M25 ..... **89** D3
ROCH OL11 ..... **39** F4
Queensgate BOL BL1 ..... **45** F1
Queensgate Dr ROY/SHW OL2 ..... **60** A3
Queensland Rd GTN M18 ..... **126** C4
Queen's Park Rd HEY OL10 ..... **37** E4
Queens Rd AUL OL6 ..... **113** E2
BOLS/LL BL3 ..... **45** E5
BRAM/HZG SK7 ..... **184** C4
CHAD OL9 ..... **77** E4
CHD/CHDH SK8 ..... **181** D3
CHD/CHDH SK8 ..... **181** D4
CHH M8 ..... **106** C2
HALE/TIMP WA15 ..... **174** C4
LIT OL15 ..... **12** C6
MPL/ROM SK6 ..... **169** E2
NEWH/MOS M40 ..... **107** F3
OLDS OL8 ..... **79** E6
SALE M33 ..... **159** D1
URM M41 ..... **138** B2
WILM/AE SK9 ..... **203** E5
Queenston Rd DID/WITH M20 ..... **163** D1
Queen St AUL OL6 ..... **113** E4

BOL BL1 ..... **46** C2 🔟
BURY BL9 ..... **34** B5
CHD/CHDH SK8 ..... **180** C1
CMANW M2 ..... **2** C4
CSLFD M3 ..... **2** B1
DTN/ASHW M34 ..... **129** F5 🔟
DTN/ASHW M34 ..... **129** F5 🔟
DUK SK16 ..... **112** C6
ECC M30 ..... **102** A6 🔟
FAIL M35 ..... **93** F6
FWTH BL4 ..... **66** B3
HEY OL10 ..... **37** E5
HYDE SK14 ..... **150** C2
LHULT M38 ..... **82** C2
LIT OL15 ..... **12** C6
MDTN M24 ..... **76** A3
MOSL OL5 ..... **99** D4
MPL/ROM SK6 ..... **187** D1 🔟
OLD OL1 ..... **79** D4
OLDE OL4 ..... **81** D5 🔟
RAD M26 ..... **70** A1
RAMS BL0 ..... **6** C5 🔟
ROY/SHW OL2 ..... **60** B5
ROY/SHW OL2 ..... **61** F5
SLFD M6 ..... **103** E2
STKP SK1 ..... **167** E3 🔟
STLY SK15 ..... **114** B5 🔟
TOT/BURYW BL8 ..... **32** B2 🔟
WHIT OL12 ..... **23** D5 🔟
Queen St West DID/WITH M20 ..... **143** F4 🔟
Queens Vw LIT OL15 ..... **25** E2 🔟
Queensway BNG/LEV M19 ..... **164** B3
CHD/CHDH SK8 ..... **194** A1
DUK SK16 ..... **132** A2
FWTH BL4 ..... **67** D5
IRL M44 ..... **135** D1
MOSL OL5 ..... **99** E6
POY/DIS SK12 ..... **198** B6
ROCH OL11 ..... **39** E4
SWIN M27 ..... **86** B3
URM M41 ..... **119** F5
WALK M28 ..... **82** C5
Queen Victoria St ECC M30 ..... **101** D5 🔟
ROCH OL11 ..... **40** B4
Quenby St HULME M15 ..... **123** E3 🔟
Quendon Av BRO M7 ..... **105** E3 🔟
Quick Edge La OLDE OL4 ..... **98** C1
Quickedge Rd MOSL OL5 ..... **99** D3
Quick Rd OLDE OL4 ..... **99** D1
Quick Vw MOSL OL5 ..... **99** F2
Quilter Gv BKLY M9 ..... **99** F2
Quinney Crs OLDTF/WHR M16 ..... **124** A6
Quinn St OP/CLY M11 ..... **108** B6
Quixall St OP/CLY M11 ..... **108** B5

R

Raby St OLDTF/WHR M16 ..... **123** F5
RUSH/FAL M14 ..... **124** A5
Racecourse Pk WILM/AE SK9 ..... **203** D5 🔟
Racecourse Rd WILM/AE SK9 ..... **202** C5
Racefield Rd ALT WA14 ..... **174** A3
The Race WILM/AE SK9 ..... **204** B1
Rachel St WGTN/LGST M12 ..... **125** D1 🔟
Rackhouse Rd NTHM/RTH M23 ..... **161** F4
Radbourne Cl
WGTN/LGST M12 ..... **126** B3 🔟
Radcliffe Moor Rd BOLS/LL BL3 ..... **49** E4
Radcliffe New Rd WHTF M45 ..... **70** A1
Radcliffe Park Crs SLFD M6 ..... **103** D2 🔟
Radcliffe Park Rd SLFD M6 ..... **102** C2
Radcliffe Rd BOLE BL2 ..... **47** F2 🔟
BOLS/LL BL3 ..... **49** E5
BURY BL9 ..... **52** B2
OLDE OL4 ..... **80** B1
Radcliffe St OLD OL1 ..... **79** D3
OLDE OL4 ..... **81** E5 🔟
ROY/SHW OL2 ..... **60** C5
Radclyffe St CHAD OL9 ..... **77** F3
MDTN M24 ..... **75** E1
Radclyffe Ter MDTN M24 ..... **75** E1 🔟
Radnor Av DTN/ASHW M34 ..... **128** C6
Radnor Dr BKLY M9 ..... **91** F5 🔟
IRL M44 ..... **116** B6
Radford St BRO M7 ..... **89** D5
Radium St ANC M4 ..... **3** H1
Radlet Dr HALE/TIMP WA15 ..... **159** E5
Radley Cl BOL BL1 ..... **26** B6 🔟
SALE M33 ..... **158** B2 🔟
Radley St DROY M43 ..... **127** F1
Radnor Av SWIN M27 ..... **86** C3
WHTF M45 ..... **71** F4
Radan Cl RUSH/FAL M14 ..... **143** F2 🔟
Radstock Cl RUSH/FAL M14 ..... **143** F2 🔟
Radstock Rd STRET M32 ..... **140** A1
Raeburn Dr MPL/ROM SK6 ..... **171** F5 🔟
Rae St EDGY/DAV SK3 ..... **166** A5
Raglan Av SWIN M27 ..... **86** C3
WHTF M45 ..... **71** F4

Raglan Dr *ALT* WA14 .... 158 C5 4
Raglan Rd *SALE* M33 .... 159 D2
  STRET M32 .... 120 C6
Raglan St *BOL* BL1 .... 27 E5
  HYDE SK14 .... 150 A1
  ROCH OL11 .... 39 D6
Ragley Cl *POY/DIS* SK12 .... 199 D5 4
Raikes La *BOLS/LL* BL3 .... 47 F5
Raikes Rd *BOLS/LL* BL3 .... 48 B4
Raikes Wy *BOLS/LL* BL3 .... 48 B4
Railgate *BCUP* OL13 .... 5 D1
Railton Av *OLDTF/WHR* M16 .... 123 E6
Railton Ter *BKLY* M9 .... 92 A6 8
Railway Ap *ROCH* OL11 .... 39 D5 11
Railway Brow *ROCH* OL11 .... 39 D5 12
Railway Rd *CHAD* OL9 .... 78 B5
  CHAD OL9 .... 94 B3
  EDGY/DAV SK3 .... 166 C5
  STRET M32 .... 122 A4
  URM M41 .... 138 B1
Railway St *ALT* WA14 .... 174 B3
  DUK SK16 .... 112 C6
  DUK SK16 .... 130 C1
  FWTH BL4 .... 66 C2 7
  GTN M18 .... 127 D3
  HEY OL10 .... 37 F6
  HTNM SK4 .... 166 C3 8
  LIT OL15 .... 12 C6
  MILN OL16 .... 40 B1
  MILN OL16 .... 42 C3
  MILN OL16 .... 43 D3 11
  RAD M26 .... 69 E1
  RAMS BL0 .... 7 D5
  TOT/BURYW BL8 .... 18 C3
Railway Vw *OLDE* OL4 .... 81 D5 8
  ROY/SHW OL2 .... 43 D6 8
Raimond St *BOL* BL1 .... 27 D4
Rainbow Cl *CCHDY* M21 .... 141 F4 6
Raincliff Av *BRUN/LGST* M13 .... 145 D1
Raines Crest *MILN* OL16 .... 42 B1
Rainford Av *DID/WITH* M20 .... 143 E3
  HALE/TIMP WA15 .... 175 E2
Rainford St *BOLE* BL2 .... 29 D1
Rainforth St *BRUN/LGST* M13 .... 126 A6 3
Rainham Dr *BOL* BL1 .... 27 F6 11
  CHH M8 .... 90 B6
Rainham Wy *CHAD* OL9 .... 77 F5 5
  RDSH SK5 .... 147 F5
Rainow Av *DROY* M43 .... 127 F1 8
Rainow Rd *EDGY/DAV* SK3 .... 182 A3 7
Rainshaw St *BOL* BL1 .... 28 A3
  OLDE OL4 .... 80 B3 6
  ROY/SHW OL2 .... 60 B5 6
Rainsough Av *PWCH* M25 .... 88 A4
Rainsough Brow *PWCH* M25 .... 88 A4
Rainsough Cl *PWCH* M25 .... 88 A4
Rainwood *CHAD* OL9 .... 76 C3 8
Raja Cl *CHH* M8 .... 90 C6
Rake *ROCH* OL11 .... 20 B6
Rake Av *SWIN* M27 .... 86 A2
Rake St *BURY* BL9 .... 34 A3
Rake Ter *LIT* OL15 .... 13 D5
Rakewood Dr *OLE* OL4 .... 62 C5
Rakewood Rd *LIT* OL15 .... 25 F2
Raleigh Cl *DID/WITH* M20 .... 143 E6
  OLD OL1 .... 79 D3
Raleigh Gdns *LIT* OL15 .... 13 D2 4
Raleigh Rd *RDSH* SK5 .... 166 C1 8
  STRET M32 .... 140 B1
Ralli Cts *CSLFD* M3 .... 2 A3 11
Ralph Av *HYDE* SK14 .... 150 C4
Ralph Green St *CHAD* OL9 .... 94 C2
Ralphs La *DUK* SK16 .... 131 D2
Ralph St *BOL* BL1 .... 27 E5
  OP/CLY M11 .... 109 E6 8
  WHIT OL12 .... 23 E4
Ralston Cl *BRO* M7 .... 90 A5 7
Ralstone Av *OLD* OL8 .... 96 A1
Ramillies Av *CHD/CHDH* SK8 .... 181 D5
Ramp Rd East *MANAIR* M90 .... 192 A2
Ramp Rd South *MANAIR* M90 .... 191 D2
Ramp Rd West *MANAIR* M90 .... 191 F2
Ramsay Av *FWTH* BL4 .... 65 F4
Ramsay Pl *MILN* OL16 .... 23 E5 12
Ramsay St *BOL* BL1 .... 27 F3 19
  MILN OL16 .... 23 E5
Ramsay Ter *MILN* OL16 .... 23 E5 13
Rambottom La *RAMS* BL0 .... 7 D4
Ramsbottom Rd *BOLE* BL2 .... 16 A3
  TOT/BURYW BL8 .... 16 A5
Ramsbury Dr *NEWH/MOS* M40 .... 93 E3 10
Ramsdale Rd *BRAM/HZG* SK7 .... 196 C1
Ramsdale St *CHAD* OL9 .... 77 F4
Ramsden Cl *OLD* OL1 .... 78 C4 8
Ramsden Crs *OLD* OL1 .... 78 C4 8
Ramsden Rd *WHIT* OL12 .... 11 D4
Ramsden St *AUL* OL6 .... 112 C3 4
  BOLS/LL BL3 .... 48 B4 3
  OLD OL1 .... 78 C4
Ramsey Av *BNG/LEV* M19 .... 146 B2
Ramsey Gv *TOT/BURYW* BL8 .... 32 C5
Ramsey St *CHAD* OL9 .... 77 F6
  NEWH/MOS M40 .... 92 C6
  OLD OL1 .... 79 F3
Ramsgate Rd *NEWH/MOS* M40 .... 109 D3

RDSH SK5 .... 147 D4
Ramsgate St *BRO* M7 .... 105 F2
Ramsgill Cl *NTHM/RTH* M23 .... 160 C3
Ramsgreave Cl *BURY* BL9 .... 52 B2 3
Ram St *LHULT* M38 .... 82 A1 2
Ramwells Brow *EDGW/EG* BL7 .... 14 A5
Ranbys Av *BKLY* M9 .... 92 A1
Randale Dr *BURY* BL9 .... 71 E1
Randal St *BOLS/LL* BL3 .... 46 A5
Randerson St
  WGTN/LGST M12 .... 125 D2 12
Randlesham St *PWCH* M25 .... 89 D1 10
Randolph Pl *EDGY/DAV* SK3 .... 166 C6
Randolph Rd *FWTH* BL4 .... 67 D4
Randolph St *BNG/LEV* M19 .... 145 E1
  BOLS/LL BL3 .... 46 B3 14
  OLDS OL8 .... 95 D3 8
Rand St *OLD* OL1 .... 80 B2 7
Ranelagh Rd *SWIN* M27 .... 87 D6
Ranelagh St *OP/CLY* M11 .... 108 C5 10
Raneley Gv *ROCH* OL11 .... 40 B5
Ranford Rd *BNG/LEV* M19 .... 145 E3
Range Dr *MPL/ROM* SK6 .... 150 A5
Rangemore Av *WYTH/NTH* M22 .... 162 B5 8
Range Rd *DUK* SK16 .... 132 C3
  EDGY/DAV SK3 .... 182 A5
  OLDTF/WHR M16 .... 123 F6
  STLY SK15 .... 132 C1
Range St *BOLS/LL* BL3 .... 46 B5
  OP/CLY M11 .... 127 D1
Rankine Ter *BOLS/LL* BL3 .... 46 B3 10
Rannoch Rd *BOLE* BL2 .... 49 D2
Ransfield Rd *CCHDY* M21 .... 141 E1
Ranworth Av *HTNM* SK4 .... 165 D3
Ranworth Cl *BOL* BL1 .... 28 B1
Raper St *OLDE* OL4 .... 80 A3
Raphael St *BOL* BL1 .... 27 E5
Rappax Rd *HALE/TIMP* WA15 .... 189 E1
Rasbottom St *BOLS/LL* BL3 .... 46 C4 16
Raspberry La *IRL* M44 .... 116 A5
Rassbottom Brow *STLY* SK15 .... 114 A5 7
Rassbottom St *STLY* SK15 .... 114 A5
Ratcliffe Av *IRL* M44 .... 135 E1
Ratcliffe St *BNG/LEV* M19 .... 145 E2
  STKP SK1 .... 167 D5 14
Rathan Rd *URM* M41 .... 119 D5
Rathbone St *MILN* OL16 .... 24 A6
Rathbourne Av *BKLY* M9 .... 91 E2
Rathen Rd *DID/WITH* M20 .... 143 F6
Rathmel Rd *NTHM/RTH* M23 .... 161 D3
Rathmore Av *NEWH/MOS* M40 .... 107 F2 8
Rathvale Dr *WYTH/NTH* M22 .... 192 A1 8
Rattenbury Ct *SLFD* M6 .... 103 D2 7
Raveden Cl *BOL* BL1 .... 27 D4
Raveley Av *RUSH/FAL* M14 .... 144 B3 9
Ravelston Dr *BKLY* M9 .... 107 E1
Raven Av *CHAD* OL9 .... 77 F6
Raven Cl *DROY* M43 .... 111 D4 8
Ravendale Cl *WHIT* OL12 .... 21 E4 7
Raven Dr *IRL* M44 .... 116 B6
Ravenhead Cl *RUSH/FAL* M14 .... 144 B3 8
Ravenhead Sq *STLY* SK15 .... 115 F2
Ravenhurst Dr *BOL* BL1 .... 44 B4
Ravenna Av *NTHM/RTH* M23 .... 160 B6 2
Ravennak Av *BNG/LEV* M19 .... 145 F3
Ravennak Dr *FAIL* M35 .... 94 B5
Ravennak Park Rd
  CHD/CHDH SK8 .... 195 F1
Ravennak Rd *CHD/CHDH* SK8 .... 182 A6 8
  EDGY/DAV SK3 .... 183 E3
Raven Rd *BOLS/LL* BL3 .... 45 E5 13
  HALE/TIMP WA15 .... 159 F4
Ravennak St *OP/CLY* M11 .... 108 C5
Ravenscar Crs *WYTH/NTH* M22 .... 192 B1
Ravens Cl *PWCH* M25 .... 89 F3
Ravenscraig Rd *LHULT* M38 .... 65 F5
Ravensdale Gdns *ECC* M30 .... 101 F4 8
Ravensdale Rd *RUSH/FAL* M14 .... 125 D6
Ravens Holme *BOL* BL1 .... 44 C2
Ravenside Pk *CHAD* OL9 .... 77 E6
Ravenstonedale Dr *ROY/SHW* OL2 .... 60 C4
Ravenstone Dr *SALE* M33 .... 140 C6
Raven St *BURY* BL9 .... 34 A3
  ROCH OL11 .... 20 B4
  WGTN/LGST M12 .... 125 D1
Ravensway *PWCH* M25 .... 89 E3
Ravens Wd *BOL* BL1 .... 44 C2
Ravenswood Av *HTNM* SK4 .... 165 E4 8
Ravenswood Dr *BKLY* M9 .... 91 F2 8
  BOL BL1 .... 44 C2
  CHD/CHDH SK8 .... 195 F1 8
Ravenswood Rd *STRET* M32 .... 122 A4
  WILM/AE SK9 .... 198 C4
Ravenwood *CHAD* OL9 .... 76 B4
Ravenwood Dr *DTN/ASHW* M34 .... 129 F3
  HALE/TIMP WA15 .... 190 B2
Ravine Av *BKLY* M9 .... 91 F6
Rawcliffe Av *BOLE* BL2 .... 49 D2
Rawcliffe St *RUSH/FAL* M14 .... 124 C6 13
Rawdon Cl *BNG/LEV* M19 .... 145 F2 8
Rawkin Cl *HULME* M15 .... 123 F4 8
Rawlyn Rd *BOL* BL1 .... 26 A6
Rawpool Gdns *NTHM/RTH* M23 .... 161 E6

Rawson Av *FWTH* BL4 .... 66 C2 8
Rawson Rd *BOL* BL1 .... 27 D6
Rawsons Rake *TOT/BURYW* BL8 .... 6 B5
Rawson St *FWTH* BL4 .... 66 A2
Rawsthorne St *BOL* BL1 .... 27 F5 28
Rawstron St *WHIT* OL12 .... 9 D2
Rayburn Wy *CHH* M8 .... 106 B2
Raycroft Av *BKLY* M9 .... 92 B3
Raydon Av *NEWH/MOS* M40 .... 107 E2 13
Rayleigh Av *OP/CLY* M11 .... 128 A2 7
Raymond Av *BURY* BL9 .... 34 A2
  CHAD OL9 .... 94 C1
Raymond Rd *NTHM/RTH* M23 .... 161 F3
Raymond St *SWIN* M27 .... 86 A4 8
Rayner La *AULW* OL7 .... 111 E5
Rayners Cl *STLY* SK15 .... 114 A6
Rayner St *STKP* SK1. .... 167 F5
Raynham Av *DID/WITH* M20 .... 163 F2
Raynham St *AUL* OL6 .... 113 D4 17
Rayson Hill Dr *BKLY* M9 .... 91 D3 8
Rayson St *BKLY* M9 .... 91 D3
Reabrook Av *WGTN/LGST* M12 .... 126 A3
The Reach WALK M28 .... 83 F3
Read Cl *BURY* BL9 .... 52 B2 8
Reade Av *URM* M41 .... 136 C2
Reading Cl *OP/CLY* M11 .... 127 D1
Reading Dr *SALE* M33 .... 158 B1
Reading St *SLFD* M6 .... 104 C2
Read St *HYDE* SK14 .... 131 D6
Read St West *HYDE* SK14 .... 131 D6
Reather Wk *NEWH/MOS* M40 .... 107 D4 12
Rebecca St *CHH* M8 .... 90 B5 8
Recreation Rd *FAIL* M35 .... 94 B4
Recreation St *BOLE* BL2 .... 29 F2 8
  BOLS/LL BL3 .... 46 C5 10
  PWCH M25 .... 89 D1 11
Rectory Av *CHH* M8 .... 90 B4 8
  PWCH M25 .... 88 C1
Rectory Cl *DTN/ASHW* M34 .... 149 E1 8
  RAD M26 .... 52 B5 8
Rectory Flds *STKP* SK1. .... 167 E4
Rectory Gdns *PWCH* M25 .... 88 C1
Rectory Gn *PWCH* M25 .... 88 B1
  STKP SK1 .... 167 E4 7
Rectory Gv *PWCH* M25 .... 88 C2
Rectory La *BURY* BL9 .... 35 E3
  PWCH M25 .... 88 B1
  RAD M26 .... 51 F6
Rectory Rd *CHH* M8 .... 90 A4
Rectory St *MDTN* M24 .... 75 D2
Redacre *POY/DIS* SK12 .... 199 D3
Redacre Rd *GTN* M18 .... 127 F4
Red Bank *ANC* M4 .... 106 B4
Red Bank Rd *RAD* M26 .... 51 D4
Redbarn Cl *MPL/ROM* SK6 .... 169 D1
Redbourne Dr *URM* M41 .... 118 A5 8
Redbrick Ct *AULW* OL7 .... 112 B6 8
Redbrook Av *NEWH/MOS* M40 .... 107 F2
Redbrook Cl *FWTH* BL4 .... 66 C2 8
Redbrook Rd *HALE/TIMP* WA15 .... 176 B1
  PART M31 .... 154 C3
Red Brook St *ROCH* OL11 .... 22 B6
Redburn Rd *NTHM/RTH* M23 .... 161 F6
Redby St *OP/CLY* M11 .... 126 C2 8
Redcar Av *URM* M41 .... 118 B5
Redcar Cl *BRAM/HZG* SK7 .... 185 E6
Redcar Rd *BOL* BL1 .... 26 C3
  BOLS/LL BL3 .... 49 E6
  SWIN M27 .... 87 D6
Redcar St *WHIT* OL12 .... 22 C5 16
Redclyffe Av *RUSH/FAL* M14 .... 125 D6 11
Redclyffe Rd *URM* M41 .... 119 D1
Redcote St *NEWH/MOS* M40 .... 92 B5 8
Redcourt Av *DID/WITH* M20 .... 163 F1 8
Redcroft Gdns *BNG/LEV* M19 .... 164 C1 8
Redcroft Rd *SALE* M33 .... 138 C5
Redcross St *WHIT* OL12 .... 23 D5
Redcross St North *WHIT* OL12 .... 23 D4 10
Reddaway Cl *SLFD* M6 .... 104 B2 8
Reddish Cl *BOLE* BL2 .... 29 F1
Reddish La *GTN* M18 .... 127 F6
Reddish Rd *RDSH* SK5 .... 147 D5
Reddish Vale Rd *RDSH* SK5 .... 147 E4
Redesmere Cl *DROY* M43 .... 110 C6
  HALE/TIMP WA15 .... 176 B1
Redesmere Dr *CHD/CHDH* SK8 .... 181 D3
  WILM/AE SK9 .... 209 D4
Redesmere Pk *URM* M41 .... 137 F3
Redfearn Wd *WHIT* OL12 .... 21 F3
Redfern Av *SALE* M33 .... 160 C2
Redfern St *ANC* M4 .... 3 E1
Redfern Wy *ROCH* OL11 .... 20 B4
Redfield Cl *OP/CLY* M11 .... 108 A6
Redford Dr *BRAM/HZG* SK7 .... 183 E5
Redford Rd *CHH* M8 .... 90 A1 8
Redford St *TOT/BURYW* BL8 .... 37 D3
Redgate *HYDE* SK14 .... 150 B3
Redgate La *WGTN/LGST* M12 .... 126 A4
Redgate Wy *FWTH* BL4. .... 65 D2
Redgrave Pas *OLDE* OL4 .... 80 B3
Redgrave St *OLDE* OL4 .... 80 B3
Red Hall St *OLDE* OL4 .... 80 A5
Redhill Dr *MPL/ROM* SK6 .... 168 B2
Redhill St *ANC* M4 .... 3 H3

Red House La ALT WA14 .... 156 A5
Redhouse La MPL/ROM SK6 .... 169 D1
Redisher Cft TOT/BURYW BL8 .... 18 A2
Redisher La TOT/BURYW BL8 .... 17 F2
Redland Av RDSH SK5 .... 147 D6
Redland Cl LIT OL15 .... 12 C5
Redland Crs CCHDY M21 .... 141 F5
Red La BOLE BL2 .... 29 E6
POY/DIS SK12 .... 201 F4
WHIT OL12 .... 23 F3
Red Lion St ANC M4 .... 3 F2
Redmere Gv RUSH/FAL M14 .... 144 A3
Redmire Ms DUK SK16 .... 132 A2
Redmond Cl DTN/ASHW M34 ...... 129 F2
Red Pike Wk OLD OL1 .... 79 E3
Redpoll Cl WALK M28 .... 82 C6
Red Rock La RAD M26 .... 68 B5
Red Rose Ct SALE M33 .... 139 F5
Red Rose Crs BNG/LEV M19 ...... 146 A4
Redruth St RUSH/FAL M14 .... 143 F1
Redshaw Av BOLE BL2 .... 28 C1
Redshaw Cl RUSH/FAL M14 .... 144 B2
Redstone Rd BNG/LEV M19 .... 164 B2
Redvales Rd BURY BL9 .... 52 C2
Redvers St OLD OL1 .... 78 B3
OP/CLY M11 .... 125 F1
Redwing Rd TOT/BURYW BL8 ..... 18 A3
SALE M33 .... 158 A1
Redwood CHAD OL9 .... 76 B4
SALE M33 .... 158 A1
Redwood Cl WHIT OL12 .... 21 F2
Redwood Dr CHH M8 .... 106 C2
DTN/ASHW M34 .... 129 F3
MPL/ROM SK6 .... 169 D2
Redwood La OLDE OL4 .... 80 C4
Redwood Park Gv MILN OL16 ...... 24 B6
Redwood St SLFD M6 .... 104 B3
Reedbank Rd RAD M26 .... 69 E3
Reedham Cl BOL BL1 .... 46 A3
Reed Hi MILN OL16 .... 23 D5
Reedley Dr WALK M28 .... 83 F4
Reedmace Cl WALK M28 .... 83 F4
Reedshaw Bank OFTN SK2 .... 184 B2
Reedshaw Rd BKLY M9 .... 107 D1
Reed St GTN M18 .... 127 E3
Reeman Cl MPL/ROM SK6 .... 169 E1
Reeve Cl OFTN SK2 .... 185 D2
Reeves Rd CCHDY M21 .... 141 F4
Reevey Av BRAM/HZG SK7 .... 184 A5
Reform St WHIT OL12 .... 23 D4
Refuge St RYNE/SHW OL2 .... 61 F3
Regal Cl WHTF M45 .... 71 F3
Regan Av CCHDY M21 .... 142 B4
Regan St BOL BL1 .... 27 E4
RAD M26 .... 69 F1
Regatta Cl CHAD OL9 .... 94 B2
Regatta St SLFD M6 .... 104 A1
Regency Ct NEWH/MOS M40 .... 107 E2
OLDS OL8 .... 95 E1
Regency Pk WILM/AE SK9 .... 203 D6
Regent Av LHULT M38 .... 83 D1
RUSH/FAL M14 .... 143 D1
Regent Cl BRAM/HZG SK7 .... 196 B5
CHD/CHDH SK8 .... 182 A3
WILM/AE SK9 .... 203 D6
Regent Crs FAIL M35 .... 109 F1
OLD OL1 .... 78 B1
Regent Dr DTN/ASHW M34 .... 148 B2
Regent Pl RUSH/FAL M14 .... 125 D5
Regent Rd WA14 .... 174 B3
OFTN SK2 .... 183 E1
SALQ/ORD M5 .... 122 C1
Regents Dr MOSL OL5 .... 99 E6
Regent Sq SALQ/ORD M5 .... 122 C1
Regent St BURY BL9 .... 34 A3
ECC M30 .... 102 A5
HEY OL10 .... 36 C6
LIT OL15 .... 12 C6
MDTN M24 .... 75 D1
NEWH/MOS M40 .... 109 E2
OLD OL1 .... 79 E4
RAMS BL0 .... 6 B6
WHIT OL12 .... 23 D4
Regent Wk FWTH BL4 .... 66 B3
Regina Av STLY SK15 .... 114 B5
Reginald St ECC M30 .... 118 B1
OP/CLY M11 .... 128 A2
SWIN M27 .... 85 E4
Reid Cl DTN/ASHW M34 .... 149 E3
Reigate Cl TOT/BURYW BL8 ...... 32 C6
Reigate Rd URM M41 .... 136 C3
Reins Lee Av OLDS OL8 .... 96 B3
Reins Lee Rd AULW OL7 .... 112 B1
Reliance St NEWH/MOS M40 .... 109 D1
Rembrandt Wk OLD OL1 .... 62 B4
Rena Cl HTNM SK4 .... 166 B2
Rendel Cl STRET M32 .... 140 B1
Renfrew Dr BOLS/LL BL3 .... 45 D6
Rennie Cl STRET M32 .... 140 B1
Renshaw Av ECC M30 .... 101 E6
Renshaw Dr BURY BL9 .... 35 D4
Renshaw St ECC M30 .... 101 E6
Renton Rd BOLS/LL BL3 .... 45 F6
STRET M32 .... 140 C1
WYTH/NTH M22 .... 178 B3

Repton Av DROY M43 .... 109 E4
DTN/ASHW M34 .... 128 B6
HYDE SK14 .... 131 F6
NEWH/MOS M40 .... 93 F4
OLDS OL8 .... 95 E2
URM M41 .... 136 B1
Reservoir Rd EDGY/DAV SK3 .... 166 B6
EDGY/DAV SK3 .... 182 B1
Reservoir St CSLFD M3 .... 105 F4
MILN OL16 .... 24 A5
SLFD M6 .... 104 A5
Retford Av MILN OL16 .... 40 C3
Retford Cl TOT/BURYW BL8 ...... 33 F2
Retford St OLDS OL8 .... 95 F6
Retiro St OLD OL1 .... 79 D4
The Retreat MPL/ROM SK6 .... 169 F4
Reuben St HTNM SK4 .... 166 C1
Revers St TOT/BURYW BL8 .... 33 E4
Reveton Gn BRAM/HZG SK7 .... 183 E5
Reynard Av CCHDY M21 .... 141 F4
Reynard St HYDE SK14 .... 131 E6
Reynell Rd BRUN/LGST M13 .... 145 D1
Reyner St AUL OL6 .... 113 F5
CMANE M1 .... 3 E5
Reynolds Dr GTN M18 .... 127 E3
MPL/ROM SK6 .... 171 F5
Reynolds Ms WILM/AE SK9 ...... 204 C3
Reynolds Rd OLDTF/WHR M16 .. 123 D5
Reynold St HYDE SK14 .... 150 B1
Rhine Cl TOT/BURYW BL8 .... 18 A6
Rhine Dr CHH M8 .... 105 F2
Rhiwlas Dr BURY BL9 .... 53 D1
Rhodes Av OLDE OL4 .... 80 C6
Rhodes Bank OLD OL1 .... 79 D5
Rhodes Crs ROCH OL11 .... 40 A4
Rhodes Dr BURY BL9 .... 71 E1
Rhodes Hl OLDE OL4 .... 81 D6
Rhodes St HYDE SK14 .... 131 D6
NEWH/MOS M40 .... 107 F3
OLD OL1 .... 79 D4
WHIT OL12 .... 23 F2
Rhodes St North HYDE SK14 .... 131 D6
Rhode St TOT/BURYW BL8 .... 32 A1
Rhos Av CHD/CHDH SK8 .... 181 D6
MDTN M24 .... 75 E4
RUSH/FAL M14 .... 144 C3
Rhos Dr BRAM/HZG SK7 .... 184 B1
Rhosleigh Av BOL BL1 .... 27 F3
Ribble Av BOLE BL2 .... 48 C2
CHAD OL9 .... 77 D2
LIT OL15 .... 12 A5
Ribble Dr FWTH BL4 .... 67 F6
WHTF M45 .... 71 E2
Ribble Rd OLDS OL8 .... 95 D2
Ribblesdale Dr
NEWH/MOS M40 .... 107 D2
Ribblesdale Rd BOLS/LL BL3 .... 46 B5
Ribble St BCUP OL13 .... 4 B1
ROCH OL11 .... 39 E3
Ribbleton Cl TOT/BURYW BL8 .. 32 A6
Ribchester Dr BURY BL9 .... 52 B2
Ribchester Gv BOLE BL2 .... 29 F6
Richelieu St BOLS/LL BL3 .... 47 E5
Richmond Av CHAD OL9 .... 94 B1
PWCH M25 .... 89 D4
ROY/SHW OL2 .... 60 B5
URM M41 .... 138 C1
WILM/AE SK9 .... 194 B5
Richmond Cl DUK SK16 .... 131 E3
MILN OL16 .... 41 D4
MOSL OL5 .... 99 F5
ROY/SHW OL2 .... 61 F3
SALE M33 .... 161 D2
STLY SK15 .... 114 B6
TOT/BURYW BL8 .... 32 A1
WHTF M45 .... 70 B4
Richmond Crs MOSL OL5 .... 99 F5
Richmond Dr WALK M28 .... 85 D5
Richmond Gdns BOLS/LL BL3 .. 47 F6
Richmond Gn ALT WA14 .... 173 D5
Richmond Gv BRUN/LGST M13 . 125 E5
CHD/CHDH SK8 .... 182 B3
ECC M30 .... 101 F4
FWTH BL4 .... 65 E2
Richmond Gv East
WGTN/LGST M12 .... 125 F4
Richmond Hill Rd CHD/CHDH SK8 .. 180 A2
Richmond Rd ALT WA14 .... 173 F5
DTN/ASHW M34 .... 128 B6
DUK SK16 .... 131 E3

FAIL M35 .... 94 B5
HTNM SK4 .... 165 D3
MPL/ROM SK6 .... 170 A2
RUSH/FAL M14 .... 144 B3
TRPK M17 .... 120 B2
Richmond St AULW OL7 .... 112 A3
BURY BL9 .... 52 C1
CMANE M1 .... 3 F5
CSLFD M3 .... 105 F4
DROY M43 .... 111 D5
DTN/ASHW M34 .... 129 F3
HYDE SK14 .... 150 C1
STLY SK15 .... 114 C5
Richmond Wk CHAD OL9 .... 78 B5
Ricroft Rd MPL/ROM SK6 .... 171 F2
Ridding Av WYTH/NTH M22 ...... 178 C4
Ridding Cl OFTN SK2 .... 184 B1
Riddings Ct HALE/TIMP WA15 ... 159 D5
Riddings Rd HALE/TIMP WA15 .. 159 E5
HALE/TIMP WA15 .... 175 D5
Ridge Av HALE/TIMP WA15 ..... 190 A3
MPL/ROM SK6 .... 187 E4
Ridge Cl MPL/ROM SK6 .... 170 C3
Ridge Crs MPL/ROM SK6 .... 187 D4
WHTF M45 .... 71 F3
Ridgecroft AULW OL7 .... 112 C1
Ridge End Fold MPL/ROM SK6 .. 187 E6
Ridgefield CMANW M2 .... 2 C3
CMANW M2 .... 2 C4
Ridgefield St FAIL M35 .... 109 F1
Ridge Gv WHTF M45 .... 71 F3
Ridge Hill La STLY SK15 .... 114 B4
Ridgemont Av HTNM SK4 .... 165 F3
Ridge Pk BRAM/HZG SK7 .... 196 B5
Ridgeway BOL BL1 .... 47 D2
SWIN M27 .... 86 C4
WILM/AE SK9 .... 205 D4
Ridgeway Rd HALE/TIMP WA15 . 176 A2
Ridgeway St NEWH/MOS M40 .. 107 F5
Ridgewood CHAD OL9 .... 76 C3
Ridgewood Av NEWH/MOS M40 .. 107 E2
Ridgmont Rd BRAM/HZG SK7 .. 196 C5
The Ridgway MPL/ROM SK6 .... 169 E4
Riding Fold La WALK M28 .... 100 B2
Riding Ga BOLE BL2 .... 29 F1
Riding Gate Ms BOLE BL2 .... 29 F1
Ridings St NEWH/MOS M40 .... 108 A2
OP/CLY M11 .... 126 C1
Riding St CSLFD M3 .... 2 A2
Ridings Wy CHAD OL9 .... 77 F6
Ridley Dr ALT WA14 .... 158 C4
Ridley Gv SALE M33 .... 161 D2
Ridley St OLDE OL4 .... 79 E5
Ridling La HYDE SK14 .... 150 C1
Ridsdale Av DID/WITH M20 ...... 143 E5
Ridyard St LHULT M38 .... 83 D1
Riefield BOL BL1 .... 26 C4
Rifle Rd SALE M33 .... 141 D6
Rifle St OLD OL1 .... 79 D3
Riga Rd RUSH/FAL M14 .... 144 A2
Riga St ANC M4 .... 3 F1
Rigby Av RAD M26 .... 52 A4
Rigby Ct BOLS/LL BL3 .... 47 D5
Rigby La BOLE BL2 .... 29 F1
Rigby St ALT WA14 .... 174 B4
BOLS/LL BL3 .... 47 D5
BRO M7 .... 89 E6
Rigel Pl BRO M7 .... 105 D4
Rigel St ANC M4 .... 107 D4
Rigton Cl WGTN/LGST M12 ..... 157 F4
Riley Cl SALE M33 .... 161 D2
Riley Ct BOL BL1 .... 28 A6
Riley Wood Cl MPL/ROM SK6 .. 169 D4
Rilldene Wk ROCH OL11 .... 20 B5
Rimington Fold MDTN M24 .... 56 B6
Rimmer Cl OP/CLY M11 .... 125 F1
Rimmington Cl BKLY M9 .... 92 B3
Rimsdale Cl CHD/CHDH SK8 .. 179 E4
Rimworth Dr NEWH/MOS M40 .. 107 D3
Ringcroft Gdns NEWH/MOS M40 .. 92 C4
Ringfield Cl OLDTF/WHR M16 .. 123 F5
Ringley Cha WHTF M45 .... 70 C3
Ringley Cl WHTF M45 .... 70 B3
Ringley Dr WHTF M45 .... 70 B4
Ringley Gv BOL BL1 .... 27 F2
Ringley Hey WHTF M45 .... 70 B3
Ringley Mdw RAD M26 .... 68 A4
Ringley Old Brow RAD M26 .... 68 A4
Ringley Pk WHTF M45 .... 70 B3
Ringley Rd RAD M26 .... 67 F5
WHTF M45 .... 70 C3
Ringley Rd West RAD M26 .... 68 A4
Ringley St BKLY M9 .... 91 E5
Ringlow Av SWIN M27 .... 85 D6
Ringlow Park Rd SWIN M27 ..... 101 D3
Ring Lows La WHIT OL12 .... 23 D1
Ringmer Dr WYTH/NTH M22 .... 178 A6
Ringmore Rd BRAM/HZG SK7 .. 183 D5
Rings Cl FAIL M35 .... 110 A1
Ringstead Cl WILM/AE SK9 ...... 204 B2
Ringstead Dr NEWH/MOS M40 .. 107 D3
WILM/AE SK9 .... 204 B2
Ringstone PWCH M25 .... 88 B2
Ringway Gv SALE M33 .... 160 C3

Ringway Rd *MANAIR* M90 ..... 192 A2
  WYTH/NTH M22 ..... 192 C2
Ringway Rd West *MANAIR* M90 ..... 192 A1
Ringwood Av *BRAM/HZG* SK7 ..... 185 F6
  DTN/ASHW M34 ..... 111 D6
  HYDE SK14 ..... 151 E2
  RAD M26 ..... 69 F2
  RAMS BL0 ..... 18 D1 [1]
  WGTN/LGST M12 ..... 145 F1
Rink St *RUSH/FAL* M14 ..... 144 C4 [7]
  OFTN SK2 ..... 183 F5
Ripley Cl *ANC* M4 ..... 125 E1
  BRAM/HZG SK7 ..... 198 C1
Ripley Crs *URM* M41 ..... 118 A4
Ripley St *BOL* BL1 ..... 28 C3
Ripon Av *BOL* BL1 ..... 26 A6
  WHTF M45 ..... 71 D1
Ripon Cl *BOLS/LL* BL3 ..... 49 D6
  CHAD OL9 ..... 77 F5
  HALE/TIMP WA15 ..... 176 A6
  RAD M26 ..... 52 B4
  WHTF M45 ..... 71 D1
Ripon Crs *STRET* M32 ..... 120 A6
Ripon Gv *SALE* M33 ..... 139 D5
Ripon Hall Av *RAMS* BL0 ..... 18 C1
Ripon Rd *STRET* M32 ..... 120 A6
Ripon St *AUL* OL6 ..... 113 D4
  OLD OL1 ..... 78 B5
Rippenden Av *CCHDY* M21 ..... 141 E1 [2]
Rippingham Rd *DID/WITH* M20 ..... 143 F4
Rippleton Rd *WYTH/NTH* M22 ..... 178 C3
Ripponden Rd *OLDE* OL4 ..... 80 B2
Ripponden St *OLD* OL1 ..... 80 A2
The Rise *OLDE* OL4 ..... 81 D4
Rishton Av *BOLS/LL* BL3 ..... 65 D1
Rishton La *BOLS/LL* BL3 ..... 47 D5
Rishworth Cl *OFTN* SK2 ..... 184 B2
Rishworth Dr *NEWH/MOS* M40 ..... 93 F5
Rishworth Ri *ROY/SHW* OL2 ..... 42 A6
Rising La *OLDS* OL8 ..... 95 F3
Risley Av *BKLY* M9 ..... 91 E5
Risley St *OLD* OL1 ..... 79 D3
Rissington Av *WYTH/NTH* M23 ..... 177 F1
Rita Av *RUSH/FAL* M14 ..... 124 C6 [2]
Ritson Cl *GTN* M18 ..... 126 C3
Riva Rd *BNG/LEV* M19 ..... 164 B3
Riverbank Dr *TOT/BURYW* BL8 ..... 33 E3
The Riverbank *RAD* M26 ..... 67 E5
Riverdale Rd *BKLY* M9 ..... 90 B2
River La *PART* M31 ..... 155 D1
Rivermead *MILN* OL16 ..... 42 C4
Rivermead Av *HALE/TIMP* WA15 ..... 189 F3
Rivermead Cl *DTN/ASHW* M34 ..... 149 E4
Rivermead Rd *DTN/ASHW* M34 ..... 149 E4
Rivermead Wy *WHTF* M45 ..... 71 E3
Riverpark Rd *NEWH/MOS* M40 ..... 108 B4
River Pl *HULME* M15 ..... 123 F2
  MILN OL16 ..... 42 A1
Riversdale Dr *OLDS* OL8 ..... 96 B4 [3]
Riversdale Rd *CHD/CHDH* SK8 ..... 180 A2 [1]
Riversdale Vw *MPL/ROM* SK6 ..... 149 E6
Rivershill *SALE* M33 ..... 139 E5
Rivershill Dr *HEY* OL10 ..... 36 C6
Rivershill Gdns *HALE/TIMP* WA15 ..... 190 A3
Riverside *BRO* M7 ..... 105 D4
  DUK SK16 ..... 113 D5
  OLD OL1 ..... 76 C2
Riverside Av *IRL* M44 ..... 135 E2
Riverside Dr *MILN* OL16 ..... 23 F5
  RAD M26 ..... 67 F3
  RAMS BL0 ..... 18 C2
  URM M41 ..... 137 E3
Riverside Rd *RAD* M26 ..... 52 B5
Rivers La *URM* M41 ..... 119 E5
Riversleigh Cl *BOL* BL1 ..... 26 A4
Riverstone Dr *NTHM/RTH* M23 ..... 160 B6
River St *BOLE* BL2 ..... 47 E3
  HEY OL10 ..... 37 E3
  HULME M15 ..... 124 A2
  MILN OL16 ..... 23 D1 [19]
  RAD M26 ..... 51 F6
  RAMS BL0 ..... 7 D5
  STKP SK1 ..... 167 F2
  WGTN/LGST M12 ..... 125 D1 [12]
  WILM/AE SK9 ..... 203 F3
Riverton Rd *DID/WITH* M20 ..... 163 F6
River Vw *RDSH* SK5 ..... 147 E4
River View Pl *PWCH* M25 ..... 88 A3 [3]
Riviera Ct *ROCH* OL11 ..... 20 A3
Rivington Av *SWIN* M27 ..... 87 D5 [1]
Rivington Dr *ROY/SHW* OL2 ..... 62 B2
  TOT/BURYW BL8 ..... 32 B6
Rivington Gv *DTN/ASHW* M34 ..... 129 D1
  IRL M44 ..... 134 B5
Rivington Rd *HALE/TIMP* WA15 ..... 175 D5
  OLDE OL4 ..... 81 A4
  SLFD M6 ..... 103 D3
Rivington St *OLD* OL1 ..... 79 D2
  WHIT OL12 ..... 23 D4 [3]
Rivington Wk *WGTN/LGST* M12 ..... 126 A4 [3]
Rixson St *OLDE* OL4 ..... 80 B1 [3]
Rix St *BOL* BL1 ..... 27 F5 [3]
Riverside Dr *MILN* OL16 ..... 24 A3

Roaches Ms *MOSL* OL5 ..... 99 E2 [1]
Roaches Wy *MOSL* OL5 ..... 99 F2
Roachill Cl *ALT* WA14 ..... 173 F2
Roach Pl *MILN* OL16 ..... 23 E5
Roach St *BURY* BL9 ..... 35 D6
  BURY BL9 ..... 53 D5
Roach V *MILN* OL16 ..... 24 A3 [3]
Roachwood Cl *CHAD* OL9 ..... 76 C4
Roading Brook Rd *BOLE* BL2 ..... 30 B4
Road La *WHIT* OL12 ..... 22 B1
Roads Ford Av *MILN* OL16 ..... 25 D6
Roan Wy *WILM/AE* SK9 ..... 209 F5
Roaring Gate La *HALE/TIMP* WA15.. 196 C4
Robert Hall St *SALQ/ORD* M5 ..... 122 C1
Robert Lawrence Ct *URM* M41 ..... 137 E2 [3]
Robert Malcolm Cl
  NEWH/MOS M40 ..... 107 E2 [15]
Robert Owen Gdns
  WYTH/NTH M22 ..... 182 B5 [2]
Robert Salt Ct *ALT* WA14 ..... 174 C1 [3]
Robertscroft Cl
  WYTH/NTH M22 ..... 178 A3 [2]
Robertshaw Av *CCHDY* M21 ..... 141 F5 [2]
Robertson St *RAD* M26 ..... 51 E5
Roberts St *ECC* M30 ..... 101 E6
Robert St *BOLE* BL2 ..... 29 F2 [3]
  CSLFD M3 ..... 106 A4
  DUK SK16 ..... 130 C1 [3]
  FAIL M35 ..... 94 B4 [4]
  HEY OL10 ..... 56 C1
  HYDE SK14 ..... 150 A1
  NEWH/MOS M40 ..... 108 A2
  OLDS OL8 ..... 94 C3
  PWCH M25 ..... 89 D1 [12]
  RAMS BL0 ..... 7 D2
  SALE M33 ..... 160 C1 [2]
  TOT/BURYW BL8 ..... 33 D4 [19]
  WHIT OL12 ..... 23 D5
Robeson Wy *WYTH/NTH* M22 ..... 179 D1
Robin Cft *MPL/ROM* SK6 ..... 168 B2
Robin Dr *IRL* M44 ..... 116 B6
Robin Hood St *CHH* M8 ..... 90 A5 [3]
Robinia Cl *ECC* M30 ..... 118 A1
Robin Rd *RAMS* BL0 ..... 18 C2
Robinsbay Rd *WYTH/NTH* M22 ..... 192 C2
Robins Cl *BRAM/HZG* SK7 ..... 196 C2
  DROY M43 ..... 111 D4
Robin's La *BRAM/HZG* SK7 ..... 196 B2
Robinson La *AULW* OL7 ..... 112 A4
Robinson St *CHAD* OL9 ..... 77 F5
  EDGY/DAV SK3 ..... 166 B6 [10]
  HYDE SK14 ..... 132 A6 [4]
  MILN OL16 ..... 23 E6
  OLDS OL8 ..... 96 A2
  STLY SK15 ..... 114 A6
Robin St *OLD* OL1 ..... 78 C3 [3]
Robinsway *ALT* WA14 ..... 174 A6 [3]
Robinswood Rd *WYTH/NTH* M22 ..... 178 D3
Robson Av *URM* M41 ..... 119 F2
Robson St *OLD* OL1 ..... 79 D5
Roby Rd *ECC* M30 ..... 119 D1 [3]
Roby St *CMANE* M1 ..... 3 G4
Roch Av *HEY* OL10 ..... 36 B5
Rochbury Cl *ROCH* OL11 ..... 38 A1
Roch Cl *WHTF* M45 ..... 71 F2
Roch Crs *WHTF* M45 ..... 71 F2
Rochdale La *HEY* OL10 ..... 37 E5 [16]
  ROY/SHW OL2 ..... 60 B4
Rochdale Old Rd *BURY* BL9 ..... 35 D4
Rochdale Rd *ANC* M4 ..... 3 C1
  BKLY M9 ..... 91 E2
  BURY BL9 ..... 34 C5
  HEY OL10 ..... 37 E5
  MDTN M24 ..... 57 F6
  MILN OL16 ..... 24 B6
  NEWH/MOS M40 ..... 107 D3
  ROY/SHW OL2 ..... 60 A3
Rochdale Rd East *HEY* OL10 ..... 37 F5
Roche Gdns *CHD/CHDH* SK8 ..... 195 F3
Rochester Av *BOLE* BL2 ..... 29 F6
  PWCH M25 ..... 89 D3
  WALK M28 ..... 83 D4
Rochester Cl *AUL* OL6 ..... 97 D6
  DUK SK16 ..... 132 B2 [2]
Rochester Dr *ALT* WA14 ..... 158 C4 [2]
Rochester Gv *BRAM/HZG* SK7 ..... 184 C4 [2]
Rochester Rd *URM* M41 ..... 119 E5
Rochford Av *WYTH/NTH* M22 ..... 192 B1
Rochford Rd *ECC* M30 ..... 118 A1 [2]
Roch Mills Crs *ROCH* OL11 ..... 39 D2
Roch St *MILN* OL16 ..... 23 F4
Roch Valley Wy *ROCH* OL11 ..... 39 D1
Rock Wy *WHTF* M45 ..... 71 F2 [2]
Rock Av *BOL* BL1 ..... 27 D5
Rockdove Av *HULME* M15 ..... 124 A2 [2]
Rocket St *CSLFD* M3 ..... 105 E4
Rockfield Dr *BKLY* M9 ..... 91 F5 [2]
Rockhampton St *GTN* M18 ..... 127 F4 [2]
Rockhouse Cl *ECC* M30 ..... 119 E1 [2]
Rockingham Cl *ROY/SHW* OL2 ..... 60 C1 [2]
  WGTN/LGST M12 ..... 125 E3 [2]
Rocklyn Av *NEWH/MOS* M40 ..... 93 D5
Rocklynes *MPL/ROM* SK6 ..... 169 F3 [2]
Rockmead Dr *BKLY* M9 ..... 91 F2
Rock Rd *URM* M41 ..... 139 D1

Rock St *AULW* OL7 ..... 112 B2
  BRO M7 ..... 105 E1
  HEY OL10 ..... 37 F6 [2]
  HYDE SK14 ..... 150 C4
  OLD OL1 ..... 79 D4
  OP/CLY M11 ..... 127 F2
  RAD M26 ..... 69 F1 [2]
  RAMS BL0 ..... 7 F4 [2]
Rock Ter *EDGW/EG* BL7 ..... 14 A4
  MOSL OL5 ..... 99 D2
The Rock *BURY* BL9 ..... 33 F5 [20]
Rocky La *ECC* M30 ..... 101 E3
Roda St *BKLY* M9 ..... 92 A6 [2]
Rodborough Rd *NTHM/RTH* M23 ..... 177 D4
Rodeheath Cl *WILM/AE* SK9 ..... 204 B4 [2]
Rodenhurst Dr *NEWH/MOS* M40 ..... 108 B1
Rodepool Cl *WILM/AE* SK9 ..... 204 B1 [2]
Rodmell Av *NEWH/MOS* M40 ..... 107 E2 [16]
Rodmell Cl *EDGW/EG* BL7.. ..... 14 A6
Rodmill Ct *RUSH/FAL* M14 ..... 144 A2
Rodmill Dr *CHD/CHDH* SK8.. ..... 179 E3
Rodney Dr *MPL/ROM* SK6 ..... 149 E6
Rodney St *ANC* M4 ..... 107 D5 [2]
  AUL OL6 ..... 113 E3
  CSLFD M3 ..... 105 E6 [11]
  ROCH OL11 ..... 38 C5
Roeacre St *HEY* OL10 ..... 37 F5
Roebuck La *OLDE* OL4 ..... 63 E6
  SALE M33 ..... 139 E1
Roedean Gdns *URM* M41 ..... 136 B1
Roefield Ter *ROCH* OL11 ..... 22 A5 [1]
Roe Gn *WALK* M28 ..... 84 B5
Roe Green Av *WALK* M28 ..... 84 B5
Roe La *OLDE* OL4 ..... 80 B6
Roe St *ANC* M4 ..... 107 D4
  WHIT OL12 ..... 22 A4
Rogate Dr *NTHM/RTH* M23 ..... 177 E2
Roger Cl *MPL/ROM* SK6 ..... 169 D4
Roger St *ANC* M4 ..... 106 B4
Rokeby Av *STRET* M32 ..... 140 B2
Roker Av *BRUN/LGST* M13 ..... 145 D1
Roker Park Av *DTN/ASHW* M34 ..... 129 E2
Roland Rd *BOLS/LL* BL3 ..... 46 A5 [32]
  RDSH SK5 ..... 147 D3 [3]
Rolla St *CSLFD* M3 ..... 2 B1
Rollesby Cl *TOT/BURYW* BL8 ..... 33 E2
Rolleston Av *ANC* M4 ..... 107 E5
Rollins La *MPL/ROM* SK6 ..... 171 E4
Rollis Crs *HULME* M15 ..... 124 A5
Rollswood Dr *NEWH/MOS* M40 ..... 108 B1 [2]
Roman Rd *FAIL* M35 ..... 94 B5 [2]
  HTNM SK4 ..... 166 C3 [2]
  OLDS OL8 ..... 94 C4
  PWCH M25 ..... 88 A4
  ROY/SHW OL2 ..... 60 B6
Roman St *ANC* M4 ..... 3 F1
  RAD M26 ..... 50 C6 [13]
Romer Av *NEWH/MOS* M40 ..... 93 F4 [2]
Rome Rd *NEWH/MOS* M40 ..... 107 D4
Romer St *BOLE* BL2 ..... 48 A2
Romford Av *DTN/ASHW* M34 ..... 130 B5 [2]
Romford Cl *OLDS* OL8 ..... 78 C6 [2]
Romford Rd *SALE* M33 ..... 138 C5
Romiley Crs *BOLE* BL2 ..... 48 B1
Romiley Dr *BOLE* BL2 ..... 48 B1
Romiley St *SLFD* M6 ..... 103 E2 [2]
  STKP SK1 ..... 167 F3
Romiley Rd *URM* M41 ..... 119 E5
Romney Av *ROCH* OL11 ..... 38 B5
Romney St *AUL* OL6 ..... 113 D4
  NEWH/MOS M40 ..... 92 B5
  SLFD M6 ..... 104 B2
Romney Wy *RDSH* SK5 ..... 147 E5
Romsey Av *MDTN* M24 ..... 57 D6
Romsey Dr *CHD/CHDH* SK8 ..... 195 F3
Romsley Cl *WGTN/LGST* M12 ..... 126 B3
Romsley Dr *BOLS/LL* BL3 ..... 46 A5 [29]
Ronaldsay Gdns *SALQ/ORD* M5 ..... 103 F6 [2]
Ronald St *OLDE* OL4 ..... 80 A4
  OP/CLY M11 ..... 109 E6
  ROCH OL11 ..... 39 D6 [2]
Rondin Cl *WGTN/LGST* M12 ..... 125 F2
Rondin Rd *WGTN/LGST* M12 ..... 125 F2
Roocroft Ct *BOL* BL1 ..... 27 E6
Roods La *ROCH* OL11 ..... 20 A4
Rookery Av *GTN* M18 ..... 128 A3
Rookery Cl *STLY* SK15 ..... 133 F2
Rookerypool Cl *WILM/AE* SK9 ..... 204 B1 [3]
Rooke St *ECC* M30 ..... 118 B1
Rookfield Av *SALE* M33 ..... 140 A6
Rook St *OLDE* OL4 ..... 80 A6 [3]
  RAMS BL0 ..... 7 D5
Rookswood Dr *ROCH* OL11 ..... 38 C4 [2]
Rookway *MDTN* M24 ..... 75 D4
Rookwood *CHAD* OL9 ..... 76 C2 [2]
Rookwood Av *NTHM/RTH* M23 ..... 161 D6 [2]
Rookwood Hl *BRAM/HZG* SK7 ..... 182 C6 [2]
Rooley Moor Rd *WHIT* OL12 ..... 21 F3
Rooley St *WHIT* OL12 ..... 22 A4
Roosevelt Rd *FWTH* BL4 ..... 67 D4 [2]
Rooth St *HTNM* SK4 ..... 166 B3
Ropefield Wy *WHIT* OL12 ..... 22 C1 [2]
Rope St *WHIT* OL12 ..... 22 D5
Rope Wk *CSLFD* M3 ..... 105 F4 [2]
Rosa Gv *BRO* M7 ..... 105 E1

Rosamond Dr CSLFD M3 .... 105 E5
Rosamond St BOLS/LL BL3 .... 46 A5
Rosamond St West HULME M15.. 124 B3
Rosary Cl OLDS OL8........................... 96 A4
Rosary Rd OLDS OL8 .... 96 B4
Roscoe Rd IRL M44.......................... 134 C2
Roscoe St EDGY/DAV SK3 .... 166 B5 🔟
OLD OL1 .... 79 D5 🔟
Roscow Av BOLE BL2 .... 48 C1
Roscow Rd FWTH BL4 .... 67 E5
Roseacre Dr CHD/CHDH SK8 .... 180 A6
Rose Av IRL M44 .... 135 D2
LIT OL15 .... 25 D2
ROCH OL11 .... 20 B3
Rosebank HOR/BR BL6...................... 44 A2
Rosebank Cl BOLE BL2 .... 31 D6 🔟
Rosebank Rd IRL M44....................... 154 A2
NEWH/MOS M40 .... 108 C3
Roseberry Av BOL BL1 .... 19 D2 🔟
Roseberry St BOLS/LL BL3 .... 46 A5 🔟🔟
OLDS OL8 .... 78 B5 🔟
Rosebery St OFTN SK2 .... 184 B3
RUSH/FAL M14 .... 124 A6
Rosebury Av BOL BL1 .... 79 F2 🔟
Rose Cottage Rd DID/WITH M20 .. 143 F4
Rose Crs IRL M44 .... 135 D2
Rosecroft Cl EDGY/DAV SK3 .... 182 C5
Rosedale Av BOL BL1 .... 27 F2 🔟
Rosedale Cl OLD OL1........................ 79 F2
Rosedale Ct DTN/ASHW M34 .... 129 F6 🔟
Rosedale Rd HTNM SK4 .... 146 B6
RUSH/FAL M14 .... 143 E1
Rosedale Wy DUK SK16 .... 131 D3 🔟
Rosefield Crs MILN OL16 .... 24 A6
Rosegarth Av DID/WITH M20 ...... 162 B1 🔟
Rosegate Cl OLDTF/WHR M16 .... 124 A6 🔟
Rose Gv FWTH BL4 .... 67 D4 🔟
TOT/BURYW BL8 .... 32 B5
Rosehay Av DTN/ASHW M34 .... 149 D1
Rose Hl BOLE BL2 .... 47 E4
DTN/ASHW M34 .... 129 E6
STLY SK15 .... 132 A1
Rose Hill Av NEWH/MOS M40 ...... 108 C3 🔟
Rose Hill Cl EDGW/EG BL7 .... 14 B6
Rosehill Cl SLFD M6........................ 104 A5
Rose Hill Dr EDGW/EG BL7 .... 14 B6
Rose Hill Rd AUL OL6...................... 114 A2
Rosehill Rd SWIN M27 .... 86 A3 🔟🔟
Rose Hill St HEY OL10 .... 36 C5
Roseland Av DID/WITH M20 .... 163 F1
Roseland Dr PWCH M25 .... 72 A5 🔟
Roselands Av SALE M33 .... 159 D3
Rose La MPL/ROM SK6 .... 186 C2
Rose Lea BOLE BL2 .... 29 F3
Rosemary Dr HYDE SK14 .... 150 B4
LIT OL15 .... 12 A5
Rosemary Gv BRO M7 .... 105 D2 🔟
Rosemary La STKP SK1 .... 167 E4 🔟
Rosemount HYDE SK14 .... 131 E4 🔟
Rose Mt MDTN M24 .... 75 D1
Rosemount Crs HYDE SK14 .... 131 E4 🔟
Roseneath BRAM/HZG SK7 .... 182 B6 🔟
Roseneath Av BNG/LEV M19....... 146 A2
Roseneath Gv BOLS/LL BL3 .... 64 B1 🔟
Roseneath Rd BOLS/LL BL3 .... 46 B6
URM M41.. 119 D3
Rose St BOLE BL2 .... 47 E4 🔟
CHAD OL9 .... 94 B2
MDTN M24 .... 76 A3
RDSH SK5 .... 167 D2 🔟
Rose Ter STLY SK15 .... 114 B6 🔟🔟
Rosethorns Cl MDTN M24 .... 57 D5 🔟
Rosevale Av BNG/LEV M19 .... 144 C6
Roseway BRAM/HZG SK7 .... 183 D5
Rosewell Cl NEWH/MOS M40 ...... 107 E3 🔟
Rose Wd DTN/ASHW M34.............. 129 E6
Rosewood ROCH OL11 .... 20 C4 🔟
Rosewood Av DROY M43 .... 110 C5
HTNM SK4 .... 165 E4
TOT/BURYW BL8 .... 32 B2
Rosewood Cl DUK SK16 .... 131 E3
Rosewood Crs CHAD OL9 .... 77 F2 🔟
Rosewood Gdns
CHD/CHDH SK8 .... 179 D1 🔟
Rosford Av RUSH/FAL M14 .... 143 F1 🔟
Rosgill Cl HTNM SK4 .... 164 C3
Rosina St OP/CLY M11 .... 128 A2
Roslin St OP/CLY M11 .... 109 E5 🔟
Roslyn Av URM M41 .... 136 C3
Roslyn Rd EDGY/DAV SK3........... 182 C2
Rossall Av RAD M26 .... 70 A3
STRET M32 .... 121 D6
Rossall Cl BOLE BL2 .... 48 A1 🔟
Rossall Dr BRAM/HZG SK7 .... 197 D3
Rossall Rd WHIT OL12 .... 23 E3
Rossall St BOLE BL2 .... 48 A1 🔟
Rossall Wy SLFD M6....................... 104 B4
Ross Av CHAD OL9 .... 94 A2 🔟
EDGY/DAV SK3 .... 182 C2
WHTF M45 .... 71 D5
Ross Dr SWIN M27 .... 85 F3
Rossenclough Rd WILM/AE SK9 .. 204 B2 🔟

Rossendale Av BKLY M9 .... 92 A4 🔟
Rossendale Cl ROY/SHW OL2 .... 62 B2 🔟
Rossendale Rd CHD/CHDH SK8.. 194 A1
Rossendale Wy WHIT OL12 .... 8 A3
Rossett Av HALE/TIMP WA15....... 159 F5 🔟
WYTH/NTH M22 .... 178 B6
Rossett Dr URM M41 .... 118 A5
Ross Gv URM M41 .... 138 A1
Rossington St NEWH/MOS M40 ... 109 E2
Rossini St BOL BL1 .... 27 E4 🔟
BOL BL1 .... 27 E4 🔟
Rosslare Rd WYTH/NTH M22 ...... 178 C5
Ross Lave La DTN/ASHW M34 ..... 148 A3
Rosslyn Gv HALE/TIMP WA15 ...... 175 E1
Rosslyn Rd CHD/CHDH SK8 .... 180 B6
NEWH/MOS M40 .... 92 B4
OLDTF/WHR M16 .... 141 E1
Rossmere Av ROCH OL11 .... 39 D1
Rossmill La HALE/TIMP WA15 ..... 189 F2
Ross St OLDS OL8 .... 78 B6
Rostherne Av MPL/ROM SK6 ..... 200 C1
RUSH/FAL M14 .... 143 E2
Rostherne Gdns BOLS/LL BL3 .. 45 F5 🔟🔟
Rostherne Rd EDGY/DAV SK3..... 182 C2
SALE M33 .... 161 D2
WILM/AE SK9 .... 202 C6
Rostherne St ALT WA14 .... 174 B4 🔟
SLFD M6 .... 103 F6 🔟
Rosthernmere Rd CHD/CHDH SK8.. 181 D3
Rosthwaite Cl MDTN M24 .... 74 A2
Roston Rd BRO M7 .... 89 F5 🔟
Rostrevor Rd EDGY/DAV SK3....... 182 C2
Rostron Av WGTN/LGST M12 ...... 125 F3
Rostron Rd RAMS BL0 .... 6 C5
Rostron St BNG/LEV M19 .... 145 F2 🔟
Rothay Cl BOLE BL2 .... 30 A6
Rothay Dr MDTN M24...................... 56 C3
RDSH SK5 .... 147 D3
Rothbury Av AULW OL7 .... 111 F2 🔟
Rothbury Cl TOT/BURYW BL8 .... 32 A5
Rothbury Ct BOLS/LL BL3 .... 45 F6 🔟🔟
Rotherby Rd WYTH/NTH M22 ...... 178 C3
Rotherdale Av HALE/TIMP WA15 .. 176 B3
Rotherwood Av STRET M32 .... 121 F6 🔟
Rotherwood Rd WILM/AE SK9 .... 202 B6
Rothesay Av DUK SK16 .... 131 D2
Rothesay Crs SALE M33 .... 158 A3
Rothesay Rd BOLS/LL BL3 .... 45 F6 🔟🔟
CHH M8 .... 89 F3
OLD OL1 .... 80 A2
Rothesay Ter MILN OL16 .... 41 D3
Rothiemay Rd URM M41 .... 136 C2
Rothley Av WYTH/NTH M22.......... 178 B2
Rothman Cl FAIL M35 .... 109 D1
Rothwell Crs LHULT M38 .... 64 C6 🔟
Rothwell La LHULT M38 .... 64 C6
Rothwell St BOLS/LL BL3 .... 46 C4 🔟🔟
FAIL M35 .... 109 F1
NEWH/MOS M40 .... 6 C5 🔟
RAMS BL0 .... 6 C5 🔟
ROY/SHW OL2 .... 60 B5 🔟🔟
WALK M28 .... 84 A2
WHIT OL12 .... 23 E4
Rottingdene Dr
WYTH/NTH M22 .... 178 A6 🔟
Roughey Gdns WYTH/NTH M22 .. 178 A3
Rough Hill La BURY BL9 .... 35 E3
Roughlee Av SWIN M27 .... 85 E6
Roughtown Rd MOSL OL5 .... 99 E3
Roundcroft MPL/ROM SK6 .... 170 B2
Roundhey CHD/CHDH SK8........... 193 F1
Round Hey MOSL OL5 .... 99 D5 🔟
Roundhill Wy OLDE OL4 .... 80 C2
Round Thorn Rd MDTN M24 .... 74 A4
Roundthorn Rd NTHM/RTH M23 ... 177 D1
OLDE OL4 .... 79 F6
Roundthorn Wk
NTHM/RTH M23 .... 177 D1 🔟
Roundway BRAM/HZG SK7 .... 196 B3
Roundwood Rd WYTH/NTH M22 .. 162 B6
Rousdon Cl NEWH/MOS M40 ..... 107 E3 🔟
Rouse St ROCH OL11 .... 39 D3
Rowan Av SALE M33 .... 160 A3
URM M41 .... 119 E6 🔟
Rowan Cl FAIL M35 .... 110 A2
SLFD M6 .... 104 B5 🔟
WHIT OL12 .... 21 E2
Rowan Crs DUK SK16 .... 132 A2
Rowan Dr CHD/CHDH SK8 .... 196 A1
Rowan Pl PWCH M25 .... 88 C2 🔟
Rowanside Dr WILM/AE SK9 ...... 204 C3 🔟
Rowans St TOT/BURYW BL8 .... 33 D3
The Rowans BOL BL1 .... 44 C2 🔟
MOSL OL5 .... 99 E4
Rowan St HYDE SK14 .... 151 D2
Rowansweod Dr HYDE SK14 .... 132 B6
Rowan Tree Dr SALE M33 .... 159 F4
Rowan Tree Rd OLDS OL8 .... 95 E4
Rowanwood CHAD OL9 .... 76 C4 🔟
Rowany Cl PWCH M25 .... 88 B3
Rowarth Av DTN/ASHW M34 ..... 149 E3 🔟
Rowarth Rd NTHM/RTH M23 .... 177 D5
Rowcon Cl DTN/ASHW M34 ...... 129 F3 🔟
DTN/ASHW M34 .... 129 F4 🔟
Rowden Rd OLDE OL4 .... 97 F1

Rowe Gn DTN/ASHW M34 .... 130 A6
Rowena St BOLS/LL BL3 .... 66 A2
Rowendale St CMANE M1 .... 2 C6 🔟
Rowfield Dr NTHM/RTH M23 ...... 177 D4 🔟
Rowland Av URM M41 .... 119 F6 🔟
Rowlands Rd BURY BL9 .... 19 F4
Rowland St MILN OL16 .... 40 C1 🔟
SALQ/ORD M5................................... 122 B1
Rowlandsway WYTH/NTH M22 .... 178 B5
Rowland Wy OLDE OL4 .... 80 C4 🔟
Rowley Rd BRAM/HZG SK7 .... 198 C1 🔟
Rowley St AUL OL6 .... 113 E1
Rowood Av CHH M8 .... 106 C1
RDSH SK5 .... 147 D1 🔟
Rowrah Crs MDTN M24 .... 73 F2
Rowsley Av BOL BL1 .... 26 B6 🔟🔟
DID/WITH M20 .... 162 C1
Rowsley Gv RDSH SK5 .... 146 C4
Rowsley Rd ECC M30 .... 119 D1
STRET M32 .... 120 B6
Rowsley St OP/CLY M11 .... 107 F5 🔟
SLFD M6 .... 104 C2 🔟
Rowson Dr IRL M44 .... 134 B5
Rowton St BOLE BL2 .... 28 C4 🔟
Roxalina St BOLS/LL BL3 .... 46 C5
Roxburgh St GTN M18 .... 127 E4 🔟
Roxbury Av OLDE OL4..................... 80 B6
Roxby Cl WALK M28 .... 82 C2 🔟
Roxholme Wk NTHM/RTH M22 ... 192 A1
Royal Av BURY BL9 .... 34 A2
CCHDY M21 .... 141 E4
DROY M43 .... 110 C5
HEY OL10 .... 37 E6
URM M41 .... 138 B1
Royal Gdns ALT WA14 .... 173 D5
Royal George St EDGY/DAV SK3 .. 166 C5
Royal Oak Rd NTHM/RTH M23 .... 161 D6
Royal Oak Yd STKP SK1 .... 167 D4 🔟
Royal St MILN OL16......................... 24 A3
Royalthorn Dr WYTH/NTH M22 .. 178 A1 🔟
Royalthorn Rd WYTH/NTH M22 .. 178 B1
Royce Av HALE/TIMP WA15 .... 174 C2
Royce Rd HULME M15 .... 123 F3
Roydale St NEWH/MOS M40 .... 107 F4
Royden Av BKLY M9 .... 74 B6
IRL M44 .... 135 D3 🔟
Roydes St MDTN M24 .... 75 F1 🔟
Royds Cl BRUN/LGST M13 .... 125 E4 🔟
Royds Pl MILN OL16 .... 40 B2 🔟🔟
Royds St BURY BL9 .... 35 E3 🔟
LIT OL15 .... 13 D6 🔟
MILN OL16 .... 40 C2
MILN OL16 .... 41 D5
TOT/BURYW BL8............................... 18 A6
Royds St West MILN OL16 .... 40 B2
Royd St OLDS OL8 .... 95 D1 🔟
Royland Av BOLS/LL BL3 .... 47 E6
Royle Barn Rd ROCH OL11 .... 39 D5
Royle Cl OFTN SK2 .... 183 E2 🔟
OLDS OL8 .... 96 A2
Royle Green Rd WYTH/NTH M22 .. 162 C5
Royle Rd ROCH OL11 .... 39 E4
Royle St DTN/ASHW M34 .... 130 A4
RUSH/FAL M14 .... 144 B4
SLFD M6 .... 104 A6 🔟
STKP SK1 .... 167 D6 🔟
WALK M28 .... 83 E3 🔟
Royley ROY/SHW OL2..................... 60 A6
Royley Crs ROY/SHW OL2.............. 60 A6
Royley Rd OLDS OL8 .... 95 F1
Royon Dr EDGY/DAV SK3 .... 165 F6
Royston Av BOLE BL2 .... 47 F1
DTN/ASHW M34 .... 130 A4
OLDTF/WHR M16 .... 123 E6
Royston Cl TOT/BURYW BL8 .... 18 A4
Royston Rd OLDTF/WHR M16 ..... 122 C6
URM M41 .... 119 F6
Roy St BOLS/LL BL3 .... 45 F5
ROY/SHW OL2 .... 60 B5 🔟🔟
Royton Av SALE M33 .... 160 B3
Ruabon Rd DID/WITH M20 .... 164 A3
Ruby St BOL BL1 .... 28 A4
DTN/ASHW M34 .... 124 B3 🔟🔟
HULME M15 .... 124 B3 🔟🔟
RAMS BL0 .... 19 D2
Rudcroft Cl BRUN/LGST M13 ..... 124 C3 🔟
Rudding St ROY/SHW OL2 .... 79 E1
Ruddpark Rd WYTH/NTH M22..... 178 B6
Rudd St NEWH/MOS M40............... 92 B6
Rudford Av OP/CLY M11 .... 127 F1 🔟
Rudgwick Dr TOT/BURYW BL8 ...... 19 D6
Rudheath Av DID/WITH M20 .... 143 E4
Rudman Dr SALQ/ORD M5 .... 123 D1
Rudman St WHIT OL12 .... 22 C3
Rudolph St BOLS/LL BL3 .... 47 D6 🔟🔟
Rudston Av NEWH/MOS M40 ...... 92 C3 🔟
Rudyard Av MDTN M24 .... 58 A6
Rudyard Gv HTNM SK4 .... 146 B5
ROCH OL11 .... 40 A5
SALE M33.. 158 C3
Rudyard Rd SLFD M6 .... 103 D2 🔟
Rudyard St BRO M7 .... 105 E1 🔟
Rufford Av HYDE SK14 .... 151 D1
ROCH OL11 .... 39 E3 🔟

Rufford Cl *AUL* OL6 .... **97** D6
  ROY/SHW OL2 .... **61** D2
  WHTF M45 .... **71** E1
Rufford Dr *BOLS/LL* BL3 .... **64** B1
  WHTF M45 .... **71** D1
Rufford Gv *OLDTF/WHR* M16 .... **123** E6
Rufford Pl *GTN* M18 .... **128** A5 🔟
Rufford Rd *OLDTF/WHR* M16 .... **123** E6
Rugby Dr *SALE* M33 .... **159** E3
Rugby Rd *SLFD* M6 .... **102** B4 🔟
  WHIT OL12 .... **23** L4
Rugby St *BRO* M7 .... **105** F3
Rugeley St *SLFD* M6 .... **104** C2 🔟
Ruins La *BOLE* BL2 .... **29** F3
Ruislip Av *NEWH/MOS* M40 .... **107** F2
Ruislip Cl *OLDS* OL8 .... **96** C1
Rumworth Rd *HOR/BR* BL6 .... **44** A3
Rumworth St *BOLS/LL* BL3 .... **46** B5 🔟
Runger La *MANAIR* M90 .... **191** D2
Runhall Cl *WGTN/LGST* M12 .... **126** B3 🔟
Runnymeade *SLFD* M6 .... **102** B1
Runnymede Cl *EDGY/DAV* SK3 .... **166** A6
Runnymede Ct *BOLS/LL* BL3 .... **46** B4 🔟
  ROY/SHW OL2 .... **60** C5 🔟
Rupert St *BOLS/LL* BL3 .... **47** D5 🔟
  NEWH/MOS M40 .... **109** F3
  RAD M26 .... **69** F2
  RDSH SK5 .... **146** C4
  WHIT OL12 .... **22** A4 🔟
Ruscombe Fold *MDTN* M24 .... **56** B6 🔟
Rush Acre Cl *RAD* M26 .... **50** C6
Rush Bank *ROY/SHW* OL2 .... **61** D1
Rushbrooke Av *OP/CLY* M11 .... **109** D5 🔟
Rushbury Dr *ROY/SHW* OL2 .... **61** E5
Rushcroft Rd *ROY/SHW* OL2 .... **61** D1
Rushden Rd *BNG/LEV* M19 .... **145** F1 🔟
Rushen St *OP/CLY* M11 .... **109** D6 🔟
Rushey Av *HALE/TIMP* WA15 .... **190** B2
Rushey Fld *EDGW/EG* BL7 .... **14** A5
Rushey Fold La *BOL* BL1 .... **27** E5
Rushey Rd *WYTH/NTH* M22 .... **178** A2
Rushfield Dr *BRUN/LGST* M13 .... **126** A6 🔟
Rushfield Rd *CHD/CHDH* SK8 .... **195** E3
Rushford Av *BNG/LEV* M19 .... **145** E1
Rushford Gv *BOL* BL1 .... **28** A3
Rushford St *WGTN/LGST* M12 .... **126** B5
Rushlake Dr *BOL* BL1 .... **27** F6 🔟
Rushley Av *BRO* M7 .... **88** C6
Rushmere *AUL* OL6 .... **113** F1
Rushmere Av *BNG/LEV* M19 .... **145** F2
Rushmere Dr *TOT/BURYW* BL8 .... **33** D2
Rushmoor Cl *IRL* M44 .... **135** E1 🔟
Rush Mt *ROY/SHW* OL2 .... **42** A6
Rusholme Gv *RUSH/FAL* M14 .... **125** D6 🔟
Rusholme Pl *RUSH/FAL* M14 .... **125** D5
Rushside Rd *CHD/CHDH* SK8 .... **195** D3
Rush St *DUK* SK16 .... **132** A1 🔟
Rushton Cl *MPL/ROM* SK6 .... **187** E2 🔟
Rushton Dr *BRAM/HZG* SK7 .... **182** B6
  MPL/ROM SK6 .... **170** A2
  MPL/ROM SK6 .... **187** B2
Rushton Gv *OLDE* OL4 .... **62** C6 🔟
  OP/CLY M11 .... **127** E2
Rushton Rd *BOL* BL1 .... **26** C6 🔟🔟
  CHD/CHDH SK8 .... **195** E5 🔟
  EDGY/DAV SK3 .... **165** F6
Rushwick Av *NEWH/MOS* M40 .... **107** F2
Rushyfield Crs *MPL/ROM* SK6 .... **170** B2
Rushy Hill Vw *WHIT* OL12 .... **21** F4 🔟
Ruskin Av *CHAD* OL9 .... **94** A2 🔟
  DTN/ASHW M34 .... **129** D2
  DTN/ASHW M34 .... **148** C2
  FWTH BL4 .... **67** D4
  RUSH/FAL M14 .... **124** C5
Ruskin Crs *PWCH* M25 .... **88** A2
Ruskin Gdns *MPL/ROM* SK6 .... **169** E2 🔟
Ruskin Gv *MPL/ROM* SK6 .... **169** E2
Ruskington Dr *BKLY* M9 .... **91** E6
Ruskin Rd *DROY* M43 .... **110** B5
  OLDTF/WHR M16 .... **123** D6
  PWCH M25 .... **87** F2
  RDSH SK5 .... **146** C2
  ROCH OL11 .... **39** F5
Ruskin St *CHAD* OL9 .... **78** B3
  RAD M26 .... **52** A5
Rusland Dr *BOLE* BL2 .... **29** F5
Russell Av *MPL/ROM* SK6 .... **200** C2
  OLDTF/WHR M16 .... **122** B1 🔟
  SALE M33 .... **140** B6
Russell Ct *FWTH* BL4 .... **66** C3 🔟
  LHULT M38 .... **80** D2
Russell Dr *IRL* M44 .... **135** E1 🔟
Russell Rd *OLDTF/WHR* M16 .... **123** E6
  PART M31 .... **155** E2
  SLFD M6 .... **102** C2
Russell St *AUL* OL6 .... **113** E3
  BOL BL1 .... **46** B1
  BURY BL9 .... **34** A3 🔟🔟
  CHAD OL9 .... **77** F4 🔟
  CHH M8 .... **106** A3 🔟
  DTN/ASHW M34 .... **130** A6 🔟🔟
  DUK SK16 .... **131** D1

ECC M30 .... **101** F5
  FWTH BL4 .... **66** B4
  HEY OL10 .... **37** F5
  LHULT M38 .... **83** D2 🔟
  MOSL OL5 .... **99** D4
  OFTN SK2 .... **183** E1
  OLDTF/WHR M16 .... **124** A6
  PWCH M25 .... **89** D1
Russet Rd *BKLY* M9 .... **91** E4
Ruth Av *NEWH/MOS* M40 .... **93** F4
Ruthen La *OLDTF/WHR* M16 .... **122** C5 🔟
Rutherford Av *RUSH/FAL* M14 .... **124** C6 🔟🔟
Rutherford Cl *HYDE* SK14 .... **150** B1 🔟🔟
Rutherglade Cl
  NEWH/MOS M40 .... **107** D1 🔟
Rutherglen Dr *BOLS/LL* BL3 .... **44** C3
Rutherglen Wk
  NEWH/MOS M40 .... **107** F2 🔟
Ruthin Av *BKLY* M9 .... **74** A6
  CHD/CHDH SK8 .... **180** C5
  MDTN M24 .... **75** E5
Ruthin Cl *OLDS* OL8 .... **94** C3
  WHIT OL12 .... **9** D2 🔟
Ruth St *BOL* BL1 .... **46** C1 🔟🔟
  BURY BL9 .... **34** A3 🔟🔟
  GTN M18 .... **127** E6
  OLD OL1 .... **79** D3
  WHIT OL12 .... **9** D2 🔟
Rutland Av *DID/WITH* M20 .... **143** E6
  OLDTF/WHR M16 .... **122** B6
  SWIN M27 .... **86** A3
  WALK M28 .... **138** C1
Rutland Cl *AUL* OL6 .... **113** E5 🔟
  BOLS/LL BL3 .... **49** F5 🔟
  CHD/CHDH SK8 .... **179** F1
Rutland Crs *RDSH* SK5 .... **148** B6
Rutland Dr *BRO* M7 .... **89** D5
  BURY BL9 .... **53** E3
Rutland Gv *BOL* BL1 .... **27** D6 🔟🔟
  FWTH BL4 .... **66** A4 🔟
Rutland La *SALE* M33 .... **141** D6
Rutland Rd *ALT* WA14 .... **174** B1
  BRAM/HZG SK7 .... **198** C1
  DROY M43 .... **109** F5
  ECC M30 .... **102** A4
  IRL M44 .... **134** B6
  PART M31 .... **154** C3
  WALK M28 .... **83** D4
Rutland St *AUL* OL6 .... **113** E5
  BOLS/LL BL3 .... **46** B5 🔟🔟
  CHAD OL9 .... **78** A6
  FAIL M35 .... **94** A5 🔟
  GTN M18 .... **127** F5 🔟🔟
  HEY OL10 .... **37** E4 🔟
  HYDE SK14 .... **131** E4
  SWIN M27 .... **85** F4
Rutland Wy *ROY/SHW* OL2 .... **62** A1
Rutter's La *BRAM/HZG* SK7 .... **184** A5
Ryall Av *SALQ/ORD* M5 .... **122** C1 🔟🔟
Ryall Av South *SALQ/ORD* M5 .... **122** C1
Ryan St *OP/CLY* M11 .... **127** E2
Rydal Av *BRAM/HZG* SK7 .... **184** A4
  CHAD OL9 .... **76** C2
  DROY M43 .... **109** F6
  ECC M30 .... **100** C3
  HYDE SK14 .... **131** D4
  MDTN M24 .... **75** D5
  MPL/ROM SK6 .... **200** C1
  ROY/SHW OL2 .... **60** A1 🔟
  SALE M33 .... **139** D6
  URM M41 .... **137** E3
Rydal Cl *BURY* BL9 .... **53** C2
  CHD/CHDH SK8 .... **179** F3 🔟
  DTN/ASHW M34 .... **147** F1
Rydal Crs *SWIN* M27 .... **102** A1
  WALK M28 .... **83** E4
Rydal Dr *HALE/TIMP* WA15 .... **190** B1
Rydal Gv *AULW* OL7 .... **112** A3
  FWTH BL4 .... **65** D4
  HEY OL10 .... **56** B1
  WHTF M45 .... **71** E3 🔟
Rydal Rd *BOL* BL1 .... **26** B6
  BOLS/LL BL3 .... **64** C1
  STRET M32 .... **121** E6 🔟
Ryde Av *DTN/ASHW* M34 .... **149** F3
  HTNM SK4 .... **165** F3
Ryder Av *ALT* WA14 .... **158** C6 🔟
Ryder Brow *GTN* M18 .... **127** F5
Ryderbrow Rd *GTN* M18 .... **127** E5
Ryder St *BOL* BL1 .... **27** D5
  HEY OL10 .... **37** E5 🔟🔟
  NEWH/MOS M40 .... **107** E3 🔟🔟
Ryde St *BOLS/LL* BL3 .... **45** E5 🔟🔟
Rydings La *WHIT* OL12 .... **10** B5
Rydings Rd *WHIT* OL12 .... **23** F1
Ryebank Gv *AUL* OL6 .... **113** E2
Ryebank Rd *CCHDY* M21 .... **141** D2
Rye Bank Rd *OLDTF/WHR* M16 .... **122** C6
Reyburn Av *WYTH/NTH* M22 .... **178** B4 🔟
Ryeburn Dr *BOLE* BL2 .... **28** C2 🔟
Reyburne St *OLDE* OL4 .... **80** A4
Ryeburn Wk *URM* M41 .... **118** A5
Rye Cft *WHTF* M45 .... **70** A4
Ryecroft Av *HEY* OL10 .... **37** F5
Rye Croft Av *SLFD* M6 .... **103** D4
Ryecroft Av *TOT/BURYW* BL8 .... **32** A1

Ryecroft Cl *CHAD* OL9 .... **94** A2
Ryecroft Gv *NTHM/RTH* M23 .... **161** E6
Ryecroft La *DTN/ASHW* M34 .... **129** F2 🔟
  WALK M28 .... **100** A3
Ryecroft Rd *STRET* M32 .... **140** A2
Ryecroft St *AULW* OL7 .... **112** A6
Ryecroft Vw *DTN/ASHW* M34 .... **129** D1 🔟
Ryedale Av *NEWH/MOS* M40 .... **107** F2 🔟
Ryedale Cl *HTNM* SK4 .... **165** F2
Ryefield Cl *HALE/TIMP* WA15 .... **176** A2 🔟
Ryefield Rd *SALE* M33 .... **158** A3 🔟
Ryefield St *BOL* BL1 .... **28** B6
Ryeland Cl *MILN* OL16 .... **40** C3
Rye St *HEY* OL10 .... **37** F4
Rylance St *OP/CLY* M11 .... **107** F6
Rylands St *GTN* M18 .... **127** E5 🔟🔟
Rylane Wk *NEWH/MOS* M40 .... **107** F2 🔟
Ryley Av *BOLS/LL* BL3 .... **45** F4 🔟🔟
Ryleys La *WILM/AE* SK9 .... **209** D4
Rylstone Av *CCHDY* M21 .... **162** B2
Ryther Gv *BKLY* M9 .... **73** F6 🔟
Ryton Av *GTN* M18 .... **127** D6

S

Sabden Cl *HEY* OL10 .... **36** B5
  NEWH/MOS M40 .... **107** F4
Sabrina St *CHH* M8 .... **105** F2 🔟🔟
Sackville Cl *ROY/SHW* OL2 .... **42** B6
Sackville St *AUL* OL6 .... **112** C4 🔟
  BOLE BL2 .... **48** A2 🔟🔟
  CMANE M1 .... **3** E5
  CSLFD M3 .... **2** A2
  ROCH OL11 .... **39** D5 🔟🔟
Saddle Gv *DROY* M43 .... **111** E4
Saddle St *BOLE* BL2 .... **28** C5 🔟
Saddlewood Av *BNG/LEV* M19 .... **164** B3
Sadie Av *STRET* M32 .... **120** B5
Sadler St *BOLS/LL* BL3 .... **47** E5 🔟
  MDTN M24 .... **75** D2
Saffron Dr *OLDE* OL4 .... **80** B1
Sagars Rd *WILM/AE* SK9 .... **194** A5
Sagar St *CHH* M8 .... **106** A3
St Agnes Rd *BRUN/LGST* M13 .... **145** D1 🔟
St Agnes St *RDSH* SK5 .... **128** A6 🔟
St Aidan's Cl *ROCH* OL11 .... **39** D2 🔟
St Aidan's Gv *BRO* M7 .... **104** C1
St Albans Av *AUL* OL6 .... **112** C1
  HTNM SK4 .... **146** A6 🔟
  NEWH/MOS M40 .... **108** C2
St Albans Cl *OLDS* OL8 .... **96** A1
St Albans Crs *ALT* WA14 .... **158** A5
St Alban's St *MILN* OL16 .... **39** F1
St Alban's Ter *CHH* M8 .... **106** A2 🔟
St Aldates *MPL/ROM* SK6 .... **169** D3
St Ambrose Rd *OLD* OL1 .... **80** A2
St Andrew's Av *DROY* M43 .... **109** F6
  ECC M30 .... **101** F6 🔟
  HALE/TIMP WA15 .... **158** C6
St Andrews Cl *ALT* WA14 .... **158** A4
  HTNM SK4 .... **165** F1
Saint Andrew's Cl *MPL/ROM* SK6 .... **169** F4
St Andrew's Cl *RAMS* BL0 .... **7** D6
St Andrew's Dr *HEY* OL10 .... **37** E5
St Andrews Rd *CHD/CHDH* SK8 .... **180** A6
  HTNM SK4 .... **165** F1
  RAD M26 .... **51** D3
  STRET M32 .... **139** F1
St Andrew's Sq *CMANE* M1 .... **125** D1 🔟🔟
  CMANE M1 .... **125** D1
St Andrew's Vw *RAD* M26 .... **51** D3
  SLFD M6 .... **103** F4 🔟
St Anne's Av *ROY/SHW* OL2 .... **60** B6
  SLFD M6 .... **103** F4 🔟
St Anne's Ct *DTN/ASHW* M34 .... **130** A3 🔟
  SALE M33 .... **160** A1 🔟
St Anne's Dr *DTN/ASHW* M34 .... **130** B5
St Anne's Gdns *HEY* OL10 .... **38** A5
St Annes Meadow
  TOT/BURYW BL8 .... **18** A6 🔟
St Annes Rd *CCHDY* M21 .... **141** F4
  DTN/ASHW M34 .... **130** A3
St Annes St *HYDE* SK14 .... **153** E3 🔟
  NEWH/MOS M40 .... **108** A1
St Anns Cl *PWCH* M25 .... **88** A2
St Ann's Rd *BRAM/HZG* SK7 .... **184** A6 🔟
  MILN OL16 .... **24** A5
  PWCH M25 .... **88** A2
St Ann's Rd North *CHD/CHDH* SK8 .... **179** F6
St Ann's Rd South *CHD/CHDH* SK8 .... **180** A6
St Ann's Sq *CHD/CHDH* SK8 .... **194** A1 🔟
  CMANW M2 .... **2** D3
St Anns St *SALE* M33 .... **161** D2 🔟
  SWIN M27 .... **85** F5 🔟
St Ann St *CMANW* M2 .... **2** C3
St Asaphs Dr *AUL* OL6 .... **96** C6
St Aubin's Rd *BOLE* BL2 .... **47** F3 🔟
St Augustine's Rd
  EDGY/DAV SK3 .... **165** F5 🔟
St Augustine St *BOL* BL1 .... **27** E5
  NEWH/MOS M40 .... **107** F2 🔟
St Austell Dr *CHD/CHDH* SK8 .... **193** F1
  TOT/BURYW BL8 .... **18** A3 🔟🔟
St Austell Rd *OLDTF/WHR* M16 .... **142** C2

St Austells Dr *PWCH* M25 .... **71** F6
  SWIN M27 .... **103** D1
St Barnabas's Dr *LIT* OL15 .... **12** B5
Saint Bartholomew's Dr
  SALQ/ORD M5 .... **123** D1 🔢
Saint Bartholomew St
  BOLS/LL BL3 .... **47** E5 🔢
St Bees Cl *CHD/CHDH* SK8 .... **179** F4
  RUSH/FAL M14 .... **124** B5
St Bees Rd *BOLE* BL2 .... **29** D5
St Benedict's Sq
  WGTN/LGST M12 .... **126** A3 🔢
St Bernard's Av *SLFD* M6 .... **105** D2 🔢
St Boniface Rd *SLFD* M6 .... **105** D3
St Brannock's Rd *CCHDY* M21 .... **142** A2
  CHD/CHDH SK8 .... **195** F2 🔢
St Brelades Dr *BRO* M7 .... **90** A5
St Brendan's Rd *DID/WITH* M20 .... **143** F4
St Brendan's Rd North
  DID/WITH M20 .... **143** F4
St Brides Wy *OLDTF/WHR* M16 .... **123** E4
St Catherine's Rd *DID/WITH* M20 .... **143** F4
St Chad's Av *NEWH/MOS* SK6 .... **170** A3
St Chad's Cl *MILN* OL16 .... **23** D6 🔢
St Chads Crs *OLDS* OL8 .... **95** E4
St Chad's Gv *MPL/ROM* SK6 .... **170** A3
St Chad's Rd *DID/WITH* M20 .... **144** B4
St Chad's Rd *CHH* M8 .... **106** B3 🔢
St Christopher's Av *AUL* OL6 .... **113** F1
St Christophers Cl
  DID/WITH M20 .... **143** D5 🔢
St Christopher's Dr *MPL/ROM* SK6 .... **169** E3
St Christopher's Rd *AUL* OL6 .... **113** E1
St Clair Rd *TOT/BURYW* BL8 .... **18** A2 🔢
St Clement's Av *SALQ/ORD* M5 .... **122** C2 🔢
St Clements Fold *URM* M41 .... **138** C1 🔢
St Clement's Rd *CCHDY* M21 .... **91** E3
Saint Cuthberts Fold *OLDS* OL8 .... **96** B4
St David's Av *MPL/ROM* SK6 .... **169** F3
St David's Cl *AUL* OL6 .... **97** E6
  SALE M33 .... **159** E2 🔢
St David's Rd *BRAM/HZG* SK7 .... **184** A6 🔢
St Dominics Ms *BOLS/LL* BL3 .... **46** A6 🔢
St Dominics Wy *MDTN* M24 .... **75** F6
St Edmund Hall Cl *RAMS* BL0 .... **19** D1 🔢
St Edmund's Rd *NEWH/MOS* M40 .... **107** F1
St Edmund St *BOL* BL1 .... **46** C2
St Elisabeth's Wy *RDSH* SK5 .... **146** C4
St Elmo Av *OFTN* SK2 .... **168** B6
St Elmo Pk *POY/DIS* SK12 .... **200** A5
St Ethelbert's Av *BOLS/LL* BL3 .... **45** F4 🔢
St Gabriel's Cl *ROCH* OL11 .... **39** E6
St George's Av
  HALE/TIMP WA15 .... **159** E5 🔢
  HYDE SK14 .... **150** B1 🔢
St George's Crs *HALE/TIMP* WA15 .... **159** E5 🔢
  SLFD M6 .... **102** D4 🔢
  WALK M28 .... **83** E3
St Georges Dr *HYDE* SK14 .... **150** B2
  NEWH/MOS M40 .... **92** C6
St George's Gdns *DTN/ASHW* M34 .... **149** E2
St George's Rd *BOL* BL1 .... **46** C2
  BURY BL9 .... **53** F5
  BURY BL9 .... **54** A5 🔢
  DROY M43 .... **110** A4
  PART M31 .... **136** B5
  ROCH OL11 .... **21** D5
  RUSH/FAL M14 .... **144** C4
  STRET M32 .... **139** F1
St Georges Sq *BOL* BL1 .... **47** D1 🔢
  CHAD OL9 .... **93** F2
St George's St *BOL* BL1 .... **47** D1 🔢
  STLY SK15 .... **114** B1
St George's Wy *SLFD* M6 .... **104** B3 🔢
St Germain St *FWTH* BL4 .... **66** B3
St Giles Dr *HYDE* SK14 .... **151** D1
St Gregorys Cl *FWTH* BL4 .... **66** A3
St Helena Rd *BOL* BL1 .... **46** C2
St Helens Rd *BOLS/LL* BL3 .... **46** A5
St Helier's Dr *BRO* M7 .... **90** A5 🔢
St Heliers St *BOLS/LL* BL3 .... **46** B5 🔢
St Hilda's Dr *OLD* OL1 .... **78** B3 🔢
St Hilda's Rd *DTN/ASHW* M34 .... **129** F3
  OLDTF/WHR M16 .... **122** C4
  WYTH/NTH M22 .... **162** B4
St Hilda's Vw *DTN/ASHW* M34 .... **129** F4 🔢
St Hugh's Cl *ALT* WA14 .... **158** C5 🔢
St Ives Av *CHD/CHDH* SK8 .... **181** E1 🔢
St Ives Crs *SALE* M33 .... **159** E4
St Ives Rd *RUSH/FAL* M14 .... **143** F1 🔢
St James Av *BOLE* BL2 .... **48** C1 🔢
  TOT/BURYW BL8 .... **32** C4
St James' Cl *MILN* OL16 .... **60** A1
St James Ct *HALE/TIMP* WA15 .... **174** C3
  SLFD M6 .... **102** C4 🔢
St James Dr *SALE* M33 .... **159** E2
  WILM/AE SK9 .... **203** E5 🔢
St James Rd *BRO* M7 .... **105** F1
St James's Gv *ALT* WA14 .... **159** D4
St James's Rd *BRO* M7 .... **105** F1
St James's Sq *CMANW* M2 .... **2** D4 🔢
St James's St *OLD* OL1 .... **79** E4
St James's Ter *HEY* OL10 .... **37** D5 🔢
St James St *AUL* OL6 .... **113** E5

CMANE M1 .... **3** E4 🔢
CMANE M1 .... **3** E5 🔢
ECC M30 .... **101** F5 🔢
FWTH BL4 .... **65** F4
HEY OL10 .... **37** D5 🔢
MILN OL16 .... **42** A1
ROY/SHW OL2 .... **61** F2 🔢
St James' Wy *CHD/CHDH* SK8 .... **195** D3 🔢
St John's Av *DROY* M43 .... **110** C5
St John's Cl *BRO* M7 .... **105** E1 🔢
  DUK SK16 .... **131** F1 🔢
  MPL/ROM SK6 .... **169** F3
St John's Ct *HYDE* SK14 .... **132** A6 🔢
  OLDE OL4 .... **81** D4 🔢
  RAD M26 .... **69** F1
St John's Dr *HYDE* SK14 .... **132** A6 🔢
  MILN OL16 .... **40** C1
St John's Gdns *MOSL* OL5 .... **99** D3
St John's Rd *ALT* WA14 .... **174** A4
  BRAM/HZG SK7 .... **183** F6
  BRUN/LGST M13 .... **126** A5
  DTN/ASHW M34 .... **130** A4
  HTNM SK4 .... **164** C3 🔢
  HTNM SK4 .... **164** C3 🔢
  OLDTF/WHR M16 .... **123** D5
  WILM/AE SK9 .... **208** C2
St John's St *BRO* M7 .... **105** E1 🔢
  CHAD OL9 .... **78** A6 🔢
  FWTH BL4 .... **66** C3
  RAD M26 .... **69** F1
St John St *CSLFD* M3 .... **2** B5
  DUK SK16 .... **131** F1 🔢
  ECC M30 .... **101** E6 🔢
  IRL M44 .... **135** E1
  OLDE OL4 .... **80** C5
  SWIN M27 .... **103** E1
  WALK M28 .... **83** D1 🔢
St John's Wk *CHAD* OL9 .... **78** A5 🔢
St Josephs Av *WHTF* M45 .... **71** F4
St Joseph's Dr *MILN* OL16 .... **40** C3 🔢
  SALQ/ORD M5 .... **122** C1 🔢
St Joseph St *BOL* BL1 .... **27** E5 🔢
St Kilda Av *FWTH* BL4 .... **67** D5
St Kilda's Av *DROY* M43 .... **110** A4
Saint Lawrence Quay
  SALQ/ORD M5 .... **122** A2
St Lawrence Rd *DTN/ASHW* M34 .... **130** A4
St Leonard's Ct *SALE* M33 .... **159** D1 🔢
St Leonards Dr *HALE/TIMP* WA15 .... **175** D1
St Leonard's Rd *HTNM* SK4 .... **146** B6
St Leonard's St *MDTN* M24 .... **75** E2
St Lesmo Rd *EDGY/DAV* SK3 .... **165** F5
St Lukes Ct *CHAD* OL9 .... **77** E4 🔢
St Luke's Rd *SLFD* M6 .... **103** E5
St Luke St *ROCH* OL11 .... **40** A2 🔢
St Margaret's Av *BNG/LEV* M19 .... **145** D5 🔢
St Margaret's Cl *BOL* BL1 .... **45** F1 🔢
  PWCH M25 .... **72** A5
St Margaret's Rd *ALT* WA14 .... **174** A3
  BOL BL1 .... **45** F1 🔢
  CHD/CHDH SK8 .... **181** E1 🔢
  NEWH/MOS M40 .... **93** E2
  PWCH M25 .... **72** A6
St Mark's Av *ALT* WA14 .... **173** E2
  ROY/SHW OL2 .... **61** E5
St Mark's Cl *ROY/SHW* OL2 .... **61** E5
St Mark's Crs *WALK* M28 .... **83** E4 🔢
St Mark's La *CHH* M8 .... **90** A5 🔢
St Mark's St *BNG/LEV* M19 .... **146** A2
  BOLS/LL BL3 .... **47** D4
  MPL/ROM SK6 .... **169** E1 🔢
St Mark St *DUK* SK16 .... **112** C6
St Mark's Vw *BOLS/LL* BL3 .... **47** D4 🔢
St Martin's Av *HTNM* SK4 .... **166** A3
St Martin's Cl *DROY* M43 .... **110** A4 🔢
  HYDE SK14 .... **151** D1 🔢
St Martin's Dr *BRO* M7 .... **90** A5 🔢
St Martin's Rd *MPL/ROM* SK6 .... **87** E1 🔢
  OLDS OL8 .... **96** B3
  SALE M33 .... **138** B5
St Martin's St *ROCH* OL11 .... **39** D6
St Mary's Cl *MILN* OL16 .... **40** C2
  PWCH M25 .... **88** B1 🔢
  STKP SK1 .... **167** E4 🔢
St Mary's Ct *NEWH/MOS* M40 .... **92** C5 🔢
St Mary's Dr *CHD/CHDH* SK8 .... **181** D1 🔢
  RDSH SK5 .... **147** D6
St Mary's Ga *CMANE* M1 .... **2** D2 🔢
  ROY/SHW OL2 .... **61** F2 🔢
  WHIT OL12 .... **22** C6
St Mary's Hall Rd *CHH* M8 .... **90** A4
St Mary's Parsonage *CSLFD* M3 .... **2** C3 🔢
St Mary's Pl *BURY* BL9 .... **33** F5 🔢
St Mary's Rd *ALT* WA14 .... **173** F5
  ECC M30 .... **102** A5
  HYDE SK14 .... **131** F4 🔢
  NEWH/MOS M40 .... **92** C6
  PWCH M25 .... **88** B1 🔢
  SALE M33 .... **139** D6
  WALK M28 .... **83** D1 🔢
St Mary's St *CSLFD* M3 .... **2** C3 🔢
  HULME M15 .... **123** F4 🔢
  OLD OL1 .... **79** D3

St Mary's Wy *OLD* OL1 .... **78** C4
  STKP SK1 .... **167** E3 🔢
St Matthew's Dr *OLD* OL1 .... **77** E1
St Matthew's Rd *EDGY/DAV* SK3 .... **166** B5
St Mawes Ct *RAD* M26 .... **50** A4 🔢
St Michael's Av *BOLS/LL* BL3 .... **65** F1
  BRAM/HZG SK7 .... **196** C2
St Michaels Cl *SALE* M33 .... **138** C5 🔢
St Michael's Rd *HYDE* SK14 .... **151** D1
St Michael's Sq *ANC* M4 .... **106** B4 🔢
St Modwen Rd *STRET* M32 .... **120** A4
St Osmund's Dr *BOLE* BL2 .... **48** C2
St Osmund's Gv *BOLE* BL2 .... **48** C2 🔢
St Oswald's Rd *BNG/LEV* M19 .... **145** F1
St Pauls Cl *STLY* SK15 .... **115** D5 🔢
St Paul's Ct *RAD* M26 .... **69** E2 🔢
St Paul's Hill Rd *HYDE* SK14 .... **151** D1
St Paul's Rd *BRO* M7 .... **89** D4
  DID/WITH M20 .... **144** A5
  HTNM SK4 .... **165** F1
  WALK M28 .... **83** F1 🔢
St Paul's Ter *BURY* BL9 .... **34** B4
  HYDE SK14 .... **131** F6 🔢
  RAMS BL0 .... **7** D4 🔢
  STKP SK1 .... **167** E2 🔢
  STLY SK15 .... **115** D5
St Peter's Av *BOL* BL1 .... **26** B5 🔢
St Peters Cl *AULW* OL7 .... **112** A5
St Peter's Dr *HYDE* SK14 .... **151** D1 🔢
St Petersgate *STKP* SK1 .... **166** C4 🔢
St Peter's Rd *BURY* BL9 .... **53** D3 🔢
  SWIN M27 .... **85** F6
St Peter's Sq *CMANW* M2 .... **2** D5 🔢
  STKP SK1 .... **166** C4 🔢
  STKP SK1 .... **167** D4 🔢
St Peter's St *AUL* OL6 .... **112** B5 🔢
  MILN OL16 .... **40** C1
St Peter's Ter *FWTH* BL4 .... **66** B4
St Peter's Wy *BOL* BL1 .... **47** D1 🔢
  BOLS/LL BL3 .... **47** D5 🔢
St Philip's Av *BOLS/LL* BL3 .... **46** B5
St Philip's Pl *CSLFD* M3 .... **105** D5 🔢
St Philip's Rd *GTN* M18 .... **127** E5 🔢
St Phillip's Dr *ROY/SHW* OL2 .... **78** C2
St Saviour's Rd *OFTN* SK2 .... **184** A3 🔢
Saintsbridge Rd
  WYTH/NTH M22 .... **178** A5 🔢
St Simons Cl *OFTN* SK2 .... **168** A5
St Simon St *CSLFD* M3 .... **105** E4
St Stephen's Av
  DTN/ASHW M34 .... **129** F1 🔢
St Stephen's Cl *BOLE* BL2 .... **48** A4 🔢
  BRUN/LGST M13 .... **125** E4
St Stephen St *CSLFD* M3 .... **2** A2
  OLD OL1 .... **79** E3 🔢
St Stephens Vw *DROY* M43 .... **110** B5
St Teresa's Rd *OLDTF/WHR* M16 .... **122** B6 🔢
St Thomas Ct *BURY* BL9 .... **34** B5 🔢
St Thomas' Pl *CHH* M8 .... **106** B3 🔢
St Thomas's Cir *OLDS* OL8 .... **78** B6 🔢
St Thomas's Pl *STKP* SK1 .... **167** D5 🔢
St Thomas St *BOL* BL1 .... **27** E5 🔢
  BOL BL1 .... **27** E5 🔢
St Thomas St North *OLDS* OL8 .... **78** B6 🔢
St Thomas St South *OLDS* OL8 .... **78** B6 🔢
St Vincent St *ANC* M4 .... **107** D5 🔢
  HALE/TIMP WA15 .... **174** B3
St Werburgh's Rd *CCHDY* M21 .... **142** A3
St Wilfred's Dr *WHIT* OL12 .... **22** B1 🔢
St Wilfrids St *HULME* M15 .... **123** F3 🔢
St Williams Av *BOLS/LL* BL3 .... **46** C6
Salcombe Av *BOLE* BL2 .... **31** E6 🔢
Salcombe Cl *SALE* M33 .... **138** C6 🔢
Salcombe Gv *BOLE* BL2 .... **49** D3 🔢
Salcombe Rd *OFTN* SK2 .... **168** A5
  OP/CLY M11 .... **127** E1 🔢
Sale Heys Rd *SALE* M33 .... **159** D2 🔢
Salem Gv *OLDE* OL4 .... **80** B5
Sale Rd *NTHM/RTH* M23 .... **161** E3 🔢
Sale St *LIT* OL15 .... **12** C5
Salford Ap *CSLFD* M3 .... **2** C1 🔢
Salford Rd *WHTN* BL5 .... **64** A4
Salford St *BURY* BL9 .... **34** B3
  OLDE OL4 .... **80** A6 🔢
Salik Gdns *ROCH* OL11 .... **40** A2 🔢
Salisbury Av *HEY* OL10 .... **56** A1
Salisbury Crs *AUL* OL6 .... **97** E6
Salisbury Dr *DUK* SK16 .... **132** B2 🔢
  PWCH M25 .... **89** D3 🔢
Salisbury Rd *ALT* WA14 .... **158** B6
  CCHDY M21 .... **142** A2 🔢
  ECC M30 .... **102** A3
  OLDE OL4 .... **79** F5 🔢
  RAD M26 .... **50** C4 🔢
  SWIN M27 .... **85** F6
  URM M41 .... **119** E5 🔢
  WHTF M45 .... **71** D3 🔢
Salisbury St *BOLS/LL* BL3 .... **46** B3 🔢
  MDTN M24 .... **75** F2 🔢
  RDSH SK5 .... **147** D3 🔢
  ROY/SHW OL2 .... **61** D1
  RUSH/FAL M14 .... **124** B5 🔢
Salisbury Ter *BOLS/LL* BL3 .... **50** A6
Salkeld St *ROCH* OL11 .... **40** A2

Salmon Flds ROY/SHW OL2 .... 61 D6
Salmon St ANC M4 .... 3 F2
Salmsbury Hall CI RAMS BL0 .... 18 C1
Salop St BOLE BL2 .... 47 E2
  SLFD M6 .... 104 B3
Saitash CI WYTH/NTH M22 .... 178 B6
Saltdene Rd WYTH/NTH M22 .... 178 A6
Saltergate BOLS/LL BL3 .... 45 E5
Salteye Rd ECC M30 .... 100 B6
Saltford Av ANC M4 .... 107 D5
Salthill Av HEY OL10 .... 56 C2
Salthill Dr WYTH/NTH M22 .... 178 C5
Salthouse CI TOT/BURYW BL8 .... 33 D1
Saltire Gdns BRO M7 .... 89 F5
Saltney Av DID/WITH M20 .... 143 D4
Saltram CI BOLS/LL BL3 .... 50 A4
Saltrush Rd WYTH/NTH M22 .... 178 B5
Salts Dr LIT OL15 .... 12 B5
Salts St ROY/SHW OL2 .... 61 F2
Salutation St HULME M15 .... 124 B3
Sam Cowan CI RUSH/FAL M14 .... 124 B6
Samian Gdns BRO M7 .... 105 D2
Samlesbury CI DID/WITH M20 .... 163 D2
  ROY/SHW OL2 .... 61 D2
Sammy Cookson CI
  RUSH/FAL M14 .... 124 B6
Samouth CI NEWH/MOS M40 .... 107 E4
Samson St MILN OL16 .... 24 A5
Sam Swire St HULME M15 .... 123 F4
Samuel La ROY/SHW OL2 .... 60 C1
Samuel Ogden St CMANE M1 .... 3 F6
Samuel St BNG/LEV M19 .... 145 F3
  BURY BL9 .... 34 B4
  FAIL M35 .... 94 A5
  HEY OL10 .... 37 D5
  HTNM SK4 .... 166 B2
  ROCH OL11 .... 39 D5
Sanby Av GTN M18 .... 127 D5
Sanby St GTN M18 .... 127 D5
Sanctuary CI HULME M15 .... 124 C4
Sandacre Rd NTHM/RTH M23 .... 161 F6
Sandal St NEWH/MOS M40 .... 107 F4
Sandbach Av RUSH/FAL M14 .... 143 D3
Sandbach Rd RDSH SK5 .... 146 C1
  SALE M33 .... 161 D2
Sandbank Gdns WHIT OL12 .... 9 D1
Sand Banks BOL BL1 .... 28 A1
Sandbed La MOSL OL5 .... 99 D3
Sandbrook Wy DTN/ASHW M34 .... 130 A4
Sandby Dr MPL/ROM SK6 .... 171 F5
Sanderling Rd OFTN SK2 .... 185 E2
Sanderson CI WALK M28 .... 84 C6
Sanderson St BURY BL9 .... 34 B4
  NEWH/MOS M40 .... 107 F2
Sanderstead Dr BKLY M9 .... 91 F2
Sandfield Dr HOR/BR BL6 .... 44 A3
Sandfield Rd MILN OL16 .... 40 C2
Sandford Av GTN M18 .... 127 E5
Sandford CI BOLE BL2 .... 29 F4
Sandford Rd SALE M33 .... 161 D2
Sandford Station La RDSH SK5 .... 146 B1
Sandford St RAD M26 .... 52 B5
Sandgate Av OP/CLY M11 .... 109 E5
Sandgate Dr URM M41 .... 119 D5
Sandgate Rd CHAD OL9 .... 77 F5
  WHTF M45 .... 71 F4
Sandham St BOLS/LL BL3 .... 47 E5
Sandheys DTN/ASHW M34 .... 130 A4
Sandheys Gv GTN M18 .... 127 F5
Sandhill CI HYDE SK14 .... 132 A6
Sandhill Wk WYTH/NTH M22 .... 177 F5
  ROCH OL11 .... 40 A6
Sand Hole Rd FWTH BL4 .... 67 E5
Sandhurst Av DID/WITH M20 .... 143 E5
Sandhurst CI TOT/BURYW BL8 .... 32 C4
Sandhurst Ct BOLE BL2 .... 48 C3
Sandhurst Dr BOLE BL2 .... 48 C3
  WILM/AE SK9 .... 204 A2
Sandhurst Rd DID/WITH M20 .... 163 F3
  OFTN SK2 .... 183 F2
Sandhutton Rd BKLY M9 .... 91 E4
Sandilands Rd NTHM/RTH M23 .... 160 B5
Sandileigh Av CHD/CHDH SK8 .... 181 E1
  DID/WITH M20 .... 143 F6
  HALE/TIMP WA15 .... 175 D4
  RDSH SK5 .... 167 F1
Sandileigh Dr HALE/TIMP WA15 .... 175 D4
Sandiway BRAM/HZG SK7 .... 182 C5
  HEY OL10 .... 37 F5
  IRL M44 .... 135 E1
  MPL/ROM SK6 .... 169 D2
Sandiway CI MPL/ROM SK6 .... 171 D5
Sandiway Dr DID/WITH M20 .... 163 E2
Sandiway PI ALT WA14 .... 174 B2
Sandiway Rd ALT WA14 .... 174 B1
  SALE M33 .... 159 D1
  WILM/AE SK9 .... 194 B4
Sandon St BOLS/LL BL3 .... 46 B5
Sandown Av SLFD M6 .... 103 F5
Sandown CI OLD OL1 .... 79 E2
  WILM/AE SK9 .... 204 B3
Sandown Crs BOLS/LL BL3 .... 67 E1
  GTN M18 .... 127 E6
Sandown Dr DTN/ASHW M34 .... 149 F3

HALE/TIMP WA15 .... 190 B3
SALE M33 .... 158 C2
Sandown Gdns URM M41 .... 137 E1
Sandown Rd BOLE BL2 .... 29 F4
  BRAM/HZG SK7 .... 185 E6
  BURY BL9 .... 71 E1
  EDGY/DAV SK3 .... 165 F5
Sandown St GTN M18 .... 131 F2
Sandpiper CI DUK SK16 .... 65 D4
  FWTH BL4 .... 21 D6
  ROCH OL11 .... 21 D6
Sandpiper Dr EDGY/DAV SK3 .... 182 B1
Sandray CI BOLS/LL BL3 .... 45 D4
Sandray Gv SALQ/ORD M5 .... 103 F6
Sandridge CI FWTH BL4 .... 66 C3
Sandringham Av
  DTN/ASHW M34 .... 128 B6
  STLY SK15 .... 114 B4
Sandringham CI ALT WA14 .... 173 D6
Sandringham Dr DUK SK16 .... 132 A2
  HTNM SK4 .... 165 E4
  MILN OL16 .... 42 B1
  POY/DIS SK12 .... 198 B6
  TOT/BURYW BL8 .... 18 B4
Sandringham Gra PWCH M25 .... 89 F2
Sandringham Rd BRAM/HZG SK7 .... 185 D5
  CHD/CHDH SK8 .... 181 E4
  HYDE SK14 .... 150 C4
  MPL/ROM SK6 .... 168 A2
Sandringham St GTN M18 .... 127 D5
Sandringham Wy ROY/SHW OL2 .... 60 A3
  WILM/AE SK9 .... 203 E5
Sands Av CHAD OL9 .... 76 B3
Sands CI HYDE SK14 .... 152 B2
Sandsend CI CHH M8 .... 105 F2
Sandsend Rd URM M41 .... 119 D6
Sandstone Rd MILN OL16 .... 25 D6
Sandstone Wy CCHDY M21 .... 142 B5
Sand St NEWH/MOS M40 .... 107 D3
  STLY SK15 .... 132 A1
Sandwell Dr SALE M33 .... 139 F5
Sandwich Rd ECC M30 .... 102 A4
Sandwich St WALK M28 .... 83 E3
Sandwick Crs BOLS/LL BL3 .... 46 B4
Sandwood Av BOLS/LL BL3 .... 44 C4
Sandy Acre MOSL OL5 .... 99 D5
Sandy Bank ROY/SHW OL2 .... 61 D1
Sandy Bank Av HYDE SK14 .... 152 B2
Sandy Bank Rd CHH M8 .... 90 A5
Sandy Bank Wk HYDE SK14 .... 152 B2
Sandybrook CI TOT/BURYW BL8 .... 32 A1
Sandy Brow BKLY M9 .... 91 E3
Sandy CI BURY BL9 .... 53 D6
Sandygate CI SWIN M27 .... 85 F6
Sandy Gv DUK SK16 .... 131 E1
  SLFD M6 .... 103 F4
  SWIN M27 .... 86 A5
Sandy Haven CI WALK M28 .... 152 B2
Sandyhill Rd BKLY M9 .... 90 B2
Sandyhills BOLS/LL BL3 .... 46 C5
Sandylands Dr PWCH M25 .... 88 A4
Sandy La CCHDY M21 .... 141 F3
  DROY M43 .... 111 D4
  DUK SK16 .... 131 E1
  IRL M44 .... 116 B6
  MDTN M24 .... 75 F4
  MPL/ROM SK6 .... 170 A2
  NTHM/RTH M23 .... 160 B6
  PWCH M25 .... 88 B3
  RDSH SK5 .... 166 C2
  ROCH OL11 .... 22 A6
  ROY/SHW OL2 .... 60 B5
  SLFD M6 .... 103 F4
  STRET M32 .... 139 F2
  WILM/AE SK9 .... 202 B3
Sandy Meade PWCH M25 .... 88 B2
Sandyway PWCH M25 .... 88 B2
Sandywell CI OP/CLY M11 .... 127 E2
Sandywell St OP/CLY M11 .... 127 E1
Sanfold La BNG/LEV M19 .... 146 A1
Sangster Ct SALQ/ORD M5 .... 122 B1
Sankey Gv BKLY M9 .... 90 C2
Sankey St BURY BL9 .... 33 E5
Santiago St RUSH/FAL M14 .... 124 C6
Santley St WGTN/LGST M12 .... 126 B6
Santon Av RUSH/FAL M14 .... 144 C3
Sapling Gv SALE M33 .... 158 B3
Sapling Rd BOLS/LL BL3 .... 64 A1
  SWIN M27 .... 101 E2
Sarah Ann St OP/CLY M11 .... 108 A6
Sarah Butterworth St
  MILN OL16 .... 40 C1
Sarah St BCUP OL13 .... 5 D1
  ECC M30 .... 100 C6
  MDTN M24 .... 75 D3
  OP/CLY M11 .... 126 A1
  ROCH OL11 .... 40 B1
  ROY/SHW OL2 .... 61 F4
Sargent Dr OLDTF/WHR M16 .... 123 F5
Sargent Rd MPL/ROM SK6 .... 168 B3
Sark Rd CCHDY M21 .... 141 E1
Sarn Av WYTH/NTH M22 .... 178 B3
Saturn Gv SLFD M6 .... 105 D2
Saunton Av BOLE BL2 .... 30 A4
Saunton Rd OP/CLY M11 .... 127 E4

Sautridge CI MDTN M24 .... 58 B2
Savernake Rd MPL/ROM SK6 .... 150 A6
Savick Av BOLE BL2 .... 48 C2
Saville Rd CHD/CHDH SK8 .... 179 F1
  RAD M26 .... 51 D2
Saville St BOLE BL2 .... 47 E2
  MDTN M24 .... 76 B4
Savio Wy MDTN M24 .... 75 E4
Savoy Dr ROY/SHW OL2 .... 78 B1
Savoy St OLDE OL4 .... 79 F6
  ROCH OL11 .... 22 A5
Sawley Av LIT OL15 .... 12 B4
  OLDE OL4 .... 97 E1
  WHTF M45 .... 71 D1
Sawley Dr CHD/CHDH SK8 .... 195 F3
Sawley Rd NEWH/MOS M40 .... 107 E3
Sawpit St LYMM WA13 .... 155 E6
Sawyer Brow HYDE SK14 .... 132 A5
Sawyer St TOT/BURYW BL8 .... 32 C3
  WHIT OL12 .... 23 D4
Saxby Av EDGW/EG BL7 .... 14 A5
Saxby St SLFD M6 .... 103 D2
Saxelby Dr CHH M8 .... 106 C1
Saxfield Dr NTHM/RTH M23 .... 178 A1
Saxon Av CHH M8 .... 90 B3
  DUK SK16 .... 131 D1
Saxon CI TOT/BURYW BL8 .... 32 C5
Saxon Dr CHAD OL9 .... 76 C3
  DROY M43 .... 110 B5
  DTN/ASHW M34 .... 129 F2
Saxonholme Rd ROCH OL11 .... 58 A1
Saxon St DROY M43 .... 110 C5
  DTN/ASHW M34 .... 130 A6
  MDTN M24 .... 75 F3
  NEWH/MOS M40 .... 107 F4
  OLDE OL4 .... 80 A4
  RAD M26 .... 51 D6
Saxthorpe CI SALE M33 .... 158 B1
Saxwood Av BKLY M9 .... 91 E4
Saxwood CI WHIT OL12 .... 21 D4
Scafell Av AULW OL7 .... 112 A5
Scafell CI MPL/ROM SK6 .... 200 C1
  OLD OL1 .... 79 D2
Scale St SALQ/ORD M5 .... 104 C6
Scarborough St
  NEWH/MOS M40 .... 92 B5
Scarcroft Rd WGTN/LGST M12 .... 126 B4
Scardale Av BOL BL1 .... 26 B6
Scarfield Dr ROCH OL11 .... 20 C4
Scargill CI RUSH/FAL M14 .... 144 A3
Scargill Rd BOLS/LL BL3 .... 45 E5
Scarisbrick Av DID/WITH M20 .... 164 B2
Scarisbrick Rd BNG/LEV M19 .... 145 D3
Scarr Av RAD M26 .... 70 A1
Scarr Dr WHIT OL12 .... 23 D3
Scarr La ROY/SHW OL2 .... 62 A2
Scarsdale Rd RUSH/FAL M14 .... 125 F5
Scarsdale St SLFD M6 .... 104 C4
Scarthwood CI BOLE BL2 .... 29 F2
Scawfell Av BOLE BL2 .... 28 C5
Schofield Av DROY M43 .... 110 C6
  ECC M30 .... 100 B6
Schofield St CSLFD M3 .... 105 E6
  FAIL M35 .... 94 A5
  HEY OL10 .... 37 E6
  LIT OL15 .... 13 D5
  MILN OL16 .... 42 B2
  OLDS OL8 .... 95 F2
  OP/CLY M11 .... 109 D5
  ROCH OL11 .... 40 B3
  ROY/SHW OL2 .... 60 B4
Scholars Dr DID/WITH M20 .... 143 E4
Scholars Wy MDTN M24 .... 75 D2
Scholes Dr NEWH/MOS M40 .... 93 F3
Scholes La PWCH M25 .... 89 D2
Scholes St CHAD OL9 .... 94 B1
  FAIL M35 .... 94 B4
  OLD OL1 .... 79 E4
  ROCH OL11 .... 39 D6
  SWIN M27 .... 86 B5
  TOT/BURYW BL8 .... 33 D4
Scholes Wk PWCH M25 .... 88 C2
Scholey St BOLE BL2 .... 47 E4
Scholfield Av URM M41 .... 139 D2
School Av AUL OL6 .... 113 E1
  STRET M32 .... 122 A6
School Brow BURY BL9 .... 34 A5
  MPL/ROM SK6 .... 169 E3
  WALK M28 .... 100 A1
School CI POY/DIS SK12 .... 197 D6
School Ct ANC M4 .... 107 D5
  EDGY/DAV SK3 .... 183 D1
  RAMS BL0 .... 7 E2
School Crs STLY SK15 .... 114 A4
School Gv DID/WITH M20 .... 144 B5
  PWCH M25 .... 88 B3
School Gv West DID/WITH M20 .... 144 A5
School HI BOL BL1 .... 46 C1
School La ALT WA14 .... 172 B5
  BKLY M9 .... 91 D3
  BURY BL9 .... 19 F5
  CHD/CHDH SK8 .... 195 E1
  DID/WITH M20 .... 144 A6
  HTNM SK4 .... 146 A6
  HYDE SK14 .... 150 C4

IRL M44	134	B6
IRL M44	135	D1
MILN OL16	23	D6
MPL/ROM SK6	151	F6
MPL/ROM SK6	151	F6
PART M31	136	C5
POY/DIS SK12	199	D5
ROCH OL11	20	A5
STLY SK15	119	F6
School Rd ECC M30	119	D1
FAIL M35	94	A6
HALE/TIMP WA15	175	D4
OLDS OL8	94	C3
SALE M33	139	E6
STRET M32	140	A1
WILM/AE SK9	194	B5
Schools Hi CHD/CHDH SK8	180	B4
Schoolside La MDTN M24	73	F4
Schools Rd GTN M18	127	F4
School St BOLS/LL BL3	49	F6
BRAM/HZG SK7	184	C5
BRO M7	105	F3
BURY BL9	34	C6
ECC M30	100	C4
EDGW/EG BL7	14	A6
HEY OL10	37	D5
LIT OL15	24	C1
OLDE OL4	81	E5
OLDS OL8	78	B6
RAD M26	51	D6
RAMS BL0	6	C6
WHIT OL12	23	D5
Schwabe St MDTN M24	74	A3
Scobell St TOT/BURYW BL8	32	A2
Score St OP/CLY M11	108	B6
Scorton Av BOLE BL2	49	D2
Scorton St BOL BL1	46	A1
Scotforth CI HULME M15	123	F2
Scotland ANC M4	106	B4
Scotland Hall Rd		
NEWH/MOS M40	108	C2
Scotland St AUL OL6	113	D5
NEWH/MOS M40	109	D2
Scott Av BURY BL9	53	D3
CCHDY M21	141	F1
ECC M30	101	D4
Scott CI RDSH SK5	167	D1
Scott Dr MPL/ROM SK6	171	F5
Scottfield OLDS OL8	79	D6
Scott Ga DTN/ASHW M34	129	F2
Scottia Rd ECC M30	118	C1
Scott Rd DROY M43	110	B5
DTN/ASHW M34	148	C2
PWCH M25	88	A2
Scott St OLDS OL8	79	D6
RAD M26	68	B4
SLFD M6	105	D5
Scout Dr NTHM/RTH M23	177	D5
Scout Rd BOL BL1	26	B1
Scout Vw TOT/BURYW BL8	32	B1
Scovell St BRO M7	105	E1
Scowcroft La ROY/SHW OL2	61	E3
Scowcroft St BOLE BL2	28	C6
Scroggins La PART M31	154	C1
Scropton St NEWH/MOS M40	107	E1
Seabrook Crs URM M41	119	E5
Seabrook Rd NEWH/MOS M40	109	D2
Seacombe Gv EDGY/DAV SK3	165	F5
Seaford Rd BOLE BL2	29	F1
SLFD M6	104	C2
Seaforth Av BOL BL1	27	F1
Seaham Dr TOT/BURYW BL8	33	D2
Sealand CI SALE M33	160	C3
Sealand Dr ECC M30	118	B1
Sealand Rd NTHM/RTH M23	161	D5
Seale Av DTN/ASHW M34	129	E2
Seal Rd BRAM/HZG SK7	197	D1
Seamon's Dr ALT WA14	173	E1
Seamon's Rd ALT WA14	173	E1
Searby Rd GTN M18	126	C5
Searness Rd MDTN M24	74	A1
Seatoller Dr MDTN M24	74	A2
Seaton CI BRAM/HZG SK7	184	B6
Seaton Ms AULW OL7	111	F3
Seaton Rd BOL BL1	27	D5
Second Av BOL BL1	45	F2
BURY BL9	35	E3
OLDS OL8	95	D3
OP/CLY M11	109	E5
STLY SK15	115	F2
SWIN M27	101	E2
TRPK M17	121	E4
Second St BOL BL1	26	A3
Sedan CI SALO/ORD M5	104	B6
Sedburgh CI SALE M33	158	B2
Sedbury CI NTHM/RTH M23	161	D4
Seddon CI GTN M18	127	E5
RAD M26	52	C4
Seddon Gdns RAD M26	67	E3
Seddon La RAD M26	67	E3
Seddon Rd ALT WA14	174	B5
Seddons Av TOT/BURYW BL8	51	E3
Seddon St BNG/LEV M19	145	F1
BOLS/LL BL3	49	F6
LHULT M38	65	D6

RAD M26	51	E6
Sedgeborough Rd		
OLDTF/WHR M16	123	F6
Sedge CI RDSH SK5	147	E3
Sedgefield CI SALQ/ORD M5	104	B5
Sedgefield Dr BOL BL1	26	C4
Sedgefield Pk OLDE OL4	80	B5
Sedgefield Rd RAD M26	69	D3
Sedgeford CI WILM/AE SK9	204	B2
Sedgeford Rd NEWH/MOS M40	107	E2
Sedgemoor CI CHD/CHDH SK8	181	F5
Sedgemoor V BOLE BL2	30	A5
Sedgley Av MILN OL16	40	C3
PWCH M25	89	D3
Sedgley CI MDTN M24	76	A4
Sedgley Park Rd PWCH M25	89	D3
Sedgley Rd CHH M8	90	B5
Sedgley St MDTN M24	76	A4
Seedfield Rd BURY BL9	34	A2
Seedley Av LHULT M38	82	C1
Seedley Park Rd SLFD M6	103	F5
Seedley Rd SLFD M6	104	A4
Seedley St RUSH/FAL M14	124	C6
Seedley Ter SLFD M6	103	F4
Seedley View Rd		
SALQ/ORD M5	103	F5
Seed St BOL BL1	46	A2
Seel St MOSL OL5	98	C4
Sefton CI BRUN/LGST M13	124	C3
MDTN M24	74	C3
Sefton Crs SALE M33	139	F5
Sefton Dr BURY BL9	34	B1
SWIN M27	101	E1
WALK M28	100	B1
WILM/AE SK9	204	A1
Sefton Rd BOL BL1	26	C5
CCHDY M21	141	E3
MDTN M24	74	C3
SALE M33	139	F6
SWIN M27	86	A4
Sefton St BURY BL9	34	A1
CHAD OL9	94	B3
CHH M8	90	B5
HEY OL10	37	F6
RAD M26	70	A2
ROCH OL11	39	F2
WHTF M45	71	D4
Selborne Rd CCHDY M21	141	F2
Selby Av CHAD OL9	77	D2
WHTF M45	71	D1
Selby CI MILN OL16	41	F1
POY/DIS SK12	198	B4
RAD M26	52	B4
STRET M32	120	A6
Selby Dr SLFD M6	102	C4
URM M41	118	A4
Selby Gdns CHD/CHDH SK8	196	A3
Selby Rd MDTN M24	57	D6
STRET M32	120	B6
Selby St HTNM SK4	166	B1
MILN OL16	23	F5
OP/CLY M11	126	B1
Selden St OLDS OL8	78	B6
Selhurst Av OP/CLY M11	109	D5
Selkirk Av OLDS OL8	95	E1
Selkirk Dr BKLY M9	91	E2
Selkirk Rd BOL BL1	27	E2
CHAD OL9	94	A1
Sellars Sq DROY M43	128	B1
Sellers Wy CHAD OL9	90	A3
Selsby Av ECC M30	100	C5
Selsey Av EDGY/DAV SK3	165	D6
SALE M33	159	D2
Selsey Dr DID/WITH M20	164	A5
Selstead Rd WYTH/NTH M22	178	A6
Selston Rd BKLY M9	90	C1
Selworth Av SALE M33	160	C1
Selworth CI HALE/TIMP WA15	174	C1
Selworthy Rd OLDTF/WHR M16	123	F5
Selwyn Av BKLY M9	91	E5
Selwyn Dr CHD/CHDH SK8	196	A2
Selwyn St BOLE BL2	47	E3
Senior Av RUSH/FAL M14	144	C4
Senior Rd ECC M30	118	A1
Senior St CSLFD M3	105	F4
Sepal CI RDSH SK5	147	E2
Sepia Gv MDTN M24	75	D2
Sequoia St BKLY M9	91	F5
BKLY M9	92	A5
Sergeants La WHTF M45	70	A4
Serin CI OFTN SK2	185	D3
Service St HTNM SK4	165	F5
Set St STLY SK15	114	A6
Settle CI TOT/BURYW BL8	32	A5
Settle St BOLS/LL BL3	46	C6
BOLS/LL BL3	68	A1
Seven Acres La WHIT OL12	20	C3
Seven Acres Rd WHIT OL12	20	C3
Sevenoaks Av HTNM SK4	145	E6
URM M41	119	E5
Sevenoaks Dr BOLS/LL BL3	46	C6
SWIN M27	102	B1
Sevenoaks Rd CHD/CHDH SK8	179	F1
Seven Stiles Dr MPL/ROM SK6	170	C6
Seventh Av OLDS OL8	95	D4

Severn CI ALT WA14	174	A1
Severn Dr BRAM/HZG SK7	196	A3
MILN OL16	42	B1
Severn Rd CHAD OL9	77	D3
HEY OL10	36	B4
OLDS OL8	94	C4
Severn Wy FWTH BL4	67	F5
RDSH SK5	147	D6
Seville St ROY/SHW OL2	61	E4
ROY/SHW OL2	78	C1
Sewerby CI OLDTF/WHR M16	124	A3
Sexa St OP/CLY M11	127	E1
Sexton St HEY OL10	37	D5
Seymour Av OP/CLY M11	109	E5
Seymour CI OLDTF/WHR M16	123	D4
Seymour Dr BOLE BL2	29	D1
Seymour Gv FWTH BL4	65	E2
HALE/TIMP WA15	175	E2
MILN OL16	40	C4
MPL/ROM SK6	186	C1
OLDTF/WHR M16	122	C5
SALE M33	159	F1
Seymour Rd BOL BL1	28	A4
CHD/CHDH SK8	195	E1
CHH M8	90	A4
OFTN SK2	183	F1
Seymour Rd South OP/CLY M11	109	E5
Seymour St BOLE BL2	29	D1
DTN/ASHW M34	129	E5
GTN M18	127	E3
HEY OL10	36	C6
RAD M26	51	F6
Shackleton St ECC M30	101	D4
Shackliffe Rd NEWH/MOS M40	92	C3
Shaddock Av ROCH OL11	21	D4
Shade Av OLDE OL4	81	D6
Shadowmoss Rd WYTH/NTH M22	192	C5
Shadows La MOSL OL5	99	F1
Shadwell St East HEY OL10	37	E4
Shadwell St West HEY OL10	37	E4
Shady La BOLE BL2	28	C1
NTHM/RTH M23	160	B6
Shady Oak Rd OFTN SK2	185	D1
Shaftesbury Av CHD/CHDH SK8	181	F6
ECC M30	119	D3
HALE/TIMP WA15	175	F2
LIT OL15	25	E3
Shaftesbury Dr WHIT OL12	11	E5
Shaftesbury Gdns URM M41	136	A1
Shaftesbury Rd CHH M8	90	B6
EDGY/DAV SK3	181	E1
SWIN M27	86	A6
Shaftsbury Dr HEY OL10	56	A1
Shakespeare Av BURY BL9	53	D3
DTN/ASHW M34	149	D3
RAD M26	50	C5
STLY SK15	115	F4
Shakespeare CI LIT OL15	13	D2
Shakespeare Crs DROY M43	110	B5
ECC M30	101	E5
Shakespeare Dr CHD/CHDH SK8	181	D1
Shakespeare Rd DROY M43	110	B5
MPL/ROM SK6	168	C2
OLD OL1	79	F1
PWCH M25	88	A2
SWIN M27	85	E5
Shakleton Av BKLY M9	92	B2
Shalbourne Rd WALK M28	83	D2
Shaldon Dr NEWH/MOS M40	109	F3
Shalfleet CI BOLE BL2	29	F2
Shalford Rd WYTH/NTH M22	192	B1
Shandon Av WYTH/NTH M22	162	B4
Shanklin Av URM M41	138	A1
Shanklin CI CCHDY M21	141	E2
DTN/ASHW M34	149	F3
Shanley Ct CHAD OL9	77	F3
Shannon CI HEY OL10	36	B4
Shannon Rd WYTH/NTH M22	178	C4
Shap Av HALE/TIMP WA15	176	B2
Shap Dr WALK M28	84	A3
Shargate CI WILM/AE SK9	204	A2
Sharman St BOLS/LL BL3	47	F4
Sharnford CI BOLE BL2	47	F3
Sharon CI AULW OL7	111	F6
Sharples Av BOL BL1	27	F1
Sharples Dr TOT/BURYW BL8	32	A3
Sharples Hall Dr BOL BL1	28	A2
Sharples Hall Fold BOL BL1	28	A2
Sharples Hall Ms BOL BL1	28	A1
Sharples Pk BOL BL1	27	E3
Sharples St HTNM SK4	166	C2
Sharp St ANC M4	106	C4
MDTN M24	75	E3
PWCH M25	88	B1
WALK M28	83	F2
Sharrington Dr NTHM/RTH M23	176	C1
Sharston Rd WYTH/NTH M22	162	C6
Shaving La WALK M28	83	E4
Shaw Av HYDE SK14	151	D3
Shawbrook Av WALK M28	82	C5
Shawbrook Rd BNG/LEV M19	145	E6
Shawbury Gv SALE M33	159	D3
Shawbury Rd NTHM/RTH M23	177	D3
Shawbury St MDTN M24	76	A4

Shawclough Cl WHIT OL12 .... 22 B2 🔢
Shawclough Dr WHIT OL12 .... 22 A2 🔢
Shawclough Rd WHIT OL12 .... 22 A2
Shawclough Wy WHIT OL12 .... 22 A2
Shawcroft Cl ROY/SHW OL2 .... 61 E4
Shawcross La WYTH/NTH M22 .... 163 D5
Shawcross St HYDE SK14 .... 151 D3
   SLFD M6 .... 104 A6
   STKP SK1 .... 167 D5
Shawdene Rd WYTH/NTH M22 .... 162 A5
Shawe Hall Av URM M41 .... 137 E3
Shawe Hall Crs URM M41 .... 137 E3
Shawe Rd URM M41 .... 137 E1
Shawe Vw URM M41 .... 137 E1
Shawfield Cl DID/WITH M20 .... 143 E3 🔢
Shawfield La WHIT OL12 .... 21 E3
Shawfields STLY SK15 .... 115 E4 🔢
Shawford Rd NEWH/MOS M40 .... 93 D3
Shawgreen Cl HULME M15 .... 123 E3
Shaw Hall Av HYDE SK14 .... 132 C4
Shaw Head Dr FAIL M35 .... 110 A1
Shaw Heath EDGY/DAV SK3 .... 166 C5
Shawheath Cl HULME M15 .... 123 E3
Shaw La MILN OL16 .... 25 D4
Shawlea Av BNG/LEV M19 .... 144 C5 🔢
Shaw Moor Av STLY SK15 .... 115 D6
Shaw Rd HTNM SK4 .... 145 F6
   MILN OL16 .... 40 C6
   MILN OL16 .... 42 C4
   OLD OL1 .... 79 E2
   ROY/SHW OL2 .... 61 D5
Shaw Rd South EDGY/DAV SK3 .. 167 D6 🔢
Shaw's Rd ALT WA14 .... 174 B5
Shaw St AUL OL6 .... 113 E4
   BOLS/LL BL3 .... 46 C4 🔢
   BURY BL9 .... 34 C4
   CSLFD M3 .... 106 A4
   FWTH BL4 .... 66 A1 🔢
   OLD OL1 .... 79 D3
   OLDE OL4 .... 81 E5
   ROY/SHW OL2 .... 60 C5
   WHIT OL12 .... 23 F5 🔢
Shay Av HALE/TIMP WA15 .... 176 C6
Shayfield Av CHAD OL9 .... 76 C3
   WYTH/NTH M22 .... 178 B2 🔢
Shayfield Dr WYTH/NTH M22 .... 178 B2
Shayfield Rd WYTH/NTH M22 .... 178 B2
Shay La HALE/TIMP WA15 .... 176 B6
Sheader Dr SALQ/ORD M5 .... 103 D5
Sheard Av AUL OL6 .... 113 E1
Shearsby Cl HULME M15 .... 123 F3
Shearwater Av BOL BL1 .... 26 C5
Shearwater Dr WALK M28 .... 83 D2
Shearwater Gdns ECC M30 .... 118 B1
Shearwater Rd OFTN SK2 .... 185 D2
The Sheddings BOLS/LL BL3 .... 47 E5 🔢
Shed St WHIT OL12 .... 9 E2 🔢
Sheepfoot La OLD OL1 .... 78 B2
   PWCH M25 .... 89 E2
Sheep Gap WHIT OL12 .... 10 A4 🔢
Sheep Gate Dr TOT/BURYW BL8 .... 31 F2
Sheerness St GTN M18 .... 127 E4 🔢
Sheffield Rd HYDE SK14 .... 132 A6
Sheffield St CMANE M1 .... 3 H5
   HTNM SK4 .... 166 C2
Shefford Cl OP/CLY M11 .... 126 A1
Sheiling Ct ALT WA14 .... 174 A3
Shelbourne Av BOL BL1 .... 26 C5
Shelderton Cl NEWH/MOS M40 ...... 92 B6 🔢
Sheldon Cl PART M31 .... 155 D2 🔢
Sheldon Ct AULW OL7 .... 112 C2
Sheldon Rd BRAM/HZG SK7 .... 198 C2
Sheldon St OP/CLY M11 .... 108 C5 🔢
Sheldrake Cl DUK SK16 .... 131 F2 🔢
Sheldrake Rd ALT WA14 .... 157 F5
Shelfield Cl ROCH OL11 .... 21 D4 🔢
Shelfield La ROCH OL11 .... 21 D4
Shelford Av GTN M18 .... 126 C5
Shelley Av MDTN M24 .... 57 F6
Shelley Ct CHD/CHDH SK8 .... 181 E6
Shelley Gv DROY M43 .... 110 B6
   HYDE SK14 .... 131 E5
   STLY SK15 .... 115 F3
Shelley Ri DUK SK16 .... 132 C2
Shelley Rd CHAD OL9 .... 94 A2
   LHULT M38 .... 65 E6 🔢
   OLD OL1 .... 80 A2
   PWCH M25 .... 88 A2
   RDSH SK5 .... 146 B2
   SWIN M27 .... 85 E5
Shelley Wk BOL BL1 .... 27 E6 🔢
Shelton Av SALE M33 .... 158 B3
Shenhurst Cl WILM/AE SK9 .... 208 C1 🔢
Shentonfield Rd WYTH/NTH M22 .. 178 C1
Shenton Park Av SALE M33 .... 154 A1 🔢
Shenton St HYDE SK14 .... 131 D5 🔢
Shepherd Cross St BOL BL1 .... 27 D6
Shepherds St TOT/BURYW BL8 ..... 18 A4 🔢
Shepherd St BKLY M9 .... 91 F4 🔢
   BURY BL9 .... 34 A6
   HEY OL10 .... 37 D5 🔢
   ROCH OL11 .... 20 B4 🔢
   ROY/SHW OL2 .... 60 C5 🔢

   ROY/SHW OL2 .... 60 C6 🔢
   TOT/BURYW BL8 .... 18 A5
   WHIT OL12 .... 23 D5 🔢
Shepley Av BOLS/LL BL3 .... 46 A4 🔢
Shepley Cl BRAM/HZG SK7 .... 198 B1
   DUK SK16 .... 131 E1 🔢
Shepley Dr BRAM/HZG SK7 .... 184 B6
Shepley La MPL/ROM SK6 .... 187 D3
Shepley Rd DTN/ASHW M34 .... 130 A3
Shepley St CMANE M1 .... 3 G5
   DTN/ASHW M34 .... 130 A3
   FAIL M35 .... 94 B4 🔢
   HYDE SK14 .... 150 C1 🔢
   OLDE OL4 .... 80 C5 🔢
   STLY SK15 .... 114 D5
Shepton Dr NTHM/RTH M23 .... 177 E5 🔢
Shepton Rd NTHM/RTH M23 .... 177 D2 🔢
Sheraton Rd OLDS OL8 .... 95 F1 🔢
   MDTN M24 .... 57 D6
   URM M41 .... 119 F6
Sherborne St CHH M8 .... 106 A2
   CSLFD M3 .... 106 A3
Sherborne St West CSLFD M3 ...... 105 F4
Sherbourne Cl CHD/CHDH SK8 ... 195 F3 🔢
   OLDS OL8 .... 97 D1 🔢
   RAD M26 .... 50 B4 🔢
Sherbourne Dr HEY OL10 .... 36 B4
Sherbourne Rd BOL BL1 .... 26 B6
Sherbourne St PWCH M25 .... 88 B1 🔢
Sherbrook Cl SALE M33 .... 159 D2 🔢
Sherdley Ct CHH M8 .... 90 B4 🔢
Sherdley Rd CHH M8 .... 90 B4
Sherford Cl BRAM/HZG SK7 .... 183 E5
Sheridan Wy CHAD OL9 .... 76 C3 🔢
Sheriff St BOLE BL2 .... 28 C6 🔢
   MILN OL16 .... 42 B2
   WHIT OL12 .... 22 C4
Sheringham Dr HYDE SK14 .... 132 B6
   SWIN M27 .... 102 A1
   TOT/BURYW BL8 .... 33 D2
Sheringham Pl BOLS/LL BL3 .... 46 B4 🔢
Sheringham Rd RUSH/FAL M14 ... 144 B4 🔢
Sherlock St RUSH/FAL M14 .... 144 C4 🔢
Sherratt St ANC M4 .... 3 H1
Sherrington St
   WGTN/LGST M12 .... 126 B6 🔢
Sherway Dr HALE/TIMP WA15 ...... 176 A1
Sherwell Rd BKLY M9 .... 90 C2
Sherwin Wy ROCH OL11 .... 39 E6
Sherwood Av BRO M7 .... 88 C6 🔢
   DROY M43 .... 111 D5
   HTNM SK4 .... 165 E4
   RAD M26 .... 51 D1
   RUSH/FAL M14 .... 144 A3 🔢
   SALE M33 .... 140 B6 🔢
Sherwood Cl AUL OL6 .... 97 D6
   MPL/ROM SK6 .... 187 D3 🔢
   SALQ/ORD M5 .... 103 E4 🔢
   TOT/BURYW BL8 .... 18 A6 🔢
Sherwood Dr SWIN M27 .... 86 C6
Sherwood Rd DTN/ASHW M34 .... 128 C6
   MPL/ROM SK6 .... 149 F6
Sherwood St BOL BL1 .... 28 A4 🔢
   OLD OL1 .... 78 B3
   ROCH OL11 .... 39 E5
   RUSH/FAL M14 .... 144 A3
Sherwood Wy ROY/SHW OL2 .... 60 C1
Shetland Rd NEWH/MOS M40 .... 107 E4 🔢
Shetland Wy RAD M26 .... 51 E4
   URM M41 .... 119 E4
Shevington Gdns
   NTHM/RTH M23 .... 161 F4 🔢
Shieldborn Dr BKLY M9 .... 91 E4
Shield Cl OLDS OL8 .... 78 C5
Shield Dr WALK M28 .... 81 F5
Shield St EDGY/DAV SK3 .... 166 C5
Shiel St WALK M28 .... 83 E2 🔢
Shiers Dr CHD/CHDH SK8 .... 180 C3
Shiffnall St BOLE BL2 .... 47 E3
Shilford Dr ANC M4 .... 106 C4
Shillingford Rd FWTH BL4 .... 66 A3 🔢
Shillingstone Cl BOLE BL2 .... 30 A4
Shillington Cl LHULT M38 .... 82 A2 🔢
Shiloh La OLDE OL4 .... 81 F1
Shilton St RAMS BL0 .... 6 C1
Shipla Cl CHAD OL9 .... 78 C4
Ship La OLDE OL4 .... 63 E4
   UPML SL3 .... 63 E4
Shipley Av SLFD M6 .... 103 D4
Shipley Vw URM M41 .... 118 A4
Shipper Bottom La RAMS BL0 .... 7 E6
Shippey St RUSH/FAL M14 .... 144 D4 🔢
Shipston Cl TOT/BURYW BL8 .... 32 C4
Shipton St BOL BL1 .... 26 C6
Shirebrook Dr RAD M26 .... 51 F5
Shireburn Av BOLE BL2 .... 48 A1
Shiredale Cl CHD/CHDH SK8 .... 181 F3
Shiredale Dr BKLY M9 .... 91 E6
Shiregreen Av NEWH/MOS M40 ... 107 D2 🔢
Shirehills PWCH M25 .... 88 B3
Shireoak Rd DID/WITH M20 .... 144 B4
The Shires DROY M43 .... 111 E4
   RAD M26 .... 51 E4

Shirley Av BRO M7 .... 88 B6
   CHAD OL9 .... 93 F3
   CHD/CHDH SK8 .... 194 A3
   DTN/ASHW M34 .... 128 A6
   DTN/ASHW M34 .... 129 D1
   ECC M30 .... 119 D1
   HYDE SK14 .... 131 E4
   MPL/ROM SK6 .... 186 C1 🔢
   STRET M32 .... 122 A6 🔢
   SWIN M27 .... 87 D6
Shirley Cl BRAM/HZG SK7 .... 184 A5 🔢
Shirley Gv EDGY/DAV SK3 .... 182 C2
Shirley Rd CHH M8 .... 90 B6
Shirley St ROCH OL11 .... 39 D5
Shoecroft Av DTN/ASHW M34 ...... 148 C1
Sholver Hill Cl OLD OL1 .... 62 C5
Sholver La OLD OL1 .... 62 B5
Shone Av WYTH/NTH M22 .... 179 D5
Shore Av ROY/SHW OL2 .... 43 D6
Shoreditch Cl HTNM SK4 .... 145 F6
Shorefield Cl MILN OL16 .... 25 D6 🔢
Shore Fold LIT OL15 .... 12 A5
Shore Hl LIT OL15 .... 13 D5 🔢
Shore Lea LIT OL15 .... 12 A5 🔢
Shore Mt LIT OL15 .... 12 A5
Shore Rd LIT OL15 .... 12 A4
Shore St MILN OL16 .... 42 A1
   OLD OL1 .... 79 E4 🔢
Shoreswood BOL BL1 .... 27 E1
Shorland St SWIN M27 .... 85 D6 🔢
Shorrocks St TOT/BURYW BL8 ..... 32 A4
Short Av DROY M43 .... 128 A1 🔢
Shortcroft St HULME M15 .... 124 A2 🔢
Shortland Crs BNG/LEV M19 .... 164 B2
Shortlands Av BURY BL9 .... 53 D1 🔢
Short St ANC M4 .... 3 F3
   BRAM/HZG SK7 .... 184 B4
   BRO M7 .... 105 F4
   HEY OL10 .... 36 C6
   HTNM SK4 .... 166 C2
Short St East HTNM SK4 .... 166 C2 🔢
Shrewsbury Gdns
   CHD/CHDH SK8 .... 196 A3 🔢
Shrewsbury Rd BOL BL1 .... 45 F1 🔢
   DROY M43 .... 110 B5
   PWCH M25 .... 88 B2
   SALE M33 .... 159 E3
Shrewsbury St OLD OL1 .... 80 A3
   OLDTF/WHR M16 .... 123 E4
Shrigley Cl WILM/AE SK9 .... 204 B2
Shropshire Av RDSH SK5 .... 148 A5
Shropshire Rd FAIL M35 .... 110 B1 🔢
Shudehill ANC M4 .... 3 E2
Shurmer St BOLS/LL BL3 .... 46 A5 🔢
Shuttle St ECC M30 .... 102 A5 🔢
   RAD M26 .... 70 A2
Shuttleworth St
   OLDTF/WHR M16 .... 142 C3 🔢
Shutts La STLY SK15 .... 133 E1
Siam St OP/CLY M11 .... 126 A1 🔢
Sibley Rd HTNM SK4 .... 165 F2
Sibley St GTN M18 .... 127 E2
Sibson Rd CCHDY M21 .... 141 E2 🔢
   SALE M33 .... 159 E2
Sickle St CMANW M2 .... 3 E5 🔢
   OLDE OL4 .... 79 E6
Sidbury Rd CCHDY M21 .... 142 A3
Sidcup Rd NTHM/RTH M23 .... 177 D2
Siddall St HEY OL10 .... 56 C1
   OLD OL1 .... 79 D5 🔢
   RAD M26 .... 51 E5 🔢
   ROY/SHW OL2 .... 61 F2 🔢
   WGTN/LGST M12 .... 145 E1
Siddington Av EDGY/DAV SK3 .... 182 A1
Siddington Rd WILM/AE SK9 ...... 194 B4 🔢
Side Av ALT WA14 .... 174 A6 🔢
Sidebotham St MPL/ROM SK6 .... 169 D1
Sidebottom St DROY M43 .... 110 A6 🔢
   OLDE OL4 .... 80 C5 🔢
   STLY SK15 .... 114 B5
Side St OLDS OL8 .... 95 D3
   OP/CLY M11 .... 108 C6 🔢
Sidford Cl BOLS/LL BL3 .... 48 B4
The Sidings BCUP OL13 .... 4 B1
   WALK M28 .... 100 B2 🔢
Sidley Av BKLY M9 .... 92 A1
Sidley St HYDE SK14 .... 132 A6 🔢
Sidmouth Av URM M41 .... 117 F6
Sidmouth Dr BKLY M9 .... 91 E3
Sidmouth Gv CHD/CHDH SK8 .... 195 D2 🔢
Sidmouth Rd SALE M33 .... 138 C6
Sidmouth St CHAD OL9 .... 78 A6 🔢
   DTN/ASHW M34 .... 129 D3 🔢
Sidney Rd BKLY M9 .... 91 E4
Sidney St BOLS/LL BL3 .... 47 D4
   CMANE M1 .... 124 B2 🔢
   CSLFD M3 .... 2 C4 🔢
   OLD OL1 .... 79 E2
Siemens Rd IRL M44 .... 134 C6
Sienna Cl IRL M44 .... 134 C5 🔢
Signal Cl ECC M30 .... 100 C5 🔢
Signet Wk CHH M8 .... 106 C2
Silas St AUL OL6 .... 113 E2 🔢
Silburn Wy MDTN M24 .... 74 A4
Silchester Dr NEWH/MOS M40 .... 107 E1

Silchester Wy *BOLE* BL2 .... 29 F6
Silfield Cl *OP/CLY* M11 .... 107 F6 🔟
Silkhey Gv *WALK* M28 .... 83 E4 🔟
Silkin Cl *BRUN/LGST* M13 .... 124 C2 🔟
Silkstone St *OP/CLY* M11 .... 127 D2 🔟
Silk St *ANC* M4 .... 3 H1
　CSLFD M3 .... 105 E4
　ECC M30 .... 102 A6
　MDTN M24 .... 75 D3
　NEWH/MOS M40 .... 109 D1
　ROCH OL11 .... 39 E3
Sillavan Wy *CSLFD* M3 .... 2 A2
Silsden Av *BKLY* M9 .... 73 F6
Silton St *BKLY* M9 .... 92 A6
Silverbirch Cl *SALE* M33 .... 158 B3 🔟
Silver Birch Gv *SWIN* M27 .... 102 C1
Silverbirch Wy *FAIL* M35 .... 94 A6 🔟
Silver Cl *DUK* SK16 .... 130 C2
Silvercroft St *HULME* M15 .... 123 F2
Silverdale *SWIN* M27 .... 86 B3
Silverdale Av *CHAD* OL9 .... 77 E5
　DTN/ASHW M34 .... 149 E1
　IRL M44 .... 116 C5
　PWCH M25 .... 89 F3
Silverdale Cl *MPL/ROM* SK6 .... 200 C1
Silverdale Dr *OLDE* OL4 .... 81 D5
　WILM/AE SK9 .... 209 E1
Silverdale Rd *BOL* BL1 .... 46 A2 🔟
　CCHDY M21 .... 142 A2 🔟
　CHD/CHDH SK8 .... 179 F3
　FWTH BL4 .... 65 E2
　HTNM SK4 .... 166 A1
Silverdale St *OP/CLY* M11 .... 128 A2
Silver HI *MILN* OL16 .... 42 A1 🔟
Silver Hill Rd *HYDE* SK14 .... 150 C2
Silverlea Dr *BKLY* M9 .... 91 D3
Silvermere *AUL* OL6 .... 113 F1
Silver Spring *HYDE* SK14 .... 151 D3
Silverstone Dr *NEWH/MOS* M40 .... 109 E3
Silver St *BURY* BL9 .... 33 F5 🔟
　CMANE M1 .... 3 E5 🔟
　IRL M44 .... 119 A6 C5
　OLD OL1 .... 78 C5
　RAMS BL0 .... 7 D5
　WHIT OL12 .... 22 B5 🔟
　WHTF M45 .... 70 C2 🔟
Silverthorne Cl *STLY* SK15 .... 114 B6
Silverton Cl *HYDE* SK14 .... 152 B1
Silverton Gv *BOL* BL1 .... 28 A3
　MDTN M24 .... 56 B5 🔟
Silverwell La *BOL* BL1 .... 47 D2
Silverwell St *BOL* BL1 .... 47 D2
　NEWH/MOS M40 .... 109 E2 🔟
Silverwood *CHAD* OL9 .... 76 C4 🔟
Silverwood Av *CCHDY* M21 .... 141 F3
Simeon St *ANC* M4 .... 106 C4 🔟
Simister Dr *BURY* BL9 .... 71 E1 🔟
Simister Gn *PWCH* M25 .... 72 C3
Simister La *PWCH* M25 .... 72 B3
Simister Rd *FAIL* M35 .... 94 A6
Simister St *BKLY* M9 .... 91 F5 🔟
Simkin Wy *OLDS* OL8 .... 96 B4
Simms Cl *CSLFD* M3 .... 105 E5 🔟
Simonbury Cl *TOT/BURYW* BL8 .... 32 A5 🔟
Simon Freeman Cl
　BNG/LEV M19 .... 146 A5 🔟
Simon La *MDTN* M24 .... 73 E1
Simons Cl *SALE* M33 .... 159 E2 🔟
Simon St *MILN* OL16 .... 42 A1
Simonsway *NTHM/RTH* M23 .... 177 E4
　WYTH/NTH M22 .... 177 F4
Simpson Av *SWIN* M27 .... 87 D3 🔟
Simpson Hill Cl *HEY* OL10 .... 38 A4 🔟
Simpson St *CHAD* OL9 .... 94 C1 🔟
　EDGY/DAV SK3 .... 166 C5 🔟
　HYDE SK14 .... 131 D6
　OP/CLY M11 .... 108 B6
　WILM/AE SK9 .... 203 D5 🔟
Sinclair St *ROCH* OL11 .... 39 E4
Sinderland La *ALT* WA14 .... 156 A4
　LYMM WA13 .... 155 F5
Sinderland Rd *ALT* WA14 .... 156 A4
　PART M31 .... 156 A2
Sindsley Gv *BOLS/LL* BL3 .... 46 C6 🔟
Sindsley Rd *SWIN* M27 .... 85 E3
Singapore Av *MANAIR* M90 .... 191 E1
Singleton Av *BOLE* BL2 .... 48 C2
Singleton Cl *BRO* M7 .... 89 D4 🔟
Singleton Rd *BRO* M7 .... 89 D4
　HTNM SK4 .... 165 F1
Singleton St *RAD* M26 .... 50 B5
Sion St *RAD* M26 .... 69 D1
Sirdar St *OP/CLY* M11 .... 128 A1 🔟
Sirius Pl *BRO* M7 .... 105 E4 🔟
Sir Matt Busby Wy
　OLDTF/WHR M16 .... 122 A4
Sir Richard Fairey Rd *HTNM* SK4 .... 145 F5
Siskin Rd *RDSH* SK5 .... 185 D3
Sisson St *FAIL* M35 .... 94 A6 🔟
Sisters' St *DROY* M43 .... 128 B1
Sixpools Gv *WALK* M28 .... 83 D5 🔟
Sixth Av *BOL* BL1 .... 65 F2
　BURY BL9 .... 35 E3
　OLDS OL8 .... 95 D4
Sixth St *TRPK* M17 .... 121 E4 🔟

Size St *WHIT* OL12 .... 9 E2 🔟
Skagen Ct *BOL* BL1 .... 27 F6
Skaife Rd *SALE* M33 .... 160 C1
Skarratt Cl *WGTN/LGST* M12 .... 126 A3 🔟
Skegness Cl *TOT/BURYW* BL8 .... 33 E2
Skelton Gv *BOLE* BL2 .... 49 D1
　BRUN/LGST M13 .... 145 D1
Skelton Rd *ALT* WA14 .... 158 C6
　STRET M32 .... 121 E6
Skelwith Av *BOLS/LL* BL3 .... 65 D1 🔟
Skelwith Cl *URM* M41 .... 118 B5 🔟
Skerry Cl *BRUN/LGST* M13 .... 124 C2
Skerton Rd *OLDTF/WHR* M16 .... 122 C5
Skip Pl *CSLFD* M3 .... 106 B4
Skipton Av *CHAD* OL9 .... 77 D2
　NEWH/MOS M40 .... 93 E4 🔟
Skipton Cl *BRAM/HZG* SK7 .... 198 A1
　TOT/BURYW BL8 .... 32 A5
Skipton Dr *URM* M41 .... 118 A4 🔟
Skipton St *BOLE* BL2 .... 48 A2
　OLDS OL8 .... 96 C1
Skye Cl *HEY* OL10 .... 36 A6
Skye Crs *MPL/ROM* SK6 .... 170 D2
Skye Rd *URM* M41 .... 119 E4
Slackey Brow *FWTH* BL4 .... 68 A6
Slack Fold La *FWTH* BL4 .... 64 B2
Slack Ga *WHIT* OL12 .... 9 F3
Slack La *BOLE* BL2 .... 15 F6
　SWIN M27 .... 86 B3 🔟
Slack Rd *BKLY* M9 .... 91 E4
Slack St *HYDE* SK14 .... 132 A5
　MILN OL16 .... 23 D6 🔟
Slade Gv *BRUN/LGST* M13 .... 126 A6
Slade Hall Rd *WGTN/LGST* M12 .... 145 E1
Slade La *BNG/LEV* M19 .... 145 D3
Sladen St *WHIT* OL12 .... 23 D4
Slade St *BOLS/LL* BL3 .... 49 E6
Sladen Av *BOLS/LL* BL3 .... 49 D5
Slaidburn Cl *MILN* OL16 .... 42 A2 🔟
Slaidburn Dr *TOT/BURYW* BL8 .... 31 F4
Slaithwaite Dr *OP/CLY* M11 .... 109 D5 🔟
Slateacre Rd *HYDE* SK14 .... 151 D4
Slate La *AULW* OL7 .... 111 F6
　DTN/ASHW M34 .... 129 F1
Slaterfield *BOLS/LL* BL3 .... 46 C4 🔟
Slater La *BOL* BL1 .... 28 B6
Slater St *BOL* BL1 .... 46 C1
　CHAD OL9 .... 78 C5 🔟
　ECC M30 .... 100 C5 🔟
　FAIL M35 .... 94 A4
　FWTH BL4 .... 66 B3 🔟
Slawson Wy *HEY* OL10 .... 38 A4 🔟
Sleaford Cl *NEWH/MOS* M40 .... 107 E4 🔟
　TOT/BURYW BL8 .... 33 E2
Sleddale Cl *OFTN* SK2 .... 184 B2
Sledmere Cl *BOL* BL1 .... 28 A5 🔟
　OP/CLY M11 .... 108 B6 🔟
Sledmoor Rd *NTHM/RTH* M23 .... 161 D4
Slimbridge Cl *BOLE* BL2 .... 30 B6
Sloane Av *OLDE* OL4 .... 80 C3
Sloane St *AUL* OL6 .... 113 E4 🔟
　BOLS/LL BL3 .... 45 F6 🔟
　BOLS/LL BL3 .... 46 A6 🔟
　OP/CLY M11 .... 108 B5 🔟
Smallbridge Cl *WALK* M28 .... 83 D5 🔟
Smallbrook Cl *ROY/SHW* OL2 .... 42 C5
Smalldale Av *OLDTF/WHR* M16 .... 124 A6
Smalley St *ROCH* OL11 .... 39 D5
Smallfield Dr *BKLY* M9 .... 91 E5 🔟
Smallridge Cl *NEWH/MOS* M40 .... 107 E4 🔟
Smallshaw La *AUL* OL6 .... 113 D2
Smallshaw Rd *WHIT* OL12 .... 21 E1
Smallwood St *NEWH/MOS* M40 .... 109 D1 🔟
Smart St *WGTN/LGST* M12 .... 126 B6
Smeaton Cl *STRET* M32 .... 140 C1 🔟
Smeaton St *CHH* M8 .... 107 D1 🔟
Smedley Av *BOLS/LL* BL3 .... 47 E6
Smedley La *CHH* M8 .... 90 C6
Smedley Rd *CHH* M8 .... 106 C1
　NEWH/MOS M40 .... 107 D2
Smedley St *CHH* M8 .... 106 B1
Smethurst Hall Rd *BURY* BL9 .... 35 F3
Smethurst St *BKLY* M9 .... 91 E4 🔟
　HEY OL10 .... 36 C5 🔟
　MDTN M24 .... 76 B4
　TOT/BURYW BL8 .... 32 C3 🔟
Smith Farm Cl *OLDE* OL4 .... 81 D3
Smith Fold La *WALK* M28 .... 82 B2
Smith HI *MILN* OL16 .... 42 A1
Smithies Av *MDTN* M24 .... 75 E1
Smithies St *HEY* OL10 .... 37 F5 🔟
Smithills Croft Rd *BOL* BL1 .... 26 B4
Smithills Dean Rd *BOL* BL1 .... 26 B2
Smithills Dr *BOL* BL1 .... 26 B3 🔟
Smithills Hall Cl *RAMS* BL0 .... 7 D6 🔟
Smith La *EDGW/EG* BL7 .... 14 A5
Smiths Lawn *WILM/AE* SK9 .... 203 E6 🔟
Smith's Rd *BOLS/LL* BL3 .... 48 B6
Smith St *AULW* OL7 .... 112 A6
　BURY BL9 .... 34 B4 🔟
　CHD/CHDH SK8 .... 181 D1 🔟
　DTN/ASHW M34 .... 149 D1
　DUK SK16 .... 130 B1 🔟
　HEY OL10 .... 37 E5 🔟
　HYDE SK14 .... 131 E4

Smithy Bridge Rd *LIT* OL15 .... 25 E3 🔟
Smithy Cft *EDGW/EG* BL7 .... 14 A5
Smithy Fold *WHIT* OL12 .... 21 F4
Smithy Fold Rd *HYDE* SK14 .... 150 C3 🔟
Smithy Gn *MPL/ROM* SK6 .... 149 F6
Smithy Gv *AUL* OL6 .... 113 D3
Smithy HI *BOLS/LL* BL3 .... 45 E5 🔟
Smithy La *ALT* WA14 .... 172 B4
　CSLFD M3 .... 2 C3 🔟
　HYDE SK14 .... 150 C2 🔟
　PART M31 .... 155 D2
Smithy St *BRAM/HZG* SK7 .... 184 B4 🔟
　RAMS BL0 .... 7 D5 🔟
Smyrna St *HEY* OL10 .... 37 D6 🔟
　OLDE OL4 .... 80 A6 🔟
　RAD M26 .... 51 D6
　SALQ/ORD M5 .... 103 F6
Snape St *RAD* M26 .... 51 D3
Snell St *ANC* M4 .... 107 E6
Snipe Av *ROCH* OL11 .... 21 D6
Snipe Cl *POY/DIS* SK12 .... 197 E6
Snipe Rd *OLDS* OL8 .... 96 C3
Snipe St *BOLS/LL* BL3 .... 47 D4
Snipe Wy *DTN/ASHW* M34 .... 111 E6
Snowden Av *URM* M41 .... 137 F3
Snowden St *BOL* BL1 .... 46 C1
　HEY OL10 .... 56 C1 🔟
　OLDS OL8 .... 96 A1 🔟
Snowdon Rd *ECC* M30 .... 102 A4
Snowdon St *ROCH* OL11 .... 40 B5
Snow Hill Rd *BOLS/LL* BL3 .... 48 B4
Soap St *ANC* M4 .... 3 F2
Sofa St *BOL* BL1 .... 26 C2
Soho St *BOL* BL1 .... 47 D4 🔟
　OLD OL1 .... 79 F4 🔟
Solent Av *CHH* M8 .... 90 B3
Solent Dr *BOLS/LL* BL3 .... 48 A4
Solness St *BURY* BL9 .... 34 A1 🔟
Solway Cl *BOLS/LL* BL3 .... 46 B6 🔟
　OLDS OL8 .... 78 C6
　SWIN M27 .... 85 F1
Solway Rd *WYTH/NTH* M22 .... 178 C3
Somerby Dr *WYTH/NTH* M22 .... 178 A6 🔟
Somerdale Av *BOL* BL1 .... 45 E1
Somerfield Rd *BKLY* M9 .... 91 E4
Somerford Av *DID/WITH* M20 .... 143 E3 🔟
Somerford Rd *RDSH* SK5 .... 147 E1
Somersby Dr *EDGW/EG* BL7 .... 14 A5
Somerset Av *ROY/SHW* OL2 .... 61 D2 🔟
Somerset Cl *IRL* M44 .... 134 B5 🔟
　RDSH SK5 .... 168 A1
Somerset Dr *BURY* BL9 .... 53 D1
Somerset Gv *ROCH* OL11 .... 21 E5
Somerset Pl *SALE* M33 .... 139 F5 🔟
Somerset Rd *ALT* WA14 .... 174 B1 🔟
　BOL BL1 .... 45 F1
　DROY M43 .... 110 B4
　ECC M30 .... 102 B3
　FAIL M35 .... 109 F1 🔟
Somerset St *OLDE* OL4 .... 80 A5 🔟
Somers Rd *RDSH* SK5 .... 147 D2
Somerton Av *SALE* M33 .... 160 A2 🔟
　WYTH/NTH M22 .... 178 A4 🔟
Somerton Rd *BOLE* BL2 .... 49 D4
Somerville Gdns
　HALE/TIMP WA15 .... 159 D6 🔟
Somerville Sq *BOL* BL1 .... 27 D4 🔟
Somerville St *BOL* BL1 .... 27 D4 🔟
Sopwith Dr *RUSH/FAL* M14 .... 143 E2
Sorbus Cl *SLFD* M6 .... 104 C5
Sorby Rd *IRL* M44 .... 135 E4
Sorrel Bank *SLFD* M6 .... 104 A3
Sorrel Dr *LIT* OL15 .... 12 A5
Sorrell Bank *RDSH* SK5 .... 147 E2
Sorrel St *HULME* M15 .... 123 G2
Soudan Rd *OFTN* SK2 .... 183 E1
Soudan St *MDTN* M24 .... 76 A2
Souracre Fold *STLY* SK15 .... 114 C4 🔟
South Acre Dr *WILM/AE* SK9 .... 194 B6
Southall St *CSLFD* M3 .... 106 A4
Southampton Cl *BRO* M7 .... 105 E2 🔟
Southam St *BRO* M7 .... 90 A6 🔟
South Av *BNG/LEV* M19 .... 145 D4
　FWTH BL4 .... 67 D5
　HEY OL10 .... 36 C5 🔟
　SWIN M27 .... 101 E2
　WHTF M45 .... 70 C2
South Back Rock *BURY* BL9 .... 33 F5 🔟
　BURY BL9 .... 34 A5 🔟
South Bank Cl *WILM/AE* SK9 .... 209 F3 🔟
Southbank Rd *BNG/LEV* M19 .... 144 B6
South Bank Rd *BURY* BL9 .... 33 F6
Southbourne Av *URM* M41 .... 139 D1
Southbourne St *SLFD* M6 .... 103 F5 🔟
Southbrook Av *CHH* M8 .... 90 A2 🔟
Southbrook Gv *BOLS/LL* BL3 .... 47 D6 🔟
Southcliffe Rd *RDSH* SK5 .... 147 D5 🔟
South Cliffe St *OP/CLY* M11 .... 128 A2 🔟

South Cl *BURY* BL9 .... 53 E6
  WILM/AE SK9 .... 203 D5
South Crs *NEWH/MOS* M40 .... 93 E2
  OP/CLY M11 .... 109 E5
South Cft *OLDS* OL8 .... 96 C2
Southcross Rd *CTN* M18 .... 127 E6 ⑦
South Cross St *BURY* BL9 .... 34 A5
South Croston St
  OLDTF/WHR M16 .... 123 E5 ⑩
Southdene Av *DID/WITH* M20 .. 162 C1
Southdown Cl *HTNM* SK4 .... 166 B3
  ROCH OL11 .... 39 D2
Southdown Crs *BKLY* M9 .... 92 B3
  CHD/CHDH SK8 .... 169 H5
Southdowns Cl *ROY/SHW* OL2 ... 61 D1 ⑩
South Downs Dr *ALT* WA14 ...... 188 B1
South Downs Rd *ALT* WA14 ...... 174 A6
South Dr *BOLE* BL2 .... 29 F4
  CCHDY M21 .... 141 F5
  CHD/CHDH SK8 .... 179 E3
  HALE/TIMP WA15 .... 159 E6
Southend Av *HULME* M15 .... 123 E3 ⑫
Southend St *BOLS/LL* BL3 .... 46 A6 ②
Southern Av *DID/WITH* M20 .... 162 C1
Southern Cl *BRAM/HZG* SK7 .. 183 D5
  DTN/ASHW M34 .... 148 C3
Southern Crs *BRAM/HZG* SK7 . 183 D6
Southern St *CSLFD* M3 .... 2 B6 ②
  SLFD M6 .... 103 F5
  WALK M28 .... 66 B6
Southey Cl *LIT* OL15 .... 25 D3 ③
Southfield Av *BURY* BL9 .... 33 F1
Southfield Cl *HYDE* SK14 .... 131 E3
Southfield Rd *TOT/BURYW* BL8 .... 18 D3
Southfields Dr
  HALE/TIMP WA15 .... 159 F6 ①
Southfield St *BOLS/LL* BL3 .... 47 F5 ⑪
Southgarth Rd *SLFD* M6 .... 103 F4
Southgate *BOLE* BL2 .... 29 F3 ⑦
  CCHDY M21 .... 141 F4
  CSLFD M3 .... 2 C5 ⑩
  HTNM SK4 .... 146 A6 ③
  URM M41 .... 137 F3
  WHIT OL12 .... 8 C4
Southgate College Land *CSLFD* M3 .... 2 C3
Southgate St *OLD* OL1 .... 79 D5
South Gv *BRUN/LGST* M13 ...... 129 F2
  SALE M33 .... 139 F2
  WALK M28 .... 83 D3
  WILM/AE SK9 .... 209 E4 ⑩
Southgrove Av *BOL* BL1 .... 27 F1
South Hl *OLDE* OL4 .... 81 D6
South Hill St *OLDE* OL4 .... 79 E5
South King St *CMANW* M2 .... 2 C3
  ECC M30 .... 100 C5
Southlands Av *ECC* M30 .... 118 A1
South Langworthy Rd
  SALQ/ORD M5 .... 104 A6
Southlea Rd *DID/WITH* M20 .... 144 B6
Southleigh Dr *BOLE* BL2 .... 49 E3
South Lonsdale St *STRET* M32 . 121 F6 ②
South Md *POY/DIS* SK12 .... 197 F4
South Meade *CCHDY* M21 ...... 141 F4
  HALE/TIMP WA15 .... 159 E6
  PWCH M25 .... 89 E3
  SWIN M27 .... 101 F1
South Meadway *MPL/ROM* SK6 . 201 D2
Southmere Cl *BKLY* M9 .... 92 C3
South Mesnefield Rd *BRO* M7 .. 88 B6
Southmill St *CMANW* M2 .... 2 C5 ④
Southmoor Rd *NTHM/RTH* M23 . 161 D6
South Oak La *WILM/AE* SK9 ... 203 D5
South Pde *BRAM/HZG* SK7 ..... 183 D5
  MILN OL16 .... 23 D6
South Park Dr *POY/DIS* SK12 .. 198 C5
South Park Rd *CHD/CHDH* SK8 . 179 F1
South Pine St *BURY* BL9 .... 34 C5
Southpool Cl *BRAM/HZG* SK7 . 183 E5 ⑩
South Pump St *CMANE* M1 .... 3 G5 ⑦
South Radford St *BRO* M7 .... 88 B6
South Rdg *DTN/ASHW* M34 .... 130 A4
South Rdg *ALT* WA14 .... 174 A5
  STRET M32 .... 120 B5
  SWIN M27 .... 87 E3
South Row *PWCH* M25 .... 88 A4 ③
South Royd St *TOT/BURYW* BL8 . 18 A6
Southsea St *OP/CLY* M11 .... 127 E2 ⑦
Southside *MPL/ROM* SK6 .... 148 C5
South St *AULW* OL7 .... 129 F1
  BOLS/LL BL3 .... 46 C6 ⑭
  MILN OL16 .... 23 E5
  OLDS OL8 .... 94 C3
  OP/CLY M11 .... 126 C1
  RAMS BL0 .... 7 E5 ⑩
  WGTN/LGST M12 .... 125 F4
  WILM/AE SK9 .... 209 E4
South Terrace St *MILN* OL16 ... 40 B2
South Vale Crs *HALE/TIMP* WA15 . 175 D2
South Vw *MPL/ROM* SK6 .... 150 A5
  RDSH SK5 .... 128 A6 ⑩
  ROCH OL11 .... 37 F1

South View Rd *MILN* OL16 ...... 24 C2
South View St *BOLE* BL2 .... 48 A2 ⑩
South View Ter *MILN* OL16 ...... 24 C1
Southview Wk *OLDE* OL4 .... 80 C2 ⑩
Southwark Dr *DUK* SK16 .... 131 E3 ②
Southway *ALT* WA14 .... 174 C1 ①
  AULW OL7 .... 112 B1
  DROY M43 .... 128 B1 ③
  NEWH/MOS M40 .... 94 A3
South Wy *OLDS* OL8 .... 95 F3
Southwell Cl *BOL* BL1 .... 46 B1 ⑩
  MPL/ROM SK6 .... 169 E4 ②
Southwell Gdns *AUL* OL6 .... 96 C6
Southwell St *BKLY* M9 .... 91 F6
Southwick Rd *NTHM/RTH* M23 . 161 E3
South William St *CSLFD* M3 .. 105 E6 ⑬
Southwood Cl *BOLS/LL* BL3 ...... 47 D6
Southwood Dr *BKLY* M9 .... 73 E6 ⑩
Southwood Rd *OFTN* SK2 .... 183 F5
Southyard St *BNG/LEV* M19 .. 143 F5 ⑫
Sovereign St *SLFD* M6 .... 104 B5 ④
Sowerby Cl *TOT/BURYW* BL8 ... 32 A5 ⑩
Spa Cl *BOLT* M35 .... 146 C3
Spa Crs *LHULT* M38 .... 65 E5
Spa Gv *LHULT* M38 .... 65 E5
Spa La *LHULT* M38 .... 65 E5
  OLDE OL4 .... 80 C6 ⑩
Spalding Dr *NTHM/RTH* M23 .. 177 E5 ⑩
Sparkford Av *NTHM/RTH* M23 . 160 B4
Sparkle St *CMANE* M1 .... 3 H4
Spark Rd *NTHM/RTH* M23 ...... 161 D6
Spa Rd *BOL* BL1 .... 46 C2
  BOLS/LL BL3 .... 46 B3
Sparrow Cl *RDSH* SK5 .... 146 C1
Sparrowfield Cl *STLY* SK15 ...... 99 F6 ⑬
Sparrow Hl *MILN* OL16 .... 22 C6
Sparrow St *ROY/SHW* OL2 ...... 78 C1 ③
Sparta Av *WALK* M28 .... 83 E3 ⑩
Sparth Bottoms Rd *ROCH* OL11 . 39 E1
Sparthfield Av *ROCH* OL11 .... 39 F2
Sparthfield Rd *HTNM* SK4 .... 166 B2
Sparth La *HTNM* SK4 .... 166 B2
Sparth Rd *NEWH/MOS* M40 ... 109 E2
Spath La *WILM/AE* SK9 .... 194 B4
Spath La East *CHD/CHDH* SK8 . 195 F4
Spath Rd *DID/WITH* M20 .... 163 E2
Spath Wk *CHD/CHDH* SK8 ..... 195 F4
Spaw St *CSLFD* M3 .... 2 A2
Spear Dr *ANC* M4 .... 3 G3
Spectator St *ANC* M4 .... 107 E5 ⑫
Spencer Av *BOLS/LL* BL3 .... 50 A6
  HYDE SK14 .... 131 E4 ⑦
  OLDTF/WHR M16 .... 142 A1
  WHTF M45 .... 70 C1
Spencer La *ROCH* OL11 .... 37 F2
Spencer St *CHAD* OL9 .... 94 C1
  DUK SK16 .... 131 D1 ④
  ECC M30 .... 101 D6 ⑩
  MOSL OL5 .... 98 C4
  OLD OL1 .... 79 E4
  RAD M26 .... 52 A5 ⑫
  RAMS BL0 .... 6 C6 ⑬
  RDSH SK5 .... 147 D3
  TOT/BURYW BL8 .... 33 D4 ⑩
  TOT/BURYW BL8 .... 33 D4 ⑩
Spender Av *CHH* M8 .... 106 B1
Spen Fold *TOT/BURYW* BL8 ..... 51 E1
Spenleach La *TOT/BURYW* BL8 . 17 D1
Spennithorne Rd *URM* M41 .... 137 F1
Spenser Av *DTN/ASHW* M34 .. 149 E3 ⑩
  RAD M26 .... 50 C5
Spenwood Rd *LIT* OL15 .... 12 A6
Spey Cl *ALT* WA14 .... 174 A1 ②
Speyside Cl *WHTF* M45 .... 71 E3 ⑩
Spindle Av *STLY* SK15 .... 115 D4
Spindlepoint Dr *WALK* M28 ..... 83 D5 ⑩
The Spindles *MOSL* OL5 .... 99 E5
Spindlewood Cl *STLY* SK15 ..... 115 E5
Spiningdale *LHULT* M38 .... 64 B5 ⑪
Spinkingfield Wy *HEY* OL10 ...... 56 B2
Spinks St *OLDE* OL4 .... 79 F6
Spinners Gdns *WHIT* OL12 .... 24 A1
Spinners Gn *WHIT* OL12 .... 23 D3
Spinners La *POY/DIS* SK12 .... 197 F5
Spinners Ms *BOL* BL1 .... 46 C1 ②
Spinners Wy *OLDE* OL4 .... 63 D5
Spinney Dr *BURY* BL9 .... 34 A1
  SALE M33 .... 158 B2
Spinney Gv *DTN/ASHW* M34 .. 130 A4
Spinney Nook *BOLE* BL2 .... 29 E5 ⑩
Spinney Rd *NTHM/RTH* M23 .. 161 F6
The Spinney *CHD/CHDH* SK8 .. 180 C4
  EDGW/EG BL7 .... 15 D3
  OLDE OL4 .... 81 E3 ⑩
  URM M41 .... 137 E1 ⑩
  WHIT OL12 .... 22 B2 ②
  WHTF M45 .... 70 A4 ②
Spinning Meadow *BOL* BL1 ...... 46 B2 ⑩
Spirewood Gdns *MPL/ROM* SK6 . 169 E4 ③
Spodden Fold *WHIT* OL12 .... 9 D3
Spodden St *WHIT* OL12 .... 22 B5 ⑪
Spod Rd *WHIT* OL12 .... 22 A4
Spokeshave Wy *MILN* OL16 ..... 24 A3 ⑩
Sportside Av *WALK* M28 .... 83 F1
Sportside Cl *WALK* M28 .... 83 E1

Sportside Gv *WALK* M28 .... 83 E1
Sportsmans Dr *OLDS* OL8 .... 96 B2
Spotland Rd *WHIT* OL12 .... 22 B5
Spotland Tops *WHIT* OL12 .... 21 E4
Spreadbury St *NEWH/MOS* M40 . 92 B6 ⑩
Spring Av *HYDE* SK14 .... 151 D3
  WHTF M45 .... 70 C1 ⑩
Spring Bank *STLY* SK15 .... 114 C6 ⑩
Spring Bank Av *AUL* OL6 .... 112 C2 ⑩
  DTN/ASHW M34 .... 129 E2
Spring Bank La *ROCH* OL11 ...... 20 C5
  STLY SK15 .... 115 D2
Spring Bank Pl *EDGY/DAV* SK3 . 166 C5 ⑫
Springbank Rd *MPL/ROM* SK6 . 150 A5
Spring Bank St *OLDS* OL8 .... 95 D1 ⑩
Spring Bridge Rd
  OLDTF/WHR M16 .... 143 D1
Spring Cl *OLDE* OL4 .... 80 B6
  RAMS BL0 .... 6 C5
  TOT/BURYW BL8 .... 31 F1
Spring Clough *SWIN* M27 .... 100 C2
Spring Clough Av *WALK* M28 .... 84 A3
Spring Clough Dr *OLDS* OL8 ...... 96 C1
  WALK M28 .... 84 A3 ⑩
Springdale Gdns *DID/WITH* M20 . 163 E2
Springfield *RAD* M26 .... 68 A5 ③
Springfield Av *BRAM/HZG* SK7 . 184 B4 ⑩
  HTNM SK4 .... 146 C4
  LIT OL15 .... 12 B4
  MPL/ROM SK6 .... 187 D1 ⑩
Springfield Cl *FAIL* M35 .... 93 F5 ⑩
Springfield Dr *WILM/AE* SK9 .. 202 B6
Springfield Gdns *FWTH* BL4 ..... 67 E5 ⑩
Springfield La *CSLFD* M3 .... 105 F4
  IRL M44 .... 135 D1
  MILN OL16 .... 24 B2
  ROY/SHW OL2 .... 60 A2
Springfield Rd *ALT* WA14 ...... 174 B2
  CHD/CHDH SK8 .... 179 F2
  DROY M43 .... 110 A4
  FWTH BL4 .... 65 E2 ③
  FWTH BL4 .... 67 D5
  MDTN M24 .... 75 D1
  SALE M33 .... 159 F1
  TOT/BURYW BL8 .... 18 B5 ③
Springfield St *AUL* OL6 .... 113 F2 ②
  BOLS/LL BL3 .... 47 E5 ㉗
  DTN/ASHW M34 .... 130 A3 ⑦
  HEY OL10 .... 36 B5
Spring Gdns *BOLE* BL2 .... 30 A3 ②
  BRAM/HZG SK7 .... 184 B4
  CMANW M2 .... 3 E3
  HALE/TIMP WA15 .... 176 A2
  HYDE SK14 .... 131 E5
  MDTN M24 .... 75 E1
  SLFD M6 .... 104 A4
  STKP SK1 .... 167 E4
Spring Hall Ri *OLDE* OL4 .... 63 D5
Springhead Av *DID/WITH* M20 . 143 E4 ⑩
  OLDE OL4 .... 81 D6
Springhill *ROY/SHW* OL2 .... 60 B5
Spring La *OLDE* OL4 .... 80 B6
  RAD M26 .... 51 F6
Spring Mill Wk *MILN* OL16 ...... 24 A3
Spring Pl *WHIT* OL12 .... 5 E6 ⑪
  WHIT OL12 .... 9 E1 ⑩
Spring Ri *ROY/SHW* OL2 .... 42 B6
Spring Rd *ALT* WA14 .... 174 B5
Springside *HTNM* SK4 .... 146 B4
Spring Side *WHIT* OL12 .... 5 E5
Springside Av *WALK* M28 .... 83 F2
Springside Cl *WALK* M28 .... 83 F2 ⑩
Springside Gv *WALK* M28 .... 83 F2 ⑦
Springside Rd *BURY* BL9 .... 19 E5
Springside Vw *TOT/BURYW* BL8 . 19 D6
Springs La *STLY* SK15 .... 114 A3
Springs Rd *MDTN* M24 .... 76 C5
The Springs *ALT* WA14 .... 173 F5
Spring St *BOLS/LL* BL3 .... 47 D4 ⑪
  BURY BL9 .... 34 A5
  FWTH BL4 .... 66 B2
  MOSL OL5 .... 99 D3 ④
  OLDE OL4 .... 80 A3
  RAMS BL0 .... 7 E4 ③
  STLY SK15 .... 114 B5
  TOT/BURYW BL8 .... 18 A6 ③
  TOT/BURYW BL8 .... 33 F1 ⑩
  WGTN/LGST M12 .... 145 E1 ⑩
  WILM/AE SK9 .... 203 E4
Spring Ter *MILN* OL16 .... 42 C4 ⑩
Spring V *BRAM/HZG* SK7 .... 184 C5 ⑩
  MDTN M24 .... 75 E3
  PWCH M25 .... 88 B3
Springvale Cl *AULW* OL7 .... 112 A2
Spring Vale Dr *TOT/BURYW* BL8 . 17 F6
Spring Vale St *TOT/BURYW* BL8 . 31 F1
Spring Vale Ter *LIT* OL15 .... 12 C6
Spring Vale Wy *ROY/SHW* OL2 . 61 E4
Springville Av *BKLY* M9 .... 92 A6 ⑩
Springwater Av *TOT/BURYW* BL8 . 18 B2
Springwater Cl *BOLE* BL2 .... 29 F4 ③
Springwater La *WHTF* M45 .... 70 C1
Springwell Cl *SLFD* M6 .... 103 F5 ②
Springwell Gdns *HYDE* SK14 .. 152 C2

Springwood Av CHAD OL9 ... 76 C2
SWIN M27 ... 102 C1
Springwood Crs MPL/ROM SK6 ... 170 C3
Springwood Hall Rd OLDS OL8 ... 96 B3
Springwood La MPL/ROM SK6 ... 171 D3
Spring Wood St RAMS BL0 ... 6 C4
Spruce Av BURY BL9 ... 34 C5
Spruce St HULME M15 ... 123 F3
RAMS BL0 ... 18 B1
Sprucewood CHAD OL9 ... 76 B3
The Spur OLDS OL8 ... 96 B3
Square St RAMS BL0 ... 7 D5
The Square HTNM SK4 ... 166 A3
SWIN M27 ... 101 F2
Squire Rd CHH M8 ... 90 A6
Squirrel Dr ALT WA14 ... 158 A5
Squirrel's Jump WILM/AE SK9 ... 209 F4
Stablefold MOSL OL5 ... 99 D5
Stable Fold RAD M26 ... 51 E5
Stablefold WALK M28 ... 100 B2
Stableford Av ECC M30 ... 101 D5
The Stables DROY M43 ... 111 E4
Stable St CHAD OL9 ... 94 B3
The Stablings WILM/AE SK9 ... 203 E6
Stack La BCUP OL13 ... 4 C1
Stafford Rd ECC M30 ... 101 E4
FAIL M35 ... 110 B2
SWIN M27 ... 86 A5
WALK M28 ... 83 D4
Stafford St CHAD OL9 ... 95 D1
TOT/BURYW BL8 ... 33 E3
Stag Pasture Rd OLDS OL8 ... 95 E4
Stainburne Rd OFTN SK2 ... 184 A1
Stainburn Rd OP/CLY M11 ... 126 C1
Staindale OLDE OL4 ... 80 B5
Stainer St WGTN/LGST M12 ... 126 B6
Stainforth Cl TOT/BURYW BL8 ... 32 A4
Stainforth St OP/CLY M11 ... 126 A1
Stainmoor Ct OFTN SK2 ... 184 B1
Stainmore Av AUL OL6 ... 97 D6
Stainsbury St BOLS/LL BL3 ... 46 A5
Stainton Av GTN M18 ... 127 F5
Stainton Cl RAD M26 ... 50 C5
Stainton Dr MDTN M24 ... 56 B6
Stainton Rd RAD M26 ... 50 C4
Staithes Rd WYTH/NTH M22 ... 192 B1
Stakeford Dr CHH M8 ... 91 D5
Stakehill La MDTN M24 ... 58 C4
Staley Cl STLY SK15 ... 115 F3
Staley St OLDE OL4 ... 80 A5
OLDE OL4 ... 81 D5
Stalham Cl NEWH/MOS M40 ... 107 E4
Stalmine Av CHD/CHDH SK8 ... 193 F2
Staly Hall Rd STLY SK15 ... 115 D5
Stalyhill Dr STLY SK15 ... 133 F2
Stamford Av ALT WA14 ... 173 E1
STLY SK15 ... 113 F3
Stamford Cl STLY SK15 ... 113 F5
STLY SK15 ... 113 F5
Stamford Dr FAIL M35 ... 110 C2
STLY SK15 ... 113 F5
Stamford Gv STLY SK15 ... 114 A5
Stamford New Rd ALT WA14 ... 174 B3
Stamford Park Rd
HALE/TIMP WA15 ... 174 C4
Stamford Pl SALE M33 ... 160 A1
Stamford Rd ALT WA14 ... 173 F5
BRO M7 ... 104 C1
BRUN/LGST M13 ... 126 A6
DTN/ASHW M34 ... 129 E2
MOSL OL5 ... 99 D3
OLDE OL4 ... 81 D3
PART M31 ... 136 B5
URM M41 ... 137 F1
WILM/AE SK9 ... 203 E2
Stamford Sq AUL OL6 ... 113 C5
Stamford St ALT WA14 ... 174 B2
AUL OL6 ... 113 F5
HEY OL10 ... 37 F6
MILN OL16 ... 40 C1
MOSL OL5 ... 98 C4
OLDE OL4 ... 80 C5
OLDTF/WHR M16 ... 125 E5
SALE M33 ... 139 E5
STLY SK15 ... 114 B5
SWIN M27 ... 86 B4
Stamford Street Central AUL OL6 ... 112 C5
Stamford St East AUL OL6 ... 113 D5
Stamford St West AUL OL6 ... 112 C5
AULW OL7 ... 112 A4
Stamford Wy ALT WA14 ... 174 B2
Stampstone St OLD OL1 ... 79 F3
Stanage Av BKLY M9 ... 92 A1
Stanbank St HTNM SK4 ... 166 C1
Stanbourne Dr BOL BL1 ... 28 A3
Stanbrook St BNG/LEV M19 ... 146 A2
Stanbury Cl HEY OL10 ... 35 E6
Stanbury Dr DUK SK16 ... 131 E1
Stancliffe Rd WYTH/NTH M22 ... 178 C2
Stancross Rd NTHM/RTH M23 ... 160 A4
Stand Av WHTF M45 ... 70 C2
Stand Cl WHTF M45 ... 70 A3
Standfield Dr WALK M28 ... 82 B6
Standish Rd RUSH/FAL M14 ... 144 B3
Stand La RAD M26 ... 69 F1
Standmoor Rd WHTF M45 ... 70 B4

Standring Av TOT/BURYW BL8 ... 51 E1
Stand Ri RAD M26 ... 69 F3
Stanedge Cl RAMS BL0 ... 19 D1
Stanford Cl RAD M26 ... 68 A4
Stanford Hall Crs RAMS BL0 ... 18 C1
Stanhope Av DTN/ASHW M34 ... 129 F4
PWCH M25 ... 71 E6
Stanhope Cl WILM/AE SK9 ... 204 B3
Stanhope Ct PWCH M25 ... 71 E6
Stanhope Rd ALT WA14 ... 173 E5
SLFD M6 ... 103 F2
Stanhope St AUL OL6 ... 113 E3
BNG/LEV M19 ... 145 F2
DTN/ASHW M34 ... 129 F4
MOSL OL5 ... 99 D5
RDSH SK5 ... 146 C4
ROCH OL11 ... 40 A2
Stanhope Wy FAIL M35 ... 93 F5
Stanhorne Av CHH M8 ... 90 B3
Stanier Av ECC M30 ... 101 E4
Stanion Gv DUK SK16 ... 131 D1
Stan Jolly Wk OP/CLY M11 ... 127 D1
Stanley Av BRAM/HZG SK7 ... 184 B4
HYDE SK14 ... 131 F5
MPL/ROM SK6 ... 170 B6
RUSH/FAL M14 ... 125 D6
Stanley Av North PWCH M25 ... 71 E5
Stanley Av South PWCH M25 ... 71 E5
Stanley Cl WHTF M45 ... 71 F2
Stanley Ct BURY BL9 ... 34 A4
OLDTF/WHR M16 ... 123 D4
Stanley Dr CHD/CHDH SK8 ... 194 B3
HALE/TIMP WA15 ... 175 E2
WHTF M45 ... 71 D5
Stanley Gv GTN M18 ... 126 C5
HTNM SK4 ... 165 F1
URM M41 ... 138 B1
WGTN/LGST M12 ... 126 A5
Stanley Ms SALE M33 ... 159 E2
Stanley Mt SALE M33 ... 159 E2
Stanley Pl WHIT OL12 ... 22 C5
Stanley Rd BOL BL1 ... 26 C6
BRO M7 ... 89 F5
CHAD OL9 ... 94 C1
CHAD OL9 ... 95 D2
CHD/CHDH SK8 ... 194 B3
DTN/ASHW M34 ... 128 C6
ECC M30 ... 101 D6
FWTH BL4 ... 64 C3
HTNM SK4 ... 165 F1
OLDTF/WHR M16 ... 122 C4
RAD M26 ... 50 C3
SWIN M27 ... 86 B5
WALK M28 ... 83 E3
WHTF M45 ... 71 D2
Stanley St BKLY M9 ... 91 F5
CHAD OL9 ... 77 F4
CHH M8 ... 106 B3
CSLFD M3 ... 2 A3
HEY OL10 ... 37 E6
NEWH/MOS M40 ... 108 A2
OLDE OL4 ... 80 C6
OLDE OL4 ... 81 E5
OP/CLY M11 ... 127 F2
PWCH M25 ... 89 D1
RAMS BL0 ... 6 C6
SALQ/ORD M5 ... 122 B1
STKP SK1 ... 167 E3
STLY SK15 ... 114 A6
WHIT OL12 ... 22 C4
WHTF M45 ... 71 D2
Stanley St South BOLS/LL BL3 ... 46 C3
Stanmore Av STRET M32 ... 139 F1
Stanmore Dr BOLS/LL BL3 ... 46 A4
Stannard Rd ECC M30 ... 100 A6
Stanneybrook Cl MILN OL16 ... 23 F5
Stanney Cl MILN OL16 ... 41 F2
Stanneylands Cl WILM/AE SK9 ... 204 A1
Stanneylands Dr WILM/AE SK9 ... 203 F1
Stanneylands Rd WILM/AE SK9 ... 193 F5
Stanney Rd MILN OL16 ... 23 F5
Stansbury Pl OFTN SK2 ... 184 C1
Stansby Gdns WGTN/LGST M12 ... 125 F3
Stansfield Dr ROCH OL11 ... 13 D2
Stansfield Hall LIT OL15 ... 13 D2
Stansfield Rd FAIL M35 ... 94 B4
HYDE SK14 ... 131 F5
Stansfield St CHAD OL9 ... 77 F6
NEWH/MOS M40 ... 109 E3
OLD OL1 ... 78 C3
OP/CLY M11 ... 127 E1
Stanthorne Av DID/WITH M20 ... 143 E4
Stanton Av BRO M7 ... 104 C1
DID/WITH M20 ... 162 C1
Stanton St CHAD OL9 ... 94 C2
OP/CLY M11 ... 109 D5
STRET M32 ... 121 E2
Stanway Cl BOLS/LL BL3 ... 46 B3
MDTN M24 ... 75 F5
Stanway Dr HALE/TIMP WA15 ... 175 D4
Stanway Rd WHTF M45 ... 71 F3
Stanway St BKLY M9 ... 91 F5
STRET M32 ... 121 E6
Stanwell Rd NEWH/MOS M40 ... 93 F6
SWIN M27 ... 85 F6

Stanwick Av BKLY M9 ... 90 B1
Stanworth Av BOLE BL2 ... 48 C2
Stanworth Cl OLDTF/WHR M16 ... 123 F6
Stanyard Ct SALQ/ORD M5 ... 122 B1
Stanycliffe La MDTN M24 ... 57 F3
Stapleford Cl NTHM/RTH M23 ... 177 D3
SALE M33 ... 140 C3
Stapleford Gv TOT/BURYW BL8 ... 32 B5
Staplehurst Rd
NEWH/MOS M40 ... 108 B3
Stapleton Av BOL BL1 ... 44 C1
Starbeck Cl TOT/BURYW BL8 ... 32 A5
Starcliffe St BOLS/LL BL3 ... 66 B1
Starfield Av LIT OL15 ... 20 B5
Star Gv BRO M7 ... 105 F1
Starkey St HEY OL10 ... 37 E4
Starkie Rd BOLE BL2 ... 28 C6
Starkie St WALK M28 ... 84 B5
Starling Cl DROY M43 ... 111 E4
Starling Dr FWTH BL4 ... 65 D4
Starling Rd RAD M26 ... 50 C1
TOT/BURYW BL8 ... 31 F6
Starmoor Dr CHH M8 ... 106 B1
Starmount Cl BOLE BL2 ... 49 E3
Starring La LIT OL15 ... 11 F6
Starring Rd WHIT OL12 ... 11 F6
Starring Wy LIT OL15 ... 12 A6
Stash Gv NTHM/RTH M23 ... 161 F6
Statford Av ECC M30 ... 119 D1
Statham Cl DTN/ASHW M34 ... 130 B6
Statham Fold HYDE SK14 ... 132 B5
Statham St SLFD M6 ... 104 C5
Station Ap CMANE M1 ... 3 E6
Station Cl HYDE SK14 ... 150 A1
Stationers Entry MILN OL16 ... 23 D6
Station La OLDE OL4 ... 81 F6
Station Rd CHD/CHDH SK8 ... 181 F5
CHH M8 ... 90 B4
ECC M30 ... 101 D6
EDCW/EG BL7 ... 15 D1
EDGY/DAV SK3 ... 166 C5
FWTH BL4 ... 67 D4
HTNM SK4 ... 164 C4
HYDE SK14 ... 151 F1
IRL M44 ... 134 C4
LIT OL15 ... 12 C6
MILN OL16 ... 42 D1
MOSL OL5 ... 99 E4
MPL/ROM SK6 ... 149 F6
MPL/ROM SK6 ... 187 D1
OLDE OL4 ... 81 E6
RDSH SK5 ... 146 C1
ROCH OL11 ... 40 A1
STRET M32 ... 121 E6
SWIN M27 ... 86 A4
TOT/BURYW BL8 ... 18 A4
URM M41 ... 138 B2
WHIT OL12 ... 5 E6
WHIT OL12 ... 8 C6
WILM/AE SK9 ... 193 E6
WILM/AE SK9 ... 196 B6
WILM/AE SK9 ... 203 F4
Station St AULW OL7 ... 112 C6
BRAM/HZG SK7 ... 184 B5
OLDE OL4 ... 81 D5
Station Vw BNG/LEV M19 ... 145 E2
Staton Av BOLE BL2 ... 48 A1
Staton St OP/CLY M11 ... 127 D1
Statter St BURY BL9 ... 53 E5
Staveley Av BOL BL1 ... 27 F1
STLY SK15 ... 114 B4
Staveley Cl ROY/SHW OL2 ... 62 B3
Staverton Cl BRUN/LGST M13 ... 125 D2
Staveton Cl BRAM/HZG SK7 ... 183 D4
Staycott Cl OLDTF/WHR M16 ... 124 A5
Stayley Dr STLY SK15 ... 115 E3
Stayley Rd MOSL OL5 ... 99 E5
Stead St RAMS BL0 ... 7 D5
Stedman Cl OP/CLY M11 ... 107 F6
Steele Gdns BOLE BL2 ... 48 C4
Steeles Av HYDE SK14 ... 131 F6
Steeple Dr SALQ/ORD M5 ... 122 B1
Steeple Vw ROY/SHW OL2 ... 60 B5
Stelfox Av HALE/TIMP WA15 ... 160 A6
RUSH/FAL M14 ... 143 F2
Stelfox La DTN/ASHW M34 ... 130 A2
Stelfox St ECC M30 ... 118 C1
Stella St BKLY M9 ... 90 C1
Stelling St GTN M18 ... 127 E4
Stenbury Cl RUSH/FAL M14 ... 125 D6
Stephanie Av DROY M43 ... 110 B6
Stephenson Rd STRET M32 ... 140 B2
Stephenson St FAIL M35 ... 94 B4
OLDE OL4 ... 80 B3
Stephens Rd DID/WITH M20 ... 144 A5
STLY SK15 ... 114 A3
Stephens St BOLE BL2 ... 48 B1
Stephen St CSLFD M3 ... 106 A3
STKP SK1 ... 167 F5
TOT/BURYW BL8 ... 33 D5
URM M41 ... 138 C1
Stephen St South
TOT/BURYW BL8 ... 33 D5
Steps Meadow WHIT OL12 ... 24 A1
Stern Av SALQ/ORD M5 ... 122 B1

Sterndale Rd *EDGY/DAV* SK3 .... 182 C2
  MPL/ROM SK6 .... 169 F4
Sterratt St *BOL* BL1 .... 46 A3
Stetchworth Dr *WALK* M28 .... 82 C6
Stevenson Dr *OLD* M41 .... 62 C5
Stevenson Pl *CMANE* M1 .... 3 G3 🔟
Stevenson Rd *SWIN* M27 .... 85 F5
Stevenson Sq *CMANE* M1 .... 3 G3 🔟
Stevenson St *CSLFD* M3 .... 105 E6 🔟
  WALK M28 .... 82 C2 🔟
Stevens St *WILM/AE* SK9 .... 209 E4
Stewart Av *FWTH* BL4 .... 65 F4
Stewart St *AULW* OL7 .... 112 A5 🔟
  BOL BL1 .... 27 F6
  MILN OL16 .... 42 C4
  TOT/BURYW BL8 .... 33 D3 🔟
Steynton Cl *BOL* BL1 .... 45 D1
Stile Cl *URM* M41 .... 136 A1
Stiles Av *MPL/ROM* SK6 .... 170 C6
Stilton Dr *OP/CLY* M11 .... 126 B1 🔟
Stirling Dr *BRAM/HZG* SK7 .... 184 B6
  DID/WITH M20 .... 143 D3
  MPL/ROM SK6 .... 187 D2
Stirling Cl *EDGY/DAV* SK3 .... 182 A1 🔟
Stirling Dr *STLY* SK15 .... 114 B4
Stirling Gv *WHTF* M45 .... 71 E3
Stirling Rd *BOL* BL1 .... 27 F2
  CHAD OL9 .... 94 A1
Stirling St *CHAD* OL9 .... 78 A4
Stirrup Ga *WALK* M28 .... 100 B2 🔟
Stitch La *HTNM* SK4 .... 166 B2
Stitch-mi-lane *BOLE* BL2 .... 29 F5
Stiups La *MILN* OL16 .... 40 C3
Stobart Av *PWCH* M25 .... 89 D4 🔟
Stockburn Dr *FAIL* M35 .... 94 C6
Stockdale Av *EDGY/DAV* SK3 ...... 183 D3 🔟
Stockdale Gv *BOLE* BL2 .... 30 A6 🔟
Stockdale Rd *BKLY* M9 .... 91 F1
Stockfield Rd *CHAD* OL9 .... 77 F4
Stock Gv *MILN* OL16 .... 25 D6
Stockholm Rd *EDGY/DAV* SK3 .... 182 B1
Stockholm St *OP/CLY* M11 ...... 108 C5 🔟
Stock La *CHAD* OL9 .... 77 F6
Stockley Av *BOLE* BL2 .... 29 F5
Stockport Rd *AULW* OL7 .... 130 A1
  BRUN/LGST M13 .... 126 A5
  DTN/ASHW M34 .... 129 F5
  EDGY/DAV SK3 .... 165 E6
  HALE/TIMP WA15 .... 178 F1
  HYDE SK14 .... 150 C2
  MOSL OL5 .... 99 D3
  MPL/ROM SK6 .... 169 F3
  WGTN/LGST M12 .... 125 E3
Stockport Rd East *MPL/ROM* SK6 . 169 D1
Stockport Rd West *MPL/ROM* SK6 . 168 A2
Stocksfield Dr *BKLY* M9 .... 91 F2 🔟
  LHULT M38 .... 65 D6
Stocks Gdns *STLY* SK15 .... 115 D6
Stocks La *STLY* SK15 .... 114 C6
Stocks St *CHH* M8 .... 106 B3
Stocks St East *CHH* M8 .... 106 B3
Stock St *TOT/BURYW* BL8 .... 33 F2 🔟
Stockton Av *EDGY/DAV* SK3 ...... 165 F5 🔟
Stockton Dr *TOT/BURYW* BL8 ...... 32 C2
Stockton Pk *OLDE* OL4 .... 80 B5
Stockton St *CCHDY* M21 .... 141 E3
  FWTH BL4 .... 66 A1
  WILM/AE SK9 .... 209 D1
Stockton St *LIT* OL15 .... 12 B6
  SWIN M27 .... 85 F5 🔟
Stoke Abbott Cl *BRAM/HZG* SK7 . 196 C2
Stokesay Cl *BURY* BL9 .... 53 D4
  ROY/SHW OL2 .... 61 E5
Stokesay Dr *BRAM/HZG* SK7 ...... 184 A6
Stokesay Rd *SALE* M33 .... 138 C6
Stokes St *OP/CLY* M11 .... 109 E6
Stoke St *MILN* OL16 .... 40 C1
Stokoe Av *ALT* WA14 .... 173 E1
Stonall Av *HULME* M15 .... 123 E3 🔟
Stoneacre Ct *SWIN* M27 .... 86 A6 🔟
Stoneacre Rd *WYTH/NTH* M22 ...... 179 F4
Stone Breaks Rd *OLDE* OL4 .... 81 F4
Stonebridge Cl *HOR/BR* BL6 ...... 44 A3 🔟
Stonechat Cl *DROY* M43 .... 111 D4 🔟
  WALK M28 .... 82 C5 🔟
Stonecliffe Av *STLY* SK15 .... 114 B5
Stone Cl *RAMS* BL0 .... 18 B1 🔟
Stoneclough Rd *FWTH* BL4 .... 67 D4
Stonedelph Cl *BOLE* BL2 .... 31 E6
Stonefield Dr *CHH* M8 .... 105 F2
Stonefield St *MILN* OL16 .... 42 A2
Stoneflat Ct *WHIT* OL12 .... 22 B5 🔟
Stonehead St *BKLY* M9 .... 92 A6 🔟
Stonehewer St *RAD* M26 .... 69 F1 🔟
Stonehill Crs *WHIT* OL12 .... 21 E2
Stonehill Dr *WHIT* OL12 .... 21 E2
Stone Hill La *WHIT* OL12 .... 21 E3
Stone Hill Rd *FWTH* BL4 .... 66 B5
Stonehill Rd *WHIT* OL12 .... 21 E2
Stonehouse *EDGW/EG* BL7 .... 14 C6
Stonehurst Cl
  WGTN/LGST M12 .... 126 B3 🔟
Stonelands Wy *OLDE* OL4 .... 98 B1
Stoneleigh Av *SALE* M33 .... 138 B6
Stoneleigh Dr *RAD* M26 .... 67 F4 🔟

Stoneleigh Rd *OLDE* OL4 .... 81 E4
Stoneleigh St *OLD* OL1 .... 79 F2
Stonelow Cl *HULME* M15 .... 124 A3 🔟
Stone Md *MPL/ROM* SK6 .... 170 C2
Stone Mead Av *HALE/TIMP* WA15 . 190 A2
Stonemead Cl *BOLS/LL* BL3 .... 47 D5 🔟
Stonepail Cl *CHD/CHDH* SK8 ...... 179 D2
Stonepail Rd *CHD/CHDH* SK8 ...... 179 E2 🔟
Stone Pale *WHTF* M45 .... 71 D4
Stone Pi *RUSH/FAL* M14 .... 125 D6 🔟
Stone Rw *MPL/ROM* SK6 .... 187 F1
Stonesby Cl *OLDTF/WHR* M16 ...... 123 E5 🔟
Stonesdale Cl *ROY/SHW* OL2 .... 60 C3
Stonesteads Dr *EDGW/EG* BL7 ...... 14 B5 🔟
Stonesteads Wy *EDGW/EG* BL7 .... 14 B5
Stone St *BOLE* BL2 .... 28 C6
  CSLFD M3 .... 2 B6
Stoneswood Dr *MOSL* OL5 .... 99 E3
Stoney Bank *RAD* M26 .... 68 A4
Stoneyfield *STLY* SK15 .... 114 B3
Stoneyfield Cl *OLDTF/WHR* M16 . 143 D2 🔟
Stoneygate Wk *OP/CLY* M11 ...... 127 E2
Stoneyhurst Cl *HULME* M15 .... 124 A3
Stoney La *WILM/AE* SK9 .... 203 D6
Stoneyroyd *WHIT* OL12 .... 9 E1 🔟
Stoneyside Av *WALK* M28 .... 83 F1
Stoneyside Gv *WALK* M28 .... 83 F2 🔟
Stonie Heyes Av *WHIT* OL12 .... 23 F3
Stonyford Rd *SALE* M33 .... 160 B1 🔟
Stonyhurst Av *BOL* BL1 .... 27 F2
Stopes Rd *BOLS/LL* BL3 .... 50 A6 🔟
Stopford Av *LIT* OL15 .... 24 C1
Stopford St *EDGY/DAV* SK3 .... 166 B5 🔟
  OP/CLY M11 .... 127 D3
Stores St *PWCH* M25 .... 89 D1 🔟
Store St *AULW* OL7 .... 112 B2
  OFTN SK2 .... 184 A3
  OP/CLY M11 .... 126 C2 🔟
  RAD M26 .... 52 B5 🔟
  ROCH OL11 .... 20 C4 🔟
  ROY/SHW OL2 .... 62 A1 🔟
Storeton Cl *WYTH/NTH* M22 ...... 178 C5 🔟
Stortford Dr *NTHM/RTH* M23 ..... 161 F5 🔟
Stothard Rd *STRET* M32 .... 139 F2
Stott Dr *URM* M41 .... 136 B1
Stottfield Rd *ROY/SHW* OL2 .... 59 F6
Stott La *BOLE* BL2 .... 28 C6 🔟
  MDTN M24 .... 57 D4
  SLFD M6 .... 102 C4
Stott Milne St *CHAD* OL9 .... 77 F6
Stott Rd *CHAD* OL9 .... 93 F2
  SWIN M27 .... 101 E1
Stott's La *NEWH/MOS* M40 .... 109 E1
Stott St *MILN* OL16 .... 24 B2
  MILN OL16 .... 42 A3 🔟
  NEWH/MOS M40 .... 109 E1
  OP/CLY M11 .... 108 A6 🔟
  WHIT OL12 .... 23 D4
Stourbridge Av *LHULT* M38 .... 65 E5 🔟
Stour Cl *ALT* WA14 .... 174 A1
Stourport Cl *MPL/ROM* SK6 .... 169 E4 🔟
Stourport St *OLD* OL1 .... 79 E2 🔟
Stovell Av *WGTN/LGST* M12 ...... 145 E1
Stovell Rd *NEWH/MOS* M40 .... 92 B5
Stow Cl *TOT/BURYW* BL8 .... 33 E2
Stowell Ct *BOL* BL1 .... 27 F6 🔟
Stowell St *BOL* BL1 .... 27 F6 🔟
  SALO/ORD M5 .... 103 F6 🔟
Stowfield Cl *BKLY* M9 .... 90 C1
Stow Gdns *DID/WITH* M20 .... 143 E5
Stracey St *NEWH/MOS* M40 .... 107 F4 🔟
Stradbroke Cl *GTN* M18 .... 126 C4
Strain Av *BKLY* M9 .... 91 E1
Strand Ct *STRET* M32 .... 140 A3 🔟
The Strand *ROCH* OL11 .... 40 A5
Strand Wy *ROY/SHW* OL2 .... 78 B1
Strangford St *RAD* M26 .... 50 B5 🔟
Strang St *RAMS* BL0 .... 7 D5 🔟
Stranton Dr *WALK* M28 .... 85 D5
Stratfield Av *NTHM/RTH* M23 ...... 160 B4
Stratford Av *BOL* BL1 .... 26 C6
  BURY BL9 .... 19 F5 🔟
  DID/WITH M20 .... 143 D6 🔟
  OLDS OL8 .... 95 F2
  ROCH OL11 .... 39 F2
Stratford Cl *FWTH* BL4 .... 65 D2
Stratford Gdns *MPL/ROM* SK6 ... 169 D2
Stratford Rd *MDTN* M24 .... 75 F6
Strathblane Cl *DID/WITH* M20 .... 143 F4 🔟
Strathfield Dr *OP/CLY* M11 .... 108 C5 🔟
Strathmere Av *STRET* M32 .... 121 E6
Strathmore Av *DTN/ASHW* M34 . 149 F1 🔟
  OLDTF/WHR M16 .... 141 F1 🔟
Strathmore Cl *RAMS* BL0 .... 19 D2
Strathmore Rd *BOLE* BL2 .... 29 F6 🔟
Stratton Rd *OFTN* SK2 .... 168 A5 🔟
  OLDTF/WHR M16 .... 141 F1
  SWIN M27 .... 86 A4
Strawberry Bank *SLFD* M6 .... 104 C4 🔟
Strawberry Cl *ALT* WA14 .... 157 F6 🔟
Strawberry HI *SLFD* M6 .... 104 C4
Strawberry Hill Rd *BOLE* BL2 .... 47 F4
Strawberry La *WILM/AE* SK9 ...... 202 C5
Strawberry Rd *SLFD* M6 .... 104 B4
Stray St *OP/CLY* M11 .... 127 F1 🔟

The Stray *BOL* BL1 .... 28 C3
Streamside Cl *HALE/TIMP* WA15 . 175 F3
Stream Ter *STKP* SK1 .... 167 F4
Street Bridge Rd *OLD* OL1 .... 77 E1
Streetgate *LHULT* M38 .... 65 D6 🔟
Street Kirklees *TOT/BURYW* BL8 .. 18 A6
Street La *RAD* M26 .... 50 C1
Stretford Rd *HULME* M15 .... 123 F3
  OLDTF/WHR M16 .... 123 D4
  URM M41 .... 138 B2
Stretton Av *DID/WITH* M20 .... 164 A2
  SALE M33 .... 158 C1
  STRET M32 .... 120 B6
Stretton Cl *NEWH/MOS* M40 ..... 107 E2 🔟
Stretton Rd *BOLS/LL* BL3 .... 45 F5 🔟
  TOT/BURYW BL8 .... 18 B3
Strines Rd *MPL/ROM* SK6 .... 187 E2
Stringer Av *HYDE* SK14 .... 153 D1
Stringer Cl *HYDE* SK14 .... 153 D1
Stringer St *STKP* SK1 .... 167 E3
Stroma Gdns *URM* M41 .... 119 D4
Strong St *BRO* M7 .... 105 F3 🔟
Strongstry Rd *RAMS* BL0 .... 7 D1
Stroud Av *ECC* M30 .... 100 C4
Stroud Cl *MDTN* M24 .... 75 E6
Stuart Av *IRL* M44 .... 135 D1
Stuart Dr *MPL/ROM* SK6 .... 170 A6
Stuart Rd *STRET* M32 .... 121 E6
Stuart St *MDTN* M24 .... 76 A3
  MILN OL16 .... 40 C1
  OLDS OL8 .... 78 C6
  OP/CLY M11 .... 108 A5
Stuart St East *OP/CLY* M11 .... 108 B5 🔟
Stubbins Cl *NTHM/RTH* M23 ...... 160 C4
Stubbins La *RAMS* BL0 .... 7 D3
Stubbins St *RAMS* BL0 .... 7 D2
Stubbins Vale Rd *RAMS* BL0 .... 6 C2
Stubbylee La *BCUP* OL13 .... 4 A1
Stubley La *LIT* OL15 .... 25 D1
Stubley Mill Rd *LIT* OL15 .... 12 B6
Studland Rd *WYTH/NTH* M22 ..... 179 D4
Studley Cl *ROY/SHW* OL2 .... 61 E5 🔟
Styal Av *RDSH* SK5 .... 147 D6
  STRET M32 .... 120 B6
Styal Gv *CHD/CHDH* SK8 .... 179 E4
Styal Rd *WILM/AE* SK9 .... 203 E2
Styal Vw *WILM/AE* SK9 .... 203 F1 🔟
Styhead Dr *MDTN* M24 .... 56 B6
Style St *ANC* M4 .... 106 B4 🔟
Styperson Wy *POY/DIS* SK12 ..... 198 C2 🔟
Sudbury Dr *CHD/CHDH* SK8 ...... 194 A2
  HOR/BR BL6 .... 44 A3
Sudbury Rd *BRAM/HZG* SK7 ...... 198 C1
Sudden Cl *ROCH* OL11 .... 39 D3
Sudell St *ANC* M4 .... 106 C4
Sudley Rd *ROCH* OL11 .... 39 D2
Sudlow St *MILN* OL16 .... 23 F3
Sudren St *TOT/BURYW* BL8 .... 32 A4 🔟
Suffield St *MDTN* M24 .... 75 D3 🔟
Suffolk Av *DROY* M43 .... 110 B4
Suffolk Cl *BOLS/LL* BL3 .... 49 F4
Suffolk Dr *RDSH* SK5 .... 148 A5
  WILM/AE SK9 .... 203 F2
Suffolk Rd *ALT* WA14 .... 173 F5
Suffolk St *CHAD* OL9 .... 94 C1
  ROCH OL11 .... 40 A1
  SLFD M6 .... 104 B2
Sugden St *AUL* OL6 .... 113 E4
Sulby Av *STRET* M32 .... 140 C1
Sulby St *NEWH/MOS* M40 .... 92 B5
  RAD M26 .... 67 F3
Sulgrave Av *POY/DIS* SK12 .... 199 D5
Sullivan St *WGTN/LGST* M12 ...... 126 B6 🔟
Sultan St *BURY* BL9 .... 53 D1
Sulway Cl *SWIN* M27 .... 86 B5 🔟
Sumac St *OP/CLY* M11 .... 109 E5 🔟
Summer *URM* M41 .... 138 C1
Summer Castle *MILN* OL16 .... 23 D6 🔟
Summercroft *CHAD* OL9 .... 94 C2 🔟
Summerdale Dr *TOT/BURYW* BL8 . 18 C3
Summerfield Av *DROY* M43 .... 109 F4 🔟
Summerfield Dr *MDTN* M24 .... 76 A1
Summerfield Pl *WILM/AE* SK9 .... 203 E6
Summerfield Rd *BOLS/LL* BL3 ...... 47 F5
  WALK M28 .... 81 D5
  WYTH/NTH M22 .... 178 A5
Summerfields Vw *OLDS* OL8 .... 97 D3
Summerlea *CHD/CHDH* SK8 .... 195 F1 🔟
Summer Pl *RUSH/FAL* M14 .... 144 A1 🔟
Summers Av *STLY* SK15 .... 115 D5
Summerseat Cl *OLDE* OL4 .... 81 E4 🔟
  SALO/ORD M5 .... 122 B1 🔟
Summerseat La *TOT/BURYW* BL8 . 18 B3
Summers St *CHAD* OL9 .... 78 A4
Summer St *MILN* OL16 .... 23 E6 🔟
Summerville Av *BKLY* M9 .... 92 A6 🔟
Summerville Rd *SLFD* M6 .... 103 F2
Summit Cl *BURY* BL9 .... 36 A3
Summit St *HEY* OL10 .... 36 A5
Sumner Av *BOLE* BL2 .... 31 E6
Sumner Rd *SLFD* M6 .... 103 E2
Sumner St *ROY/SHW* OL2 .... 61 F4
Sumner Wy *URM* M41 .... 138 A1
Sunadale Cl *BOLS/LL* BL3 .... 45 F4 🔟

Sunbank Cl WHIT OL12 ...... 22 B3
Sunbank La HALE/TIMP WA15 .. 190 B3
Sunbury Cl DUK SK16 ...... 132 A1
  WILM/AE SK9 ...... 204 C1
Sunbury Dr NEWH/MOS M40 .. 109 E5 ⑤
Sunderland Av AUL OL6 ...... 113 D3 ⑩
Sundew Pl MDTN M24 ...... 76 B4 ⑧
Sundial Cl HYDE SK14 ...... 133 E6
Sundial Rd OFTN SK2 ...... 184 B1
Sunfield MPL/ROM SK6 ...... 169 F2
Sunfield Av OLDE OL4 ...... 62 C6
Sunfield Crs ROY/SHW OL2 .. 60 C5 ⑦
Sunfield Dr ROY/SHW OL2 ...... 61 D6
Sunfield Rd OLD OL1 ...... 78 C3
Sunfield Wy OLDE OL4 ...... 80 C4
Sunhill Cl MILN OL16 ...... 40 C5
Sunk La MDTN M24 ...... 75 E4
Sunlight Rd BOL BL1 ...... 46 A2 ⑬
Sunningdale Av OP/CLY M11 .. 108 C5 ⑭
  RAD M26 ...... 50 B4
  SALE M33 ...... 160 C2
  WHTF M45 ...... 70 A4
Sunningdale Cl HYDE SK14 ...... 131 F2
  SLFD M6 ...... 51 E1
Sunningdale Dr BRAM/HZG SK7 .. 197 E2
  HEY OL10 ...... 56 B1
  IRL M44 ...... 116 A6
  PWCH M25 ...... 71 E6
  SLFD M6 ...... 102 B2
Sunningdale Rd CHD/CHDH .. 195 E2
  DTN/ASHW M34 ...... 149 E3
  URM M41 ...... 137 F2
Sunning Hill St BOLS/LL BL3 .. 46 B3 ⑬
Sunny Av BURY BL9 ...... 34 A2 ⑬
Sunny Bank OLDE OL4 ...... 80 C6
  RAD M26 ...... 67 E3
  WILM/AE SK9 ...... 208 B1
Sunny Bank Av DROY M43 ...... 110 A6
Sunnybank Av ECC M30 ...... 102 A4
  HTNM SK4 ...... 165 D1
Sunny Bank Rd ALT WA14 ...... 188 A1
Sunnybank Rd BOL BL1 ...... 27 D5
Sunny Bank Rd BRUN/LGST M13 .. 125 F6
  BURY BL9 ...... 53 E6
  DROY M43 ...... 110 A6
Sunny Bower St TOT/BURYW BL8 .. 31 F1
Sunny Brow Rd GTN M18 ...... 127 D4
  MDTN M24 ...... 74 C3
Sunny Dr PWCH M25 ...... 88 A1
Sunnyfield Rd HTNM SK4 ...... 165 D2
  PWCH M25 ...... 72 A4
Sunnylea Av BNG/LEV M19 .. 144 C6 ⑩
Sunnymead Av BOL BL1 ...... 28 A3
Sunnymede V TOT/BURYW BL8 .. 18 B2
Sunnyside AULW OL7 ...... 111 F2
Sunnyside Av DROY M43 ...... 110 A3
Sunnyside Gv AUL OL6 ...... 113 E5 ⑤
Sunnyside Rd BOL BL1 ...... 27 D5 ②⑨
  DROY M43 ...... 110 A4
Sunnywood Dr TOT/BURYW BL8 .. 32 B1
Sunnywood La TOT/BURYW BL8 .. 32 B1
Sunset Av WYTH/NTH M22 ...... 162 B5
Sun St MOSL OL5 ...... 99 D4
  RAMS BL0 ...... 6 C4
Sunwell Ter MPL/ROM SK6 .. 187 D3 ⑬
Surbiton Rd NEWH/MOS M40 .. 108 C2 ⑥
Surma Cl MILN OL16 ...... 40 C2
Surrey Av DROY M43 ...... 110 A4
  ROY/SHW OL2 ...... 61 D2
Surrey Cl BOLS/LL BL3 ...... 64 B3
Surrey Dr BURY BL9 ...... 53 D1
Surrey Park Cl ROY/SHW OL2 .. 61 F1 ⑩
Surrey Rd BKLY M9 ...... 91 E3
Surrey St AUL OL6 ...... 113 E2
  BKLY M9 ...... 91 D2 ②
  CHAD OL9 ...... 78 A6 ③
Surtees Rd NTHM/RTH M23 .. 161 E3
Sussex Av DID/WITH M20 ...... 163 F1
  HEY OL10 ...... 35 F6
Sussex Cl CHAD OL9 ...... 77 E5
  SWIN M27 ...... 86 B3 ②
Sussex Dr BURY BL9 ...... 53 D1
  DROY M43 ...... 110 B4
Sussex Pl HYDE SK14 ...... 132 A4 ⑧
Sussex Rd EDGY/DAV SK3 ...... 165 F5
  IRL M44 ...... 134 A5
  PART M31 ...... 154 C3 ⑤
Sussex St BRO M7 ...... 105 E3
  CMANW M2 ...... 2 D3
  ROCH OL11 ...... 40 A1 ⑭
Sutcliffe Av WGTN/LGST M12 .. 145 E2
Sutcliffe St AULW OL7 ...... 112 A6
  BCUP OL13 ...... 5 D1 ③
  BOL BL1 ...... 27 F5
  LIT OL15 ...... 12 C5
  MDTN M24 ...... 76 A3 ⑧
  OLDS OL8 ...... 78 C6
  ROY/SHW OL2 ...... 61 E6
Sutherland Cl OLDS OL8 ...... 96 A4 ⑧
Sutherland St BOLS/LL BL4 .. 66 A3 ⑧
Sutherland Rd BOL BL1 ...... 45 E1
  HEY OL10 ...... 36 A6
  OLDTF/WHR M16 ...... 122 B6

Sutherland St AUL OL6 ...... 113 F4
  ECC M30 ...... 100 C4
  FWTH BL4 ...... 66 A3
  SWIN M27 ...... 85 F4
Suthers St CHAD OL9 ...... 78 A5
  RAD M26 ...... 70 A2
Sutton Dr DROY M43 ...... 109 F4
Sutton Rd BOLS/LL BL3 ...... 45 D5
  GTN M18 ...... 127 D6
  HTNM SK4 ...... 166 A2
  WILM/AE SK9 ...... 209 D4
Suttons La MPL/ROM SK6 ...... 187 E2
Swailes St OLDE OL4 ...... 79 F5 ⑧
Swaindrod La LIT OL15 ...... 13 F4
Swaine St EDGY/DAV SK3 .. 166 C4 ⑬
Swainsthorpe Dr BKLY M9 .. 91 F5 ⑭
Swain St WHIT OL12 ...... 22 C4 ⑧
Swalecliff Av NTHM/RTH M23 .. 160 B4
Swale Cl WILM/AE SK9 ...... 204 C1
Swaledale Cl ROY/SHW OL2 .. 60 C4
Swale Dr ALT WA14 ...... 174 A1
Swallow Bank Dr ROCH OL11 .. 38 C4 ③
Swallow Dr BURY BL9 ...... 34 C3
  IRL M44 ...... 116 B6
  ROCH OL11 ...... 21 D6
Swallow St OLDS OL8 ...... 95 E3
  OP/CLY M11 ...... 108 A6
  STKP SK1 ...... 167 D6
  WGTN/LGST M12 .. 145 E1 ⑪
Swanage Av NTHM/RTH M23 .. 160 B4
  OFTN SK2 ...... 184 B1
Swanage Cl TOT/BURYW BL8 .. 33 D1
Swanage Rd ECC M30 ...... 100 C4 ⑩
Swan Cl POY/DIS SK12 ...... 197 F5
Swan Ct ROY/SHW OL2 ...... 61 F3 ⑬
Swanhill Cl GTN M18 ...... 128 A3 ⑦
Swan La BOLS/LL BL3 ...... 46 B5
Swanley Av NEWH/MOS M40 .. 107 F2
Swann Gv CHD/CHDH SK8 ...... 195 F1
Swann La CHD/CHDH SK8 ...... 181 F6
Swan Rd HALE/TIMP WA15 ...... 159 E4
  TOT/BURYW BL8 ...... 18 A3
Swansea St OLDS OL8 ...... 96 C1
Swan St ANC M4 ...... 3 F1
  AUL OL6 ...... 113 D4
  RAD M26 ...... 69 F1
  WILM/AE SK9 ...... 203 F4
Swarbrick Dr PWCH M25 ...... 88 A3
Swayfield Av BRUN/LGST M13 .. 126 A6
Swaylands Dr SALE M33 ...... 159 F4
Sweetbriar Cl ROY/SHW OL2 .. 61 F2 ⑩
Sweet Briar Cl WHIT OL12 .. 22 C5 ⑦
Sweet Briar La WHIT OL12 .. 22 C5 ⑧
Sweetloves Gv BOL BL1 ...... 27 F2
Sweetloves La BOL BL1 ...... 27 F2
Sweetnam Dr OP/CLY M11 .. 108 C5 ⑬
Swettenham Rd WILM/AE SK9 .. 194 B4 ⑧
Swift Cl MPL/ROM SK6 ...... 150 A6
Swift Rd OLD OL1 ...... 62 C4
  ROCH OL11 ...... 21 D6
Swift St AUL OL6 ...... 113 E2 ⑤
Swinburne Av DID/WITH M20 .. 144 A4
Swinburne Av DROY M43 ...... 110 B4 ⑧
Swinburne Gn RDSH SK5 ...... 146 B2
Swinburn St BKLY M9 ...... 92 A4 ⑧
Swindells St HYDE SK14 .. 131 F4 ⑧
  OP/CLY M11 ...... 127 F2 ⑱
Swindon Cl GTN M18 ...... 127 E4
Swinfield Av CCHDY M21 .. 141 D5 ⑤
Swinford Gv ROY/SHW OL2 .. 61 E4
Swinley Cha WILM/AE SK9 .. 205 D2
Swinside Cl MDTN M24 ...... 74 A1
Swinside Rd BOLE BL2 ...... 49 D1
Swinstead Av
  NEWH/MOS M40 ...... 107 F2 ⑩
Swinton Crs BURY BL9 ...... 71 E2
Swinton Gv BRUN/LGST M13 .. 125 D4
Swinton Hall Rd SWIN M27 .. 86 B5
Swinton Park Rd SLFD M6 .. 102 C2
Swinton St BOLE BL2 ...... 48 C2 ⑬
  OLDE OL8 ...... 80 A6
Swiss Hl WILM/AE SK9 ...... 209 F4
Swithin Rd WYTH/NTH M22 .. 192 C1
Swythamley Rd EDGY/DAV SK3 .. 165 E5 ③
Swythamley Rd EDGY/DAV SK3 .. 165 E5 ⑤
Sybil St LIT OL15 ...... 12 B5
Sycamore Av ALT WA14 ...... 173 E2 ⑧
  CHAD OL9 ...... 94 A1 ⑥
  DTN/ASHW M34 ...... 149 D1 ⑦
  HEY OL10 ...... 41 D2
  MILN OL16 ...... 42 B4
  OLDE OL4 ...... 80 B3
  RAD M26 ...... 69 D3
Sycamore Cl AUL OL6 ...... 113 F5 ⑬
  DUK SK16 ...... 132 A1
  LIT OL15 ...... 12 A6
  WILM/AE SK9 ...... 203 F1
Sycamore Crs AUL OL6 ...... 113 D2
Sycamore Dr DROY M43 ...... 111 D5
  RAD M26 ...... 51 E4
Sycamore Gv FAIL M35 ...... 94 C6
Sycamore Pl WHTF M45 ...... 71 D5 ⑧
Sycamore Rd ECC M30 ...... 100 B3
  MPL/ROM SK6 ...... 169 E1
  PART M31 ...... 154 B2

  TOT/BURYW BL8 ...... 32 A2
The Sycamores MOSL OL5 ...... 99 F4
  OLDE OL4 ...... 81 D3
  RAD M26 ...... 67 F5 ②
  STLY SK15 ...... 132 C1 ⑪
Sycamore St EDGY/DAV SK3 .. 165 F5 ⑬
  SALE M33 ...... 160 C1
Sycamore Wk CHD/CHDH SK8 .. 180 B1 ⑬
Sydall St DTN/ASHW M34 .. 130 A6 ⑪
Syddal Cl BRAM/HZG SK7 ...... 196 B4
Syddal Crs BRAM/HZG SK7 .. 196 B5
Syddal Gn BRAM/HZG SK7 .. 196 B4
Syddall Av CHD/CHDH SK8 .. 194 B1
Syddall St HYDE SK14 ...... 150 B1
Syddal Rd BRAM/HZG SK7 .. 196 B4
Sydenham St OLD OL1 ...... 79 F2
Sydney Av ECC M30 ...... 101 E5
  MANAIR M90 ...... 191 E1
Sydney Gdns LIT OL15 ...... 13 D2
Sydney Jones Ct NEWH/MOS M40 .. 93 D4
Sydney Rd BRAM/HZG SK7 .. 197 D4
Sydney St FAIL M35 ...... 93 F6 ⑪
  OFTN SK2 ...... 168 A6
  SLFD M6 ...... 103 F5
  STRET M32 ...... 140 B1
  SWIN M27 ...... 85 E5
Syke La WHIT OL12 ...... 23 D1
Syke Rd WHIT OL12 ...... 23 D1
Sykes Av BURY BL9 ...... 53 F5
Sykes Meadow EDGY/DAV SK3 .. 182 A1
Sykes St BURY BL9 ...... 34 B4
  MILN OL16 ...... 40 C1 ⑧
  MILN OL16 ...... 42 B3
  RDSH SK5 ...... 147 D3 ③
Sylvan Av FAIL M35 ...... 109 F2
  HALE/TIMP WA15 ...... 159 D5
  SALE M33 ...... 160 A2
  URM M41 ...... 119 E6
  WILM/AE SK9 ...... 203 D6
Sylvan Cl MDTN M24 ...... 74 B1 ⑧
Sylvan Gv ALT WA14 ...... 174 B2
Sylvan St CHAD OL9 ...... 78 A4
Sylvester Av STKP SK1 ...... 183 F1
Sylvester Cl HYDE SK14 ...... 152 C1
Sylvia Gv RDSH SK5 ...... 146 C4 ⑫
Symms St SLFD M6 ...... 104 C3 ③
Symond Rd BKLY M9 ...... 74 C6
Symons Rd SALE M33 ...... 139 F6
Symons St BRO M7 ...... 89 F6
Syndall Av WGTN/LGST M12 .. 125 E3 ⑦
Syndall St WGTN/LGST M12 .. 125 E3 ⑧

T

Tabley Av RUSH/FAL M14 ...... 143 F1
Tabley Gdns MPL/ROM SK6 .. 187 E3
Tabley Gv BRUN/LGST M13 .. 145 D2
  HALE/TIMP WA15 ...... 159 E5
  RDSH SK5 ...... 146 C4 ⑬
Tabley Mere Gdns CHD/CHDH SK8 .. 181 D4
Tabley Rd BOLS/LL BL3 ...... 45 F5
  SALE M33 ...... 160 C5 ⑧
  WILM/AE SK9 ...... 194 B4
Tabley St DUK SK16 ...... 131 F1 ③
  MOSL OL5 ...... 99 F5
  SLFD M6 ...... 104 C2 ⑦
Tabor St MDTN M24 ...... 75 D1
Tackler Cl SWIN M27 ...... 86 A6 ⑧
Tadman Gv ALT WA14 ...... 173 E1
Tadmor Cl LHULT M38 ...... 82 A1
Tagore Cl BRUN/LGST M13 .. 125 F5 ⑧
Tahir Cl CHH M8 ...... 90 C6 ③
Talavera St BRO M7 ...... 105 E2
Talbenny Cl BOL BL1 ...... 45 D1 ②
Talbot Cl OLDE OL4 ...... 80 A3
Talbot Ct BOL BL1 ...... 28 A3 ③
Talbot Gv BURY BL9 ...... 34 B1 ②
Talbot Pl OLDTF/WHR M16 .. 122 C4 ⑧
Talbot Rd ALT WA14 ...... 173 F5
  HYDE SK14 ...... 131 F4
  RUSH/FAL M14 ...... 144 C4
  SALE M33 ...... 160 C1 ⑩
  STRET M32 ...... 122 A5
  WILM/AE SK9 ...... 209 F4
Talbot St AUL OL6 ...... 112 B4 ⑧
  BRAM/HZG SK7 ...... 184 B3
  ECC M30 ...... 101 F6 ⑧
  MDTN M24 ...... 75 E1
  ROCH OL11 ...... 40 A1 ⑬
Talford Gv DID/WITH M20 .. 143 E6 ⑧
Talgarth Rd NEWH/MOS M40 .. 107 D3
Talkin Dr MDTN M24 ...... 56 C6
Tallarn Cl DID/WITH M20 .. 144 A4 ⑧
Tallis St WGTN/LGST M12 .. 126 B6
Tall Trees Cl ROY/SHW OL2 .. 60 C5
Tall Trees Pl OFTN SK2 ...... 184 A1
Talmine Av NEWH/MOS M40 .. 107 F2 ⑪
Tamar Cl FWTH BL4 ...... 67 F6
Tamar Dr NTHM/RTH M23 .. 177 E3 ⑧
Tamarin Cl SWIN M27 ...... 85 D4 ③
Tamebank MOSL OL5 ...... 99 E2 ③
Tame Barn Cl MILN OL16 .. 42 B1 ③
Tame Cl STLY SK15 ...... 115 D4

Tamerton Dr CHH M8 ... 106 B1
Tame St ANC M4 ... 107 E6 [15]
  DTN/ASHW M34 ... 130 A2
  MOSL OL5 ... 99 F2
Tamworth Av SALQ/ORD M5 ... 122 C1 [10]
  WHTF M45 ... 71 F4
Tamworth Ave West
  SALQ/ORD M5 ... 122 B1 [10]
Tamworth Cl BRAM/HZG SK7 ... 198 B1 [2]
  HULME M15 ... 123 F4 [3]
Tamworth Dr TOT/BURYW BL8 ... 33 D2
Tamworth St CHAD OL9 ... 78 A6
  STKP SK1 ... 167 F3
Tandle Hill Rd ROY/SHW OL2 ... 59 F3
Tandlewood Ms
  NEWH/MOS M40 ... 109 D2 [10]
Tandlewood Pk ROY/SHW OL2 ... 59 F3
Tanfield Dr RAD M26 ... 67 F4 [1]
Tanfield Rd DID/WITH M20 ... 163 F6
Tangmere Cl NEWH/MOS M40 ... 93 D2 [2]
Tanhill Cl OFTN SK2 ... 184 C1
Tanhill La OLDS OL8 ... 96 B3
Tanhouse Rd URM M41 ... 117 E6
Tanners Cft RAMS BL0 ... 6 C5 [11]
Tanners Fold OLDS OL8 ... 96 B3
Tanners St RAMS BL0 ... 6 C5
Tanner St HYDE SK14 ... 131 E6 [7]
Tannery Wy ALT WA14 ... 158 C6 [1]
Tannock Rd BRAM/HZG SK7 ... 185 D6
Tanpits Rd BURY BL9 ... 33 F4
Tansey Gn BRO M7 ... 90 A6
Tansley Rd CHH M8 ... 90 B3
Tan Yard Brow GTN M18 ... 127 F5
Tanyard Dr HALE/TIMP WA15 ... 190 A3
Tanyard Gn RDSH SK5 ... 147 D6 [5]
Tanyard La HALE/TIMP WA15 ... 189 D4
Tape St RAMS BL0 ... 6 C5 [12]
Taplin Dr GTN M18 ... 127 D4 [3]
Taplow Gv CHD/CHDH SK8 ... 181 D5
Tarbet Dr BOLE BL2 ... 49 D3
Tarbet Rd DUK SK16 ... 131 D2
Tarbolton Crs HALE/TIMP WA15 ... 176 A4
Tariff St CMANE M1 ... 3 H3
Tarleton Pl BOLS/LL BL3 ... 45 E6
Tarnbrook Cl WHTF M45 ... 72 A3 [8]
Tarn Dr BURY BL9 ... 52 C3
Tarn Gv WALK M28 ... 84 A4
Tarnside Cl MILN OL16 ... 24 A2
  OFTN SK2 ... 185 D1
The Tarns CHD/CHDH SK8 ... 179 F4
Tarporley Av RUSH/FAL M14 ... 143 E3
Tarporley Cl EDGY/DAV SK3 ... 182 A2 [3]
Tarran Gv DTN/ASHW M34 ... 149 F2
Tarran Pl ALT WA14 ... 174 C1
Tarrington Cl WGTN/LGST M12 ... 126 B4
Tartan St OP/CLY M11 ... 108 C5
Tarvin Av DID/WITH M20 ... 143 E4
  HTNM SK4 ... 146 B4
Tarvin Dr MPL/ROM SK6 ... 168 C1
Tarvington Cl NEWH/MOS M40 ... 107 D1 [3]
Tarvin Rd CHD/CHDH SK8 ... 181 E3
Tasle Ay CMANW M2 ... 2 D4 [2]
Tatchbury Rd FAIL M35 ... 105 E1
Tate St OLDS OL8 ... 96 C1
Tatham Cl BRUN/LGST M13 ... 126 A6 [8]
Tatham St MILN OL16 ... 23 E6
Tatland Dr WYTH/NTH M22 ... 179 D4 [3]
Tattersall St CHAD OL9 ... 78 B5 [9]
Tatton Cl BRAM/HZG SK7 ... 185 D3
  CHD/CHDH SK8 ... 181 E3
Tatton Gdns MPL/ROM SK6 ... 150 B6
Tatton Gv DID/WITH M20 ... 143 E3
Tatton Mere Dr DROY M43 ... 110 C6
Tattonmere Gdns CHD/CHDH SK8 ... 181 E3
Tatton Pl SALE M33 ... 139 F6
  DTN/ASHW M34 ... 149 E2
  SALE M33 ... 139 F6 [5]
  WILM/AE SK9 ... 194 C4
Tatton Rd HTNM SK4 ... 146 A6
Tatton Rd North HTNM SK4 ... 166 A1
Tatton Rd South HTNM SK4 ... 123 E3
  HULME M15 ... 150 C4 [10]
  SALQ/ORD M5 ... 122 C1
  STKP SK1 ... 167 D4 [25]
  STLY SK15 ... 114 C3
Taunton Av AULW OL7 ... 112 B3
  ECC M30 ... 100 C4
  RDSH SK5 ... 148 A6
  ROCH OL11 ... 21 F6
  URM M41 ... 137 F3 [2]
Taunton Cl BRAM/HZG SK7 ... 185 E5
Taunton Dr FWTH BL4 ... 65 D2 [3]
Taunton Gn AULW OL7 ... 112 A2 [2]
Taunton Gv WHTF M45 ... 71 E5
Taunton Hall Cl AULW OL7 ... 112 A3
Taunton Lawns AULW OL7 ... 112 B3
Taunton Pl AULW OL7 ... 112 A2 [2]
Taunton Rd AULW OL7 ... 112 B2 [2]
  CHAD OL9 ... 77 D2
  SALE M33 ... 158 B1
Taunton St ANC M4 ... 107 E6
Taurus St OLDE OL4 ... 80 A3
Tavern Court Av FAIL M35 ... 94 B6
Tavery Cl ANC M4 ... 107 D5 [12]
Tavistock Cl HYDE SK14 ... 152 C1

Tavistock Dr CHAD OL9 ... 77 D2
Tavistock Rd BOL BL1 ... 46 B3 [57]
  ROCH OL11 ... 40 A4
  SALE M33 ... 138 B6
Tawton Av HYDE SK14 ... 152 C1
Taxi Rd MANAIR M90 ... 191 F2
Tay Cl OLDS OL8 ... 78 C6
Tayfield Rd WYTH/NTH M22 ... 178 A5
Taylor Av ROCH OL11 ... 21 D5
Taylor Green Wy OLDE OL4 ... 81 D4
Taylor La DTN/ASHW M34 ... 129 E5
Taylor Rd ALT WA14 ... 173 E2
  URM M41 ... 119 F2
Taylor's La BOLE BL2 ... 49 F2
Taylorson St SALQ/ORD M5 ... 122 C2
Taylorson St South SALQ/ORD M5 ... 122 B3
Taylor's Rd STRET M32 ... 121 F5
Taylor St BURY BL9 ... 34 A3
  CHAD OL9 ... 77 F4
  DROY M43 ... 110 B6
  DTN/ASHW M34 ... 130 A3
  GTN M18 ... 127 D3
  HEY OL10 ... 37 D5
  HYDE SK14 ... 132 A6
  MDTN M24 ... 75 E3 [6]
  OLD OL1 ... 80 A3 [3]
  OLDE OL4 ... 80 C5
  PWCH M25 ... 89 D1
  RAD M26 ... 51 E6
  ROY/SHW OL2 ... 60 B4 [3]
  RUSH/FAL M14 ... 125 D6
  STLY SK15 ... 114 C6
  WHIT OL12 ... 9 E3
  WHIT OL12 ... 23 D4
Teak Dr FWTH BL4 ... 85 E1
Teak St BURY BL9 ... 34 C5
Teal Av POY/DIS SK12 ... 197 E5
Tealby Av OLDTF/WHR M16 ... 123 D5
Tealby Rd CTN M18 ... 126 C5
Teal Cl ALT WA14 ... 157 F5
  OFTN SK2 ... 185 D2
Teal Ct ROCH OL11 ... 21 D6
Teal St BOLS/LL BL3 ... 47 D5 [8]
Teasdale Cl CHAD OL9 ... 93 F2 [3]
Tebbutt St ANC M4 ... 106 C4 [13]
Tedder Cl BURY BL9 ... 71 F1
Tedder Dr WYTH/NTH M22 ... 193 D2
Teddington Rd NEWH/MOS M40 ... 93 D4
Teer St NEWH/MOS M40 ... 107 E5 [7]
Teesdale Av URM M41 ... 118 B3
Teesdale Cl OFTN SK2 ... 184 C1 [3]
Tees St MILN OL16 ... 40 C1 [10]
Teignmouth St
  NEWH/MOS M40 ... 107 D3 [4]
Telfer Av BRUN/LGST M13 ... 144 C1 [1]
Telfer Rd BRUN/LGST M13 ... 144 C1 [3]
Telford Cl DTN/ASHW M34 ... 129 F2
Telford Rd MPL/ROM SK6 ... 187 E3
Telford St CHH M8 ... 107 D2
Telford Wy ROCH OL11 ... 40 B5
Telison St SLFD M6 ... 103 E1 [3]
Telson Crs SLFD M6 ... 103 E1
Tell St WHIT OL12 ... 22 B6
Temperance St BOLS/LL BL3 ... 46 B4
  HYDE SK14 ... 153 E3 [3]
  WGTN/LGST M12 ... 125 D2
Tempest Cl HOR/BR BL6 ... 44 A4
Tempest St BOLS/LL BL3 ... 45 F5 [2]
Temple Cl OLDE OL4 ... 80 C3
Templecombe Dr BOL BL1 ... 27 E1
Temple Dr BOL BL1 ... 27 D4
  SWIN M27 ... 86 C6
Temple La LIT OL15 ... 13 D2
Temple Rd BOL BL1 ... 27 D4
  SALE M33 ... 160 B1
Temple St HEY OL10 ... 37 E5 [1]
  MDTN M24 ... 75 F2 [3]
  OLD OL1 ... 79 F4 [20]
Templeton Cl ALT WA14 ... 173 F1
Ten Acre Dr WHTF M45 ... 70 B4
Ten Acres La NEWH/MOS M40 ... 108 B2
Tenax Rd TRPK M17 ... 120 C2
Tenbury Cl SLFD M6 ... 104 A4 [12]
Tenbury Dr MDTN M24 ... 75 E2
Tenby Av BOL BL1 ... 26 B6 [17]
  STRET M32 ... 121 F5
Tenby Dr CHD/CHDH SK8 ... 181 E3
  SLFD M6 ... 103 F2 [2]
Tenby Gv EDGY/DAV SK3 ... 165 F6
  OLDS OL8 ... 94 C3
Tenby St WHIT OL12 ... 22 A4 [11]
Tenement La CHD/CHDH SK8 ... 182 A4
Teneriffe St BRO M7 ... 105 E2 [15]
Tennis St BOL BL1 ... 27 E4 [10]
  OLDTF/WHR M16 ... 122 C5
Tennyson Av BURY BL9 ... 53 D5
  DTN/ASHW M34 ... 149 E4 [3]
  DUK SK16 ... 130 C2
  RAD M26 ... 50 C5
Tennyson Cl HTNM SK4 ... 165 E4
Tennyson Gdns PWCH M25 ... 88 A2 [8]
Tennyson Rd CHD/CHDH SK8 ... 181 D1
  DROY M43 ... 110 B5
  FWTH BL4 ... 65 F5

  MDTN M24 ... 57 F6
  RDSH SK5 ... 146 B2
  SWIN M27 ... 85 E5
Tennyson St BOL BL1 ... 27 F6
  BRUN/LGST M13 ... 125 D4 [4]
  OLD OL1 ... 80 A2
  ROCH OL11 ... 40 B2 [10]
  SLFD M6 ... 105 D3
Tensing Av AULW OL7 ... 112 C2 [3]
Tensing St OLDS OL8 ... 96 B5
Tenterden St BURY BL9 ... 33 E5
Tenterhill La WHIT OL12 ... 20 B3
Tenters St BURY BL9 ... 33 E5
Tenth St TRPK M17 ... 121 E3
Terence St NEWH/MOS M40 ... 109 E2
Terminal Rd East MANAIR M90 ... 191 F2 [2]
Terminal Rd North MANAIR M90 ... 191 F2
Terminal Rd South
  MANAIR M90 ... 191 F2 [2]
Tern Av FWTH BL4 ... 65 D3
Tern Cl ALT WA14 ... 157 F5
  DUK SK16 ... 131 F2
  ROCH OL11 ... 21 D6
Tern Dr POY/DIS SK12 ... 197 F5
Ternhill Ct FWTH BL4 ... 66 B3 [10]
Terrace St OLDE OL4 ... 79 F4 [13]
The Terrace PWCH M25 ... 88 C2 [4]
Terrington Cl CCHDY M21 ... 142 C4 [3]
Tetbury Dr BOLE BL2 ... 49 D1
Tetbury Rd WYTH/NTH M22 ... 177 F3
Tetlow Gv ECC M30 ... 101 D6
Tetlow La BRO M7 ... 89 F5
Tetlow St HYDE SK14 ... 131 F4 [2]
  MDTN M24 ... 75 E3 [10]
  NEWH/MOS M40 ... 109 E2 [11]
Teviot St BRUN/LGST M13 ... 125 F5 [4]
Teviot Wy STKP SK1 ... 167 D2
Tewkesbury Av AUL OL6 ... 107 F2 [2]
  DROY M43 ... 110 B4 [5]
  HALE/TIMP WA15 ... 176 A4
  MDTN M24 ... 57 F6
  URM M41 ... 119 E5
Tewkesbury Cl CHD/CHDH SK8 ... 195 F3
  POY/DIS SK12 ... 198 B5 [3]
Tewkesbury Dr PWCH M25 ... 89 D3
Tewkesbury Rd EDGY/DAV SK3 ... 181 F1 [3]
  NEWH/MOS M40 ... 107 E4
Texas St DUK SK16 ... 113 D5
Textile St WGTN/LGST M12 ... 126 B2
Textilose Rd TRPK M17 ... 120 C4
Thackeray Cl CHH M8 ... 106 B1 [1]
Thackeray Gv DROY M43 ... 110 B5
Thackeray Rd OLD OL1 ... 80 A2
Thames Cl OP/CLY M11 ... 126 C1
Thames Dr URM M41 ... 119 D3
Thames Rd MILN OL16 ... 42 B1
Thames Steet MILN OL16 ... 40 C1
Thames St OLD OL1 ... 79 E3
Thanet Cl BRO M7 ... 105 F2 [8]
Thankerton Av DTN/ASHW M34 ... 111 E6
Thatcher Cl ALT WA14 ... 188 A1
Thatcher St OLDS OL8 ... 96 B2
Thatch Leach CHAD OL9 ... 77 D6
Thatch Leach La WHTF M45 ... 71 E4
Thaxmead Dr NEWH/MOS M40 ... 109 E3 [5]
Thaxted Dr OFTN SK2 ... 185 E2
Thaxted Pl BOL BL1 ... 46 A1 [43]
Thbeechwood La STLY SK15 ... 115 D3
Theatre St OLD OL1 ... 79 D4 [9]
Thekla St CHAD OL9 ... 78 B3 [9]
Thelma St RAMS BL0 ... 6 C5 [13]
Thelwall Av BOLE BL2 ... 48 B1
  RUSH/FAL M14 ... 143 D3
Thelwall Cl HALE/TIMP WA15 ... 174 C1 [2]
Thelwall Rd SALE M33 ... 160 C2
Theobald Rd ALT WA14 ... 174 B6
Thetford Cl TOT/BURYW BL8 ... 33 E2 [3]
Thetford Dr CHH M8 ... 90 C6 [2]
Thicketford Brow BOLE BL2 ... 29 E6
Thicketford Cl BOLE BL2 ... 29 D5
Thicketford Rd BOLE BL2 ... 28 C6 [10]
  BOLE BL2 ... 29 D6 [1]
Thimble Cl WHIT OL12 ... 24 B1
The Thimbles WHIT OL12 ... 24 B1
Third Av BOL BL1 ... 45 F2
  BOLS/LL BL3 ... 49 D3
  OLDS OL8 ... 95 D3
  OP/CLY M11 ... 109 D5
  STLY SK15 ... 115 F1
  SWIN M27 ... 101 F2
  TRPK M17 ... 121 E4
Third St BOL BL1 ... 26 A3
Thirlby Dr WYTH/NTH M22 ... 178 B6
Thirlemere Rd STKP SK1 ... 167 F6 [3]
Thirlmere Av AULW OL7 ... 112 A3
  STRET M32 ... 121 D6
  SWIN M27 ... 86 B6 [3]
Thirlmere Cl WILM/AE SK9 ... 209 D4 [3]
Thirlmere Dr BURY BL9 ... 52 C2 [3]
  LHULT M38 ... 65 E6
  MDTN M24 ... 74 C1
Thirlmere Gv FWTH BL4 ... 64 C3 [3]
  ROY/SHW OL2 ... 60 B3
Thirlmere Rd PART M31 ... 154 C1
  ROCH OL11 ... 38 C3
  URM M41 ... 117 F6

WYTH/NTH M22 .... 177 F5
Thirlspot Cl BOL BL1 .... 27 F1
Thirlstone Av OLDE OL4 .... 63 D5
Thirsfield Dr OP/CLY M11 .... 109 D5
Thirsk Av CHAD M8 .... 77 D2
  SALE M33 .... 158 A2
Thirsk Cl TOT/BURYW BL8 .... 32 C2
Thirsk Rd BOLS/LL BL3 .... 67 E1
Thirsk St WGTN/LGST M12 .... 125 D2
Thistle Cl STLY SK15 .... 133 F2
Thistledown Cl ECC M30 .... 119 D1
Thistle Sq PART M31 .... 154 C3
Thistleton Rd BOLS/LL BL3 .... 45 D6
Thistlewood Dr WILM/AE SK9 .... 204 B4
Thomas Cl DTN/ASHW M34 .... 130 B5
Thomas Dr BOLS/LL BL3 .... 46 B4
Thomas Gibbon Cl STRET M32 .... 140 A2
Thomas Holden St BOL BL1 .... 46 B1
Thomas Johnson Cl ECC M30 .... 101 D6
Thomas More Cl FWTH BL4 .... 67 D5
Thomas St ANC M4 .... 3 F2
  BOLS/LL BL3 .... 46 B4
  CHH M8 .... 90 A5
  FWTH BL4 .... 66 C4
  HALE/TIMP WA15 .... 174 C3
  MILN OL16 .... 23 E5
  MPL/ROM SK6 .... 169 E2
  MPL/ROM SK6 .... 171 F3
  OLDE OL4 .... 80 C6
  RAD M26 .... 51 F6
  ROY/SHW OL2 .... 61 D6
  ROY/SHW OL2 .... 62 A3
  STKP SK1 .... 167 D6
  STRET M32 .... 121 E6
Thomas St West OFTN SK2 .... 167 D6
Thompson Av BOLE BL2 .... 31 E6
  WHTF M45 .... 71 E4
Thompson Cl DTN/ASHW M34 .... 129 D6
Thompson Ct DTN/ASHW M34 .... 128 C6
Thompson Dr BURY BL9 .... 35 D4
Thompson Fold STLY SK15 .... 114 A5
Thompson La CHAD OL9 .... 94 B1
Thompson Rd BOL BL1 .... 26 C6
  DTN/ASHW M34 .... 128 C6
  TRPK M17 .... 119 F1
Thompson St ANC M4 .... 3 G1
  BOLS/LL BL3 .... 47 D4
  CHAD OL9 .... 78 B4
  CSLFD M3 .... 106 A4
  NEWH/MOS M40 .... 108 A2
Thomson Rd GTN M18 .... 127 D5
Thomson St BRUN/LGST M13 .... 125 D3
  EDGY/DAV SK3 .... 166 C5
Thoralby Cl WGTN/LGST M12 .... 126 B4
Thorburn Rd WHIT OL12 .... 8 C4
Thoresby Cl BOLS/LL BL3 .... 50 A4
Thoresway Rd BRUN/LGST M13 .... 125 F6
  WILM/AE SK9 .... 203 D6
Thor Gv SALQ/ORD M5 .... 123 D1
Thorley Cl CHAD OL9 .... 93 F3
Thorley Dr HALE/TIMP WA15 .... 175 F1
  URM M41 .... 138 D1
Thorley Ms BRAM/HZG SK7 .... 197 D2
Thorley St FAIL M35 .... 94 A5
Thornage Dr NEWH/MOS M40 .... 107 D3
Thorn Av FAIL M35 .... 110 A1
Thornbank Dr HEY OL10 .... 56 C2
Thornbeck Dr BOL BL1 .... 26 A6
Thornbeck Rd BOL BL1 .... 26 A6
Thornbridge Av CCHDY M21 .... 141 F3
Thornbury Av HYDE SK14 .... 152 C1
Thornbury Cl CHD/CHDH SK8 .... 182 A6
Thornbury Rd STRET M32 .... 121 F5
Thornbury Wy GTN M18 .... 127 D4
Thornbush Wy MILN OL16 .... 24 A5
Thorncliff Av OLDS OL8 .... 95 F2
Thorncliffe Av DUK SK16 .... 131 D2
  ROY/SHW OL2 .... 60 A3
Thorncliffe Gv BNG/LEV M19 .... 146 A2
Thorncliffe Rd ROY/SHW OL2 .... 60 A3
Thorncliffe Rd BOL BL1 .... 26 A6
Thorn Cl HEY OL10 .... 36 C4
Thorncombe Rd OLDTF/WHR M16... 123 F6
Thorndale Cl ROY/SHW OL2 .... 60 C4
Thorndale Gv HALE/TIMP WA15 .... 175 E2
Thorn Dr WYTH/NTH M22 .... 193 E1
Thorne Av URM M41 .... 118 B6
Thorneside DTN/ASHW M34 .... 130 A4
Thorne St FWTH BL4 .... 66 A2
Thorneycroft Av CCHDY M21 .... 141 F6
Thorneycroft Rd
  HALE/TIMP WA15 .... 175 F2
Thorney Dr BRAM/HZG SK7 .... 196 A3
Thorney Hill Cl OLDE OL4 .... 79 E5
Thorneyholme Cl HOR/BR BL6 .... 44 A3
Thorneylea WHIT OL12 .... 9 E2
Thornfield Crs LHULT M38 .... 65 D6
Thornfield Dr SWIN M27 .... 85 F6
Thornfield Gv CHD/CHDH SK8...... 181 E5
  LHULT M38 .... 65 D6
Thornfield Hey WILM/AE SK9 .... 204 C3
Thornfield Rd BNG/LEV M19 .... 144 C6
  HTNM SK4 .... 165 E2
  TOT/BURYW BL8 .... 17 E6

Thornfield St SALQ/ORD M5 .... 103 E6
Thorngate Rd CHH M8 .... 106 B2
Thorn Gv CHD/CHDH SK8 .... 195 F2
  HALE/TIMP WA15 .... 174 C4
  RUSH/FAL M14 .... 144 B3
  SALE M33 .... 158 A2
Thorngrove Av NTHM/RTH M23 .... 160 B6
Thorngrove Dr WILM/AE SK9 .... 204 A5
Thorngrove Hl WILM/AE SK9 .... 204 A5
Thorngrove Rd WILM/AE SK9 .... 204 A5
Thornham Cl TOT/BURYW BL8 .... 33 D1
Thornham Ct WILM OL16 .... 60 A1
Thornham Dr BOL BL1 .... 28 A1
Thornham La MDTN M24 .... 58 B3
  ROY/SHW OL2 .... 60 A1
Thornham New Rd ROCH OL11... 40 A6
Thornham Old Rd MDTN M24 .... 59 D2
  ROY/SHW OL2 .... 59 E2
Thornham Rd ROY/SHW OL2 .... 60 B2
  SALE M33 .... 158 C3
Thornhill Cl DTN/ASHW M34 .... 147 E1
Thornhill Dr WALK M28 .... 83 F5
Thornhill Rd DROY M43 .... 110 C5
  TOT/BURYW BL8 .... 18 B4
Thornholme Cl GTN M18 .... 126 C6
Thornholme Rd MPL/ROM SK6.... 187 D3
Thorniley Brow ANC M4 .... 3 E2
Thornlea Av OLDS OL8 .... 94 C4
  SWIN M27 .... 101 E1
Thornlea Dr WHIT OL12 .... 21 F3
Thornleigh Rd RUSH/FAL M14 .... 143 F2
Thornley Av BOL BL1 .... 27 E4
Thornley Cl OLDE OL4 .... 81 E6
Thornley Crs MPL/ROM SK6 .... 169 E1
  OLDE OL4 .... 81 E6
Thornley La OLDE OL4 .... 81 E6
Thornley La North RDSH SK5 .... 128 A6
Thornley La South RDSH SK5 .... 147 E2
Thornley Park Rd OLDE OL4 .... 81 E6
Thornley Rd DTN/ASHW M34 .... 130 B5
  PWCH M25 .... 72 A4
Thornley St HYDE SK14 .... 150 C2
  MDTN M24 .... 75 F2
  RAD M26 .... 69 F1
Thornmere Cl SWIN M27 .... 85 D3
Thorn Rd BRAM/HZG SK7 .... 196 B4
  OLDS OL8 .... 97 D2
  SWIN M27 .... 101 F1
Thorns Av BOL BL1 .... 27 E4
Thorns Cl BOL BL1 .... 27 E4
Thornsett Cl BKLY M9 .... 91 F5
Thornsgreen Rd WYTH/NTH M22... 192 B1
Thorns Rd BOL BL1 .... 27 E4
The Thorns CCHDY M21 .... 141 E4
Thorn St BOL BL1 .... 28 A5
  RAMS BL0 .... 19 D2
Thornton Av BOL BL1 .... 26 A6
  DTN/ASHW M34 .... 129 D1
  URM M41 .... 137 E1
Thornton Cl BOLS/LL BL3 .... 50 A6
  FWTH BL4 .... 65 F4
Thornton Dr WILM/AE SK9 .... 194 B6
Thornton Ga CHD/CHDH SK8 .... 179 E6
Thornton Pl HTNM SK4 .... 165 F1
Thornton Rd CHD/CHDH SK8...... 180 A6
  RUSH/FAL M14 .... 143 E1
Thornton St BOLE BL2 .... 47 E2
  NEWH/MOS M40 .... 107 D3
  OLDS OL8 .... 79 D6
  ROCH OL11 .... 40 A2
Thornton St North
  NEWH/MOS M40 .... 107 E2
Thorntree Cl BKLY M9 .... 91 F6
Thorn Vw BURY BL9 .... 35 D4
Thornway BRAM/HZG SK7 .... 196 A1
  MPL/ROM SK6 .... 201 D2
  WALK M28 .... 82 B5
Thornwood Av GTN M18 .... 127 F5
Thorndyke Av BOL BL1 .... 27 F3
Thorold Gv SALE M33 .... 160 C1
Thorpe Av RAD M26 .... 52 B4
  SWIN M27 .... 84 A2
Thorpebrook Rd NEWH/MOS M40... 108 B1
Thorpe Cl DTN/ASHW M34 .... 130 A5
  OLDE OL4 .... 81 E3
Thorpe Gv HTNM SK4 .... 146 B5
Thorpe Hall Gv HYDE SK14 .... 132 A3
Thorpe La OLDE OL4 .... 81 E3
Thorpeness Sq GTN M18 .... 127 E3
Thorpe St BOLE BL2 .... 27 E5
  MDTN M24 .... 74 A4
  OLDTF/WHR M16 .... 123 D5
  RAMS BL0 .... 6 C6
  WALK M28 .... 83 E1
Thorp Rd NEWH/MOS M40 .... 108 B2
  ROY/SHW OL2 .... 60 B5
Thorp St ECC M30 .... 118 C1
  WHTF M45 .... 70 C2
Thorp Vw ROY/SHW OL2 .... 60 A3
Thorsby Av HYDE SK14 .... 151 D1
Thorsby Cl EDGW/EG BL7 .... 14 A5
Thorsby Rd HALE/TIMP WA15 .... 174 C2
Thrapston Av DTN/ASHW M34 .... 111 E6
Threaphurst La BRAM/HZG SK7 .... 186 A5

Threapwood Rd WYTH/NTH M22... 178 C6
Three Acre Av ROY/SHW OL2 .... 61 E5
Threlkeld Cl MDTN M24 .... 74 A2
Threlkeld Rd MDTN M24 .... 74 A2
Thresher Cl SALE M33 .... 161 D2
Threshfield Dr HALE/TIMP WA15... 160 A6
Throstle Bank St HYDE SK14 .... 131 D5
Throstle Gv MPL/ROM SK6 .... 186 C2
  TOT/BURYW BL8 .... 33 D2
Throstle Hall Ct MDTN M24 .... 75 D2
Throstles Cl DROY M43 .... 111 D4
Thrum Fold WHIT OL12 .... 22 B1
Thrum Hall La WHIT OL12 .... 22 C2
Thrush Av FWTH BL4 .... 65 D3
Thrush Dr BURY BL9 .... 34 C3
Thrush St WHIT OL12 .... 22 A4
Thruxton Cl OLDTF/WHR M16 .... 123 F6
Thurland Rd OLDE OL4 .... 80 A5
Thurland St CHAD OL9 .... 76 C3
Thurlby Av BKLY M9 .... 74 C6
Thurlby St BRUN/LGST M13 .... 125 E5
Thureigh Rd DID/WITH M20 .... 163 F1
Thurlestone Av BOLE BL2 .... 31 E6
Thurlestone Dr BRAM/HZG SK7 .... 183 F5
  URM M41 .... 119 D6
Thurlestone Rd ALT WA14 .... 173 F1
Thurloe St RUSH/FAL M14 .... 125 D6
Thurlow St SALQ/ORD M5 .... 122 A1
Thurlston Crs CHH M8 .... 90 C6
Thurlwood Av DID/WITH M20 .... 143 E4
Thurnham St BOLS/LL BL3 .... 46 A5
Thursfield St SLFD M6 .... 104 C2
Thurstane St BOL BL1 .... 27 D5
Thurston Cl BURY BL9 .... 71 E1
Thurston Gn WILM/AE SK9 .... 209 E4
Thynne St BOLS/LL BL3 .... 47 D4
  FWTH BL4 .... 66 A2
Tiber Av OLDS OL8 .... 95 D4
Tib La CMANW M2 .... 2 D4
Tib St ANC M4 .... 3 F3
  DTN/ASHW M34 .... 149 D1
  RAMS BL0 .... 6 C6
Tideswell Av NEWH/MOS M40 .... 107 E4
Tideswell Cl CHD/CHDH SK8 .... 194 B1
Tideswell Rd BRAM/HZG SK7 .... 198 C1
  DROY M43 .... 109 F4
Tideway Cl SWIN M27 .... 88 A5
Tidworth Av ANC M4 .... 107 E5
Tiflis St WHIT OL12 .... 22 C5
Tig Fold Rd FWTH BL4 .... 64 C3
Tilbury St OLD OL1 .... 78 C3
Tilby Cl URM M41 .... 136 C1
Tildsley St BOLS/LL BL3 .... 46 C5
Tile St BURY BL9 .... 34 A4
Tillard Av EDGY/DAV SK3 .... 165 F5
Tillhey Rd WYTH/NTH M22 .... 178 B5
Tilney Av STRET M32 .... 140 C2
Tilson St WHIT OL12 .... 22 C5
Tilton St OLD OL1 .... 80 A1
Timberbottom BOLE BL2 .... 29 D3
Times St MDTN M24 .... 75 F3
Timothy Cl SLFD M6 .... 102 C4
Timperley Cl OLDS OL8 .... 96 B3
Timperley Fold AUL OL6 .... 113 D1
Timperley Rd AUL OL6 .... 112 C1
Timperley St CHAD OL9 .... 78 B4
  OP/CLY M11 .... 127 D3
Timpson Rd NTHM/RTH M23 .... 160 C6
Timsbury Cl BOLE BL2 .... 49 D4
Timson St FAIL M35 .... 94 A6
Tindall St ECC M30 .... 107 D2
  RDSH SK5 .... 128 A6
Tindle St WALK M28 .... 84 A2
Tinline St BURY BL9 .... 34 B5
Tinningham Cl OP/CLY M11 .... 127 F2
Tinshill Cl WGTN/LGST M12 .... 126 B4
Tinsley Cl NEWH/MOS M40 .... 107 F5
Tin St BOLS/LL BL3 .... 46 C4
Tintagel Ct RAD M26 .... 50 A4
  STLY SK15 .... 114 A5
Tintern Av BOLE BL2 .... 28 C5
  DID/WITH M20 .... 143 D6
  HEY OL10 .... 37 D3
  LIT OL15 .... 12 B4
  URM M41 .... 137 E3
  WHIT OL12 .... 22 C3
  WHTF M45 .... 71 D2
Tintern Cl POY/DIS SK12 .... 198 B4
Tintern Dr HALE/TIMP WA15 .... 176 A5
Tintern Gv STKP SK1 .... 167 F4
Tintern Pl HEY OL10 .... 37 D3
Tintern Rd CHD/CHDH SK8...... 195 F3
  MDTN M24 .... 57 D6
Tintern St RUSH/FAL M14 .... 143 F1
Tipperary St STLY SK15 .... 115 F2
Tipping St ALT WA14 .... 174 B4
  HALE/TIMP WA15 .... 174 B4
Tipton Cl CHD/CHDH SK8 .... 181 F3
  RAD M26 .... 50 B4
Tipton Dr NTHM/RTH M23 .... 161 E3
Tiree Cl BRAM/HZG SK7 .... 185 D6
Tirza Av BNG/LEV M19 .... 145 D4
Titanian Ri OLD OL1 .... 62 B4
Titchfield Rd OLDS OL8 .... 97 D1
Tithe Barn Cl WHIT OL12 .... 24 B1

Tithe Barn Crs *BOL* BL1 .... 28 C3
Tithebarn Rd *HALE/TIMP* WA15 .... 190 A1
Tithe Barn Rd *HTNM* SK4 .... 165 D1 🔟
Tithebarn St *BURY* BL9 .... 34 A5 🔢
Titherington Cl *RDSH* SK5 .... 146 B2 🔢
Titterington La *CCHDY* M21 .... 141 F1
Tiverton Av *SALE* M33 .... 159 D2
Tiverton Cl *RAD* M26 .... 50 B4
Tiverton Dr *SALE* M33 .... 159 D2
Tiverton Pl *AULW* OL7 .... 112 B2
Tiverton Rd *URM* M41 .... 119 F5
Tiviot Dl *STKP* SK1 .... 167 D3
Tiviot Wy *RDSH* SK5 .... 167 D2
Tivoli St *CSLFD* M3 .... 2 B4
Toad La *MILN* OL16 .... 23 D5 🔢
   WHIT OL12 .... 22 C5
Tobermory Cl *OP/CLY* M11 .... 109 E6 🔢
Tobermory Rd *CHD/CHDH* SK8 .. 180 A5
Todd St *ANC* M4 .... 3 E1
   BRO M7 .... 105 F1
   BURY BL9 .... 34 A3
   HEY OL10 .... 36 B5
   MILN OL16 .... 23 E6
Todmorden Rd *LIT* OL15 .... 13 D5
Toft Rd *GTN* M18 .... 127 D5
Toledo St *OP/CLY* M11 .... 109 E6
Tolland La *HALE/TIMP* WA15 .... 189 D1
Tollard Av *NEWH/MOS* M40 .... 107 E2 🔢
Tollard Cl *CHD/CHDH* SK8 .... 195 F2
Toll Bar St *WGTN/LGST* M12 .... 125 F3 🔢
Tollesbury Cl *NEWH/MOS* M40 .. 107 E3 🔢
Toll Gate Cl *BRUN/LGST* M13 .... 125 F5
Tollgate Wy *MILN* OL16 .... 24 A5 🔢
Tolworth Dr *CHH* M8 .... 90 C6
Tomcroft La *DTN/ASHW* M34 .... 148 B1
Tomlinson Cl *OLDS* OL8 .... 78 C6
Tomlinson St *NEWH/MOS* M40 .. 93 D2 🔢
   ROCH OL11 .... 39 D3
Tomlin Sq *BOLE* BL2 .... 48 A2 🔢
Tommy Taylor Cl
   NEWH/MOS M40 .... 109 D2 🔢
Tom Shepley St *HYDE* SK14 ...... 150 C1
Tonacliffe Rd *WHIT* OL12 .... 9 D5
Tonacliffe Ter *MDTN* M24 .... 9 D4
Tonacliffe Wy *WHIT* OL12 .... 9 D5
Tonbridge Cl *TOT/BURYW* BL8 .. 19 D6
Tonbridge Rd *BNG/LEV* M19 .... 145 E3
   RDSH SK5 .... 147 D3 🔢
Tonge Bridge Wy *BOLE* BL2 ...... 47 F1
Tonge Cl *WHTF* M45 .... 71 F2
Tonge Fold Rd *BOLE* BL2 .... 47 F2
Tonge Gn *STLY* SK15 .... 133 F3 🔢
Tonge Hall Cl *MDTN* M24 .... 75 D3
Tonge Moor Rd *BOLE* BL2 .... 28 C6
Tonge Roughs *MDTN* M24 .... 76 B3 🔢
Tonge St *HEY* OL10 .... 37 E5
   ROCH OL11 .... 40 D1 🔢
   WGTN/LGST M12 .... 125 E2 🔢
Tongfields *EDGW/EG* BL7 .... 14 A5
Tong Head Av *BOL* BL1 .... 28 C3
Tong La *WHIT* OL12 .... 9 D2
Tong Rd *BOLS/LL* BL3 .... 49 E5
Tong St *FWTH* BL4 .... 68 A6 🔢
Tonman St *CSLFD* M3 .... 2 B5
Toon Crs *TOT/BURYW* BL8 .... 33 D1
Tootal Dr *SLFD* M6 .... 103 D4
Tootal Gv *SLFD* M6 .... 103 D5
Tootal Rd *SALQ/ORD* M5 .... 103 D5
Topaz St *OP/CLY* M11 .... 108 A6
Topcroft Cl *WYTH/NTH* M22 .... 162 C5
Topfield Rd *WYTH/NTH* M22 .... 178 A4
Topham St *BURY* BL9 .... 53 D1
Topley St *BKLY* M9 .... 107 D1
Top O' Th' Gn *CHAD* OL9 .... 95 D1
Top O' Th' La *BOLS/LL* BL3 .... 48 D4 🔢
Top O' Th' Meadows La *OLDE* OL4 .. 81 E2
Topping Fold Rd *BURY* BL9 .... 35 D4
Toppings Gn *EDGW/EG* BL7 ...... 14 B6 🔢
The Toppings *MPL/ROM* SK6 .... 169 E2
Topping St *BOL* BL1 .... 27 F6 🔢
   BURY BL9 .... 34 B4 🔢
Topp St *FWTH* BL4 .... 66 C4
Topp Wy *BOL* BL1 .... 46 C1
Top Schwabe St *MDTN* M24 ...... 74 A3
Top St *MDTN* M24 .... 74 C2
   OLDE OL4 .... 80 B3
Torah St *CHH* M8 .... 106 B3
Tor Av *TOT/BURYW* BL8 .... 18 A3
Torbay Dr *OFTN* SK2 .... 167 F6
Torbay Dr *OFTN* SK2 .... 167 F6
Torbay Rd *CCHDY* M21 .... 142 A3
   URM M41 .... 138 C2
Torcross Rd *BKLY* M9 .... 73 F6
Torkington Av *SWIN* M27 .... 86 A4 🔢
Torkington La *BRAM/HZG* SK7 .. 186 B4
Torkington Rd *BRAM/HZG* SK7 .. 185 E5
   CHD/CHDH SK8 .... 179 F2
   WILM/AE SK9 .... 204 A5
Torkington St *EDGY/DAV* SK3 .. 166 B3
Toronto Av *MANAIR* M90 .... 191 F3
Toronto Rd *OFTN* SK2 .... 183 E1 🔢
Toronto St *BOLE* BL2 .... 48 C1
Torquay Cl *BRUN/LGST* M13 .... 125 D4 🔢

Torquay Gv *OFTN* SK2 .... 183 F3
Torrax Cl *SLFD* M6 .... 102 C1 🔢
Torre Cl *MDTN* M24 .... 57 E6
Torrens St *SLFD* M6 .... 103 E2 🔢
Torridon Rd *BOLE* BL2 .... 49 D2 🔢
Torrin Cl *EDGY/DAV* SK3 .... 183 D2
Torrington Av *BKLY* M9 .... 92 B3 🔢
   BOL BL1 .... 27 F5
Torrington Dr *HYDE* SK14 .... 152 B1
Torrington Rd *SWIN* M27 .... 102 C1
Torrington St *HEY* OL10 .... 56 C1
Torrisdale Cl *BOLS/LL* BL3 .... 45 F4 🔢
Torver Dr *BOLE* BL2 .... 49 D1
   MDTN M24 .... 74 B1
Torwood Dr *CHAD* OL9 .... 76 C2
Totland Cl *WGTN/LGST* M12 .... 126 B6
Totnes Av *BRAM/HZG* SK7 ...... 183 E5
   CHAD OL9 .... 77 D2
Totnes Rd *CCHDY* M21 .... 142 A3
   SALE M33 .... 138 B6
Totridge Cl *OFTN* SK2 .... 184 B2
Tottenham Dr *NTHM/RTH* M23 .. 160 B6
Totland Av *OLDE* OL4 .... 81 D4
Tottington Av *BOLE* BL2 .... 16 A3
   BOLE BL2 .... 29 F2
   TOT/BURYW BL8 .... 32 C3
Tottington St *OP/CLY* M11 ...... 109 D5 🔢
Totton Rd *FAIL* M35 .... 94 A6
Touchet Hall Rd *MDTN* M24 ...... 58 B5
Tours Av *NTHM/RTH* M23 .... 161 E3 🔢
Towcester Cl *ANC* M4 .... 107 E6 🔢
Tower Ct *EDGW/EG* BL7 .... 15 D1
Towers Av *BOLS/LL* BL3 .... 45 E5
Towers Rd *POY/DIS* SK12 .... 199 D3
Towers St *OLDE* OL4 .... 80 B2
Tower St *DUK* SK16 .... 113 C6
   EDGW/EG BL7 .... 15 D1 🔢
   HEY OL10 .... 37 D5
   HYDE SK14 .... 150 B2 🔢
   RAD M26 .... 52 B5
Towey Cl *GTN* M18 .... 127 E3
Towncroft *DTN/ASHW* M34 ...... 130 B5 🔢
Towncroft Av *MDTN* M24 .... 75 D1
Towncroft La *BOL* BL1 .... 44 C1
Townend St *HYDE* SK14 .... 150 C1
Townfield *URM* M41 .... 137 F2
Townfield Gdns *ALT* WA14 ...... 174 B2
Townfield La *LYMM* WA13 .... 154 A6
Townfield Rd *ALT* WA14 .... 174 B2 🔢
Town Fields Cl *BURY* BL9 .... 34 A6 🔢
Townfield St *OLDE* OL4 .... 79 F4 🔢
Town Fold *MPL/ROM* SK6 .... 171 F6 🔢
Town Gate Dr *URM* M41 .... 136 A1
Town Hall La *CMANW* M2 .... 2 D4 🔢
Town House Rd *LIT* OL15 .... 12 C5
Town La *DTN/ASHW* M34 .... 148 B2
   DUK SK16 .... 131 D1
Townley Fold *HYDE* SK14 .... 132 C3
Townley Rd *MILN* OL16 .... 42 A1
Townley St *CHH* M8 .... 106 A2 🔢
   MDTN M24 .... 75 E2
   OP/CLY M11 .... 126 A1 🔢
Townrow St *HEY* OL10 .... 37 E5 🔢
Townscliffe La *MPL/ROM* SK6 .. 187 F1
Townsend Rd *SWIN* M27 .... 86 A4
Townside Rw *BURY* BL9 .... 34 A6
Townsley Gv *AUL* OL6 .... 113 F2
Town St *MPL/ROM* SK6 .... 171 F6
Towton St *BKLY* M9 .... 91 F5
Towyn Av *SALQ/ORD* M5 .... 104 B5 🔢
Toxteth St *OP/CLY* M11 .... 127 C1
Tracey St *CHH* M8 .... 90 B4 🔢
Traders Av *URM* M41 .... 119 F3
Trafalgar Cl *POY/DIS* SK12 ...... 199 E6
Trafalgar Gv *BRO* M7 .... 105 E2 🔢
Trafalgar Pl *DID/WITH* M20 ...... 163 E1
Trafalgar Rd *SALE* M33 .... 140 A5 🔢
   SLFD M6 .... 102 B4
Trafalgar Sq *AULW* OL7 .... 112 A6 🔢
   AULW OL7 .... 112 A6 🔢
Trafalgar St *AULW* OL7 .... 112 A6
   BRO M7 .... 105 F2
   MILN OL16 .... 23 E5
   OLD OL1 .... 78 C3
Trafford Av *URM* M41 .... 119 F6 🔢
Trafford Bank Rd
   OLDTF/WHR M16 .... 123 D4 🔢
Trafford Dr *HALE/TIMP* WA15 .. 159 F5
   LHULT M38 .... 65 F6
Trafford Gv *FWTH* BL4 .... 66 C2 🔢
   STRET M32 .... 140 B2 🔢
Trafford Park Rd *TRPK* M17 .... 120 C1
Trafford Pl *HULME* M15 .... 123 E3
Trafford Rd *ECC* M30 .... 119 E1
   SALQ/ORD M5 .... 122 B3
   WILM/AE SK9 .... 203 E2
   WILM/AE SK9 .... 209 E4
Trafford St *CSLFD* M3 .... 2 B6
   FWTH BL4 .... 66 B3
   OLDS OL8 .... 78 C6 🔢
   ROCH OL11 .... 39 F2 🔢
Trafford Wharf Rd *TRPK* M17 .. 121 D2

Tragan Cl *OFTN* SK2 .... 184 B1 🔢
Tragan Dr *OFTN* SK2 .... 184 B1
Trail St *SLFD* M6 .... 103 F5
Tram St *OP/CLY* M11 .... 127 D2
Tramway Rd *IRL* M44 .... 135 D4
Tranby Cl *WYTH/NTH* M22 ...... 179 D3
Tranmere Cl *GTN* M18 .... 126 C4 🔢
Tranmere Dr *WILM/AE* SK9 .... 194 C6
Tranmere Rd *EDGY/DAV* SK3 .. 165 F5 🔢
Transvaal St *OP/CLY* M11 ...... 109 E6
Travis Brow *HTNM* SK4 .... 166 B4
Travis St *CMANE* M1 .... 125 D1
   HYDE SK14 .... 150 C1
   MILN OL16 .... 42 C3 🔢
   ROY/SHW OL2 .... 61 F2
Trawden Av *BOL* BL1 .... 27 D5
Trawden Dr *BURY* BL9 .... 19 F5
Trawden Gn *OFTN* SK2 .... 184 B3 🔢
Traylen Wy *WHIT* OL12 .... 21 E4 🔢
Tree Av *DROY* M43 .... 110 B4
Tree Cl *OLDE* OL4 .... 80 B3
Tree House Av *AULW* OL7 .... 112 A1
Tree Tops *BOLE* BL2 .... 29 D1 🔢
Treetops Av *TOT/BURYW* BL8 .... 18 B2
Trefoil Wy *LIT* OL15 .... 12 A5
Tregaer Fold *MDTN* M24 .... 76 A3
Trenam Pl *SALQ/ORD* M5 .... 104 C5
Trenant Rd *SLFD* M6 .... 103 F2
Trenchard Dr *WYTH/NTH* M22 .. 193 D2
Trencherbone *RAD* M26 .... 50 C4 🔢
Trengrove St *WHIT* OL12 .... 22 A4 🔢
Trent Av *CHAD* OL9 .... 76 C3
   HEY OL10 .... 36 B4
   MILN OL16 .... 43 D3
Trent Cl *BRAM/HZG* SK7 .... 196 A3
   RDSH SK5 .... 148 A6
Trent Dr *WALK* M28 .... 82 C3
Trentham Av *FWTH* BL4 .... 66 A2
   HTNM SK4 .... 165 D2 🔢
Trentham Cl *FWTH* BL4 .... 66 A2
Trentham Gv *NEWH/MOS* M40 .. 92 B4
Trentham Rd *OLDTF/WHR* M16 .. 122 B6 🔢
Trentham St *FWTH* BL4 .... 66 A2
   HULME M15 .... 123 D2
   SWIN M27 .... 85 F4 🔢
Trent Rd *ROY/SHW* OL2 .... 61 E1
Trent St *MILN* OL16 .... 40 C1 🔢
Trent Wy *FWTH* BL4 .... 67 F6
Tresco Av *STRET* M32 .... 140 C2
Trevelyan St *ECC* M30 .... 102 B5 🔢
Trevor Av *SALE* M33 .... 159 D3
Trevor Dr *NEWH/MOS* M40 ...... 93 F3
Trevor Rd *ECC* M30 .... 100 C4
   SWIN M27 .... 101 F1
   URM M41 .... 118 A6
Trevor St *OP/CLY* M11 .... 127 F2 🔢
   ROCH OL11 .... 38 C4
The Triangle *HALE/TIMP* WA15 .. 159 F6
Tribune Av *ALT* WA14 .... 157 F6 🔢
Trident Rd *ECC* M30 .... 118 A2
Trimdon Cl *OP/CLY* M11 .... 108 C5
Trimingham Dr *TOT/BURYW* BL8 .. 33 E1
Trimley Av *NEWH/MOS* M40 .. 107 E2 🔢
Trinity Av *SALE* M33 .... 160 B1
Trinity Cl *DUK* SK16 .... 131 F1
Trinity Crs *WALK* M28 .... 83 F3
Trinity Gdns *EDGY/DAV* SK3 .. 183 D4
Trinity Gn *TOT/BURYW* BL8 ...... 18 C5 🔢
Trinity Rd *SALE* M33 .... 160 A1
Trinity St *BOLS/LL* BL3 .... 46 C3
   BURY BL9 .... 34 A6 🔢
   MDTN M24 .... 75 D3 🔢
   MPL/ROM SK6 .... 187 D2 🔢
   OLD OL1 .... 78 C3
   STLY SK15 .... 114 B6
Trinity Wy *CSLFD* M3 .... 2 A5
Trippier Rd *ECC* M30 .... 118 A1 🔢
Tripps Ms *DID/WITH* M20 .... 163 D1 🔢
Tristam Cl *BRUN/LGST* M13 .... 125 D3 🔢
Trojan Gdns *BRO* M7 .... 105 D2 🔢
Troon Cl *BOLS/LL* BL3 .... 45 D6
   BRAM/HZG SK7 .... 197 E2 🔢
Troon Dr *CHD/CHDH* SK8 .... 180 A6 🔢
Troon Rd *NTHM/RTH* M23 .... 177 D1
Trough Ga *OLDS* OL8 .... 95 D3
Troutbeck Av *ANC* M4 .... 107 E5 🔢
Troutbeck Cl *TOT/BURYW* BL8 .. 16 C3
Troutbeck Dr *RAMS* BL0 .... 7 D4 🔢
Troutbeck Rd *CHD/CHDH* SK8 .. 179 F4
   HALE/TIMP WA15 .... 176 B2 🔢
Troutbeck Wy *ROCH* OL11 .... 38 C3 🔢
Trowbridge Dr *NEWH/MOS* M40 .. 93 D4
Trowbridge Rd *DTN/ASHW* M34 .. 149 E2 🔢
Trows La *ROCH* OL11 .... 39 E6
Trowtree Av *WGTN/LGST* M12 .. 125 F3
Troydale Dr *NEWH/MOS* M40 .. 108 B2 🔢
Trumpet St *CMANE* M1 .... 2 C6
Truro Av *AUL* OL6 .... 97 F6
   RDSH SK5 .... 148 A6
   STRET M32 .... 140 C1
Truro Cl *BRAM/HZG* SK7 .... 197 D2 🔢
   TOT/BURYW BL8 .... 33 E4
Truro Dr *SALE* M33 .... 158 B1
Truro Rd *CHAD* OL9 .... 77 E2 🔢
Trust Rd *GTN* M18 .... 127 D6

Tudbury Wy CSLFD M3 .... 105 E5 20
Tudor Av BKLY M9 .... 91 F4
 BOL BL1 .... 45 F2
 CHAD OL9 .... 93 E2
 FWTH BL4 .... 65 F4
 STLY SK15 .... 115 E4
Tudor Cl MOSL OL5 .... 99 F4 9
 RDSH SK5 .... 146 C4
Tudor Ct PWCH M25 .... 89 D2
Tudor Gv WILM/AE SK9 .... 204 C2
Tudor Gv MDTN M24 .... 56 B6
Tudor Hall St ROCH OL11 .... 39 D5 13
Tudor Rd ALT WA14 .... 157 F6
 WILM/AE SK9 .... 204 C2
Tudor St BOLS/LL BL3 .... 46 A5 63
 MDTN M24 .... 75 F3 8
 OLDS OL8 .... 78 B6
 ROY/SHW OL2 .... 61 F2
Tuffley Rd NTHM/RTH M23 ...... 177 E3
Tuley St OP/CLY M11 .... 126 A2
Tulip Av FWTH BL4 .... 65 E2
 FWTH BL4 .... 67 D6
Tulip Cl CHAD OL9 .... 76 C4
 EDGY/DAV SK3 .... 182 B2
 SALE M33 .... 158 A1
Tulip Dr HALE/TIMP WA15 ...... 175 D1
Tulip Gv WHIT OL12 .... 22 C2
Tulip Rd PART M31 .... 154 C3
Tully Pl CSLFD M3 .... 105 F3 6
Tully St BRO M7 .... 105 F1 13
Tully St South BRO M7 .... 105 F1
Tulpen Sq OLD9 .... 77 F4 7
Tulworth Rd POY/DIS SK12 ...... 198 B5
Tumblewood Dr
 CHD/CHDH SK8 .... 180 C3 1
Tunshill Rd NTHM/RTH M23 .... 160 C4
Tuns Rd OLDS OL8 .... 96 C3
Tunstall Rd OLDE OL4 .... 80 A5
Tunstall St HTNM SK4 .... 166 C3 13
 OP/CLY M11 .... 127 F2 13
Tunstead Av DID/WITH M20 .... 143 D5
Turf Cl ROY/SHW OL2 .... 60 C6
Turf Hill Rd MILN OL16 .... 40 C3
Turf House Cl LIT OL15 .... 12 A4 1
Turfland Av ROY/SHW OL2 ...... 60 C6
Turf La CHAD OL9 .... 94 A2
 ROY/SHW OL2 .... 60 C6
Turf Lea Rd MPL/ROM SK6 ...... 187 F6
Turf Park Rd ROY/SHW OL2 ...... 60 C6
Turf Pit La OLDE OL4 .... 62 A5
Turf St RAD M26 .... 51 D6 2
Turf Ter LIT OL15 .... 12 B5
Turfton Rd ROY/SHW OL2 .... 61 D5
Turks Rd RAD M26 .... 50 B4
Turk St BOL BL1 .... 46 A1 40
Turley St CHH M8 .... 106 C1 9
Turnberry BOLS/LL BL3 .... 45 D6
Turnberry Dr WILM/AE SK9 ...... 204 B3
Turnberry Rd CHD/CHDH SK8 .. 180 A6
Turnbull Av PWCH M25 .... 72 A4
Turnbull Rd BRUN/LGST M13 .. 145 D1
 GTN M18 .... 128 A6
Turnbury Cl SALE M33 .... 139 F5 8
Turnbury Rd WYTH/NTH M22 .. 178 C3
Turncliff Crs MPL/ROM SK6 .... 170 B6
Turncroft La STKP SK1 .... 167 E5
Turncroft Wy WALK M28 .... 82 A6
Turnell Wy WALK M28 .... 100 B2
Turner Av FAIL M35 .... 109 F1
 IRL M44 .... 116 B6
Turner Bridge Rd BOLE BL2 .... 48 A1
Turner Dr URM M41 .... 139 D1
Turner Gdns HYDE SK14 .... 131 F5
Turner La AUL OL6 .... 112 C3
 HYDE SK14 .... 132 A5
 MPL/ROM SK6 .... 149 D5
Turner Rd MPL/ROM SK6 .... 187 D1
Turner's Pl WHIT OL12 .... 22 C2
Turner St ANC M4 .... 3 F7
 AUL OL6 .... 112 C3
 BOL BL1 .... 47 E1
 BRO M7 .... 89 F6 2
 DTN/ASHW M34 .... 129 F4
 GTN M18 .... 127 E4 13
 OLDE OL4 .... 80 C3
 OLDTF/WHR M16 .... 123 D3 6
 OP/CLY M11 .... 109 D6
 WHIT OL12 .... 22 C4 7
Turnfield Cl MILN OL16 .... 24 B2 13
Turnfield Rd CHD/CHDH SK8 .. 180 A4
Turnhill Rd MILN OL16 .... 40 C4 8
Turn Moss Rd STRET M32 .... 141 D3
Turnough Rd MILN OL16 .... 25 D6 2
The Turnpike MPL/ROM SK6 .... 170 B6
Turn Rd RAMS BL0 .... 7 F3
Turnstone Rd BOLE BL2 .... 47 E3 2
 OFTN SK2 .... 185 E2
Turn St AUL OL6 .... 113 E3 10
Turton Cl HEY OL10 .... 36 B5 3
 TOT/BURYW BL8 .... 51 F1
Turton Hts BOLE BL2 .... 28 C1
Turton Rd BOLE BL2 .... 29 D1
 TOT/BURYW BL8 .... 16 B3
Turton St BOL BL1 .... 47 D1
 OP/CLY M11 .... 127 E2 4

Turves Rd CHD/CHDH SK8 ...... 180 C6
Tuscan Rd DID/WITH M20 ...... 163 F5
Tuscany Vw BRO M7 .... 88 C5
Tutbury St ANC M4 .... 107 E6
Tuxford Wk NEWH/MOS M40 .. 107 E2 22
Tweedale Av BKLY M9 .... 74 A6
Tweedale St ROCH OL11 .... 39 F2
Tweedale Wy CHAD OL9 .... 94 B3
 FAIL M35 .... 94 B4
Tweed Cl ALT WA14 .... 174 A1
 OLDS OL8 .... 78 C6
Tweedle Hill Rd BKLY M9 .... 90 C1
Tweenbrook Av NTHM/RTH M23 .. 177 E4
Tweesdale Cl WHTF M45 .... 71 F2 3
Twelve Yards Rd ECC M30 .... 117 E2
Twigworth Rd WYTH/NTH M22 . 178 A5 7
Twillbrook Dr CSLFD M3 .... 105 F4 10
Twinegate WHIT OL12 .... 22 C2
Twining Brook Rd CHD/CHDH SK8 .. 181 F4
Twining Rd TRPK M17 .... 119 F1
Twinnies Rd WILM/AE SK9 ...... 203 F2
Twin St HEY OL10 .... 37 F6 11
Twirl Hill Rd AUL OL6 .... 97 F4
Twisse Rd BOLE BL2 .... 49 D2 8
Twoacre Av WYTH/NTH M22 .... 178 A2
Two Acre Dr ROY/SHW OL2 ...... 61 D1
Two Acre La OLDE OL4 .... 81 E1
Two Bridges Rd MILN OL16 ...... 42 C4
Two Brooks La TOT/BURYW BL8 .. 16 C3
Two Trees La DTN/ASHW M34 .. 149 E2
Twyford Cl DID/WITH M20 ...... 163 D2 2
Tybyrne Cl WALK M28 .... 82 A6
Tydden St OLDS OL8 .... 96 A2 8
Tydeman Wk MILN OL16 .... 42 B2 8
Tyler St WILM/AE SK9 .... 209 E4
Tyndall Av NEWH/MOS M40 .... 92 B4
Tyndall St OLDE OL4 .... 80 A5
Tyne Ct WALK M28 .... 83 D2
Tynedale Cl RDSH SK5 .... 146 C6
Tynesbank WALK M28 .... 83 D3
Tyne St OLDE OL4 .... 80 A4 8
Tynwald St OLDE OL4 .... 80 A4
Tyrone Cl NTHM/RTH M23 ...... 160 B5
Tyrone Dr ROCH OL11 .... 38 A2
Tyro St OLDS OL8 .... 96 A2 7
Tyrrell Gv HYDE SK14 .... 151 E2
Tyrrel Rd RDSH SK5 .... 147 D2 7
Tysoe Gdns CSLFD M3 .... 105 E5 21
Tyson St CHH M8 .... 90 A5
Tytherington Dr RDSH SK5 ...... 146 B2

U

Uganda St BOLS/LL BL3 .... 64 A1 14
Ukraine Rd BRO M7 .... 104 B1
Uldale Dr MDTN M24 .... 74 C2
Ulleswater Cl BOLS/LL BL3 ...... 49 D6 3
Ulleswater Rd BOL BL1 .... 28 A5
Ullswater Av AULW OL7 .... 112 B3
 ROY/SHW OL2 .... 60 B3
 WHIT OL12 .... 22 A4
Ullswater Dr BURY BL9 .... 52 C2 3
 FWTH BL4 .... 64 C4
 MDTN M24 .... 57 D6
Ullswater Gv HEY OL10 .... 56 B1
Ullswater Rd STKP SK1 .... 167 F6 8
 URM M41 .... 117 F5
 WILM/AE SK9 .... 194 A5
 WYTH/NTH M22 .... 178 A5
Ullswater Ter STLY SK15 .... 114 B3
Ulster Av ROCH OL11 .... 39 F2 13
Ulundi St RAD M26 .... 51 E6
Ulverston Av CHAD OL9 .... 77 E5
 DID/WITH M20 .... 143 E4 13
Uncouth Rd MILN OL16 .... 24 C6
Underhill MPL/ROM SK6 .... 170 A2
Underhill Rd OLD OL1 .... 78 C2
Under La CHAD OL9 .... 94 C2
 OLDE OL4 .... 98 C1
Underwood Cl GTN M18 .... 128 A3
Underwood Rd DUK SK16 .... 130 C1
Underwood Wy ROY/SHW OL2 .. 62 B1
Undsworth Ct HEY OL10 .... 37 E5 20
Unicorn St ECC M30 .... 118 C3 8
Union Rd AUL OL6 .... 113 D3
 BOL BL1 .... 28 B5
 MPL/ROM SK6 .... 187 D1 8
 WHIT OL12 .... 24 C1
Union St ANC M4 .... 3 F2 13
 AUL OL6 .... 112 C3
 CHAD OL9 .... 94 C1
 GTN M18 .... 127 F5 11
 HYDE SK14 .... 150 C1
 MDTN M24 .... 75 E2
 OLD OL1 .... 79 D5
 OLDE OL4 .... 80 C5
 RAMS BL0 .... 7 D5
 ROY/SHW OL2 .... 60 B5
 RUSH/FAL M14 .... 124 C6 15
 SLFD M6 .... 104 B3 15

STKP SK1 .... 167 D5 18
 SWIN M27 .... 85 F5 13
 WGTN/LGST M12 .... 125 D2
 WHIT OL12 .... 9 D3
 WHIT OL12 .... 23 D5
Union St West CHAD OL9 .... 78 C5
 OLDS OL8 .... 78 C6
United Rd OLDTF/WHR M16 .... 121 F4
Unity Cl HEY OL10 .... 36 C6
Unity Crs HEY OL10 .... 36 C6
Unity Dr BRO M7 .... 105 F1
Unity St HEY OL10 .... 36 C6
Unity Wy STKP SK1 .... 167 D5
University Av SALQ/ORD M5 .... 104 C5 13
 SLFD M6 .... 104 C4 13
University Rd West
 SALQ/ORD M5 .... 104 C5 11
Unsworth St RAD M26 .... 51 D5
Unwin Av GTN M18 .... 127 E5
Upavon Rd WYTH/NTH M22 .... 179 D4
Upcast La WILM/AE SK9 .... 208 B2
Upland Dr LHULT M38 .... 65 D5
Upland Rd OLDS OL8 .... 95 F1
Uplands MDTN M24 .... 75 E4
Uplands Av RAD M26 .... 70 A1
Uplands Rd HYDE SK14 .... 151 E5
 URM M41 .... 136 C3
The Uplands MOSL OL5 .... 99 E4
Upper Brook St BRUN/LGST M13 .. 124 C3
 STKP SK1 .... 167 E4 10
Upper Camp St BRO M7 .... 105 E2
Upper Chorlton Rd
 OLDTF/WHR M16 .... 123 D6
Upper Cleminson St CSLFD M3 . 105 E5
Upper Conran St BKLY M9 .... 91 F3
Upper Cyrus St
 NEWH/MOS M40 .... 107 F5 7
Upper Dover St OP/CLY M11 .... 108 B6 4
Upper Downs ALT WA14 .... 174 A4 8
Upper George St WHIT OL12 .... 23 D4 13
Upper Gloucester St SLFD M6 .. 104 B4 8
Upper Hayes Cl MILN OL16 ...... 24 A5 2
Upper Helena St NEWH/MOS M40 .. 107 F5
Upper Hibbert La MPL/ROM SK6 .. 187 D3
Upper Kent Rd RUSH/FAL M14 . 125 E6
Upper Kirby St ANC M4 .... 107 D6 13
Upper Lloyd St RUSH/FAL M14 . 124 B6
Upper Md EDGW/EG BL7 .... 14 A4 1
Upper Medlock St HULME M15 . 124 C3
Uppermill Dr BNG/LEV M19 .... 164 B2
Upper Monsall St
 NEWH/MOS M40 .... 107 F1
Upper Moss La HULME M15 .... 123 F3 8
Upper Park Rd BRO M7 .... 89 E4 1
 BRO M7 .... 90 A4 8
 RUSH/FAL M14 .... 125 D5
Upper Passmonds Gv ROCH OL11 .. 21 F5
Upper Stone Dr MILN OL16 ...... 41 E1 2
Upper West Gv BRUN/LGST M13 . 125 E4 2
Upper Wilton St PWCH M25 .... 89 D1 14
Uppingham Dr RAMS BL0 .... 6 C4
Upton Av CHD/CHDH SK8 .... 195 E1 8
 HTNM SK4 .... 164 C1
Upton Cl MDTN M24 .... 75 E6 8
Upton Dr ALT WA14 .... 158 C5
Upton La TOT/BURYW BL8 .... 32 A2 2
Upton Wy TOT/BURYW BL8 ...... 32 A2 2
Urban Dr HALE/TIMP WA15 .... 174 C3
Urban Rd HALE/TIMP WA15 .... 174 C3
 SALE M33 .... 159 E1
Urmson St OLDS OL8 .... 96 A2
Urmston La STRET M32 .... 139 E2
Urmston Pk URM M41 .... 138 C1 3
Urwick Rd MPL/ROM SK6 .... 169 F4
Usk Cl WHTF M45 .... 72 A4
Uttley St BOL BL1 .... 27 E5 19
 ROCH OL11 .... 39 D3
Uxbridge St AUL OL6 .... 112 B4

V

Vaal St OLDS OL8 .... 95 D2
Valance Cl WGTN/LGST M12 .... 126 B3 13
Valdene Cl FWTH BL4 .... 66 B4 15
Valdene Dr FWTH BL4 .... 66 B4
 WALK M28 .... 83 E5
Vale Av BURY BL9 .... 52 B2
 HYDE SK14 .... 132 B6
 RAD M26 .... 68 A4
 SALE M33 .... 140 C6
 SWIN M27 .... 86 B4
 URM M41 .... 136 C2
Vale Cl BRAM/HZG SK7 .... 184 C3
 HTNM SK4 .... 165 D3
 MPL/ROM SK6 .... 171 D3
Vale Cottages LIT OL15 .... 12 B6 3
Vale Cresent CHD/CHDH SK8 .. 181 D5
Vale Dr CHAD OL9 .... 78 B5
 PWCH M25 .... 88 B3
Vale Edge RAD M26 .... 69 F3
Vale Head WILM/AE SK9 .... 204 B1
Vale La FAIL M35 .... 110 B2
Valencia Rd BRO M7 .... 104 C1 2

Valentia Rd BKLY M9 .... 91 E1
Valentine St FAIL M35 .... 93 F6
  OLDE OL4 .... 80 A5 10
Vale Rd ALT WA14 .... 173 F6
  DROY M43 .... 110 C4
  HALE/TIMP WA15 .... 165 D4
  HTNM SK4 .... 165 D4
  MPL/ROM SK6 .... 169 F5
  ROY/SHW OL2 .... 62 B3
  STLY SK15 .... 115 F1 8
  WILM/AE SK9 .... 202 C3
Vale Side MOSL OL5 .... 99 D4
Vale St AULW OL7 .... 112 B1
  BOLE BL2 .... 49 E2
  HEY OL10 .... 37 F5
  MDTN M24 .... 75 F3
  OP/CLY M11 .... 109 D5
The Vale MOSL OL5 .... 98 C4
Vale Top Av BKLY M9 .... 92 A6 13
Valetta Cl RUSH/FAL M14 .... 143 F2
Valewood Av HTNM SK4 .... 165 E4
Valletts La BOL BL1 .... 27 D6
Valley Av TOT/BURYW BL8 .... 32 C3
Valley Cl CHD/CHDH SK8 .... 180 C4
  MOSL OL5 .... 98 C3
Valley Dr WILM/AE SK9 .... 194 A6
Valley Gv DTN/ASHW M34 .... 149 F1
Valley New Rd ROY/SHW OL2 .... 60 C5
Valley Ri ROY/SHW OL2 .... 42 B6
Valley Rd BRAM/HZG SK7 .... 183 D6
  CHD/CHDH SK8 .... 180 C4
  HYDE SK14 .... 152 C3
  MDTN M24 .... 75 F1
  MPL/ROM SK6 .... 168 B1
  ROCH OL11 .... 39 F3
  ROY/SHW OL2 .... 60 C6
  URM M41 .... 117 E5
Valley Rd South URM M41 .... 136 A1
Valley Vw HYDE SK14 .... 132 B5
  WHIT OL12 .... 5 E5
Valley Wy STLY SK15 .... 115 D6
Valpy Av BOLE BL2 .... 34 C5
Vancouver Quay SALQ/ORD M5 .... 122 A2 8
Vandyke Av SLFD M6 .... 102 C4
Vandyke St ROCH OL11 .... 21 D4
Vane St ECC M30 .... 101 E5 8
Vantomme St BOL BL1 .... 27 F3
Varden Gv EDGY/DAV SK3 .... 182 B2
Varden Rd POY/DIS SK12 .... 198 C6
Vardon Dr WILM/AE SK9 .... 204 B5
Varey St GTN M18 .... 127 E4 14
Varley Rd BOLS/LL BL3 .... 45 E3
Varley St NEWH/MOS M40 .... 107 E3
Varna St OP/CLY M11 .... 127 D1
Vauban Dr SLFD M6 .... 102 C4
Vaudrey Dr BRAM/HZG SK7 .... 184 C5
  CHD/CHDH SK8 .... 181 E4
  HALE/TIMP WA15 .... 159 E4
Vaudrey La DTN/ASHW M34 .... 149 E1
Vaudrey Rd MPL/ROM SK6 .... 149 E6
Vaudrey St STLY SK15 .... 132 B1 9
Vaughan Av NEWH/MOS M40 .... 92 B5 8
Vaughan Gv OLDE OL4 .... 81 D5 10
Vaughan Rd CCHDY M21 .... 142 B3
  HTNM SK4 .... 166 D2 8
Vaughan St ECC M30 .... 100 C4
  ROY/SHW OL2 .... 60 D1
  WGTN/LGST M12 .... 126 A2
Vauxhall St NEWH/MOS M40 .... 106 C3
Vavasour St MILN OL16 .... 40 C1
Vawdrey Dr NTHM/RTH M23 .... 161 D3 9
Vega St CHH M8 .... 105 F3 9
Velmere Av BKLY M9 .... 73 E6
Velour Cl BRO M7 .... 105 E4
Vendale Av SWIN M27 .... 101 E1
Venetia St NEWH/MOS M40 .... 109 D2 13
Venice St BOLS/LL BL3 .... 46 A5 57
  CMANE M1 .... 3 F6 8
Venlow Gdns CHD/CHDH SK8 .... 181 F6
Ventnor Cl DTN/ASHW M34 .... 149 F3 8
Ventnor Rd DID/WITH M20 .... 164 A2 8
  HTNM SK4 .... 165 E3 8
Ventnor St BKLY M9 .... 91 E5
  ROCH OL11 .... 40 A2
  SLFD M6 .... 104 C2 8
Venture Scout Wy BRO M7 .... 106 A1 17
Venwood Rd PWCH M25 .... 88 A3
Verbena Av FWTH BL4 .... 65 E2 8
Verbena Cl PART M31 .... 155 D2
Verdant La ECC M30 .... 118 A1
Verdant Wy MILN OL16 .... 41 D4
Verdon St ANC M4 .... 106 B4
Verdun Av SLFD M6 .... 102 C4
Verdun Crs ROCH OL11 .... 22 A5
Verdun Rd ECC M30 .... 100 C3
Verdure Av BOL BL1 .... 44 C1
  SALE M33 .... 160 A4
Verdure Cl FAIL M35 .... 94 C5
Vere St SALQ/ORD M5 .... 104 A6
Verity Cl DID/WITH M20 .... 143 E1
  ROY/SHW OL2 .... 78 B1

Vermont St BOL BL1 .... 46 B1 29
Verne Av SWIN M27 .... 85 F5
Verne Dr OLD OL1 .... 62 C4
Verney Rd ROY/SHW OL2 .... 78 C1
Vernon Av ECC M30 .... 102 A5 10
  STKP SK1 .... 167 F3
  STRET M32 .... 140 B2
Vernon Cl CHD/CHDH SK8 .... 180 C6
Vernon Dr MPL/ROM SK6 .... 170 A6
  PWCH M25 .... 88 B3
Vernon Gv SALE M33 .... 160 C2
Vernon Pk HALE/TIMP WA15 .... 159 E6
Vernon Rd BRO M7 .... 89 D4
  DROY M43 .... 109 F5 4
  MPL/ROM SK6 .... 168 C2
  TOT/BURYW BL8 .... 18 A4
Vernon St AUL OL6 .... 113 D3 11
  BKLY M9 .... 91 F6
  BOL BL1 .... 46 C1 30
  BRAM/HZG SK7 .... 184 B4 18
  BRO M7 .... 105 D2
  BURY BL9 .... 34 A3
  FWTH BL4 .... 66 C3
  HYDE SK14 .... 150 C1
  MOSL OL5 .... 99 D5 8
Verona Dr NEWH/MOS M40 .... 109 D5
Veronica Rd DID/WITH M20 .... 164 A2 8
Verrill Av NTHM/RTH M23 .... 162 A4 8
Vesper St FAIL M35 .... 94 B5
Vesta St ANC M4 .... 107 D6
  RAMS BL0 .... 6 C5 14
Vestris Dr SLFD M6 .... 102 C4
Viaduct Rd ALT WA14 .... 158 B6
Viaduct St CSLFD M3 .... 2 B1
  EDGY/DAV SK3 .... 166 C4
  WGTN/LGST M12 .... 125 F1
Vicarage Av CHD/CHDH SK8 .... 195 F1
Vicarage Cl BURY BL9 .... 19 F5 3
  DUK SK16 .... 131 F1 8
  OLDE OL4 .... 81 D4
  SLFD M6 .... 102 C4
Vicarage Crs AUL OL6 .... 113 E2
  MILN OL16 .... 24 A2 8
Vicarage Gdns HYDE SK14 .... 151 D1 8
Vicarage Gv ECC M30 .... 102 A5
Vicarage La ALT WA14 .... 150 C2
  MDTN M24 .... 76 B4
  POY/DIS SK12 .... 198 C4
Vicarage Rd AULW OL7 .... 112 C2
  EDGY/DAV SK3 .... 182 C1
  IRL M44 .... 135 E1
  SWIN M27 .... 85 F5
  URM M41 .... 118 C5
  WALK M28 .... 83 D7
Vicarage Rd North ROCH OL11 .... 39 D6
Vicarage Rd South ROCH OL11 .... 39 D6 11
Vicarage Rd OLDS OL8 .... 95 D3
  RAD M26 .... 51 E6 7
  ROY/SHW OL2 .... 61 F2
Vicarage Vw ROCH OL11 .... 39 E6 5
Vicarage Wy ROY/SHW OL2 .... 61 F2
Vicar's Dr MILN OL16 .... 23 D6
Vicar's Ga MILN OL16 .... 23 D6
Vicars Rd CCHDY M21 .... 141 E3
Vicars St ECC M30 .... 102 A5
Vicker Cl SWIN M27 .... 86 A3 11
Vicker Gv DID/WITH M20 .... 143 D6
Vickerman St BOL BL1 .... 27 F3 50
Vickers Rw FWTH BL4 .... 65 F3 7
Vickers St BOLS/LL BL3 .... 46 B4 55
  NEWH/MOS M40 .... 107 F4
Victor Av BURY BL9 .... 33 F3
Victoria Av BKLY M9 .... 74 A6
  BNG/LEV M19 .... 145 E2
  BRAM/HZG SK7 .... 184 C4 8
  CHD/CHDH SK8 .... 181 D5
  DID/WITH M20 .... 163 E2
  ECC M30 .... 102 A4 2
  HALE/TIMP WA15 .... 158 C6
  MPL/ROM SK6 .... 169 D2
  SWIN M27 .... 86 B5 3
  WHTF M45 .... 71 E3
Victoria Av East BKLY M9 .... 92 A1
Victoria Bridge St CSLFD M3 .... 2 C1
Victoria Cl BRAM/HZG SK7 .... 196 B5 8
  EDGY/DAV SK3 .... 166 C6 7
Victoria Ct AULW OL7 .... 112 B6 8
  FWTH BL4 .... 66 A1 10
Victoria Crs ECC M30 .... 102 A5
Victoria Dr SALE M33 .... 160 B2
Victoria Gdns HYDE SK14 .... 132 A5
  ROY/SHW OL2 .... 61 F2 7
Victoria Gv BOL BL1 .... 27 D6
  HTNM SK4 .... 146 A6
  RUSH/FAL M14 .... 144 A4
Victoria La SWIN M27 .... 85 E5
  WHTF M45 .... 71 D4
Victoria Ldg BRO M7 .... 105 D2 18
Victoria Ms BURY BL9 .... 71 F1 3
Victoria Rd BOL BL1 .... 44 B2
  DUK SK16 .... 131 D3
  ECC M30 .... 101 F4
  FWTH BL4 .... 67 E5 2
  HALE/TIMP WA15 .... 174 C5

HALE/TIMP WA15 .... 175 E1
  IRL M44 .... 135 D2
  OLDTF/WHR M16 .... 142 B1
  RUSH/FAL M14 .... 143 F3
  SALE M33 .... 160 B2
  SLFD M6 .... 102 B3
  STKP SK1 .... 167 E1
  STRET M32 .... 140 B1
  URM M41 .... 137 F1
  WILM/AE SK9 .... 203 E5
  WYTH/NTH M22 .... 162 B5
Victoria Station Ap CSLFD M3 .... 2 D1
Victoria St ALT WA14 .... 174 B2
  AULW OL7 .... 112 B6
  CHAD OL9 .... 77 F4
  CSLFD M3 .... 2 D1
  DTN/ASHW M34 .... 131 E1
  DTN/ASHW M34 .... 130 A6 12
  DUK SK16 .... 131 E1
  FAIL M35 .... 109 E1
  FWTH BL4 .... 65 F1 7
  HEY OL10 .... 37 F6 8
  HYDE SK14 .... 132 A5
  LIT OL15 .... 12 C6
  MDTN M24 .... 75 E1 11
  OLDE OL4 .... 79 E5
  OLDE OL4 .... 80 C5
  OLDS OL8 .... 96 A5 8
  OP/CLY M11 .... 127 D1
  RAD M26 .... 51 E6 8
  RAMS BL0 .... 6 C5
  ROY/SHW OL2 .... 114 A5 8
  STLY SK15 .... 114 A5 8
  STLY SK15 .... 115 E3 8
  TOT/BURYW BL8 .... 17 F6
  TOT/BURYW BL8 .... 33 E5
  WHIT OL12 .... 9 D3 9
  WHIT OL12 .... 23 D4 24
Victoria St East AULW OL7 .... 112 B5 7
Victoria Ter WGTN/LGST M12 .... 126 A5
Victoria Wy BRAM/HZG SK7 .... 196 B5
Victor Mann St OP/CLY M11 .... 128 B2
Victor St CSLFD M3 .... 105 E3 22
  HEY OL10 .... 56 C1
  NEWH/MOS M40 .... 107 D3 8
  OLDS OL8 .... 94 C4
Victory Gv DTN/ASHW M34 .... 129 D2 8
Victory Rd BOLS/LL BL3 .... 49 E5
  IRL M44 .... 154 A1
Victory St BOL BL1 .... 46 A1 57
  RUSH/FAL M14 .... 125 D6
Vienna Rd EDGY/DAV SK3 .... 182 A5
Vienna Rd East EDGY/DAV SK3 .... 182 B1
Viewlands Dr WILM/AE SK9 .... 204 B1 8
View St BOLS/LL BL3 .... 46 B4
Vigo Av BOLS/LL BL3 .... 45 F4
Vigo St HEY OL10 .... 37 E6 10
  OLDE OL4 .... 80 B5 8
Viking Cl OP/CLY M11 .... 108 A6 10
Viking St BOLS/LL BL3 .... 47 E5
  ROCH OL11 .... 22 A5
Village Ct TRPK M17 .... 121 D3
Village St BRO M7 .... 105 D2 17
The Village URM M41 .... 137 D3
Village Wy WILM/AE SK9 .... 201 D3
Village Way (Ashburton Road East)
  TRPK M17 .... 120 C3
Villa Rd OLDS OL8 .... 96 A1
Villdale Av OFTN SK2 .... 168 A6
Villiers Dr OLDS OL8 .... 78 C6
Villiers St AUL OL6 .... 113 C5
  BURY BL9 .... 34 B4
  HYDE SK14 .... 151 D1 8
Vinca Gv BRO M7 .... 105 E1 15
Vincent Av CCHDY M21 .... 141 E2 2
  OLDE OL4 .... 80 A3
Vincent St BOL BL1 .... 46 B3 53
  BRO M7 .... 89 E6
  HYDE SK14 .... 151 D3 4
  MDTN M24 .... 75 E1 10
  MILN OL16 .... 40 B1 17
  OP/CLY M11 .... 127 D1
Vine Av SWIN M27 .... 86 C5
Vine Cl ROY/SHW OL2 .... 61 F2
  SALE M33 .... 138 A6
Vine Ct STRET M32 .... 140 B2
Vine Fold NEWH/MOS M40 .... 94 A4 1
Vine Gv OFTN SK2 .... 184 A1
Vine Pl ROCH OL11 .... 40 A2
Vinery Gv DTN/ASHW M34 .... 129 F3
Vine St BRAM/HZG SK7 .... 184 C4 8
  BRO M7 .... 88 C5
  CHAD OL9 .... 94 C2
  ECC M30 .... 101 D2
  OP/CLY M11 .... 127 F2
  RAMS BL0 .... 18 B1
Vineyard Cl WHIT OL12 .... 11 D4
Vineyard St OLDE OL4 .... 79 D1 14
Viola St OP/CLY M11 .... 109 E5
Violet Av FWTH BL4 .... 65 E2
Violet St GTN M18 .... 128 A3 7
  OFTN SK2 .... 183 E1
Violet Wy MDTN M24 .... 76 B4
Virginia Cha CHD/CHDH SK8 .... 195 D1
Virginia Cl NTHM/RTH M23 .... 160 B6

Virginia St BOLS/LL BL3 ..... 45 F5
ROCH OL11 ..... 39 F5
Viscount Dr CHD/CHDH SK8 ..... 194 B2
MANAIR M90 ..... 191 D2
Viscount Pk RUSH/FAL M14 ..... 125 D6
The Vista IRL M44 ..... 154 A1
Vivian St ROCH OL11 ..... 39 F2
Vixen CI CCHDY M21 ..... 142 C4
Voltaire Av SLFD M6 ..... 102 C4
Vorlich Dr CHAD OL9 ..... 77 D5
Vulcan St HYDE SK14 ..... 150 B1
OLD OL1 ..... 79 F2
Vyner Gv SALE M33 ..... 139 D5

W

Waddicor Av AUL OL6 ..... 113 F1
Waddington CI TOT/BURYW BL8 ..... 31 F5
Waddington Fold MILN OL16 ..... 41 D5
Waddington St BOL BL1 ..... 26 B6
Waddington St CHAD OL9 ..... 78 B3
Wadebridge Av NTHM/RTH M23 ..... 160 B6
Wadebridge Dr TOT/BURYW BL8 ..... 32 A5
Wadeford CI ANC M4 ..... 107 D4
ANC M4 ..... 107 D5
Wadeson Rd BRUN/LGST M13 ..... 124 C2
Wade St BOLS/LL BL3 ..... 47 D6
MDTN M24 ..... 76 B3
Wade Wk OP/CLY M11 ..... 126 B1
Wadham Gdns MPL/ROM SK6 ..... 150 A6
Wadham Wy HALE/TIMP WA15 ..... 175 D6
Wadlow CI SLFD M3 ..... 105 F4
Wadsley St BOL BL1 ..... 46 C1
Wadsworth CI WILM/AE SK9 ..... 194 C6
Wadsworth Ms DROY M43 ..... 110 A6
Waggoners CI SWIN M27 ..... 86 A6
Waggon Rd BOLE BL2 ..... 48 B1
MOSL OL5 ..... 99 D5
Wagner St BOL BL1 ..... 27 E4
Wagstaffe Dr FAIL M35 ..... 94 A6
Wagstaffe St MDTN M24 ..... 75 E2
Wagtail CI SLFD M6 ..... 83 E5
Waincliffe Av CCHDY M21 ..... 162 B1
Wain CI ECC M30 ..... 100 C5
Waingap Crs WHIT OL12 ..... 9 E3
Waingap Ri WHIT OL12 ..... 23 D1
Waingap Vw WHIT OL12 ..... 9 E4
Wainman St SLFD M6 ..... 104 C2
Wainwright Av DTN/ASHW M34 ..... 128 A6
Wainwright CI OFTN SK2 ..... 167 E5
OLDE OL4 ..... 81 E4
Wainwright Rd ALT WA14 ..... 173 F2
Wainwright St DUK SK16 ..... 113 E6
OLDS OL8 ..... 78 C6
Waithlands Rd MILN OL16 ..... 40 C1
Wakefield Dr OLD OL1 ..... 78 A2
SWIN M27 ..... 85 E1
Wakefield Rd STLY SK15 ..... 114 C5
Wakeling Rd DTN/ASHW M34 ..... 148 C3
Walcott CI BRUN/LGST M13 ..... 125 E4
Wald Av RUSH/FAL M14 ..... 144 C4
Waldeck St BOL BL1 ..... 46 A1
Walden Av OLDE OL4 ..... 80 B1
Walden Crs BRAM/HZG SK7 ..... 184 A6
Walderton Av NEWH/MOS M40 ..... 108 B5
Waldon CI BOLS/LL BL3 ..... 45 F4
Waldon Av CHD/CHDH SK8 ..... 180 B2
Wales St OLD OL1 ..... 80 A2
Walkdene Dr WALK M28 ..... 82 C2
Walkden Rd WALK M28 ..... 83 F6
Walker Av BOLS/LL BL3 ..... 47 D6
FAIL M35 ..... 110 C1
STLY SK15 ..... 115 D3
WHTF M45 ..... 71 E5
Walker CI FWTH BL4 ..... 67 E5
HYDE SK14 ..... 151 D1
Walker La HYDE SK14 ..... 150 C1
Walker Rd BKLY M9 ..... 91 F1
CHAD OL9 ..... 94 A3
ECC M30 ..... 100 B3
IRL M44 ..... 135 D2
Walkers Ct FWTH BL4 ..... 66 B3
Walker's Cft CSLFD M3 ..... 2 D1
Walker's La OLDE OL4 ..... 81 E5
Walker's Rd OLDS OL8 ..... 95 D3
Walker St BOL BL1 ..... 46 B3
BURY BL9 ..... 52 C1
DTN/ASHW M34 ..... 129 F5
HEY OL10 ..... 37 D6
MDTN M24 ..... 73 F4
MILN OL16 ..... 23 E6
OLDS OL8 ..... 78 B5
RAD M26 ..... 70 A2
STKP SK1 ..... 166 C4
Walkerwood Dr STLY SK15 ..... 115 E5
Walk Mill CI WHIT OL12 ..... 24 B1
The Walk MILN OL16 ..... 23 D6
The Walkway BOLS/LL BL3 ..... 45 D4
Wallace Av RUSH/FAL M14 ..... 125 E6
Wallace St OLDS OL8 ..... 96 A1
Wallbank Dr WHIT OL12 ..... 8 C4

Wallbank Rd BRAM/HZG SK7 ..... 183 E6
Wallbrook Crs LHULT M38 ..... 65 E5
Waller Av RUSH/FAL M14 ..... 144 A3
Walley St BOL BL1 ..... 27 F4
Wallingford Rd URM M41 ..... 119 F6
WILM/AE SK9 ..... 194 A4
Wallis St CHAD OL9 ..... 94 B1
NEWH/MOS M40 ..... 109 D2
Wallness La SLFD M6 ..... 105 D2
Wallshaw PI OLD OL1 ..... 79 E4
Wallshaw St OLD OL1 ..... 79 E4
Wall St OLDS OL8 ..... 79 D6
SLFD M6 ..... 104 A5
Wall Wy GTN M18 ..... 127 F5
Wallwork CI ROCH OL11 ..... 20 C4
Wallwork St OP/CLY M11 ..... 127 F1
RDSH SK5 ..... 147 D1
Wallworth Av GTN M18 ..... 127 E4
Wally Sq BRO M7 ..... 105 F1
Walmer Dr BRAM/HZG SK7 ..... 183 E6
Walmersley Rd BURY BL9 ..... 19 F4
NEWH/MOS M40 ..... 93 F3
Walmer St GTN M18 ..... 127 F3
RUSH/FAL M14 ..... 124 C6
Walmer St East RUSH/FAL M14 ..... 125 D6
Walmley Gv BOLS/LL BL3 ..... 46 A6
Walmsley Av LIT OL15 ..... 25 D2
Walmsley Gv URM M41 ..... 138 B1
Walmsley St RDSH SK5 ..... 167 D2
STLY SK15 ..... 132 B1
TOT/BURYW BL8 ..... 32 C3
Walney Rd WYTH/NTH M22 ..... 178 B3
Walnut Av BURY BL9 ..... 38 C4
OLDE OL4 ..... 80 B3
Walnut Gv ECC M30 ..... 100 B3
PART M31 ..... 154 B2
Walnut St BOL BL1 ..... 28 A4
GTN M18 ..... 127 E3
Walnut Tree Rd EDGY/DAV SK3 ..... 165 E6
Walnut Wk STRET M32 ..... 140 A3
Walpole St MILN OL16 ..... 23 E6
Walsall St SLFD M6 ..... 104 B2
Walsden St OP/CLY M11 ..... 109 D5
Walsh Av BKLY M9 ..... 91 E3
Walshaw Brook CI TOT/BURYW BL8 ..... 32 A3
Walshaw Dr SWIN M27 ..... 86 A6
Walshaw La TOT/BURYW BL8 ..... 32 A3
Walshaw Rd TOT/BURYW BL8 ..... 33 E4
Walshe St BURY BL9 ..... 53 E5
Walsh St SHD OL8 ..... 77 F5
Walsingham Av DID/WITH M20 ..... 163 D3
MDTN M24 ..... 75 E6
Walter Scott St OLD OL1 ..... 79 F3
Walters Dr OLDS OL8 ..... 96 B2
Walter St BKLY M9 ..... 91 E5
GTN M18 ..... 127 F3
OLDTF/WHR M16 ..... 123 D5
PWCH M25 ..... 88 A1
WALK M28 ..... 83 E7
Waltham Av CHD/CHDH SK8 ..... 195 F5
Waltham Rd OLDTF/WHR M16 ..... 142 C1
Waltham St OLDS OL8 ..... 97 D1
Walton CI MDTN M24 ..... 74 A2
Walton Ct BOLS/LL BL3 ..... 47 D5
Walton Dr BURY BL9 ..... 19 F5
MPL/ROM SK6 ..... 170 B6
Walton Hall Dr RDSH SK5 ..... 146 B2
Walton PI FWTH BL4 ..... 66 C4
Walton Rd ALT WA14 ..... 173 F2
BKLY M9 ..... 74 B6
SALE M33 ..... 159 D4
Walton St AULW OL7 ..... 112 A2
HEY OL10 ..... 56 B1
MDTN M24 ..... 75 E1
STKP SK1 ..... 167 D6
Walwyn CI STRET M32 ..... 140 C1
Wandsworth Av OP/CLY M11 ..... 109 E5
Wansbeck CI STRET M32 ..... 140 C2
Wansford St RUSH/FAL M14 ..... 124 B6
Wanstead Av BKLY M9 ..... 92 B2
Wapping St BOL BL1 ..... 27 E5
Warbeck CI RDSH SK5 ..... 147 E1
Warbeck Rd NEWH/MOS M40 ..... 93 E3
Warbreck Gv SALE M33 ..... 160 B2
Warburton CI HALE/TIMP WA15 ..... 190 B2
MPL/ROM SK6 ..... 169 E4
Warburton La HALE/TIMP WA15 ..... 190 B2
Warburton La LYMM WA13 ..... 154 B5
PART M31 ..... 155 D2
Warburton Rd WILM/AE SK9 ..... 194 B5
Warburton St BOL BL1 ..... 28 A5
DID/WITH M20 ..... 163 F2
ECC M30 ..... 101 D2
SALQ/ORD M5 ..... 122 C3
Warcock Rd OLDE OL4 ..... 80 A4
Wardend CI LHULT M38 ..... 65 E5
Warden St NEWH/MOS M40 ..... 108 C1
Warde St HULME M15 ..... 123 F3
Wardle Brook Av HYDE SK14 ..... 133 E6
Wardle CI RAD M26 ..... 50 C4

STRET M32 ..... 140 C1
Wardle Edge WHIT OL12 ..... 23 F2
Wardle Fold WHIT OL12 ..... 11 D4
Wardle Gdns WHIT OL12 ..... 24 A2
Wardle Rd SALE M33 ..... 159 F2
WHIT OL12 ..... 11 D6
Wardle St BOLE BL2 ..... 47 E5
LIT OL15 ..... 12 B5
NEWH/MOS M40 ..... 107 F4
OLDE OL4 ..... 79 F5
Wardley Av CCHDY M21 ..... 142 C3
WALK M28 ..... 82 C3
Wardley Hall La WALK M28 ..... 84 B5
Wardley Hall Rd WALK M28 ..... 84 C4
Wardley St SWIN M27 ..... 86 A5
Wardlow Av BOLS/LL BL3 ..... 45 F5
Ward Rd DROY M43 ..... 110 C6
Ward St BKLY M9 ..... 91 D3
CHAD OL9 ..... 78 A4
FAIL M35 ..... 93 F5
HYDE SK14 ..... 150 C1
MPL/ROM SK6 ..... 169 D2
NEWH/MOS M40 ..... 92 A5
OLD OL1 ..... 78 B3
STKP SK1 ..... 167 E6
Wareham Gv ECC M30 ..... 101 D4
Wareham St CHH M8 ..... 90 C4
Wareings Yd ROCH OL11 ..... 40 B3
Warford St ANC M4 ..... 106 C3
Warham St WILM/AE SK9 ..... 203 F4
Warley CI CHD/CHDH SK8 ..... 180 C1
Warley Gv DUK SK16 ..... 131 D1
Warley Rd OLDTF/WHR M16 ..... 122 B6
Warley St LIT OL15 ..... 12 C6
Warlingham CI TOT/BURYW BL8 ..... 32 C6
Warmington Dr WGTN/LGST M12 ..... 125 F3
Warmley Rd NTHM/RTH M23 ..... 160 B2
Warne Av DROY M43 ..... 111 D5
Warnford CI NEWH/MOS M40 ..... 109 E3
War Office Rd ROCH OL11 ..... 37 F1
Warren Av CHD/CHDH SK8 ..... 180 B2
Warren Bank BKLY M9 ..... 91 E2
Warren Bruce Rd TRPK M17 ..... 121 E3
Warren CI BRAM/HZG SK7 ..... 182 B5
DTN/ASHW M34 ..... 148 B1
POY/DIS SK12 ..... 197 F5
Warren Dr BCUP OL13 ..... 5 D1
HALE/TIMP WA15 ..... 190 B2
SWIN M27 ..... 101 E2
Warrener St SALE M33 ..... 160 B2
Warren Hey WILM/AE SK9 ..... 204 C5
Warren La OLDS OL8 ..... 96 C1
Warren Lea MPL/ROM SK6 ..... 171 F5
POY/DIS SK12 ..... 198 C4
Warren Rd CHD/CHDH SK8 ..... 181 F5
EDGY/DAV SK3 ..... 182 C1
TRPK M17 ..... 120 C3
WALK M28 ..... 83 F2
Warren St BKLY M9 ..... 91 D3
BRO M7 ..... 90 A5
STKP SK1 ..... 167 D3
TOT/BURYW BL8 ..... 32 C6
Warre St AUL OL6 ..... 112 C4
Warrington Rd BKLY M9 ..... 91 D1
Warrington St AUL OL6 ..... 112 C5
OLDE OL4 ..... 80 C6
STLY SK15 ..... 114 C6
Warslow Dr SALE M33 ..... 160 C4
Warsop Av WYTH/NTH M22 ..... 178 C2
Warth Fold Rd RAD M26 ..... 52 A3
Warth Rd BURY BL9 ..... 52 A2
Warton CI BRAM/HZG SK7 ..... 197 E2
TOT/BURYW BL8 ..... 32 A6
Warton Dr NTHM/RTH M23 ..... 177 D2
Warwick Av DID/WITH M20 ..... 163 D1
DTN/ASHW M34 ..... 149 D2
SWIN M27 ..... 85 E3
WHTF M45 ..... 71 F4
Warwick CI CHD/CHDH SK8 ..... 181 E3
DUK SK16 ..... 131 D3
HTNM SK4 ..... 166 A2
MDTN M24 ..... 75 E6
ROY/SHW OL2 ..... 61 D2
TOT/BURYW BL8 ..... 18 B4
TOT/BURYW BL8 ..... 32 C3
WHTF M45 ..... 71 E4
Warwick Ct OLDTF/WHR M16 ..... 122 B6
Warwick Dr BRAM/HZG SK7 ..... 198 B1
HALE/TIMP WA15 ..... 174 C6
SALE M33 ..... 160 B1
URM M41 ..... 118 C5
Warwick Gv DTN/ASHW M34 ..... 129 D1
Warwick Rd AUL OL6 ..... 113 D2
CCHDY M21 ..... 141 F2
FAIL M35 ..... 110 A2
HALE/TIMP WA15 ..... 174 C6
HTNM SK4 ..... 166 A2
IRL M44 ..... 134 B6
MDTN M24 ..... 75 F6
MPL/ROM SK6 ..... 169 E3
OLDTF/WHR M16 ..... 122 B5
RAD M26 ..... 51 D3
STRET M32 ..... 122 B5
WALK M28 ..... 83 D4

Warwick Rd South
 OLDTF/WHR M16 .... **122** B6
Warwick St ANC M4 .... **3** C2
 BOL BL1 .... **27** F3
 CHAD OL9 .... **95** D1 ⊡
 HULME M15 .... **123** F3
 PWCH M25 .... **88** A1 ⊡
 SWIN M27 .... **86** A4
 WHIT OL12 .... **23** F3
Wasdale Av BOLE BL2 .... **30** A6
 URM M41 .... **118** C6
Wasdale Dr CHD/CHDH SK8 ... **179** F4 ⊡
 MDTN M24 .... **74** C1
Wasdale St ROCH OL11 .... **39** D6
Wasdale Ter STLY SK15 .... **114** B3
Wash Brook CHAD OL9 .... **94** C1
Washbrook Av WALK M28 .... **82** C4
Washbrook Dr STRET M32 .... **139** F2
Wash Ford TOT/BURYW BL8 ...... **32** C3
Washford Dr NTHM/RTH M23 ... **160** B5
Washington Ct BURY BL9 .... **34** A4 ⊡
Washington St BOLS/LL BL3 ... **46** A3 ⊡
 CHAD OL9 .... **78** A4 ⊡
Wash La BURY BL9 .... **34** B5
Washway Rd ALT WA14 .... **158** C4 ⊡
Washwood Cl LHULT M38 .... **65** F3 ⊡
Wasp Av ROCH OL11 .... **40** B4
Wastdale Av BURY BL9 .... **53** E6 ⊡
Wastdale Rd NTHM/RTH M23 .... **177** D3
Wastwater St OL1 .... **79** E2
Watchgate Cl MDTN M24 .... **56** B6 ⊡
Waterbridge WALK M28 .... **100** B2
Watercroft ROCH OL11 .... **20** B4 ⊡
Waterdale Dr WHTF M45 .... **71** E3
Waterfield Wy FAIL M35 .... **110** B1
Waterfold La BURY BL9 .... **35** D6
Waterford Av DID/WITH M20 .... **162** B2
 MPL/ROM SK6 .... **170** C3
Waterfront Quay SALQ/ORD M5 **122** A2
Watergate DTN/ASHW M34 ..... **129** E1 ⊡
Watergate La WHTN BL5 .... **64** A4
Watergate La WHTN BL5 .... **64** A3
Water Grove Rd DUK SK16 ...... **132** A2
Waterhouse Cl WHIT OL12 .... **11** D6
Waterhouse Rd GTN M18 .... **127** F5
Waterhouse St WHIT OL12 .... **23** D5 ⊡⊡
Water La DROY M43 .... **109** F6
 FWTH BL4 .... **66** C4 ⊡⊡
 MILN OL16 .... **42** B2
 RAMS BL0 .... **7** E1
 WILM/AE SK9 .... **203** E4
Water Lane RAD M26 .... **51** D6 ⊡⊡
Waterloo Ct BURY BL9 .... **52** C1 ⊡
 BKLY M9. .... **91** D4
 BRAM/HZG SK7 .... **183** D6
 CHH M8 .... **105** F3 ⊡⊡
 MPL/ROM SK6 .... **170** C3
 STKP SK1 .... **167** D4
 STLY SK15 .... **114** B5
Waterloo Rd AUL OL6 .... **113** E3
 BOL BL1 .... **28** A6
 CHH M8 .... **91** D5
 CMANE M1 .... **3** E5 ⊡
 OLD OL1 .... **79** D4
 OLDE OL4 .... **79** E6
Waterman Vw MILN OL16 ...... **24** A5 ⊡
Watermead Cl EDGY/DAV SK3 . **182** C3
Watermeetings La MPL/ROM SK6 . **170** C3
Watermill Cl MILN OL16 .... **41** E1 ⊡
Watermill Ct AULW OL7 .... **112** B2 ⊡
Watermillock Gdns BOL BL1 ... **28** B1 ⊡
Waterpark Rd BRO M7 .... **89** F5
Water's Edge FWTH BL4 .... **65** E1
 MPL/ROM SK6 .... **171** E5
Watersedge Cl CHD/CHDH SK8 **181** F4 ⊡
Watersfield Cl CHD/CHDH SK8 **195** D1 ⊡
Watersheddings Wy OLDE OL4 ... **80** B2
Waterside HYDE SK14 .... **152** B1
 MPL/ROM SK6 .... **187** D2
 TRPK M17 .... **137** D2
Waterside Av MPL/ROM SK6 ... **187** D2 ⊡
Waterside Cl CCHDY M21 ...... **162** B1 ⊡
 HYDE SK14 .... **152** B1 ⊡
 RAD M26 .... **52** B5
Waterside La MILN OL16 .... **23** F5 ⊡
Waterside Rd BURY BL9 .... **19** D3
Waterslea ECC M30 .... **101** D5
Waterslea Dr BOL BL1 .... **45** D2
Watersmead Cl BOL BL1 .... **28** A5 ⊡⊡
Watersmead St BOL BL1 ...... **28** A5 ⊡⊡
Watersmeet STRET M32 .... **121** D5
Waters Meeting Rd BOL BL1 ..... **28** A6
Waterson Av NEWH/MOS M40 . **92** B6
Waters Reach POY/DIS SK12 ... **199** D4
 TRPK M17 .... **122** A3
Water Sreet RAD M26 .... **51** E6
Water St AUL OL6 .... **112** C4
 BKLY M9. .... **91** E5
 BOL BL1 .... **47** D2
 CSLFD M3 .... **123** F1
 DTN/ASHW M34 .... **129** F2
 HYDE SK14 .... **131** E6
 MDTN M24 .... **75** D3

Welbeck Rd BOL BL1 .... **45** E1
 ECC M30 .... **101** F3
 HYDE SK14 .... **151** D1
 MILN OL16 .... **40** C3
 RDSH SK5 .... **147** D3 ⊡
 WALK M28 .... **100** C1
Welbeck St GTN M18 .... **127** E3
Welbeck St South AUL OL6 ..... **112** B5
 AULW OL7 .... **112** B5
Welburn Av WYTH/NTH M22 ... **178** C4
Welburn St ROCH OL11 .... **40** A2 ⊡
Welbury Rd NTHM/RTH M23 .... **161** D4
Welby St BRUN/LGST M13 .... **125** E5
Welch Rd HYDE SK14 .... **132** A5
Welcomb Cl MPL/ROM SK6 ... **169** D1 ⊡
Welcomb St OP/CLY M11 .... **126** C2
Welcome Pde OLDS OL8 .... **97** D2
Welcroft St STKP SK1 .... **167** D5
Weldon Crs EDGY/DAV SK3 ... **182** C3
Weldon Dr BKLY M9 .... **74** B6
Weldon Rd ALT WA14 .... **174** A1
Weld Rd DID/WITH M20 .... **144** B4 ⊡
Welford Cl WILM/AE SK9 ...... **204** C3 ⊡⊡
Welford Gn RDSH SK5 .... **147** D6 ⊡
Welford Rd CHH M8 .... **90** A1
Welford St SLFD M6 .... **104** C3
Welkin Rd MPL/ROM SK6 .... **168** A2
Wellacre Av URM M41 .... **136** B1 ⊡
Welland Av HEY OL10 .... **36** A4
Welland Cl HULME M15 .... **123** E3 ⊡
Welland Rd ROY/SHW OL2 .... **61** E1
 WILM/AE SK9 .... **204** B1
Welland St OP/CLY M11 .... **127** E1
 RDSH SK5 .... **147** D2
Wellbank STLY SK15 .... **133** D1
Wellbank Av AUL OL6 .... **113** F1
Wellbank Cl OLDS OL8 .... **96** B1 ⊡
Wellbank St TOT/BURYW BL8 ... **32** A1
Wellbank Vw WHIT OL12 .... **21** D3
Wellbrow Ter WHIT OL12 .... **22** B4
Wellens Wy MDTN M24 .... **74** A1 ⊡
Weller Av CCHDY M21 .... **142** B4
Wellesbourne Dr
 NTHM/RTH M23 .... **161** D6 ⊡
Wellesley Av GTN M18 .... **127** E3 ⊡⊡
Wellfield Cl BURY BL9 .... **52** C3
Wellfield La HALE/TIMP WA15 . **176** A3
Wellfield Pl ROCH OL11 ...... **40** B2 ⊡⊡
Wellfield Rd BOLS/LL BL3 .... **46** A4
 CHH M8 .... **90** B5 ⊡⊡
 NTHM/RTH M23 .... **161** E6
 OFTN SK2 .... **184** A1
Wellfield St ROCH OL11 .... **40** B2
Wellgate Av BNG/LEV M19 .... **145** F3 ⊡⊡
Wellgreen Cl HALE/TIMP WA15 . **176** A4
Well Gv WHTF M45 .... **52** C5
Wellhead Cl HULME M15 ...... **124** A4 ⊡
Wellhouse Dr BKLY M9 .... **92** C2
Welling Rd NEWH/MOS M40 ..... **93** F5
Welling St BOLE BL2 .... **28** C6 ⊡⊡
Wellington Av OLDTF/WHR M16 . **142** B1 ⊡
Wellington Cl SALE M33 .... **140** A5
Wellington Clough ALUW OL7 .. **112** A1 ⊡
Wellington Crs OLDTF/WHR M16 . **123** D6
Wellington Gv HULME M15 .... **123** E3 ⊡⊡
 OFTN SK2 .... **167** D6
Wellington Ms EDGW/EG BL7 ... **15** E1
Wellington Pl ALT WA14 .... **174** B4
 MILN OL16 .... **23** E5 ⊡⊡
Wellington Rd AUL OL6 .... **112** A4
 BRAM/HZG SK7 .... **199** F1
 BURY BL9 .... **34** A6
 CHH M8 .... **90** C5 ⊡
 DID/WITH M20 .... **144** A4 ⊡
 ECC M30 .... **101** F5
 EDGW/EG BL7 .... **15** E1
 OLDS OL8 .... **78** B6
 OLDTF/WHR M16 .... **142** C1
 RUSH/FAL M14 .... **144** A4
 SWIN M27 .... **86** A5
Wellington Rd North HTNM SK4 . **145** F4
Wellington Rd South HTNM SK4 . **166** C4
 OFTN SK2 .... **167** D6
Wellington St AUL OL6 .... **112** C5
 BOLS/LL BL3 .... **46** B3
 BRAM/HZG SK7 .... **185** D4 ⊡
 CHAD OL9 .... **77** F3
 CSLFD M3 .... **105** E5
 DTN/ASHW M34 .... **130** A3
 FAIL M35 .... **94** B4 ⊡
 FWTH BL4 .... **66** B3
 GTN M18 .... **127** E4
 HYDE SK14 .... **131** D6
 LIT OL15 .... **12** C6
 MILN OL16 .... **42** B1
 OLDE OL4 .... **79** D5
 RAD M26 .... **52** A5 ⊡
 STKP SK1 .... **167** D4
 STRET M32 .... **140** A2
 TOT/BURYW BL8. .... **33** D6
 WHIT OL12 .... **23** D4 ⊡⊡
 WHIT OL12 .... **23** D4 ⊡⊡
Wellington St East BRO M7 .... **89** E6
Wellington St West BRO M7 ... **105** E1
Wellington Ter SALQ/ORD M5 ... **103** E5 ⊡⊡

 MILN OL16 .... **23** D6 ⊡⊡
 ROY/SHW OL2 .... **61** E5
 STKP SK1 .... **167** E2
 STLY SK15 .... **114** B5 ⊡
 WHIT OL12 .... **9** D3 ⊡
Waterton Av MOSL OL5 .... **98** C3
Waterton La MOSL OL5 .... **98** C3
Waterview Cl MILN OL16 .... **42** C4 ⊡
Waterworks Rd OLDE OL4 .... **80** C2
Watford Av RUSH/FAL M14 .... **143** F1 ⊡⊡
Watkin Cl BRUN/LGST M13 ..... **124** C3
Watkins Dr PWCH M25 .... **89** F2
Watkin St CSLFD M3 .... **105** E4 ⊡⊡
 HYDE SK14 .... **132** B4
 MILN OL16 .... **40** C3
Watling St TOT/BURYW BL8 ..... **16** A3
 TOT/BURYW BL8. .... **32** A6
 TOT/BURYW BL8. .... **51** D1
Watlington Cl OL1 .... **62** B6
Watson Rd FWTH BL4 .... **65** D3
Watson Sq STKP SK1 .... **167** D4 ⊡⊡
Watson St CMANW M2 .... **2** C6
 DTN/ASHW M34 .... **130** C6
 ECC M30 .... **101** D5
 OLDE OL4 .... **80** A3 ⊡
 RAD M26 .... **51** E5
 SWIN M27 .... **86** A4
Watts St BNG/LEV M19 .... **145** F3
 CHAD OL9 .... **77** F4
 OLDS OL8 .... **95** E3
 WHIT OL12 .... **23** E5
Waugh Av FAIL M35 .... **110** A1
Wavell Dr BURY BL9 .... **71** E2
Wavell Rd WYTH/NTH M22 ..... **178** B5
Waveney Dr ALT WA14 .... **174** A1
 WILM/AE SK9 .... **204** B1
Waveney Rd ROY/SHW OL2 ...... **61** E1
 WYTH/NTH M22 .... **178** C3
Waverley Av FWTH BL4 .... **67** D5
 STRET M32 .... **122** A6 ⊡
Waverley Crs DROY M43 .... **110** B4
Waverley Dr CHD/CHDH SK8 .. **195** F3
Waverley Rd BKLY M9 .... **92** A6
 BOL BL1 .... **27** F4
 EDGY/DAV SK3 .... **166** A6
 HYDE SK14 .... **150** B3
 MDTN M24 .... **57** E6
 SALE M33 .... **140** A5
 SWIN M27 .... **87** D5
 WALK M28 .... **82** C4
Waverley Rd West
 NEWH/MOS M40 .... **108** A1
Waverley St OLD OL1 .... **79** F3
 ROCH OL11 .... **39** D6
Waverton Av HTNM SK4 .... **146** B4
Waverton Rd RUSH/FAL M14 .. **143** F3
Wavertree Rd BKLY M9 .... **91** D1
Wayfarers Wy SWIN M27 .... **85** F6
Wayland Rd GTN M18 .... **127** E6
Wayland Rd South RDSH SK5 .. **127** E5
Wayne Cl DROY M43 .... **111** D3 ⊡
Wayne St OP/CLY M11 .... **127** F1 ⊡
Wayside Dr POY/DIS SK12 ...... **198** A5
Wayside Gdns BRAM/HZG SK7 . **185** E5 ⊡
Wayside Gv WALK M28 .... **83** F1 ⊡
Weald Cl BRUN/LGST M13 .... **125** D3 ⊡⊡
Weardale Rd BKLY M9 .... **73** F6
Weaste Av LHULT M38 .... **65** F2
Weaste Dr SLFD M6 .... **103** E4
Weaste La SALQ/ORD M5 ...... **105** E6 ⊡
 SLFD M6. .... **103** E4
Weaste Rd SALQ/ORD M5 ...... **103** E6
Weatherall St North BRO M7 .... **90** A6
Weatherley Cl OLDS OL8 .... **96** A4 ⊡
Weatherley Dr MPL/ROM SK6. **186** B1
Weaver Av WALK M28. .... **82** B3
Weaver Cl ALT WA14 .... **174** A6 ⊡
Weaver Ct BOLS/LL BL3 .... **46** C4 ⊡⊡
 MDTN M24 .... **75** D2 ⊡
Weavers Gn FWTH BL4 .... **66** B4
Weavers La BRAM/HZG SK7 ... **196** B5
Weavers Rd MDTN M24 .... **75** D2
Webb Gv HYDE SK14 .... **152** C2
Webb La STKP SK1 .... **167** E5
Webb St TOT/BURYW BL8 .... **33** E4
Webdale Dr NEWH/MOS M40 .... **92** B6 ⊡
Weber Dr BOLS/LL BL3 .... **46** B4 ⊡⊡
Webster Gv PWCH M25 .... **88** A5
Webster St BOLS/LL BL3 .... **47** F4 ⊡
 MOSL OL5 .... **99** D3 ⊡
 OLDS OL8 .... **79** E6
Wedgewood St
 NEWH/MOS M40 .... **108** A3 ⊡
Wedgwood Rd SWIN M27 .... **86** C3
Wedhurst St OLDE OL4 .... **80** A4 ⊡⊡
Weedall Av SALQ/ORD M5 ...... **122** B3
Weedon St MILN OL16 .... **23** F5 ⊡
Weeton Av BOLE BL2 .... **49** D2 ⊡
Weir Rd MDTN M24 .... **24** C6
Weir St FAIL M35 .... **93** F6
Welbeck Av CHAD OL9 .... **93** E2
 LIT OL15 .... **12** B5
 URM M41 .... **119** F6
Welbeck Cl WHTF M45 .... **71** D1
Welbeck Gv BRO M7 .... **89** F6

Well I' Th' La *ROCH* OL11 .... 40 B2
Well La *WHTF* M45 .... 71 D1
Well Md *MPL/ROM* SK6 .... 168 C2
Wellmead Cl *CHH* M8 .... 106 A2
Well Meadow *HYDE* SK14 .... 131 E5
Wellock St *NEWH/MOS* M40 .... 108 A1
Well Rw *HYDE* SK14 .... 153 E5
Wells Av *CHAD* OL9 .... 73 F2
  PWCH M25 .... 89 D3
Wells Cl *CHD/CHDH* SK8 .... 44 A4
  MDTN M24 .... 74 A4
  OP/CLY M11 .... 128 C3 *2*
Wells Ct *DUK* SK16 .... 131 D3
Wells Dr *DUK* SK16 .... 131 D3
  HTNM SK4 .... 164 C3 *2*
Wells Rd *OLD* OL1 .... 62 C4
Wells St *BOLS* BL9 .... 33 E6
Wellstock La *LHULT* M38 .... 65 D5
Well St *ANC* M4 .... 3 E2
  BOL BL1 .... 47 E2
  BOLE BL2 .... 31 D6
  HEY OL10 .... 37 F6
  ROCH OL11 .... 40 B2
Well St West *RAMS* BL0 .... 6 C6 *1*
Wellwood Dr *NEWH/MOS* M40 .... 92 B6 *1*
Wellyhole St *OLD* OL4 .... 80 B5
Welney Rd *OLDTF/WHR* M16 .... 122 C6
Welshpool Cl *NTHM/RTH* M23 .... 161 F5 *1*
Welton Av *DID/WITH* M20 .... 164 A5
Welton Cl *WILM/AE* SK9 .... 209 D1
Welton Dr *WILM/AE* SK9 .... 208 C1
Welton Gv *WILM/AE* SK9 .... 208 C1
Welwyn Cl *URM* M41 .... 119 D4
Welwyn Dr *SLFD* M6 .... 102 B2
Wembley Gv *RUSH/FAL* M14 .... 144 A3
Wembley Rd *GTN* M18 .... 127 D5
Wembury St *BKLY* M9 .... 91 F5 *16*
Wembury St North *BKLY* M9 .... 91 F5 *17*
Wemsley Gv *BOLE* BL2 .... 28 C6 *20*
Wem St *CHAD* OL9 .... 94 B1
Wemyss Av *RDSH* SK5 .... 147 D2 *2*
Wendlebury Cl *ROY/SHW* OL2 .... 61 E4
Wendon Rd *NTHM/RTH* M23 .... 177 F2
Wendover Dr *BOLS/LL* BL3 .... 44 C4
Wendover Rd *NTHM/RTH* M23 .... 160 A6
  URM M41 .... 138 A1
Wenfield Dr *BKLY* M9 .... 92 B2
Wenlock Av *UNS* OL2 .... 112 C2
Wenlock Cl *OFTN* SK2 .... 185 E1
Wenlock Rd *SALE* M33 .... 159 E3
Wenlock St *SWIN* M27 .... 85 E5
Wenlock Wy *WGTN/LGST* M12.......... 126 B3
Wenning St *WHTF* M45 .... 72 A2
Wensleydale Av *CHD/CHDH* SK8 .... 180 A1 *2*
Wensleydale Cl *BURY* BL9 .... 53 E6 *3*
  NTHM/RTH M23 .... 177 D4 *3*
  ROY/SHW OL2 .... 60 A4
Wensley Dr *BRAM/HZG* SK7 .... 198 B2
  DID/WITH M20 .... 143 F6
Wensley Rd *BRO* M7 .... 88 B2
  CHD/CHDH SK8 .... 180 A1
  RDSH SK5 .... 167 D1
Wensley Wy *MILN* OL16 .... 40 C1
Wentbridge Rd *BOL* BL1 .... 46 B1
Wentworth Av *FWTH* BL4 .... 66 A4
  GTN M18 .... 127 F4 *8*
  HALE/TIMP WA15 .... 175 E1
  HEY OL10 .... 56 B1
  IRL M44 .... 116 B6 *8*
  SLFD M6 .... 103 D4
  TOT/BURYW BL8 .... 32 C5 *14*
  WHTF M45 .... 70 B4
Wentworth Cl *MDTN* M24 .... 73 E3 *3*
  MPL/ROM SK6 .... 171 D5 *2*
  RAD M26 .... 50 B5 *3*
Wentworth Dr *BRAM/HZG* SK7 .... 197 E2
  SALE M33 .... 139 D6
Wentworth Rd *ECC* M30 .... 102 A3
  RDSH SK5 .... 147 D2 *3*
  SWIN M27 .... 101 E1 *10*
Wenworth Av *URM* M41 .... 137 F2
Werneth Av *HYDE* SK14 .... 151 D3
  RUSH/FAL M14 .... 143 F1 *13*
Werneth Cl *OFTN* SK2 .... 185 E1
  DTN/ASHW M34 .... 149 D1
Werneth Crs *OLDS* OL8 .... 95 D1
Werneth Hall Rd *OLDS* OL8 .... 78 B6
Werneth Hollow *MPL/ROM* SK6 .... 149 F5
Werneth Low Rd *MPL/ROM* SK6 .... 170 B1
Werneth Ri *HYDE* SK14 .... 151 D1
Werneth Rd *HYDE* SK14 .... 151 D1
  MPL/ROM SK6 .... 150 A6
Werneth St *DTN/ASHW* M34 .... 130 A4 *1*
  STKP SK1 .... 167 F3 *3*
Wesley Cl *WHIT* OL12 .... 23 F3
Wesley Dr *AUL* OL6 .... 113 E1
  WALK M28 .... 81 F5
Wesley Sq *URM* M41 .... 137 E1 *3*
Wesley St *BOLS/LL* BL3 .... 46 C4 *22*
  BRAM/HZG SK7 .... 184 C4 *7*
  ECC M30 .... 101 D5 *3*
  EDGW/EG BL7 .... 14 B5 *4*
  FAIL M35 .... 94 B4 *5*
  FWTH BL4 .... 66 C4 *13*
  HEY OL10 .... 37 D5

MILN OL16 .... 41 F1 *8*
OP/CLY M11 .... 126 B1 *15*
ROY/SHW OL2 .... 60 C6
STKP SK1 .... 167 D4 *27*
STRET M32 .... 121 F5
SWIN M27 .... 86 A5
TOT/BURYW BL8 .... 17 F6
WHIT OL12 .... 23 F2 *2*
Wessenden Bank East
  OFTN SK2 .... 184 B2 *8*
Wessenden Bank West *OFTN* SK2 .... 184 B2
Wessex Park Cl *ROY/SHW* OL2 .... 61 F1 *11*
Westage Gdns *NTHM/RTH* M23 .... 161 E6
West Ashton St *SALQ/ORD* M5 .... 122 A4
West Av *ALT* WA14 .... 173 E2
  BNG/LEV M19 .... 145 D4 *3*
  CHD/CHDH SK8 .... 180 A6
  FWTH BL4 .... 65 F3
  GTN M18 .... 127 F4 *10*
  NEWH/MOS M40 .... 93 E4
  STLY SK15 .... 114 B5
  WALK M28 .... 83 D2
  WHTF M45 .... 70 C1
West Bank *OP/CLY* M11 .... 128 B3
  WILM/AE SK9 .... 209 E5 *8*
Westbank Rd *DID/WITH* M20 .... 144 B6
  HOR/BR BL6 .... 44 B5
West Bank Rd *SALQ/ORD* M5 .... 123 D1
Westbourne Av *BOLS/LL* BL3 .... 47 E6
  FWTH BL4 .... 68 B6
  WHTF M45 .... 70 B2 *1*
Westbourne Gv *BKLY* M9 .... 91 E5 *3*
  RDSH SK5 .... 147 D3 *7*
  SALE M33 .... 159 E1 *3*
Westbourne Pk *URM* M41 .... 119 E6
Westbourne Range *GTN* M18 .... 128 A6
Westbourne Rd *DTN/ASHW* M34 .... 148 C1
  ECC M30 .... 100 C3
  RUSH/FAL M14 .... 144 B3
  URM M41 .... 138 B1
Westbourne St *CHAD* OL9 .... 78 B4
Westbrook Cl *BOLE* BL2 .... 47 E3 *8*
Westbrook Rd *SWIN* M27 .... 85 F6
  TRPK M17 .... 121 D2
Westbrook Sq
  WGTN/LGST M12 .... 126 B3 *14*
Westbrook St *BOLE* BL2 .... 47 E3 *8*
Westbury Av *SALE* M33 .... 158 A4
Westbury Cl *TOT/BURYW* BL8 .... 32 B6
Westbury Dr *MPL/ROM* SK6 .... 186 C1
Westbury Rd *CHH* M8 .... 90 B4
Westbury St *AUL* OL6 .... 113 C4
  HYDE SK14 .... 131 D4
Westbury Wy *ROY/SHW* OL2 .... 78 B1
Westby Cl *BRAM/HZG* SK7 .... 197 E2
West Canteen Rd *TRPK* M17 .... 121 F1
West Central Dr *SWIN* M27 .... 86 C6 *3*
West Charles St *SALQ/ORD* M5 .... 104 C6 *3*
West Church St *HEY* OL10 .... 37 D5 *23*
Westcliffe Rd *BOL* BL1 .... 28 A1 *2*
Westcombe Dr *TOT/BURYW* BL8 .... 33 D3
Westcott Av *DID/WITH* M20 .... 143 E5
Westcott Cl *BOLE* BL2 .... 29 F2
Westcott Gv *ROY/SHW* OL2 .... 61 E4 *3*
Westcourt Rd *BOLS/LL* BL3 .... 46 B6
  SALE M33 .... 139 D6 *3*
Westcraig Av *NEWH/MOS* M40 .... 93 D2
West Craven St *SALQ/ORD* M5 .... 122 C2
Westcroft Rd *DID/WITH* M20 .... 164 B1
West Crown Av *SALQ/ORD* M5 .... 122 C1 *17*
Westdale Gdns *BNG/LEV* M19 .... 145 E6
Westdean Crs *BNG/LEV* M19 .... 145 D6
West Dean St *SALQ/ORD* M5 .... 105 D6 *12*
West Downs Rd *CHD/CHDH* SK8 .... 181 D4
West Dr *BURY* BL9 .... 33 F3
  CHD/CHDH SK8 .... 179 E3
  DROY M43 .... 110 A6
  SLFD M6 .... 103 F1
  SWIN M27 .... 86 C1
West Duke St *SALQ/ORD* M5 .... 105 E6 *15*
West Egerton St *SALQ/ORD* M5 .... 104 C6
West End Av *CHD/CHDH* SK8 .... 179 E1
West End St *CHAD* OL9 .... 78 B4
Westend St *FWTH* BL4 .... 65 F3 *8*
Westerdale *OLDE* OL4 .... 80 A5 *11*
Westerdale Dr *BOLS/LL* BL3 .... 45 E4
  ROY/SHW OL2 .... 60 A4
Westerham Av *SALQ/ORD* M5 .... 104 B6 *12*
Westerham Cl *TOT/BURYW* BL8 .... 19 D6 *2*
Wester Hill Rd *OLDS* OL8 .... 96 B4
Western Av *SWIN* M27 .... 87 E3
Western Cir *BNG/LEV* M19 .... 145 D5
Western Rd *URM* M41 .... 136 C2
Western St *GTN* M18 .... 127 F3
  SLFD M6 .... 103 F4
Westerton Ct *BOLS/LL* BL3 .... 46 B4 *57*
Westfield *SLFD* M6 .... 103 F3
Westfield Av *MDTN* M24 .... 75 D4
Westfield Cl *ROCH* OL11 .... 21 D4
Westfield Dr *MPL/ROM* SK6 .... 150 A6
Westfield Gv *DTN/ASHW* M34 .... 129 F4 *11*
Westfield Rd *CCHDY* M21 .... 141 F2
  CHD/CHDH SK8 .... 195 D1
  DROY M43 .... 109 F5 *3*
Westfields *HALE/TIMP* WA15 .... 189 D1

Westfield St *BRO* M7 .... 89 E4
  CHAD OL9 .... 78 A3
Westgate *HALE/TIMP* WA15 .... 174 C5
  SALE M33 .... 159 E1 *5*
  URM M41 .... 137 F2
  WHIT OL12 .... 8 C4
  WILM/AE SK9 .... 203 E6
Westgate Av *BKLY* M9 .... 91 D3 *3*
  BOL BL1 .... 46 A2
  BURY BL9 .... 33 F6 *7*
  TOT/BURYW BL8 .... 18 A3
Westgate Cl *WHIT* OL12 .... 8 C3
Westgate Dr *SWIN* M27 .... 102 A1
Westgate Rd *SLFD* M6 .... 102 C3
Westgate St *AULW* OL7 .... 112 B6 *10*
West Gn *MDTN* M24 .... 73 F4
West Gv *BRUN/LGST* M13 .... 125 E4
  MOSL OL5 .... 99 D5
  SALE M33 .... 159 F2
Westgrove Av *BOL* BL1 .... 27 F1 *8*
West High St *SALQ/ORD* M5 .... 104 B5
Westholm Av *HTNM* SK4 .... 145 F4
Westholme Ct *WILM/AE* SK9 .... 209 E5 *3*
Westholme Rd *DID/WITH* M20 .... 143 F6
  PWCH M25 .... 72 A3
West Hope St *SALQ/ORD* M5 .... 104 C6
Westhulme Av *OLD* OL1 .... 78 B2
Westhulme St *OLD* OL1 .... 78 B2
Westinghouse Rd *TRPK* M17 .... 120 C5
West King St *CSLFD* M3 .... 2 A1
Westlake St *OP/CLY* M11 .... 127 D2 *3*
Westland Av *BOL* BL1 .... 26 B6
  FWTH BL4 .... 66 A5
  STKP SK1 .... 167 F4 *5*
Westland Dr *BKLY* M9 .... 91 E1
Westlands *WHTF* M45 .... 71 D5
The Westlands *SWIN* M27 .... 102 C1
West Lea *DTN/ASHW* M34 .... 130 B6
Westlea Dr *GTN* M18 .... 127 E6
Westleigh Dr *PWCH* M25 .... 89 E2
Westleigh St *BKLY* M9 .... 91 F4
West Marwood St *BRO* M7 .... 105 F1 *13*
Westmead Dr *CHH* M8 .... 105 F2 *18*
  HALE/TIMP WA15 .... 159 F6
West Meade *BOLS/LL* BL3 .... 64 C1
  CCHDY M21 .... 141 E4
  PWCH M25 .... 89 E3 *2*
  SWIN M27 .... 101 F1
Westmeade Rd *WALK* M28 .... 66 A6
West Meadow *RDSH* SK5 .... 147 E2
Westmere Dr *BKLY* M9 .... 91 D2
Westminister Cl *ROY/SHW* OL2 .... 61 F1 *12*
Westminster Av *AUL* OL6 .... 97 E6
  FWTH BL4 .... 66 C4
  HTNM SK4 .... 146 C4
  OLDTF/WHR M16 .... 142 A1 *8*
  RAD M26 .... 50 B5
  ROY/SHW OL2 .... 60 A3
  WHTF M45 .... 70 C1
Westminster Cl *MPL/ROM* SK6 .... 170 B6 *3*
  SALE M33 .... 158 B2
Westminster Dr *CHD/CHDH* SK8 .... 195 F3
  WILM/AE SK9 .... 209 F1 *8*
Westminster Rd *BOL* BL1 .... 27 F2
  ECC M30 .... 101 F4
  FAIL M35 .... 94 C5
  HALE/TIMP WA15 .... 175 E4
  URM M41 .... 119 E5
  WALK M28 .... 83 D2
Westminster St *BNG/LEV* M19 .... 145 F2 *8*
  BURY BL9 .... 33 F6 *8*
  FWTH BL4 .... 66 A3 *10*
  OLD OL1 .... 79 F3
  ROCH OL11 .... 39 E2 *3*
  SWIN M27 .... 85 E4
Westminster Wy *DUK* SK16 .... 131 E3
Westmoreland Cl *BURY* BL9 .... 52 C3 *3*
Westmorland Av *AULW* OL7 .... 112 B3
  DUK SK16 .... 131 F1 *3*
Westmorland Cl *RDSH* SK5 .... 148 A5 *3*
Westmorland Dr *RDSH* SK5 .... 147 F5
  WHIT OL12 .... 11 E5
Westmorland Rd *DID/WITH* M20 .... 163 E3
  ECC M30 .... 102 B2
  PART M31 .... 154 C3 *3*
  SALE M33 .... 160 A3
  URM M41 .... 138 A2
West Mosley St *CMANW* M2 .... 3 E4
Westmount Cl *NEWH/MOS* M40 .... 107 D1 *8*
West Oak Pl *CHD/CHDH* SK8 .... 181 D6 *3*
Weston Av *MILN* OL16 .... 40 C3
  NEWH/MOS M40 .... 93 F4
  SWIN M27 .... 86 A1 *1*
  URM M41 .... 137 F2 *3*
Weston Dr *CHD/CHDH* SK8 .... 182 B3
  DTN/ASHW M34 .... 130 B6
Weston Gv *HTNM* SK4 .... 146 A5
  WYTH/NTH M22 .... 162 C5
Weston Rd *IRL* M44 .... 135 E1 *7*
  WILM/AE SK9 .... 204 B5
Weston St *BOLS/LL* BL3 .... 47 D5
  MILN OL16 .... 41 F1 *3*
  MILN OL16 .... 42 A1 *3*
  NEWH/MOS M40 .... 107 E5 *10*
  RDSH SK5 .... 166 C1 *7*

West Over MPL/ROM SK6 .... 169 E5
Westover Rd URM M41 .... 119 D6
Westover St SWIN M27 .... 85 F4
West Pk HYDE SK14 .... 150 C4
West Park Av DTN/ASHW M34 ... 149 C4
POY/DIS SK12 .... 197 C5
West Park Rd BRAM/HZG SK7 ... 182 B5
STKP SK1 .... 167 F3
West Park St SALQ/ORD M5 .... 122 C2
West Pl BNG/LEV M19 .... 145 D4
Westray Crs SALQ/ORD M5 .... 103 F6
Westray Rd BRUN/LGST M13 ..... 144 C1
West Rd ALT WA14 .... 174 A5
PWCH M25 .... 71 D6
STRET M32 .... 120 B5
West Rw PWCH M25 .... 88 A4
West Starkey St HEY OL10 .... 37 D4
West St AUL OL6 .... 112 C4
BOL BL1 .... 46 A2
CHAD OL9 .... 78 B5
DUK SK16 .... 112 C6
EDGY/DAV SK3 .... 166 B4
FAIL M35 .... 93 F6
FWTH BL4 .... 66 C2
HEY OL10 .... 37 E5
HYDE SK14 .... 131 E4
LIT OL15 .... 12 C6
MDTN M24 .... 75 E1
MILN OL16 .... 24 B6
OLD OL1 .... 78 C4
OLDE OL4 .... 80 C6
OP/CLY M11 .... 108 C5
RAMS BL0 .... 6 C6
STLY SK15 .... 114 A5
WILM/AE SK9 .... 209 E4
West Towers St SLFD M6 .... 104 A6
West V RAD M26 .... 51 E4
West Vale HALE/TIMP WA15 ...... 175 D2
West Vw LIT OL15 .... 13 D6
RAMS BL0 .... 7 D1
West View Gv WHTF M45 .... 70 B5
West View Rd WYTH/NTH M22 .. 162 C5
Westville Gdns BNG/LEV M19 ... 144 C6
Westward Ho MILN OL16 .... 42 A1
Westward Rd WILM/AE SK9 ...... 203 D5
Westway BKLY M9 .... 73 E5
Westway DROY M43 .... 128 B2
West Wy BOL BL1 .... 28 C4
West Wy LHULT M38 .... 65 E6
Westway OLDE OL4 .... 80 C6
ROY/SHW OL2 .... 61 F3
Westwood Av BRO M7 .... 89 F5
HALE/TIMP WA15 .... 159 D6
NEWH/MOS M40 .... 92 B4
URM M41 .... 139 D2
WALK M28 .... 82 B3
Westwood Cl FWTH BL4 .... 66 B3
SALE M33 .... 159 F3
SWIN M27 .... 103 D1
Westwood Dr CHAD OL9 .... 78 B4
SALE M33 .... 159 F3
SWIN M27 .... 103 D1
Westwood Rd BOL BL1 .... 46 A1
CHD/CHDH SK8 .... 193 F1
OFTN SK2 .... 183 F3
STRET M32 .... 139 F1
Westwood St RUSH/FAL M14 .... 124 B5
West Works Rd TRPK M17 .... 121 D5
Westworth Cl BOL BL1 .... 46 B1
Wetheral Dr BOLS/LL BL3 .... 46 C6
Wetherall St BNG/LEV M19 .... 145 F2
Wetherby Dr BRAM/HZG SK7 .... 185 E2
ROY/SHW OL2 .... 60 A4
Wetherby St OP/CLY M11 .... 127 F2
Weybourne Av BKLY M9 .... 92 B3
Weybourne Dr MPL/ROM SK6 ... 169 D1
Weybourne Gv BOLE BL2 .... 28 C5
Weybridge Rd ANC M4 .... 107 D5
Weybrook Rd HTNM SK4 .... 145 F4
Weycroft Cl BOLE BL2 .... 49 E5
Wey Gates Dr HALE/TIMP WA15 ... 190 A3
Weyhill Rd NTHM/RTH M23 .... 177 E3
Weylands Gv SLFD M6 .... 102 C2
Weymouth Rd AUL OL6 .... 113 F1
ECC M30 .... 100 C4
Weymouth St BOL BL1 .... 27 F3
Weythorne Dr BOL BL1 .... 28 A3
BURY BL9 .... 36 A2
Whalley Av BNG/LEV M19 .... 145 F1
BOL BL1 .... 26 A4
CCHDY M21 .... 142 A4
LIT OL15 .... 12 B5
OLDTF/WHR M16 .... 123 E6
SALE M33 .... 140 A6
URM M41 .... 119 F6
WHTF M45 .... 71 D2
Whalley Cl HALE/TIMP WA15 .... 159 D6
Whalley Dr TOT/BURYW BL8 ...... 32 A5
Whalley Gdns WHIT OL12 .... 21 F4
Whalley Gv AUL OL6 .... 97 D6
OLDTF/WHR M16 .... 142 A1
Whalley Rd HALE/TIMP WA15 ... 175 E5
HEY OL10 .... 36 B5
MDTN M24 .... 57 D6
OFTN SK2 .... 168 A6
OLDTF/WHR M16 .... 123 E6

RAMS BL0 .... 7 F2
WHIT OL12 .... 21 F4
WHTF M45 .... 71 D2
Wham Bar Dr HEY OL10 .... 36 B5
Wham Bottom La WHIT OL12 ...... 22 B1
Wham St HEY OL10 .... 36 C5
Wharfedale Av NEWH/MOS M40 ... 92 B4
Wharfedale Rd RDSH SK5 .... 146 C3
Wharf End TRPK M17 .... 122 B5
Wharf Rd ALT WA14 .... 158 B6
SALE M33 .... 140 A6
Wharfside Av ECC M30 .... 119 E1
Wharfside Way (Trafford Park Road)
TRPK M17 .... 121 F3
Wharf St CHAD OL9 .... 121 D5
DUK SK16 .... 112 C6
HTNM SK4 .... 166 C2
Wharmton Vw MOSL OL5 .... 99 F2
Wharton Av CCHDY M21 .... 142 B4
Wharton La LHULT M38 .... 64 C6
Wharton Ldg ECC M30 .... 101 F4
Wheat Cl BRUN/LGST M13 .... 125 D4
Wheat Cft EDGY/DAV SK3 .... 183 D2
Wheater's Crs BRO M7 .... 105 E4
Wheater's St BRO M7 .... 105 E3
Wheater's Ter BRO M7 .... 105 E3
Wheatfield STLY SK15 .... 133 F2
Wheatfield Cl MPL/ROM SK6 ..... 169 E1
Wheatfield Crs ROY/SHW OL2 ... 60 A6
Wheatfield St BOLE BL2 .... 47 F4
Wheathill St ROCH OL11 .... 40 B3
Wheeldale OLDE OL4 .... 80 B5
Wheeldale Cl BOL BL1 .... 27 F5
Wheelock Cl WILM/AE SK9 .... 204 B2
Wheelton Cl TOT/BURYW BL8 .... 32 B6
Wheelwright Cl MPL/ROM SK6 .. 171 D5
ROCH OL11 .... 38 C2
Wheelwright Dr MILN OL16 .... 24 A2
Whelan Av BURY BL9 .... 52 C2
Whelan Cl BURY BL9 .... 52 C2
Wheler St OP/CLY M11 .... 127 E1
Whernside Av AUL OL6 .... 97 D6
NEWH/MOS M40 .... 92 B4
Whernside Cl HTNM SK4 .... 166 C3
Whetstone Hill Cl OLD OL1 .... 80 A1
Whetstone Hill La OLD OL1 .... 80 A2
Whetstone Hill Rd OLD OL1 .... 79 F1
Whewell Av RAD M26 .... 52 B4
Whickham Cl RUSH/FAL M14 .... 124 C6
Whiley St BRUN/LGST M13 .... 126 A5
Whimberry Cl SALQ/ORD M5 .... 122 C2
Whimbrel Rd OFTN SK2 .... 185 E2
Whinberry Rd ALT WA14 .... 157 F6
Whinberry Wy OLDE OL4 .... 62 C5
Whinchat Cl OFTN SK2 .... 185 E3
Whinfell Dr MDTN M24 .... 73 F2
Whins Av FWTH BL4 .... 64 C3
Whins Crest HOR/BR BL6 .... 44 A2
Whinslee Dr HOR/BR BL6 .... 44 A2
Whinstone Wy CHAD OL9 .... 76 C2
Whipp St HEY OL10 .... 36 C4
Whirley Cl HTNM SK4 .... 146 B6
Whiston Dr BOLE BL2 .... 48 A3
Whiston Rd CHH M8 .... 90 C5
Whitaker St MDTN M24 .... 75 D3
Whitbrook Wy MDTN M24 .... 58 A4
Whitburn Av BRUN/LGST M13 .. 144 C1
Whitburn Cl BOLS/LL BL3 .... 44 C5
Whitburn Dr TOT/BURYW BL8 .... 33 D2
Whitburn Rd NTHM/RTH M23 .... 177 E3
Whitby Av HEY OL10 .... 37 D4
OLDTF/WHR M16 .... 123 E6
RUSH/FAL M14 .... 144 C3
SLFD M6 .... 103 D4
URM M41 .... 138 C1
Whitby Cl CHD/CHDH SK8 .... 182 C5
POY/DIS SK12 .... 198 A4
TOT/BURYW BL8 .... 32 A5
Whitby Rd OLDS OL8 .... 97 D2
RUSH/FAL M14 .... 144 B3
Whitby St MDTN M24 .... 76 A2
ROCH OL11 .... 40 B2
Whitchurch Dr
OLDTF/WHR M16 .... 123 E4
Whitchurch Rd DID/WITH M20 ... 143 D4
Whitchurch St BRO M7 .... 105 F4
Whiteacre Rd AUL OL6 .... 113 E5
White Bank Av RDSH SK5 .... 168 A1
White Bank Rd OLDS OL8 .... 95 E4
Whitebarn Rd WILM/AE SK9 ..... 209 F5
Whitebeam Cl HALE/TIMP WA15 ... 176 C2
MILN OL16 .... 42 B4
SLFD M6 .... 104 B4
White Birk Cl TOT/BURYW BL8 .. 18 A5
Whitebrook Rd RUSH/FAL M14 .. 143 F2
Whitecar Av NEWH/MOS M40 .... 93 E4
Whitecarr La HALE/TIMP WA15 . 176 B4
Whitechapel St DID/WITH M20 .. 163 F2
White City Wy OLDTF/WHR M16 . 122 B4
Whitecliff Cl RUSH/FAL M14 ...... 125 D4
Whitecroft Av ROY/SHW OL2 ...... 62 B2
Whitecroft Dr TOT/BURYW BL8 .. 32 A5
Whitecroft Gdns BNG/LEV M19 . 164 C1

Whitecroft Rd BOL BL1 .... 26 B6
Whitecroft St OLD OL1 .... 80 A2
Whitefield HTNM SK4 .... 166 B2
Whitefield Av ROCH OL11 .... 21 D5
Whitefield Rd BURY BL9 .... 52 C2
MPL/ROM SK6 .... 168 C1
SALE M33 .... 139 D6
Whitegate LIT OL15 .... 24 C1
Whitegate Av CHAD OL9 .... 94 A1
Whitegate Cl NEWH/MOS M40 ... 93 F4
Whitegate Dr BOL BL1 .... 28 A3
SALQ/ORD M5 .... 103 E5
SWIN M27 .... 86 C3
Whitegate La CHAD OL9 .... 94 A1
Whitegate Pk URM M41 .... 136 C1
Whitegate Rd CHAD OL9 .... 93 F2
Whitegates Cl HALE/TIMP WA15 . 175 F2
Whitegates La OLDE OL4 .... 81 F1
Whitegates Rd CHD/CHDH SK8 . 180 B2
MDTN M24 .... 58 A5
Whitehall Cl WILM/AE SK9 .... 203 E6
Whitehall La BOL BL1 .... 27 E1
OLDE OL4 .... 63 D5
Whitehall Rd DID/WITH M20 ...... 164 A3
SALE M33 .... 159 F3
Whitehall St OLD OL1 .... 79 D3
WHIT OL12 .... 23 D5
White Hart Meadow
MDTN M24 .... 75 E1
White Hart St HYDE SK14 .... 131 E5
Whitehaven Gdns DID/WITH M20 . 163 E3
Whitehaven Rd BRAM/HZG SK7 . 196 A4
Whitehead Crs RAD M26 .... 67 F4
TOT/BURYW BL8 .... 33 D2
Whitehead Rd CCHDY M21 .... 141 D3
SWIN M27 .... 86 C3
Whitehead St MILN OL16 .... 24 C6
ROY/SHW OL2 .... 61 D3
WALK M28 .... 85 E1
White Hill Cl WHIT OL12 .... 22 B1
Whitehill Dr NEWH/MOS M40 ..... 92 B6
Whitehill St HTNM SK4 .... 167 D1
RDSH SK5 .... 147 D6
Whitehill St West HTNM SK4 ..... 166 B1
Whiteholme Av CCHDY M21 ...... 162 B1
White Horse Mdw MILN OL16 ..... 41 D5
White House Av CHH M8 .... 89 F2
Whitehouse Av OLDE OL4 .... 80 A5
White House Cl HEY OL10 .... 56 B2
Whitehouse Dr HALE/TIMP WA15 . 189 F1
NTHM/RTH M23 .... 177 E2
Whitehouse La ALT WA14 .... 156 B6
Whitehurst Rd HTNM SK4 .... 165 D1
Whitekirk Cl BRUN/LGST M13 ... 124 C3
White Lady Cl LHULT M38 .... 82 A3
Whiteland Av BOLS/LL BL3 .... 46 A4
Whitelands DUK SK16 .... 113 D5
Whitelands Rd AUL OL6 .... 113 D5
Whitelea Dr EDGY/DAV SK3 ...... 182 B2
Whitelees Rd LIT OL15 .... 12 B6
Whitelegge St TOT/BURYW BL8 . 32 C3
Whiteley Dr MDTN M24 .... 76 A3
Whiteley Pl ALT WA14 .... 174 B1
Whiteley St CHAD OL9 .... 94 C1
OP/CLY M11 .... 108 C5
White Lion Brow BOL BL1 .... 46 C2
Whitelow Rd CCHDY M21 .... 141 E3
HTNM SK4 .... 165 E2
RAMS BL0 .... 7 F6
Whitemead St DTN/ASHW M34 . 130 A2
Whitemoss WHIT OL12 .... 21 F3
White Moss Av CCHDY M21 ...... 142 A3
White Moss Rd BKLY M9 .... 92 A1
Whitemoss Rd BKLY M9 .... 92 A1
Whiteoak Cl MPL/ROM SK6 .... 170 C6
Whiteoak Rd RUSH/FAL M14 .... 144 A3
Whiteoak Vw BOLS/LL BL3 .... 48 B4
Whites Cft SWIN M27 .... 86 A5
Whiteside Cl SALQ/ORD M5 ...... 103 E5
Whiteside Fold WHIT OL12 .... 21 E4
Whitestone Cl HOR/BR BL6 .... 44 B3
White St HULME M15 .... 123 E5
SLFD M6 .... 103 F6
TOT/BURYW BL8 .... 32 C6
White Swallows Rd SWIN M27 ... 102 C1
Whitethorn Av
OLDTF/WHR M16 .... 123 E6
Whitethorn Cl MPL/ROM SK6 .... 170 C6
Whitewater Dr BRO M7 .... 88 A6
Whiteway St BKLY M9 .... 91 F6
Whitewell Cl BURY BL9 .... 52 B2
Whitewillow Cl FAIL M35 .... 110 B1
Whitfield Crs MILN OL16 .... 42 C4
Whitfield Dr MILN OL16 .... 41 F2
Whitfield Ri ROY/SHW OL2 .... 42 B6
Whitfield St SLFD M6 .... 106 B3
Whiting Gv BOLS/LL BL3 .... 44 C1
Whitland Av BOL BL1 .... 45 D1
Whitland Dr OLDS OL8 .... 94 C3
Whit La SLFD M6 .... 104 A1
Whitley Gdns HALE/TIMP WA15 . 159 F6
Whitley Pl HALE/TIMP WA15 .... 159 F6
Whitley Rd HTNM SK4 .... 165 F2

NEWH/MOS M40 .... **107** D3
Whitley St FWTH BL4 .... **66** B1 ⑪
Whitlow Av ALT WA14 .... **157** F5
Whitman St BKLY M9 .... **92** A5
Whitmore Rd RUSH/FAL M14 .... **143** F2
Whitnall Cl OLDTF/WHR M16 .... **123** F6
Whitnall St HYDE SK14 .... **131** E4 ②
Whitsand Rd WYTH/NTH M22 .... **178** C2
Whitsbury Av GTN M18 .... **127** E6
Whitstable Cl OLDE OL9 .... **77** F5
Whitstable Rd NEWH/MOS M40 ... **93** D4 ③
Whitsters Hollow BOL BL1 .... **26** C4
Whittaker Dr LIT OL15 .... **25** D3
Whittaker La PWCH M25 .... **89** D1
ROCH OL11 .... **20** B4
Whittaker St CHAD OL9 .... **77** F4
NEWH/MOS M40 .... **92** B5 ⑦
RAD M26 .... **51** F5 ⑤
ROCH OL11 .... **20** C4 ③
WGTN/LGST M12 .... **125** E1
Whittingham Dr RAMS BL0 .... **19** D1 ③
RAMS BL0 .... **19** D1 ③
Whittingham St AULW OL7 .... **112** B6 ⑪
Whittlebrook Gv HEY OL10 .... **56** C2
Whittle Dr ROY/SHW OL2 .... **62** B1
WALK M28 .... **66** B6 ②
Whittle Gv BOL BL1 .... **26** C6
WALK M28 .... **83** F2 ②
Whittle La HEY OL10 .... **55** E4
Whittles Av DTN/ASHW M34 ..... **130** B6
Whittle's Cft CMANE M1 .... **3** H4 ③
Whittles St BCUP OL13 .... **5** E5 ⑪
WHIT OL12 .... **3** C2 ③
Whittle St ANC M4 .... **12** A6
LIT OL15 .... **12** A6
SWIN M27 .... **85** F6
TOT/BURYW BL8 .... **33** D4 ②
TOT/BURYW BL8 .... **33** D4 ②
WALK M28 .... **83** F2
Whitwell Wy GTN M18 .... **127** E6 ⑩
Whitworth Cl AUL OL6 .... **113** D3 ⑫
Whitworth La RUSH/FAL M14 .... **144** B2
Whitworth Rake WHIT OL12 .... **9** E3
Whitworth Sq WHIT OL12 .... **23** D3
Whitworth St CMANE M1 .... **3** F6
MILN OL16 .... **24** A3 ③
MILN OL16 .... **42** A1
OP/CLY M11 .... **126** C2
Whitworth St East OP/CLY M11 ... **127** D2
Whixhall Av WGTN/LGST M12 ... **125** F3 ⑥
Whoolden St FWTH BL4 .... **66** A2 ③
Whowell Fold BOL BL1 .... **27** D4 ⑩
Whowell St BOLS/LL BL3 .... **46** C3 ⑦
Wibbersley Pk URM M41 .... **137** D1 ③
Wichbrook Rd WALK M28 .... **82** A2 ⑪
Wicheaves Crs WALK M28 .... **82** A2
The Wicheries LHULT M38 .... **82** A2 ⑫
Wicken Bank HEY OL10 .... **56** C2
Wickenby Dr SALE M33 .... **159** E1 ⑩
Wicken St OFTN SK2 .... **168** A6
Wickentree Holt WHIT OL12 .... **21** E4 ⑩
Wickentree La FAIL M35 .... **94** A4 ③
FAIL M35 .... **94** B4 ③
Wicker La HALE/TIMP WA15 ...... **189** F1
Wicket Gv SWIN M27 .... **85** F1 ②
Wickliffe St BOL BL1 .... **46** C1 ③
Wicklow Av EDGY/DAV SK3 ..... **165** F6 ③
Wicklow Dr WYTH/NTH M22 .... **178** C3
Widcombe Dr BOLS/LL BL3 .... **49** D4
Widdop St CHAD OL9 .... **78** B4
Widecombe Cl URM M41 .... **118** C5 ③
Widgeon Cl POY/DIS SK12 .... **197** F5 ③
RUSH/FAL M14 .... **143** F3 ⑫
Widgeon Rd ALT WA14 .... **157** F5
Widnes St OP/CLY M11 .... **127** D2 ⑧
Wigan Rd BOLS/LL BL3 .... **44** C6
Wigley St WGTN/LGST M12 ..... **125** F2
Wigmore Rd CHH M8 .... **90** C6 ⑩
Wigmore St AUL OL6 .... **113** D4
Wigsby Av NEWH/MOS M40 ...... **93** D4
Wigwam Cl POY/DIS SK12 .... **198** A5
Wike St TOT/BURYW BL8 .... **33** D4
Wilbraham St CCHDY M21 .... **141** D3
OLDTF/WHR M16 .... **142** C2
WALK M28 .... **83** E2
Wilburn St SALQ/ORD M5 .... **125** E1 ⑩
Wilby Av BOLS/LL BL3 .... **49** E4
Wilby Cl TOT/BURYW BL8 .... **33** E2 ③
Wilby St CHH M8 .... **106** C1
Wilcock Cl OLDTF/WHR M16 .... **125** F5 ⑪
WILM/AE SK9 .... **209** D2
Wilcott Rd CHD/CHDH SK8 ...... **179** E2
Wildbank Cha STLY SK15 .... **133** F2
Wildbrook Crs OLDS OL8 .... **96** B2
Wild Clough HYDE SK14 .... **151** D2 ③
Wildcroft Av NEWH/MOS M40 .... **92** B4 ⑩
Wilderswood Cl DID/WITH M20 . **144** A6 ③
Wilde St DTN/ASHW M34 .... **130** A6 ③
Wildhouse La LIT OL15 .... **25** D3
Wildman La FWTH BL4 .... **65** D3
Wildmoor Av OLDE OL4 .... **97** F2
Wilds Pl RAMS BL0 .... **6** C6 ②

Wild St BRAM/HZG SK7 .... **184** B5 ③
DUK SK16 .... **131** E1
HEY OL10 .... **37** F5
MPL/ROM SK6 .... **169** D3
OLD OL1 .... **79** E4
OLDE OL4 .... **80** C5
ROY/SHW OL2 .... **62** A3
Wildwood Cl RAMS BL0 .... **18** B1 ⑳
Wilford Av SALE M33 .... **159** E3
Wilfred Dr BURY BL9 .... **34** C3 ③
Wilfred Rd ECC M30 .... **118** B1
WALK M28 .... **83** E3
Wilfred St EDGW/EG BL7 .... **14** B6 ⑧
NEWH/MOS M40 .... **92** B5
Wilfrid St SWIN M27 .... **86** A5 ③
Wilkes St OLD OL1 .... **62** B6
Wilkin Cft CHD/CHDH SK8 .... **180** C6
Wilkins La WILM/AE SK9 .... **192** C6
Wilkinson Av BOLS/LL BL3 .... **49** E5
Wilkinson Rd BOL BL1 .... **27** E2
HTNM SK4 .... **146** C3
Wilkinson St AUL OL6 .... **112** B4
MDTN M24 .... **75** D2 ③
SALE M33 .... **160** B1 ③
Wilks Av WYTH/NTH M22 .... **179** D5
Willand Cl BOLE BL2 .... **49** E3
Willand Dr BOLS/LL BL3 .... **49** E3
Willan Rd BKLY M9 .... **91** D1
ECC M30 .... **101** F5 ③
Willard St BRAM/HZG SK7 .... **184** B4 ③
Willaston Cl CCHDY M21 .... **141** E4
Willbutts La ROCH OL11 .... **22** A5
Willdale Cl OP/CLY M11 .... **108** B5
Willdor Gv EDGY/DAV SK3 ...... **181** F1 ③
Willenhall Rd NTHM/RTH M23 ... **162** A3
Willerby Rd BRO M7 .... **105** F2 ⑩
Willesden Av BRUN/LGST M13 . **125** F6 ③
William Chadwick Cl
   NEWH/MOS M40 .... **107** D4 ⑩
William Cl URM M41 .... **138** A2
William Greenwood Cl
   HEY OL10 .... **37** D5 ②
William Henry St ROCH OL11 ..... **40** B3 ⑬
William Kay Cl OLDTF/WHR M16 **123** F3 ⑦
William Lister Cl
   NEWH/MOS M40 .... **109** E3 ⑦
Williams Av CHAD OL9 .... **94** A2
Williamson Av MPL/ROM SK6 ... **169** E1 ⑦
   RAD M26 .... **51** D3
Williamson La DROY M43 .... **106** C1
Williamson St ANC M4 .... **108** C1
   AUL OL6 .... **112** C4 ②
   RDSH SK5 .... **146** C4 ⑪
   RDSH SK5 .... **147** D4 ⑪
Williams Rd GTN M18 .... **127** D4
   NEWH/MOS M40 .... **92** C6
Williams St BOLS/LL BL3 .... **49** F6
   GTN M18 .... **127** D5
William St AULW OL7 .... **112** B6
   BCUP OL13 .... **5** D1 ③
   CSLFD M3 .... **2** A2
   DID/WITH M20 .... **163** F2
   FAIL M35 .... **94** B4
   LIT OL15 .... **12** B6
   MDTN M24 .... **75** F3
   MILN OL16 .... **24** B1 ⑪
   RAD M26 .... **51** F5 ③
   RAMS BL0 .... **7** D2
   ROCH OL11 .... **40** A1
   STKP SK1 .... **167** F6 ⑩
   WGTN/LGST M12 .... **125** E1
   WHIT OL12 .... **9** D2 ③
Willingdon Cl TOT/BURYW BL8 .. **19** D6
Willingdon Dr PWCH M25 .... **71** F6
Willis Rd EDGY/DAV SK3 .... **182** C1
Willis St BOLS/LL BL3 .... **46** A5
Willock St BRO M7 .... **105** F1
Willoughby Av DID/WITH M20 ... **164** A1
Willoughby Cl SALE M33 .... **139** E6
Willow Av CHD/CHDH SK8 .... **181** D5
   MDTN M24 .... **76** A4
   RDSH SK5 .... **167** D1
   URM M41 .... **138** C1
Willow Bank CHD/CHDH SK8 ... **195** E3
   OLDE OL4 .... **80** C3
Willowbank RAD M26 .... **69** D3 ③
Willow Bank RUSH/FAL M14 .... **144** A3
Willowbank Av BOLE BL2 .... **49** F1
Willowbrook Av
   NEWH/MOS M40 .... **92** B6 ③
Willow Cl BOLS/LL BL3 .... **45** F5
   DUK SK16 .... **132** A2 ③
   POY/DIS SK12 .... **198** C6
Willow Ct MPL/ROM SK6 .... **187** D2 ③
   SALE M33 .... **140** C6 ③
Willowdale Av CHD/CHDH SK8 . **179** F5 ③
Willowdene Cl EDGW/EG BL7 .... **14** A5
   NEWH/MOS M40 .... **107** D2 ③
Willow Dr SALE M33 .... **158** C3
   WILM/AE SK9 .... **194** B6
Willowfield Rd OLDE OL4 .... **80** B1 ③
Willow Fold DROY M43 .... **128** C1
Willow Gv CHAD OL9 .... **77** F3 ③
   DTN/ASHW M34 .... **129** F6
   GTN M18 .... **127** F5 ⑦

MPL/ROM SK6 .... **187** D2
Willow Hill Rd CHH M8 .... **90** B3
Willowmead Wy WHIT OL12 .... **21** E3 ③
Willowmoss Cl WALK M28 .... **83** F4
Willow Ri LIT OL15 .... **25** D2 ⑩
Willow Rd ECC M30 .... **100** B3
   MPL/ROM SK6 .... **201** D2
   PART M31 .... **154** C3
   PWCH M25 .... **71** E5
Willows Dr FAIL M35 .... **110** A3
Willows La BOLS/LL BL3 .... **46** A5
   MILN OL16 .... **24** C6 ②
Willows Rd SALO/ORD M5 .... **103** E5 ⑬
The Willows BOLS/LL BL3 .... **49** E4
   CCHDY M21 .... **141** E4 ②
   MOSL OL5 .... **99** F4
   PART M31 .... **155** D2
Willow St BURY BL9 .... **34** C5
   CHH M8 .... **105** F3 ⑪
   HEY OL10 .... **37** E5
   OP/CLY M11 .... **108** B6
   SWIN M27 .... **85** D6 ③
   SWIN M27 .... **101** E2 ③
Willow Tree Ms CHD/CHDH SK8 . **179** F6 ③
Willow Tree Rd ALT WA14 .... **174** B5
Willow Wy BRAM/HZG SK7 ...... **196** A2
   DID/WITH M20 .... **164** A2
Willow Wood Cl AUL OL6 .... **113** F4
Wilma Av BKLY M9 .... **91** D1
Wilmcote Cl HOR/BR BL6 .... **44** B3 ③
Wilmcote Rd NEWH/MOS M40 .. **107** E3 ⑫
Wilmington Rd STRET M32 .... **139** F1 ③
Wilmot St BOL BL1 .... **27** D4
Wilmott St HULME M15 .... **124** A2
Wilmslow Av BOL BL1 .... **27** F2 ⑯
Wilmslow Old Rd
   HALE/TIMP WA15 .... **191** D3
Wilmslow Park Rd WILM/AE SK9 **204** A4
Wilmslow Rd BRAM/HZG SK7 ... **205** F2 ③
   CHD/CHDH SK8 .... **180** B4
   DID/WITH M20 .... **143** F6
   HALE/TIMP WA15 .... **191** D3
   MCFLDN SK10 .... **206** A5
   RUSH/FAL M14 .... **125** D5
   WILM/AE SK9 .... **194** B6 ③
   WILM/AE SK9 .... **209** E5
Wilmur Av BRO M7 .... **105** F1
   WHTF M45 .... **71** E4
Wilpshire Av WGTN/LGST M12 . **126** C6 ③
Wilshaw Gv AULW OL7 .... **112** B1
Wilshaw La AULW OL7 .... **112** B2
Wilson Av HEY OL10 .... **36** B5
   SWIN M27 .... **86** C3
Wilson Crs AUL OL6 .... **113** F3 ③
Wilson Rd BKLY M9 .... **91** E4
   HTNM SK4 .... **165** F1
Wilson St BRUN/LGST M13 ...... **125** D3
   BURY BL9 .... **34** B6
   FWTH BL4 .... **66** C3 ③
   HYDE SK14 .... **150** C1
   OLDS OL8 .... **95** F1
   OP/CLY M11 .... **126** B1
   RAD M26 .... **51** D5 ③
   SALE M33 .... **139** F6 ③
   STRET M32 .... **121** F5
   WHIT OL12 .... **23** D5 ⑳
Wilsthorpe Cl BNG/LEV M19 ..... **146** A5
Wilton Av CHD/CHDH SK8 .... **194** A2
   OLDTF/WHR M16 .... **122** B6 ③
   PWCH M25 .... **89** E3
   SWIN M27 .... **87** D6
Wilton Ct DTN/ASHW M34 .... **128** B5
Wilton Crs WILM/AE SK9 .... **209** D3
Wilton Dr BURY BL9 .... **53** E4 ③
   HALE/TIMP WA15 .... **190** A1
Wilton Gdns RAD M26 .... **52** A4
Wilton Gv DTN/ASHW M34 ...... **128** B5
   HEY OL10 .... **37** E6
Wilton Paddock DTN/ASHW M34 **128** B5
Wilton Pl CSLFD M3 .... **105** E5 ②③
Wilton Rd BOL BL1 .... **27** F2
   CCHDY M21 .... **141** F3
   CHH M8 .... **90** B3
   SLFD M6 .... **102** C3
Wilton St BOL BL1 .... **28** A4 ⑳
   CHAD OL9 .... **94** C2
   DTN/ASHW M34 .... **129** F5
   HEY OL10 .... **37** D5
   MDTN M24 .... **73** F4
   PWCH M25 .... **89** D1 ⑩
   RDSH SK5 .... **147** D1
   WHTF M45 .... **71** D4
Wilton Ter WHIT OL12 .... **22** C5 ⑲
Wiltshire Av RDSH SK5 .... **168** A1
Wiltshire Cl BURY BL9 .... **53** E1
Wiltshire Rd CHAD OL9 .... **77** F6
   FAIL M35 .... **110** A1
   PART M31 .... **154** C3 ③
Wiltshire St BRO M7 .... **105** F1
Wimbledon Dr EDGY/DAV SK3 . **182** A1 ③
Wimbledon Lawns ALT WA14 ... **174** A4
Wimbledon Rd FAIL M35 .... **94** C5
Wimborne Av URM M41 .... **119** E5
Wimborne Cl CHD/CHDH SK8 .. **182** A3 ②
Wimpole St AUL OL6 .... **113** D4 ⑲

OLD OL1 .... 79 E2
Wimpory St OP/CLY M11 .... 127 E2
Winbolt St OFTN SK2 .... 184 A3 ⑤
Winby St ROCH OL11 .... 40 B2 ②
Wincanton Av NTHM/RTH M23 ... 160 B5
Wincanton Pk OLDE OL4 .... 80 B5 ⑯
Wince Cl ANC M4 .... 76 A5
Wincham Rd SALE M33 .... 158 C3
Winchester Av AUL OL6 .... 97 E6
  CHAD OL9 .... 77 D2
  DTN/ASHW M34 .... 149 D2
  HEY OL10 .... 56 A1
  PWCH M25 .... 89 D3 ⑧
Winchester Cl ROCH OL11 .... 21 D6
  TOT/BURYW BL8 .... 19 D6
  WILM/AE SK9 .... 202 C6 ⑪
Winchester Dr HTNM SK4 .... 166 A3 ⑬
  SALE M33 .... 158 B1
Winchester Pk OLDE OL4 .... 163 D2
Winchester Rd DUK SK16 .... 132 C2
  ECC M30 .... 102 B3
  HALE/TIMP WA15 .... 176 A6
  RAD M26 .... 50 B4
  SLFD M6 .... 103 D3
  URM M41 .... 119 E6
Winchester Wy BOLE BL2 .... 29 E6 ⑧
Wincombe St RUSH/FAL M14 ... 143 F1 ⑯
Windale WALK M28 .... 82 C2
Windcroft Cl OP/CLY M11 .... 126 A1
Winder Dr ANC M4 .... 107 D6
Windermere Av BOLS/LL BL3 ...... 49 E5
  DTN/ASHW M34 .... 147 E1
  SALE M33 .... 160 B3 ②
  SWIN M27 .... 86 B6 ⑨
Windermere Cl OP/CLY M11 ... 126 B3 ⑪
  STRET M32 .... 121 D6 ②
Windermere Crs AULW OL7 ...... 112 A3 ③
Windermere Dr BURY BL9 .... 52 C2
  RAMS BL0 .... 7 D4
  WILM/AE SK9 .... 209 D4
Windermere Rd FWTH BL4 .... 64 C4
  HYDE SK14 .... 131 D4
  MDTN M24 .... 74 C1
  MPL/ROM SK6 .... 186 B6
  ROY/SHW OL2 .... 60 B2
  STKP SK1 .... 167 F6
  STLY SK15 .... 114 B4
  URM M41 .... 138 A2 ⑦
  WILM/AE SK9 .... 194 A5
Windermere St BOL BL1 .... 28 A5 ⑨
Winders Wy SLFD M6 .... 104 C3
Windfields Cl CHD/CHDH SK8 ... 181 F4 ②
Windham St MILN OL16 .... 10 C6
Windle Av CHH M8 .... 90 A2
Windle Ct OFTN SK2 .... 184 C2
Windlehurst Dr WALK M28 .... 82 C6
Windlehurst Old Rd
  MPL/ROM SK6 .... 187 D5
Windlehurst Rd MPL/ROM SK6 ... 200 B3
Windley St BOLE BL2 .... 47 E1
Windmill Av SALQ/ORD M5 .... 122 C2 ⑬
Windmill Cl DTN/ASHW M34 .... 147 F1 ②
  WALK M28 .... 66 A6 ②
Windmill La DTN/ASHW M34 .... 147 E1
  RDSH SK5 .... 147 D2
Windmill Rd SALE M33 .... 161 D2 ⑫
  WALK M28 .... 66 A6
Windmill St CMANW M2 .... 2 C5
  MILN OL16 .... 40 C1
Windover St BOLS/LL BL3 ...... 45 E5 ⑫
Windrush Av TOT/BURYW BL8 ...... 18 B3
Windrush Dr BKLY M9 .... 91 E6 ④
The Windrush WHIT OL12 .... 22 A1
Windsor Av BOLS/LL BL3 .... 49 E6 ⑪
  CHAD OL9 .... 94 B1
  CHD/CHDH SK8 .... 179 D2
  FAIL M35 .... 94 C5 ⑥
  HEY OL10 .... 36 C5
  HTNM SK4 .... 165 E2 ②
  IRL M44 .... 116 C6
  LHULT M38 .... 65 F6
  SALE M33 .... 139 F5 ⑦
  SWIN M27 .... 86 B3
  URM M41 .... 137 D1
  WHTF M45 .... 71 E4
  WILM/AE SK9 .... 203 D5
Windsor Cl POY/DIS SK12 .... 198 B5
  TOT/BURYW BL8 .... 18 B3 ②
Windsor Dr ALT WA14 .... 159 D5
  AULW OL7 .... 112 A3 ⑤
  DTN/ASHW M34 .... 129 E1
  DUK SK16 .... 132 A2
  MPL/ROM SK6 .... 186 C2 ②
  STLY SK15 .... 114 B4
  TOT/BURYW BL8 .... 51 F1
Windsor Gv AUL OL6 .... 97 D6
  BOL BL1 .... 27 D6 ②
  CHD/CHDH SK8 .... 195 D1
  MPL/ROM SK6 .... 170 C3 ⑪
  RAD M26 .... 67 F4 ⑤
Windsor Rd BKLY M9 .... 91 F6
  BNG/LEV M19 .... 145 D3
  BRAM/HZG SK7 .... 185 D5
  DROY M43 .... 109 E5
  DTN/ASHW M34 .... 128 B6

EDGW/EG BL7 .... 14 B6
HYDE SK14 .... 150 B4
MPL/ROM SK6 .... 168 A2
NEWH/MOS M40 .... 109 F3
OLDS OL8 .... 78 B6
PWCH M25 .... 89 F2
Windsor St FAIL M35 .... 94 B5 ④
  GTN M18 .... 127 D5
  NEWH/MOS M40 .... 109 F3 ⑧
  OFTN SK2 .... 183 E1 ⑤
  ROCH OL11 .... 40 D2 ②
  SALQ/ORD M5 .... 104 C6
Windybank BKLY M9 .... 74 A6
Windy Harbour La EDGW/EG BL7 ... 14 C5
Windyhill Dr BOLS/LL BL3 .... 45 E6
Winfell Dr NEWH/MOS M40 .... 107 E4 ⑰
Winfield Av DID/WITH M20 .... 144 B6
Winfield Dr GTN M18 .... 127 E3 ⑪
Winfield Gv MPL/ROM SK6 .... 171 F4 ③
Winford St HYDE SK14 .... 151 D1
Winford St BKLY M9 .... 91 F5 ⑬
Wingate Av TOT/BURYW BL8 .... 32 C5
Wingate Dr DID/WITH M20 ...... 164 A3 ②
  HALE/TIMP WA15 .... 175 E2
  WHTF M45 .... 70 C2
Wingate Rd HTNM SK4 .... 166 A1
  LHULT M38 .... 82 C1
Wingate St ROCH OL11 .... 20 C4
Wingfield Av WILM/AE SK9 .... 202 C5
Wingfield Dr SWIN M27 .... 102 B3
  WILM/AE SK9 .... 202 C5
Wingfield St STRET M32 .... 121 E5
Wings Gv HEY OL10 .... 56 B2
Winifred Av BURY BL9 .... 36 A3 ⑬
Winifred Rd DID/WITH M20 .... 163 F2
  FWTH BL4 .... 65 E2
  NEWH/MOS M40 .... 92 C6
  OFTN SK2 .... 183 E2
  URM M41 .... 119 D6
Winifred St ECC M30 .... 100 C6 ⑧
  HYDE SK14 .... 150 C4 ⑪
  RAMS BL0 .... 6 C2 ③
  WHIT OL12 .... 21 F4
Winmarith Dr HALE/TIMP WA15 ... 190 B2
Winmarleigh Cl TOT/BURYW BL8 ... 32 A6 ⑦
Winnie St NEWH/MOS M40 .... 92 B5
Winnington Gn OFTN SK2 .... 184 B5
Winnington Rd MPL/ROM SK6 ... 171 D5
Winnipeg Quay SALQ/ORD M5 ... 122 A2 ①
The Winnows DTN/ASHW M34 ... 129 E6
Winscombe Dr
  NEWH/MOS M40 .... 107 D3 ⑦
Winser St CMANE M1 .... 3 E6
Winsfield Rd BRAM/HZG SK7 ... 198 B3
Winsford Dr ROCH OL11 .... 38 A2
Winsford Gv BOLS/LL BL3 .... 45 D4
Winsford Rd RUSH/FAL M14 ...... 143 E2
Winskill Rd IRL M44 .... 135 E3
Winslade Cl BRAM/HZG SK7 ... 183 E5 ④
Winslade Ms FWTH BL4 .... 66 B2 ②
Winsley Rd NTHM/RTH M23 ...... 161 D3
Winslow Av HYDE SK14 .... 153 D1
Winslow St OP/CLY M11 .... 126 B1
Winstanley Rd NEWH/MOS M40 ... 107 E4
  SALE M33 .... 140 A6
Winster Av BRO M7 .... 104 C1
  DID/WITH M20 .... 162 C1
  STRET M32 .... 120 B6
Winster Cl BOLE BL2 .... 30 A6
  WHTF M45 .... 71 F3
Winster Dr BOLE BL2 .... 29 F6
  MDTN M24 .... 74 C1 ⑧
Winster Gv OFTN SK2 .... 183 E1
Winster Rd ECC M30 .... 118 C1
Winston Av BOLS/LL BL3 .... 50 A6 ③
  ROCH OL11 .... 37 F1
Winston Cl MPL/ROM SK6 .... 170 B6
  RAD M26 .... 50 B4
Winston Rd BKLY M9 .... 92 A4 ⑩
  BKLY M9 .... 92 A5 ⑫
  SALE M33 .... 139 D6
Winterbottom Gv HYDE SK14 .... 153 D1 ②
Winterbottom St CHAD OL9 .... 78 A4 ⑦
Winterburn Av BOLE BL2 .... 29 D1 ⑤
Winterburn Gn OFTN SK2 .... 184 C2
Winterdyne St BKLY M9 .... 91 F6 ⑪
Winterfield Dr BOLS/LL BL3 .... 45 D3
Winterford Av BRUN/LGST M13 ... 125 E4
Winterford Rd CHH M8 .... 90 A6
  MOSL OL5 .... 99 F4
Wintermans Rd CCHDY M21 ...... 142 A5
Winterslow Av NTHM/RTH M23 ... 160 B4
Winter St BOL BL1 .... 33 F2
Winterton Rd RDSH SK5 .... 147 E2 ③
Winthrop Av NEWH/MOS M40 .... 107 E2 ⑬
Winton Av DTN/ASHW M34 .... 129 E4
  NEWH/MOS M40 .... 93 E4 ③
Winton Cl BRAM/HZG SK7 .... 182 A5
Winton Gv BOLS/LL BL3 .... 44 C5
Winton Rd ALT WA14 .... 174 A5
  SLFD M6 .... 103 D2
Winton St AUL OL6 .... 112 C4
  LIT OL15 .... 12 C6 ⑱
  STLY SK15 .... 114 C6
Winward St BOLS/LL BL3 .... 45 E5 ⑱

Winwood Dr MDTN M24 .... 75 F1
Winwood Rd DID/WITH M20 ...... 164 A5
Wirral Cl SWIN M27 .... 86 B3 ③
Wirral Crs EDGY/DAV SK3 .... 165 E5
Wisbech Dr NTHM/RTH M23 ... 161 D4 ②
Wisbeck Rd BOLE BL2 .... 48 A1
Wiseley St OP/CLY M11 .... 125 F1 ⑤
Wiseman Ter PWCH M25 .... 89 D1 ⑯
Wishaw Sq CCHDY M21 .... 142 C4 ⑥
Wisley Cl RDSH SK5 .... 147 D3
Wistaria Rd GTN M18 .... 127 E4
Witham Av WYTH/NTH M22 ..... 178 C2 ⑤
Witham Cl HEY OL10 .... 36 B4 ②
Witham St AUL OL6 .... 113 F3
Withenfield Rd NTHM/RTH M23 ... 161 D5
Withens Gn OFTN SK2 .... 184 C1
Withington Gn MDTN M24 .... 57 E5 ①
Withington Rd CCHDY M21 ...... 142 B3 ①
  OLDTF/WHR M16 .... 123 E6
Withington St HEY OL10 .... 56 C1 ⑩
  SLFD M6 .... 106 C5
Withins Av RAD M26 .... 52 A4
Withins Cl BOLE BL2 .... 48 C1 ③
Withins Dr BOLE BL2 .... 48 C1
Withins Gv BOLE BL2 .... 48 C1
Withins La BOLE BL2 .... 29 F6
  RAD M26 .... 52 A4
Withins Rd OLDS OL8 .... 94 C3
Withins St RAD M26 .... 52 A5
Withnell Dr TOT/BURYW BL8 .... 32 B6
Withnell Rd DID/WITH M20 ...... 164 B2
Withycombe Pl SLFD M6 .... 104 B2 ⑨
Withy Gv ANC M4 .... 3 E2
Withypool Dr OFTN SK2 .... 183 F2
Withy Tree Gv DTN/ASHW M34 ... 149 E1 ②
Witley Dr SALE M33 .... 138 B5
Witley Rd MILN OL16 .... 23 F6
Wittenbury Rd HTNM SK4 .... 158 C5
Witterage Cl WGTN/LGST M12 ... 126 A3 ⑪
Woburn Av BOLE BL2 .... 29 D4 ②
  OLDTF/WHR M16 .... 124 A6
Woburn Cl MILN OL16 .... 41 F1 ⑩
  OLDTF/WHR M16 .... 124 A6
Woburn Dr BURY BL9 .... 53 D4
  HALE/TIMP WA15 .... 175 F5
Woburn Rd OLDTF/WHR M16 ... 141 E1 ③
Woden's Av SALQ/ORD M5 .... 123 D2 ③
Woking Back Gdns BOL BL1 .... 27 F6 ⑩
Woking Rd CHD/CHDH SK8 ...... 195 E3
Wolfenden St BOL BL1 .... 27 F5
Wolfreton Crs SWIN M27 .... 86 B2
Wolseley Pl DID/WITH M20 .... 143 F6
Wolseley Rd SALE M33 .... 139 F5
Wolseley St MILN OL16 .... 42 C3 ⑪
  TOT/BURYW BL8 .... 32 C6 ③
Wolsey Dr ALT WA14 .... 173 E6
Wolsey St HEY OL10 .... 37 D6
  RAD M26 .... 51 F6
Wolstenholme Av BURY BL9 .... 34 A1 ③
Wolstenholme La ROCH OL11 .... 20 A3 ⑧
Wolstenvale Cl MDTN M24 .... 75 F2
Wolver Cl LHULT M38 .... 65 F5 ③
Wolverton Av OLDS OL8 .... 95 D4
Wolverton Dr WILM/AE SK9 ...... 204 A2 ②
Woodacres CI WILM/AE SK9 ...... 203 D5
Woodall Cl SALE M33 .... 160 B1
Woodark Cl OLDE OL4 .... 81 D6
Woodbank BOLE BL2 .... 29 E5
Woodbank Av MPL/ROM SK6 .... 168 C2
  STKP SK1 .... 168 A5 ⑧
Woodbank Dr TOT/BURYW BL8 ... 33 D3
Wood Bank Rd LIT OL15 .... 25 E2
Woodbine Av IRL M44 .... 154 B2 ②
Woodbine Crs OFTN SK2 .... 167 D6 ⑭
Woodbine Rd BOLS/LL BL3 .... 46 A5 ⑮
  BOLS/LL BL3 .... 46 A5 ⑯
Woodbine St MILN OL16 .... 40 D2
Woodbine St East MILN OL16 ..... 40 C2 ⑨
Woodbourne Rd HTNM SK4 ...... 146 A5 ③
  SALE M33 .... 159 E3
Woodbray Av BNG/LEV M19 ... 144 C6 ⑬
Woodbridge Av DTN/ASHW M34 ... 129 E3
Woodbridge Gdns WHIT OL12 ... 22 A3 ④
Woodbridge Rd NTHM/RTH M23 ... 161 E4 ③
Woodbridge Rd URM M41 .... 117 E6
Woodbrook Av OLDE OL4 .... 81 F4
Wood Brook La OLDE OL4 .... 81 F4
Wood Brook Rd OLDE OL4 .... 81 F4
Woodbrook Rd WILM/AE SK9 ... 209 F4
Woodburn Dr BOL BL1 .... 26 C4
Woodburn Rd WYTH/NTH M22 ... 162 B5
Woodbury Crs DUK SK16 .... 130 C2 ③
Woodbury Rd EDGY/DAV SK3 ... 165 F6 ④
Woodcock Cl DROY M43 .... 111 D4 ③
  ROCH OL11 .... 21 D6 ③
Woodcote Av BRAM/HZG SK7 ... 182 A6
Woodcote Rd ALT WA14 .... 157 F3
Woodcote Vw WILM/AE SK9 ..... 205 D2 ②
Wood Cottage La WALK M28 .... 82 A2 ⑬
Wood Crs OLDE OL4 .... 97 F2
Woodcroft OFTN SK2 .... 184 B1
Woodcroft Av BNG/LEV M19 ... 164 C1 ③
Wooded Cl BURY BL9 .... 38 A2
Wood Edge Cl BOLS/LL BL3 ..... 48 A6 ①
Wood End BRAM/HZG SK7 .... 182 B5

Woodend Dr *STLY* SK15 .... 133 E3
Woodend La *HYDE* SK14 .... 150 A2
   STLY SK15 .... 133 E2
   WHIT OL12 .... 11 E5
Woodend Rd *EDGY/DAV* SK3 ...... 183 D3
   WYTH/NTH M22 .... 178 B3
Woodend St *OLD* OL1 .... 78 C2 ▣
   OLDE OL4 .... 81 D6 ▣
Woodfield *WYTH/NTH* M22 .... 178 A4
Woodfield Av *HYDE* SK14 .... 150 B3
   MPL/ROM SK6 .... 169 E1 ▣
   WHIT OL12 .... 22 C3 ▣
Woodfield Cl *OLDS* OL8 .... 95 D1
Woodfield Crs *MPL/ROM* SK6 ... 169 D3 ▣
Woodfield Gv *ECC* M30 .... 101 D6
   FWTH BL4 .... 66 A5 ▣
   SALE M33 .... 139 E5 ▣
Woodfield Ms *HYDE* SK14 .... 150 B3 ▣
Woodfield Rd *ALT* WA14 .... 174 A1
   CHD/CHDH SK8 .... 195 F2
   CHH M8 .... 90 B4 ▣
   MDTN M24 .... 74 C5
   SLFD M6 .... 103 E3 ▣
Woodfield St *BOLS/LL* BL3 .... 47 E6 ▣
Wood Fold *BOLE* BL2 .... 29 D1
Woodfold Av *BNG/LEV* M19 ...... 145 E1
Woodfold Rd *FAIL* M35 .... 94 B5
Woodford Av *DTN/ASHW* M34 .. 130 A5
   ECC M30 .... 100 C5
   ROY/SHW OL2 .... 62 B2 ▣
Woodford Dr *SWIN* M27 .... 85 F3
Woodford Gdns *DID/WITH* M20 .. 163 E3
Woodford Gv *BOLS/LL* BL3 .... 46 A5
Woodford La *MCFLDN* SK10 ...... 206 A5
Woodford Rd *BRAM/HZG* SK7 .. 196 C4
   POY/DIS SK12 .... 197 F4
   WILM/AE SK9 .... 205 E3
Woodgarth Av
   NEWH/MOS M40 .... 109 E2 ▣
Woodgarth Dr *SWIN* M27 .... 101 F1
Woodgarth La *WALK* M28 .... 100 A2
Woodgate Av *BURY* BL9 .... 35 E3
Woodgate Cl *MPL/ROM* SK6 .... 169 D2
Woodgate Dr *PWCH* M25 .... 72 A5 ▣
Woodgate Hill Rd *BURY* BL9 ..... 35 E3 ▣
Woodgate Rd *OLDTF/WHR* M16 .. 142 C2
Woodgate St *BOLS/LL* BL3 .... 47 E6
Woodgrange Cl *SLFD* M6 .... 103 F5 ▣
Woodgreen Dr *RAD* M26 .... 69 E2
Wood Gv *DTN/ASHW* M34 .... 130 A5 ▣
   MPL/ROM SK6 .... 149 E6 ▣
   WHTF M45 .... 52 C6
Woodhall Av *DID/WITH* M20 ..... 143 E4 ▣
   WHTF M45 .... 70 B5
Woodhall Cl *BOLE* BL2 .... 29 D4 ▣
   BRAM/HZG SK7 .... 196 B6
   TOT/BURYW BL8 .... 33 E2 ▣
Woodhall Crs *RDSH* SK5 .... 167 E1
Woodhall Rd *RDSH* SK5 .... 167 E1
Woodhall St *FAIL* M35 .... 94 A5
Woodhalt Rd *CHH* M8 .... 90 B5 ▣
Woodham Rd *NTHM/RTH* M23 .. 161 D4
Woodhead Cl *RAMS* BL0 .... 19 D1 ▣
Woodhead Dr *HALE/TIMP* WA15 .. 175 D6
Woodhead Rd *HALE/TIMP* WA15 .. 175 D6
Wood Hey *RAD* M26 .... 50 B6 ▣
Wood Hey Gv *DTN/ASHW* M34 .. 149 E1 ▣
   WHIT OL12 .... 23 D1
Woodhey Rd *RAMS* BL0 .... 18 B2
Woodheys *HTNM* SK4 .... 165 D2
Woodheys Dr *SALE* M33 .... 153 B4
Woodheys Rd *LIT* OL15 .... 25 E3
Woodhill Cl *MDTN* M24 .... 75 D1
   WGTN/LGST M12 .... 126 C5
Woodhill Dr *PWCH* M25 .... 88 C3
Woodhill Fold *TOT/BURYW* BL8 .. 33 E4
Woodhill Gv *PWCH* M25 .... 88 C2
Woodhill Rd *TOT/BURYW* BL8 .... 33 E3
Woodhill St *TOT/BURYW* BL8 .... 33 E3
Woodhouse La *ALT* WA14 .... 157 F4
   SALE M33 .... 158 A3
   WHIT OL12 .... 20 B2
   WYTH/NTH M22 .... 178 B2
   WYTH/NTH M22 .... 192 A1
Woodhouse La East
   HALE/TIMP WA15 .... 159 F4 ▣
Woodhouse Rd *ROY/SHW* OL2 ... 43 D6 ▣
   URM M41 .... 118 A5
   WYTH/NTH M22 .... 192 B1
Woodhouse St *GTN* M18 .... 127 E4
   NEWH/MOS M40 .... 108 A2 ▣
Woodhouses *FAIL* M35 .... 109 F3
   URM M41 .... 119 D6 ▣
Woodlands Av *CHD/CHDH* SK8 .. 181 E5

   ECC M30 .... 118 A1
   IRL M44 .... 116 B6 ▣
   MPL/ROM SK6 .... 149 E6
   ROCH OL11 .... 21 E6
   STRET M32 .... 140 B1 ▣
   SWIN M27 .... 101 D1 ▣
   URM M41 .... 136 A1 ▣
   WHTF M45 .... 70 C2
Woodlands Cl *CHD/CHDH* SK8 .. 195 E1
   HYDE SK14 .... 153 D2
   STLY SK15 .... 133 E2
   WALK M28 .... 83 F6
Woodlands Dr *MPL/ROM* SK6 .. 149 F6
   OFTN SK2 .... 168 A5
   SALE M33 .... 160 A4
Woodlands Gv *HYDE* SK14 .... 153 D2
   TOT/BURYW BL8 .... 32 C4 ▣
Woodlands La *HALE/TIMP* WA15 .. 174 C2 ▣
Woodlands Park Rd *OFTN* SK2 .. 168 B5
Woodlands Pkwy
   HALE/TIMP WA15 .... 174 C2
Woodlands Rd *ALT* WA14 .... 174 C2
   AUL OL6 .... 113 F1
   CHH M8 .... 90 B5
   HTNM SK4 .... 164 B3
   MILN OL16 .... 41 F2
   OLDTF/WHR M16 .... 142 C2
   POY/DIS SK12 .... 201 E3
   RAMS BL0 .... 7 E1
   SALE M33 .... 140 A6
   STLY SK15 .... 133 E2
   WALK M28 .... 83 F6
   WILM/AE SK9 .... 194 C6
   WILM/AE SK9 .... 202 C2
Woodlands St *CHH* M8 .... 90 A5
The Woodlands *HEY* OL10 .... 54 C1 ▣
   HOR/BR BL6 .... 44 A1
   TOT/BURYW BL8 .... 33 E2
Woodland St *HEY* OL10 .... 37 E5 ▣2
   WGTN/LGST M12 .... 126 C4
   WHIT OL12 .... 23 E3
Woodlands Vw *MILN* OL16 .... 24 A5
Woodland Vw *EDGW/EG* BL7 .... 14 C5
Woodland Wy *MDTN* M24 .... 75 D5 ▣
Wood La *AULW* OL7 .... 112 C2
   HALE/TIMP WA15 .... 175 E2
   MDTN M24 .... 75 F4 ▣
   MPL/ROM SK6 .... 186 B2
   PART M31 .... 154 C2
Woodlawn Ct *OLDTF/WHR* M16 .. 125 D6
Woodlea *CHAD* OL9 .... 76 B4
Woodlea Av *BNG/LEV* M19 ...... 144 C5
Woodlea Gv *WALK* M28 .... 83 F5 ▣
Woodleigh Dr *DROY* M43 .... 111 D3
Woodleigh Rd *OLDE* OL4 .... 81 E4 ▣
Woodleigh St *BKLY* M9 .... 92 A4 ▣
Woodley Av *OFTN* SK2 .... 168 B6 ▣
Woodley Cl *OFTN* SK2 .... 168 B5 ▣
Woodley Gv *BURY* BL9 .... 53 D1
Woodman Dr *BURY* BL9 .... 33 F1
Woodman St *STKP* SK1 .... 166 C4 ▣
Woodmeadow *MOSL* OL5 .... 99 D3 ▣
Woodmere Dr *BKLY* M9 .... 91 F2 ▣
Wood Mt *HALE/TIMP* WA15 ...... 175 F2
Woodmount Cl *MPL/ROM* SK6 .. 170 C3
Woodpark Cl *OLDS* OL8 .... 96 B3 ▣
Woodpecker Pl *WALK* M28 .... 83 E5 ▣
Woodridge Dr *BOLE* BL2 .... 28 C6
Wood Rd *HALE/TIMP* WA15 ...... 159 E4
   OLDTF/WHR M16 .... 123 D6
   SALE M33 .... 159 F4
Wood Road La *TOT/BURYW* BL8 .. 18 C5
Wood Rd North *OLDTF/WHR* M16 .. 123 D6
Woodrow Wy *IRL* M44 .... 135 D3
Woodroyd Cl *BRAM/HZG* SK7 .. 182 B6
Woodroyd Dr *BURY* BL9 .... 35 D4 ▣
Woodruffe Gdns *MPL/ROM* SK6 .. 169 E5
Woodseats La *GLSP* SK13 .... 153 E4
Woodsend Cir *URM* M41 .... 117 E6 ▣
Woodsend Crescent Rd *URM* M41 .. 136 B1
Woodsend Rd *URM* M41 .... 117 F6
Woodsend Rd South *URM* M41 .. 136 C2 ▣
Woods Gv *CHD/CHDH* SK8 .... 195 F2
Woodshaw Gv *WALK* M28 .... 83 D5 ▣
Woodside *MILN* OL16 .... 43 D2
   ROY/SHW OL2 .... 62 B1 ▣
Woodside Av *BNG/LEV* M19 ...... 145 D6
   WALK M28 .... 84 A3
Woodside Dr *HYDE* SK14 .... 150 C2 ▣3
   MPL/ROM SK6 .... 200 C2
   SLFD M6 .... 103 D4 ▣
Woodside La *POY/DIS* SK12 ...... 198 C5
Woodside Rd *OLDTF/WHR* M16 .. 141 F1
Woodside St *STLY* SK15 .... 115 F1 ▣
Woods La *CHD/CHDH* SK8 .... 195 F2
Woods Lea *BOL* BL1 .... 45 D2
Woodsley Rd *BOL* BL1 .... 26 A5 ▣
Woods Moor La *EDGY/DAV* SK3 .. 183 E5
Woods Rd *SWIN* M27 .... 85 E6 ▣
Wood Sq *DROY* M43 .... 128 B3 ▣
Woods Rd *IRL* M44 .... 135 D3
The Woods *ALT* WA14 .... 174 C1
   OLDE OL4 .... 81 F5
Woodstock Av *CHD/CHDH* SK8 .. 195 E2
   RDSH SK5 .... 147 D6

Woodstock Cl *HEY* OL10 .... 37 F5 ▣2
Woodstock Crs *MPL/ROM* SK6 .. 149 E6
Woodstock Dr *BOL* BL1 .... 26 B6
   SWIN M27 .... 102 B1 ▣
   TOT/BURYW BL8 .... 17 E6
   WALK M28 .... 100 B1
Woodstock Gn *RDSH* SK5 .... 147 E6
Woodstock Rd *ALT* WA14 .... 158 A5
   NEWH/MOS M40 .... 93 D4
   OLDTF/WHR M16 .... 122 C6
Woodstock St *OLDS* OL8 .... 79 D6
   WHIT OL12 .... 22 A4 ▣3
Wood St *ALT* WA14 .... 174 B3 ▣
   CHD/CHDH SK8 .... 180 B1
   CSLFD M3 .... 2 B2
   DTN/ASHW M34 .... 130 A5
   DUK SK16 .... 112 C5
   DUK SK16 .... 131 D3
   ECC M30 .... 102 A6
   EDGY/DAV SK3 .... 166 C4
   HEY OL10 .... 37 E5 ▣5
   HYDE SK14 .... 150 C1
   LIT OL15 .... 12 B6 ▣
   MDTN M24 .... 74 C1
   MILN OL16 .... 43 D2
   OLD OL1 .... 79 F3
   OP/CLY M11 .... 126 C2
   RAD M26 .... 68 C3
   RAMS BL0 .... 6 C6 ▣2
   ROCH OL11 .... 40 B1
   ROY/SHW OL2 .... 60 C2
   STLY SK15 .... 114 A5
   TOT/BURYW BL8 .... 33 E5 ▣0
Wood Ter *BOLE* BL2 .... 31 E6 ▣
Woodthorpe Cl *PWCH* M25 .... 89 E3 ▣
Woodthorpe Dr *CHD/CHDH* SK8 .. 181 E5 ▣
Woodthorpe Gra *PWCH* M25 ..... 89 E3 ▣
Woodvale *ALT* WA14 .... 174 A5
   MDTN M24 .... 57 E5 ▣
Woodvale Av *BOLS/LL* BL3 .... 64 B1
Woodvale Dr *BOLS/LL* BL3 .... 64 B1 ▣
Woodvale Gdns *BOLS/LL* BL3 .... 64 B1 ▣
Woodvale Gv *BOLS/LL* BL3 .... 64 B1
Wood Vw *HEY* OL10 .... 37 D3
   WYTH/NTH M22 .... 162 B4
Woodview Dr *BNG/LEV* M19 ..... 145 D6 ▣
Woodville Dr *MPL/ROM* SK6 .... 186 C3
   SALE M33 .... 139 E6
   STLY SK15 .... 115 E4
Woodville Gv *RDSH* SK5 .... 147 D5
Woodville Rd *ALT* WA14 .... 174 A5
   SALE M33 .... 139 E6 ▣
Woodville Ter *NEWH/MOS* M40 .. 92 A4 ▣2
Woodward Cl *BURY* BL9 .... 34 A2
Woodward Pl *ANC* M4 .... 107 D5 ▣4
Woodward Rd *PWCH* M25 .... 88 A3
Woodward St *ANC* M4 .... 107 D5
Woodwise La *NTHM/RTH* M23 .. 160 C4 ▣
Woolden St *ECC* M30 .... 100 C4 ▣3
Woollacot St *OLD* OL1 .... 79 D5 ▣3
Woollam Pl *CSLFD* M3 .... 123 E1 ▣
Woolley Av *POY/DIS* SK12 .... 198 B6 ▣
Woolley St *CHH* M8 .... 106 A3 ▣
Wootton St *HYDE* SK14 .... 131 E5 ▣
Worcester Av *DTN/ASHW* M34 .. 149 E2
   RDSH SK5 .... 148 A6
Worcester Cl *AUL* OL6 .... 97 E5 ▣2
   BURY BL9 .... 53 E1 ▣
   MPL/ROM SK6 .... 169 E4 ▣
Worcester Rd *BOLS/LL* BL3 .... 49 D6
   CHD/CHDH SK8 .... 181 E3
   MDTN M24 .... 75 D6
   SALE M33 .... 158 B2 ▣0
   SLFD M6 .... 103 D3
   SWIN M27 .... 85 E3
Worcester St *BRO* M7 .... 105 F1 ▣8
   CHAD OL9 .... 77 F6
   ROCH OL11 .... 39 F3
   TOT/BURYW BL8 .... 33 E3
Wordsworth Av *BURY* BL9 .... 53 D3 ▣
   CHH M8 .... 106 B1 ▣0
   DROY M43 .... 110 A5
   FWTH BL4 .... 65 F4
   RAD M26 .... 50 C5
Wordsworth Cl *DUK* SK16 .... 132 B2
Wordsworth Crs *AULW* OL7 ..... 111 F2
   LIT OL15 .... 25 D3 ▣
Wordsworth Gdns *PWCH* M25 .. 88 A2 ▣
Wordsworth Rd *DTN/ASHW* M34 .. 149 E4
   LHULT M38 .... 65 F6 ▣
   MDTN M24 .... 75 F1
   OLD OL1 .... 79 F2
   OLDTF/WHR M16 .... 122 C6
   RDSH SK5 .... 146 B2
   SWIN M27 .... 85 E4
Wordsworth St *BOL* BL1 .... 27 E5 ▣2
   SLFD M6 .... 105 D3 ▣1
Wordsworth Wy *ROCH* OL11 ..... 37 F1
Workesleigh St
   NEWH/MOS M40 .... 109 D2 ▣0
World Wy *MANAIR* M90 .... 191 F1
Worrall St *EDGY/DAV* SK3 .... 166 C6 ▣
   NEWH/MOS M40 .... 108 B1 ▣3
   SALQ/ORD M5 .... 123 D2
   WHIT OL12 .... 22 B3 ▣

Worsbrough Av *WALK* M28 .... **83** D3 ④
Worsefold St *NEWH/MOS* M40 ..... **92** B5 ⑤
Worsel St *BOLS/LL* BL3 .... **46** A5 ⑱
Worsley Av *NEWH/MOS* M40............ **92** A4
  WALK M28 .... **82** B3
Worsley Ct *WALK* M28 .... **83** E2 ⑧
Worsley Crs *OFTN* SK2 .... **167** F6 ⑤
Worsley Gv *BNG/LEV* M19 .... **145** E2 ②
  WALK M28 .... **82** B3
Worsley Pl *MILN* OL16 .... **23** F6 ⑧
  ROY/SHW OL2 .... **61** E3
Worsley Rd *BOLS/LL* BL3 .... **45** E5
  ECC M30 .... **100** C5
  FWTH BL4 .... **66** B5
  WALK M28 .... **100** B2
Worsley Rd North *WALK* M28 ...... **66** B6
Worsley St *BOLS/LL* BL3 .... **46** C4 ㉓
  CSLFD M3 .... **2** B6 ③
  HULME M15 .... **123** E2
  MILN OL16 .... **23** F6
  OLDS OL8 .... **79** F6
  SWIN M27 .... **86** B3
  TOT/BURYW BL8 .... **17** F6 ②
Worston Av *BOL* BL1 .... **26** A5
Worth La *DTN/ASHW* M34 .... **149** E4
Worthing Cl *OFTN* SK2 .... **184** B1 ③
Worthing St *RUSH/FAL* M14 ...... **143** F1 ⑮
Worthington Av *HEY* OL10 .... **56** C2
  PART M31 .... **155** D2
Worthington Cl *HYDE* SK14 .... **152** C1 ③
Worthington Dr *BRO* M7 .... **89** E4 ②
Worthington Rd *DTN/ASHW* M34.... **149** F1
  SALE M33 .... **160** C1
Worthington St *AULW* OL7 .... **112** A2
  BOLS/LL BL3 .... **46** A6 ⑯
  NEWH/MOS M40 .... **93** D5
  STLY SK15 .... **114** A6 ⑥
Worth's La *DTN/ASHW* M34 .... **149** E4
Wortley Av *SLFD* M6 .... **103** D4
Wortley Gv *NEWH/MOS* M40.......... **92** A4
Wragby Cl *TOT/BURYW* BL8........... **33** E2
Wrath Cl *BOLE* BL2 .... **28** C1
Wray Pl *MILN* OL16 .... **41** D1
Wrekin Av *NTHM/RTH* M23 .... **177** E4
Wren Av *SWIN* M27 .... **86** C2
Wrenbury Av *DID/WITH* M20......... **143** D4
Wrenbury Crs *EDGY/DAV* SK3 ..... **182** A1
Wrenbury Dr *CHD/CHDH* SK8 ..... **180** C1 ②
  EDGW BL7 .... **28** A1
  MILN OL16 .... **41** D3
Wren Cl *DTN/ASHW* M34 .... **111** D5
  FWTH BL4 .... **65** D3
  OFTN SK2 .... **185** D2
Wren Dr *BURY* BL9 .... **34** C3 ⑤
  IRL M44 .... **116** B5 ③
Wren Gdns *MDTN* M24 .... **75** D2 ⑬
Wren Gn *MILN* OL16 .... **40** C1 ⑫
Wren's Nest Av *ROY/SHW* OL2 .... **62** A1 ⑤
Wren St *OLDE* OL4 .... **80** A5
Wrenswood Dr *WALK* M28 .... **83** D5 ⑪
Wrexham Cl *OLDS* OL8 .... **94** C3 ⑨
Wrigglesworth Cl
  TOT/BURYW BL8 .... **32** A4 ④
Wright Robinson Cl
  OP/CLY M11 .... **125** F1 ⑥
Wrights Bank North *OFTN* SK2 .. **184** B2
Wrights Bank South *OFTN* SK2 .. **184** C2 ③
Wright St *AULW* OL6 .... **113** E3 ⑪
  CHAD OL9 .... **77** F6
  DTN/ASHW M34 .... **129** F1
  FAIL M35 .... **94** A3 ③
  OLD OL1 .... **79** E4 ③
  OLDTF/WHR M16 .... **123** D4
  RAD M26 .... **51** D6 ⑪
Wrigley Crs *FAIL* M35 .... **94** A6
Wrigley Fold *MDTN* M24 .... **56** A5
Wrigley Head *FAIL* M35 .... **94** A5
Wrigley Head Crs *FAIL* M35 .... **94** A5
Wrigley Pl *LIT* OL15 .... **25** D2 ⑬
Wrigley St *AUL* OL6 .... **112** C3
  OLDE OL4 .... **79** F4
  OLDE OL4 .... **81** D5 ⑪
  OLDE OL4 .... **81** F3
Wroe St *CSLFD* M3 .... **105** E6
  OLDE OL4 .... **81** D5 ⑫
  SWIN M27 .... **86** A2
Wrotham Cl *SALQ/ORD* M5 .... **104** B6 ③
Wroxham Av *DTN/ASHW* M34 ..... **128** B6 ③
  URM M41 .... **118** C6
Wroxham Cl *TOT/BURYW* BL8 ...... **33** E2 ③
Wroxham Rd *BKLY* M9 .... **90** C2
Wuerdle Cl *MILN* OL16 .... **24** C1 ④
Wuerdle Farm Wy *MILN* OL16 ... **24** C1 ③
Wuerdle Pl *MILN* OL16 .... **24** C1
Wuerdle St *MILN* OL16 .... **24** C1 ①
Wyatt Av *SALQ/ORD* M5 .... **122** C2 ⑬
Wyatt St *DUK* SK16 .... **131** D1 ③
  HTNM SK4 .... **166** C3
Wybersley Rd *MPL/ROM* SK6 ..... **187** F6
Wychbury St *SALQ/ORD* M5 .... **103** F5
Wychelm Rd *PART* M31 .... **155** D2

Wycherley Rd *WHIT* OL12 .... **21** F3
Wych Fold *HYDE* SK14 .... **150** C4 ④
Wych St *AUL* OL6 .... **112** C5 ⑤
Wychwood *ALT* WA14 .... **173** F6
Wychwood Cl *MDTN* M24 .... **75** F4 ③
Wycliffe Av *WILM/AE* SK9 .... **203** E5
Wycliffe Rd *URM* M41 .... **138** A1
Wycliffe St *ECC* M30 .... **101** D5 ⑦
  HTNM SK4 .... **166** B3
Wycombe Av *GTN* M18 .... **127** F3
Wycombe Cl *URM* M41 .... **119** D4 ③
Wye Av *FAIL* M35 .... **94** A6 ③
Wyecroft Cl *MPL/ROM* SK6 .... **149** F6
Wye St *OLDS* OL8 .... **78** B6
Wykeham Gv *WHIT* OL12 .... **21** F4 ③
Wykeham Ms *BOL* BL1 .... **45** E2 ③
Wykeham St *RUSH/FAL* M14 ...... **124** B6 ⑪
Wyke Pk *OLDE* OL4 .... **80** B5
The Wylde *BURY* BL9 .... **33** F5 ㉔
Wynchgate Rd *BRAM/HZG* SK7.... **185** E4 ③
Wyndale Dr *FAIL* M35 .... **110** A2
Wyndale Rd *OLDS* OL8 .... **96** A2
Wyndcliff Dr *URM* M41 .... **136** C2
Wyndham Av *SWIN* M27 .... **86** A3
  WYTH/NTH M22 .... **162** B4
Wyndham Cl *BRAM/HZG* SK7....... **196** C2
Wyne Cl *BRAM/HZG* SK7 .... **185** E4 ①
Wynfield Av *WYTH/NTH* M22....... **193** D2
Wynford Sq *SALQ/ORD* M5 .... **104** A6 ⑧
Wyngate Rd *CHD/CHDH* SK8 ...... **181** D6
  HALE/TIMP WA15 .... **189** D2
Wynne Av *SWIN* M27 .... **86** A2
Wynne Cl *DTN/ASHW* M34 .... **149** D2
  OP/CLY M11 .... **126** A4
Wynne Gv *DTN/ASHW* M34 .... **148** C2
Wynne St *BOL* BL1 .... **27** F5
  LHULT M38 .... **82** B1 ⑦
  SLFD M6 .... **104** C3
Wynnstay Gv *RUSH/FAL* M14 ..... **144** A3
Wynnstay Rd *SALE* M33 .... **139** F6
Wynyard Cl *SALE* M33 .... **160** B3 ③
Wynyard Rd *WYTH/NTH* M22 ..... **178** A4
Wyre Dr *WALK* M28 .... **82** C6
Wyresdale Rd *BOL* BL1 .... **46** A1
Wyre St *CMANE* M1 .... **3** H6
  MOSL OL5 .... **98** C4
Wythall Av *LHULT* M38 .... **65** F5 ④
Wythburn Av *BOL* BL1 .... **26** B6 ⑲
  CHH M8 .... **107** D1 ⑩
  URM M41 .... **118** C6 ④
Wythburn Rd *MDTN* M24 .... **56** C6
  STKP SK1 .... **167** F6
Wythburn St *SALQ/ORD* M5 ...... **103** F5 ③
Wythenshawe Rd
  NTHM/RTH M23 .... **160** C5
  SALE M33 .... **160** C1
Wythens Rd *CHD/CHDH* SK8 ...... **195** F1
Wythop Gdns *SALQ/ORD* M5 ..... **104** B6 ⑥
Wyvern Av *HTNM* SK4 .... **146** C6
Wyverne Rd *CHD/CHDH* M21 ...... **142** B3
Wyville Dr *BRAM/HZG* SK7 .... **185** E5
Wyville Dr *BKLY* M9 .... **73** F5
  SLFD M6 .... **104** A4 ⑬
  SWIN M27 .... **85** E3

Y

Yale St *EDGW/EG* BL7 .... **15** E1
Yarburgh St *OLDTF/WHR* M16...... **123** F6
Yardley St *STRET* M32 .... **139** E1
Yardley Cl *STRET* M32 .... **139** E1
Yarmouth Dr *NTHM/RTH* M23 .... **161** F4 ②
Yarnton Cl *ROY/SHW* OL2 .... **61** E4 ⑦
Yarrow Cl *ROCH* OL11 .... **40** A2
Yarrow Pl *BOL* BL1 .... **27** E6
Yarwood Av *NTHM/RTH* M23 ..... **161** D6 ⑤
Yarwood Cl *HEY* OL10 .... **37** F4 ③
Yarwood St *ALT* WA14 .... **174** B4
  BURY BL9 .... **34** B5 ㉓
Yasmin Gdns *OLD* OL1 .... **78** B3
Yates Dr *WALK* M28 .... **82** B2 ②
Yates St *BOLE* BL2 .... **28** B6
  MDTN M24 .... **74** A4
  OLD OL1 .... **79** E3
  STKP SK1 .... **167** F2
Yates Ter *TOT/BURYW* BL8............ **33** E2
Yattendon Av *NTHM/RTH* M23 .... **160** B5 ①
Yealand Av *HTNM* SK4 .... **166** B3 ⑩
Yealand Cl *ROCH* OL11 .... **38** C1
Yeardsley Cl *BRAM/HZG* SK7 ..... **182** C4 ③
Yeoford Dr *ALT* WA14 .... **173** F1
Yeoman Cl *BRAM/HZG* SK7 .... **184** B4 ⑩
Yeoman's Cl *MILN* OL16 .... **25** D6
Yewbarrow Rd *OLD* OL1 .... **79** E3
Yew Cl *BOLS/LL* BL3 .... **45** F5
Yew Crs *OLDE* OL4 .... **80** B3
Yewdale *SWIN* M27 .... **86** C3 ③
Yewdale Av *BOLE* BL2 .... **30** A5

Yewdale Dr *MDTN* M24 .... **74** C2
Yewdale Gdns *BOLE* BL2 .... **30** A5
Yew Dale Gdns *ROCH* OL11 .... **38** C3
Yewdale Rd *OFTN* SK2 .... **183** F1
Yewlands Av *BKLY* M9 .... **74** B6
Yew St *BRO* M7 .... **105** D1
  BURY BL9 .... **34** C4
  DTN/ASHW M34 .... **130** A3
  HEY OL10 .... **36** C5
  HTNM SK4 .... **165** F5
  HULME M15 .... **123** F4
Yew Tree Av *BNG/LEV* M19 .... **145** E2
  BRAM/HZG SK7 .... **199** D1
  RUSH/FAL M14 .... **124** B6
  WYTH/NTH M22 .... **162** B4
Yew Tree Cl *AULW* OL7 .... **112** B1
  MPL/ROM SK6 .... **186** C2
  WILM/AE SK9 .... **204** B4 ③
Yew Tree Dr *MDTN* M24 .... **76** B4
  MPL/ROM SK6 .... **168** B2
  PWCH M25 .... **88** C1
  SALE M33 .... **160** C1
  URM M41 .... **118** A5 ③
  WYTH/NTH M22 .... **162** B4
Yew Tree La *BOL* BL1 .... **28** B2
  DUK SK16 .... **131** F3
Yewtree La *NTHM/RTH* M23 .... **161** F3
  WYTH/NTH M22 .... **162** B4
Yew Tree Park Rd *CHD/CHDH* SK8 . **195** F3
Yew Tree Rd *DTN/ASHW* M34 ..... **148** C2
  EDGY/DAV SK3 .... **183** D4
  RUSH/FAL M14 .... **143** F1
York Av *BOLS/LL* BL3..................... **49** E6
  OLDS OL8 .... **95** E1
  OLDTF/WHR M16 .... **142** A1
  PWCH M25 .... **89** E3
  ROCH OL11 .... **38** B1
  SALE M33 .... **139** F6
  SWIN M27 .... **85** E3
  URM M41 .... **119** F6 ⑧
York Cl *CHD/CHDH* SK8 .... **181** E2
York Crs *WILM/AE* SK9 .... **204** B4
Yorkdale Rd *OLDE* OL4 .... **80** B4
York Dr *ALT* WA14 .... **174** B6
  BRAM/HZG SK7 .... **185** E5
  MANAIR M90 .... **191** D2
  RAMS BL0 .... **18** B2
York Pl *AULW* OL7 .... **112** B5
York Rd *ALT* WA14 .... **174** A6
  CCHDY M21 .... **141** F3 ⑫
  CHAD OL9 .... **77** D3
  DROY M43 .... **110** A4
  DTN/ASHW M34 .... **130** A5
  HTNM SK4 .... **165** F6
  HYDE SK14 .... **150** C5
  IRL M44 .... **134** B6
  SALE M33 .... **139** E6
Yorkshire Rd *PART* M31 .... **154** C3 ③
York St *AUL* OL6 .... **112** C3
  CSLFD M3 .... **2** B2 ③
  MILN OL16 .... **23** D5
  OLD OL1 .... **79** E4
York St *BKLY* M9 .... **91** F5
  BNG/LEV M19 .... **145** E3
  BURY BL9 .... **34** B5
  CHAD OL9 .... **78** C5
  CMANE M1 .... **124** B2 ⑪
  CMANW M2 .... **3** E3
  DID/WITH M20 .... **163** F2
  DTN/ASHW M34 .... **129** F1
  EDGY/DAV SK3 .... **166** B5
  FWTH BL4 .... **66** C3 ③
  HALE/TIMP WA15 .... **174** C4
  HEY OL10 .... **37** E5
  HULME M15 .... **123** F2
  MILN OL16 .... **40** C1
  RAD M26 .... **52** C4
  WHTF M45 .... **71** D3
Young St *CSLFD* M3 .... **2** B4
  FWTH BL4 .... **66** B4
  RAMS BL0 .... **6** C5
Yulan Dr *SALE* M33 .... **158** A1
Yule St *EDGY/DAV* SK3 .... **166** B5

Z

Zama St *RAMS* BL0 .... **18** B1 ㉑
Zealand St *OLDE* OL4 .... **80** A3
Zebra St *BRO* M7 .... **90** A6 ②
Zeta St *BKLY* M9 .... **92** A6
Zetland Rd *CCHDY* M21 .... **141** F3
Zetland St *DUK* SK16 .... **113** D6
Zinnia Dr *IRL* M44 .... **134** C3
Zion Crs *HULME* M15 .... **125** F3
Zion Ter *WHIT* OL12 .... **20** C3 ⑥
Zurich Gdns *BRAM/HZG* SK7 ..... **182** C4 ⑨

Abbey Hey Primary School
  GTN M18 .... **127** F4
Abbey Independent College
  CMANW M2 .... **2** D4
Abbey Tutorial College
  CMANW M2 .... **3** E3
Abbotsford Preparatory School
  URM M41 .... **137** E1
Abbott CP School
  NEWH/MOS M40 .... **107** D4
A B C Cinema
  ROCH OL11 .... **39** F3
Abingdon Primary School
  RDSH SK5 .... **147** D4
Abraham Moss High School
  CHH M8 .... **90** B5
Acorn Business Park
  EDGY/DAV SK3 .... **166** B4
Adswood Clinic
  EDGY/DAV SK3 .... **182** C2
Adswood Primary School
  EDGY/DAV SK3 .... **182** B2
A & E Wythenshawe Hospital
  NTHM/RTH M23 .... **177** D2
Ailsa Craig Medical Practice
  BRUN/LGST M13 .... **125** F6
Ainsworth C of E Primary School
  BOLE BL2 .... **31** D6
Alastair Ross Health Centre
  BOLE BL2 .... **49** D1
Albany Trading Estate
  CCHDY M21 .... **141** F2
Albion Drive Clinic
  DROY M43 .... **110** B4
Albion Trading Estate
  SLFD M6 .... **104** B3
Alderley Edge CP School
  WILM/AE SK9 .... **209** E3
Alderley Edge Cricket Club
  WILM/AE SK9 .... **209** F4
Alderley Edge Golf Club
  WILM/AE SK9 .... **208** C2
Alderley Edge School for Girls
  WILM/AE SK9 .... **209** D3
Alderman Kay School
  MDTN M24 .... **57** E5
Alder Park CP School
  ECC M30 .... **100** C3
Aldwyn CP School
  DTN/ASHW M34 .... **111** D6
Alexandra Centre Retail Park
  OLDE OL4 .... **79** E5
The Alexandra Hospital
  CHD/CHDH SK8 .... **180** B1
Alexandra Industrial Estate
  DTN/ASHW M34 .... **130** B5
Alexandra Park Junior &
  Infant School
  EDGY/DAV SK3 .... **166** A6
Alexandra Park School
  OLDS OL8 .... **96** B1
Alexandra Practice
  CCHDY M21 .... **142** B2
Alf Kaufman School
  ROCH OL11 .... **20** C4
Alice Ingham Primary School
  MILN OL16 .... **24** A3
Al Kowsar Surgery
  OLDS OL8 .... **78** B6
Alkrington Clinic Centre
  MDTN M24 .... **75** E6
Alkrington CP School
  MDTN M24 .... **75** E5
Alkrington Moss CP School
  MDTN M24 .... **75** F6
Alkrington Physiotherapy
  Sports Injury Clinic
  MDTN M24 .... **75** E4
Alliston House Medical Centre
  URM M41 .... **138** A1
All Saints C of E Junior School
  FWTH BL4 .... **66** B2
All Saints C of E Primary School
  HTNM SK4 .... **166** B1
All Saints C of E Primary School
  MPL/ROM SK6 .... **187** E2
All Saints C of E Primary School
  WHIT OL12 .... **23** E4
All Saints C of E Primary School
  WHTF M45 .... **71** E1
All Saints Primary School
  GTN M18 .... **126** C3
All Saints Primary School
  NEWH/MOS M40 .... **109** D2

All Saints RC School
  DUK SK16 .... **131** F2
Alma Industrial Estate
  WHIT OL12 .... **23** D4
Alma Park Primary School
  BNG/LEV M19 .... **145** E3
Alt Primary School
  OLDS OL8 .... **97** E2
Altrincham & Broadheath
  CP School
  ALT WA14 .... **158** A5
Altrincham C of E
  Primary School
  ALT WA14 .... **174** A2
Altrincham General Hospital
  ALT WA14 .... **174** A3
Altrincham Grammar School
  for Boys
  ALT WA14 .... **174** B5
Altrincham Grammar School
  for Girls
  ALT WA14 .... **174** A4
Altrincham Ice Rink
  ALT WA14 .... **174** B1
Altrincham Industrial Centre
  ALT WA14 .... **173** E1
Altrincham Rugby Football Club
  HALE/TIMP WA15 .... **160** A6
Altrincham Leisure Centre
  HALE/TIMP WA15 .... **174** C2
Altrincham Preparatory School
  ALT WA14 .... **174** A6
Altrincham Preparatory School
  ALT WA14 .... **174** A5
Altrincham Priory Hospital
  HALE/TIMP WA15 .... **189** E1
Amalgamated Sports Club
  POY/DIS SK12 .... **201** F3
Ancoats Hospital
  ANC M4 .... **107** D6
Angouleme Way Retail Park
  BURY BL9 .... **34** A5
Ann Street Health Centre
  DTN/ASHW M34 .... **129** F6
Anson Medical Centre
  RUSH/FAL M14 .... **125** E5
Apollo Theatre
  WGTN/LGST M12 .... **125** D2
Aquinas Sixth Form College
  OFTN SK2 .... **183** F1
Arcadia Sports Centre
  BNG/LEV M19 .... **145** E2
The Archways Surgery
  MPL/ROM SK6 .... **169** F3
Ardath Israel Synagogue
  BRO M7 .... **89** F4
Arden Business Centre
  MPL/ROM SK6 .... **148** C5
Arden Primary School
  MPL/ROM SK6 .... **168** B2
Arlies Primary School
  AUL OL6 .... **114** B2
Armitage C of E Primary School
  WGTN/LGST M12 .... **125** F3
Arndale Shopping Centre
  ANC M4 .... **3** E2
Arrow Trading Estate
  DTN/ASHW M34 .... **129** E4
Art Gallery
  BURY BL9 .... **33** F5
Ashbury Primary School
  OP/CLY M11 .... **126** A1
Ashcroft Surgery
  BNG/LEV M19 .... **145** E2
Ashdene CP School
  WILM/AE SK9 .... **203** D6
Ash Field Primary School
  WALK M28 .... **83** F4
Ashfield Valley Primary School
  ROCH OL11 .... **39** F3
Ashley C of E Primary School
  HALE/TIMP WA15 .... **189** D4
Ashton on Mersey School
  SALE M33 .... **159** D1
Ashton Private Clinic of
  Natural Health
  AUL OL6 .... **112** B5
Ashton Swimming Pool
  AUL OL6 .... **112** C4
Ashton Under Lyne Rugby Club
  AUL OL6 .... **96** C6
Ashton Under Lyne Sixth
  Form College
  AUL OL6 .... **113** E3

Ashton United Football Club
  AUL OL6 .... **113** E1
Aspinall School
  GTN M18 .... **127** F6
Astley Bridge Cricket Club
  BOL BL1 .... **27** E3
Astra Business Park
  TRPK M17 .... **120** A1
Astra Industrial Centre
  ROCH OL11 .... **39** D4
Atlantic Business Centre
  ALT WA14 .... **158** A6
Audenshaw CP School
  DTN/ASHW M34 .... **129** D2
Audenshaw Grammar School
  DTN/ASHW M34 .... **129** F3
Audenshaw Hawthorns School
  DTN/ASHW M34 .... **129** E4
Austerlands Cricket Club
  OLDE OL4 .... **81** E3
Avenue Medical Centre
  BKLY M9 .... **74** C6
Avicenna Grammar School
  DID/WITH M20 .... **163** D1
Avondale Health Centre
  BOL BL1 .... **27** D6
Avondale Industrial Estate
  EDGY/DAV SK3 .... **165** F5
Avondale Recreation Centre
  EDGY/DAV SK3 .... **165** F6
Avondale Secondary School
  EDGY/DAV SK3 .... **166** A6
Baguley Hall Primary School
  NTHM/RTH M23 .... **177** E1
Baillie Street Health Centre
  MILN OL16 .... **23** D5
Balderstone Community School
  ROCH OL11 .... **40** B4
Bamford Primary School
  ROCH OL11 .... **37** F1
Bank Meadow Primary School
  WGTN/LGST M12 .... **125** E1
Bankside School
  HYDE SK14 .... **151** D2
Banks Lane Primary School
  STKP SK1 .... **167** F5
Baretrees CP School
  CHAD OL9 .... **77** F3
Barlow Hall Primary School
  CCHDY M21 .... **142** A6
Barlow Medical Centre
  DID/WITH M20 .... **163** F2
The Barlow RC High School
  DID/WITH M20 .... **164** A3
Barn Gallery
  CMANE M1 .... **3** E6
Barrack Hill Primary School
  MPL/ROM SK6 .... **169** E3
Barrington Medical Centre
  ALT WA14 .... **174** B1
Barton Business Park
  ECC M30 .... **101** D6
Barton Clough Primary School
  STRET M32 .... **120** A5
Barton Moss C of E
  Primary School
  ECC M30 .... **100** A6
BBC North
  CMANE M1 .... **124** B2
Bealey Community Hospital
  RAD M26 .... **52** B5
Bealey Industrial Estate
  RAD M26 .... **52** B4
Beaumont County
  Primary School
  HOR/BR BL6 .... **44** C4
Beaver Road Junior &
  Infant School
  DID/WITH M20 .... **163** F2
Beech House Group Practice
  BRAM/HZG SK7 .... **184** C5
Beech House School
  ROCH OL11 .... **39** F1
Beech Road Gallery
  CCHDY M21 .... **141** E3
Beever CP School
  OLD OL1 .... **79** E3
Belfield Community School
  MILN OL16 .... **24** A5
Benchill Junior & Infant School
  WYTH/NTH M22 .... **178** A1
Benchill Medical Practice
  WYTH/NTH M22 .... **178** B3

Bents Lane Medical Practice
MPL/ROM SK6 .... 169 D1
The Berrisford Gallery
WILM/AE SK9 .... 208 C2
Beth David School
PWCH M25 .... 88 C3
Bethesda School
CHD/CHDH SK8 .... 180 B4
Bilal Jamia Mosque
OLDE OL4 .... 80 A4
Birches Health Centre
PWCH M25 .... 72 A5
The Birches School
DID/WITH M20 .... 143 D6
Birchfields Primary School
RUSH/FAL M14 .... 144 C2
Birch Industrial Estate
HEY OL10 .... 55 E3
Birtenshaw School
BOL BL1 .... 28 C1
Birtle View Special School
HEY OL10 .... 37 D5
Bishop Bilsborrow RC Primary
School
OLDTF/WHR M16 .... 143 D1
Bishop Bridgeman C of E
Primary School
BOLS/LL BL3 .... 46 C5
B & J Leisure Centre
WILM/AE SK9 .... 203 E4
Blackburn Street Health Centre
RAD M26 .... 51 E6
Blackshaw CP School
BOLE BL2 .... 49 E3
Blackshaw Lane CP School
ROY/SHW OL2 .... 61 E5
Blind School
BOLE BL2 .... 47 F2
Blue Chip Business Park
ALT WA14 .... 157 F6
Blue Coat C of E
Secondary School
OLD OL1 .... 79 D4
Bnos Yisroel School
BRO M7 .... 89 F6
Boarshaw CP School
MDTN M24 .... 57 F6
Bodmin Road Clinic
SALE M33 .... 138 B6
Bollin CP School
ALT WA14 .... 173 F6
Bolshaw Primary School
CHD/CHDH SK8 .... 193 F2
Bolton Business Centre
BOLE BL2 .... 47 E3
Bolton Cricket Club
BOLS/LL BL3 .... 65 F1
Bolton District Hospital
FWTH BL4 .... 65 D2
Bolton Health Authority
BOL BL1 .... 46 B1
Bolton Little Theatre
BOL BL1 .... 46 C3
Bolton Metropolitan
Borough Council
BOL BL1 .... 27 E5
Bolton Metropolitan
Borough Council
BOL BL1 .... 27 E3
Bolton Metropolitan
Borough Council
BOL BL1 .... 45 E2
Bolton Metropolitan
Borough Council
BOL BL1 .... 46 C2
Bolton Metropolitan
Borough Council
BOL BL1 .... 46 A2
Bolton Metropolitan
Borough Council
BOL BL1 .... 47 D2
Bolton Metropolitan
Borough Council
BOLS/LL BL3 .... 46 B4
Bolton Metropolitan
Borough Council
BOLS/LL BL3 .... 49 E6
Bolton Metropolitan College
BOLE BL2 .... 47 E3
Bolton Open Golf Club
BOLE BL2 .... 29 E4
Bolton Rugby Union Football Club
BOL BL1 .... 46 B1

Bolton School
BOL BL1 .... 45 F2
Bolton Trophy & Sports Centre
BOLE BL2 .... 47 F1
Bolton Wyresdale Associated
Football Club
BOLE BL2 .... 49 E3
Bond Street Industrial Estate
WGTN/LGST M12 .... 125 D1
Booth Hall Childrens Hospital
BKLY M9 .... 92 A2
The Borchardt Medical Centre
DID/WITH M20 .... 143 D5
Boundary Industrial Estate
BOLE BL2 .... 49 E2
Boundary Medical Practice
HULME M15 .... 124 B3
Boundary Trading Estate
ECC M30 .... 117 D5
Bowdon Cricket Club
ALT WA14 .... 174 A6
Bowdon Rugby Union
Football Club
HALE/TIMP WA15 .... 176 A3
Bowdon Vale Cricket Club
ALT WA14 .... 188 A1
Bowker Vale Primary School
BKLY M9 .... 90 A1
Bowness CP School
BOLS/LL BL3 .... 49 D6
Brabyns School
MPL/ROM SK6 .... 171 E6
Bradley Fold Trading Estate
BOLE BL3 .... 50 A3
Bradley Green CP School
HYDE SK14 .... 132 A3
Bradshaw Cricket Club
BOLE BL2 .... 29 D2
Bradshaw Hall Infant &
Junior School
CHD/CHDH SK8 .... 180 C6
Bramhall Hall
BRAM/HZG SK7 .... 182 C6
Bramhall Health Centre
BRAM/HZG SK7 .... 196 C3
Bramhall High School
BRAM/HZG SK7 .... 197 D1
Bramhall Park Medical Centre
BRAM/HZG SK7 .... 182 C5
Brandlesholme CP School
TOT/BURYW BL8 .... 33 D1
Brandwood County
Infant School
BOLS/LL BL3 .... 46 A5
Branwood Preparatory School
ECC M30 .... 101 A3
Braunhill Park Golf Course
BRAM/HZG SK7 .... 196 A3
Bredbury Clinic
MPL/ROM SK6 .... 169 D1
Bredbury Green Primary School
MPL/ROM SK6 .... 169 D4
Breeze Hill Comprehensive
School
OLDE OL4 .... 80 B6
Breightmet CP School
BOLE BL2 .... 30 A6
Breightmet Football Club
BOLE BL2 .... 49 D2
Breightmet Industrial Estate
BOLE BL2 .... 49 D2
Brentnall Primary School
BRO M7 .... 89 E6
Brentwood School
ALT WA14 .... 158 C6
Bridge College
OFTN SK2 .... 168 B5
Bridge Hall Primary School
EDGY/DAV SK3 .... 182 B1
Bridge House Medical Centre
CHD/CHDH SK8 .... 181 F4
Bridge Trading Estate
TOT/BURYW BL8 .... 33 E5
Bridgewater Concert Hall
CMANW M2 .... 2 D6
Bridgewater Primary School
LHULT M38 .... 82 C1
Bridgewater School
WALK M28 .... 100 B1
Brimrod CP School
ROCH OL11 .... 39 E2
Brindale Primary School
RDSH SK5 .... 168 A1

Brindle House Community
Mental Health Centre
HYDE SK14 .... 150 B1
Brinnington Health Centre
RDSH SK5 .... 148 A6
Briscoe Lane Junior
& Infant School
NEWH/MOS M40 .... 108 C2
Britannia County Primary School
BCUP OL13 .... 5 D1
Britannia Mill Industrial Estate
HEY OL10 .... 36 C5
Broadbent Fold Primary School
DUK SK16 .... 132 B2
Broadbottom C of E
Primary School
HYDE SK14 .... 153 D3
Broadfield County Primary
School
OLDS OL8 .... 79 D6
Broadfield Industrial Estate
HEY OL10 .... 36 C6
Broadhurst CP School
NEWH/MOS M40 .... 93 D6
Broadoak Business Park
TRPK M17 .... 120 A2
Broadoak County Infant School
AUL OL6 .... 113 D1
Broadoak County Primary
School
SWIN M27 .... 101 D1
Broadoak CP School
AUL OL6 .... 113 D2
Broadoak High School
BURY BL9 .... 34 C5
Broadoak High School
PART M31 .... 154 C3
Broad Oak Primary School
DID/WITH M20 .... 163 F5
Broadstone Hall Primary School
HTNM SK4 .... 146 B5
Broadway Industrial Estate
SALQ/ORD M5 .... 122 B1
Brookburn Primary School
CCHDY M21 .... 141 E4
Brook Dean CP School
WILM/AE SK9 .... 194 B4
Brookhead Junior School
CHD/CHDH SK8 .... 181 D2
Brooks Bar Medical Centre
OLDTF/WHR M16 .... 123 E5
Brookside Business Park
MDTN M24 .... 76 B5
Brookside Primary School
MPL/ROM SK6 .... 200 C3
Brookway High School
NTHM/RTH M23 .... 160 C5
Broomwood CP School
HALE/TIMP WA15 .... 176 B2
Broughton Baths
BRO M7 .... 105 E1
Broughton Cricket Club
BRO M7 .... 105 E1
Broughton Recreation Centre
BRO M7 .... 105 E2
Brownhall Moor Industrial
Estate
BRAM/HZG SK7 .... 183 F5
Brownhill School
WHIT OL12 .... 22 C4
Brownlow Business Centre
BOL BL1 .... 27 E6
Brownlow Fold CP School
BOL BL1 .... 27 E6
Brunswick Health Centre
BRUN/LGST M13 .... 124 C3
Bruntwood Primary School
CHD/CHDH SK8 .... 180 C5
Buchanan Pet Surgery
ECC M30 .... 101 E4
Buckley Road Industrial Estate
WHIT OL12 .... 23 F3
Buile Hill High School
SLFD M6 .... 103 E3
Bullough Moor CP School
HEY OL10 .... 36 C6
Burgess Becker Primary School
BKLY M9 .... 91 F6
Burnage High School for Boys
BNG/LEV M19 .... 145 D6
Burnage Rugby Club
HTNM SK4 .... 164 C4
Burnden Industrial Estate
BOLS/LL BL3 .... 47 F5

Bury Business Centre
 BURY BL9................................ **34** B3
Bury Catholic Preparatory
 School
 BURY BL9................................ **52** C1
Bury C of E High School
 BURY BL9................................ **52** C1
Bury College
 WHTF M45.............................. **70** C2
Bury Football Club Co
 BURY BL9................................ **53** D2
Bury General Hospital
 BURY BL9................................ **34** A1
Bury Grammar Boys School
 BURY BL9................................ **33** F6
Bury Health Care Nhs Trust
 BURY BL9................................ **34** B2
Bury Industrial Estate
 BOLE BL2................................ **49** D1
Bury Metropolitan
 Borough Council
 BURY BL9................................ **33** F2
Bury Metropolitan
 Borough Council
 BURY BL9................................ **33** E5
Bury Metropolitan
 Borough Council
 RAD M26................................ **50** A4
Bury Metropolitan
 Borough Council
 RAD M26................................ **51** F6
Bury & Rochdale
 Health Authority
 BURY BL9................................ **33** F5
Bury & Rochdale
 Health Authority
 MILN OL16............................. **23** D6
Bury Sports Club
 BURY BL9................................ **52** C1
Bury Whitefield Jewish Primary
 School
 BURY BL9................................ **53** F6
Bus Depot
 OLD OL1................................. **79** E4
Butterstile County Primary
 School
 PWCH M25............................. **88** B3
Button Lane Primary School
 NTHM/RTH M23...................... **161** D3
CAB
 ANC M4.................................. **3** G1
Cadishead Junior School
 IRL M44.................................. **134** B5
Cadishead Recreation Centre
 IRL M44.................................. **134** B6
Caius House School
 URM M41................................ **138** A2
Calderbank Surgery
 EDGY/DAV SK3........................ **183** D3
Caldershaw Primary School
 WHIT OL12............................. **21** E4
Cale Green Primary School
 EDGY/DAV SK3........................ **166** C6
Cale Green Surgery
 EDGY/DAV SK3........................ **183** D1
Cambridge Industrial Estate
 BRO M7.................................. **105** F3
Cams Lane Primary School
 RAD M26................................ **51** D6
Canalside Industrial Estate
 MILN OL16............................. **40** C2
Cannon Street Health Centre
 BOLS/LL BL3........................... **46** B4
Canon Johnson C of E
 Primary School
 AULW OL7............................... **112** C3
Canon Slade School
 BOLE BL2............................... **28** C3
Canterbury Road Junior &
 Infant School
 URM M41................................ **119** E6
Canterbury Road Surgery
 URM M41................................ **119** F6
Capital Business Centre
 BRAM/HZG SK7....................... **196** B3
Capital Road Surgery
 OP/CLY M11............................ **127** F2
Cardinal Langley Grammar
 School
 MDTN M24.............................. **58** A3
Cariocca Business Park
 WGTN/LGST M12..................... **125** E3
Carlton Industrial Centre
 BOLE BL2............................... **47** D3

Carrington Business Park
 PART M31............................... **136** A5
Carver Theatre
 MPL/ROM SK6......................... **187** D2
Castlebrook High School
 BURY BL9................................ **54** A6
Castlefield Gallery
 CSLFD M3............................... **2** B6
Castle Hill School
 RDSH SK5.............................. **148** A5
Castle Leisure Centre
 BURY BL9................................ **33** F5
Castle Park Industrial Estate
 OLD OL1................................. **79** F4
Castleton CP School
 ROCH OL11............................. **39** E5
Castleton Swimming Pool
 ROCH OL11............................. **39** D4
Castiton Gabriels Football Club
 ROCH OL11............................. **38** B6
Cavendish Industrial Estate
 AUL OL6................................. **112** B4
Cavendish Road Primary School
 DID/WITH M20........................ **143** E6
Cellar Vie the Ginnel Gallery
 CMANW M2............................. **2** C4
Central Industrial Estate
 BOLS/LL BL3........................... **47** D4
Central Industrial Estate
 MDTN M24.............................. **75** E3
Central Leisure Centre
 MILN OL16............................. **23** E6
Central Retail Park
 ANC M4.................................. **107** D6
Century Mill Industrial Estate
 FWTH BL4............................... **65** F3
Chadderton A F C
 CHAD OL9............................... **77** F3
Chadderton Industrial Estate
 MDTN M24.............................. **76** A6
Chadderton Public Baths
 CHAD OL9............................... **77** F4
Chadderton Town Health Centre
 CHAD OL9............................... **77** F4
Chalfont Street CP School
 BOL BL1................................. **28** A5
Chantlers CP School
 TOT/BURYW BL8...................... **32** B5
Chapelfield School
 RAD M26................................ **70** A2
Chapel Medical Centre
 IRL M44.................................. **135** E1
Chapel Street CP School
 BNG/LEV M19......................... **145** F2
Charleston Industrial Estate
 AULW OL7............................... **112** C3
Charlestown CP School
 SLFD M6................................. **104** B3
Charlestown Health Centre
 BKLY M9................................. **92** B3
Charlestown Primary School
 BKLY M9................................. **92** C2
Cheadle Cricket Club
 CHD/CHDH SK8....................... **180** A2
Cheadle Golf Course
 CHD/CHDH SK8....................... **180** C3
Cheadle Heath Clinic
 EDGY/DAV SK3........................ **165** E5
Cheadle Heath Junior &
 Infant School
 EDGY/DAV SK3........................ **165** E6
Cheadle Heath Sports Centre
 CHD/CHDH SK8....................... **181** E1
Cheadle Hulme College
 CHD/CHDH SK8....................... **195** F2
Cheadle Hulme Medical Centre
 CHD/CHDH SK8....................... **195** E1
Cheadle Hulme School
 CHD/CHDH SK8....................... **195** E1
Cheadle Medical Practice
 CHD/CHDH SK8....................... **180** B1
Cheadle Primary School
 CHD/CHDH SK8....................... **180** B1
Cheadle RC Junior
 & Infants School
 CHD/CHDH SK8....................... **180** C5
Cheadle Royal Hospital
 CHD/CHDH SK8....................... **180** A5
Cheadle Royel Shopping Centre
 CHD/CHDH SK8....................... **180** B5
Cheadle Swimming &
 Recreation Centre
 CHD/CHDH SK8....................... **180** C3

Cheadle Town Football Club
 CHD/CHDH SK8....................... **180** C2
Cheetham Community C of E
 School
 BRO M7.................................. **90** A6
Cheetham Hill Cricket Club
 CHH M8.................................. **89** F4
Cheethwood Community &
 Sports Centre
 CHH M8.................................. **106** A1
Cheetwood Primary School
 CHH M8.................................. **105** F3
Cherry Manor Primary School
 SALE M33............................... **158** A3
Cherry Tree Hospital
 OFTN SK2............................... **184** A2
Cherry Tree School
 FWTH BL4............................... **64** C3
Chesham CP School
 BURY BL9................................ **34** B1
Chesham Industrial Estate
 BURY BL9................................ **34** B3
Cheshire County Council
 WILM/AE SK9.......................... **194** B6
Cheshire County Council
 WILM/AE SK9.......................... **203** E5
Chethams School of Music
 CSLFD M3............................... **2** D1
Chevassut Primary School
 HULME M15............................ **123** F2
Chichester Business Centre
 MILN OL16............................. **23** E6
Child Health Clinic
 MDTN M24.............................. **75** D2
Chinese Medical Centre
 CSLFD M3............................... **2** B5
Chinese Traditional Health
 Centre
 URM M41................................ **137** F2
Chiropody Surgery
 OLD OL1................................. **79** E5
Chorlton Cum Hardy C of E
 Junior School
 CCHDY M21............................ **141** E3
Chorlton Cum Hardy Cricket Club
 CCHDY M21............................ **141** F5
Chorlton Leisure Centre
 CCHDY M21............................ **141** F2
Chorlton Park Junior School
 CCHDY M21............................ **142** A4
Christ Church C of E Primary
 School
 CHAD OL9............................... **77** E5
Christ Church School
 BURY BL9................................ **19** F5
Christie Hospital & Holt Radium
 Institute
 DID/WITH M20........................ **143** F5
Christie Street Industrial Estate
 STKP SK1............................... **167** E6
Christs Church C of E School
 BOLE BL2............................... **30** A5
Christ the King RC School
 NEWH/MOS M40...................... **109** D2
Christ the King School
 WALK M28.............................. **83** F3
Church Road CP School
 BOL BL1................................. **26** C5
City College Manchester
 CHH M8.................................. **90** C5
City College Manchester
 DID/WITH M20........................ **163** D1
City College Manchester
 NTHM/RTH M23...................... **160** B5
City College Manchester
 NTHM/RTH M23...................... **161** D5
City College Manchester
 NTHM/RTH M23...................... **162** A4
City Course Trading Estate
 OP/CLY M11............................ **126** B2
City Court Trading Estate
 ANC M4.................................. **107** D5
Civic Centre
 BOL BL1................................. **46** C2
Civic Centre
 OLD OL1................................. **78** C4
Civic Centre
 SWIN M27............................... **85** F5
Civic Hall
 BRAM/HZG SK7....................... **184** C5
Claremont road Junior
 and Infant School
 RUSH/FAL M14........................ **124** B6

Clarendon Clinic
SWIN M27 .... 86 A5
Clarendon Cottage School
ECC M30 .... 102 A4
Clarendon Fields School
DUK SK16 .... 130 C1
Clarendon Medical Practice
HYDE SK14 .... 131 E6
Clarendon Primary School
ECC M30 .... 102 A4
Clarendon Street CP School
BOLS/LL BL3 .... 46 C4
Clarke Industrial Estate
STRET M32 .... 120 B4
Clarksfield Junior School
OLDE OL4 .... 80 A5
Clayton Health Centre
OP/CLY M11 .... 108 C5
Clayton Industrial Estate
OP/CLY M11 .... 127 E2
Clevelands Preparatory School
BOL BL1 .... 45 E2
Clifton Cricket Club
SWIN M27 .... 85 F1
Clifton Primary School
SWIN M27 .... 86 A2
Club Theatre
ALT WA14 .... 174 B3
Cobden Mill Industrial Estate
FWTH BL4 .... 66 A2
C of E Primary School
BOLE BL2 .... 47 F2
Coldhurst Industrial Estate
OLD OL1 .... 78 C3
Coliseum Theatre
OLD OL1 .... 79 D4
Collegiate Medical Centre
CHH M8 .... 90 B6
Collyhurst Police Station
ANC M4 .... 106 C4
Concord Business Park
WYTH/NTH M22 .... 178 A6
Concord Business Park
WYTH/NTH M22 .... 178 C6
Coney Green High School
RAD M26 .... 51 F5
Constellation Trading Estate
RAD M26 .... 51 D3
Co-operative Museum
WHIT OL12 .... 22 C5
Copley Comprehensive School
STLY SK15 .... 115 D5
Copper Beeches School
SALE M33 .... 159 D1
Coppice Industrial Estate
OLDS OL8 .... 78 B6
Coppice Junior School
OLDS OL8 .... 95 F1
Cornbrook Estate
HULME M15 .... 123 E2
Corpus Christi Junior &
Infant School
CHAD OL9 .... 94 C1
Corrie CP School
DTN/ASHW M34 .... 149 D2
Counthill Comprehensive School
OLDE OL4 .... 80 B1
County Galleries
ALT WA14 .... 174 B3
County Primary School
BOL BL1 .... 28 C4
County Primary School
RAD M26 .... 67 F3
Crab Lane Primary School
BKLY M9 .... 90 C1
Craft Centre
ANC M4 .... 3 F2
Cravewood Primary School
CHH M8 .... 90 A4
Croft Industrial Estate
BURY BL9 .... 53 E4
Cromer Industrial Estate
MDTN M24 .... 75 F2
Cromford Business Park
OLD OL1 .... 79 F3
Crompton Buckstones Primary
School
ROY/SHW OL2 .... 62 B1
Crompton Cricket Club
ROY/SHW OL2 .... 61 F1
Crompton Fold CP School
BOLE BL2 .... 48 C2
Crompton Health Centre
ROY/SHW OL2 .... 61 F3

Crompton House C of E
High School
ROY/SHW OL2 .... 61 E1
Crompton Swimming Pool
ROY/SHW OL2 .... 61 F3
Cromwell House Community
Mental Health Centre
ECC M30 .... 101 E5
Cromwell Special School
DTN/ASHW M34 .... 147 D1
Crosland Industrial Estate
MPL/ROM SK6 .... 168 C1
Crossacres Junior &
Infant School
WYTH/NTH M22 .... 179 D3
Crosslee County Primary School
BKLY M9 .... 92 A1
Crowcroft Park Primary School
WGTN/LGST M12 .... 126 B6
Crown Business Centre
FAIL M35 .... 94 A5
Crown Court
CMANE M1 .... 3 G4
Crown Industrial Estate
ALT WA14 .... 158 C6
Crown Industrial Estate
ANC M4 .... 107 D4
Crown Royal Industrial Park
STKP SK1 .... 167 D5
Crumpsall Lane Primary School
CHH M8 .... 90 B4
Cuba Industrial Estate
RAMS BL0 .... 7 D3
Culcheth Hall School
ALT WA14 .... 174 A4
Curzon Ashton Football Club
AULW OL7 .... 112 A5
Dale Grove School
AULW OL7 .... 112 B2
The Dale Primary School
MPL/ROM SK6 .... 170 B6
Dancehouse Theatre & Northern
Ballet Scool
CMANE M1 .... 124 B2
Dane Bank Primary School
DTN/ASHW M34 .... 147 E1
Darnhill CP School
HEY OL10 .... 36 A6
Davaar Medical Centre
DUK SK16 .... 131 D1
David Cuthbert Business Centre
OP/CLY M11 .... 127 D2
David Medical Centre
CCHDY M21 .... 142 A5
David Roger Galleries
HYDE SK14 .... 150 C4
The Dawes Family Practice
WHIT OL12 .... 22 C5
Deane C of E School
BOLS/LL BL3 .... 45 D5
Deane Comprehensive School
BOLS/LL BL3 .... 45 D5
Deane & Derby Cricket Club
BOLS/LL BL3 .... 46 B6
Deane Medical Practice
BOLS/LL BL3 .... 46 B3
Deane Sports Centre
BOLS/LL BL3 .... 45 D5
Dean Lane Medical Centre
BRAM/HZG SK7 .... 198 B1
Dean Row County Junior School
WILM/AE SK9 .... 204 C2
The Deans CP School
SWIN M27 .... 85 F5
Delamere School
URM M41 .... 136 B1
De La Salle College
SLFD M6 .... 103 D4
Demmings Infant School
CHD/CHDH SK8 .... 181 D2
Denton Central CP School
DTN/ASHW M34 .... 129 F6
Denton Cricket & Sports Club
DTN/ASHW M34 .... 129 F4
Denton St Lawrence Cricket Club
DTN/ASHW M34 .... 149 D1
Denton West End Junior &
Infant School
DTN/ASHW M34 .... 128 B6
Department of Clinical
Psychology
ROY/SHW OL2 .... 78 C1
Derby High School
BURY BL9 .... 52 B1

Derby Shopping Centre
BOLS/LL BL3 .... 46 B4
Derby Street Junior
& Infant School
ROCH OL11 .... 40 B2
Devonshire Road CP School
BOL BL1 .... 45 F1
Dial Park Primary School
OFTN SK2 .... 184 B3
Didsbury C of E Primary School
DID/WITH M20 .... 163 F2
Didsbury Cricket Club
DID/WITH M20 .... 164 A4
Didsbury Medical Centre
DID/WITH M20 .... 163 F1
Didsbury Road Primary School
HTNM SK4 .... 165 D3
3 D Medical Centre
CMANE M1 .... 3 F5
The Dogs Surgery
CMANE M1 .... 3 F5
Donnybrook House Group
Practice
HYDE SK14 .... 150 B1
Doocot Theatre of Objects &
Figures
OLDTF/WHR M16 .... 123 F6
Downing Street Industrial Estate
WGTN/LGST M12 .... 124 C2
Dowry Park Industrial Estate
OLDE OL4 .... 80 C4
Dowson County Primary School
HYDE SK14 .... 150 C3
Droylsden Associated Football
Club
DROY M43 .... 110 B6
Droylsden High School for Girls
DROY M43 .... 109 F5
Droylsden Swimming Pool
DROY M43 .... 128 B1
Ducie High School
RUSH/FAL M14 .... 124 C5
Ducie Sports Centre
RUSH/FAL M14 .... 124 C5
Dukesgate Primary School
LHULT M38 .... 65 E6
Dukinfield Astley High School
DUK SK16 .... 131 F3
Dunstan Medical Centre
BOLE BL2 .... 47 F2
Durnford Medical Centre
MDTN M24 .... 75 D2
Durn Street Industrial Estate
LIT OL15 .... 13 D5
Eagley County Infant School
EDGW/EG BL7 .... 14 B5
East Crompton St Georges C of E
Primary School
ROY/SHW OL2 .... 62 A2
East Crompton St James C of E
Junior School
ROY/SHW OL2 .... 61 F2
East Ward CP School
BURY BL9 .... 34 C5
Eaton Place Business Centre
SALE M33 .... 159 E1
Ebbefone Galleria
DID/WITH M20 .... 144 B6
Ebbe Fonte Galleria
WILM/AE SK9 .... 203 F4
Eccles College
ECC M30 .... 102 A3
Eccles Health Centre
ECC M30 .... 102 A6
Eccles Recreation Centre
ECC M30 .... 102 A6
Edenfield Road Surgery
ROCH OL11 .... 21 F5
Edgeley Medical Practice
EDGY/DAV SK3 .... 166 A5
Egerton & Dunscar Health Centre
EDGW/EG BL7 .... 14 A6
Egerton Park High School
DTN/ASHW M34 .... 129 F4
Elk Mill Central Retail Park
OLD OL1 .... 59 F6
Ellenbrook Primary School
WALK M28 .... 82 C5
Ellen Wilkinson High School
WGTN/LGST M12 .... 125 E2
Ellesmere Bowling & Tennis Club
WALK M28 .... 83 F5
Ellesmere Shopping Centre
LHULT M38 .... 83 D2

Elmridge Primary School
HALE/TIMP WA15 .... **190** A1

Elms Medical Centre
WHTF M45 .... **70** C2

Elm Street CP School
MDTN M24 .... **76** A3

Elsinore Business Centre
OLDTF/WHR M16 .... **122** B5

Elton County Primary School
TOT/BURYW BL8 .... **33** D3

Elton High School
TOT/BURYW BL8 .... **32** B3

English Martyrs RC School
URM M41 .... **138** A1

Enterprise Trading Estate
TRPK M17 .... **120** B1

Etchells Primary School
CHD/CHDH SK8 .... **180** A6

Europa Business Park
EDGY/DAV SK3 .... **181** F1

Europa Trading Estate
RAD M26 .... **67** F4

Eustace Street CP School
CHAD OL9 .... **78** A3

Express Trading Estate
FWTH BL4 .... **66** B5

The Eye Clinic
CMANW M2 .... **2** D4

Failsworth County Upper School
FAIL M35 .... **94** B6

Failsworth Health Centre
FAIL M35 .... **93** F6

Failsworth Industrial Estate
FAIL M35 .... **109** D1

Fairfield CP School
BURY BL9 .... **35** E4

Fairfield Girls High School
DROY M43 .... **128** B1

Fairfield Road CP School
DROY M43 .... **128** A1

Fairhill Industrial Estate
IRL M44 .... **135** D4

Fairview Medical Centre
URM M41 .... **138** A1

Fairway Primary School
OFTN SK2 .... **168** C6

Falinge Park High School
WHIT OL12 .... **22** B4

Fallowfield Medical Centre
RUSH/FAL M14 .... **144** B3

Fallowfield Shopping Centre
RUSH/FAL M14 .... **144** C2

Family Surgery
RDSH SK5 .... **146** C2

Farjo Medical Centre
CMANE M1 .... **3** F4

Farnworth Health Centre
FWTH BL4 .... **66** B3

Farnworth Leisure Centre
FWTH BL4 .... **66** B3

Farnworth Little Theatre
FWTH BL4 .... **66** B3

Farnworth Park Industrial Estate
FWTH BL4 .... **66** B2

Farnworth Social Circle
Cricket Club
FWTH BL4 .... **66** A4

Farrowdale House
Preparatory School
ROY/SHW OL2 .... **61** E3

Ferneyfield School
CHAD OL9 .... **77** D4

Fiddlers Lane Primary School
IRL M44 .... **116** C6

Fieldhouse Cricket Club
ROCH OL11 .... **37** F1

Fieldhouse Industrial Estate
WHIT OL12 .... **23** D3

Firbank County School
ROY/SHW OL2 .... **60** B2

Fire Station
ANC M4 .... **3** H1

Fire Station
ANC M4 .... **106** C4

Firgrove Business Park
MILN OL16 .... **24** B5

Firs CP School
SALE M33 .... **158** B1

Fir Tree Primary School
RDSH SK5 .... **146** C1

Firwood Industrial Estate
BOLE BL2 .... **29** D5

Firwood School
BOLE BL2 .... **29** D5

Fishbrook Industrial Estate
FWTH BL4 .... **67** D4

Fishpool County Infant School
BURY BL9 .... **53** D1

Fitton Hill Infant School
OLDS OL8 .... **96** C2

Fitton Hill Junior School
OLDS OL8 .... **96** B2

F K Bassis Surgery
STLY SK15 .... **114** C6

Flixton County Junior School
URM M41 .... **137** D1

Flixton Cricket Club
URM M41 .... **117** F6

Flixton Football Club
URM M41 .... **117** E6

Flixton Girls High School
URM M41 .... **137** E1

Flixton Health Clinic
URM M41 .... **136** B1

Flixton Infant School
URM M41 .... **137** D1

Florence Nightingale
Hospital Lodge
TOT/BURYW BL8 .... **33** D6

The Flower Gallery
RAMS BL0 .... **7** D5

Flowery Field Primary School
HYDE SK14 .... **131** E5

Forest Park School
SALE M33 .... **159** E1

Forest School
HALE/TIMP WA15 .... **175** D1

Forge Industrial Estate
OLDE OL4 .... **79** F4

Forum Leisure Centre
WYTH/NTH M22 .... **178** A4

Fourways Trading Estate
TRPK M17 .... **120** B3

The Framing Studio & Gallery
STKP SK1 .... **167** D5

Freehold Community School
CHAD OL9 .... **78** A6

Fulshaw C of E CP School
WILM/AE SK9 .... **203** D5

Gainsborough Galleries
MPL/ROM SK6 .... **170** A3

Gainsbourgh Galleries
MPL/ROM SK6 .... **187** D1

The Gallery Bistro
WGTN/LGST M12 .... **125** E3

The Gallery Furnishings
OFTN SK2 .... **183** F2

The Gallery
ALT WA14 .... **174** B4

The Gallery
AUL OL6 .... **113** D4

The Gallery
IRL M44 .... **134** C6

The Gallery
WGTN/LGST M12 .... **125** D2

Garrick Theatre
EDGY/DAV SK3 .... **166** C4

Gaskell Street CP School
BOL BL1 .... **46** C1

The Gates Shopping Centre
BOL BL1 .... **47** D2

Gateway Industrial Estate
CMANE M1 .... **3** H4

Gatley Health Centre
CHD/CHDH SK8 .... **179** E1

Gatley Primary School
CHD/CHDH SK8 .... **179** E2

Gee Cross C of E Primary School
HYDE SK14 .... **151** D3

Gee Cross Social & Sports Club
HYDE SK14 .... **150** C3

George H Carnall Leisure Centre
URM M41 .... **119** F5

George Tomlinson School
FWTH BL4 .... **66** C5

Gill Medical Centre
WALK M28 .... **83** E2

Gilnow CP School
BOL BL1 .... **46** A3

Glen Trading Estate
OLDE OL4 .... **80** B5

Globe Industrial Estate
RAD M26 .... **51** F6

Globe Lane CP School
DUK SK16 .... **130** C3

Globe Lane Industrial Estate
DUK SK16 .... **130** C3

Glodwick Health Centre
OLDE OL4 .... **79** F5

Glodwick Infant School
OLDE OL4 .... **79** F6

Gloucester House Medical Centre
URM M41 .... **138** B1

Gmex Centre
CMANW M2 .... **2** C6

Golden Mosque
WHIT OL12 .... **22** C5

Gordon Street Medical Centre
AUL OL6 .... **113** F3

Gorrells Industrial Estate
ROCH OL11 .... **39** F4

Gorse Bank School
CHAD OL9 .... **77** D6

Gorsefield CP School
RAD M26 .... **51** E5

Gorse Hall Primary School
STLY SK15 .... **114** A6

Gorse Hill Health Centre
STRET M32 .... **121** F6

Gorse Hill Primary School
STRET M32 .... **121** F5

Gorsey Bank CP School
WILM/AE SK9 .... **203** D4

Gorton Brook First School
WGTN/LGST M12 .... **126** B3

Gorton Medical Centre
GTN M18 .... **127** E4

Gorton Mount Infant School
GTN M18 .... **126** C6

Granada Studios Tour
CSLFD M3 .... **2** A4

Granada Superbowl
WALK M28 .... **85** D5

Grange Arts Centre
(Oldham College)
CHAD OL9 .... **78** B4

Grange Road C of E
Primary School
ALT WA14 .... **174** A6

Grange School
CHAD OL9 .... **78** C4

Grange School
RUSH/FAL M14 .... **125** E6

Greater Manchester
Museum of Science & Industry
CSLFD M3 .... **2** A5

Great Moor Clinic
OFTN SK2 .... **184** A2

Great Moor Primary School
OFTN SK2 .... **183** F3

Greave Primary School
MPL/ROM SK6 .... **170** A1

Greenacres Junior & Infant School
OLDE OL4 .... **80** A4

Greenbank CP School
WHIT OL12 .... **23** D4

Greenbank School
CHD/CHDH SK8 .... **181** E6

Greencourts Business Park
WYTH/NTH M22 .... **193** E2

Green End Junior School
BNG/LEV M19 .... **144** C6

Greenfield Primary School
HYDE SK14 .... **150** C1

Green Fold School
FWTH BL4 .... **65** D3

Greenhill CP School
TOT/BURYW BL8 .... **32** A6

Greenland Road Surgery
BOLS/LL BL3 .... **65** D1

Green Lane High School
HALE/TIMP WA15 .... **175** E4

Greenmount CP School
TOT/BURYW BL8 .... **17** F3

Greenmount Cricket Club
TOT/BURYW BL8 .... **18** A4

Green Room Theatre
CMANE M1 .... **2** D6

Greenside Primary School
DROY M43 .... **110** A5

Greenside Trading Centre
DROY M43 .... **110** B6

Greenwood Primary School
ECC M30 .... **101** F3

Greyland Medical Centre
PWCH M25 .... **71** F5

Grosvenor Business Park
MPL/ROM SK6 .... **149** D5

Grosvenor Industrial Estate
AULW OL7 .... **112** B6

Grosvenor Road County
Junior & Infant School
SWIN M27 .... **86** C6

Grove Galleries
HULME M15 .... **123** D2

Guardian Angels RC
Primary School
TOT/BURYW BL8 .... **32** C4

Guide Bridge Industrial Estate
DTN/ASHW M34 .... **129** F1

Guide Bridge Theatre
DTN/ASHW M34 .... **129** F1

Guide Bridge Trading Estate
DTN/ASHW M34 .... **129** F1

Guinness Road Trading Estate
TRPK M17 .... **120** A1

Hale Barns Cricket Club
HALE/TIMP WA15 .... **190** C1

Halebarns Cricket Club
HALE/TIMP WA15 .... **190** B3

Hale Preparatory School
HALE/TIMP WA15 .... **174** C4

Halliwell Health Centre &
School Clinic
BOL BL1 .... **27** F6

Halliwell Industrial Estate
BOL BL1 .... **27** E4

Halliwell Surgery
BOL BL1 .... **28** A6

Handforth Health Centre
WILM/AE SK9 .... **194** B6

Hardman Fold School
FAIL M35 .... **93** E6

Harehill Primary School
HYDE SK14 .... **152** A1

Hare Krishna Temple
BOL BL1 .... **46** A2

Harper Green Comprehensive
School
FWTH BL4 .... **65** F2

Harper Mount Primary School
BKLY M9 .... **91** D5

Harphurey Business Centre
BKLY M9 .... **91** E4

Harp Industrial Estate
ROCH OL11 .... **39** E5

Harp Trading Estate
TRPK M17 .... **120** B1

Harpurhey Health Centre
BKLY M9 .... **91** E5

Harrytown RC High School
MPL/ROM SK6 .... **169** E3

Hartford Industrial Estate
CHAD OL9 .... **78** A5

Hartshead High School
AUL OL6 .... **97** F6

Harwood Health Centre
BOLE BL2 .... **29** E2

Harwood Meadows CP School
BOLE BL2 .... **30** A4

Haslam Park CP School
BOLS/LL BL3 .... **45** F4

Hathershaw Secondary School
OLDS OL8 .... **95** F3

Hattersley Health Clinic
HYDE SK14 .... **152** C1

Hattersley High School
HYDE SK14 .... **152** B1

Haveley Hey Junior
& Infant School
WYTH/NTH M22 .... **178** A3

Hawkins Clinic
MILN OL16 .... **23** D6

Hayward School
& Bolton South
6th Form College
BOLS/LL BL3 .... **64** A1

Hayward Sports Centre
BOLS/LL BL3 .... **64** B1

Hazeldene Medical Centre
NEWH/MOS M40 .... **93** F4

Hazel Grove Clinic
BRAM/HZG SK7 .... **184** C4

Hazel Grove High School
BRAM/HZG SK7 .... **184** A6

Hazel Grove Primary
& Infant School
BRAM/HZG SK7 .... **184** C4

Hazelhurst CP School
RAMS BL0 .... **18** B1

Heald Green Medical Centre
CHD/CHDH SK8 .... **193** F1

Heald Place Primary School
RUSH/FAL M14 .... **124** C6

Healey Primary School
WHIT OL12 .... **22** C2

Healey Surgery
WHIT OL12 .... **22** C2

The Health Centre
ALT WA14 .... **174** B2

Heap Bridge CP School
BURY BL9 .... **35** E6

Heathside Primary School
WALK M28 .... **83** F2

Heaton Cricket Club
BOL BL1 .... **26** B5

Heaton Hall
PWCH M25 .... **72** C6

Heaton Medical Centre
BOL BL1 .... **26** A6

Heaton Moor Medical Centre
HTNM SK4 .... **146** A6

Heaton Moor Rugby Union
Football Club
HTNM SK4 .... **165** F2

Heaton Norris Health Centre
HTNM SK4 .... **166** B2

Heaton Park CP School
PWCH M25 .... **71** F5

Heaton Park Synagogue
CHH M8 .... **90** A3

Heaton School
HTNM SK4 .... **145** F6

Hempshaw Business Centre
STKP SK1 .... **167** F6

Henry Donn Galleries
WHTF M45 .... **70** A4

Henry Donn Galleries
WHTF M45 .... **71** D3

Hertford Industrial Estate
AULW OL7 .... **112** B6

Heybrook CP School
WHIT OL12 .... **23** E4

Heyes Lane Junior
& Infant School
HALE/TIMP WA15 .... **159** F5

Heys CP School
AUL OL6 .... **113** E3

Hey with Zion Primary School
OLDE OL4 .... **80** C4

Heywood All Souls School
HEY OL10 .... **38** A4

Heywood Sports Centre
HEY OL10 .... **37** D4

Higginshaw Sports Club
OLD OL1 .... **79** E3

Highbank Trading Estate
OP/CLY M11 .... **127** E2

Highbarn Primary School
ROY/SHW OL2 .... **60** C5

High Birch School
ROCH OL11 .... **38** C2

High Crompton St Marys C of E
School
ROY/SHW OL2 .... **61** D1

Higher Broughton Health Centre
BRO M7 .... **105** F1

Higher Crumpsall & Higher
Broughton Synagogue
BRO M7 .... **89** F5

Higher Lane County Junior &
Infant School
WHTF M45 .... **70** C3

Higher Openshaw
Community School
OP/CLY M11 .... **127** E1

Highfield CP School
FWTH BL4 .... **65** E3

Highfield Hospital
ROCH OL11 .... **39** F1

Highfield Primary School
URM M41 .... **139** D1

The Highlands Group Practice
AULW OL7 .... **130** A1

High Lane Medical Centre
MPL/ROM SK6 .... **200** C2

High Lane Primary School
MPL/ROM SK6 .... **200** C1

High Lawn CP School
BOL BL1 .... **27** F1

Hillcrest Grammar School
EDGY/DAV SK3 .... **183** D1

Hillgate Business Centre
STKP SK1 .... **167** D5

Hilltop School
OLDE OL4 .... **63** E5

Hilton Lane CP School
WALK M28 .... **82** C2

Hm Manchester Prison
CHH M8 .... **106** A3

Hodge Clough Junior School
OLD OL1 .... **62** B6

Holcombe Brook CP School
TOT/BURYW BL8 .... **18** B3

Holcombe Brook Sports Club
TOT/BURYW BL8 .... **18** B2

Holcombe C of E Primary School
TOT/BURYW BL8 .... **6** B5

Holden Clough Primary School
AUL OL6 .... **97** D6

Hollies Surgery
DUK SK16 .... **131** E1

Hollin CP School
MDTN M24 .... **57** E6

Hollins County Secondary School
MOSL OL5 .... **99** F4

Hollins Grundy CP School
BURY BL9 .... **53** E4

Hollinwood Cricket Club
OLDS OL8 .... **95** D5

Holly Bank Industrial Estate
RAD M26 .... **51** D6

Holly Mount School
TOT/BURYW BL8 .... **17** E4

Hollywood Bowl
NEWH/MOS M40 .... **93** E4

Holy Cross & All Saints R C
Primary School
ECC M30 .... **119** E1

Holy Cross College
BURY BL9 .... **52** C1

Holy Family Primary School
ROCH OL11 .... **40** B4

Holy Family RC Primary School
OLDS OL8 .... **95** E5

Holy Family RC Primary School
SALE M33 .... **160** C1

Holy Infant RC Primary School
BOL BL1 .... **27** F3

Holy Name RC Primary School
HULME M15 .... **124** B4

Holy Rosary RC Primary School
OLDS OL8 .... **96** A3

Holy Trinity C of E Primary School
BKLY M9 .... **91** F5

Holy Trinity C of E School
AUL OL6 .... **112** B4

Holy Trinity Primary School
BURY BL9 .... **34** A6

Hong Sing Chinese
Medical Centre
BRAM/HZG SK7 .... **184** B4

Hopwood CP School
HEY OL10 .... **56** C1

Hopwood Hall College
WHIT OL12 .... **22** C6

Hopwood Medical Centre
HEY OL10 .... **37** F6

Horton Mill Primary School
OLDE OL4 .... **79** F5

Houldsworth Golf Club
RDSH SK5 .... **146** C3

Houldsworth Medical Centre
RDSH SK5 .... **147** D4

Hubert House Jewish
Boys School
BRO M7 .... **89** E5

Hulme Grammar School
OLDS OL8 .... **95** E1

Hulme Hall School
CHD/CHDH SK8 .... **181** E6

Hulton Hospital
BOLS/LL BL3 .... **45** E5

Hurst Clough CP School
HYDE SK14 .... **152** C2

Hurstfield Industrial Estate
HTNM SK4 .... **146** C5

Hursthead Infant
& Primary School
CHD/CHDH SK8 .... **196** A3

Hurst Knoll Junior
& Infant School
AUL OL6 .... **113** D3

Hurst Methodist Junior School
AUL OL6 .... **97** E6

Huvys Gallery
BRO M7 .... **89** F6

Hyde Cricket Club
HYDE SK14 .... **151** D5

Hyde Little Theatre
HYDE SK14 .... **150** C2

Hyde Technology School
  HYDE SK14.................................. **131** D5
Hyde 6th Form College
  HYDE SK14.................................. **131** F5
Hyde United Football Club
  HYDE SK14.................................. **151** D1
Independent British Hospitals
  RUSH/FAL M14............................ **125** D5
Industrial Estate
  HEY OL10...................................... **55** E1
The Industrial Estate
  BOL BL1... **27** D5
Inland Revenue Office
  CSLFD M3... **2** B3
Innes School
  WHIT OL12..................................... **22** A4
The Instructor College
  STKP SK1..................................... **167** D4
International Convention
  Centre U/c
  CMANW M2....................................... **2** C5
Irlam & Cadishead Community
  High School
  IRL M44....................................... **134** C4
Irlam County Primary School
  IRL M44....................................... **135** D2
Irlam Endowed Primary School
  IRL M44....................................... **135** E1
Irlam Industrial Estate
  IRL M44....................................... **134** C4
Irlam Swimming Pool
  IRL M44....................................... **135** E2
Irwell Park High School
  SLFD M6....................................... **104** B2
Jacksons Lane Recreation Centre
  BRAM/HZG SK7............................ **183** E6
Jalalia Mosque
  MILN OL16...................................... **23** E5
James Brindley Infant & Junior
  School
  WALK M28....................................... **83** D4
Jamia Mosque
  HYDE SK14................................... **150** B1
Jeff Joseph Sale Moor
  Technology College
  SALE M33..................................... **160** B3
Jewish High School for Girls
  BRO M7... **89** E5
Jewish Museum
  CHH M8....................................... **106** B3
Jewish Synagogue
  WHTF M45....................................... **71** D4
John Rylands University
  CSLFD M3... **2** C4
Johnson Fold CP School
  BOL BL1... **26** A4
Joseph Adamson Industrial
  Estate
  HYDE SK14................................... **150** A1
Joseph Eastham Primary School
  WALK M28....................................... **82** C3
Jubilee Surgery
  OLDTF/WHR M16......................... **122** C5
Kaskenmoor School
  OLDS OL8....................................... **94** C5
Kayley Industrial Estate
  AULW OL7..................................... **112** A4
Kearsley Cricket Club
  FWTH BL4....................................... **67** E5
Kearsley Medical Centre
  FWTH BL4....................................... **67** D4
Kearsley Sports Centre
  FWTH BL4....................................... **66** C5
Kearsley West CP School
  FWTH BL4....................................... **66** C4
Kenmore Medical Centre
  WILM/AE SK9............................... **203** E5
Kenyon Business Park
  BOLS/LL BL3.................................. **46** C4
Kersal High School
  BRO M7... **88** B5
Kiely Business Park
  BURY BL9....................................... **34** B3
King David High School
  CHH M8... **90** A4
King David Junior School
  CHH M8... **90** A4
Kings Road Primary School
  OLDTF/WHR M16......................... **122** B6
King Street Remedial Clinic
  DUK SK16..................................... **112** C6
Kingsway CP School
  URM M41....................................... **119** F5

Kingsway School
  CHD/CHDH SK8............................ **180** A3
Kingsway Secondary School
  CHD/CHDH SK8............................ **180** A2
Kingsway West Business Park
  MILN OL16...................................... **41** D2
Kingsway West Business Park
  ROCH OL11..................................... **40** B2
Knowsley Junior Mixed School
  OLDE OL4....................................... **81** E4
Lacey Green CP School
  WILM/AE SK9............................... **203** E2
Lady Barn House School
  CHD/CHDH SK8............................ **180** B4
Ladybarn Primary School
  DID/WITH M20............................. **144** B5
Ladybridge CP School
  BOLS/LL BL3.................................. **45** D4
Ladybridge CP School
  CHD/CHDH SK8............................ **181** F2
Ladybrook Primary School
  BRAM/HZG SK7............................ **197** D2
Ladywell Hospital
  SALQ/ORD M5.............................. **102** B5
Ladywell Hospital Lodge
  SALQ/ORD M5.............................. **102** B5
Lancashire County Cricket Club
  STRET M32................................... **122** A5
Lancasterian School
  DID/WITH M20............................. **142** C6
Lance Burn Health Centre
  SLFD M6....................................... **104** B5
Lane End Primary School
  CHD/CHDH SK8............................ **182** A5
Langley CP School
  MDTN M24....................................... **56** C6
Langley Furrow Community
  School
  MDTN M24....................................... **74** A1
Langley Group Surgery
  MDTN M24....................................... **74** B1
Langley Junior High School
  MDTN M24....................................... **74** A1
Langworthy Clinic
  SLFD M6....................................... **104** A5
Langworthy Medical Practice
  SLFD M6....................................... **104** A4
Langworthy Road School
  SLFD M6....................................... **104** A4
Larkhill Junior & Infant School
  EDGY/DAV SK3............................ **166** A5
Lawnhurst Trading Estate
  CHD/CHDH SK8............................ **181** F2
Leesbrook Surgery
  OLDE OL4....................................... **80** C5
Leigh Street Primary School
  HYDE SK14................................... **151** D1
Lemon Park Industrial Estate
  HEY OL10....................................... **37** F6
Lemon Park Industrial Estate
  HEY OL10....................................... **56** C1
Levenshulme Baths
  BNG/LEV M19............................... **145** F2
Levenshulme Health Centre
  BNG/LEV M19............................... **145** F2
Levenshulme High School
  BNG/LEV M19............................... **145** E4
Lever Edge Lane CP School
  BOLS/LL BL3.................................. **64** C1
Library
  OLD OL1... **79** D5
Light Oaks Infant School
  SLFD M6....................................... **102** C3
Lily Lane Junior & Infant School
  NEWH/MOS M40........................... **92** B5
Lime Tree Primary School
  SALE M33..................................... **160** C2
Linden Road Primary School
  DTN/ASHW M34........................... **130** B6
Lindow CP School
  WILM/AE SK9............................... **208** B2
Linguard Business Park
  ROCH OL11..................................... **40** B1
Lisburne School
  OFTN SK2..................................... **184** C1
Littleborough CP School
  LIT OL15... **12** C4
Littleborough Cricket Club
  LIT OL15... **12** C5
Little Heaton C of E Primary
  School
  MDTN M24....................................... **74** A4

Little Hulton Community School
  LHULT M38..................................... **82** B1
Little Hulton Cricket Club
  LHULT M38..................................... **64** C6
Little Lever Comprehensive School
  BOLS/LL BL3.................................. **48** C6
Little Lever Cricket Club
  BOLS/LL BL3.................................. **49** F5
Little Lever Health Centre
  BOLS/LL BL3.................................. **49** E6
Littlemoor Infant School
  OLDE OL4....................................... **80** A3
Little Moss High School
  DROY M43..................................... **111** D3
Livingstone CP School
  MOSL OL5....................................... **98** C5
L & M Business Park
  ALT WA14..................................... **173** F1
Lockside Medical Centre
  STLY SK15..................................... **114** C5
Longford Park School
  STRET M32................................... **141** D1
Longford Street Group Practice
  HEY OL10....................................... **37** D5
Longford Trading Estate
  STRET M32................................... **121** E6
Longsight CP School
  BOLE BL2... **29** F3
Longsight Cricket Club
  WGTN/LGST M12......................... **126** B6
Longsight Health Centre
  BRUN/LGST M13......................... **126** A5
Longsight Industrial Estate
  WGTN/LGST M12......................... **126** A5
Longsight Park School
  WGTN/LGST M12......................... **125** F4
Lords College
  BOLS/LL BL3.................................. **47** E3
Loreto College
  HULME M15................................... **123** F4
Loreto Convent Grammar School
  ALT WA14..................................... **174** A2
Lostock Clinic
  STRET M32................................... **120** B6
Lostock CP School
  HOR/BR BL6.................................. **44** A3
Lostock Hall CP School
  POY/DIS SK12.............................. **197** F6
Lower Broughton Health Centre
  BRO M7... **105** E3
Lowercroft CP School
  TOT/BURYW BL8........................... **31** F5
Lower Kersal Primary School
  BRO M7... **104** C1
Lower Park CP School
  POY/DIS SK12.............................. **198** A5
Lower Place School
  MILN OL16...................................... **40** C3
Lowry Heritage Centre
  (Art Gallery & Museum)
  SALQ/ORD M5.............................. **105** D5
Lowry School
  BRO M7... **105** E2
Ludworth Primary School
  MPL/ROM SK6.............................. **171** E5
Lum Head Primary School
  CHD/CHDH SK8............................ **179** F4
The Lyceum Musical Theatre
  OLD OL1... **79** D5
Lyndhurst Primary School
  DUK SK16..................................... **113** D6
Lyndhurst Primary School
  OLDS OL8....................................... **95** F2
Lyon Industrial Estate
  ALT WA14..................................... **157** F6
Macclesfield Borough Council
  POY/DIS SK12.............................. **198** C5
Macdonald Road Medical Centre
  IRL M44....................................... **134** C3
Mackenzie Industrial Estate
  CHD/CHDH SK8............................ **181** F1
Magda House Medical Centre
  OFTN SK2..................................... **184** B3
Makki Mosque
  BOL BL1... **27** E5
Malbern Industrial Estate
  DTN/ASHW M34........................... **129** D5
Manchester Air & Space Museum
  CSLFD M3... **2** B5
Manchester Cathedral
  CSLFD M3... **2** D1

Manchester Central Hospitals &
Community Care NHS Trust
BRUN/LGST M13 .... 125 D4
Manchester Centre for the Deaf
BRUN/LGST M13 .... 124 C3
Manchester Centre for Vision
BRUN/LGST M13 .... 124 C4
Manchester City Art Galleries
CMANW M2 .... 2 D4
Manchester City Co
CMANW M2 .... 2 D4
Manchester City Council
BKLY M9 .... 91 F5
Manchester City Council
BNG/LEV M19 .... 144 C6
Manchester City Council
CHH M8 .... 90 B5
Manchester City Council
CMANE M1 .... 3 E6
Manchester City Council
DID/WITH M20 .... 143 D5
Manchester City Council
GTN M18 .... 127 D4
Manchester City Council
NEWH/MOS M40 .... 93 D3
Manchester City Council
NEWH/MOS M40 .... 108 C2
Manchester City Council
NTHM/RTH M23 .... 161 F3
Manchester City Council
NTHM/RTH M23 .... 177 F1
Manchester City Council
OLDTF/WHR M16 .... 124 A6
Manchester City Council
OP/CLY M11 .... 127 F2
Manchester City Council
SALE M33 .... 158 A3
Manchester City Council
WCTN/LGST M12 .... 125 F2
Manchester City Council
WYTH/NTH M22 .... 178 B2
Manchester City Football Club
RUSH/FAL M14 .... 143 F1
Manchester City
Magistrates Court
CSLFD M3 .... 2 B4
Manchester College of Arts &
Technology
BKLY M9 .... 92 A5
Manchester College of Arts &
Technology
CMANE M1 .... 3 G3
Manchester College of Arts &
Technology
OP/CLY M11 .... 126 C2
Manchester Computing School
BRUN/LGST M13 .... 124 C3
Manchester Conference Centre
CMANE M1 .... 3 G6
Manchester Evening News
(MEN) Arena
CSLFD M3 .... 106 A4
Manchester Grammar School
RUSH/FAL M14 .... 144 B1
Manchester High School for Girls
RUSH/FAL M14 .... 144 A2
Manchester Industrial Centre
SALQ/ORD M5 .... 123 E1
Manchester Islamic High
School for Girls
CCHDY M21 .... 141 E3
Manchester Jewish
Grammar School
PWCH M25 .... 88 C2
Manchester Junior Girls School
BRO M7 .... 89 E4
Manchester Metropolitan
University
CMANE M1 .... 3 G5
Manchester Metropolitan
University
DID/WITH M20 .... 163 F3
Manchester Metropolitan
University
HULME M15 .... 124 B2
Manchester Metropolitan
University
OLDTF/WHR M16 .... 143 D1
Manchester Metropolitan
University
PART M31 .... 137 E5
Manchester Metropolitan
University
RUSH/FAL M14 .... 144 B1

Manchester Preparatory
School
DID/WITH M20 .... 163 F1
Manchester Reform Synagogue
CSLFD M3 .... 2 C4
Manchester Road CP School
DROY M43 .... 109 F6
Manchester Royal Infirmary
BRUN/LGST M13 .... 125 D5
Manchester United Football Club
OLDTF/WHR M16 .... 121 F4
Manchester University
BRUN/LGST M13 .... 125 D4
Manchester Watersports Centre
HULME M15 .... 123 E2
Manchester Youth Theatre
HULME M15 .... 124 A3
Mancunian Community
Health NHS Trust
CCHDY M21 .... 141 F2
Mancunian Community
Health Nhs Trust
HULME M15 .... 123 F4
Mancunian Community
Health NHS Trust
NEWH/MOS M40 .... 108 C1
Mancunian Community
Health NHS Trust
OLDTF/WHR M16 .... 123 F5
Mancunian Community
Health NHS Trust
WYTH/NTH M22 .... 162 A5
Mandelay Health Centre
BOLE BL1 .... 27 F1
Manley Park Infant School
OLDTF/WHR M16 .... 142 A1
Manley Park Junior School
OLDTF/WHR M16 .... 142 A1
Manor Green Junior
& Infant School
DTN/ASHW M34 .... 149 E3
Manway Business Park
ALT WA14 .... 158 C6
The Maples Medical Centre
NTHM/RTH M23 .... 177 D3
Marcliffe Industrial Estate
BRAM/HZG SK7 .... 185 D6
Marjory Lees Health Centre
OLD OL1 .... 79 D4
Market
ANC M4 .... 3 E2
Market Hall
OLD OL1 .... 78 C4
Markland Hill CP School
BOL BL1 .... 45 D1
Mark Street Surgery
WHIT OL12 .... 23 F4
Marland Fold School
OLDS OL8 .... 96 B4
Marland Hill CP School
ROCH OL11 .... 39 D2
Marlborough Road School
BRO M7 .... 106 A1
Marple Clinic
MPL/ROM SK6 .... 187 D1
The Marple Cottage Surgery
MPL/ROM SK6 .... 187 D2
Marple Gallery
MPL/ROM SK6 .... 187 D1
Marple Hall School
MPL/ROM SK6 .... 170 A6
Masefield CP School
BOLS/LL BL3 .... 49 F5
Mather Street Primary School
FAIL M35 .... 93 E5
Matthew Moss High School
ROCH OL11 .... 38 B3
Mauldeth Medical Centre
DID/WITH M20 .... 144 B4
Mauldeth Road Primary School
DID/WITH M20 .... 144 B4
Maycroft Junior & Infant School
RDSH SK5 .... 148 A5
Mayfield Industrial Park
IRL M44 .... 117 D6
Mayfield Primary School
OLD OL1 .... 79 F2
Maypole Farm Estate
PART M31 .... 136 B5
Mcilvride Medical Practice
POY/DIS SK12 .... 198 B5
Meadow Industrial Estate
FAIL M35 .... 109 E1

The Meadows School
MDTN M24 .... 92 A1
Meadway Health Centre
SALE M33 .... 158 C3
Meanwood CP School
WHIT OL12 .... 22 A4
Mecca Mosque
BOLS/LL BL3 .... 47 D5
Medlock Infant School
BRUN/LGST M13 .... 124 C2
Medlock Leisure Centre
DROY M43 .... 110 C5
Megabowl
OLDTF/WHR M16 .... 122 B4
Melland School
RDSH SK5 .... 146 B1
Menorah Synagogue
WYTH/NTH M22 .... 178 C1
Mental Health Centre
BOLE BL2 .... 30 A6
Meridian Clinic
BURY BL9 .... 33 F5
Mersey Drive Primary School
WHTF M45 .... 72 A1
Mersey Road Industrial Estate
OLDS OL8 .... 94 C4
Mersey Vale Primary School
HTNM SK4 .... 165 E4
Mesne Lea CP School
WALK M28 .... 83 F4
Metropolitan College
BOL BL1 .... 27 F5
Micklehurst All Saints C of E
Primary School
MOSL OL5 .... 99 E4
Micklehurst Cricket Club
MOSL OL5 .... 99 F4
Middleton Cricket Club
MDTN M24 .... 75 D1
Middleton Parish Primary School
MDTN M24 .... 75 D1
Middleton Public Baths
MDTN M24 .... 75 E3
Mill 5 Belgrave Industrial Estate
OLDS OL8 .... 96 B2
Millbrook Business Centre
NTHM/RTH M23 .... 176 C1
Millbrook Industrial Estate
NTHM/RTH M23 .... 176 C1
Millbrook Primary School
STLY SK15 .... 115 F2
Mills Hill CP School
CHAD OL9 .... 76 C3
Mills Hill Junior School
CHAD OL9 .... 76 C3
Mill Street Industrial Estate
BOL BL1 .... 47 E2
Millwood School
BURY BL9 .... 53 D3
Milnrow Cricket Club
MILN OL16 .... 42 A2
Milnrow Crossgates School
MILN OL16 .... 25 E6
Milnrow Health Centre
MILN OL16 .... 42 A2
Milton CP School
MOSL OL5 .... 99 D3
Minden Medical Centre
BURY BL9 .... 34 A5
MMU
HULME M15 .... 124 B2
Moat House School
HTNM SK4 .... 166 C2
Monde Trading Estate
TRPK M17 .... 120 B3
Montague Business Park
OLDTF/WHR M16 .... 122 B5
Monton Bowling Club
ECC M30 .... 101 F3
Monton Cricket Club
ECC M30 .... 101 F3
Monton Medical Centre
ECC M30 .... 101 D3
Moor Allerton School
DID/WITH M20 .... 163 D1
Moorfield County Primary School
IRL M44 .... 116 B6
Moorfield Junior & Infant School
BRAM/HZG SK7 .... 184 A6
Moorgate CP School
BOLE BL2 .... 47 F1
Moorhouse CP School
MILN OL16 .... 41 F1

Moorlands Junior School
SALE M33 .... **140** C6

Moorside High School
SWIN M27 .... **85** E6

Moorside Primary School
SWIN M27 .... **85** E6

Moravian College
DROY M43 .... **128** B1

Morris Green Business Park
BOLS/LL BL3 .... **46** A5

Mosque
AUL OL6 .... **112** C5

Mosque
CHAD OL9 .... **78** A6

Mosque
CHH M8 .... **90** B6

Mosque
OLDTF/WHR M16 .... **123** E5

The Mosques
OLDE OL4 .... **79** F6

The Mosque
BURY BL9 .... **34** A5

The Mosque
MILN OL16 .... **23** E5

Moss CP School
BOLE BL2 .... **49** D3

Mossfield CP School
HEY OL10 .... **37** D4

Mossfield Primary School
SWIN M27 .... **86** A4

Moss Hey Primary School
BRAM/HZG SK7 .... **196** A4

Moss Industrial Estate
MILN OL16 .... **40** C2

Moss Lane Industrial Estate
ROY/SHW OL2 .... **61** E6

Mossley Associated Football Club
MOSL OL5 .... **99** D4

Mossley Health Centre
MOSL OL5 .... **99** D4

Moss Park Junior & Infant School
STRET M32 .... **139** F1

Moss Side Health Centre
RUSH/FAL M14 .... **124** B5

Moss Side Leisure Centre
HULME M15 .... **124** A4

Moss View Primary School
PART M31 .... **155** E2

Moston Brook High School
NEWH/MOS M40 .... **108** A1

Moston Fields Primary School
NEWH/MOS M40 .... **92** B4

Moston Indoor Market
NEWH/MOS M40 .... **92** A5

Moston Lane Primary School
NEWH/MOS M40 .... **92** A5

Mount Carmel RC Junior School
BKLY M9 .... **91** E3

Mount Pleasant Business Centre
OLDE OL4 .... **79** F5

Mount St Joseph RC School
BOLS/LL BL3 .... **45** F5

Mount St Josephs School
FWTH BL4 .... **65** D1

Museum of Transport
CHH M8 .... **106** C1

Muslim Girls School
WHIT OL12 .... **22** C5

Mytham CP School
BOLS/LL BL3 .... **49** F6

National Industrial Estate
AULW OL7 .... **112** B5

National Museum of Labour
History
CMANE M1 .... **3** E5

National Trading Estate
BRAM/HZG SK7 .... **184** A4

Natural History
OLDS OL8 .... **78** A6

Navigation Primary School
ALT WA14 .... **174** B1

Navigation Trading Estate
NEWH/MOS M40 .... **108** B2

Nelson Business Centre
DTN/ASHW M34 .... **130** A5

Neville Street Industrial Estate
CHAD OL9 .... **78** A4

Nevill Road Junior and
Infant School
BRAM/HZG SK7 .... **182** C5

Newall Green High School
NTHM/RTH M23 .... **177** D3

Newall Green Primary School
NTHM/RTH M23 .... **177** F3

New Ardwick Sports Centre
BRUN/LGST M13 .... **125** E3

Newbarn Infant School
ROY/SHW OL2 .... **61** E3

New Barn Junior School
ROY/SHW OL2 .... **61** E3

Newby Road Industrial Estate
BRAM/HZG SK7 .... **184** B5

New Church College
RAD M26 .... **70** A1

New Croft High School
SLFD M6 .... **104** A4

New Hall Road Synagogue/Pinto
Talmudical Centre
BRO M7 .... **89** D5

Newhaven Business Park
ECC M30 .... **101** F6

Newhey County School
MILN OL16 .... **42** B4

New Kingsway Health Centre
DID/WITH M20 .... **164** B1

Newlands Medical Centre
BOL BL1 .... **45** E2

New Line Industrial Estate
BCUP OL13 .... **4** B1

New Moston Primary School
NEWH/MOS M40 .... **93** F3

New Museum
OLD OL1 .... **78** C3

Newton Business Park
HYDE SK14 .... **132** B4

Newton Heath Cricket Club
NEWH/MOS M40 .... **109** C2

Newton Street Police Museum
CMANE M1 .... **3** G3

Newtown Street Mosque
AUL OL6 .... **113** D4

New Wellington School
HALE/TIMP WA15 .... **175** D1

Nicholas Varley Community
School
NEWH/MOS M40 .... **107** F3

Noorul Islam Mosque
BOL BL1 .... **27** F6

Noor Ul Islam Mosque
BURY BL9 .... **34** A5

Norbury Hall Primary School
BRAM/HZG SK7 .... **184** C6

Norden CP School
WHIT OL12 .... **21** D3

Norden Cricket Club
WHIT OL12 .... **20** C3

Norman House School
NEWH/MOS M40 .... **93** E2

Norris Bank Medical Centre
HTNM SK4 .... **166** A4

Norris Bank Primary School
HTNM SK4 .... **165** F2

Nortex Business Centre
BOL BL1 .... **46** A1

North Area Sixth Form College
HTNM SK4 .... **145** F5

North Bolton Sixth Form College
BOL BL1 .... **26** C3

North Chadderton
Comprehensive Lower School
CHAD OL9 .... **77** E3

North Chadderton
Comprehensive School
CHAD OL9 .... **77** E1

North Cheshire Jewish
Primary School
CHD/CHDH SK8 .... **179** F5

Northenden Primary School
WYTH/NTH M22 .... **162** B4

Northern A & O Medical Centre
BURY BL9 .... **33** F4

Northern Moor Clinic
NTHM/RTH M23 .... **161** D4

North Grecian Street Primary
School
BRO M7 .... **105** D2

North Heaton Primary School
HTNM SK4 .... **146** A5

North Manchester General
Hospital
CHH M8 .... **91** D4

North Manchester High
School for Girls
BKLY M9 .... **92** B3

North Manchester Reform
Synagogue
WHTF M45 .... **71** D2

North Manchester Synagogue
BRO M7 .... **89** F5

North Reddish Health Centre
RDSH SK5 .... **146** C2

North Reddish Infant School
RDSH SK5 .... **147** D2

North Trafford College
STRET M32 .... **122** A5

North Walkden Primary School
WALK M28 .... **66** A6

North West Regional Health
Authority
DID/WITH M20 .... **143** D6

Oakenclough CP School
WILM/AE SK9 .... **204** B2

Oakenrod Primary School
ROCH OL11 .... **22** B6

Oakfield CP School
HYDE SK14 .... **131** F4

Oakhill Trading Estate
WALK M28 .... **66** A5

Oaklands County Infant School
WILM/AE SK9 .... **204** C2

Oakleigh Medical Centre
CHH M8 .... **90** C4

The Oaks CP School
BOL BL1 .... **28** A1

Oakwood High Lower School
CCHDY M21 .... **141** F6

Oakwood High School
SLFD M6 .... **103** D2

Oakwood Primary School
PART M31 .... **154** B2

Octagon Theatre
BOL BL1 .... **47** D2

Odeon Theatre
CMANW M2 .... **2** D5

Offerton Green Clinic
OFTN SK2 .... **185** D2

Offerton Health Centre
STKP SK1 .... **167** F5

Offerton High School
OFTN SK2 .... **168** C6

Old Hall Clinic
CHD/CHDH SK8 .... **179** F1

Old Hall CP School
TOT/BURYW BL8 .... **18** C6

Old Hall Drive Junior &
Infant School
GTN M18 .... **127** E5

Oldham Athletic Association
Football Club
OLD OL1 .... **78** A1

Oldham Central Clinic
CHAD OL9 .... **78** C5

Oldham College
CHAD OL9 .... **78** C4

Oldham County Court
OLD OL1 .... **78** C4

Oldham Cricket Club
OLD OL1 .... **80** A2

Oldham Golf Club
OLDE OL4 .... **98** A1

Oldham Metropolitan
Borough Council
CHAD OL9 .... **77** F4

Oldham Metropolitan
Borough Council
CHAD OL9 .... **78** B4

Oldham Metropolitan
Borough Council
FAIL M35 .... **94** A6

Oldham Metropolitan
Borough Council
OLD OL1 .... **62** C4

Oldham Metropolitan
Borough Council
OLD OL1 .... **78** C3

Oldham Metropolitan
Borough Council
OLDS OL8 .... **96** C4

Oldham Owls Disabled
Sports Club
CHAD OL9 .... **78** A3

Oldham Rugby Union
Football Club
OLDS OL8 .... **96** A5

Oldham Sixth Form College
CHAD OL9 .... **78** C5

Oldhams Lane CP School
BOL BL1 .... **27** D2

Oldham Sports Centre
OLD OL1 .... **79** D4

Oldham Theatre Workshop
ROY/SHW OL2 .... **60** B5

Oldham West Business Centre
CHAD OL9 .... **77** F4

Old Mill Hotel & Leisure Centre
RAMS BL0 .... **6** C4

Old Moat Junior & Infant School
DID/WITH M20 .... **143** E4

Oldwood Primary School
WYTH/NTH M22 .... **177** F5

Olympia Trading Estate
HULME M15 .... **123** F2

The Open University
CCHDY M21 .... **141** F2

Opera House
CSLFD M3 .... **2** B4

The Operating Theatre
STRET M32 .... **121** F6

Optimax Eye Care Clinic
CMANW M2 .... **2** D4

Orchard House Day Hospital
ROY/SHW OL2 .... **60** C5

Orchard Trading Estate
SLFD M6 .... **104** A2

Ordsall Hall Museum
SALQ/ORD M5 .... **122** C3

Ordsall Health Centre
SALQ/ORD M5 .... **122** C1

Oriel Bank High School
EDGY/DAV SK3 .... **183** D2

Orion Trading Estate
TRPK M17 .... **120** B1

Orrismere Primary School
CHD/CHDH SK8 .... **181** E4

Orsall Sports Centre
SALQ/ORD M5 .... **122** B2

Ortenbrook School
PART M31 .... **154** C3

Osborne Trading Estate
CHAD OL9 .... **78** A3

Oswald Road Primary School
CCHDY M21 .... **141** E2

Oulder Hill School
ROCH OL11 .... **21** F6

Our Lady of Lourdes RC
Junior & Infant School
FWTH BL4 .... **65** E3

Our Lady of Lourdes RC
Primary School
PART M31 .... **154** B2

Our Lady of Mount RC
High School
SLFD M6 .... **103** E4

Our Lady & St Pauls
Primary School
HEY OL10 .... **36** A6

Our Ladys High School
BKLY M9 .... **74** B5

Our Ladys RC High School
ROY/SHW OL2 .... **60** B6

Our Ladys RC Primary School
EDGY/DAV SK3 .... **166** C5

Our Ladys RC Primary School
OLDE OL4 .... **62** C6

Our Ladys RC Primary School
OLDTF/WHR M16 .... **123** E6

Our Lady & the Lancashire
Martyrs School
WALK M28 .... **82** B2

Outwood Primary School
CHD/CHDH SK8 .... **194** A2

Overdale Primary School
MPL/ROM SK6 .... **169** D4

Owl Business Centre 49-51
OLDE OL4 .... **80** B5

Oxford Grove CP School
BOL BL1 .... **27** D6

O Y Y Lubavitch Girls School
BRO M7 .... **89** E4

Palace Theatre
CMANE M1 .... **3** E6

Palm Business Centre
CHAD OL9 .... **77** F4

Paragon Industrial Estate
LIT OL15 .... **25** D2

Parish Church C of E Junior School
OLD OL1 .... **79** D3

Park Dean School
OLDS OL8 .... **96** C3

Parker International Estate
DUK SK16 .... **130** C2

Parkfield Industrial Estate
MDTN M24 .... **74** C3

Parkfield School
MDTN M24 .... **74** C2

Park Galleries
BOL BL1 .... **46** B2

Parklands High School
WYTH/NTH M22 .... **178** A4

Parkl Lane Gallery
POY/DIS SK12 .... **199** D6

Park Medical Practice
HALE/TIMP WA15 .... **159** E5

Park Road CP School
SALE M33 .... **139** E5

Park School
NTHM/RTH M23 .... **161** D5

Parkside Industrial Estate
ROY/SHW OL2 .... **60** C5

Park Surgery
OLDTF/WHR M16 .... **123** F6

Park View County Primary
School
PWCH M25 .... **88** C2

Park View Practice
RDSH SK5 .... **147** D2

Parkway Business Centre
OLDTF/WHR M16 .... **143** D2

Parkway Trading Estate
STRET M32 .... **120** B4

Parochial C of E Primary School
AUL OL6 .... **113** D4

Parr Lane CP School
BURY BL9 .... **71** E1

Parrs Wood High School
DID/WITH M20 .... **164** B4

Partington CP School
PART M31 .... **155** D2

Partington Health Centre
PART M31 .... **155** D2

Partington Shopping Centre
PART M31 .... **155** D2

Partington Sports Centre
PART M31 .... **155** D3

Patricroft C of E School
ECC M30 .... **101** D5

Peacefield Primary School
MPL/ROM SK6 .... **186** C2

Peacock County Primary School
GTN M18 .... **127** D3

Pear Mill Industrial Estate
MPL/ROM SK6 .... **168** A3

Peel Brow County Primary
School
RAMS BL0 .... **7** E5

Peel College
BURY BL9 .... **33** F6

Peel Hall Primary School
LHULT M38 .... **82** A2

Peel Hall Primary School
WYTH/NTH M22 .... **179** D4

Peel Health Centre
BURY BL9 .... **33** F6

Peel Moat Recreation Centre
HTNM SK4 .... **145** F6

Peerglow Industrial Estate
ALT WA14 .... **158** C5

Pendlebury Health Centre
SWIN M27 .... **86** B3

Pendleton Medical Centre
SLFD M6 .... **104** B5

Pennant Industrial Estate
OLD OL1 .... **79** F3

Pennine Business Park
HEY OL10 .... **55** F1

Peoples History Museum
CSLFD M3 .... **2** A3

Peterloo Medical Centre
MDTN M24 .... **74** C3

Phil Hughes Practice
CHD/CHDH SK8 .... **181** E4

Philips High School
WHTF M45 .... **70** C3

Phoenix Medical Centre
STKP SK1 .... **167** D5

Phoenix Park Industrial Estate
HEY OL10 .... **38** A6

Phoenix Park Industrial Estate
HEY OL10 .... **57** D1

Pictor School
SALE M33 .... **159** D1

Pike Fold Primary School
BKLY M9 .... **91** D2

Pikes Lane Infant School
BOLS/LL BL3 .... **46** B3

Pilot Industrial Estate
BOLS/LL BL3 .... **47** F5

Pinfold Junior & Infant School
HYDE SK14 .... **152** B2

Pinnacle Business Centre
HTNM SK4 .... **166** C2

Piper Hill School
NTHM/RTH M23 .... **161** F3

Plant Hill High School
BKLY M9 .... **91** D1

Plasman Industrial Centre
BNG/LEV M19 .... **145** E2

Plodder Lane CP School
FWTH BL4 .... **65** F2

Plymouth Court Business Centre
BRUN/LGST M13 .... **125** D4

Plymouth Grove Primary School
BRUN/LGST M13 .... **125** F4

Poland Industrial Estate
ANC M4 .... **107** D5

Portland Basin Museum
AULW OL7 .... **112** B6

Portland Industrial Estate
BURY BL9 .... **34** B3

Po Sorting Office
ANC M4 .... **106** C4

Poundswick Primary School
WYTH/NTH M22 .... **178** A5

Pownall Green Primary School
BRAM/HZG SK7 .... **196** C2

Pownall Hall School
WILM/AE SK9 .... **203** D3

Poynton Clinic
POY/DIS SK12 .... **198** C5

Poynton County High School
POY/DIS SK12 .... **199** D6

Poynton Parish Council
POY/DIS SK12 .... **198** C5

Poynton Sports Club
POY/DIS SK12 .... **198** C5

Prestwich Health Centre
PWCH M25 .... **71** E6

Prestwich Hebrew Congregation
Synagogue
PWCH M25 .... **88** C3

Prestwich High School
PWCH M25 .... **71** F6

Prestwich Hospital
PWCH M25 .... **71** D6

Prestwich Preparatory School
PWCH M25 .... **72** A6

Priestnall School
HTNM SK4 .... **165** D2

Primary School
BNG/LEV M19 .... **145** D4

Primary School
BRUN/LGST M13 .... **125** F5

Primary School
OLDTF/WHR M16 .... **122** B6

Princess Christian College
RUSH/FAL M14 .... **144** A2

Priorsleigh Medical Centre
POY/DIS SK12 .... **198** C5

Propps Hall Primary School
FAIL M35 .... **109** F1

Prospect Vale Primary School
CHD/CHDH SK8 .... **179** F6

Python Industrial Estate
LIT OL15 .... **13** D5

Queen Elizabeth School
MDTN M24 .... **57** D5

Queensgate Primary School
BRAM/HZG SK7 .... **196** C5

Queens Park Art Gallery
BKLY M9 .... **107** D1

Queens Road Primary School
CHD/CHDH SK8 .... **181** E4

Queen Street CP Infant School
FWTH BL4 .... **66** B3

Queensway CP School
ROCH OL11 .... **40** A4

Rackhouse Primary School
NTHM/RTH M23 .... **161** E4

Radcliffe Ainsworth C of E School
BOLE BL2 .... **31** D6

Radcliffe Borough
Associated Football Club
RAD M26 .... **50** C5

Radcliffe CP School
RAD M26 .... **50** C5

Radcliffe Cricket Club
RAD M26 .... **51** D5

Radcliffe Hall C of E
  Methodist Primary School
  RAD M26 .... 52 B5
Radcliffe High School
  RAD M26 .... 51 D6
Radcliffe Swimming Pool
  RAD M26 .... 51 E6
Radclyffe County Primary School
  SALQ/ORD M5 .... 122 B2
The Radclyffe School
  CHAD OL9 .... 77 D5
Raikes Lane Industrial Estate
  BOLS/LL BL3 .... 47 F5
Ralph Williams Clinic
  WHIT OL12 .... 24 A2
Ramillies Hall School
  CHD/CHDH SK8 .... 182 A5
Ramsbottom Cottage Hospital
  RAMS BL0 .... 7 D6
Ramsbottom Health Centre
  RAMS BL0 .... 6 C4
Ramsbottom Swimming Pool
  RAMS BL0 .... 7 D4
Ravensbury CP School
  OP/CLY M11 .... 108 B4
Ravensfield Industrial Estate
  DUK SK16 .... 112 B6
Ravenside Retail Park
  BOLS/LL BL3 .... 47 D3
Recreation Centre
  CHD/CHDH SK8 .... 195 F2
Red Bank Health Centre
  RAD M26 .... 51 D5
Reddish Vale School
  RDSH SK5 .... 147 D4
Red Lane CP School
  BOLE BL2 .... 30 A6
Regal Industrial Estate
  WGTN/LGST M12 .... 126 A2
Regent Trading Estate
  SALQ/ORD M5 .... 105 D6
The Regimental Museum of XX
  Lancashire Fusiliers
  TOT/BURYW BL8 .... 32 C6
Registry Office
  CSLFD M3 .... 2 C4
Ribble Drive CP School
  WHTF M45 .... 71 E2
Ribblesdale House Medical Centre
  BURY BL9 .... 33 F5
Richmond Junior School
  CHAD OL9 .... 78 B5
The Ridge College
  MPL/ROM SK6 .... 186 C2
Ridge Danyers College
  CHD/CHDH SK8 .... 181 D4
Ridge Danyers College
  MPL/ROM SK6 .... 187 D2
Ridge Hill Primary & Infant School
  STLY SK15 .... 114 A4
Ripon Avenue School
  BURY BL9 .... 53 D6
Roaches Industrial Estate
  MOSL OL5 .... 99 F1
The Robert Darbishire Practice
  RUSH/FAL M14 .... 124 C6
Rochdale Association
  Football Club
  ROCH OL11 .... 22 A5
Rochdale Council
  ROCH OL11 .... 21 F5
Rochdale Curtain Theatre
  ROCH OL11 .... 39 F1
Rochdale Healthcare NHS Trust
  LIT OL15 .... 12 B6
Rochdale Healthcare NHS Trust
  WHIT OL12 .... 11 E6
Rochdale Industrial Centre
  ROCH OL11 .... 39 E1
Rochdale Infirmary
  WHIT OL12 .... 22 C4
Rochdale Metropolitan
  Borough Council
  MDTN M24 .... 75 E2
Rochdale Metropolitan
  Borough Council
  MILN OL16 .... 23 D6
Rochdale Metropolitan
  Borough Council
  ROCH OL11 .... 40 A5
Rochdale Metropolitan
  Borough Council
  WHIT OL12 .... 23 D5

Roch House Fairfield
  General Hospital
  BURY BL9 .... 35 F3
Roe Green Cricket Club
  WALK M28 .... 84 A5
Roker Industrial Estate
  OLD OL1 .... 79 F4
Roman Fort
  CSLFD M3 .... 2 A6
Romiley CP School
  MPL/ROM SK6 .... 170 B3
Romiley Health Centre
  MPL/ROM SK6 .... 170 A3
Rosedale Shopping Centre
  NEWH/MOS M40 .... 109 D2
Rose Hill Primary School
  MPL/ROM SK6 .... 186 C1
Roundthorn Primary School
  OLDE OL4 .... 80 A5
Roundwood Upper School
  WYTH/NTH M22 .... 162 A6
Royal Exchange Clinic
  CMANW M2 .... 2 D3
Royal Exchange Theatre
  ANC M4 .... 3 F1
Royal Exchange Theatre Co
  ANC M4 .... 2 D2
Royal Manchester
  Childrens Hospital
  SWIN M27 .... 86 C6
Royal Oak Industrial Estate
  STKP SK1 .... 167 D5
Royal Oak Primary School
  NTHM/RTH M23 .... 161 E6
Royal Oldham Hospital
  OLD OL1 .... 78 B2
Royal Pennine Trading Estate
  ROCH OL11 .... 38 C4
Royce Primary School
  HULME M15 .... 123 F4
Royce Trading Estate
  TRPK M17 .... 120 A2
Royle Pennine Trading Estate
  ROCH OL11 .... 39 E4
Royton & Crompton School
  ROY/SHW OL2 .... 61 E5
Royton Medical Centre
  ROY/SHW OL2 .... 60 B5
Royton Public Baths
  ROY/SHW OL2 .... 60 C5
Rushcroft CP School
  ROY/SHW OL2 .... 61 F1
Russell Leite Theatre School
  RUSH/FAL M14 .... 124 C5
Russell Scott Primary School
  DTN/ASHW M34 .... 129 F5
Rycroft Park Sports Club
  CHD/CHDH SK8 .... 181 D6
Rydings School
  WHIT OL12 .... 23 F1
Ryecroft Business Park
  AULW OL7 .... 111 F6
Ryleys Preparatory School
  WILM/AE SK9 .... 209 D4
Sacred Heart RC Primary School
  MILN OL16 .... 41 D1
Sacred Heart RC Primary School
  NTHM/RTH M23 .... 176 C1
Sacred Heart RC Primary School
  OLD OL1 .... 80 A1
St Agnes C of E School
  OLDE OL4 .... 81 E6
St Agnes Primary School
  BRUN/LGST M13 .... 126 A6
St Aidan RC Primary School
  NTHM/RTH M23 .... 161 F4
St Albans RC High School
  GTN M18 .... 146 B1
St Alphonsus RC Infant School
  OLDTF/WHR M16 .... 123 E4
St Ambrose Barlow RC
  High School
  SWIN M27 .... 86 A6
St Ambrose College
  HALE/TIMP WA15 .... 175 F6
St Ambrose RC Primary School
  CCHDY M21 .... 162 B1
St Ambrose RC Primary School
  EDGY/DAV SK3 .... 182 B2
St Andrews C of E
  Primary School
  BNG/LEV M19 .... 145 F3

St Andrews C of E
  Primary School
  RAMS BL0 .... 6 C6
St Andrews C of E
  Primary School
  WHIT OL12 .... 24 C1
St Andrews C of E School
  ECC M30 .... 101 F6
St Andrews C of E School
  RAD M26 .... 51 D3
St Andrews Medical Centre
  ECC M30 .... 101 F5
St Andrews Methodist School
  WALK M28 .... 82 C2
St Andrews RC Primary School
  BOLE BL2 .... 48 C1
St Annes C of E (Aided)
  Primary School
  SALE M33 .... 160 A1
St Annes CP School
  DTN/ASHW M34 .... 130 B5
St Annes Ear Nose &
  Throat Hospital
  ALT WA14 .... 174 A4
St Annes Primary School
  DTN/ASHW M34 .... 128 B2
St Annes RC Primary School
  OLDE OL4 .... 80 A4
St Annes RC School
  ANC M4 .... 107 E6
St Annes RC School
  HTNM SK4 .... 166 B1
St Anns RC Infant School
  STRET M32 .... 140 B1
St Anns RC Junior School
  STRET M32 .... 140 B1
St Anselms RC School
  WHIT OL12 .... 9 E1
St Anthonys RC Junior School
  WYTH/NTH M22 .... 178 B6
St Antony High School
  URM M41 .... 139 D1
St Augustine of Canterbury
  RC School
  OLDS OL8 .... 95 E2
St Augustines C of E Primary
  School
  NEWH/MOS M40 .... 107 F2
St Augustines C of E School
  SWIN M27 .... 86 C5
St Barnabas C of E
  Primary School
  OP/CLY M11 .... 126 C1
St Bartholomews C of E
  Primary School
  WHIT OL12 .... 9 D3
St Bedes C of E Primary School
  BOLS/LL BL3 .... 64 A1
St Bedes College
  OLDTF/WHR M16 .... 123 F6
St Benedicts RC Primary School
  CHD/CHDH SK8 .... 194 C5
St Benedicts RC Primary School
  WILM/AE SK9 .... 194 C6
St Bernadettes RC Primary School
  BURY BL9 .... 53 D6
St Bernadettes RC Primary School
  RDSH SK5 .... 167 F1
St Bernards Primary School
  BNG/LEV M19 .... 145 D5
St Bernards RC Primary School
  BOLS/LL BL3 .... 44 C4
St Boniface RC Junior
  & Infant School
  BRO M7 .... 105 D1
St Brendans RC School
  BOLE BL2 .... 29 F2
St Brigids RC School
  OP/CLY M11 .... 108 B6
St Catherines Preparatory School
  MPL/ROM SK6 .... 171 F6
St Chads RC Primary School
  CHH M8 .... 106 B2
St Charles RC Primary School
  SWIN M27 .... 85 E5
St Christophers RC Primary School
  MPL/ROM SK6 .... 169 E3
St Christophers School
  AUL OL6 .... 113 E1
St Chrysostoms C of E Primary
  School
  BRUN/LGST M13 .... 125 E4
St Clares R C Primary School
  BKLY M9 .... 74 A6

St Patricks RC Primary School
WHIT OL12 .... 23 E4

St Pauls C of E Junior School
ROY/SHW OL2 .... 60 A6

St Pauls C of E Primary School
BOL BL1 .... 28 A4

St Pauls C of E Primary School
BURY BL9 .... 34 C3

St Pauls C of E Primary School
DID/WITH M20 .... 143 F5

St Pauls C of E Primary School
SALQ/ORD M5 .... 104 B6

St Pauls C of E Primary School
STLY SK15 .... 115 D5

St Pauls C of E School
RAMS BL0 .... 7 D4

St Pauls C of E School
WALK M28 .... 83 F3

St Pauls Junior School
LHULT M38 .... 65 D6

St Pauls Primary School
RDSH SK5 .... 167 F1

St Pauls RC High School
NTHM/RTH M23 .... 177 F3

St Pauls RC Primary School
HYDE SK14 .... 132 A5

St Peter & St. John RC Primary
School
CSLFD M3 .... 105 E4

St Peters C of E Primary School
AULW OL7 .... 112 A6

St Peters C of E School
FWTH BL4 .... 66 B4

St Peters C of E School
MILN OL16 .... 41 D2

St Peters Primary School
BURY BL9 .... 52 C3

St Peters Primary School
NTHM/RTH M23 .... 177 F4

St Peters RC Primary School
BRAM/HZG SK7 .... 184 B6

St Peters RC Primary School
MDTN M24 .... 75 E4

St Peters School C of E
Primary School
SWIN M27 .... 85 F5

St Peters Smithills Dean
C of E Primary School
BOL BL1 .... 26 C3

St Philips C of E Primary School
CSLFD M3 .... 105 E6

St Philips RC Primary School
OFTN SK2 .... 184 B1

St Phillips C of E Primary School
HULME M15 .... 124 A3

St Phillips RC Primary School
BRO M7 .... 89 D4

St Raphaels RC School
STLY SK15 .... 115 F3

St Roberts RC School
BRUN/LGST M13 .... 126 A6

St Saviour Ringley C of E
Primary School
RAD M26 .... 68 A4

St Sebastians RC School
SLFD M6 .... 104 B2

St Simon & St. Judes C of E Primary
School
BOLS/LL BL3 .... 47 D6

St Simons RC Primary School
BRAM/HZG SK7 .... 184 C4

St Stephen & All Martyrs School
BOLE BL2 .... 48 A3

St Stephens C of E Primary School
BRAM/HZG SK7 .... 185 D3

St Stephens C of E Primary School
DTN/ASHW M34 .... 129 F1

St Stephens C of E Primary School
OLD OL1 .... 79 E3

St Stephens C of E Primary School
TOT/BURYW BL8 .... 32 B6

St Stephens C of E Primary School
FWTH BL4 .... 67 E5

St Stephens RC School
DROY M43 .... 110 B5

St Teresa Junior School
BOLS/LL BL3 .... 49 E6

St Teresas RC School
IRL M44 .... 134 C3

St Thomas Aquinas RC
High School
OLDTF/WHR M16 .... 142 C2

St Thomas Aquinas RC
High & Upper School
CCHDY M21 .... 142 B4

St Thomas C of E Primary School
OLD OL1 .... 62 C5

St Thomas C of E Primary School
STKP SK1 .... 167 D5

St Thomas C of E School
BOL BL1 .... 27 E5

St Thomas Hospital
EDGY/DAV SK3 .... 166 C6

St Thomas More RC High School
DTN/ASHW M34 .... 149 D1

St Thomas More RC Primary
School
MDTN M24 .... 75 E6

St Thomas of Canterbury
RC Primary School
BOL BL1 .... 45 E1

St Thomas Primary School
BURY BL9 .... 34 C6

St Thomas Primary School
CHH M8 .... 91 D5

St Thomas's C of E School
MILN OL16 .... 42 C3

St Vincent De Paul High School
RUSH/FAL M14 .... 125 E6

St Vincent RC Infant School
HALE/TIMP WA15 .... 174 C2

St Vincents School
WHIT OL12 .... 21 D4

St Wilfrids C of E Primary School
WYTH/NTH M22 .... 162 C5

St Williams RC School
BOLS/LL BL3 .... 46 C6

St Willibrords RC School
OP/CLY M11 .... 109 D4

St Winifreds RC Primary School
HTNM SK4 .... 165 E3

Sale Cricket Club
SALE M33 .... 140 B6

Sale Football Club
SALE M33 .... 159 F2

Sale Grammar School
SALE M33 .... 160 A2

Sale Leisure Centre
SALE M33 .... 140 A6

Salford City Council
BRO M7 .... 89 E6

Salford City Council
CSLFD M3 .... 105 F4

Salford City Council
ECC M30 .... 102 A5

Salford City Council
IRL M44 .... 135 D3

Salford City Council
LHULT M38 .... 82 C1

Salford City Council
SALQ/ORD M5 .... 103 D5

Salford City Council
SALQ/ORD M5 .... 122 B2

Salford City Council
SLFD M6 .... 102 C4

Salford City Council
SLFD M6 .... 104 C2

Salford City Council
SWIN M27 .... 86 A5

Salford City Council
WALK M28 .... 83 D2

Salford College
ECC M30 .... 100 B5

Salford College
SALQ/ORD M5 .... 122 B3

Salford College
SLFD M6 .... 104 C3

Salford College
SWIN M27 .... 85 D3

Salford College
WALK M28 .... 83 E4

Salford County Council
WALK M28 .... 83 D2

Salford County Court
SALQ/ORD M5 .... 104 B6

Salford Medical Centre
SLFD M6 .... 103 F4

Salford Royal Hospitals
NHS Trust
SLFD M6 .... 102 C4

Salford Rugby Club
SALQ/ORD M5 .... 103 E5

Salford Town Hall
CSLFD M3 .... 105 E5

Salford & Trafford Health
Authority
ECC M30 .... 102 A5

Salford University Business Park
SLFD M6 .... 104 C3

Salvation Army
BRUN/LGST M13 .... 124 C2

Samuel Laycock Special School
STLY SK15 .... 114 A3

Sandifords Gallery
MILN OL16 .... 23 D6

Sandilands Primary School
NTHM/RTH M23 .... 160 A5

Saviour C of E Primary School
NEWH/MOS M40 .... 107 D2

School Lane Farm
MPL/ROM SK6 .... 171 F2

Seaford Industrial Estate
SLFD M6 .... 104 C3

Sedgley Park CP School
PWCH M25 .... 89 E3

Sedgley Park Rugby
Union Football Club
WHTF M45 .... 70 B5

Seedley Primary School
SLFD M6 .... 103 F5

Severnside Trading Estate
TRPK M17 .... 120 C4

Seymour Park Primary School
OLDTF/WHR M16 .... 122 C5

Seymour Road Primary School
OP/CLY M11 .... 109 E6

Shaare Sedek Synagogue
DID/WITH M20 .... 163 D1

Shandon Clinic
HULME M15 .... 124 B4

Sharples CP School
BOL BL1 .... 28 B2

Shawclough CP School
WHIT OL12 .... 22 C2

Shawclough Trading Estate
WHIT OL12 .... 22 B2

Shawgrove School
DID/WITH M20 .... 143 D5

Shaw Heath Health Centre
EDGY/DAV SK3 .... 166 C6

Shay Lane Medical Centre
HALE/TIMP WA15 .... 176 A6

Shena Simon College
CMANE M1 .... 3 F5

Sherwood Business Park
ROCH OL11 .... 39 E5

Shiv Lodge Medical Centre
BRUN/LGST M13 .... 126 A6

Showcase Cinemas Belle Vue
GTN M18 .... 126 C4

Shree Swaminarayan Temple
OLDS OL8 .... 78 C6

Siddall Surgery
HEY OL10 .... 56 C1

Sikh Temple
OLDTF/WHR M16 .... 123 E5

Silverdale Primary School
SWIN M27 .... 86 C3

Smallbridge Health Centre
WHIT OL12 .... 24 A2

Smallbridge Industrial Park
MILN OL16 .... 23 F3

Smallbridge St Johns C of E School
WHIT OL12 .... 23 F1

Smallbridge School
WHIT OL12 .... 23 F2

Smithills Museum
BOL BL1 .... 26 C3

Smithy Bridge Primary School
LIT OL15 .... 25 D2

Sorrel Group Practice
SLFD M6 .... 102 B4

South Chadderton
Secondary School
CHAD OL9 .... 94 A2

Southern Cross School
CCHDY M21 .... 142 A6

South Failsworth County School
FAIL M35 .... 109 F2

Southfield Industrial Estate
TRPK M17 .... 121 D4

Southfields School
SALE M33 .... 159 D2

Southgate Industrial Estate
HEY OL10 .... 38 A6

Southlink Business Park
Workshops
OLDE OL4 .... 79 E5

South Manchester High School
WYTH/NTH M22 .... 178 B4

South Manchester Synagogue
RUSH/FAL M14 .... 144 A2

South Manchester
University Hospitals NHS Trust
NTHM/RTH M23 .... 177 D3

Southmoor Business Park
NTHM/RTH M23 .... 160 C6

South Reddish Medical Centre
RDSH SK5 .... 167 D1

South Trafford College
ALT WA14 .... 158 B5

South Trafford College
SALE M33 .... 138 A6

South West Manchester
Cricket Club
CCHDY M21 .... 142 A2

Spa Road Industrial Estate
BOL BL1 .... 46 B2

Sparrow Hill Community School
MILN OL16 .... 22 C6

Spindle Point CP School
FWTH BL4 .... 68 A6

The Spindles Shopping Centre
OLD OL1 .... 78 C5

Sports Centre
MPL/ROM SK6 .... 171 E6

Sports Hall
OLDS OL8 .... 78 C5

Spotland Primary School
WHIT OL12 .... 22 B4

Springfield Business Centre
CSLFD M3 .... 105 F4

Springfield House Medical Centre
OLD OL11 .... 80 A3

Springfield Primary School
SALE M33 .... 159 F1

Springfield Surgery
BRAM/HZG SK7 .... 184 B4

Springhead County Infant School
OLDE OL4 .... 81 E5

Springhill High School
MILN OL16 .... 40 C2

Springside CP School
BURY BL9 .... 19 F6

Spring View Medical Centre
BOLS/LL BL3 .... 49 E6

Springwood Primary School
MPL/ROM SK6 .... 170 C2

Spurley Hey High School
GTN M18 .... 146 A1

Stag Industrial Estate
ALT WA14 .... 173 F1

Stakehill Industrial Estate
MDTN M24 .... 58 B5

Stalybridge Celtic Associated
Football Club
STLY SK15 .... 133 D1

Stalybridge Cricket Club
DUK SK16 .... 131 F1

Stalybridge Millbrook
Cricket Club
STLY SK15 .... 115 E3

Stalybridge St Pauls
Cricket Club
DUK SK16 .... 132 A2

Stalyhill Junior School
STLY SK15 .... 133 E2

Stalyhill Primary School
STLY SK15 .... 133 F2

Staly Industrial Estate
STLY SK15 .... 114 C5

Stamford High School
AUL OL6 .... 113 F3

Stamford Park Junior
& Infant School
HALE/TIMP WA15 .... 174 C4

Stanley Road Primary School
CHAD OL9 .... 94 C1

Stansfield Hall CP School
LIT OL15 .... 13 D3

Stansfield Road Junior School
FAIL M35 .... 94 B5

Star Industrial Estate
OLDS OL8 .... 78 C6

Station Approach Business Estate
ROCH OL11 .... 40 A1

Staveleigh Medical Centre
STLY SK15 .... 114 B5

Stella Maris School
HTNM SK4 .... 164 C3

Stepping Hill Hospital
OFTN SK2 .... 183 F3

Stockport Acute Services
NHS Trust
OFTN SK2 .... 184 A3

Stockport College of Further & Higher
Education
EDGY/DAV SK3 .... 166 C5

Stockport County Court
STKP SK1 .... 167 D4

Stockport County Football Club
EDGY/DAV SK3 .... 166 B6

Stockport Cricket Club
EDGY/DAV SK3 .... 182 C1

Stockport Grammar School
OFTN SK2 .... 183 F2

Stockport Metropolitan
Borough Council
CHD/CHDH SK8 .... 181 E5

Stockport Metropolitan
Borough Council
EDGY/DAV SK3 .... 181 F2

Stockport Metropolitan
Borough Council
MPL/ROM SK6 .... 171 E3

Stockport Metropolitan
Borough Council
MPL/ROM SK6 .... 187 E1

Stockport Metropolitan
Borough Council
OFTN SK2 .... 184 B1

Stockport Metropolitan
Borough Council
RDSH SK5 .... 147 D4

Stockport Metropolitan
Borough Council
STKP SK1 .... 167 D5

Stockport Road Medical
Practice
MPL/ROM SK6 .... 187 D1

Stockport Rugby Union
Football Club
BRAM/HZG SK7 .... 183 D6

Stockport School
OFTN SK2 .... 183 F2

Stockport Super Bowl
EDGY/DAV SK3 .... 166 C5

Stockport Trading Estate
HTNM SK4 .... 165 F5

Stonecourt Great
& New Synagogue
BRO M7 .... 89 E4

Stonefield Street Surgery
MILN OL16 .... 42 A2

Stonehill Medical Centre
FWTH BL4 .... 66 A4

Stoneleigh Junior & Infant
School
OLD OL1 .... 79 F1

The Strand Medical Centre
ROCH OL11 .... 40 A5

Stretford Grammar School
STRET M32 .... 140 C2

Stretford High School
STRET M32 .... 122 A5

Stretford Memorial Hospital
OLDTF/WHR M16 .... 122 C6

Stubbins CP School
RAMS BL0 .... 7 E2

Styal Primary School
WILM/AE SK9 .... 192 A5

Sudden Health Centre
ROCH OL11 .... 39 D3

Sughar Mosque
FWTH BL4 .... 66 A1

Summerseat Methodist
Primary School
BURY BL9 .... 19 E3

Summerville Primary School
SLFD M6 .... 103 E2

Sunning Hill CP School
BOLS/LL BL3 .... 46 B5

Sunnybank Clinic
BURY BL9 .... 53 E6

Sunnybank Primary School
BURY BL9 .... 53 E6

Sunset Business Centre
FWTH BL4 .... 68 A6

Surrey Lodge Group Practice
RUSH/FAL M14 .... 125 E5

Swaminarayan Temple
BOLS/LL BL3 .... 46 B3

Swan Lane Medical Centre
BOLS/LL BL3 .... 46 B5

Swinton Cricket Club
SWIN M27 .... 86 B6

Swinton High School
SWIN M27 .... 85 F4

Swinton Industrial Estate
SWIN M27 .... 86 B5

Swinton Leisure Centre
SWIN M27 .... 86 A5

Syddal Park School
BRAM/HZG SK7 .... 196 B4

Synagogue
BRO M7 .... 88 C5

Synagogue
DID/WITH M20 .... 163 D1

Talbot Court Medical Practice
STRET M32 .... 121 F6

Talmah Torah Jewish School
BRO M7 .... 89 E6

Tameside Business Park
DUK SK16 .... 130 C2

Tameside College of Technology
AUL OL6 .... 113 E4

Tameside College of Technology
HYDE SK14 .... 150 B4

Tameside County Court
AUL OL6 .... 113 D5

Tameside General Hospital
AUL OL6 .... 113 F4

Tameside & Glossop
Health Authority
DROY M43 .... 128 B1

Tameside & Glossop
Health Authority
DTN/ASHW M34 .... 129 F2

Tameside & Glossop
Health Authority
HYDE SK14 .... 131 D4

Tameside & Glossop
Health Authority
HYDE SK14 .... 150 B1

Tameside Metropolitan
Borough Council
AUL OL6 .... 112 C4

Tameside Metropolitan
Borough Council
DTN/ASHW M34 .... 129 F6

Tameside Metropolitan
Borough Council
DTN/ASHW M34 .... 129 D1

Tameside Metropolitan
Borough Council
DUK SK16 .... 130 C3

Tameside Metropolitan
Borough Council
STLY SK15 .... 114 A5

Tameside Private Specialist
Medical Centre
AUL OL6 .... 113 F3

Tame Valley Primary School
MPL/ROM SK6 .... 148 A4

Tavistock Industrial Estate
OP/CLY M11 .... 127 E3

Taylors Sports Club
ECC M30 .... 101 F6

Telford School
BKLY M9 .... 91 D1

Temple Junior School
CHH M8 .... 106 B1

Temple Street Infant School
CHH M8 .... 106 B1

Tennis Club
WILM/AE SK9 .... 208 B1

Thames Industrial Estate
WGTN/LGST M12 .... 125 E2

Thames Trading Centre
IRL M44 .... 135 D4

Thomasson Memorial
Special School
BOL BL1 .... 45 F1

Thornfield School
HTNM SK4 .... 165 D2

Thorn Grove Primary School
CHD/CHDH SK8 .... 195 E3

Thornham Cricket Club
MDTN M24 .... 58 B2

Thornham St James C of E
Primary School
ROY/SHW OL2 .... 60 B1

Thornleigh Salesian College
BOL BL1 .... 27 E3

Thorp County Primary School
ROY/SHW OL2 .... 60 A4

Tian Guan Temple
NEWH/MOS M40 .... 107 F3

Tib Lane Gallery
CMANW M2 .... 2 D4

Times Retail Park
HEY OL10 .... **37** D4
Timperley Health Centre
HALE/TIMP WA15 .... **159** E6
Timperley Park Road CP School
ALT WA14 .... **158** C5
Tip Toes Complimentary Health
Centre
MILN OL16 .... **42** A1
Tonacliffe School
WHIT OL12 .... **9** D5
Tone Up & Tan Health Centre
BRAM/HZG SK7 .... **184** B4
Tonge Bridge Industrial Estate
BOLE BL2 .... **47** F2
Tonge Cricket Club
BOLE BL2 .... **28** C4
Tonge Fold Health Centre
BOLE BL2 .... **48** A2
Tonge Moor County School
BOLE BL2 .... **28** C6
Tonge Moor Health Centre
BOLE BL2 .... **29** D6
Tootal Drive County Primary
School
SALQ/ORD M5 .... **103** D5
Top O' Th' Brow CP School
BOLE BL2 .... **29** E5
Torkington Primary School
BRAM/HZG SK7 .... **185** E5
Tottington CP School
TOT/BURYW BL8 .... **32** A2
Tottington Health Centre
TOT/BURYW BL8 .... **17** F6
Tottington High School
TOT/BURYW BL8 .... **32** A1
Towers Business Park
DID/WITH M20 .... **162** C1
Townfield Industrial Estate
OLDE OL4 .... **79** F4
Town Square Shopping Centre
OLD OL1 .... **79** D5
Trafalgar Business Park
BRO M7 .... **105** F3
Trafford Area Health Authority
SALE M33 .... **139** F6
Trafford Football Club
URM M41 .... **137** E2
Trafford Health Authority
HALE/TIMP WA15 .... **174** C5
Trafford Healthcare NHS Trust
SALE M33 .... **160** B2
Trafford Healthcare NHS Trust
URM M41 .... **118** B6
Trafford Metropolitan
Borough Council
ALT WA14 .... **174** A3
Trafford Metropolitan
Borough Council
OLDTF/WHR M16 .... **122** C5
Trafford Metropolitan
Borough Council
PART M31 .... **155** D2
Trafford Metropolitan
Borough Council
SALE M33 .... **139** F6
Trafford Metropolitan
Borough Council
SALE M33 .... **159** F1
Trafford Metropolitan
Borough Council
STRET M32 .... **121** D6
Trafford Metropolitan
Borough Council
STRET M32 .... **140** A1
Trafford Metropolitan
Borough Council
URM M41 .... **138** B1
Trafford M V R F C C
SALE M33 .... **139** E4
Tregenna Health
Centre & Dental Surgery
WYTH/NTH M22 .... **178** C6
Tregenna Surgery
WYTH/NTH M22 .... **192** B1
Trinity C of E High School
HULME M15 .... **124** B3
Trinity Retail Park
BOLE BL2 .... **47** E4
Trinity School
STLY SK15 .... **114** A6
Tudor Industrial Estate
DUK SK16 .... **130** B3

Turton Eagley County Junior School
EDGW/EG BL7 .... **14** C5
Turton Harwood Hardy Mill County
Primary School
BOLE BL2 .... **30** A3
Turton High School
EDGW/EG BL7 .... **14** C6
Turton Tower
EDGW/EG BL7 .... **15** D2
Two Trees High School
DTN/ASHW M34 .... **149** F2
Tyldesley Highfield School
TYLD M29 .... **82** A6
Tyntesfield CP School
SALE M33 .... **158** C4
UMIST
CMANE M1 .... **3** G6
The Unicorn Gallery
WILM/AE SK9 .... **203** F5
United Synagogue
CHH M8 .... **89** F2
University
BRUN/LGST M13 .... **124** C3
University
RUSH/FAL M14 .... **144** B2
University of Manchester
BRUN/LGST M13 .... **124** C4
University of Manchester
ECC M30 .... **117** E3
University of Manchester
HULME M15 .... **124** C4
University of Manchester
RUSH/FAL M14 .... **125** E6
University of Manchester
RUSH/FAL M14 .... **144** B1
University of Manchester
Institute of Science
& Technology
BRUN/LGST M13 .... **124** C2
University of Salford
SALQ/ORD M5 .... **105** D5
University of Salford
SLFD M6 .... **105** D4
Unsworth Medical Centre
BURY BL9 .... **54** A6
Urmston Grammar School
URM M41 .... **119** D6
Urmston Group Practice
URM M41 .... **138** A2
Urmston Infant School
URM M41 .... **138** A1
Urmston Junior School
URM M41 .... **138** A1
Urmston Leisure Centre
URM M41 .... **137** F1
Urmston Town Football Club
URM M41 .... **137** D2
Vaishali Medical Centre
CCHDY M21 .... **141** F2
Valley School
BRAM/HZG SK7 .... **196** A4
Varley Street Clinic
NEWH/MOS M40 .... **107** E3
Vauxhall Industrial Estate
RDSH SK5 .... **146** C5
Vauxhall Industrial Estate
RDSH SK5 .... **167** D1
Vernon County Infant School
POY/DIS SK12 .... **198** C6
Vernon County Junior School
POY/DIS SK12 .... **198** C6
Vernon Industrial Estate
STKP SK1 .... **167** D3
Vernon Park Primary School
STKP SK1 .... **167** E4
Vernon Road Medical Centre
TOT/BURYW BL8 .... **18** B4
Victoria Avenue Primary School
BKLY M9 .... **74** B6
Victoria Industrial Estate
ANC M4 .... **107** E6
Victoria Medical Centre
URM M41 .... **138** B1
Victoria Park Infant School
STRET M32 .... **140** A1
Victoria Park Junior School
STRET M32 .... **140** B1
Victoria Trading Estate
CHAD OL9 .... **94** C2
Victory Trading Estate
BOLS/LL BL3 .... **47** E4
Village Medical Centre
LIT OL15 .... **12** C6

The Village Surgery
BRAM/HZG SK7 .... **196** C3
Virgin Cinemas
EDGY/DAV SK3 .... **166** C4
Virgin Cinemas
SALQ/ORD M5 .... **122** B3
Wadeson Junior School
BRUN/LGST M13 .... **125** D2
Walkden Cricket Club
WALK M28 .... **83** E2
Walkden High School
WALK M28 .... **83** F3
Walshaw C of E School
TOT/BURYW BL8 .... **32** A3
Walshaw Sports Club
TOT/BURYW BL8 .... **32** A2
Walton Park Leisure Centre
SALE M33 .... **159** E3
Wardle High School
WHIT OL12 .... **11** E6
Wardley C of E School
SWIN M27 .... **85** E3
Wardley Industrial Estate
WALK M28 .... **85** D4
Warren Wood Primary School
OFTN SK2 .... **185** E1
Warth Park Industrial Estate
BURY BL9 .... **52** B2
Washway Road Medical Centre
SALE M33 .... **159** E1
The Watergate Clinic
MILN OL16 .... **23** D6
Waterloo Industrial Park
STKP SK1 .... **167** D4
Waterloo Primary School
AULW OL7 .... **112** A2
Waters Edge Business Park
OLDTF/WHR M16 .... **123** D3
Waters Edge Business Park
SALQ/ORD M5 .... **122** C3
Waterside Hotel & Galleon
Leisure Centre
DID/WITH M20 .... **164** A5
Watersports Centre
SALQ/ORD M5 .... **122** A2
Waybridge Industrial Estate
SALQ/ORD M5 .... **121** E1
Weaste Trading Estate
SALQ/ORD M5 .... **103** E5
Webster Junior School
RUSH/FAL M14 .... **124** B5
Welfare Clinic
MDTN M24 .... **74** B1
Wellacre County Junior
& Primary School
URM M41 .... **136** B1
Wellacre High Boys School
URM M41 .... **136** B1
Wellfield Junior School
SALE M33 .... **139** D5
Wellfield Medical Centre
CHH M8 .... **90** A5
Wellfield Surgery
ROCH OL11 .... **40** B2
Well Green Primary School
HALE/TIMP WA15 .... **175** F5
Wellington Road Industrial Estate
AUL OL6 .... **112** B4
Wensley Gallery
RAMS BL0 .... **7** D5
Wentworth High School
ECC M30 .... **102** A3
Werneth Cricket Bowling
& Tennis Club
OLDS OL8 .... **95** E1
Werneth Infant School
OLDS OL8 .... **95** E1
Werneth Jamia Mosque
OLDS OL8 .... **78** A6
Werneth Private
Preparatory School
OLDS OL8 .... **78** B6
Werneth School
MPL/ROM SK6 .... **169** D3
Wesley Methodist
Primary School
RAD M26 .... **51** D4
Westbrook Trading Estate
TRPK M17 .... **121** E2
West Croft Industrial Estate
MDTN M24 .... **74** A4
West End Medical Centre
AULW OL7 .... **112** A6

West End Primary School
AULW OL7 112   A5
West End Trading Estate
SWIN M27 86   A4
Westernlea Clinic
DTN/ASHW M34 129   F4
West Gorton Medical Centre
WGTN/LGST M12 126   A3
West Hill School
STLY SK15 114   A5
West Liverpool Street School
SLFD M6 104   A5
Westpoint Medical Centre
BNG/LEV M19 145   D2
Westwood Business Centre
CHAD OL9 78   B5
Westwood Industrial Estate
CHAD OL9 78   A4
Westwood Park Primary School
ECC M30 100   C4
Westwood Primary School
CHAD OL9 78   B4
Whalley Range Football Club
CCHDY M21 142   B2
Whalley Range High School
for Girls
OLDTF/WHR M16 143   D3
Wharfside Business Centre
TRPK M17 122   A3
Wheatfield Industrial Estate
ROY/SHW OL2 60   B6
White City Retail Park
OLDTF/WHR M16 122   B4
Whitefield County Primary School
WHTF M45 71   E3
Whitefield Medical Centre
WHTF M45 70   C3
Whitegate End Primary School
CHAD OL9 93   F2
Whitehill Primary School
HTNM SK4 166   C1
White Swan Industrial Estate
OLD OL1 80   A3
Whitley Road Medical Centre
NEWH/MOS M40 107   D3
Whittaker Moss Primary School
ROCH OL11 20   C4
Whitworth Art Gallery
HULME M15 124   C5
Whitworth Football & Cricket Club
WHIT OL12 9   D2
Whitworth High School
WHIT OL12 9   D2
Whitworth Park School
RUSH/FAL M14 124   B5
Whitworth Swimming Pool
WHIT OL12 9   E1
Whitworth Town Council Offices
WHIT OL12 9   E2
Wigan & Bolton Health Authority
BOL BL1 28   A5

Wilbraham Infant School
RUSH/FAL M14 143   E2
Wild Bank Primary School
STLY SK15 115   E5
Willan Industrial Estate
SALQ/ORD M5 104   A6
William Andrews Swimming Baths
DUK SK16 131   E2
William Hulmes Grammar School
OLDTF/WHR M16 143   D2
The Willows Primary School
HALE/TIMP WA15 175   D1
Wilmslow Albion Football Club
WILM/AE SK9 193   E6
Wilmslow Grange County Primary
School
WILM/AE SK9 194   A5
Wilmslow Health Centre
WILM/AE SK9 203   E5
Wilmslow High School
WILM/AE SK9 203   F5
Wilmslow Leisure Centre
WILM/AE SK9 203   F5
Wilmslow Preparatory School
WILM/AE SK9 203   F4
Wilmslow Road Medical Centre
RUSH/FAL M14 125   D6
Wilmslow Road Medical Centre
WILM/AE SK9 194   B5
Wilmslow Rugby Club
WILM/AE SK9 203   D2
Wilton Villa Surgery
DTN/ASHW M34 129   F5
Windmill Medical Practice
DTN/ASHW M34 128   A6
Windsor High School
SLFD M6 104   B5
Withington Bowling Club
RUSH/FAL M14 144   A4
Withington Girls School
RUSH/FAL M14 143   F3
Withington Hospital
DID/WITH M20 143   D5
Withington Swimming Baths
DID/WITH M20 143   F5
Withins Comprehensive School
BOLE BL2 29   F5
Woodbank County Primary School
TOT/BURYW BL8 33   E3
Woodbank Cricket Club
TOT/BURYW BL8 33   E3
Woodbank Surgery
TOT/BURYW BL8 33   E2
Woodfields Retail Park
BURY BL9 33   F4
Woodford Aerodrome
MCFLDN SK10 207   F1
Woodford Cricket Club
BRAM/HZG SK7 196   C6
Woodford Preparatory School
BRAM/HZG SK7 206   B1

Woodhey High School
RAMS BL0 18   B2
Woodheys Primary School
SALE M33 158   C3
Woodhouse Park Primary School
WYTH/NTH M22 192   B1
Woodhouse Primary School
URM M41 118   B5
Woodhouses School
FAIL M35 111   D1
Woodlands Hospital
WALK M28 82   B1
Woodley Health Centre
MPL/ROM SK6 149   E6
Woodley Infants & Junior School
MPL/ROM SK6 149   F6
Woodley Sports Centre
MPL/ROM SK6 149   E5
Woodsend Primary School
URM M41 117   D6
Woodside Junior School
BOL BL1 44   C2
Woodside School
WYTH/NTH M22 179   D3
Woolfold Industrial Estate
TOT/BURYW BL8 32   C3
Woolworths Sports Club
ROCH OL11 39   D4
Wordsworth Industrial Estate
BOL BL1 27   E5
Worsley Business Park
TYLD M29 82   A5
Worsley Road Industrial Estate
FWTH BL4 66   A5
Worsley Trading Estate
LHULT M38 64   C6
Worsley Wharton School
LHULT M38 64   C5
Worth County Primary School
POY/DIS SK12 199   D6
Wright Robinson High School
GTN M18 128   A3
Wythenshawe Hall
NTHM/RTH M23 161   F5
Xaverian College
RUSH/FAL M14 125   D6
Yeargate Industrial Estate
BURY BL9 35   E5
Yew Tree Junior & Infant School
CHAD OL9 94   A1
Yew Tree Primary School
DUK SK16 131   F3
YHA
CSLFD M3 123   E1
Y Sport & Leisure Centre
CSLFD M3 2   A5
Zakaria Mosque
OLDTF/WHR M16 142   B1

Page 2

C3
1 Back College Land
2 Butter La
3 Dunlop St
4 Garden La
5 Ridgefield
6 St Mary's St
7 Smithy La
8 Southgate

D4
1 Clarence St
2 County St
3 Four Yards
4 Mosley St
5 St James's Sq
6 Tasle Alley
7 Town Hall La

Page 3

E4
1 Back George St
2 Charlotte St
3 St James St

F2
1 Back Thomas St
2 Back Turner St
3 Brick St
4 Catlow La
5 Hare St
6 Red Lion St
7 Union St

F6
1 Bombay St
2 Donald St
3 Galbraith St
4 Holbrook St
5 Makin St
6 Pritchard St
7 Samuel Ogden St
8 Venice St

G2
1 Back Spear St
2 Bradley St
3 Dorsey St
4 Faraday St
5 Houldsworth St
6 Little Ancoats St
7 Oak St
8 Whittle St

G3
1 Back Piccadilly
2 Bradleys Court
3 Bunsen St
4 Cavell St
5 Faraday St
6 Little Lever St
7 Postal St
8 Stevenson Pl
9 Stevenson Sq

G5
1 Auburn St
2 Aytoun St
3 Back Acton St
4 Bladon St
5 Lower Brook St
6 Minshull St South
7 South Pump St

Page 7

D6
1 Smithills Hall Cl

E6
1 Beechacre

Page 14

A5
1 Back Cox Green Rd North
2 Back Darwen Rd North
3 Back King St North
4 Back Mill St North
5 Back Mill St South
6 King St
7 Mill St

Page 18

A3
1 Chisholme Cl
2 Coleridge Rd
3 Conway Crs
4 Dunedin Rd
5 Glenmore Rd
6 Greenmount Cl
7 Holcombe Ct
8 Jackdaw Rd
9 Redwing Rd
10 St Austell Dr
11 White Birk Cl

B1
1 Adelaide St
2 Annie St
3 Balm St
4 Bloom St
5 Butler St
6 Canron St
7 Cato St
8 The Coppice
9 Dalton Cl
10 Dora St
11 Elsie St
12 Flax St
13 Crime St
14 Hall St
15 Hill Rl
16 Isa St
17 Mill St
18 Ringwood Av
19 Stone St
20 Wildwood Cl
21 Zama St

Page 21

D5
1 Bagslate Moor La
2 Chepstow Cl
3 Moorland Av

Page 22

A5
1 Roefield Ter
2 Savoy St

B4
1 Beaufort St
2 Belvoir St
3 Madeley Gdns

C3
1 Bassett Wy
2 Blackthorn Cl
3 Bradley Smithy Cl
4 Campbell St
5 Dew Meadow Cl
6 Heights Cl
7 Sweet Briar Cl
8 Sweet Briar La
9 Woodfield Av

C4
1 Augusta St
2 Headlands St
3 Henley St
4 Moorfield Pl
5 Moorland St
6 Swain St
7 Turner St

C5
1 Ashworth St
2 Beswicke St
3 Brook's Pl
4 Clement Royds St
5 Cromer St
6 Daisy St
7 Failinge Mas
8 Greenhill Av
9 Green La
10 Hallwell St
11 Jane St
12 Knowsley St
13 Leamington St
14 Littledale St
15 Mount St
16 Redcar St
17 Stanley Pl
18 Tiflis St
19 Wilton Ter

C6
1 Fenwick St

Page 23

D5
1 Bell St
2 Blossom Pl
3 Cheetham St
4 East Gate St
5 Goose La
6 Greenlees St
7 Howard Pl
8 Hunter's La
9 New Buildings Pl
10 Oldmill St
11 Park La
12 Petrie St
13 Queen St
14 Reed Hl
15 School St
16 Shepherd St
17 Toad La
18 Waterhouse St
19 Whitehall St
20 Wilson St

D6
1 Baillie St
2 The Butts Av
3 Chancel Pl
4 Church La
5 Constantine Rd
6 Faulkner St
7 Fleece St
8 Great George St
9 Greenwood St
10 Ink St
11 Junction Alley
12 Kenion St
13 Lyceum Pas
14 Mason St
15 Moore St
16 Nelson St
17 Oak St
18 Packer St
19 River St
20 St Chad's Cl
21 Slack St
22 Stationers Entry
23 Summer Castle
24 Water St

E6
1 Guildford St
2 Hill St
3 Pickup St
4 Summer St

F5
1 Aboukir St
2 Cooper Ter
3 Heybrook St
4 Lower Wheat End
5 Waterside La
6 Weedon St

Page 24

A2
1 Holmes St
2 Howarth Farm Wy
3 Louise Cl
4 Maitland Cl
5 Martha's Ter
6 Mitchell St
7 Old Brow La
8 Vicarage Dr

Page 27

D4
1 Back Ainsworth St
2 Back Mcdonna St
3 Back Raimond St
4 Back Rock Av
5 Back Somerville St
6 Back Wilmot St
7 Booth St
8 Ellen St
9 Elliot St
10 Hillbank Cl
11 Mcdonna St
12 Somerville Sq
13 Somerville St
14 Whowell Fold

D5
1 Ainsworth St
2 Back Adrian Rd East
3 Back Bennett's La
4 Back Bennett's La East
5 Back Canada St
6 Back Canada St South
7 Back Church Rd
8 Back Church Rd North
9 Back Cloister St
10 Back Canada St
11 Back Huxley St
12 Back Ivy Rd
13 Back Ivy Rd West
14 Back Keighley St
15 Back Packer St
16 Back Sunnyside St
17 Barnet Rd
18 Bede St
19 Dudwell Cl
20 Frankford Sq
21 Garside Cv
22 Holy Harbour St
23 Kingscourt Av
24 Knowles Edge St
25 Lawson Rd
26 Longford Av
27 Oscar St
28 Packer St
29 Sunnyside Rd
30 Thurstane St

D6
1 Arkwright Cl
2 Back Avondale St
3 Back Cundey St
4 Back Ivy Rd
5 Back Northern Cv
6 Back Osborne Gv
7 Back Oxford Cv North
8 Back Pedder St
9 Back Rawson Rd
10 Back Rawson Rd North
11 Back Rutland Cv
12 Back Victoria Cv
13 Back Victoria Cv North
14 Back Windsor Cv
15 Cundey St
16 Kingswear Dr
17 Lovalle St
18 Northern Cv
19 Rutland Cv
20 Windsor Cv

E5
1 Back Ainsworth St
2 Back Apple Ter
3 Back Boundary St
4 Back Chaucer St
5 Back Cotton St
6 Back Darwin St
7 Back Elgin St
8 Back Eskrick St
9 Back Eskrick St East
10 Back Frances St
11 Back Frank St
12 Back Glen Bott St
13 Back Grove St
14 Back Hallwell Rd
15 Back Hallwell Rd South
16 Back Haydn St
17 Back Kingsley St
18 Back Lytton St
19 Back Nut St
20 Back Olga St North
21 Back St Augustine St
22 Back St Thomas St
23 Back Uttley St
24 Back Vickerman St
25 Back Wapping St
26 Back Wordsworth St
27 Blake Gdns
28 Blake St
29 Boundary St
30 Broughton St
31 Carl St
32 Chaucer St
33 Dobson St
34 Duxbury St
35 Frances St
36 Frank St
37 Glen Bott St
38 Hallwell St
39 Harold St
40 Horace St
41 Libra St
42 Lytton St
43 Miles St
44 Norway St
45 Peak St
46 St Joseph St
47 St Thomas St
48 Uttley St
49 Vickerman St
50 Wapping St
51 Wordsworth St

F3
1 Back Baxendale St
2 Back Birley St
3 Back Blackburn Rd West
4 Back Drummond St
5 Back Holland St
6 Back Holly St
7 Back Maxwell St
8 Back Miller St
9 Baxendale St
10 Drummond St
11 East Rd
12 Hillview Rd
13 Lawson St
14 Manley Ter
15 Maxwell St
16 Miller St
17 Park Av
18 Pemberton St
19 Ramsay St
20 Rhosleigh Av

F4
1 Ashbee St
2 Back Ashbee St
3 Back Blackburn Rd West
4 Back Crumpsall St North
5 Back Eckersley St
6 Back Eden St
7 Back Irlam St
8 Back Irlam St North
9 Back Palm St
10 Back Waverley Rd
11 Bloomfield St
12 Derbyshire Rw
13 Duty St
14 Eden Av
15 Eden Cv
16 Greenwood V
17 Grierson St
18 Irlam St
19 Mold St

F5
1 Back Astley St
2 Back Ewart St
3 Back Hargreaves St
4 Back Newton St
5 Back Stewart St
6 Back Wolfenden St
7 Back Wynne St
8 Belgrave St
9 Boardman St
10 Bridle St
11 Brooklyn St
12 Byland Cl
13 Canning St
14 Canning St
15 Cardwell Gdns
16 Charlotte St
17 Chesham Av
18 Cowanlock's St
19 Hargreaves St
20 Hazelhurst Cl
21 Irving St
22 Lomax St
23 Maplewood Gdns
24 Newton St
25 Newton Wk
26 Paulette St
27 Pinewood Cl
28 Rawsthorne St
29 Rix St
30 Wheeldale Cl

F6
1 Back Grantham Cl
2 Back Nevada St
3 Back St Ann St
4 Back Thomasson Cl
5 Back Worcester St
6 Barnwood Dr
7 Cromford Cl
8 Glenthorne St
9 Nebraska St
10 Nottingham Dr
11 Rainham Dr
12 Rushlake Dr
13 Stowell Ct
14 Stowell St
15 Topping St
16 Woking Back Gdns

Page 28

A1
1 The Gardens
2 Holden Av
3 Kellett St
4 Lakenheath Cl
5 Northland Rd
6 Ollerton St
7 Playfair St
8 Sand Banks
9 Sharples Hall Ms

A2
1 Back Florence Av
2 Back Poplar Av
3 Back Primula St
4 Cowley Rd
5 Daffodil St
6 Ornatus St
7 Poplar Av
8 Primrose St
9 Primula St

A4
1 Almond Cv
2 Anson St
3 Back Baytorpe St North
4 Back Blackburn St
5 Back Coniston St
6 Back Fairhaven Rd
7 Back Gaythorne St
8 Back Gresham St
9 Back Seymour St
10 Back Sherwood St
11 Back Wilton St
12 Beryl St
13 Canisbrooke Dr
14 Coniston
15 Dormer St
16 Eagley Brook Wy
17 Emerald St
18 Gaythorne St
19 Greenwood's Hollow
20 Heywood's Hollow
21 Norton St
22 Orchard Av
23 Palm St
24 Sherwood St
25 Ventnor Av
26 Wilton St

A6
1 Adisham Dr
2 Back Blackbank St
3 Back Blackburn Rd
4 Back Hawley St
5 Back Progress St
6 Kingsdown Dr
7 Mulliver St
8 Newington Dr
9 Peterborough St
10 Progress St
11 Prospect St
12 Riley Ct

B1
1 Ashfield Cv
2 Crundale Rd
3 Littlebourne Wk

B2
1 Denham Cl
2 Eleanor St
3 Fitzhugh St
4 Hatton Cv

C6
1 Back Beaconsfield Ter
2 Back George Barton St
3 Back Horsa St North
4 Back Olaf St
5 Back Scowcroft St
6 Back Stone St
7 Back Thicketford Rd West
8 Back Tonge Moor Rd East
9 Eccleston Av
10 George Barton St
11 Harner St
12 Harwood Cl
13 Lansdowne Rd
14 Le Cendre St
15 Lowerwood La
16 Sheriff St
17 Stott La
18 Thicketford Rd
19 Welling St
20 Wemsley Cv

Page 29

D1
1 Back Rigby La North
2 Back Rigby La South
3 Hardcastle Ct
4 Seymour St
5 Tree Tops
6 Winterburn Av

D4
1 Hartwell Cl
2 Woburn Av
3 Woodhall Cl

D6
1 Alexander Rd
2 Back Abingdon Rd
3 Back Alexander Rd
4 Back Banbury St
5 Back Bristol Av
6 Back Cromer Av
7 Back Thicketford Rd
8 Banbury St
9 Canute St
10 Castlewood Sq
11 Gibson St
12 Huntroyde Av
13 Jack St
14 Kingston Av
15 Kirkham St
16 Montrose Av
17 Parkside St
18 Thicketford Rd

F4
1 Brook House Cl
2 Carlton Cl
3 Fair Acres
4 Greenheys
5 Hazelwood Av
6 High Mt
7 Hillsdale Gv
8 Springwater Cl

Page 32

C4
1 Greenway Cl
2 Hamilton Cl
3 Northleach Cl
4 Oakwood Cl
5 Sandhurst Cl
6 Woodlands Cv

C6
1 Beckenham Cl
2 Chirnside St
3 Chislehurst Cl
4 Luton St
5 Reigate Cl
6 Warlingham Cl
7 Warren St
8 Wolseley St

Page 33

D5
1 Arthur St
2 Back Ainsworth Rd North
3 Back Belbeck St
4 Back Horbury St
5 Back Knight St
6 Back Stephen St
7 Belbeck St South
8 Knight St

D6
1 Back Bolton Rd North
2 Back Hulbert St
3 Back Proctor St
4 Fountain St
5 Hulbert St
6 Stephen St South

F1
1 Arbour Cl
2 Burnswood Dr

F5
1 Back Bolton St South
2 Back Broad St
3 Back Knowsley St
4 Back Manchester Rd
5 Back Market St
6 Back Market St West
7 Back Phoenix St
8 Back Silver St
9 Back St Mary's Pl
10 Bank St
11 Castle St
12 Cooper St
13 Crompton St
14 Edwin St
15 Lower Bank St
16 Manchester Rd
17 Market Pl
18 North Back Rock
19 Parks Yd
20 The Rock
21 St Mary's Pl
22 Silver St
23 South Back Rock
24 The Wylde

F6
1 Back Manchester Old Rd
2 Back Wells St
3 Barker St
4 Belle Vue Ter
5 Glenmore St
6 Manchester Old Rd
7 Westgate Av
8 Westminster St

Page 34

A1
1 Back Walmersley Rd East
2 Halvard Av
3 Halvard Ct
4 Lime St
5 Newton St
6 Purdon St
7 Soiness St
8 Wolstenholme Av

A2
1 Back Argyle St
2 Back Linton Av
3 Back Malvern Av
4 Back Milner Av
5 Back Monmouth Av
6 Back Mostyn Av
7 Back Raymond Av
8 Back Royal Av
9 Back Walmersley Rd East
10 Back Walmersley Rd West
11 Littlewood Av
12 Monmouth Av
13 Sunny Av

A4
1 Back Birch St
2 Back Cateaton St
3 Back Hornby St West
4 Back Moorgate
5 Back Parsons La
6 Back Richard Burch St
7 Badger St
8 Brunswick St
9 Charles St
10 Fernhill St
11 Fox St
12 John St
13 Marsden St
14 Richard Burch St
15 Stanley Ct
16 Washington Ct

A5
1 Back Derby St
2 Back Foundry St
3 Bediam Gn
4 Clerke St
5 Earl St
6 Eden St
7 The Haymarket
8 Hilton Rd
9 School Brow
10 South Back Rock
11 Tithebarn St

C6
1 Back Cedar St North
2 Back Huntley Mount Rd
3 Back Percy St
4 Back Rochdale Old Rd South
5 Back Shaw-Street
6 Brighton St
7 Crabtree St
8 Higher Av
9 Huntley Mount Rd
10 Huntley St
11 Pearson St

C5
1 Back Deal St
2 Back Elm St
3 Back Fir St
4 Back Laurel St
5 Back Myrtle St
6 Back Myrtle St South
7 Back Pine St
8 Back Teak St
9 Eastwood Cl
10 Elm St
11 Greywood Av
12 Larch St
13 Maple Av
14 Myrtle Gdns
15 Myrtle St North

Page 37

D6
1 Betley St
2 Cleves Ct
3 Clifton Cl
4 Coverdale Cl
5 Cranmer Ct
6 Denton St
7 Smyrna St
8 Walker St

E4
1 Brown St
2 Millers Brook Cl
3 Prospect Pl
4 Rutland St
5 Shadwell St West

F3
1. Cedar Gv
2. Cheetham Hl
3. Dawn St
4. Diggle St
5. Durden Ms
6. Fardale
7. Hawthorn Crs
8. Henthorn St
9. High St
10. Margaret St
11. Milne St
12. Newtown St
13. Osborne St
14. Richmond Cl
15. Swan Ct
16. Westway

Page 62

A1
1. Bridge St
2. Copley St
3. Dunwood Av
4. Park Side Av
5. Store St
6. Wren's Nest Av

A2
1. Belgravia Ms
2. Buckley St
3. Chancery La
4. Cyril St
5. Edmund St
6. Gillemere Gv
7. Greaves St
8. Moorlands St

Page 64

A1
1. Back Fair St
2. Back Morris Green La
3. Back Morris Green La East
4. Back Partington St
5. Back Sapling Rd South
6. Back Uganda St
7. Bulteel St
8. Cranford St
9. Curtis St
10. Fair St
11. Lambton St
12. Morris Gn
13. Partington St
14. Uganda St

Page 65

E6
1. Alderminster Av
2. Ayrton Gv
3. Brynheys Cl
4. Clegg's La
5. Duke St
6. Lackwell Gv
7. Owenington Gv
8. Shelley Rd

Page 66

A1
1. Back Manchester Rd
2. Back Marion St South
3. Back Rowena St
4. Brentwood Dr
5. Campbell St
6. Dover St
7. Ivanhoe St
8. Marion St
9. Shaw St
10. Victoria Ct

A2
1. Bentinck St
2. Gladstone Pl
3. Thorne St
4. Trentham Cl
5. Trentham St
6. Whoolden St

A4
1. Brookside Av
2. Edale Rd
3. Langdale St
4. Lower St
5. Manor St
6. Parks Nook
7. Prospect Pl
8. Rutland Gv

B2
1. Bentley St
2. Bridgeman St
3. Carlton Pl
4. Entwisle St
5. Joseph St
6. Limefield Av
7. Osbourne St
8. Park Vw
9. Winslade Ms

B3
1. Albert Gv
2. Albert Rd
3. Arthur St
4. Barnes Ct
5. Byng St
6. Dial Ct
7. Dobhill St
8. Doodson Sq
9. Duckshaw La
10. Entwisle Rw
11. Finlay St
12. Fletcher St
13. Greenwood St
14. Leigh St
15. Princess Gv
16. Regent Wk
17. Slater St
18. Ternhill Ct
19. Walkers St
20. Westwood Cl

B6
1. Enfield St
2. Whittle Dr

C5
1. Bridgewater St
2. Chapel St
3. Couill Sq
4. Danebridge Cl
5. Garden St
6. John St
7. Russell St
8. Wilson St
9. York St

Page 67

D5
1. Clammerclough Av
2. Dorning St

Page 71

F1
1. Dempsey Dr
2. Pilkington St
3. Victoria Ms

Page 73

E6
1. Beadham Dr
2. Brynford Av
3. Darliston Av
4. Heaton Park Rd West
5. Southwood Dr

Page 74

A4
1. Booth Bridge Cl
2. Chapel St
3. Egerton St
4. Great Heaton St
5. High Hurst Cl
6. Pool Bank St
7. Wellens Wy

Page 75

D5
1. Barton Rd
2. Beech St
3. Burton St
4. Henry St
5. Michael St
6. Suffield St
7. Trinity St

E2
1. Bardsley St
2. Cemetery St
3. King St

E5
1. Ledbury Cl

Page 76

C5
1. Abbotsford Rd
2. Amberwood
3. Lindenwood
4. Owens Cl
5. Rainwood
6. Sheridan Wy
7. Thurland St

Page 78

A5
1. Berne St
2. Castleton St
3. Charles St
4. Commercial St
5. St John's Wk

B1
1. Palace Gdns
2. Regent Crs

B4
1. Bay St
2. Harold St
3. Hurst St
4. Mark St
5. Neath St
6. Thompson St
7. Timperley St
8. Westwood St
9. Winterbottom St

B6
1. Bright St
2. Burnaby St
3. Hornby St
4. St Thomas's Cir
5. St Thomas St North
6. St Thomas St South

C1
1. Dan Fold
2. Fountain St
3. King St
4. Kirkham St
5. Ramsden Cl
6. Ramsden Crs
7. West St

C5
1. Back King St
2. Cannon St
3. Cavendish St
4. Connaught St
5. Crossbank St
6. Garlick St
7. George St
8. Slater St

C6
1. Jackson Cl
2. Kennedy St
3. Poorfield St
4. Romford St
5. Trafford St
6. Wainwright St

Page 79

D6
1. Back Scott St
2. Havelock St
3. Hinton St
4. Scottfield
5. Thornton St

E4
1. Bailey St
2. Hardcastle St
3. Medlock St
4. Partington St
5. Prince St
6. Scholes St
7. Shore St
8. Wright St

E5
1. East Hill St
2. Greenhill Pas
3. Hooper St
4. Jarvis St
5. Picton Sq
6. Ridley St
7. Thorney Hill Cl

F6
1. Calderbrook Wy
2. Clifton Av
3. Cranberry St
4. Delamere St
5. Kingsbridge Rd
6. Retford St

Page 80

A2
1. Brooklyn St
2. Ena St
3. Filbert St
4. French Av
5. Ivanhoe St
6. Keston Rd
7. Otago St
8. Ripponden St
9. Whetstone Hill La
10. Whitecroft

A5
1. Chancery St
2. Chesham Rd
3. Easterdale
4. Frome St
5. Gibson St
6. Goss Hall St
7. Kentucky St
8. Somerset St
9. Staley St
10. Valentine St
11. Westerdale
12. Whitehouse St

B6
1. Ceylon St
2. Cyprus Cl
3. Vigo St

C4
1. Further Hey Cl
2. Milford Brow
3. Rowland Wy

C5
1. Ancoats St
2. Booth St
3. Chapel St
4. Cross St
5. Pearson Av
6. Shepley St
7. Stamford St

C6
1. Albert St
2. Bardsley St
3. Belmont St
4. Buckley St
5. Dawson St
6. Heywood Av
7. Nelson St
8. Spa La
9. Stanley St
10. Westway

Page 81

D6
1. John Booth St
2. Woodend St

E5
1. Clegg St
2. Glade Brow
3. Helsby St
4. Leadale Rl
5. Oldcroft
6. Radcliffe St
7. Stanley St

Page 82

A2
1. Ashawe Gv
2. Buttercup Av
3. Clock Tower Cl
4. Freesia Av
5. Harebell Av
6. Helias Cl
7. Ice House Cl
8. Mortlake Cl
9. Shillingten Cl
10. White Lady Cl
11. Wichbrook Rd
12. The Wicheries
13. Wood Cottage Cl

B2
1. Engine Fold Rd
2. Fleetwood Cl
3. Gibson Av
4. Yates Dr

C6
1. Blackcap Cl
2. Cannel Fold
3. Chapel Meadow
4. Crombooke Fold
5. Goldcrest Cl
6. Herevale Gra
7. Ingles Fold
8. Penrice Fold
9. Redpoll Cl

Page 83

D1
1. Gratten Ct
2. Mountain Ash
3. Phipps St
4. Plantation Av
5. Regent Av
6. St John St
7. Vicarage Rd

D3
1. Barrowshaw Cl
2. Bickershaw Dr
3. Kiveton Cl
4. Worsbrough Av

D6
1. The Chanters
2. Habergham Cl

E2
1. Alfred St
2. Egerton Rd
3. Harriet St
4. Malvern Gv
5. Mayfield Av
6. Old Vicarage Gdns
7. Shiel St
8. Smith St
9. Worsley Ct

Page 84

A3
1. Arthur St
2. Crosby Av
3. Grundy St
4. How Clough Av
5. Kendal Gv
6. Marsh St
7. Oakwood Av
8. Spring Clough Dr

Page 86

A3
1. Brindley St
2. Centaur Ct
3. Dryad Cl
4. Dumbell St
5. Gaskell St
6. Grosvenor St
7. Hall St
8. Holt St
9. Kent St
10. Mimosa Dr
11. Newtown Cl
12. Pott St
13. Rosehill Rd
14. Vicker St

C3
1. Dewes Av
2. Falcon Crs
3. Glendale
4. Heywood Av
5. Yewdale

C4
1. Greenwood Av

Page 89

D1
1. Albert St
2. Brandram Rd
3. Countess Pl
4. Egerton St
5. Grey St
6. Infant St
7. Naseby Pl
8. Park St
9. Princess Rd
10. Randlesham St
11. Recreation St
12. Robert St
13. Stores St
14. Upper Wilton St
15. Wilton St
16. Wiseman St

F6
1. Bispham Gv
2. Bower St
3. Carnarvon St
4. Cleveleys Gv
5. Kimberley St
6. Marie St
7. Norman Rd
8. Turner St

Page 90

A6
1. Back Halliwell La
2. Barry Lawson Cl
3. Broomfield Dr
4. Carstairs Cl
5. Crookhill Dr
6. Dorothy St
7. Guy St
8. Halliwell St West
9. Highshore Dr
10. Hovey Cl
11. Inghamwood Cl
12. Lanbury Dr
13. Lanfield Dr
14. Masboro St
15. Morrowfield Av
16. Moston St
17. Narbuth Dr
18. Overstone Dr
19. Southam St
20. Zebra St

B2
1. Glanford Av

B5
1. Balfour St
2. Crescent Av
3. Cromhurst St
4. Greenhill Rd
5. Hillcroft Cl
6. Limestead Av
7. Maureen Av
8. Parslow Av
9. Rebecca St
10. Wellfield Rd
11. Woodhalt Rd

C6
1. Blanwood Dr
2. Frome Dr
3. Harland Dr
4. Humber St
5. Lichfield Dr
6. Tahir Cl
7. Thetford Dr
8. Thurlston Crs
9. Wigmore Rd

Page 91

D4
1. Limbert Cir

E5
1. Baywood St
2. Bernard St
3. Brewster St
4. Coniston Av
5. Highfield Ter
6. Ringley St
7. Smallfield Dr
8. Walter St
9. Westbourne Gv

F3
1. Augustine Webster Cl
2. Caversham Dr
3. Cicero St
4. Elsie St
5. Jonas St
6. Lubeck St
7. Monkwood Dr
8. Radford Dr
9. Rockfield Dr
10. Sequoia St
11. Simister St
12. Stanley St
13. Stanway St
14. Swainsthorpe Dr
15. Thomsett St
16. Wembury St
17. Wembury St North
18. Winford St

F6
1. Beechwood Gv
2. Conran St
3. Durham St
4. Glenwood Dr
5. Mossdough Ct
6. Nethervale Dr
7. Norbet Wk
8. Ockendon Dr
9. Orpington Rd
10. Osborne Rd
11. Winterdyne St

Page 92

A1
1. Clement Scott Cl
2. Daneswood Av
3. Fulwood Av
4. Ingleby Av
5. Kingston Gv
6. Newburn Av
7. Stanage Av
8. White Moss Rd

A6
1. Carnaby St
2. Grimscott Cl
3. Kennard Cl
4. Lordship Cl
5. Melton St
6. Merville Av
7. Nettleton Gv
8. Rossendale Av
9. Swinburn St
10. Winston Rd
11. Woodleigh St
12. Woodville Ter

Page 93

E4
1. Greenhloth Cl
2. Greenways
3. Skipton Av
4. Winton Av

Page 94

A6
1. Casson St
2. Clayton St
3. Francis St
4. Henry St
5. Laycock Gv
6. Richard St
7. Silverbirch Wy
8. Sisson St
9. Wye Av

C3
1. Alford St
2. Barmouth Wk
3. Brecon Wk
4. Chelbourne Dr
5. Irving St
6. Moorfield Av
7. Parkfield Av
8. Whitland Dr
9. Wrexham Cl

C6
1. Argyll Cl
2. Elsinore Cl
3. Gore Av
4. Holborn Av
5. Lime Tree Gv

Page 95

D1
1. Agnes Cl
2. Durham St
3. Fernholme Ct
4. Norfolk St
5. Royd St
6. Spring Bank St
7. Warwick St

D6
1. Arkendale Cl
2. Margrove Cl

Page 96

A1
1. Belgrave Rd
2. Blunn St
3. Columbia St
4. Dartmouth Cl
5. Estate St South
6. Isaiah St
7. Macdonald St
8. Noble St
9. Panmure St
10. Snowden St
11. Wallace St

A6
1. Denbigh St
2. Emma St
3. Holden St
4. Kenyon Av
5. Marion St
6. Tydden St
7. Tyro St

Page 99

D3
1. Carrhill Quarry Cl
2. Cross St
3. Lees St
4. Spring St
5. Stamford Rd
6. Vernon St
7. Webster St
8. Woodmeadow Ct

A6
1. Benton St
2. Brantwood Ter
3. Elmwood Gv
4. Larchwood Av
5. Lila St
6. Margaret Ashton Cl
7. Norman Rd West
8. Railton Ter
9. Roda St
10. Springville Av
11. Stonehead St
12. Summerville Av
13. Vale Top Av

B6
1. Brocklehurst St
2. Douglas St
3. Joan St
4. Moorsholme Av
5. Shelderton Cl
6. Spreadbury St
7. Webdale Dr
8. Wellwood Dr
9. Willowbrook Av

Page 100

C5
1. Annisdale Cl
2. Brodie Cl
3. Bromsgrove Av
4. Cleavley St
5. Corran Cl
6. Egerton St
7. Kearsley St
8. Langholme Pl
9. Lavinia St
10. Medford Av
11. Nameplate Cl
12. Pollitts Cl
13. Portree Cl
14. Selsby Av
15. Signal Cl
16. Slater St
17. Wain Cl

Page 101

D1
1. Colwyn Rd
2. Lambton St
3. Larch Av
4. Lime Av
5. Merlewood Dr
6. Moorfield Rd
7. Woodlands Av

D5
1. Cook St
2. Cromwell Rd
3. King Edward St
4. Princess St
5. Queen Victoria St
6. Wesley St
7. Wycliffe St

E1
1. Brooklands Rd
2. Dales Park Dr
3. Ewhurst Av
4. Fulmere Ct
5. Galloway Wy
6. Greenbank Av
7. Lyndale Av
8. Midgley St
9. Thornlea Av
10. Wentworth Rd

F1
1. Acacia Av
2. Anson Av
3. Chilham St
4. Dales Brow
5. Dale St
6. Laburnam Av
7. Marlow Dr
8. Meredew Av
9. Morley Av

F4
1. Cavendish Gv
2. Claybar Dr
3. Gienart
4. Hopwood Av
5. Ravensdale Gdns
6. Richmond Gv

F5
1. Abbey Gv
2. Devonshire Rd
3. Ellesmere Av
4. Francis Av
5. Mather Av
6. Richardson Rd
7. St James St
8. Willan Rd

Page 102

A1
1. Brondgate Meadow
2. Buttermere Av
3. Ennerdale Av
4. Hawes Av
5. Lichfield Dr

A6
1. Bentcliffe Wy
2. Irwell Pl
3. King St
4. Queen St

B5
1. College Rd
2. Millers Ct
3. Trevelyan St

C5
1. Canterbury Gdns

Page 103

D2
1. Ashbourne Rd
2. Helena St
3. Kendal Rd
4. New Herbert St
5. Pomfret St
6. Radcliffe Park Crs
7. Rattenbury Ct
8. Rudyard St

E6
1. Belmont St
2. Foster St
3. Kerrera Dr
4. Oronsay Gv
5. Thornfield St
6. Weaste La

F5
1 Alexander St
2 Baltic St
3 Cressington Cl
4 Derby Av
5 Emaline Gra
6 Fram St
7 Glendinning St
8 Greenland St
9 Hersey St
10 Horsham St
11 Littlewood St
12 Lyndhurst St
13 Mere Av
14 Middlebourne St
15 Nona St
16 Northbourne St
17 Sandown St
18 Seedley View Rd
19 Southbourne St
20 Springwell Cl
21 Woodgrange Cl
22 Wythburn St

F6
1 Cardigan St
2 Cumbrae Gdns
3 Dolbey St
4 Haven St
5 Heyworth St
6 Pembroke St
7 Ronaldsay Gdns
8 Rostherne St
9 Sandray Gv
10 Stowell St
11 Westray Crs

Page 104

A5
1 Iceland St
2 Langham Rd
3 Wall St

B4
1 Eades St
2 Gloucester Pl
3 Gore St
4 Hankinson Wy
5 Higham Vw
6 Loganberry Av
7 Mulberry Rd
8 Upper Gloucester St

C1
1 Mackenzie Rd
2 Valencia Rd

C4
1 Belvedere St
2 Nichols St
3 Peel Mt
4 Scarsdale St
5 Strawberry Bank
6 University Rd

C5
1 Aldred St
2 Canute St
3 Caxton Wy
4 Chevron Cl
5 Clementine Cl
6 Coconut Gv
7 Elior St
8 Melksham Cl
9 Melon Pl
10 University Rd
11 University Rd West

C6
1 Caxton Wy
2 Christopher St
3 Scale St
4 West Charles St

Page 105

D5
1 Aquarius La
2 Baroness Gv
3 Capricorn Wy
4 Harry Hall Gdns
5 Longfellow St
6 Myrtle Pl
7 Paton Cl
8 Pluto Cl
9 Saturn Gv
10 Scott St
11 Wordsworth St

D6
1 Back Hulme St
2 Barlow Rd
3 Blackburn Pl
4 Canal St
5 Clare St
6 Cranbourne St
7 Craven St
8 Hulme Pl
9 Joiner St
10 Massey St
11 Muslin St
12 West Dean St

E2
1 Back Camp St
2 Burland Cl
3 Carter St
4 Countess Gv
5 Enid Cl
6 Gosport Sq
7 Nelson St
8 Nile Ter
9 Southampton Cl
10 Teneriffe St
11 Trafalgar Gv

E4
1 Alexandra St
2 Antares Av
3 Briggs St
4 Brocade Cl
5 Calico Cl
6 Elton's Yd
7 Flax St
8 Linen St
9 Mistletoe Gv
10 Sirius Pl
11 Watkin St

E6
1 Barrow St
2 Egerton St
3 Factory La
4 Firefly Cl
5 Gibbs St
6 Islington Wy
7 Mason St
8 Nangreave St
9 North Star Dr
10 Oldham St
11 Rodney St
12 Schofield St
13 South William St
14 Stevenson St
15 West Duke St

F1
1 Back Roman Rd
2 Bannerman St
3 Becket Av
4 Bevendon Sq
5 Bond Sq
6 Brighton Av
7 Centurion Gv
8 Duncombe St
9 Fenney St
10 Fenney St East
11 Hadfield St
12 Ivyleaf Sq
13 Kenneth Sq
14 Legion Gv
15 Maleham St
16 Pembroke St
17 Star Gv
18 Tully St
19 Wally Sq
20 West Marwood St
21 Worcester St

F2
1 Ashworth St
2 Benson Cl
3 Canonsleigh Cl
4 Cascade Dr
5 Colina Dr
6 Forum Gv
7 Hilton St
8 Holberton Cl
9 Melbourne St
10 Otter Dr
11 Richborough Cl
12 Sabrina St
13 Sandsend Cl
14 Thanet Cl
15 Westmead Dr
16 Willerby Rd

F3
1 Caroline St
2 Chatford Cl
3 Cheetwood St
4 Clement St
5 Lampson St
6 Neill St
7 Strong St
8 Tully St
9 Vega St
10 Waterloo Rd
11 Willow St

F4
1 Carding Gv
2 Evans St
3 Half St
4 Hothersall St
5 Poplin Dr
6 Reservoir St
7 Richmond St
8 Rope Wk
9 Twillbrook Dr
10 Wadlow Cl

F5
1 Blossom St
2 Browncross St
3 Cable St
4 Caxton St
5 Deal St
6 Edmund St
7 Garden La
8 Griffin Ct
9 Hodson St
10 Hopwood St
11 Johnson St
12 Lamb Ct
13 Linsley St
14 North Broughton St
15 Rolla St
16 Sackville St
17 Wood St
18 Worsley St
19 Yorkshire St

F6
1 Atherton St
2 Atkinson St
3 Back Quay St
4 Beck St
5 Bolton St
6 Brown St
7 Crown Sq
8 Dolefield
9 Hardman St
10 Joddrell St
11 Left Bank
12 Little John St
13 Little Quay St
14 Lower Hardman St
15 Riding St
16 Water St

Page 106

A1
1 Avebury Cl
2 Axford Cl
3 Brakenhurst Dr
4 Chisledon Av
5 Cranlington Dr
6 Dalmain Cl
7 Errington Dr
8 Everleigh Dr
9 Greywood Av
10 Highclere Av
11 Kilmington Dr
12 Linstead Dr
13 Marlborough Av
14 Oscroft Cl
15 Peach Tree Cl
16 Percival Cl
17 Venture Scout Wy

A4
1 Breslin St
2 Briddon St
3 Langston St
4 Newcombe St
5 Thompson St

A5
1 Boond St
2 Cannon St
3 Cathedral Ap
4 Cathedral Gates
5 Cathedral St
6 Dawson St
7 Gorton St
8 Greengate
9 Hanging Ditch
10 Harding St
11 Longridge Pl
12 New Kings Head Yd
13 Norton St
14 Parsonage La
15 Viaduct St
16 Victoria Bridge St
17 Victoria Station Ap
18 Victoria St

B1
1 Brinsworth St
2 Dameral Cl
3 Dinnington Dr
4 Hansdon Cl
5 Holmbrook Wk
6 Huxley Av
7 Magnolia Dr
8 Starmoor Dr
9 Thackeray Cl
10 Wordsworth Av

B2
1 Thorngate Rd

B5
1 Amber St
2 Back Balloon St
3 Back Thomas St
4 Bradshaw St
5 Brick St
6 Carpenters La
7 Catlow La
8 Copperas St
9 Edgehill St
10 Federation St
11 Hare St
12 Kelvin St
13 Long Millgate
14 Mayes St
15 Newbeck St
16 Newgate St
17 Redfern St
18 Red Lion St
19 Roman St
20 Soap St
21 Thornley Brow
22 Union St
23 Well St

B6
1 Back George St
2 Back Piccadilly
3 Birchin La
4 Bridgewater Pl
5 Chain St
6 Charlotte St
7 Concert La
8 Gold St
9 Hart St
10 Joiner St
11 New Market La
12 Nicholas St
13 Phoenix St
14 Piccadilly
15 Pine St
16 St James St
17 Short St
18 Silver St
19 Spear St
20 Sussex St
21 West Mosley St

C3
1 Almond St
2 Davy St

C4
1 Back Ashley St
2 Back St George's Rd
3 Baptist St
4 Burstock St
5 Clive St
6 Dulwich St
7 Durant St
8 Flag Rw
9 Hinton St
10 Jason St
11 Moorhead St
12 Simeon St
13 Tebbutt St

C5
1 Back Spear St
2 Bradley St
3 Chadderton St
4 Coop St
5 Cornell St
6 Cross Keys St
7 Faraday St
8 Hatter St
9 Henry St
10 Houldsworth St
11 Little Ancoats St
12 Little Lever St
13 Luna St
14 Mason St
15 Oak St
16 Primrose St
17 Sherratt St
18 Warwick St
19 Whittle St

C6
1 Auburn St
2 Back China La
3 Back Junction St
4 Back Piccadilly
5 Binns Pl
6 Bradleys Count
7 Brock St
8 Bunsen St
9 Cavell St
10 Chatham St
11 China La
12 Circus St
13 Faraday St
14 Gore St
15 Hilton St
16 Houldsworth St
17 Lena St
18 Leycroft St
19 Little Lever St
20 Little Pitt St
21 Lizard St
22 Mangle St
23 Paton St
24 Peak St
25 Pigeon St
26 Plant St
27 Postal St
28 Roby St
29 Stevenson Pl
30 Stevenson Sq
31 Whittle's Cft

Page 107

D1
1 Derwent St
2 Gransden Dr
3 Highstone Dr
4 Lanhill Dr
5 Reedshaw Rd
6 Rutherglade Cl
7 Smeaton St
8 Tarvington Cl
9 Westmount Cl
10 Wythburn Av

D5
1 Cinder St
2 Downley Dr
3 Holkham Cl
4 Kingham Dr
5 Mozart Cl
6 Naval St
7 New Islington
8 Portugal St
9 Rodney St
10 Salford Av
11 School Ct
12 Tavery Cl
13 Wadeford Cl
14 Woodward Pl

E2
1 Ailsa St
2 Aldbourne Cl
3 Anslow Cl
4 Bishop Marshall Cl
5 Burnett Cl
6 Foreland Cl
7 Foynes Cl
8 Gervis Cl
9 Hillman Cl
10 Johnny King Cl
11 Needwood Cl
12 Overbrook Av
13 Raydon Av
14 Regency Cl
15 Robert Malcolm Cl
16 Rodmell Av
17 Rousdon Cl
18 Stretton Cl
19 Thornton St North
20 Toliard Av
21 Trimley Av
22 Tuxford Wk
23 Winthrop Av

E3
1 Back Hampson St
2 Birt St
3 Falkland Av
4 Ferdinand St
5 Hampson St
6 Helga St
7 Johnson's Sq
8 Lashbrook Cl
9 Rosewell Cl
10 Ryder St
11 Tollesbury Cl
12 Wilmcote Rd

E5
1 Audlem Cl
2 Cowan St
3 Cranfield Cl
4 Halmore Rd
5 Layton St
6 Spectator St
7 Teer St
8 Tidworth Av
9 Troutbeck Av
10 Weston St

F2
1 Aldsworth Dr
2 Cheetham St
3 Evan St
4 Lodge St
5 Rathmore Av
6 Rutherglen Wk
7 Ryedale Av
8 Rylane Wk
9 St Augustine St
10 Swinstead Av
11 Talmine Av

F3
1 Kirkhaven Sq
2 Lifton Av
3 Princess St

F4
1 Barbeck Cl
2 Barking St
3 Brookhill St
4 Danson St
5 Eastfield Av
6 Granshaw St
7 Kenyon St
8 Lanchester St
9 Padstow St
10 Penzance St
11 Pochin St
12 Stracey St

F5
1 Adswood St
2 Charnley Cl
3 Lanstead Dr
4 Lind St
5 Millhead Av
6 Tinsley Cl
7 Upper Cyrus St

F6
1 Baslow St
2 Bellis Cl
3 Euclid Cl
4 Gaitskell Cl
5 Hassop Cl
6 Longham Cl
7 Orme Cl
8 Silfield Cl

Page 108

A2
1 Cramer St
2 Fletcher St
3 Hague St
4 Lancashire St
5 Mansford St
6 Partington St
7 Thompson St
8 Woodhouse St

B1
1 Copenhagen St
2 Jessie St
3 Lowcross Rd
4 Rollswood Dr
5 Worrall St

C1
1 Boringdon Cl
2 Colclough Cl
3 Dixon St
4 Oulverton St
5 Erwin St
6 Glemsford Cl
7 Harold Priestnall Cl
8 John Foran Cl

C5
1 Alpine St
2 Buchan St
3 Coghlan Cl
4 Flint Cl
5 Frankland Cl
6 Franton Rd
7 Homebury Dr
8 Hurstbourne Av
9 Midlothian St
10 Ranelagh St
11 Sheldon St
12 Stockholm St
13 Strathfield Dr
14 Sunningdale Av
15 Sweetnam Dr

C6
1 Aintree St
2 Cantrell St
3 Side St

Page 109

D1
1 Bridlington Cl
2 Cowley St
3 Greenhalgh St
4 Lastingham St
5 Linwood St
6 Newton St
7 Smallwood St

D3
1 Aldham Av
2 Camden Av
3 Clough St
4 Dymchurch St
5 Finchley Av
6 Finsbury Av
7 Hackney Av
8 Lambeth Rd

D4
1 East Gra
2 Goldenhill Av

D6
1 Bebbington St
2 Braddon St
3 Eswick St
4 Foxlake St
5 Iredine St
6 John William St
7 Kintyre Cl
8 Langness St
9 Parrot St
10 Rushen St

E2
1 Bardsley St
2 Charfield St
3 Clovelly St
4 Deal Cl
5 Devonshire St East
6 Graver La
7 Leaholme St
8 Mabel St
9 Marguerita Rd
10 Silverwell St
11 Tetlow St
12 Woodgarth Av

F6
1 Brook Av
2 Charles St
3 Clay Bank
4 Cooper St
5 Davenport St

Page 110

C1
1 Walker Av

Page 111

D5
1 Hazel Cl
2 Jasmine Av
3 Kempton Cl
4 Langfield Crs
5 Marlborough Gv
6 Moorside Av
7 Moss Bank Ct
8 Myrtle Gv
9 Park St
10 Pipit Cl
11 Richmond St

Page 112

A2
1 Belsay Cl
2 Earnshaw Cl
3 Inglewood Cl
4 Patterdale Av
5 Taunton Gn
6 Taunton Hall Cl
7 Taunton Pl

B1
1 Colwyn St
2 Limehurst Av
3 Limehurst Rd

B6
1 Bradgate St
2 Cecil St
3 Eastgate St
4 Grosvenor Ct
5 John St East
6 Marlborough St
7 Redbrick Ct
8 Victoria St
9 Westgate St
10 Whittington St

C5
1 Booth St
2 Charles St
3 Coulthart St
4 Delamere St
5 Duke St
6 Higher Wharf St
7 Stamford St West
8 Warrington St
9 Wych St

Page 113

D4
1 Adam St
2 Albemarle St
3 Albemarle Ter
4 Albion St
5 Arlington St
6 Ashvinne
7 Athol St
8 Cricket's La
9 Cross Glebe St
10 Enville St
11 Gower St
12 Harper Pl
13 Mount Pleasant St
14 Mulberry St
15 Newton St
16 Old Cross St
17 Raynham St
18 Ripon St
19 Wimpole St

E4
1 Grey St

E5
1 Addison Av
2 Bowman Crs
3 Caroline St
4 Sloane St

Page 114

A5
1 Crossley St
2 Cumberland St
3 Harrop St
4 Huilly St
5 Newton St
6 Off Ridge Hill La
7 Rassbottom Brow
8 Thompson Fold
9 Victoria St

B6
1 Back Grosvenor St
2 Back Melbourne St
3 Bennett St
4 Borough St
5 Canal St
6 Castle Hall Ct
7 Crosvenor St
8 Kay St
9 Kensington Gv
10 Kenworthy St
11 Rose Ter

Page 119

D1
1 Adamson Rd
2 Ashford Av
3 Calver Av
4 Chesham Rd
5 Darley Av
6 Driffield St
7 Matlock St
8 Mount St
9 Roby Rd
10 School Rd
11 Stafford Av

E4
1 Arran Gdns

Page 122

B2
1 Archie St
2 Aubrey St
3 Glen St

B3
1 Wharf End

C2
1 Buckfield Av
2 Chetham Ct
3 Clarke Av
4 Colman Gdns
5 Fallowfield Av
6 Gurner Av
7 Guy Fawkes St
8 Hillgate Av
9 Napier Gn
10 New Park Rd
11 Nine Acre Dr
12 Percy Dr
13 St Clement's Dr
14 Windmill Av
15 Wyatt Av

C4
1 Carver Cl
2 Talbot Pl

C6
1 Abbey Lawn

Page 123

D1
1 Asgard Gv
2 Carmel Av
3 Carmel Cl
4 Chancel Av
5 Freya Gv
6 Garden Wall Cl
7 Parsonage Cl
8 Saint Bartholomew's Dr
9 Thor Gv

D3
1 Bath Crs
2 Blackley St
3 Darwen St
4 Farwood Cl
5 Lango St
6 Manchester St
7 Northumberland St
8 Northumberland Crs
9 Nuttall St
10 Seymour Ct
11 Stanley Ct
12 Trafford Bank Rd

E3
1 Fernleigh Dr
2 Globe Ct
3 Gordon St
4 Whitchurch Dr

F2
1 Alpha Pl
2 Commercial St
3 Crown St
4 Galgate Cl
5 Gilbert St
6 Melbourne St
7 Pryme St
8 Scotforth Cl

F3
1 Barrhill Cl
2 Charles Barry Crs
3 Eliza St
4 Hornchurch St
5 Mallow St
6 St Wilfrids St
7 Sorrel St
8 Upper Moss La

F5
1 Bishop Cl
2 Gladstone Ct
3 Merriman St
4 Portstone Cl
5 Ringfield Cl
6 Rinyfield Cl
7 Wilcock Cl
8 William Kay Cl

Page 169

D1
1 Cheetham Pl
2 Crown St
3 Elderfield Dr
4 Forbes St
5 Kerridge Dr
6 Lombard Cl
7 Welcomb Cl

E2
1 Barrack Hill Cl
2 Hardman Av
3 King's Rd
4 Prince's Av
5 Ruskin Gdns
6 Thomas St

Page 178

B1
1 Hollycroft Av
2 Marford Cl

C3
1 Ashgate Av
2 Briardene Gdns
3 Ebor Rd

C5
1 Hockenhull Cl
2 Storeton Cl

C6
1 Green Meadows Wk
2 Kepwick Dr

Page 181

F5
1 Sedgemoor Cl
2 Station Rd
3 Warren Rd

F6
1 Bellfield Av
2 Butterfield Cl
3 Chase Briar Wd
4 Hill Top Ct
5 Ravenoak Rd

Page 182

B3
1 Adswood Old Hall Rd

Page 183

D1
1 Anglesea Av
2 Beech Av
3 Chatswood Av
4 Lytham St
5 Meyer St
6 School Ct

Page 184

A2
1 Archer St
2 Castle Farm La
3 Castlewood Gdns
4 Eltham Av
5 Frome Av
6 Garden St
7 Hollymount Av
8 Meadow St

B2
1 Ashway Clough North
2 Ashway Clough South
3 Reedshaw Bank
4 Rishworth Cl
5 Wessenden Bank East

B4
1 Albert St
2 Albion Pl
3 Angel St
4 Ash St
5 Brewer's Gn
6 Buxton St
7 Charles St
8 Crown Ct
9 Gordon Av
10 Grosvenor St
11 John St
12 Lyme St
13 Newbourne Cl
14 Pownall St
15 Smithy St
16 Springfield Av
17 Stanley Av
18 Vernon St
19 Willard St
20 Yeoman Cl

C5
1 The Boulevard
2 Brook St
3 Daniel St
4 Grundey St
5 Spring V